# The GALE
## ENCYCLOPEDIA of
# PSYCHOLOGY
### SECOND EDITION

# The GALE ENCYCLOPEDIA of PSYCHOLOGY

## SECOND EDITION

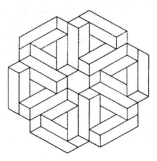

BONNIE STRICKLAND, EXECUTIVE EDITOR

GALE GROUP

Detroit
New York
San Francisco
London
Boston
Woodbridge, CT

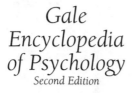

# Gale
# Encyclopedia
# of Psychology
### Second Edition

Bonnie R. Strickland, *Executive editor*

**GALE GROUP STAFF**

Kristine Krapp, *Coordinating senior editor*
Christine Jeryan, *Managing editor*
Melissa C. McDade, *Assistant editor*
Deirdre Blanchfield, *Assistant editor*
Mark Springer, *Editorial Technical Trainer*

Barbara J. Yarrow, *Manager, Multimedia and imaging content*
Robyn V. Young, *Senior editor, Imaging acquisitions*
Robert Duncan, *Senior imaging specialist*

Kenn Zorn, *Product design manager*
Marie Claire Krzewinski, *Cover design*
Marie Claire Krzewinski and Michelle DiMercurio, *Page design*
Mike Logusz, *Graphic artist*

Mary Beth Trimper, *Manager, Composition and electronic prepress*
Evi Seoud, *Assistant manager, Composition and electronic prepress*
Stacy L. Melson, *Buyer*

Tables by Mark Berger, Standley Publishing, Ferndale, Michigan
First Edition by Eastword Publication Development, Pepper Pike, Ohio

Copyright 2001
Gale Group
27500 Drake Rd.
Farmington Hills, MI 48331-3535

ISBN 0-7876-4786-1

Printed in the United States of America
10 9 8 7 6 5 4 3 2 1

Library of Congress Cataloging-in-Publication Data

The Gale encyclopedia of psychology / Bonnie R. Strickland, executive editor.–2nd ed.
    p. cm.
    Includes bibliographical references and index.
    ISBN 0-7876-4786-1
      1. Psychology–Encyclopedias. I. Strickland, Bonnie R.

BF31.G35 2000
150'.3–dc21    00-34736

# EDITORS AND CONTRIBUTORS

## EXECUTIVE EDITOR

Bonnie Ruth Strickland, Ph.D
Professor of Psychology
University of Massachusetts/Amherst

## COORDINATING EDITOR

Kristine M. Krapp

## CONTRIBUTORS

Margaret Alic
Doreen Arcus
Howard Baker
Bernard Beins
Karen L. Bierman
Hallie Bourne
James Calland
Kenneth Chiacchia
Dianne Daeg de Mott
Jill De Villiers
Marie Doorey
Catherine Dybiec Holm
Lindsay Evans
Alan Feldman
Paula Ford-Martin

Susan Gall
Lauri R. Harding
Jim Henry
D. George Joseph
Jerome Kagan
Kyung Lim Kalasky
Mary Anne Klasen
Judson Knight
Peter LaFreniere
Johnna Laird
Lara Lynn Lane
Patricia Martin
Mary McNulty
George A. Milite
Zoran Minderovic
Nancy Moore
Timothy E. Moore
Patricia Skinner
Gail B. Slap
Jane Spear
Laurence Steinberg
Judith Turner
Cindy Washabaugh
Janet A. Welsh
Rosalie Wieder
Angela Woodward

# ABOUT THE ENCYCLOPEDIA

The *Gale Encyclopedia of Psychology, Second Edition* includes over 650 entries on people and subjects important to the study of psychology. This number represents one-third more entries than the first edition. The book has been designed so the reader can easily find and access the information needed.

- Entries are alphabetically arranged.

- Length of entries ranges from brief explanations of a concept in one or two paragraphs to longer, more detailed entries on more complex topics. Almost 65% of the entries are entirely new or updated from the first edition.

- A brief definition of the entry term appears between the entry title and the full text of the entry.

- Over 175 photos, illustrations, and tables accompany the text and enhance the reader's understanding of the subject covered.

- Bolded cross-references direct the reader to entries on terms mentioned in the text of other entries.

- *See also* references at the end of entries point the reader to related entries.

- Further Reading and Further Information sections follow entries, directing the reader to other sources of information on the topic.

- A new and improved glossary of over 350 essential terms is included to help the reader understand key concepts.

- An updated appendix lists psychological organizations that the reader may contact for further inquiries.

- An updated and expanded general subject index points the reader to concepts and people covered in the encyclopedia.

# CONTENTS

# INTRODUCTION

Psychology is one of the most fascinating fields of study. Almost everyone seems interested in understanding his or her own behavior, as well as the actions of others. Psychology is, by far, the most popular of the social and behavioral sciences and one of the most attractive to those who are interested in knowing more about people and their behavior. In college and universities, psychology has been one of the most popular majors for over three decades, and students are more likely to take an elective course in psychology than one from any other field. Not surprisingly, psychology has also become a popular high school offering.

Initially, psychology courses at the secondary school level tried to meet the needs of rapidly maturing adolescents who were interested in the changes they were experiencing in themselves and in their relationships with others—family, friends, the world of adults. We are living in times of dramatic social change. Each of us continually faces new challenges about how we will make our place in the world. As the discipline of psychology matured, adjustment courses gave way to substantive content courses that offered not just psychology's latest findings about developmental and identity issues, but also featured those more traditional areas of cognitive, experimental, physiological, and social psychology. These courses were joined by newly developed offerings such as neuropsychology and psycholinguistics. The advances in the scientific side of psychology were paralleled by the remarkable growth of counseling, clinical, and school psychology.

To keep up with the rapidly expanding field, the newly revised second edition of the *Gale Encyclopedia of Psychology* has added about a third more entries and biographies. Coverage includes the key concepts on which the science is built, as well as major theoretical advances in psychology. Clinical information is broadly covered, noting the various psychological theories and techniques currently in use and the scientific evidence that supports then. Biographical profiles of major figures in the field of psychology are included, ranging from the earliest historical pioneers to current clinicians.

Psychology is one of our youngest sciences. People first looked at the stars to predict and control their destiny and the science of astronomy was born. Mathematics was necessary to count and measure, and eventually the physical sciences, such as physics, chemistry, and biology, emerged. The study of human psychology, however, developed later. It has only been a bit over a century since scientists and philosophers turned their eyes from the planets to people and tried to understand human behavior in a systematic, scientific way. In the late 19th century, philosophers and physiologists began to examine the ways people perceive and interact with the world around them. How do individuals use their senses of sight, hearing, and touch to make sense of the world? How do people remember what has happened to them or know how to plan for the future?

In the late second half of the 1800s, a number of young North American men and a few women traveled to Germany to study with Wilhelm Wundt, who had established a laboratory and the first graduate program of study in psychology at the University of Leipzig in Germany. They returned to teach psychology and train other students in the major universities of this country with the intent of quantifying individual differences and important elements of human perception and memory.

About the same time (1896), Lightner Witmer established a Psychological Clinic at the University of Pennsylvania to help children who were having difficulty in school.

Being a psychologist, he assumed that his new profession—dedicated to learning and memory—would help him assist children who were having trouble reading, writing, spelling, and remembering information. Unfortunately, Witmer could find no help from the complex, theoretical notions within the experimental laboratories, and he turned to schoolteachers and social workers for practical advice.

Thus began the long struggle between the scientific study and practice of psychology, theory and action. Scientists want to know that the data that they gather in their experiments are valid and replicable (that is, others pursuing the same questions with appropriate methods would find the same results). They sometimes feel that clinicians, for example, use psychotherapy techniques that have not been proven to be useful and may even be harmful. Practitioners, on the other hand, faced with pressing and immediate problems of clients who are anxious, depressed, or psychotic, need immediate treatments to relieve suffering and may use methods that have not have been fully proven in the laboratories.

The earliest psychologists worked primarily with children, usually those who were delinquent or having trouble in school. They were particularly taken with assessing intelligence and translated a test developed by a Frenchman, Alfred Binet, to quantify "mental age." Unfortunately, they moved well beyond the limitations of the test that had been designed to identify children who were having trouble in school. They began testing soldiers recruited for the First World War and immigrants who wanted to come to this country. According to their tests, they found almost half of the young, white male recruits and some 80% of Eastern European immigrants to be "morons." This led them to rethink the uses of intelligence tests, especially because of opinions like that of journalist Walter Lippman, who recommended that the "intelligence testers and their tests should be sunk without warning in the... sea." But serious harm had been done. Some six million immigrants were denied entrance into this country, and intelligence testing laid the base for human eugenics laws that allowed individuals who were found "intellectually unfit" to be sterilized.

Nonetheless, psychology became something of a national mania in the 1920s. With the introduction of psychoanalysis into this country, people wanted to "adjust" through self-examination and the probing of the unconscious. The scientific psychologists were dismayed at the excesses of pseudopsychologists, whose ranks included mind readers and charlatans. Psychological clinicians were concerned as well and took steps to develop a standard of ethics and ways of identifying appropriately trained psychologists.

With the advent of the Second World War, psychologists joined the military effort and were surprised themselves by how much they had to offer. Human factors psychologists designed airplane cockpits and the lighting on runways that we still use today. Gestalt psychologists taught American citizens how to identify enemy planes should they fly overhead. B.F. Skinner taught pigeons to guide missiles toward enemy targets. Psychologists worked for the Office of Strategic Services (which eventually became the CIA) to develop propaganda and disinformation. This group also developed assessments to determine who might be good officers (or spies). On the battlefield, clinicians were helping troops who were experiencing "traumatic neurosis, " originally called "shell shock" in the First World War and now known as post-traumatic stress disorder. When the soldiers returned home, they led therapy groups for wounded military personnel.

At the end of the Second World War, the National Research Council urged the American Psychological Association (APA) to heal the schism between scientists and clinicians and reorganize with full membership benefits for all doctoral psychologists. The Veteran's Hospitals, in particular, needed well-trained personnel to provide mental health services for their patients. A major 1949 conference held in Boulder, Colorado established standards of education and training for clinical psychologists. Their recommendations were that clinical psychologists should be trained as generalists who were both scientists and clinicians. Doctoral students would complete at least a year of internship and receive the Ph. D. (doctor of philosophy) degree. These standards are still in place today, although newer of training are available for students who want to place more emphasis on practice and less on doing research. In addition to university graduate programs, a large number of professional schools have been established, often offering a Psy. D (doctor of psychology) degree. Currently, some 4,000 students graduate each year with a doctoral degree in psychology and perhaps three times that many receive a master's degree. The overwhelming majority of these graduates go into clinical or applied work, although changing conditions in the health fields, such as the growth of HMOs, have raised concerns about job opportunities for clinical psychologists.

A field as broad as psychology, which stretches from the study of brain cells to that of prison cells, is an active, argumentative, and exciting adventure that offers opportunities in science, practice, and social policy. Most of the pressing economic and social issues of our generation, such as the environment, health needs, poverty, and violence, will only be alleviated if we understand the ways in which people create or creatively solve the problems that we bring upon ourselves. The student who is interested in unraveling the secrets of the human brain to see the mind at work, who is fascinated about how children grow up and become competent adults, who is dedicated to bringing people together to resolve conflict, who is committed to helping people with physical, emotional, or behavioral difficulties, or who is challenged by the desire to develop social policy in the public interest is welcomed in psychology. We hope this encyclopedia will provide useful information that will help students and others understand this fascinating field and its opportunities.

Bonnie R. Strickland, Ph.D.

Bonnie Ruth Strickland received her Ph.D. in Clinical Psychology from The Ohio State University in 1962. She has been on the faculties of Emory University and the University of Massachusetts in Amherst as a teacher, researcher, administrator, clinician, and consultant. A Diplomate in Clinical Psychology, she has also been in practice for over 35 years. Dr. Strickland has served as President of the American Psychological Association, the Division of Clinical Psychology and the American Association for Applied and Preventive Psychology; she was a Founder and on the first Board of Directors of the American Psychological Society. An advocate for minority concerns, she has published more than a hundred scholarly works including two Citation Classics in psychology.

A

# Ability

Knowledge or skill, including the potential to acquire knowledge or skills and those already acquired.

The capacity to learn, commonly known as aptitude, and the demonstration of skills and knowledge already learned, called achievement, are among the factors used to evaluate **intelligence**. When evaluating or comparing subjects, two kinds of abilities are considered: verbal ability, including reading comprehension, ability to converse, vocabulary, and the use of language; and problem-solving ability, which includes a person's capacity to make good decisions given a set of circumstances.

Relatively straightforward tests of ability are often used by employers to determine an applicant's skills. For example, a person applying for a job as a word processor may be given a keyboarding test, while a bus-driving applicant would be given a driving test. Tests to evaluate more complex abilities, such as **leadership, motivation,** and social skills tend to be less precise.

Developed around the turn of the twentieth century, formal tests used by psychologists and educators to measure aptitude and achievement remain controversial. Intelligence, or IQ, tests are faulted for ignoring cultural or social biases, particularly with regard to schoolchildren, and critics contend such standardized measures cannot adequately predict a person's future performance.

*See also* Achievement tests; Scholastic Assessment Test; Stanford-Binet intelligence scales; Vocational Aptitude Test

## Further Reading

Atkinson, Rita L.; Richard C. Atkinson; Edward E. Smith; and Ernest R. Hilgard. *Introduction to Psychology.* 9th ed. San Diego: Harcourt Brace Jovanovich, 1987.

Zimbardo, Philip G. *Psychology and Life.* 12th ed. Glenview, IL: Scott, Foresman, 1988.

# Abnormal psychology

The subfield of psychology concerned with the study of abnormal behavior.

Abnormal behavior is defined as behavior that is considered to be maladaptive or deviant by the social culture in which it occurs. Though disagreement exists regarding which particular behaviors can be classified as abnormal, psychologists have defined several criteria for purposes of classification. One is that the behavior occurs infrequently and thus deviates from statistical norms. Another is that the behavior deviates from social norms of acceptable behavior. A third is that the behavior is maladaptive, that it has adverse affects on the individual or on the individual's social group. Lastly, abnormality may be defined based on the subjective feelings of misery, **depression,** or anxiety of an individual rather than any behavior he exhibits.

The ***Diagnostic and Statistical Manual of Mental Disorders,*** 4th edition (DSM-IV), is a classification system of abnormal behaviors which aids psychologists and other **mental health** professionals in diagnosing and treating mental disorders. *DSM-IV* includes the major categories of abnormal behavior which are anxiety disorders, such as **obsessive-compulsive disorders** and **phobias;** affective disorders, which are disturbances of **mood** such as depression; schizophrenic disorders, which are characterized by major disturbances in **personality** and distortion of reality; and various **personality disorders.**

While psychologists use similar criteria to diagnose abnormal behavior, their perspectives in understanding and treating related disorders vary greatly. For instance, a psychologist with a psychoanalytic approach would explain depression as a reaction to loss, worsened by **anger** turned inward. A behavioral psychologist would assume a lack of positive **reinforcement** to be a significant cause in the disease. A cognitive theorist would focus on the negative thought patterns and attitudes of an individual in contributing to his depression. And a psychologist with a biological perspective would consider a chemical imbalance in the **nervous system** of a depressed individual to be responsible for his disorder. Many studies have shown that a number of these factors may come into play in the life of an individual suffering from a mental disorder characterized by abnormal behavior.

*See also* Mental illness; Psychotic disorders

**Further Reading**
Oldham, John M. *The New Personality Self-Portrait.* New York: Bantam, 1995.
*Personality Disorders and the Five-Factor Model of Personality.* Washington, DC: American Psychological Association, 1994.

# Abortion

Invasive procedure resulting in pregnancy termination and death of the fetus.

Abortion is the final consequence of a woman's decision to terminate her pregnancy. In the U.S., more than 50% of the pregnancies are unintended, and 50% of these end in abortion. More than half (53%) of the unplanned pregnancies happen among the 10% of women who practice no contraception. Most women getting abortions are young: 55% are under 25, including 21% teenagers.

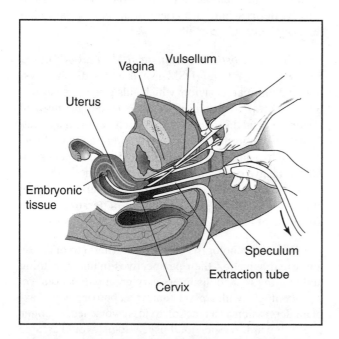

**Between five and seven weeks, a pregnancy can be ended by a procedure called menstrual extraction, shown above.** *(Electronic Illustrations Group. Reproduced with permission.)*

While abortion is practiced throughout society, in all socioeconomic strata, poor women are three times more likely to have an abortion than their well-off counterparts.

White women have 63% of all abortions, but the non-white abortion rate is more than twice the white rate—54 per 1,000 versus 20 per 1,000. About 93% of all abortions are performed for social, not medical, reasons; in other words, most abortions are, from the medical point of view, unnecessary: the mother's health and life are not in jeopardy, and there are no abnormalities which would justify the termination of the fetus's life. Social reasons include **fear** of motherhood, fear of losing a partner who doesn't want children, fear of parental and social disapproval, financial difficulties, lack of support, and psychological problems, among others.

Abortion is a complex issue that raises a plethora of medical, ethical, political, legal, and psychological questions, and is viewed by proponents and opponents as one of society's fundamental problems. "Abortion," Paul D. Simmons has written (Butler and Walbert, 1992), "is related to life and death, **sexuality** and procreation—all of which are integrally related in the human psyche." While the "pro-choice" camp defends a woman's right to terminate her pregnancy, "pro-life" forces define abortion as murder. As commentators have noted, dialogue between the two camps has been difficult, seemingly impossible, because opinions are often based on strong feelings and beliefs. An additional obstacle to dialogue is the fact that the two opposing sides use fundamentally different discourses. Pro-life discourse often draws its strength from the Christian axiom about the sanctity of life, while pro-choice thinking proceeds from the belief that an individual woman has the freedom to act in her best interest.

While vulnerable to moral condemnation, and even harassment, adult women have the protection of liberal legislation in seeking an abortion (in *Roe v. Wade,* 1973, the U.S. Supreme Court ruled that abortion is a constitutional right). Teenagers, however, are subject to state laws; in 25 states, a minor cannot seek an abortion without parental consent. Traditionally, any medical treatment of a minor requires parental consent, and as the Planned Parenthood Fact Sheet "Teenagers, Abortion, and Government Intrusion Laws" points out, a physician treating a minor without parental consent is committing the common law equivalent of battery. However, "in the area of abortion, there have never been criminal penalties for treating a minor on her own consent."

Zoran Minderovic

**Further Reading**
Butler, J. Douglas, and David F. Walbert, eds. *Abortion, Medicine, and the Law.* 4th rev. ed. New York: Facts On File, 1992.

Darroch Forrest, Jacqueline, and Jennifer J. Frost. "The Family Planning Attitudes and Experiences of Low-Income Women." *Family Planning Perspectives* 28, no. 6. (November-December 1996): 246-55.

Hern, Warren M. *Abortion Practice*. Philadelphia: J. B. Lippincott, 1984.

Matthews, Stephen, David Ribar, and Mark Wilhelm. "The Effects of Economic Conditions and Access to Reproductive Health Services on State Abortion Rates and Birthrates." *Family Planning Perspectives* 29, no. 2. (March-April 1997): 52-60.

"Teenagers, Abortion, and Government Intrusion Laws." (Planned Parenthood Fact Sheet). New York: Planned Parenthood Federation of America, October 1992.

Torres, Aida, and Jacqueline Darroch Forrest. "Why Do Women Have Abortions?" *Family Planning Perspectives* 20, no. 4. (July-August 1988).

# Absolute threshold

> The minimal amount of energy necessary to stimulate the sensory receptors.

The method of testing for the absolute threshold is similar for different sensory systems. Thus, the tester can briefly present a light or a sound (or any other kind of stimulus) at different, low intensities until the observer is unable to detect the presence of the stimulus. In such a task, the person may undergo thousands of trials before the researcher can determine the threshold.

While the absolute threshold is a useful concept, it does not exist in reality. That is, on one occasion, an individual might be unable to detect a certain faint light but on a subsequent occasion, may detect it. In addition, scientists cannot determine with absolute certainty how much energy is present in a light because of limits to the physics of **measurement**. As a result, psychologists often define the threshold as the lowest intensity that a person can detect 50 percent of the time.

A number of different factors can influence the absolute threshold, including the observer's motivations and expectations, and whether the person is adapted to the stimulus. Scientists have discovered that cognitive processes can influence the measurement of the threshold and that it is not as simple as once understood. Psychologists have also studied how different two stimuli have to be in order to be noticed as not being the same. Such an approach involves what are called difference thresholds.

**Further Reading**
Galantner, E. "Contemporary Psychophysics." In *New Directions in Psychology*, edited by R. Brown. New York: Holt, Rinehart & Winston, 1962.

# Acculturation

> The process of adapting to or adopting the practices of a culture different from one's own.

Acculturation is the process of learning about and adapting to a new culture. A new culture may require adjustments in all or some of the aspects of daily living, including language, work, shopping, housing, children's schooling, health care, recreation, and social life. Relo-

| EXAMPLES OF ABSOLUTE THRESHOLDS | |
| --- | --- |
| **Sense** | **Example of threshold** |
| Vision | The amount of light present if someone held up a single candle 30 mi (48 km) away from us, if our eyes were used to the dark. If a person in front of you held up a candle and began backing up at the rate of one foot (30 cm) per second, that person would have to back up for 44 hours before the flame became invisible. |
| Hearing | The ticking of a watch in a quiet environment at 20 ft (6 m). |
| Taste | One drop on quinine sulfate (a bitter substance) in 250 gal (946 l) of water. Quinine is one of the components of tonic water. |
| Smell | One drop of perfume in a six-room house. This value will change depending on the type of substance we are smelling. |
| Touch | The force exerted by dropping the wing of a bee onto your cheek from a distance of one centimeter (0.5 in). This value will vary considerably depending on the part of the body involved. |

cation to a society that is similar to one's own requires less acculturation than moving to a society where cultural norms are unfamiliar. For example, moving to a society where women's roles are different from those of one's home culture can cause feelings of isolation and confusion for the adult women of the **family**.

Acculturation is different in subtle ways from **assimilation**: assimilation involves being absorbed into the new culture. A popular metaphor for this process was introduced in 1908 by the playwright Israel Zangwill with his work, *The Melting Pot*. Acculturation, on the other hand, is the process of learning the practices and customs of a new culture. People can assimilate without being acculturated. The distinctively dressed Hasidim of Brooklyn or the Mormons of Utah are not completely acculturated to contemporary American society, but they are assimilated. Understanding the distinction between acculturation and assimilation is important for public policy and for society's ability to grow and function smoothly.

A homogeneous consumer culture worldwide has changed the nature of acculturation. People all over the globe watch the same news reports on CNN, rent the same movies, watch the same television programs, eat the same pizzas and burgers from fast food franchises, and many of the world's families have made at least one visit to a Disney theme park. Immigrants to a new country may already be very familiar with the customs and lifestyle of their new home.

### Cultural pluralism and multiculturalism

American sociologist Horace Kallen argues that it is unrealistic and counterproductive to force new immigrants to abandon their familiar, lifelong cultural attributes when they arrive in the United States. Instead of the concept of the "melting pot," Kallen prescribed what he called "cultural pluralism." Cultural pluralism views U.S. society as a federation rather than a union. Sometimes referred to as multiculturalism, this approach suggests that each group of ethnic Americans has rights, such as representation in government according to their percentage of the total population, and the right to speak and work in their native language. However, English-language culture and social influences continue to dominate, but African American, Hispanic, Jewish, Italian, Asian, and other ethnic influences are certainly apparent.

### Further Reading

Gordon, Milton Myron. *Assimilation in American Life: The Role of Race, Religion, and National Origins.* New York: Oxford University Press, 1964.

Jacobson, Adam R. "Changing With the Times." *Hispanic* 7, (March 1994): 20+.

Portes, Alejandro and Min Zhou. "Should Immigrants Assimilate?" *The Public Interest*, (Summer 1994): 18+.

Richey, Marilyn. "Global Families: Surviving an Overseas Move." *Management Review* 85, (June 1996): 57+.

Salins, Peter D. *Assimilation, American Style.* New York: Basic Books, 1997.

# Achievement motivation

See **Motivation**

# Achievement tests

Standardized tests, administered to groups of students, intended to measure how well they have learned information in various academic subjects.

Spelling tests, timed arithmetic tests, and map quizzes are all examples of achievement tests. Each measures how well students can demonstrate their knowledge of a particular academic subject or skill. Achievement tests on a small scale like these are administered frequently in schools. Less frequently, students are given more inclusive achievement tests that cover a broader spectrum of information and skills. For instance, many states now require acceptable scores on "proficiency" tests at various grade levels before advancement is allowed. Admission to colleges and graduate studies depends on achievement tests such as the **Scholastic Assessment Test** (SAT), which attempts to measure both aptitude and achievement, the Graduate Record Exam (GRE), the Law School Admissions Test (LSAT), and the Medical College Admissions Test (MCAT). The Iowa Test of Basic Skills (ITBS) and the California Achievement Test (CAT) are examples of achievement tests given to many elementary school students around the United States.

Useful achievement tests must be both reliable and valid. Reliable tests are consistent and reproducible. That is, a student taking a similar test, or the same test at a different time, must respond with a similar performance. Valid tests measure achievement on the subject they are intended to measure. For example, a test intended to measure achievement in arithmetic—but filled with difficult vocabulary—may not measure arithmetic achievement at all. The students who score well on such a test may be those who have good vocabularies or above-average reading **ability** in addition to appropriate arithmetic skills. Students who fail may have achieved the same arithmetic skills, but did not know how to demonstrate them. Such tests would not be considered valid. In order for reliable comparisons to be made, all standardized tests, including achievement tests, must be given under similar conditions and with similar time limitations and scoring procedures. The difficulty of maintaining consistency in these administration procedures makes the reliability of such tests questionable, critics contend.

Many researchers point to another problem with achievement tests. Because it is difficult to distinguish in test form the difference between aptitude—innate ability—and achievement—learned knowledge or skills—the results of tests that purport to measure achievement alone are necessarily invalid to some degree. Also, some children attain knowledge through their experiences, which may assist them in tests of academic achievement. The presence of cultural biases in achievement tests is a frequent topic of discussion among educators, psychologists, and the public at large. Political pressure to produce high scores and the linking of achievement to public funds for schools have also become part of the achievement-test controversy.

Yet further skepticism about achievement test results comes from critics who contend that teachers frequently plan their lessons and teaching techniques to foster success on such tests. This "teaching to the test" technique used by some teachers makes comparisons with other curricula difficult; thus, test scores resulting from the different methods become questionable as well. **Test anxiety** may also create unreliable results. Students who experience excessive anxiety when taking tests may perform below their level of achievement. For them, achievement tests may prove little more than their aversion to test-taking.

### Further Reading

Houts, Paul L., ed. *The Myth of Measurability.* New York: Hart Publishing Co., 1977.

Wallace, Betty, and William Graves. *Poisoned Apple: The Bell-Curve Crisis and How Schools Create Mediocrity and Failure.* New York: St. Martin's Press, 1995.

# Nathan Ward Ackerman

**1908-1971**
Psychologist and educator noted for his work as a family therapist, particularly for his ability to look beyond the traditional assessment of families and to accurately assess the way that family members relate to each other.

Nathan Ward Ackerman was born in Bessarabia, Russia on November 22, 1908. His parents were pharmacist David Ackerman and Bertha (Greenberg) Ackerman. They came to the United States in 1912, and were naturalized in 1920. He was married to Gwendolyn Hill on October 10, 1937. They had two daughters, Jeanne and Deborah.

Ackerman attended a public school in New York City. In 1929 he was awarded a B.A. from Columbia University, and in 1933 earned his M.D. from the same university. After a short spell (1933–34) as an intern at the Montefiore Hospital in New York, he interned at the Menninger Clinic and Sanitorium in Topeka, Kansas. He joined their psychiatric staff in 1935.

He assumed the post of chief psychiatrist at the Menninger Child Guidance Clinic in 1937. For the next fourteen years, Ackerman was also chief psychiatrist to the Jewish Board of Guardians in New York City. During this period, he had numerous positions at a variety of institutions in New York City. Ackerman acted as psychiatrist to the Red Cross Rehabilitation Clinic during World War II, and also worked as a consultant to the department of scientific research when it was first established by Max Horkheimer in 1944. After the war, Ackerman assumed the post of clinical professor of psychiatry at Columbia University, and later lectured at the New York School of Social Work, a part of Columbia University. He also lectured (1944–48) at the Visiting Nurse Service and the Community Service Society.

In addition to his active career in New York City, Ackerman served as visiting professor of psychiatry for a number of universities, including Tulane University and the University of North Carolina. In 1952 Ackerman served as a member of the White House Conference on Children in Washington D.C.

### Pioneers field of family psychology

Ackerman published *The Unity of the Family* and *Family Diagnosis: An Approach to the Preschool Child* in 1938, both of which contributed to the initial promotion of the theory of **family therapy**. In 1950 Ackerman wrote a book on anti-Semitism in collaboration with Marie Jahoda. Sponsored by the American Jewish Committee, *Anti-Semitism and Emotional Disorder, a Psychoanalytic Interpretation* examines and analyzes the phenomenon and offers possible solutions. He went on to write many books during his career, including *The Psychodynamics of Family Life* (1958) and *Treating the Troubled Family* (1966). He coauthored several books, including *Exploring the Base for Family Therapy* and published more than 100 articles in professional journals.

Ackerman is widely acknowledged as a pioneer in his field and credited with developing the concept of family psychology. In 1955 he was the first to initiate a debate on family therapy at a meeting of the American Orthopsychiatric Association, with the intention of opening lines of communication in this new branch of psychiatry. He believed that the mental or physical disposition of one family member would affect other family members, and that often the best way to treat the individual was to treat the family as a whole. In fact he was a very strong advocate of treating the whole family in order to solve the problems of the individual. He devoted most of his career to family **psychotherapy**.

Ackerman's work was deeply appreciated by his peers, as evidenced by the number of awards bestowed upon him. He received the Rudolph Meyer award from the Association for Improvement to Mental Health in 1959. He was also the recipient of the Wilfred Hulse award for group psychotherapy in 1965.

### Founds institute to study the family

In 1960, Ackerman opened the Institute for Family Studies and Treatment, a nonprofit organization devoted to promoting family mental health. The Institute's premise was (and is) that if the family is healthy, the individual will be healthy and ultimately produce a healthier society. Ackerman developed a program for research that greatly furthered the effectiveness of the Institute.

He served as the director of this establishment up until his death, when it was renamed the Nathan W. Ackerman Institute (usually known as the Ackerman Institute) in his honor. The Institute has its own journal, *Family Process,* which was the first ever family therapy journal, started by Ackerman in association with Don Jackson. This journal remains a principal reference for other professionals in the field. Today the Ackerman Institute is considered perhaps the finest facility for family psychology in the world.

In addition to being a fellow of the American Board of Psychiatry and the New York Academy of Medicine, Ackerman was also president (1957–59) of the Association of Psychoanalytic Medicine, as well as a member of the Academy of Child Psychiatry, the American Psychopathalogical Society, and the New York Council of Child Psychiatry.

Ackerman died on June 12, 1971, and was buried in Westchester Hills Cemetery, Hastings on Hudson, New York.

Patricia Skinner

### Further Reading
*Ackerman Institute* www.ackerman.org.

# Acquired Immune Deficiency Syndrome (AIDS)

A progressive, degenerative disease involving several major organ systems, including the immune system and central nervous system. Uniformly fatal, it is associated with human immunodeficiency virus (HIV), a viral infection that progressively weakens the immune system.

Since Acquired Immune Deficiency Syndrome (AIDS) manifests itself in a number of different diseases and conditions, it has been difficult to arrive at a formal definition. In an attempt to standardize the definition of AIDS, the Centers for Disease Control in 1992 included among its diagnostic criteria a count of 200 or fewer CD4T lymphocyte cells per cubic ml of blood (a sign of severe immune system suppression). AIDS was first recognized in 1981 as a cluster of symptoms in homosexual men in New York City and San Francisco. Eventually, similar symptoms were found among intravenous drug users, hemophiliacs, and other recipients of blood transfusions. In 1984, the human immunodeficiency virus (HIV) was isolated and subsequently determined as the probable cause of AIDS.

HIV is transmitted through sexual intercourse, contact with infected blood and blood products, and the **birth** process. However, casual social contact—even if close and prolonged—has not been found to spread HIV. The greatest number of HIV cases are sexually transmitted, through both homosexual and heterosexual intercourse. Screening of donated blood and blood products since 1985 has drastically reduced the risk of transfusion-related HIV. Children may be infected *in utero* or by exposure to blood and vaginal secretions during childbirth. The child of an infected mother has a 25 to 35 percent chance of acquiring the virus.

Persons infected with HIV initially show no symptoms. Within three to six weeks after infection they may exhibit flu-like symptoms that last up to three weeks and resolve spontaneously. According to long-term studies, all or almost all persons infected with HIV eventually become ill with full-blown AIDS, although the incubation period varies from less than a year to as long as 15 years. AIDS is considered full-blown when the immune system is seriously suppressed. At this point, the patient becomes vulnerable to opportunistic infections and diseases that are able to attack because of reduced immune system defenses. These include candiasis, pneumocystis carinii pneumonia (PCP), herpes and other viral infections, toxoplasmosis, and tuberculosis. AIDS also weakens the body's defenses against carcinomas, and conditions such as lymphoma and Kaposi's sarcoma are common complications of the disease. AIDS also attacks the **nervous system**. Neurological disorders such as encephalitis and **dementia** occur in over two-thirds of AIDS patients. HIV/AIDS patients are also prone to blood abnormalities, respiratory infections, and gastrointestinal problems, including diarrhea, which is partly responsible for the weight loss that occurs in the course of the disease.

Comforting a person with AIDS or any other fatal illness is challenging for friends, **family**, and others around him. Isolation is one of the most difficult aspects of this disease, often resulting from misinformation and **fear** about how the disease is spread. There is no scientific evidence that AIDS is spread through casual contact, and there is no reason to avoid gestures of **friendship** and comfort, such as a personal visit, a hug, or holding the patient's hand.

According to the World Health Organization, an estimated five to ten million people worldwide are infected with HIV. The highest incidence of AIDS is in major cities in Asia, Africa, and the United States. In the United States alone, there are thought to be over one million infected with HIV, and over 250,000 cases of full-blown AIDS have been reported. AIDS has become a leading cause of death in men and women under the age of 45 and children under the age of five. Originally thought of as a "gay men's disease," in 1993 AIDS was the nation's fourth leading cause of death in women between the ages of 15 and 44.

HIV is usually diagnosed through a test called ELISA (enzyme-linked immunosorbent assay), which screens the blood for HIV antibodies. If the test is positive, a more specific test, the Western blot assay, is administered. Most patients will test positive for HIV one to three months after being infected, and 95 percent will test positive after five months. There is no effective vaccine against the HIV virus, and no known cure for AIDS, but antiviral drugs have been effective in slowing the progression of the disease, particularly the suppression of the immune system. One of the earliest of these medications to be effective was azidothymidine (AZT), which inhibits viral DNA polymerase.

The best method of containing the AIDS epidemic is education and prevention. Much of the anti-AIDS effort both in the United States and globally has been directed toward promoting safer sex practices, including abstinence (especially among young people) and the use of latex condoms, which greatly reduce the chance of infection. The threat of HIV among intravenous drug users has been addressed by programs offering education, **rehabilitation**, and the free dispension of sterile needles. Modification of sexual behavior among homosexuals has been successful in reducing the incidence of new HIV infections among the gay population. However, risk-re-

lated behavior is increasing among young homosexuals under the mistaken belief that the threat of AIDS applies mostly to older gay men. Risky sexual behavior has also remained widespread among heterosexual teenagers in the 1990s, especially among African-American and Hispanic males.

**Further Reading**

Anonymous. *It Happened to Nancy.* New York: Avon Books, 1994.
*A Conversation With Magic.* Lucky Duck Productions, 1992. Videorecording.
Foster, Carol, et al., eds. *AIDS.* Wylie, TX: Information Plus, 1992.
Siegel, Larry. *AIDS, The Drug and Alcohol Connection.* Center City, MN: Hazelden, 1989.

# Action potential

Behavior that enables an organism to function effectively in its environment.

A momentary electrical event occurring through the membrane of a nerve cell fiber in response to a stimulus, forming a nerve impulse.

An action potential is transmitted along a **nerve** fiber as a wave of changing electrical charge. This wave travels at a speed that ranges from about five feet (1.5 m) per second to about 350 feet (107 m) per second, depending on various properties of the nerve fiber involved and other factors.

An action potential occurs in about one millisecond. During an action potential, there is a change in voltage across the nerve cell membrane of about 120 millivolts, and the negative electrical charge inside the resting nerve cell is reversed to a positive electrical charge. This change in voltage and reversal of electrical charge results from the movement of sodium ions, which carry a positive charge, into the nerve cell fiber. This is followed by the movement of potassium ions, which also carry a positive charge, out of the nerve cell fiber, allowing the nerve cell to return to its resting state. The temporarily increased permeability of the nerve cell fiber membrane, first to sodium ions and then to potassium ions, is caused by a chemical transmitter substance.

**Further Reading**

Adams, Raymond. *Principles of Neurology.* New York: McGraw-Hill, 1993.

# Adaptation

Behavior that enables an organism to function effectively in its environment.

Adaptation describes the process of change in organisms or species to accommodate to a particular **environment**, enabling their survival. Adaptation is crucial to the process of natural selection. Ethologists, scientists who study the behavior of animals in their natural habitats from an evolutionary perspective, have documented two main types of adaptive behavior. Some behaviors, known as "closed programs," transmit from one generation to the next relatively unchanged. "Open genetic programs" involve greater degrees of environmental influence.

Adaptation occurs in individual organisms as well as in species. Sensory adaptation consists of physical changes that occur in response to the presence or cessation of stimuli. Examples include the adjustment eyes make when going from broad daylight into a darkened room and the way bodies adjust to the temperature of cold water after an initial plunge. Once a steady level of stimulation (such as light, sound, or odor) is established, we no longer notice it. However, any abrupt changes require further adaptation.

The adrenalin-produced reaction to environmental dangers called the "fight or flight" syndrome (including rapid breathing, increased heart rate, and sweating) can also be considered a form of adaptation. The psychological responses involved in classical and operant **conditioning**, which involve learned behaviors motivated by either positive **reinforcement** or **fear** of **punishment**, can also be considered adaptation.

**Further Reading**

Bateson, P.P.G. *Perspectives in Ethology: Behavior and Evolution.* New York: Vintage Books, 1993.

Lorenz, Konrad. *The Foundations of Ethology.* New York: Springer-Verlag, 1981.

Weiner, Jonathan. *The Beak of the Finch: A Story of Evolution in Our Time.* New York: Vintage Books, 1995.

# Addiction/Addictive personality

A wide spectrum of complex behaviors that ranges from patterns of behavior to physical addiction.

Addiction has come to refer to a wide and complex range of behaviors. In addition to familiar addictions, such as alcohol dependence, drug dependence, and smoking, addictive behavior has also been associated with food, exercise, work, and even relationships with others (codependency). Some experts describe the spectrum of behaviors designated as addictive in terms of five interrelated concepts: patterns, habits, compulsions, **impulse control disorders**, and physical addiction. Compulsions differ from patterns and habits in that they originate for the purpose of relieving anxiety. Impulse control disorders, such as overeating, constitute a specific type of compulsive behavior that provides short-term gratification but is harmful in the long run. In contrast to these various types of potentially addictive behavior, physical addiction involves dependence on a habit-forming substance characterized by tolerance and well-defined physiological withdrawal symptoms.

In spite of the variety of activities that can be considered addictive, people who engage in them tend to have certain attitudes and types of behavior in common. An addiction is generally associated with relieving anxiety or blocking out other types of uncomfortable feelings. To a greater or lesser extent, people engaged in addictive behavior tend to plan their lives around it; in extreme cases they will do almost anything to obtain the substance or engage in the behavior. The addiction makes them neglect other areas of their lives. They are commonly secretive about it, either out of shame or to protect their access to a substance. When confronted, they generally deny that they have a problem, although privately they regret their addictive behavior, which in many cases they have tried without success to discontinue. They tend to rationalize engaging in the behavior and tell themselves they can stop whenever they want. They may also blame others for their addiction and often experience frequent and uncontrollable **mood** swings.

Substance abuse and dependence (substance-related disorders) are among the psychological disorders in the list of major clinical syndromes (Axis I) found in the **American Psychiatric Association**'s *Diagnostic and Statistical Manual of Mental Disorders*. Alcohol, which is classified as a depressant, is probably the most frequently abused psychoactive substance. Alcohol abuse and dependence affects over 20 million Americans—about 13 percent of the adult population. An alcoholic has been defined as a person whose drinking impairs his or her life adjustment, affecting health, personal relationships, and/or work. Alcohol dependence, sometimes called alcoholism, is about five times more common in men than women, although alcohol abuse by women and by teenagers of both sexes is growing.

When blood alcohol level reaches 0.1 percent, a person is considered to be intoxicated. Judgment and other rational processes are impaired, as well as motor coordination, speech, and **vision**. Alcohol abuse typically progresses through a series of stages from social drinking to chronic alcoholism. Danger signs that indicate the probable onset of a drinking problem include the frequent desire to drink, increased alcohol consumption, **memory** lapses ("blanks"), and morning drinking. Among the most acute reactions to alcohol are four conditions referred to as alcoholic psychoses: alcohol idiosyncratic intoxication (an acute reaction in persons with an abnormally low tolerance for alcohol); alcohol withdrawal **delirium** (delirium tremens); **hallucinations**; and Korsakoff's **psychosis**, an irreversible **brain** disorder involving severe memory loss.

Aside from alcohol, other psychoactive substances most frequently associated with abuse and dependence are barbiturates (which, like alcohol, are depressants); narcotics (opium and its derivatives, including heroin); stimulants (amphetamines and cocaine); antianxiety drugs (tranquilizers such as Librium and Valium); and psychedelics and **hallucinogens** (**marijuana**, mescaline, psilocybin, LSD, and PCP). While drug abuse and dependence can occur at any age, they are most frequent in **adolescence** and early adulthood.

The causes of substance abuse are multiple. Some people are at high risk for dependence due to genetic or physiological factors. Researchers have found the sons of alcoholics to be twice as prone to alcoholism as other people. Among pairs of identical **twins**, if one is an alcoholic, there is a 60 percent chance that the other will be also. In spite of an apparent inherited tendency toward alcoholism, the fact that the majority of people with alcoholic parents do not become alcoholics themselves demonstrates the influence of psychosocial factors, including **personality** factors and a variety of environmental stressors, such as occupational or marital problems.

Variations in the incidence of alcoholism among different ethnic groups show that social learning also plays a role in addiction. Parental influence, especially in terms of **modeling** the use of alcohol and other drugs, has a strong influence on the behavior of children and adolescents, as does peer behavior. Although positive experiences with one drug may lead to experimentation with another, the "stepping stone" theory of drug use— for example, using marijuana leads to the use of hard drugs—is highly speculative as the majority of marijuana smokers do not go on to use other drugs. Only heavy marijuana use has been linked to the use of other drugs.

Not all addictive behavior involves the use of drugs or alcohol. One such potentially life-threatening type of behavior is compulsive overeating associated with **obesity**. While obesity is viewed as a physiological condition in some cases, it is commonly linked to a long-standing pattern of overeating and an addictive relationship to food that can generally be traced to personality factors in combination with learned responses. Another type of non-drug-related addictive behavior is compulsive gambling. While about half of all persons engage in some form of gambling at some point in their lives, compulsive gamblers carry this activity to the extent that it disrupts their lives psychologically and financially.

**Crack users. Crack, a form of cocaine, is one of the most addictive drugs.** *(Photo by Roy Morsch. Stock Market. Reproduced with permission.)*

Addictions are difficult to treat. Addictive behavior often involves long-term psychological problems or ongoing stressors in a person's life. Rates of initial "cure" followed by relapse are very high, and many consider recovery to be an ongoing, lifelong process. Physical addictions alter a person's brain chemistry in ways that make it difficult to be exposed to the addictive substance again without lapsing back into addiction; abstinence is generally necessary for recovery from substance dependency. People addicted to a type of activity—such as compulsive spending or eating—from which it is impossible to abstain entirely must learn to understand and alter their behaviors.

The first step in the recovery process is admitting that there is a problem and seeking help. Biological intervention may be necessary, including medication to treat withdrawal symptoms and treatment for malnutrition. (Many heroin addicts are given methadone, a synthetic opiate that is addictive but less harmful than heroin). There are many kinds of psychological intervention available, offered in forms ranging from counseling to inpatient programs. Among the most effective are **group therapy**; environmental intervention (which deals with negative factors in an addict's social **environment**); **behavior therapy**, including **aversive conditioning**; and 12-step programs based on the approach pioneered by Alcoholics Anonymous.

*See also* Alcohol dependence and abuse; Codependence; Drugs/Drug abuse; Gambling, pathological

### Further Reading
Cohen, Irving A. *Addiction: The High-Low Trap.* Santa Fe, NM: Health Press, 1995.

Engel, Joel. *Addicted: In Their Own Words. Kids Talk About Drugs.* New York: Tom Doherty Associates, 1990.

Porterfield, Kay Marie. *Focus on Addictions: A Reference Handbook.* Santa Barbara: ABC-CLIO, 1992.

# Adjustment disorders

The development of significant emotional or behavioral symptoms in response to an identifiable event that precipitated significant psychological or social stress.

Adjustment disorders are maladpative, or unhealthy, responses to stressful or psychologically distressing life events, such as the end of a romantic relationship or being terminated from a job.

The **American Psychiatric Association** has identified and categorized several varieties of adjustment disorders, depending on accompanying symptoms and their duration. These subtypes include adjustment disorder with depressed **mood**, with anxiety, with anxiety and depressed mood, and with disturbances of conduct. The disorders can additionally be classified as acute or chronic. It is thought that adjustment disorders are fairly common; recent figures estimate that 5 to 20 percent of persons seeking outpatient psychological treatment suffer from one of these disorders. Psychiatrists rigidly define the time frames in which these disorders can occur to differentiate them from other types of responses to stressful events, such as **post-traumatic stress disorder** and acute stress disorder. Adjustment disorders must occur within three months of the stressful event and can, by definition, last no longer than six months.

Symptoms of these various adjustment disorders include a decrease in performance at work or school, and withdrawal from social relationships. These disorders can lead to suicide or suicidal thinking and can complicate the course of other diseases when, for instance, a sufferer loses interest in taking medication as prescribed or adhering to difficult diets or exercise regimens.

Adjustment disorders can occur at any stage of life. In early **adolescence**, individuals with adjustment disorders tend to be angry, aggressive, and defiant. Temper tantrums are common and are usually well out of balance with the event that caused them. Other adolescents with adjustment disorders may, alternately, become passive and withdrawn, and older teens often experience intense anxiety or **depression**. They may experience what psychologists call "depersonalization," a state in which a person feels he or she can observe their body interacting with others, but feels nothing.

Many psychological theorists and researchers consider adjustment disorders in adolescents as a stage in establishing an identity. Adolescents may develop adjustment disorders as part of a **defense mechanism** meant to break their feelings of dependence on their parents. This sort of psychological maneuver may precipitate problems in families as adolescents begin seeking individuals outside the **family** as replacements for their parents. This can be particularly destructive when these feelings of dependence are transferred to involvement with **gangs** or **cults**.

### Further Reading
*Diagnostic and Statistical Manual of Mental Disorders.* 4th ed. Washington, D.C.: American Psychiatric Association, 1994.

Nicholi, Armand, ed. *The New Harvard Guide to Psychiatry.* Cambridge, MA: Harvard University Press, 1988.

"The Not-So Maddening Crowd: Crowding Stress Leads to Coping Behavior in Primates." *Discover* (February 1994): 14.

Shanok, Rebecca. "Coping with Crisis." *Parents Magazine* (October 1991): 169.

# Alfred Adler

**1870-1937**
Psychiatrist known for his theory of individual psychology and for his pioneering work with children and families.

Alfred Adler was born in a suburb of Vienna, Austria, in 1870. After graduating from the University of Vienna medical school in 1895, he at first practiced ophthalmology but later switched to psychiatry. In 1902, Adler joined the discussion group that later became the Vienna Psychoanalytic Society. **Sigmund Freud** was also a member. Adler eventually became president and editor of its journal. After 1907, however, Adler's growing disagreement with Freud's theories, especially with their heavy emphasis on the role of **sexuality** in **personality** formation, alienated him from the ranks of Freudians.

In 1911, Adler and his followers left the Psychoanalytic Society to form their own group, The Society of Individual Psychology, and developed the system of individual psychology, a holistic, humanistic, therapeutic approach. Adlerian psychology views the individual as primarily a social rather than a sexual being and places more emphasis on choices and values than Freudian psychology. Adler saw the individual striving toward perfection and overcoming feelings of inferiority (a concept later popularized as the "**inferiority complex**"). After serving in military hospitals during World War I, Adler became interested in **child psychology**. He established a network of public child guidance clinics in the Vienna school system, offering what was probably the very first **family** counseling. There were 28 of these facilities in operation until the Nazis ordered them closed in 1934. Adlerian parent study groups still meet throughout the United States and Canada.

In 1926 Adler began dividing his time between Vienna and the United States. He was appointed visiting lecturer at Columbia University in New York in 1927. In 1932 he became a lecturer at the Long Island College of Medicine and emigrated to the United States with his wife. Adler died suddenly in 1937 in Aberdeen, Scotland, while on a lecture tour. There are more than 100 professional Adlerian organizations and 34 training institutes in the United States, Canada, and Europe.

### Further Reading

Adler, Alfred. *Co-operation Between the Sexes: Writings on Women and Men, Love and Marriage, and Sexuality.* New York: Norton, 1982.

———. *The Individual Psychology of Alfred Adler: A Systematic Presentation in Selections From His Writings.* New York: Harper & Row, 1964.

**Alfred Adler** *(Archive Photos, Inc. Reproduced with permission.)*

dicate that the percent of the U.S. population between the ages of 14 and 17 will peak around the year 2005.

There is no single event or boundary line that denotes the end of childhood or the beginning of adolescence. Rather, experts think of the passage from childhood into and through adolescence as composed of a *set of transitions* that unfold gradually and that touch upon many aspects of the individual's behavior, development, and relationships. These transitions are biological, cognitive, social, and emotional.

# Adolescence

Sometimes referred to as teenage years, youth, or puberty, adolescence covers the period from roughly age 10 to 20 in a child's development.

In the study of **child development**, adolescence refers to the second decade of the life span, roughly from ages 10 to 20. The word adolescence is Latin in origin, derived from the verb *adolescere,* which means "to grow into adulthood." In all societies, adolescence is a time of growing up, of moving from the immaturity of **childhood** into the maturity of adulthood. Population projections in-

## Puberty

The *biological transition* of adolescence, or **puberty**, is perhaps the most salient sign that adolescence has begun. Technically, puberty refers to the period during which an individual becomes capable of sexual reproduction. More broadly speaking, however, puberty is used as a collective term to refer to all the physical changes that occur in the growing girl or boy as the individual passes from childhood into adulthood.

The timing of physical maturation varies widely. In the United States today, menarche, the first menstrual period, typically occurs around age 12, although some youngsters start puberty when they are only eight or nine, others when they are well into their teens. The duration of puberty also varies greatly: eighteen months to six years in girls and two to five years in boys.

The physical changes of puberty are triggered by **hormones**, chemical substances in the body that act on specific organs and tissues. In boys a major change is the increased production of testosterone, a male sex hormone, while girls experience increased production of the female hormone estrogen. In both sexes, a rise in growth hormone produces the adolescent growth spurt, the pronounced increase in height and weight that marks the first half of puberty.

Perhaps the most dramatic changes of puberty involve **sexuality**. Internally, through the development of primary sexual characteristics, adolescents become capable of sexual reproduction. Externally, as secondary sexual characteristics appear, girls and boys begin to look like mature women and men. In boys primary and secondary sexual characteristics usually emerge in a predictable order, with rapid growth of the testes and scrotum, accompanied by the appearance of pubic hair. About a year later, when the growth spurt begins, the penis also grows larger, and pubic hair becomes coarser, thicker, and darker. Later still comes the growth of facial and body hair, and a gradual lowering of the voice. Around mid-adolescence internal changes begin making a boy capable of producing and ejaculating sperm.

In girls, sexual characteristics develop in a less regular sequence. Usually, the first sign of puberty is a slight elevation of the breasts, but sometimes this is preceded by the appearance of pubic hair. Pubic hair changes from sparse and downy to denser and coarser. Concurrent with these changes is further breast development. In teenage girls, internal sexual changes include maturation of the uterus, vagina, and other parts of the reproductive system. Menarche, the first menstrual period, happens relatively late, not at the start of puberty as many people believe. Regular ovulation and the ability to carry a baby to full term usually follow menarche by several years.

For many years, psychologists believed that puberty was stressful for young people. We now know that any difficulties associated with adjusting to puberty are minimized if adolescents know what changes to expect and have positive attitudes toward them. Although the immediate impact of puberty on the adolescent's self-image and **mood** may be very modest, the *timing* of physical maturation does affect the teen's social and **emotional development** in important ways. Early-maturing boys tend to be more popular, to have more positive self-conceptions, and to be more self-assured than their later-maturing peers, whereas early-maturing girls may feel awkward and self-conscious.

## Cognitive transition

A second element of the passage through adolescence is a *cognitive transition*. Compared to children, adolescents think in ways that are more advanced, more efficient, and generally more complex. This can be seen in five ways.

First, during adolescence individuals become better able than children to think about what is possible, instead of limiting their thought to what is real. Whereas children's thinking is oriented to the here and now—that is, to things and events that they can observe directly, adolescents are able to consider what they observe against a backdrop of what is possible—they can think hypothetically.

Second, during the passage into adolescence, individuals become better able to think about abstract ideas. For example, adolescents find it easier than children to comprehend the sorts of higher-order, abstract logic inherent in puns, proverbs, metaphors, and analogies. The adolescent's greater facility with abstract thinking also permits the application of advanced reasoning and logical processes to social and ideological matters. This is clearly seen in the adolescent's increased facility and interest in thinking about interpersonal relationships, politics, philosophy, religion, and morality—topics that involve such abstract concepts as **friendship**, faith, democracy, fairness, and honesty.

Third, during adolescence individuals begin thinking more often about the process of thinking itself, or metacognition. As a result, adolescents may display increased introspection and self-consciousness. Although improvements in metacognitive abilities provide important intellectual advantages, one potentially negative by-product of these advances is the tendency for adolescents to develop a sort of egocentrism, or intense preoccupation with the self. Acute adolescent egocentrism sometimes leads teenagers to believe that others are constantly watching and evaluating them, much as an audience glues its **attention** to an actor on a stage. Psychologists refer to this as the *imaginary audience*.

A fourth change in **cognition** is that thinking tends to become multidimensional, rather than limited to a single issue. Whereas children tend to think about things one aspect at a time, adolescents can see things through more complicated lenses. Adolescents describe themselves and others in more differentiated and complicated terms and find it easier to look at problems from multiple perspectives. Being able to understand that people's personalities are not one-sided, or that social situations can have different interpretations, depending on one's point of view, permits the adolescent to have far more sophisticated—and complicated—relationships with other people.

Finally, adolescents are more likely than children to see things as relative, rather than absolute. Children tend to see things in absolute terms—in black and white. Adolescents, in contrast, tend to see things as relative. They are more likely to question others' assertions and less likely to accept "facts" as absolute truths. This increase in relativism can be particularly exasperating to parents, who may feel that their adolescent children question everything just for the sake of argument. Difficulties often arise, for example, when adolescents begin seeing their parents' values as excessively relative.

## Emotional transition

In addition to being a time of biological and cognitive change, adolescence is also a period of *emotional transition* and, in particular, changes in the way individuals view themselves and in their capacity to function independently.

During adolescence, important shifts occur in the way individuals think about and characterize themselves—that is, in their self-conceptions. As individuals mature intellectually and undergo the sorts of cognitive changes described earlier, they come to perceive themselves in more sophisticated and differentiated ways. Compared with children, who tend to describe themselves in relatively simple, concrete terms, adolescents are more likely to employ complex, abstract, and psychological self-characterizations. As individuals' self-conceptions become more abstract and as they become more able to see themselves in psychological terms, they become more interested in understanding their own personalities and why they behave the way they do.

Conventional wisdom holds that adolescents have low **self-esteem** —that they are more insecure and self-critical than children or adults—but most research indicates otherwise. Although teenagers' feelings about themselves may fluctuate, especially during early adolescence, their self-esteem remains fairly stable from about age 13 on. If anything, self-esteem increases over the course of middle and late adolescence. Most researchers today believe that self-esteem is multidimensional, and that young people evaluate themselves along several different dimensions. As a consequence, it is possible for an adolescent to have high self-esteem when it comes to his academic abilities, low self-esteem when it comes to athletics, and moderate self-esteem when it comes to his physical appearance.

One theorist whose work has been very influential on our understanding of adolescents' self-conceptions is **Erik Erikson**, who theorized that the establishment of a coherent sense of identity is the chief psychosocial task of adolescence. Erikson believed that the complications inherent

**During adolescence, most American girls experiment with make-up.** *(Photo by Robert J. Huffman. Field Mark Publications. Reproduced with permission.)*

in identity development in modern society have created the need for a psychosocial moratorium—a time-out during adolescence from the sorts of excessive responsibilities and obligations that might restrict the young person's pursuit of self-discovery. During the psychosocial moratorium, the adolescent can experiment with different roles and identities, in a context that permits and encourages this sort of exploration. The experimentation involves trying on different personalities and ways of behaving. Sometimes, parents describe their teenage children as going through "phases." Much of this behavior is actually experimentation with roles and personalities.

For most adolescents, establishing a sense of autonomy, or independence, is as important a part of the emotional transition out of childhood as is establishing a sense of identity. During adolescence, there is a movement away from the dependency typical of childhood toward the autonomy typical of adulthood. One can see this in several ways.

First, older adolescents do not generally rush to their parents whenever they are upset, worried, or in need of assistance. Second, they do not see their parents as all-knowing or all-powerful. Third, adolescents often have a great deal of emotional energy wrapped up in relationships outside the **family**; in fact, they may feel more attached to a boyfriend or a girlfriend than to their parents. And finally, older adolescents are able to see and interact with their parents as people—not just as their parents. Many parents find, for example, that they can confide in

Adolescence

their adolescent children, something that was not possible when their children were younger, or that their adolescent children can easily sympathize with them when they have had a hard day at work.

Some theorists have suggested that the development of independence be looked at in terms of the adolescent's developing sense of individuation. The process of individuation, which begins during **infancy** and continues well into late adolescence, involves a gradual, progressive sharpening of one's sense of self as autonomous, as competent, and as separate from one's parents. Individuation, therefore, has a great deal to do with the development of a sense of identity, in that it involves changes in how we come to see and feel about ourselves.

The process of individuation does not necessarily involve **stress** and internal turmoil. Rather, individuation entails relinquishing childish dependencies on parents in favor of more mature, more responsible, and less dependent relationships. Adolescents who have been successful in establishing a sense of individuation can accept responsibility for their choices and actions instead of looking to their parents to do it for them.

Being independent means more than merely *feeling* independent, of course. It also means being able to make your own decisions and to select a sensible course of action by yourself. This is an especially important capability in contemporary society, where many adolescents are forced to become independent decision makers at an early age. In general, researchers find that decision-making abilities improve over the course of the adolescent years, with gains continuing well into the later years of high school.

Many parents wonder about the susceptibility of adolescents to **peer pressure**. In general, studies that contrast parent and peer influences indicate that in some situations, peers' opinions are more influential, while in others, parents' are more influential. Specifically, adolescents are more likely to conform to their peers' opinions when it comes to short-term, day-to-day, and social matters—styles of dress, tastes in music, and choices among leisure activities. This is particularly true during junior high school and the early years of high school. When it comes to long-term questions concerning educational or occupational plans, however, or values, religious beliefs, and ethical issues, teenagers are influenced in a major way by their parents.

Susceptibility to the influence of parents and peers changes with development. In general, during childhood, boys and girls are highly oriented toward their parents and less so toward their peers; peer pressure during the early elementary school years is not especially strong. As they approach adolescence, however, children become somewhat less oriented toward their parents and more oriented toward their peers, and peer pressure begins to escalate. During early adolescence, **conformity** to parents continues to decline and conformity to peers and peer pressure continues to rise. It is not until middle adolescence, then, that genuine behavioral independence emerges, when conformity to parents as well as peers declines.

### Social transition

Accompanying the biological, cognitive, and emotional transitions of adolescence are important changes in the adolescent's social relationships, or the *social transition of adolescence*. Developmentalists have spent considerable time charting the changes that take place with friends and with family members as the individual moves through the adolescent years.

One of the most noteworthy aspects of the social transition into adolescence is the increase in the amount of time individuals spend with their peers. Although relations with agemates exist well before adolescence, during the teenage years they change in significance and structure. Four specific developments stand out.

First, there is a sharp increase during adolescence in the sheer amount of time individuals spend with their peers and in the relative time they spend in the company of peers versus adults. In the United States, well over half of the typical adolescent's waking hours are spent with peers, as opposed to only 15% with adults—including parents. Second, during adolescence, peer groups function much more often without adult supervision than they do during childhood. Third, during adolescence increasingly more contact with peers is with opposite-sex friends.

Finally, whereas children's peer relationships are limited mainly to pairs of friends and relatively small groups—three or four children at a time, for example—adolescence marks the emergence of larger groups of peers, or crowds. Crowds are large collectives of similarly stereotyped individuals who may or may not spend much time together. In contemporary American high schools, typical crowds are "jocks," "brains," "nerds," "populars," "druggies," and so on. In contrast to **cliques**, crowds are not settings for adolescents' intimate interactions or friendships, but, instead, serve to locate the adolescent (to himself and to others) within the social structure of the school. As well, the crowds themselves tend to form a sort of social hierarchy or map of the school, and different crowds are seen as having different degrees of status or importance.

The importance of peers during early adolescence coincides with changes in individuals' needs for intimacy. As children begin to share secrets with their friends, a new sense of loyalty and commitment grows, a belief that friends can trust each other. During adolescence, the search for intimacy intensifies, and self-disclosure between best friends becomes an important pastime. Teenagers, especially girls, spend hours discussing their innermost thoughts and feelings, trying to understand one another. The discovery that they tend to think and feel the same as someone else becomes another important basis of friendship.

One of the most important social transitions that takes place in adolescence concerns the emergence of sexual and romantic relationships. In contemporary society, most young people begin dating sometime during early adolescence.

Dating during adolescence can mean a variety of different things, from group activities that bring males and females together (without much actual contact between the sexes); to group dates, in which a group of boys and girls go out jointly (and spend part of the time as couples and part of the time in large groups); to casual dating as couples; and to serious involvement with a steady boyfriend or girlfriend. More adolescents have experience in mixed-sex group activities like parties or dances than dating, and more have experience in dating than in having a serious boyfriend or girlfriend.

Most adolescents' first experience with sex falls into the category of "autoerotic behavior"—sexual behavior that is experienced alone. The most common autoerotic activities reported by adolescents are erotic fantasies and masturbation. By the time most adolescents have reached high school, they have had some experience with sex in the context of a relationship. About half of all American teenagers have had sexual intercourse by the time of high school graduation.

Estimates of the prevalence of sexual intercourse among American adolescents vary considerably from study to study, depending on the nature of the sample surveyed and the year and region in which the study was undertaken. Although regional and ethnic variations make it difficult to generalize about the "average" age at which American adolescents initiate sexual intercourse, national surveys of young people indicate that more adolescents are sexually active at an earlier age today than in the recent past.

For many years, researchers studied the psychological and social characteristics of adolescents who engaged in premarital sex, assuming that sexually active teenagers were more troubled than their peers. This view has been replaced as sexual activity has become more prevalent. Indeed, several recent studies show that sexual activity during adolescence is decidedly not associated with psychological disturbance.

Although it is incorrect to characterize adolescence as a time when the family ceases to be important, or as a time of inherent and inevitable family conflict, early adolescence is a period of significant change and reorganization in family relationships. In most families, there is a movement during adolescence from patterns of influence and interaction that are asymmetrical and unequal to ones in which parents and their adolescent children are on a more equal footing. Family relationships change most around the time of puberty, with increasing conflict between adolescents and their parents—especially between adolescents and their mothers—and closeness between adolescents and their parents diminishing somewhat. Changes in the ways adolescents view family rules and regulations, especially, may contribute to increased disagreement between them and their parents.

Although puberty seems to distance adolescents from their parents, it is not associated with familial "storm and stress," however. Family conflict during this stage is more likely to take the form of bickering over day-to-day issues than outright fighting. Similarly, the diminished closeness is more likely to be manifested in increased privacy on the part of the adolescent and diminished physical affection between teenagers and parents, rather than any serious loss of love or respect between parents and children. Research suggests that this distancing is temporary, though, and that family relationships may become less conflicted and more intimate during late adolescence.

Generally speaking, most young people are able to negotiate the biological, cognitive, emotional, and social transitions of adolescence successfully. Although the mass media bombard us with images of troubled youth, systematic research indicates that the vast majority of individuals move from childhood into and through adolescence without serious difficulty.

Laurence Steinberg, Ph.D.

**Further Reading**

Feldman, S., and G. Elliott, eds. *At the Threshold: The Developing Adolescent.* Cambridge: Harvard University Press, 1990.

Pipher, Mary. *Reviving Ophelia.* New York: Ballantine Books, 1994.

Steinberg, L. *Adolescence.* 4th ed. New York: McGraw-Hill, 1996.

Steinberg, L., and A. Levine. *You and Your Adolescent: A Parent's Guide for Ages 10 to 20.* New York: HarperPerennial, 1991.

# Adoption

A practice in which an adult assumes the role of parent for a child who is not his or her biological offspring.

An adult assumes the role of parent for a child other than his or her own biological offspring in the process of adoption. Informal adoptions occur when a relative or stepparent assumes permanent parental responsibilities without court involvement. However, legally recognized adoptions require a court or other government agency to award permanent custody of a child (or, occasionally, an older individual) to adoptive parents. Specific requirements for adoption vary among states and countries. Adoptions can be privately arranged through individuals or agencies, or arranged through a public agency such as a state's child protective services. Adoptees may be infants or older children; they may be adopted singly or as sibling groups; and they may come from the local area or from other countries. Adoptive parents may be traditional married couples, but they may also be single men or women or non-traditional couples. Parents may be childless or have other children.

Adoption is a practice that dates to ancient times, although there have been fundamental changes in the process. Ancient Romans, for example, saw adoption as a way of ensuring male heirs to childless couples so that **family** lines and religious traditions could be maintained. In contrast, modern American adoption laws are written in support of the best interests of the child, not of the adopter.

Modern American adoption laws evolved during the latter half of the 19th century, prompted by changes due to the Industrial Revolution, large numbers of immigrant children who were often in need of care, and a growing concern for child welfare. Because of the poor health conditions in the tenements of large cities, many children were left on their own at early ages. These dependent children were sometimes placed in almshouses with the mentally ill, and sometimes in foundling homes plagued by high mortality rates. In the 1850s the Children's Aid Society of New York City began to move dependent children out of city institutions. Between 1854 and 1904 orphan trains carried an estimated 100,000 children to the farms of the Midwest where they were placed with families and generally expected to help with farm work in exchange for care.

Massachusetts became the first state to pass legislation mandating judicial supervision of adoptions in 1851, and by 1929 all states had passed some type of adoption legislation. During the early part of the 20th century it was standard practice to conduct adoptions in secret and with records sealed, in part to protect the parties involved from the social stigma of illegitimate **birth**. After WWI two factors combined to increase interest in the adoption of infants. The development of formula feeding allowed for the raising of infants without a ready supply of breast milk, and psychological theory and research about the relative importance of training and **condition-** ing in child rearing eased the concerns of childless couples about potential "bad seeds." Because of the burgeoning interest in infant adoptions, many states legislated investigations of prospective adoptive parents and court approval prior to finalization of the adoption.

Until about mid-century the balance of infant supply and parent demand was roughly equal. However during the 1950s the demand for healthy white infants began to outweigh the supply. Agencies began to establish matching criteria in an attempt to provide the best fit between characteristics of the child or birth parents and the adoptive parents, matching on items such as appearance, ethnicity, education, and religious **affiliation**. By the 1970s it was not uncommon for parents to wait 3-5 years after their initial application to a private adoption agency before they had a healthy infant placed with them. These trends resulted from a decrease in the numbers of infants surrendered for adoption following the increased availability of birth control, the legalization of **abortion**, and the increasingly common decision of unmarried mothers to keep their infants.

In response to this dearth of healthy, same-race infants, prospective adoptive parents turned increasingly to international and transracial adoptions. Children from Japan and Europe began to be placed with American families by agencies after WWII, and since the 1950s Korea has been the major source of international adoptions (except in 1991 with the influx of Romanian children). The one child policy of the Chinese government has provided a new source of infants to American families, and recently many adoptees have come from Peru, Colombia, El Salvador, Mexico, the Philippines, and India.

The civil rights movement of the 1960s was accompanied by an increase in the number of transracial adoptions involving black children and white parents. These adoptions peaked in 1971, and one year later the National Association of Black Social Workers issued a statement opposing transracial adoption. They argued that white families were unable to foster the growth of psychological and cultural identity in black children. Transracial adoptions now account for a small percentage of all adoptions, and these most frequently involve Korean-born children and white American families.

While healthy infants have been much in demand for adoption during the last 50 years, the number of other children waiting for adoptive homes has grown. In response, the U.S. Congress passed the federal Adoption Assistance Child Welfare Act (Public Law 96-272) in 1980, giving subsidies to families adopting children with special needs that typically make a child hard to place. Although individual states may define the specific parameters, these characteristics include older age, medical disabilities, minority group status, and certain physical, mental, or emotional needs.

## Types of adoption

Adoption arrangements are typically thought of as either closed or open. Actually, they may involve many varying degrees of openness about identity and contact between the adoptive family and the birth family. At one extreme is the closed adoption in which an intermediary third party is the only one who knows the identity of both the birth and adoptive parents. The child may be told he or she is adopted, but will have no information about his or her biological heritage. When the stigma attached to births out of wedlock was greater, most adoptions were closed and records permanently sealed; however, a move to open records has been promoted by groups of both adoptees and by some birth mothers. Currently about half of the states allow access to sealed records with the mutual consent of adoptee and birth parent, and others have search processes through intermediary parties available. Why search? Some research and clinical observation suggests that, especially during **adolescence**, healthy identity formation depends on full awareness of one's origins (Where do I get my freckles? Why do I have this musical **ability**? Why did they give me up?). Other important medical history may be critical to the adoptee's health care planning. For birth mothers, sometimes they simply want to know that their child turned out okay.

The move to open records lead to an increase in open adoptions in which information is shared from the beginning. Open adoptions may be completely open, as is the case when the birth parents (usually the mother) and adoptive parents meet beforehand and agree to maintain contact while the child is growing up. The child then has full knowledge of both sets of parents.

Other open adoptions may include less contact, or periodic letters sent to an intermediary agency, or continued contact with some family members but not others. It can be a complex issue. In the case of an older child who is removed from the family by protective services because of abuse or neglect, the child clearly knows his birth parents as well as any other siblings. If these siblings are also removed and placed in different adoptive homes, it may be decided that periodic visits between the the children—once every few months, perhaps—should be maintained, but that contact with the abusive parents should be terminated until the child reaches adulthood and may choose to search. Siblings may know each other's placements, but the birth parents may have no knowledge of the children's whereabouts. However, if a child is ultimately adopted by the foster family with whom he or she was initially placed prior to the termina-

tion of parental rights or visitation, then the birth parents might have knowledge of the child's placement and whereabouts even though continued contact may not be deemed in the best interests of the child.

Children removed from families for protective issues are sometimes reunited with their parents after a stay in temporary foster homes and after the parents have had the chance to rehabilitate and are able to care adequately for their children. On the other hand, it may be decided that reunification is not a feasible objective for a particular family and a permanent home is then sought. The foster family then plays a major role in the child's transition to his or her "forever family." The desire to provide children with permanent homes and the resulting sense of security and **attachment** as soon as possible gives rise to another type of adoption, the legal risk adoption.

Legal risk adoptions involve placement in the prospective adoptive home prior to the legal termination of parental rights and subsequent freeing of the child for adoption. In these cases, child protective services are generally involved and relatively certain that the courts will ultimately decide in favor of the adoptive placement. The legal process can be drawn out if birth parents contest the agency's petition for termination. Although there is the risk that the adoption may not be finalized and that the child will be returned to his or her birth parents, social service agencies generally do not recommend such placements unless, in their best judgments, the potential benefits to child and family far outweigh the legal risk.

Whether the child is free for adoption or a legal risk placement, there is generally a waiting period before the adoption is finalized or recognized by the courts. Although estimates vary, about 10% of adoptions disrupt, that is, the child is removed from the family before finalization. This figure has risen with the increase in older and special needs children being placed for adoption. The risk of disruption increases with the age of the child at placement, a history of multiple placements prior to the adoptive home, and acting-out behavior problems. Interestingly, many children who have experienced disruption go on to be successfully adopted, suggesting that disruption is often a bad fit between parental expectations, skills, or resources and the child's needs. Many agencies conduct parent support groups for adoptive families, and some states have instituted training programs to alert prospective adoptive parents to the challenges—as well as the rewards—of adopting special needs children, thereby attempting to minimize the risk of disruption.

## Who gets adopted?

Estimating the total number of children adopted in the United States is difficult because private and independent adoptions are reported only voluntarily to census centers. According to the National Committee for Adoption, there were just over 100,000 domestic adoptions in the U.S. in 1986, roughly an even split between related and unrelated adoptions. Of unrelated domestic adoptees, about 40% were placed by public agencies, 30% by private agencies, and 30% by private individuals. Almost half of these adoptees were under the age of two, and about one-quarter had special needs. There were also just over 10,000 international adoptions, the majority of these children under the age of two and placed by private agencies.

The American Public Welfare Association has collected data through the Voluntary Cooperative Information System on children in welfare systems across the U.S. who are somewhere in the process of being adopted. Of children in the public welfare systems, about one-third had their adoptions finalized in 1988, one-third were living in their adoptive home waiting for finalization, and one-third were awaiting adoptive placements. Key statistics on these adoptions appear in the accompanying table.

Adoptions may be arranged privately through individuals, or a public or private agency may be involved. Although adopting parents may have certain expenses if the adoption is privately arranged, adoptions are assumed to be a gratuitous exchange by law. No parties may profit improperly from adoption arrangements and children are not to be brokered. The objectives of public and private agencies can differ somewhat. Private agencies generally have prospective adoptive parents as their clients and the agency works to find a child for them. Public agencies, on the other hand, have children as their clients and the procurement of parents as their primary mission.

## Outcomes of adoption

There is general agreement that children who are adopted and raised in families do better than children raised in institutions or raised with birth parents who are neglectful or abusive. Compared to the general population, however, the conclusions are less robust and the interpretation of the statistics is not clear. Adopted adolescents, for example, receive **mental health** services more often than their non-adopted peers, but this may be because adoptive families are more likely to seek helping services or because once referring physicians or counselors know that a child is adopted they assume there are likely to be problems warranting professional attention.

When adjustment problems are manifested by adoptees, they tend to occur around school age or during adolescence. D. M. Brodzinsky and his colleagues have conducted a series of studies from which they conclude that adopted infants and toddlers generally do not differ from non-adopted youngsters, but greater risks for problems such as **aggression** or **depression** emerge as the 5-7-year-old child begins to understand the salience and implications of being adopted. Still, it should be noted that *the absolute incidence of adjustment problems in adoptees is low even though it may be statistically higher than the corresponding figures for non-adoptees.*

In the course of **normal** development, adolescence is seen as a time of identity formation and emerging independence. Adopted adolescents are faced with the challenge of integrating disparate sources of identity— their biological origins and their family of rearing—as they establish themselves as individuals. For some this is a difficult task and may result in rebellious or depressive behavior, risks for all adolescents. Many adoption experts feel that families who do not acknowledge the child's birth heritage from the beginning may increase the likelihood that their child will experience an especially difficult adolescence.

Problems associated with adoption may not always be the result of psychological adjustment to adoption status or a reflection of less than optimal family dynamics. **Attention deficit/hyperactivity disorder (ADHD)** was found to be more prevalent in adoptees than non-adoptees, both among children adopted as infants and children removed from the home at older ages. C. K. Deutsch suggests that ADHD in children adopted as infants may be genetically inherited from the birth parents and perhaps reflected in the impulsive behavior that resulted in the child's birth in the first place. In the case of children who have been removed from the home because of the trauma of abuse, the hypervigilance used to cope with a threatening **environment** may compromise the child's ability to achieve normal attention regulation

Many of the studies addressing the outcomes of adoption fail to consider important factors such as the pre-placement history of the child, the structure and dynamic of the adopting family, or the courses of individual children's development. Many studies are cross-sectional rather than longitudinal by design, meaning that different groups of children at different ages are studied rather than the same children being followed over a period of time. It is also difficult to establish what control or comparison groups should be used. Should adopted children be compared to other children in the types of families into which they have been adopted or should they be compared to children in the types of families from which they have been surrendered? These are complex issues because adoptees are a heterogeneous group, and it is as important to understand their individual differences as it is their commonalities.

Doreen Arcus, Ph.D.

## Further Reading

Brodzinsky, D. M., and M. D. Schechter, eds. *The Psychology of Adoption*. New York: Oxford University Press, 1990.

Brodzinsky, D. M. "Long-Term Outcomes in Adoption." *The Future of Children* 3, 1993, pp. 153-66.

Caplan. L. *An Open Adoption*. Boston: Houghton-Mifflin, 1990.

Deutsch, D. K., J. M. Swanson, and J. H. Bruell. "Overrepresentation of Adoptees in Children with Attention Deficit Disorder." *Behavior Genetics* 12, 1982, pp. 231-37.

Lancaster, K. *Keys to Adopting a Child*. Hauppauge, NY: Barron's Educational Series, 1994.

Melina, L. R. *Making Sense of Adoption*. New York: Harper & Row, 1989.

National Committee for Adoption (NCFA). *1989 Adoption Factbook*. Washington, DC: National Committee for Adoption, 1989.

Stolley, K. S. "Statistics on Adoption in the United States." *The Future of Children* 3, pp. 26-42.

Tatara, T. *Characteristics of Children in Substitute and Adoptive Care: A Statistical Summary of the VCIS National Child Welfare Base*. Washington, DC: American Public Welfare Association, 1992.

## Further Information

AASK (Adopt A Special Kid). 2201 Broadway, Suite 702, Oakland, CA 94612, (510) 451–1748.

Adopted Child. P.O. Box 9362, Moscow, ID 83842, (208) 882–1794, fax: (208) 883–8035.

Adoptive Families of America. 3333 North Highway 100, Minneapolis, MN 55422, (800) 372–3300.

American Adoption Congress. 1000 Connecticut Ave., N.W., Suite 9, Washington, DC 20036, (202) 483–3399 (Public information center.)

Child Welfare League of America. P.O. Box 7816, 300 Raritan Center Pkwy, Edison, NJ 08818-7816, (800) 407–6273.

National Adoption Center. 1500 Walnut Street, Philadelphia, PA 19102 (Provides information especially with regard to special needs adoption.)

National Adoption Information Clearinghouse. 11426 Rockville Pike, Rockville, MD 20852, (202) 842–1919 (Resource for information and referral. Maintains copies of all state and federal adoption laws, including Public Law 96-272, *The Adoption Assistance and Child Welfare Act of 1980*.)

National Council for Single Adoptive Parents. P.O. Box 15084, Chevy Chase, MD 20825, (202) 966–6367.

# Affective disorders

See **Bipolar disorder; Depression; Mania**

# Affect

A psychological term for an observable expression of emotion.

A person's affect is the expression of **emotion** or feelings displayed to others through facial expressions, hand gestures, voice tone, and other emotional signs such as laughter or tears. Individual affect fluctuates according to emotional state. What is considered a **normal** range of affect, called the *broad effect*, varies from culture to culture, and even within a culture. Certain individuals may gesture prolifically while talking, and display dramatic facial expressions in reaction to social situations or other stimuli. Others may show little outward response to social environments, expressing a narrow range of emotions to the outside world.

Persons with psychological disorders may display variations in their affect. A *restricted* or *constricted affect* describes a mild restriction in the range or intensity of display of feelings. As the reduction in display of emotion becomes more severe, the term *blunted affect* may be applied. The absence of any exhibition of emotions is described as *flat affect* where the voice is monotone, the face expressionless, and the body immobile. *Labile affect* describes emotional instability or dramatic **mood** swings. When the outward display of emotion is out of context for the situation, such as laughter while describing **pain** or sadness, the affect is termed inappropriate.

*See also* Mood

## Further Reading

Moore, Bert S. and Alice M. Isen, eds. *Affect and Social Behavior*. New York: Cambridge University Press, 1990.

Thayer, S. *The Origin of Everyday Moods*. New York Oxford University Press, 1995.

# Affiliation

The need to form attachments to other people for support, guidance, and protection.

The need to form attachments with others is termed affiliation. **Attachment** is one of 20 psychological needs measured by the **Thematic Apperception Test**, a projective **personality** test developed at Harvard University in 1935 by **Henry Murray**. Subjects look at a series of up to 20 pictures of people in a variety of recognizable settings and construct a story about what is happening in each one. The need for affiliation (referred

**Facial expressions are an important part of a person's affect.** *(Photo by Robert J. Huffman. Field Mark Publications. Reproduced with permission.)*

to as "n Aff") is scored when a test-taker's response to one of the pictures demonstrates concern over "establishing, maintaining, or restoring a positive affective relationship with another person." In the hierarchy of needs outlined by **Abraham Maslow**, the need for affiliation (or "belongingness") appears midway between the most basic physical needs and the highest-level need for **self-actualization**.

Anxiety has been observed to strengthen one's need for affiliation. In addition, females generally show a higher need for affiliation than males. Traditionally, affiliation has been negatively correlated with achievement. While achievement centers on one's personal self-improvement, affiliation focuses on concern for others, even to the extent of deliberately suppressing competitive tendencies or accomplishments that may make others less comfortable.

**Further Reading**

Harvey, Terri L., Ann L. Orbuch, and John H. Weber, eds. *Attributions, Accounts, and Close Relationships.* New York: Springer-Verlag, 1992.

Meinhold, Patricia. *Child Psychology: Development and Behavior Analysis.* Dubuque, IA: Kendall/Hunt, 1993.

# Aggression

Any act that is intended to cause pain, suffering, or damage to another person.

Aggressive behavior is often used to claim status, precedent, or access to an object or territory. While aggression is primarily thought of as physical, verbal attacks aimed at causing psychological harm also constitute aggression. In addition, fantasies involving hurting others can also be considered aggressive. The key component in aggression is that it is deliberate—accidental injuries are not forms of aggression.

Theories about the nature and causes of aggression vary widely in their emphases. Those with a biological orientation are based on the idea that aggression is an innate human **instinct** or drive. **Sigmund Freud** explained aggression in terms of a death wish or instinct (Thanatos) that is turned outward toward others in a process called displacement. Aggressive impulses that are not channeled toward a specific person or group may be expressed indirectly through safe, socially acceptable activities such as sports, a process referred to in psychoanalytic theory as **catharsis**. Biological theories of aggression have also been advanced by ethologists, researchers who study the behavior of animals in their natural environments. Several have advanced views about aggression in humans based on their observations of animal behavior. The view of aggression as an innate instinct common to both humans and animals was popularized in three widely read books of the 1960s—*On Aggression* by **Konrad Lorenz**, *The Territorial Imperative* by Robert Ardrey, and *The Naked Ape* by Desmond Morris. Like Freud's Thanatos, the aggressive instinct postulated by these authors builds up spontaneously—with or without outside provocation—until it is likely to be discharged with minimal or no provocation from outside stimuli.

Today, instinct theories of aggression are largely discredited in favor of other explanations. One is the frustration-aggression hypothesis first set forth in the 1930s by John Dollard, Neal Miller, and several colleagues. This theory proposes that aggression, rather than occurring spontaneously for no reason, is a response to the frustration of some goal-directed behavior by an outside source. Goals may include such basic needs as food, water, **sleep**, sex, love, and recognition. Contributions to frustration-aggression research in the 1960s by Leonard Berkowitz further established that an environmental stimulus must produce not just frustration but **anger** in order for aggression to follow, and that the anger can be the result of stimuli other than frustrating situations (such as verbal abuse).

In contrast to instinct theories, **social learning theory** focuses on aggression as a learned behavior. This approach stresses the roles that social influences, such as models and **reinforcement**, play in the acquisition of aggressive behavior. The work of **Albert Bandura**, a prominent researcher in the area of social learning, has demonstrated that aggressive behavior is learned through a combination of **modeling** and reinforcement. Children are influenced by observing aggressive behavior in their parents and peers, and in cultural forms such as movies, television, and comic books. While research has shown that the behavior of live models has a more powerful effect than that of characters on screen, film and television are still pervasive influences on behavior. Quantitative studies have found that network television averages 10 violent acts per hour, while on-screen deaths in movies such as *Robocop* and *Die Hard* range from 80 to 264. Some have argued that this type of **violence** does not cause violence in society and may even have a beneficial cathartic effect. However, correlations have been found between the viewing of violence and increased interpersonal aggression, both in **childhood** and, later, in **adolescence**. In addition to its modeling function, viewing vio-

lence can elicit aggressive behavior by increasing the viewer's arousal, desensitizing viewers to violence, reducing restraints on aggressive behavior, and distorting views about **conflict resolution**.

As Bandura's research demonstrates, what is crucial in the modeling of violence—both live and on screen—is seeing not only that aggressive behavior occurs, but also that it works. If the violent parent, playmate, or superhero is rewarded rather than punished for violent behavior, that behavior is much more likely to serve as a positive model: a child will more readily imitate a model who is being rewarded for an act than one who is being punished. In this way, the child can learn without actually being rewarded or punished himself—a concept known as vicarious learning.

The findings of social learning theory address not only the acquisition, but also the instigation, of aggression. Once one has learned aggressive behavior, what environmental circumstances will activate it? The most obvious are adverse events, including not only frustration of desires but also verbal and physical assaults. Modeling, which is important in the learning of aggression, can play a role in instigating it as well. Seeing other people act in an aggressive manner, especially if they are not punished for it, can remove inhibitions against acting aggressively oneself. If the modeled behavior is rewarded, the reward can act vicariously as an incentive for aggression in the observer. In addition, modeled aggression may serve as a source of emotional arousal.

Some aggression is motivated by reward: aggressive behavior can be a means of obtaining what one wants. Another motive for aggression is, paradoxically, obedience. People have committed many violent acts at the bidding of another, in both military and civilian life. Other possible motivating factors include stressors in one's physical **environment**, such as crowding, noise, and temperature, and the delusions resulting from **mental illness**. In addition to the acquisition and instigation of aggression, various types of reinforcement, both direct and vicarious, help determine whether aggression is maintained or discontinued.

Researchers have attempted to learn whether certain childhood characteristics are predictors of aggression in adults. **Traits** found to have connections with aggressive behavior in adulthood include maternal deprivation, lack of identification with one's father, **pyromania**, cruelty to animals, and parental abuse. A 22-year **longitudinal study** found patterns of aggression to be established by the age of eight—the aggressive behavior of both boys and girls at this age was a strong predictor of their future aggression as adults. Other factors cited in the same study include the father's upward social mobility, the child's degree of identification with parents, and preference for violent television programs.

*See also* Television and aggression

**Further Reading**
*Aggression and Peacefulness in Humans and Other Primates.* New York: Oxford University Press, 1992.
*Aggressive Behavior: Current Perspectives.* New York: Plenum Press, 1994.
Bandura, Albert. *Aggression: A Social Learning Analysis.* New York: Prentice-Hall, 1973.
*Of Mice and Women: Aspects of Female Aggression.* New York: Academic Press, 1992.

# Aging

The process by which the human body changes and matures over time, especially the means by which dying cells are not replaced in sufficient numbers to maintain current levels of function; the process by which human behavior alters with time.

Psychological studies of aging populations began in earnest in the late nineteenth century when psychologists found that mental abilities deteriorated with age. These abilities included **memory** and the types of mental performance measured in IQ tests. In some individuals, verbal abilities were shown to deteriorate with advanced age, although at a slower rate than other skills; with others, verbal abilities, especially vocabulary, may increase with age. Such data have often been corroborated in tests with chimpanzees, where younger animals perform better in tests of memory and other such areas of mental functioning. For decades, then, it was assumed that the physical deterioration of the body, so evident in the elderly, was surely matched by a similar decline in the mind.

Recent studies, however, have begun to cast doubt on these assumptions. One area where current research has disproved a long-held belief about the aging of the mind is in the death of neurons, formally thought to necessarily lead to diminished mental functioning. It is now known that the **brain** has far more neurons than it could ever use, and that as they die their functions are taken over by nearby neurons. Scientists have recently proven that while abilities like short-term memory and performing certain specific tasks within a time constraint often deteriorate after mid-life, other areas of mental activity, such as wisdom and judgment, become more acute and powerful. Still other studies have shown that brains in older subjects are capable of performing many tasks as quickly and efficiently as brains in younger subjects, although the tasks are performed using different areas of

the brain. For instance, research conducted at the Georgia Institute of Technology studied typing speeds in accomplished typists of college age and another group in their sixties. Common sense suggests that the older typists would perform less well because of decreased **hand-eye coordination** and slower **reaction time**. Surprisingly, both groups typed at the same speed. Researchers explained the results by pointing out that the assumptions about dexterity and response time were correct, but that the older typists had made clever, efficient adjustments, such as making fewer finger movements and to read ahead in the text, to compensate for their deficiency in those areas.

Fifty seems to be a crucial age in determining the brain's pattern of aging. Once a person has passed that age, brain functioning and mental **ability** are thought to be determined by essentially three factors: mental habits, chronic disease, and the mind's flexibility.

The elderly populations of many Western countries are the fastest growing segment of the population. In the United States, it is estimated that by the year 2030 there will be 50 million persons over age 65. Among the elderly, the fastest growing population is people over 85. Such demographic data will continue to focus attention on the process of aging and the psychological problems faced by the elderly. Perhaps the most common **psychological disorder** often associated with aging is **depression**. According to the National Institute of Mental Health, depression among the elderly range from 10 to 65 percent. Suicide rates among the elderly have been increasing at alarming rates. A study conducted by the federal government found that between 1980 and 1986, suicides by persons aged 65 and older increased 23 percent among white men, 42 percent among black men, and 17 percent among white women. The highest suicide rates are for white men over age 85. The elderly comprise about 13 percent of the nation's population (one in eight Americans) and account for about 20 percent of all suicides.

With the increase in the aging population, more focus is being placed on geriatric mental health issues, including disabilities since more than half the population has at least one, chronic health problems, living alone or in assisted housing, depression, loss, **pain**, Alzheimer's and **dementia**, among others. The nation's 78 million American baby boomers are expected to crave more vitality and longer life, which could contribute to a healthier version of aging.

**Further Reading**
Cadoff, Jennifer. "Feel Your Best at Every Age." *McCall's* (February 1994): 128.
Kahn, Ada, and Jan Fawcett, eds. *The Encyclopedia of Mental Health.* New York: Facts on File, 1993.

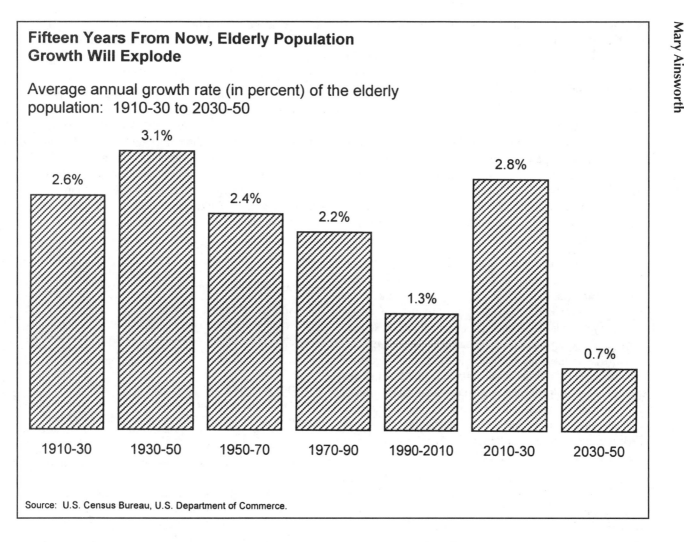

**Fifteen Years From Now, Elderly Population Growth Will Explode**

Average annual growth rate (in percent) of the elderly population: 1910-30 to 2030-50

- 1910-30: 2.6%
- 1930-50: 3.1%
- 1950-70: 2.4%
- 1970-90: 2.2%
- 1990-2010: 1.3%
- 2010-30: 2.8%
- 2030-50: 0.7%

Source: U.S. Census Bureau, U.S. Department of Commerce.

**Average annual growth rate of the elderly population.** *(Dana Hansen. Gale Group. Reproduced with permission.)*

Schrof, Joannie M. "Brain Power." *U.S. News and World Report* (28 November 1994): 88+.

White, Kristin. "How the Mind Ages: Aging: Getting It Right." *Psychology Today* (November/December 1993): 38+.

# Mary Ainsworth

**1913-**
American psychologist specializing in the study of infant attachment.

Mary D. Satler Ainsworth graduated from the University of Toronto in 1935 and earned her Ph.D. in psychology from that same institution in 1939. She is best known for her landmark work in assessing the security of infant **attachment** and linking attachment security to aspects of maternal caregiving.

Ainsworth began her career teaching at the University of Toronto before joining the Canadian Women's Army Corp in 1942 during World War II. After a brief period of post-war government service as the superintendent of Women's Rehabilitation in the Canadian Department of Veteran's Affairs, Ainsworth returned to Toronto to teach **personality** psychology and conduct research in the assessment of security. She married Leonard Ainsworth in 1950. Since he was a graduate student in the same department in which she held a faculty appointment, the couple decided to move to London where he could finish his degree at University College.

In England Mary Ainsworth began work at the Tavistock Clinic on a research project investigating the effects of early maternal separation on children's **personality development**. The project director, **John Bowlby**, had studied children's reactions to separations during the war years in England, and brought an evolutionary and ethological perspective to understanding the problems of attachment, separation, and loss. Her work with Bowlby brought Ainsworth's earlier interest in security into the developmental realm, and she planned to conduct a **longitudinal study** of mother-infant interaction in a natural setting at her earliest opportunity.

That opportunity came when Ainsworth's husband accepted a position in the East African Institute of Social Research in Kampala, Uganda. It was in Uganda that Mary Ainsworth studied mothers and infants in their natural **environment**, observing and recording as much as possible, and analyzing and publishing the data years later after joining the faculty at Johns Hopkins University in Baltimore.

Based on her original observations in Uganda and subsequent studies in Baltimore, Ainsworth concluded that there are qualitatively distinct patterns of attachment that evolve between infants and their mothers over the opening years of life. Although a majority of these patterns are marked by comfort and security, some are tense or conflicted, and Ainsworth found evidence suggesting that these relationships were related to the level of responsiveness that mothers showed toward their infants from the earliest months. In one study she found mothers who responded more quickly to their infants' cries at three months were more likely to have developed secure attachments with their babies by one year.

How could the security of a relationship be measured? Ainsworth and her colleagues devised a system for assessing individual differences in infants' reactions to a series of separations and reunions with their mothers. This method, the "**Strange Situation**," has become one of the most widely used procedures in **child development** research.

In this scenario, an observer takes a mother and child of about one year to an unfamiliar room containing toys. There are a series of separations and reunions. For example, mother and child are alone in the room for several minutes, the observer re-enters, remains, and after a few minutes, the mother leaves and returns after a few more minutes. Both observer and mother may comfort the distressed child.

Ainsworth found that key individual differences among children are revealed by the child's reaction to the mother's return. She categorized these responses into three major types: (A) Anxious/avoidant—the child may not be distressed at the mother's departure and may avoid or turn away from her on return; (B) Securely attached—the child is distressed by mother's departure and easily soothed by her on her return; (C) Anxious/resistant—the child may stay extremely close to the mother during the first few minutes and become highly distressed at her departure, only to seek simultaneously comfort and distance from the mother on her return by such behaviors as crying and reaching to be held and then attempting to leave once picked up.

The development of this procedure has spawned an enormous body of literature examining the development of mother-child attachment, the role of attachments to other caregivers, and the correlates and consequences of secure and insecure attachments. Ainsworth's work has not been without controversy. Attempts to replicate her link between response to early crying and later attachment have met with mixed success, and there is much debate about the origins of children's reactions in the Strange Situation. Still, Mary Ainsworth has made a lasting contribution to the study of children's affective growth and the role of supportive relationships in many aspects of development.

*See also* Bowlby, John

Doreen Arcus

## Further Reading

Ainsworth, M. *Infancy in Uganda: Infant Care and the Growth of Love.* Baltimore: Johns Hopkins University Press, 1967.

Ainsworth, M., M. C. Blehar, E. Waters, and S. Wall. *Patterns of Attachment: A Psychological Study of the Strange Situation.* Hillsdale, NJ: Erlbaum, 1978.

Karen, Robert. "Becoming Attached: What Experiences in Infancy Will Allow Children to Thrive Emotionally and to Come to Feel That the World of People Is a Positive Place?" *Atlantic* 265 (February 1990): 35+.

# Alcohol dependence and abuse

The abuse of alcohol in any of its various forms, exhibited by repeated episodes of excessive drinking often to the point of physical illness during which increasing amounts of alcohol must be consumed to achieve the desired effects.

The **American Psychiatric Association** ranks alcohol dependence and abuse into three categories (what society normally thinks of as "alcoholics"): 1) individuals who consume alcohol regularly, usually daily, in large amounts 2) those who consume alcohol regularly and heavily, but, unlike the first group, have the control to confine their excessive drinking to times when there are fewer social consequences, such as the weekend and 3) drinkers defined by the APA who endure long periods of sobriety before going on a binge of alcohol consumption. A binge can last a night, a weekend, a week, or longer. People in the latter two categories often resist seeking help because the control they exercise over their intake usually allows them to maintain a **normal** daily schedule and function well at work or at school aside from binges.

Other psychologists categorize alcohol dependence and abuse into "species." There are several species currently recognized by some in the medical community, including *alpha*, a minor, controllable dependence; *beta*, a dependence that has brought on physical complaints; *epsilon*, a dependence that occurs in sprees or binges; *gamma*, a severe biological dependence; and *delta*, an advanced form of *gamma* where the drinker has great difficulty going 24 to 48 hours without getting drunk. It should be noted, however, that many psychologists dispute these particular subdivisions on the grounds that the original data behind their creation has been shown to be flawed.

Alcohol dependence and abuse in adolescents and persons under 30 years of age is often accompanied by abuse of other substances, including **marijuana**, cocaine, amphetamines, and nicotine, the primary drug in cigarettes. These conditions may also be accompanied by **depression**, but current thinking is unclear as to whether depression is a symptom or a cause of alcohol dependence and abuse. **Heredity** appears to play a major role in the contraction of this disorder, with recent discoveries of genes that influence vulnerability to alcoholism. Studies of adopted children who are genetically related to alcohol abusers but raised in families free of the condition suggest that **environment** plays a smaller role in alcoholism's onset than heredity. Recent studies suggest that between 10 to 12 percent of the adult population of the United States suffers from some form of alcohol abuse or dependence.

Alcohol dependence and abuse typically appear in males and females at different ages. Males are more likely to begin heavy drinking as teenagers, while females are more likely to begin drinking in their mid-to-late twenties. In males, the disease is likely to progress rapidly; debilitating symptoms in females can take years to develop. According to the U.S. Department of Health and Human Services, 14 percent of males aged 18 to 29 report symptoms of alcohol dependence, and 20 percent revealed that their drinking has brought about negative consequences in their lives. As age progresses, these figures drop steadily. In females aged 18 to 29, similar statistics demonstrated that 5 to 6 percent admit to symptoms of dependence and that this number stays essentially the same until age 49, at which point it plummets to one percent. Females reporting negative consequences of drinking, however, begins at 12 percent but drops to statistical insignificance after age 60.

## QUESTIONS TO ASK BEFORE ALCOHOL OR SUBSTANCE ABUSE TREATMENT

The following key issues should be considered in determining which option is the most appropriate for given circumstances:

• How severe is the substance abuse problem and is there any evidence (e.g., suicide attempts) to suggest that there may be other problems (e.g., depression)?

• What are the credentials of the staff and what form(s) of therapy (e.g., family, group, medications) are to be used?

• How will the family be involved in the treatment and how long will it be from treatment entry to discharge? Is there a follow-up phase of treatment?

• How will the adolescent continue his/her education during the treatment?

• How much of the treatment will our insurance cover and how much will we need to pay "out of pocket?"

A key physiological component of alcohol dependence is what is referred to as neurological **adaptation**, or, more commonly, tolerance, whereby the **brain** adapts itself to the level of alcohol contained in the body and in the bloodstream. This process occurs over time as the drinker drinks more regularly while increasing intake in order to achieve the desired effect. In some cases, however, high levels of tolerance to alcohol is an inborn physical trait, independent of drinking history.

There is considerable debate as to the exact nature of alcoholism (the biological disease) and alcohol dependence and abuse (the psychological disorders). The disease model, which has been embraced by physicians and Alcoholics Anonymous for more than 50 years, is undergoing reexamination, particularly for its view that total abstinence is the only method for recovery. Many psychologists now believe that some victims of alcohol dependence and abuse can safely return to controlled drinking without plunging back into self-destructive binges. Experiments have been conducted that indicate the consumption of a few drinks after a lengthy period of abstinence can lessen the resolve to remain totally abstinent, but that a devastating return to abusive drinking is not the inevitable result. In fact, some psychologists contend that the binge drinking that occurs after initially "falling off the wagon" is less a result of the return of alcohol to the body than to the feelings of uselessness and self-pity that typically accompany such a failure to keep a promise to oneself.

## CHILDREN OF ALCOHOLICS

A number of researchers have studied children of alcoholics (COAs) and their counterparts, children of non-alcoholic parents (nonCOAs). These points summarize their findings:

COAs and non-COAs are most likely to differ in cognitive performance: scores on tests of abstract and conceptual reasoning and verbal skills were lower among children of alcoholic fathers than among children of non-alcoholic fathers in one study (Ervin, Little, Streissguth, and Beck).

A research team (Johnson and Rolf) found that both COAs and mothers of COAs were found to underestimate the child's abilities.

School records indicate that COAs are more likely to repeat grades, fail to graduate from high school, and require referral to the school psychologist than their non-COA classmates. (Miller and Jang; Knop and Teasdale)

Researchers (West and Prinz) found that COAs exhibit behavior problems such as lying, stealing, fighting, truancy, and are often diagnosed as having conduct disorders.

Although it may be premature to suggest that a paradigm shift has occurred in the psychological community regarding alcohol dependence and abuse, many researchers do in fact believe that the disease model, requiring total, lifelong abstinence, no longer adequately addresses the wide variety of disorders related to excessive, harmful intake of alcohol. It is important to note, however, that the human body has no physical requirement for alcohol and that persons with a history of uncontrollable drinking should be very careful in experimenting with alcohol after having achieved a hard-won abstinence. Other factors to keep in mind are problems alcohol can cause to the fetuses of pregnant women, a condition known as **fetal alcohol syndrome** (FAS). Some researchers believe that children born with FAS are prone to learning disabilities, behavior problems, and cognitive deficits, although others feel the evidence is insufficient to establish a reliable link between these problems and FAS. Alcohol also has a negative effect on human organs, especially the liver, and a lifetime of drinking can cause terminal illnesses of the liver, stomach, and brain. Finally, drunk driving is a tremendous problem in the United States, as are violent crimes committed by people who are under the influence of alcohol. Findings for alcohol expectancies among school-age children indicate increasingly positive alcohol expectancies across the grade levels. By fourth grade children

tended to believe that use of alcohol led to positive outcomes, such as higher levels of acceptance and liking by peers and a good **mood** with positive feelings about oneself. Findings also indicate that 25% of fourth graders studied reported feeling at least some **peer pressure** to consume alcoholic beverages; this figure increased to 60% among seventh graders

Dr. John Ewing developed a four-question test, known as the "CAGE" test, that therapists and the medical community frequently use as a first step to evaluate alcohol dependence and/or abuse. The test takes its name from a key word in each question: 1) Have you ever felt you should Cut down on your drinking? 2) Have people Annoyed you by criticizing your drinking? 3) Have you ever felt bad or Guilty about your drinking? And 4) Have you ever had a drink first thing in the morning to steady your nerves or to get rid of a hangover (Eye opener)? One yes suggests a possible alcohol problem.

Treatment modalities vary. Professionals frequently employ a combination of modalities. Studies indicate cognitive behavioral therapies improve self-control and social skills. Behavioral and **group therapy** have also proven effective. Self-help programs include Alcoholics Anonymous, Smart Recovery, and Rational Recovery. In some cases medications designed to ease drug cravings or block the effects of alcohol are prescribed. To reduce cravings, even acupuncture is being tried. The managed care environment has contributed to a belief that treatment should occur in the least restrictive settings that provide safety and effectiveness. Treatment settings vary from hospitalization to partial hospital care to outpatient treatment to **self-help groups**.

*See also* Addiction/Addictive Personality; Self-help groups

### Further Reading

Barlow, David H. and V. Mark Durand, eds. *Abnormal Psychology*. Pacific Grove, CA: Brooks/Cole, 1995.

Knapp, Caroline. "My Passion for Liquor." *New Woman* (August 1995): 80-83.

Noble, Ernest P. "Moderate Drinking Is Not for People in Recovery." *Addiction Letter* (September 1995): 1-2.

Sheed, Wilfrid. "Down in the Valley." *Psychology Today* (November 1995): 26-28.

Szpir, Michael. "Alcoholism, Personality, and Dopamine." *American Scientist* (September 1995): 425-26.

## Alienation

The state of being emotionally separated from others and from one's own feelings.

**Compound of the Branch Davidians in Waco, Texas. Feelings of alienation sometimes lead people to form small, close-knit groups such as cults.** *(AP/Wide World Photos. Reproduced with permission.)*

Alienation is a powerful feeling of isolation and loneliness, and stems from a variety of causes. Alienation may occur in response to certain events or situations in society or in one's personal life. Examples of events that may lead to an individual's feeling of alienation include the loss of a charismatic group leader, or the discovery that a person who served as a role model has serious shortcomings. Examples of personal events are a death in the **family**, a job change, **divorce**, or leaving home for the first time. Although most people may find that such occurrences trigger temporary feelings of disillusionment or loneliness, a small percentage will be unable to overcome these events, and will feel hopelessly adrift and alone.

Many sociologists have observed and commented upon an increase in this feeling of alienation among young people since the 1960s. They attribute this alienation to a variety of societal conditions: the rapid changes in society during this period, the increase in alcohol and drug abuse, **violence** in the media, or the lack of communal values in the culture at large. Some sociologists observe that individuals become alienated when they perceive government, employment, or educational institutions as cold and impersonal, unresponsive to those who need their services. Entire groups may experience alienation—for example, ethnic minorities or residents of inner city neighborhoods who feel the opportunities and advantages of mainstream society are beyond their reach.

Feeling separated from society is not the only way a person experiences alienation: sometimes the individual feels alienation as disharmony with his or her true self. This condition develops when a person accepts societal expectations (to take over a family business, for example) that are counter to the person's true goals, feelings, or desires (perhaps to be a teacher). He may appear to be successful in the role others expect him to assume, but his true wish is hidden, leaving him feeling deeply conflicted and alone.

In the workplace, jobs have become increasingly specialized since the 1700s and the Industrial Revolution. Workers may see little connection between the tasks they perform and the final product or service, and may thus feel intense loneliness while in the midst of a busy work environment. In the 1840s, American writer and philosopher Henry David Thoreau (1817-1862) observed that "the mass of men lead lives of quiet desperation. What is called resignation is confirmed desperation." Thoreau dealt with his own feelings of alienation by retreating to a solitary, simple life on the banks of Walden Pond in rural Massachusetts. He felt less isolated there—even though he lived in solitude—than when he lived in a town, surrounded by people. When living in town, his feelings of alienation confronted him daily, since his activities did not reflect his true feelings and desires.

Alienation is expressed differently by different people. Some become withdrawn and lethargic; others may react with **hostility** and violence; still others may become disoriented, rejecting traditional values and behavior by adopting an outlandish appearance and erratic behavior patterns. As society undergoes rapid changes, and traditional values and behavioral standards are challenged, some people find little they can believe in and so have difficulty constructing a reality in which they can find a place for themselves. It is for this reason that social and cultural beliefs play such an important role in bringing about or averting a feeling of alienation.

Psychologists help people cope with feelings of alienation by developing exercises or designing specific tasks to help the person become more engaged in society. For example, by identifying the alienated individual's true feelings, the psychologist may suggest a volunteer activity or a job change to bring the individual into contact with society in a way that has meaning for him or her.

Some have proposed treating the epidemic of alienation among America's young people by fostering social solutions rather than individual solutions. One such social solution is the idea of communitarianism, a movement begun early in the 1990s by Amitai Etzioni, a sociology professor from George Washington University in Washington, D.C. Etzioni became a popular speaker and writer in the mid-1990s with the publication of his book, *The Spirit of Community*. Etzioni advocates a return to community values to replace the rampant alienation of contemporary culture, education to reinforce shared societal morals focusing on family values, and strictly enforcing anti-crime measures. This movement has met serious criticism, however; civil libertarian groups are concerned about communitarian beliefs that certain rights can and should be restricted for the good of the community.

**Further Reading**

D'Antonio, Michael. "I or We." *Mother Jones* (May-June 1994): 20+.

Foster, Hal. "Cult of Despair." *New York Times* (30 December 1994): A3.

Guinness, Alma, ed. *ABCs of the Human Mind*. Pleasantville, NY: Reader's Digest Association, 1990.

Jackson, Richard. "Alone in the Crowd: Breaking the Isolation of Childhood." *School Library Journal* (November 1995): 24.

Upton, Julia. "A Generation of Refugees." *The Catholic World* (September-October 1995): 204+.

*See also* Loss and grief

# Gordon Willard Allport

### 1897-1967
American humanist psychologist who developed a personality theory that emphasized individuality.

Gordon Willard Allport was one of the great **personality** theorists of the twentieth century. His work was a synthesis of individual personality **traits** and the traditional psychology of **William James**, which emphasized psychological traits that are common among humans. He also examined complex social interactions. As a humanistic psychologist, he opposed both behavioral and psychoanalytical theories of psychology. Above all, Allport believed in the uniqueness of the individual. A prolific and gifted writer, he was the recipient of numerous professional awards.

Allport, born in 1897 in Montezuma, Indiana, was the youngest of four sons in the family of John Edwards and Nellie Edith (Wise) Allport. He was educated in Cleveland, Ohio, where the family moved when he was six years old. John Allport was a physician with a clinic in the family home and, as they were growing up, his sons assisted him in his practice. Gordon Allport's mother, a former school teacher, maintained a home environment that emphasized religion and intellectual development. As a teenager, Allport ran his own printing business and edited his high school newspaper. Following graduation in 1915, scholarships enabled him to join his brother Floyd at Harvard College. Although his education was interrupted for military service during the First World War, Allport earned his A.B. degree in 1919, with majors in philosophy and economics. Following a year of teaching English and sociology at Robert College in Istanbul, Turkey, Allport returned to Harvard with a fellowship to study psychology. He was influenced both by his brother Floyd and by the noted experimental psychologist Hugo Münsterberg. He coauthored his first publication, "Personality Traits: Their Classification and Measurement," with his brother in 1921. Allport received his M.A. degree in 1921 and his Ph.D. in 1922, for his study of personality traits under the direction of Herbert S. Langfeld.

A Sheldon Traveling Fellowship enabled Allport to spend two years studying in Berlin and Hamburg, Germany, and in Cambridge, England. He then returned to Harvard as an instructor in social **ethics** from 1924 to 1926. Allport married Ada Lufkin Gould in 1925. Their son, Robert Bradlee Allport, grew up to become a pediatrician. After four years as an assistant professor of psychology at Dartmouth College, Allport returned to Harvard where he remained for the rest of his career. He became an associate professor of psychology in 1937 and a full professor in 1942. He served as chairman of the Psychology Department and helped found Harvard's Department of Social Relations. In 1939 he was elected president of the American Psychological Association and, in 1964, received the Distinguished Scientific Contribution Award of that society. In 1963, he was awarded the Gold Medal of the American Psychological Foundation.

## Publishes theory of personality

Allport's first major book, *Personality: A Psychological Interpretation* (1937), distinguished between traits that are common to many people, such as assertiveness, and personal dispositions which are traits that are characteristic of the individual. The latter were classified according to their degree of influence on an individual personality. Allport also identified how individuals develop self-awareness throughout **childhood** and **adolescence**. One of Allport's most important concepts, functional autonomy, encompassed his theories of **motivation**. Finally, he attempted to define the mature personality. *Personality: A Psychological Interpretation* remained the standard text on personality theory for many years. In 1961, following years of study and research, Allport published a major revision of this work, *Pattern and Growth in Personality*. He also helped to develop methods of personality assessment, including the *A-S Reaction Study* (1928), with his brother Floyd Allport.

## Examines the nature of prejudice

Allport was a man of diverse interests. During World War II, as a member of the National Research Council, he began studying the social problem of spreading rumors. In 1947 he published *The Psychology of Rumor* with Leo Postman. Allport also was concerned with racial and religious prejudice. His 1954 book, *The Nature of Prejudice*, was a milestone study. As a visiting consultant at the University of Natal in South Africa in 1956, Allport predicted that the white supremacist cultures of both South Africa and the American South would be overthrown. Like his predecessor William James, Allport also examined the psychology of religion in *The Individual and his Religion: A Psychological Interpretation* (1950), in which he warned of the prejudices that could be fostered by institutionalized religions.

**Gordon W. Allport** *(Archives of the History of American Psychology. Reproduced with permission.)*

During his career, Allport published 12 books and more than 200 papers on psychology and held important positions in American and foreign psychological associations. Allport was editor of the *Journal of Abnormal and Social Psychology* from 1937 until 1949. Boston University awarded him an honorary L.H.D. degree in 1958. He also held honorary doctorates from Ohio Wesleyan University, Colby College, and the University of Durham in England. He died of lung cancer in Cambridge, Massachusetts, in 1967.

*See also* Personality development; Prejudice and discrimination; Religion and psychology

Margaret Alic

### Further Reading
Allport, G. W. "Autobiography." In *A History of Psychology in Autobiography,* edited by E. Boring and G. Lindzey. Boston: Beacon Press, 1967.

Evans, Richard I. *Gordon Allport, the Man and his Ideas.* New York: Dutton, 1971.

Maddi, Salvatore R. and Paul T. Costa. *Humanism in Personalogy: Allport, Maslow, and Murray.* Chicago: AldineAtherton, 1972.

# Alzheimer's disease

An irreversible, progressive condition in which nerve cells in the brain degenerate, and the size of the brain decreases.

Alzheimer's disease is the most common degenerative **brain** disorder, although onset of the disease is rare before the age of 60. After that age, the incidence of Alzheimer's disease increases steadily, and more than one-quarter of all individuals above the age of 85 have this disease. In addition, Alzheimer's disease is the cause of about three-quarters of all cases of **dementia** in individuals above the age of 65. General interest and research focusing on the cause and treatment of this condition have grown in recent years because the number of elderly persons in the population is increasing.

The cause of Alzheimer's disease is not known, but several theories of causality have been advanced. These theories propose genetic, environmental, viral, immunological, biochemical, and other causes for the disease. The specific features of Alzheimer's disease vary from individual to individual, but the general course of the disease is fairly consistent in most cases. The symptoms of the disease tend to be more severe at night. The first stage of Alzheimer's disease is usually forgetfulness, accompanied by some anxiety and mild **depression**. This usually develops into a more serious loss of **memory**, especially of recent events, moderate spatial and temporal disorientation, loss of **ability** to concentrate, **aphasia**, and increased anxiety. This set of symptoms is usually followed by profound spatial and temporal disorientation, delusions, **hallucinations**, incontinence, general physical decline, and death.

*See also* Dementia

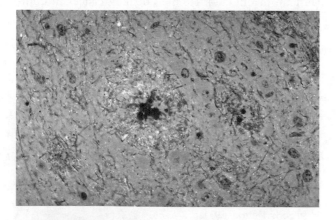

**Brain tissue damaged by Alzheimer's disease.** *(Photo by Cecil Fox/Science Source. National Audubon Society Collection/Photo Researchers, Inc. Reproduced by permission.)*

## Further Reading

Edwards, Allen. *When Memory Fails.* New York: Plenum, 1994.

Gregg, Daphna. *Alzheimer's Disease.* Boston: Harvard Medical School Health Publications, 1994.

# American Academy of Child and Adolescent Psychiatry

The American Academy of Child and Adolescent Psychiatry (AACAP) represents over 6,500 child and adolescent psychiatrists, all of whom have at least five years of additional training beyond medical school in the fields of general and child and adolescent psychiatry. The members of the Academy actively research, diagnose, and treat psychiatric disorders affecting children and adolescents and their families and support their activities through a variety of programs.

The Academy was established in 1953 as the American Academy of Child Psychiatry with fewer than 100 members. Today the AACAP is a dynamic, growing organization whose mission is to direct and respond quickly to new developments in the health care environment, particularly as they affect the needs of children, adolescents, and their families.

The Academy sponsors over 45 committees which work to increase the areas of knowledge for Academy members and the public, and to disseminate information, including position statements on various issues such as adolescent psychiatric hospitalization, pregnancy prevention, and substance abuse.

The Academy's strong commitment to furthering the understanding and treatment of children and adolescents is also reflected in the wide range of their activities, which include publishing the bi-monthly *Journal* of the American Academy of Child and Adolescent Psychiatry and a quarterly *Newsletter;* promoting support for research careers; providing a national continuing medical education program and participating in the American Medical Association regarding innovations in treatment; and providing public information in the form of *Facts for Families,* a collection of informational sheets providing the most up-to-date material discussing current psychiatric issues concerning children, adolescents, and their families.

## Further Information

American Academy of Child and Adolescent Psychiatry. 3615 Wisconsin Ave., N.W., Washington, DC 20016, (202) 966–7300. www.aacap.org/about/introduction.html.

# Americans with Disabilities Act (ADA)

U.S. federal legislation (PL 101-336; 42 U.S.C. 12101) enacted in 1990 and designed to prohibit certain forms of discrimination against individuals with disabilities.

In 1990, approximately 40 million Americans could be classified as having one or more physical or mental disabilities. The Americans with Disabilities Act (ADA) was enacted to legally address the widespread and serious social problem of discrimination against these individuals in employment, housing, public accommodations, education, transportation, communication, public service, and other areas. In addition to establishing enforceable standards in reference to discrimination against individuals with disabilities and ensuring that the federal government enforces those standards, the intent of this legislation was to provide a clear national mandate for the elimination of discrimination against individuals with disabilities and to allow these individuals into the economic and social mainstream of American life.

*See also* Disability

**Further Reading**
Bowe, Frank. *Equal Rights for Americans with Disabilities.* New York: Franklin Watts, 1992.

# Ames Room

Specially constructed space that demonstrates aspects of visual perception.

People make sense out of visual scenes by relying on various cues. The Ames Room is a specially constructed space that demonstrates the power of these cues. Normally, people use monocular depth cues such as relative size and height in the visual plane as indicators of depth. If two people of similar size stand a distance part, the one closer to the viewer appears larger. Similarly, the person farther away appears higher in the visual plane.

An Ames Room is constructed to look like a normal room. In reality, the floor slants up on one side and, at the same time, slopes up from front to back. Finally, the back wall is slanted so that one side is closer to the viewer than the other. The figure below shows a top view of the shape of the room and the spot from which the viewer looks at the scene.

If one person stands at the back right corner of the room (Person B), and another person at the left corner (Per-

son A), Person A should appear somewhat smaller than Person B because Person A is farther from the viewer. However, because the room is constructed so that the back wall looks normal, the viewer has no depth cues and Person A appears unusually small, while Person B appears very large. If a person moves from one corner to the other, he gives the illusion of shrinking or growing as he moves. That is, the cues that people normally use for size are so powerful that viewers see things that could not possibly be true.

# Amnesia

A partial or total loss of memory.

There are numerous causes of amnesia, including stroke, injury to the **brain**, surgery, alcoholism, encephalitis, and **electroconvulsive therapy**. Contrary to the popular notion of amnesia—in which a person suffers a severe blow to the head, for example, and cannot recall his or her past life and experiences—the principal symptom of amnesia is the inability to retain new information, beginning at the point at which the amnesia began. The capacity to recall past experiences may vary, depending on the severity of the amnesia.

There are two types of amnesia: retrograde and anterograde. Retrograde amnesia refers to the loss of **memory** of one's past, and can vary from person to person. Some retain virtually full recall of things that happened prior to the onset of amnesia; others forget only their recent past, and still others lose all memory of their past lives. Anterograde amnesia refers to the inability to recall events or facts introduced since the amnesia began.

Amnesiacs often appear perfectly **normal**. Motor skills such as tying laces and bows and bike riding are retained, as is the **ability** to read and comprehend the meaning of words. Because of this phenomenon, researchers have suggested that there is more than one area of the brain used to store memory. General knowledge and perceptual skills may be stored in a memory separate from the one used to store personal facts.

The most famous study of amnesia involves a patient called H.M., who in 1953 underwent brain surgery designed to treat his **epilepsy**. Following the surgery, he could recall all the events of his past life up until three weeks before the operation. However, H.M. could no longer function normally because he had lost the ability to learn new facts and associations. For example, he could not recognize his doctor from day to day or hour to hour.

**Childhood** amnesia, a term coined by **Anna Freud** in the late 1940s, refers to the fact that most people cannot recall childhood experiences during the first three to five years of life. It has been suggested that this type of amnesia occurs because children and adults organize memories in different ways based on their brain's physical development. Others believe children begin remembering facts and events once they have accumulated enough experience to be able to relate experiences to each other.

*See also* Fugue

### Further Reading

Atkinson, Rita L.; Richard C. Atkinson; Edward E. Smith; and Ernest R. Hilgard. *Introduction to Psychology* . 9th ed. San Diego: Harcourt Brace Jovanovich, 1987.

Bolles, Edmund Blair. *Remembering and Forgetting: An Inquiry into the Nature of Memory.* New York: Walker and Co., 1988.

Zimbardo, Philip G. *Psychology and Life.* 12th ed. Glenview, IL: Scott, Foresman, 1989.

# American Psychiatric Association

A national medical society whose approximately 40,500 members—physicians and medical students—specialize in the diagnosis and treatment of mental and emotional disorders.

The oldest medical specialty society in the United States, the American Psychiatric Association was founded in October 1844, when thirteen physicians who specialized in the treatment of mental and emotional disorders met in Philadelphia and founded the Association of Medical Superintendents of American Institutions for the Insane. (It is interesting to note that this forerunner of the American Psychiatric Association preceded the American Medical Association, which was founded in 1847.) The goals of the physicians meeting in Philadelphia were to communicate professionally, cooperate in the collection of data, and improve the treatment of the mentally ill.

The American Psychiatric Association's objectives are still designed to advance care for people with mental illnesses: to improve treatment, **rehabilitation**, and care of the mentally ill and emotionally disturbed; to promote research, professional education in psychiatry and allied fields, and the prevention of psychiatric disabilities; to advance the standards of psychiatric services and facilities; to foster cooperation among those concerned with the medical, psychological, social and legal aspects of **mental health**; to share psychiatric knowledge with other practitioners of medicine, scientists, and the public; and to promote the best interests of patients and others actually or potentially using mental health services.

The American Psychiatric Association supports psychiatrists and their service to patients through publications such as the *American Journal of Psychiatry,* the oldest specialty journal in the United States, and the *Psychiatric News,* the Association's official newsletter, as well as numerous books, journals, and reports. The Association's annual meeting attracts more than 15,000 attendees and features hundreds of sessions and presenters. Additionally, the Association schedules more than 200 meetings each year among its councils, committees, and task forces to advance the cause of mental health. The American Psychiatric Association also offers a comprehensive continuing medical education program to its members. The ***Diagnostic and Statistical Manual of Mental Disorder***s *(DSM-IV),* an authoritative reference work, is published by American Psychiatric Association.

*See also Diagnostic and Statistical Manual of Mental Disorders*

### Further Information

American Psychiatric Association. 1400 K Street, NW, Washington, D.C. 20005, (202) 682–6000.

# American Psychological Association (APA)

The American Psychological Association (APA) was founded in July 1892, and by the 1990s, it was both the world's largest association of psychologists and the major organization representing psychology in the United States. APA has 159,000 members and affiliates (students and high school teachers) from around the world. APA sponsors approximately 50 specialty divisions.

The program of the APA is organized in four directorates, namely Science, Practice, Public Interest, and Education, all of which contribute to the goal of seeking ways to increase human wellness through an understanding of behavior. The Science Directorate promotes the exchange of ideas and research findings through conventions, conferences, publications, and traveling museum exhibits. It also helps psychologists locate and obtain research funding. The Practice Directorate promotes the practice of psychology and the availability of psychological care. It lobbies both federal and state legislatures on issues such as health care reform, regulatory activities such as state licensure, and public service such as the pro bono services provided through the Disaster Response Network. The Public Interest Directorate supports the application of psychology to the advancement of human welfare through program and policy development, conference planning, and support of research, training, and advocacy in areas such as minority affairs, women's issues, and lesbian and gay concerns. The Education Directorate serves to advance psychology in its work with educational institutions, professional agencies, and programs and initiatives in education.

APA publishes books as well as more than 24 scientific and professional journals and newsletters, including *APA Monitor* and *American Psychologist*. Since 1970, *PsychINFO*, a worldwide computer database, has provided references in psychology and related behavioral and social sciences. The week-long APA annual convention is the world's largest meeting of psychologists. More than 15,000 psychologists attend, and have opportunities to attend the presentation of more than 3,000 papers, lectures, and symposia.

*See also* American Psychological Society (APS); National Association for Mental Health; National Institute of Mental Health

**Further Information**

American Psychological Association. 1200 Seventeenth Street NW, Washington, D.C. 20036, (202) 336–5500.

# American Psychological Society (APS)

Organization devoted to academic, applied, and science-oriented psychology.

The American Psychological Society was founded in 1988 to represent the interests of academic, applied, and science-oriented psychology and psychologists. The formation of APS originated from the Assembly for Scientific and Applied Psychology (ASAP), a group that attempted to reform the **American Psychological Association (APA)** to give the scientists greater representation and autonomy. As of early 1996, the APS had about 15,000 members.

Headquartered in Washington, D.C., APS prides itself on its strong, committed **leadership** and minimal bureaucracy. It publishes two bimonthly journals, *Psychological Science* and *Current Directions in Psychological Science*, and produces a monthly newsletter. The APS holds annual conventions and actively lobbies Congress for funds to support scientifically oriented research projects in psychology. In 1991, it initiated a national behavioral science research agenda known as the Human Capital Initiative (HCI). The goal of HCI is to apply the knowledge gained from scientific psychology to address such social ills as illiteracy, substance abuse, **violence**, as well as mental and physical health.

**Further Information**

American Psychological Society. 1010 Vermont Avenue, Suite 1100, Washington, D.C. 20005, (202) 783–2077.

# Anaclitic depression

See **Depression**

# Anal stage

See **Psychosexual development**

# Anne Anastasi

**1908-**
American psychologist instrumental in developing psychometrics—how psychological traits are influenced, developed, and measured.

In her long and productive career, Anne Anastasi has produced not only several classic texts in psychology but has been a major factor in the development of psychology as a quantitative behavioral science. To psychology professionals, the name Anastasi is synonymous with psychometrics, since it was she who pioneered understanding how psychological **traits** are influenced, developed, and measured. In 1987 she was rated by her peers as the most prominent living woman in psychology in the English-speaking world.

Anne Anastasi was born December 19, 1908, in New York City, the only child of Anthony and Theresa Gaudiosi. Her father, who died when she was only one year old, worked for the New York City Board of Education. Soon after his death, her mother experienced such a deep split with her father's relatives that they would never be a part of her life. From then on, she was raised by her mother, grandmother, and great uncle. Her mother was compelled to find a job, and eventually she became office manager of one of the largest foreign newspapers in New York, *Il Progresso Italo-Americano*. Meanwhile, the precocious and intelligent young Anastasi was educated at home by her grandmother, and it was not until the sixth grade that she entered the public school system. After graduating from P.S. 33 in the Bronx at the top of her class, she attended Evander Childs High School, but found the entire experience dispiriting and dropped out after two months.

## Skips high school and discovers psychology at Barnard College

The dilemma of a 13-year old girl leaving high school after only two months was solved by an insightful family friend, Ida Stadie, who suggested that she prepare to skip high school and go directly to college. Since Barnard College in New York City did not specify a high school degree as an admissions requirement, Anastasi decided she need only submit the results of her College Entrance Examination Board tests. After taking two years to prepare at the Rhodes Preparatory School in Manhattan, she took the tests and was admitted to Barnard College in 1924 at the age of 15.

Mathematics had been her first love since elementary school, and at Barnard she was placed in all the advanced math classes. During her sophomore year, however, she took a course in **developmental psychology** with the department chairman, Harry L. Hollingworth, whose stimulating lectures made her intellectually curious about the discipline. In that course, she encountered a psychology article by **Charles Spearman**, whose intriguing work on correlation coefficients showed her that it was possible to combine mathematics and psychology. Convinced she had found the best of both worlds, she enrolled in the Barnard's Honors Program in psychology for her last two years, and received her B.A. in 1928 at the age of 19, having been elected to Phi Beta Kappa and having won the Caroline Duror Graduate Fellowship, "awarded to the member of the graduating class showing the greatest promise of distinction in her chosen line of work."

## Receives Ph.D., teaches at 21, and writes classic text at 29

Having taken graduate courses at Columbia University while still at Barnard, she applied there after graduation and was allowed to skip the master's degree and to go directly for her Ph.D. in general **experimental psychology**. At this time, Columbia's psychology department provided a stimulating and lively environment, made more enlightening by its summer sessions that were visited by eminent psychologists. During her second year at Columbia, Anastasi began to specialize, and it was then that she decided on the complex field of **differential psychology**. As the branch of psychology that deals with individual and group differences in behavior, it is a highly quantitative field of study, and therefore much to her liking.

As she had planned, Anastasi received her Ph.D. from Columbia in only two years, and in 1930 returned to Barnard to begin teaching. Three years later, she married psychologist John Porter Foley Jr., a fellow Columbia Ph.D. student. In 1939 she left Barnard to become assistant professor and sole member of the newly created Psychology Department at Queens College of the City of New York. After the war, she left Queens College in 1947 to become associate professor of psychology in the Graduate School of Arts and Sciences at Fordham University, and full professor in 1951. She remained there until her retirement in 1979, when she became a professor emeritus.

The focus of her research, writing, and teaching has been on the nature and **measurement** of psychological traits. In her landmark work, *Psychological Testing*, Anastasi emphasizes the ways education and **heredity** influence trait development, and then goes on to demonstrate how the measurement of those traits is affected by such variables as training, culture, and language differences. Throughout her work, the "nature-nurture" controversy is dominant, and typically, she argues that psychologists have been incorrect seeking to explain behavior by using one or the other. She states, rather, that neither exists apart from the other, and that psychologists should be questioning how the two interact.

At least two of Anastasi's other books are considered classics in the field and are found in many translations around the world. The recipient of several honorary degrees, she became in 1972 the first woman to be elected president of the American Psychological Association in 50 years. In 1987 her career achievements were recognized when she was presented the National Medal of Science by President Ronald Reagan.

Anastasi's life has not been entirely trouble-free, as she had to survive a diagnosis of cervical cancer in 1934. When the successful radiation therapy left her unable to have children, she looked only at the positive aspects of her condition and stated that she was able to focus solely on her career without **guilt**. A well-rounded individual with an avocational interest in art, she continued her professional writing, speaking, and organizational activities long past the time when most people have fully retired.

*See also* Nature-nuture controversy

Leonard C. Bruno

### Further Reading

"American Psychological Foundation Awards for 1984." *American Psychologist* (March 1985): 340-341.
"Distinguished Scientific Award for the Applications of Psychology: 1981." *American Psychologist* (January 1982): 52-59.
Metzger, Linda and Deborah A. Straub, editors. *Contemporary Authors*. New Revision Series, Volume 17. Detroit, MI: Gale Research Co., p 21.
O'Connell, Agnes N. and Nancy Felipe Russo, editors. *Women in Psychology*. New York: Greenwood Press, 1990, pp. 13-22.

Sheehy, Noel, Antony J. Chapman, and Wendy A. Conroy, editors. *Biographical Dictionary of Psychology.* New York: Routledge Reference, 1997, pp. 13-14.

# Anger

*One of the primordial emotions, along with fear, grief, pain, and joy.*

Anger is usually caused by the frustration of attempts to attain a goal, or by hostile or disturbing actions such as insults, injuries, or threats that do not come from a feared source. The sources of anger are different for people at different periods in their lives. The most common cause of anger in infants, for example, is restraint of activity. Children commonly become angry due to restrictive rules or demands, lack of **attention**, or failure to accomplish a task. As children reach **adolescence** and adulthood, the primary sources of anger shift from physical constraints and frustrations to social ones. In adults, the basis of anger include disapproval, deprivation, exploitation, manipulation, betrayal, and humiliation, and the responses to it become less physical and more social with age. The tantrums, fighting, and screaming typical of **childhood** give way to more verbal and indirect expressions such as swearing and sarcasm. Physical **violence** does occur in adults, but in most situations it is avoided in deference to social pressures.

Like **fear**, anger is a basic **emotion** that provides a primitive mechanism for physical survival. The physiological changes that accompany anger and fear are very similar and include increased heart rate and blood pressure, rapid breathing, and muscle tension. However, anger produces more muscle tension, higher blood pressure, and a lower heart rate, while fear induces rapid breathing. Unlike the adrenalin-produced "fight or flight" response that characterizes fear, anger is attributed to the secretion of both adrenalin and another hormone, noradrenalin. Other physical signs of anger include scowling, teeth grinding, glaring, clenched fists, chills and shuddering, twitching, choking, flushing or paling, and numbness.

People use a number of **defense mechanisms** to deal with anger. They may practice denial, refusing to recognize that they are angry. Such repressed anger often finds another outlet, such as a physical symptom. Another way of circumventing anger is through passive **aggression**, in which anger is expressed covertly in a way that prevents retaliation. Both sarcasm and chronic lateness are forms of passive aggression. In the classroom, a passive aggressive student will display behavior that is subtly uncooperative or disrespectful but which provides no concrete basis for disciplinary action. Passive aggressive acts may even appear in the guise of a service or favor, when in fact the sentiments expressed are those of **hostility** rather than altruism. Some of the more extreme defenses against anger are **paranoia**, in which anger is essentially projected onto others, and bigotry, in which such a projection is targeted at members of a specific racial, religious, or ethnic group.

*See also* Aggression

## Further Reading
Carter, William Lee. *The Angry Teenager.* Nashville: Thomas Nelson, 1995.

Dentemaro, Christine. *Straight Talk About Anger.* New York: Facts on File, 1995.

Ellis, Albert. *Anger: How to Live With and Without It.* New York: Citadel Press, 1977.

*Letting Go of Anger: The 10 Most Common Anger Styles and What To Do About Them.* Oakland, CA: New Harbinger Publications, 1995.

Licata, Renora. *Everything You Need to Know About Anger.* New York: Rosen Publishing Group, 1994.

Luhn, Rebecca R. *Managing Anger: Methods for a Happier and Healthier Life.* Los Altos, CA: Crisp Publications, 1992.

# Animal experimentation

*The use of destructive and nondestructive testing upon various animal species in order to better understand the mechanisms of human and animal behaviors, emotions, and thought processes.*

Biologists believe that chimpanzees share at least 98.4 percent of the same DNA as humans. Gorillas have a genetic composition which is at least 97 percent consistent with that of humans. Because the advancement of scientific technology has increasingly demonstrated similarities between animals and people, popular attitudes toward the use of animals in research and scientific experimentation have changed considerably. Ironically, this knowledge of the close genetic bond between species has enhanced the interest in animal experimentation. Nevertheless, evidence of animals as "sentient" beings, capable of a wide range of emotions and thought processes, has led scientists and animal activists to search for alternative ways to study behavior without victimizing animals. Although most psychology research does not involve deadly disease or experimental pathology, it often involves unrelenting or quantitative mental, physical, and psychological stress—all of which animals are capable of experiencing.

Animal rights activists, protesting the use of animals in laboratory experiments by dressing in monkey suits, block the entrance to the Department of Health and Human Services in Washington, D.C. *(Corbis-Bettmann. Reproduced with permission.)*

## History

Charles Darwin's theory of evolution in 1859 became the scientific rationale for using animal experiments to learn more about humans. In the late nineteenth century, **Ivan Pavlov**'s experiments in the development of "conditioned" responses in dogs (salivation) helped to foster an increasingly authoritative school of psychology known as **behaviorism**. The contemporary human treatment regimen known as **behavior modification** is fashioned from parallels drawn on these early experiments in **operant conditioning**.

In 1876, England passed the British Cruelty to Animals Act, which regulated animal experimentation. Still, behaviorist thinking at that time denied animals any **psyche** or **emotion**. Academic journals described animal behavior only in terms of physiologic response to stimuli, with no mention of any psychological consequence.

In later years, the behaviorist theories were overshadowed by the development and spread (from Europe to the United States) of **ethology** which concerns itself with genetic predisposition, or innate/instinctive behavior and knowledge. This theory continues to prevail in the United States, but in terms of relevance, it is tempered by the reality that between 85 and 90 percent of all animal experimentation is conducted on species not sufficiently similar to humans to draw dispositive parallels. The majority of all animal research in the field of psychology is conducted on various rodent species (rats, mice, hamsters, etc.) or birds as laboratory subjects.

Australian philosopher Peter Singer made the case for an end to animal experimentation with his 1975 book, *Animal Liberation*. Coinciding with his book was the comprehensive and sensitive research of such ethologists as Jane Goodall and Dian Fossey, who suggested that primates were capable of a full spectrum of emotions, including love, sorrow, **jealousy**, **humor**, and deceit. These animals also learned to communicate with humans by using over 300 learned signs in American Sign Language. Studies with other species produced similar results. During the late 1990s, an African gray parrot named Alex, who was being studied at the Arizona State University, fell ill and was required to spend the night alone at a veterinary clinic. When his keeper attempted to leave the room at the clinic, Alex cried out, "Come here, I love you, I'm sorry. Wanna go back."

Such examples of the yet-unknown extent of emotional, psychological, and behavioral capacity in other species have cast new doubts on the scientific rationale for the continuation of captive animal experimentation.

## Current trends

Animal experimentation is still widely used in psychological research. Animals are used in projects of many types from alcohol-induced **aggression** to **pain** medication. A 1999 medical study questioned whether animal experimentation on the neuroendocrine mechanisms in laboratory rats might provide a better understanding of human **bisexuality**. However, the trend in academia seems to be following the popular distaste for animal experimentation. A British study of undergraduate students enrolled in psychology classes during the 1990s showed that students in psychology were less in favor of animal testing than students in medicine, and second-year students were less in favor of such research than first-year students. Several articles have been published which address the general lack of acknowledgment, in leading introductory psychology textbooks, of contributions made by animal subjects.

According to the **American Psychological Association (APA)**, less than 10 percent of pure psychological research uses animals as subjects. This estimate does not include animal subjects used for cross-over medical experimentation, such as in the related field of neuropsychology. Best estimates for the total number of animal subjects in all medical/psychological research is about 20 million per year. Of the animals used in psychological research, 90 percent are rodents and birds.

Concerns about animal cruelty have led to the search for alternative methodologies. Of great promise in this regard is computer simulation technology. As early as 1996, psychology students were able to study "**shaping**" and partial **reinforcement** in operant conditioning, by using a computer-created "virtual rat" named Sniffy. Commensurate with such technological developments and their refinements, statistics have shown a slow but consistent yearly decline in animal experimentation through 1999.

Lauri R. Harding

## Further Reading

Baluch, Bahman; and Baljit Kaur. "Attitude Change Toward Animal Experimentation in an Academic Setting." *Journal of Psychology* (July 1995): 477.

McElroy, Susan Chernak. *Animals as Teachers and Healers.* New York: Ballantine, 1997.

Mukerjee, Madhusree. "Trends in Animal Research," *Scientific American* (February 1997): 86.

## Further Information

Humane Society of the United States, Animal Research Issues Section. Washington, DC.

# Anorexia

An eating disorder where preoccupation with dieting and thinness leads to excessive weight loss while the individual continues to feel fat and fails to acknowledge that the weight loss or thinness is a problem.

Symptoms of anorexia, or anorexia nervosa, include significant weight loss, continuation of weight loss despite thinness, persistent feeling of being fat even after weight loss, exaggerated **fear** of gaining weight, loss of menstrual periods, preoccupation with food, calories, nutrition and/or cooking, dieting in secret, compulsive exercising, **sleep** disorders, and a pattern of binging and purging. The condition also has psychosexual effects. The sexual development of anorexic adolescents is arrested, while adults who have the disease generally lose interest in sex. While the term *anorexia* literally means "loss of appetite," anorexics generally do feel hunger but still refuse to eat.

The great majority of anorexics (about 95 percent) are women. Risk factors for the disorder may include a history of alcoholism and/or **depression**, early onset of **puberty**, tallness, **perfectionism**, low **self-esteem**, and certain illnesses such as juvenile diabetes. Psychosocial factors associated with the disease are over-controlling parents, an upwardly mobile **family**, and a culture that places excessive value on female thinness. Emotionally, anorexia often involves issues of control; the typical anorexic is often a strong-willed adolescent whose aversion to food is a misdirected way of exercising autonomy to compensate for a lack of control in other areas of his or her life.

Medical consequences of anorexia may include infertility, osteoporosis, lower body temperatures, lower blood pressure, slower pulse, a weakened heart, lanugo (growth of fine body hair), bluish hands and feet, constipation, slowed metabolism and **reflexes**, loss of muscle mass, and kidney and heart failure. Anorexics also have been found to have abnormal levels of several neurotransmitters, which can, in turn, contribute further to depression. People suffering from anorexia often must be hospitalized for secondary medical effects of the condition. Sometimes the victim must be force-fed in order to be kept alive. Due to medical complications as well as emotional distress caused by the disorder, anorexia nervosa is one of the few mental disorders that can be fatal. The

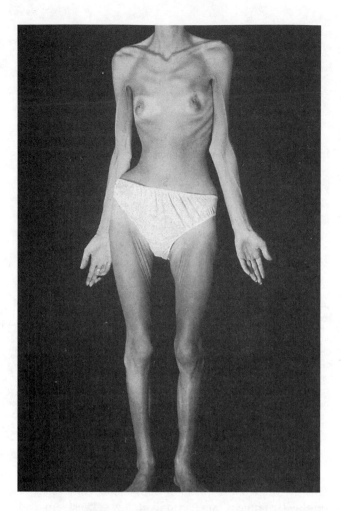

**The body of a woman with anorexia.** *(Biophoto Associates/ Science Source. Photo Researchers, Inc. Reproduced with permission.)*

**American Psychiatric Association** estimates that mortality rates for anorexia may be as high as 5 to 18 percent.

According to the National Association of Anorexia Nervosa and Associated Disorders (ANAD), anorexia nervosa and its related disorders, **bulimia** and binge eating disorder, afflict an estimated seven million women and one million men in the United States. The peak times of onset are ages 12 to 13 and age 17. The American Anorexia and Bulimia Association (AABA) calculates that as many as 1 percent of teenage girls become anorexic and 10 percent of those may die as a result.

In order to reduce the risks of **eating disorders**, cultural ideals connecting thinness and beauty to self-worth and happiness must change so that children establish healthier attitudes and eating behaviors, and learn to value themselves and others for intrinsic qualities, rather than extrinsic ones focusing on appear-

ance. Treatment and cure for anorexia are possible through skilled psychiatric intervention that includes medical evaluation, **psychotherapy** for the individual and family group, nutritional counseling, and possibly medication and/or hospitalization. With treatment and the passage of time, about 70 percent of anorexics eventually recover and are able to maintain a **normal** body weight.

The American Anorexia and Bulimia Association is the principal and oldest national non-profit organization working for the prevention, treatment, and cure of eating disorders. Its mission is inclusive of sufferers, their families, and friends. The AABA publishes a quarterly newsletter reviewing developments in research and programming. It also organizes a referral network which includes educational programs and public information materials, professional services and outpatient programs, patient and parent support groups, and training of recovered patients as support group facilitators.

*See also* Body image; Bulimia

**Further Reading**

Epling, W. Rank. *Solving the Anorexia Puzzle.* Toronto: Hogrefe and Hubers, 1991.

Maloney, Michael. *Straight Talk About Eating Disorders.* New York : Facts on File, 1991.

**Further Information**

American Anorexia and Bulimia Association (AABA). 418 E. 78th Street, New York, New York 10021, (212) 734–1114.

American Dietetic Association (ADA) NCDC-Eating Disorders. 216 W. Jackson Blvd., Chicago, Illinois 60606, (800) 366–1655.

National Anoretic Aid Society. 445 E. Dublin-Granville Road, Worthington, Ohio 43229, (614) 436–1112.

National Association of Anorexia Nervosa and Associated Disorders (ANAD). Box 7, Highland Park, Illinois 60035, (708) 831–3438.

# Antidepressants

Medications used to treat depression.

The two most common types of antidepressants are tricyclic antidepressants (TCAs) and selective serotonin re-uptake inhibitors (SSRIs). Examples of TCAs include nortriptyline (also known by the brand name Pamelor), imipramine (Tofranil), and desipramine (Norpramin). Examples of SSRIs include fluoxetine (Prozac), sertraline (Zoloft), and paroxetine (Paxil). Clinical studies have shown that some people benefit from these medications.

## Tricyclic antidepressants (TCAs)

Before using TCAs, it is necessary to have a medical history and examination of the patient, including an electrocardiogram (EKG). Not everyone develops side effects when taking TCAs, but the most common side effects include: dry mouth, impaired **ability** to focus **vision** at close range, constipation, urinary hesitation, dizziness, weight gain, and sedation. TCAs may produce minor cardiovascular changes such as orthostatic hypotension (low blood pressure when the person stands up, often causing light-headedness), hypertension, rapid heart beat, and minor changes in the electrical activity of the heart, which may show in the electrocardiogram (EKG). Most of these side effects can be minimized by slowly adjusting the dose of the drug.

During treatment with TCAs, patients should be monitored by a physician trained in the management of these medications. It is recommended that he or she perform regular blood pressure, heart rate, and EKG monitoring. TCAs may interact with other medications the patient is taking, so it is important to consult a doctor before doing so. Finally, the TCAs should not be stopped abruptly, as this may induce mild withdrawal side effects (malaise, chills, stomachache, flu-like symptoms). Though they are safe if carefully monitored and taken as prescribed, TCAs can be lethal if taken in overdose.

## Selective serotonin re-uptake inhibitors (SSRIs)

The reports that SSRIs are effective in treating adults with major depressive disorder (MDD), together with the findings that SSRIs have a relatively benign side effect profile, low lethality after an overdose, and once-a-day administration, have encouraged the use of SSRIs.

Several studies have reported 70-90% response rate to fluoxetine or sertraline for the treatment of adolescents with major depressive disorder, but the results of these studies are not conclusive because they have methodological limitations. A recent, large, well-performed investigation showed that fluoxetine was more effective for the treatment of depressed children and adolescents than a placebo. Despite the significant response to fluoxetine, many patients had only partial improvement.

Overall, the SSRIs have similar effectiveness and side effects as TCAs. The most common side effects include nausea, stomachache, diarrhea, headaches, mild tremors, sweating, **sleep** disturbance, sedation, restlessness, lack of appetite, decreased weight, vivid **dreams**, and **sexual dysfunction** (inability to have an orgasm or delayed ejaculation). Most of these side effects are temporary and may be diminished by reducing the dose or discontinuing the medication. There are no specific laboratory tests required before administering SSRIs. These drugs do have potentially harmful interactions with several commonly prescribed drugs; therefore, all physicians should be informed if someone is taking an SSRI.

## Patients who do not respond to treatment

The most common reasons for failure of treatment are inadequate medication dosage or length of medication trial, lack of compliance with treatment, exposure to chronic or severe life events that require different modalities of therapy, existence of other psychiatric disorders (e.g., substance abuse, anxiety disorder), and misdiagnosis. In adults with resistant **depression**, several types of combinations of medications and ECT (**electroconvulsive therapy**) have been found to be useful.

# Antisocial behavior

A pattern of behavior that is verbally or physically harmful to other people, animals, or property, including behavior that severely violates social expectations for a particular environment.

Antisocial behavior can be broken down into two components: the presence of antisocial (i.e., angry, aggressive, or disobedient) behavior and the absence of prosocial (i.e., communicative, affirming, or cooperative) behavior. Most children exhibit some antisocial behavior during their development, and different children demonstrate varying levels of prosocial and antisocial behavior. Some children may exhibit high levels of both antisocial and prosocial behaviors; for example, the popular but rebellious child. Some, however, may exhibit low levels of both types of behaviors; for example, the withdrawn, thoughtful child. High levels of antisocial behavior are considered a clinical disorder. Young children may exhibit **hostility** towards authority, and be diagnosed with **oppositional-defiant disorder**. Older children may lie, steal, or engage in violent behaviors, and be diagnosed with **conduct disorder**. **Mental health** professionals agree, and rising rates of serious school disciplinary problems, delinquency, and violent crime indicate, that antisocial behavior in general is increasing. Thirty to 70% of **childhood** psychiatric admissons are for disruptive behavior disorders, and diagnoses of behavior disorders are increasing overall. A small percentage of antisocial children grow up to become adults with **antisocial personality disorder**, and a greater proportion suffer from the social, academic, and occupational failures resulting from their antisocial behavior.

## Causes and characteristics

Factors that contribute to a particular child's antisocial behavior vary, but usually they include some form of **family** problems (e.g., marital discord, harsh or inconsistent disciplinary practices or actual **child abuse**, frequent changes in primary caregiver or in housing, learning or cognitive disabilities, or health problems). **Attention deficit/hyperactivity disorder** is highly correlated with antisocial behavior. A child may exhibit antisocial behavior in response to a specific stressor (such as the death of a parent or a **divorce**) for a limited period of time, but this is not considered a psychiatric condition. Children and adolescents with antisocial behavior disorders have an increased risk of accidents, school failure, early alcohol and substance use, **suicide**, and criminal behavior. The elements of a moderate to severely antisocial personality are established as early as kindergarten. Antisocial children score high on **traits** of impulsiveness, but low on anxiety and reward-dependence—that is, the degree to which they value, and are motivated by, approval from others. Yet underneath their tough exterior antisocial children have low **self-esteem**.

A salient characteristic of antisocial children and adolescents is that they appear to have no feelings. Besides showing no care for others' feelings or remorse for hurting others, they tend to demonstrate none of their own feelings except **anger** and hostility, and even these are communicated by their aggressive acts and not necessarily expressed through **affect**. One analysis of antisocial behavior is that it is a defense mechanism that helps the child to avoid painful feelings, or else to avoid the anxiety caused by lack of control over the **environment**.

Antisocial behavior may also be a direct attempt to alter the environment. **Social learning theory** suggests that negative behaviors are reinforced during childhood by parents, caregivers, or peers. In one formulation, a child's negative behavior (e.g., whining, hitting) initially serves to stop the parent from behaving in ways that are aversive to the child (the parent may be fighting with a partner, yelling at a sibling, or even crying). The child will apply the learned behavior at school, and a vicious cycle sets in: he or she is rejected, becomes angry and attempts to force his will or assert his pride, and is then further rejected by the very peers from whom he might learn more positive behaviors. As the child matures, "mutual avoidance" sets in with the parent(s), as each party avoids the negative behaviors of the other. Consequently, the child receives little care or supervision and, especially during **adolescence**, is free to join peers who have similarly learned antisocial means of expression.

Different forms of antisocial behavior will appear in different settings. Antisocial children tend to minimize the frequency of their negative behaviors, and any reliable assessment must involve observation by mental health professionals, parents, teachers, or peers.

## Treatment

The most important goals of treating antisocial behavior are to measure and describe the individual child's or adolescent's actual problem behaviors and to effectively teach him or her the positive behaviors that should be adopted instead. In severe cases, medication will be administered to control behavior, but it should not be used as substitute for therapy. Children who experience explosive rage respond well to medication. Ideally, an interdisciplinary team of teachers, social workers, and guidance counselors will work with parents or caregivers to provide universal or "wrap-around" services to help the child in all aspects of his or her life: home, school, work, and social contexts. In many cases, parents themselves need intensive training on **modeling** and reinforcing appropriate behaviors in their child, as well as in providing appropriate discipline to prevent inappropriate behavior.

A variety of methods may be employed to deliver social skills training, but especially with diagnosed antisocial disorders, the most effective methods are systemic therapies which address communication skills among the whole family or within a peer group of other antisocial children or adolescents. These probably work best because they entail actually developing (or redeveloping) positive relationships between the child or adolescent and other people. Methods used in social skills training include modeling, role playing, corrective feedback, and token **reinforcement** systems. Regardless of the method used, the child's level of cognitive and **emotional development** often determines the success of treatment. Adolescents capable of learning communication and problem-solving skills are more likely to improve their relations with others.

Unfortunately, conduct disorders, which are the primary form of diagnosed antisocial behavior, are highly resistant to treatment. Few institutions can afford the comprehensiveness and intensity of services required to support and change a child's whole system of behavior; in most cases, for various reasons, treatment is terminated (usually by the client) long before it is completed. Often, the child may be fortunate to be diagnosed at all. Schools are frequently the first to address behavior problems, and regular classroom teachers only spend a limited amount of time with individual students. **Special education** teachers and counselors have a better chance at instituting long-term treatment programs—that is, if the student stays in the same school for a period of years. One study showed teenage boys with conduct disorder had had an average of nine years of treatment by 15 different institutions. Treatments averaged seven months each.

Studies show that children who are given social skills instruction decrease their antisocial behavior, especially when the instruction is combined with some form of supportive peer group or **family therapy**. But the long-term effectiveness of any form of therapy for antisocial behavior has not been demonstrated. The fact that peer groups have such a strong influence on behavior suggests that schools that employ collaborative learning and the mainstreaming of antisocial students with regular students may prove most beneficial to the antisocial child. Because the classroom is a natural environment, learned skills do not need to be transferred. By judiciously dividing the classroom into groups and explicitly stating procedures for group interactions, teachers can create opportunities for positive interaction between antisocial and other students.

*See also* Antisocial personality disorder; Conduct disorder; Oppositional-defiant disorder; Peer acceptance

### Further Reading

Evans, W. H., et al. *Behavior and Instructional Management: An Ecological Approach*. Boston: Allyn and Bacon, 1989.
Landau, Elaine. *Teenage Violence*. Englewood Cliffs, NJ: Julian Messner, 1990.
McIntyre, T. *The Behavior Management Handbook: Setting Up Effective Behavior Management Systems*. Boston: Allyn and Bacon, 1989.
Merrell, K. W. *School Social Behavior Scales*. Bradon, VT: Clinical Psychology Pub. Co., 1993.
Redl, Fritz. *Children Who Hate: The Disorganization and Breakdown of Behavior Controls*. New York: Free Press, 1965.
Shoemaker, Donald J. *Theories of Delinquency: An Examination of Explanations of Delinquent Behavior*, 2nd ed. New York: Oxford UP, 1990.
Whitehead, John T. and Steven P. Lab. *Juvenile Justice: An Introduction*. Cincinnati, OH: Anderson Pub. Co., 1990.
Wilson, Amos N. *Understanding Black Adolescent Male Violence: Its Prevention and Remediation*. Afrikan World Infosystems, 1992.

# Antisocial personality disorder

A behavior disorder developed by a small percentage of children with conduct disorder whose behavior does not improve as they mature. Also known as sociopathy or psychopathy.

About 3% of males and 1% of females develop antisocial personality disorder, which is essentially the adult version of childhood **conduct disorder**. Antisocial personality disorder is only diagnosed in people over age 18, the symptoms are similar to those of conduct disorder, and the criteria for diagnosis include the onset of conduct disorder before the age of 15. According to the ***Diagnostic and Statistical Manual of Mental Disorders*** (DSM-IV), people with antisocial personality disorder demonstrate a pattern of **antisocial behavior** since age 15.

The adult with antisocial personality disorder displays at least three of the following behaviors:

• Fails to conform to social norms, as indicated by frequently performing illegal acts, and pursuing illegal occupations.
• Is deceitful and manipulative of others, often in order to obtain money, sex, or drugs.
• Is impulsive, holding a succession of jobs or residences.
• Is irritable or aggressive, engaging in physical fights.
• Exhibits reckless disregard for safety of self or others, misusing motor vehicles or playing with fire.
• Is consistently irresponsible, failing to find or sustain work or to pay bills and debts.
• Demonstrates lack of remorse for the harm his or her behavior causes others.

An individual diagnosed with antisocial personality disorder will demonstrate few of his or her own feelings beyond contempt for others. This lack of **affect** is strangely combined with an inflated sense of self-worth and often a superficial charm, which tends to mask their inner apathy. Authorities have linked antisocial personality disorder with abuse, either physical or sexual, during childhood, neurological disorders (which are often undiagnosed), and low IQ. Those with a parent with an antisocial personality disorder or substance abuse problem are more likely to develop the disorder. The antisocially disordered person may be poverty-stricken, homeless, a substance abuser, or have an extensive criminal record. Antisocial personality disorder is associated with low socioeconomic status and urban settings.

### Treatment

Antisocial personality disorder is highly unresponsive to any form of treatment. Although there are medications available that could quell some of the symptoms of the disorder, noncompliance or abuse of the drugs prevents their widespread use. The most successful treatment programs are long-term, structured residential settings in which the patient systematically earns privileges as he or she modifies behavior. Some form of dynamic **psychotherapy** is usually given along with the **behavior modification**. The therapist's primary task is to establish a relationship with the patient, who has usually had very few relationships in his or her life and is unable to trust, fantasize, feel, or learn. The patient should be given the opportunity to establish positive relationships with as many people as possible and be encouraged to join **self-help groups** or prosocial reform organizations.

*See also* Antisocial behavior; Conduct disorder; Oppositional-defiant disorder; Peer acceptance

### Further Reading
Cleckley, Hervey M. *The Mask of Sanity*. Rev. ed. New York: New American Library; St. Louis: Mosby, 1982.
Magid, Ken, and Carole A. McKelvey. *High Risk*. New York: Bantam Books, 1988.
Winnicott, D. W. *Deprivation and Delinquency*. New York: Tavistock Publications, 1984.

### Further Information
Antisocial and Violent Behavior Branch. Division of Biometry and Applied Sciences. National Institute of Mental Health. 18-105 Parklawn Bldg., 5600 Fishers Lane, Rockville, MD 20857, (301) 443–3728.

# Anxiety/Anxiety disorders

An unpleasant emotion triggered by anticipation of future events, memories of past events, or ruminations about the self.

Stimulated by real or imagined dangers, anxiety afflicts people of all ages and social backgrounds. When the anxiety results from irrational fears, it can disrupt or disable **normal** life. Some researchers believe anxiety is synonymous with **fear**, occurring in varying degrees and in situations where people feel threatened by some danger. Others describe anxiety as an unpleasant **emotion** caused by unidentifiable dangers or dangers that, in reality, pose no threat. Unlike fear, which is caused by realistic, known dangers, anxiety can be more difficult to identify and to alleviate.

Rather than attempting to formulate a strict definition of anxiety, most psychologists simply make the distinction between normal anxiety and neurotic anxiety, or anxiety disorders. Normal (sometimes called objective) anxiety occurs when people react appropriately to the situation causing the anxiety. For example, most people feel anxious on the first day at a new job for any number of reasons. They are uncertain how they will be received by co-workers, they may be unfamiliar with their duties, or they may be unsure they made the correct decision in taking the job. Despite these feelings and any accompanying physiological responses, they carry on and eventually adapt. In contrast, anxiety that is characteristic of

anxiety disorders is disproportionately intense. Anxious feelings interfere with a person's **ability** to carry out normal or desired activities. Many people experience stage fright—the fear of speaking in public in front of large groups of people. There is little, if any, real danger posed by either situation, yet each can stimulate intense feelings of anxiety that can affect or derail a person's desires or obligations. **Sigmund Freud** described neurotic anxiety as a danger signal. In his id-ego-superego scheme of human behavior, anxiety occurs when **unconscious** sexual or aggressive tendencies conflict with physical or moral limitations.

Anxiety disorders afflict millions of people. Symptoms of these disorders include physiological responses: a change in heart rate, trembling, dizziness, and tension, which may range widely in severity and origin. People who experience generalized anxiety disorder and panic disorders usually do not recognize a specific reason for their anxiety. **Phobias** and **obsessive-compulsive disorders** occur as people react to specific situations or stimuli. Generalized anxiety disorder is characterized by pervasive feelings of worry and tension, often coupled with fatigue, rapid heart rate, impaired **sleep**, and other physiological symptoms. Any kind of **stress** can trigger inappropriate, intense responses, and panic attacks can result. People suffering from generalized anxiety experience "free-floating" fears, that is, no specific event or situation triggers the response. People keep themselves on guard to ward against unknown dangers.

It is believed that generalized anxiety disorder is, at least to some extent, inherited, or is caused by chemical imbalances in the body. Depending on the severity of the symptoms and the responsiveness of the patient, treatment may vary. Often, drugs in the benzodiazepine family (Valium, Librium, and Xanax) are prescribed. These drugs combat generalized anxiety by relaxing the **central nervous system**, thus reducing tension and relaxing muscles. They can cause drowsiness, making them an appropriate treatment for insomnia. In proper dosages, they can relieve anxiety without negatively affecting thought processes or alertness. Medication is most effective when combined with psychological therapies to reduce the risk of recurrence. **Behavior therapy** is designed to help modify and gain control over unwanted behaviors by learning to cope with difficult situations, often through controlled exposures to those situations. **Cognitive therapy** is designed to change unproductive thought patterns by learning to examine feelings and distinguish between rational and irrational thoughts. Relaxation techniques focus on breathing retraining to relax and resolve the stresses that contribute to anxiety.

Controlling or eliminating the physical symptoms of anxiety without medication is another method of treatment.

| APGAR SCORING SYSTEM | | | |
|---|---|---|---|
| Factor | 0 points | 1 point | 2 points |
| Heart rate | No heartbeat | Under 100 beats per minute | Over 100 beats per minute |
| Respiration | Not breathing | Irregular, with weak cry | Regular with strong cry |
| Muscle tone | Limp, no movement | Limited movement of the limbs | Active movement of the limbs |
| Color | Completely blue, pale | Pink body with blue hands and feet | All pink |
| Reflexes | No response to being poked in the nose | Grimace when poked | Cry, cough, or sneeze when poked |

For example, practiced breathing techniques can slow the heart rate. Access to fresh air can ease sweating. Effective control of such symptoms can be useful in controlling the anxiety itself. **Psychotherapy** is another method of treating generalized anxiety disorder and is used in conjunction with **drug therapy** or in cases where medication proves ineffective. While there is no definitive cause for the disorder, communicating their feelings to a sympathetic therapist helps some people reduce their anxiety.

### Further Reading

Amen, Daniel G. *Change Your Brain, Change Your Life: The Breakthrough Program for Conquering Anxiety, Depression, Obsessiveness, Anger, and Impulsiveness.* New York: Crown Publishing Group, 2000.

Goodwin, Donald W. *Anxiety.* New York: Oxford University Press, 1986.

Zimbardo, Philip G. *Psychology and Life.* 12th ed. Glenview, IL: Scott, Foresman, 1988.

# Apgar score

An indication of a newborn infant's overall medical condition.

The Apgar Score is the sum of numerical results from tests performed on newborn infants. The tests were devised in 1953 by pediatrician Virginia Apgar (1909-1974). The primary purpose of the Apgar series of tests is to determine as soon as possible after **birth** whether an infant requires any medical attention, and to determine whether transfer to a neonatal (newborn infant) intensive care unit is necessary. The test is administered one minute after birth and again four minutes later. The newborn infant's condition is evaluated in five categories: heart rate, breathing, muscle tone, color, and **reflexes**. Each category is given a score between zero and two, with the highest possible test score totaling ten (a score of 10 is rare, see chart). Heart rate is assessed as either under or over 100 beats per minute. Respiration is evaluated according to regularity and strength of the newborn's cry. Muscle tone categories range from limp to active movement. Color—an indicator of blood supply—is determined by how pink the infant is (completely blue or pale; pink body with blue extremities; or completely pink). Reflexes are measured by the baby's response to being poked and range from no response to vigorous cry, cough, or sneeze. An infant with an Apgar score of eight to ten is considered to be in excellent health. A score of five to seven shows mild problems, while a total below five indicates that medical intervention is needed immediately.

# Aphasia

A condition, caused by neurological damage or disease, in which a person's previous capacity to understand or express language is impaired. The ability to speak, listen, read, or write may be affected depending on the type of aphasia involved.

In contrast to neurological problems that affect the physical **ability** to speak or perform other linguistic functions, aphasia involves the mental ability to manipulate speech sounds, vocabulary, grammar, and meaning. There are several different types of aphasia. Each has different symptoms and is caused by damage to a different part of the **brain**.

The great majority of aphasias are caused by damage to the left hemisphere of the brain, which is the dom-

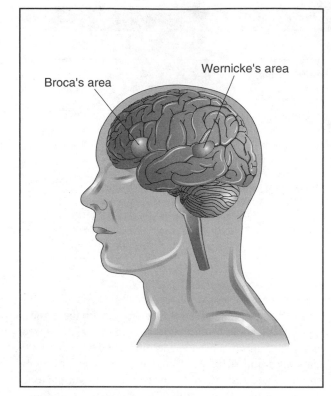

Broca's area

Wernicke's area

**Broca's aphasia results from damage to the frontal lobe of the language-dominant area of the brain. Wernicke's aphasia is caused by damage to the temporal lobe of the same language-dominant area.** *(Electronic Illustrations Group. Reproduced with permission.)*

inant language hemisphere for approximately 95 percent of right-handed people and 60 to 70 percent of left-handed people. Two areas in the left hemisphere—Broca's area and Wernicke's area—and the pathways connecting them are especially important to linguistic ability, and damage to these areas is the most common cause of aphasia. Broca's area, located in the frontal lobe of the left hemisphere, is named for the 19th-century French physician **Paul Broca** (1824-1880), an early pioneer in the study of lateralization (the specialized functioning of the right and left sides of the brain). Aphasia resulting from damage to this area, called Broca's aphasia, is characterized by slow, labored, "telegraphic" speech, from which common grammatical function words, such as prepositions and articles, are missing ("I went doctor"). In general, however, comprehension of spoken and written language is relatively unaffected.

Wernicke's area, in the upper rear part of the left temporal lobe, is named for **Carl Wernicke** (1848-1905), who first described it in 1874. Aphasia associated with this area—called Wernicke's aphasia—differs dramatically from Broca's aphasia. While speech in Broca's

aphasia is overly concise, in Wernicke's aphasia it is filled with an abundance of words (logorrhea), but they are words which fail to convey the speaker's meaning. Even though their pitch and rhythm sound normal, many of the words are used incorrectly or are made-up words with no meaning (aphasic jargon). Besides their speech difficulties, persons with Wernicke's aphasia also have trouble comprehending language, repeating speech, naming objects, reading, and writing. An interesting exception to their comprehension impairment is their ability to respond readily to direct commands that involve bodily movement, such as "Close your eyes."

Certain types of aphasia—called disconnection aphasias—are caused by damage to the connections of Broca's or Wernicke's areas to each other or to other parts of the brain. Conduction aphasia results from damage to the fiber bundles connecting the two language areas and is characterized by fluent but somewhat meaningless speech and an inability to repeat phrases correctly. In transcortical sensory aphasia, the connections between Wernicke's area and the rest of the brain are severed, but the area itself is left intact. Persons with this condition have trouble understanding language and expressing their thoughts but can repeat speech without any trouble. Another type of aphasia, word deafness, occurs when auditory information is prevented from reaching Wernicke's area. Persons affected by word deafness can hear sounds of all kinds and understand written language, but spoken language is incomprehensible to them, since the auditory signals cannot reach the part of the brain that decodes them.

Most types of aphasia are accompanied by some difficulty in naming objects. However, when this problem is the only symptom, the condition is called anomic aphasia. Persons with anomic aphasia can comprehend and repeat the speech of others and express themselves fairly well, although they are unable to find some of the words they need. However, they do poorly when asked to name specific objects. Anomic aphasia is caused by left hemisphere damage that does not affect either Broca's or Wernicke's area. It commonly occurs after a head injury and also in **Alzheimer's disease**. Global aphasia is caused by widespread damage to the dominant cerebral hemisphere, either left or right. This condition is characterized by an almost total loss of all types of verbal ability—speech, comprehension, reading, and writing.

It is possible for people suffering from aphasia following a stroke or head injury to recover some of their language abilities with the aid of a speech therapist. However, there is little chance of recovery from severe cases of aphasia.

*See also* Left-brain hemisphere; Right-brain hemisphere

## Further Reading

Browning, Elizabeth. *I Can't See What You're Saying.* New York: Coward, McCann & Geoghegan, 1973.

Hughes, Kathy. *God Isn't Finished With Me Yet.* Nashville: Winston-Derek, 1990.

Howard, David. *Aphasia Therapy: Historical and Contemporary Issues.* Hillsdale, NJ: Erlbaum, 1987.

# Applied psychology

The area of psychology in which basic theory and research are applied to the actual problems faced by individuals on a daily basis.

Applied psychology can be best understood by comparing it to the area of psychology known as basic psychology, which is concerned with answering questions about behavior through psychological theory and research. Applied psychology utilizes this knowledge to actively intervene in the treatment of individuals with mental or emotional disorders, and is also employed in business, education, and government.

Approximately two-thirds of American psychologists work in applied fields. Many are involved in clinical or **counseling psychology**, diagnosing and treating individuals with various problems of adjustment. Approximately one-third of the psychologists in practice in the United States today are clinical psychologists, and most people are referred to them for treatment of a wide range of problems, including developmental, medical, and rehabilitative as well as psychiatric. These professionals use a wide range of therapies, ranging from Freudian **psychoanalysis** to Rogerian **client-centered therapy** to newer cognitive approaches. Clinical psychologists may go into private practice, either alone or in groups, or work in hospitals or clinics. They may also practice in a variety of other settings, including community mental-health centers, university medical schools, centers for the mentally and physically handicapped, prisons, state institutions and hospitals, judicial courts, and probation offices. A subfield within **clinical psychology** is community psychology, which investigates environmental factors that contribute to mental and emotional disorders. Health psychologists deal with the psychological aspects of physical illness, investigating the connections between the mind and a person's physical condition.

Applied psychology also includes the areas of school and **educational psychology**. School psychologists are state certified and work in public school settings, often with children who have learning, behavioral, and emotional problems. They perform individualized assessments of each child, consult with his or her par-

ents, and advise the school system on methods to best facilitate the child's education. Educational psychologists, by comparison, study the process of education itself; how people learn and which educational methods and materials are most successful. Applied research in this field focuses on how to improve teaching, solve learning problems, and measure learning **ability** and progress. Educational psychologists may devise **achievement tests**, evaluate teaching methods, develop learning aids and curricula, and investigate how children of various ages learn. They often serve as researchers and educators at teacher training institutions, in university psychology departments, and on the staffs of educational research organizations. Educational psychologists also work in government agencies, business, and the military.

Applied psychology has many applications in business and industry. Organizational and industrial psychologists are concerned with the relationships between people and their jobs. They study and advise employers in such areas as employee morale, job-related **stress**, job enrichment, **leadership** qualities, and the effects of flex time in productivity. Personnel psychologists screen job applicants, assess job performance, and recommend employees for promotion. Consumer psychologists study the preferences and buying habits of consumers as well as their responses to advertising, often working together with advertising copywriters, public relations experts, and statisticians. They are employed not only by business but also by government agencies such as the Food and Drug Administration and the Federal Trade Commission.

Engineering psychology applies information about human behavior to the design of machines, tools, jobs, and work environments to provide the best possible match with the abilities and limitations of the human beings who will use them. It is part of a broader area known as human-factors engineering (also called ergonomics) that has links to anatomy, anthropometry, environmental medicine, and toxicology. One very specific work environment that provides the arena for another specialization is the military. Military psychologists applying psychological research to the operations of the armed forces are involved in personnel selection, testing, and training; evaluating morale; analyzing job performance; studying social interaction among troops; and exploring the dynamics of combat situations. Psychology has also contributed to the exploration of space in areas including the selection and training of astronauts; the study of alterations in work-rest cycles; the design of space vehicles, space suits, and equipment used in space; and research on the operational problems of space flight.

A relatively new specialty is **forensic psychology**, which involves the application of psychology to law enforcement and the judicial system. While some forensic psychologists perform research in academic settings, others work in police departments, participating in officer training and assisting in criminal investigations. Forensic psychologists may help create **personality** profiles of criminals; formulate principles for jury selection; hypnotize victims, eyewitnesses, or defendants to enhance their memories; or study the problems involved in eyewitness testimony. Yet another emerging area is program evaluation, whose practitioners evaluate the effectiveness and cost efficiency of government programs for the Congressional Budget Office, the General Accounting Office, and other government offices and agencies.

Like psychologists engaged in research, the majority of those who practice applied psychology hold Ph.D. degrees in the field. Doctoral programs generally require completion of a four- to six-year program offered by a university psychology department. The course of study includes a broad overview (including courses in such areas as statistics, personality theory, and **psychotherapy**), as well as specialization in a particular subfield and completion of a practicum, internship, and dissertation. Some clinical psychologists hold a Psychology Doctorate (Psy.D.), a degree that was introduced at the University of Illinois in 1968 and is geared exclusively toward the training of clinicians rather than researchers. Offered at universities and at independent, "free-standing" professional schools of psychology, the Psy.D. program stresses course work in applied methods of assessment and intervention and eliminates the dissertation requirement.

### Further Reading
Beck, Robert C. *Applying Psychology: Critical and Creative Thinking.* 3rd ed. Englewood Cliffs, NJ: Prentice-Hall, 1992.
Wise, Paula Sachs. *The Use of Assessment Techniques by Applied Psychologists.* Belmont, CA: Wadsworth Publishing Co., 1989.

# Aptitude tests

See **Vocational Aptitude Test**

# Archetype

A central concept in the theory of personality developed by Swiss psychiatrist Carl Jung.

Archetypes are primordial images and symbols found in the collective **unconscious**, which—in contrast to the personal unconscious—gathers together and passes on the experiences of previous generations, preserving traces of humanity's evolutionary development over time.

**Carl Jung** began to evolve his theory of archetypes around 1910 while working with patients at the Burghölzli Mental Hospital. Noting the presence of universal symbols from religion and mythology in the **dreams** and fantasies of uneducated patients, who would have had no conscious way of learning them, he concluded that these images belonged to a part of the unconscious not derived from personal experience. Jung proposed that universal images and ideas can be passed from generation to generation like biological **traits**, and he formulated the concept of the collective unconscious, whose contents become conscious when called forth by appropriate experiences in one's life. In formulating his ideas about archetypes, Jung supplemented his clinical observations with a comprehensive study of myths and symbols that later included investigations into the religions and mythologies of preliterate peoples in Africa and the southwestern United States.

Jungian archetypes are like prototypes or molds that each person fills in differently depending on his or her individual experience. For example, although the term "mother" has certain universal connotations that come to mind for most people, the details of this archetype will be different for everyone. For Jung, archetypes were more than a theoretical construct—his interest in them was primarily therapeutic. He claimed that his patients improved when they understood the ways in which their difficulties were related to archetypes. There is no limit to the number of possible archetypes: they are as varied as human experience itself. Many take the form of persons, such as the hero, the child, the trickster, the demon, and the earth mother. Others are expressed as forces of nature (sun, moon, wind, fire) or animals. They may also occur as situations, events (**birth**, rebirth, death), or places.

Jung considered four archetypes, in particular, important enough to form separate systems within the **personality**. These include the persona, the anima and animus, the shadow, and the self. The persona is a person's public image, the self he or she shows to others ("persona" is derived from the Latin word for mask). The persona is necessary for survival, as everyone must play certain roles, both socially and professionally, to get along in society. However, management of the persona can cause emotional difficulties. A common problem occurs when a person comes to identify too strongly with the persona that he or she has created, a condition that Jung called inflation. Victims of this problem are often highly successful, accomplished people who have become so preoccupied with projecting a certain image—often for professional advancement—that their lives become empty and alienated.

The anima and animus are the opposite of the persona—they represent a person's innermost self. They are also distinguished by gender: the anima is a man's feminine side, and the animus is a woman's masculine side. Jung theorized that in order for persons of both sexes to understand and respond to each other, each sex had to incorporate and be able to express elements of the other, a belief that foreshadowed both the feminist and men's movements in the United States by over half a century. The shadow is associated with a person's animal instincts, the "dark side" that is outside the control of the conscious personality. However, it is also potentially a source of spontaneity, **creativity**, and insight. In contrast to the anima and animus, the shadow is involved in one's relationships to persons of the same sex. Perhaps the most important archetype is that of the Self, which organizes and unites the entire personality. However, rather than combining all the other archetypes or aspects of personality, the Self has a dynamic all its own, which governs both inner harmony and harmony with the external world. It is closely related to the ability of human beings to reach their highest potential, a process that Jung called individuation, which he considered every person's ultimate goal.

## Further Reading

Hall, Calvin S. and Vernon J. Nordby. *A Primer of Jungian Psychology.* New York: Mentor, 1973.

Hopcke, Robert. *A Guided Tour of the Collected Works of C. G. Jung.* Shambhala; distributed in the U.S. by Random House, 1989.

# Artificial intelligence

Computer-based technology intended to replicate the complicated processes of human cognition, including such complex tasks as reasoning, and machine learning, whereby a man-made device actually incorporates its experiences into new endeavors, learning from its mistakes and engaging in creative problem solving.

The study of artificial **intelligence**, referred to as AI, has accelerated in recent years as advancements in computer technology have made it possible to create more and more sophisticated machines and software programs. The field of AI is dominated by computer scientists, but it has important ramifications for psychologists as well because in creating machines that replicate human thought, much is learned about the processes the human **brain** uses to "think."

Creating a machine to think highlights the complexities and subtleties of the human mind. For instance, cre-

ating a machine to recognize objects in photographs would seem, at first thought, rather simple. Yet, when humans look at a photograph, they do so with expectations about the limitations of the media. We fill in the missing third dimension and account for other missing or inconsistent images with our sense of what the real world looks like. To program a computer to make those kinds of assumptions would be a gargantuan task. Consider, for instance, all the information such a computer would need to understand that the array of images all pressed up against a flat surface actually represent the three-dimensional world. The human mind is capable of decoding such an image almost instantaneously.

This process of simulating human thought has led to the development of new ideas in information processing. Among these new concepts are fuzzy logic, whereby a computer is programmed to think in broader terms than either/or and yes/no; expert systems, a group of programming rules that describe a reasoning process allowing computers to adapt and learn; data mining, detecting patterns in stimuli and drawing conclusions from them; genetic algorithm, a program that provides for random mutation for the machine to improve itself; and several others.

Recent applications of AI technology include machines that track financial investments, assist doctors in diagnoses and in looking for adverse interactions in patients on multiple medications, and spotting credit card fraud. An Australian scientist working in Japan is attempting to create a silicon brain using newly developed quantum resistors. Reported in a 1995 article in *Business Week*, Hugo de Garis is leading a team of scientists to create a computing system capable of reproducing itself. As *Business Week* reports, the project will attempt to "not only coax silicon circuits into giving birth to innate intelligence but imbue them with the power to design themselves—to control their own destiny by spawning new generations of ever improving brains at electronic speeds." This type of technology is called evolvable hardware.

Other recent advances in AI have been the creation of artificial neural systems (ANS) which has been described as "an artificial-intelligence tool that attempts to simulate the physical process upon which intuition is based—that is, by simulating the process of adaptive biological learning." ANS, essentially, is a network of computers that are grouped together in ways similar to the brain's configuration of biological processing lobes.

Even considering all of these advancements, many people are skeptical that a machine will ever replicate human **cognition**. Marvin Minsky, a scientist at the Massachusetts Institute of Technology, states that the hardest thing of all in the creation of artificial intelligence is building a machine with common sense.

**Further Reading**

Anthes, Gary H. "Great Expectations: Award Winning AI Scientist Raj Reddy . . ." *Computer World* (3 April 1995): 82.

Chartrand, Sabra. "A Split in Thinking among Keepers of Artificial Intelligence." *New York Times* (18 July 1993).

Port, Otis. "Computers That Think Are Almost Here." *Business Week* (17 July 1995): 68-73.

Wright, Robert. "Can Machines Think?" *Time* (25 March 1996): 50-58.

# Art therapy

The use of art to express feelings, emotions, and perceptions through the creation and analysis of visual and other sensory symbols and works.

Art therapy, sometimes called expressive art or art psychology, encourages self-discovery and emotional growth. It is a two-part process, involving both the creation of art and the discovery of its meaning. Rooted in **Sigmund Freud** and **Carl Jung**'s theories of the subconscious and **unconscious**, art therapy is based on the premise that visual symbols and images are the most accessible and natural form of communication to the human experience. Patients are encouraged to visualize, and then create, the thoughts and emotions that they can't express verbally. The resulting artwork is then reviewed, and its meaning interpreted by the patient. The analysis of the artwork typically enables a patient to gain some level of insight into their feelings and allows them to work through these issues in a constructive manner. Art therapy is typically practiced in conjunction with individual, group, or **family psychotherapy** (or verbal therapy). While a therapist may provide critical guidance for these activities, an important feature of effective talk therapy is that the patient/artist, not the therapist, direct the interpretation of their artwork.

Some **mental health** professionals also view art therapy as an effective diagnostic tool for the identification of specific types of **mental illness** or traumatic events. In the late 19th century, French psychiatrists Ambrose Tardieu and Paul-Max Simon both published studies on the visual characteristics of and symbolism in the artwork of the mentally ill. They found that there were recurring themes and visual elements in the drawings of patients with specific types of mental illness. More recently, psychiatric literature has explored common themes and symbols in the artwork of **sexual abuse** survivors and victims of trauma.

## Applications

Art therapy can be a particularly useful treatment tool for children, who often have limited language and communications skills. By drawing or visually expressing their feelings, even if they can't identify or label the emotions, younger patients have a starting point from which to address these issues. Art therapy is also valuable for adolescents and adults who are unable or unwilling to verbalize thoughts and feelings.

Beyond its use in mental health treatment, art therapy is also employed as an adjunct (or complementary) therapy to traditional medicine for the treatment of biologically based diseases and conditions. The correlation between mental health and physical health is well documented. Art therapy has been used in the healing process to relieve **stress** and develop coping mechanisms, in an effort to treat both the physical and mental needs of the patient.

Although art therapy has traditionally centered on visual mediums (paintings, sculptures, drawings, etc.), some mental healthcare providers have broadened the definition to include music, film, dance, writing, and other artistic genres.

## Benefits

- *Self-discovery.* At its most successful, art therapy triggers an emotional **catharsis** (a sense of relief and well-being through the recognition and acknowledgement of subconscious feelings).

- *Personal fulfillment.* The creation of a tangible reward can build confidence and nurture feelings of self-worth. Personal fulfillment comes from both the creative and the analytical components of the process.

- *Empowerment.* Art therapy can help individuals visually express emotions and fears that they were never able to articulate through conventional means, and give them some sense of control over these feelings.

- *Relaxation and stress relief.* Chronic stress can be harmful to both mind and body. It can weaken and damage the immune system, cause insomnia and **depression**, and trigger a host of circulatory problems (e.g., high blood pressure, atherosclerosis, and cardiac arrhythmia). When used alone or in combination with other relaxation techniques such as guided imagery, art therapy can be a potent stress reliever.

- *Symptom relief and physical rehabilitation.* Art therapy can also help individuals cope with **pain** and promote physiological healing by identifying and working through **anger** and resentment issues and other emotional stresses.

*See also* Music therapy

Paula Ford-Martin

## Further Reading

Ganim, Barbara. *Art and healing: using expressive art to heal your body, mind, and spirit.* New York: Three Rivers Press, 1999.

# Assessment, psychological

*The assessment of personality variables.*

Psychological assessment is used for a variety of purposes, ranging from screening job applicants to providing data for research projects. Most assessment methods fall into one of three categories: observational methods, **personality** inventories, or **projective techniques**.

Observational assessment is performed by a trained professional either in the subject's natural setting (such as a classroom), an experimental setting, or during an interview. Interviews may be either structured with a standard agenda, or unstructured, allowing the subject to determine much of what is discussed and in what order. Impressions gained from interviews are often recorded using rating scales listing different personality **traits**. Expectations of the observer, conveyed directly or through body language and other subtle cues, may influence how the interviewee performs and how the observer records and interprets his or her observations.

Personality inventories consist of questionnaires on which people report their feelings or reactions in certain situations. They may assess a particular trait, such as anxiety, or a group of traits. One of the oldest and best known personality inventories is the **Minnesota Multiphasic Personality Inventory** (MMPI), a series of 550 questions used to assess a number of personality traits and psychological disturbances for people over age 16. The MMPI is scored by comparing the subject's answers to those of people known to have the traits or disturbances in question. While initially designed to aid in the diagnosis of serious **personality disorders**, the MMPI is now widely used for persons with less severe problems, as enough data has been collected from this population to allow for reliable interpretation of test results. One problem with personality inventories is that people may try to skew their answers in the direction they think will help them obtain their objective in taking the test, whether it is being hired for a job or being admitted to a therapy program. Validity scales and other methods are commonly used to help determine whether an individual has answered the test items carefully and honestly.

A projective test gives the subject a greater opportunity for imaginative freedom of expression than does a **personality inventory**, where the questions are fixed before-hand. Projective tests present individuals with ambiguous situations which they must interpret, thus projecting their own personalities onto those situations. The best known projective test is the Rorschach Psychodiagnostic Test, or inkblot, test first devised by the Swiss psychologist Hermann Rorschach in the 1920s. The test subject describes his or her reactions to elaborate inkblots presented on a series of ten cards. Responses are interpreted with attention to three factors: what parts or parts of each inkblot the subject responds to; what aspects of the inkblot are stressed (color, shape, etc.); and content (what the inkblot represents to the subject). Another widely used projective test is the **Thematic Apperception Test** (TAT), developed at Harvard University in the 1930s. In this test, the subject is shown a series of pictures, each of which can be interpreted in a variety of ways, and asked to construct a story based on each one. Responses tend to reflect a person's problems, motives, preoccupations, and interpersonal skills. Projective tests require skilled, trained examiners, and the reliability of these tests is difficult to establish due to their subjective nature. Assessments may vary widely among different examiners. Scoring systems for particular traits have been fairly reliable when used with the Thematic Apperception Test.

*See also* Personality inventory; Rorschach technique

## Further Reading

*Handbook of Psychological Assessment.* New York: Wiley, 1990.
*Personality and Ability: The Personality Assessment System.* Lanham, MD: University Press of America, 1994.

# Assimilation

*An aspect of adaptation proposed by French psychologist Jean Piaget.*

In the **cognitive development** theory of **Jean Piaget**, assimilation is one of two complementary activities involved in **adaptation**, the process of learning from and adjusting to one's **environment**. Assimilation consists of taking in new information and incorporating it into existing ways of thinking about the world. Conversely, accommodation is the process of changing one's existing ideas to adapt to new information. When an infant first learns to drink milk from a cup, for example, she tries to assimilate the new experience (the cup) into her existing way of ingesting milk (sucking). When she finds that this doesn't work, she then changes her way of drinking milk by accommodating her actions to the cup. The dual process of accommodation and assimilation leads to the formation and alteration of schemas, generalizations about the world which are formed from past experience and used to guide a person through new experiences. According to Piaget, cognitive development involves the constant search for a balance between assimilation and accommodation, which he referred to as equilibration.

In the context of **personality**, the term "assimilation" has been used by **Gordon Allport** (1897-1967) to describe the tendency to fit information into one's own attitudes or expectations. In the study of **attitudes and attitude change**, it means adopting the attitudes of people with whom we identify strongly.

**Further Reading**

Allport, G. *Pattern and Growth in Personality.* New York: Holt, Rinehart, and Winston, 1961.

Piaget, Jean, and Bärbel Inhelder. *The Psychology of the Child.* New York: Basic Books, 1969.

# Associationism

The view that mental processes can be explained in terms of the association of ideas.

Advanced primarily by a succession of 18th- and 19th-century British philosophers, associationism anticipated developments in the modern field of psychology in a variety of ways. In its original empiricist context, it was a reaction against the Platonic philosophy of innate ideas that determined, rather than derived from, experience. Instead, the associationists proposed that ideas originated in experience, entering the mind through the senses and undergoing certain associative operations.

The philosopher **John Locke** (1632-1704) introduced the term "association of ideas" in the fourth edition of his *Essay Concerning Human Understanding* (1700), where he described it as detrimental to rational thought. George Berkeley (1685-1753), an Irish bishop, applied associationist principles to visual **depth perception**, arguing that the capacity to see things in three dimensions is the result of learning, not of innate **ability**. The British physician David Hartley (1705-1757) also dealt with the biological implications of associationism, formulating a neurophysiological theory about the transmission of ideas and also describing physical activity in terms of association (a concept that anticipated subsequent principles of **conditioning**). Hartley also developed a comprehensive theory of associationism that encompassed **memory, imagination, dreams**, and morality. The Scottish philosopher **David Hume** (1711-1776) proposed the principles of similarity and contiguity, asserting that ideas that are similar or experienced simul-

taneously (or in rapid succession) become associated with each other.

James and John Stuart Mill (father and son philosophers) continued to examine associationism into the 19th century. The elder Mill proposed a mechanistic theory that linked ideas together in "compounds," especially through the principle of contiguity. The younger Mill, whose defining metaphor for the association of ideas was "mental chemistry," differed from his father in claiming that the mind played an active rather than a passive role in forming associations. He also suggested that a whole idea may amount to more than the sum of its parts, a concept similar to that later advocated by psychologists of the Gestalt school. Other 19th-century figures known for associationist ideas were Thomas Browne, who proposed several secondary laws of association, and Alexander Bain (1818-1903), who formulated a comprehensive psychological system based on association.

Aside from similarity and contiguity, other governing principles have been proposed to explain how ideas become associated with each other. These include temporal contiguity (ideas or sensations formed close together in time), repetition (ideas that occur together repeatedly), recency (associations formed recently are the easiest to remember), and vividness (the most vivid experiences form the strongest associative bonds). In the 20th century, the clearest heir to associationism is **behaviorism**, whose principles of conditioning are based on the association of responses to stimuli (and on one's association of those stimuli with positive or negative **reinforcement**). Also, like associationism, behaviorism emphasizes the effects of **environment** (nurture) over innate characteristics (nature). Association appears in other modern contexts as well: the **free association** of ideas is a basic technique in the theory and practice of **psychoanalysis**, and association plays a prominent role in more recent cognitive theories of memory and learning.

**Further Reading**

Locke, John. *An Essay Concerning Human Understanding.* Buffalo: Prometheus Books, 1995.

Russell, Bertrand. *A History of Western Philosophy.* New York: Simon and Schuster, 1945.

Schultz, D. P. *A History of Modern Psychology.* 3rd ed. New York: Academic Press, 1981.

# Attachment

An emotional bond between an infant or animal and its caregiver, contributing to the infant or animal's experience of safety, comfort, and security while in the caregiver's presence and distress when temporarily separated.

Many developmental psychologists view attachment—the special relationship between infant and caregiver—as an important building block for later relationships and adult **personality**. Since attachment plays a central role in theories of social and **emotional development**, the scientific study of attachment has remained in the forefront of **developmental psychology** for the past several decades.

**John Bowlby**, a psychoanalytically trained clinician, developed modern attachment theory in the 1950s as a variant of object-relations, which was a variant of Freud's theory that the infant's tie to the mother is the cornerstone of adult personality.

Bowlby integrated a number of approaches into his theory, including systems and evolutionary theories to formulate a modern attachment theory.

Before widespread acceptance of Bowlby's theory, psychologists viewed attachment as a secondary drive, derived from primary drives like hunger. It was thought that attachment to the mother occurred because she supplied food and became the object of the infant's attachment through association with feeding and the reduction of other primary needs. Prior to Bowlby's theory, behaviorist psychologists theorized that the need for attachment arose from an infant's physical needs for food and warmth, both of which were provided by the mother. They believed that a baby's preference for the mother was the result of **conditioning**. A child was thought to be overly attached if crying and clingy behavior occurred frequently.

Research in the 1950s, however, cast these theories into doubt. One of the most famous research studies in this area was performed by **Harry Harlow**. He placed infant monkeys in a cage with two surrogate mother dolls: one made of wire holding a bottle of milk and the other made of soft cloth. According to the behaviorist view, the monkey should have developed an attachment to the wire mother because she was the source of food. But the infant monkeys developed attachments to the cloth mothers, suggesting that the need for comfort and warmth are more important, or more psychologically ingrained, than the need for food.

Later experiments with monkeys also revealed the effects secure attachments had on infants. In one experiment, strange foreign objects were introduced to a cage with an infant monkey. When alone, the monkey would react with **fear**. When the cloth mother was present, however, the infant would first retreat to the mother in fear, but then, having been reassured, it would begin to explore the foreign object. Human infants, too, are much more likely to react with fear to unknowns if a mother is not in the vicinity. With a mother present, however, an infant is much more exploratory—even if the mother is not within sight but nearby.

Bowlby became one of the first to map out stages of attachment, addressed in his writings, including his 1980 book, *Attachment and Loss*. Bowlby suggested that from **birth** until about the age of three months, babies are in the initial pre-attachment phase. Here, infants simply need to be held and demonstrate no preference for who does the holding. The next phase, attachment-in-the-making phase, takes place from three to four months and is marked by an infant's emerging preference to be held by familiar figures, although it is important to note that the figure does not necessarily have to be the mother. According to Bowlby, the final stage of attachment is the clear-cut attachment phase. Beginning at about six months, this phase features an infant's clear insistence on its mother or its primary caregiver.

**Mary Ainsworth**, a prominent researcher in attachment and an associate of Bowlby's, devised a test to measure the type and degree of attachment a child feels for his mother. The test, called the Ainsworth **Strange Situation** test, involves a mother leading her child into a strange room, which the child is free to explore with the mother present. A stranger then enters the room and the mother leaves. If the infant becomes distressed, the stranger will try and console her. The mother then returns and the stranger leaves. In another scenario, the mother leaves again after the stranger returns. Finally, the mother returns for good and the stranger leaves. Based on the infants' response to their mothers' return, children are labeled "securely attached," "avoidant," or "ambivalent."

Psychologists believe that attachment serves to help children begin exploring the world. As the above studies show, if presented with a strange situation, an infant will either avoid or engage in exploration, chiefly dependent upon whether an attachment figure is present. Additionally, it has been shown that lack of attachment in early life can have a negative impact on exploratory propensity in later life. In 1971, researchers separated a group of monkeys from their mothers for six days and then analyzed their behaviors two years later in comparison to a **control group** that had not undergone separation. The group that had been separated was observed to be far more reticent in exploratory behaviors than the control group. Still other studies indicate that cognitive functioning in children is enhanced among "securely attached" (according to the Ainsworth scale) infants.

*See also* Behaviorism; Stranger anxiety

## Further Reading

Karen, Robert. *Becoming Attached: Unfolding the Mysteries of the Infant-Mother Bond and Its Impact on Later Life.* New York: Warner Books., 1994.

Thompson, Andrea. "The Affection Factor." *Working Mother* (April 1995): 63.

Wise, Nicole. "What's in Passion?" *Parenting* (May 1993): 131.

# Attention

Selective concentration or focus on a particular stimulus.

Attention describes the focusing of perceptive awareness on a particular stimulus or set of stimuli that results in the relative exclusion of other stimuli and is often accompanied by an increase in the readiness to receive and to respond to the stimulus or set of stimuli involved. A state of attention may be produced initially in many ways, including as a conscious, intentional decision, as a **normal** function of social interaction, or as a reaction to an unexpected event. In any case, attention is a fundamental component of learning. There is evidence that very young human infants have an innate **ability** and inclination to attend to, however briefly, particular instances of auditory or visual stimulation. Children often demonstrate the effects of their attention in the form of apparent misperceptions. For example, the relative size of objects near the center of a child's visual stimulus field is regularly overestimated by the child. In human adults, generally, attention seems to be directly related to the novelty, incongruity, complexity, or personal significance of the situation. As situations become increasingly familiar or similar to situations previously experienced by an individual, the actions of that individual become increasingly routine, and the individual becomes less attentive. There are distinct and measurable neurological and physiological, bioelectric and biochemical aspects and correlates of attention, and the capacity to achieve or to maintain a state of attention may be limited by a number of mental or physical dysfunctions.

In psychology, the term "attention span" is used technically and specifically to mean the number of separate stimulus elements, or the amount of stimulus material, that can be perceived and remembered after a brief presentation. In popular usage, the term attention span is used to mean the amount of time that can be continuously spent in a state of attention.

## Further Reading

Hans, James. *The Mysteries of Attention.* Albany: SUNY Press, 1993.

# Attention deficit/hyperactivity disorder (ADHD)

Disorder characterized by attentional deficit and/or hyperactivity—impulsivity more severe than expected for a developmental age.

Attention deficit/hyperactivity disorder (ADHD) refers to a combination of excessive motor restlessness, difficulty in controlling or maintaining attention to relevant events, and impulsive responding that is not adaptive. Children and adults experience the symptoms of ADHD in most areas of their life. It affects their performance in school or at work, depending on their age, and it affects them socially. In some cases, however, ADHD sufferers experience the disorder in only one arena, such as a child who may be hyperactive only in school, or an adult who finds it impossible to concentrate during meetings or while socializing with friends after work. Particularly stressful situations, or those requiring the sufferer to concentrate for prolonged periods of time, often will exacerbate a symptom or a series of symptoms.

Studies indicate that ADHD affects 3-5% of all children. For some children hyperactivity is the primary feature of their ADHD diagnosis. These children may be unable to sit quietly in class. They may fidget in their chairs, sharpen their pencils multiple times, flip the corners of the pages back and forth, or talk to a neighbor. On the way up to the teacher's desk they may take several detours.

Most children with ADHD have both attentional and hyperactivity-impulsivity components, and so they may experience difficulties regulating both attention and activity. Although many children who do not have ADHD seem periodically inattentive or highly active, children with ADHD experience these difficulties more severely than others at the same developmental level. Moreover, these difficulties interfere with age-appropriate behavioral expectations across settings such as home, playground, and school.

Psychologists have not always used the label ADHD to describe this constellation of behaviors. In the 1950s and 60s, children exhibiting these symptoms were either diagnosed as minimally **brain** damaged or labeled as behavior problems. The fourth edition of the *Diagnostic and Statistical Manual (DSM-IV)*, which is used to classify psychiatric disorders, describes ADHD as a pattern of inattention and/or impulsivity-hyperactivity more severe than expected for the child's developmental level. The symptoms must be present before age seven, although diagnosis is frequently made only after the disor-

**ADHD affects people throughout their lives. This man is performing memory-improving exercises to overcome his attention deficit difficulties.** *(AP/Wide World Photos. Reproduced with permission.)*

der interferes with school activities. Symptoms must be present in at least two settings, and there must be clear evidence of interference with academic, social, or occupational functioning. Finally, the symptoms must not be due to other neuropsychiatric disorders such as **pervasive developmental disorder**, **schizophrenia** or other psychoses, or anxiety disorder or other neuroses.

Inattention may be evident in (a) failing to attend closely to tasks or making careless errors, (b) having difficulty in persisting with tasks until they are completed, (c) appearing not to be listening, (d) frequently shifting tasks or activities, (e) appearing disorganized, (f) avoiding activities that require close or sustained attention, (g) losing or damaging items by not handling them with sufficient care, (h) being distracted by background noises or events, or (i) being forgetful in daily activities. According to the *DSM-IV,* six or more of these symptoms must persist for six months or more for a diagnosis of ADHD with inattention as a major component.

Hyperactivity may be seen as (a) fidgety behavior or difficulty sitting still, (b) excessive running or climbing when not appropriate, (c) not remaining seated when asked to, (d) having difficulty enjoying quiet activities,

(e) appearing to be "constantly on the go," or (f) excessive talking. Impulsivity may be related to hyperactive behavior and may be manifest as (a) impatience or blurting out answers before the question has been finished, (b) difficulty in waiting for one's turn, and (c) frequent interruptions or intrusions. Impulsive children frequently talk out of turn or ask questions seemingly "out of the blue." Their impulsivity may also lead to accidents or engaging in high risk behavior without consideration of the consequences. According to the *DSM-IV,* six or more of these symptoms must persist for six months or more for a diagnosis of ADHD with hyperactivity-impulsivity as a major component.

The *DSM-IV* recognizes subtypes of ADHD. The most prevalent type is the Combined Type, in which individuals show at least six of the symptoms of inattention as well as of hyperactivity or impulsivity. The Predominantly Inattentive Type and the Predominantly Hyperactive-Impulsive type are distinguished by which of the major pattern of symptoms predominate.

It is important that a careful diagnosis be made before proceeding with treatment, especially with medication. Often symptoms of inattention or hyperactivity may cause parents to seek professional help, but these symptoms may not necessarily indicate the presence of ADHD. Paul Dworkin, a physician with special interests in school failure, reports that out of 245 children referred for evaluation due to parental or school concerns about inattention, impulsivity, or overactivity, only 38% received a diagnosis of ADHD, although almost all (91%) were diagnosed with some kind of academic problem.

## Who gets ADHD?

Boys outnumber girls by at least a factor of four; studies have found prevalence ranging from four to nine times as many boys with ADHD compared to girls. The **family** members (first degree relatives) of children with ADHD are more likely to have the disorder, as well as a higher prevalence of **mood** and anxiety disorders, learning disabilities, and substance abuse problems. Children who have a history of abuse or neglect, multiple foster placements, infections, prenatal drug exposure, or low birth weight are also more likely to have ADHD. Although there is no definitive laboratory test for ADHD nor a distinctive biological marker, children with ADHD do have a higher rate of minor physical anomalies than the general population.

Children may develop problems because of the consequences of ADHD. If the causes of a child's disruptive or inattentive behavior are not understood, the child may be punished, ridiculed, or rejected, leading to potential reactions in the areas of **self-esteem**, conduct, academic performance, and family and social relations. A child who feels that he or she is unable to perform to expectations no matter what type of effort is put forth may begin to feel helpless or depressed. Often, the reaction can exacerbate the inattention or hyperactivity or diminish the child's capacity to compensate, and a vicious cycle can develop.

The course of the disorder may vary. For many ADHD children, symptoms remain relatively stable into the early teen years and abate during later **adolescence** and adulthood. About 30-40% of cases persist into the late teens. Some individuals continue to experience all of their symptoms into adulthood and others retain only some.

## What causes ADHD?

The exact cause of ADHD is not known. The increased incidence of the disorder in families suggests a genetic component in some cases. Brain chemistry is implicated by the actions of the medications that reduce ADHD symptoms, suggesting that there may be a dysfunction of the norepinephrine and dopamine systems. Brain imagining techniques have been used with mixed success. Positron emission tomography (PET) scans show some reduced metabolism in certain areas (prefrontal and premotor cortex) in ADHD adults, but findings on younger patients are less clear. One complication in conducting these imagining studies is the necessity for patients to remain still for a period of time, something that is, of course, difficult for ADHD children to do.

## Treatment

Treatment for ADHD takes two major forms: treating the child and treating the **environment**. Pharmacological treatment can be effective in many cases. Stimulant medications (Ritalin/methylphenidate, Dexedrine/dextroamphetimine, and Cylert/magnesium pemoline) have positive effect in 60-80% of cases and are the most common type of drugs used for ADHD. The benefits include enhancement of attention span, decrease in impulsivity and irrelevant behavior, and decreased activity. Vigilance and discrimination increase and handwriting and math skills frequently improve. These gains are most striking when pharmacological treatment is combined with educational and behavioral interventions.

Stimulant medications, however, may have side effects that may make them inappropriate choices. These side effects include loss of appetite, insomnia, mood disturbance, headache, and gastro-intestinal distress. Tics may also appear and should be monitored carefully. Psychotic reactions are among the more severe side effects. There is some evidence that long-term use of stimulant medication may interfere with physical growth and weight gain. These effects are thought to be ameliorated by "medication breaks" over school vacations and weekends, and the like.

When stimulant medications are not an appropriate choice, non-stimulants or tricyclic **antidepressants** may be prescribed. The use of tricyclic antidepressants, especially, has to be monitored carefully due to possible cardiac side effects. Combined pharmacologic treatment is used for patients who have ADHD in addition to another psychiatric disorder.

It is important that drug treatment not be used exclusively in the management of ADHD. Each child should have an individual educational plan that outlines modifications to the regular mode of instruction that will facilitate the child's academic performance. Teachers need to consider the needs of the ADHD child when giving instructions, making sure that they are well paced with cues to remind the child of each one. They must also understand the origins of impulsive behavior—that the child is not deliberately trying to ruin a lesson or activity by acting unruly. Teachers should be structured, comfortable with the remedial services the child may need, and able to maintain good lines of communication with the parent.

Special assistance may not be limited to educational settings. Families frequently need help in coping with the demands and challenges of the ADHD child. Inattention, shifting activities every five minutes, difficulty completing homework and household tasks, losing things, interrupting, not listening, breaking rules, constant talking, **boredom**, and irritability can take a toll on any family.

Support groups for families with any ADHD member are increasingly available through school districts and health care providers. Community colleges frequently offer courses in discipline and behavior management. Counseling services are available to complement any type of pharmacological treatment that the family obtains for its member. There are also a number of popular books that are informative and helpful. Some of these are listed below.

Doreen Arcus, Ph.D.

**Further Reading**

Barkley, R.A. *Attention Deficit Hyperactivity Disorder: A Handbook for Diagnosis and Treatment.* New York: Guildord Press, 1990.

Hallowell, E.M. and J.J. Ratey. *Driven to Distraction: Recognizing and Coping with Attention Deficit Disorder from Childhood through Adulthood.* New York: Simon and Schuster, 1994.

Manuzza, S., R.G. Klein, A. Bessler, P. Malloy, and M. LaPadula. "Adult Outcome of Hyperactive Boys: Educational Achievement, Occupational Rank, and Psychiatric Status." *Archives of General Psychiatry,* 50, (1993): 565-76.

Weiss, G. *Attention Deficit Hyperactivity Disorder.* Philadelphia: W.B. Saunders, 1992.

Wender, P. *The Hyperactive Child, Adolescent, and Adult: Attention Deficit Disorder through the Lifespan.* New York: Oxford University Press, 1987.

Wilens, T.E. and J. Biederman. "The Stimulants." *Psychiatric Clinics of North America.* D. Shafer, ed. Philadelphia: W.B. Saunders, 1992.

Zametkin, A.J. and J.L. Rappaport. "Neurobiology of Attention Deficit Disorder with Hyperactivity: Where Have We Come in 50 Years?" *Journal of the American Academy of Child and Adolescent Psychiatry* 26, (1987): 676-86.

**Further Information**

Attention Deficit Disorder Association. P.O. Box 972, Mentor, OH 44061, (800) 487–2282.

CHADD (Children and Adults with Attention Deficit Disorder). 499 NW 70th Ave., Suite 308, Plantation, FL 33317, (305) 587–3700 (A national and international non-profit organization for children and adults with ADHD).

# Attitude and behavior

Attitude is a feeling, belief, or opinion of approval or disapproval towards something. Behavior is an action or reaction that occurs in response to an event or internal stimuli (i.e., thought).

People hold complex relationships between attitudes and behavior that are further complicated by the social factors influencing both. Behaviors usually, but not always, reflect established beliefs and attitudes. For example, a man who believes strongly in abstinence before marriage may choose to remain a virgin until his wedding night. Under other circumstances, that same man may engage in premarital sex despite his convictions after being influenced by social messages that his masculinity is dependent on sexual activity.

Ideally, positive attitudes manifest well-adjusted behaviors. However, in some cases healthy attitudes may result in harmful behavior. For example, someone may remain in an abusive and potentially deadly domestic situation because they hold negative attitudes towards **divorce**.

Behavior can be influenced by a number of factors beyond attitude, including preconceptions about self and others, monetary factors, social influences (what peers and community members are saying and doing), and convenience. Someone may have strong convictions about improving the public school system in their town, but if it means a hefty increase to their property taxes, they may vote against any improvements due to the potential for monetary loss. Or, they may simply not vote at all because their polling place is too far from their home, or the weather is bad on election day.

Studies have demonstrated that, in some cases, pointing out inconsistencies between attitudes and behavior can redirect the behavior. In the case of the school supporter, showing that their actions (i.e., not voting, not attending parent-teacher organization meetings) are harming rather than helping efforts to improve education in their town may influence them to reevaluate their behavior so that it reflects their attitudes.

For those in need of psychological treatment, there are several treatment approaches that focus on changing attitudes in order to change behavior. **Cognitive therapy** and cognitive-behavior therapy are two of those techniques. Cognitive therapy attempts to change irrational ways of thinking. Cognitive-behavioral therapy tries to correct the resulting inappropriate behavior.

## Changing attitudes to change behavior

Attitude and behavior are woven into the fabric of daily life. Research has shown that individuals register an immediate and automatic reaction of "good" or "bad" towards everything they encounter in less than a second, even before they are aware of having formed an attitude. Advertising, political campaigns, and other persuasive media messages are all built on the premise that behavior follows attitude, and attitude can be influenced with the right message delivered in the right way.

The fields of social and behavioral psychology have researched the relationship between attitude and behavior extensively. The more psychologists can understand the relationship between attitude and behavior and the factors that influence both, the more effectively they can treat mental disorders, and contribute to the dialogue on important social problems such as **racism**, **gender bias**, and age discrimination.

The concept of "social marketing" combines cognitive-behavioral components of psychology with social science and commercial marketing techniques to encourage or discourage behaviors by changing the attitudes that cause them. It is also a key part of public health education initiatives, particularly in the case of preventive medicine. Campaigns promoting positive attitudes towards prenatal care, abstinence from drug use, smoking cessation, sunscreen use, organ donations, safe sex, cancer screening, and other healthcare initiatives are all examples of social marketing in action. In effect, social marketing is "selling" attitudes and beliefs and ideally influencing associated behavior.

### Changing behavior to influence attitudes

In 1955, clinical psychologist and educator **George Kelly** introduced his psychology of personal constructs. Kelly's constructs were based on the idea that each individual looks at the world through his or her own unique set of preconceived notions about it (i.e., constructs). These constructs change and adapt as the individual is exposed to new and different situations. At the heart of Kelly's theory is the idea that individuals can seek new experiences and practice and adapt new behaviors in order to change their attitudes (or constructs) towards the world. He recommended that therapists encourage their patients to try out new behaviors and coping strategies; he and others that followed frequently found that patients would adapt these useful new behavior patterns and subsequently change their attitudes.

When behavior is inconsistent with attitude, it is sometimes a result of social or **peer pressure**. While adult behavior generally follows from held attitudes, for children, attitudes are often shaped by observed behavior. From a very young age, children copy the actions of others and, to a degree, build their attitudes and beliefs from this learned behavior. As children grow into **adolescence**,

the behavior of their peers can have a significant impact. Sometimes this peer pressure factor can be used to an advantage. One research study found that antismoking campaigns targeted at teenagers can have a higher success rate when adolescent peers are used as instructors.

Paula Ford-Martin

**Further Reading**

Byrne, Donn and Robert A. Baron. *Social psychology.* 8th edition. Boston, MA: Allyn & Bacon, Inc., 1997.

Eagly, Alice and Shelly Chaiken. Dawn Youngblood, ed. *The psychology of attitudes.* Forth Worth, TX: Harcourt Brace Jovanovich College Publishers, 1993.

Kelly, George. *The psychology of personal constructs.* 2 vols. New York: Norton, 1955.

## Attitudes and attitude change

An attitude is a predisposition to respond cognitively, emotionally, or behaviorally to a particular object, person, or situation in a particular way.

Attitudes have three main components: cognitive, affective, and behavioral. The cognitive component concerns one's beliefs; the affective component involves feelings and evaluations; and the behavioral component consists of ways of acting toward the attitude object. The cognitive aspects of attitude are generally measured by surveys, interviews, and other reporting methods, while the affective components are more easily assessed by monitoring physiological signs such as heart rate. Behavior, on the other hand, may be assessed by direct observation.

Behavior does not always conform to a person's feelings and beliefs. Behavior which reflects a given attitude may be suppressed because of a competing attitude, or in deference to the views of others who disagree with it. A classic theory that addresses inconsistencies in behavior and attitudes is **Leon Festinger**'s theory of **cognitive dissonance**, which is based on the principle that people prefer their cognitions, or beliefs, to be consistent with each other and with their own behavior. Inconsistency, or dissonance, among their own ideas makes people uneasy enough to alter these ideas so that they will agree with each other. For example, smokers forced to deal with the opposing thoughts "I smoke" and "smoking is dangerous" are likely to alter one of them by deciding to quit smoking, discount the evidence of its dangers, or adopt the view that smoking will not harm them personally. Test subjects in hundreds of experiments have reduced cognitive dissonance by changing their attitudes. An alternative explanation of attitude change is provided by Daryl Bem's self-perception theory, which asserts that people adjust their attitudes to match their own previous behavior.

Attitudes are formed in different ways. Children acquire many of their attitudes by **modeling** their parents' attitudes. **Classical conditioning** using pleasurable stimuli is another method of attitude formation and one widely used by advertisers who pair a product with catchy music, soothing colors, or attractive people. **Operant conditioning**, which utilizes rewards, is a mode of attitude formation often employed by parents and teachers. Attitudes are also formed through direct experience. It is known, in fact, that the more exposure one has toward a given object, whether it is a song, clothing style, beverage, or politician, the more positive one's attitude is likely to be.

One of the most common types of communication, *persuasion,* is a discourse aimed at changing people's attitudes. Its success depends on several factors. The first of these is the source, or communicator, of a message. To be effective, a communicator must have credibility based on his or her perceived knowledge of the topic, and also be considered trustworthy. The greater the perceived similarity between communicator and audience, the greater the communicator's effectiveness. This is the principle behind politicians' perennial attempts to portray themselves in a folksy, "down home" manner to their constituency. This practice has come to include distinguishing and distancing themselves from "Washington insiders" who are perceived by the majority of the electorate as being different from themselves.

In analyzing the effectiveness of the persuasive message itself, the method by which the message is presented is at least as important as its content. Factors influencing the persuasiveness of a message include whether it presents one or both sides of an argument; whether it states an implicit or explicit conclusion; whether or not it provokes **fear**; and whether it presents its strongest arguments first or last. If the same communicator were to present an identical message to two different groups, the number of people whose attitudes were changed would still vary because audience variables such as age, sex, and **intelligence** also affect attitude change. Many studies have found women to be more susceptible to persuasion than men, but contrasting theories have been advanced to account for this phenomenon. Some have attributed it to the superior verbal skills of females which may increase their **ability** to understand and process verbal arguments. Others argue that it is culturally determined by the greater pressure women feel to conform to others' opinions and expectations.

The effect of intelligence on attitude change is inconclusive. On one hand, it has been hypothesized that the greater one's intelligence, the more willing one is to consider differing points of view. On the other hand, people with superior intelligence may be less easily persuaded because they are more likely to detect weaknesses in another person's argument. There is, however, evidence of a direct link between **self-esteem** and attitude change. People with low self-esteem are often not attentive enough to absorb persuasive messages, while those with high self-esteem are too sure of their own opinions to be easily persuaded to change them. The most easily persuaded individuals tend to be those with moderate levels of self-esteem, who are likely to pay a reasonable amount of **attention** to what those around them say and remain open enough to let it change their minds.

The medium of persuasion also influences attitude change ("the medium is the message"). Face-to-face communication is usually more effective than mass communication, for example, although the effectiveness of any one component of communication always involves the interaction of all of them. The effects of persuasion may take different forms. Sometimes they are evident right away; at other times they may be delayed (the so-called "sleeper effect"). In addition, people may often change their attitudes only to revert over time to their original opinions, especially if their environment supports the initial opinion.

The information-processing model of persuasion, developed by psychologist William McGuire, focuses on a chronological sequence of steps that are necessary for successful persuasion to take place. In order to change listeners' attitudes, one must first capture their attention, and the listeners must comprehend the message. They must then yield to the argument, and retain it until there is an opportunity for action—the final step in attitude change.

## Further Reading
Chapman, Elwood N. *Attitude: Your Most Priceless Possession.* 2nd ed. Los Altos, CA: Crisp Publications, 1990.
Eiser, J. Richard *Social Psychology: Attitudes, Cognition, and Social Behaviour.* New York: Cambridge University Press, 1986.
Zimbardo, Philip G. *The Psychology of Attitude Change and Social Influence.* Philadelphia: Temple University Press, 1991.

# Attraction, interpersonal

A favorable attitude toward, or a fondness for, another person.

Both personal characteristics and environment play a role in interpersonal attraction. A major determinant of attraction is propinquity, or physical proximity. People who come into contact regularly and have no prior negative feelings about each other generally become attracted to each other as their degree of mutual familiarity and comfort level increases. The situation in which people first meet also determines how they will feel about each other. One is more likely to feel friendly toward a person first encountered in pleasant, comfortable circumstances.

People are generally drawn to each other when they perceive similarities with each other. The more attitudes and opinions two people share, the greater the probability that they will like each other. It has also been shown that disagreement on important issues decreases attraction. One of the most important shared attitudes is that liking and disliking the same people creates an especially strong bond between two individuals. The connection between interpersonal attraction and similar attitudes is complex because once two people become friends, they begin to influence each other's attitudes.

**Personality** type is another determinant of interpersonal attraction. In areas involving control, such as dominance, **competition**, and self-confidence, people tend to pair up with their opposites. Thus, for example, the complementary pairing of a dominant person with a submissive one. People gravitate to others who are like themselves in terms of characteristics related to **affiliation**, including sociability, friendliness, and warmth. Another important factor in interpersonal attraction, especially during the initial encounter, is that of physical appearance, even among members of the same sex. Each culture has fairly standard ideas about physical appearance that serve as powerful determinants in how we perceive **character**. Kindness, sensitivity, **intelligence**, modesty, and sociability are among those characteristics that are often attributed to physically attractive individuals in research studies. In one study, attractive job applicants (both male and female) were given markedly preferential treatment by prospective employers compared with equally qualified candidates who were less attractive. There is also evidence that physical appearance has a greater role in the attraction of males to females than vice versa. Behavior, as well as appearance, influences interpersonal attraction. No matter what the circumstances are, behavior is often seen as reflecting a person's general **traits** (such as kindness or **aggression**) rather than as a response to a specific situation.

The type of interpersonal attraction that has particular interest to most people is attraction to the opposite sex. To a certain extent, romantic attraction is influenced by evolutionary considerations: the survival of the species. Some experts claim that when people select potential mates, they look for someone whose status, physical attractiveness, and personal qualities are roughly equivalent to their own. According to another theory, a person will choose a partner who will enhance his or her own self-image or persona. Researchers generally acknowledge a specific set of courting or flirting behaviors, employed by both sexes to attract each other. Initially, both men and women use varied repertoires of body language to signal interest and/or availability. Men may stretch, exaggerate ordinary motions (such as stirring a drink), or engage in preening motions, such as smoothing the hair or adjusting neckties, and younger men often affect a swagger. Women draw attention to themselves by tossing or playing with their hair, tilting their heads, raising their eyebrows, giggling, or blushing. The first connection is generally made through eye contact, often an intent gaze which is then lowered or averted. If the eye contact is positively received, a smile often follows and a conversation is initiated.

Conversations initiated by romantic attraction are generally light and often include laughter. If the attraction progresses, the next step is casual touching in innocuous areas such as the shoulder, wrist, or forearm. The final step in the initial romantic attraction is known as mirroring or body synchrony, which is a matching of nonverbal body language. With bodies aligned and facing each other, the couple begins to move in tandem, leaning toward each other, crossing their legs, or tilting their heads. By these actions, the couple mutually transmit the messages that they like and are like each other. This mirroring activity is not confined to romantic relationships. Infants begin to mirror adult behavior shortly after **birth**, and the technique is consciously practiced by therapists, salespeople, and others whose work depends on establishing a sense of closeness with others. Generally, the adoption of each other's postures may be seen in virtually any grouping of individuals who feel comfortable with and are close to each other.

**Further Reading**

Berscheid, Ellen. *Interpersonal Attraction.* 2nd ed. Reading, MA: Addison-Wesley, 1978.

Bull, Ray. *The Social Psychology of Facial Appearance.* New York: Springer-Verlag, 1988.

# Attribution theory

An area of cognitive therapy that is concerned with how people explain the causes of behavior, both their own and those of others.

A major concept in the study of attribution theory is **locus of control**: whether one interprets events as being caused by one's own behavior or by outside circumstances. A person with an internal locus of control, an "internal," for example, will believe that her performance on a work project is governed by her **ability** or by how hard she works. An "external" will attribute success or failure by concluding that the project was easy or hard, the boss was helpful or unhelpful, or some other rationale. In general, an internal locus of control is associated with optimism and physical health. People with an internal locus of control also tend to be more successful at delaying gratification.

Internal or external attribution is also made with respect to other people (i.e., is another person personally responsible for a certain event, or is it caused by something beyond his or her control?). We make this sort of attribution when we decide whether or not to blame a friend for failing to pay back a loan. If we blame it on her personal qualities, the attribution is internal. If we blame it on a problem she is having, then the attribution is external. Three factors influence whether the behavior of others is attributed to internal or external causes: consensus, consistency, and distinctiveness. Consensus refers to whether other people exhibit similar behavior; consistency refers to whether the behavior occurs repeatedly; and distinctiveness is concerned with whether the behavior occurs in other, similar, situations. For example, if a friend consistently fails to repay a loan, an internal attribution may be ascribed.

### Further Reading
Douglas, Tom. *Scapegoats: Transferring Blame.* New York: Routledge, 1995.

Hewstone, Miles, ed. *Attribution Theory: Social and Functional Extensions.* Oxford, England: B. Blackwell, 1983.

Lamb, Sharon. *The Trouble with Blame: Victims, Perpetrators, and Responsibility.* Cambridge: Harvard University Press, 1996.

McLaughlin, Mary L., Michael J. Cody, and Stephen Reed, eds. *Explaining Oneself to Others: Reason-Giving in a Social Context.* Hillsdale, NJ: Lawrence Erlbaum Assoc., 1992.

## Authoritarian personality

A personality pattern described in detail in the 1950 book of the same name that grew out of a study of anti-Semitism.

**Adolf Hitler and his troops. Authoritarian personality types project their own weaknesses onto groups they denigrate as inferior.** *(Reproduced with permission.)*

Theodor Adorno (1903-1969) led a team of researchers at the University of California, Berkeley, to determine whether there was a correlation between anti-Semitism and certain **personality traits**. While the original goal had been the identification of an "anti-Semitic" personality, the scope was widened, first from anti-Semitic to "Fascist" then to "authoritarian," when the study found that people prejudiced against one ethnic or racial group were likely to be prejudiced against others as well.

A major determining factor in the formation of the authoritarian personality was found to be a pattern of strict and rigid parenting, in which obedience is instilled through physical **punishment** and harsh verbal discipline. Little parental praise or affection is shown, independence is discouraged, and the child's behavior is expected to meet a set standard. Significantly, such parents instill in children not only obedience to themselves but also a deeply entrenched sense of social hierarchy which entails obedience to all persons of higher status. When they reach adulthood, people with this personality structure discharge the **hostility** accumulated by their harsh upbringing against those whom they perceive to be of lower status by forming negative stereotypes of them and discriminating against or overtly persecuting them. It is also thought that they may be projecting their own weaknesses and fears onto the groups they denigrate as inferior. Other traits associated with this personality type include dependence on authority and rigid rules, **conformity** to group values, admiration of powerful figures, compulsiveness, concreteness, and intolerance of ambiguity.

## Further Reading

Eiser, J. Richard *Social Psychology: Attitudes, Cognition, and Social Behaviour.* New York: Cambridge University Press, 1986.
Stone, William F., Gerda Lederer, and Richard Christie, eds. *Strength and Weakness: the Authoritarian Personality Today.* New York: Springer-Verlag, 1993.

# Autism

A severe psychological disorder that first appears in early childhood and is characterized by impaired social interaction and language development, and other behavioral problems.

First described by Dr. Leo Kanner in 1943, autism is a severe **psychological disorder** that affects an estimated four children in 10,000. Autism manifests itself in early **childhood**. The autistic child is impaired socially, in **language development**, and exhibits other behavioral problems. This disorder is also known as infantile or childhood autism and Kanner's autism.

The occurrence of autism is four times higher in boys than girls. It is now believed that some of the "wild" or "feral" children found living outdoors on their own may have been autistic children abandoned by their parents. The most famous of these was Victor, the "wild boy of Aveyron," discovered in 1799 at the age of approximately 11. Although he remained almost totally unable to speak, Victor showed great improvements in **socialization** and cognitive **ability** after working for several years with Jean-Marc-Gaspard Itard, a physician and teacher of the deaf.

Contrary to earlier beliefs, autism is not thought to have psychological origins, such as inadequate parenting. Several possible causes of autism have been proposed, including phenylketonuria (an inherited metabolic disease), exposure to rubella or certain chemicals *in utero*, and hereditary predisposition. There is no accurate test for autism, although CT scans of autistic children sometimes reveal abnormalities in the ventricles of the **brain**. Autism is usually diagnosed in children between the ages of two and three years based on clinical observation and parental reports. Until this point, manifestations of the disorder are difficult to detect, and in some cases an autistic child will develop normally for the first year or two of life. However, a break usually occurs before the age of two and a half, when speech development (if it has begun) stops and social responses fail to develop.

Children and adults with autism demonstrate a marked impairment in social interaction. Generally, it first appears in children as an inability to form a close **attachment** to their parents. As infants, they may refuse to cuddle and may react to physical contact by stiffening their bodies and attempting to slide away. Often, autistic children do not develop other feelings that commonly accompany emotional attachments, such as grief, sadness, **guilt**, or shame, and when older, they are generally impervious to being left with strangers. There is also a lack of interest in or a failure to form peer relationships, and the ordinary desire to share experiences and interests with others tends to be lacking. Autistic children lack interest and skill in games and other typical kinds of reciprocal child's **play**, including imitative play. Standard nonverbal behaviors that support social interactions—eye contact, facial expressions, and body language—are generally not used appropriately.

Language difficulties are the single symptom that most often leads parents to seek diagnosis and help for autistic children. The development of spoken language is either delayed or totally absent in children with autism. Those who can speak still have trouble listening to others and initiating or carrying on a conversation. The speech of autistic persons often lacks normal grammatical structures and is also nonstandard in terms of such characteristics as pitch, speed, rhythm, or stress on syllables. **Echolalia** (echoing other people's voices or voices heard on television) is also common.

Besides social and language impairments, the other major symptom of autism is the presence of repetitive, ritualized patterns of behavior. These may be repeated physical movements, such as rocking, swaying, flapping one's arms, or clapping. Autistic behavior may also take such forms as arranging objects in specific patterns or quantities, mimicking a particular action, or performing a routine activity exactly the same way every day. Other behavioral characteristics associated with autism are a preoccupation with a single interest (often one for which a large number of facts may be collected); resistance to trivial changes in routine; fascination with a moving object (such as revolving doors) or a particular part of an object; and a strong attachment to an inanimate object. Persons with autism may exhibit oversensitivity to certain stimuli (such as light or **touch**), unusual pickiness in eating, inappropriate **fear** and/or fearlessness, and self-injuring behavior, such as head banging. As many as 25 percent of autistic children develop epileptic seizures later in life, often in **adolescence**, although this particular symptom appears only in those who are mentally retarded.

Three-fourths of autistic children are mentally retarded, and 60 percent have IQ scores below 50. However, many demonstrate skill in music, mathematics, long-term memorization of trivial data, and specialized tasks such as assembling jigsaw puzzles. Autistic children with IQ scores of 70 and above have the best prognosis for living and working independently as adults, although only one in six children with autism becomes a well-adjusted adult, with another one out of six achieving a fair degree of adjustment. Even those autistic adults who function relatively well will still experience difficulty with social interaction and communication, and highly restricted interests and activities. Besides IQ, other predictors of future adjustment for autistic children are their degree of language development, the overall severity of their symptoms, and the types of treatment they receive. While **psychotherapy** has not been of value in treating persons with autism, **behavior modification**, medication, and dietary recommendations have been proven effective in controlling specific symptoms. **Special education** programs are able to improve the social interaction of autistic children and enhance their academic skills. Developmental work that includes parents has been found to be especially helpful.

## Further Reading

*Autism: Nature, Diagnosis, and Treatment.* New York: Guilford Press, 1989.

Cunninghame, Karen. *Autism: A World Apart.* Fanlight Productions, 1988.

Frith, Uta. *Autism: Explaining the Enigma.* Basil Blackwell, 1989.

Jordan, Rita. *Understanding and Teaching Children with Autism.* New York: Wiley, 1995.

## Further Information

Autism Society of America (formerly National Society for Autistic Children). 7910 Woodmont Avenue, Suite 650, Bethesda, MD 20814-3015, (301) 657–0881, (800) 3328–8476.

# Autoeroticism

Manual stimulation (usually self-stimulation) of the genital organs with the intention, typically, of producing sexual arousal and orgasm.

Autoeroticism is the scientific term used to describe masturbation, the stimulation of the genital organs to achieve orgasm. Although masturbation was widely condemned in most premodern societies, and has been the subject of remarkable and persistent superstitions and extreme taboos, there is evidence that contemporary attitudes toward masturbation are becoming increasingly tolerant of this behavior. Studies in the United States and Europe indicate that about 90 percent of adolescent and adult males and about 80 percent of adolescent and adult females have engaged in masturbation. While masturbation is usually a private, solitary activity, it is often accompanied by fantasies of sexual activity that involve another person. Relatively few individuals consistently prefer masturbation to sexual activity that involves another person. It has been shown that masturbation is not physically harmful, and the psychological significance of masturbation depends on how it is regarded by the individual.

## Further Reading

Marcus, Irwin M., and John J. Francis, eds. *Masturbation: From Infancy to Senescence.* New York: International Universities Press, 1975.

# Autonomic nervous system

The nervous system responsible for regulating automatic bodily processes, such as breathing and heart rate. The autonomic system also involves the processes of metabolism, or the storage and expenditure of energy.

The **nervous system** consists of two main structures, the **central nervous system** (the **brain** and the spinal cord) and the peripheral nervous system (the sense organs and the nerves linking the sense organs, muscles, and glands to the central nervous system). The structures of the peripheral nervous system are further subdivided into the autonomic nervous system (automatic bodily processes) and the somatic nervous system.

The part of the autonomic nervous system that controls the storage of energy (called anabolism) is the parasympathetic division. Parasympathetic (or anabolic) activities involve bodily functions that occur in normal, nonstressful situations. For example, after eating, the digestive process begins, whereby nutrients are taken from the food and stored in the body. The flow of blood increases to the stomach and intestines while at the same time the heart rate decreases and saliva is secreted. The parasympathetic division also mediates sexual arousal, even though most parasympathetic functions lead to lower overt arousal levels. Sexual climax is controlled by the sympathetic division.

In general, sympathetic processes reverse parasympathetic responses. The sympathetic division is activated when the body mobilizes for defense or in response to **stress**. Such processes use energy stored during anabolism; this use of energy is referred to as catabolism. In defensive situations, the heart rate increases, the lungs expand to hold more oxygen, the pupils dilate, and blood flows to the muscles.

While the autonomic nervous system normally functions quite appropriately, abnormalities can appear. In anxiety disorders, for example, certain somatic (bodily) symptoms such as muscular tension, hyperventilation, increased heart rate, and high blood pressure are increased, posing the body for attack. This physiological response can lead to such additional maladies as headaches and digestive problems. At times, parasympathetic responses occur simultaneously. In extreme stressful situations, for example, an individual may experience involuntary discharge of the bladder and bowels. Some research has also indicated deficiencies in autonomic arousal processes in psychiatric patients prior to schizophrenic breakdown.

For decades, scientists believed that autonomic processes were not amenable to voluntary control. In recent years, however, people with heart problems have learned to modify heart rates, and headache sufferers have learned to modify blood flow to relieve **pain** through **biofeedback** techniques.

**Further Reading**
*Biofeedback and Behavioral Medicine.* New York: Aldine Pub. Co., published annually since 1981.

# Aversive conditioning

Also referred to as aversion therapy, a technique used in behavior therapy to reduce the appeal of behaviors one wants to eliminate by associating them with physical or psychological discomfort.

In aversive conditioning, the client is exposed to an unpleasant stimulus while engaging in the targeted behavior, the goal being to create an aversion to it. In adults, aversive conditioning is often used to combat addictions such as smoking or alcoholism. One common method is the administration of a nausea-producing drug while the client is smoking or drinking so that unpleasant associations are paired with the addictive behavior. In addition to smoking and alcoholism, aversive therapy has also been used to treat nail biting, sex addiction, and other strong habits or addictions. In the past, **electroconvulsive therapy** was sometimes administered as a form of aversion therapy for certain disorders, but this practice has been discontinued.

In children aversive conditioning plays a role in one of the most effective treatments for enuresis (bedwetting): the bell and pad method. A pad with a wetness sensor is placed in the child's bed, connected to a bell that sounds at the first sign of wetness. When the bell rings, the child must then get out of bed and go to the bathroom instead of continuing to wet the bed. This method is successful in part because it associates bedwetting with the unpleasantness of being awakened and inconvenienced in the middle of the night. A related technique that further reinforces the inconvenience of bedwetting is having the child change his own sheets and pajamas when he wakes up wet at night.

In a variation of aversive conditioning called **covert sensitization**, the client imagines the undesirable behavior instead of actually engaging in it, and then either imagines or is exposed to an unpleasant stimulus.

*See also* Behavior therapy

**Further Reading**
Doft, Norma. *When Your Child Needs Help: A Parent's Guide to Therapy for Children.* New York: Crown Paperbacks, 1992.

Feindler, Eva L., and Grace R. Kalfus, eds. *Adolescent Behavior Therapy Handbook.* New York: Springer, 1990.

**Further Information**
American Academy of Child and Adolescent Psychiatry. 3615 Wisconsin Avenue NW., Washington, DC 20016–3007, (202) 966–7300, (800) 333–7636.

Association for the Advancement of Behavior Therapy. 15 W. 36th St., New York, NY 10018, (212) 647–1890.

Federation of Families for Children's Mental Health. 1021 Prince St., Alexandria, VA 22314–2971, (703) 684–7710.

# Avoidance learning

An individual's response to avoid an unpleasant or stressful situation; also known as escape learning.

Avoidance learning is the process by which an individual learns a behavior or response to avoid a stressful or unpleasant situation. The behavior is to avoid, or to remove oneself from, the situation. Researchers have found avoidance behavior challenging to explain, since the **reinforcement** for the behavior is to not experience the negative reinforcer, or **punishment**. In other words, the reinforcement is the absence of punishment. To explain this, psychologists have proposed two stages of learning: in stage one, the learner experiences **classical conditioning**; a warning, or stimulus, paired with a punishment. The learner develops a **fear** response when he experiences the stimulus. In stage two, the learner experiences **operant conditioning**; whereby he realizes that an action response to the stimulus eliminates the stressful outcome.

In a common laboratory experiment conducted to demonstrate avoidance learning, a rat is placed in a confined space with an electrified floor. A warning signal is given, followed by an electric current passing through the floor. To avoid being shocked, the rat must find an escape, such as a pole to climb or a barrier to jump over onto a nonelectric floor. At first, the rat responds only when the shock begins, but as the pattern is repeated, the rat learns to avoid the shock by responding to the warning signal. An example of avoidance learning in humans is the situation when a person avoids a yard where there is a barking dog. This learning is particularly strong in individuals who have been attacked by a dog.

*See also* Drive reduction theory; Stress

## Further Reading

Archer, Trevor, and Lars-Gvran Nilsson. *Aversion, Avoidance, and Anxiety: Perspective on Aversively Motivated Behavior.* Hillsdale, NJ: L. Erlbaum Associates, 1989.

Ruben, Douglas H. *Avoidance Syndrome: Doing Things Out of Fear.* St. Louis, MO: W.H. Green, 1993.

# Avoidant personality

A disorder characterized by the avoidance of both social situations and close interpersonal relationships due to an excessive fear of rejection by others.

## Causes and symptoms

The cause of avoidant personality disorder is not clearly defined, and may be influenced by a combination of social, genetic, and biological factors. Avoidant personality **traits** typically appear in **childhood**, with the appearance of excessive **shyness** and **fear** of new people and situations. However, these characteristics are also developmentally appropriate emotions for children, and do not necessarily mean that a pattern of avoidant personality disorder will continue into adulthood. When shyness, unfounded fear of rejection, hypersensitivity to criticism, and a pattern of social avoidance persists and intensifies through **adolescence** and young adulthood, avoidant personality disorder is often indicated. Between 0.5% and 1.0% of the general population suffers from avoidant personality disorder.

## Diagnosis

Many individuals experience avoidant personality characteristics at one point or another in their lives. The occasional feelings of self-doubt and fear in new and unfamiliar social or personal relationships is not unusual, nor is it unhealthy, as these situations may cause feelings of inadequacy and social avoidance in even the most self-confident individuals. Avoidant personality traits only emerge as a disorder when they begin to have a long-term, negative impact on the individual, cause functional impairment by significantly altering lifestyle and impacting quality of life, and trigger feelings of distress for the individual.

The *Diagnostic and Statistical Manual of Mental Disorders, Fourth Edition (DSM-IV)*, the standard diagnostic reference for **mental health** professionals in the United States, states that at least four of the following criteria (or symptoms) must be present in an individual for a diagnosis of avoidant personality disorder:

- The avoidance of occupational or school activities that involve significant interpersonal contact due to an unreasonable or excessive fear of rejection or criticism.
- An unwillingness to enter into an interpersonal relationship unless there are assurances of acceptance.
- Restraint in interpersonal situations because of an unreasonable fear of being ridiculed.
- Preoccupation with criticism and the possibility of rejection in social situations.
- Inhibition with others in interpersonal relationships due to feelings of inadequacy.
- Self-perception of social inadequacy and inferiority to others.
- Reluctance to participate in new activities or take any personal risks because of a perceived risk of embarrassment.

Avoidant personality disorder can occur in conjunction with other social phobias, **mood** and anxiety disorders, and **personality disorders**. Diagnosis may be complicated by the fact that avoidant personality disorder can either be the cause or result of other mood and anxiety disorders. For example, individuals who suffer from major depressive disorder may begin to withdraw from social situations and experience feelings of worthlessness, symptoms that are also prominent features of avoidant personality disorder. On the other hand, the insecurity and isolation that are symptoms of avoidant personality disorder can naturally trigger feelings of **depression**.

## Treatment

**Cognitive therapy** may be helpful in treating individuals with avoidant personality disorder. This therapy assumes that the patient's faulty thinking is causing the personality disorder, and therefore focuses on changing distorted cognitive patterns by examining the validity of the assumptions behind them. If a patient feels he is inferior to his peers, unlikable, and socially unacceptable, a cognitive therapist would test the reality of these assumptions by asking the patient to name friends and **family** who enjoy his company, or to describe past social encounters that were fulfilling to him. By showing the patient that others value his company and that social situations can be enjoyable, the irrationality of his social fears and insecurities are exposed. This process is known as *cognitive restructuring*.

Paula Ford-Martin

## Further Reading

American Psychiatric Association. *Diagnostic and Statistical Manual of Mental Disorders* 4th ed. Washington, DC: American Psychiatric Press, Inc., 1994.

## Further Information

National Mental Health Association. 1021 Prince Street, Alexandria, VA, USA. 22314-2971, fax: (703)684-5968, (703)684-7722, (800)969-NMHA. Email: infoctr@nmha.org. http://www.nmha.org.

# B

## Albert Bandura

**1925-**
American psychologist whose work is concentrated in the area of social learning theory.

Albert Bandura was born in the province of Alberta, Canada, and received his B.A. from the University of British Columbia. He earned his M.A. and Ph.D. in **clinical psychology** at the University of Iowa, focusing on social learning theories in his studies with **Kenneth Spence** and Robert Sears. Graduating in 1952, Bandura completed a one-year internship at the Wichita Guidance Center before accepting an appointment to the department of psychology at Stanford University, where he has remained throughout his career. In opposition to more radical behaviorists, Bandura considers cognitive factors as causal agents in human behavior. His area of research, social cognitive theory, is concerned with the interaction between **cognition**, behavior, and the **environment**.

Much of Bandura's work has focused on the acquisition and modification of **personality traits** in children, particularly as they are affected by observational learning, or **modeling**, which, he argues, plays a highly significant role in the determination of subsequent behavior. While it is common knowledge that children learn by imitating others, little formal research was done on this subject before Neal Miller and John Dollard published *Social Learning and Imitation* in 1941. Bandura has been the single figure most responsible for building a solid empirical foundation for the concept of learning through modeling, or **imitation**. His work, focusing particularly on the nature of **aggression**, suggests that modeling plays a highly significant role in determining thoughts, feelings, and behavior. Bandura claims that practically anything that can be learned by direct experience can also be learned by modeling. Moreover, learning by modeling will occur although neither the observer nor the model is rewarded for performing a particular action, in contrast

**Albert Bandura** *(Archives of the History of American Psychology. Reproduced with permission.)*

to the behaviorist learning methods of **Ivan Pavlov** and **B.F. Skinner**, with their focus on learning through **conditioning** and **reinforcement**. However, it has been demonstrated that **punishment** and reward can have an effect on the modeling situation. A child will more readily imitate a model who is being rewarded for an act than one who is being punished. Thus, the child can learn without actually being rewarded or punished himself—a concept known as *vicarious learning*. Similarly, Bandura has shown that when a model is exposed to stimuli intended to have a conditioning effect, a person who simply observes this process, even without participating in it directly, will tend to become conditioned by the stimuli as well.

Based on his research, Bandura has developed modeling as a therapeutic device. The patient is encouraged to modify his or her behavior by identifying with and imitating the behavior of the therapist. Although modeling was first studied in relation to children, it has been found to be effective in treating phobias in adults as well. The patient watches a model in contact with a feared object, at first under relatively non-threatening conditions. The patient is encouraged to perform the same actions as the model, and the situation is gradually made more threatening until the patient is able to confront the feared object or experience on his or her own.

Bandura has also focused on the human capacity for symbolization, which can be considered a type of inverse modeling. Using their symbolic capacities, people construct *internal* models of the world which provide an arena for planning, problem-solving, and reflection and can even facilitate communication with others. Another area of social cognition theory explored by Bandura is self-regulatory activity, or the ways in which internal standards affect **motivation** and actions. He has studied the effects of beliefs people have about themselves on their thoughts, choices, motivation levels, perseverance, and susceptibility to **stress** and **depression**. Bandura is the author of many books, including *Adolescent Aggression* (1959), *Social Learning and Personality* (1963), *Principles of Behavior Modification* (1969), *Aggression* (1973), *Social Learning Theory* (1977), and *Social Foundations of Thought and Action* (1985).

*See also* Modeling

**Further Reading**

Decker, Philip J. *Behavior Modeling Training.* New York: Praeger, 1985.

# Battered child syndrome

A group of physical and mental symptoms arising from long-term physical violence against a child.

Battered child syndrome occurs as the result of long-term physical **violence** against a child or adolescent. An estimated 2,000 children die each year in the United States from confirmed cases of physical abuse and 14,000 more are seriously injured. The battering takes many forms, including lacerations, bruises, burns, and internal injuries. In addition to the physical harm inflicted, battered children are at risk for an array of behavioral problems, including school difficulties, drug abuse, sexual acting out, running away, **suicide**, and becoming abusive themselves. **Dissociative identity disorder**, popularly known as multiple personality, is also common among abused children.

Detecting and preventing battered child syndrome is difficult because society and the courts have traditionally left the **family** alone. Out of **fear** and **guilt**, victims rarely report abuse. Nearly one-half of **child abuse** victims are under the age of one and therefore unable to report what is happening to them. The parents or guardians who bring a battered child to a hospital emergency room rarely admit that abuse has occurred. Instead, they offer complicated, often obscure, explanations of how the child hurt himself. However, a growing body of scientific literature on pediatric injuries is simplifying the process of differentiating between intentional and accidental injuries. For instance, a 1991 study found that a child needs to fall from a height of 10 ft (3m) or more to sustain the life-threatening injuries that accompany physical abuse. Medical professionals have also learned to recognize a spiral pattern on x rays of broken bones, indicating that the injury was the result of twisting a child's limb.

Once diagnosed, the treatment for battered children is based on their age and the potential for the parents or guardians to benefit from therapy. The more amenable the parents are to entering therapy themselves, the more likely the child is to remain in the home. For infants, the treatment ranges from direct intervention and hospital care to foster care to home monitoring by a social service worker or visiting nurse. Ongoing medical assessment is recommended in all types of treatment. For the preschool child, treatment usually takes place outside the home, whether in a day care situation, a therapeutic preschool, or through individual therapy. The treatment includes speech and language therapy, physical therapy, **play** therapy, **behavior modification**, and specialized medical care.

By the time the child enters school, the physical signs of abuse are less visible. Because these children may not yet realize that their lives are different from those of other children, very few will report that their mothers or fathers are subjecting them to gross physical injury. It is at this stage that psychiatric and behavioral disorders begin to surface. In most cases the children are removed from the home, at least initially. The treatment, administered through either group or individual therapy, focuses on establishing trust, restoring **self-esteem**, expressing emotions, and improving cognitive and problem-solving skills.

Recognizing and treating physical abuse in the adolescent is by far the most difficult. By now the teen is an expert at hiding bruises. Instead, teachers and health care professionals should be wary of exaggerated responses to being touched, provocative actions, extreme aggressiveness or withdrawal, assaulting behavior, fear of adults, self-destruction, inability to form good peer relationships, alertness to danger, and/or frequent **mood** swings. Detection is exacerbated by the fact that all teenagers exhibit some of these signs at one time or another.

Abused teens do not evoke as much sympathy as younger victims, for society assumes that they are old enough to protect themselves or seek help on their own. In truth, all teenagers need adult guidance. The behavior that the abused adolescent often engages in—delinquency, running away, and failure in school—usually evokes **anger** in adults but should be recognized as symptoms of underlying problems. The abused teen is often resistant to therapy, which may take the form of individual **psychotherapy**, **group therapy**, or residential treatment.

While reporting child abuse is essential, false accusations can also cause great harm. It is a good idea for anyone who suspects that a child is being physically abused to seek confirmation from another adult, preferably a non-relative but one who is familiar with the family. If the second observer concurs, the local child protective services agency should be contacted. The agency has the authority to verify reports of child abuse and make decisions about protection and intervention.

Unlike many other medical conditions, child abuse is preventable. Family support programs can provide parenting information and training, develop family skills, offer social support, and provide psychotherapeutic assistance before abuse occurs.

*See also* Child abuse

Mary McNulty

**Further Reading**

Ackerman, Robert J., and Dee Graham. *Too Old to Cry: Abused Teens in Today's America.* Blue Ridge Summit, PA: TAB Books, 1990.
Helfer, Ray E., M.D., and Ruth S. Kempe, M.D., eds. *The Battered Child.* Chicago: The University of Chicago Press, 1987.
Arbetter, Sandra. "Family Violence: When We Hurt the Ones We Love," *Current Health* 22, November 1995, p. 6.

**Further Information**

National Committee for Prevention of Child Abuse. 332 S. Michigan Avenue, Chicago, IL 60605, (312) 663-3520.

# Nancy Bayley

**1899-1994**

American developmental psychologist known for her "Scales of Mental and Motor Development."

Nancy Bayley was a pioneer in the field of human development. She devoted her life to documenting and measuring intellectual and motor development in infants, children, and adults. Her studies of the rates of physical and mental maturation have greatly influenced our understanding of developmental processes. Her "Bayley Scales of Mental and Motor Development" are used throughout the world as standardized measurements of infant development. Bayley was the recipient of numerous honors and awards throughout her career. In 1966, she became the first woman to win the Distinguished Scientific Contribution Award of the **American Psychological Association (APA)**.

The third of five children of Prudence Cooper and Frederick W. Bayley, Nancy Bayley was born in The Dalles, Oregon, in 1899. She and her siblings were delivered by her aunt who had become a country physician after her husband died. Bayley's father was head of the grocery in a department store in The Dalles. **Childhood** illness prevented Bayley from attending school until she was eight, but she quickly made up the missed grades and completed high school in The Dalles.

## Defines her niche in developmental psychology

Although she entered the University of Washington in Seattle with plans to become an English teacher, Bayley quickly switched to psychology after taking an introductory course with E. R. Guthrie. She earned her B.S. degree in 1922 and her M.S. degree two years later, while serving as a research assistant at the Gatzert Foundation for Child Welfare at the university. For her master's thesis under Stevenson Smith, Bayley devised performance tests for preschoolers, a subject that would occupy her for the rest of her life. A graduate fellowship then took Bayley to the State University of Iowa (now the University of Iowa) in Iowa City where she earned her doctoral degree in 1926. For her Ph.D. dissertation, Bayley used the newly invented galvanometer to measure electrical skin responses to **fear** in children. It was one of the first studies of its kind.

In 1926, as an instructor at the University of Wyoming, Bayley published the first of her nearly 200 contributions to the literature of psychology. Two years later, Harold Jones invited her to become a research associate at the Institute of Child Welfare (now the Institute of Human Development) at the University of California at Berkeley. Bayley was to remain there for most of her career. At Berkeley she met John R. Reid, a doctoral candidate in philosophy. They married in 1929, and Reid joined Bayley at the Institute. While at Berkeley, Bayley taught a course on developmental assessment of infants and small children in the Department of Psychology and held concurrent research positions in psychology and anatomy at Stanford University.

## Initiates major study of infant development

At the Institute, Bayley began a major study of **normal** and handicapped infant development. It became famous as the Berkeley Growth Study. Her 1933 publication, *The California First-year Mental Scale*, was followed in 1936 by *The California Infant Scale of Motor Development*. In these works, Bayley introduced methodologies for assessing infant development. Likewise, her 1933 publication, *Mental Growth During the First Three Years*, became a milestone in **developmental psychology**. Bayley earned the G. Stanley Hall Award of the APA's Division of Developmental Psychology in 1971.

In 1954, Bayley became head of **child development** in the Laboratory of Psychology at the National Institute of Mental Health in Bethesda, Maryland. There she worked on the National Collaborative Perinatal Project, a study of 50,000 children from **birth** to age eight. The study examined neurological and psychological disorders, including cerebral palsy and **mental retardation**. The newly revised Bayley Mental and Motor Scales were used to assess the development of hundreds of children from one to eighteen months of age. Many surviving subjects of this study continued to participate in follow-up studies. Among her many findings, Bayley demonstrated that there were no sex-related differences in physical and mental development. She continued to work on this project after returning to Berkeley as the first head of the Harold E. Jones Child Study Center at the Institute of Human Development. She also acted as consultant on a study of infants with **Down syndrome** at the Sonoma State Hospital in California.

Bayley's work was remarkable for its interdisciplinary nature. In 1951 she co-authored a paper with Mary Cover Jones on the relationships between physical development and behavior. Bayley also was the first scientist to correlate infant size with eventual adult size and in 1946 she published tables for predicting adult height. She was very interested in physical differences between the sexes and in androgynous characteristics that were intermediate between male and female **traits**. She studied the development of emotions in children and the maintenance of intellectual abilities throughout adulthood. Bayley also studied the impact of maternal behaviors on children. She argued forcefully that poor development in children was the result of poverty and other social factors, rather than psychological factors.

Bayley was active in a number of professional organizations. She was a fellow of the APA and of the Ameri-

can Association for the Advancement of Science. From 1961 to 1963 Bayley served as president of the Society for Research in Child Development and in 1983 she earned their distinguished contribution award. She received the Gold Medal Award of the American Psychological Foundation in 1982. Bayley died of respiratory failure in Carmel, California, in 1994.

*See also* Bayley Scales of Infant Development

Margaret Alic

## Further Reading
O'Connell, A. N. and N. F. Russo. "Models for achievement: eminent women in psychology." *Psychology of Women Quarterly* 5 (1980): 6-54.

Lipsitt, Lewis P. and Dorothy H. Eichorn. "Nancy Bayley (1899-)." In *Women in Psychology: A Bio-Bibliographic Sourcebook,* edited by Agnes N. O'Connell and Nancy Felipe Russo. New York: Greenwood Press, 1990.

Rosenblith, J. F. "A singular career: Nancy Bayley." *Developmental Psychology* 28 (1992): 747-58.

Stevens, G. and S. Gardner. *The women of psychology. Vol. 2, Expansion and Refinement.* Cambridge, MA: Schenkman, 1982.

# Bayley Scales of Infant Development

A comprehensive developmental test for infants and toddlers from two to 30 months of age.

The Bayley Scales of Infant Development measure mental and physical, as well as emotional and social, development. The test, which takes approximately 45 minutes, is administered individually by having the child respond to a series of stimuli. The Mental Scales, which measure intellectual development, assess functions such as **memory**, learning, problem-solving **ability**, and verbal communication skills. The Motor Scales evaluate the child's ability to sit and stand, perform other activities requiring coordination of the large muscles (**gross motor skills**), and perform more delicate manipulations with fingers and hands (**fine motor skills**). Finally, the Infant Behavior Record (IBR) assesses the child's social and **emotional development** through a standardized description of his or her behavior during the testing session. Scores are measured against norms for each of the 14 different age groups. Often, the Bayley scales are used to determine whether a child is developing normally and provide for early diagnosis and intervention in cases of **developmental delay**, where there is significant tardiness in acquiring certain skills or performing key activities. Additionally, they can be used to qualify a child for special services and/or demonstrate the effectiveness of those services. Most recently, the Bayley scales have been used to insure compliance with legislation that requires identification of at-risk children and provision of services for them.

*See also* Bayley, Nancy

## Further Reading

Cohen, Libby G., and Loraine J. Spenciner. *Assessment of Young Children.* New York: Longman, 1994.

McCullough, Virginia. *Testing and Your Child: What You Should Know About 150 of the Most Common Medical, Educational, and Psychological Tests.* New York: Plume, 1992.

Walsh, W. Bruce, and Nancy E. Betz. *Tests and Assessment.* 2nd ed. Englewood Cliffs, NJ: Prentice Hall, 1990.

Wortham, Sue Clark. *Tests and Measurement in Early Childhood Education.* Columbus, OH: Merrill Publishing Co., 1990.

# Aaron T. Beck

1921-
American neurologist and father of cognitive therapy.

## A pragmatic approach to therapy

Aaron T. Beck was born in Providence, Rhode Island, on July 18, 1921, the third son of Russian Jewish immigrants. His father was a printer by trade who seriously abided by his socialist ideals. His rather overbearing mother was known for her extreme **mood** swings. Beck had two siblings who died before he was born. Beck's **childhood** typified middle-class America, complete with his involvement in Boy Scouts and athletics.

From this mediocrity rose one of America's groundbreaking psychotherapists. Beck developed what is known as **cognitive therapy**, which is used for cases ranging from **depression** and panic attacks to addictions, **eating disorders**, and even the most severe psychiatric illnesses. Beck's childhood strongly influenced his approach to therapy. A life-threatening staph infection at the age of eight changed his life. At this point, Beck was transformed from a very active young man to a quiet one who preferred reading to playing football. As a child, he developed a **fear** of hospitals, blood, and even the scent of ether, which made him feel as if he would faint. Eventually, he overcame those fears rationally. "I learned not to be concerned about the faint feeling, but just to keep active," he later recounted.

Beck graduated from Brown University in 1942. In 1946 he received his Ph.D. in psychiatry from Yale Uni-

versity. During his residency in neurology he began to investigate **psychotherapy** and **cognition**. Beck served as Assistant Chief of Neuropsychology at Valley Forge Hospital in Pennsylvania during the Korean War (1950–53). Even with his doubts about Freud and **psychoanalysis**, Beck attended the Philadelphia Institute of Psychoanalysis, graduating in 1958. Not long into his work with patients using psychoanalysis, Beck began to alter his approach. Beck joined the faculty of the University of Pennsylvania (Penn) in 1954, where he began to search for empirical evidence supporting Freud's theories. In his research, Beck attempted to discover a correlation between depression and masochism. Beck and his colleagues failed to find this correlation. Within two years his cognitive approach to therapy had taken shape.

Beck would go on to establish the Beck Institute for Cognitive Therapy and Research in Bala Cynwyd, a suburb of Philadelphia. Beck's determination was simple. For him, the **unconscious** does not play the role that Freud proposed. One of Beck's favorite maxims is "there's more to the surface than meets the eye." The cognitive method involves a person using rational thoughts to overcome fears rather than delving into the unconscious causes of those fears. In cognitive therapy the fears of the client are carefully examined and confronted rationally.

## A family affair

Beck and his wife, Phyllis, a Superior Court Judge in Philadelphia, have four children and eight grandchildren. One of his children, Dr. Judith Beck, became director at the Beck Institute, working closely with her father. As a younger man he was driven by his work. As an older man he became more driven by his **family**. For years his main supporter was his wife, at a time when his beliefs were not popular. Throughout his career he has continued to meet his critics by encouraging them to test his theories and his results. Rather than being a boorish scientist too smug to be proven wrong, Beck welcomes any challenges in his pursuit of what is best for his patients.

What was originally a method to solve depression has now evolved further. According to his daughter, Prozac and other modern anti-depressant drugs have changed the clientele they see at the Institute. More complicated problems bring people to their doors at the beginning of the twenty-first century. These are problems that might take more than the usual eight to ten sessions a relatively simple case of depression would take to resolve. Beck insists that his cognitive approach can be used to treat **psychotic disorders**, even those as serious as **schizophrenia**. Beck's research conducted with Dr. Neil A. Rector of the University of Toronto has indicated that patients suffering from schizophrenia showed greater improvement through a combination of drug and cognitive therapies than patients receiving **drug therapy** alone.

Beck's theories are constantly evolving through his continued research efforts. A prolific writer, Beck has authored several books and articles both on his own as well as under collaboration. His books include *Prisoners of Hate* (1999), *Depression: Clinical, Experimental, and Theoretical* (1980), *Cognitive Therapy and the Emotional Disorders* (1979), and *Depression: Causes and Treatment* (1972). The *Beck Depression Inventory* and *Scale for Suicide Ideation* are among two of the widely used tools that he developed for use by therapists. The *Beck Depression Inventory II* in 1996 followed his long-successful original as an assessment tool for clinicians in diagnosing depression.

Jane Spear

## Further Reading

Beck, Aaron T., M.D. *Prisoners of Hate: The Cognitive Basis of Anger, Hostility, and Violence.* New York: HarperCollins Publishers, 1999.

Goode, Erica. "A therapy modified for patient and times." *The New York Times* (January 11, 2000).

Goode, Erica. "Pragmatist embodies his no-nonsense therapy. (Dr. Aaron T. Beck and his 'cognitive therapy.')" *The New York Times* (January 11, 2000).

**Clifford Beers** *(AP/Wide World Photos. Reproduced with permission.)*

## Clifford Beers

### 1876-1943
American reformer and founder of the mental hygiene movement.

Clifford Whittingham Beers was born in New Haven, Connecticut, studied at Yale University, and began a professional career in the insurance industry. In 1900 he was institutionalized for a mental breakdown after a suicide attempt and diagnosed as manic-depressive. Confined to both public and private institutions over a three-year period, Beers found the treatment of mental patients inhumane and ineffective. When his efforts to complain directly to hospital administrators were ignored, Beers smuggled letters out to state officials, and his efforts met with some success. By 1903 Beers was able to return to his career, but continued to work on behalf of reforming the treatment of the mentally ill.

In 1908 Beers published *A Mind That Found Itself,* a popular autobiographical study of his confinement and recovery, which was praised by the prominent psychologist and philosopher **William James**. After the publication of this work, and with the general support of the medical community, Beers became a leading figure in the movement to reform the treatment of, and attitudes toward, **mental illness**. In the same year his book was published, Beers founded the Connecticut Society for Mental Hygiene (a name suggested by the psychologist **Adolf Meyer**, another supporter of Beers's efforts). This organization lobbied for improved treatment of mental patients and heightened public awareness of mental illness. In 1909, Beers organized the National Committee for Mental Hygiene and served as its secretary until 1939. He also helped establish the American Foundation for Mental Hygiene in 1928.

Beers's influence eventually spread beyond the United States. In 1918 he helped Clarence M. Hincks found a mental hygiene society in Canada, the Canadian National Committee for Mental Hygiene. Beers was active in organizing the International Congress on Mental Health in 1930, and three years later received an award for his achievements in the mental health field from the National Institute of Social Science. Beers's autobiography remained popular and influential, having gone into 26 printings by the time of his death in 1943.

# Behavior modification

*A treatment approach, based on the principles of operant conditioning, that replaces undesirable behaviors with more desirable ones through positive or negative reinforcement.*

Behavior modification is based on the principles of **operant conditioning**, which were developed by American behaviorist B.F. Skinner (1904-1990). In his research, he put a rat in a cage later known as the Skinner Box, in which the rat could receive a food pellet by pressing on a bar. The food reward acted as a **reinforcement** by strengthening the rat's bar-pressing behavior. Skinner studied how the rat's behavior changed in response to differing patterns of reinforcement. By studying the way the rats "operated on" their **environment**, Skinner formulated the concept of operant conditioning, through which behavior could be shaped by reinforcement or lack of it. Skinner considered his discovery applicable to a wide range of both human and animal behaviors and introduced operant conditioning to the general public in his 1938 book, *The Behavior of Organisms.*

Today, behavior modification is used to treat a variety of problems in both adults and children. Behavior modification has been successfully used to treat **obsessive-compulsive disorder** (OCD), **attention deficit/hyperactivity disorder** (ADHD), phobias, enuresis (bedwetting), anxiety disorder, and **separation anxiety** disorder, among others. One behavior modification technique that is widely used is positive reinforcement, which encourages certain behaviors through a system of rewards. In **behavior therapy**, it is common for the therapist to draw up a contract with the client setting out the terms of the reward system.

In addition to rewarding desirable behavior, behavior modification can also discourage unwanted behavior, through either negative reinforcement, or **punishment**. In children, this could be removal of television privileges. The removal of reinforcement altogether is called **extinction**. Extinction eliminates the incentive for unwanted behavior by withholding the expected response. A widespread parenting technique based on extinction is the time-out, in which a child is separated from the group when he or she misbehaves. This technique removes the expected reward of parental attention.

*See also* Behaviorism

## Further Reading

Martin, Garry. *Behavior Modification: What It Is and How to Do It.* Englewood Cliffs, NJ: Prentice-Hall, 1988.

## Further Information

Association for the Advancement of Behavior Therapy. 15 W. 36th St., New York, NY 10018, (212) 279–7970.

## DID SKINNER RAISE HIS OWN CHILD IN A SKINNER BOX?

This famous urban legend was perpetuated by a photo that appeared in *Life* magazine of behavioral psychologist B.F. Skinner's two-year old daughter standing up in a glass-fronted box. The box was, in fact, a climate-controlled, baby-sized room that Skinner built, called the "aircrib." The aircrib was made of sound-absorbing wood, had a humidifier, an air filter, and was temperature-controlled by a thermostat. Dissatisfied with traditional cribs, Skinner built the box to keep his new daughter warm, safe, and quiet without having to wrap her in clothes and blankets. Skinner was quoted in *New Yorker* magazine as saying his daughter "...spent most of the next two years and several months there, naked and happy." Deborah was so happy in the box, Skinner reported, that she rarely cried or got sick and showed no signs of agoraphobia when removed from the aircrib or claustrophobia when placed inside. The box-like structure and people's misunderstandings about behavioral psychology contributed to the misconception that Skinner was experimenting on his daughter and also probably prevented the crib from becoming a commercial success. People got the impression that Skinner was raising his child in a box similar to the kind he used to study animal behavior—with levers for releasing food.

# Behavior therapy

*A goal-oriented, therapeutic approach that treats emotional and behavioral disorders as maladaptive learned responses that can be replaced by healthier ones with appropriate training.*

In contrast to the psychoanalytic method of **Sigmund Freud** (1856-1939), which focuses on **unconscious** mental processes and their roots in the past, behavior therapy focuses on observable behavior and its modification in the present. Behavior therapy was developed during the 1950s by researchers and therapists critical of the psychodynamic treatment methods that prevailed at the time. It drew on a variety of theoretical work, including the **classical conditioning** principles of the Russian physiologist **Ivan Pavlov** (1849-1936), who became famous for experiments in which dogs were trained to salivate at the sound of a bell, and the work of American **B.F. Skinner** (1904-1990), who pioneered the concept of **operant conditioning**, in which behavior is modified by changing the response it elicits. By the 1970s, behavior therapy enjoyed widespread popularity as a treatment approach. Over the past two decades, the attention of behavior therapists has focused increasingly on their clients' cognitive processes, and many therapists have begun to use **cognitive behavior therapy** to change clients' unhealthy behavior by replacing negative or self-defeating thought patterns with more positive ones.

As an initial step in many types of behavioral therapy, the client monitors his or her own behavior carefully, often keeping a written record. The client and therapist establish a set of specific goals that will result in gradual behavior change. The therapist's role is often similar to that of a coach or teacher who gives the client "homework assignments" and provides advice and encouragement. Therapists continuously monitor and evaluate the course of the treatment itself, making any necessary adjustments to increase its effectiveness.

A number of specific techniques are commonly used in behavioral therapy. Human behavior is routinely motivated and rewarded by positive **reinforcement**. A more specialized version of this phenomenon, called systematic positive reinforcement, is used by behavior-oriented therapists. Rules are established that specify particular behaviors that are to be reinforced, and a reward system is set up. With children, this sometimes takes the form of tokens that may be accumulated and later exchanged for certain privileges. Just as providing reinforcement strengthens behaviors, withholding it weakens them. Eradicating undesirable behavior by deliberately withholding reinforcement is another popular treatment method called **extinction**. For example, a child who habitually shouts to attract attention may be ignored unless he or she speaks in a conversational tone.

**Aversive conditioning** employs the principles of classical conditioning to lessen the appeal of a behavior that is difficult to change because it is either very habitual or temporarily rewarding. The client is exposed to an unpleasant stimulus while engaged in or thinking about the behavior in question. Eventually the behavior itself becomes associated with unpleasant rather than pleasant feelings. One treatment method used with alcoholics is the administration of a nausea-inducing drug together with an alcoholic beverage to produce an aversion to the **taste** and **smell** of alcohol by having it become associated with nausea. In **counterconditioning**, a maladaptive response is weakened by the strengthening of a response that is incompatible with it. A well-known type of counterconditioning is systematic **desensitization**, which counteracts the anxiety connected with a particular behavior or situation by inducing a relaxed response to it instead. This method is often used in the treatment of people who are afraid of flying. **Modeling**, another treatment method, is based on the human tendency to learn through observation and **imitation**. A desired behavior is performed by another person while the client watches. In some cases, the client practices the behavior together with a model, who is often the therapist.

## Further Reading

Ammerman, Robert T. and Michel Hersen, eds. *Handbook of Behavior Therapy with Children and Adults: A Developmental and Longitudinal Perspective.* New York: Allyn and Bacon, 1993.

Craighead, Linda W. *Cognitive and Behavioral Interventions: An Empirical Approach to Mental Health Problems.* Boston: Allyn and Bacon, 1994.

O'Leary, K. Daniel and G. Terence Wilson. *Behavior Therapy: Application and Outcome.* Englewood Cliffs, NJ: Prentice-Hall, 1975.

Wolpe, Joseph. *The Practice of Behavior Therapy.* Tarrytown, NY: Pergamon Press, 1996.

## Further Information

Association for the Advancement of Behavior Therapy. 15 W. 36th St., New York, NY 10018, (212) 647-1890.

# Behaviorism

A theory of human development initiated by American educational psychologist Edward Thorndike, and developed by American psychologists John Watson and B.F. Skinner.

Behaviorism is a psychological theory of human development that posits that humans can be trained, or conditioned, to respond in specific ways to specific stimuli and that given the correct stimuli, personalities and behaviors of individuals, and even entire civilizations, can be codified and controlled.

**Edward Thorndike** (1874-1949) initially proposed that humans and animals acquire behaviors through the association of stimuli and responses. He advanced two laws of learning to explain why behaviors occur the way they do: The **Law of Effect** specifies that any time a behavior is followed by a pleasant outcome, that behavior is likely to recur. The Law of Exercise states that the more a stimulus is connected with a response, the stronger the link between the two. **Ivan Pavlov**'s (1849-1936) groundbreaking work on **classical conditioning** also provided an observable way to study behavior. Although most psychologists agree that neither Thorndike nor Pavlov were strict behaviorists, their work paved the way for the emergence of behaviorism.

The birth of modern behaviorism was championed early in the 20th century by a psychologist at Johns Hopkins University named **John Watson**. In his 1924 book, *Behaviorism,* Watson made the notorious claim that, given a dozen healthy infants, he could determine the adult personalities of each one, "regardless of his talents, penchants, tendencies, abilities, vocations and the race of his ancestors." While making such a claim seems ridiculous today, at the time Watson was reacting to emerging Freudian psychoanalytical theories of development, which many people found threatening. Watson's scheme rejected all the hidden, **unconscious**, and suppressed longings that Freudians attributed to behaviors and posited that humans respond to punishments and rewards. Behavior that elicits positive responses is reinforced and continued, while behavior that elicits negative responses is eliminated.

Later, the behaviorist approach was taken up by **B.F. Skinner** (1904-1990) who deduced the evolution of human behavior by observing the behavior of rats in a maze. Skinner even wrote a novel, *Walden Two*, about a Utopian society where human behavior is governed totally by self-interested decisions based on increasing pleasure. The book increased Skinner's renown and led many to believe that behaviorism could indeed produce such a society.

In the 1950s, however, the popularity of behaviorism began to decline. The first sustained attack on its tenets was made by **Noam Chomsky** (1928-), a renowned linguist, who demonstrated that the behaviorist model simply could not account for the acquisition of language. Other psychologists soon began to question the role of **cognition** in behavior.

Today, many psychologists debate the extent to which cognitive learning and behavioral learning affect the development of **personality**.

*See also* Behavior modification; Behavior therapy

**Further Reading**

Donahoe, John W., and David C. Palmer. *Learning and Complex Behavior.* Boston: Allyn and Bacon, 1994.

Nye, Robert D. *Three Psychologies: Perspectives from Freud, Skinner, and Rogers.* 4th ed. Pacific Grove, CA: Brooks/Cole Pub. Co., 1992.

Rachlin, Howard. *Introduction to Modern Behaviorism.* 3rd ed. New York: Freeman, 1991.

Sapolsky, Robert M. *Biology and Human Behavior: The Neurological Origins of Individuality.* Springfield, VA: The Teaching Company, 1996. (Four audio cassettes and one 32-page manual).

Staddon, John. *Behaviorism: Mind, Mechanism and Society.* London: Duckworth, 1993.

Todd, James T., and Edward K. Morris. *Modern Perspectives on B.F. Skinner and Contemporary Behaviorism.* Westport, CT: Greenwood Press, 1995.

Todd, James T., and Edward K. Morris. *Modern Perspectives on John B. Watson and Classical Behaviorism.* Westport, CT: Greenwood Press, 1994.

Westen, Drew. *Is Anyone Really Normal?: Perspectives on Abnormal Psychology.* Kearneysville, WV: The Teaching Company, 1991. (Four audio cassettes and one 13-page booklet).

# Bender-Gestalt Test

Diagnostic assessment test to identify learning disability, neurological disorders, and developmental delay.

The complete name of this test is Bender Visual Motor Gestalt Test. It is a test used with all age groups to help identify possible **learning disabilities**, neurological disorders, **mental retardation**, or **developmental delay**. Test results also provide information about specific abilities, including motor coordination, **memory**, and organization. The test-taker is given a series of nine designs, each on a separate card, and asked to reproduce them on a blank sheet of paper. There is no time limit. The test is scored by professionals who consider a variety of factors, including form, shape, pattern, and orientation on the page.

*See also* Learning disability

**Further Reading**

Lacks, Patricia. *Bender Gestalt Screening for Brain Dysfunction.* New York: Wiley, 1984.

# Bestiality

See **Paraphilias**

# Bruno Bettelheim

**1903-1990**
Austrian-born American psychologist known for his treatment of emotionally disturbed children, particularly autistic children.

Bruno Bettelheim was born in Vienna in 1903. He was trained as a psychoanalyst, receiving his Ph.D. from the University of Vienna in 1938. In the same year, the Nazis conquered Austria, and Bettelheim was interned in the Dachau and Buchenwald concentration camps. He was released in 1939 and emigrated to the United States, where he first became a research associate of the Pro-

**Bruno Bettelheim** *(AP/Wide World Photos, Inc. Reproduced with permission.)*

gressive Education Association at the University of Chicago, and then an associate professor at Rockford College from 1942 to 1944.

In 1943, Bettelheim gained widespread recognition for his article, "Individual and Mass Behavior in Extreme Situations," a study of human adaptability based on his concentration camp experiences. In 1944, he was granted a dual appointment by the University of Chicago as assistant professor and head of the Sonia Shankman Orthogenic School, a residential treatment center for 6 to 14-year-old children with severe emotional problems. Here he successfully treated many children unresponsive to previous therapy, using the technique—which has been both lauded and criticized—of unconditionally accepting their behavior. Bettelheim was also concerned with the emotional lives and upbringing of **normal** children, and with applying psychoanalytic principles to social problems.

In three decades as an author of works for both scholarly and popular audiences, Bettelheim covered a broad range of topics. *Love Is Not Enough* (1950), *Truants from Life* (1954), and *The Empty Fortress* (1967) are based on his work at the Orthogenic School. *The Informed Heart* (1960) deals with Bettelheim's concentra-

tion camp experiences. *Children of the Dream* (1969) analyzes communal childrearing methods on an Israeli kibbutz and their implications for American **family** life. *The Uses of Enchantment* (1976) argues for the importance of fairy tales in a child's development. Bettelheim's later books include *On Learning to Read: The Child's First Fascination with Meaning* (1981) and *Freud and Man's Soul* (1982). A full professor at the University of Chicago from 1952, Bettelheim retired from both teaching and directorship of the Orthogenic School in 1973. Following the death of his wife in 1984 and after suffering a stroke in 1987, Bettelheim committed suicide in 1990.

*See also* Adaptation; Autism

**Further Reading**

Sutton, Nina. *Bettelheim, A Life and a Legacy.* New York: Basic Books, 1996.

# Bilingualism/Bilingual education

Use of a language other than English in public school classrooms.

The language rights of ethnic minorities in the United States have been a source of public controversy for close to two decades. The 1970s saw record levels of immigration, bringing an estimated 4 million legal and 8 million illegal immigrants into the country. To accommodate this dramatic surge in the nation's population of foreign language speakers, language assistance has been mandated on the federal, state, and local levels in areas ranging from voting and tax collection to education, social services, disaster assistance, and consumer rights. Today Massachusetts offers driver's license tests in 24 languages; residents of California can choose one of six different languages when they vote; street signs in some parts of Miami are printed in both English and Spanish; and classroom instruction is taught in 115 different languages in New York City schools. Altogether, over 300 languages are spoken in the United States. As of 1990, 31.8 million Americans spoke a language other than English at home, and the country's population included 6.7 million non-English speakers. Nationwide, one-third of the children enrolled in urban schools speak a language other than English at home as their first language. Around 2.6 million schoolchildren throughout the country do not speak English at all.

Organized opposition to bilingualism, which collectively became known as the English-Only movement, began in the 1980s. In 1980 voters in Dade County,

Florida, designated English as their official language. The following year, U.S. Senator S.I. Hayakawa of California introduced a constitutional amendment to make English the country's official language. Two influential English-Only lobbying groups were formed: U.S. English, in 1983, and English First, in 1986. In 1986, with the passage of Proposition 63, English became the official language of California. By the mid-1990s, 22 states had passed similar measures. In August 1996, the U.S. House of Representatives, by a margin of 259-169, passed a bill to make English the official language of the federal government. (However, President Bill Clinton vowed to veto the bill if it passed the Senate.) Observers attribute the English-Only movement to backlash against immigration and affirmative action, spurred by **fear** of **competition** for jobs and resentment of government spending on bilingual programs.

The government program that has drawn the most fire is bilingual education, which costs taxpayers an estimated $200 million a year in federal funds and billions of dollars in state and local expenditures. Bilingual education programs, which allow students to pursue part of their study in their first language and part in English, were first mandated by Congress in 1968. The constitutionality of bilingual education was upheld in a 1974 Supreme Court ruling affirming that the city of San Francisco had discriminated against 18,000 Chinese-American students by failing to make special provisions to help them overcome the linguistic barriers they faced in school. However, the court did not specify what these provisions should be, and educators have evolved several different methods of instruction for students with first languages other than English. With the immersion (or "sink or swim") approach, nearly all instruction is in English, and the students are expected to pick up the language through intensive exposure. If the teacher is bilingual, the students may be allowed to ask questions in their native language, but the teacher is supposed to answer them in English. The English as a Second Language (ESL) approach, often used in a class where students speak more than one foreign language, takes a more gradual approach to mastering English, using it in conjunction with the student's first language. English-only instruction may be offered, but only in some, rather than all, classes.

The remaining methods rely more heavily on the student's first language. Even though, technically, all teaching methods aimed at meeting the needs of foreign language speakers are considered bilingual education, participants in debates about bilingual education often single out the following methods as targets of praise or criticism. In Transitional Bilingual Education (TBE), students study English but are taught all other academic subjects in their native languages until they are considered ready to switch to English. In some cases, bilingual teachers also help the students improve their skills in their native language. Bilingual/bicultural programs use the students' native languages not only to teach them the standard curriculum but also for special classes about their ethnic heritage and its history and culture. Two-way or dual language programs enroll students from different backgrounds with the goal of having all of them become bilingual, including those who speak only English. For example, Spanish-speaking children may learn English while their English-speaking classmates learn Spanish.

Critics of bilingual education (or of those methods that rely heavily on the students' native languages) claim that it fails to provide children with an adequate knowledge of English, thus disadvantaging them academically, and they cite high dropout rates for Hispanic teenagers, the group most likely to have received instruction in their native language. They accuse school systems of continuing to promote bilingual programs to protect the jobs of bilingual educators and receive federal funding allocated for such programs. As evidence of this charge, they cite barriers placed in the way of parents who try to remove their children from bilingual programs. Hispanic parents in New York City have claimed that their children are being railroaded into bilingual programs by a system that requires all children with Spanish surnames, as well as children of any nationality who have non-English-speaking **family** members, to take a language proficiency exam. Children scoring in the bottom 40% are then required to enroll in bilingual classes even if English is the primary language spoken at home. Critics of bilingual instruction also cite a 1994 New York City study that reported better results for ESL instruction than for methods that taught children primarily in their native languages.

In spite of the criticism it has aroused, bilingual education is strongly advocated by many educators. Defenders cite a 1991 study endorsed by the National Academy of Sciences stating that children who speak a foreign language learn English more rapidly and make better overall academic progress when they receive several years of instruction in their native language. A later study, conducted at George Mason University, tracked 42,000 children who had received bilingual instruction and reported that the highest scores on standardized tests in the eleventh grade were earned by those students who had had six years of bilingual education. Programs with two-way bilingual education have had particularly impressive results. Oyster Bilingual Elementary School in Washington, D.C., (whose student body is 58% Hispanic, 26% white, 12% black, and 4% Asian) is admiringly cited as a model for bilingual education. Its sixth graders read at a ninth-grade level and have tenth-grade-level math skills. Experts on both sides of the controversy agree that for any teaching method to be successful, the teaching must be done by qualified instructors equipped with adequate teaching materials in appropriately assigned classes with a reasonable ratio of students to teachers.

## Further Reading

Chavez, Linda. *Out of the Barrio: Toward a New Politics of Hispanic Assimilation.* New York: Basic Books, 1991.

Crawford, James. *Hold Your Tongue: Bilingualism and the Politics of "English-Only."* Reading, MA: Addison-Wesley Publishing Co., 1992.

Harlan, Judith. *Bilingualism in the United States: Conflict and Controversy.* New York: Franklin Watts, 1991.

Lang, Paul. *The English Language Debate: One Nation, One Language!* Springfield, NJ: Enslow Publishers, Inc., 1995.

Porter, Rosalie Pedalino. *Forked Tongue: The Politics of Bilingual Education.* New York: Basic Books, 1990.

Rodriguez, Richard. *Hunger of Memory: The Education of Richard Rodriguez.* New York: Bantam Books, 1983.

Simon, Paul. *The Tongue-Tied American: Confronting the Foreign Language Crisis.* New York: Continuum, 1980.

## Further Information

Multicultural Education, Training, and Advocacy, Inc. (META). 240A Elm Street, Suite 22, Somerville, MA 02144.

National Association for Bilingual Education (NABE). Union Center Plaza, 1220 L Street NW, Suite 605, Washington, DC 20005.

U.S. English. 818 Connecticut Ave. NW, Suite 200, Washington, DC 20006.

**Alfred Binet**

# Alfred Binet

### 1857-1911

French psychologist and founder of experimental psychology in France and a pioneer in intelligence testing.

Alfred Binet was born in Nice, France, in 1857. After studying both law and medicine in Paris, he earned a doctorate in natural science. Binet's psychological training—mostly at Jean-Martin Charcot's neurological clinic at the Salpetriere Hospital—was in the area of **abnormal psychology**, particularly hysteria, and he published books on **hypnosis** (*Le magnetisme animal,* with C.S. Fere in 1886) and suggestibility (*La suggestibilite,* 1900). From 1895 until his death in 1911, Binet served as director of France's first psychological laboratory at the Sorbonne of the University of Paris. Also in 1895, he established the journal *L'Annee psychologique.* Binet had been interested in the psychology of—and individual differences in— **intelligence** since the 1880s and published articles on **emotion**, **memory**, **attention**, and problem solving. In 1899 he set up a special laboratory where he devised a series of tests which he used to evaluate the intellectual development of his two daughters. His 1903 book, *L'Etude experimentale de l'intelligence,* was based on his studies of them.

In 1905, Binet and Theodore Simon created the first intelligence test to aid the French government in establishing a program to provide **special education** for mentally retarded children. In 1908 they revised the test, expanding it from a single scale of **measurement** to a battery of tests for children in different age groups, with the focus now shifted from identifying retardation to the general measurement of intelligence. A further test revision in 1911 introduced the concept of **mental age**. In 1916, the American psychologist **Lewis Terman** used the 1908 Binet-Simon scale as the basis for the Stanford-Binet Intelligence Scale, the best-known and most researched intelligence test in the United States. Binet co-authored *Les enfants anormaux (Abnormal Children)* (1907) with Simon and published *Les idees modernes sur les enfants (Modern Ideas on Children)* in 1909. He died in Paris in 1911.

*See also* Intelligence quotient; Mental retardation

## Further Reading

Wolf, Theta Holmes. *Alfred Binet.* Chicago: University of Chicago Press, 1973.

# Binocular depth cues

Properties of the visual system that facilitate depth perception by the nature of messages that are sent to the brain.

Binocular depth cues are based on the simple fact that a person's eyes are located in different places. One cue, binocular disparity, refers to the fact that different optical images are produced on the retinas of both eyes when viewing an object. By processing information about the degree of disparity between the images it receives, the **brain** produces the impression of a single object that has depth in addition to height and width.

The second cue, called binocular convergence, is based on the fact that in order to project images on the retinas, the two eyes must rotate inward toward each other. The closer the perceived object is, the more they must rotate, so the brain uses the information it receives about the degree of rotation as a cue to interpret the distance of the perceived objects. Yet another cue to **depth perception** is called binocular accommodation, a term that refers to the fact that the lens of the eye changes shape when it brings an image into focus on the retina. The muscular activity necessary for this accommodation acts as a signal for the brain to generate **perception** of depth and distance.

*See also* Vision

## Further Reading

Bennett, Jill. *Sight.* Morristown, NJ: SilverBurdett, 1986.
Chalkley, Thomas. *Your Eyes.* 3rd ed. Springfield, IL: C.C. Thomas, 1995.
Elkins, James. *The Object Stares Back: On the Nature of Seeing.* New York: Simon & Schuster, 1996.

# Biofeedback

A technique that allows individuals to monitor their own physiological processes so they can learn to control them.

Biofeedback originated with the field of psychophysiology, which measures physiological responses as a way of studying human behavior. Types of behavior that may be studied in this way range from basic emotional responses to higher cognitive functions. Today, biofeedback is also associated with behavioral medicine, which combines behavioral and biomedical science in both clinical and research settings. In biofeedback training, the monitoring of physiological responses is performed for therapeutic instead of (or in addition to) in-

## BINOCULAR DISPARITY DEMONSTRATION

This simple experiment demonstrates binocular disparity. Hold a pencil about 12 inches (30 cm) from your face. With one eye closed, align the pencil with the edge of a doorway, window, or other vertical line in the room. Close the eye, open the other, and observe the position of the pencil: it will have jumped. Binocular disparity describes this phenomenon of different images of the pencil in each eye.

vestigative purposes. Biofeedback has been applied with success to a variety of clinical problems, ranging from migraine headaches to hypertension.

The technique provides people with continuous information about physiological processes of which they are normally unaware, such as blood pressure or heart rate. Through special equipment, these processes are recorded, and the information is relayed back to the person through a changing tone or meter reading. With practice, people learn strategies that enable them to achieve voluntary control over the processes involved. For example, persons trying to control their blood pressure levels may see a light flash whenever the pressure drops below a certain level. They may then try to remember and analyze what their thoughts or emotions were at that moment and deliberately repeat them to keep the pressure level low. Initially, they may simply be asked to try and keep the light flashing for as long as possible and given verbal **reinforcement** for their efforts.

The biofeedback training may continue for several days or weeks, with the subjects trying to keep the light flashing for longer periods in subsequent sessions. Eventually they will need to produce the desired response without electronic feedback, a goal which can be accomplished through various methods. They may practice the learned response at the end of the training session or at home between sessions. There can also be random trials without feedback during the sessions. An alternate strategy is the gradual and systematic removal of the feedback signal during the training sessions over a period of time. After the initial training is completed, subjects may return to the biofeedback facility to assess their retention of the skills they have learned or for additional training.

Biofeedback training has been used in treating a number of different clinical problems. Monitoring of patients' heart rates has been used with some success to help people suffering from heartbeat irregularities, including premature ventricular contractions (PVCs) and tachycardia, while hypertensive individuals have been

**A patient undergoing biofeedback.** *(Photo by Will & Deni McIntyre. Photo Researchers, Inc. Reproduced with permission.)*

able to control high blood pressure through the use of biofeedback. Clinicians have been particularly successful in their use of neuromuscular feedback to treat complaints arising from tension in specific muscles or muscle groups. Tension headaches have been alleviated through the reduction of frontalis (forehead) tension, and relaxation of the face and neck muscles has been helpful to stutterers. Feedback from muscle groups has been helpful in the **rehabilitation** of stroke patients and other persons with neuromuscular disorders such as foot drop. These patients may be unable to relax or contract muscles at will, and biofeedback can make them aware of small, otherwise imperceptible changes in the desired direction and allow them to repeat and eventually increase such changes.

In addition to its alleviation of physical complaints, neuromuscular biofeedback has been an effective tool in the treatment of chronic anxiety, even when it has resisted **psychotherapy** and medication. By learning deep muscle relaxation, anxious patients, including those suffering from related conditions such as insomnia, have seen a reduction in their symptoms. Even for patients who have been able to achieve relaxation through other means, such as meditation or progressive relaxation, biofeedback can be a valuable supplementary technique that offers special advantages, such as allowing a therapist to track closely the points at which a patient tenses up and try to learn what thoughts are associated with the tension. Biofeedback-induced relaxation of forehead muscles has also been effective in treating asthma.

Another type of biofeedback involves the monitoring of **brain** activity through electroencephalographs (EEGs). A reduction of seizures in epileptics has been reported through biofeedback techniques involving EEG activity near the sensorimotor cortex, known as sensory motor rhythm. Brain wave activity has also been of interest in connection with alpha waves, which are thought to characterize a desirable state of relaxed alertness. Patients have been taught to increase their alpha rhythms in three or four 30-minute **conditioning** sessions.

### Further Reading

Andreassi, John L. *Psychophysiology: Human Behavior and Physiological Response.* New York: Oxford University Press, 1980.

Beatty, J., and H. Legewie, eds. *Biofeedback and Behavior.* New York: Plenum Press, 1977.

## Bipolar disorder

A condition (traditionally called manic depression) in which a person alternates between the two emotional extremes of depression and mania (an elated, euphoric mood).

Bipolar disorder is classified among affective disorders in the **American Psychiatric Association**'s *Diagnostic and Statistical Manual of Mental Disorders* . The National Institute of Mental Health (NIMH) estimates that about one in one hundred people will develop the disorder, which affects some two million Americans. While this condition occurs equally in both males and females and in every ethnic and racial groups, it is more common among well-educated, middle- and upper-income persons. Those suffering from untreated bipolar disorder will generally experience an average of four depression/ **mania** episodes in a ten-year period. However, some people go through four or more **mood** swings a month, while others may only experience a mood swing every five years. The onset of bipolar disorder usually occurs in the teens or early twenties.

Of all types of depressive illness, bipolar disorder is the one that is most likely to have biological origins, specifically an imbalance in the brain's chemistry. Genetic factors play an important role in the disease. In one study, one-fourth of the children who had one manic-depressive parent became manic-depressive themselves, and three-fourths of those with two manic-depressive parents developed the disorder. The likelihood of bipolar disorder being shared by identical **twins** is also exceptionally high. Manic **depression** has also been associated with the "biological clock" that synchronizes body rhythms and external events.

The depressed state of a person suffering from bipolar disorder resembles major depression. It is characterized by feelings of sadness, apathy, and loss of energy. Other possible symptoms include **sleep** disturbances; significant changes in appetite or weight; languid movements; feelings of worthlessness or inappropriate **guilt**; lack of concentration; and preoccupation with death or **suicide**. When they shift to a manic state, people with bipolar disorder become elated and overly talkative, speaking loudly and rapidly and abruptly switching from one topic to another. Plunging into many work, social, or academic activities at once, they are in constant motion and are hyperactive. They also demonstrate grandiosity—an exaggerated sense of their own powers, which leads them to believe they can do things beyond the power of ordinary persons. Other common symptoms include excessive and/or promiscuous sexual behavior and out-of-control shopping sprees in which large amounts of money are spent on unnecessary items. People in a manic phase typically become irritable or angry when others try to tone down their ideas or behavior, or when they have difficulty carrying out all the activities they have begun. Mania may also be accompanied by delusions and **hallucinations**.

Mania creates enormous turmoil in the lives of its victims, many of whom turn to drugs or alcohol as a way of coping with the anxiety generated by their condition—61 percent of persons with bipolar disorder have substance abuse or dependency problems. In addition, 15 percent of those who fail to receive adequate treatment for bipolar disorder commit suicide. The disease may be misdiagnosed as **schizophrenia**, unipolar depression, a **personality** disorder, or drug or alcohol dependence. Individuals commonly suffer from it for as long as seven to ten years without being diagnosed or treated.

However, effective treatment is available. Lithium, which stabilizes the **brain** chemicals involved in mood swings, is used to treat both the mania and depression of bipolar disorder. This drug, which is taken by millions of people throughout the world, halts symptoms of mania in 70 percent of those who take it, usually working within one to three weeks—sometimes within hours. Antipsychotic drugs or benzodiazepines (tranquilizers) may initially be needed to treat cases of full-blown mania until lithium can take effect. Persons taking lithium must have their blood levels, as well as kidney and thyroid functions, monitored regularly, as there is a relatively narrow gap between toxic and therapeutic levels of the drug. Since lithium also has the ability to prevent future manic episodes, it is recommended as maintenance therapy even after manic-depressive symptoms subside. Some persons

resist remaining on medication, however, either because they **fear** of becoming dependent on the drug or because they are reluctant to give up the "highs" or alleged **creativity** of the manic state. However, psychiatrists have reported instances in which lithium was not as effective after being discontinued as it had been initially.

Many great artists, writers, musicians, and other people prominent in both creative and other fields have suffered from bipolar disorder, including composers Robert Schumann and Gustav Mahler, painter Vincent van Gogh, writers Virginia Woolf and Sylvia Plath, and actresses Patty Duke and Kristy McNichol. The NIMH reports that 38 percent of all Pulitzer Prize-winning poets have had the symptoms of bipolar disorder.

**Further Reading**
Duke, Patty. *Call Me Anna*. New York: Bantam, 1987.
Jamison, Kay. *Touched with Fire: Manic-Depressive Illness and the Artistic Temperament*. New York: Free Press, 1993.

# Birth order

*A chronological sequence of the birth of children in a family.*

Research has correlated birth order with such aspects of life as **temperament** and behavior. For example, first-born children, when compared to their siblings, tend to score slightly higher on **intelligence** tests and to attain a slightly higher socioeconomic status. Some psychologists believe that birth order is a significant factor in the development of **personality**.

The psychologist **Alfred Adler** pioneered a study of relationships between birth order and personality. As part of his view that patients need to be understood in the context of their family environments, Adler hypothesized that a child's position in the family is associated with certain problems that are responded to in similar ways by other children in the same birth position. Adler stressed that it was not the numerical birth position itself that mattered but rather the situation that tended to accompany that position, and the child's reaction to it. Thus, for example, first-born children, when compared to their siblings, tend to have a greater chance of developing feelings of inferiority as their focal position in the family structure is altered by the birth of a sibling. Later-born children, on the other hand, tend to have stronger social skills, having had to deal with siblings throughout their lives, as opposed to first-borns, who have their parents to themselves initially and thus have their first **socialization** experiences with adults only. Later-borns, having had to compromise more at home, are better equipped to develop the flexibility that

# SIBLING RIVALRY

Sibling rivalry is a normal part of family life. All children become jealous of the love and attention that siblings receive from parents and other adults. When a new baby is brought home, older children feel betrayed by their parents and become angry, directing their anger first toward the parents and later toward the intruder who is usurping their position. Jealousy, resentment, and competition are most intense between siblings spaced less than three years apart. Although a certain amount of sibling rivalry is unavoidable, there are measures that parents can take to reduce its severity and its potential effects on their children.

An older child should be prepared for a new addition to the family by having the situation explained and being told in advance about who will take care of her while her mother is in the hospital having the baby. The child's regular routine should be disturbed as little as possible; it is preferable for the child to stay at home and under the care of the father or another close family member. If there is to be a new babysitter or other caretaker unknown to the child, it is helpful for them to meet at least once in advance. If sibling visits are allowed, the child should be taken to visit the mother and new baby in the hospital.

Once the new baby is home, it is normal for an older child to feel hurt and resentful at seeing the attention lavished on the newcomer by parents, other relatives, and family friends. It is not uncommon for the emotional turmoil of the experience to cause disturbances in eating or sleeping. Some children regress developmentally, temporarily losing such attainments as weaning, bowel and bladder control, or clear speech, in an attempt to regain lost parental attention by becoming babies again themselves.

There are a number of ways to ease the unavoidable jealousy of children whose lives have been disrupted by the arrival of a younger sibling. When friends or relatives visit to see the new baby, parents can make the older child feel better by cuddling him or giving him special attention, including a small present to offset the gifts received by the baby. The older child's self-esteem can be bolstered by involving him in the care of newborn in modest ways, such as helping out when the baby is being diapered or dressed, or helping push the carriage. The older child should be made to feel proud of the attainments and responsibilities that go along with his more advanced age—things the new baby can't do yet because he is too young. Another way to make older children feel loved and appreciated is to set aside some "quality time" to spend alone with each of them on a regular basis. It is also important for parents to avoid overtly comparing their children to each other, and every effort should be made to avoid favoritism.

In general, the most stressful aspect of sibling rivalry is fighting. (Physical—as opposed to verbal—fights usually peak before the age of five). It is important for parents not to take sides but rather to insist that the children work out disagreements themselves, calling for a temporary "time out" for feelings to cool down, if necessary. Any form of parental involvement in squabbling by siblings can create a triangle that perpetuates hostilities. Over-insistence that siblings share can also be harmful: to retain a sense of individuality, children need some boundaries from their siblings in terms of possessions, territory, and activities. Furthermore, it is especially difficult for very young children to share their possessions.

Parents should take time to praise cooperation and sharing between siblings as a means of positive reinforcement. The fact that siblings quarrel with each other does not necessarily mean that they will be inconsiderate, hostile, or aggressive in their dealings with others outside the family. The security of family often makes children feel free to express feelings and impulses they are unable to in other settings.

can make their subsequent relationships more successful. It has also been posited that birth order influences one's choice of a marriage partner. The "duplication hypothesis" advanced by Walter Toman (1976) states that people seek to duplicate their sibling relationships in marriage, a duplication that includes birth order.

More specific research on the effects of birth order has generally focused on five ordinal birth positions: first-born, second-born, middle, last, and only-born child in a family. Studies have consistently linked first-born children and academic achievement. The number of first-born National Merit Scholarship winners was found to equal the number of second- and third-borns combined. Separate studies have found high academic achievement levels among first-borns in both urban ghettoes in the United States and at British universities. First-born children are generally responsible, assertive, and task-oriented, often rising to **leadership** positions as adults. They are more frequently mentioned in *Who's Who* publications than individuals in any other birth position and are overrepresented among members of Congress and U.S. presidents. Studies have also found that first-born students are especially vulnerable to **stress** and tend to seek the approval of others. Adler found that there were more first-borns than later-borns among problem children.

Second-born and/or middle children tend to feel inferior to the older child or children, since they do not realize that their lower level of achievement is a function of age. They often try to succeed in areas not excelled in by their elder siblings. Middle-born children have shown a relatively high level of success in team sports, and both they and last-borns have been found to be better adjusted emotionally if from large families. Studies have also found middle children to be sensitive to injustice and likely to have aesthetic interests. Generally trusting, accepting, and other-centered, they tend to maintain relationships successfully.

The last-born child, never dethroned as the "baby" of the family, often exhibit a strong sense of security and non-competitiveness. As a group, last-borns are most successful socially and have the highest self-esteem levels of all the birth positions. One study found last-borns more likely than first-borns or only children to join a fraternity or sorority. Like youngest children, only children are never displaced as the youngest in the family. With only adult models to emulate within the family, only children are achievement-oriented and most likely to attain academic success and attend college. However, studies show that only children have the most problems with close relationships and the lowest need for **affiliation**. They are also the most likely to be referred for help with psychiatric disorders.

Sibling rivalry frequently erupts in households with two or more children, competing for the time, attention and affection of parents. The ages of children, and the years between them, can influence the degree and intensity of of fighting and arguing. First borns may resent responsibility placed upon them for their siblings. Middle children may feel "squeezed out" while last-borns may play on their baby position in the family. Mental health experts advise parents to listen to their children's feelings rather than deny their feelings or convince them to feel differently. To lessen the tensions, experts suggest that parents find time to spend with each child and share in each child's interests.

## Further Reading

Leman, Kevin. *The New Birth Order Book: Why You Are the Way You Are.* Grand Rapids, Mich.: F.H. Revell, 1998.
Toman, Walter. *Family Constellation: Its Effects on Personality and Social Behavior.* New York: Springer Pub. Co., 1993
Wallace, Meri. *Birth Order Blues: How Parents Can Help Their Children Meet the Challenges of Birth Order.* New York: H. Holt, 1999.

## Birth trauma

*In psychoanalysis, birth provides the first experience of anxiety in an individual's life.*

In psychoanalytical theory, birth trauma is the first major occasion of great anxiety in the life of an individual experienced at **birth** as the infant moves from the gentle comfort of the womb into a new **environment** full of harsh and unfamiliar stimuli. While most psychoanalytical psychologists assign a moderate degree of importance to the birth trauma in terms of its effects, some believe that the birth trauma is the prototypical basis of all later anxiety neuroses. The universality of the birth experience presents obvious difficulties in the precise determination of the nature and effects of the birth trauma. The term birth trauma may also mean any physical injury to an infant that occurs during birth.

## Further Reading

Hotchner, Tracy. *Pregnancy and Childbirth: The Complete Guide for a New Life.* 2nd ed. New York: Avon, 1990
Martin, Margaret. *The Illustrated Book of Pregnancy and Childbirth.* New York: Facts on File, 1991.

## Birth

*In humans, the process of delivering a child from the uterus, usually by passage through the birth canal at the end of pregnancy, normally after a gestation period of about 267 days; also called parturition, or labor.*

Childbearing is often viewed as the transition to adult female **sexuality**. Birth labor is divided into several stages. During the latent phase (Stage 0), which lasts from several hours to as long as three days, uterine contractions (either regular or irregular) are present, but the cervix has not dilated more than three or four centimeters. The mucus plug may be passed at this stage. The first stage of labor begins with uterine contractions accompanied by mild **pain** at intervals of about 10 to 20 minutes and sensations of discomfort in the small of the back which eventually become stronger and spread to the entire abdominal area. The cervix, or neck of the uterus, dilates rapidly from three or four centimeters until its opening is large enough to allow the passage of the child (10 centimeters). By the end of the first stage (although sometimes much earlier), the sac containing the amniotic fluid which surrounds the child breaks. The first stage can take up to 12 hours with first-time mothers, although it may be very rapid in women who have had several children. It can last many hours in obstructed labor, where the baby is unusually large or badly angled.

The second stage of labor begins with the complete dilation and effacement (thinning) of the cervix and ends when the baby is born. At this stage, the contractions are

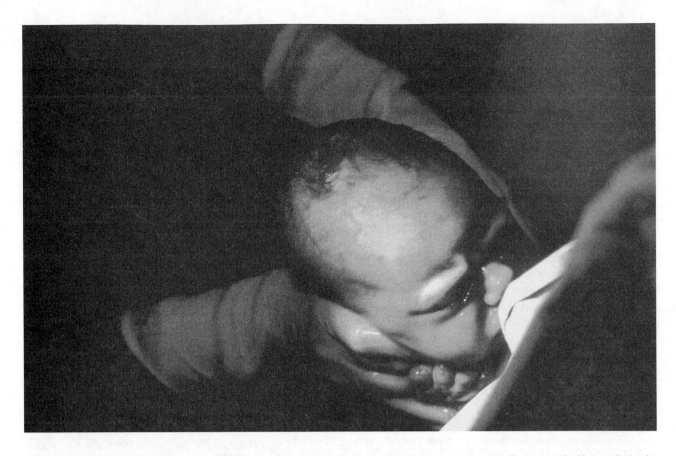

**Baby emerging from the womb.** *(SIU, National Audubon Society Collection/ Photo Researchers, Inc. Reproduced with permission.)*

increasingly frequent and intense, ultimately recurring at intervals of two to three minutes and lasting about a minute. The mother begins contracting her abdominal muscles voluntarily ("bearing down"), and the baby is expelled, usually head first, by a combination of this voluntary contraction and the involuntary contractions of the uterine muscles. The physician aids in the delivery by guiding the infant's head and shoulders out of the birth canal. About 2 to 3 percent of babies are born feet first (breech babies). Obstetrical forceps may be applied during the second stage of labor to speed delivery in order to ease either maternal exhaustion or infant distress. Other medical techniques utilized include the episiotomy, a surgical incision along the back of the vagina to enlarge the opening. (This procedure is now performed less frequently than it was in the past.)

When the baby is born, mucus and blood are removed from the nose and mouth by means of suctioning. The umbilical cord is clamped and cut, and the child is given to the mother to hold. The infant's physical condition is then assessed by the **Apgar score**, which evaluates the overall level of health based on heart rate, skin color, muscular activity and respiratory effort, and response to stimuli. During the third stage of labor, which occurs within the first hour after the child is born, placental material, or afterbirth, is expelled through the birth canal by strong uterine contractions called afterbirth pains. These contractions also help the uterus to return to its normal size. The doctor examines the placenta and amniotic sac to confirm that all tissue has been expelled from the uterus, as serious complications may result if fragments remain inside, especially hemorrhaging. If parts of the placenta or sac are missing, the doctor removes them by hand. Finally, the episiotomy (if one has been performed) is sutured with absorbable stitches. The total duration of labor averages about 13 hours for first deliveries and about eight hours for subsequent deliveries, although there are large individual variances from these figures.

The pain of the birth process can be relieved by drugs, but many of these drugs also have the effect of slowing uterine contractions or depressing the respiratory system of the child. Drugs are either not used—or used with special care—in the case of **twins** or premature infants. Moderate doses of narcotic analgesics may be given to the mother, which are metabolized quickly and nearly absent by the time of delivery. Local anesthetics similar to Novocaine may be administered to provide pain relief in the cervical and vaginal areas, offering more localized relief with fewer side effects than narcotics. Methods of childbirth have been developed in which the use of drugs is kept to a minimum.

The natural childbirth movement begun by Fernand Lamaze, which advocates birth without drugs or medical intervention, departed from the practices of the 1940s and 1950s, when the administration of drugs and medical procedures such as episiotomies were standard obstetrical procedure. Natural childbirth methods use nonmedical relaxation techniques for pain control and allow for more active participation in labor by the mother and a lay coach, usually the husband. They typically include prenatal classes for the mother and coach. Women who use the Lamaze method are taught to perform three activities simultaneously during contractions: breathing in a special pattern, chanting a nonsense or meaningless phrase coordinated with the rhythm of her breathing, and staring intently at an object.

The home delivery movement, which became popular in the United States during the 1970s, gave way to the establishment of birthing centers (in or affiliated with hospitals) staffed by nurse-midwives and obstetricians in an attempt to duplicate the family-centered, drug-free experience of home birth but without the risks posed by the absence of medical professionals. The natural childbirth movement has also focused on easing the birth experience for the infant. In *Birth Without Violence,* the physician Frederick Leboyer described modern hospital birth as "torture of the innocent" and proposed measures to make the transition to life outside the womb a more gentle one for the newborn. These measures include dim lights and a quiet atmosphere in the delivery room, postponing cutting of the umbilical cord, and bathing the infant in lukewarm water. Psychologists **Otto Rank** and R.D. Laing have elaborated on the idea of **birth trauma** as a factor in adult mental and emotional problems, and Leonard Orr developed rebirthing in the 1970s as a holistic healing technique for eliminating negative beliefs that influence an adult's behavior and attitudes.

Occasionally, complicating factors that can affect the mother, the child, or both are encountered in the birth process. These factors include, for example, poor health, anatomical abnormalities, prematurity, and unusual orientation of the child in the uterus, such as breech presentation, in which the child moves through the birth canal head last, and (rarely) transverse presentation, in which the child is positioned sideways. In some women, the pelvic space is too small for spontaneous birth of a baby, and the delivery of the child is accomplished through a surgical opening made in the mother's abdominal wall and uterus, in a procedure called a cesarean section. For a healthy mother and child, the risks of childbirth are extremely low. Premature labor, which occurs in about one pregnancy out of 20, is the primary danger to mother and child during the last trimester of pregnancy and the major cause of newborn death. About 40 to 50 percent of mothers—especially first-time mothers—experience mild postpartum **depression**, thought to be caused by a combination of biochemical factors and adjustment to the pressures and demands of parenthood. A smaller percentage—between 5 and 10 percent—become severely depressed. Postpartum depression usually lasts up to 90 days.

Abnormalities present at the time of birth, known as birth defects or congenital defects, occur in one of every 14 babies born in the United States. More than 3,000 birth defects have been identified, ranging from minor dark sports or a birthmarks to serious disfigurements or limited lifespans. Congenital heart defects occur to one of every 125 to 150 infants born in the U.S., making heart defects among the most common birth defects and the leading cause of birth defect-related deaths. **Down syndrome** is the most frequently occurring chromosomal abnormality, occurring to one of every 800 to 1,000 infants born in the United States. Annually, care of children with birth defects in the U.S. costs billions of dollars.

Birth defects have two causes: **heredity** and **environment**. Environment includes maternal illness, such as German measles. Other environmental factors include: alcohol and drugs, consumed during the pregnancy, and exposure to certain medicines or chemicals. Heavy alcohol consumption during pregnancy can trigger **fetal alcohol syndrome** in newborns, characterized by underweight, small eyes, a short upturned nose with a broad bridge, and often a degree of **mental retardation**. Thalidomide, prescribed in the 1950s as a mild sedative, led to the birth of 7,000 severely deformed babies, suffering from a condition called phocomelia, characterized by extremely short limbs that were often without fingers or toes.

For some diseases, like spina bifida, the causes are unknown but believed to be a combination of heredity and environment. Spina bifida, a neural tube defect, is the most frequently occurring permanently disabling birth defect in the United States, affecting one out of every 1,000 newborns. In spina bifida, the spine fails to close properly during the first month of pregnancy. In worst cases, the spinal cord protrudes through the back. A large percentage of children born with spina bifida have hydrocephalus, an accumulation of fluid in the **brain** which requires a surgical procedures called "shunting" to relieve the fluid build up and redirect it into the abdominal area. Sophisticated medical techniques allow most children with spina bifida to live well into adulthood. Based on research, the U.S. Public Health Service recommends that women of childbearing age in the U.S. consume 0.4 mg of folic acid daily to reduce the risk of having a pregnancy with spinal bifida or the other two neural two defects: anencephaly or encephalocele. Amniocentesis or ultrasound testing can diagnose spina bifida before birth.

Sickle-cell anemia, Tay-Sachs, color blindness, deafness, and extra digits on the hand or feet are hereditary birth defects passed on through generations by abnormal genes. Birth defects may not impact each generation, but the abnormal gene is passed on.

### Further Reading
Hotchner, Tracy. *Pregnancy and Childbirth: The Complete Guide for a New Life.* 2nd ed. New York: Avon, 1990.
Martin, Margaret. *The Illustrated Book of Pregnancy and Childbirth.* New York: Facts on File, 1991.
Nathaniels, Peter. *Life Before Birth and a Time to Be Born.* Ithaca, NY: Promethean Press, 1992.
    *See also* Fetal alcohol effect and syndrome

## Bisexuality

Sexual orientation defined as sexual involvement with members of both sexes concurrently (within the period of one year) or any sexual attraction to or involvement with members of both sexes at any time in one's life.

There is no single accepted definition of bisexuality. Some define it narrowly as sexual involvement with members of both sexes concurrently (within a twelve-month period or less). Others define bisexuality more broadly as any sexual attraction to or involvement with members of both sexes at any time in one's life. However, few people qualify as bisexual in its narrow definition. A comprehensive study, "Sex in America," conducted in 1992 by the University of Chicago, found that less than 1% of either males (0.7%) or females (0.3%) had engaged in sexual activity with both males and females within the previous year. While no statistics exist on the numbers of Americans who fit the broad definition of bisexuality, estimates range from the millions to tens of millions.

**Sigmund Freud** believed that bisexuality was a "disposition" common to all humans. He contended that every individual has a masculine and feminine side, and that each side is heterosexually attracted to members of the opposite sex. Most people, however, according to Freud, repress one side, becoming either hetero- or homosexual. **Alfred Kinsey** posited a scale for human **sexuality** ranging from zero, representing exclusive heterosexual behavior, to six, representing exclusive homosexual behavior. Between the two poles is a spectrum of bisexual activity.

Dr. Fritz Klein, a noted psychiatrist, has expanded on Kinsey's work, creating the Klein Sexual Orientation Grid, which takes into account seven different variables and the passage of time in defining one's sexual orientation. Klein's variables provide a more detailed look at one's sexuality, examining preferences in attraction, behavior, fantasies, emotional involvement, social involvement, lifestyle, and self-identification. Klein also allows for sexual development over time, an important element missing from Kinsey's work.

Martin S. Weinberg, Colin J. Williams, and Douglas W. Pryor, in their book *Dual Attraction: Understanding Bisexuality*, have developed a simplified version of Klein's grid, exploring only three, rather than seven, variables: sexual feelings, sexual activities, and romantic feelings. Sexual feelings include attraction, fantasies, arousal, etc. Sexual activities are actual behaviors such as kissing, fellatio, and intercourse. Romantic feelings are the experience of "falling in love." Self-identified bisexuals can be more or less hetero- or homosexual in each of these categories.

Some studies of fraternal and identical **twins** show that identical twins are more likely to be bisexual than are fraternal twins, suggesting a genetic basis for bisexual predisposition. These studies have yet to be tested adequately to be considered conclusive, however. The fact is that without a single accepted definition of bisexuality, no single conclusion can be reached concerning its origins.

Debate over why people are hetero-, homo-, or bisexual is a fairly recent phenomenon. Identification by sexual preference only began in the 19th century, and before then, it was rarely discussed. Today, however, there is tremendous pressure for a person to declare a sexual preference. The idea of bisexuality is threatening to some people because sexuality is no longer clearly defined between **homosexuality** and **heterosexuality**.

Bisexuals are often accused of being "homosexuals in disguise." As a result, they often feel confused about their sexuality. They are considered "too gay" to be straight, and "too straight" to be gay. Few resources exist to help bisexuals understand themselves. Homosexual support groups may reject them if they reveal their heterosexual sides; heterosexuals may reject them if they reveal their homosexual feelings. Many bisexuals remain in the closet, hiding their gender-encompassing feelings from others, and sometimes even from themselves. Others lead dual lives, expressing their homosexual sides with one group of friends, while reserving their heterosexual selves for a totally separate social circle.

Life, and love, can become quite complicated for a bisexual person. The pressures can be tremendous, creating a great deal of **stress** and **pain**. A 1989 U.S. Department of Health and Human Services report determined that 30% of teenage **suicide**s occur among gay and lesbian youths, but the number of bisexual victims is unknown. Fortunately, however, a movement has begun in recent years to promote a greater acceptance and understanding of bisexuality. More studies are being done specifically on bisexuality or that include bisexuality as a distinct category.

Unfortunately, concern over the spread of AIDS has caused another backlash against bisexuality, based on the assumption that all bisexuals are promiscuous. Most bisexuals are monogamous for all or part of their lives, and those who engage in promiscuous behavior are not necessarily at greater risk of contracting AIDS. It has been suggested that of women who contract AIDS through sexual intercourse, only 10-20% were infected by bisexual males.

Dianne K. Daeg de Mott

## Further Reading

Bass, Ellen, and Kate Kaufman. *Free Your Mind: The Book for Gay, Lesbian, and Bisexual Youth—and Their Allies.* New York: HarperPerennial, 1996.

D'Augelli, Anthony R., and Charlotte J. Patterson. *Lesbian, Gay, and Bisexual Identities Over the Lifespan: Psychological Perspectives.* New York: Oxford University Press, 1995.

Ehrenreich, Barbara. "The Gap Between Gay and Straight." *Time* 141, no. 19, May 10, 1993, p. 76.

Garber, Marjorie. *Vice Versa: Bisexuality and the Eroticism of Everyday Life.* New York: Simon & Schuster, 1995.

Gelman, David. "Tune In, Come Out." *Newsweek* 122, no. 19, November 8, 1993, pp. 70-71.

Hutchins, Loraine, and Lani Kaahumanu, eds. *Bi Any Other Name: Bisexual People Speak Out.* Boston: Alyson Publications, 1991.

Klein, Fritz, M.D. *The Bisexual Option,* 2nd ed. New York: The Haworth Press, 1993.

Leland, John. "Bisexuality." *Newsweek* 126, no. 3, July 17, 1995, pp. 44-50.

Rose, Sharon, et al. *Bisexual Horizons: Politics, Histories, Lives.* London: Lawrence & Wishart, 1996.

Weinberg, Martin S., Colin J. Williams, and Douglas W. Pryor. *Dual Attraction: Understanding Bisexuality.* New York: Oxford University Press, 1994.

# Body image

The subjective conception of one's own body, based largely on evaluative judgments about how one is perceived by others.

Humans have the unique **ability** to form abstract conceptions about themselves and to gaze at themselves as both the seer and the object seen. Conflict occurs when the seer places unrealistic demands on him or herself and the body. Body image considers physical appearance and may include body functions or other features. Body image is linked to internal sensations, emotional experiences, fantasies, feedback from others, and plays a key role in a person's **self-concept**. Self-perceptions of physical inferiority can strongly affect all areas of one's life and may lead to avoidance of social or sexual activities or result in **eating disorders**.

How one's physical characteristics correspond to cultural standards plays a crucial role in the formation of body image. In the South Pacific island of Tonga, for example, corpulence is considered a sign of wealth and elevated social status, but would be termed **obesity** in Western societies, particularly in the United States where the slim and firm athletic form is idealized. Deference to cultural standards and concepts can be very damaging, as few people attain an "ideal body," no matter how it is defined, and those who depart drastically from the ideal can suffer a sharply reduced sense of self-worth.

Psychologists are interested in body image primarily to determine whether the image held reasonably agrees with reality. A seriously distorted or inappropriate body image characterizes a number of mental disorders. For **anorexia** nervosa, a seriously distorted body image is a classic symptom and major diagnostic criterion. The anorexic, most likely an adolescent female, perceives herself as "fat" even when she is emaciated. A distorted sense of body image may comprise a disorder in itself, known as body dysmorphic disorder. People affected by this condition generally become preoccupied with a specific body part or physical feature and exhibit signs of anxiety or **depression**. Commonly, the victim mentally magnifies a slight flaw into a major defect, sometimes erroneously believing it the sign of a serious disease, such as cancer, and may resort to plastic surgery to relieve distress due to the person's perceived appearance.

A healthy body image, according to some in the **mental health** field, is one that does not diverge too widely from prevailing cultural standards but leaves room for a person's individuality and uniqueness.

Humans start to recognize themselves in mirrors in meaningful ways at about 18 months and begin perceiving themselves as physical beings in toddlerhood. By school-age, children often face prejudices based on their appearances. Children spend much of their early lives in schools, an **environment** that is highly social and competitive with notoriously rigid hierarchies often based on physical appearances. Studies have found that teachers are also drawn to the most attractive children, which can further compound a child's poor body image. In a

**Constant exposure to very thin models in the media can lead to unrealistic body images.** *(Photo by David Karp. AP/Wide World Photos. Reproduced with permission.)*

school-age child, a poor body image may result in social withdrawal and poor **self-esteem**.

As **puberty** nears, children become increasingly focused on the appearance of their bodies. An adolescent may mature too quickly, too slowly, in a way that is unattractive, or in a way that makes the adolescent stand out in the crowd. Any deviation from the ideal can result in a negative body image, and adolescents may diet or use steroids to counter a negative self-concept. As people age, most revise their views of the ideal body so that they can continue to feel reasonably attractive at each stage of their lives.

*See also* Anorexia; Bulimia

## Further Reading

Cash, Thomas F. *What Do You See When You Look in the Mirror?: Helping Yourself to a Positive Body Image.* New York: Bantam Books, 1995.

Costin, Carolyn. *Your Dieting Daughter: Is She Dying for Attention?* New York: Brunner/Mazel, 1997.

# Bonding

The process by which parents form a close personal relationship with their newborn child.

Bonding is the process by which parents form a close personal relationship with their newborn child. The term "bonding" is often used interchangeably with " attachment," a related phenomenon. For the purposes of this essay, bonding is confined to the newborn period. **Attachment** develops over the larger period of **infancy** and is treated in a separate entry.

The way parents feel about a new child is highly subjective and emotional, and can be very difficult to measure. Some researchers in the United States and elsewhere have attempted to show that there is a "sensitive period" soon after **birth**, in which the newborn is quietly alert and interested in engaging the mother, and the mother is able to attune to the new child. It is assumed, but not proven, that if mothers are given the opportunity to interact with their infants at this time, they are most likely to become bonded to the child—to begin to respond to him, love him, and take care of him. Fathers who are with their partners at the birth also respond to the infant in characteristic ways immediately after birth.

American pediatricians John Kennell and Marshall Klaus pioneered scientific research on bonding in the 1970s. Working with infants in a neonatal intensive care unit, they often observed that infants were often taken away from their mothers immediately after birth for emergency medical procedures. These babies often remained in the nursery for several weeks before being allowed to go home with their families. Although the babies did well in the hospital, a troubling percentage of them seemed not to prosper at home, and were even victims of battering and abuse. Kennell and Klaus also noted that the mothers of these babies were often uncomfortable with them, and did not seem to believe that their babies had survived birth. Even mothers who had successfully raised previous infants seemed to have special difficulties with their children that had been treated in the intensive care nursery. Kennell and Klaus surmised that the separation immediately after birth interrupted some fundamental process between the mother and the new baby. They experimented with giving mothers of both premature and healthy full-term babies extra contact with their infants immediately after birth and in the few days following birth. Mothers who were allowed more access to their babies in the hospital seemed to develop better rapport with their infants, to hold them more comfortably, smile and talk to them more.

Studies conducted in the 1970s making these claims have come under attack in the 1980s and 1990s. Much of

**GALE ENCYCLOPEDIA OF PSYCHOLOGY, 2ND EDITION**

Research shows that instinctive behaviors in new mothers facilitate bonding with their infants. *(Goujon/Jerrican. Photo Researchers, Inc. Reproduced with permission.)*

the earlier research has been difficult to duplicate, and many mitigating factors in **parent-child relationships** make the lasting effects of early bonding experience difficult to pin down with scientific rigor. Nevertheless, bonding research brought about widespread changes in hospital obstetrical practice in the United States. Fathers and **family** members were allowed to remain with the mother during labor and delivery in many cases. Mothers were allowed to hold their infants immediately after birth, and in many cases babies remained with their mothers throughout their hospital stay. Bonding research has also led to increased awareness of the natural capabilities of the infant at birth, and so has encouraged many others to deliver their babies without anesthesia (which depresses mother and infant responsiveness).

One important factor in the parents' **ability** to bond with the infant after birth is that the healthy, undrugged newborn is often in what is called a "quiet alert" state for 45 to 60 minutes after birth. Research has demonstrated that immediately after birth the newborn can see and has visual preferences, can hear and will turn his head toward a spoken voice, and will move in rhythm to his mother's voice. Mothers and fathers allowed to interact

with their newborns in this time frame often exhibit characteristic behaviors, such as stroking the baby, first with fingertips, then with the palm, looking in the baby's eyes, and speaking to the baby in a high-pitched voice. Researchers have also found physical changes in the mother right after birth, such as hormonal increases triggered by the infant licking or sucking her nipples, and increased blood flow to her breasts when hearing the infant cry. Some scientists speculate that there are instinctual behaviors triggered in the mother in response to the infant immediately after birth that facilitate her bonding with the infant, and thus promote the infant's survival.

Research on the bonding process has been scrutinized. Detractors call attention to the often poor research design of early studies and reject bonding as a scientific fallacy thrust on women to make them feel that they must react to their infants in certain prescribed fashions. Some people have misinterpreted bonding to mean that if the early sensitive period is missed, they cannot become successful parents. Obviously, parents can form close attachments to infants they did not see at birth, either because of medical emergencies or because their children are adopted. Thus, early experience with the newborn is only one factor in the complex relations of parents to children.

Despite some problems with quantifying bonding as a scientific phenomenon, there is a wealth of anecdotal evidence on the positive effects of an after-birth bonding experience. Most hospitals are now much more sensitive to parents' desire to be with their newborn than in the past. Parents-to-be may wish to find out their hospital's policies regarding the period immediately after birth. Questions to ask may include: Will the mother be allowed to hold the baby immediately if there is no problem? If tests are needed, can they be delayed until after the first hour? What family members can be present at the birth? Can family members be present at a cesarean birth? Will the baby stay in the same room with the mother or be sent to a central nursery? Some hospitals reportedly score mothers on how well they seem to bond with their infants, allegedly to flag potential future **child abuse**. This in effect makes early and rapid bonding a test, with failure potentially criminal, and egregiously violates the spirit of the hospital reform that bonding research brought about. If a hospital admits to "testing" for bonding, parents may ask if they may decline the test, or if they can have access to the test results. Ideally, both the birth and the period immediately after should be handled according to the parents' wishes.

A. Woodward

### Further Reading

Eyer, Diane E. *Mother-Infant Bonding: A Scientific Fiction.* New Haven, CT: Yale University Press, 1992.

Gaskin, Ina May. *Babies, Breastfeeding and Bonding.* South Hadley, MA: Bergin & Garvey, 1987.

Klaus, Marshall H., John H. Kennell, and Phyllis H. Klaus. *Bonding: Building the Foundations of Secure Attachment and Independence.* Reading, MA: Addison-Wesley, 1995.

# Borderline personality

Mental illness characterized by erratic and impulsive self-destructive behavior and an intense fear of abandonment.

## Characteristics

Borderline individuals have a history of unstable interpersonal relationships. They have difficulty seeing the "shades of gray" in the world, and view significant people in their lives as either completely flawless or extremely unfair and uncaring (a phenomena known as *splitting*). These alternating feelings of idealization and devaluation are the hallmark feature of borderline personality disorder. Because borderline patients set up such excessive and unrealistic expectations for others, they are bound to be disappointed when their expectations aren't realized.

The term "borderline" was originally coined by psychologist Adolf Stern in the 1930s to describe patients who bordered somewhere between **psychosis** and **neurosis**. It has also been used to describe the borderline states of **consciousness** these patients sometimes feel when they experience dissociative symptoms (a feeling of disconnection from oneself).

## Causes and symptoms

Borderline personality disorder accounts for 30–60% of all **personality disorders**, and is present in approximately 2% of the general population. The disorder appears to affect women more frequently than men, and 75% of all diagnosed patients are female.

Adults with borderline personalities often have a history of significant traumas such as emotional and physical abuse, neglect, or the loss of a parent in **childhood**. Feelings of inadequacy and self-loathing that arise from these situations may be key in developing the borderline personality. It has also been theorized that these patients are trying to compensate for the care they were denied in childhood through the idealized demands they now make on themselves and on others as an adult.

In its *Diagnostic and Statistical Manual of Mental Disorders, Fourth Edition (DSM-IV)*, a reference standard for **mental health** professionals, the **American Psychiatric Association** defines borderline personality as a long-standing pattern of instability and impulsive behavior beginning in early adulthood. DSM-IV states that at least five of the following criteria (or symptoms) must be present in an individual for a diagnosis of borderline disorder:

- Frantic efforts to avoid real or perceived abandonment.
- A pattern of unstable, and intense interpersonal relationships, characterized by alternating between idealization and devaluation (i.e., a "love-hate" relationship).
- Identity disturbance characterized by an extreme, persistently unstable self-image and sense of self.
- Impulsive behavior in at least two areas (e.g., spending, sex, substance abuse, reckless driving, binge eating).
- Recurrent suicidal behavior, gestures, or threats, or recurring acts of self-mutilation (e.g., cutting or burning oneself).
- Affective (**mood**) instability due to brief but intense episodes of dysphoria (**depression**), irritability, or anxiety.

- Chronic feelings of emptiness.
- Inappropriate and intense **anger**, or difficulty controlling anger displayed through temper outbursts, physical fights, and/or sarcasm.
- Transient, stress-related **paranoia** and/or severe dissociative symptoms (a separation from the subconscious, sometimes characterized by a "dream-like" state and physical symptoms such as flashbacks).

### Diagnosis

Borderline personality disorder typically first appears in early adulthood. Although the disorder may occur in **adolescence**, it may be difficult to diagnose, as "borderline symptoms" such as impulsive and experimental behaviors, insecurity, and mood swings are also common, developmentally appropriate occurrences at this age.

Borderline symptoms may also be the result of chronic substance abuse and biologically based medical conditions (specifically, disorders of the **central nervous system**). These should be ruled out as causes before making the diagnosis of borderline personality disorder.

The disorder commonly occurs together with mood disorders (i.e., depression and anxiety), **post-traumatic stress disorder**, **eating disorders**, **attention deficit/hyperactivity disorder** (ADHD), and other personality disorders. It has also been suggested by some researchers that borderline personality disorder is not a true pathological condition in and of itself, but rather a number of overlapping personality disorders; however, it is commonly recognized as a separate and distinct disorder by the **American Psychological Association** and by most mental health professionals.

### Treatment

Individuals with borderline personality disorder seek psychiatric help and hospitalization at a much higher rate than people with other personality disorders, probably due to their **fear** of abandonment and need to seek out idealized interpersonal relationship. These patients represent the highest percentage of diagnosed personality disorders (up to 60%).

Providing effective therapy for the borderline personality patient is a necessary, but difficult, challenge. The therapist-patient relationship is subject to the same inappropriate and unrealistic demands that borderline personalities place on all their significant interpersonal relationships. They are chronic "treatment seekers" who become easily frustrated with their therapist if they feel they are not receiving adequate attention or **empathy**, and symptomatic anger, impulsivity, and self-destructive behavior can impede the therapist-patient relationship.

However, their fear of abandonment, and of ending the therapy relationship, may actually cause them to discontinue treatment as soon as progress is made.

**Psychotherapy**, typically in the form of cognitive behavioral therapy, is usually the treatment of choice for borderline personalities. Dialectical **behavior therapy** (DBT), a cognitive-behavioral technique, has emerged as an effective therapy for borderline personalities with suicidal tendencies. The treatment focuses on giving the borderline patient self-confidence and coping tools for life outside of treatment through a combination of social skill training, mood awareness and meditative exercises, and education on the disorder. **Group therapy** is also an option for some borderline patients, although some may feel threatened by the idea of "sharing" a therapist with others.

Medication is not considered a front-line treatment choice, but may be useful in treating some symptoms of the disorder, and in alleviating the symptoms of mood disorders that have been diagnosed in conjunction with borderline personality disorder. Recent clinical studies have indicated that naltrexone, an opiate antagonist, may be helpful in relieving physical discomfort related to dissociative episodes.

### Prognosis

The disorder usually peaks in young adulthood and frequently stabilizes after age 30. Approximately 75-80% of borderline patients attempt or threaten **suicide**, and between 8-10% are successful. If the borderline patient suffers from depressive disorder, the risk of suicide is much higher. For this reason, swift diagnosis and appropriate interventions are critical.

*See also* Dissociation/Dissociative disorders

Paula Ford-Martin

### Further Reading
American Psychiatric Association. *Diagnostic and Statistical Manual of Mental Disorders*, 4th ed. Washington, D.C.: American Psychiatric Press, Inc., 1994.
Moskovitz, Richard A. *Lost in the Mirror: An Inside Look at Borderline Personality Disorder.* Dallas, TX: Taylor Publishing, 1996.

### Further Information
BPD Central. http://www.bpdcentral.com.
National Alliance for the Mentally Ill (NAMI). 200 North Glebe Road, Suite 1015, Arlington, VA, USA. 22203-3754, (800)950-6264. http://www.nami.org.
National Institute of Mental Health (NIMH). 6001 Executive Boulevard, Rm. 8184, MSC 9663, Bethesda, MD, USA. 20892-9663, fax: (301)443-4279, (301)443-4513. Email: nimhinfo@nih.gov. http://www.nimh.nih.gov.

# Boredom

A state of weariness with, and disinterest in, life.

Everyone, at one time or another, feels bored. Children, however, may report boredom more frequently because they have not yet learned to alleviate it for themselves. Infants and toddlers rarely experience boredom. Infants spend large blocks of time asleep and much of their waking time feeding. Toddlers have a nearly unlimited curiosity to explore a world that is still new to them. Preschool and school-aged children, though, are fickle in their **attention**s. The child may be engrossed in an activity one minute and, seconds later, lose interest and complain of boredom.

Adults who complain of boredom may be expressing their frustration at being unchallenged by their present activities. People who complain about being bored at work, for example, may feel that they are not being used to their potential. Boredom in adults is often a sign of a lack of intellectual stimulation. In rare instances, people who repeatedly complain of boredom might be suffering from a clinical condition such as **depression**. Depressed people may withdraw from formerly interesting activities and complain of boredom. Such a person may need to talk to a psychologist about the factors that are causing the depression.

## Further Reading

Wester-Anderson, Joan. "Overcoming Life's Little Doldrums," *Current Health* 19, (February 1993): 4+.

# Medard Boss

### 1903-1990

Swiss psychotherapist who helped build the concept of existential psychology.

The idea of combining psychology and philosophy may seem to run counter to the idea of psychology as a science. But psychology is a science of the mind, and the releationship between the mind and ideas is critically important to psychological study. Medard Boss, trained as a physician, used his knowledge of philosophy to help humanize psychology. He spent his career developing the concept he called *Daseinanalysis*. "Dasein" is a German word meaning "being there," and it forms a critical element of the philosophy of Martin Heidigger (who became a friend of Boss).

Boss was born in St. Gallen, Switzerland on October 4, 1903 and raised in Zurich. Zurich during the early years of the twentieth century. was one of the leading cities for psychological research. Trained as a physician, Boss received his medical degree from the University of Zurich in 1928. Before that, however, he had spent time in Vienna, where he had met (and been analyzed by) **Sigmund Freud**.

It was Boss's exposure to the writings of Ludwig Binswanger and Heidigger that prompted him to formulate a psychological model. Binswanger (1881-1966) has been called the first existential psychologist. In 1946, Boss met Heidigger, and it was then that he was able to fully grasp the concepts that led to his later work.

Essentially, Boss believed that Dasein was a means of opening the mind—of bringing light to a situation. The symbolism of light played an important role in Boss's work: the idea of "coming out of the darkness," of "illuminating an idea," and ultimately, of "enlightenment." Boss further believed that **mood** played an important part in how people reacted to their **environment**. An angry person, for example, would be attuned primarily to things that create feelings of **anger**. Boss also felt that **dreams** were important—more so than other existential thinkers. What made his interpretation of dreams different from those of Freud or Jung, however, was that he believed that dreams created their own message rather than displaying symbols of deeper feelings.

Boss's books include *Existential Foundations of Medicine and Psychology, Psychoanalysis and Daseinanalysis*, and *The Analysis of Dreams*. He died in 1990.

George A. Milite

# Murray Bowen

### 1913-1990

American psychiatrist who pioneered family therapy.

Murray Bowen grew up in a small town that he believed gave him the foundation for his theories on **family therapy**. To Bowen, the family was an emotional unit; although it was made up of individuals who had their own thoughts and needs, much of how they behaved was the result of how they functioned as part of the family.

Bowen, the oldest of five children, was born in Waverly, Tennessee, on January 31, 1913. His parents were Jesse and Maggie Bowen; their families had lived in Tennessee since the days of the American Revolution. Jesse Bowen was mayor of Waverly, and he also ran several small businesses there, including the funeral parlor.

Bowen attended the University of Tennessee, graduating with a bachelor's degree in 1934. He then went to the University of Tennessee Medical School, where he received his M.D. in 1937. He completed internships in New York and in 1941 enlisted in the Army. Before his military experience he had planned to become a cardiac surgeon. His observation of soldiers in the midst of war, however, convinced him that **mental illness** was a more pressing and worthwhile goal. Upon leaving the Army in 1946, he accepted a fellowship at the Menninger Foundation in Topeka, Kansas, where he studied **psychoanalysis** for several years. Eventually he came to believe that, despite Freud's success, his methods fell short in one important regard: recognizing the family as a unit with its own emotional needs and behaviors. Whereas Freud focused on the self, Bowen saw the family as a source of much of the behavior its members expressed. Each member operated as an individual, but within the family structure with its own set of rules. In other words, Bowen's approach took a more pragmatic look at human relationships. As one of five siblings, and as a husband and father of four children, he no doubt observed much of what he was writing about in his own family structure.

Bowen moved to the National Institute of Mental Health in 1954, and then to Georgetown University Medical Center in 1959, where he remained for the rest of his career. In the late 1950s he further developed what he called his "Family Systems Theory." Bowen believed that family members would adopt certain types of behavior based on their place in the family; with this knowledge, a therapist could grapple with behavioral issues more effectively and accurately.

In his later years, Bowen remained active in family therapy. He published his book, *Family Therapy in Clinical Practice,* in 1978, and he was a founder and first president of the American Family Therapy Association from 1978 to 1982. He died of lung cancer at his home in Chevy Chase, Maryland, on October 9, 1990.

George A. Milite

# John Bowlby

**1907-1990**
British psychiatrist who discovered insights into the mother-child bond.

John Bowlby's pioneering work on the relationship between mothers and children was instrumental in shaping **child psychology** in the twentieth century. His research focusing on the mother-child bond—what it meant, and what happened when it did not or could not exist—formed the basis for groundbreaking work that culminated in his "attachment theory" about maternal **bonding**. More important, he made practical as well as theoretical use of his research, working directly with patients and taking young and talented researchers under his wing.

Born in London on February 26, 1907, Edward John Mostyn Bowlby was the son of Major Sir Anthony Bowlby and the former May Mostyn. Sir Anthony was a physician who served as surgeon to King George V. When John, one of six children, was born, his father was 52 and his mother was 40. His **childhood** was typical of many middle- and upper-class children in Britain; early years spent with a nanny or governess, then boarding school. Bowlby did not feel that his own upbringing was out of the ordinary, although one could conclude that his own reserved demeanor may have been formed at an early age.

Bowlby attended the Royal Naval College and Cambridge, where he prepared for medical school. He volunteered for a year in a hospital for maladjusted children, an experience that set the stage for his later work. Two children in particular intrigued Bowlby: an adolescent loner who had been expelled from school for stealing, and a nervous seven-year-old who was called Bowlby's shadow because he followed him around. These two children left a lasting impression on the researcher.

Bowlby entered University College Medical School in London for his medical training. He became interested in psychiatry, attending the British Psychoanalytic Institute and also training at the prestigious Maudsley Hospital. At the Institute he was supervised by the innovative child psychoanalyst Melanie Klein. Although Bowlby did not agree with many of Klein's theories, her guidance helped him to ground his later research.

After graduating from medical school, Bowlby stayed on at Maudsley. Initially he worked with adult patients, but his work gradually turned to children. His first empirical study, in fact, tracked 44 children whose behavior patterns included anxiety and petty crime. He discovered a common thread among these children: they had been deprived of their mothers at some point during their childhood.

During the Second World War, Bowlby moved away from child research and conducted studies on officer selection criteria for the military. This gave him a chance to gain solid experience with statistics, which aided his research after the war. In 1946 he joined the staff of the Tavistock Clinic in London, where he spent the remainder of his career. During his years at Tavistock, Bowlby was intrigued by the work of **Konrad Lorenz**, who researched "imprinting" (for example, how young birds identify the first creature they see upon hatching as their mother), and his belief that early experience influenced later behavior grew stronger. From 1950 to 1952, Bowlby served as a consultant for the World Health Organization, in which he worked with orphaned and institutionalized children who had been separated by their mothers. His report, *Maternal Child Care and Child Health* (1951), said that children who were deprived of their mothers needed a mother figure to substitute; lack of a mother or a substitute mother figure would adversely affect children later in life.

In the 1960s, Bowlby began working on his most important work, his "Attachment and Loss" trilogy. The books included *Attachment* (1969), *Separation* (1973), and *Loss* (1980). Initially, his theories were attacked by traditional psychoanalysts (including **Anna Freud**) who claimed that he had misinterpreted Freud's ideas. But as psychologists and psychiatrists revised Freud's theories, they realized that Bowlby's theories were both innovative and accurate.

Although Bowlby officially retired in 1972, he remained active in research and writing. He continued his association with Tavistock, but he also spent more time at his vacation home on the Isle of Skye, off the Scottish coast, with his **family**. (He married Ursula Longstaff in 1938 and had four children.) His last book, a biography of **Charles Darwin**, was published in 1990, only months before his death of a stroke on September 2 on Skye.

George A. Milite

**Further Reading**

Bowlby, John. *Attachment and Loss, vols. 1-3*. New York, Basic Books, 1969, 1973, 1980.

Holmes, Jeremy. *John Bowlby and Attachment Theory*. London, Routledge, 1993.

# Brain disorders

Any of the various disorders associated with the human brain, including stroke, trauma, and tumors.

It has recently been reported that neurology, the study of the **brain**, is the fastest growing specialty in the life sciences. With this growth has come a wealth of new information about the origins of and treatments for some of the more prevalent brain disorders. There are many varieties of brain disorders that affect humans, including **Alzheimer's disease**, **Parkinson's disease**, **epilepsy**, and other disorders that are more generally thought of as being "behavioral" rather than biological. These types of disorders that could be termed disorders of the brain in a broad sense include **depression**, **schizophrenia**, and **bipolar disorder**. Beyond these, however, are several other types of disorders of the brain, including stroke, trauma, brain tumors, and developmental disorders such as muscular dystrophy and cerebral palsy.

Strokes are the third leading cause of death in the United States and are one of the leading causes of **disability** among older adults. According to the most recent statistics, a staggering 1,200 people suffer from strokes each day in this country. "Stroke" is technically a lay term; when physicians speak of strokes, they are referring to thromboses, hemorrhages, or embolisms. Basically, the term stroke refers to the loss of blood to a part of the brain and the resulting tissue damage. Because of the variables involved, strokes are often not correctly diagnosed. Often, especially with very mild events, a patient will attribute odd sensations to something else. The effects of a stroke may vary, based on its origins and the area of the brain that was deprived of blood. Generally speaking, if tissue damage occurred in the right brain hemisphere, the victim may experience some degree of paralysis on the left side of the body, a distortion of **vision**, especially the **ability** to perceive depth and distance, and a loss of **memory**. If the tissue affected is on the left side of the brain, patients may experience some degree of paralysis on the right side of the body, minor memory loss, and some degree of language loss.

Other common brain disorders include the array of conditions caused by head trauma. Injuries to the head can, obviously, vary tremendously, but such injuries all result in biochemical abnormalities in the brain. After the head has been injured in some way, a tremendous amount of chemicals travel through the brain, which often have detrimental effects on brain cells, including paralysis and behavioral and cognitive losses. Recent medical advances have uncovered some drugs and treatments that can offset this after-effect of trauma, and physicians now know that brain cells can be replaced in adults, a procedure that was thought impossible only a decade ago. Doctors now have the ability to procure accurate images of the brain from magnetic resonance imaging (MRI) machines, allowing them to pinpoint damaged areas for treatment.

The incidence of brain tumors has increased in recent years, although it is not certain if this trend is simply a result of better diagnostic technology, such as MRIs. Nonetheless, treatments devised thus far have generally been less than stellar. Researchers have found that certain genes inside tumors are capable of creating resistance to drugs being used to destroy the tumor.

Often, if drug treatment of brain tumors is ineffective, surgery is required to remove the tumor, which can further damage the brain.

Developmental neurologic disorders of the brain include well-known brain diseases such as Alzheimer's, Parkinson's, muscular dystrophy, and cerebral palsy. Most of these disorders are now known to be inheritable, passed from one generation to another genetically. Recent research has isolated the gene that causes strains of Alzheimer's, Huntington's disease, and several other muscular disorders. Cerebral palsy, a devastating developmental neurologic disorder involving severe muscle and coordination deterioration, has been attributed to stroke in newborn infants.

In 1995, the National Institutes of Health (NIH) spent the following studying brain disorders: Alzheimer's disease, $305 million; stroke, $116 million; multiple sclerosis, $80 million; Parkinson's disease, $72 million; epilepsy, $55 million; and head injury, $51 million. As a way of comparison, NIH spent $199 million studying arthritis in 1995.

## Further Reading

"Cognitive Impairment to Dementia." *The Lancet* (25 February 1995): 465.
"Combating Disorders of the Brain." *New York Times* (30 August 1994).
Connaughton, P. Noel. "Decade of the Brain: A Midpoint Status Report." *Patient Care* (15 July 1995).
Guiness, Alma E., ed. *The Reader's Digest ABCs of the Human Mind.* Pleasantville, NY: Reader's Digest Association, 1990.
Mattson, Sarah N. "MRI and Prenatal Alcohol Exposure: Images Provide Insight into FAS." *Alcohol Health and Research World* (Winter 1994): 49.

# Brain

Part of the central nervous system located in the skull. Controls mental and physical actions of the organism.

The brain, with the spinal cord and network of nerves, controls information flow throughout the body, voluntary actions, such as walking, reading, and talking, and involuntary reactions, such as breathing and heartbeat. The human brain is a soft, shiny, grayish white, mushroom-shaped structure. Encased within the skull, the brain of an average adult weight about 3 lb (1.4 kg). At **birth**, the average human infant's brain weighs 13.7 oz (390 g); by age 15, the brain has nearly reached full adult size. The brain is protected by the skull and by a three-layer membrane called the meninges. Many bright red arteries and bluish veins on the surface of the brain penetrate inward. Glucose, oxygen, and certain ions pass easily from the blood into the brain, whereas other substances, such as antibiotics, do not. The four principal sections of the human brain are the brain stem, the diencephalon, the cerebrum, and the cerebellum.

### The brain stem

The brain stem connects the brain with the spinal cord. All the messages that are transmitted between the brain and spinal cord pass through the medulla—a part of the brain stem—via fibers. The fibers on the right side of the medulla cross to the left and those on the left cross to the right. As a result, each side of the brain controls the opposite side of the body. The medulla also controls the heartbeat, the rate of breathing, and the diameter of the blood vessels and helps to coordinate swallowing, vomiting, hiccupping, coughing, and sneezing. Another component of the brain stem is the pons (meaning bridge). It conducts messages between the spinal cord and the rest of the brain, and between the different parts of the brain. Conveying impulses between the cerebral cortex, the pons, and the spinal cord is a section of the brain stem known as the midbrain, which also contains visual and audio reflex centers involving the movement of the eyeballs and head.

Twelve pairs of cranial nerves originate in the underside of the brain, mostly from the brain stem. They leave the skull through openings and extend as peripheral nerves to their destinations. Among these cranial nerves are the olfactory nerves that bring messages about **smell** and the optic nerves that conduct visual information.

### The diencephalon

The diencephalon lies above the brain stem and embodies the **thalamus** and **hypothalamus**. The thalamus is an important relay station for sensory information, interpreting sensations of sound, smell, **taste**, **pain**, pressure, temperature, and **touch**; the thalamus also regulates some emotions and **memory**. The hypothalamus controls a number of body functions, such as heartbeat rate and digestion, and helps regulate the endocrine system and normal body temperature. The hypothalamus interprets hunger and thirst, and it helps regulate **sleep, anger,** and **aggression**.

### The cerebrum

The cerebrum constitutes nearly 90% of the brain's weight. Specific areas of the cerebrum interpret sensory impulses. For example, spoken and written language are transmitted to a part of the cerebrum called Wernicke's

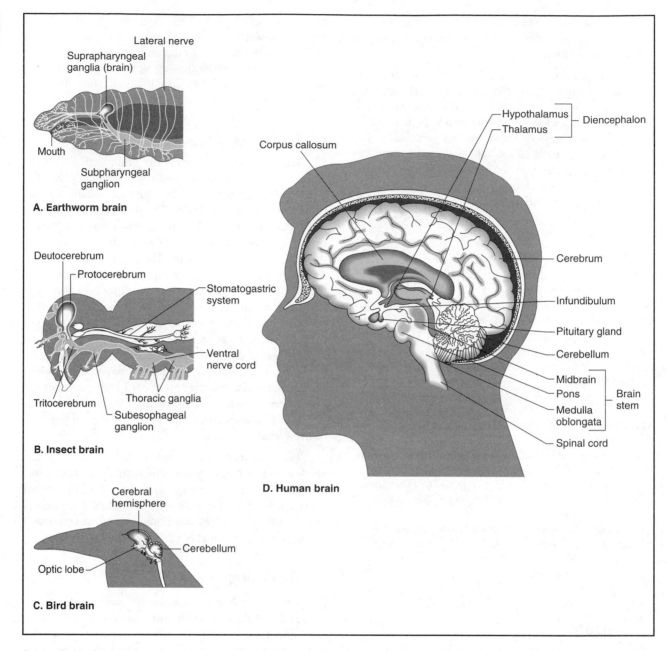

**Comparison of the brains of an earthworm, an insect, a bird, and a human.** *(Hans & Cassidy. Gale Research. Reproduced with permission.)*

area where meaning is extracted. Motor areas of the cerebrum control muscle movements. Broca's area translates thoughts into speech, and coordinates the muscles needed for speaking. Impulses from other motor areas direct hand muscles for writing and eye muscles for physical movement necessary for reading. The cerebrum is divided into two hemispheres—left and right. In general, the left half of the brain controls the right side of the body, and vice versa. For most right-handed people (and many left-handed people as well), the left half of the brain is dominant. By studying patients whose cor-

pus callosum had been destroyed, scientists realized that differences existed between the left and right sides of the cerebral cortex. The left side of the brain functions mainly in speech, logic, writing, and arithmetic. The right side of the brain, on the other hand, is more concerned with **imagination**, art, symbols, and spatial relations.

The cerebrum's outer layer, the cerebral cortex, is composed of gray matter made up of **nerve** cell bodies. The cerebral cortex is about 0.08 in (2 mm) thick and its surface area is about 5 sq ft (0.5 sq m)—around half the size of an office desk. White matter, composed of nerve fibers covered with myelin sheaths, lies beneath the gray matter. During embryonic development, the gray matter grows faster than the white matter and folds on itself, giving the brain its characteristic wrinkly appearance. The folds are called convolutions or gyri, and the grooves between them are known as sulci.

A deep fissure separates the cerebrum into a left and right hemisphere, with the corpus callosum, a large bundle of fibers, connecting the two.

## The cerebellum

The cerebellum is located below the cerebrum and behind the brain stem. It is butterfly-shaped, with the "wings" known as the cerebellar hemispheres. The cerebellum controls many subconscious activities, such as balance and muscular coordination. Disorders related to damage of the cerebellum are ataxia (problems with co-ordination), dysarthria (unclear speech resulting from problems controlling the muscles used in speaking), and nystagmus (uncontrollable jerking of the eyeballs). A brain tumor that is relatively common in children known as medullablastoma grows in the cerebellum.

## Studying the brain

Researchers have discovered that neurons carry information through the **nervous system** in the form of brief electrical impulses called **action potential**s. When an impulse reaches the end of an axon, neurotransmitters are released at junctions called **synapse**s. The neurotransmitters are chemicals that bind to receptors on the receiving neurons, triggering the continuation of the impulse. Fifty different neurotransmitters have been discovered since the first one was identified in 1920. By studying the chemical effects of neurotransmitters in the brain, scientists are developing treatments for mental disorders and are learning more about how drugs affect the brain.

Scientists once believed that brain cells do not regenerate, thereby making brain injuries and brain diseases untreatable. Since the late 1990s, researchers have been testing treatment for such patients with **neuron** transplants, introducing nerve tissue into the brain. They have also been studying substances, such as nerve growth factor (NGF), that someday could be used to help regrow nerve tissue.

Technology provides useful tools for researching the brain and helping patients with **brain disorders**. An electroencephalogram (EEG) is a record of brain waves, electrical activity generated in the brain. An EEG is obtained by positioning electrodes on the head and amplifying the waves with an electroencephalograph and is valuable in diagnosing brain diseases such as **epilepsy** and tumors.

Scientists use three other techniques to study and understand the brain and diagnose disorders:

(1) Magnetic resonance imaging (MRI) uses a magnetic field to display the living brain at various depths as if in slices.

(2) Positron emission tomography (PET) results in color images of the brain displayed on the screen of a monitor. During this test, a technician injects a small amount of a substance, such as glucose, that is marked with a radioactive tag. The marked substance shows where glucose is consumed in the brain. PET is used to study the chemistry and activity of the normal brain and to diagnose abnormalities such as tumors.

(3) Magnetoencephalography (MEG) measures the electromagnetic fields created between neurons as electrochemical information is passed along. When under the machine, if the subject is told, "wiggle your toes," the readout is an instant picture of the brain at work. Concentric colored rings appear on the computer screen that pinpoint the brain signals even before the toes are actually wiggled.

Using an MRI along with MEG, physicians and scientists can look into the brain without using surgery. They foresee that these techniques could help paralysis victims move by supplying information on how to stimulate their muscles or indicating the signals needed to control an artificial limb.

## Further Reading

Bear, Mark F., Barry W. Connors, and Michael A. Paradiso. *Neuroscience: Exploring the Brain*. Baltimore: Williams & Wilkins, 1996.

Burstein, John. *The Mind by Slim Goodbody*. Minneapolis, MN: Fairview Press, 1996.

Carey, Joseph, ed. *Brain Facts*. Washington, D.C.: Society for Neuroscience, 1993.

Greenfield, Susan A., ed. *The Human Mind Explained: An Owner's Guide to the Mysteries of the Mind*. New York: Henry Holt, 1996.

Howard, Pierce J. *The Owner's Manual for the Brain: Everyday Applications from Mind-Brain Research*. Austin, TX: Leornian Press, 1994.

Jackson, Carolyn, ed. *How Things Work: The Brain*. Alexandria, VA: Time-Life Books, 1990.

*The Mind*. Alexandria, VA: PBS Video, 1988. (Series of nine 1-hour videocassettes.)

*The Nature of the Nerve Impulse*. Films for the Humanities and Sciences, 1994-95. (Videocassette.)

# Brainwashing

A systematic, coercive effort to alter an individual's beliefs and attitudes, usually by physical and/or psychological means; also referred to as "thought control."

Brainwashing has been used predominantly in reference to severe programs of political indoctrination, although it is used occasionally in connection with certain religious, especially cultic, practices. Brainwashing works primarily by making the victim's existing beliefs and attitudes nonfunctional and replacing them with new ones that will be useful in the environment created by the captor.

Basically, the techniques of brainwashing involve the complete removal of personal freedom, independence, and decision-making prerogatives; the radical disruption of existing routine behavior; the total isolation from, and destruction of loyalties to, former friends and associates; the absolute obedience to authority in all matters; intense physical abuse and threats of injury, death, and permanent imprisonment; and the constant presentation of the new beliefs as the only correct and acceptable alternative to continuing an unenlightened life. These techniques are intended to induce in the victim a state of childlike trust in, and dependency on, the captor. Confessions of imagined past crimes are often part of the brainwashing process, with the victim admitting to trivial or absurd shortcomings and errors, and sometimes implicating others falsely. Other captives who have already been brainwashed may be used to reinforce the process, criticizing the victim and supporting the captors and their value system. Once the process begins to take hold, threats and punishments are replaced by rewards. The victim is allowed increased physical comfort and given psychological **reinforcement** in the form of approval and **friendship**. All efforts are directed toward cementing his or her new identity, based on the new set values and beliefs provided by the captor.

The study of the techniques and effects of brainwashing grew markedly in the 1950s, after a number of U.S. soldiers appeared to have become indoctrinated when taken prisoner during the Korean War. They confessed to imagined crimes, including the waging of germ warfare, and refused to be repatriated when the war ended. Studies of these prisoners of war and of individuals who had undergone ideological conversion in Chinese prisons during the same period revealed connections between the radical changes in attitude caused by brainwashing and existing knowledge about attitude and identity formation and change in ordinary circumstances. While some brainwashed individuals may actually be re-leased and allowed to return home, researchers have expressed doubts about whether the process can be completely effective or really last for a prolonged period. Its short-term and long-term effectiveness in actually altering an individual's beliefs—both within the brainwashing environment and removed from that environment— vary from individual to individual, depending on **personality** characteristics and many other factors. Intense effort and complete control over the victim are required, and must be exercised over a period of years. Consequently, many of the brainwashing efforts made during the Korean War were ineffective, with the prisoners either resisting change or merely becoming confused instead of indoctrinated. In addition, certain attitudes on the part of prisoners proved particularly resistant to change. Due to these limitations, many psychologists believe it would be impossible to brainwash large populations, even with the use of mass media.

A classic literary example of brainwashing is found in George Orwell's novel, *1984*. The protagonist, Winston Smith, is subjected to isolation, humiliation, physical deprivation and **violence**, and constant threats of further violence. He is also forced to make false confessions which include implicating and denouncing others. His captors express their intent to "squeeze you empty and fill you with ourselves." Their ultimate success in forcing Smith to adapt to whatever beliefs they choose is most memorably demonstrated in his final capitulation to the view that two plus two equals five.

*See also* Cults

## Further Reading
Hyde, Margaret. *Brainwashing and Other Forms of Thought Control.* New York: McGraw-Hill, 1977.

# T. Berry Brazelton

### 1918-
Well-known pediatrician, writer, researcher, and educator.

Like Dr. **Benjamin Spock** (1903- ) before him, T. Berry Brazelton has earned a nationwide reputation as a trusted expert on child care, reaching a mass audience through books, personal appearances, newspaper columns, videos, and a cable-TV program. His research on infant behavior and development led him to formulate the Neonatal Behavioral Assessment Scale (NBAS), a series of clinical tests used in hospitals worldwide. Brazelton's efforts on behalf of children have also been extended to the public policy arena through congressional appearances and lobbying efforts.

**Dr. T. Berry Brazelton** *(Photo by Elise Amendola. AP/Wide World Photos. Reproduced with permission.)*

found the Child Development Unit at Children's Hospital Medical Center in Boston in 1972, together with Edward Tronick. The unit provides medical students and other professionals the opportunity to research early child development and also prepare for clinical work with parents and children. Brazelton's first book, *Infants and Mothers* (1969), has sold more than a million copies and has been translated into 18 languages. It has been followed by a dozen more, including *Toddlers and Parents* (1974), *On Becoming a Family* (1981), and *Working and Caring* (1984), as well as a series of videotapes on child development. Brazelton also writes a syndicated newspaper advice column and since 1984 has had his own program, *What Every Baby Knows,* on cable television.

Rosalie Wieder

# Josef Breuer

**1842-1925**
Austrian physician, physiologist, and a founder of psychoanalysis.

Thomas Berry Brazelton II was born in Waco, Texas, in 1918. By the sixth grade he had decided on a career in pediatrics. He earned his undergraduate degree from Princeton in 1940 and his M.D. from Columbia in 1943. He remained there another year as an intern and then served for a year in the Naval Reserves. His residency was served at Massachusetts General Hospital in Boston, where he completed an additional residency in child psychiatry at the James Jackson Putnam Children's Center in Roxbury. Brazelton opened his own private practice in Cambridge, Massachusetts, in 1950 and became an instructor at Harvard Medical School the following year. He also began research on newborns, toddlers, and parents with the goal of helping parents better understand and interact with their children. Among other areas, he has focused on individual differences among newborns; parent-infant **attachment** during the first four months of life; and the effects of early intervention on at-risk infants. Based on his research, Brazelton developed the NBAS, first published in 1973. The test, popularly called "the Brazelton," uses visual, auditory, and tactile stimuli to assess how newborns respond to their **environment**. It is widely used both clinically and as a research tool.

Brazelton's interest in shifting the focus of pediatric study from disease to infant development led him to

Josef Breuer made the crucial observations upon which early psychoanalytic theory was based. He discovered that neuroses could arise from **unconscious** processes and, furthermore, that the neurotic symptoms could disappear when these underlying causes became part of the conscious mind. He communicated these findings to **Sigmund Freud** and the two men entered into a collaboration. Breuer emphasized **hypnosis**. He also believed that differing levels of **consciousness** are very important in both **normal** and abnormal mental processes. Although Freud eventually rejected this concept, it is now believed to be of great significance. Breuer also was among the most important physiologists of the nineteenth century.

Breuer was born in Vienna, Austria, in 1842. His father, Leopold Breuer, taught religion in Vienna's Jewish community. Breuer's mother died when he was quite young, and he was raised by his maternal grandmother and educated by his father until the age of eight. He graduated from the Akademisches Gymnasium of Vienna in 1858 and then studied at the university for one year, before enrolling in the medical school of the University of Vienna. He passed his medical exams in 1867 and went to work as assistant to the internist Johann Oppolzer at the university.

## Studies physiological processes

Breuer's first important scientific work was published in 1868. With Ewald Hering, a physiology professor at the military medical school in Vienna, he demonstrated the reflex nature of respiration. It was one of the first examples of a feedback mechanism in the **autonomic nervous system** of a mammal. Their experiments changed the way scientists viewed the relationship of the lungs to the **nervous system**, and the mechanism is still known as the Hering-Breuer reflex.

In 1868, Breuer married Matilda Altmann, and they eventually had five children. Following Oppolzer's death in 1871, Breuer entered private practice. Still, he found time for scientific study. He worked in his home, with funds derived from his medical practice. Turning his attention to the physiology of the ear, he discovered the function of the semicircular canals. This work provided the foundation for our modern understanding of how sensory receptors detect position and movement. In all, Breuer published approximately 20 papers on physiology over a period of 40 years. Although he joined the faculty of internal medicine at the University of Vienna in 1875, his relationships there were strained; he resigned his position in 1885.

### The story of Anna O.

It was in 1880 that Breuer first observed the development of a severe **mental illness** in one of his patients, "Anna O." Breuer found that he could reduce the severity of Anna's symptoms by encouraging her to describe her fantasies and **hallucinations**. He began using hypnosis to facilitate these sessions. He found that when she recalled a series of memories back to a traumatic **memory**, one of her many symptoms would disappear, a process that Breuer called cathartic. Soon, Breuer was treating Anna with hypnosis twice a day and eventually all of her symptoms were gone. Breuer drew two important conclusions from his work with Anna: that her symptoms were the result of thoughts that were buried in her unconscious and that when these thoughts were spoken and became conscious, the symptoms disappeared. Breuer's treatment of Anna O. is the first example of "deep psychotherapy" carried out over an extended time period.

Breuer did not publish the results of Anna's treatment. However, he taught his methods to Sigmund Freud and, together, they began to develop this new form of **psychotherapy**. Breuer did not continue to treat patients such as Anna. Although he claimed that the demands of his busy medical practice prevented him from pursuing psychotherapy, Freud believed that he was upset by the strong **attachment** that Anna developed for Breuer towards the end of her treatment, a phenomenon that became known as **transference**. When Freud began to use Breuer's methods of **psychoanalysis**, Breuer and Freud discussed Freud's patients and the techniques and results

of their treatments. In 1893, they published an article on their work and, two years later, the book which marked the beginning of psychanalytic theory, *Studien über Hysterie*. At about the same time, their collaboration—and their friendship—came to an end. Apparently Breuer's ambivalence concerning the value of their work fueled their discord. However their final break came about over the question of **childhood** memories of seduction. At the time, Freud believed that most of his patients had actually been seduced as children. Only later did he realize that Breuer was correct in believing these to be memories of childhood fantasies.

Breuer dropped his study of psychoanalysis, whereas Freud continued to develop his theories independently. However, among other concepts, Breuer usually is credited with having first suggested that **perception** and memory are different psychic processes and with having developed a theory of hallucinations. Breuer's background in physiology had a profound influence on the development of his theories and it is likely that his influence on the work of Sigmund Freud has been underestimated. Some physicians, the "Breuerians," continued for a time to use Breuer's original cathartic techniques without adopting Freud's modifications and amplifications.

Breuer was regarded as one of the finest physicians and scientists in Vienna. In 1894, he was elected to the Viennese Academy of Science. Breuer died in Vienna in 1925. His daughter Dora later committed suicide rather than be deported by the Nazis. Likewise, one of his granddaughters died at the hands of the Nazis. Other members of his family emigrated.

Margaret Alic

### Further Reading
Cranefield, Paul F. "Breuer, Josef." In *Dictionary of Scientific Biography*, edited by Charles Coulston Gillispie, vol. 2. New York: Charles Scribner's Sons, 1970.
Hirschmüller, Albrecht. *The Life and Work of Josef Breuer: Physiology and Psychoanalysis*. New York: New York University Press, 1989.

# Brief reactive psychosis

An uncommon acute mental disorder precipitated by an event that causes intense psychological stress.

Episodes that are classified as brief reactive psychoses may last more than two hours but less than one month. Typical triggering events can be the death of a spouse or other loved one, combat trauma, financial disaster, or any other major event involving psychosocial **stress**. Brief reactive psychosis has a sudden onset, typically in late **adolescence** and early adulthood, and is characterized by delusions, **hallucinations**, incoherent speech, disorganized or catatonic behavior, and possibly aggressive or suicidal impulses. Although episodes of brief reactive psychosis occur in a short period of time, the degree of cognitive impairment during these episodes may be very severe, and often individuals with this condition must be prevented from acting in dangerously inappropriate or self-destructive ways. Complete recovery usually follows, however, and the patient is restored to his or her prior level of functioning.

# Pierre Paul Broca

**1824-1880**
French medical doctor and anthropologist known for his role in the discovery of specialized functions in different areas of the brain.

Pierre Paul Broca, the son of a Huguenot doctor, was born near Bordeaux, France, in 1824. After studying mathematics and physical science at the local university, he entered medical school at the University of Paris in 1841. He received his M.D. in 1849. Though trained as a pathologist, anatomist, and surgeon, Broca's interests were not limited to the medical profession. His versatility and tireless dedication to science permitted him to make significant contributions to other fields, most notably to anthropology.

The application of his expertise in anatomy outside the field of medicine began in 1847 as a member of a commission charged with reporting on archaeological excavations of a cemetery. The project permitted Broca to combine his anatomical and mathematical skills with his interests in anthropology.

The discovery in 1856 of Neanderthal Man once again drew Broca into anthropology. Controversy surrounded the interpretation of Neanderthal. It was clearly a human skull, but more primitive and apelike than a modern skull and the soil stratum in which it was found indicated a very early date. Neanderthal's implications for evolutionary theory demanded thorough examination of the evidence to determine decisively whether it was simply a congenitally deformed *Homo sapiens* or a primitive human form. Both as an early supporter of **Charles Darwin** and as an expert in human anatomy, Broca supported the latter view. Broca's view eventually prevailed, though not until the discovery of the much more primitive Java Man (then known as *Pithecanthropus*, but later *Homo erectus*).

Broca is best known for his role in the discovery of specialized functions in different areas of the **brain**. In 1861, he was able to show, using post-mortem analysis of patients who had lost the **ability** to speak, that such loss was associated with damage to a specific area of the brain. The area, located toward the front of the brain's left hemisphere, became known as Broca's convolution. Aside from its importance to the understanding of human physiology, Broca's findings addressed questions concerning the evolution of language.

All animals living in groups communicate with one another. Non-human primates have the most complex communication system other than human language. They use a wide range of gestures, facial expressions, postures, and vocalizations, but are limited in the variety of expressions and are unable to generate new signals under changing circumstances. Humans alone possess the capacity for language rather than relying on a body language vocabulary. Language permits humans to generate an infinite number of messages and ultimately allows the transmission of information—the learned and shared patterns of behavior characteristic of human social groups, which anthropologists call culture—from generation to generation. The development of language spurred human evolution by permitting new ways of social interaction, organization, and thought.

Given the importance assigned to human speech in human evolution, scientists began to look for the physical preconditions of speech. The fact that apes have the minimal parts necessary for speech indicated that the shape and arrangement of the vocal apparatus was insufficient for the development of speech. The vocalizations produced by other animals are involuntary and incapable of conscious alteration. However, human speech requires codifying thought and transmitting it in patterned strings of sound. The area of the brain isolated by Broca sends the code to another part of the brain that controls the muscles of the face, jaw, tongue, palate, and larynx, setting the speech apparatus in motion. This area and a companion area that controls the understanding of language, known as Wernicke's area, are detectable in early fossil skulls of the genus *Homo*. The brain of *Homo* was evolving toward the use of language, although the vocal chamber was still inadequate to articulate speech. Broca discovered one piece in the puzzle of human communication and speech, which permits the transmission of culture.

Equally important, Broca contributed to the development of physical anthropology, one of the four subfields of anthropology. Craniology, the scientific **measurement** of the skull, was a major focus of physical anthropology during this period. Mistakenly considering contemporary human groups as if they were living fossils, anthropologists became interested in the nature of

Pierre Paul Broca

human variability and attempted to explain the varying levels of technological development observed worldwide by looking for a correspondence between cultural level and physical characteristics. Broca furthered these studies by inventing at least twenty-seven instruments for making measurements of the human body, and by developing standardized techniques of measurement.

Broca's many contributions to anthropology helped to establish its firm scientific foundation at a time when the study of nature was considered a somewhat sinister science.

# Jerome S. Bruner

## 1915-

American psychologist and educator whose principal areas of study are in the fields of cognitive psychology and language development.

Jerome S. Bruner was born in New York City and educated at Duke University. During World War II, Bruner worked on the subject of propaganda and popular attitudes for U.S. Army intelligence at General Dwight D. Eisenhower's headquarters in France. He obtained his Ph.D. from Harvard University in 1947, after which he became a member of the faculty, serving as professor of psychology, as well as cofounder and director of the Center for Cognitive Studies. In 1972 Bruner left Harvard to teach for several years at Oxford University. He returned to Harvard as a visiting professor in 1979 and two years later joined the faculty of the new School for Social Research in New York City. Bruner's early work in **cognitive psychology** focused on the sequences of decisions made by subjects as part of their problem-solving strategies in experimental situations.

Beginning in the 1940s, Bruner, together with his colleague Leo Postman, did important work on the ways in which needs, motivations, and expectations (or "mental sets") affect **perception**. Their approach, sometimes referred to as the "New Look," contrasted a functional perspective with the prevailing "formal" one that treated perception as a self-sufficient process to be considered separately from the world around it. When Bruner and Postman showed young children toys and plain blocks of equal height, the children, expecting toys to be larger than blocks, thought the toys were taller. The toys also seemed to increase in size when the researchers made them unavailable. In further experiments involving mental sets, the two scientists used an instrument called a tachistoscope to show their subjects brief views of playing cards, including some nonstandard cards, such as a red ace of

**Jerome S. Bruner** *(Archives of the History of American Psychology. Reproduced with permission.)*

spades. As long as the subjects were not alerted to the presence of the abnormal cards, almost none saw them.

Bruner's work in cognitive psychology led to an interest in the **cognitive development** of children and related issues of education, and in the 1960s he developed a theory of cognitive growth. Bruner's theories, which approach development from a different angle than those of **Jean Piaget**, focus on the environmental and experiential factors influencing each individual's specific development pattern. His argument that human intellectual **ability** develops in stages from **infancy** to adulthood through step-by-step progress in how the mind is used has influenced experimental psychologists and educators throughout the world. Bruner is particularly interested in language and other representations of human thought. In one of his best-known papers, Bruner defines three modes of representing, or "symbolizing," human thought. The *enactive* mode involves human motor capacities and includes activities such as using tools. The *iconic* mode pertains to sensory capacities. Finally, the *symbolic* mode involves reasoning, and is exemplified by language, which plays a central role in Bruner's theories of **cognition** and development. He has called it "a means, not only for representing experience, but also for transforming it."

Bruner's view that the student should become an active participant in the educational process has been widely accepted. In *The Process of Education* (1960) he asserts that, given the appropriate teaching method, every child can successfully study any subject at any stage of his or her intellectual development. Bruner's later work involves the study of the pre-speech developmental processes and linguistic communication skills in children. *The Relevance of Education* (1971) applied his theories to infant development. Bruner was appointed a visiting member of the Institute for Advanced Study at Princeton University. In 1963, he received the Distinguished Scientific Award from the **American Psychological Association**, and in 1965 he served as its president. Bruner's expertise in the field of education led to his appointment to the President's Advisory Panel of Education, and he has also advised agencies of the United Nations. Bruner's books include *A Study of Thinking* (1956), *On Knowing: Essays For the Left Hand* (1962), *On Knowing* (1964), *Toward a Theory of Instruction* (1966), *Processes of Cognitive Growth* (1968), *Beyond the Information Given* (1973), and *Child's Talk* (1983).

*See also* Child development; Cognitive development; Developmental psychology

## Further Reading
Bruner, Jerome S. *In Search of Mind: Essays in Autobiography.* New York: Harper & Row, 1983.

# Bulimia

An eating disorder in which a person indulges in recurrent episodes of binge eating, followed by purging through self-induced vomiting or by the use of laxatives and/or diuretics in order to prevent weight gain.

The symptoms of bulimia, or bulimia nervosa, include eating uncontrollably (binging) and then purging by dieting, fasting, exercising, vomiting, or abusing laxatives or diuretics. A binge involves a large amount of food, for example, several boxes of cookies, a loaf of bread, a half gallon of ice cream, and a bucket of fried chicken, eaten in a short and well-defined time period. Specific behaviors associated with bulimia include: 1) eating high-calorie "junk food" (candy bars, cookies, ice cream, etc.); 2) eating surreptitiously; 3) eating until stopped by a stomach ache, drowsiness, or external interruption; 4) a tendency to go on "crash diets"; and 5) weight that varies over a 10-pound (4.5 kg) range. Although all of these behaviors are not present in all bulimics, the presence of at least three makes it likely that an individual is suffering from the disorder. In general, binging episodes occur at least twice a week, and may take place two or more times a day.

Unlike anorexics, bulimics may be close to normal weight or overweight (within 15 percent of normal standards) and do not suffer from amenorrhea or lose interest in sex. Bulimics feel out of control, realize that their eating patterns are abnormal, and experience intense feelings of **guilt** and shame over their binging. Their preoccupation with body weight and secretive eating behaviors may combine with **depression** or **mood** swings. Possible warning signals of bulimia may include irregular periods, dental problems, swollen cheeks, heartburn, bloating, and alcohol or drug abuse.

The American Anorexia/Bulimia Association estimates that up to 5 percent of college-age women are bulimic and more than 90 percent of all bulimics are women. The onset of the disorder commonly occurs in the late teens or early twenties and can begin after a period of dieting or weight loss. Risk factors for the disorder involve a pattern of excessive dieting in an attempt to weigh less, a history of depression or alcoholism, low **self-esteem**, obese parents or siblings, and a history of **anorexia** nervosa. It has also been suggested that bulimia may have physiological causes, including a defective satiety mechanism.

In order to reduce the risks of developing an eating disorder, cultural attitudes associating thinness and beauty with personal worth and happiness must change to reflect a greater emphasis on developing healthier attitudes and eating behaviors in early **childhood**. Individuals must learn to value themselves and others for intrinsic rather than extrinsic qualities such as appearance.

Although bulimia is seldom life-threatening, it is a serious illness with severe medical consequences, including abdominal **pain**, vomiting blood, electrolyte imbalance possibly leading to weakness or cardiac arrest, muscle weakness, and intestinal damage. Bulimics and anorexics rarely cure themselves and the longer the behavior continues, the more difficult it is to help the individual change. The most effective treatment involves a team approach consisting of medical evaluation, individual and/or group **psychotherapy**, nutritional counseling, anti-depressant medication, and possible hospitalization. Psychotherapy generally consists of investigating the patient's **unconscious** motivations for binging in combination with **behavior modification** techniques to help cope with the disease. Commonly recommended medications include diphenylhydantoin (Dilantin), an anticonvulsant, and tricyclic **antidepressants**. Even with treatment, only about one-third of bulimics appear to recover while another third show some improvement in their eating behavior. The remaining third do not respond to treatment and 10 to 20 percent of these people eventually die of the disease.

*See also* Anorexia; Body image

**Further Information**

American Anorexia/Bulimia Association (AABA). 418 E. 76th St., New York, New York 10021, (212) 734–1114.

American Dietetic Association (ADA) NCND-Eating Disorders. 216 W. Jackson Blvd., Chicago, Illinois 60606, (800) 366–1655.

National Anorexic Aid Society. 445 E. Dublin-Granville Rd., Worthington, Ohio 43229, (614) 436–1112.

National Association of Anorexia Nervosa and Associated Disorders (ANAD). Box 7, Highland Park, Illinois 60035, (708) 831–3438.

# Bullies

An aggressive child who repeatedly victimizes a less powerful child with physical and/or emotional abuse.

Bullying usually involves an older or larger child (or several children) victimizing a single child who is incapable of defending himself or herself. Although much bullying goes unreported, it is estimated that in the average school an incident of bullying occurs approximately once every seven minutes. Bullying occurs at about the same rate regardless of class size or school size, but, for an unknown reason, rural schools appear to have a higher rate of bullying than urban or suburban schools. Even when bullying is reported, it is not always taken seriously by teachers and parents because many adults believe that children should learn to "stand up for themselves" or "fight back."

Although the stereotypical bully is male, girls engage in bullying behavior almost as often as boys. Their tactics differ, however, in that they are less visible. Boy bullies tend to resort to one-on-one physical **aggression**, while girls tend to bully as a group through social exclusion and the spreading of rumors. Girls who would never bully individually will often take part in group bullying activities such as "slam books," notebooks that are circulated among the peer group in which comments and criticisms are written about particular individuals.

Bullying begins at a very early age; it is not uncommon to find bullies in preschool classrooms. Up until about age seven, bullies appear to choose their victims at random. After that, they single out specific children to torment on a regular basis. Nearly twice as much bullying goes on in grades two to four as in grades six to eight, and, as bullies grow older, they use less physical abuse and more verbal abuse.

Until about sixth grade, bullies are not necessarily unpopular. They average two or three friends, and other children seem to admire them for their physical toughness. By high school, however, their social acceptance has diminished to the point that their only "friends" are other bullies. Despite their unpopularity, bullies have relatively high **self-esteem**. Perhaps this is because they process social information inaccurately.

For example, bullies attribute hostile intentions to people around them and therefore perceive provocation where it does not exist. "What are you staring at?" is a common opening line of bullies. For the bully, these perceived slights serve as justification for aggressive behavior.

In general, children who become the targets of bullies have a negative view of **violence** and go out of their way to avoid conflict. They tend to be "loners" who exhibit signs of vulnerability before being singled out by a bully. Being victimized leads these children—who are already lacking in self-esteem—to feel more anxious and thereby increase their vulnerability to further victimization. Being the target of a bully leads to social isolation and rejection by peers, and victims tend to internalize others' negative views, further eroding their self-esteem. Although bullying actually lessens during **adolescence**, that is the period when peer rejection is most painful for victims. In a number of well-publicized cases (in Scandinavia, Japan, and Australia, as well as the United States), adolescents tormented by bullies have been driven to **suicide**.

Evidence indicates that bullying is not a phase a child will outgrow. In a long-term study of more than 500 children, University of Michigan researchers discovered that children who were viewed as the most aggressive by their peers at age eight grew up to commit more (and more serious) crimes as adults. Other studies indicate that, as adults, bullies are far more likely to abuse their spouses and children.

**Further Reading**

Olweus, Dan. *Bullying at School: What We Know and What We Can Do.* Cambridge, MA: Blackwell, 1993.

**Further Information**

Bullies and Scapegoats Project.

Educators for Social Responsibility. 23 Garden Street, Cambridge, MA 02138, (617) 492–1764.

National School Safety Center. 4165 Thousand Oaks Blvd., Westlake Village, CA 91362, (805) 777–9977.

# Bystander effect

The effect of the presence of others on an individual's perception of and response to a situation.

The term bystander effect, or bystander apathy, was first employed by psychologists in the early 1960s. The 1964 murder of New Yorker Kitty Genovese provides an illustration of this phenomenon. Genovese, who was being savagely attacked outside her apartment building, screamed for help for over 30 minutes. Although 40 neighbors heard Genovese's desperate cries, no one came to her aid or even called the police. Researchers have explained several components of the bystander effect. First, witnesses must perceive the situation as an emergency. When others are present, not taking action or behaving as if nothing were wrong, all observers tend to view the situation as a nonemergency. Psychologists describe this as *pluralistic ignorance*, in which the behavior of the group causes each individual to be lulled into inaction. In the case of Genovese's murder, her neighbors were not hearing her cries for help as a group. Each person, isolated in his or her own apartment, heard the disturbance and had no way of knowing the reactions of others who were hearing Genovese's screams. However, each person could believe that someone else was taking action, and therefore the responsibility for response fell to that other person. Psychologists call this reaction *diffusion of responsibility*.

Experiments have been developed to demonstrate the components of the bystander effect. In one experiment designed to test the power of pluralistic ignorance, male subjects were given appointments for an interview. As they wait in an outer room, smoke begins to pour through a ventilation duct. Researchers observed the subjects through a one-way mirror for three minutes. Seventy-five percent of the subjects who were alone in the waiting room reported the smoke within two minutes, while 13 percent of those tested in groups reported the smoke. Those who did not report the smoke ex-

## TIPS FOR PREVENTING BULLYING BEHAVIOR

Parents and teachers can do a number of things to prevent bullying:

- All children should be given regular opportunities to discuss bullying and ways to deal with bullies. in role-playing exercises, for example, children can practice saying, "Leave me alone" and walking away.

- Children can be taught simple measures to lessen the likelihood of becoming the target of a bully. Looking people in the eye, speaking up, and standing straight are just a few behaviors that communicate self-confidence.

- Children who tend to be loners (potential targets of bullies) can be paired up with socially competent "models." Some children need a little help learning how to make friends.

- Because bullies are most likely to strike during unsupervised times such as recess, children should be provided with as much structured activity as possible.

plained that, since others in the room did not seem to be concerned, the smoke must have been air conditioning vapors or steam. This experiment illustrates that bystanders can contribute significantly to an individual's interpretation of a situation.

## Further Reading

Latani, Bibb. The *Unresponsive Bystander: Why Doesn't He Help?* New York: Appleton-Century Crofts, 1970.
Palma, Giuseppe. *Apathy and Participation: Mass Politics in Western Societies.* New York: Free Press, 1970.

# C

## Mary Whiton Calkins

**1863-1930**

American psychologist and philosopher who became the first woman president of both the American Psychological Association (1905) and the American Philosophical Association (1918).

The eldest of five children born to Reverend Wolcott Calkins, a strong-willed, intellectually gifted evangelical minister, and Charlotte Grosvenor Whiton, a daughter of an established New England Puritan family, Mary Whiton Calkins grew up in a close-knit family that valued education. As her mother's mental and physical health began to deteriorate, Calkins took on increased responsibilities for her younger siblings as well as her mother.

After earning a B.A. from Smith College with a concentration in the classics, Calkins began teaching Greek at Wellesley College in 1887. In 1888, she was offered the new position of instructor in psychology there, which was contingent upon a year's training in the discipline. Consistent with university policy toward women in 1890, Calkins was granted special permission to attend classes in psychology and philosophy at Harvard University and in laboratory psychology at Clark University in Worcester, but was denied admission to their graduate studies programs. She was also denied permission to attend regular Harvard seminars until faculty members **William James** and Josiah Royce (1855-1916), as well as Calkins's father, intervened on her behalf. After she was enrolled in James's seminar, four men enrolled in the class dropped it in protest. Attendance at James's seminar led to individual study with him, and within a year Calkins had published a paper on association, suggesting a modification to James's recently published *Principles of Psychology*. Her paper was enthusiastically received by her mentor, who referred to it when he later revised his book.

Returning to Wellesley in the fall of 1891, Calkins established the first psychology laboratory at a women's

**Mary Whiton Calkins** *(Archives of the History of American Psychology. Reproduced with permission.)*

college in the United States with help from Edmund Sanford, a faculty member at Clark, with whom she collaborated on an experimental study of **dreams** published in the *American Journal of Psychology*. In 1893, seeking further laboratory training, Calkins returned to Harvard to work with James's protégé, Hugo Münsterberg (1863-1916), investigating the factors influencing **memory**. During the course of this work, Calkins originated the "paired associates" technique, a method of testing memory by presenting test subjects with paired numbers and colors. Her findings revealed that numbers paired with bright colors were retained better than those associated with neutral colors. However, the prime factor influencing memory was frequency of exposure. The results of this research were published as a supplement to *Psychological Review* in 1896.

In 1895, Calkins requested and took an examination equivalent to the official Ph.D. exam. Her performance was praised by James as "the most brilliant examination for the Ph.D. that we have had at Harvard," surpassing that of his junior colleague, George Santayana (1863-1952). Nevertheless, Calkins was still denied admission to candidacy for the degree. With the creation of Rad-cliffe College in April 1902, Calkins was one of the first four women to be offered the Ph.D., but she refused it in protest.

Calkins taught at Wellesley College until her retirement in 1929, and had published four books and more than 100 papers in psychology and philosophy. In 1901, she published a well-received *Introduction to Psychology* and spent the early 1900s developing a psychology of the self that anticipated later theories of **personality**. In 1909, Columbia University awarded Calkins a honorary Doctor of Letters (Litt.D.) and in 1910, Smith College granted her the Doctor of Laws (LL.D.). Calkins died in 1930.

### Further Reading
Scarborough, Elizabeth and Laurel Furumoto. *Untold Lives: The First Generation of American WomenPsychologists*, 17-51. New York: Columbia University Press, 1987.

# Case study methodologies

Research procedures that focuses on a particular individual or group.

A case study (or case history) consists of an intensive, detailed description and analysis of a particular individual, group, or event. Information may be obtained by means of careful observation, interviews, psychological tests, or archival records. Case study research is useful when the researcher is starting to investigate a new area in which there is little information available. Case studies are a rich source of ideas and hypotheses for future research. They can also be used to disconfirm a generally accepted principle. For example, the motor theory of speech **perception** was based on the claim that decoding and interpreting speech was dependent on the listener's **ability** to produce speech. In other words, an inability to speak should be accompanied by an inability to comprehend speech. In 1962, Eric Lenneberg reported the outcome of extensive tests over a five-year period on a young boy who was totally inarticulate because of an inborn defect of his vocal tract. Testing showed that he had **normal** and complete understanding of spoken language. This single counterexample was sufficient to invalidate the theory's basic assumption.

Another widely cited case study is that of Phineas Gage. He was a railway construction foreman who suffered a bizarre accident in 1848 when a three-foot-long iron rod was driven into his skull. The inch-thick rod entered beneath his left eye and exited through the top of his head, destroying much of the prefrontal cortex. Because Gage survived, it provided an opportunity to investigate the effects of **brain** damage on outward behavior. Although he could still speak and move normally, his friends reported a big change in his **personality**. The accident transformed him from an amiable, dependable worker into an inconsiderate, foul-mouthed lout. This case, and others like it, suggest that parts of the frontal lobes control social judgment, decision-making, and goal-setting.

While findings from case studies can be valuable, the method has limitations. One major weakness is poor representativeness. Because of the exclusive focus on a particular individual or group, the researcher has no way of knowing whether that individual is typical of people in general. Does the case of Phineas Gage tell us how everyone with a similar injury might be affected? The answer is no, because no two people could ever suffer from precisely identical injuries. Definitive statements about the relationship between brain damage and behavior can only be obtained by means of controlled investigative procedures. Moreover, case studies, by their very nature, do not permit the researcher to draw any conclusions as to causality. In a conventional experiment, the researcher usually has one or more specific hypotheses that are tested by the controlled manipulation of the specific variables of interest. Case studies do not permit careful control, thus it is impossible to identify a specific causal association.

The difficulty of drawing causal inferences from individual case studies is further illustrated by the case of Genie. Genie was a 13-year-old girl who had been grievously neglected by her parents for most of her **childhood**. From the age of 18 months she was confined to a small room and denied any opportunity for social interactions or normal human contact. No one spoke to her, and she was punished for making any sounds herself. This sad case permitted researchers to test the hypothesis that there is a **critical period** of language acquisition. The critical period hypothesis maintained that a child's ability to learn its native language effectively ends at the onset of **puberty**. Genie was 13 when she was rescued. Of particular interest to scientists interested in language learning was the fact that she could not speak. Her only sounds were high-pitched whimpers. Placed in a nurturing **environment**, would Genie learn to speak? If so, the critical period hypothesis would be refuted. After several years, Genie was able to use words to convey some of her needs, but her grammar and pronunciation remained abnormal and impoverished. While this case is supportive of the critical period hypothesis, crucial information is missing from the picture. We cannot know if Genie was born with mental deficits that might have prevented normal **language development**, even in the absence of her social isolation.

Because of their very narrow focus, case studies can sometimes be very misleading. John was a normal baby whose penis was burned beyond repair due to a surgical accident in 1963. His doctors persuaded John's parents to have him undergo sex reassignment. At the age of seventeen months, John became "Joan," and from then on the child was treated as a girl. When Joan was evaluated eight years later, the reassignment was judged a success. The case received widespread publicity in textbooks and the mass media. The John/Joan story was heralded as an important demonstration of the influence of social factors in determining **gender identity**. By age 14, however, Joan suspected that she was a boy. Increasingly dissatisfied with her plight, she became depressed and suicidal. Eventually, Joan underwent plastic surgery and was given male hormone treatments. Today, John is married and reasonably well adjusted. This case clearly illustrates the importance of constitutional factors in establishing gender identity. It also shows us how risky it is to make sweeping generalizations based on observations of a single individual.

Timothy E. Moore

**Further Reading**
Christensen, L. *Experimental methodology.* Boston: Allyn & Bacon, 1997.

# Catharsis

The release of repressed psychic energy.

The term catharsis originated from the Greek word *katharsis,* meaning to purge, or purgation. In psychology, the term was first employed by Sigmund Freud's colleague **Josef Breuer** (1842-1925), who developed a "cathartic" treatment for persons suffering from hysterical symptoms through the use of **hypnosis**. While under hypnosis, Breuer's patients were able to recall traumatic experiences, and through the process of expressing the original emotions that had been repressed and forgotten, they were relieved of their symptoms. Catharsis was also

central to Freud's concept of **psychoanalysis**, but he replaced hypnosis with **free association**.

In other schools of **psychotherapy**, catharsis refers to the therapeutic release of emotions and tensions, although not necessarily **unconscious** ones such as Freud emphasized. Certain types of therapy in particular, such as psychodrama and primal scream therapy, have stressed the healing potential of cathartic experiences.

*See also* Repression

**Further Reading**
Jenson, Jean C. *Reclaiming Your Life: A Step-by-Step Guide to Using Regression Therapy to Overcome the Effects of Childhood Abuse.* New York: Dutton, 1995.

# Cathexis

In classic psychoanalysis, the investment of psychic energy in a person or object connected with the gratification of instincts.

The English word for cathexis—which replaces the German besetzung—is derived from the Greek word for "I occupy." Through the process of cathexis, which **Sigmund Freud** saw as analogous to the channeling of an electrical charge, the psychic energy of the **id** is bound to a selection of objects. An infant's earliest cathected objects are his mother's breast, his own mouth, and the process of sucking.

When a cathected object becomes a source of conflict, as parents do during the Oedipal stage, anti-cathexes redirect all thoughts about the object to the **unconscious** level in order to relieve anxiety. Thus, cathexes originate in the id, while anti-cathexes are formed by the **ego** and the **superego**.

Freud believed that most **personality** processes are regulated by cathexes and anti-cathexes. He considered anti-cathexes as an internal form of frustration, paralleling the external frustration of instincts that one encounters from environmental factors over which one has no control. In the case of anti-cathexis, this frustration is provided internally by one's own psychic mechanisms. However, it cannot occur until one has experienced external frustration, generally in the form of parental discipline. Having been subjected to external controls, one becomes able to develop inner ones.

Cathexes are involved in the repression of memories, which can be recalled either by weakening the anti-cathexis or strengthening the cathexis. Either process is difficult and may be facilitated by the use of special techniques, including **hypnosis**, **free association**, and the interpretation of **dreams**.

## Further Reading

Freud, Sigmund. *The Standard Edition of the Complete Psychological Works of Sigmund Freud*. London: Hogarth Press, 1962.

Firestone, Robert. *Psychological Defenses in Everyday Life*. New York: Human Sciences Press, 1989.

Goleman, Daniel. *Vital Lies, Simple Truths: the Psychology of Self-Deception*. New York : Simon and Schuster, 1985.

Hall, Calvin S. *A Primer of Freudian Psychology*. New York: Harper and Row, 1982.

# James McKeen Cattell

### 1860-1944
American pioneer in psychological research techniques and founder of a psychological testing company.

James McKeen Cattell developed an approach to psychological research that continues to dominate the field of psychology today. During psychology's early years, most research focused on the sensory responses of single individuals studied in depth because **Wilhelm Wundt** (1832-1920), the first experimental psychologist, favored this approach. As Cattell's ideas developed, his perspective diverged greatly from Wundt's, and Cattell developed techniques that allowed him to study groups of people and the individual differences among them.

Cattell's career was quite varied. He traveled to the University of Göttingen to study with the philosopher Rudolf Hermann Lotze (1817-1881) and later with Wundt at Leipzig. Following that, he returned home to the United States and worked with **G. Stanley Hall** (1844-1924), one of America's most famous psychologists. Apparently, Cattell's relationship with Hall was less than positive, and Cattell did not complete his doctoral work at that time. When he was with Hall, however, Cattell developed an interest in studying psychological processes.

Subsequently, he returned to Leipzig and earned his doctorate with Wundt, although his correspondence with his parents revealed that Cattell did not hold Wundt in high esteem as a scientist. According to some, those letters also depict Cattell as arrogant, self-confident, and disrespectful of others. While in Germany, Cattell improved on existing psychological instrumentation and invented new ways to study psychological processes.

After leaving Germany, Cattell taught briefly in the United States, then traveled to England and worked with

Sir **Francis Galton** (1822-1911). Cattell was highly impressed with Galton's use of statistics and quantification of research, and he also supported some of Galton's other ideas, such as the importance of individual differences and the application of scientific knowledge to create a **eugenics** movement.

Ultimately, Cattell adopted the practice of testing a large number of research subjects and using statistics to understand his results. Cattell coined the term "mental test" and devoted a significant amount of time trying to develop a useful **intelligence** test. He recorded the results of simple tasks (e.g., the speed of a person's response to a simple sound, the **ability** to detect slight differences in weights of stimuli, and simple **memory** for letters of the alphabet), hoping to find a correlation between sensory response and academic performance, or intelligence. He was disappointed to find that, not only did sensory performance fail to relate to academic success, the different sensory measures did not even correlate with one another. As a result, he abandoned such an approach to mental testing.

Even though Cattell's research on intelligence was unsuccessful, he nonetheless exerted a dramatic influence on other American psychologists. During his career at Columbia University, more students earned doctorates in psychology with him than with any other psychologist. Cattell also affected psychology in the United States in other ways. For example, he founded the journal *Psychological Review* with another prominent psychologist, J. Mark Baldwin (1861-1934), then resurrected the financially troubled journal *Science*, which he acquired from Alexander Graham Bell. Cattell also helped start the American Association for the Advancement of Science, one of the premier scientific organizations in America today. He also published *Scientific Monthly* and *School and Society*. Not surprisingly, as his editing and publishing increased, his research diminished.

Cattell left the academic world in 1917 when Columbia University dismissed him because of his unpopular opposition to sending draftees into battle in the first World War. He sued the University for libel and won $40,000 in court, but he did not return to the institution. Instead, he attempted further application of psychological testing when he founded the Psychological Corporation, a company organized to promote commercial psychological tests. His entrepreneurial abilities failed him in this endeavor, however; the company earned only about $50 during its first two years. After he left, the organization began to prosper, and today, the Psychological Corporation is a flourishing business. Cattell continued his work as a spokesperson for **applied psychology** until his death.

## Further Reading

Benjamin, L. T., Jr. *A History of Psychology: Original Sources and Contemporary Research.* New York: McGraw-Hill, 1988.

Schultz, D. P., and S.E. Schultz. *A History of Modern Psychology.* 6th ed. Fort Worth, TX: Harcourt Brace College Publishers, 1996.

# Raymond Bernard Cattell

### 1905-1998
American psychologist who designed personality and intelligence tests and espoused controversial theories of eugenics.

Raymond B. Cattell was one of psychology's most prolific scholars. In a career spanning over half a century he wrote more than 50 books and 500 research articles, and his contributions to **personality** and **intelligence** testing are widely regarded as invaluable. Yet some of his theories about natural selection, particularly as put forth in a philosophy known as Beyondism, were attacked as racist and caused a bitter controversy only months before his death.

Cattell was born in Hilltop, England, on March 20, 1905. He grew up in Devon, where he developed a lifelong love of sailing and the sea. He attended the University of London, where he received his undergraduate degree in chemistry in 1924 and his Ph.D. in psychology in 1929. He taught briefly and worked at a psychology clinic until 1937, when he moved to the United States to take a teaching position at Columbia University. From there he moved on to Clark University and Harvard before arriving in 1946 at the University of Illinois, where he stayed for 27 years.

### Innovator of personality tests

During the Second World War, in addition to his teaching duties, Cattell worked in the Adjutant General's office, where he devised psychological tests for the military. Throughout his career, Cattell created a number of such tests to measure intelligence and to assess personality **traits**. The best known of these is the Sixteen Personality Factor questionnaire (16PF). First published in 1949, the 16PF profiles individuals using 16 different personality traits, such as emotional stability (easily upset vs. calm), impulsiveness (sober vs. enthusiastic), and **conformity** (expedient vs. conscientious). These are measured with what Cattell calls "second-order factors," including **extroversion**, anxiety, and independence. The test is still widely used by corporations and institutions to determine an individual's compatibility with different occupations and overall psychological **character**.

**Raymond Cattell** *(Archives of the History of American Psychology. Reproduced with permission.)*

Cattell retired from the University of Illinois in 1973 and after five years in Colorado moved to Hawaii. There, he accepted a part-time position at the University of Hawaii, where he continued to teach, conduct research, and write. He also took the opportunity to spend leisure time with his third wife and enjoyed visits from his five children and two stepchildren.

### Beyondism and a storm of controversy

The publication of *Beyondism: Religion from Science* in 1987 dramatically altered the remainder of Cattell's life as well as his scientific legacy. Cattell intended the book to be a discussion of his theories on evolution and natural selection. He believed that natural selection among humans was governed by individual genetic and cultural selection. However, his advocacy of **eugenics** (the study of improving the human race), was extremely controversial, particularly because eugenics was the pseudo-scientific rationale for Nazi genocide. Cattell claimed, for example, that among the tenets of Beyondism was the idea that races as we know them today would not exist in the future. "The genetic groupings (races) of the future," he wrote, "will arise from self-conscious selection by each cultural group." The question many critics asked was whether Cattell's theories were simply his approbation for natural selection or a call for something more ominous. The fact that Cattell had acknowledged **Arthur Jensen** and William Shockley—two scientists who had claimed that blacks were genetically less intelligent than whites—in his book only furthered people's suspicions.

The issue came to a head in the summer of 1997, when Cattell was scheduled to receive a lifetime achievement award from the American Psychological Foundation (APF). Almost as soon as APF had announced its decision, there were protests, some from prominent citizens and organizations. The APF trustees postponed the award presentation so they could further investigate. Cattell, ninety-two years old and in failing health, attempted to resolve the furor by declining the award. He then wrote an open letter to the **American Psychological Association (APA)** defending himself and his work. He asserted that he detested **racism**, and that he had only ever advocated voluntary eugenics. His health declined further, and he died quietly on February 2, 1998, at home in Hawaii.

George A. Milite

### Further Reading

Cattell, Raymond B. *Beyondism: Religion from Science.* New York Praeger Publishers, 1987.

Cattell, Raymond B. *Factor Analysis: An Introduction and Manual for the Psychologist and Social Scientist.* New York: Harper, 1952.

Cattell, Raymond B. *General Psychology.* Cambridge, MA: Sci-Art Publishers, 1941.

"Lifetime Achievement Award is Questioned." *APA Monitor,* (October 1997).

# Central nervous system

In humans, that portion of the nervous system that lies within the brain and spinal cord; it receives impulses from nerve cells throughout the body, regulates bodily functions, and directs behavior.

The central nervous system contains billions of **nerve** cells, called neurons, and a greater number of support cells, or glia. Until recently, scientists thought that the only function of glial cells—whose name means "glue"—was to hold the neurons together, but current research suggests a more active role in facilitating communication. The neurons, which consist of three elements—dendrites, cell body, and axon—send electrical impulses from cell to cell along pathways which receive, process, store, and retrieve information. The dendrites are the

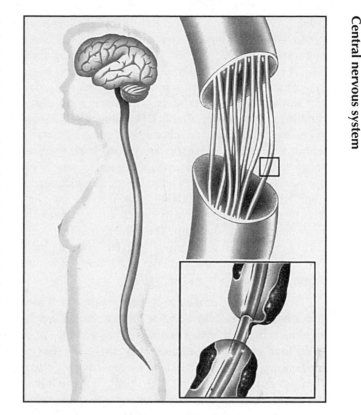

The brain and spinal cord comprise the central nervous system. At the right is a magnified view of the spinal cord showing the individual nerves. The inset shows an individual axon covered with a myelin sheath. *(John Bavosi. Photo Researchers, Inc. Reproduced with permission.)*

message-receiving portions of the **neuron** and the axons are the message-sending part of the cell. Both are branching fibers that reach out in many extensions to join the neuron to other neurons. The junction between the axon of one cell and the **dendrite** of another is a minute gap, eighteen millionths of an inch wide, which is called a **synapse**.

The spinal cord is a long bundle of neural tissue continuous with the **brain** that occupies the interior canal of the spinal column and functions as the primary communication link between the brain and the rest of the body. It is the origin of 31 bilateral pairs of spinal nerves which radiate outward from the central nervous system through openings between adjacent vertebrae. The spinal cord receives signals from the peripheral senses and relays them to the brain. Its sensory neurons, which send sense data to the brain, are called afferent, or receptor, neurons; motor neurons, which receive motor commands from the brain, are called efferent, or **effector**, neurons.

The brain is a mass of neural tissue that occupies the cranial cavity of the skull and functions as the center of instinctive, emotional, and cognitive processes. Twelve pairs of cranial nerves enter the brain directly. It is composed of three primary divisions: the forebrain, midbrain, and hindbrain, which are divided into the left and right hemispheres and control multiple functions such as receiving sensory messages, movement, language, regulating involuntary body processes, producing emotions, thinking, and **memory**. The first division, the forebrain, is the largest and most complicated of the brain structures and is responsible for most types of complex mental activity and behavior. It is involved in a huge array of responses, including initiating movements, receiving sensations, emoting, thinking, talking, creating, and imagining. The forebrain consists of two main divisions: the diencephalon and the cerebrum. The cerebrum is the larger part of the forebrain. Its parts, which are covered by the cerebral cortex, include the corpus callosum, striatum, septum, hippocampus, and amygdala.

The midbrain, or mesencephalon, is the small area near the lower middle of the brain. Its three sections are the tectum, tegmentum, and crus cerebri. Portions of the midbrain have been shown to control smooth and reflexive movements, and it is important in the regulation of **attention**, **sleep**, and arousal. The hindbrain (rhombencephalon), which is basically a continuation of the spinal cord, is the part of the brain that receives incoming messages first. Lying beneath the cerebral hemispheres, it consists of three structures: the cerebellum, the medulla, and the pons, which control such vital functions of the **autonomic nervous system** as breathing, blood pressure, and heart rate. The cerebellum, a large convoluted structure attached to the back surface of the brain stem, receives information from hundreds of thousands of sensory receptors in the eyes, ears, skin, muscles, and joints, and uses the information to regulate coordination, balance, and movement, especially finely coordinated movements such as threading a needle or tracking a moving target. The medulla, situated just above the spinal cord, controls heartbeat and breathing and contains the reticular formation which extends into and through the pons. The pons, a band of nerve fibers connecting the midbrain, medulla (hindbrain), and cerebrum, controls sleep and dreaming. The pons and medulla, because of their shape and position at the base of the brain, are often referred to as the brainstem.

**Further Reading**
Changeux, Jean-Pierre. *Neuronal Man.* New York: Pantheon Books, 1985.

# Cerebellum

See **Brain**

# Cerebral cortex

See **Brain**

# Character

General term in psychology used to describe behavior motivations and personality traits that make each person an individual.

Character is most often used in reference to a set of basic innate, developed, and acquired motivations that shape an individual's behavior. These qualities of an individual's **motivation** are shaped during all stages of **childhood**. By late **adolescence**, around age 17, the **traits** that make up individual's character are normally integrated into a unique and distinctive whole. The term character is sometimes used as roughly synonymous with the term **personality**, although such usage does little to reduce the imprecision of either term. Some psychologists believe that differences in character among individuals largely reflect affective, or emotional, differences, that are the result of biochemical or other organic variations. Many psychologists claim that character, to some extent, is a function of experience. These psychologists, generally, believe that, as the early behavior of an individual directed toward a primary, instinctive goal is modified by environmental circumstances, the motivational system of the individual is also modified, and the character of the individual is affected. There is some dispute among psychologists about whether, or to what extent, character may be controlled by conscious or rational decisions, and about whether, or to what extent, character may be dominated by **unconscious** or irrational forces. At the same time, there is widespread agreement among psychologists that, while much research remains to be done to delineate the genetic, instinctive, organic, cognitive, and other aspects of character, the development of a reasonably stable and harmonious character is an essential part of a psychologically healthy existence.

Character education, a periodic but recurring theme for schools to teach basic values and moral reasoning to primary and secondary students, attracted renewed popularity in the 1990s. Character education initiatives have developed at the local and state levels, but reflect a national trend. In 1995, President Bill Clinton and the U.S. Congress declared October 16-22 "National Character Counts Week." In character education, teachers confront students with moral dilemmas and ask them to formulate and defend courses of action.

Many prominent educators, politicians, and academics support character education. Opponents, including the American Civil Liberties Union, object to character education because it could lead to teaching religious beliefs. Some religious groups oppose it as well, since public school teachers must avoid teaching religion and could make character a virtue that is anti-religious.

*See also* Personality development

### Further Reading
Lockwood, Anne Turnbaugh. *Character Education: Controversy and Consensus.* Thousand Oaks, California: Corwin Press, 1997.

Murphy, Madonna M. *Character Education in America's Blue Ribbon Schools: Best Practices for Meeting the Challenge.* Lancaster, PA.: Technomic Publishing Co. Inc., 1998.

# Jean Martin Charcot

### 1825-1893
French psychiatrist who specialized in the study of hysteria, using hypnosis as a basis for treatment.

Jean Martin Charcot was born in Paris on Nov. 29, 1825, the son of a carriage maker. He took his medical degree at the University of Paris in 1853 and was appointed professor of pathological anatomy there in 1860. In 1862 he was appointed senior physician at the Salpêtrière, a hospital for the treatment of the mentally ill. It became a center for psychiatric training and psychiatric care, for Charcot had a flair for theatrics in addition to his reputation for sound science, and his lectures and demonstrations attracted students from all over Europe.

Charcot's contributions fall largely into three categories. First, he studied the **etiology** and cure of hysterical disorders (psychoneuroses). These disorders involve what appear to be physiological disturbances such as convulsions, paralyses, blindness, deafness, anesthesias, and amnesias. However, there is no evidence of physiological abnormalities in psychoneuroses since the root of the problem is psychological. In Charcot's time hysteria was thought to be a disorder found only in women (the Greek word *hystera* means uterus), but his demonstrations were eventually influential in correcting this idea. Charcot, however, continued to think of hysteria as a female disorder. Freud was later to associate hysterical symptoms with sexual problems.

Charcot's second area of contribution was the correlation of various behavioral symptoms with physiological abnormalities of the **nervous system**. One of the major problems for early psychiatry was that of determining whether certain behavioral abnormalities had their origins

Jean Charcot *(The Library of Congress. Reproduced with permission.)*

in psychological or in physiological disturbances and, if physiological, where in the **central nervous system** the abnormality might be located. Charcot became noted for his **ability** to diagnose and locate the physiological disturbances of nervous system functioning.

Finally, Charcot made popular the use of **hypnosis** as a part of diagnosis and therapy. Hypnosis, known at the time as "mesmerism" (named for Franz Anton Mesmer), was regarded by the medical profession as charlatanism. Charcot found hypnotism useful in distinguishing true psychoneurotics from fakers and, like Mesmer, found that hysterical symptoms could be relieved through its use. In the hypnotic state the patient falls into an apparent **sleep**. While in this condition, the patient can sometimes recall events in his life which are not recalled in the waking state, and he is susceptible to the suggestions of the therapist. In 1882 Charcot presented a summary of his findings to the French Academy of Sciences, where they were favorably received. Scientific psychiatry was thus well on its way to being accepted by the medical profession. Charcot died on Aug. 16, 1893.

### Further Reading
Guillian, Georges. *J.M. Charcot, 1825-1893: his life-his work.* trans. 1959.

Garrison, Fielding H. *An introduction to the history of medicine*. 1913. 4th ed. 1929.

Goetz, Christopher G. *Charcot*. New York: Oxford University Press, 1995.

# Child abuse

The act of harming children by neglect, physical force, violence, sexual attack, or by inflicting psychological or emotional distress.

For much of history, children were considered the property of parents. The family system was rarely, if ever, intervened upon by society. If a mother or father routinely abused their children, the abuse went unnoticed, or if noticed, merely ignored. It was largely considered a parent's prerogative to do whatever he or she wanted with their child.

Over the past several decades, however, the issue and, seemingly, the prevalence of child abuse have become widespread. Psychologists question whether the number of child abuse cases indicates increased occurrences of abuse or increased public awareness that encourages more reporting.

The first detailed account of the abuse of children was published in 1962 by Harry Hemke in an article titled "The Battered Child Syndrome," and since then there have been numerous articles and books published on this subject.

Over the years, child abuse has been categorized into four types, although many psychologists dispute the usefulness of doing so. In compiling statistics on abuse, the

## HOTLINES

The following organizations operate hotlines or provide advice for family members where there are problems related to physical or other abuse.

- Childhelp National Abuse Hotline
  **Telephone:** toll-free (800) 422-4453

- National Coalition Against Domestic Violence
  **Telephone:** (303) 839-1852

- National Council on Child Abuse and Family Violence
  **Telephone:** toll-free (800) 222-2000

- National Victim Center
  **Telephone:** toll-free (800) FYI-CALL [394-2255]

- National Runaway Switchboard
  **Telephone:** toll-free (800) 621-4000

United States Department of Health and Human Services (HHS) considers four categories of abuse: neglect, physical abuse, **sexual abuse**, and emotional maltreatment. Obviously, these categories are not mutually exclusive (that is, any given child can experience one or all, and all types of abuse are forms of "emotional maltreatment").

Statistically, it is difficult to find reliable national figures for cases of child abuse because each state keeps its own records and has its own definitions of what constitutes abuse. Nonetheless, several organizations do compile national estimates of abuse and neglect. One of the most commonly cited reports comes from Prevent Child Abuse America, formerly known as the National Committee for the Prevention of Child Abuse headquartered in Chicago, which conducts an annual national survey of the 50 states to acquire the most current data available.

An estimated 3,154,000 children were reported to child protective service agencies as alleged victims of child abuse or neglect in 1998, with about 1 million of the reports confirmed. This means that 45 children out of 1,000 were reported as abused or neglected and 14 confirmed as abused or neglected in 1998. On average, three children died each day in the United States from abuse or neglect in 1997. While the nation's overall crime rate fell from 1993 to 1997 by 22 percent, reports of child abuse and neglect increased by 8 percent with confirmed cases increasing by 4 percent.

In 1998, 51 percent of the cases reported involved neglect, 25 percent involved physical abuse, 10 percent involved sexual abuse, 3 percent involved emotional abuse and 11 percent related to other forms of child maltreatment. These figures represent substantiated cases, meaning they were investigated by child protection services and found valid. Like any statistics on child abuse, these must be considered incomplete, since not all cases of abuse are reported.

Strong social and familial pressure may continue to exist to avoid the issue when abuse is seen; however, requirements that professionals, such as doctors, teachers, and therapists who work with children, report suspicions of abuse have helped to make public health system intervention more widely accepted by society.

Still, newly arrived immigrants not yet acculturated in the United States may, to their surprise, face social service intervention for their cultural practices toward children, deemed as child abuse in the United States.

Despite myths about its prevalence among lower-income populations, child abuse occurs throughout all strata of society. Physical abuse does appear more frequently in poor families. Since middle-class and wealthy families are more likely to have their children treated by a sympathetic personal physician who may be less likely

# CHILD ABUSE: SIGNS AND SYMPTOMS

Although these signs do not necessarily indicate that a child has been abused, they may help adults recognize that something is wrong. The possibility of abuse should be investigated if a child shows a number of these symptoms, or any of them to a marked degree:

## Sexual Abuse

Being overly affectionate or knowledgeable in a sexual way inappropriate to the child's age
Medical problems such as chronic itching, pain in the genitals, venereal diseases
Other extreme reactions, such as depression, self-mutilation, suicide attempts, running away, overdoses, anorexia
Personality changes such as becoming insecure or clinging
Regressing to younger behavior patterns such as thumb sucking or bringing out discarded cuddly toys
Sudden loss of appetite or compulsive eating
Being isolated or withdrawn
Inability to concentrate
Lack of trust or fear someone they know well, such as not wanting to be alone with a babysitter
Starting to wet again, day or night/nightmares
Become worried about clothing being removed
Suddenly drawing sexually explicit pictures
Trying to be "ultra-good" or perfect; overreacting to criticism

## Physical Abuse

Unexplained recurrent injuries or burns
Improbable excuses or refusal to explain injuries
Wearing clothes to cover injuries, even in hot weather
Refusal to undress for gym
Bald patches
Chronic running away
Fear of medical help or examination
Self-destructive tendencies
Aggression towards others
Fear of physical contact—shrinking back if touched
Admitting that they are punished, but the punishment is excessive (such as a child being beaten every night to "make him/her study")
Fear of suspected abuser being contacted

## Emotional Abuse

Physical, mental, and emotional development lags
Sudden speech disorders
Continual self-depreciation ("I'm stupid, ugly, worthless, etc.")
Overreaction to mistakes
Extreme fear of any new situation
Inappropriate response to pain ("I deserve this")
Neurotic behavior (rocking, hair twisting, self-mutilation)
Extremes of passivity or aggression

## Neglect

| | | |
|---|---|---|
| Constant hunger | Poor personal hygiene | No social relationships |
| Constant tiredness | Poor state of clothing | Compulsive scavenging |
| Emaciation | Untreated medical problems | Destructive tendencies |

A child may be subjected to a combination of different kinds of abuse. It is also possible that a child may show no outward signs and hide what is happening from everyone.

**Source: Kidscape, http://www.solnet.co.uk/kidscape/kids5.htm. Reprinted by permission.**

**Child abuse symptoms.** *(Stanley Publishing. Reproduced with permission.)*

to diagnose and report injuries as child abuse, numbers reported may be biased. Even with such reporting bias, however, poverty seems strongly linked to abuse.

Child abuse is also linked to parental use of alcohol or other drugs. Several studies conducted during the 1970s confirmed that nearly 70 percent of substantiated cases of abuse were related to alcohol.

**Anger** most frequently triggers abuse by parents. Abusive parents appear to have a lower threshold for childish behaviors than nonabusive parents. The same child cues triggers more upset in abusive parents than in nonabusive parents. Most abusers are likely to have been abused themselves and generally resort to **violence** to cope with life stressors. Their abusive actions can be seen as subconscious reactions to an array of stressful aspects of parenting, including disappointment in the gender or appearance of a child; a jealous reaction to the **attention** a child diverts from themselves; an attempt by the abuser to hurt the other parent; or a reaction against the child for failing to meet unrealistic expectations.

Pedophiles, or sexual abusers of children, occur across all economic and cultural groups. Psychologically, however, they share certain **traits**. Pedophiles often have a history of being abused themselves, and abusing other children seems to be triggered by increased life stressors, such as marital problems, job layoffs, or abuse of drugs.

About 60 percent of the major physical injuries inflicted by caregivers occur in children ages birth to 4, the age group most likely to be injured from abuse.

Typically, abused children show developmental delays by preschool age. It is unclear whether these delays occur due to cumulative neurological damage or due to inadequate stimulation and uncertainty in the child about the learning **environment** and the absence of positive parental interactions that would stimulate language and motor processes. These delays, in concert with their parents' higher-than-normal expectations for their children's self-care and self-control abilities, may provoke additional abuse. Abused preschoolers respond to peers and other adults with more **aggression** and anger than do non-abused children. A coercive cycle frequently develops where parents and children mutually control one another with threats of negative behavior.

School-aged children who are abused typically have problems academically with poorer grades and performance on standardized **achievement tests**. Studies of abused children's intellectual performance find lower scores in both verbal and performance (e.g., math, visual-spatial) areas. Abused children also toward distractibility and overactivity, making school a very difficult environment for them. With their peers, abused children are often more aggressive and more likely to be so-

cially rejected than nonabused children. Less mature socially, abused children show difficulty in developing trusting relationships with others.

Within the home, abused children are more disruptive and aggressive, frequently viewed by their parents as defiant and noncompliant. Although observational measures confirm higher levels of disruptiveness, the number and intensity of the problem behaviors seen by abusive parents in their children may be partially a function of the parents' lower threshold of tolerance for children's noncompliance.

As adolescents, abused children are more likely to be in contact with the juvenile justice system than nonabused children of comparable family constellation and income level. Many of these children are labeled "ungovernable" for committing offenses such as running away and truancy. A higher proportion of abused than nonabused delinquent youth are also involved in crimes of assault.

Follow-up studies on abused children in later **adolescence** show that in addition to having problems with the law, they are also more likely to be substance abusers or to have emotional disturbances such as **depression**.

Over the last several years, many consider the number of child abuse reportings to be at epidemic levels. As reported in *The CQ Researcher* in 1993, "Almost overnight, the national consciousness has been jolted into confronting a disturbing possibility: **Incest** and child molestation may be far more common than previously thought." This increased reporting of sexual abuse has become a highly contentious topic among the psychological community and in the media as well. Many find the reports a reflection of a sexually disturbed society, while others believe that increased reporting is the result of sensationalist media accounts, celebrity pronouncements about their own abuse, and over-zealous therapists who too readily suggest to patients that episodes of sexual abuse may lay at the heart of their other problems.

Another disturbing trend shows an increase in reports of ritual abuse, or **satanic ritual abuse** (SRA), in which, it is alleged, children are systematically and repeatedly tortured by friends and family members in elaborate Satanic ceremonies often involving human sacrifice and ritual **rape**. Writing in *The Journal of Psychohistory* in 1994, psychoanalyst David Lotto reported that at a recent convention of the **American Psychological Association**, 800 therapists reported that they were currently treating cases of ritual abuse. A 1988 study conducted by University of New Hampshire researcher David Finkelhor found that as many as 13% of child abuse allegations occurring at day care centers involved ritual abuse. Another report followed the cases of 24 ritual abuse trials and found that 23 people had been convicted of some kind of abuse. In looking at this phenomenon critically, however, please note, as did an FBI investigator at a 1991 conference of the American Psychological Association, that in several years of intensive investigation by local and federal law enforcement, there has never been any evidence of a network of satanic child abusers. Victims often report the existence of elaborate underground sacrificial altars where their abuse occurred, and yet no trace has ever been found of such a construction.

Putting aside the current controversy over the prevalence of child sexual abuse in this country, no one disputes that sexual abuse does in fact occur and takes a devastating toll on those abused. Sexually abused children may still be preoccupied in adulthood with events, trying to understand and repair the damage. Frequently, sexual abuse is a cited cause, for instance, of **dissociative identity disorder**. Sexual abuse, like severe physical and emotional abuse, can lead to other psychological disorders as well, such as depression, **mood** disorders, anxiety and panic disorders, and substance abuse.

**Further Reading**

"Child Sexual Abuse: Does the Nation Face an Epidemic Or a Wave of Hysteria?" *The CQ Researcher* (15 January 1993).
Cockburn, Alexander. "Out of the Mouths of Babes: Child Abuse and the Abuse of Adults." *The Nation* (12 February 1990): 190.
Interview with National Committee for the Prevention of Child Abuse, April 17, 1996.
Lotto, David. "On Witches and Witch Hunts: Ritual and Satanic Cult Abuse." *Journal of Psychohistory* (Spring 1994): 373.
Lowry, Richard. "How Many Battered Children?" *National Review* (12 April 1993): 46.
Smith, Timothy. "You Don't Have to Molest That Child." Pamphlet published by the National Committee for the Prevention of Child Abuse, 1987.
Terry, Sara. "Children Are Falling Victim to a New Kind of Sexual Offender: Other Children." *Rolling Stone* (31 October 1991): 68.

**Further Information**

Prevent Child Abuse America. 200 S. Michigan, 17th Floor, Chicago, Illinois 60604-2404, (312) 663–3520.

# Child development

The study of the sequential physical, cognitive, emotional, and social changes a child undergoes between birth and adolescence or adulthood.

The first detailed scientific study of child development was probably **Charles Darwin**'s *Biographical Sketch of an Infant* (1877), based on a log he had kept on the devel-

## LANDMARK PUBLICATIONS ON CHILD DEVELOPMENT

**1877** Charles Darwin's *Biographical Sketch of an Infant,* observations on development of his eldest child.

**1880** G. Stanley Hall, the "father of child psychology in America," publishes *The Contents of Children's Minds.*

**1914** John Broadus Watson publishes his most important work, *Behavior—An Introduction to Comparative Psychology.*

**1926** Jean Piaget publishes *The Child's Conception of the World,* followed ten years later by *The Orgin of Intelligence in Children.*

**1934** Arnold Gesell publishes *An Atlas of Infant Behavior,* followed by *Child in the Culture of Today* (1943), *The Child from Five to Ten* (1946), and *Child Development* (1949).

**1946** Benjamin Spock publishes *The Common Sense Book of Baby and Child Care.*

**1950** Erik Erikson publishes *Childhood and Society.*

opment of his eldest child. In this work, Darwin advanced the hypothesis that each individual's development from **birth** to adulthood parallels or recapitulates the phylogenetic development of the human species as a whole (he had made a similar observation about the development of the fetus). Darwin's ideas influenced the early study of child development, also known as the child study movement.

In the United States, the most famous figure associated with Darwin's evolutionary approach was **G. Stanley Hall**, who was labeled "the father of child psychology in America." The development of **intelligence** testing around World War I directed attention to the intellectual development of children, especially those considered either gifted or mentally retarded. As the century progressed, emphasis shifted from the study of children as a source of scientific knowledge to a more altruistic endeavor aimed at improving their welfare. From **Sigmund Freud** and **Jean Piaget** to **Benjamin Spock** and **T. Berry Brazelton**, child development has been studied and written about to better understand of children in order to promote their well-being during the various stages of **childhood**, and to help them mature into healthy adults.

Freud developed many theories about the enormous influence of childhood experiences on adult behavior and also proposed a five-stage chronological model of childhood psychosexual development. The oral stage (birth to 1.5 years), in which primary gratification is through sucking, is followed by the anal stage (1.5 to 3 years), in which control of elimination is a primary concern. Next comes the phallic stage (3 to 7 years), during which a child experiences and resolves the Oedipal crisis and assumes his or her sexual identity. During the latency stage (ages 7 to 12) **sexuality** is dormant, and the primary love objects are people outside the home. With the genital stage, which begins at age 12 and lasts into adulthood, instinctual sexual drives increase and parental attachments are dissolved.

**Arnold Gesell** was among the first psychologists to undertake a thorough quantitative study of **normal** human development from birth through **adolescence**. Based on his work at Yale's Child Development Clinic and his own Institute, Gesell produced reports that had a widespread influence on both parents and educators, and created the Gesell Development Schedules, which are still used today to assess motor and **language development**, adaptive behavior, and personal-social behavior in children between four weeks and six years of age.

Probably the most famous theory of child development is the **cognitive development** model pioneered by the Swiss psychologist Jean Piaget. Piaget divided child development between birth and late adolescence into four stages of increasingly complex and abstract thought, each qualitatively different from the ones preceding it but still dependent on them. The first, or sensorimotor, stage (birth to approximately 2 years) is a time of nonverbal, experimental basic learning when infants experience the world primarily through their senses and gradually gain mastery of their own bodies and external objects. The preoperational stage (ages 2 to 6 years) involves the association of objects with words and the **ability** to solve more complex problems, although the child's focus at this stage remains egocentric, a term that refers to the inability to consider things from another person's perspective. The third, or concrete operations, stage (6 to 11 years of age) is a period during which categorizing activities and the earliest logical operations occur. The fourth, or formal operations, stage (ages 12 and higher) is characterized by the gradual emergence of a mature ability to reason and deal with abstract relationships.

Another well-known development theory structured in stages is the one proposed by neo-Freudian **Erik Erikson** in *Childhood and Society* (1950). While Erikson's eight-stage theory encompasses the entire human life span, much of it is centered on childhood and adolescence. Each developmental stage in Erikson's scheme is concerned with a central conflict: trust versus mistrust in **infancy**; autonomy versus doubt and shame in early childhood; initiative versus **guilt** in the preschool period; and industry versus inferiority during the early school years. The goals of the first

four stages create the foundation for the successful negotiation of the fifth stage, in which the adolescent must form a stable identity and achieve a sense of self.

**Lawrence Kohlberg**'s work on the development of moral reasoning approaches childhood from a different perspective. After studying the different ways in which children aged 7 through adolescence respond to moral dilemmas, Kohlberg determined that there are universal stages in **moral development**, which, like the cognitive stages delineated by Piaget, differ from each other qualitatively. Children from the ages of 7 through about 10 act on the preconventional level, which involves deferring to adults and obeying rules based on the immediate prospect of **punishment** or reward. At around age 10, they progress to the conventional level, where their behavior is guided by the opinions of other people and the desire to conform. During adolescence, children become capable of postconventional morality, which entails the ability to formulate abstract moral principles and act on motives that transcend self-interest and even social norms that conflict with one's personal sense of justice.

In recent years, researchers in child development have focused increasingly on the developmental patterns and needs of minorities and women. Carol Gilligan, Kohlberg's colleague at Harvard University, found fault with Kohlberg's exclusive focus on white males in his initial research, and in her own study, *In a Different Voice*, Gilligan differentiates between male and female moral development. In contrast to the male problem-solving approach to moral dilemmas based on an "ethic of justice," she describes a female "ethic of care" that is based on **empathy** and involves the **perception** of moral dilemmas in terms of conflicting responsibilities rather than competing rights.

**Further Reading**
Bee, Helen L. *The Developing Child*. 5th ed. New York: Harper & Row, 1989.
Dworetzky, John. *Introduction to Child Development*. 5th ed. Minneapolis: West Publishing Co., 1993.
Meinhold, Patricia. *Child Psychology: Development and Behavior Analysis*. Dubuque, IA: Kendall/Hunt Publishing Co., 1993.
Owens, Karen. *The World of the Child*. New York: Holt, Rinehart, and Winston, 1987.
Papalia, Diane E. *A Child's World: Infancy through Adolescence*. 5th ed. New York : McGraw-Hill, 1990.

# Childhood

The period between birth and adulthood, during which a person develops physically, intellectually, and socially.

## History of childhood

Childhood has been defined differently across the ages. The Greek philosopher Plato (427?-347 B.C.) believed children were born with certain dispositions that could be changed by their **environment**. Ancient Romans expressed great affection for their children in letters and on tombstones. During the Middle Ages, little distinction was made between adults and children, who worked from a very young age. The Renaissance saw the beginning of the nuclear **family** in Europe, with an increased focus on childhood as a time for education and training. **John Locke** (1632-1704), founder of the empirical school of philosophy, believed the child enters the world as a *tabula rasa* or blank slate, and learns through experience. Jean-Jacques Rousseau (1712-1778) took the opposite tack, recommending that education should follow nature since infants automatically prefer goodness. According to **Sigmund Freud**'s (1856-1939) psychoanalytic theory, children must pass through five **psychosexual stages** to achieve healthy adulthood. In contrast behaviorist **John Watson** (1878-1935) asserted that, given a controlled environment, he could train a child to be anything from doctor to thief. The emphasis on environment, particularly the behavior of parents, continued through the twentieth century until studies of identical and fraternal **twins**, reared together or apart, began to show the effect of genes on the journey from **infancy** to adulthood.

## Prenatal development

The future adult begins not at **birth** but at conception, with the creation of a unique set of genes, half from the mother, half from the father. This genetic blueprint is called the *genotype*; its outward manifestation is the *phenotype*. Sometimes the phenotype is controlled directly by the genotype, for example, eye color. More often, the phenotype represents the interaction of the genotype and the environment. It is even possible for the genotype to be altered by the environment, as happens when men exposed to certain toxins suffer an increased risk of fathering children with genetic abnormalities.

Fewer than half of fertilized eggs, called *zygotes*, survive the first two weeks during which the zygote moves from the fallopian tube where it was fertilized to the uterus where it is implanted. During the next six weeks, the zygote differentiates into an *embryo* with internal organs, skin, nerves, and rudimentary limbs, fingers, and toes. In the final seven months of gestation, the maturing skeletal, muscular, and nervous systems of what is now called the *fetus* make movement possible. Babies born at 28 weeks can survive, although often with chronic health problems.

As each system undergoes its most rapid growth, it is especially vulnerable to damage. In addition to genetic abnormalities like **Down syndrome**, environmental agents called *teratogens* can affect the fetus. These might be maternal viruses such as rubella (German measles) or chemicals such as nicotine, alcohol, and cocaine. Exposure to nicotine is linked to premature birth, low birth weight, and cleft (malformed) palate and lips, while exposure to alcohol is linked to intellectual and behavioral impairments. An inadequate maternal diet also puts the fetus at risk, especially its **brain** and **nervous system**. Prenatal teratogens can cause lifelong problems or even death. The vast majority of babies, however, are born healthy and **normal**.

## Infancy

Newborns enter the world with many skills. In addition to a range of adaptive **reflexes** such as grasping, sucking, and *rooting* (turning the head when the cheek is touched), they are able to recognize their mothers' face, voice, and **smell**. Even more impressive, less than one hour after birth, babies can imitate gestures such as sticking out the tongue.

## Physical development

The average healthy newborn is 7.5 pounds (3.4 kg) and 20 inches (52 cm). It triples its weight and grows 10 to 12 inches (24-30 cm) its first year. By age two for girls and two-and-a-half for boys, babies reach half their adult height. Physical development is largely programmed by a genetically determined timetable called *maturation*, which proceeds in predictable stages. For healthy, well-nourished babies, progress is influenced only slightly by environment, although they need opportunities to practice new skills.

The rate of physical growth slows after the second year, not accelerating again until **puberty**. Both size and rate of growth are genetically determined. In industrialized societies, puberty begins at 10 for girls and 12 for boys, ages that have declined significantly over the past 150 years due to improved health and nutrition.

## Intellectual development

The Swiss researcher **Jean Piaget** (1896-1980) pioneered the field of cognitive, or intellectual, development. On the basis of his observations and ingenious questions, he divided children's thinking into four qualitatively distinct stages, moving from a direct sensory understanding of the world, to the symbolic representation of objects, to mental manipulation of objects, to **logical thinking** about abstract concepts. Using new techniques such as changes in sucking and heart-rate, contemporary researchers have found that, contrary to Piaget's theory, even babies seem to understand basic principles like *object permanence*, the concept that objects continue to exist when hidden. And although his middle stages of development have been confirmed, far fewer people attain Piaget's final stage of logical reasoning than he predicted.

Other theories of learning attribute **cognitive development** not to the child's own construction of knowledge, but to *conditioning*, the effect of environment on the child. **Conditioning** works by encouraging behavior through **reinforcement** or discouraging it through **punishment**. **Social learning theory** adds another mechanism, **modeling**, or learning by observation.

### Intelligence

The **measurement** of **intelligence**, *psychometrics*, began with Sir **Francis Galton** (1822-1911). Although his measures of **vision**, **reaction time**, and grip strength proved poor predictors of academic success, his model of multiple indicators of intelligence has remained useful. *IQ*, or **intelligence quotient**, was originally a way to identify children who needed remedial teaching. It compares **mental age** to chronological age, with average intelligence set at 100. Modern IQ tests are quite successful in predicting school success, but have been criticized as culturally biased and limited in scope. IQ tends to remain the same when measured after the age of 4, an indication of its reliability.

### Language learning

Perhaps the most crucial task of childhood is learning to communicate. Researchers have found that humans are attuned to language even before birth. Following a universal sequence, even deaf babies first cry, then coo, then babble. Around eight months, babies begin to copy the sounds and intonations of their native language and speak their first words around one year of age. Vocabulary expands to over 200 words by age two, expressed in phrases such as "want cookie." The speech of three-year-olds reflects knowledge of plurals, past tense, negatives, and questions, along with an increased vocabulary. Grammatical complexity and vocabulary continue to expand throughout the school years. Children who are spoken and read to more are linguistically advanced, although late talkers tend to catch up with early talkers in the absence of other problems. Children who are read to also have less trouble learning to read.

## Personality development

**Personality** is what makes each person unique. Where do individual differences come from and how sta-

ble are they from birth to adulthood? There is strong evidence for a biological component to personality dimensions like sociability, irritability, neuroticism, and conscientiousness, but environmental effects are also present. A baby's innate sociability, for example, can be squelched by a depressed mother, or a child's innate irritability increased by a punitive teacher. In general, however, personality characteristics remain stable from infancy to **adolescence**.

## Social development

Children grow up in a web of social relationships. The first and most important is the bond between infant and mother called **attachment**. Attachment is crucial because securely attached babies tend to become sociable, confident, independent, and emotionally mature children. Adolescents who feel close to their parents also enjoy more friendships and higher **self-esteem**. Another predictor of social success is physical attractiveness. Even infants prefer attractive faces, as do older children. Boys who physically mature early are also more popular. Not surprisingly, aggressive, disruptive, and uncooperative behaviors are predictors of social rejection. A cycle of **aggression** and rejection often persists into adulthood.

## Nature and nurture

The most contentious issue in the study of childhood is the relative importance of genetics (nature) and environment (nurture). Purely environmental models such as **behaviorism** have been contradicted by numerous studies showing a strong genetic influence for everything from intelligence to **shyness** to sexual orientation. On the other hand, even clearly genetic **traits** interact with environment. Tall children, for example, are often treated as more mature. Intelligence is even more complicated. Twin studies show that between 50 and 60 percent of IQ is determined by genes. A child's genetic intellectual potential, then, is actually a range that can be maximized by a rich environment or minimized by a deprived one. In general, a child's development follows a genetic blueprint, but the final result is constrained by the building materials of the environment.

## Cultural differences

Most research on childhood is conducted in Western, industrial cultures. However, there is a growing body of cross-cultural studies highlighting both similarities and differences in childhood around the world. Secure maternal attachment, for example, is less common in Germany, a culture that values autonomy, than in Japan, a culture that values community. Guatemalan mothers always **sleep** with their babies, who fall asleep without the rituals and problems typical among American babies. Attitudes toward school achievement also vary. Japanese and Chinese mothers expect more from their children than do American mothers, and their children outperform Americans. Some children spend their first years in constant proximity to their mother, some in day care centers. Some children watch younger siblings or work in factories, some attend school. Some children live in extended families, an increasing number live with a single parent. Despite these differences, however, children everywhere show a zest for learning, **play**, and **friendship**, and a drive to make sense out of their ever-changing world.

Lindsay Evans

**Further Reading**
Bee, Helen. *The Developing Child*. Addison-Wesley Educational Publishers, Inc., 1997.
Casey, James. *The History of the Family*. Basil Blackwell Inc., 1989.
Harris, Judith Rich. *The Nurture Assumption*. The Free Press, 1998.
Kagan, Jerome. *The Nature of the Child*. Basic Books, Inc., 1984.
Kalat, James W. *Introduction to Psychology, 5th ed.* Wadsworth Publishing Company, 1999.
"Linking Cleft Palates and Smoking Moms." *New York Times*, (11 April 2000): D8.
Monastersky, Richard. "A New Round of Research Rattles Old Ideas of How Infants Interpret the World." *The Chronical of Higher Education*, (24 March 2000): A22.
Nairne, James S. *The Adaptive Mind*. Brooks/Cole Publishing Company, 1997.
Rawson, Beryl, ed. *Marriage, Divorce, and Children in Ancient Rome*. Oxford University Press, Inc., 1996.
Wood, Samuel E. and Ellen Green Wood. *The World of Psychology*. Allyn and Bacon, 1996.
http://www.nichd.nih.gov/ *Home page of the National Institute of Child Health and Human Development*. Last modified: April 12, 2000.

# Child psychology

Disciplines and theories concerned with the cognitive, psychological, physiological, and social/interpersonal aspects of human development.

Child psychologists study human development from the earliest stages of life through **adolescence** and adulthood. These scientists focus on many areas of growth. In the early years of life they include motor skills, percep-

tual analysis and inference, language and speech, social behavior, and the emergence of basic emotions of **fear**, sadness, anxiety, shame, and **guilt**.

The two important strategies for studying development include the **longitudinal study** in which a particular group of children is studied over a long period of time, sometimes from **infancy** through adulthood. The second method, which is more popular because it is less expensive, is called the cross-sectional method. In this strategy a group of children or adolescents at a particular age are studied at that age. In order to compare different ages, different samples would be studied but no group would be studied over time.

The major question that developmental psychologists wish to understand is how the maturational forces that are inevitable interact with experience to produce the behaviors, skills, and motives that we observe. For example, all children will develop an **ability** to speak and understand language before they are three years of age. However, in some cultural settings, children display this skill soon after the first birthday, while in others it might be delayed until the second or third birthday.

A related problem that puzzles child psychologists has to do with the temperamental factors children inherit that make a contribution to their individual personalities. Here, too, the puzzle is to understand how these inherited temperamental biases and experience in the **family** and with other children contribute to the **traits** the child develops.

Prior to **Sigmund Freud**'s writings which became popular after the turn of the century, most Western explanations of the differences among children were attributed to **temperament** or constitution. Freud changed this by arguing that family experience was the more important determinant of differences in children's moods, emotions, and symptoms. Freud believed that those experiences in the family made the child vulnerable to conflicts over **hostility** and **sexuality**. The intensity of the conflict and the defenses the child learned to deal with those conflicts were the main determinant of the child's **personality**. These view were very popular in the United States for the period from 1930 to 1960. However, because of the lack of strong scientific support for these theories, loyalty to these ideas has eroded in a major way.

**Erik Erikson** substituted for Freud's famous stages on oral, anal, phallic, and genital a more humane set of stages which emphasized the development of **attachment** relations in the first year of life and more generative and creative aspects of human nature, rather than the more narcissistic and destructive.

**Jean Piaget**'s contribution was to motivate child psychologists to pay more attention to the child's intellectual and **cognitive development**.

However, it is fair to say that at the present time there is no overarching theory of **child development**. Child psychologists are working on a series of problems that cover all of the important areas of growth. It is hoped that as these facts are gathered, brilliant theorists sometime in the future will be able to synthesize this information into a coherent theory that clarifies the child's growth.

Jerome Kagan

### Further Reading

Bee, Helen L. *The Developing Child.* 7th ed. New York: HarperCollins College Publishers, 1995.

Gemelli, Ralph J. *Normal Child and Adolescent Development.* Washington, DC: American Psychiatric Press, 1996.

Kagan, Jerome. *The Nature of the Child.* New York: Basic Books, 1994.

Roberts, Michael C. *Handbook of Pediatric Psychology.* 2nd ed. New York: Guilford Press, 1995.

Sroufe, L. Alan, Robert G. Cooper, and Mary E. Marshall. *Child Development.* New York: Random House, 1987.

Thomas, R. Murray. *Comparing Theories of Child Development.* 3rd ed. Belmont, CA: Wadsworth Publishing Company, 1992.

Vasta, Ross, Marshall M. Haith, and Scott A. Miller. *Child Psychology: the Modern Science.* New York: J. Wiley & Sons, 1992.

**Noam Chomsky** *(UPI/Corbis-Bettmann. Reproduced with permission.)*

# Noam Chomsky

### 1928-

American linguist whose theory of transformational or generative grammar has had a profound influence on the fields of both linguistics and psychology.

Noam Chomsky was born in Philadelphia and educated at the University of Pennsylvania, where he received his B.A. (1949), M.A. (1951), and Ph.D. (1955). In 1955, he was appointed to the faculty of the Massachusetts Institute of Technology (MIT), where he has served as professor of foreign languages and linguistics. He has also taught courses and lectured at many universities throughout the world, including Oxford University. Besides his work in the field of psycholinguistics, Chomsky is also well-known as a leftist activist and social critic. He was an outspoken opponent of the Vietnam War and has remained critical of media coverage of politics. Although Chomsky's work is primarily of interest to linguistics scholars, several of his theories have had popular applications in psychology.

Chomsky was a pioneer in the field of psycholinguistics, which, beginning in the 1950s, helped establish a new relationship between linguistics and psychology. While Chomsky argued that linguistics should be understood as a part of **cognitive psychology**, in his first book, *Syntactic Structures* (1957), he opposed the traditional **learning theory** basis of language acquisition. In doing so, his expressed a view that differed from the behaviorist view of the mind as a *tabula rasa;* his theories were also diametrically opposed to the verbal learning theory of **B. F. Skinner**, the foremost proponent of **behaviorism**. In Chomsky's view, certain aspects of linguistic knowledge and **ability** are the product of a universal innate ability, or "language acquisition device" (LAD), that enables each **normal** child to construct a systematic grammar and generate phrases. This theory claims to account for the fact that children acquire language skills more rapidly than other abilities, usually mastering most of the basic rules by the age of four. As evidence that an inherent ability exists to recognize underlying syntactical relationships within a sentence, Chomsky cites the fact that children readily understand transformations of a given sentence into different forms—such as declarative and interrogative—and can easily transform sentences of their own. Applying this principle to adult mastery of language, Chomsky has devised the now-famous nonsense sentence, "Colorless green ideas sleep furiously." Although the sentence has no coherent meaning, English speakers regard it as still more nonsensical if the syntax, as well as the meaning, is deprived of underlying logic, as in "Ideas furiously green colorless sleep." (The same idea underlies Lewis Carroll's well-known poem "Jabberwocky" from his *Alice in Wonderland.*) Chomsky's approach is also referred to as "generative" because of the idea that rules generate the seemingly infinite variety of orders and sentences existing in all languages. Chomsky argues that the underlying logic, or *deep structure*, of all languages is the same and that human mastery of it is genetically determined, not learned. Those aspects of language that humans have to study are termed *surface structures.*

Chomsky's work has been highly controversial, rekindling the age-old debate over whether language exists in the mind before experience. His theories also distinguish between language *competence* (knowledge of rules and structure) and *performance* (how an individual uses language in practice). Besides *Syntactic Structures*, Chomsky's books include *Current Issues in Linguistics Theory* (1964), *Aspects of the Theory of Syntax* (1965), *Topics in the Theory of Generative Grammar* (1966), *Cartesian Linguistics* (1966), *Language and Mind* (1968), *Reflections on Language* (1975), *Logical Structure of Linguistic Theory* (1975), and *Knowledge of Language* (1986).

## Further Reading

D'Agostino, F. *Chomsky's System of Ideas.* Oxford: Oxford University Press, 1986.

# Kenneth Bancroft Clark

**1914-**
American psychologist who studied the psychological effects of racial segregation.

Many psychologists have made history within their profession; few, however, have had an impact on the laws of a nation. Such was the case with Kenneth Bancroft Clark, whose work the Supreme Court cited in its historic *Brown v. Board of Education* ruling. In the 1954 case, which overturned racial segregation in public schools, the Court referred to a 1950 paper by Clark, and described him as a "modern authority" on the psychological effects of segregation. His recognition by the highest court in the land made Clark an instant celebrity, and on the heels of this success, he set out to develop a prototype community action program for young people in Harlem in 1962. However, political workings brought an early end to his vision. Disillusioned by this experience, Clark penned the most well-known of his many books, *Dark Ghetto: Dilemmas of Social Power* (1965), which

would become an important text for sociologists studying inner-city life in America.

## A world of opportunities in Harlem

Clark was born on July 24, 1914, in the Panama Canal Zone. His father, Arthur Bancroft Clark, had come from the West Indies and worked as a cargo superintendent for the United Fruit Company, a major employer in Central America at that time. Clark's mother, Miriam Hanson Clark, was from Jamaica, and she and his father disagreed over their children's upbringing. Miriam wanted to move the **family** to the United States, where Kenneth and his younger sister Beulah would have greater educational and career opportunities than they would in Panama. But the father refused to go with them. He had a good position at United Fruit, and under the harsh **racism** and segregation that prevailed even in the northern United States at that time, he did not believe he could obtain a similar job in America. Therefore Miriam and her two children boarded a boat for New York harbor, leaving the children's father behind.

In New York City, Miriam got a job as a seamstress in the New York garment district, and the family settled in Harlem. At that time Harlem was a mixed community, and besides other black families, the Clarks found themselves living alongside Irish and Jewish neighbors. This experience undoubtedly had an effect on Clark's later commitment to integrated education. In school, he told the *New Yorker* magazine in 1982, all students were expected to excel, regardless of skin color: "When I went to the board in Mr. Ruprecht's algebra class," he recalled, "…I had to do those equations, and if I wasn't able to do them he wanted to find out why. He didn't expect any less of me because I was black."

In spite of this positive educational **environment**, the rest of the world was filled with people who had low expectations for black students. Hence when Clark finished junior high and had to choose a high school, counselors urged him to enroll in a vocational school. In spite of his strong academic record, he was black, and therefore he could only hope to gain employment in a limited range of jobs, all of which involved working with one's hands. That, at least, was the logic, and to many people it would have made sense—but not to Miriam Clark. When her son told her what the school counselor had suggested, she went to the counselor's office and informed him that she had not struggled to bring her family from Panama so that her son could become a factory worker.

She enrolled Kenneth in George Washington High School, an academic school where he performed well in all subjects. He was particularly interested in economics, and had begun to consider becoming an economist. But when he earned an award for his outstanding performance in the class, the teacher refused to give it to him. This example of racial discrimination, Clark's first clear-cut experience with it, would have enormous impact on his life. Because of it, he decided not to study economics, and it may have led to his lifelong interest in the psychology of racism.

## Meetings with remarkable men—and a woman

Clark had not yet decided to become a psychologist; in fact, when he entered Washington, D.C.'s Howard University in 1931, he planned to study medicine. But in his sophomore year, he took a psychology course taught by Professor Frances Sumner. Sumner's method of psychological study, Clark recalled in his 1982 *New Yorker* interview, offered "the promise of...systematic understanding of the complexities of human behavior and human interaction"—including insight into "the seemingly intractable nature of racism." Intrigued, Clark switched his major to psychology. Another professor at Howard who had an influence on Clark was Ralph Bunche. Bunche, who would later gain fame as a diplomat and winner of the Nobel Peace Prize in 1950, taught Clark in several political science courses.

After graduating in 1935, Clark went on to obtain his M.S. in psychology the next year, then accepted a teaching position at Howard. But Sumner, recognizing his great potential, encouraged him to obtain his doctorate at Columbia University. Therefore Clark returned to New York City and enrolled in the doctoral program at Columbia. On April 14, 1938, he married Mamie Phipps, a psychology student from Arkansas whom he had met at Howard. The couple would eventually have two children, Kate Miriam and Hilton. Clark, the first black doctoral candidate in Columbia's psychology program, earned his Ph.D. degree in 1940.

For a short period of time, Clark taught at Hampton Institute in Virginia, an old and highly conservative black college. But Clark had strong differences of opinion with the administration at Hampton, and resigned after one semester. From 1941 to 1942, Clark worked for the federal government's Office of War Information, studying morale conditions of America's black population as the country entered World War II. In 1942, he accepted a position as an instructor at City College of New York (CCNY), and in 1949 became an assistant professor.

Clark and his mentor Bunche had worked together on research for renowned Swedish economist Gunnar Myrdal, another future Nobel laureate. Myrdal's study of conditions among African Americans in the United States would be published in 1944 as *An American Dilemma: The Negro Problem and Modern Democracy.* But his work with Bunche and Myrdal would not prove to be the most significant collaboration of Clark's career; his most important partner was closer to home, in the person of his wife Mamie.

## The rising young social scientist

In 1946, the Clarks established the Northside Testing and Consultation Center in Harlem. In time this would become the Northside Center for Child Development, and the name change reflected a shift of emphasis. In the course of their research and therapy for troubled black youngsters, the Clarks had discovered evidence that racism helped to create a pervasive negative self-image. For instance, when given a choice between a brown doll and a white one and told "Give me the doll that looks bad," black children would usually choose the brown doll; told to point out "the doll that is a nice color," they would select the white one.

The Clarks had been conducting such studies for some time. Between 1939 and 1950, they published five articles on the effect that segregated schooling had on kindergartners in Washington, D.C. For the Midcentury White House Conference on Children and Youth in 1950, Clark wrote another article that summed up his and Mamie's research, as well as the work of other social scientists who had studied the psychological effects of segregation.

Up to that time, the law of the land regarding segregated schooling had been governed by the Supreme Court's decision in *Plessy v. Ferguson* (1896). In that case, the Court held that the establishment of separate schools for blacks and whites—as long as the schools were of equal quality—did not violate the concept of equal protection under the law guaranteed by the Fourteenth Amendment to the Constitution. In practice, of course, schools for blacks were certainly separate, but rarely equal. Furthermore, Clark's research had shown that even if they *were* equal in quality, the very fact of enforced separation created an inherent inequity.

When the National Association for the Advancement of Colored People (NAACP) began to challenge institutionalized segregation in the nation's courts, the organization turned to Clark. In three of the four cases that led to the Supreme Court's review of the segregation issue, Clark testified as an expert witness. When the case went before the Supreme Court, the NAACP presented a special paper, prepared by Clark and others, called "The Effects of Segregation and the Consequences of Desegregation: A Social Science Statement." It was the first time in American legal history that a brief prepared by a social scientist, illustrating the human consequences of a law in terms of its social and psychological impact, had been presented before the Supreme Court.

In its ruling on *Brown v. Board of Education,* the historic 1954 case which struck down institutionalized segregation, the Court cited Clark's work as valuable evidence. More important, it reiterated the theme he had presented as the evidence mounted from his studies: "Separate educational facilities are inherently unequal."

## Highs and lows, disappointment and hope

On the heels of the May 17, 1954, Supreme Court decision, Clark became a celebrity in the community of social scientists. He was feted and honored at universities around the country, bestowed with honorary degrees and described in glowing terms by his colleagues. A generation later, three young graduate students writing in the *Journal of Applied Behavioral Science* would sum up the extent of his reputation: "We approached our telephone interview with Dr. Kenneth Clark with awe. After all, his contribution to U.S. history had enabled our own education to occur in an integrated society."

For the next decade, Clark went from triumph to triumph. In 1960, CCNY made him a full professor, and he thus became the first African American awarded a permanent position at any of New York's city colleges. The next year, the NAACP gave him its Spingarn Award for his contributions to race relations. With the support of the federal government, Clark in June 1962 established Harlem Youth Opportunities Unlimited, or HARYOU. With HARYOU, he planned to reorganize the schools of Harlem by integrating classes, enforcing higher standards on teachers, and involving members of the community—especially parents—in the education of its young people. It was to be the prototype for the sort of community-action programs which come into increasing prominence in the 1980s and 1990s.

HARYOU outlined these principles in a 620-page report, which took two years to prepare; unfortunately, as Clark would later say in his *New Yorker* profile, "As it turned out, all we did at HARYOU was to produce a document." Clark's dream for the organization would never become a reality, and his opposition came not from white racists but from a black politician. The federal government in May 1964 allocated $110 million for the program, and arranged a merger of HARYOU with Associated Community Teams (ACT), a group in which Democratic Congressman Adam Clayton Powell had a hand. Clark and Powell disagreed over who should lead the program, and when Clark accused Powell of trying to take it over for political purposes, Powell claimed that Clark was profiting financially from the program. In disgust, Clark resigned from the organization on July 31, 1964.

As a result of his disappointing experience, Clark wrote *Dark Ghetto,* which would become the most well-known of his more than 16 books. In 1967 he formed the Metropolitan Applied Research Center, or MARC, with a group of other social scientists. Three years later, in 1970, MARC attempted to resurrect a program similar to that of HARYOU, this time in Washington, D.C. Yet again, however, power politics defeated Clark's dream. Teachers' unions rejected Clark's attempts to hold educators to higher standards, and the city school board chairman disagreed with Clark's central idea that black children should be expected to do as well in school as their white counterparts. To add to his misfortunes, in the late 1960s, Clark was subjected to scorn by black militants who rejected his integrationist approach.

Just as the decade leading up to the HARYOU debacle had been characterized by triumphs, the decade that followed had proven to be one of disappointments. In 1975, Clark retired from teaching and with his wife and children founded Clark, Phipps, Clark & Harris, Inc., a consulting firm that assisted corporations such as AT&T in setting up affirmative action programs. Clark continued with this work after he lost his most important partner, Mamie, when she died in 1983.

Meanwhile, the idealist who had dreamed of fully integrated schools watched with disappointment as society became more segregated. This time the segregation was not a matter of law, but of choice, and the growing gap between the performance of black students and those in the mainstream only threatened to increase the division. But Clark managed to retain his hope that society could make a change. The key, as he wrote in *Newsweek* in 1993, was to teach genuine respect for humankind: "We have not yet made education a process whereby students are taught to respect the inalienable dignity of other human beings.... [But] by encouraging and rewarding empathetic behavior in all of our children.... [w]e will be helping them to understand the commonality of being human. We will be *educating* them."

*See also* Prejudice and discrimination

Judson Knight

## Further Reading
Bigelow, Barbara Carlisle, ed. *Contemporary Black Biography,* Volume 5. Detroit: Gale, 1994, pp. 51-55.
*Contemporary Authors,* Volume 36. Detroit: Gale, 1978.
Guthrie, Robert V. *Even the Rat Was White,* Harper's (1976): 150-1
Hentoff, N. "Profiles," *New Yorker,* (August 23, 1982): 37-40.
Keppel, Ben. *The Work of Democracy: Ralph Bunche, Kenneth B. Clark, Lorraine Hansberry, and the Cultural Politics of Race.* Harvard University Press, 1995.

Latting, Jean Kantambu et al., "Dr. Kenneth Bancroft Clark: A Biography," *Journal of Applied Behavioral Sciences,* (September 1991): 263-64.

"Light in the Ghetto," *Newsweek,* (May 31, 1965): 78.

Markowitz, Gerald and Rosner, David. *Children, Race, and Power: Kenneth and Mamie Clark's Northside Center.* University Press of Virginia, 1996.

McGuire, William and Wheeler, Leslie. *American Social Leaders.* ABC-Clio, 1993, pp. 99-100.

Sammons, Vivian Ovelton. *Blacks in Science and Medicine.* Hemisphere Publishing, 1990.

"10 Forces Behind U.S. Education," *Scholastic Update,* (February 3, 1984): 9.

Willie, C.V., "Five Black Scholars," *Change,* (September 1983): 27.

Young, Margaret. *Black American Leaders.* Watts, 1969, pp. 28-30.

# Classical conditioning

The process of closely associating a neutral stimulus with one that evokes a reflexive response so that eventually the neutral stimulus alone will evoke the same response.

Classical conditioning is an important concept in the school of psychology known as **behaviorism**, and it forms the basis for some of the techniques used in **behavior therapy**.

Classical conditioning was pioneered by the Russian physiologist **Ivan Pavlov** (1849-1936) in the 1890s in the course of experiments on the digestive systems of dogs (work which won him the Nobel Prize in 1904). Noticing that the dogs salivated at the mere sight of the person who fed them, Pavlov formulated a theory about the relationship between stimuli and responses that he believed could be applied to humans as well as to other animals. He called the dogs' salivation in response to the actual **taste** and **smell** of meat an *unconditioned response* because it occurred through a natural reflex without any prior training (the meat itself was referred to as an *unconditioned stimulus*). A normally neutral act, such as the appearance of a lab assistant in a white coat or the ringing of a bell, could become associated with the appearance of food, thus producing salivation as a *conditioned response* (in response to a *conditioned stimulus*).Pavlov believed that the conditioned reflex had a physiological basis in the creation of new pathways in the cortex of the **brain** by the conditioning process. In further research early in the 20th century, Pavlov found that in order for the **conditioned response** to be maintained, it had to be paired periodically with the unconditioned stimulus or the learned association would be forgotten (a process known as **extinction**). However, it could quickly be relearned if necessary.

In humans, classical conditioning can account for such complex phenomena as a person's emotional reaction to a particular song or perfume based on a past experience with which it is associated. Classical (sometimes called Pavlovian) conditioning is also the basis for many different types of fears or phobias, which can occur through a process called stimulus generalization (a child who has a bad experience with a particular dog may learn to **fear** all dogs). In addition to causing fears, however, classical conditioning can also help eliminate them through a variety of therapeutic techniques. One is systematic **desensitization**, in which an anxiety-producing stimulus is deliberately associated with a positive response, usually relaxation produced through such techniques as deep breathing and progressive muscle relaxation. The opposite result (making a desirable stimulus unpleasant) is obtained through aversion therapy, in which a behavior that a person wants to discontinue—often an addiction, such as alcoholism—is paired with an unpleasant stimulus, such as a nausea-producing drug.

**Further Reading**

Gormezano, Isidore, William F. Prokasy, and Richard F. Thompson. *Classical Conditioning.* 3rd ed. Hillsdale, NJ: L. Erlbaum, 1987.

Lieberman, David A. *Learning: Behavior and Cognition.* Belmont, CA: Wadsworth Publishing Co., 1990.

Mackintosh, N.J. *Conditioning and Associative Learning.* New York: Oxford University, 1983.

# Client-centered therapy

An approach to counseling and psychotherapy that places much of the responsibility for the treatment process on the patient, with the therapist taking a non-directive role.

Developed in the 1930s by the American psychologist **Carl Rogers**, client-centered therapy—also known as non-directive or Rogerian therapy—departed from the typically formal, detached role of the therapist common to **psychoanalysis** and other forms of treatment. Rogers believed that therapy should take place in the supportive **environment** created by a close personal relationship between client and therapist. Rogers's introduction of the term "client" rather than "patient" expresses his rejection of the traditionally authoritarian relationship between therapist and client and his view of them as equals. The client determines the general direction of therapy, while the therapist seeks to increase the client's insightful self-understanding through informal clarifying questions.

Rogers believed that the most important factor in successful therapy was not the therapist's skill or training, but rather his or her attitude. Three interrelated attitudes on the part of the therapist are central to the success of client-centered therapy: congruence, unconditional positive regard, and **empathy**. Congruence refers to the therapist's openness and genuineness—the willingness to relate to clients without hiding behind a professional facade. Therapists who function in this way have all their feelings available to them in therapy sessions and may share significant ones with their clients. However, congruence does not mean that therapists disclose their own personal problems to clients in therapy sessions or shift the focus of therapy to themselves in any other way.

Unconditional positive regard means that the therapist accepts the client totally for who he or she is without evaluating or censoring, and without disapproving of particular feelings, actions, or characteristics. The therapist communicates this attitude to the client by a willingness to listen without interrupting, judging, or giving advice. This creates a nonthreatening context in which the client feels free to explore and share painful, hostile, defensive, or abnormal feelings without worrying about personal rejection by the therapist.

The third necessary component of a therapist's attitude is empathy ("accurate empathetic understanding"). The therapist tries to appreciate the client's situation from the client's point of view, showing an emotional understanding of and sensitivity to the client's feelings throughout the therapy session. In other systems of therapy, empathy with the client would be considered a preliminary step enabling the therapeutic work to proceed, but in client-centered therapy, it actually constitutes a major portion of the therapeutic work itself. A primary way of conveying this empathy is by active listening that shows careful and perceptive **attention** to what the client is saying. In addition to standard techniques, such as eye contact, that are common to any good listener, client-centered therapists employ a special method called reflection, which consists of paraphrasing and/or summarizing what a client has just said. This technique shows that the therapist is listening carefully and accurately and gives clients an added opportunity to examine their own thoughts and feelings as they hear them repeated by another person. Generally, clients respond by elaborating further on the thoughts they have just expressed.

Two primary goals of client-centered therapy are increased **self-esteem** and greater openness to experience. Some of the related changes that it seeks to foster in clients include increased correspondence between the client's idealized and actual selves; better self-understanding; decreases in defensiveness, **guilt**, and insecuri-

## CLIENT-CENTERED THERAPY

### QUALITIES OF THE THERAPIST

**Congruence:** therapist's openness to the client

**Unconditional positive regard:** therapist accepts the client without judgement

**Empathy:** therapist tries to convey an appreciation and understanding of the client's point of view

### GOALS OF THE THERAPY

**Increase self-esteem**

**Expand openness** to life experiences.

ty; more positive and comfortable relationships with others; and an increased capacity to experience and express feelings at the moment they occur. Beginning in the 1960s, client-centered therapy became allied with the **human potential movement**. Rogers adopted terms such as "person-centered approach" and "way of being" and began to focus on personal growth and **self-actualization**. He also pioneered the use of encounter groups, adapting the **sensitivity training** (T-group) methods developed by **Kurt Lewin** (1890-1947) and other researchers at the National Training Laboratories in 1950s.

While client-centered therapy is considered one of the major therapeutic approaches, along with psychoanalytic and cognitive-behavioral therapy, Rogers's influence is felt in schools of therapy other than his own, and the concepts and methods he developed are drawn on in an eclectic fashion by many different types of counselors and therapists.

### Further Reading
Rogers, Carl. *Client-Centered Therapy.* Boston: Houghton Mifflin, 1951.
———. *On Becoming a Person.* Boston: Houghton Mifflin, 1961.
———. *A Way of Being.* Boston: Houghton Mifflin, 1980.

# Clinical psychology

The application of psychological principles to diagnosing and treating persons with emotional and behavioral problems.

Clinical psychologists apply research findings in the fields of mental and physical health to explain dysfunctional behavior in terms of **normal** processes. The problems they address are diverse and include **mental illness**, **mental retardation**, marital and **family** issues, criminal behavior, and chemical dependency. The clinical psychologist may also address less serious problems of adjustment similar to those encountered by the counseling psychologist.

Approximately one-third of the psychologists working in the United States today are clinical psychologists. A number of clinical psychologists are in private practice, either alone or in group practice with other **mental health** professionals. Others may practice in a variety of settings, including community mental-health centers, university medical schools, social work departments, centers for the mentally and physically handicapped, prisons, state institutions and hospitals, juvenile courts, and probation offices. Clinical psychologists use psychological assessment and other means to diagnose psychological disorders and may apply **psychotherapy** to treat clients individually or in groups. In the United States, they are governed by a code of professional practice drawn up by the **American Psychological Association**.

Individuals consult clinical psychologists for treatment when their behaviors or attitudes are harmful to themselves or others. Many different treatment types and methods are employed by psychologists, depending on the setting in which they work and their theoretical orientation. The major types of therapy include psychodynamic therapies, based on uncovering **unconscious** processes and motivations, of which the most well known is Freudian **psychoanalysis**; phenomenological, or humanistic, therapies (including the Rogerian and Gestalt methods) which view psychotherapy as an encounter between equals, abandoning the traditional doctor-patient relationship; and behavior-oriented therapies geared toward helping clients see their problems as learned behaviors that can be modified without looking for unconscious motivations or hidden meanings. These therapies, derived from the work of **Ivan Pavlov** and **B.F. Skinner**, include methods such as **behavior modification** and cognitive-behavior therapy, which may be used to alter not only overt behavior but also the thought patterns that drive it.

The work of the clinical psychologist is often compared with that of the psychiatrist, and although there is overlap in what these professionals do, there are also specific distinctions between them. As of 1996, clinical psychologists cannot prescribe drugs to treat psychological disorders, and must work in conjunction with a psychiatrist or other M.D. who is authorized to administer controlled substances. However, a movement is underway for prescription privileges for psychologists. The clinical psychologist has extensive training in research methods and in techniques for diagnosing, treating, and preventing various disorders. Most psychologists earn a Ph.D. degree in the field, which requires completion of a four- to six-year program offered by a university psychology department. The course of study includes a broad overview of the field (including courses in such areas as statistics, **personality** theory, and psychotherapy), as well as specialization in a particular subfield and completion of a practicum, internship, and dissertation.

A new training program for psychologists was developed and introduced at the University of Illinois, which offered the first Psychology Doctorate (Psy.D.) in 1968. This degree program is geared exclusively toward the training of clinicians rather than researchers. It stresses course work in applied methods of assessment and intervention and eliminates the dissertation requirement. The number of Psy.D. programs in the United States has grown since 1968, with some programs offered at universities and others at independent, "free-standing" professional schools of psychology.

Assessment plays a prominent role among the functions of clinical psychology. The term "clinical psychology" itself was first used at the end of the nineteenth century in connection with the testing of mentally retarded and physically handicapped children. The discipline soon expanded with the growing interest in the application of assessment techniques to the general population following Robert Yerkes's revision of the Stanford Binet **Intelligence** scales in 1915, creating a widely used point scale for the **measurement** of human mental **ability**. Clinical psychologists must be familiar with a variety of techniques of assessing patients through interviews, observation, tests, and various forms of **play**. Assessment may be used to compare an individual with others in a reliable way using standardized norms; determine the type and circumstances of symptomatic behaviors; understand how a person functions in a given area (**cognition**, social skills, **emotion**); or match a patient to a particular diagnostic category for further treatment.

While the clinical psychologist does not specialize in research, the two disciplines often overlap. With their varied experiences, clinicians are qualified to participate in research on, for example, cost effectiveness in health care, design of facilities, doctor-patient communication, or studies of various treatment methods. Clinical psychologists routinely contribute to the training of mental health professionals and those in other areas of health care, serving on the faculties of universities and independent institutes of psychology, where they teach courses, supervise practicums and internships, and oversee dissertation research. They also carry out administrative appointments which call for them to assist in the planning and implementation of health care services and are represented in international groups such as the World Health Organization.

**Further Reading**

Bernstein, Douglas A. *Introduction to Clinical Psychology.* New York: McGraw-Hill, 1980.

Lilienfeld, Scott O. *Seeing Both Sides: Classic Controversies in Abnormal Psychology.* Pacific Grove, CA: Brooks/Cole, 1995.

Nietzel, Michael T. *Introduction to Clinical Psychology.* 3rd ed. Englewood Cliffs, NJ: Prentice Hall, 1991.

# Cliques

A group of people who identify with each other and interact frequently.

The term clique has two levels of significance. In its neutral usage by social researchers, it denotes a group of people who interact with each other more intensively than with other peers in the same setting. In its more popular form it has negative connotations. It is used to describe an adolescent social group that excludes others on the basis of superficial differences, exercising greater than average amount of **peer pressure** upon its members. The numerous terms teenagers use to describe themselves and others—such as jocks, druggies, populars, brains, nerds, normals, rappers, preps, stoners, rockers, punks (punx), freaks (phreaks), and skaters—exemplify both levels of meaning in the word "clique." These terms both accurately refer to the activities or qualities the group members share as well as to the exclusiveness of the groups.

A clique consists of a particular group of people within a particular location. Cliques are characterized by a pattern of relationships in which each member is either directly or indirectly connected with every other member, and in each pair relationship the members exchange social overtures (phone calls, get-togethers, etc.) on a fairly equal basis. Joining cliques, having the desire to join a particular clique, and being excluded from cliques are considered a **normal** part of adolescent development. Joining cliques helps children to develop, identify, and regulate social interaction. Generally children begin to be more aware of differences and form cliques in late elementary school, between the ages of 8 and 10 years old. As they begin to separate emotionally from their parents, young adolescents' identification with their peers is greatly exaggerated between ages 10 and 12 years old, when a child's clique may change on a daily basis.

The issue of belonging is extremely important during middle school and high school, and membership in cliques can have a strong effect on the adolescent's sense of self-worth. During high school, cliques become more consistent, though their composition may change. Research shows that the way an adolescent or teen behaves is better predicted by the behavior of cliques in which he is a part than by the behavior of individual friends.

Most cliques are fairly complex and have a mixture of positive and negative qualities. Cliques may be judged according to the degree to which they exert positive or negative peer pressure, accept diversity among members, and appreciate individuality. Even if a group exerts positive peer pressure, it may also be exerting negative peer pressure by being exclusive on the basis of race, class, religion, sexual orientation, or ethnicity.

**Further Reading**

Peck, Lee A. *Coping with Cliques.* New York: Rosen Publishing Group, 1992.

Sciacca, Fran. *Cliques and Clones: Facing Peer Pressure.* Grand Rapids, MI: Zondervan, 1992.

Shellenberger, Susie. *Lockers, Lunch Lines, Chemistry, and Cliques.* Minneapolis, MN: Bethany House Publishers, 1995.

# Cocaine

See **Drugs/Drug abuse**

# Codependence

A term used to describe a person who is intimately involved with a person who is abusing or addicted to alcohol or another substance.

The concept of codependence was first developed in relation to alcohol and other substance abuse addictions. The alcoholic or drug abuser was the *dependent,* and the person involved with the dependent person in any intimate way (spouse, lover, child, sibling, etc.) was the codependent. The definition of the term has been expanded to include anyone showing an extreme degree of certain **personality traits**: denial, silent or even cheerful tolerance of unreasonable behavior from others, rigid loyalty to **family** rules, a need to control others, finding identity through relationships with others, a lack of personal boundaries, and low **self-esteem**. Some consider it a progressive disease, one which gets worse without treatment until the codependent becomes unable to function successfully in the world. Progressive codependence can lead to **depression**, isolation, self-destructive behavior (such as **bulimia**, **anorexia**, self-mutilation) or even **suicide**. There is a large self-help movement to help codependents take charge of themselves and heal their lives.

There is some criticism of the "codependence movement" by those who feel it is only a fad that encourages labeling and a weak, dependent, victim mentality that obscures more important underlying truths of oppression. Many critics claim the definition of codependence is too vague and the list of symptoms too long and broad to be meaningful. These critics believe that all families fit the "dysfunctional" label; by diagnosing a person as "codependent," all responsibility for the individual's dissatisfaction, shortcomings, and failures comes to rest on the individual and his or her family. Larger issues of cultural, societal, or institutional responsibility are ignored. However, some proponents of the codependence definition are widening their perspective to look at how society as a whole, as well as separate institutions within society, function in an addictive, dysfunctional, or codependent way.

## Further Reading

Beattie, Melody. *Codependent No More: How to Stop Controlling Others and Start Caring for Yourself.* San Francisco: Hazelden/HarperCollins, 1987.

Johnson, Sonia. *Wildfire: Igniting the She/Volution.* Albuquerque, NM: Wildfire Books, 1989.

Katz, Dr. Stan J., and Eimee E. Liu. *The Codependency Conspiracy: How to Break the Recovery Habit and Take Charge of Your Life.* New York: Warner Books, 1991.

# Cognitive behavior therapy

A therapeutic approach based on the principle that maladaptive moods and behavior can be changed by replacing distorted or inappropriate ways of thinking with thought patterns that are healthier and more realistic.

**Cognitive therapy** is an approach to **psychotherapy** that uses thought patterns to change moods and behaviors. Pioneers in the development of cognitive **behavior therapy** include **Albert Ellis** (1929-), who developed rational-emotive therapy (RET) in the 1950s, and **Aaron Beck** (1921-), whose cognitive therapy has been widely used for **depression** and anxiety. Cognitive behavior therapy has become increasingly popular since the 1970s. Growing numbers of therapists have come to believe that their patients' cognitive processes play an important role in determining the effectiveness of treatment. Currently, almost 70% of the members of the Association for the Advancement of Behavior Therapy identify themselves as cognitive behaviorists.

Like behavior therapy, cognitive behavior therapy tends to be short-term (often between 10 and 20 sessions), and it focuses on the client's present situation in contrast to the emphasis on past history that is a promi-

nent feature of Freudian **psychoanalysis** and other psychodynamically oriented therapies. The therapeutic process begins with identification of distorted perceptions and thought patterns that are causing or contributing to the client's problems, often through detailed record keeping by the client. Some self-defeating ways of thinking identified by Aaron Beck include all-or-nothing thinking; magnifying or minimizing the importance of an event; overgeneralization (drawing extensive conclusions from a single event); personalization (taking things too personally); selective abstraction (giving disproportionate weight to negative events); arbitrary inference (drawing illogical conclusions from an event); and automatic thoughts (habitual negative, scolding thoughts such as "You can't do anything right").

Once negative ways of thinking have been identified, the therapist helps the client work on replacing them with more adaptive ones. This process involves a repertoire of techniques, including self-evaluation, positive self-talk, control of negative thoughts and feelings, and accurate assessment of both external situations and of the client's own emotional state. Clients practice these techniques alone, with the therapist, and also, wherever possible, in the actual settings in which stressful situations occur (*in vivo*), gradually building up confidence in their **ability** to cope with difficult situations successfully by breaking out of dysfunctional patterns of response.

Today cognitive behavior therapy is widely used with children and adolescents, especially for disorders involving anxiety, depression, or problems with social skills. Like adult clients, children undergoing cognitive behavior therapy are made aware of distorted perceptions and errors in logic that are responsible for inaccurate or unrealistic views of the world around them. The therapist then works to change erroneous beliefs and perceptions by instruction, **modeling**, and giving the child a chance to rehearse new attitudes and responses and practice them in real-life situations. Cognitive behavior therapy has been effective in treating a variety of complaints, ranging from minor problems and developmental difficulties to severe disorders that are incurable but can be made somewhat more manageable. It is used either alone or together with other therapies and/or medication as part of an overall treatment plan.

Cognitive behavioral therapy has worked especially well, often in combination with medication, for children and adolescents suffering from depression. It can help free depressed children from the pervasive feelings of helplessness and hopelessness that are supported by self-defeating beliefs. Children in treatment are assigned to monitor their thoughts, and the therapist points out ways that these thoughts (such as "nothing is any fun" or "I never do anything right") misrepresent or distort reality.

Other therapeutic techniques may include the completion of graded task assignments, and the deliberate scheduling of pleasurable activities.

Cognitive behavioral therapy is also used for children with **conduct disorder**, which is characterized by aggressive, antisocial actions, including hurting animals and other children, setting fires, lying, and theft. Through a cognitive behavioral approach (which generally works better with adolescents than with younger children because of the levels of thinking and control involved), young people with this disorder are taught ways to handle **anger** and resolve conflicts peacefully. Through instruction, modeling, role playing, and other techniques, they learn to react to events in socially appropriate, nonviolent ways. Other **childhood** conditions for which cognitive behavior therapy has been effective include generalized anxiety disorder and **attention deficit/hyperactivity disorder**. It can help children with ADHD become more controlled and less impulsive; often, they are taught to memorize and internalize the following set of behavior guidelines: "Stop—Listen—Look—Think—Act."

Cognitive behavioral therapy has also been successful in the treatment of adolescents with **eating disorders**, who, unlike those with conduct disorders, hurt themselves rather than hurting (or attempting to hurt) others. The cognitive approach focuses on the distorted perceptions that young women with **anorexia** or **bulimia** have about food, eating, and their own bodies. Often administered in combination with medication, therapy for eating disorders needs to be continued for an extended period of time—a year and a half or longer in the case of anorexia.

Cognitive therapy is generally not used for disorders, such as **schizophrenia** or **autism**, in which thinking or communication are severely disturbed.

## Further Reading

Beck, Aaron. *Cognitive Therapy and the Emotional Disorders*. New York: International Universities Press, 1976.

Dryden, Windy, ed. *The Essential Albert Ellis: Seminal Writings on Psychotherapy*. New York: Springer, 1990.

Feindler, Eva L. *Adolescent Anger Control: Cognitive-Behavioral Techniques*. New York: Pergamon Press, 1986.

Fishman, Katharine Davis. *Behind the One-Way Mirror: Psychotherapy and Children*. New York: Bantam Books, 1995.

Mahoney, Michael J., ed. *Cognition and Psychotherapy*. New York: Plenum Press, 1985.

Martorano, Joseph T., and John P. Kildahl. *Beyond Negative Thinking: Breaking the Cycle of Depressing and Anxious Thoughts*. New York: Insight Books, 1989.

Wolpe, Joseph. *Life Without Fear*. Oakland, CA: Harbinger, 1988.

## Further Information

American Academy of Child and Adolescent Psychiatry. 3615 Wisconsin Avenue NW, Washington, DC 20016, (202) 966–7300.

American Society for Adolescent Psychiatry. 4330 East West Highway, Suite 1117, Bethesda, MD 20814, (301) 718–6502.

Association for Advancement of Behavior Therapy. 15 West 36th St., New York, NY 10018, (212) 279–7970.

Albert Ellis Institute (formerly the Institute for Rational-Emotive Behavior Therapy). 45 East 65th St., New York, NY 10021, (212) 535–0822. http://www.rebt.org.

# Cognitive development

The development of thought processes, including remembering, problem solving, and decision-making, from childhood through adolescence to adulthood.

Historically, the cognitive development of children has been studied in a variety of ways. The oldest is through **intelligence** tests, such as the widely used Stanford Binet **Intelligence Quotient**, or IQ, test first adopted for use in the United States by psychologist **Lewis Terman** (1877-1956) in 1916 from a French model pioneered in 1905. IQ scoring is based on the concept of "mental age," according to which the scores of a child of average intelligence match his or her age, while a gifted child's performance is comparable to that of an older child, and a slow learner's scores are similar to those of a younger child. IQ tests are widely used in the United States, but they have come under increasing criticism for defining intelligence too narrowly and for being biased with regard to race and gender. In contrast to the emphasis placed on a child's native abilities by intelligence testing, **learning theory** grew out of work by behaviorist researchers such as **John Watson** and **B.F. Skinner** (1904-1990), who argued that children are completely malleable. Learning theory focuses on the role of environmental factors in shaping the intelligence of children, especially on a child's **ability** to learn by having certain behaviors rewarded and others discouraged.

The most well-known and influential theory of cognitive development is that of French psychologist **Jean Piaget**. Piaget's theory, first published in 1952, grew out of decades of extensive observation of children, including his own, in their natural environments as opposed to the laboratory experiments of the behaviorists. Although Piaget was interested in how children reacted to their **environment**, he proposed a more active role for them than that suggested by learning theory. He envisioned a child's knowledge as composed of *schemas*, basic units of knowledge used to organize past experiences and serve as a basis for understanding new ones. Schemas are continually being modified by two complementary processes that Piaget termed **assimilation** and accommodation. Assimilation refers to the process of taking in new information by incorporating it into an existing schema. In other words, we assimilate new experiences by relating them to things we already know. On the other hand, accommodation is what happens when the schema itself changes to accommodate new knowledge. According to Piaget, cognitive development involves an ongoing attempt to achieve a balance between assimilation and accommodation that he termed equilibration.

## Piaget's stages of cognitive development

At the center of Piaget's theory is the principle that cognitive development occurs in a series of four distinct, universal stages, each characterized by increasingly sophisticated and abstract levels of thought. These stages always occur in the same order, and each builds on what was learned in the previous stage. During the first, or sensorimotor, stage (birth to 24 months), knowledge is gained primarily through sensory impressions and motor activity. Through these two modes of learning, experienced both separately and in combination, infants gradually learn to control their own bodies and objects in the external world. The ultimate task at this stage is to achieve a sense of object constancy, or permanence—the sense that objects go on existing even when we cannot see them. This developing concept can be seen in the child's keen enjoyment of games in which objects are repeatedly made to disappear and reappear.

The preoperational stage (ages two to six years) involves the manipulation of images and symbols. One object can represent another, as when a broom is turned into a "horsey" that can be ridden around the room, and a child's **play** expands to include "pretend" games. Language acquisition is yet another way of manipulating symbols. Key concepts involved in the logical organization of thoughts—such as causality, time, and perspective—are still absent, as is an awareness that substances retain the same volume even when shifted into containers of different sizes and shapes. The child's focus remains egocentric throughout both the preoperational and sensorimotor stages.

During the third, or concrete operational, stage (six or seven to 11 years of age), children can perform logical operations, but only in relation to concrete external objects rather than ideas. They can add, subtract, count, and measure, and they learn about the conservation of length, mass, area, weight, time, and volume. At this stage, children can sort items into categories, reverse the direction

of their thinking, and think about two concepts, such as length and width, simultaneously. They also begin to lose their egocentric focus, becoming able to understand a situation from the viewpoint of another person.

The fourth, or formal operations, stage begins in early **adolescence** (age 11 or 12) with the development of the ability to think logically about abstractions, including speculations about what might happen in the future. Adolescents are capable of formulating and testing hypotheses, understanding causality, and dealing with abstract concepts like probability, ratio, proportion, and analogies. They become able to reason scientifically and speculate about philosophical issues. Abstract concepts and moral values become as important as concrete objects.

## Modern views

In the decades since Piaget's theory of cognitive development became widely known, other researchers have contested some of its principles, claiming that children's progress through the four stages of development is more uneven and less consistent than Piaget believed. It has been found that children do not always reach the different stages at the age levels he specified, and that their entry into some of the stages is more gradual than was first thought. However, Piaget remains the most influential figure in modern **child development** research, and many of his ideas are still considered accurate, including the basic notion of qualitative shifts in children's thinking over time, the general trend toward greater logic and less egocentrism as they get older, the concepts of assimilation and accommodation, and the importance of active learning by questioning and exploring.

The most significant alternative to the work of Piaget has been the information-processing approach, which uses the computer as a model to provide new insight into how the human mind receives, stores, retrieves, and uses information. Researchers using **information-processing theory** to study cognitive development in children have focused on areas such as the gradual improvements in children's ability to take in information and focus selectively on certain parts of it and their increasing **attention** spans and capacity for **memory** storage. For example, they have found that the superior memory skills of older children are due in part to memorization strategies, such as repeating items in order to memorize them or dividing them into categories.

Today it is widely accepted that a child's intellectual ability is determined by a combination of **heredity** and environment. Thus, although a child's genetic inheritance is unchangeable, there are definite ways that parents can enhance their children's intellectual development through environmental factors. They can provide stimulating learning materials and experiences from an early age, reading to and talking with their children and helping them explore the world around them. As children mature, parents can both challenge and support the child's talents. Although a supportive environment in early **childhood** provides a clear advantage for a child, it is possible to make up for early losses in cognitive development if a supportive environment is provided at some later period, in contrast to early disruptions in physical development, which are often irreversible.

## Further Reading

Bruner, Jerome S. *Studies in Cognitive Growth: A Collaboration at the Center for Cognitive Studies.* New York: Wiley, 1966.

Ginsburg, Herbert, and Sylvia Opper. *Piaget's Theory of Intellectual Development.* 3rd ed. Englewood Cliffs, NJ: Prentice-Hall, 1988.

Lee, Victor, and Prajna Das Gupta., eds. *Children's Cognitive and Language Development.* Cambridge, MA: Blackwell Publishers, 1995.

McShane, John. *Cognitive Development: An Information Processing Approach.* Oxford, Eng.: B. Blackwell, 1991.

Piaget, Jean, and Barbel Inhelder. *The Growth of Logical Thinking from Childhood to Adolescence.* New York: Basic Books, 1958.

Sameroff, Arnold J., and Marshall M. Haith, eds. *The Five to Seven Year Shift: The Age of Reason and Responsibility.* Chicago: University of Chicago Press, 1991.

# Cognition

A general term for the higher mental processes by which people acquire knowledge, solve problems, and plan for the future.

Cognition depends on the **ability** to imagine or represent objects and events that are not physically present at a given moment. Cognitive functions include **attention**, **perception**, thinking, judging, decision making, problem solving, **memory**, and linguistic ability.

One of the most basic cognitive functions is the ability to conceptualize, or group individual items together as instances of a single concept or category, such as "apple" or "chair." Concepts provide the fundamental framework for thought, allowing people to relate most objects and events they encounter to preexisting categories. People learn concepts by building prototypes to which variations are added and by forming and testing hypotheses about which items belong to a particular category. Most thinking combines concepts in different forms. Examples of different forms concepts take include propositions (proposals or possibilities), mental

models (visualizing the physical form an idea might take), schemas (diagrams or maps), scripts (scenarios), and images (physical models of the item). Other fundamental aspects of cognition are reasoning, the process by which people formulate arguments and arrive at conclusions, and problem solving—devising a useful representation of a problem and planning, executing, and evaluating a solution.

Memory—another cognitive function—is crucial to learning, communication, and even to one's sense of identity (as evidenced by the effects of **amnesia**). Short-term memory provides the basis for one's working model of the world and makes possible most other mental functions; long-term memory stores information for longer periods of time. The three basic processes common to both short- and long-term memory are encoding, which deposits information in the memory; storage; and retrieval. Currently, the question of whether short- and long-term memory are qualitatively and biologically distinct is a matter of debate.

The cognitive function that most distinctively sets humans apart from other animals is the ability to communicate through language, which involves expressing propositions as sentences and understanding such expressions when we hear or read them. Language also enables the mind to communicate with itself. The interaction between language and thought has been a topic of much speculation. Of historical interest is the work of Benjamin Whorf (1897-1941), the proponent of the idea that the language people use determines the way in which they view the world. As of the late 1990s, most psychologists view the Whorfian hypothesis with skepticism, believing that language and perception interact to influence one another.

Language acquisition is another topic of debate, with some—including psycholinguist **Noam Chomsky**—arguing that all humans have innate language abilities, while behaviorists stress the role of **conditioning** and social learning theorists stress the importance of **imitation and reinforcement**.

Since the 1950s, **cognitive psychology**, which focuses on the relationship between cognitive processes and behavior, has occupied a central place in psychological research. The cognitive psychologist studies human perceptions and the ways in which cognitive processes operate on them to produce responses. One of the foremost cognitive psychologists is **Jerome Bruner**, who has done important work on the ways in which needs, motivations, and expectations (or "mental sets") affect perception. In 1960, Bruner and his colleague, George A. Miller, established the Harvard Center for Cognitive Studies, which was influential in the "cognitive revolution" of the following years. In the area of linguistics, the work of Noam Chomsky has rekindled the age-old debate over whether language exists in the mind before experience. Other well-known work in cognitive psychology includes that of D.E. Berlyne on curiosity and information seeking; George Kelly's theory of personal constructs; and investigations by Herman Witkin, Riley Gardner, and George Klein on individual perceptual and cognitive styles.

The development of the modern computer has influenced current ways of thinking about cognition through computer simulation of cognitive processes for research purposes and through the creation of information-processing models. These models portray cognition as a system that receives information, represents it with symbols, and then manipulates the representations in various ways. The senses transmit information from outside stimuli to the **brain**, which applies perceptual processes to interpret it and then decides how to respond to it. The information may simply be stored in the memory or it may be acted on. Acting on it usually affects a person's **environment** in some way, providing more feedback for the system to process. Major contributions in the area of information processing include D.E. Broadbent's information theory of attention, learning, and memory; and Miller, Galanter, and Pribram's analysis of planning and problem solving.

*See also* Artificial intelligence; Cognitive development

### Further Reading

Anderson, John R. *Cognitive Psychology and Its Implications.* New York: W.H. Freeman, 1985.
Ashcraft, Mark H. *Human Memory and Cognition.* New York: HarperCollins College Publishers, 1994.
Broadbent, Donald E. *Perception and Communication.* New York: Oxford University Press, 1987.
Halpern, Diane F. *Sex Differences in Cognitive Abilities.* Hillsdale, NJ: L. Erlbaum Associates, 1992.

# Cognitive dissonance

An influential concept in the study of the relationship between attitudes and behavior.

First proposed by **Leon Festinger** in 1957, the theory of cognitive dissonance is based on the principle that people prefer their cognitions, or beliefs, to be consistent with each other and with their own behavior.

Inconsistency, or dissonance, among their own ideas makes people uneasy enough to alter these ideas so that they will agree with each other. For example, smokers

forced to deal with the opposing thoughts "I smoke" and "smoking is dangerous" are likely to alter one of them by deciding to quit smoking. Alternatively, one can diffuse dissonance by reducing its importance (discounting the evidence against smoking or adopting the view that smoking will not harm you personally); adding new information that gives more weight to one of the dissonant beliefs or appears to reconcile them (deciding that smoking is less dangerous than the stresses it helps alleviate).

In a classic study of cognitive dissonance, subjects were asked to perform a dull task and then to persuade others that this task was interesting and enjoyable. Some were paid one dollar to do this, while others were paid $20, and all of their attitudes toward the task were measured at the conclusion of the experiment. The subjects who had been paid one dollar showed a marked improvement in their attitude toward the task, while the more highly paid subjects did not. The designers of the experiment interpreted their results in the following way. Cognitive dissonance was created in all of the subjects by the conflicting facts that the task had been boring and that they were saying it was interesting—their statements and beliefs did not match. However, those who were paid $20 had been given a justification for lying: they could tell themselves that their actions made some kind of sense. However, the actions of the other group made no sense unless they could persuade themselves that the task had indeed been interesting. Thus they acted to reduce the dissonance by changing their original belief.

Children have shown similar responses to experimental situations involving cognitive dissonance. In one case, children were asked not to play with an appealing toy. One experimenter made this request mildly and politely while another one made it in a threatening fashion. Those children who had accommodated the polite request also became less attracted to the toy, since liking the toy and giving it up were conflicting experiences that created dissonance. However, the children who were threatened felt no pressure to change their opinions about the toy since they had a logical reason for giving it up.

Several types of cognitive dissonance have been identified. In post-decision dissonance, a person must decide between two choices, each of which has both positive and negative components (in other contexts, this type of situation is called a multiple approach-avoidance conflict). Forced compliance dissonance occurs when people are forced to act in ways that conflict with their beliefs and can not find any way to justify their actions to themselves. Dissonance also occurs when people are exposed to new information that threatens or changes their current beliefs. Various group situations also generate cognitive dissonance. It occurs when a person must abandon old beliefs or adopt new ones in order to join a group, when

Group situations sometimes create cognitive dissonance. A potential member of a group will change his or her opinions to conform to the group's collective opinion. In Hitler's Germany, this had tragic consequences. *(Bildarchiv Preussischer Kulturbursitz. Reproduced with permission.)*

members disagree with each other, and when the group as a whole has its central beliefs threatened by an external event or by the receipt of new information.

Festinger proposed that some individuals have a higher tolerance for cognitive dissonance than others. Subsequent researchers have found correlations between various **personality traits**, such as **extroversion**, and the ability to withstand dissonance.

**Further Reading**
Festinger, Leon. *A Theory of Cognitive Dissonance.* Stanford, CA: Stanford University Press, 1957.

# Cognitive psychology

An approach to psychology which focuses on the relationship between cognitive or mental processes and behavior.

The cognitive psychologist studies human perceptions and the ways in which cognitive processes operate to produce responses. Cognitive processes (which may involve language, symbols, or imagery) include perceiving, recognizing, remembering, imagining, conceptualizing, judging, reasoning, and processing information for planning, problem-solving, and other applications. Some cognitive psychologists may study how internal cognitive operations can transform symbols of the external world, others on the interplay between genetics and **environment** in determining individual **cognitive development** and capabilities. Still other cognitive psychologists may focus their studies on how the mind detects, selects, recognizes, and verbally represents features of a particular stimulus. Among the many specific topics investigated by cognitive psychologists are language acquisition; visual and auditory **perception**; information storage and retrieval; altered states of **consciousness**; cognitive restructuring (how the mind mediates between conflicting, or dissonant, information); and individual styles of thought and perception.

The challenges of studying human **cognition** are evident when one considers the work of the mind in processing the simultaneous and sometimes conflicting information presented in daily life, through both internal and external stimuli. For example, an individual may feel hunger pangs, the external heat of the sun, and sensations of bodily movement produced by walking while simultaneously talking, listening to a companion, and recalling past experiences. Although this **attention** to multiple stimuli is a common phenomenon, complex cognitive processing is clearly required to accomplish it.

At its inception as a discipline in the nineteenth century, psychology focused on mental processes. However, the prevailing structuralist methods, which analyzed consciousness introspectively by breaking it down into sensations, images, and affective states, fell out of favor early in the twentieth century and were superseded by those of the behaviorists, who replaced speculation about inner processes with the study of external, observable phenomena. Although important inroads continued to be made into the study of mental processes—including the work of the Würzburg School, the Gestalt psychologists, the field theory of **Kurt Lewin**, and **Jean Piaget**'s theories of cognitive development in children—the behaviorist focus remained dominant in the United States through the middle of the twentieth century.

Since the 1950s, cognitive approaches have assumed a central place in psychological research and theorizing. One of its foremost pioneers is **Jerome Bruner**, who, together with his colleague Leo Postman, did important work on the ways in which needs, motivations, and expectations (or "mental sets") affect perception. Bruner's work led him to an interest in the cognitive development of children and related issues of education, and he later developed a theory of cognitive growth. His theories, which approached development from a different angle than—and mostly complement—those of Piaget, focus on the environmental and experiential factors influencing each individual's specific development pattern.

In 1957, **Leon Festinger** advanced his classic theory of **cognitive dissonance**, which describes how people manage conflicting cognitions about themselves, their behavior, or their environment. Festinger posited that conflict among such cognitions (which he termed dissonance) will make people uncomfortable enough to actually modify one of the conflicting beliefs to bring it into line with the other belief. Thus, for example, the conflicting cognitions "I smoke" and "smoking is bad" will lead a smoker either to alter the first statement by quitting, or the second one by telling himself or herself that smoking is not bad. In 1960, Jerome Bruner and George A. Miller established the Harvard Center for Cognitive Studies, which became influential in the "cognitive revolution." As a result, an increasing number of experimental psychologists abandoned behaviorist studies of rats and mazes for research involving the higher mental processes in human beings. This trend in psychology paralleled advances in several other fields, including neuroscience, mathematics, anthropology, and computer science.

Language became an important area of study for cognitive psychologists. In 1953, the term "psycholinguistics" was coined to designate an emerging area of common interest, the psychology of language, and **Noam Chomsky**, a professor at the Massachusetts Institute of Technology, became its most famous proponent. Chomsky argued that the underlying logic, or deep structure, of all languages is the same and that human mastery of it is genetically determined, not learned. His work has been highly controversial, rekindling the age-old debate over whether language exists in the mind before experience. Other well-known studies in cognitive psychology includes that of D.E. Berlyne's work on curiosity and information seeking; George Kelly's theory of personal constructs, and investigations by Herman Witkin, Riley Gardner, and George Klein on individual perceptual and cognitive styles.

The emergence of cybernetics and computer science have been central to contemporary advances in cognitive psychology, including computer simulation of cognitive processes for research purposes and the creation of information-processing models. Herbert Simon and Allen Newell created the first computer simulation of human thought, called Logic Theorist, at Carnegie-Mellon University in 1956, followed by General Problem Solver (GPS) the next year. Other major contributions in this area include D.E. Broadbent's information theory of attention, learning, and **memory**, and Miller, Galanter, and

Pribram's analysis of planning and problem solving. Despite skepticism that computer-generated "thought" will ever match human cognition, the study of **artificial intelligence** has helped scientists learn more about the human mind. In turn, this type of psychological research is expected to aid in the development of more sophisticated computers in the future through links between the psychological study of cognition and research in electrophysiology and computer science. This subfield of cognitive engineering focuses on the application of knowledge about human thought processes to the design of complex systems for aviation, industry, and other areas.

At one time, the study of cognitive processes was specific to cognitive psychology. As research began to yield information regarding the applicability of these processes to all areas of psychology, the study of cognitive processes was taken up and applied in many other subfields of psychology, such as abnormal and **developmental psychology**. Today, the term "cognitive perspective" or "cognitive approach" is applied in a broader sense to these and other areas of psychology.

*See also* Abnormal psychology; Cognitive behavior therapy; Cognitive development; Information-processing approach

# Cognitive therapy

Cognitive therapy is a psychosocial therapy that assumes that faulty cognitive, or thought, patterns cause maladaptive behavior and emotional responses. The treatment focuses on changing thoughts in order to adjust psychological and personality problems.

## Purpose

Psychologist **Aaron Beck** developed the cognitive therapy concept in the 1960s. The treatment is based on the principle that maladaptive behavior (ineffective, self-defeating behavior) is triggered by inappropriate or irrational thinking patterns, called automatic thoughts. Instead of reacting to the reality of a situation, an individual automatically reacts to his or her own distorted viewpoint of the situation. Cognitive therapy focuses on changing these thought patterns (also known as cognitive distortions), by examining the rationality and validity of the assumptions behind them. This process is termed cognitive restructuring.

Cognitive therapy is a treatment option for a number of mental disorders, including agoraphobia, **Alzheimer's disease**, anxiety or panic disorder, **attention deficit-hy-**

peractivity disorder (ADHD), **eating disorders**, **mood** disorders, **obsessive-compulsive disorder** (OCD), **personality** disorders, **post-traumatic stress disorder (PTSD)**, **psychotic disorders**, **schizophrenia**, social **phobia**, and substance abuse disorders. It can be useful in helping individuals with **anger** management problems, and has been reported to be effective in treating insomnia. It is also frequently prescribed as an adjunct, or complementary, therapy for patients suffering from back **pain**, cancer, rheumatoid arthritis, and other chronic pain conditions.

## Treatment techniques

Cognitive therapy is usually administered in an outpatient setting (clinic or doctor's office) by a therapist trained or certified in cognitive therapy techniques. Therapy may be in either individual or group sessions, and the course of treatment is short compared to traditional **psychotherapy** (often 12 sessions or less). Therapists are psychologists (Ph.D., Psy.D., Ed.D., or M.A. degree), clinical social workers (M.S.W., D.S.W., or L.S.W. degree), counselors (M.A. or M.S. degree), or psychiatrists (M.D. trained in psychiatry).

Therapists use several different techniques in the course of cognitive therapy to help patients examine thoughts and behaviors. These include:

- *Validity testing.* The therapist asks the patient to defend his or her thoughts and beliefs. If the patient cannot produce objective evidence supporting his or her assumptions, the invalidity, or faulty nature, is exposed.

- *Cognitive rehearsal.* The patient is asked to imagine a difficult situation he or she has encountered in the past, and then works with the therapist to practice how to successfully cope with the problem. When the patient is confronted with a similar situation again, the rehearsed behavior will be drawn on to deal with it.

- *Guided discovery.* The therapist asks the patient a series of questions designed to guide the patient towards the discovery of his or her cognitive distortions.

- *Journaling.* Patients keep a detailed written diary of situations that arise in everyday life, the thoughts and emotions surrounding them, and the behavior that accompany them. The therapist and patient then review the journal together to discover maladaptive thought patterns and how these thoughts impact behavior.

- *Homework.* In order to encourage self-discovery and reinforce insights made in therapy, the therapist may ask the patient to do homework assignments. These may include note-taking during the session, journaling (see above), review of an audiotape of the patient session, or reading books or articles appropriate to the therapy. They may also be more behaviorally focused, applying a newly learned strategy or coping mechanism to a situation, and then recording the results for the next therapy session.

- *Modeling.* Role-playing exercises allow the therapist to act out appropriate reactions to different situations. The patient can then model this behavior.

Cognitive-behavioral therapy (CBT) integrates features of behavioral modification into the traditional cognitive restructuring approach. In cognitive-behavioral therapy, the therapist works with the patient to identify the thoughts that are causing distress, and employs behavioral therapy techniques to alter the resulting behavior. Patients may have certain fundamental core beliefs, known as schemas, which are flawed, and are having a negative impact on the patient's behavior and functioning. For example, a patient suffering from **depression** may develop a social phobia because he/she is convinced he/she is uninteresting and impossible to love. A cognitive-behavioral therapist would test this assumption by asking the patient to name family and friends that care for him/her and enjoy his/her company. By showing the patient that others value him/her, the therapist exposes the irrationality of the patient's assumption and also provides a new model of thought for the patient to change his/her previous behavior pattern (i.e., I am an interesting and likeable person, therefore I should not have any problem making new social acquaintances). Additional behavioral techniques such as **conditioning** (the use of positive and/or negative reinforcements to encourage desired behavior) and systematic **desensitization** (gradual exposure to anxiety-producing situations in order to extinguish the **fear** response) may then be used to gradually reintroduce the patient to social situations.

## Preparation

Cognitive therapy may not be appropriate for all patients. Patients with significant cognitive impairments (e.g., patients with traumatic **brain** injury or organic brain disease) and individuals who are not willing to take an active role in the treatment process are not usually good candidates.

Because cognitive therapy is a collaborative effort between therapist and patient, a comfortable working relationship is critical to successful treatment. Individuals interested in cognitive therapy should schedule a consultation session with their prospective therapist before starting treatment. The consultation session is similar to an interview session, and it allows both patient and therapist to get to know one another. During the consultation, the therapist gathers information to make an initial assessment of the patient and to recommend both direction and goals for treatment. The patient has the opportunity to learn about the therapist's professional credentials, his/her approach to treatment, and other relevant issues.

In some managed-care settings, an intake interview is required before a patient can meet with a therapist. The intake interview is typically performed by a psychiatric nurse, counselor, or social worker, either face-to-face or over the phone. It is used to gather a brief background on treatment history and make a preliminary evaluation of the patient before assigning them to a therapist.

## Typical results

Because cognitive therapy is employed for such a broad spectrum of illnesses, and is often used in conjunction with medications and other treatment interventions, it is difficult to measure overall success rates for the therapy. Cognitive and cognitive behavior treatments have been among those therapies not likely to be evaluated, however, and efficacy is well-documented for some symptoms and problems.

Some studies have shown that cognitive therapy can reduce relapse rates in depression and in schizophrenia, particularly in those patients who respond only marginally to antidepressant medication. It has been suggested that this is because cognitive therapy focuses on changing the thoughts and associated behavior underlying these disorders rather than just relieving the distressing symptoms associated with them.

Paula Ford-Martin

## Further Reading

Alford, B.A. and Beck, A.T. *The integrative power of cognitive therapy.* New York: Guilford, 1997.

Beck, A.T. *Prisoners of hate: the cognitive basis of anger, hostility, and violence.* New York: Harper Collins Publishers, 1999.

Greenberger, Dennis and Christine Padesky. *Mind over mood: a cognitive therapy treatment manual for clients.* New York: Guilford Press, 1995.

## Further Information

Beck Institute For Cognitive Therapy And Research. GSB Building, City Line and Belmont Avenues, Suite 700, Bala Cynwyd, PA, USA. 19004-1610, fax: (610)664-4437, (610)664-3020. Email: beckinst@gim.net. http://www.beckinstitute.org.

# Robert Martin Coles

### 1929-
American psychiatrist and author.

Psychiatrist and author Robert Coles pioneered the use of oral history as a method of studying children. His

**Robert Coles** *(AP/Wide World Photos, Inc. Reproduced with permission.)*

five-volume series of books called *Children in Crisis*, published from 1967-1978, won a Pulitzer Prize in recognition of its wide-ranging examination of children throughout the world and how they cope with war, poverty, and other crises. Trained as a pediatrician as well as a psychiatrist, Coles became a professor of psychiatry and medical humanities at Harvard University Medical School in 1978. His lifelong interest in children has generated more than 50 books.

Coles was born in 1929 in Boston to parents who encouraged him to read what he has called "spiritually alert" novelists such as Tolstoy and George Eliot. His mother was a lifelong community worker; his father's values were exemplified in his work from the mid-1960s to the mid-1980s as an advocate for poor, elderly residents of Boston. Coles studied medicine and psychiatry in Boston before serving two years as a U.S. Air Force physician. During advanced training in **psychoanalysis** in New Orleans, Coles reached a turning point. Deeply moved by the sight of a young black girl being heckled by white segregationists, in 1960 Coles began his examination of children and their hopes and fears by studying school desegregation in New Orleans. "History had knocked on the city's door—a city whose people were frightened and divided. Had I not been there, driving by the mobs that heckled six-year-old Ruby Bridges, a black first-grader, as she tried to attend the Frantz School, I might have pursued a different life," Coles writes in the introduction to *The Spiritual Life of Children*." I had planned until then to enter the profession of psychoanalytic child psychiatry. Instead, I became a 'field worker,' learning to talk with children going through their everyday lives amid substantial social and educational stress."

Traveling from the Deep South to Appalachia, from New Mexico to Alaska, Coles eventually traveled overseas to Europe, Africa, Central and South America, and the Middle East. His wife, Jane, and their three sons began to share in some of the research, as they talked to children of all races and social status about religion, race, poverty, and war. During his career, Coles has written for various medical, psychiatric, and psychoanalytic journals, in addition to seeing patients when possible. He has also volunteered as a tutor in a school for underprivileged children. Besides *Children in Crisis*, Coles's prominent books include *The Moral Life of Children*, *The Political Life of Children*, *The Spiritual Life of Children,* and *Women of Crisis*.

## Further Reading

Coles, Robert. *The Mind's Fate: A Psychiatrist Looks at His Profession*. Boston: Little, Brown and Co., 1975.
Gordon, Mary. "What They Think About God." *The New York Times Book Review*, November 25, 1990, p.1+.
Gray, Francine du Plessix. "When We Are Good We Are Very, Very Good." *The New York Times Book Review*, November 21, 1993, p. 9.

# Color vision

The ability to perceive color.

Color **vision** is a function of the **brain**'s ability to interpret the complex way in which light is reflected off every object in nature. What the human eye sees as color is not a quality of an object itself, nor a quality of the light reflected off the object; it is actually an effect of the stimulation of different parts of the brain's visual system by the varying wavelengths of light.

Each of three types of light receptors called cones, located in the retina of the eye, recognizes certain ranges of wavelengths of light as blue, green, or red. From the cones, color signals pass via neurons along the visual pathway where they are mixed and matched to create the **perception** of the full spectrum of 5 million colors in the world.

Because each person's neurons are unique, each of us sees color somewhat differently. Color blindness, an

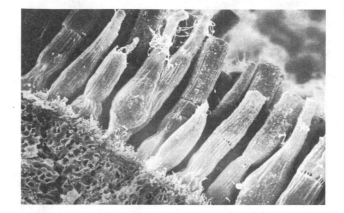

**Scanning electron micrograph (SEM) of the eye's rods and cones.** *(Omikron/Photo Researchers, Inc. Reproduced with permission.)*

inherited condition which affects more men than women, has two varieties: monochromats lack all cone receptors and cannot see any color; dichromats lack either red-green or blue-yellow cone receptors and cannot perceive hues in those respective ranges. Another phenomenon, known as color weakness or anomalous trichromat, refers to the situation where a person can perceive a given color, but needs greater intensity of the associated wavelength in order to see it normally.

*See also* Vision

# Coma

An abnormal state of profound unconsciousness accompanied by the absence of all voluntary behavior and most reflexes.

A coma may be induced by a severe neurological injury—either temporary or permanent—or by other physical trauma. A comatose individual cannot be aroused by even the most intense stimuli, although he or she may show some automatic movements in response to **pain**. Comas often occur just before death in the course of many diseases. The affected **brain** cells may be either near the surface (cerebral cortex) or deeper in the brain (diencephalon or brainstem). Specific conditions that produce comas include cerebral hemorrhage; blood clots in the brain; failure of oxygen supply to the brain; tumors; intracranial infections that cause meningitis or encephalitis; poisoning, especially by carbon monoxide or sedatives; concussion; and disorders involving electrolytes. Comas may also be caused by metabolic abnormalities that impair the functioning of the brain through a sharp drop in the blood sugar level, such as diabetes.

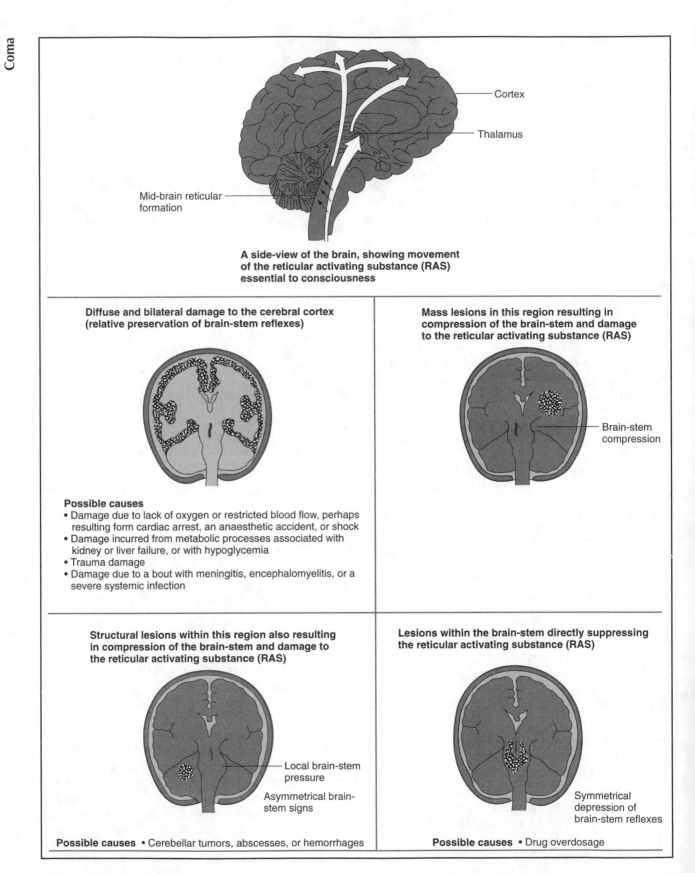

A side-view of the brain, showing movement of the reticular activating substance (RAS) essential to consciousness

Cortex

Thalamus

Mid-brain reticular formation

**Diffuse and bilateral damage to the cerebral cortex (relative preservation of brain-stem reflexes)**

**Possible causes**
- Damage due to lack of oxygen or restricted blood flow, perhaps resulting form cardiac arrest, an anaesthetic accident, or shock
- Damage incurred from metabolic processes associated with kidney or liver failure, or with hypoglycemia
- Trauma damage
- Damage due to a bout with meningitis, encephalomyelitis, or a severe systemic infection

**Mass lesions in this region resulting in compression of the brain-stem and damage to the reticular activating substance (RAS)**

Brain-stem compression

**Structural lesions within this region also resulting in compression of the brain-stem and damage to the reticular activating substance (RAS)**

Local brain-stem pressure

Asymmetrical brain-stem signs

**Possible causes** • Cerebellar tumors, abscesses, or hemorrhages

**Lesions within the brain-stem directly suppressing the reticular activating substance (RAS)**

Symmetrical depression of brain-stem reflexes

**Possible causes** • Drug overdosage

**The four brain conditions that result in coma.** *(Hans & Cassidy. Gale Group. Reproduced with permission.)*

The passage from wakefulness to coma can be rapid and/or gradual. Often, it is preceded by lethargy and then a state resembling light **sleep**. In general, treatment of a coma involves avoiding further damage to the brain by maintaining the patient's respiratory and cardiac functions, and by an intravenous (usually glucose) nutritional supply to the brain.

## Combat neurosis

The preferred term to describe mental disturbances related to the stress of military combat; also known by such alternative terms as combat fatigue syndrome, shell shock, operational or battle fatigue, combat exhaustion, and war neurosis.

Combat neurosis describes any **personality** disturbance that represents a response to the **stress** of war. It is closely related to **post-traumatic stress disorder**, and is often characterized under that term. Symptoms of the disturbance may appear during the battle itself, or may appear days, weeks, months, or even years later. An estimated ten percent of all personnel who fought in World War II experienced symptoms of combat neurosis, known then according to the **American Psychiatric Association** as "gross stress reaction." (The term was applied to personality disturbances resulting from catastrophes other than war as well.) More recently, considerable attention from both the general public and the medical community has focused on the combat neuroses experienced by those who fought during the Vietnam and Persian Gulf Wars. There is no specific set of symptoms that are triggered by war or combat; rather, in most cases, the disturbance begins with feelings of mild anxiety.

Symptoms of combat neuroses vary widely. The first signs are typically increased irritability and problems with sleeping. As the disturbance progresses, symptoms include **depression**, bereavement-type reactions (characterized as **guilt** over having survived when others did not), **nightmares**, and persistent, terrifying daydreams. The inability to concentrate and loss of **memory** are also common. Emotional indifference, withdrawal, lack of attention to personal hygiene and appearance, and self-endangering behaviors are also possible signs of combat neurosis. Individuals suffering from combat neurosis often react to these symptoms by abusing alcohol or drugs.

Combat neuroses can be a severe mental disorder and the potential success of treatment varies considerably. Some patients are treated successfully with antidepressant and antianxiety medications. For a small percentage, however, hospitalization may be required.

*See also* Post-traumatic stress disorder

### Further Reading
Herman, Judith Lewis. *Trauma and Recovery.* New York: Basic Books, 1992.
Porterfield, Kay Marie. *Straight Talk About Post-traumatic Stress Disorder: Coping With the Aftermath of Trauma.* New York: Facts on File, 1996.
Waites, Elizabeth A. *Trauma and Survival: Post-traumatic and Dissociative Disorders in Women.* New York: Norton, 1993.

## Communication skills and disorders

The skills needed to use language (spoken, written, signed, or otherwise communicated) to interact with others, and problems related to the development of these skills.

Language employs symbols—words, gestures, or spoken sounds—to represent objects and ideas. Communication of language begins with spoken sounds combined with gestures, relying on two different types of skills. Children first acquire the skills to receive communications, that is, listening to and understanding what they hear (supported by accompanying gestures). Next, they will begin experimenting with expressing themselves through speaking and gesturing. Speaking will begin as repetitive syllables, followed by words, phrases, and sentences. Later, children will acquire the skills of reading and writing, the written forms of communication. Although milestones are discussed for the development of these skills of communication, many children begin speaking significantly earlier or later than the milestone date. Parents should refrain from attaching too much significance to either deviation from the average. When a child's deviation from the average milestones of development cause the parents concern, they may contact a pediatrician or other professional for advice.

Spoken language problems are referred to by a number of labels, including **language delay**, language **disability**, or a specific type of language disability. In general, experts distinguish between those people who seem to be slow in developing spoken language (language delay) and those who seem to have difficulty achieving a milestone of spoken language (language disorders). Language disorders include stuttering; articulation disorders, such as substituting one sound for another (tandy for candy), omitting a sound (canny for candy), or distorting a sound (shlip for sip); and voice disorders, such as inappropriate pitch, volume, or quality. Causes can be related to **hear-**

## COMMUNICATION MILESTONES

| Age | Milestone |
|---|---|
| 0–12 months | • Responds to speech by looking at the speaker; responds differently to aspects of speakers voice (such as friendly or angry, male or female).<br>• Turns head in direction of sound.<br>• Responds with gestures to greetings such as "hi," "bye-bye," and "up" when these words are accompanied by appropriate gestures by speaker.<br>• Stops ongoing activity when told "no," when speaker uses appropriate gesture and tone.<br>• May say two or three words by around 12 months of age, although probably not clearly.<br>• Repeats some vowel and consonant sounds (babbles) when alone or spoken to; attempts to imitate sounds. |
| 12–24 months | • Responds correctly when asked "where?"<br>• Understands prepositions *on, in,* and *under;* and understands simple phrases (such as "Get the ball.")<br>• Says 8–10 words by around age 18 months; by age two, vocabulary will include 20–50 words, mostly describing people, common objects, and events (such as "more" and "all gone").<br>• Uses single word plus a gesture to ask for objects.<br>• Refers to self by name; uses "my" or "mine." |
| 24–36 months | • Points to pictures of common objects when they are named.<br>• Can identify objects when told their use.<br>• Understands questions with "what" and "where" and negatives "no." "not," "can't," and don't."<br>• Responds to simple directions.<br>• Selects and looks at picture books; enjoys listening to simple stories, and asks for them to be read aloud again.<br>• Joins two vocabulary words together to make a phrase.<br>• Can say first and last name.<br>• Shows frustration at not being understood. |
| 36–48 months | • Begins to understand time concepts, such as "today," "later," "tomorrow," and "yesterday."<br>• Understands comparisons, such as "big" and "bigger."<br>• Forms sentences with three or more words.<br>• Speech is understandable to most strangers, but some sound errors may persists (such as "t" sound for "k" sound). |
| 48–60 months | • By 48 months, has a vocabulary of over 200 words.<br>• Follows two or three unrelated commands in proper order.<br>• Understands sequencing of events, for example, "First we have to go to the grocery store, and then we can go to the playground."<br>• Ask questions using "when," "how," and why." Talks about causes for things using "because." |

ing, nerve/muscle disorders, head injury, viral diseases, **mental retardation**, drug abuse, or cleft lip or palate.

### Further Reading

Bates, Elizabeth, and Jeffrey Elman. "Learning Rediscovered." *Science* 274, (December 13, 1996): 1849+.

Berko-Gleason, J. *The Development of Language.* New York: Macmillan, 1993.

Cowley, Geoffrey. "The Language Explosion." *Newsweek* 129, (Spring-Summer 1997): 16+.

Goodluck, H. *Language Acquisition: A Linguistic Introduction.* Cambridge, MA: Blackwell Publishers, 1991.

Pinker, S. *The Language Instinct.* New York: Morrow, 1994.

### Further Information

American Speech-Language-Hearing Association. 1801 Rockville Pike, Rockville, MD 20852, voice or TTY(301) 897–8682, voice or TTY (800) 638–8255. Email: ir-casha.org. www.asha.org. (Publishes brochures, booklets, and fact sheets on speech-language pathology.)

National Institute on Deafness and Other Communication Disorders. National Institutes of Health, Bethesda, MD 20892. Email: webmaster@ms.nih.gov. www.nih.gov/nidcd/.

# Comparative psychology

A subfield of experimental psychology which focuses on the study of animals for the purpose of comparing the behavior of different species.

Studies of animal behavior have taken two main directions in the twentieth century. The type of research most often practiced in the United States has been animal research, involving the study of animals in laboratories and emphasizing the effects of **environment** on behavior. European research, by comparison, has been more closely associated with the area of inquiry known as **ethology**, which concentrates on studying animals in their natural environment and emphasizes the evolution of behavioral patterns which are typical of a particular species. Prompting an increase in the study of animal behavior, ethology has laid the groundwork for an understanding of species-typical behavior and also led to progress in relating and contrasting behaviors among different species. Comparative psychology serves a number of functions. It provides information about the genetic relations among different species, furthers understanding of human behavior, tests the limitations of psychological theories, and aids in the conservation of the natural environment.

# Competence to stand trial

The ability of a person charged with a crime to understand the nature and purpose of the criminal proceedings.

Defendants in a criminal trial must have the **ability** (i.e., the competence) to understand the charges, to consult with an attorney, and to have a rational grasp of the courtroom proceedings. This requirement is a longstanding and fundamental principle of criminal law. Its purpose is to ensure that defendants can participate meaningfully in their own defense. The requirement refers to the defendant's competence at the time of the trial, rather than their psychological state at the time of the alleged offense. Rationality is a key issue in competency determinations. People judged to be incompetent usually lack the ability to understand, communicate, or

make rational decisions. The legal requirement, however, does not indicate how judgments about competency should be make. Furthermore, some cases are more complex than others. Consequently it is possible for a defendant to be competent for certain kinds of legal proceedings, but not for others.

There are a number of questions that evaluators might seek to answer when making a competency determination. Does the defendant understand the charges? Does he appreciate the possible penalties? Does he appreciate the adversarial nature of the courtroom? Can he discuss legal strategy with his lawyer? Can he behave appropriately in the courtroom? Can he provide meaningful testimony in his own defense? The issue of competence can arise at any point during criminal proceedings, and may be initiated by the defense, by the prosecutor, or by the judge. Prior to 1972, defendants found to be incompetent could be confined to **mental hospitals** for very lengthy periods of time—sometimes for a longer period than they would have served if they had been found guilty. A U. S. Supreme Court ruling in 1972 restricted the length of time a defendant could be hospitalized because of incompetence to stand trial.

Once the question of competence arises, a competency evaluation will be conducted. The evaluation typically takes place in a special hospital or clinic. A number of professionals may be qualified to conduct such examinations, including physicians, psychiatrists, psychologists, and social workers. There are several different psychological tests or procedures that designed to assist in the assessment of competence to stand trial. One of these is the Competency Screening Test (CST). It is a 22-item sentence completion test that requires the test-taker to complete sentence stems, such as: "When I go to court, the lawyer will _____." Answers are scored as indicating competence, questionable competence, or incompetence. Total scores are calculated with a cutoff score that indicates possible incompetence. Another assessment test is the Competency Assessment Instrument (CAI). It consists of a detailed face-to-face interview about various aspects of competent functioning, including an appreciation of the charges and an understanding of the various roles of the judge, witnesses, jury, prosecutor, etc.

Research has shown that when competency evaluations occur, most (70%) of the defendants who are assessed are judged competent. As a group, those judged incompetent tend to have been charged with more serious crimes, compared to defendants in general. They also are likely to have a history of **psychosis**, to have a serious current mental disorder, and to be poorly educated. Once a defendant is judged to be competent, the legal proceedings are resumed and a trial takes place. If the defendant is found incompetent, the charges may be dropped for crimes that are not serious. Otherwise the defendant is returned to an institution until competency can be restored. Until then, all legal proceedings are postponed. If competency cannot be restored within a reasonable period of time (e.g., within a year or so), defendants may be committed to a hospital through involuntary civil (i.e., noncriminal) proceedings.

Theodore Kaczynski was accused in April, 1996 of being the serial bomber who built homemade bombs that killed three people and injured many others between 1978 and 1995. At the beginning of his trial he disrupted the proceedings because of a dispute with his lawyers about his defense. His request to represent himself and an attempted suicide provoked concerns about his competence. The court requested a competency assessment. Kaczynski (also known as the Unabomber) was judged by the psychiatrist who conducted the assessment to be legally competent to stand trial. In her report to the court, the psychiatrist said that Kaczynski was not suffering from any mental defect that could prevent him from understanding the nature of the charges, or from assisting his lawyers in mounting a defense. On the other hand, she noted that he was suffering from paranoid **schizophrenia**. Ultimately, a trial was averted when he agreed to plead guilty to numerous charges in exchange for a promise that prosecutors would not seek the death penalty during his sentencing. He was sentenced to four life terms plus 30 years with no possibility of parole. The Unabomber case provides a good illustration of a situation in which a **psychological disorder** did not necessarily harm the defendant's ability to participate meaningfully in the trial proceedings.

Timothy Moore

## Further Reading
Wrightsman, L., Nietzel, M., & Fortune, W. *Psychology and the Legal System.* New York: Brooks Cole, 1998.

# Competition

An adaptive strategy that pits one person's interests against another's.

Psychologists have long been in disagreement as to whether competition is a learned or a genetic component of human behavior. Perhaps what first comes to mind when thinking of competition is athletics. It would be a mistake, however, not to recognize the effect competition has in the areas of academics, work, and many other areas of contemporary life. This is especially true in the United States, where individual rigor and competition appear to be nationalistic qualities Americans cherish and praise. It has often been suggested that the American capitalist-driven society thrives because of the spirited competition for a limited amount of resources available.

Psychologically speaking, competition has been seen as an inevitable consequence of the psychoanalytic view of human drives and is a natural state of being. According to **Sigmund Freud**, humans are born screaming for attention and full of organic drives for fulfillment in various areas. Initially, according to this view, we compete for the attention of our parents—seeking to attract it either from siblings or from the other parent. Thereafter, we are at the mercy of a battle between our base impulses for self-fulfillment and social and cultural mores which prohibit pure indulgence.

Current work in anthropology has suggested, however, that this view of the role of competition in human behavior may be incorrect. Thomas Hobbes (1588-1679), one of the great philosophers of the seventeenth century, is perhaps best remembered for his characterization of the "natural world," that is, the world before the imposition of the will of humanity, as being "nasty, brutish, and short." This image of the pre-rational world is still widely held, reinforced by **Charles Darwin**'s seminal work, *The Origin of Species,* which established the doctrine of natural selection. This doctrine, which posits that those species best able to adapt to and master the natural **environment** in which they live will survive, has suggested to many that the struggle for survival is an inherent human trait which determines a person's success. Darwin's theory has even been summarized as "survival of the fittest"—a phrase Darwin himself never used—further highlighting competition's role in success. As it has often been pointed out, however, there is nothing in the concept of natural selection that suggests that competition is the most successful strategy for "survival of the fittest." Darwin asserted in *The Origin of Species* that the struggles he was describing should be viewed as metaphors and could easily include dependence and cooperation.

Many studies have been conducted to test the importance placed on competition as opposed to other values, such as cooperation—by various cultures, and generally conclude that Americans uniquely praise competition as natural, inevitable, and desirable. In 1937, the world-renowned anthropologist **Margaret Mead** published *Cooperation and Competition among Primitive Peoples,* based on her studies of several societies that did not prize competition, and, in fact, seemed at times to place a negative value on it. One such society was the Zuni Indians of Arizona, and they, Mead found, valued cooperation far more than competition. For example, the Zuni held a ritu-

**Dominique Dawes on the uneven bars during competition. Psychologists disagree as to whether competition is a learned or genetic component of human behavior.** *(AP/Wide World Photos. Reproduced with permission.)*

al footrace that anyone could participate in, the winner of which was never publicly acknowledged and, in fact, if one person made a habit of winning the race, that person was prevented from participating in the future. After studying dozens of such cultures, Mead's final conclusion was that competitiveness is a culturally created aspect of human behavior, and that its prevalence in a particular society is relative to how that society values it.

### Further Reading

Boyd, David. "Strategic Behaviour in Contests: Evidence from the 1992 Barcelona Olympic Games." *Applied Economics* (November 1995): 1037.

Clifford, Nancy. "How Competitive Are You?" *Teen Magazine* (September 1995): 56.

Epstein, Joseph. *Ambition: The Secret Passion.* New York: E.P. Dutton, 1980.

Freud, Anna. *The Writings of Anna Freud.* Vol. 6, *Normality and Pathology in Childhood: Assessments of Development.* International Universities Press, 1965.

Kohn, Alfie. *No Contest: The Case Against Competition.* Boston: Houghton Mifflin, 1986.

Mithers, Carol. "The Need to Compete: Why Competition Is Good for You." *Ladies Home Journal* (February 1995): 136.

# Concept formation

Learning process by which items are categorized and related to each other.

A concept is a generalization that helps to organize information into categories. For example, the concept "square" is used to describe those things that have four equal sides and four right angles. Thus, the concept categorize things whose properties meet the set requirements. The way young children learn concepts has been studied in experimental situations using so-called artificial concepts such as "square." In contrast, real-life, or natural, concepts have characteristic rather than defining features. For example, a robin would be a prototypical or "good" example of the concept "bird." A penguin lacks an important defining feature of this category—flight, and thus is not as strong an example of a "bird." Similarly, for many children the concept "house" represents a squarish structure with walls, windows, and a chimney that provides shelter. In later development, the child's concept of house would be expanded to include nontypical examples, such as "teepee" or "igloo," both of which have some but not all of the prototypical characteristics that the children have learned for this concept.

Natural concepts are often learned through the use of prototypes, highly typical examples of a category—like the robin cited above. The other major method of concept learning is through the trial-and-error method of testing hypotheses. People will guess or assume that a certain item is an instance of a particular concept; they then learn more about the concept when they see whether their hypothesis is correct or not.

People learn simple concepts more readily than complex ones. For example, the easiest concept to learn is one with only a single defining feature. The next easiest is one with multiple features, all of which must be present in every case, known as the conjunctive concept. In conjunctive concepts, *and* links all the required attributes. For example, the concept square is defined by four sides *and* four 90-degree angles. It is more difficult to master a so-called disjunctive concept, when either one feature or another must be present. People also learn concepts more easily when they are given positive rather than negative examples of a concept (e.g., shown what it is rather than what it is not).

### Further Reading

Bruner, Jerome S. *Studies in Cognitive Growth: A Collaboration at the Center for Cognitive Studies.* New York: Wiley, 1966.

Ginsburg, Herbert, and Sylvia Opper. *Piaget's Theory of Intellectual Development.* 3rd ed. Englewood Cliffs, NJ: Prentice-Hall, 1988.

Lee, Victor, and Prajna Das Gupta. (eds.) *Children's Cognitive and Language Development.* Cambridge, MA: Blackwell Publishers, 1995.

McShane, John. *Cognitive Development: An Information Processing Approach.* Oxford, Eng.: B. Blackwell, 1991.

Piaget, Jean, and Barbel Inhelder. *The Growth of Logical Thinking from Childhood to Adolescence.* New York: Basic Books, 1958.

Sameroff, Arnold J., and Marshall M. Haith. (eds.) *The Five to Seven Year Shift: The Age of Reason and Responsibility.* Chicago: University of Chicago Press, 1991.

# Conditioned response

In classical conditioning, behavior that is learned in response to a particular stimulus.

Reflexive behaviors occur when an animal encounters a stimulus that naturally leads to a reflex. For example, a loud noise generates a fright response. If an initially neutral stimulus is paired with the noise, that neutral or **conditioned stimulus** produces a fright response. In

**classical conditioning**, the response to the conditioned stimulus is called a conditioned response.

Conditioned responses develop in a process called acquisition, in which the natural or unconditioned stimulus is paired with the conditioned stimulus. Some responses develop more quickly than others; similarly, some responses are stronger than others. The nature of the conditioned response depends on the circumstances in which acquisition occurs. The conditioned response emerges most effectively if the conditioned stimulus appears slightly before the unconditioned stimulus. This process is called "delayed conditioning" because the unconditioned stimulus is delayed relative to the conditioned stimulus. The response is weaker if the conditioned and unconditioned stimuli begin together, and becomes even weaker if the unconditioned stimulus precedes the conditioned stimulus. In general, the conditioned response resembles the unconditioned response (e.g., the normal fright response) very closely. Psychologists have shown, however, that the conditioned response is not identical to the unconditioned response and may be very different.

An animal usually produces a conditioned response to stimuli that resemble the conditioned stimulus, a process called stimulus generalization. Balancing this is a complementary tendency not to respond to anything but the conditioned stimulus itself; the process of ignoring stimuli is called stimulus discrimination. The combination of generalization and discrimination leads to appropriate responses.

# Conditioned stimulus

In classical conditioning, a stimulus leads to a learned response.

In **Ivan Pavlov**'s experimentations with **classical conditioning**, a sound was paired with the placement of meat powder in a dog's mouth, and the powder naturally induced salivation. After the powder and the sound had co-occurred a few times, the dog salivated when the sound occurred, even when the meat powder was not administered. Although most research in classical conditioning has involved reflexive behaviors that are typically involuntary, other nonreflexive behaviors have also been classically conditioned. The effects of the conditioned stimulus can vary widely in different circumstances. For example, if the unconditioned stimulus is more intense, the conditioned stimulus will have a greater effect. On the other hand, if the conditioned stimulus does not always occur when the natural, unconditioned stimulus does, the conditioned stimulus will have less effect. Further, if an animal has associated a particular conditioned stimulus with a certain unconditioned stimulus and a new conditioned stimulus is presented, the animal will typically not develop a response to the new conditioned stimulus. Psychologists refer to this lack of a response to the new stimulus as blocking.

The conditioned stimulus seems to exert its effect by providing information to the animal. If the animal has already gained information through an initial conditioned stimulus, the second one will not be very useful. Similarly, if the potential conditioned stimulus does not always occur with the unconditioned stimulus, the information provided by the conditioned stimulus is less useful to the animal. If the conditioned stimulus occurs without the unconditioned stimulus, **extinction** will occur; that is, the conditioned stimulus will no longer have an effect. The reflex can be conditioned more easily the second time around if the two are again paired. Sometimes, after extinction has taken place, the conditioned stimulus will produce the reflexive behavior without the unconditioned stimulus, a process called spontaneous recovery.

Psychologists have applied knowledge of classical conditioning to human behavior. For example, people with allergies may rely on drugs that have unwanted side effects. Their allergies have been alleviated by pairing a unique odor (the conditioned stimulus) with the drug (the unconditioned stimulus). Over time, presentation of the odor by itself may alleviate the allergic symptoms.

**During potty training, children are conditioned to associate the urge to urinate with sitting on the toilet.** (Photo by Elizabeth Hathon. Stock Market. Reproduced with permission.)

# Conditioning

A broad term to describe techniques used by psychologists to study the process of learning.

Psychology has often been defined as the study of behavior. As such, psychologists have developed a diverse array of methods for studying both human and animal activity. Two of the most commonly used techniques are **classical conditioning** and **operant conditioning**. They have been used to study the process of learning, one of the key areas of interest to psychologists in the early days of psychology. Psychologists also attach considerable significance to conditioning because it has been effective in changing human and animal behavior in predictable and desirable ways.

The Russian physiologist **Ivan Pavlov** developed the principles of classical conditioning. In his Nobel Prize-winning research on the digestive processes, he placed meat powder in the mouths of his research animals and recorded their levels of salivation. At one point,

he noticed that some of his research animals began to salivate in the absence of food. He reasoned that the presence of the animal caretakers led the animals to anticipate the meat powder, so they began to salivate even without the food.

When classical conditioning occurs, an animal or person initially responds to a naturally occurring stimulus with a natural response (e.g., the food leads to salivation). Then the food is systematically paired with a previously neutral stimulus (e.g., a bell), one that does not lead to any particular response. With repeated pairings, the natural response occurs when the neutral stimulus appears.

Pavlovian (i.e., classical) conditioning influenced psychologists greatly, even though Pavlov himself was skeptical of the work psychologists performed. In the United States, **John Watson**, the first widely known behaviorist, used the principles of classical conditioning in his research. For example, in a widely cited study, Watson tried to develop a classically conditioned **phobia** in an infant.

Although classical conditioning became the dominant Russian model for the study of **behaviorism**, another form of conditioning took hold in the United States. This version, which became known as operant or instrumental conditioning, initially developed from the ideas of the psychologist **Edward Thorndike**. Thorndike began his psychological research by studying learning in chickens, then in cats. Based on the problem solving of these animals, he developed the **Law of Effect**, which in simple form states that a behavior that has a positive outcome is likely to be repeated. Similarly, his Law of Exercise states that the more a response occurs in a given situation, the more strongly it is linked with that situation, and the more likely it is to be repeated in the future.

Operant conditioning was popularized by the psychologist **B.F. Skinner**. His research and writings influenced not only psychologists but also the general public. Operant conditioning differs from classical conditioning in that, whereas classical conditioning relies on an organism's response to some stimulus in the **environment**, operant conditioning relies on the organism's initiating an action that is followed by some consequence.

For example, when a hungry person puts money into a vending machine, he or she is rewarded with some product. In psychologists' terms, the behavior is reinforced; in everyday language, the person is satisfied with the outcome. As a result, the next time the person is hungry, he or she is likely to repeat the behavior of putting money into the machine. On the other hand, if the machine malfunctions and the person gets no food, that individual is less likely to repeat the behavior in the future. This refers to **punishment**.

Any time a behavior leads to a positive outcome that is likely to be repeated, psychologists say that behavior has been reinforced. When the behavior leads to a negative outcome, psychologists refer to it as punishment. Two types of **reinforcement** and punishment have been described: positive and negative.

Positive reinforcement is generally regarded as synonymous with reward: when a behavior appears, something positive results. This leads to a greater likelihood that the behavior will recur. Negative reinforcement involves the termination of an unpleasant situation. Thus, if a person has a headache, taking some kind of **pain** reliever leads to a satisfying outcome. In the future, when the person has a headache, he or she is likely to take that pain reliever again. In positive and negative reinforcement, some behavior is likely to recur either because something positive results or something unpleasant stops.

Just as reinforcement comes in two versions, punishment takes two forms. Psychologists have identified positive punishment as the presentation of an unpleasant result when an undesired behavior occurs. On the other hand, when something positive is removed, this is called negative punishment. In both forms of punishment, an undesired behavior results in a negative consequence. As a result, the undesired behavior is less likely to recur in the future.

Many people mistakenly equate negative reinforcement with punishment because the word "negative" conjures up the idea of punishment. In reality, a situation involving negative reinforcement involves the removal of a negative stimulus, leading to a more satisfying situation. A situation involving punishment always leads to an unwanted outcome.

Beginning with Watson and Skinner, psychology in the United States adopted a behavioral framework in which researchers began to study people and animals through conditioning. From the 1920s through the 1960s, many psychologists performed conditioning experiments with animals with the idea that what was true for animals would also be true for humans. Psychologists assumed that the principles of conditioning were universal. Although many of the principles of learning and conditioning developed in animal research pertain to human learning and conditioning, psychologists now realize that each species has its own behavioral characteristics. Consequently, although the principles of conditioning may generalize from animals to humans, researchers must consider the differences across species as well.

*See also* Aversive conditioning; Classical conditioning; Operant conditioning

### Further Reading
Mackintosh, N. J. *Conditioning and Associative Learning.* New York: Oxford University Press, 1983.
Walker, James T. *The Psychology of Learning.* Upper Saddle River, NJ: Prentice-Hall, 1996.

# Conduct disorder

A childhood antisocial behavior disorder characterized by aggressive and destructive actions that harm other human beings, animals, or property, and which violate the socially expected behavior for the child's age.

Along with anxiety and **depression**, conduct disorder is one of the most frequently diagnosed **childhood** psychological disorders. Depending on the population, rates of the disorder range from 6-16% in males and 2-9% in females and are expected to increase as **antisocial behavior** increases. Symptoms of conduct disorder include **aggression**, destruction of property, deceitfulness or theft, and serious violations of rules. The specific manner in which these activities are carried out may vary with age as cognitive and physical development occur. The child may exhibit opposition to authority (characteristic of **oppositional-defiant disorder**) during early childhood, gradually adopt the more serious behaviors of lying, shoplifting, and fighting during school age years, and then develop the most extreme behaviors such as burglary, confrontative theft, and **rape** during **puberty** and teenage years. Males tend to demonstrate more confrontative behaviors, such as fighting, theft, vandalism, and discipline problems, than females, who are more likely demonstrate lying, truancy, substance abuse, and prostitution.

Depending on the age it first appears, two forms of conduct disorder are identified: childhood-onset type and adolescent-onset type. In childhood-onset conduct disorder, the individual, usually a male, will have exhibited at least one criteria for the disorder before age 10 and will usually have full-blown conduct disorder by puberty. These children are more likely to develop adult **antisocial personality disorder**. Adolescent-onset conduct disorder tends to be milder, with no exhibiting symptoms before age 10. Adolescents with this type of conduct disorder are only slightly more frequently male than female, have more normal peer relationships, and are less likely to progress to antisocial personality disorder as adults. Their antisocial behaviors may be much more marked when in the presence of others.

## Diagnosis

According to the ***Diagnostic and Statistical Manual of Mental Disorders (DSM IV)***, conduct disorder is present when a child or adolescent (1) repetitively violates the rights of others or violates age-appropriate social norms and rules, and (2) this pattern of behavior causes significant impairment in social, academic, or occupational functioning. Three or more of the following criteria must have been present within the past 12 months, with one present within the past six months:

## Aggression

The child or adolescent:

• bullies, threatens, or intimidates others;
• initiates physical fights;
• uses a weapon with potential to cause serious harm;
• is physically cruel to people;
• is physically cruel to animals;
• steals while confronting the victim (mugging, extortion, robbery);
• forces another person into sexual activity.

## Destruction of property

The child or adolescent:

• deliberately engages in fire-setting with the intention of doing serious damage;
• deliberately destroys others' property (other than by fire).

## Deceitfulness or theft

The child or adolescent:

• breaks into someone else's house, building, or car;
• lies to obtain goods, favors, or to avoid obligations;
• steals objects of non-trivial value without confronting the victim.

## Serious violations of rules

The child or adolescent:

• stays out late at night against parental prohibition before age 13;
• runs away once for a lengthy period of time or twice overnight;
• is truant from school before age 13.

Because children and adolescents with conduct disorder often attempt to minimize the seriousness of their behavior, diagnosis is based on observations by parents, teachers, other authorities, peers, and by victims of the child's abuse. Generally, the child will present an exterior of toughness which actually conceals low **self-esteem**, and will demonstrate little **empathy** for the feelings of others or remorse for his or her actions. The disorder is associated with early sexual activity, substance abuse, reckless acts, and suicidal ideation. Chronic health problems, **attention deficit/hyperactivity disorder**, poverty, **family** conflict or a family history of alcohol dependence, **mood** disorders, antisocial disorders, and **schizophrenia** are also linked to the disorder.

There is some concern that the behaviors associated with conduct disorder may potentially be considered "normal" responses in the context of certain highly violent social conditions, for example war-zones (a concern when treating some immigrants) and high-crime urban neighborhoods. In these areas, the routine threats posed to life and property may encourage aggressive and deceptive behaviors as protective responses. Thus, the social and economic context in which the behaviors occurred should be taken into account, and in some cases a model based on trauma may be helpful.

A majority of children with conduct disorder no longer exhibit the extreme behaviors by the time they reach adulthood, but a substantial number do go on to develop antisocial personality disorder. For information about treatment, see entry on antisocial behavior.

*See also* Antisocial behavior; Oppositional-defiant disorder

### Further Reading

Kazdin, Alan E. *Conduct Disorders in Childhood and Adolescence.* Newbury Park, CA: Sage Publications, 1995.

Kernberg, Paulina F., et al. *Children with Conduct Disorders: A Psychotherapy Manual.* New York: Basic Books, 1991.

Sholevar, G. Pirooz, ed. *Conduct Disorders in Children and Adolescents.* Washington, DC: American Psychiatric Press, 1995.

### Further Information

American Academy of Child and Adolescent Psychiatry. 3615 Wisconsin Avenue, NW, Washington, DC 20016-3007, (202) 966–7300. http://www.aacap.org. (A professional association whose mission includes educating parents and families about psychiatric disorders affecting children and adolescents, educating child and adolescent psychiatrists, and developing guidelines for treatment of childhood and adolescent mental health disorders.)

The Federation of Families for Children's Mental Health. 1021 Prince Street, Alexandria, VA 22314–2971, (703)684-7710 (A national parent-run organization focused on the needs of children and youth with emotional, behavioral, or mental disorders and their families.)

## Conflict resolution

The process of defusing antagonism and reaching agreement between conflicting parties, especially through some form of negotiation. Also, the study and practice of solving interpersonal and intergroup conflict.

"Conflict" from the Latin root "to strike together" can be defined as any situation where incompatible activities, feelings, or intentions occur together. Conflict may take place within one person, between two or more people who know each other, or between large groups of people who do not know each other. It may involve actual confrontation between persons, or merely symbolic confrontation through words and deeds. The conflict may be expressed through verbal denigration, accusations, threats, or through physical **violence** to persons or property. Or the conflict may remain unexpressed, as in avoidance and denial.

A given conflict may be defined in terms of the *issues* that caused it, the *strategies* used to address it, or the *outcomes* or consequences that follow from it. The issues of the conflict may be varied, ranging from the simple to the complex. Strategies for resolving or pre-

venting the development of conflict can be classified as avoidance, diffusion, or confrontation. Turning on the TV rather than discussing an argument is a form of avoidance. Two workers who talk to their boss about a dispute is an example of diffusion. Insulting a person or physically harming someone are examples of confrontation. Courtroom litigation, like the trial and indictment of a person who has violated the law, also represents a form of confrontation.

The phrase conflict resolution refers specifically to strategies of diffusion developed during the second half of the twentieth century as alternatives to traditional litigation models of settling disputes. Based on the idea that it is better to expose and resolve conflict before it damages people's relationships or escalates into violence, methods of conflict resolution were developed in business management and gradually adopted in the fields of international relations, legal settings, and, during the 1980s, educational settings. Conflict resolution in education includes any strategy that promotes handling disputes peacefully and cooperatively outside of, or in addition to, traditional disciplinary procedures. The rise of violence and disciplinary problems, along with an increasing awareness of need for behavioral as well as cognitive instruction, spurred the development of conflict resolution programs in schools during the 1980s. These programs received national attention in 1984 with the formation of the National Association for Mediation in Education (NAME). By the late 1990s most major cities had instituted some form of large-scale conflict resolution program. According to a 1994 National School Boards study, 61% of schools had some form of conflict resolution program.

Most conflict resolution programs employ some form of negotiation as the primary method of communication between parties. In the negotiation process, parties with opposing interests hold conversations to settle a dispute. Negotiation can be distributive, where each party attempts to win as many concessions to his or her own self-interest as possible (win-lose), or integrative, where parties attempt to discover solutions that embody mutual self-interest (win-win). Research on games theory and the decision-making process suggest that the face-to-face conversation involved in direct negotiation may actually influence people to act in the interest of the group (including the opposing party), or some other interest beyond immediate self-interest. Certainly the simple act of talking with the opposition sends a message that the parties are committed to positive resolution, and face-to-face negotiation inherently tends to be integrative in its consequences.

The success of a given instance of conflict resolution depends on the attitudes and skills of the disputants and of the mediator or arbitrator. In the workplace, for example, two people may have different ideas about how to accomplish a project. If one person decides to begin the project without the input of the other person, this person's attitude has already jeopardized the conflict resolution process. It is the mediator's role to clearly lay out the issues of the conflict and to help the disputants arrive at the appropriate response to the conflict. There are several responses to a conflict: withdrawing from a conflict; demanding or requesting the opposing party to concede; providing reasons the opposing party should concede (appealing to norms); proposing alternatives to the opposing party; and proposing "if" statements, suggesting willingness to negotiate. Perspective taking, or articulating and validating the feelings and thoughts of the other party ("I see that you want…."), reflects the higher orders of conflict resolution skills. Integration of interests ("We both want…") reflects the highest level, leading to a consensual settlement of negotiations. According to the principles of conflict resolution, the only true solution to a conflict is one that attempts to satisfy the inherent needs of all the parties involved.

## Further Reading

Deutsch, M. *The Resolution of Conflict: Constructive and Destructive Processes.* New Haven, CT: Yale University Press, 1989.

Girard, K. and S. Koch. *Conflict Resolution in the Schools: A Manual for Educators.* San Francisco: Jossey-Bass, Inc., 1996.

## Further Information

Institute for Mediation and Conflict Resolution (IMCR). Automation House, 4th Floor, 49 East 68th St., New York, NY 10021.

National Institute for Dispute Resolution. 1726 M Street, NW, Suite 500, Washington, DC 20036, (202) 466–4764.

# Conformity

Adaptation of one's behavior or beliefs to match those of the other members of a group.

Conformity describes the **adaptation** of behavior that occurs in response to unspoken group pressure. It differs from compliance, which is adaptation of behavior resulting from overt pressure. Individuals conform to or comply with group behavior in an attempt to "fit in" or to follow the norms of the social group. In most cases, conforming to social norms is so natural that people aren't even aware they are doing it unless someone calls it to their attention or violates the norms.

Researchers have studied conformity using controlled experiments. The first classic experiment in con-

These troubled teens are in a military-style camp, where conformity and compliance work to make them adhere to social norms. *(Photo by Pete Cosgrove. UPI/Corbis-Bettmann. Reproduced with permission.)*

formity was carried out in the 1930s by Muzafer Sherif. It made use of an optical illusion called the autokinetic phenomenon—the fact that a small stationary point of light in a darkened room will appear to move. The autokinetic phenomenon affects individuals differently, i.e., the amount of movement experienced by different people varies. In Sherif's experiment, several subjects were placed together in a room with a stationary light. Each was asked to describe its movement aloud. As the individuals listened to the descriptions of others, their answers became increasingly similar as they unconsciously sought to establish a group **norm**. The power of social norms was demonstrated even more strikingly when the subjects continued to adhere to the norm later when they were retested individually. Sherif's experiment demonstrates one of the important conditions that produces conformity: ambiguity. There was no clear-cut right answer to the question asked of the subjects, so they were more vulnerable to reliance on a norm.

In the 1950s another researcher, Solomon Asch, devised a conformity experiment that eliminated the ambiguity factor. Subjects were asked to match lines of different lengths on two cards. In this experiment, there was one obvious right answer. However, each subject was tested in a room full of "planted" peers who deliberately gave the wrong answer in some cases. About three-fourths of the subjects tested knowingly gave an incorrect answer at least once in order to conform to the group.

Asch's experiment revealed other factors—notably unanimity and size of the majority—that influence conformity even when ambiguity isn't an issue. Unanimity of opinion is extremely powerful in influencing people to go along with the group. Even one dissenter decreases the incidence of conformity markedly. Individuals are much more likely to diverge from a group when there is at least one other person to share the potential disapproval of the group. People who follow the lead of an initial dissenter may even disagree with that person and be dissenting from the group for a totally different reason. However, knowing there is at least one other dissenting voice makes it easier for them to express their own opinions.

Individual differences also determine the degree to which conformity will occur. Although the ambiguity and unanimity of the situation are powerful contributors to the incidence of conformity, they are not the sole determinants. Personal characteristics and the individual's position within the group play a role as well. Individuals who have a low status within a group or are unfamiliar with a particular situation are the ones most likely to conform. Thus, students who are new to a class, new members of a study or activity group, or new residents to a community are more likely to be affected by the pressure to conform. **Personality traits**, such as concern with being liked or the desire to be right, also play a role.

Cultural factors are also influential. Certain cultures are more likely than others to value group harmony over individual expression. In fact, school administrators, organization managers, and even parents can establish an atmosphere or "culture" that either fosters conformity or allows for dissension and individuality.

### Further Reading

Feller, Robyn M. *Everything You Need to Know About Peer Pressure*. New York: Rosen Publishing Group, 1995.
Friar, Linda and Penelope B. Grenoble. *Teaching Your Child to Handle Peer Pressure*. Chicago: Contemporary Books, 1988.
Goldhammer, John. *Under the Influence: The Destructive Effects of Group Dynamics*. Amherst, NY: Prometheus Books, 1996.

# Conscience

The moral dimension of human consciousness, the means by which humans modify instinctual drives to conform to laws and moral codes.

**Sigmund Freud** viewed the conscience as one of two components of the **superego**, the other being the ego-ideal. In this scheme, the conscience prevents people from doing things that are morally wrong, and the ego-ideal motivates people to do things that are considered morally right. This theory suggests that the conscience is developed by parents, who convey their beliefs to their children. They in turn internalize these moral codes by a process of identification with a parent.

Other psychologists have proposed different theories about the development of the conscience.

*See also* Moral development

### Further Reading

Weissbud, Bernice. "How Kids Develop a Conscience." *Parents' Magazine* (December 1991): 156.

# Consciousness

Awareness of external stimuli and of one's own mental activity.

**Wilhelm Wundt**'s investigations of consciousness, begun in 1879, were central to the development of psychology as a field of study. Wundt's approach, called structuralism, sought to determine the structure of consciousness by recording the verbal descriptions provided by laboratory subjects to various stimuli, a method that became known as introspection. The next major approach to the study of consciousness was the **functionalism** of **William James**, who focused on how consciousness helps people adapt to their **environment**. **Behaviorism**, pioneered by **John B. Watson** in the early 1900s, shifted interest from conscious processes to observable behaviors, and the study of consciousness faded into the background for almost half a century, especially in the United States, until it was revived by the "cognitive revolution" that began in the 1950s and 1960s.

The existence of different levels of consciousness was at the heart of **Sigmund Freud**'s model of human mental functioning. In addition to the conscious level, consisting of thoughts and feelings of which one is aware, Freud proposed the existence of the **unconscious**, a repository for thoughts and feelings that are repressed because they are painful or unacceptable to the conscious mind for some other reason. He also formulated the concept of the **preconscious**, which functions as an intermediate or transitional level of mind between the unconscious and the conscious. A preconscious thought can quickly become conscious by receiving **attention**, and a conscious thought can slip into the preconscious when attention is withdrawn from it. In contrast, the repressed material contained in the unconscious can only be retrieved through some special technique, such as **hypnosis** or dream interpretation. (What Freud called the unconscious is today referred to by many psychologists as the subconscious.) Freud's contemporary, **Carl Jung**, posited the existence of a collective unconscious shared by all people which gathers together the experiences of previous generations. The collective unconscious contains images and symbols, called **archetypes**, that Jung found are shared by people of diverse cultures and tend to emerge in **dreams**, myths, and other forms. In Jung's view, a thorough analysis of both the personal and collective unconscious was necessary to fully understand the individual **personality**.

People experience not only different levels, but also different states of consciousness, ranging from wakefulness (which may be either active or passive) to deep **sleep**. Although sleep suspends the voluntary exercise of both bodily functions and consciousness, it is a much more active state than was once thought. Tracking **brain** waves with the aid of electroencephalograms (EEGs), researchers have identified six stages of sleep (including a pre-sleep stage), each characterized by distinctive brain-wave frequencies. In **rapid eye movement (REM)** sleep, which makes up 20% of sleep time, the same fast-frequency, low-amplitude beta waves that characterize waking states occur, and a person's physiological signs—heart rate, breathing, and blood pressure—also resemble those of a waking state. It is during REM sleep that dreams are experienced. Delta waves demarcate the deepest levels of sleep, when heart rate, respiration, temperature, and blood flow to the brain are reduced and growth hormone is secreted.

Certain waking states, which are accompanied by marked changes in mental processes, are considered states of altered consciousness. One of these is hypnosis, a highly responsive state induced by a hypnotist through the use of special techniques. While the term "hypnosis" comes from the Greek word for sleep (*hypnos*), hypnotized people are not really asleep. Their condition resembles sleep in that they are relaxed and out of touch with ordinary environmental demands, but their minds remain active and conscious. Other characteristics of hypnosis include lack of initiative, selective redistribution of attention, enhanced **ability** to fantasize, reduced reality testing, and increased suggestibility. Also, hypnosis is often followed by post-hypnotic **amnesia**, in which the person is unable to remember what happened during the hypnotic session. Hypnosis has proven useful in preventing or controlling various types of **pain**, including pain from dental work, childbirth, burns, arthritis, **nerve** damage, and migraine headaches.

In meditation, an altered state of consciousness is achieved by performing certain rituals and exercises. Typical characteristics of the meditative state include intensified **perception**, an altered sense of time, decreased distraction from external stimuli, and a sense that the experience is pleasurable and rewarding. While meditation is traditionally associated with Zen Buddhism, a secular form called Transcendental Meditation (TM) has been widely used in the United States for purposes of relaxation. It has been found that during this type of meditation, people consume less oxygen, eliminate less carbon dioxide, and breathe more slowly than when they are in an ordinary resting state.

Consciousness may be altered in a dramatic fashion by the use of **psychoactive drugs**, which affect the interaction of neurotransmitters and receptors in the brain. They include illegal "street drugs," tranquilizers and other prescription medications, and such familiar substances as alcohol, tobacco, and coffee. The major categories of psychoactive drugs include depressants, which reduce activity of the **central nervous system**; sedatives, another type of depressant that includes barbiturates such as Seconal and Nembutal; anxiolytics (traditionally referred to as tranquilizers); narcotics—including heroin and its derivatives—which are addictive drugs that cause both drowsiness and euphoria, and are also pain-killers; psychostimulants, such as amphetamines and cocaine, which stimulate alertness, increase excitability, and elevate moods; and psychedelics or **hallucinogens**, such as **marijuana** and LSD. Psychedelics, which affect moods, thought, **memory**, and perception, are particularly known for their consciousness-altering properties. They can produce distortion of one's **body image**, loss of identity, dreamlike fantasies, and **hallucinations**. LSD (lysergic acid diethylamide), one of the most powerful psychedelic drugs, can cause hallucinations in which time is distorted, sounds produce visual sensations, and an out-of-body feeling is experienced.

Various states of consciousness are viewed differently by different cultures and even subcultures. In the United States, for example, hallucinations are devalued by mainstream culture as a bizarre sign of insanity, whereas the youth counterculture of the 1960s viewed drug-induced hallucinations as enlightening, "mind-expanding" experiences. In certain other societies, hallucinations are respected as an important therapeutic tool used by ritual healers.

## Further Reading

Dennett, D.C. *Brainstorms*. Cambridge, MA: Bradford Books, 1980.
Freud, Sigmund. "The Unconscious." In *The Standard Edition of the Complete Psychological Works of Sigmund Freud*. London: Hogarth Press, 1962.

# Consumer psychology

The study of the behavior of consumers of goods and services regarding their buying patterns and reactions to advertising and marketing.

Consumer psychology seeks to explain human, or *consumer* behavior, in two basic ways: what the consumer *wants* and what the consumer *needs*. The logical explanation for fulfilling the needs is a simple one. If a person lives in New York, that person needs a winter coat to survive the cold outside. But why the person buys a particular style or color hinges on the more complex issues of why a particular choice is made. The Society for Consumer Psychology is a division of the **American Psychological Association (APA)**. The group's main focus is conducting scientific research, development and practice in the field. Its quarterly journal, *Journal of Consumer Psychology* as well as another publication, *Journal of Consumer Research and Psychology and Marketing,* periodically serves as the voice of those engaged in the understanding of why people buy what they buy.

## What the consumer wants

The key to unlocking consumer psychology is understanding that desires rule over needs when it comes to consumer purchase. In a modern world with hundreds of brands of toothpaste, where new food products and electronic gadgets emerge daily, it is the interest of psychologists, as well as those marketing the products, to understand the relationship between financial and psychological factors that make people buy what they buy. In fact, consumer psychology utilizes more than simply psychology. It must study economics and culture too. Accordingly, there are several principles at play when examining this issue.

Psychology views certain factors that include: 1) The Gestalt principle. If you want to know why a particular restaurant is popular, it is important to understand what cultural implications are present beside the food; 2) The Iceberg principle. What could be the superficial or seemingly rational reason a person might have for making a purchase (the need)? What other factors (wants) influence it? For instance, even if shoes are purchased as foot protection, the desired shoe may be open-toed, strapless, and come with six- inch heels; 3) The Dynamic principle.

**Consumer psychology studies issues like why the need for transportation is coupled with the want for a luxury vehicle, like this BMW.** *(AP/Wide World Photos. Reproduced with permission.)*

People and their motivations constantly change, whether influenced by social, economic, or psychological factors. The millionaire who grew up in dire poverty might still buy the cheapest margarine because the psychological **motivation** takes time to catch up to the economic status; and 4) Image and Symbolism. From product spokespersons to the picture on a candy bar wrapper, the ever-elusive association people make with a product might be a big factor in whether or not they buy it, more than the nature or quality of the product itself.

### What consumer psychologists know

In 1957, a writer named Vance Packard started a minor revolution with his book, *The Hidden Persuader*. Packard uncovered the manipulations of the advertising community, done to ensure a certain brand of a product becomes a best-selling item. He urged consumers to be cautious and not fall prey to hidden meanings or symbols in advertising, and pointed out less-than-honest representations of what a product could do for the buyer. The book was popular, and people started looking for the subtle messages in everything from liquor ads to spaghetti packages. What they also did, and often, is buy the product anyway. Their awareness did not necessarily combat their emotional needs.

Psychologists understand that in the burgeoning economy of the early twenty-first century people's needs and wants are continually growing too. In the 1970s and early 1980s, household items such as computers and video recorders were new, and counted as luxuries. By 1999, by virtue of a changing society, those items had become more than simple luxuries, as schools and businesses often came to require their use. Complex human behavior can take one invention and create a hierarchy of needs around it. Whereas economists or marketing strategists might look to numbers—wages or interest levels—psychologists know that something more motivates the consumer purchase trends. They have discovered that often in the most depressed economic times, the sales of luxury items go up.

Consumer psychology is a pursuit that is likely to expand now that an estimated $5 billion worth of products were purchased online by the spring of 2000. Online shopping habits might differ drastically from catalogue sales or in-store purchases. These trends are just beginning to be studied, and certainly consumer psychologists will be studying buying habits well into the twenty-first century.

Jane Spear

### Further Reading

Asker, Jennifer L. "The malleable self: the role of self-expression in persuasion." *Journal of Marketing Research*, (February 1999).

Bidlake, Suzanne. "Scents of real purpose." *Marketing*, (October 15, 1992).

Dawar, Niraj. "Product-harm crises and the signaling ability of brands." *International Studies of management & Organization*, (Fall 1998).

Dichter, E. "Consumer Psychology." In *Encyclopedia of Psychology, Second Edition*. Ray Corsini, ed. New York: John Wiley & Sons 1994.

Krugman, Herbert E. "Pavlov's dog and the future of consumer psychology." *Journal of Advertising Research*, (Nov-Dec 1994).

LaFreniere, Andrea. "Buyer psychology, consumer confidence: how to post sales in today's marketplace (housing market)." *Professional Builder and Remodeler*, (May 1, 1991).

McKenna, Joseph F. "Brand management: just do it." *Industry Week*, (March 20, 1995).

### Further Information

Society for Consumer Psychology of the American Psychological Association. c/o 313 Commerce West Building, 1206 South 6th Street, Champaign, IL, USA. 61820, (217) 333-4550.

# Contrast

The relative difference in intensity between two stimuli and their effect on each other.

Contrast, or contrast effect, is the effect a visual stimulus has on another. When one stimulus is present, it affects the other. As can be seen in this illustration, two gray boxes of equal intensity are surrounded by, in one case, a white field, and in the other, a black field. The perceived shade of gray is affected by the contrasting field.

Psychologists also study the contrast threshold, the point at which differences in two stimuli can be detected. These tests are used in the study of visual **perception** and the **ability** to perceive spatial relationships. Understanding contrast effect has practical applications. For example, black and yellow have the lowest contrast effect, which means the largest percentage of the population can clearly detect the difference between these two colors. Therefore, black and yellow are the colors used to mark school buses and many traffic signs.

# Control group

In an experiment that focuses on the effects of a single condition or variable, the group that is exposed to all the conditions or variables except the one being studied.

Scientists often study how a particular condition or factor influences an outcome. In such an experiment, in which there are two groups of subjects, the group that is exposed to the condition or factor is called the **experimental group**. The other group, which provides a basis for comparison, is called the control group. For example, in a hypothetical study of the influence of the presence of loud music on the test performances of children, the control group would consist of the group of children not exposed to the loud music during the test. Their test scores would be compared with the experimental group, the group of children who were exposed to loud music during the test. In this type of **experimental design**, subjects would be randomly assigned to each group to ensure a reliable comparison.

### Further Reading

Atkinson, Rita L.; Richard C. Atkinson; Edward E. Smith; and Ernest R. Hilgard. *Introduction to Psychology.* 9th ed. San Diego: Harcourt Brace Jovanovich, 1987.

Zimbardo, Philip G. *Psychology and Life.* 12th ed. Glenview, IL: Scott, Foresman, 1988.

# Convergent thinking

The ability to narrow the number of possible solutions to a problem by applying logic and knowledge.

The term convergent thinking was coined J. P. Guilford, a psychologist well-known for his research on **creativity**. Guilford posited that a prime component of creativity is **divergent thinking**, the capacity to arrive at unique and original solutions and the tendency to consider problems in terms of multiple solutions rather than just one. Convergent thinking, which narrows all options to one solution, corresponds closely to the types of tasks usually called for in school and on standardized multiple-choice tests. In contrast, creativity tests designed to assess divergent thinking often ask how many different answers or solutions a person can think of to a specific question or problem. Some researchers have claimed that creative achievement actually involves both divergent and convergent thinking—divergent thinking to generate new ideas and convergent thinking to "reality test" them in order to determine if they will work.

### Further Reading

Amabile, Teresa M. *Growing Up Creative: Nurturing a Lifetime of Creativity.* New York: Crown Publishers, 1989.

Guilford, J. P. *The Nature of Human Intelligence.* New York: McGraw-Hill, 1967.

# Conversion reaction

A psychological disorder characterized by physical symptoms for which no physiological cause can be found.

This condition was first described by **Sigmund Freud** as conversion hysteria because it involved the conversion of a repressed emotional problem to a physiological form. Today, conversion reaction is classified as a somatoform disorder in the **American Psychiatric Association**'s *Diagnostic and Statistical Manual of Mental Disorders* (DSM-IV ).

Conversion reaction is a very rare condition, accounting for about 2 percent of all psychiatric diagnoses, and usually first appears during **adolescence** or early adulthood, generally when an individual is under severe **stress**. Symptoms tend to be both specific and severe, and generally interferes with daily activities. A conversion disorder may serve as a way for a patient to avoid activities or situations associated with a source of emotional conflict or even shut down conscious awareness of the conflict itself. Another source of "secondary gain" is the attraction of attention, sympathy, and support that the patient may need but is unable to obtain in other ways.

Some of the most common symptoms of conversion disorder are paralysis, blindness or tunnel **vision**, seizures, loss of sensation, and disturbance of coordinated movements, such as walking. Other physical complaints include tremors, abdominal **pain**, and speech impairments such as aphonia, the inability to speak above a whisper. Sometimes a person will experience anesthesia in only one part of the body, such as "glove anesthesia," which affects the hand only up to the wrist, although such a problem could have no physiological origin since there is no cut-off point between the nerves of the hand and arm. Symptoms may also involve the **endocrine glands** or **autonomic nervous systems**. If the symptoms of a conversion disorder are prolonged, they may produce physiological damage by interrupting the **normal** functioning of the body, and psychological damage by inducing excessive dependence on **family** members and other persons.

### Further Reading

Freud, Sigmund. *The Standard Edition of the Complete Psychological Works of Sigmund Freud.* London: Hogarth Press, 1962.

——. *Dora: An Analysis of a Case of Hysteria.* New York: Collier, 1963.

# Correlational method

A technique used to measure the likelihood of two behaviors relating to each other.

Psychologists are often interested in deciding whether two behaviors tend to occur together. One means of making this assessment involves using correlations. Sometimes two measurements are associated so that when the value of one increases, so does the other—a positive correlation. On the other hand, one value may increase systematically as the other decreases—a negative correlation.

For example, the number of correct answers on a student's test is generally positively related to the number of hours spent studying. Students who produce more correct answers have spent more hours studying; similarly, fewer correct answers occur with fewer hours spent studying.

One could also see whether the number of wrong answers on a test is associated with study time. This pattern is likely to produce a negative correlation: a greater number of wrong answers is associated with less study time. That is, the value of one variable increases (wrong answers) as the other decreases (hours spent studying).

Correlations allow an assessment of whether two variables are systematically related within a group of individuals. A single person may show behavior that differs from most of the rest of the group. For example, a given student might study for many hours and still not perform well on a test. This does not mean that study time and test grades are not related; it only means that exceptions exist for individuals, even if the rest of the group is predictable.

It is critical to remember that correlational approaches do not allow us to make statements about causation. Thus, greater study time may not necessarily cause higher grades. Students who are interested in a particular subject do better because of their interest; they also study more because they like the material. It may be their interest that is more important than the study time. One of the limitations of the correlational method is that although one variable (such as study time) may have a causal role on the other (such as test scores), one does not know that for certain because some other important factor (such as interest in the material) may be the most important element associated with both greater study time and higher test scores. When a third element is responsible for both variables (increase in study time and increase in grades), psychologists refer to this as the third variable problem.

The British scientist Sir **Francis Galton** developed the concept of the correlational method. The British statistician Karl Pearson (1857-1936) worked out the mathematical formulation. There are several different types of correlations; the most commonly used is called the Pearson Product-Moment Correlation.

*See also* Research methodology; Scientific method

# Cortex

See **Neocortex**

# Counseling psychology

An area of psychology which focuses on nurturing the development potential of relatively healthy individuals in all areas of their lives.

While the counseling psychologist may diagnose, assess, and treat adjustment difficulties, they often address problems which are more moderate than those encountered by the clinical psychologist. Clients of counseling psychologists are people who need help coping with the stresses of everyday life, and the focus is on strengthening their existing resources rather than overcoming disorders or deficits in particular areas. The counseling psychologist may use a number of tools in treating clients, including **psychotherapy**, workshops in such areas as assertiveness training or communications skills, and psychological assessments . These tests are used to measure a person's aptitudes, interests, or **personality** characteristics and provide feedback which can facilitate the counseling process. Clients may be treated individually, in **group therapy**, or in **family** groups, depending on the nature of the problems and the specialization of the counselor. In contrast to a clinical psychotherapist, the counseling psychologist may intervene in the client's immediate **environment**. Also, unlike traditional psychotherapy, the relationship between counselor and client may extend to situations outside the office setting.

Counseling psychology has its roots in education and vocational guidance and has been closely linked with the use of mental testing, which is central to these fields. It has traditionally followed an educational rather than a medical model, considering those it helps as clients rather than patients. Its educational context is also evident in its emphasis on developmental models derived from the work of **Erik Erikson**, Robert Havighurst, Daniel Levinson, Roger Gould, and other theorists. Counseling psychologists work on helping clients remove obstacles to optimal development. A focus on adult development is helpful to many types of clients, such as women returning to the work force, or individuals undertaking second careers. Counseling psychology, paralleling a growing trend among health care providers, also advocates preventive as well remedial approaches to problems, seeking to identify "at risk" individuals and groups and intervene before a crisis occurs.

Of the psychotherapeutic models available to counseling psychology at its inception in the 1940s, Rogerian, or **client-centered therapy** has had the most influence. **Carl Rogers**, whose methods were more readily understood and adapted by counselors than those of **Sigmund Freud**, had a lasting influence on the techniques of vocational counseling and counseling psychology, which focus more on the process than on the outcome of the counseling relationship. Two other theoretical models that have been especially influential are decision-making theory and the **social influence** model. The former attempts to teach clients procedures and strategies for effective decision making, including such techniques as weighing the factors in a decision according to a numerical point system. Decision-making is related to counseling psychology's overall emphasis on problem solving.

Social influence theory, currently one of the prevailing theories in the field, involves the counselor's influence over the client based on how the client perceives him or her in terms of such factors as credibility and degree of expertise. Researchers have studied the behaviors that contribute to the counselor's social influence; the ways in which social influence can be maximized; and social influence in relation to such factors as race, gender, age, and social class. Over the years, the fields of counseling psychology and psychotherapy have begun to overlap as clinical psychologists have concentrated more on relatively healthy clients and counselors have grown to rely more heavily on psychotherapeutic techniques. There has also been a growing overlap between counseling and social work, as social workers have moved in the direction of therapeutic counseling themselves. Thus, there has been an overlap between these professions.

Most counselor training programs are offered by colleges of education rather than psychology departments. As the establishment of credentials has become more and more important (particularly with regard to payments by insurance companies), counseling psychology programs are offering (and requiring) an increased amount of training in basic psychology, which can include rigorous internship programs. Counseling psychology has its own division, Division 17, of the **American Psychological Association**, and its own professional publications, including *The Counseling Psychologist,* a quarterly, and the *Journal of Counseling Psychology,* which appears bimonthly.

**Further Reading**

Brammer, Lawrence M. *Therapeutic Psychology: Fundamentals of Counseling and Psychotherapy.* 5th ed. Englewood Cliffs, NJ: Prentice Hall, 1989.

Ronch, Judah L, William van Ornum, and Nicholas C. Stilwell, eds. *The Counseling Sourcebook: A Practical Reference on Contemporary Issues.* New York: Crossroad, 1994.

Vernon, Ann, ed. *Counseling Children and Adolescents.* Denver, CO: Love, 1993.

# Counterconditioning

An aspect of behavior therapy that involves weakening or eliminating an undesired response by introducing and strengthening a second response that is incompatible with it.

The type of counterconditioning most widely used for therapeutic purposes is systematic **desensitization**, which is employed to reduce or eliminate **fear** of a particular object, situation, or activity. An early example of systematic desensitization was an experiment that is also the first recorded use of **behavior therapy** with a child. In a paper published in 1924, Mary Cover Jones, a student of the pioneering American behaviorist **John Watson**, described her treatment of a three-year-old with a fear of rabbits. Jones countered the child's negative response to rabbits with a positive one by exposing him to a caged rabbit while he sat some distance away, eating one of his favorite foods. The boy slowly became more comfortable with the rabbit as the cage was gradually moved closer, until he was finally able to pet it and **play** with it without experiencing any fear.

In the 1950s South African psychiatrist **Joseph Wolpe** (1915- ) pioneered a prototype for systematic desensitization as it is generally practiced today. Like Cover's experiment, Wolpe's technique involved gradually increasing the intensity of exposure to a feared experience. However, instead of countering the fear with a pleasurable stimulus such as food, Wolpe countered it with deliberately induced feelings of relaxation. He had the client imagine a variety of frightening experiences and then rank them in order of intensity. The client was then trained in deep muscle relaxation and instructed to practice it as he pictured the experiences he had described, progressing gradually from the least to the most frightening. Today systemic desensitization of the type pioneered by Wolpe is widely used with both adults and children. In adults its uses range from combating phobias, such as a fear of snakes or flying, to increasing tolerance of **pain** from chronic illnesses or natural childbirth. In children, it is used to overcome a wide variety of fears, such as fear of certain animals or fear of the dark.

Another type of counterconditioning is **aversive conditioning**, which makes a particular behavior less appealing by pairing it with an unpleasant stimulus. Aversive conditioning has been used in adults to break addictions to substances such as tobacco and alcohol. Alcoholics are sometimes given an alcoholic drink together with a drug that induces nausea to weaken the positive feelings they associate with drinking.

# Covert sensitization

An aversion therapy that reduces unwanted behaviors by repeated, imagined associations with an unpleasant consequence.

Covert sensitization was first described in the mid-1960s by psychologist Joseph Cautela as a new treatment for people who engage in undesirable behaviors. In the past 30 years it has been researched as a treatment for alcoholism, smoking, **obesity**, and various sexual deviations including **pedophilia** and exhibitionism.

Covert sensitization discourages people from engaging in unwanted behaviors by creating an association between those behaviors and an unpleasant consequence. Because of this, it is classified as a type of aversion therapy. What is unique about covert sensitization, however, is that the unwanted consequence is never actually present in therapy. This is best illustrated with an example. If a person was undergoing covert sensitization to stop using alcohol, for instance, a typical therapy session would involve the therapist instructing the client to imagine himself drinking and becoming very nauseous. Then the client would be encouraged to imagine himself becoming so nauseous that he starts vomiting all over himself, the room he is in, and in the beer mug from which he was drinking. By imagining this disgusting scene over and over again, the client starts associating alcohol with vomit, and drinking becomes much less appealing. Finally, the therapist would instruct the client to imagine accepting a drink, becoming nauseous again, and then deciding to refuse the drink. In the imagined scene, the nausea (which is an unpleasant stimulus for almost everyone) goes away as a consequence of the client's choice not to drink.

The major advantage covert sensitization has over other methods of aversion therapy is that it works without the presence of the unwanted behavior and the unpleasant consequence. This has practical and ethical ad-

vantages. For example, when treating exhibitionists, it would be difficult to justify encouraging people to expose themselves to others while a therapist administered a shock or some other unpleasant stimulus. It is important to note that aversion therapy is not the only way to break bad habits. Large-scale studies comparing several methods have found that other techniques, such as behavioral family counseling and self-management techniques, are also effective.

Timothy Moore

## Further Reading

Rimmele, C., Howard, M., & Hilfrink, M. "Aversion Therapies." In Hester, R., Miller, W., et al., eds. *Handbook of Alcoholism Treatment Approaches: Effective Alternatives.* Boston: Allyn & Bacon, 134-147,1995

Plaud, J. & Gaither, G. "A clinical investigation of the possible effects of long-term habituation of sexual arousal in assisted covert sensitization." *Journal of Behavior Therapy and Experimental Psychiatry*, 28 no. 4 (1997): 281-290.

# Creativity

The ability to juxtapose ideas in a new and unusual way to find solutions to problems, create new inventions, or produce works of art.

Any human endeavor can involve creativity and is not limited to just the arts. Numerous theories of creativity were proposed by 20th-century psychologists, educators and other social scientists. Howard Gruber, who worked to understand creativity by studying the lives of famous innovators, found broad common characteristics: 1) they engaged in a variety of activities within their chosen fields; 2) they held a strong sense of purpose about their work; 3) they had a profound emotional attachment to their work; and 4) they tended to conceptualize problems in terms of all encompassing images. Graham Wallas's 1962 study of well-known scientists and other innovators yielded a widely used four-stage breakdown of the creative process. The preparation stage consists of formulating a problem, studying previous work on it, and thinking intensely about it. In the incubation stage, there is no visible progress on the problem; it may be periodically "mulled over," but it is largely left dormant, allowing subconscious ideas about it to emerge. At the illumination stage, an important insight about the problem is reached, often in a sudden, intuitive fashion. In the final, or verification, stage, the idea is tested and evaluated.

Creativity differs from the kinds of abilities measured by standard **intelligence** tests. Creative people tend to

**Creativity, often associated with fine and performing arts, can be an important factor in human relations.** *(Index Stock Imagery. Reproduced with permission.)*

have average or above-average scores on IQ tests. Beyond an IQ of 120, there is little correlation between intelligence and creativity. J.P. Guilford first distinguished the thought processes of creative people from those of other people in terms of convergent and **divergent thinking**. Convergent thinking—the type required for traditional IQ tests—involves the application of logic and knowledge to narrow the number of possible solutions to a problem until one's thoughts "converge" on the most appropriate choice. In contrast, divergent thinking—the kind most closely associated with creativity and originality—involves the **ability** to envision multiple ways to solve a problem. Guilford identified three aspects of divergent thinking: fluency entails the ability to come up with many different solutions to a problem in a short amount of time; flexibility is the capacity to consider many alternatives at the same time; and originality refers to the difference between a person's ideas and those of most other people.

Special tests, such as the Consequences Test, have been designed to assess creativity. Instead of based on one correct answer for each question, as in conventional intelligence tests, the scoring on these tests is based on the number of different plausible responses generated for each question, or the extent to which a person's answers differ from those of most other test takers. Typical questions asked on such tests include "Imagine all of the things that might possibly happen if all national and local laws were suddenly abolished" and "Name as many uses as you can think of for a paper clip." While divergent thinking is important to the creative process, it is not the sole element necessary for creative achievement. Researchers have found little correlation between the scores of fifth and tenth graders on divergent thinking tests and their actual achievements in high school in such fields as art, drama, and science.

It appears that creative accomplishment requires both divergent and **convergent thinking**. Originality is not the only criterion of a successful solution to a problem: it must also be appropriate for its purpose, and convergent thinking allows one to evaluate ideas and discard them if they are inappropriate in the light of existing information. In addition, studies of people known for their creative accomplishments show that certain **personality traits** that may be impossible to measure on a test—such as **motivation**, initiative, tolerance for ambiguity, and independent judgment—are commonly associated with creativity. Other traits known to be shared by highly creative people include self-confidence, nonconformity, ambition, and perseverance. Albert Einstein (1879-1955) once remarked that for every hundred thoughts he had, one turned out to be correct.

In a 1986 study, a group of researchers identified three essential criteria for creative achievement: expertise in a specific field, which must be learned; creative skills, including divergent thinking; and the motivation to engage in creative activity for its own sake regardless of external reward. In this study, items created by people who were told that their work would be judged and possibly rewarded for creativity were found to be less creative than the results produced by those who were simply asked to work on a project with no prospect of external reward.

Creativity does not appear to be inherited. Studies with identical **twins** raised separately show that environmental influences play at least as great a role in the development of creativity as intelligence. Creative skills of identical twins reared apart vary more than their intellectual abilities. Studies have shown that reinforcing novel ideas in both children and adults leads to increased creativity. The originality of block arrangements produced by four-year-olds increased dramatically when novel designs were praised by adults; when this positive **reinforcement** was stopped, the children reverted to producing unimaginative patterns. Other studies have used similar techniques to boost creativity scores of fifth graders, improve the originality of stories written by sixth graders, and increased the ability of college students to produce novel word associations. One interesting finding in studies such as these is that positively reinforcing one kind of creative activity encourages original thinking in other areas as well. The play of children is closely related to the development of creativity. The sensory stimulation that results from exposure to new objects and activities reinforces the exploratory impulse in both children and adults and results in an openness to new experiences and ideas that fosters creative thinking.

Schools as well as families can encourage creativity by offering children activities that give them an active role in their learning, allow them freedom to explore within a loosely structured framework and participation in creative activities for enjoyment rather than an external reward.

*See also* Intelligence quotient

## Further Reading

Briggs, John. *Fire in the Crucible: The Alchemy of Creative Genius.* New York: St. Martin's Press, 1988.
Dacey, John S. *Understanding Creativity: The Interplay of Biological, Psychological, and Social Factors.* San Francisco: Jossey-Bass, 1998.

# Creativity tests

Tests designed to measure creativity in children or adults.

Creativity tests, mostly devised during the past 30 years, are aimed at assessing the qualities and abilities that constitute **creativity**. These tests evaluate mental abilities in ways that are different from—and even diametrically opposed to—conventional **intelligence** tests. Because the kinds of abilities measured by creativity tests differ from those measured by **intelligence quotient** (IQ) tests, persons with the highest scores on creativity tests do not necessarily have the highest IQs. Creative people tend to have IQs that are at least average if not above average, but beyond a score of 120 there is little correlation between performance on intelligence and creativity tests.

Most creativity tests in use today are based at least partially on the theory of creativity evolved by J.P. Guilford in the 1950s. Guilford posited that the **ability** to envision multiple solutions to a problem lay at the core of creativity. He called this process **divergent thinking** and its opposite—the tendency to narrow all options to a single solution—**convergent thinking**. Guilford identified three components of divergent thinking: fluency (the ability to quickly find multiple solutions to a problem); flexibility (being able to simultaneously consider a variety of alternatives); and originality (referring to ideas that differ from those of other people). Early tests designed to assess an individual's aptitude for divergent thinking included the Torrance (1962) and Meeker (1969) tests.

The most extensive work on divergent thinking was done under Guilford's direction at the University of Southern California by the Aptitudes Research Project (ARP), whose findings between the 1950s and 1970s produced a broad structure-of-intellect (SI) model which encompassed all intellectual functions, including divergent thinking. A number of the ARP divergent thinking tests, which were originally devised as research instruments for the study of creativity, have been adapted by a variety of testing companies for use by educators in placing gifted students and evaluating gifted and talented programs. The ARP tests are divided into verbal and figural categories. Those that measure verbal ability include:

- *Word fluency* : writing words containing a given letter

- *Ideational fluency*: naming things that belong to a given class (i.e., fluids that will burn)

- *Associational fluency*: writing synonyms for a specified word

- *Expressional fluency*: writing four-word sentences in which each word begins with a specified letter
- *Alternate uses*: listing as many uses as possible for a given object
- *Plot titles*: writing titles for short-story plots
- *Consequences*: listing consequences for a hypothetical event ("What if no one needed to sleep?")
- *Possible jobs*: list all jobs that might be symbolized by a given emblem.

The figural ARP tests, which measure spatial aptitude, include the following:

- *Making objects*: drawing specified objects using only a given set of shapes, such as a circle, square, etc.
- *Sketches*: elaborating on a given figure to produce sketches of recognizable items
- *Match problems*: removing a specified number of matchsticks from a diagram to produce a specified number of geometric shapes
- *Decorations*: using as many different designs as possible to outline drawings of common objects.

Divergent thinking tests are generally evaluated based on the number and variety of answers provided; the originality of the answers; and the amount of detail they contain (a characteristic referred to as elaboration). A number of creativity tests currently in use include sections that measure divergent thinking.

Rather than ways of thinking, some creativity tests evaluate attitudes, behavior, creative **perception**, or creative activity. Some creativity tests specifically address the problem of assessing creativity in minority populations, who are at a disadvantage in tests that place a strong emphasis on verbal and semantic ability. The Eby Gifted Behavior Index reflects the growing view of creativity as specific to different domains. It is divided into six talent fields: verbal, social/leadership, visual/spatial, math/science problem-solving, mechanical/technical, and musical. The Watson-Glaser Critical Thinking Appraisal is a more analytical assessment of **giftedness** based on five components of critical thinking: inference, deduction, interpretation, awareness of assumptions, and evaluation of arguments.

Creativity tests have been found reliable in the sense that one person's scores tend to remain similar across a variety of tests. However, their validity has been questioned in terms of their ability to predict the true creative potential of those who take them. In one study, there was little correlation between the scores of both elementary and secondary students on divergent thinking tests and their actual achievements in high school in such creative fields as art, drama, and science. Creativity tests have also been criticized for unclear instructions, lack of suit-

ability for different populations, and excessive narrowness in terms of what they measure. In addition, it may be impossible for any test to measure certain personal **traits** that are necessary for success in creative endeavors, such as initiative, self-confidence, tolerance of ambiguity, **motivation**, and perseverance. Tests also tend to create an anxiety-producing situation that may distort the scores of some test takers.

Rosalie Wieder

**Further Reading**

Amabile, Teresa. *The Social Psychology of Creativity*. New York: Springer-Verlag, 1983.
———. *Growing Up Creative: Nurturing a Lifetime of Creativity*. New York: Crown Publishers, 1989.
Guilford, J.P. *The Nature of Human Intelligence*. New York: McGraw-Hill, 1967.
Sternberg, R.J. *The Nature of Creativity*. New York: Cambridge University Press, 1988.
Torrance, E.P. *Guiding Creative Talent*. Englewood Cliffs, NJ: Prentice-Hall, 1962.

# Crisis intervention

Brief, preventative psychotherapy administered following a crisis.

The term crisis intervention can refer to several different therapeutic approaches, which are applied in a variety of situations. The common denominator among these interventions, however, is their brief duration and their focus on improving acute psychological disturbances rather than curing long-standing mental disorders. Some common examples of crisis intervention include **suicide** prevention telephone hotlines, hospital-based crisis intervention, and community-based disaster **mental health**.

The theoretical basis for crisis intervention programs reflects an approach that stresses the public health and preventative components of mental health. Two psychiatrists in particular heavily influenced our approach to crisis intervention with their crisis theory. Erich Lindemann and Gerald Caplan believed that, when people are in a state of crisis, they are anxious, open to help, and motivated to change. The rationale for crisis intervention programs is therefore the belief that providing support and guidance to people in crisis will avert prolonged mental health problems.

Crisis or suicide hotlines offer immediate support to individuals in acute distress. Since they are usually anonymous, individuals in difficulty may find themselves less embarrassed than in face-to-face interaction. Most hotlines are staffed by volunteers who are supervised by mental health professionals. Suicidal callers are provided with information about how to access mental health resources in the community. Further, some centers will arrange referrals to clinicians. Typically, crisis hotlines do not offer therapy directly. If a volunteer feels a caller is at immediate risk, however, confidentiality will be broken and a mental health worker will be called upon to intervene.

Although crisis hotlines are numerous, whether they effectively reduce suicide has not clearly been demonstrated. Some researchers fear that the people who call may not be those at highest risk. For many centers a small fraction of callers appear to represent a large fraction (estimated up to 50%) of the total phone contacts. Since the major role of the telephone operators is education about mental health resources in the community, not therapy, these frequent callers, who are often already involved in ongoing outpatient psychiatric treatment, represent an ineffective use of resources. A further problem is that there appears to be significant discrepancies in the training of telephone operators at these hotlines.

Hospital-based crisis intervention usually refers to the treatment of people suffering psychiatric emergencies that typically arise in the context of a crisis. The aim of this type of crisis intervention is usually the normalization of some type of extreme behavior. Professionals regard patients who are suicidal, homicidal, extremely violent, or suffering from severe adverse drug reactions as major psychiatric emergencies. In the United States, when individuals appear to represent imminent danger to themselves or others, they may be committed to a psychiatric facility against their will. In Canada, you can be involuntarily committed and never receive treatment. When treatment is administered, however, it is usually in the form of psychotropic drugs with follow-up outpatient therapy scheduled upon release.

A relatively recent type of crisis intervention involves the mobilization of mental health professionals following plane crashes, school shootings, natural disasters, and other traumatic events affecting several people. The professionals who arrive on the scene attempt to administer preventative procedures to avert mental disorders such as **post-traumatic stress disorder**, which may develop following exposure to upsetting experiences. The most popular of these is psychological debriefing, or CISD (critical incident stress debriefing), which originated in the military. People are encouraged to relive the traumatic moments, with the belief that re-experiencing the emotions will facilitate healing and prevent psychological disturbance. Unfortunately, this technique is based on assumptions held by clinicians, rather than on any research evidence; the efficacy of this technique has not been demonstrated.

Some investigations of CISD suggest that we should be more cautious about its use. Recent research in Europe indicates that this type of counseling often has no demonstrable benefits and may even make things worse. It is possible that having people focus on the upsetting event emphasizes the victimization that has already taken place, rather than people's innate abilities to overcome these challenges. In other words, the CISD may make people feel worse by making them question their own coping abilities. These studies serve as reminders that a particular psychological intervention may be intuitively appealing but at the same time counterproductive. It is crucial that interventions be subjected to appropriate evaluation research; otherwise our efforts to help may actually waste resources and harm people.

Timothy Moore

## Further Reading

Bressi, C., et al. "Crisis Intervention in Psychiatric Emergencies: Effectiveness and Limitations." *New Trends in Experimental and Clinical Psychiatry* 15, no. 2 (1999): 163-67.

Callahan, J. "Crisis Theory and Crisis Intervention in Emergencies." In *Emergencies in Mental Health Practice: Evaluation and Management,* edited by M. Kleespies, et al. New York: The Guilford Press, 1998.

Canterbury, R. and W. Yule. "Debriefing and Crisis Intervention." In *Post-Traumatic Stress Disorders: Concepts and Therapy,* edited by W. Yule, et al. Chinchester: John Wiley and Sons Ltd., 1999.

# Critical period

A specified time span, also referred to as the optimal or sensitive period, during which certain events or experiences must occur in order for the development of an organism to proceed normally.

Although this term is used in a variety of contexts, the term is most closely associated with **ethology**, the study of animal behavior in its natural **environment** from the perspective of evolutionary **adaptation**. The critical period plays an important role in the concept of **imprinting**, first used by **Konrad Lorenz** in connection with the earliest process of social **attachment** in young animals. (However, the term imprinting is also applicable to any irreversible behavioral response acquired early in life and normally released by a specific triggering stimulus or situation.) In the most famous example of imprinting, Lorenz demonstrated that exposure to an appropriately maternal object during a critical period would activate the "following" **instinct** of newborn goslings: he successfully had a group of goslings follow him after he "impersonated" their absent mother.

Other examples of critical periods include the initial four months of life during which puppies must be exposed to humans in order to make good pets and the early months in which birds must be exposed to the characteristic song of their species in order to learn it. Critical periods vary in length: the period for identifying one's mother may last only a few hours, while the period for learning to identify a mate may take several months.

The specifically human phenomenon of **language development** also appears to be subject to a critical period. So-called "wild" or "feral" children deprived of human society for an extended period show that they have been unable to catch up on language due to lack of exposure early in life.

The term "critical period" is also used to describe physiological as well as behavioral phenomena. For example, the embryonic stage in humans is a critical period for certain types of growth (such as the appearance of the heart, eyes, ears, hands, and feet) which must occur for prenatal development to proceed normally.

### Further Reading

Denny, M. Ray. *Comparative Psychology: Research in Animal Behavior.* New York:Dorset Press, 1970.

Lorenz, Konrad. *The Foundation of Ethology.* New York: Springer-Verlag, 1981.

# Cross-cultural psychology

A subfield of psychology concerned with observing human behavior in contrasting cultures.

Studies in this discipline attempt to expand the compass of psychological research beyond the few highly industrialized nations on which it has traditionally focused. While definitions of what constitutes a culture vary widely, most experts concur that "culture" involves patterns of behavior, symbols, and values. The prominent anthropologist Clifford Geertz has described culture as ". . . a historically transmitted pattern of meanings embodied in symbols, a system of inherited conceptions expressed in symbolic forms by means of which men communicate, perpetuate, and develop their knowledge about and attitudes toward life."

While cross-cultural psychology and anthropology often overlap, both disciplines tend to focus on different aspects of a culture. For example, many issues of interest to psychologists are not addressed by anthropologists, who have their own concerns traditionally, including such topics as kinship, land distribution, and ritual. When anthropologists do concentrate on areas of psychology, they focus on activities whereby data can be collected through direct observation, such as the age of children at weaning or child rearing practices. However, there is no significant body of anthropological data on many of the more abstract questions commonly addressed by psychologists, such as cultural conceptions of **intelligence**.

Cross-cultural research can yield important information on many topics of interest to psychologists. In one of the best known studies, researchers found evidence that human perceptual processes develop differently depending on what types of shapes and angles people are exposed to daily in their **environment**. People living in countries such as the United States with many buildings containing 90-degree angles are susceptible to different optical illusions than those in rural African villages, where such buildings are not the **norm**. Cross-cultural studies have also discovered that the symptoms of most psychological disorders vary from one culture to another, and has led to a reconsideration of what constitutes **normal** human **sexuality**. For example, **homosexuality**, long considered pathological behavior in the United States, is approved of in other cultures and is even encouraged in some as a normal sexual outlet before marriage.

Collection of cross-cultural data can also shed new light on standard psychological theories. In the 1920s, the anthropologist Bronislaw Malinowski observed that young boys living in the Trobriand islands exhibited the type of **hostility** that **Sigmund Freud** had described in his formulation of the **Oedipus complex**, only it was directed not at their fathers but at a maternal uncle who was assigned the role of **family** disciplinarian. This observation posed a challenge to Freud's oedipal theory by raising the possibility that boys' tense relations with their fathers at a certain period in their lives may be a reaction to discipline rather than a manifestation of sexual **jealousy**. The questions raised by Malinowski's observation demonstrate a particularly valuable type of contribution that cross-cultural research can make to psychology. Psychological research often confounds, or merges, two variables in a situation in this case, the boy's **anger** toward his father and the father's sexual role in relation to the mother. A cross-cultural perspective can untangle such confounded variables when it finds them occurring separately in other cultures—e.g., the disciplinarian (the uncle), and the mother's lover (the father), as two separate persons.

Cross-cultural psychology may also be practiced within a given society by studying the contrasts between its dominant culture and subcultures. A subculture—defined as a group of people whose experiences differ from those of the majority culture—may be constituted in different ways. Often, it is an ethnic, racial, or religious group. Any group that develops its own customs, norms, and jargon may be considered a subculture, however, including such deviant groups as drug or gang subcultures. A prominent area of intersection between psychological inquiry and subcultures within the United States has been the issue of cultural bias in testing. Today, testing experts assert that there is no evidence for bias across race or social class in "standardized" intelligence and **achievement tests**. However, children whose primary language is not English should be tested in their primary language.

### Further Reading

Barnouw, Victor. *Culture and Personality.* 4th ed. Homewood, IL: Dorsey Press, 1985.

Bock, Philip K. *Rethinking Psychological Anthropology: Continuity and Change in the Study of Human Action.* New York: W.H. Freeman, 1988.

# Cross-sectional study

Research that collects data simultaneously from people of different ages, in contrast to a longitudinal study, which follows one group of subjects over a period of time.

A cross-sectional study is a research method where data are collected at the same time from people in different age categories. It contrasts with the method, known as **longitudinal study**, where the same group of subjects is studied over time. One weakness, or confounding variable, of the cross-sectional study is that its subjects, in addition to being different ages, are also born in different years, and their behavior may thus be influenced by differences in education, cultural influences, and medical treatment. In the longitudinal study, data can be obtained from subjects of different ages born within the same period of time. However, a confounding variable in longitudinal studies is the degree to which each person's environmental influences will vary from those of others over the period of time covered by the experiment.

# Cults

Highly organized groups led by a dynamic leader who exercises strong control.

A cult is a structured group, most of whose members demonstrate unquestioned loyalty to a dynamic

leader. The cult leader governs most, if not all, aspects of the lives of his or her followers, often insisting that they break all ties with the world outside of the cult. Such groups are usually thought of in terms of religion, although other types of cults can and do exist.

The proliferation of religious cults in the United States is considered by many experts as symptomatic of the general social discordance that has plagued postwar Western society. Cults offer the allure of an ordered world that is easily understood. Clear rules of behavior are enforced and nagging questions about meaning and purpose are dispelled by the leader, who defines members' lives in service to the cult's interest. It is probably most useful to examine the phenomenon of cults without dwelling on the sensationalistic practices of the flamboyant, the infamous, and the suicidal. When a psychologist examines a cult and its dynamics, what is actually observed is the mental condition of the member; in other words, what is it about the individual that allows them to willingly relinquish themselves to such rigid and dogmatic ways of thinking and living?

To understand this process, consider that many social organizations other than what we traditionally think of as cults require strict adherence to a set of beliefs and, in turn, provide a sense of meaning and purpose to their followers. Behavior that is not normally considered as being cult-like can be seen as having some of the main characteristics of cults. The rigid social contract of the military, for instance, is considered by many psychologists as being cult-like. Other social organizations that have had a profound impact on the lives of its followers include **self-help groups**, such as Alcoholics Anonymous, where selflessness and devotion to the group are highly valued and rewarded. Certain types of political groups and terrorist organizations are still other examples of "cults" that defy the common definition of the term. Dr. Arthur Deikman, clinical professor of psychiatry at the University of California at San Francisco, is one of many psychologists who has observed cultic behavior in many areas of society other than in extremist religious groups. In the introduction to his 1990 book, *The Wrong Way Home: Uncovering the Patterns of Cult Behavior in American Society,* Deikman asserted that "behavior similar to that which takes place in extreme cults takes place in all of us," and suggested that "the longing for parents persists into adulthood and results in cult behavior that pervades **normal** society."

Because cultic behavior underlies more than extremist religious sects, many psychologists refer to these groups as charismatic groups. Marc Galanter, professor of psychiatry at New York University, defines the characteristics of charismatic groups in his study *Cults: Faith, Healing, and Coercion* (1989). According to Galanter, charismatic group members "1) have a shared belief system; 2) sustain a high level of social cohesiveness; 3) are strongly influenced by the group's behavioral norms, and 4) impute charismatic (or sometimes divine) **power** to the group or its leadership." Other psychologists have devised additional theories to explain the drawing power of charismatic groups, and some conclude that people who devote themselves to such groups have not yet achieved the developmental stage of individuation. Still other experts, drawing on the field of **sociobiology**, suggest that the need to be part of a group has biological, evolutionary roots traceable to that period in human history when to be banned from the dominant hunter-gatherer group meant almost certain death.

Whatever the origins of the psychological need to be a part of a defined group, the fact is most people do not fall under the sway of charismatic groups. Typically, such groups find recruits among young people. Usually, such a young person is approached by friendly, outgoing recruiters for the cult who express a deep interest in the person's life and offer **empathy** and understanding for the difficulties they may be experiencing. These difficulties may be in relation to a failed romance, an unhappy **family** life, or an existential crisis of the sort usually associated with late **adolescence** in which a young person has no idea how they fit in the world. The recruiters are often trained to provide a "friendly ear" to troubled young people, to validate their experiences as being common, and, finally, to suggest that other people (such as themselves) have found solace in their groups.

During the process of initiation, recruits may experience severe psychological disorders as they at once begin and resist immersion into an entirely new system. Abandoning old allegiances and belief systems can bring about intense **guilt** before the recruit completely immerses him or herself into the charismatic group. Some psychologists believe that such mental illnesses as **dissociative identity disorders**, pathologic adjustment reactions, major depressive disorders, and others may be attributed to the agonizing process of joining a charismatic group. Once immersed in the cult, members will often cut all ties with their past lives, ending contact with their families and friends as they join a new social order that seems to give them meaning and purpose. This kind of behavior is obviously less true of charismatic groups such as the military and some types of self-help groups, but these symptoms can nonetheless appear in less extreme forms.

Interviews with former cult members have revealed that in extremist religious cults, there are often tremendous obstacles to leaving. These obstacles can come in the form of **peer pressure**, where loyal cult members will intervene in the case of a member who has doubts about the cult and longs for his or her old life, or the obstacles may be physical ones for those whose cult lives communally in an isolated area. Often, family members of persons in religious cults hire what are called "deprogrammers" to kidnap their loved ones and take them to some neutral place where they can be reasoned with sensibly without the interference of other cult members espousing the group's prevailing ideology.

Most psychologists would probably acknowledge that there exists a deep human need to belong to a group. Often, this need leads people to form what might be viewed as unhealthy allegiances to a person or group who, ultimately, does not truly have the person's interest at heart.

Followers of American-born cult leader Jim Jones left the U.S. to set up the Jonestown commune in the Guyana jungle in South America. After a U.S. Congressman and three journalists investigating the cult were killed, Jones persuaded 911 members of his People's Temple flock to kill themselves with cyanide-laced potions in a mass suicide on Nov. 18, 1978. David Koresh, leader of the Branch Davidians, a group that originally split from the Seventh Day Adventist Church during the Depression, led 82 people to their death, when he refused to be served with a search and arrest warrant at the Davidian compound in Waco, Texas. Koresh's followers believed he was the Messiah, despite reports of **child abuse** and other questionable behaviors. After an initial gunfight that killed four agents and six Davidians, a 51-day stand-off occurred between federal agents and the Davidians holed up in the compound. When agents launched a tear gas attack on April 19, 1993, to end the siege, a fire burned the compound and killed 82 Davidians, probably in a deliberate mass **suicide**.

Bodies of 39 similarly dressed men and women were found in San Diego on March 26, 1997, after a mass suicide led by Marshall Applewhite, cult leader of Heaven's Gate. The deaths were triggered by the cult's belief that a flying saucer traveled behind comet Hale-Bopp to take them home, an evolutionary existence above the human level. Articles have appeared about the use of the Internet to recruit Heaven's Gate followers.

## Further Reading

Ankerberg, John and Weldon, John. *Encyclopedia of Cults and New Religions* Eugene, Ore.: Harvest House Publishers, 1999.

Deikman, Arthur J. *The Wrong Way Home: Uncovering Patterns of Cult Behavior in American Society.* Boston: Beacon Press, 1990.

Deutsch, A. "Tenacity of Attachment to a Cult Leader: A Psychiatric Perspective." *American Journal of Psychiatry* 137 (1980): 1569-73.

Dolan, Sean. *Everything you need to know about cults.* New York: Rosen Pub. Group, 2000.

Hall, J.R. "The Apocalypse at Jonestown." *In Gods We Trust: New Patterns of Religious Pluralism in America,* edited by T. Robbins and D. Anthony. New Brunswick, NJ: Transaction Books, 1981.

*See also* Military psychology

# Culture-fair test

An intelligence test in which performance is not based on experience with or knowledge of a specific culture.

Culture-fair tests, also called culture-free tests, are designed to assess **intelligence** (or other attributes) without relying on knowledge specific to any individual cultural group. The first culture-fair test, called Army Examination Beta, was developed by the United States military during World War II to screen soldiers of average intelligence who were illiterate or for whom English was a second language. Beginning in the postwar period, culture-fair tests, which rely largely on nonverbal questions, have been used in public schools with Hispanic students and other non-native-English speakers whose lack of familiarity with both English language and American culture have made it impossible to assess their intelligence level using standard IQ tests. Culture-fair tests currently administered include the Learning Potential Assessment Device (DPAD), the Culture-Free Self-Esteem Inventories, and the Cattell Culture Fair Series consisting of scales one to three for ages four and up. The Cattell scales are intended to assess intelligence independent of cultural experience, verbal **ability**, or educational level. They are used for **special education** placement and college and vocational counseling. The tests consist mostly of paper-and-pencil questions involving the relationships between figures and shapes. Parts of scale one, used with the youngest age group, utilize various objects instead of paper and pencil. Activities in scales two and three, for children age eight and up, include completing series, classifying, and filling in incomplete designs.

Culture-fair testing is a timely issue given current debate over bias in intelligence and educational testing as it affects students who can speak and write English, but who are unfamiliar with white middle-class culture. Bias in intelligence testing has a historical precedent in early tests designed to exclude immigrants from Southern and Eastern Europe from admission to the United States on grounds of mental inferiority. Critics of current tests claim that they discriminate against ethnic minorities in similar ways by calling for various types of knowledge unavailable to those outside the middle-class cultural mainstream. To dramatize the discriminatory nature of most intelligence testing, Professor Robert L. Williams devised the Black Intelligence Test of Cultural Homogeneity that requires a command of vocabulary items widely known among African Americans but not familiar to most whites (such as "do rag" and "four corners") and a knowledge of black history and culture ("Who wrote the Negro National Anthem?"). Williams claimed that the difficulties faced by white persons attempting to take this test are comparable to those that confront many blacks taking standardized IQ tests.

Critics of standardized tests claim that minority test takers are also penalized in ways other than their unfamiliarity with specific facts. A pervasive negative attitude toward such tests may give children from minority groups less **motivation** than whites to perform well on them, further reduced by low levels of trust in and identification with the person administering the test. In addition, students from a minority culture may be more likely to interpret and answer a question in ways that differ from the prescribed answer. (In the field of **educational psychology**, this phenomenon is referred to as **divergent thinking** and also tends to penalize gifted children.) Studies have shown that culture-fair tests do reduce differences in performance between whites and members of minority groups. However, they lag behind the standard tests in predicting success in school, suggesting that in their quest for academic success, members of minority groups must overcome cultural barriers that extend beyond those encountered in IQ tests.

**Further Reading**

Fraser, Steven. *The Bell Curve Wars: Race, Intelligence, and the Future of America.* New York: Basic Books, 1995.

Herrnstein, Richard J., and Charles Murray. *The Bell Curve: Intelligence and Class Structure in American Life.* New York: Free Press, 1994.

Mensh, Elaine, and Harry Mensh. *The IQ Mythology: Class, Race, Gender, and Inequality.* Carbondale, IL: Southern Illinois University Press, 1991.

Seligman, Daniel. *A Question of Intelligence: The IQ Debate in America.* New York: Birch Lane Press, 1992.

# D

## Charles Robert Darwin

### 1809-1882
British naturalist whose theory of organic evolution through natural selection revolutionized science.

Charles Robert Darwin was born in Shrewsbury, England. His father was a successful provincial physician, and his grandfather, Erasmus Darwin (1731-1802), had been a distinguished intellectual figure. Young Darwin attended the Shrewsbury School, and his early failure to achieve academic distinction continued at Edinburgh University, where he studied medicine, and at Cambridge University, where he studied theology. While at Cambridge, however, Darwin enthusiastically pursued natural history as an avocation, drawing the attention of botanist John Stevens Henslow (1796-1861) and geologist Adam Sedgwick (1785-1873). In 1831, through his connection with Henslow, Darwin joined the expedition team aboard the survey ship H.M.S. *Beagle* headed for the coasts of South America, the Galápagos Islands, New Zealand, and Tasmania. There is some indication that Darwin went on the voyage in order to accompany Captain FitzRoy. FitzRoy, as captain, was not to socialize with the lower status crew members on the ship, and he was worried about maintaining his **mental health** during the long, solitary voyage. (FitzRoy later committed suicide.) During what turned out to be a five-year voyage, Darwin, a creationist, recorded his observations. Upon his return to England, Darwin developed his theory of evolution, one of the major intellectual achievements of the nineteenth century. However, because of his creationist perspective, some of the observations made during the voyage were not useful in the development of his evolutionary ideas. In 1858, when another scientist, Alfred Russell Wallace (1823-1913) shared his observations gathered in the Malay Archipelago, Darwin hastened to publish *The Origin of Species* to ensure his own work would receive recognition.

Darwin's theory of evolution postulates that all species on earth change over time, and that process is

**Charles Darwin** *(The Library of Congress. Reproduced by permission.)*

governed by the principles of natural selection. These principles hold that in the struggle for existence, some individuals, because of advantageous biological **adaptation**, are better able to occupy effectively a given ecological niche and therefore will produce more offspring than individuals who are less able. Realizing that his theory challenged biblically oriented views about the nature and origins of humans and animals, Darwin was extremely cautious and continued his research for another 18 years before publishing it in 1859 as *On the Origin of Species by Means of Natural Selection; or, the Preservation of Favoured Races in the Struggle for Life.* Every copy of the book was sold on the first day of publication. Within a few years, scientists were convinced of the soundness of the theory, although popular debate about its ideological and theological implications has continued to the present.

Although psychology was one of the fields for which Darwin's theory had revolutionary implications, it was largely left to others—notably Darwin's cousin **Francis Galton**—to expand them publicly. However, toward the end of his career, Darwin published three books in which he explored how human mental qualities could be understood as the result of evolution. In *The Descent of Man* (1871), he supported the controversial position that human beings are descended from animal ancestors. In line with this idea, he argued that the mental activities of humans and animals are fundamentally similar. He identified the presence in animals of "human" qualities such as courage and devotion, and "human" emotions, including pride, **jealousy**, and shame. After examining these and other common mental functions, such as **memory**, **attention**, and dreaming, Darwin concluded that the mental difference between humans and the higher animals is one of degree rather than kind.

In *The Expression of the Emotionsin Man and Animals* (1872), Darwin posited that human emotional expressions have evolved over time because of their link with reactions that have had adaptive or survival value. For example, an animal baring its teeth in rage is literally preparing to fight; thus its **emotion** gives it a physical advantage. Similarly, Darwin postulated that the "fight or flight" reaction, a heightened state of nervous arousal, was a mechanism that aided survival. He also put forth that human reactions which no longer have any clear survival value probably did in the past and that the similarity of emotional expression among all known human groups suggests a common descent from an earlier prehuman ancestor.

Darwin's final contribution to psychology was the publication in 1877 of *Biographical Sketch of an Infant*, based on a detailed log he had kept on the development of his eldest child, who was born in 1840. This milestone in the history of **child psychology** was probably the first publication of its type. One seminal idea expressed in this short work is that the individual's development parallels the development of the species to which it belongs. (Darwin had earlier made a similar observation about the development of the fetus before birth.)

Darwin's work had far-reaching influences on the theory and practice of psychology. Its emphasis on the individual's adaptation to the **environment** helped establish the "functional" view of the mind and of human behavior, influencing such thinkers as **John Dewey**

and James Angell (1869-1949) in the United States, who together founded the functionalist movement at the University of Chicago. Darwin's conception of the continuity between humans and other species gave the study of animal behavior a new importance. Sigmund Freud's younger colleague, George J. Romanes (1848-1894), to whom Darwin turned over his notes on animal behavior shortly before his death, established the field of **comparative psychology**. Paralleling the science of comparative anatomy, this field seeks to provide insights about human beings by studying the similarities and differences between human and animal psychological functioning. In addition, Darwin's principle of natural selection led to a greater interest in variation and individual differences among members of the same species.

Darwin's other books include *The Variations of Animals and Plants under Domestication* (1868), *Insectivorous Plants* (1875), and *The Power of Movement in Plants* (1880). He was awarded membership in the London Geological Society in 1836 and won election to the Royal Society in 1839.

**Further Reading**
Clark, Ronald W. *The Survival of Charles Darwin: A Biography of a Man and an Idea*. New York: Random House, 1984.
Darwin, Charles. *The Autobiography of Charles Darwin*, 1809-1882. Edited by Nora Barlow. New York: Norton, 1969.
De Beer, Gavin. *Charles Darwin: Evolution by Natural Selection*. London: Doubleday, 1963.
Gruber, Howard E. *Darwin on Man: A Psychological Study of Scientific Creativity*. London: Wildwood House, 1974.
Ridley, Mark. *The Darwin Reader*. New York: Norton, 1987.

# Daydreaming

A temporary escape from daily reality by forming mental pictures, usually in spontaneous, brief episodes, of other experiences.

Daydreams are a form of **imagination**. In daydreams, the person forms a mental image of a past experience or of a situation that he or she has never actually experienced. Some psychologists use the acronym TUIT (Task-Unrelated Images and Thoughts) to describe episodes of daydreaming. A daydream may be triggered by a situation, a **memory**, or a sensory input (sight, **taste**, **smell**, sound, **touch**).

The daydreamer may use these mental pictures to escape from reality temporarily, to overcome a frustrating situation, or to satisfy hidden wishes. Almost all people daydream, although the frequency of daydreaming varies considerably from individual to individual. Psychologists estimate that one-third to one-half of a person's thoughts while awake are daydreams, although a single daydream rarely last more than a few minutes.

When the daydreamer begins to confuse the mental images with reality, the daydream is called an **hallucination**. Daydreaming is generally not harmful, unless the daydreaming episodes interfere with activities of daily living. When the daydreamer's daily routine is disrupted—a driver misses an exit on the freeway continuously, or a student does not hear the teacher assigning homework—he or she may want to consider whether the daydreams are a symptom of a psychological problem.

Although most psychologists view daydreams as generally healthy and natural, this was not always the case. In the 1960s, for example, textbooks used for training teachers provided strategies for combating daydreaming, using language similar to that used in describing drug use. **Sigmund Freud** felt that only unfulfilled individuals created fantasies, and that daydreaming and **fantasy** were early signs of **mental illness**. By the late 1980s, most psychologists considered daydreams a natural component of the mental process for most individuals.

Similar to **dreams** experienced during **sleep**, daydreams occur in cycles set by biological cycles of temperature and hormone levels (psychologists estimate that the average person daydreams about every 90 minutes), and peak around the lunch hour (noon to 2 p.m.). Daydreaming first occurs for most people during **childhood**, sometime before age three, and these early daydreams set the pattern for adult daydreaming. Children who have positive, happy daydreams of success and achievement generally continue these types of mental images into adulthood; these daydreamers are most likely to benefit from the positive aspects of **mental imagery**. Daydreams become the impetus for problem-solving, **creativity**, or accomplishment. On the other hand, children whose daydreams are negative, scary, or visualize disasters are likely to experience anxiety, and this pattern will carry over into adulthood as well. A child's daydreams may take a visible or public form—the daydreamer talks about his mental images while he is experiencing them, and may even act out the scenario she or he is imagining. After age ten, however, the process of internalizing daydreaming begins.

It is not unusual for a daydream, or series of daydreams, to precede an episode of creative writing or invention. Athletes, musicians, and other performers use a form of daydreaming known as visualization. As the individual prepares for a **competition** or performance, he or she forms a mental picture of him- or herself executing and completing the task with the desired successful outcome.

## Further Reading

Hogan, John. "Daydreaming: Experiments Reveal Links Between Memory and Sleep." *Scientific American* (October 1994): 32+.

Seligson, Susan V. "What Your Daydreams Really Mean." *Redbook* (July 1995): 51+.

# Deductive reasoning

Way of thinking that relates ideas to one another in reaching conclusions.

Deductive reasoning is a way of reasoning that relates two or more general concepts or conditions to a specific case. For example, a child learns that birds fly south in October, and that a robin is a bird, he will use deductive reasoning to conclude that a robin will fly south in October. Deductive reasoning is often confused with **inductive reasoning**, which uses a specific observation to reach a general conclusion.

# Defense mechanisms

Unconscious strategies for avoiding or reducing threatening feelings, such as fear and anxiety.

The concept of the defense mechanism originated with **Sigmund Freud** (1856-1939) and was later elaborated by other psychodynamically oriented theorists, notably his daughter **Anna Freud** (1895-1982). Defense mechanisms allow negative feelings to be lessened without an alteration of the situation that is producing them, often by distorting the reality of that situation in some way. While they can help in coping with **stress**, they pose a danger because the reduction of stress can be so appealing that the defenses are maintained and become habitual. They can also be harmful if they become a person's primary mode of responding to problems. In children, excessive dependence on defense mechanisms may produce social isolation and distortion of reality and hamper the **ability** to engage in and learn from new experiences.

Defense mechanisms include denial, repression, suppression, projection, displacement, reaction formation, regression, **fixation**, identification, introjection, rationalization, isolation, sublimation, compensation, and humor. *Denial* and *repression* both distort reality by keeping things hidden from **consciousness**. In the case of denial, an unpleasant reality is ignored, and a realistic interpretation of potentially threatening events is replaced by a benign but inaccurate one. Either feelings or events (or both) may be denied. In very young children, a degree of denial is **normal**. One way of coping with the relative powerlessness of **childhood** is for young children to sometimes act as if they can change reality by refusing to acknowledge it, thereby ascribing magical powers to their thoughts and wishes. For example, a child who is told that her parents are divorcing may deny that it is happening or deny that she is upset about it. Denial has been shown to be effective in reducing the arousal caused by a threatening situation. In life-threatening or other extreme situations, denial can temporarily be useful in helping people cope, but in the long term painful feelings and events must be acknowledged in order to avoid further psychological and emotional problems. Related to denial is avoidance, which involves avoiding situations that are expected to elicit unwanted emotions and impulses.

In repression, painful feelings are conscious initially and then forgotten. However, they are stored in the **unconscious**, from which, under certain circumstances, they can be retrieved (a phenomenon Freud called "the return of the repressed"). Repression can range from momentary **memory** lapses to forgetting the details of a catastrophic event, such as a murder or an earthquake. Complete **amnesia** can even occur in cases where a person has experienced something very painful. The **Oedipus complex** by which Sigmund Freud explained the acquisition of **gender identity** relies on a child's repression of incestuous desires toward the parent of the opposite sex and feelings of rivalry toward the parent of the same sex. Other situations may also occasion the repression of hostile feelings toward a loved one (especially a parent). Possibly the most extreme is **child abuse**, the memory of which may remain repressed long into adulthood, sometimes being deliberately retrieved in therapy through **hypnosis** and other techniques.

A third defense mechanism, related to denial and repression, is *suppression,* by which unpleasant feelings are suppressed through a conscious decision not to think about them. Suppression differs from repression and denial in that the undesirable feelings are available but deliberately ignored (unlike repression and denial, where the person is completely unaware of these feelings). Suppression generally works by replacing unpleasant thoughts with others that do not produce stress. This may be done instinctively, or it may be done deliberately in a therapeutic context. **Cognitive behavior therapy** in particular makes use of this technique to help people combat negative thought patterns that produce maladaptive emotions and behavior. For example, a child may be in-

structed to block feelings of **fear** by thinking about a pleasant experience, such as a party, an academic achievement, or a victory in a sporting event. Suppression is considered one of the more mature and healthy defense mechanisms.

*Projection* and *displacement* allow a person to acknowledge anxiety-producing feelings but transfer them to either another source or another object. In projection, the undesirable feelings are attributed to another person or persons. An angry person believes others are angry at her; a person who is critical of others believes they are critical of him. Very young children are especially prone to projection because of their egocentric orientation, which blurs the boundary between themselves and others, making it easier to also blur the distinction between their feelings and those of others.

Displacement is a defense by which an impulse perceived as dangerous is displaced, either through redirection toward a different object or replacement by another impulse. In the first type, known as object displacement, **anger** or another **emotion** is initially felt toward a person against whom it is unsafe to express it (in children, for example, toward a parent). Displacement functions as a means by which the impulse can still be expressed—allowing a **catharsis** of the original emotion—but toward a safer target, such as a sibling, peer, or even a toy. In the second type of displacement, known as drive displacement, the object of the emotion remains the same but the emotion itself is replaced by a less threatening one.

*Reaction formation,* another defense mechanism, involves behavior that is diametrically opposed to the impulses or feelings that one is repressing. For example, a parent who is repressing feelings of resentment or rejection toward a child may overcompensate by appearing to be lavishly generous and solicitous of the child's welfare. In this type of situation, the child generally senses the true **hostility** underlying the parent's behavior. A child who is being toilet trained may show an exaggerated sense of fastidiousness to counter conflicts over controlling elimination. The Freudian stage of sexual latency in middle childhood is yet another example of reaction formation: in order to repress their sexual feelings, children at this age evince a strong sense of indifference or even hostility toward the opposite sex. Sometimes a distinction is drawn between feelings that are diametrically opposed to a repressed impulse and the actual behavior that expresses them, with the former called reaction formation and the latter referred to as undoing.

Two defense mechanisms—*regression* and *fixation*—are associated with developmental disturbances in children. In regression, a child, confronted with a situation that produces conflict, anxiety, or frustration, reverts to the behavior of an earlier stage of development, such as thumb-sucking or bed-wetting, in an attempt to regain the lost sense of safety that characterized the earlier period. In fixation, the child doesn't lose any previously gained developmental ground but refuses to move ahead because developmental progress has come to be associated with anxiety in some way.

*Identification,* which is basic to human development and an essential part of the learning process, can also serve as a defense mechanism. Taking on the characteristics of someone else can enable a person to engage in impulses or behavior that she sees as forbidden to her but acceptable for the person with whom she is identifying. Another motive for identification is a fear of losing the person with whom one identifies. One particularly well-known variety of identification is identification with the aggressor, where someone who is victimized in some way takes on the **traits** of the victimizer to combat feelings of powerlessness. This type of projection occurs when a child who is abused by his parents abuses others in turn. In some cases, however, this type of projection may occur in response to **aggression** that is imagined rather than real and create a self-perpetuating cycle by actually eliciting in others the aggression that was only imaginary initially. In *introjection,* which is related to identification, only a particular aspect of someone else's **personality** is internalized.

*Rationalization,* another type of defense mechanism, is an attempt to deny one's true motives (to oneself or others) by using a reason (or rationale) that is more logical or socially acceptable than one's own impulses. Typical rationalizations include such statements as "I don't care if I wasn't chosen for the team; I didn't really want to play soccer anyway" and "I couldn't get my homework done because I had too many other things to do." Adolescents, caught between their own unruly impulses and adult expectations that seem unreasonable, are especially prone to rationalizing their behavior. Their advanced **cognitive development** makes many adolescents adept at this strategy.

Like rationalization, *isolation* is a rather complicated defense. It involves compartmentalizing one's experience so that an event becomes separated from the feelings that accompanied it, allowing it to be consciously available without the threat of painful feelings. Isolation can take on aspects of a *dissociative disorder,* with children separating parts of their lives to the point that they think of themselves as more than one person (for example, a good child and a bad one who only appears under certain circumstances). By compartmentalizing they can be relieved of feeling responsible for the actions of the "bad child."

*Sublimation,* one of the healthiest defense mechanisms, involves rechanneling the energy connected with an unacceptable impulse into one that is more socially acceptable. In this way, inappropriate sexual or aggressive impulses can be released in sports, creative pursuits, or other activities. Undesired feelings can also be sublimated into altruistic impulses, from which one may derive the vicarious pleasure of helping others. Other defense mechanisms generally viewed in a positive light include *compensation* —devoting unusual efforts to achievement in order to overcome feelings of inferiority—and the use of *humor* as a coping device.

## Further Reading
Firestone, Robert W., and Joyce Catlett. *Psychological Defenses in Everyday Life.* New York: Human Sciences Press, 1989.

Freud, Anna. *The Ego and the Mechanisms of Defense.* New York: International Universities Press, 1966.

Freud, Sigmund. *An Outline of Psychoanalysis.* New York: Norton, 1987.

Goleman, Daniel. *Vital Lies, Simple Truths: The Psychology of Self-Deception.* New York: Simon and Schuster, 1985.

# Delayed response

A characteristic event of an experimental procedure in which the subject is not permitted to respond to a stimulus until some time after the stimulus has been removed.

A delayed response experiment might include placing a stimulus object inside one of several similar opaque containers while the subject is watching but is restrained, and then allowing the subject to search for the object after a certain period of delay. Delayed response experiments have been conducted in the psychological study of both animals and (usually very young) humans. Some psychologists believe that the **ability** to respond appropriately after a significant delay indicates the operation of some form of advanced mental functioning, and that investigations of delayed response are useful in the comparative psychological analysis of various species.

# Delayed speech

See **Language delay**

# Delay of gratification

The ability to forgo an immediate pleasure or reward in order to gain a more substantial one later.

Almost everyone, everyday, practices delay of gratification—whether deciding to skip dessert in order to lose weight or give up smoking in order to live longer. The **ability** to delay gratification is often a sign of emotional and social maturity. Young children, for example, find it more difficult to delay gratification than older children. When kindergartners in one study were offered a choice between getting a small candy bar immediately or a larger one later, 72% chose the smaller candy bar. This number decreased to 67% among first and second graders and 49% for third and fourth graders. By the fifth and sixth grades it had fallen to 38%, nearly half the rate for kindergartners.

Although most people show an improved ability to delay gratification as they get older, some are more successful at it than others. Generally, the people who are most successful in delaying gratification are those with an internal **locus of control** (a strong belief that their actions can influence events). By contrast, people with an external locus of control are less likely to forego present pleasures for greater future gain.

# Delirium

A mental condition characterized by disorientation, confusion, uncontrolled imagination, reduced ability to focus or to maintain attention, and general inability to correctly comprehend immediate reality; often accompanied by illusions, delusions, and hallucinations.

Delirious behavior ranges from mildly inappropriate to maniacal, and is a symptom of a number of disorders. Delirium has been classified into several varieties, based primarily on causal factors. As an example, alcohol-withdrawal delirium, which is also called delirium tremens or D.T.s (because of the characteristic tremor), is an acute delirium related to physical deterioration and the abrupt lowering of blood alcohol levels upon cessation of alcohol intake after a period of abuse.

Delirium is believed to be caused by a chemical imbalance in the **brain**, which, in turn, may be caused by fever, drugs, head injury, disease, malnutrition, or other factors. The onset of delirium is usually fairly rapid, although the condition sometimes develops slowly, especially if a metabolic disorder is involved. Typically, delirium disappears soon after the underlying cause is successfully treated. Occasionally, however, recovery from delirium is limited by neurological or other damage.

# Delusion/Delusional disorders

Beliefs that are in stark contrast to reality, often having to do with persecution or an exaggerated sense of importance or glory.

Delusions are generally experienced by people suffering from a severe psychotic disorder, usually **schizophrenia**, although delusional thinking can occur in other types of patients (as the result of drug or alcohol abuse, for instance). Typical delusional ideas are categorized into delusions of grandeur, in which a person imagines for him or herself some God-given purpose or, in some cases, believe they are in fact historical personalities of great importance. Another type of delusion are delusions of persecution, in which a patient will believe that some person or group is out to harm him. Still another set of delusions involve what are referred to as "command hallucinations," in which a person hears voices telling him or her to commit an act. These delusional thoughts can lead people to acts of self-mutilation or to violent criminal acts.

Many psychological disorders feature aspects of delusional thought. People suffering from **depression** often experience delusions such as beliefs that they are worthless, sinful, or too unlikable to engage productively in society. Other forms of delusional thinking occur in people with somatoform and **dissociative identity disorder**s. These include body dysmorphic disorder, **obsessive-compulsive disorder**, and multiple **personality** disorder.

John Junginger, a clinical scientist at Indiana University, studied 138 patients who exhibited delusional beliefs and developed a scale of "bizarreness." Junginger identified the 12 types of delusional beliefs (including those mentioned above) as well as several others, such as "insertion" and "control." After categorizing delusional thoughts as such, Junginger conducted another study, attempting to discern how well his categories could predict violent behavior. Describing the study in *Omni* magazine, Steve Nadis wrote that "Junginger suspects psychotics are more likely to act out their false beliefs if they have involved, highly 'systematized' delusions." That is, elaborate delusional beliefs correlate more highly with violent behavior than vague delusional beliefs; so that someone who believes that some unidentified person is out to hurt them is less likely to act violently than someone who believes that a specific neighbor has been sending him messages to kill himself through the walls.

While researchers such as Junginger have sought out methods to predict **violence** as a result of delusions, other psychologists have been attempting to explain the occurrence of delusional thoughts. One intriguing idea, proposed by G.A. Roberts in the *British Journal of Psychiatry* in 1991, is that delusions actually help psychotic and schizophrenic patients by providing them with a detailed sense of purpose for their lives. Roberts found that people currently exhibiting delusional behavior were less depressed than those who had been delusional but were recovering.

### Further Reading
Nadis, Steve. "Dangerous Delusions: Making Sense of Senseless Behavior." *Omni* (December 1994): 32.
Starr, Cynthia. "A 'Secret Disorder' Yields to Serotonin Reuptake Inhibitors." *Drug Topics* (5 July 1993): 20.

# Dementia

A gradual deterioration of mental functioning affecting all areas of cognition, including judgment, language, and memory.

Dementia generally occurs in the elderly, although it can appear at any age. Several substantial studies have been done to determine its prevalence, and in 1991 a major study was conducted which found that dementia occurred in just over 1 percent of the population aged 65 to 74; in approximately 4 percent in ages 75 to 84; and more than doubling to 10.14 percent in persons 85 and over. Other studies have concluded that many as 47 percent of people over 85 suffer from some form of dementia. Prevalence rates tend to be comparable between the sexes and across sociocultural barriers, such as education and class. It is also worth noting that, despite what is often commonly thought, dementia is not an inevitable consequence of **aging**.

Researchers have identified many types of dementia, including dementia resulting from **Alzheimer's disease**, vascular dementia, substance induced dementia, dementia due to multiple etiologies, dementia due to other general medical conditions, and dementia not otherwise specified. More than half of the persons diagnosed with dementia are classified as having dementia resulting from Alzheimer's disease. This type of dementia occurs in more than half of dementia cases in the United States. There is no definitive method in diagnosing this kind of dementia until after the patient's death and an autopsy can be performed on the **brain**. Alzheimer-related de-

mentia is characterized by slow deterioration in the initial stages, but the rate of cognitive loss speeds up as the disease progresses. Patients with this type of dementia can generally be expected to live eight years.

Vascular dementia is the second most common type of dementia and is caused by damage to the blood vessels that carry blood to the brain, usually by stroke. Because the area of the brain that is affected differs from person to person, the pattern of cognitive deterioration in this type of dementia is unpredictable. Other diseases that can cause dementia include human immunodeficiency virus (HIV), **Parkinson's disease**, Huntington's disease, Pick's disease, and Creutzfeldt-Jakob disease. The kind of dementia induced by these diseases is known as subcortical, meaning they affect mainly the interior structures of the brain, as opposed to cortical dementia (Alzheimer's and vascular) which affect the outer layers of the brain. Many of these subcortical diseases have been known for some time to result in dementia, but HIV-related dementia has only recently been described and diagnosed. Recent studies have indicated that between 29 to 87 percent of people with AIDS show significant signs of dementia.

Generally speaking, dementia has a gradual onset and can take different routes in different people. All sufferers, however, are eventually impaired in all areas of **cognition**. Initially, dementia can appear in **memory** loss, which may result in being able to vividly remember events from many years past while not being able to remember events of the very recent past. Other symptoms of dementia are agnosia, which is the technical term for not being able to recognize familiar objects, facial agnosia, the inability to recognize familiar faces, and visiospatial impairment, the inability to locate familiar places.

Along with cognitive deterioration, sufferers of dementia often experience related emotional disorders as they recognize their deterioration and experience anxiety about its continuation and worsening. Typical among reactions are **depression**, anxiety, **aggression**, and apathy. Psychologists are uncertain to what extent these symptoms are direct results of dementia or simply responses to its devastation. Dementia progressively deteriorates the brain and eventually sufferers are completely unable to care for themselves and, ultimately, the disease results in death.

### Further Reading
Cooper, James W. Jr. "The Effects of Dementia." *American Druggist* (April 1993): 59.
Crystal, Howard. "Treating Severe Clinical Memory Disorders." *Newsweek* (3 May 1993): S6.
"Dementia: When You Suspect a Loved One's Problem." *Mayo Clinic Health Letter* (November 1995): 6

# Dendrite

Nerve cell fibers that receive signals from other cells.

Dendrites are one of two types of short, threadlike fibers that extend from the cell body of a **nerve** cell, or **neuron**. The other type are called axons. Dendrites receive electrochemical signals, which are known as postsynaptic potentials, from the axons of other neurons, and the information contained in these signals is fired across a synaptic gap or cleft about 0.02 microns or about 8 millionths of an inch wide and transmitted toward the cell body, with the signals fading as they approach their destination. A single neuron can have many dendrites, each composed of numerous branches; together, they comprise the greater part of the neuron's receptive surface.

The number of axons and dendrites increases dramatically during **infancy** and childhood—possibly to facilitate the rapid development experienced during this period—and decrease in early **adolescence**. A child of six or seven has more dendrites than an adult.

*See also* Synapse

# Deoxyribonucleic acid (DNA)

An organic substance occurring in chromosomes in the nuclei of cells, which encodes and carries genetic information, and is the fundamental element of heredity.

As the transmitter of inherited characteristics, deoxyribonucleic acid (DNA) replicates itself exactly and determines the structure of new organisms, which it does by governing the structure of their proteins. The Swiss researcher Friedrich Miescher first discovered DNA in 1869 when he extracted a substance (which he called nuclein) containing nitrogen and phosphorus from cell nuclei. The question of whether nucleic acids or proteins, or both, carried the information that make the genes of every organism unique was not answered, however, until the molecular structure of DNA was determined in 1953. This pioneering work was accomplished by an American biochemist, James D. Watson, and two British scientists, Francis Crick, a biochemist, and Maurice Wilkins, a biophysicist. The thousands of genes that make up each chromosome are composed of DNA, which consists of a five-carbon sugar (deoxyribose), phosphate, and four types of nitrogen-containing molecules (adenine, guanine, cytosine, and thymine). The sugar and phosphate combine to form the outer edges of a double helix, while

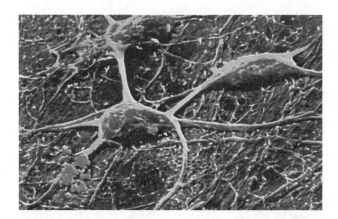

A scanning electron micrograph (SEM) of three neurons. The long thin structures connecting the cells are dendrites. *(Secchi-Lecague/Roussel-UCLAF/CNRI/Science Photo Library. National Audubon Society Collection/Photo Researchers, Inc. Reproduced with permission.)*

the nitrogen-containing molecules appear in bonded pairs like rungs of a ladder connecting the outer edges. They are matched in an arrangement that always pairs adenine in one chain with thymine in the other, and guanine in one chain with cytosine in the other. A single DNA molecule may contain several thousand pairs.

The specific order and arrangement of these bonded pairs of molecules constitute the genetic code of the organism in which they exist by determining, through the production of **ribonucleic acid (RNA)**, the type of protein produced by each gene, as it is these proteins that govern the structure and activities of all cells in an organism. Thus, DNA acts as coded message, providing a blueprint for the characteristics of all organisms, including human beings. When a cell divides to form new life, its DNA is "copied" by a separation of the two strands of the double helix, after which complementary strands are synthesized around each existing one. The end result is the formation of two new double helices, each identical to the original. All cells of a higher organism contain that organism's entire DNA pattern. However, only a small percentage of all the DNA messages are active in any cell at a given time, enabling different cells to "specialize."

Many viruses are also composed of DNA, which, in some cases, has a single-strand form rather than the two strands forming the edges of a double helix. Each particle of a virus contains only one DNA molecule, ranging in length from 5,000 to over 200,000 subunits. (The total length of DNA in a human cell is estimated at five billion subunits.) Radiation, thermal variations, or the presence of certain chemicals can cause changes, or "mistakes," in an organism's DNA pattern, resulting in a genetic mutation. In the course of evolution, such mutations provided the hereditary blueprints for the emergence of new species.

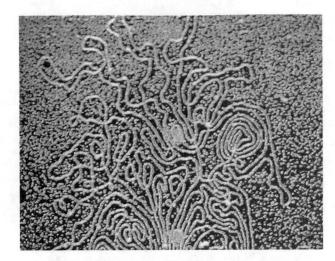

**Scan of DNA strands.** *(Photo by Howard Sochurek. Stock Market. Reproduced by permission.)*

Since the 1970s, scientists have furthered their understanding of the molecular structure of genes through experiments with recombinant DNA. As its name suggests, this technique combines fragments of DNA from two different species, allowing an experimenter to purify, or clone, a gene from one species by inserting it into the DNA of another, which replicates it together with its own genetic material. The term "recombinant DNA" also refers to other laboratory techniques, such as splitting DNA with microbial enzymes called endonucleases, splicing fragments of DNA, and even synthesizing it chemically. Although controversial, gene cloning is an important scientific accomplishment which has enabled researchers to gain new understanding of the structure of genes through the ability to produce an unlimited number of gene copies gathered from a variety of organisms, including human ones.

*See also* Heredity

**Further Reading**

Gribbin, John. *In Search of the Double Helix.* New York: McGraw-Hill, 1985.

# Dependent personality disorder

A lack of self-confidence coupled with excessive dependence on others.

Persons affected by dependent personality disorder have a disproportionately low level of confidence in their own **intelligence** and abilities and have difficulty making decisions and undertaking projects on their own. Their pervasive reliance on others, even for minor tasks or decisions, makes them exaggeratedly cooperative out of **fear** of alienating those whose help they need. They are reluctant to express disagreement with others and are often willing to go to abnormal lengths to win the approval of those on whom they rely. Another common feature of the disorder is an exaggerated fear of being left to fend for oneself. Adolescents with dependent personality disorder rely on their parents to make even minor decisions for them, such as what they should wear or how they should spend their free time, as well as major ones, such as what college they should attend.

Dependent personality disorder occurs equally in males and females and begins by early adulthood. It may be linked to either chronic physical illness or **separation anxiety** disorder earlier in life. The primary treatment for dependent personality disorder is **psychotherapy**, with an emphasis on learning to cope with anxiety, developing assertiveness, and improving decision-making skills. **Group therapy** can also be helpful.

**Further Reading**

Costa, Paul T., and Thomas A. Widiger, eds. *Personality Disorders and the Five-Factor Model of Personality.* Washington, DC: American Psychological Association, 1994.

Friedland, Bruce. *Personality Disorders.* New York: Chelsea House, 1991.

# Dependent variable

The variable measured in an experiment or study; what the experimenter measures.

When conducting research, a psychologist typically takes two or more similar groups of people or animals and exposes them to different treatments or situations. Then the researcher monitors a behavior of interest to see whether that behavior differs from one group to the next. This **measurement** is the dependent variable. A single experiment may involve more than one dependent variable.

When specifying the dependent variable, it must be clearly defined and measurable. In one experiment, researchers gathered a group of business executives who displayed evidence of Type A behavior (e.g., nonstop working, aggressiveness, and competitiveness). The researchers divided the executives into subgroups and either exposed them to a small amount of information regarding the health hazards of such behavior, provided them with support groups, or offered a course in **stress** management. The dependent variable was a score on a test that reflected Type A tendencies. Although **personality** is so complex that it cannot really be described by a single score, the test for Type A behavior provides a measurement that is objective and measurable. The executives who took the stress management course scored lower than those in the support groups; the highest test scores occurred in the group with the least exposure to information about stress management. The researchers concluded that the executives' test scores, the dependent variable, changed differently, depending on their group.

## Further Reading

Levenkron, J. C.; J. D. Cohen; H. S. Mueller; and E. B. Fisher. "Modifying the Type A Coronary-Prone Behavior Pattern." *Journal of Consulting and Clinical Psychology* 51 (1983): 192-204.

# Depression

An emotional state or mood characterized by one or more of these symptoms: sad mood, low energy, poor concentration, sleep or appetite changes, feelings of worthlessness or hopelessness, and thoughts of suicide.

Depression may signify a **mood**, a symptom, or a syndrome. As a mood, it refers to temporary feelings of sadness, despair, and discouragement. As a symptom, it refers to these feelings when they persist and are associated with such problems as decreased pleasure, hopelessness, **guilt**, and disrupted sleeping and eating patterns. The entire syndrome is also referred to collectively as a depression or depressive disorder. At any given time about 10 percent of all people suffer some of the symptoms of depression at an economic cost of more than $30 billion annually and costs in human suffering that cannot be estimated. The **American Psychiatric Association** estimates that about one in five Americans experiences an episode of depression at least once in his or her lifetime.

Depression can generally be traced to a combination of physical, psychological, and environmental factors. Depressive disorders involve a person's body, mood and thoughts.

Genetic inheritance makes some people more likely than others to suffer from depression. More than 60 percent of people who are treated for depression have family members who have been depressed at some time, and there is a 15 percent chance that immediate biological relatives of a depressed person will develop depression. Twin studies have also supported the existence of a genetic predisposition to depression, particularly bipolar depression. Researchers have found that depression is associated with changes in **brain** chemistry. The normal balance and functioning of two neurotransmitters in particular—serotonin and norepinephrine—appear to be disrupted in depressed persons, a finding that has led to the development of a variety of antidepressant drugs. Depression is also associated with an imbalance of cortisol, the main hormone secreted by the adrenal glands. Other physiological factors sometimes associated with depression include viral infections, low thyroid levels, and biological rhythms, including women's menstrual cycles—depression is a prominent symptom of **premenstrual syndrome (PMS)**.

Life events, including developmental traumas, physical illness, problems in intimate relationships, and losses may trigger a depression. According to classic psychoanalytic theory, depression is the result of losing someone through death or abandonment and turning one's feelings of **anger** and resentment inward. For behaviorists, the link between such negative events as the death of a loved one, the end of a relationship, or the loss of a job is the removal of a source of reward. Cognitive theorists claim that depressed people develop destructive ways of thinking, which include blaming themselves when things go wrong, focusing on the negative side of events, and habitually jumping to excessively pessimistic conclusions.

Another psychological explanation of depression centers on the concept of **learned helplessness**, a phenomenon first observed in a laboratory setting when animals that had no control over their situations (such as changing their situation by pressing a lever) showed signs of depression. It has been found that lack of control over their own lives is also associated with depression in humans and may be especially relevant to depression in women, whose incidence of depression is twice that of men. Another factor that may be linked to depression in women is the tendency to dwell on negative events, a cognitive style that research has shown to be more common among women than among men, who are more likely to distract themselves from negative feelings by engaging in various forms of activity.

The *Diagnostic and Statistical Manual (DSM) of Mental Disorders*, produced by the American Psychiatric Association, categorizes depression as an affective, or mood, disorder. The DSM criterion for clinical depression is the presence of at least five of the following symptoms almost every day for at least two weeks: depressed mood; loss of interest in activities; significant changes in appetite or weight; disturbed **sleep** patterns; agitated or slowed movements; fatigue; feelings of worthlessness or inappropriate guilt; trouble concentrating; and preoccupation with death or **suicide**. In a major depressive episode, these symptoms can persist for six months or longer without treatment. Usually, major depression first occurs in one's late twenties. In severe cases, people may be almost completely incapacitated, losing the ability to work, socialize, and even care for themselves. The depressive episode may eventually lift completely, or some symptoms may persist for as long as two years. More than half the people who suffer from major depression experience more than one episode. A serious complication of major depression is the threat of suicide. Some 60 percent of people who commit suicide are depressed, and 15 percent of those diagnosed with depression eventually commit suicide.

In dysthymia, a less severe form of depression, the symptoms are more prolonged but not disabling. Depressed mood is the major symptom. The depressed mood lasts at least two years for adults and one year for children with two or more of the other symptoms of clinical depression present. **Bipolar disorder** (manic depression) is characterized by the alternation of depression and **mania**, an overly elated, energetic state. Characteristic symptoms of mania include an inappropriately cheerful mood; inflated optimism and **self-esteem**; grandiose notions; excessive energy with a decreased need for sleep; racing thoughts; increased talking; and irritability when confronted by obstacles or opposition. During manic episodes, people characteristically use poor judgment, make irrational decisions and may even endanger their own lives. In bipolar disorder, manic episodes lasting days, weeks, or even months, alternate with periods of depression. There may be a period of normalcy between the two or an immediate mood swing from one mode to the other.

Cyclothymic disorder, the bipolar equivalent of dysthymia, resembles bipolar disorder but consists of a less extreme pattern of mood swings. Another type of depression, seasonal affective disorder (SAD), follows an annual cycle triggered by seasonal variations in light and usually involves depression during the winter months; it is thought to be due to an excess of the sleep-inducing hormone melatonin. Sometimes depressions become severe enough and include features of **psychosis**. These cases—which account for about 10 percent of all clinical depressions—are characterized by delusions or **hallucinations** and an especially high incidence of suicide.

Most people with clinical depression do not recognize that they have it and fail to seek treatment, blaming **stress** or physical ailments for their lack of well-being. Of those who do seek treatment either through **psychotherapy**, medication, or a combination of both, 80 percent improve, often within a matter of weeks. Psychotherapy alone is generally more effective for people with mild or moderate depression, while medication is advised for those whose depression is more severe or

who have developed physical symptoms. Most persons receiving psychotherapy for their depression undergo short-term treatment lasting between 12 and 16 weeks. Treatment methods vary among g different schools of therapy and individual therapists. **Cognitive behavior therapy** focuses on helping patients identify and change negative thought patterns; interpersonal and family therapies emphasize strategies for improving one's relationships with others; and behavioral therapy involves monitoring one's actions and modifying them through a system of incentives and rewards.

Two types of medication traditionally used to treat depression—tricyclic **antidepressants** and monoamine oxidase (MAO) inhibitors—increase the brain's supply of certain neurotransmitters, including norepinephrine and dopamine. Both medications are effective for many patients but can cause a variety of side effects, particularly MAO inhibitors. In recent years a new generation of antidepressants has been developed that affects levels of serotonin rather than norepinephrine. Among these selective serotonin reuptake inhibitors (SSRIs) is fluoxetine (Prozac), the most widely used antidepressant in the United States. It is effective in 60 to 80 percent of those who take it and has fewer side effects than previous types of antidepressants. Other SSRIs prescribed include sertraline (Zoloft) and paroxetine (Paxil). Lithium for many years has been used to treat manic episodes in persons with bipolar disorder. Other medications found to help control mood swings are: carbamazepine, which has gained wide acceptance in clinical practice, and valproate, approved by the Food and Drug Administration for first-line treatment of acute mania.

Whenever possible, persons suffering from depression should be urged to seek treatment through a private therapist, clinic, or hospital. There are special treatment centers for depression at medical centers throughout the country. A complete physical examination by a family physician or internist is the first step in getting appropriate treatment. Since certain medications and medical conditions, such as a viral infection, can cause depression-like symptoms, a physician can rule out these possibilities first.

*See also* Suicide/Suicidal behavior

## Further Reading
Persons, Jacqueline B. *Essential Components of Cognitive-Behavior Therapy for Depression.* Washington, D.C.: American Psychological Association, 2000.

Sholevar, G. Pirooz. *The Transmission of Depression in Families and Children: Assessment and Intervention.* Northvale, N.J.: Aronson, 1994.

Volkan, Vamik D. *Depressive states and their treatment.* Northvale, N.J.: J. Aronson, 1994.

# Depth perception

Ability to determine visually the distance between objects.

We can determine the relative distance of objects in two different ways. One uses cues involving only one eye; the second requires two eyes. When something is far from us, we rely on monocular cues, those that require the use of only one eye. For closer objects, we use both monocular cues and binocular cues, those that necessitate both eyes.

The **ability** to perceive depth seems to exist early in life. Research with infants has revealed that by two months of age, babies can perceive depth. Prior to that, they may be unable to do so in part because of weak eye muscles that do not let them use **binocular depth cues.**

*Monocular Depth Cues.* Psychologists have identified two different kinds of monocular cues. One comes into play when we use the muscles of the eye to change the shape of the eye's lens to focus on an object. We make use of the amount of muscular tension to give feedback about distance.

A second kind of monocular cue relates to external visual stimuli. These cues appear in the table below. Artists use these visual cues to make two dimensional paintings appear realistic. These cues may seem obvious to us now, but artistic renderings from earlier than about the sixteenth century often seem distorted because artists had not yet developed all the techniques to capture these visual cues.

*Binocular Cues.* Binocular cues require that we use both eyes. One cue makes use of the fact that when we look at a nearby object with both eyes, we bring our eyes together; the muscle tension associated with looking at close objects gives us information about their distance. The second binocular cue involves retinal disparity. This means that each eye (or, more specifically, the retina of each eye) has a slightly different perspective. The slight difference in appearance of an object in each eye when we gaze at it gives us further information about depth. Children's Viewmasters produce a three-dimensional image that has depth because of a slightly different picture that is delivered to each eye. In the natural world, because of the relatively small distance from one pupil to another (about 2.5 inches or 6.5 centimeters) binocular cues are effective only for objects that are within about 500 yards (455 m) of the viewer.

Animals that have eyes on front of the face, like primates, will be able to use binocular depth cues because the two eyes see almost, but not quite, the same scene; on the other hand, animals with eyes on the side of the head, like most birds, will be less able to use binocular cues because the visual fields of the two eyes do not overlap very much and each eye sees different scenes.

| MONOCULAR CUE—HOW IT WORKS | |
|---|---|
| Aerial Perspective | Objects that are near seem crisper and clearer; far away objects appear fuzzier. |
| Height in Plane | Objects that are farther away appear higher in the visual scene. |
| Interposition | Objects that are nearer block objects that are farther away. |
| Linear Perspective | Lines that are parallel (e.g., railroad tracks) look like they come to a point in the distance. The farther the lines, the closer they are. |
| Motion Parallax | When you are moving and you fixate on a spot, objects closer to you than that spot appear to move in the direction opposite to your motion; objects farther than that spot appear to move in the same direction as you are moving. |
| Relative Size | If two objects are of the same size, the closer one is bigger. |

# René Descartes

## 1596-1650

French philosopher and mathematician whose ideas included early and significant contributions to the field of psychology.

Descartes was born in France, near the small village of Le Haye. From the age of 10, he attended the most prestigious school in France, the Royal Collège of La Flèche, graduating at the age of 16. After spending some time sampling the amusements of Parisian society, followed by a period of solitary studies in philosophy and mathematics, Descartes briefly served as a soldier on the eve of the Thirty Years' War, joining first the Protestant and then the Catholic forces. Returning to the study of science and philosophy after the war, he spent several more years in Paris before moving to Holland at the age of 32. There Descartes wrote his most important works, *Discourse on Method* (1637), *Meditations on First Philosophy* (1642), and *Principles of Philosophy* (1644). Because his books aroused controversy among the Dutch Protestant clergy, Descartes, already wary after Galileo's condemnation by the Inquisition, published little for the remainder of his life, confining his thoughts largely to unpublished manuscripts and letters. His last published work was the *Passions of the Soul* (1649). Descartes remained in Holland for most of his life, although he moved frequently during his time there. In 1649, he left for Sweden at the invitation of Queen Christina and undertook to tutor her in philosophy. Only months after arriving in Sweden, Descartes died at the age of 53.

Descartes's philosophy is known for its glorification of human reason. He began with the premise that the only way to be sure of anything is to doubt everything ("I resolved to reject as false everything in which I could imagine the least doubt, in order to see if there afterwards remained anything that was entirely indubitable"). In so doing, Descartes arrived at the conclusion that the one thing he could be sure of was his own act of doubting—a mental process. From the certainty expressed in the famous statement, "I think, therefore I am," he built a philosophy that gave to the workings of the individual mind priority over both immediate sensory experience and received wisdom. Descartes postulated a radical mind-body dualism, claiming that the universe consisted of two utterly distinct substances: mind ("thinking substance" or *res cogitans)* and matter ("physical substance" or *res extensa* ). Thus, he separated mental phenomena from the comprehensive mechanistic explanation he gave for the workings of matter and material things, including the human body, which he divided into ten physiological systems. These included such faculties as **memory** and

**René Descartes** *(The Library of Congress. Reproduced by permission.)*

**imagination**, along with the purely physiological functions of digestion, circulation, and respiration.

Descartes believed the primary site of interaction between mind and body to be the pineal gland (which he incorrectly thought to be unique to humans). He held that the will, an aspect of the mind, can move the pineal gland and cause the transmission of what he called animal spirits, which produce mechanical changes in the body; and, similarly, that changes in the body are transmitted to the pineal gland and can there affect the mind. His rationalistic ideas provided a basis for the Enlightenment and became the dominant system of philosophy until the work of **David Hume** (1711-1776) and Immanuel Kant (1724-1804). While many of Descartes's individual arguments have since been discredited, his overall view of the dualism between mind and body has been a powerful influence on succeeding generations of philosophers and psychologists.

## Further Reading

Popper, K., and J. Eccles. *The Self and Its Brain.* London, 1977.

Smith, Norman Kemp. *New Studies in the Philosophy of Descartes.* New York: Russell and Russell, 1963.

Vrooman, J. R. *Rene Descartes: A Biography.* New York: Putnam, 1970.

# Desensitization

*A behavior modification technique used to combat phobias and other irrational fears.*

Developed by **Joseph Wolpe** in the 1950s, desensitization is a treatment method which weakens the learned association between anxiety and feared objects or situations by strengthening another response—in this case, relaxation—that is incompatible with anxiety. Relaxation responses are strengthened through progressive relaxation training, first developed by Edmund Jacobson in the 1930s. Clients first tighten and then relax 16 different muscle groups in various parts of the body, releasing the tension and focusing on the resulting feelings of relaxation. Once people learn how their muscles feel when they are truly relaxed, they develop the ability to reproduce this state voluntarily and in a variety of situations.

Next, the client outlines an "anxiety hierarchy," a list of situations or stimuli arranged in order from least to most anxiety-provoking. For a person who is afraid of flying, such a list might begin with seeing a picture of an airplane, eventually progress to driving to the airport, and end with taking an actual plane flight. With the aid of the therapist, the client then works through the list, either imagining or actually experiencing each situation while in a state of relaxation. When tolerance for each listed item is established, the client moves on to the next one. As clients face progressively more threatening situations, relaxation rather than **fear** becomes associated with the source of their anxiety, and they become gradually desensitized to it. While exposure through **mental imagery** does produce desensitization, actual real-life exposure to the feared stimulus whenever possible is more effective.

## Further Reading

Craighead, W. Edward. *Behavior Modification: Principles, Issues, and Applications.* New York: Houghton Mifflin, 1976.
Skinner, B.F. *About Behaviorism.* New York: Knopf, 1974.
Wolpe, Joseph. *The Practice of Behavior Therapy.* Tarrytown, NY: Pergamon Press, 1990.

# Determinism

*A scientific perspective which specifies that events occur in completely predictable ways as a result of natural and physical laws.*

Since ancient times, the origins of human behavior have been attributed to hidden or mystical forces. The Greek philosopher Democritus speculated, for example, that objects in our world consist of atoms; included among these "objects" was the soul, which was made of finer, smoother, and more spherical atoms than other physical objects. He rejected the concept of free will and claimed that all human behavior results from prior events. Some philosophers have advanced the argument that human behavior is deterministic, although most have resisted the idea that human beings merely react to external events and do not voluntarily select behaviors.

There is a clear dilemma in explaining human behavior through psychological principles. On the one hand, if psychology is a science of behavior, then there should be laws allowing the prediction of behavior, just as there are gravitational laws to predict the behavior of a falling object. On the other hand, objections have been raised by individuals who believe that humans control their own behaviors and possess free will. Part of the controversy relates to the concept of the mind and body as separate entities. In this view, the mind may not be subject to the same laws as the body. **Wilhelm Wundt** (1832-1920) attempted to make the distinction between determinism and indeterminism by suggesting that psychological processes could be creative and free, whereas the physiological processes in the **brain** were deterministic. This argument does not solve the problem for psychology, however, because psychologists consider mental processes appropriate for study within a scientific framework, thus subject to scientific laws.

Other psychologists like **William James**, who was interested in religion and believed in free will, recognized this conflict but was reluctant to abandon the concept that behaviors were not free. At one point, he suggested that mind and body operated in tandem, whereas on another occasion he concluded that they interacted. Clearly, James struggled with the issue and, like others, was unable to resolve it. The behaviorists were the most obvious proponents of determinism, dating back to **John B. Watson**, who claimed that **environment** was the single cause of behavior, and who made one of the most famous deterministic assertions ever: "Give me a dozen healthy infants . . . and my own specified world to bring them up in and I'll guarantee to take anyone at random and train him to become any type of specialist I might select—doctor, lawyer, artist, merchant, chief, and, yes, even beggar man and thief."

The psychologist with the greatest influence in this area, however, was **B. F. Skinner.** He adopted a stance called radical **behaviorism**, which disregarded free will and the internal causes of behavior. All behavior, Skinner maintained, was determined through **reinforcement** contingencies, that is, the pattern of reinforcements and punishments in an individual's life. Although critics have claimed that Skinner's concept of determinism denied people of their humanity, he maintained that his approach could actually lead to more humane societies. For example, if people were not responsible for negative behaviors, they should not be punished, for they had no control over their behaviors. Instead, the environment that reinforced the unwanted behaviors should be changed so that desirable behaviors receive reinforcement and increase in frequency.

**Sigmund Freud** defined determinism in terms of the **unconscious** and contended that behavior is caused by internal, mental mechanisms. In some ways, Freud was more extreme than Skinner, who acknowledged that some behaviors are not predictable. The main difference between Freud and Skinner involved the origin of causation; Freud believed in underlying physiological processes while Skinner opted to focus on external causes. Thus, even though Freudians and Skinnerians differ on almost every conceivable dimension, they have at least one commonality in their reliance on determinism.

Those scientists who believe that behaviors are determined have recognized the difficulty in making explicit predictions. Thus, they have developed the concept of statistical determinism. This means that, even though behaviors are determined by fixed laws, predictions will never be perfect because so many different factors, most of them unknown, affect actions, which result in generally accurate predictions. The recently developed theory of chaos relates to making predictions about complex events such as behaviors. This theory suggests that in a cause-effect situation, small differences in initial conditions may lead to very different outcomes. This theory supports the notion that behaviors may not be completely predictable even though they may be dictated by fixed natural laws.

**Further Reading**
Doob, Leonard William. *Inevitability: Determinism, Fatalism, and Destiny.* New York: Greenwood Press, 1988.

# Developmental delay

Any delay in a child's physical, cognitive, behavioral, emotional, or social development, due to any number of reasons.

Developmental delay refers to any significant retardation in a child's physical, cognitive, behavioral, emotional, or social development. The two most frequent reasons for classing a child as having developmental delay involve those psychological systems for which there are good norms. This is especially true for motor development and **language development**. Because it is

known that all children begin to crawl by eight months of age and walk by the middle of the second year, any child who was more than five or six months delayed in attaining those two milestones would probably be classified as developmentally delayed and the parents should consult the pediatrician.

Most children begin to speak their first words before they are eighteen months old and by three years of age the vast majority are speaking short sentences. Therefore, any child who is not speaking words or sentences by the third birthday would be considered developmentally delayed and, as in motor development delay, the parent should consult the pediatrician.

The other developmental problems that children show are more often called disabilities rather than delays. Thus, the small group of children with **autism** do not show **normal** social development but these children are usually called disabled or autistic rather than developmentally delayed. Similarly, most children are able to read single words by the second grade of elementary school. Children who cannot do that are normally labeled dyslexic or learning disabled, or in some cases academically delayed, rather than developmentally delayed.

Physical development is assessed by progress in both fine and **gross motor skills**. Possible problems are indicated by muscles that are either too limp or too tight. Jerky or uncertain movements are another cause for concern, as are abnormalities in **reflexes**. Delays in motor development may indicate the presence of a neurological condition such as mild cerebral palsy or Tourette's syndrome. Neurological problems may also be present when a child's head circumference is increasing either too fast or too slowly. Although physical and cognitive delays may occur together, one is not necessarily a sign of the other.

Important cognitive attainments that physicians look for in infants in the first 18 months include object permanence, an awareness of causality, and different reactions to strangers and family members. Cognitive delays can signal a wide variety of problems, including **fetal alcohol syndrome** and **brain** dysfunction. Developmental milestones achieved and then lost should also be investigated, as the loss of function could be sign of a degenerative neurological condition.

Delays in social and **emotional development** can be among the most difficult for parents, who feel rejected by a child's failure to respond to them on an emotional level. They expect such responses to social cues as smiling, vocalization, and cuddling, and may feel angry or frustrated when their children do not respond. However, a delay in social responses can be caused by a number of factors, including prenatal **stress** or deprivation, prematurity, **birth** difficulties, including oxygen deprivation, or a hypersensitivity of the **nervous system** (which creates an aversion to stimuli that are normally tolerated or welcomed).

Many physicians routinely include developmental screening in physical examinations. Parents concerned about any aspect of their child's development are generally advised to seek the opinion of a pediatrician or appropriate specialist. Specific assessment instruments such as the Gesell Development Scales and the **Bayley Scales of Infant Development** are used to help determine whether an infant is developing at a rate appropriate to the child's age.

### Further Reading

Haskell, Simon H. *The Education of Children with Motor and Neurological Disabilities.* New York: Nichols, 1989.

Sugden, David A. *Problems in Movement Skill Development.* Columbia, SC: University of South Carolina Press, 1990.

# Developmental reading disorder

A condition in which reading ability is significantly below the norm in relation to chronological age and overall intellectual potential.

Also referred to as reading **disability**, reading difficulty, and **dyslexia**, developmental reading disorder is the most commonly diagnosed **learning disability** in the United States. Estimates of its prevalence vary widely, ranging from 4% of children—the figure given by the **American Psychiatric Association**'s *Diagnostic and Statistical Manual*—to 20%, the figure given by a 1995 study directed by Sally E. Shaywitz of Yale University. According to the latter figure, some 10 million children in the United States have some form of reading disability.

Reading disabilities are diagnosed up to five times more frequently in boys than girls, although some sources claim that this figure is misleading because boys are more likely to be screened for learning disabilities due to their higher incidence of disruptive behavior, which draws the attention of educators and other professionals. Most reading disabilities were formerly grouped together under the term dyslexia, which has largely fallen out of favor with educators and psychologists because of confusion over widespread and inconsistent use of the term in both broad and narrower contexts. Developmental reading disorder is distinct from alexia, which is the term for reading difficulties caused by **brain** damage from injury or disease. However, neurological studies of alexia have helped researchers better understand reading disabilities.

## Types of and causes of reading disorders

Reading disabilities have been classified as either dyseidetic, dysphonetic, or mixed. Children with the dyseidetic type are able to sound out individual letters phonetically but have trouble identifying patterns of letters when they are grouped together. By comparison, dysphonic readers have difficulty relating letters to sounds, so their spelling is totally chaotic. Children with mixed reading disabilities have both the dyseidetic and dysphonic types of reading disorder.

A variety of causes have been advanced for developmental reading disorder. Researchers favoring a biological explanation have cited **heredity**, **minimal brain dysfunction**, delays in neurological development, and failure of the right and left hemispheres to function properly together.

Developmental reading disorder is often identified in the first grade, when reading instruction begins. Children with reading disabilities lag behind their peers in reading progress and have serious spelling problems. They also tend to have trouble writing (many have poor handwriting), have an unusually small vocabulary, and favor activities that do not require verbal skills. Also, like children with other learning disabilities, those with developmental reading disorder often earn poor grades and dislike school, reading, and homework. Even at the preschool stage, there are certain problems, such as trouble sounding out words and difficulty understanding words or concepts, which may foreshadow a reading disability.

The outcome of treatment for reading disabilities varies, depending on the quality of the remedial reading program, the severity of the disorder, and the **motivation** and **intelligence** of the child. Given the proper remedial help, some children with reading disabilities have been able to successfully complete high school, college, and even graduate school, while others have been forced to limit their vocational choices to fields that do not demand strong literacy skills. Factors that have been found to contribute to the success of treatment include early intervention (elementary rather than secondary school); an IQ over 90; instruction by qualified reading specialists; and a total of over 50 hours of instruction.

### Further Reading

Goldsworthy, Candace L. *Developmental Reading Disorders: A Language-Based Treatment Approach.* San Diego: Singular Publishing Group, 1996.

Lipson, Marjorie Y. and Karen K. Wixson. *Assessment and Instruction of Reading Disability: An Interactive Approach.* New York: HarperCollins, 1991.

Manzo, Ula C. *Literacy Disorders: Holistic Diagnosis and Remediation.* Fort Worth: Harcourt, Brace Jovanovitch, 1993.

## Further Information

Dyslexia Research Foundation. 600 Northern Boulevard, Great Neck, NY 11021, (516) 482–2888.

The Learning Disabilities Association of America. 4156 Library Rd., Pittsburgh, PA 15234, (412) 341–1515.

Nation Center for Learning Disabilities, Inc. (NCLD). 99 Park Ave., 6th Floor, New York, NY 10016, (212) 687–7211

Orton Dyslexia Society. 8600 LaSalle Road, Chester Building, Suite 382, Baltimore, MD 21286-2044, (410) 296–0232, information line: (800) ABC-D123.

# Developmental psychology

A field of psychology which examines how human behavior changes as a person matures through focusing on biological, emotional, physical, cognitive, and social changes that are age-related, sequential, and long-lasting.

Developmental psychologists study how characteristics and behaviors first appear and how and when they change. They study the relationships between different types of development, such as cognitive and social, as well as individual variations in development, both **normal** and deviant. Initially, developmental psychology focused on **childhood** but was subsequently expanded to cover changes that occur over the entire life span, from the intrauterine environment through childhood, **adolescence**, middle age, and maturity. Three processes that play a central role in development are growth, maturation, and learning. Growth refers to physical changes that are quantitative, such as increases in height or weight. Maturation involves anatomical, neurophysiological, and chemical transformations that change the way a person functions (such as a woman's passage into or out of childbearing age). Learning involves relatively long-term changes in behavior or performance acquired through observation, experience, or training.

One of the oldest questions in developmental psychology involves the **nature-nurture controversy**, which asks how and to what degree nature (inherited or genetic factors influencing development) contributes to a person's biological, emotional, cognitive, and social development, and to what degree it is the result of nurture (the influence of learning and experience in the **environment**). This issue has been debated for centuries by philosophers, who often argued strenuously for the predominance of one influence over the other (a famous example is the British philosopher John Locke's concept of the newborn human being as a blank slate, or *tabula rasa*, to be formed by experience). Pioneered by the American psychologist **Arnold Gesell**, the concept of maturation, which is central to developmental psychology, stresses the role of nature in human development. Gesell observed that the motor skills of children develop in a fixed order through a series of stages relatively unaffected by outside influences. The interplay of nature and nurture, rather than the importance of one over the other, however, has gained a greater emphasis in the work of more recent figures, notably the Swiss psychologist **Jean Piaget**, whose theory of **cognitive development** in children has been a model for much subsequent work in the field. Going beyond simplistic dichotomies, scientists have been able to gather substantial amounts of specific data on the effects of **heredity** and environment through **family**, twin, and **adoption** studies. Current concepts of maturation focus on models in which each stage of a developmental process is defined not only by innate characteristics but also by increased receptivity (or "readiness") toward certain environmental factors.

Another significant issue in the field of developmental psychology is the question of continuity versus stages, specifically, does an individual's development occur in a gradual and progressive (continuous) fashion, or in a distinct series of discrete stages? In his pioneering theory of cognitive development, Piaget delineated a sequence of developmental stages that occur in a fixed order with each dependent on the previous ones (sensorimotor, preoperational, concrete operational, and formal operational). Subsequent research has challenged some of his assumptions, finding in some cases that children are capable of advanced thinking at younger ages than those posited by Piaget. Observations such as these have led to the conclusion that cognitive development is more uneven and less systematic than previously thought, and that children's reasoning abilities in a specific situation may depend on variables—familiarity with certain objects, language comprehension, and prior experiences—that are not part of Piaget's system. One recent model advances the notion of cognitive development in "pockets" rather than globally uniform levels or stages. Another alternative that has been suggested is an information processing model focusing on gradual quantitative advances in **memory** and other learning abilities rather than qualitative progress through a series of stages.

In addition to Piaget, another major influence in the area of human development was **Erik Erikson**, whose eight stages of psychosocial development, encompassing the entire life span from **infancy** through old age, inspired an interest in the continuation of development past childhood. Erikson's work also popularized the concept of the adolescent "identity crisis" (a term he coined). Yet another type of development that has gained increased interest in recent years is **moral development**, which has been most extensively investigated by **Lawrence Kohlberg**. Presenting subjects with hypothetical moral dilemmas, Kohlberg found that moral reasoning in children develops through three distinct levels (consisting of two stages each) between the age of seven and adolescence. Like Piaget's theory, Kohlberg's stages do not necessarily occur at a given age but they do occur consistently in a given order. Also, not all individuals reach the final stage, at which following rules and obeying the social order is superseded by the imperative of the individual **conscience** to obey ethical principles that may transcend the law. The universality of some of Kohlberg's findings has been challenged in terms of applicability to non-Western cultures and women (Kohlberg's research focused on men). When Carol Gilligan questioned subjects about moral conflicts, the reactions of male and female respondents differed significantly, and Gilligan drew up her own model for women.

*See also* Cognitive development; Cognitive psychology; Information-processing theory

### Further Reading

Anderson, Clifford. *The Stages of Life: A Groundbreaking Discovery: the Steps to Psychological Maturity.* New York: Atlantic Monthly Press, 1995.

Berger, Kathleen Stassen. *The Developing Person Through the Life Span.* 2nd ed. New York: Worth Publishers, 1988.

Cicchetti, Dante, and Donald J. Cohen, eds. *Developmental Psychopathology.* New York: J. Wiley, 1995.

# Developmental stages, theories of

The various stages developmental psychologists theorize people go through as they develop from early life into childhood and beyond.

Developmental psychologists, by and large, study the way humans develop from an embryo into a full grown adult, focusing mainly on the factors that contribute to **intelligence**, **personality**, morality, and lifestyle. Of special interest are the effects certain stimuli have on the development of humans. For instance, does genetics pre-program a person to be introverted, or is that personality trait the result of specific life events that caused him or her to retreat inward? Or, did intense study of music from an early age make someone a gifted musician, or is that something their genes had pre-programmed from the moment of conception?

Over the past hundred years or so, several prominent psychologists and psychiatrists have devised various theories seeking to quantify the developmental stages humans pass through, and in doing so, have sought to map out this difficult process. One of the more

---

## STAGES OF DEVELOPMENT

**ERIK ERIKSON**

"Trust versus mistrust" from birth to 18 months

"Autonomy versus shame" from one-and-a-half to three years

"Initiative versus guilt" from three to six years

"Industry versus inferiority" from six to 12 years.

**JEAN PIAGET**

"Sensorimotor stage" from birth to two years

"Preoperational stage" from two to seven years

"Concrete operational stage" from seven to 12 years

"Formal operational stage" from 13 to adult.

**LAWRENCE KOHLBERG**

"Preconventional stage," where moral decisions are based on how they *themselves* are affected

"Conventional stage," where moral judgments are based on the conventions of society, family, religion, or other social order (Many people do not pass beyond this stage.)

"Post-conventional level," where moral judgments are based on personal beliefs.

---

famous theories of **developmental psychology** was put forth by the psychological theorist **Erik Erikson** in 1963 in his important work *Childhood and Society*. In this work, Erikson suggests that psychosocial development, the changing ways we perceive ourselves individually and in relation to society, occurs in eight stages—only four of which deal with **childhood**. The first of Erikson's stages is "trust versus mistrust" and occurs from birth to 1 years. The child formulates either a trusting or mistrusting relationship to the world around it, based on whether its immediate needs are met. These needs, at this young age, generally have to do with satisfaction of physical cravings (food, **sleep**, and comfort) and for feelings of **attachment**.

The second stage of development Erikson called "autonomy versus shame" and doubt—occurring between 1 and 3 years of age. Here, young children learn to be independent and autonomous on the condition that they are adequately encouraged to explore their world and given the freedom to do so. On the other hand, children with overly restrictive or anxious parents who wield too great an influence over their children's behavior, stifling **creativity** and independent exploration of their **environment**, become shameful and self doubting.

Between the ages of three and six, children pass through the stage Erikson refers to as "initiative versus guilt." During this period of development, children seek to further explore their world by initiating new experiences. The **guilt** comes about when there are unexpected consequences involved in these initiations. The final stage of childhood development is called "industry versus inferiority," and it lasts from age six to 12. Here, children seek to become industrious in all areas of life, from school to interpersonal relations. Mastery of these skills, with adequate support at home and in school, brings about a sense of overall competence, whereas failure brings about a sense of inferiority.

Another prominent theorist in developmental psychology was **Jean Piaget**, who developed the four stages of **cognitive development**. He theorized that people pass from one stage to another not just as a matter of course, but only when they are confronted with the correct type of stimulation to initiate a change. Piaget believed that in the absence of the correct kinds of stimulation, children would never reach their full potential.

According to Piaget, from birth to two years of age, children are in the "sensorimotor" stage of cognitive development. During this stage, children first begin to develop motor skills. They also have little or no **ability** for what is called symbolic representation, that is, the ability to conceive of things existing outside of their immediate vicinity. Piaget called this ability object permanence. Piaget's next stage is called "preoperational" (from ages two to seven). In this stage, children begin to use language and other representational systems to conceive of, and even discuss, things or people who are not physically present. The chief marker of this stage is what Piaget called egocentric thought. That is, preoperational children can conceive of things that are not present, but they can not conceive of others perceiving what *they* can not. The classic example of this kind of thinking is the young child who in order to hide simply covers his eyes, thinking that since he can no longer see, no one else can either.

Piaget's next stage is called "concrete operational" and covers the years 7 to 12. Here, children begin to develop clearer methods of thinking, and they start to overcome the egocentrism of the preoperational stage. They begin to better understand spatial relationships and matters of time, but they are largely bound by the concrete world and have trouble conceiving abstract thought. During the formal operational stage, from age 12 to adulthood, people develop the ability to think logically and systematically and to understand abstractions and the concepts of causality and choice. They see that different outcomes can proceed from different actions, and that they are free to choose between various actions depending on a desired outcome. According to Piaget, and to many who believe in his framework, not everyone reaches this stage of cognitive development. Some researchers assert that as few as 25 percent of the general population reaches the formal operational stage. Still others suggest that it is a culture-based phenomena and that in less technological societies, almost no one reaches the stage—mainly because such thinking is not valued or even necessary.

A final theory dealing with developmental psychology was devised by **Lawrence Kohlberg** and presented in his 1981 book *The Philosophy of Moral Development: Moral Stages and the Idea of Justice*. Kohlberg's stages deal with how children formulate moral reasoning at various stages of cognitive development. He called the earliest stage the "preconventional." Here, children base moral decisions on how they themselves are affected. Something is "right," in other words, if they are not likely to be punished for doing it. The next level is the "conventional" stage. During this stage, people base their moral judgments on the conventions of society (or of family or religion or some other social order). Something is "right" during this stage of development if it is something most people would agree is right. Many people do not pass beyond the conventional level of moral reasoning. If they do, they arrive at what Kohlberg calls the "post-conventional level," where moral judgments are based on personal beliefs. People in this stage of **moral development** will do what they consider is "right" even if it contradicts social norms.

*See also* Cognitive development; Psychosexual stages

### Further Reading
Marse, Michele Black. "Is My Child Normal?" *Parents' Magazine* (September 1991): 68.

# John Dewey

## 1859-1952
American philosopher, educator, and psychologist who made significant contributions to the establishment of the school of functional psychology.

John Dewey was born near Burlington, Vermont. After receiving his B.A. from the University of Vermont, he taught high school and studied philosophy independently before entering the graduate program in philosophy at Johns Hopkins University. After receiving his Ph.D. in 1884, Dewey served on the faculties of the University of Michigan, the University of Minnesota, the University of Chicago, and Columbia University. Dewey was a founder

**John Dewey** *(The Library of Congress. Reproduced with permission.)*

of the philosophical movement called pragmatism, and his writings on educational theory and practice were widely read and accepted. He held that the disciplines of philosophy, pedagogy, and psychology should be understood as closely interrelated. Dewey came to believe in an "instrumentalist" theory of knowledge, in which ideas are seen to exist primarily as instruments for the solution of problems encountered in the **environment**.

Dewey's work at the University of Chicago between 1894 and 1904—together with that of his colleague, Rowland Angell (1869-1949)—made that institution a world-renowned center of the functionalist movement in psychology. Dewey's **functionalism** was influenced by **Charles Darwin**'s theory of evolution, as well as by the ideas of **William James** and by Dewey's own instrumentalist philosophy. His 1896 paper, "The Reflex Arc Concept in Psychology," is generally considered the first major statement establishing the functionalist school. In this work, Dewey attacked the prevailing reductionist methods of such figures as **Wilhelm Wundt** (1832-1920) and Edward Titchener (1867-1927), who used stimulus-response analysis as the basis for psychological theories that reduced human experience to the simplest and most basic units possible. Dewey considered their approach flawed because it ignored both the continuity

of human behavior and its significance in terms of **adaptation**. In contrast, functionalism sought to consider the total organism as it functioned in the environment—an active perceiver rather than a passive receiver of stimuli.

Dewey was also an educational reformer and a pioneer in the field of **educational psychology**. Paralleling his philosophical and psychological theories, his concept of instrumentalism in education stressed learning by doing, as opposed to authoritarian teaching methods and rote learning. Dewey's ideas have remained at the center of much educational philosophy in the United States. While at the University of Chicago, Dewey founded an experimental school to develop and study new educational methods, a project that won him both fame and controversy. He experimented with educational curricula and methods, successfully combining theory and practice, and also pioneered in advocating parental participation in the educational process. His first influential book on education, *The School and Society* (1899), was adapted from a series of lectures to parents of the pupils in his school at the University of Chicago. During his time at Columbia, he continued working on the applications of psychology to problems in education, and his work influenced educational ideas and practices throughout the world.

Dewey wrote the first American psychology textbook, titled *Psychology (1886)*, which was followed by William James's *The Principles of Psychology* four years later. Dewey served as president of the **American Psychological Association** from 1899 to 1900 and was the first president of the American Association of University Professors in 1915. In 1920 he helped organize the American Civil Liberties Union. In the following years, Dewey surveyed educational practices in several foreign countries, including Turkey, Mexico, and the Soviet Union. After his retirement in 1930, Dewey continued his writing and his advocacy of political and educational causes, including the advancement of adult education. Among Dewey's large body of writings are: *Applied Psychology: An Introduction to the Principles and Practice of Education* (1889), *Interest as Related to Will* (1896), *Studies in Logical Theory* (1903), *How We Think* (1910), *Democracy and Education* (1916), *Experience and Nature* (1925), *Philosophy and Civilization* (1931), *Experience and Education* (1938), and *Freedom and Culture* (1939).

*See also* Assessment, psychological

**Further Reading**

Boydston, Jo Ann. *Guide to the Works of John Dewey.* Edwardsville, IL:Southern Illinois University Press, 1972.

Hook, Sidney. *John Dewey: An Intellectual Portrait.* New York: John Day Co., 1939.

# Diagnostic and Statistical Manual of Mental Disorders (DSM-IV)

A reference work developed by the American Psychiatric Association and designed to provide guidelines for the diagnosis and classification of mental disorders.

The **American Psychiatric Association** publishes the *Diagnostic and Statistical Manual of Mental Disorders,* widely referred to as *DSM-IV,* a reference work de-

signed to provide guidelines for psychologists and others to use in the diagnosis and classification of mental disorders. The latest edition, *DSM-IV,* serves as a reference to psychiatrists, other physicians and **mental health** professionals, psychologists, social workers, and others in clinical, educational, and social service settings.

First published in 1917, each new edition of *Diagnostic and Statistical Manual of Mental Disorders* has added new categories. With the third edition, published in 1980, the *DSM* began recommending assessment of mental disorders according to five axes, or dimensions, that together establish an overall picture of a person's mental,

## CLASSIFICATION OF MENTAL DISORDERS

**DISORDERS USUALLY FIRST DIAGNOSED IN INFANCY, CHILDHOOD, OR ADOLESCENCE**

- Mental retardation
- Learning disorders
- Motor skill disorder
- Communication disorders
- Pervasive developmental disorders
- Attention-deficit and disruptive behavior disorders
- Feeding and eating disorders of infancy or early childhood
- Tic disorders
- Elimination disorders
- Other disorders of infancy, childhood, or adolescence

**DELIRIUM, DEMENTIA, AND AMNESTIC AND OTHER COGNITIVE DISORDERS**

- Delirium
- Dementia
- Amnestic disorders
- Other cognitive disorders

**MENTAL DISORDERS DUE TO A GENERAL MEDICAL CONDITION NOT ELSEWHERE CLASSIFIED**

**SUBSTANCE-RELATED DISORDERS**

- Alcohol-related disorders
- Amphetamine use disorders
- Amphetamine-induced disorders
- Caffeine-related disorders
- Cannabis-related disorders
- Cocaine-related disorders
- Hallucinogen-related disorders
- Inhalent-related disorders

- Nicotine-related disorders
- Opioid-related disorders

**PHENCYCLIDINE-RELATED DISORDERS**

- Sedative-, hypnotic-, or anxiolytic-related disorders
- Polysubstance-related disorder
- Other, or unknown substance-related disorder

**SCHIZOPHRENIA AND OTHER PSYCHOTIC DISORDERS**

**MOOD DISORDERS**

- Depressive disorders
- Bipolar disorders

**ANXIETY DISORDERS**

- Somatoform disorders
- Factitious disorders
- Dissociative disorders

**SEXUAL AND GENDER IDENTITY DISORDERS**

- Sexual dysfunctions
- Paraphilias
- Gender identity disorders

**EATING DISORDERS**

**SLEEP DISORDERS**

- Primary sleep disorders
- Sleep disorders related to another mental disorder

**IMPULSE-CONTROL DISORDERS NOT ELSEWHERE CLASSIFIED**

**ADJUSTMENT DISORDERS**

**PERSONALITY DISORDERS**

**OTHER CONDITIONS**

emotional, and physical health, providing as complete a context as possible in which to make a proper diagnosis. The diagnostician evaluates the patient according to criteria for each axis to produce a comprehensive assessment of the patient's condition; the multiaxial system addresses the complex nature of more mental disorders.

Axis I lists 14 major clinical syndromes. These include disorders usually first diagnosed in **childhood** or **adolescence** (hyperactivity, **mental retardation**, **autism**); **dementia**, **amnesia**, and other cognitive disorders; substance-related disorders; **schizophrenia** and other conditions characterized by abnormalities in thinking, perception, and **emotion**; and sexual and **gender identity** disorders. Also listed in Axis I are **mood**, anxiety, somatoform, dissociative, eating, **sleep**, impulse control, and **adjustment disorders**, as well as factitious (false) disorders.

Axis II is for assessment of **personality** disorders—lifelong, deeply ingrained patterns of behavior that are destructive to those who display them or to others. Some examples are narcissistic, dependent, avoidant, and antisocial personality types. This axis also includes developmental disorders in children.

Axis III considers any organic medical problems that may be present. The fourth axis includes any environmental or psychosocial factors affecting a person's condition (such as the loss of a loved one, **sexual abuse**, **divorce**, career changes, poverty, or homelessness).

In Axis V, the diagnostician assesses the person's level of functioning within the previous 12 months on a scale of 1 to 100.

One notable feature of *DSM-IV* is that it dispenses with two previously ubiquitous terms in the field of psychology—"**neurosis**" and "**psychosis**"—because they are now considered too vague. The term "neurosis" was generally used for a variety of conditions that involved some form of anxiety, whereas "psychosis" referred to conditions in which the patient had lost the ability to function normally in daily life and/or had lost touch with reality. Conditions that would formerly have been described as neurotic are now found in five Axis I classifications: mood disorders, anxiety disorders, somatoform disorders, **dissociative identity disorder**s, and sexual disorders. Conditions formerly referred to as psychotic are now found in Axis I as well. Besides diagnostic criteria, the *DSM-IV* also provides information about mental and emotional disorders, covering areas such as probable cause, average age at onset, possible complications, amount of impairment, prevalence, gender ratio, predisposing factors, and **family** patterns.

*DSM-IV* contains the results of a comprehensive and systematic review of relevant published literature, in-

### MULTIAXIAL CLASSIFICATION SYSTEM

- **Axis I** – Clinical disorders; other conditions that may be a focus of clinical attention
- **Axis II** – Personality disorders; mental retardation
- **Axis III** – General medical conditions
- **Axis IV** – Psychosocial and enviromental problems
- **Axis V** – Global assessment of functioning.

cluding earlier editions of *DSM*. In cases where the evidence of a literature review was found to be insufficient to resolve a particular question, data sets were reanalyzed and issue-focused field trials were conducted. These literature reviews, data reanalyses, and field trials that form the basis of *DSM-IV* have been fully documented, condensed, and published separately as a reference record in a five-volume set entitled *DSM-IV Sourcebook*. The *DSM-IV Sourcebook* also contains executive summaries of the rationales for the final decisions relative to inclusion in *DSM-IV*.

### Further Reading

*Diagnostic and Statistical Manual of Mental Disorders,* 4th edition. Washington, DC: American Psychiatric Association, 1994.

*DSM-IV Sourcebook.* Washington, DC: American Psychiatric Association, 1994. In five volumes, contains documentation of all work leading to criteria published in *DSM-IV,* and includes executive summaries of the rationales for final decisions made in compiling the work.

# Differential psychology

The area of psychology concerned with measuring and comparing differences in individual and group behavior.

The earliest research in the field of differential psychology began in the late nineteenth century with **Francis Galton**'s investigation of the effects of **heredity** on individual **intelligence** and his pioneering work in intelligence testing, which was further advanced by **James McKeen Cattell** and **Alfred Binet**. It was Binet who developed the first standardized intelligence test. Growth in related areas such as genetics and **developmental psychology**, as well as advances in psychological testing, all broadened the scope of the field considerably. While individual differences are often conceived of, at least popularly, in terms of categories ("gifted," "slow learner"), they are actually measurable on a continuum which, for most **traits**, follows the **normal** probability or "bell" curve first derived from the study of heights of soldiers. The majority of subjects cluster near the center with a gradual decrease toward the extremes.

Some areas of research focused on today by psychologists working in differential psychology are the effect of heredity and **environment** on behavioral differences and differences in intelligence among individuals and groups. Observations about group differences can be misused and turn into stereotypes when **mean** characteristics are indiscriminately ascribed to all individuals in a group, and when differences between groups are viewed as unchangeable and solely hereditary.

## Further Reading

Eysenck, Michael W. *Individual Differences: Normal and Abnormal.* Hillsdale, NJ: L. Erlbaum Associates, 1994.

# Disability

Any physical, mental, sensory, or psychological impairment or deficiency resulting in the lack, loss, or substantial reduction of the ability to perform some normal function.

In the United States, the term disability is legally defined in the Rehabilitation Act (PL 93-112; 29 U.S.C. 794) Amendments of 1974 and the Americans with Disabilities Act (PL 101-336; 42 U.S.C. 12101) of 1990 as a physical or mental impairment that substantially limits one or more of the major life activities of an individual. Disabilities may be caused by congenital, traumatic, pathological, or other factors, and vary widely in severity. They may be temporary or permanent, correctable or irreversible. Physical disabilities include blindness, deafness, deformity, muscular and nervous disorders, paralysis, and loss of limbs. Paralysis is frequently caused by injuries to the spinal cord, with the extent of paralysis depending on the portion of the spine that is injured. Congenital disabilities include spina bifida, cystic fibrosis, and muscular dystrophy. Other causes of disabilities include cerebral hemorrhage, arthritis and other bone diseases, amputation, severe pulmonary or cardiac disease, **nerve** diseases, and the natural process of **aging**. Mental impairments are of two types: **mental illness** and **mental retardation**. Approximately 35 million people in the United States are disabled.

Professionals including physicians, physical and occupational therapists, social workers, and psychologists assist disabled persons in the **rehabilitation** process, helping them function at the highest possible physical, vocational, and social levels. Specialists in rehabilitation medicine, sometimes referred to as physiatrists, diagnose patients and plan individual treatment programs for the management of **pain** and disabilities resulting from musculoskeletal injuries. People with **hearing** or **vision** loss require **special education**, including instruction in lip reading, sign language, or Braille. Physical rehabilitation for individuals with musculoskeletal disabilities includes passive exercise of affected limbs and active exercise for parts of the body that are not affected. Occupational training, including counseling, helps persons whose disabilities make it necessary for them to find new jobs or careers. Rehabilitation also involves the services of speech pathologists, recreational therapists, home planning consultants, orthotists and prosthetists, driver educators, and dieticians.

Recent technological advances—especially those involving computer-aided devices—have aided immeasurably in mainstreaming the disabled into many areas of society. These include voice-recognition aids for the paralyzed; optical character-recognition devices for the blind; sip-and-puff air tubes that enable quadriplegics to type and control wheelchair movements with their mouths; and computerized electronic grids that translate eye movements into speech. In addition to access, mobility for the disabled has become an area of concern. The American Automobile Association (AAA) estimates that there are 500,000 licensed drivers in the United States with significant physical impairments and another 1.5 million with lesser disabilities. AAA auto clubs throughout the country are working to improve the mobility of disabled drivers and travelers through improved driver education for those with impairments and improved facilities for the handicapped traveler, including motorist rest areas on the highway.

Public attitudes toward the disabled have changed. Since the 1970s, advocates for the disabled have won passage of numerous laws on the federal, state, and local levels aimed at making education, employment, and public accommodation more accessible through the elimination of physical barriers to access, as well as affirmative action in the hiring and professional advancement of disabled people. Whereas many people with disabilities were formerly confined to their homes or to institutions, the current trend is geared toward reintegrating disabled persons into the community in ways that enable them the greatest possible amount of independence in both their living arrangements and their jobs. Wheelchair access at building entrances, curbs, and public restrooms has been greatly expanded and mandated by law. Braille signs are standard in public areas such as elevators.

Two major pieces of federal legislation have protected the rights of the disabled: a 1975 law guaranteeing

| CAUSES OF DISABILITIES IN CHILDREN UNDER AGE 17 | | |
|---|---|---|
| Condition | Number (thousands) | Percent |
| Learning disability | 1435 | 29.5% |
| Speech problems | 634 | 13.1% |
| Mental retardation | 331 | 6.8% |
| Asthma | 311 | 6.4% |
| Mental or emotional problem or disorder | 305 | 6.3% |
| Blindness or vision problem | 144 | 3.0% |
| Cerebral palsy | 129 | 2.7% |
| Epilepsy or seizure disorder | 128 | 2.6% |
| Impairment deformity of back, side, foot, or leg | 121 | 2.5% |
| Deafness or serious trouble hearing | 116 | 2.4% |
| Tonsilitis or repeated ear infections | 80 | 1.6% |
| Hay fever or other respiratory allergies | 76 | 1.6% |
| Missing legs, feet, toes, arms, hands, or fingers | 70 | 1.4% |
| Autism | 48 | 1.0% |
| Drug or alcohol problem or disorder | 48 | 1.0% |
| Head or spinal cord injury | 45 | 0.9% |
| Heart trouble | 44 | 0.9% |
| Impairment deformity of finger, hand, or arm | 27 | 0.6% |
| Cancer | 26 | 0.5% |
| Diabetes | 14 | 0.3% |
| Other | 653 | 13.4% |
| Total | 4858 | 100% |

Source: Centers for Disease Control, U.S. Department of Health and Human Services.

disabled children a right to public education in the least restrictive setting possible and the 1990 **Americans with Disabilities Act (ADA)**, which extends comprehensive civil rights protection in employment and access to public areas. Title I of the ADA, which prohibits discrimination by private employers on the basis of disability, is intended to ensure that the same performance standards and job requirements are applied to disabled persons as to persons who are not. In cases where functional limitations may interfere with job performance, employers are required to take any necessary steps to accommodate reasonably the needs of a disabled person, including adjustments to the work **environment** or to the way in which the job is customarily performed. The ADA also contains provisions ensuring nondiscrimination in state and local government services (Title II) and nondiscrimi-

nation in public accommodations and commercial facilities (Title III).

**Further Reading**
Davis, Lennard J. *Enforcing Normalcy: Disability, Deafness, and the Body.* New York: Verso, 1995.

# Dissociation/Dissociative disorders

The feeling of being detached from oneself, of being able to watch oneself as though from a distance; psychological disorders having at their core long-term periods of such feelings when a specific cause may not be identified.

Dissociation, or the feeling of being detached from the reality of one's body, can be categorized into two types: depersonalization and derealization. Depersonalization is highlighted by a sense of not knowing who you are, or of questioning long-held beliefs about who you are. In derealization, persons perceive reality in a grossly distorted way. Psychologists have identified several types of disorders based on these feelings. These include depersonalization disorder, dissociative **fugue**, dissociative **amnesia**, dissociative trance disorder, and **dissociative identity disorder** (also known as multiple personality syndrome), among others.

Depersonalization disorder is a condition marked by a persistent feeling of not being real. The ***DSM -IV*** describes its symptoms as "persistent or recurrent experiences of feeling detached from, and as if one is an outside observer of, one's mental processes or body (e.g., feeling like one is in a dream)." While many people have experienced a similar feeling, persons actually suffering from this disorder are so overwhelmed by these feelings that they are unable to function normally in society. It is also critical to point out that in order to be diagnosed as having this disorder, these feelings cannot be caused by some specific drug or event. Depersonalization disorder, by itself, is a rare disorder, and, in fact, many of its symptoms are also symptomatic of other more common disorders, such as acute **stress** disorder and panic attacks.

Dissociative fugue is a strange phenomena in which persons will be stricken with a sudden **memory** loss that prompts them to flee their familiar surroundings. These flights are usually caused by some traumatic event. People suffering from this disorder will suddenly find themselves in a new surrounding, hundreds or even thousands of miles from their homes with no memories of the weeks, months, or even years that have elapsed since their flight. Incidence of dissociative fugue rarely appear until after **adolescence** and usually before the age of 50. Once a person has fallen into the behavior, however, it is more likely that it will recur.

Dissociative amnesia describes the condition of suddenly losing major chunks of memory. There are two types of this disorder: generalized amnesia, in which a person cannot remember anything about their lives, and localized amnesia, a common disorder in which a person forgets pieces of their identity but retains an overall understanding of who they are. Dissociative amnesia is generally caused by some traumatic event, such as a natural disaster, a violent crime, or war. In these instances, it is an adaptive mechanism that allows a person to continue his or her life without having to deal with an utterly horrific memory.

Dissociative trance disorder describes the trance-state that people experience in various kinds of religious ceremonies. Such people generally perform feats that would normally cause injury or severe pain—such as walking on hot coals—but because of their dissociated mental state, they are not harmed. This is a curious subcategory in that the condition is not considered a "disorder" in many cultures of the world. Western psychiatrists are divided as to whether this should really be considered a "disorder," since the word has negative implications. It has been proposed, however, that future editions of the *DSM* specify a diagnosis of trance and possession disorder as one of several dissociative disorders.

### Further Reading

Goleman, Daniel. "Those Who Stay Calm in Disasters May Face Psychological Risk." *New York Times* (17 April 1994): 12.
Mukerjee, Madhursee. "Hidden Scars: Sexual and Other Abuse May Alter Brain Region." *Scientific American* (October 1995): 14.

# Dissociative identity disorder

Also referred to as multiple personality disorder, a condition in which a person's identity dissociates, or fragments, creating additional, distinct identities that exist independently of each other within the same person.

Persons suffering from dissociative identity disorder (DID) adopt one or more distinct identities which co-exist within one individual. Each personality is distinct from the other in specific ways. For instance, tone of voice and mannerisms will be distinct, as well as posture, vocabulary, and everything else we normally think of as marking a personality. There are cases in which a person will have as many as 100 or more identities, while some people only exhibit the presence of one or two. In either case, the criteria for diagnosis are the same. This disorder was, until the publication of *DSM-IV,* referred to as multiple personality disorder. This name was abandoned for a variety of reasons, one having to do with psychiatric explicitness (it was thought that the name should reflect the dissociative aspect of the disorder).

The *DSM-IV* lists four criteria for diagnosing someone with dissociative identity disorder. The first being the presence of two or more distinct "identities or personality states." At least two personalities must take control of the person's identity regularly. The person must exhibit aspects of amnesia—that is, he or she forgets routine personal information. And, finally, the condition must not have been caused by "direct physiological effects," such as drug abuse or head trauma.

Persons suffering from DID usually have a main personality that psychiatrists refer to as the "host." This is generally not the person's original personality, but is rather developed along the way. It is usually this personality that seeks psychiatric help. Psychiatrists refer to the other personalities as "alters" and the phase of transition between alters as the "switch." The number of alters in any given case can vary widely and can even vary across gender. That is, men can have female alters and women can have male alters. The physical changes that occur in a switch between alters is one of the most baffling aspects of dissociative identity disorder. People assume whole new physical postures and voices and vocabularies. One study conducted in 1986 found that in 37 percent of patients, alters even demonstrated different **handedness** from the host.

Statistically, sufferers of DID have an average of 15 identities. The disorder is far more common among females than males (as high as 9-to-1), and the usual age of onset is in early **childhood**, generally by the age of four. Once established, the disorder will last a lifetime if not treated. New identities can accumulate over time as the person faces new types of situations. For instance, as a sufferer confronts **sexuality** in **adolescence**, an identity may emerge that deals exclusively with this aspect of life. There are no reliable figures as to the prevalence of this disorder, although it has begun to be reported with increased frequency over the last several years. People with DID tend to have other severe disorders as well, such as **depression**, substance abuse, **borderline personality** disorder and **eating disorders**, among others.

In nearly every case of DID, horrific instances of physical or sexual child abuse—even torture—was present (one study of 100 DID patients found that 97 had suffered **child abuse**). It is believed that young children, faced with a routine of torture and neglect, create a **fantasy** world in order to escape the brutality. In this way, DID is similar to **post-traumatic stress disorder**, and recent thinking in psychiatry has suggested that the two disorders may be linked; some are even beginning to view DID as a severe subtype of post-traumatic stress disorder.

Treatment of dissociative identity disorder is a long and difficult process, and success (the complete integration of identity) is rare. A 1990 study found that of 20 patients studied, only five were successfully treated. Current treatment method involves having DID patients recall the memories of their childhoods. Because these childhood memories are often subconscious, treatment often includes **hypnosis** to help the patient remember. There is a danger here, however, as sometimes the recovered memories are so traumatic for the patient that they cause more harm.

## TWO FAMOUS CASES

The stories of two women with multiple personality disorders have been told both in books and films. A woman with 22 personalities was recounted in 1957 in a major motion picture staring Joanne Woodward and in a book by Corbett Thigpen, both titled *the Three Faces of Eve*. Twenty years later, in 1977, Caroline Sizemore, the 22nd personality to emerge in "Eve," described her experiences in a book titled *I'm Eve*. Although the woman known as "Eve" developed a total of 22 personalities, only three could exist at any one time—for a new one to emerge, an existing personality would "die."

The story of Sybil (a pseudonym) was published in 1973 by Flora Rheta Schreiber, who worked closely for a decade with Sybil and her New York psychiatrist Dr. Cornelia B. Wilbur. Sybil's sixteen distinct personalities emerged over a period of 40 years.

Both stories reveal fascinating insights—and raise thought-provoking questions—about the unconscious mind, the interrelationship between remembering and forgetting, and the meaning of personality development. The separate and distinct personalities manifested in these two cases feature unique physical traits and vocational interests. In the study of this disorder, scientists have been able to monitor unique patterns of brainwave activity for the unique multiple personalities.

There is considerable controversy about the nature, and even the existence, of dissociative identity disorder. One cause for the skepticism is the alarming increase in reports of the disorder over the last several decades. Eugene Levitt, a psychologist at the Indiana University School of Medicine, noted in an article published in *Insight on the News* (1993) that "In 1952 there was no listing for [DID] in the *DSM*, and there were only a handful of cases in the country. In 1980, the disorder [then known as multiple personality disorder] got its official listing in the *DSM*, and suddenly thousands of cases are springing up everywhere." Another area of contention is in the whole notion of suppressed memories, a crucial component in DID. Many experts dealing with **memory** say that it is nearly impossible for anyone to remember things that happened before the age three, the age when much of the abuse supposedly occurred to DID sufferers.

Regardless of the controversy, people diagnosed with this disorder are clearly suffering from some profound disorder. As Helen Friedman, a clinical psychologist in St. Louis told *Insight on the News*, "When you see it, it's just not fake."

## Further Reading

Arbetter, Sandra. "Multiple Personality Disorder: Someone Else Lives Inside of Me." *Current Health* (2 November 1992): 17.

Mesic, Penelope. "Presence of Minds." *Chicago* (September 1992): 100.

Sileo, Chi Chi. "Multiple Personalities: The Experts Are Split." *Insight on the News* (25 October 1993): 18.

Sizemore, Chris Costner. *I'm Eve*. Garden City, NY: Doubleday, 1977.

Sybil [videorecording].

Thigpen, Corbett H. *The Three Faces of Eve*. New York: Popular Library, 1957.

*The Three Faces of Eve* [videorecording]. Beverly Hills, CA: FoxVideo, 1993. Produced and directed from his screenplay by Nunnally Johnson. Originally released as motion picture in 1957.

"When the Body Remembers." *Psychology Today* (April 1994): 9.

# Divergent thinking

The ability to develop original and unique ideas and to envision multiple solutions to a problem.

The concept of divergent thinking was developed in the 1950s by psychologist J.P. Guilford, who saw it as a major component of **creativity** and associated it with four main characteristics. The characteristics were fluency (the **ability** to rapidly produce a large number of ideas or solutions to a problem); flexibility (the capacity to consider a variety of approaches to a problem simultaneously); originality (the tendency to produce ideas different from those of most other people); and elaboration (the ability to think through the details of an idea and carry it out). Guilford, whose research was oriented toward testing and **measurement** (psychometrics), believed that creative thinkers are at a disadvantage when taking standard **intelligence** tests, which penalize divergent thinking and reward its opposite, **convergent thinking**—the ability to narrow all possible alternatives down to a single solution (the type of thinking required by multiple choice tests).

Over a number of years, the Aptitudes Research Project (ARP) at the University of Southern California, under Guilford's **leadership**, devised an extensive sequence of tests to measure intellectual abilities, including creativity. Some of the ARP divergent thinking tests have been widely adapted for use in placing students in gifted programs and evaluating the success of such programs. They include a number of different assessment techniques that measure the key characteristics of fluency, flexibility, and originality. Among the fluency tests are word fluency, which asks test-takers to think of as many words as they can that contain a given letter, and ideational fluency, which involves naming things that belong to a specific category, such as fluids that will burn. Other tests included listing all the possible jobs that might be represented by a specific emblem and writing titles for short stories after having been told their plots. Another popular **creativity test** derived from the ARP project is the consequences test, in which a person is asked to list the possible consequences of an imaginary event ("What would happen if everyone were immortal?"). In addition to these verbal tests, ARP also devised tests to measure spatial aptitude, which include such tasks as drawing objects using geometrical shapes.

Although creativity is associated with the highest levels of achievement in many fields and presumably valued by society, the educational system often penalizes divergent thinkers. The typical standardized measure of intelligence is the multiple-choice test, which is diametrically opposed to the divergent thinker's problem-solving process. To a creative thinker, it may seem more productive to try finding reasons why *all* the choices on a multiple-choice question could be correct than to select the preferred answer. In addition, most classroom teaching is heavily biased toward the learning style of convergent thinkers, a fact that helps explain the dismal school performance of such legendary geniuses as Albert Einstein and Thomas Alva Edison, who was considered retarded and expelled from school.

## Further Reading

Amabile, Teresa M. *Growing Up Creative: Nurturing a Lifetime of Creativity*. New York: Crown Publishers, 1989.

Guilford, J.P. *The Nature of Human Intelligence*. New York: McGraw-Hill, 1967.

# Divorce

The legal dissolution of a marriage.

The divorce rate in the United States began rising in the 1960s and continued for more than two decades, with a decline in the trend in the 1990s. In 1960 the divorce rate per 1,000 population was 2.6. By 1980, the rate had reached 5.2 and in 1990 dropped to 4.7. This decline continued to 4.3 in 1997. Based on current societal trends, researchers project that 40 to 50 percent of all first marriages in the United States will end in divorce.

Possible factors for the high incidence of divorce include the enactment of "no-fault" divorce laws that make it easier legally to get divorced; a decline in the number of couples who stay together for religious reasons; the increased financial independence of women; conflicts resulting from the growing number of dual-career marriages; and a greater social acceptance of divorce.

Divorce is generally preceded by a breakdown in communication between the partners. Research indicates that marriages may also breakdown because of the manner in which couples argue and attempt to repair their relationship after quarreling. Other factors leading to divorce include alcoholism and drug abuse, domestic **violence**, extramarital affairs, and desertion. Divorce generally causes significant **stress** for all **family** members. After the death of one's spouse, divorce is considered the single greatest stressor on the Holmes and Rahe Social Readjustment Scale, which assigns point values to a variety of stress-producing life changes. Both partners must make financial adjustments—an area of much bitterness during divorce proceedings. Social relationships with friends and family often change, and the newly divorced person will likely face the challenges and insecurities of dating. Divorced parents have to adjust to raising children on their own, adjust or adapt to noncustodial parenthood. In adults, divorce may cause feelings of **guilt** over one's share of the responsibility for a failed marriage, **anger** toward one's spouse, and feelings of social, emotional, and financial insecurity. Also common to divorce are feelings of anxiety, incompetence, **depression**, and loneliness.

Children—who are involved in 70 percent of American divorces— may be even more severely affected than their parents, although this also depends on such factors as custody arrangements and parental attitudes. Divorce often results in economic stress and disorganization for the family. Divorce is thought to be hardest on young children, who tend to blame themselves, fantasize that their parents will get back together, and worry about being abandoned. Sometimes the effects on younger children do not become apparent until they reach **adolescence**. Children who are teenagers at the time of the divorce are strongly affected as well. In one study, subjects who were in early adolescence when their parents divorced had trouble forming committed relationships ten years later. The effects of parental divorce on children have also been linked to phenomena as diverse as emotional and behavioral problems, school dropout rates, crime rates, physical and **sexual abuse** and physical health. However, the effects of divorce must be weighed against the difficulty of continuing to live in a household characterized by conflict and estrangement. Researchers have found evidence that of the two alternatives, divorce can be the less emotionally damaging one. After an initial period of turmoil, stability generally returns to the lives of adults and children. Both may function more competently than they did before the divorce and show

improved **self-esteem**. Most divorced people remarry within three years, but many second marriages have not been found to be successful.

The prevalence of divorce has led to a number of prevention programs to train couples how to prevent divorce. Research indicates a small percentage of couples considering divorce seek counseling, usually six years after problems have developed in the marriage.

### Further Reading

Fisher, Helen E. *Anatomy of Love: The Natural History of Monogamy, Adultery, and Divorce.* New York: W. W. Norton, 1992.

Gottman, John. *Why Marriages Succeed Or Fail* New York: Simon & Schuster, 1994.

McDonough, Hanna. *Putting Children First: A Guide for Parents Breaking Up.* Toronto: University of Toronto Press, 1999.

Wallerstein, Judith S. *The Legacy of Divorce: A 25 Year Landmark Study.* New York: Hyperion, 2000.

# DNA

See **Deoxyribonucleic acid**

# Double-blind study

See **Experimental design**

# Down syndrome

A hereditary mental disorder present at birth resulting from an abnormality in the number of chromosomes; also known Trisomy 21.

Down syndrome was named after John Langdon Haydon Down, a British physician and advocate of education for the mentally retarded, who first described it in 1866. In 1959, the French pediatrician Jerome Lejeune discovered that the disorder is caused by a chromosomal abnormality. Ninety-five percent of individuals with Down syndrome have Trisomy 21, an extra chromosome in the 21st pair (altogether, they have 47 chromosomes instead of the **normal** 46); four percent have translocation, a chromosomal abnormality; and one percent have mosaicism. Down syndrome is characterized primarily by varying degrees of mental and motor retardation.

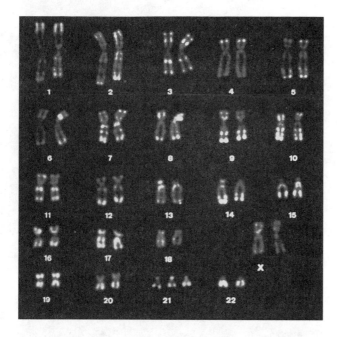

Genetic map of a person with Down syndrom. Note three copies of chromosome 21. *(Phototake/ NYC. Reproduced by permission.)*

Most people with the disorder are retarded. Individuals with Down syndrome have I.Q.s ranging from 20 to more than 90, with the **mean** being 49. They are also prone to possible heart defects, poor **vision** and **hearing**, cataracts, and a low resistance to respiratory infections. Until the discovery of antibiotics, most Down syndrome children died of pneumonia before reaching adulthood. People with Down syndrome are 20 times more likely than the general population to develop leukemia and a neurological condition similar to **Alzheimer's disease**.

Individuals with Down syndrome have a distinctive physical appearance characterized by almond-shaped eyes (on which the condition's former alternate name— mongolism—was based); a short, stocky build; a flat nose and large, protruding tongue (which makes normal speech difficult); a small skull flattened in the back; a short neck with extra skin; and small hands with short fingers. Other features include a fold of skin on the inner side of the eye; speckling at the edge of the iris; and a small amount of facial and body hair. Muscle tone is often poor, and newborns are prone to hypotonia, or "floppiness." People with Down syndrome are widely recognized to have docile temperaments; and are generally cheerful, cooperative, affectionate, and relaxed, although there are no scientific studies to confirm this. Their motor, speech, and sexual development is delayed, and their **cognitive development** may not peak until the age of 30 or 40. In **infancy**, speech development is delayed by about seven months.

Recent research has led to the conclusion that Down children are capable of expressing complex feelings, of developing richer personalities, and of mastering higher degrees of learning using adaptive strategies (such as computer-aided learning to teach reading and writing). One developmental program that began with Down children as young as 30 months old and stressed positive parent-child communication eventually enabled the children to read at a second-grade level. The theory is that early stimulation helps to develop connections in the **brain** that might otherwise not have developed.

Although most people with Down syndrome were institutionalized until the 1970s, those with only moderate retardation are capable of achieving some degree of self-sufficiency. Today, with changed social attitudes and expanded educational opportunities, many lead productive, fulfilling lives. In less than a century, the expected lifespan of a person with Down syndrome has increased from nine years of age in 1910 to 19 or 20 after the discovery of antibiotics to age 55 today, due to recent advancements in clinical treatment.

More than 350,000 people in the United States have Down syndrome; one baby is born with Down syndrome for every 800 to 1,000 births in the U.S. Down syndrome babies are found in every ethnic group and socioeconomic class. About 5,000 babies are born yearly in the United States with Down syndrome. Twenty to 25 percent of children conceived with Down syndrome survive beyond **birth**. Women over age 35 have a one in 400 chance of conceiving a child with Down syndrome. For women age 40, the incidence becomes one in 110. For mothers age 45, the incidence increases to one child in every 35. Under age 30, women give birth to Down syndrome babies at a rate of one for every 1,500 babies born. However, women under age 35 actually bear 80 percent of Down infants, and recent studies suggest that the father's age may play a role as well. Prenatal detection of Down syndrome is possible through amniocentesis and chorionic villus sampling and is recommended for pregnant women over the age of 35.

*See also* Mental retardation

## Further Reading

Cicchetti, D. & Beeghly, M. (Eds.) *Children with Down Syndrome: A Developmental Perspective.* New York: Cambridge University Press, 1990.

Cunningham, C. *Understanding Down Syndrome: An Introduction for Parents.* Cambridge, MA: Brookline Books, 1996.

## Further Information

National Down Syndrome Congress. 1800 Dempster Street, Park Ridge, Illinois 60068-1146, (708) 823–7550, (800) 232–NDSC.

National Down Syndrome Society. 666 Broadway, New York, New York 10012, (212) 460–9330, (800) 221–4602.

## Draw-a-person test

A test used to measure nonverbal intelligence or to screen for emotional or behavior disorders.

Based on children's drawings of human figures, this test can be used with two different scoring systems for different purposes. One measures nonverbal **intelligence** while the other screens for emotional or behavioral disorders. During the testing session, which can be completed in 15 minutes, the child is asked to draw three figures—a man, a woman, and him- or herself. To evaluate intelligence, the test administrator uses the Draw-a-Person: QSS (Quantitative Scoring System). This system analyzes fourteen different aspects of the drawings, such as specific body parts and clothing, for various criteria, including presence or absence, detail, and proportion. In all, there are 64 scoring items for each drawing. A separate standard score is recorded for each drawing, and a total score for all three. The use of a nonverbal, nonthreatening task to evaluate intelligence is intended to eliminate possible sources of bias by reducing variables like primary language, verbal skills, communication disabilities, and sensitivity to working under pressure. However, test results can be influenced by previous drawing experience, a factor that may account for the tendency of middle-class children to score higher on this test than lower-class children, who often have fewer opportunities to draw. To assess the test-taker for emotional problems, the administrator uses the Draw-a-Person: SPED (Screening Procedure for Emotional Disturbance) to score the drawings. This system is composed of two types of criteria. For the first type, eight dimensions of each drawing are evaluated against norms for the child's age group. For the second type, 47 different items are considered for each drawing.

*See also* Intelligence

## Dreams

The sequence of imagery, thoughts, and emotions that pass through the mind during sleep.

Dreams defy the laws of physics, the principles of logic, and personal morality, and may reflect fears, frustrations, and personal desires. Often occurring in story-form with the dreamer as participant or observer, dreams usually involve several characters, motion, and may include sensations of **taste**, **smell**, **hearing**, or **pain**. The content of dreams clearly reflects daytime activities, even though these may be distorted to various degrees. While some people report dreaming only in black and white, others dream in color. "Lucid dreaming," in which the sleeper is actually aware of dreaming while the dream is taking place, is not uncommon. Research has indicated that everyone dreams during every night of normal **sleep**. Many people do not remember their dreams, however, and most people recall only the last dream prior to awakening. The **memory** shut-down theory suggests that memory may be one of the brain's functions which rests during dreaming, hence we forget our dreams.

In order to understand how dreaming occurs, **brain** waves during sleep have been measured by an **electroencephalograph (EEG)**. Normally large and slow during sleep, these waves become smaller and faster during periods of sleep accompanied by **rapid eye movement**s (called REM sleep), and it is during these period when dreams occur. During a normal eight-hour period of sleep, an average adult will dream three to five dreams lasting ten to thirty minutes each for a total of 100 minutes.

Dreams—which **Sigmund Freud** called "the royal road to the unconscious"—have provided psychologists and psychotherapists with abundant information about the structure, dynamics, and development of the human **personality**. Several theories attempt to explain why we dream. The oldest and most well-known is Freud's psychoanalytic theory, elucidated in *The Interpretation of Dreams* (1900), in which he suggested that dreams are disguised symbols of repressed desires and therefore offer us direct insight into the **unconscious**. According to Freud, the manifest content of dreams, such as daily events and memories, serve to disguise their latent content or unconscious wishes through a process he called dream-work, consisting of four operations. *Condensation* refers to the condensing of separate thoughts into a single image in order to fit the latent content into the brief framework of a dream. *Displacement* serves to disguise the latent content by creating confusion between important and insignificant elements of the dream. *Symbolization* serves as a further effort to evade the "censor" of repressed desires by symbolizing certain objects with other objects, as in the case of phallic symbols. *Secondary revision* enables the dreamer to make the dream more coherent by additions that fill it in more intelligibly while he or she is recalling it.

Although **Carl Jung**'s system of analysis differed greatly from that of Freud, the Swiss psychologist agreed with Freud's basic view of dreams as compensating for repressed psychic elements. According to Jung's theory, significant dreams (those that involve the collective unconscious) are attempts to reveal an image, or **archetype**, that is not sufficiently "individuated" in the subject's personality. Another Swiss analyst, **Medard Boss**, offered yet another perspective on dreams as part of his system of "existential analysis." Under Boss's system, the significance of dreams lay close to their surface details rather than corresponding to an intricate symbolic pattern. Thus, for example, dreams set in a narrow, constricted room indicated that this was how the dreamer viewed his or her existence. Existential analysis was based on the feelings of the dreamer, the contents of the dream, and his or her response to them.

In contrast with the methods of these early dream analysts, modern researchers gather data from subjects in a sleep laboratory, a mode of investigation furthered in the 1950s. Calvin Hall, a pioneer in the content analysis of dreams, posits that dreams are meant to reveal rather than to conceal. Hall and his associates gathered dreams from a large and varied sampling of subjects and analyzed them for the following content categories: 1) human characters classified by sex, age, family members, friends and acquaintances, and strangers; 2) animals; 3) types of interactions among characters, such as aggressive or friendly; 4) positive and negative events; 5) success and failure; 6) indoor and outdoor settings; 7) objects; and 8) emotions. Other investigators have devised their own systems of content analysis, such as the one outlined by David Foulkes in *A Grammar of Dreams*. The dreams of children have also been extensively assessed through laboratory testing and shown to be linked to their **cognitive development**. Content analysis has also yielded longitudinal information about individuals, including the observations that an adult's dreams remain strikingly similar over time and are strongly linked to the preoccupations of waking life, a phenomenon known as the continuity principle.

Dream analysis may occur in certain therapies. In the 1970s, writers and psychologists, such as Ann Faraday, helped to take dream analysis out of the therapy room and popularize it by offering techniques anyone could use to analyze his or her own dreams. Widely recommended techniques include keeping paper and pen by the bed to write dreams down upon waking (even in the middle of the night), keeping a dream diary to recognize recurring themes, and making associations with the imagery in the dream to decode its personal meaning. Analysts, such as Robert Johnson, maintain that dreams contain the dreamer's thoughts or feelings not yet expressed or made conscious. Johnson recommends making associations to the dream to unlock ways the dream mirrors inner tensions or dynamics of the dreamer's emotional life. The dreamer uses the associations and dynamics linked to daily life to interpret or give meaning to the dream. Some psychologists recommend cultivating lucid dreaming where the dreamer is aware in the dream that he or she is dreaming and then can direct the events of dreams and the manner in which they unfold.

Not all dreams reflect daily life. Reports indicate dreams have foretold events upcoming in the dreamer's life, including death. One study reports that 70 percent of women successfully predicted the sex of their unborn child based upon dreams.

Some scientists have attempted to discount the significance of dreams entirely. The activation-synthesis hypothesis created by J. Alan Hobson and Robert W. McCarley in 1977 holds that dreaming is a simple and unimportant by-product of random stimulation of brain cells activated during REM sleep. Another dream theory, the mental housecleaning hypothesis, suggests that we dream to rid our brains of useless, bizarre, or redundant information. A current synthesis of this theory sees dreaming as analogous to a computer's process of program inspection in which sleep is similar to "down" time and the dream becomes a moment of "on-line" time, a glimpse into a program being run at that moment.

*See also* Rapid eye movement (REM)

### Further Reading
Gardner, Richard A. *Dream Analysis in Psychotherapy.* Cresskill, N.J.: Creative Therapeutics, 1996.
Hall, Kirsten. *Last Night I Danced With A Stranger.* New York: Black Do & Leventhal Publishers, 2000.

# Drive reduction theory

A popular theory of the 1940s and 1950s that attributed behavior to the desire to reduce tension produced by primary (biological) or secondary (acquired) drives.

Many psychologists believed that all **motivation** depended upon the pleasure experienced when basic needs are met. A person who is hungry, for instance, eats in order to reduce the tension that hunger produces. All human behavior could be attributed to the pleasure gained when these drive-induced tensions were reduced.

Drive reduction theory lost favor over the years because it failed to explain human actions that produced, rather than reduced, tension. Many people enjoy riding roller coasters or skydiving, for instance, despite the fact that such activity may cause **fear** and anxiety. Similarly, drive theory could not adequately explain sexual behavior in humans or animals. For example, experiments showed that rats persisted in seeking sexual gratification even when their biological urges to mate were interrupted and thus tension was not reduced.

More modern motivational theory includes the principal of optimal arousal, that is, individuals act to maintain an appropriate—rather than a minimal—level of stimulation and arousal. Optimal levels vary from person to person, which explains why some people drive race cars and others prefer an evening at the symphony.

## Further Reading

Atkinson, Rita L.; Richard C. Atkinson; Edward E. Smith; and Ernest R. Hilgard. *Introduction to Psychology.* 9th ed. San Diego: Harcourt Brace Jovanovich, 1987.

Zimbardo, Philip G. *Psychology and Life.* 12th ed. Glenview, IL: Scott, Foresman, 1988.

## Drugs/Drug abuse

Any chemical substance that alters normal biological processes.

**Psychoactive drugs** alter behavior, thought, or emotions by changing biochemical reactions in the nervous system. They can be addictive (habit-forming), and they can be legal or illegal.

Drug abuse is the self-administration of drugs in ways that depart from medical or social norms, and it can lead to psychological or physical dependence. Physical dependence, or addiction, which can occur together with psychological dependence, is characterized by withdrawal symptoms and can involve increased tolerance for the drug. The causes of substance abuse are multiple: some people are high-risk for dependence due to genetic or physiological reasons; others become dependent on drugs to cope with emotional or social problems, or physical **pain**.

*Depressants* reduce activity of the **central nervous system**. The most common depressive drug is alcohol, which calms, induces sleep, decreases inhibitions and fears, and slows **reflexes**. With continued use, the nervous system accommodates alcohol, requiring increasing amounts to achieve the alcoholic state, and produces withdrawal symptoms. Sedatives are another major category of depressants, notably barbiturates, such as Seconal and Nembutal. Overdoses can be fatal, and withdrawal symptoms are among the most severe for any drug. Anxiolytics (traditionally referred to as tranquilizers) are also sedatives and include the benzodiazepines (Librium, Valium) and meprobamate (Miltown). Many users of these drugs become both psychologically and physically dependent, and their withdrawal symptoms resemble those of barbiturate takers. Taken in combination with alcohol, anxiolytics can be fatal. Anxiolytics are still used in the clinical treatment of anxiety and are the most widely prescribed and used legal drugs. Because they pose little danger of death from overdose, the benzodiazepines have remained popular for the treatment of patients suffering from anxiety. A new member of this class of drug, Xanax, has also been widely used in the treatment of panic disorders and agoraphobia.

*Narcotics,* such as opiates which include heroin and its derivatives, are drugs with sedative properties; they are addictive and produce tolerance. They have a complex combination of effects, causing both drowsiness and euphoria, and are also pain-killers. Eaten, smoked, inhaled, or injected intravenously, heroin impairs the respiratory system, induces changes in the heart and blood vessels, constipation, and loss of appetite. It is derived from morphine, but is several times more powerful. An overdose of heroin can result in death.

*Psychedelics,* or **hallucinogens**, such as **marijuana**, are consciousness-altering drugs that affect moods, thought, **memory**, and **perception**. They can produce distortion of **body image**, loss of identity, and hallucinations. Usage can produce impaired performance on intellectual and psychomotor tasks, psychoses, and psychological dependence. LSD (lysergic acid diethylamide) is one of the most powerful psychedelic drugs. It can cause bizarre **hallucinations**, its effects are highly unpredictable, and some users suffer long-term side effects. While low doses of marijuana are considered relaxing and relieve anxiety with minimal health risks, long-term usage in larger amounts may cause major health hazards such as asthma and other respiratory disorders, suppression of the immune system, and heart problems.

*Psychostimulants,* such as amphetamines and cocaine, are drugs that in moderate or low doses increase mental and behavioral activity. They stimulate alertness, reduce fatigue, increase excitability, elevate moods, and depress appetites. Benzedrine, Dexedrine, Methedrine, (also called "uppers" or "speed"), raise the heart rate and blood pressure, constrict blood pressure, shrink mucous membranes (thus their use as decongestants), and reduce appetite. Many people abuse amphetamines in order to lose weight, remain productive and alert, or to "get high." The symptoms of severe amphetamine abuse can resemble those of paranoid **schizophrenia**. Cocaine and its derivative, "crack," are both highly addictive and take effect more rapidly than amphetamines. Overdoses, especially of crack, can be fatal, and small doses may induce cardiac arrest or stroke. Cocaine addiction is especially difficult to break.

Two popular stimulants that most people do not consider "drugs" are caffeine and nicotine. Caffeine is found in coffee, tea, chocolate, and many soft drinks. It decreases drowsiness and speeds up thought, but at high doses can produce anxiety and induce tremors. Caffeine is addictive; its withdrawal symptoms include headaches, fa-

# COCAINE

A crystalline alkaloid derived from the leaves of the South American coca plant, *Erythorxylun*. Medically, cocaine can be used as a local aesthetic because it interrupts the conduction of the nerve impulses, particularly in the mucous membranes of the eyes, nose and throat. Illegally, cocaine is widely abused. As powered cocaine hydrochloride, it is usually diluted with some other substance, such as aspirin, cornstarch lactose, or talc, and sucked into the nostrils or dissolved in water and injected intravenously. When cocaine is sniffed, it travels from the nasal tissue to the bloodstream and then to the brain, affecting the user within two or three minutes, and if injected, within 15 seconds. Its physiological effects include dilated pupils; elevated heart rate, blood pressure, and body temperature; rapid breathing; and an increased appetite. The drug may also augment norepinephrine and dopamine activity—an effect similar to the of amphetamines—and stimulate the cortex of the brain. Cocaine produces a quick but short "rush," characterized by temporary feelings of euphoria, self-confidence, well-being, and optimism, and hallucinations can also be present. The drug's pleasant effects peak in about 20 to 40 minutes and subside after about a hour, followed by a depression that induces a craving for the drug.

Cocaine can also be converted into a solid from by separating it from its hydrochloride base. This from, commonly known as "crack" cocaine, produces a high that is particularly fast and intense. It is extremely addictive, inducing constant cravings that can cost up to $500 a day to satisfy. Crack cocaine is usually smoked in a pipe or mixed with tobacco in a cigarette. As it has become cheaper to produce, its cost has dropped, and now crack cocaine costs less than one-fifth as much as regular cocaine.

Cocaine is a potent drug, and habituation and dependence may occur very quickly with its abuse. Cocaine users first become psychologically addicted to the drug, as the artificially induced optimism and confidence they feel helps them to cope with daily stresses. Soon, the cocaine user becomes physically addicted as well and often develops a secondary addiction to a depressant, such as alcohol or heroin, to help him or her "come down" from the drug's effects and to induce sleep. When taken internally in any form, cocaine has a highly toxic effect on the central nervous system. Frequent and/or long-term abuse of cocaine may cause overactivity, loss of appetite, nausea, heart problems, seizures, comas, strokes, and permanent brain damage. It can also precipitate delusional psychotic disorders.

Withdrawal from habitual cocaine abuse is characterized by severe physical and emotional discomfort and may last several weeks. Symptoms include muscle pains and spasms, and decreased energy levels and mental functioning. It is very difficult to withdraw from the drug without professional help. An overdose of cocaine stimulate the spinal cord, and may result in convulsions, depression of the entire nervous system, respiratory failure, and death. In the past 50 years, the incidence of cocaine among Americans has risen dramatically (although there has been a slight decrease since the mid-1980s). A 1988 survey found that one in ten people had used the drug with the number rising to one in four for adults between the ages of 18 and 25.

tigue, craving, and shakiness. They appear within 12 to 24 hours from the last intake, peak at around 48 hours, and continue for a week. Nicotine, the psychostimulant in tobacco, has a powerful effect on the **autonomic nervous system**. While some claim that nicotine addiction is more psychological than physical, it is associated with definite withdrawal symptoms, including cravings, restlessness, irritability, and weight gain. It can cause lung cancer, heart attack, respiratory disorders, and stroke. When used by pregnant women, it can harm their unborn children in a number of ways.

Certain classes of psychoactive drugs are used clinically to treat depression, **mania**, anxiety, and schizophrenia. Therapy for severe mental disorders was transformed in the 1950s with the discovery of neuroleptics (antipsychotics), which reduced psychotic symptoms, including delusions, paranoid suspicions, confusion, incoherence, and hallucinations. Phenothiazines, notably chlorpromazine, Thorazine, and Haldol, are the most commonly used antipsychotic drug.

Another drug, clozapine (Clozaril), has effects similar to those of phenothiazines but without the long-term side effect of movement disorders that afflicts at least 25 percent of phenothiazine users. However, about two percent of clozapine users are at risk for a different problem—agranulucytosis, a fatal blood disorder, and all patients who take the drug must be tested regularly for this side effect.

**Antidepressants**, a second class of therapeutic drugs, reduce symptoms of depression (depressed **mood**, fatigue, appetite loss, **sleep disorders**) in a majority of users. There are several types of antidepressants, including monoamine oxidase inhibitors (MAO-I), which can also relieve panic attacks; tricyclic antidepressants, which seem to be more effective for many patients; and a "second generation" of serotonin-related antidepressants. The best-known drug of this type, Prozac (fluoxetine), has become the most widely prescribed antidepressant in the United States due to its combination of effectiveness and lack of side effects. It also helps sufferers from **obsessive-compulsive disorder**. The drug lithium is used to relieve episodes of both mania and depression in patients with **bipolar disorder**.

*See also* Alcohol dependence and abuse

# Drug therapy

Medications administered to help people suffering from psychological illnesses.

Because research has shown that many psychiatric illnesses are biological in origin, drug therapy is often the prescribed treatment. Drug therapy is used to treat a variety of psychological disorders, including **attention deficit/hyperactivity disorder** (ADHD), major **depression**, **schizophrenia**, Tourette's syndrome, anxiety disorders, **autism**, panic attacks, and **obsessive-compulsive disorder**, among many others. Drug therapy can be very effective when the patient shows a high level of compliance to the recommended course of treatment. The effectiveness of various medications has enabled many people to lead a full and active life, or at a higher level of functioning than would otherwise be possible without drug therapy.

Along with the benefits derived from drug therapy, however, medications can also evoke side effects such as irritability, agitation, nausea, and headaches. The stimulants used to control ADHD, for example, can suppress growth, particularly weight gain. Schizophrenia is treated with antipsychotic agents such as chlorpromazine, thioridazine, haloperidol, and thiothlxene. Long-term use can produce tardive dyskinesia, an involuntary tongue and mouth movement disorder, stiffness, and tremors. Clomipramime, an antidepressant effective in the treatment of obsessive-compulsive disorder, can produce dry mouth, blurred **vision**, constipation, rapid heartbeat, and urinary retention. Muscle stiffness often accompanies the drug haloperidol when it is taken for Tourette's syndrome. **Antidepressants** such as nortriptyline (brand name Pamelor), imipramine (Tofranil), desipramine (Norpramin), fluoxetine (Prozac), sertraline (Zoloft), and paroxetine (Paxil) all carry a small risk of triggering a manic or hypomanic episode. When a person considers taking medication for a psychological condition, it is important to be aware of the possible side effects, as well as knowing the proper dosage, and any harmful drug interactions.

When drug therapy was first introduced, many people, including some **mental health** professionals, considered medication a simple solution to controlling undesirable behaviors. Research has shown, however, that drug therapy is most effective when used in conjunction with traditional therapy. In the early history of drug therapy, patients in psychiatric hospitals were often medicated, sometimes without receiving any other sort of treatment. Today, it is more common for patients to participate in a range of activities and therapies, such as **group therapy** and **music therapy**, while they are on medication. Indeed, sometimes medication makes it possible for some patients to participate in the therapeutic process at all.

# DSM-IV

See *Diagnostic and Statistical Manual of Mental Disorders*

# Dysfunctional family

A family whose interrelationships serve to detract from, rather than promote, the emotional and physical health and well-being of its members.

Although this term is used casually in popular culture, health care professionals define dysfunctional **family** as one where the relationships among family members are not conducive to emotional and physical health. Sexual or physical abuse, alcohol and drug addictions, delinquency and behavior problems, **eating disorders**, and extreme **aggression** are some conditions commonly associated with dysfunctional family relationships.

The concept of the dysfunctional family is based on a systems approach to **mental health** diagnosis and treatment, where the individual's symptoms are seen in the context of relationships with other individuals and groups, rather than as problems unique to the client. There is no strict definition of a "dysfunctional family," and especially in popular usage the term tends to be a catchall for many different relational disorders that take place within the family system and its subsystems (parents, children). Mental health care providers and institutions increasingly recognize family and couples therapy as effective methods of treating diverse mental health disorders, especially where children are involved.

Some of the characteristics of dysfunctional family systems are as follows:

- Blaming; failure to take responsibility for personal actions and feelings; and invalidation of other family members' feelings.

- Boundaries between family members that are either too loose or too rigid. For example, the parent may depend excessively on the child for emotional support (loose boundaries) or prevent the child from developing autonomy by making all the decisions for the child (rigid boundaries).

- Boundaries between the family as a whole and the outside world may also be too loose or too rigid.

- A tendency for family members to enact set roles—caregiver, hero, scapegoat, saint, bad girl or boy, little prince or princess—that serve to restrict feelings, experience, and self-expression.

- A tendency to have an "identified patient"—one family member who is recognized as mentally unhealthy, who may or may not be in treatment, but whose symptoms are a sign of the inner family conflict. Often the identified patient's problems function to disguise the larger family issues. For example, a child may be regarded as a bully and a troublemaker in school and labeled a "problem child," when he may in fact be expressing conflicts and problems, such as abuse from home, by acting out and being "bad."

Family therapists, like other therapists, take many different treatment approaches—psychodynamic, behavioral, cognitive, or a combination of these therapies. They may talk to members individually, together, and in subgroups. They may ask family members to reenact situations, or to do "homework" by modifying elements of their behavior and responses. As with individual therapy, one of the goals of family counseling is to reframe problems so that family members can see specific events and behaviors more clearly in a broader systems perspective.

## Further Reading

Annunziata, Jane, and Phyllis Jacobson-Kram. *Solving Your Problems Together: Family Therapy for the Whole Family.* Washington, DC: American Psychological Association, 1994.

Kaslow, Florence W., ed. *Handbook of Relational Diagnosis and Dysfunctional Family Patterns.* New York: John Wiley, 1996.

Minuchin, Salvador, and H. Charles Fishman. *Family Therapy Techniques.* Cambridge, MA: Harvard University Press, 1981.

# Dyslexia

A reading disability that is not caused by an identifiable physical problem (such as brain damage, visual or auditory problems).

Dyslexia is a specific **learning disability** characterized by a significant disparity between an individual's general **intelligence** and his or her language skills, usually reflected in school performance.

Estimates of people with dyslexia range from 2% to the National Institutes of Health figure of 15% of the U.S. population. It is a complicated disorder with no identifiable cause or cure, yet it is highly responsive to treatment in the form of special instruction. The most obvious symptoms of the dyslexic show up in reading and writing, but listening, speaking, and general organizational skills are also affected. The dyslexic may have trouble transferring information across modalities, for example from verbal to written forms. The dyslexic's characteristic reversal of letters, confusion between similar letters such as "b" and "d," omission of words when reading aloud, trouble sounding out words, and difficulty following written instructions were first thought to be the result of **vision** and perceptual problems—i.e., a failure of taking in the stimulus. Only a small percentage of dyslexics have vision disorders, however, and it is now generally agreed by physicians, researchers, and educators that dyslexia is primarily a **language disorder**. Whereas the non-dyslexic intuitively learns phonic (sound) rules while learning to read, the dyslexic needs specific, methodical drill and practice to learn the visual-auditory associations necessary for reading comprehension and written expression.

Originally it was thought that dyslexia affected more males than females (in a ratio of 5:1), but later studies found males to be only slightly more likely than females to be dyslexic. Figures for diagnosed child dyslexics are skewed because for various reasons boys tend to be referred more frequently for **special education**. Diagnosis is complicated by the fact that anywhere from 20% to 55% of dyslexics also suffer from **attention deficit/hyperactivity disorder** (ADHD), a behavioral disorder which can aggravate reading problems. There are many different theories about the causes and classifications of different types of dyslexia, but few hard conclusions. It is definitely familial, and about 40% of boys and 20% of girls with a dyslexic parent show the disorder. Several genetic studies have found gene linkages which demonstrate heterogeneous (multiple methods of) transmission. Dyslexics have average or above average intelligence, and it is speculated that they have heightened visual-spatial and motor awareness. Thomas Edison, Albert Einstein, Woodrow Wilson, General George Patton, and Auguste Rodin are thought to have been dyslexic.

There are many treatment approaches available to the public, ranging from visual stimulation to diets to enhancement of regular language education. However, it is generally agreed that specialized education is the only

**Typical writings of a dyslexic.** *(Will & Deni McIntyre/Science Source, National Audubon Society Collection/ Photo Researchers, Inc. Reproduced with permission.)*

successful remedy, and the American Academy of Ophthalmology, the American Academy of Pediatrics, and the American Association for Pediatric Ophthalmology and Strabismus have issued a policy statement warning against visual treatments and recommending a cross-disciplinary educational approach. In fact the first researcher to identify and study dyslexia, Samuel Torrey Orton, developed the core principles of such an approach in the 1920s. The work of three of his followers—teachers Bessie Stillman, Anna Gillingham, and Beth Slingerland—underlies many of the programs in wide use today such as project READ, the Wilson Reading System, and programs based on the Herman method. These and other successful programs have three characteristics in common. They are:

(1) Sound/symbol based. They break words down into their smallest visual components: letters and the sounds associated with them.

(2) Multisensory. They attempt to form and strengthen mental associations among visual, auditory, and kinesthetic channels of stimulation. The dyslexic simultaneously sees, feels, and says the sound-symbol association; for example, a student may trace the letter or letter combination with his finger while pronouncing a word out loud.

(3) Highly structured. Remediation begins at the level of the single letter-sound, works up to digraphs, then syllables, then into words and sentences in a very systematic fashion. Repetitive drill and practice serve to form necessary sound-symbol associations.

If caught early, especially before the third grade, dyslexia is highly treatable through special education.

## Further Reading

Bowler, Rosemary F., ed. *Annals of Dyslexia*. Baltimore, MD: The Orton Dyslexia Society, 1983.

Galaburda, A., ed. *Dyslexia and Development: Neurobiological Aspects of Extraordinary Brains*. Cambridge, MA: Harvard UP, 1993.

Miles. T.R. *Dyslexia*. Philadelphia: Open University Press, 1990.

Lytle, Vicky. "Edison, Rockefeller, Rodin, and the Reading Problem: Detecting Dyslexia in Students." *NEA Today* 4, (October 1985): 10-11.

Rooney, Karen. "Dyslexia Revisited: History, Educational Philosophy, and Clinical Assessment Applications." *Intervention in School and Clinic* 31, no. 1, (1995): 6-15.

Rumsey, Judith M. "The Biology of Developmental Dyslexia: Grand Rounds at the Clinical Center of the National Institutes of Health." *JAMA* 19, no. 7, (1992): 912-16.

## Further Information

Council for Learning Disabilities. P.O. Box 40303, Overland Park, KS 66204.

Foundation for Children with Learning Disabilities. 99 Park Avenue, New York, NY 10016.

Orton Dyslexia Society. 8600 LaSalle Road, Chester Building, Suite 382, Baltimore, MD 21286-2044, (410) 296–0232, information line: (800) ABC-D123.

# Eating disorders

Eating disorders are characterized by an obsessive preoccupation with food and/or body weight.

Eating disorders are rooted in complex emotional issues that center on **self-esteem** and pervasive societal messages that equate thinness with happiness. Eating disorders usually surface in **adolescence**, and more than 90% of sufferers are female, although the incidence among males appears to be growing. Because eating disorders are neither purely physical nor purely psychological, effective treatment must include both medical management and **psychotherapy**. The earlier a diagnosis is made and treatment is started, the better the chances of a successful outcome.

The two most common types of eating disorders are **anorexia** nervosa and **bulimia**, which are covered separately in this book.

Gail B. Slap, M.D.

### Further Reading
Maloney, Michael and Rachel Kranz. *Straight Talk About Eating Disorders*. New York: Facts on File, 1991.

### Further Information
National Association of Anorexia Nervosa and Associated Disorders (ANAD). P.O. Box 7, Highland Park, IL 60035, (847) 831–3438.
National Eating Disorders Organization. 6655 Yale Avenue, Tulsa, OK 74136, (918) 481–4044.

# Hermann Ebbinghaus

### 1850-1909
German psychologist whose work resulted in the development of scientifically reliable experimental methods for the quantitative measurement of rote learning and memory.

**Hermann Ebbinghaus** (Corbis-Bettmann. Reproduced with permission.)

Born in Germany, Hermann Ebbinghaus received his formal education at the universities of Halle, Berlin, and Bonn, where he earned degrees in philosophy and history. After obtaining his philosophy degree in 1873, Ebbinghaus served in the Franco-Prussian War. For the next seven years following the war, he tutored and studied independently in Berlin, France, and England. In the late 1870s, Ebbinghaus became interested in the workings of human **memory**. In spite of **Wilhelm Wundt**'s assertion in his newly published *Physiological Psychology* that memory could not be studied experimentally, Ebbinghaus decided to attempt such a study, applying to this new field the same sort of mathematical treatment that **Gustav Fechner** (1801-1887) had described in *Elements of Psychophysics* (1860) in connection with his study of sensation and **perception**.

Using himself as both sole experimenter and subject, Ebbinghaus embarked on an arduous process that involved repeatedly testing his memorization of nonsense words devised to eliminate variables caused by prior familiarity with the material being memorized. He created 2,300 one-syllable consonant-vowel-consonant combinations—such as *taz*, *bok*, and *lef*— to facilitate his study of learning independent of meaning. He divided syllables into a series of lists that he memorized under fixed conditions. Recording the average amount of time it took him to memorize these lists perfectly, he then varied the conditions to arrive at observations about the effects of such variables as speed, list length, and number of repetitions. He also studied the factors involved in retention of the memorized material, comparing the initial memorization time with the time needed for a second memorization of the same material after a given period of time (such as 24 hours) and subsequent memorization attempts. These results showed the existence of a regular **forgetting curve** over time that approximated a mathematical function similar to that in Fechner's study. After a steep initial decline in learning time between the first and second memorization, the curve leveled off progressively with subsequent efforts.

Ebbinghaus also measured immediate memory, showing that a subject could generally remember between six and eight items after an initial look at one of his lists. In addition, he studied comparative learning rates for meaningful and meaningless material, concluding that meaningful items, such as words and sentences, could be learned much more efficiently than nonsense syllables. His experiments also yielded observations about the value of evenly spaced as opposed to massed memorization. A monumental amount of time and effort went into this ground-breaking research. For example, to determine the effects of number of repetitions on retention, Ebbinghaus tested himself on 420 lists of 16 syllables 340 times each, for a total of 14,280 trials. After careful accumulation and analysis of data, Ebbinghaus published the results of his research in the volume *On Memory* in 1885, while on the faculty of the University of Berlin. Although Wundt argued that results obtained by using nonsense syllables had limited applicability to the actual memorization of meaningful material, Ebbinghaus's work has been widely used as a model for research on human verbal learning, and *Über Gedachtnis* (*On Memory)* has remained one of the most cited and highly respected sourcebooks in the history of psychology.

In 1894, Ebbinghaus joined the faculty of the University of Breslau. While studying the mental capacities of children in 1897, he began developing a sentence completion test that is still widely used in the **measurement** of **intelligence**. This test, which he worked on until 1905, was probably the first successful test of mental **ability**. Ebbinghaus also served on the faculties of the Friedrich Wilhelm University and the University of Halle. He was a cofounder of the first German psychology journal, the *Journal of Psychology and Physiology of the Sense Organs,* in 1890, and also wrote two successful textbooks, *The Principles of Psychology* (1902) and *A Summary of Psychology* (1908), both of which went into several editions. His achievements represented a major advance for psychology as a distinct scientific discipline and many of his methods continue to be followed in verbal learning research.

*See also* Forgetting curve; Intelligence quotient

# John C. Eccles

## 1903-1997
Australian neurophysiologist known for his research in nerve cell communication.

John Carew Eccles was a neurophysiologist whose research explained how **nerve** cells communicate with one another. He demonstrated that when a nerve cell is stimulated it releases a chemical that binds to the membrane of neighboring cells and activates them in turn. He further demonstrated that by the same mechanism a nerve cell can also inhibit the electrical activity of nearby nerve cells. For this research, Eccles shared the 1963 Nobel Prize for Physiology or Medicine with Alan Lloyd Hodgkin and Andrew Huxley.

Born on January 27, 1903, in Melbourne, Australia, Eccles was the son of **William James** and Mary Carew Eccles. Both of his parents were teachers, and they taught him at home until he entered Melbourne High School in 1915. In 1919, Eccles began medical studies at Melbourne University, where he participated in athletics and graduated in 1925 with the highest academic honors. Eccles's academic excellence was rewarded with a Rhodes Scholarship, which allowed him to pursue a graduate degree in England at Oxford University. In September 1925, Eccles began studies at Magdalen College, Oxford. As he had done at Melbourne, Eccles excelled academically, receiving high honors for science and being named a Christopher Welch Scholar. In 1927, he received appointment as a junior research fellow at Exeter College, Oxford.

### Embarks on neurological research

Even before leaving Melbourne for Oxford, Eccles had decided that he wanted to study the **brain** and the nervous system, and he was determined to work on these subjects with Charles Scott Sherrington. Sherrington, who would win the Nobel Prize in 1932, was then the world's leading neurophysiologist; his research had virtually founded the field of cellular neurophysiology. The following year, after becoming a junior fellow, Eccles realized his goal and became one of Sherrington's research assistants. Although Sherrington was then nearly seventy years old, Eccles collaborated with him on some of his most important research. Together, they studied the factors responsible for inhibiting a **neuron**, or a nerve cell. They also explored what they termed the "motor unit"—a nerve cell which coordinates the actions of many muscle fibers. Sherrington and Eccles conducted their research without the benefit of the electronic devices that would later be developed to measure a nerve cell's electrical activity. For this work on neural excitation and inhibition, Eccles was awarded his doctorate in 1929.

Eccles remained at Exeter after receiving his doctorate, serving as a Staines Medical Fellow from 1932 to 1934. During this period, he also held posts at Magdalen College as tutor and demonstrator in physiology. The research that Eccles had begun in Sherrington's laboratory continued, but instead of describing the process of neural inhibition, Eccles became increasingly interested in explaining the process that underlies inhibition. He and other neurophysiologists believed that the transmission of electrical impulses was responsible for neural inhibition. Bernhard Katz and Paul Fatt later demonstrated, however, that it was a chemical mechanism and not a wholly electrical phenomenon which was primarily responsible for inhibiting nerve cells.

## Returns to Australia

In 1937, Eccles returned to Australia to assume the directorship of the Kanematsu Memorial Institute for Pathology in Sydney. During the late 1930s and early 1940s, the Kanematsu Institute, under his guidance, became an important center for the study of neurophysiology. With Katz, Stephen Kuffler, and others, he undertook research on the activity of nerve and muscle cells in cats and frogs, studying how nerve cells communicate with muscle or motor cells. His team proposed that the binding of a chemical (now known to be the **neurotransmitter** acetylcholine) by the muscle cell led to a depolarization, or a loss of electrical charge, in the muscle cell. This depolarization, Eccles believed, occurred because charged ions in the muscle cell were released into the exterior of the cell when the chemical substance released by the nerve cell was bound to the muscle cell.

**Sir John Eccles** *(The Library of Congress. Reproduced with permission.)*

During World War II, Eccles served as a medical consultant to the Australian army, where he studied **vision**, **hearing**, and other medical problems faced by pilots. Returning to full-time research and teaching in 1944, Eccles became professor of physiology at the University of Otago in Dunedin, New Zealand. At Otago, Eccles continued the research that had been interrupted by the war, but now he attempted to describe in greater detail the neural transmission event, using very fine electrodes made of glass. This research continued into the early 1950s, and it convinced Eccles that transmission from nerve cell to nerve cell or nerve cell to muscle cell occurred by a chemical mechanism, not an electrical mechanism as he had thought earlier.

In 1952, Eccles left Otago for the Australian National University in Canberra. Here, along with Fatt and J. S. Coombs, he studied the inhibitory process in postsynaptic cells, which are the nerve or muscle cells that are affected by nerve cells. They were able to establish that whether nerve and muscle cells were excited or inhibited was controlled by pores in the membrane of the cells, through which ions could enter or leave. By the late 1950s and early 1960s, Eccles had turned his attention to higher neural processes, pursuing research on neural pathways and the cellular organization of the brain.

## Begins a second career in the United States

In 1966, Eccles turned sixty-three and university policy at the Australian National University required him to retire. Wanting to continue his research career, he accepted an invitation from the American Medical Association to become the director of its Institute for Biomedical Research in Chicago. He left that institution in 1968 to become professor of physiology and medicine and the Buswell Research Fellow at the State University of New York in Buffalo. The university constructed a laboratory for him where he could continue his research on transmission in nerves. Even at a late stage in his career, Eccles's work suggested important relationships between the excitation and inhibition of nerves and the storing and processing of information by the brain.

In 1975, he retired from SUNY with the title of Professor Emeritus, subsequently moving to Switzerland. During the final period of his career, Eccles focused on a variety of fundamental problems relating to **consciousness** and identity, conducting research in areas where physiology, psychology, and philosophy intersect. He died at his home in Contra, Switzerland.

Eccles received a considerable number of scientific distinctions. His memberships included the Royal Society of London, the Royal Society of New Zealand, and the American Academy of Arts and Sciences. He was awarded the Gotch Memorial Prize in 1927, and the Rolleston Memorial Prize in 1932. The Royal College of Physicians presented him with their Baly Medal in 1961, the Royal Society gave him their Royal Medal in 1962, and the German Academy awarded him the Cothenius Medal in 1963. Also in 1963, he shared the Nobel Prize for Physiology and Medicine with Alan Hodgkin and Andrew Huxley. He was knighted in 1958.

In 1928, Eccles married Irene Frances Miller of New Zealand. The marriage, which eventually ended in **divorce** in 1968, produced four sons and five daughters. One of their daughters, Rosamond, earned her doctorate and participated with her father in his research. After his divorce from Irene Eccles, Eccles married the Czech neurophysiologist Helena Tabořiková in 1968. Dr. Tabořiková also collaborated with Eccles in his scientific research.

*See also* Central nervous system

D. George Joseph

## Further Reading

Fox, D., and M. Meldrum, eds. *Nobel Laureates in Medicine or Physiology.* New York: Garland, 1990.

Fox, D., and M. Meldrum, eds. *One Hundred Most Important People in the World Today.* New York: Putnam, 1970.

# Echolalia

Repetition of another person's words or phrases.

Using a mechanical, robotlike speech pattern, an individual with certain mental disorders may repeat words or phrases spoken by others. Known as echolalia, this behavior is observed in children with **autism**, Tourette's syndrome, **schizophrenia**, and certain other **brain** disorders.

# Educational psychology

The study of the process of education, e.g., how people, especially children, learn and which teaching methods and materials are most successful.

Educational psychology departments in many universities provide training to educators, school psychologists, and other educational professionals. Applied research in this field focuses on how to improve teaching, solve learning problems, and measure learning **ability** and progress. Other concerns of educational psychology include **cognitive development**, the dynamics of pupil behavior, and the psychological atmosphere of the classroom. Educational psychologists devise **achievement tests**, evaluate teaching methods, develop learning aids and curricula, and investigate how children of different ages learn. They often serve as researchers and educators at teacher training institutions, in university psychology departments, on the staffs of educational research organizations, and also work in government agencies, business, and the military. An educational psychologist might investigate areas as diverse as the causes of **dyslexia** and the measures that can be taken to help dyslexics improve their reading and learning skills; gender differences in mathematical ability; anxiety in education; the effect of television on study habits; the identification of gifted children; how teachers affect student behavior; and creative thinking in children of a specific grade level or age.

Educational psychology in the United States has its roots in the pioneering work of the 1890s by two of the country's foremost psychologists, **William James** and **John Dewey**. James—who is known for his 1899 volume, *Talks to Teachers on Psychology* —pioneered the concept of taking psychology out of the laboratory and applying it to problems in the real world. He advocated the study of educational problems in their natural **environment**, the classroom, and viewed classroom interactions and observations as a legitimate source of scientific data. John Dewey, the country's most famous advocate of active learning, founded an experimental school at the University of Chicago to develop and study new educational methods. Dewey experimented with educational curricula and methods and advocated parental participation in the educational process. His philosophy of education stressed learning by doing, as opposed to authoritarian teaching methods and rote learning, and his ideas have had a strong impact on the theory and practice of education in the United States. Dewey's first influential book on education, *The School and Society* (1899), was adapted from a series of lectures to parents of the pupils in his school at the University of Chicago.

In the twentieth century, the theoretical and practical branches of educational psychology have developed separately from each other. The name most prominently associated with the scientific, experimental focus is that of Edward L. Thorndike, often called "the father of educational psychology." Applying the learning principles he had discovered in his animal research to humans, Thorndike became a pioneer in the application of psychological principles to such areas as the teaching of reading, **language development**, and mental testing. His *Introduction to the Theory of Mental and Social Measurements* (1904) gave users of **intelligence** tests access to statistical data about test results. Although Thorndike's emphases were on **conditioning** and scientific **measurement**, he was both directly and indirectly responsible for a number of curricular and methodological changes in education throughout the United States. Thorndike is especially well-known as an opponent of the traditional Latin and Greek classical curriculum used in secondary schools, which he helped to discontinue by demonstrating that progress in one subject did not substantially influence progress in another—the major premise on which classical education had been based.

The work of Thorndike's contemporary, Charles Hubbard Judd (1873-1946), provided a marked contrast in its more pragmatic focus on transforming contemporary educational policies and practices. Judd served as director of the University of Chicago School of Education, where he disseminated his philosophy of education. His research interests were applied to the study of school subjects and teaching methods. Concerned with school organization as well, Judd recommended the establishment of both junior high schools and junior colleges and championed equal education opportunities for students of all backgrounds. His published books include *Psychology of High School Subjects* (1915), *Psychology of Secondary Education* (1927), and *Genetic Psychology for Teachers* (1939).

Other educational psychologists have focused their work on either measurement and **learning theory** or school and curriculum reform. The contributions of **G. Stanley Hall** (1844-1924) to the field of intelligence testing were especially significant and influential. He passed on his view of intelligence as an inherited trait to two of his most famous students, **Arnold Gesell** and **Lewis Terman**. It was Terman who introduced the **Stanford-Binet Intelligence Scales** in the United States in 1916, creating new norms based on American standardizing groups. Gesell also made important contributions to the study of human development, and by the 1930s, this subject had become a part of the standard educational psychology texts, and today it is a central area in the field. The learning process, a related area that is also traditionally studied, includes such issues as hierarchies of learning activities, the relationship of learning to **motivation**, and effective instructional methods.

The study of evaluation has remained a central part of the educational psychology and includes techniques for assessing learning, achievement, and behavior; analysis of individual differences; and methods of addressing learning problems. Another relevant area is that of **mental health** in the classroom ( **personality** integration; adjustment problems; teacher-pupil interaction). In recent years, the trend has been toward a more "holistic" and humanistic approach that stresses the learner's affective needs in the context of cognitive processes. A growing area of emphasis for all education professionals is educating individuals with special needs. Current psychological theory and practice—as well as federal law—rejects the traditional exclusionary approach in dealing with disabled or emotionally troubled children and adolescents. Mainstreaming such students is now common practice, with the goal of expanding boundaries and reducing the barriers between exceptional or atypical students and mainstream students. Educational psychology must now concern itself with such issues as systems for classification of children and teenagers as mentally retarded or deviant; creation of alternative educational environments and intervention programs that promote the development of the special needs population and the requisite teaching strategies and skills; and the creation, where necessary, of individualized educational plans.

Division 15 of the **American Psychological Association (APA)** is devoted to educational psychology. Its members are mostly faculty members at universities, although some work in school settings. In 1982, nearly 14 percent of the members of the APA were members of this division and identified themselves as educational psychologists. Professional journals in educational psychology include *Journal of Educational Psychology, Educational Psycholo-*

*gist, Educational Researcher, Review of Educational Research,* and *American Educational Research Journal.*

**Further Reading**

Dembo, Myron H. *Applying Educational Psychology.* 5th ed. New York: Longman, 1994.

Eysenck, Michael W. *Individual Differences: Normal and Abnormal.* Hillsdale, NJ: L. Erlbaum Associates, 1994.

Farnham-Diggory, Sylvia. *Cognitive Processes in Education.* 2nd ed. New York: HarperCollins, 1992.

# Effector

Peripheral tissue at the outer end of an efferent neural path (one leading away from the central nervous system).

An effector acts in special ways in response to a **nerve** impulse. In humans, effectors may either be muscles, which contract in response to neural stimuli, or glands, which produce secretions. The muscles are generally divided into two groupings: somatic effectors, which are the body's striated muscles (such as those found in the arm and back), and autonomic effectors, which are smooth muscles (such as the iris of the eye).

Both types of effectors are linked to the gray matter of the spinal cord, but each system originates in a different portion of it. The somatic effectors, which are responsible for powerful motor movements, are linked to the ventral horn cell, a large **neuron** in the ventral portion of the gray matter. The autonomic effectors receive impulses from the lateral part of the gray matter. The smooth muscles that are supplied by these effectors maintain the tone of blood vessels walls, thus helping to regulate blood pressure. Glandular secretions controlled by autonomic effectors include external secretions, such as sweat, and internal ones, such as the hormone epinephrine secreted by the adrenal medulla of the **brain.** Some nerve fibers that connect with autonomic effectors also pass through the ventral roots of the spinal nerves by way of a ganglion located outside the spinal cord and are then distributed to smooth muscles and glands.

**Further Reading**

*ABC's of the Human Mind.* Pleasantville, NY: Reader's Digest Association, 1990.

# Ego

In psychoanalytic theory, the part of human personality that combines innate biological impulses

(id) or drives with reality to produce appropriate behavior.

**Sigmund Freud** believed that human **personality** has three components: the **id**, the **ego** and the **superego.** In his scheme, the id urges immediate action on such basic needs as eating, drinking, and eliminating wastes without regard to consequences. The ego is that portion of the personality that imposes realistic limitations on such behavior. It decides whether id-motivated behavior is appropriate, given the prevailing social and environmental conditions.

While the id operates on the "pleasure principle," the ego uses the "reality principle" to determine whether to satisfy or delay fulfilling the id's demands. The ego considers the consequences of actions to modify the powerful drives of the id. A person's own concept of what is acceptable determines the ego's decisions. The ego also must "negotiate" with the superego (**conscience**) in the often bitter battle between the id's drives and a person's own sense of right and wrong. Repression and anxiety may result when the ego consistently overrides the id's extreme demands.

**Further Reading**

Atkinson, Rita L.; Richard C. Atkinson; Edward E. Smith; and Ernest R. Hilgard. *Introduction to Psychology.* 9th ed. San Diego: Harcourt Brace Jovanovich, 1987.

Zimbardo, Philip G. *Psychology and Life.* 12th ed. Glenview, IL: Scott, Foresman, 1988.

# Electra complex

See **Oedipus complex**

# Electrical stimulation of the brain (ESB)

A procedure which involves the introduction of a weak electrical current into specific locations in the brain by using multiple microelectrodes to apply short pulses of electrical currents intended to mimic the natural flow of impulses through the neural pathways.

Electrical stimulation of the **brain** (ESB) is useful in a variety of situations, including neurosurgical operations and experimental research. In neurosurgery, this procedure may be used to assist physicians in determining which brain tissue should be removed. Because the patient must remain awake during the procedure, only a local anesthetic is administered. Focal **epilepsy** has been surgically treated by using electrical brain stimulation in conscious patients to determine the epileptic focus.

In experimental research, ESB does not control complex behavior patterns such as **depression**, but it can be employed quite successfully to control individual functions. Therefore, this procedure has proven useful in studying the relationships among various areas and structures of the brain and the activities they control. It has been found, for example, that stimulation of the visual cortex produces visual sensations, such as bursts of light or color (blind people have seen spots of light as a result of ESB). Similarly, stimulation of the auditory cortex results in aural sensation, while stimulating areas associated with motor control produces arm, leg, or other body movements. Stimulation of areas of the brain linked to association can induce memories of scenes or events.

In addition to research and experimental uses, electrical brain stimulation has been successfully used for some therapeutic purposes. Brain stem and cerebellar stimulation have aided in some movement disorders; peroneal **nerve** stimulation has been used to treat dropfoot in stroke victims; and transcutaneous nerve, dorsal-column, and deep-brain stimulation have proven useful in the relief of chronic severe **pain**.

Electrical brain stimulation has aided in mapping connections between different regions of the brain in animals, and has been used to induce many different types of behavior in animals, including eating, drinking, **aggression**, hoarding, and both sexual and maternal behavior. While hypothalamic stimulation is associated with such emotional responses as attack and defense, stimulation of the reticular formation in the brain stem can induce **sleep**. ESB has also confirmed the existence of a "reward center" in animals, whereby animals can be taught to stimulate their own brains mechanically by pressing a lever when such stimulation results in a pleasant sensation.

# Electroconvulsive therapy (ECT)

The application of a mild electric current to the brain to produce an epileptic-like seizure as a means of treating certain psychological disorders, primarily severe depression.

Electroconvulsive therapy, also known as ECT and electroshock therapy, was developed in the 1930s when various observations led physicians to conclude that epileptic seizures might prevent or relieve the symptoms of **schizophrenia**. After experiments with insulin and other potentially seizure-inducing drugs, Italian physicians pioneered the use of an electric current to create seizures in schizophrenic patients.

ECT was routinely used to treat schizophrenia, **depression**, and, in some cases, **mania**. It eventually became a source of controversy due to misuse and negative side effects. ECT was used indiscriminately and was often prescribed for treating disorders on which it had no real effect, such as alcohol dependence, and was used for punitive reasons. Patients typically experienced confusion and loss of **memory** after treatments, and even those whose condition improved eventually relapsed. Other side effects of ECT include speech defects, physical injury from the force of the convulsions, and cardiac arrest. Use of electroconvulsive therapy declined after 1960 with the introduction of antidepressant and antipsychotic drugs.

ECT is still used today but with less frequency and with modifications that have made the procedure safer and less unpleasant. Anesthetics and muscle relaxants are usually administered to prevent bone fractures or other injuries from muscle spasms. Patients receive approximately 4 to 10 treatments administered over a period of about two weeks. Confusion and memory loss are minimized by the common practice of applying the current only to the non-dominant **brain** hemisphere, usually the **right-brain hemisphere**. Nevertheless, some memory loss still occurs; anterograde memory (the **ability** to learn new material) returns relatively rapidly following treatment, but retrograde memory (the ability to remember past events) is more strongly affected. There is a marked memory deficit one week after treatment which gradually improves over the next six or seven months. In many cases, however, subtle memory losses persist even beyond this point, and can be serious and debilitating for some patients.

About 100,000 people in the United States receive electroconvulsive therapy annually. ECT can only be administered with the informed consent of the patient and is used primarily for severely depressed patients who have not responded to antidepressant medications or whose suicidal impulses make it dangerous to wait until such medications can take effect. ECT is also administered to patients with **bipolar disorder**. Contrary to the theories of those who first pioneered its use, ECT is not an effective treatment for schizophrenia unless the patient is also suffering from depression. The rate of relapse after administration of ECT can be greatly diminished when it is accompanied by other forms of treatment.

Researchers are still not sure exactly how electroconvulsive therapy works, although it is known that the seizures rather than the electric current itself are the basis for the treatment's effects, and that seizures can affect the functioning of neurotransmitters in the brain, including norepinephrine and serotonin, which are associated with depression. They also increase the release of pituitary **hormones**. Because of its possible side effects, as well as the public's level of discomfort with both electrical shock and the idea of inducing seizures, ECT remains a controversial treatment method. In 1982, the city of Berkeley, California, passed a referendum making the administration of ECT a misdemeanor punishable by fines of up to $500 and six months in prison, but the law was later overturned.

## Further Reading

*Electroconvulsive Therapy: Theory and Practice. New York:* Raven Press, 1979.

# Electroencephalograph (EEG)

A device used to record the electrical activity of the brain.

Electroencephalography is used for a variety of research and diagnostic purposes. It is usually conducted using electrodes, metal discs attached to the scalp or to wires connected to the skull or even to the **brain** itself. The signals obtained through the electrodes must then be amplified in order to be interpreted. EEG patterns typically take the form of waves, which may be measured according to both their frequency and size (also referred to as amplitude). The electrical activity of animals' brains had been recorded as early as 1875, but it was not until 1929 that the first human EEG was reported by Austrian psychiatrist Anton Berger. Since then, it has been used to study the effects of drugs on the brain, as well as the localization of certain behavioral functions in specific areas of the brain. EEGs have also been widely used in **sleep** research. While the deeper stages of sleep are characterized by large, slow, irregular brain waves, and, in some cases, bursts of high-amplitude waves called "sleep spindles," REM (**rapid eye movement**) sleep, during which most vivid dreaming occurs, resembles the faster brain-wave pattern of the waking state.

As a diagnostic tool, EEGs have been used to diagnose **epilepsy**, strokes, infections, hemorrhages, inadequate blood supply to the brain, and certain tumors. They are especially useful because they can pinpoint the location of tumors and injuries to the brain. EEGs are also used to monitor patients in a **coma** and, during surgery, to indicate the effectiveness of anesthetics.

## Further Reading

Cooper, R. *EEG Technology*. New York: Butterworth, 1980.

# David Elkind

1931-
American psychologist and educator.

Psychologist and educator David Elkind was born in Detroit, Michigan, to Peter and Bessie (maiden name Nelson) E. Elkind. He and his **family** moved to California when he was an adolescent. He received the Bachelor of Arts from the University of California at Los Angeles (UCLA) in 1952, and his Doctorate in Philosophy (Ph.D.) from UCLA in 1955. He also received an honorary Doctorate in Science from Rhode Island College in 1987.

Elkind's father operated machinery in a factory that built parts for the automotive industry. Elkind remembered his father complaining about how the engineers who designed the parts did not understand the machinery his father was working with and thus sometimes designed things the machines could not create. This **memory** stuck with Elkind so that he always tried to consider the relationship between theory and practice, how theory could and would be applied.

After receiving his Ph.D., Elkind was a research assistant to David Rappaport at the Austen Riggs Center in Stockbridge, Massachusetts. There he was first exposed to the research and theory of **Jean Piaget**. From 1964 to 1965, Elkind was a national Science Foundation Senior Postdoctoral Fellow at Piaget's Institut d'Epistemologie Genetique in Geneva, Switzerland.

Piaget, originally trained as a biologist, studied and observed children for over fifty years. He sought to understand how children formed knowledge of the world around them, and his theories of **cognitive development** have been extremely influential in psychology. Much of Elkind's work can be seen as an attempt to duplicate, build upon, and more fully explore Piaget's theory and research. Elkind's research has focused on cognitive, perceptual, and social development in children and adolescents, as well as the causes and effects of **stress** on children, adolescents, and families. Throughout all of his work, Elkind has tried to apply theory and research to real life arenas, such as **psychotherapy**, parenting, and education. And he uses real life experiences to shape his theory and research.

One of Elkind's most well-known contributions to psychology is his work on adolescent psychology in which he expands on Piaget's description of adolescent egocentrism (difficulty in distinguishing between the

**David Elkind** *(AP/Wide World Photos. Reproduced with permission.)*

mental occupations of the self and those of other people). Elkind looked at how this egocentrism affects adolescent thought, behavior, and **emotion**.

According to Piagetian theory, the abilities to separate oneself from one's own thoughts and analyze them, as well as conceptualizing others' thoughts is developed only at young **adolescence**. Elkind describes how young adolescents, because they are undergoing major physiological changes, are preoccupied by themselves. The egocentrism of adolescents lies in their belief that others are as preoccupied with their appearance and behavior as they are. As a consequence, the adolescent anticipates other people's responses and thoughts about herself, and is, in a way, constantly creating or reacting to an *imaginary audience.*

According to Elkind, this probably plays a role in the self-consciousness so common in early adolescence, as well as other experiences in this period of life. Elkind also introduced the idea of the *personal fable,* in which the adolescent constructs a story about herself, a version of her life stressing the uniqueness of her feelings and experiences. Indeed, these ideas of personal uniqueness are also seen in a common conviction that the adolescent will not die. Elkind stressed how he found these concepts useful in understanding and treating troubled adolescents. Elkind believes the egocentrism of early adolescence usually lessens by the age of 15 or 16 as cognitive development proceeds.

In his more recent work, Elkind has turned his attention to educational methods, and how recent changes in society and the family affect children, adolescents, and the family unit. Another aspect of Elkind's work has been his focus on learning and healthy development. He believes that children need to have many and varied experiences to develop in a healthy way, and that this is also necessary for children to truly learn about and understand things. Elkind thinks parents pushing their infants and children to learn at earlier and earlier ages does not allow a child time to have the "rich" experiences necessary to absorb and learn in a deep and meaningful way.

Elkind is a well-respected speaker and author. He has written more than 400 book chapters and articles, and several stories for children. His numerous books include *Reinventing Childhood* (1998), *All Grown Up and No Place to Go* (1998), and *Ties That Stress: The New Family Imbalance* (1994).

In line with his efforts to apply research findings to practical problems, he has tried to communicate to the general public how his research relates to education and child rearing through writing articles for popular publications such as the magazine *Good Housekeeping.* In addition, he has appeared on numerous televisions shows including the *Oprah Winfrey Show, The Today Show,* and *The CBS Morning News.* He is member of the editorial board for a number of prestigious scientific journals, including the *Journal of Youth and Adolescence, Bulletin of the Menninger Clinic, Education Digest, Journal of Science and Education,* and *Montessori Life.*

Among his professional positions, from 1966 to 1978 Elkind served as Professor and Director of Graduate Training in Developmental Psychology at the Department of Psychology at the University of Rochester, New York. He also served as President of the National Association for the Education of Young Children. He is currently a Professor in the Department of Child Development at Tufts University in Medford, Massachusetts, which he joined in 1978. He also co-hosts the Lifetime television series *Kids These Days.* He has three sons and resides in Massachusetts.

Marie Doorey

**Further Reading**

Corsini, R.J., ed. "Elkind, David (1931- )." In *Encyclopedia of psychology, 2nd ed.* V. 4. New York: John Wiley & Sons.
Elkind, D. *Reinventing Childhood.* Rosemont, NJ: Modern Learning Press, 1998.

Elkind, D. *Ties that Stress: The New Family Imbalance*. Cambridge, MA: Harvard University Press, 1994.

"Elkind, D." In *Who's Who in America, 54th Edition*. Wilmette, IL: Marquis Who's Who, 1998.

Elkind, D. *Egocentrism in Adolescence. In Readings in Developmental Psychology, 2nd Ed.*, pp. 383-90. Eds: Gardner, Judith Krieger and Gardner, Ed. Boston: Little, Brown and Company. From David Elkind. 1967. *Egocentrism in Adolescence. Child Development*, 38,1025-33. Published by the Society for Research in Child Development.

Lapsley, D.K. "Toward an integrated theory of adolescent ego development: The 'new look' at adolescent egocentrism." *American Journal of Orthopsychiatry,* 63, (1993): 562-71.

Reber, A.S. *The Penguin Dictionary of Psychology*. Middlesex, England: Penguin Books, 1985.

Sheehy, N. Chapman, A.J., and Conroy, W.A. "Elkind, D." In *Biographical dictionary of psychology*. London and New York: Routledge, 1997.

Twentieth Annual Great Plains Students' Psychology Convention Website, 3/00, Missouri Western State College, St. Joseph, MO. http://www.psych-central.com/GPconvention.biograph.htm

Tuft's Child and Family News Feature News Service for Journalists Child & Family News Advisory Board Website, http://www.tufts.edu/cfn/who.shtml

**Further Information**

Tufts University, Department of Child Development. Medford, MA, USA. 02155.

**Albert Ellis** *(AP/Wide World Photos. Reproduced with permission.)*

# Albert Ellis

**1913-**
American psychologist who originated rational-emotive therapy (RET), also known for his work as an author and counselor in the areas of marriage and sexuality.

Raised in the Bronx, New York, Albert Ellis was shy and physically frail when he was young. Although he had literary ambitions in his teens and twenties, he earned degrees in accounting and business. While in his twenties, he found that he had a gift for advising his friends on sexual matters and undertook an intensive independent study of human **sexuality**. Deciding to become a professional therapist, he earned a Ph.D. in **clinical psychology** at the Teachers College at Columbia University in 1947, followed by four years of psychoanalytic training with Charles R. Hulbeck at the Karen Horney Institute. By 1952, he had a full-time practice in Manhattan.

However, Ellis soon became dissatisfied with the limits of **psychoanalysis**. He found it slow and ineffective, and he was frustrated with the passive role it assigned to the therapist. In 1953 he began experimenting with different therapeutic techniques, and within two years he developed rational-emotive therapy (RET), which he then began to practice and advocate in writing. It was based on the idea that psychological problems are caused by self-defeating thoughts (such as "I must be loved or approved by everyone" and "If I don't find the perfect solution to this problem, a catastrophe will result"). Once such thoughts are changed, emotional and behavioral changes will follow. The therapist's task is to help the client recognize illogical and self-destructive ways of thinking and replace them with healthier, more positive ones. Ellis outlined an active role for the therapist: his own therapeutic style involved continually challenging the client's illogical and self-destructive ideas in a dynamic and provocative manner.

When Ellis first began promoting his new system of therapy, it was met with widespread professional opposition. However, the growing dissatisfaction with **behaviorism** created a climate that was more hospitable to a therapeutic method like RET that emphasized the role of **cognition** in changing behavior. Other psychologists, including **Aaron Beck** and social learning theorist **Julian Rotter**, developed their own cognitive-oriented therapies, and Ellis found himself the pioneer of a new school of therapy—the cognitive-behavioral approach. He has described himself as "the father of RET and the grandfather of cognitive-behavioral therapy." Ellis has also published numerous books on sexuality, including several popular best sellers (such as *Sex Without Guilt* ) associated with the "sexual revolution" of the 1960s, and he was an innovator in the area of sex and marital therapy.

### Further Reading

Bernard, M. E. *Staying Alive in an Irrational World: Albert Ellis and Rational-Emotive Therapy.* South Melbourne, Australia: Carlson/Macmillan, 1986.

Ellis, A., and W. Dryden. *The Essential Albert Ellis.* New York: Springer, 1990.

# Emotional development

*The process by which infants and children begin developing the capacity to experience, express, and interpret emotions.*

The study of the emotional development of infants and children is relatively new, having been studied empirically only during the past few decades. Researchers have approached this area from a variety of theoretical perspectives, including those of social constructionism, differential **emotion** theory, and **social learning theory**. Each of these approaches explores the way infants and children develop emotionally, differing mainly on the question of whether emotions are learned or biologically predetermined, as well as debating the way infants and children manage their emotional experiences and behavior.

## Early infancy (birth-six months)

### Emotional expressivity

To formulate theories about the development of human emotions, researchers focus on observable display of emotion, such as facial expressions and public behavior. A child's private feelings and experiences cannot be studied by researchers, so interpretation of emotion must be limited to signs that can be observed. Although many descriptions of facial patterns appear intuitively to represent recognizable emotions, psychologists differ on their views on the range of emotions experienced by infants. It is not clear whether infants actually experience these emotions, or if adults, using adult facial expressions as the standard, simply superimpose their own understanding of the meaning of infant facial expressions.

Between six and ten weeks, a social smile emerges, usually accompanied by other pleasure-indicative actions and sounds, including cooing and mouthing. This social smile occurs in response to adult smiles and interactions. It derives its name from the unique process by which the infant engages a person in a social act, doing so by expressing pleasure (a smile), which consequently elicits a positive response. This cycle brings about a mutually reinforcing pattern in which both the infant and the other person gain pleasure from the social interaction.

As infants become more aware of their **environment**, smiling occurs in response to a wider variety of contexts. They may smile when they see a toy they have previously enjoyed. They may smile when receiving praise for accomplishing a difficult task. Smiles such as these, like the social smile, are considered to serve a developmental function.

Laughter, which begins at around three or four months, requires a level of **cognitive development** because it demonstrates that the child can recognize incongruity. That is, laughter is usually elicited by actions that deviate from the **norm**, such as being kissed on the abdomen or a caregiver playing peek-a-boo. Because it fosters reciprocal interactions with others, laughter promotes social development.

## Later infancy (7-12 months)

### Emotional expressivity

During the last half of the first year, infants begin expressing **fear**, disgust, and **anger** because of the maturation of cognitive abilities. Anger, often expressed by crying, is a frequent emotion expressed by infants. As is the case with all emotional expressions, anger serves an adaptive function, signaling to caregivers of the infant's discomfort or displeasure, letting them know that something needs to be changed or altered. Although some infants respond to distressing events with sadness, anger is more common.

Fear also emerges during this stage as children become able to compare an unfamiliar event with what they know. Unfamiliar situations or objects often elicit fear responses in infants. One of the most common is the presence of an adult stranger, a fear that begins to appear at about seven months. The degree to which a child reacts with fear to new situations is dependent on a variety of factors. One of the most significant is the response of its mother or caregiver. Caregivers supply infants with a secure base from which to explore their world, and accordingly an exploring infant will generally not move beyond eyesight of the caregiver. Infants repeatedly check with their caregivers for emotional cues regarding safety and security of their explorations. If, for instance, they wander too close to something their caregiver perceives as dangerous, they will detect the alarm in the caregiver's facial expression, become alarmed themselves, and retreat from the potentially perilous situation.

Infants look to caregivers for facial cues for the appropriate reaction to unfamiliar adults. If the stranger is a trusted friend of the caregiver, the infant is more likely to respond favorably, whereas if the stranger is unknown to the caregiver, the infant may respond with anxiety and distress. Another factor is the infant's **temperament**.

A second fear of this stage is called **separation anxiety**. Infants seven to twelve months old may cry in fear if the mother or caregiver leaves them in an unfamiliar place.

Many studies have been conducted to assess the type and quality of emotional communication between caregivers and infants. Parents are one of the primary sources that socialize children to communicate emotional experience in culturally specific ways. That is, through such processes as **modeling**, direct instruction, and **imitation**, parents teach their children which emotional expressions are appropriate to express within their specific sub-culture and the broader social context.

**Socialization** of emotion begins in **infancy**. Research indicates that when mothers interact with their infants they demonstrate emotional displays in an exaggerated slow motion, and that these types of display are highly interesting to infants. It is thought that this process is significant in the infant's acquisition of cultural and social codes for emotional display, teaching them how to express their emotions, and the degree of acceptability associated with different types of emotional behaviors.

Another process that emerges during this stage is social referencing. Infants begin to recognize the emotions of others, and use this information when reacting to novel situations and people. As infants explore their world, they generally rely on the emotional expressions of their mothers or caregivers to determine the safety or appropriateness of a particular endeavor. Although this process has been established by several studies, there is some debate about the intentions of the infant; are infants simply imitating their mother's emotional responses, or do they actually experience a change in **mood** purely from the expressive visual cues of the mother? What is known, however, is that as infants explore their environment, their immediate emotional responses to what they encounter are based on cues portrayed by their mother or primary caregiver, to whom they repeatedly reference as they explore.

## Toddlerhood (1-2 years)

### Emotional expressivity

During the second year, infants express emotions of shame or embarrassment and pride. These emotions mature in all children and adults contribute to their development. However, the reason for the shame or pride is learned. Different cultures value different actions. One culture may teach its children to express pride upon winning a competitive event, whereas another may teach children to dampen their cheer, or even to feel shame at another person's loss.

### Emotional understanding

During this stage of development, toddlers acquire language and are learning to verbally express their feelings. In 1986, Inge Bretherton and colleagues found that 30% of American 20-month-olds correctly labeled a series of emotional and physiological states, including sleep-fatigue, **pain**, distress, disgust, and affection. This **ability**, rudimentary as it is during early toddlerhood, is the first step in the development of emotional self-regulation skills.

Although there is debate concerning an acceptable definition of emotion regulation, it is generally thought to involve the ability to recognize and label emotions, and to control emotional expression in ways that are consistent with cultural expectations. In infancy, children largely rely on adults to help them regulate their emotional states. If they are uncomfortable they may be able to communicate this state by crying, but have little hope of alleviating the discomfort on their own. In toddlerhood, however, children begin to develop skills to regulate their emotions with the emergence of language providing an important tool to assist in this process. Being able to articulate an emotional state in itself has a regulatory effect in that it enables children to communicates their feelings to a person capable of helping them manage their emotional state. Speech also enables children to self-regulate, using soothing language to talk themselves through difficult situations.

**Empathy**, a complex emotional response to a situation, also appears in toddlerhood, usually by age two. The development of empathy requires that children read others' emotional cues, understand that other people are entities distinct from themselves, and take the perspective of another person (put themselves in the position of another). These cognitive advances typically are not evident before the first birthday. The first sign of empathy in children occurs when they try to alleviate the distress of another using methods that they have observed or experienced themselves. Toddlers will use comforting language and initiate physical contact with their mothers if they are distressed, supposedly modeling their own early experiences when feeling upset.

## Preschool (3-6 years)

### Emotional expressivity

Children's capacity to regulate their emotional behavior continues to advance during this stage of development.

Parents help preschoolers acquire skills to cope with negative emotional states by teaching and modeling use of verbal reasoning and explanation. For example, when preparing a child for a potentially emotionally evocative event, such as a trip to the doctor's office or weekend at their grandparents' house, parents will often offer comforting advice, such as "the doctor only wants to help" or "grandma and grandpa have all kinds of fun plans for the weekend." This kind of emotional preparation is crucial for the child if he or she is to develop the skills necessary to regulate their own negative emotional states. Children who have trouble learning and/or enacting these types of coping skills often exhibit acting out types of behavior, or, conversely, can become withdrawn when confronted with fear or anxiety-provoking situations.

Beginning at about age four, children acquire the ability to alter their emotional expressions, a skill of high value in cultures that require frequent disingenuous social displays. Psychologists call these skills emotion display rules, culture-specific rules regarding the appropriateness of expressing in certain situations. As such, one's external emotional expression need not match one's internal emotional state. For example, in Western culture, we teach children that they should smile and say thank-you when receiving a gift, even if they really do not like the present. The ability to use display rules is complex. It requires that children understand the need to alter emotional displays, take the perspective of another, know that external states need not match internal states, have the muscular control to produce emotional expressions, be sensitive to social contextual cues that alert them to alter their expressivity, and have the **motivation** to enact such discrepant displays in a convincing manner.

It is thought that in the preschool years, parents are the primary socializing force, teaching appropriate emotional expression in children. Moreover, children learn at about age three that expressions of anger and **aggression** are to be controlled in the presence of adults. Around peers, however, children are much less likely to suppress negative emotional behavior. It appears that these differences arise as a result of the different consequences they have received for expressing negative emotions in front of adults as opposed to their peers. Further, this distinction made by children—as a function of social context—demonstrates that preschoolers have begun to internalize society's rules governing the appropriate expression of emotions.

Carolyn Saarni, an innovator in the exploration of emotional development, has identified two types of emotional display rules, prosocial and self-protective. Prosocial display rules involve altering emotional displays in order to protect another's feelings. For example, a child might not like the sweater she received from her aunt, but would appear happy because she did not want to make her aunt feel badly. On the other hand, self-protective display rules involve masking emotion in order to save face or to protect oneself from negative consequences. For instance, a child may feign toughness when he trips in front of his peers and scrapes his knee, in order to avoid teasing and further embarrassment. In 1986 research findings were mixed concerning the order in which prosocial and self-protective display rules are learned. Some studies demonstrate that knowledge of self-protective display rules emerges first, whereas other studies show the opposite effect.

There also has been research done examining how children alter their emotional displays. Researchers Jackie Gnepp and Debra Hess in 1986 found that there is greater pressure on children to modify their verbal rather than facial emotional expressions. It is easier for preschoolers to control their verbal utterances than their facial muscles.

### Emotional understanding

Beginning at about age four or five, children develop a more sophisticated understanding of others' emotional states. Although it has been demonstrated that empathy emerges at quite a young age, with rudimentary displays emerging during toddlerhood, increasing cognitive development enables preschoolers to arrive at a more complex understanding of emotions. Through repeated experiences, children begin to develop their own theories of others' emotional states by referring to causes and consequences of emotions, and by observing and being sensitive to behavioral cues that indicate emotional distress. For instance, when asked why a playmate is upset, a child might respond "Because the teacher took his toy" or by reference to some other external cause, usually one that relates to an occurrence familiar to them. Children of this age are also beginning to make predictions about others' experience and expression of emotions, such as predicting that a happy child will be more likely to share his or her toys.

## Middle childhood (7-11 years)

### Emotional expressivity

Children ages seven to eleven display a wider variety of self-regulation skills. Sophistication in understanding and enacting cultural display rules has increased dramatically by this stage, such that by now children begin to know when to control emotional expressivity as well as have a sufficient repertoire of behavioral regulation skills allowing them to effectively mask emotions in socially appropriate ways. Research has indicated that children at this age have become sensitive to the social contextual cues which serve to guide their decisions to express or control negative emotions. Several factors influence their emotion management decisions, including the type of emotion experienced, the nature of their relationship with the person involved in the emotional exchange, child age, and child gender. Moreover, it appears that children have developed a set of expectations concerning the likely outcome of expressing emotion to others. In general, children report regulating anger and sadness more to friends than mothers and fathers because they expect to receive a negative response—such as teasing or belittling—from friends. With increasing age, however, older children report expressing negative emotions more often to their mothers than their fathers, expecting dads to respond negatively to an emotional display. These emotion regulation skills are considered to be adaptive and deemed essential to establishing, developing, and maintaining social relationships.

Children at this age also demonstrate that they possess rudimentary cognitive and behavioral coping skills that serve to lessen the impact of an emotional event and in so doing, may in fact alter their emotional experience. For example, when experiencing a negative emotional event, children may respond by employing rationalization or minimization cognitive coping strategies, in which they re-interpret or reconstruct the scenario to make it seem less threatening or upsetting. Upon having their bicycle stolen or being deprived of television for a weekend, they might tell themselves, "It's only a bike, at least I didn't get hurt" or "Maybe mom and dad will make up something fun to do instead of watching TV."

### Emotional understanding

During middle **childhood**, children begin to understand that the emotional states of others are not as simple as they imagined in earlier years, and that they are often the result of complex causes, some of which are not externally obvious. They also come to understand that it is possible to experience more than one emotion at a time, although this ability is somewhat restricted and evolves slowly. As Susan Harter and Nancy Whitsell demonstrated, seven-year-old children are able to understand that a person can feel two emotions simultaneously, even if the emotions are positive and negative. Children can feel happy and excited that their parents bought them a bicycle, or angry and sad that a friend had hurt them, but they deny the possibility of experiencing "mixed feelings." It is not until age ten that children are capable of understanding that one can experience two seemingly contradictory emotions, such as feeling happy that they were chosen for a team but also nervous about their responsibility to play well.

Displays of empathy also increase in frequency during this stage. Children from families that regularly discuss the complexity of feelings will develop empathy more readily than those whose families avoid such topics. Furthermore, parents who set consistent behavioral limits and who themselves show high levels of concern for others are more likely to produce empathic children than parents who are punitive or particularly harsh in restricting behavior.

## Adolescence (12-18 years)

### Emotional expressivity

Adolescents have become sophisticated at regulating their emotions. They have developed a wide vocabulary with which to discuss, and thus influence, emotional states of themselves and others. Adolescents are adept at interpreting social situations as part of the process of managing emotional displays.

It is widely believed that by **adolescence** children have developed a set of expectations, referred to as scripts, about how various people will react to their emotional displays, and regulate their displays in accordance with these scripts. Research in this area has found that in early adolescence, children begin breaking the emotionally intimate ties with their parents and begin forming them with peers. In one study, for instance, eighth-grade students, particularly boys, reported regulating (hiding) their emotions to (from) their mothers more than did either fifth- or eleventh-grade adolescents. This dip in emotional expressivity towards mothers appeared to be due to the boys' expectations of receiving less emotional support from their mothers. This particular finding demonstrates the validity of the script hypothesis of self-regulations; children's expectations of receiving little emotional support from their mothers, perhaps based on past experience, guide their decisions to regulate emotions more strictly in their mothers' presence.

Another factor that plays a significant role in the ways adolescents regulate emotional displays is their heightened sensitivity to others' evaluations of them, a sensitivity which can result in acute self-awareness and self-consciousness as they try to blend into the dominant social structure. **David Elkind** has described adolescents as operating as if they were in front of an imaginary audience in which every action and detail is noted and evaluated by others. As such, adolescents become very aware of the impact of emotional expressivity on their social interactions and fundamentally, on obtaining peer approval. Because guidelines concerning the appropriateness of emotional displays is highly culture-specific, adolescents have the difficult task of learning when and how to express or regulate certain emotions.

As expected, gender plays a significant role in the types of emotions displayed by adolescents. Boys are less likely than girls to disclose their fearful emotions during times of distress. This reluctance was similarly supported by boys' belief that they would receive less understanding and, in fact, probably be belittled, for expressing both aggressive and vulnerable emotions.

Janice Zeman

## Further Reading

Bretherton, Inge and Janet Fritz, et al. "Learning to Talk about Emotions: A Functionalist Perspective," *Child Development* 57, (1986): 529-48.

Gnepp, Jackie, and Debra Hess. "Children's Understanding of Verbal and Facial Display Rules," *Developmental Psychology* 22, no. 1, (1986): 103-08.

Malatesta, Carol Zander, and Jeannette Haviland. "Learning Display Rules: The Socialization of Emotion Expression in Infancy." *Child Development* 53, (1982): 991-1003.

Zahn-Waxler, Carolyn, and Marian Radke-Yarrow, et al. "Development of Concern for Others," *Developmental Psychology* 28, no. 1, (1992): 126-36.

# Emotional intelligence

The ability to perceive and constructively act on both one's own emotions and the feelings of others.

## Origins

Emotional **intelligence** (EI) is sometimes referred to as emotional quotient or emotional literacy. Individuals with emotional intelligence are able to relate to others with compassion and **empathy**, have well-developed social skills, and use this emotional awareness to direct their actions and behavior. The term was coined in 1990 by psychologists John Mayer and Peter Salovey. In 1995, psychologist/journalist Daniel Goleman published the highly successful *Emotional Intelligence*, which built on Mayer and Salovey's work and popularized the EI concept.

The four areas of emotional intelligence, as identified by Mayer and Salovey, are as follows:

• *Identifying emotions*. The **ability** to recognize one's own feelings and the feelings of those around them.

• *Using emotions*. The ability to access an **emotion** and reason with it (use it to assist thought and decisions).

• *Understanding emotions*. Emotional knowledge; the ability to identify and comprehend what Mayer and Salovey term "emotional chains"—the transition of one emotion to another.

• *Managing emotions*. The ability to self-regulate emotions and manage them in others.

## Characteristics

### The brain and emotional learning

The *amygdala*, a structure of the limbic system (the behavioral center of the **brain**) located near the brainstem, is thought to be responsible for emotional learning and emotional **memory**. Studies have shown that damage to the amygdala can impair the ability to judge **fear** and other emotions in facial expressions (to "read" the emotions of others), a skill which is critical to effective social interaction. The amygdala serves as an emotional scrapbook that the brain refers to in interpreting and reacting to new experiences. It is also associated with emotional arousal.

The ability to understand the thoughts and feelings of others is also regulated by the *prefrontal cortex* of the brain, sometimes called "the executive center." This brain structure and its components store emotional memories that an individual draws on when interacting socially. Research studies have demonstrated that individuals with brain lesions in the prefrontal cortex area have difficulties in social interactions and problem-solving and tend to make poor choices, probably because they have lost the ability to access past experiences and emotions.

## Applications

The concept of emotional intelligence has found a number of different applications outside of the psychological research and therapy arenas. Professional, educational, and community institutions have integrated different aspects of the emotional intelligence philosophy into their organizations to promote more productive working relationships, better outcomes, and enhanced personal satisfaction.

In the workplace and in other organizational settings, the concept of emotional intelligence has spawned an entire industry of EI consultants, testing materials, and workshops. "People skills," another buzzword for emotional intelligence, has long been recognized as a valued attribute in employees. The popularity of the EI concept in business is easily explained—when employees, managers, and clients have mutually rewarding personal relationships, productivity increases and profits follow.

Educators and youth counselors who work with children try to help them develop emotional self-awareness and the ability to recognize and positively act on feelings. Emphasis on emotional intelligence in the classroom also focuses on problem solving, **conflict res-**

olution, empathy, coping, and communication skills, and is frequently implemented in violence-prevention programs. *Self-science*, an educational curriculum developed in the 1970s by educator Karen Stone McCown and psychologist Hal Dillehunt, was an early forerunner of emotional intelligence. The program, which focused on developing social and emotional skills to nurture unique learning styles and life skills, is still in use today.

A number of tests or assessments have been developed to "measure" emotional intelligence, although their validity is questioned by some researchers. These include the Mayer-Salovey-Caruso Emotional Intelligence Test (MSCEIT), the Multifactor Emotional Intelligence Scale (MEIS), the Emotional Competence Inventory 360 (ECI 360), the Work Profile Questionnaire-emotional intelligence version (WPQ-ei), and the Baron Emotional Quotient Inventory (EQ-i). Other psychometric measures, or tests, such as the Wechsler Intelligence Scale for Children, Revised (WISC-R), a standard intelligence test, are sometimes useful in measuring the social aptitude features of emotional intelligence.

Paula Ford-Martin

**Further Reading**

Goleman, Daniel. *Emotional Intelligence.* New York: Bantam, 1995.

Mayer, J.D. and P. Salovey. "What Is Emotional Intelligence?" In *Emotional Development, Emotional Literacy, and Emotional Intelligence: Implications for Educators,* edited by P. Salovey and D. Sluyter. New York: Basic Books, 1997.

**Further Information**

National Institute of Mental Health (NIMH). 6001 Executive Boulevard, Rm. 8184, MSC 9663, Bethesda, MD, USA. 20892-9663, fax: (301)443-4279, (301)443-4513. Email: nimhinfo@nih.gov. http://www.nimh.nih.gov.

6 Seconds. 316 Seville Way, San Mateo, CA, USA. 94402, (650)685-9885. Email: solutions@6seconds.org. http://www.6seconds.org.

# Emotion

A reaction, both psychological and physical, subjectively experienced as strong feelings, many of which prepare the body for immediate action.

In contrast to moods, which are generally longer-lasting, emotions are transitory, with relatively well-defined beginnings and endings. They also have valence, meaning that they are either positive or negative. Subjectively, emotions are experienced as passive phenomena.

Even though it is possible to exert a measure of control over one's emotions, they are not initiated—they happen *to* people. Objectively, emotions involve internal physiological responses and expressive outward displays that are both learned and innate. Certain emotions themselves, considered to be primary emotions—joy, **anger**, sadness, **fear**, and love—are thought to be innate, while complex emotions—such as altruism, shame, **guilt**, and envy—seem to arise from social learning.

The first influential theory of emotion in modern times—the James-Lange theory—was formulated independently in the 1880s by both American psychologist and philosopher **William James** and Danish physiologist C.G. Lange (1834-1900). Both scientists arrived at the view that the physiological manifestations of emotion precede the subjective ones—rather than trembling because we are afraid, we are afraid because we tremble. Even though the **brain** responds to a threatening situation by activating peripheral responses, we do not consciously experience the emotion until these responses are activated. Thus, the **central nervous system** itself does not actually produce the emotion. Over the following decades, this theory drew widespread response and criticism.

An alternative model of emotional experience was formulated in 1927 by Walter Cannon (1871-1945), who proposed that emotions do originate in the central nervous system. Cannon argued that **nerve** impulses first pass through the **thalamus**, from which subjective responses are routed through the cerebral cortex, directly creating the experience of fear at the same time that physiological responses are passing through the **hypothalamus**. The Cannon-Bard theory, whose name reflects later modifications by Phillip Bard, thus delineated the psychological and physiological components of emotion as simultaneous and argued that the experience of emotion comes directly from the central nervous system. Some more recent theorists have once again moved closer to the James-Lange model. The 1962 Schachter-Singer theory restores James's emphasis on the interpretation of physiological responses but adds another element—a cognitive evaluation of what caused the responses. This theory thus contradicts James's assertion that emotion is communicated solely on the basis of physical feedback, asserting that this feedback by itself is not clear enough to specify a particular emotion. Rather, the brain chooses one of many possible interpretations and "labels" the feedback pattern, and it is this labeling that results in the experiencing of a particular emotion.

Areas of the brain that play an important role in the production of emotions include the reticular formation, the limbic system, and the cerebral cortex. The reticular formation, within the brain stem, receives and filters sensory information before passing it on the limbic system and cortex. The limbic system includes the hypothalamus, which produces most of the peripheral responses to emotion through its control of the endocrine and autonomic nervous systems; the amygdala, which is associated with fear and aggressive behavior; the hippocampus; and parts of the thalamus. The frontal lobes of the cerebral cortex receive nerve impulses from the thalamus and play an active role in the experience and expression of emotions.

While the physiological changes associated with emotions are triggered by the brain, they are carried out by the endocrine and autonomic nervous systems. In response to fear or anger, for example, the brain signals the pituitary gland to release a hormone called ACTH, which in turn causes the adrenal glands to secrete cortisol, another hormone that triggers what is known as the fight-or-flight response, a combination of physical changes that prepare the body for action in dangerous situations. The heart beats faster, respiration is more rapid, the liver releases glucose into the bloodstream to supply added energy, fuels are mobilized from the body's stored fat, and the body generally goes into a state of high arousal. The pupils dilate, perspiration increases while secretion of saliva and mucous decreases, hairs on the body become erect, causing "goose pimples," and the digestive system slows down as blood is diverted to the brain and skeletal muscles. These changes are carried out with the aid of the sympathetic nervous system, one of two divisions of the **autonomic nervous system**. When the crisis is over, the parasympathetic nervous system, which conserves the body's energy and resources, returns things to their **normal** state.

Ways of expressing emotion may be either innate or culturally acquired. Certain facial expressions, such as smiling, have been found to be universal, even among blind persons, who have no means of imitating them. Other expressions vary across cultures. For example, the Chinese stick out their tongues to register surprise, in contrast to Americans and other Westerners, who raise their eyebrows and widen their eyes. In addition to the ways of communicating various emotions, people within a culture also learn certain unwritten codes governing emotional expression itself—what emotions can be openly expressed and under what circumstances. Cultural forces also influence how people describe and categorize what they are feeling. An emotion that is commonly recognized in one society may be subsumed under another emotion in a different one. Some cultures, for example, do not distinguish between anger and sadness. Tahitians, who have no word for either sadness or guilt, have 46 words for various types of anger.

In daily life, emotional arousal may have beneficial or disruptive effects, depending on the situation and the intensity of the emotion. Moderate levels of arousal in-

crease efficiency levels by making people more alert. However, intense emotions—either positive or negative—interfere with performance because central nervous system responses are channeled in too many directions at once. The effects of arousal on performance also depend on the difficulty of the task at hand; emotions interfere less with simple tasks than with more complicated ones.

**Further Reading**
Powell, Barbara. *The Complete Guide to Your Child's Emotional Health*. Danbury, CT: F. Watts, 1984.
*Your Child's Emotional Health: Adolescence*. New York: Macmillan, 1994.

# Empathy

The capacity to vicariously experience and understand the thoughts and feelings of another person by putting oneself in that person's place.

While most forms of **psychotherapy** require some degree of empathy on the part of the counselor or therapist, the **client-centered therapy** pioneered by **Carl Rogers** places particular emphasis on this quality as part of the therapeutic experience. Instead of looking at the client from outside (external frame of reference), the client-centered therapist attempts to see things as they actually look to the client (internal frame of reference). Throughout each therapy session, the therapist demonstrates what Rogers termed "accurate empathetic understanding," showing sensitivity to the client's feelings through active listening that shows careful and perceptive **attention** to what the client is saying. The therapist employs standard behaviors common to all good listeners, making frequent eye contact with the client, nodding in agreement or understanding, and generally showing that he or she is listening attentively.

One unique way client-centered therapists demonstrate empathy with the client is through a special method called reflection, which consists of paraphrasing and/or summarizing what a client has just said. This technique lets therapists check the accuracy of their perceptions while showing clients that they are paying careful attention to and are interested in what is being said. **Hearing** their own thoughts and feelings repeated by another person can also help clients achieve new levels of insight and self-awareness. Clients generally respond to reflection by elaborating further on the thoughts they have just expressed. Empathy constitutes a major portion of the therapeutic work in client-centered therapy. By helping clients feel better about themselves, it gives them the self-confidence and energy to deal actively with their problems.

### Further Reading

Rogers, Carl. *Client-Centered Therapy.* Boston: Houghton Mifflin, 1951.

———. *On Becoming a Person.* Boston: Houghton Mifflin, 1961.

———. *A Way of Being.* Boston: Houghton Mifflin, 1980.

# Empiricism

Type of research that is based on direct observation.

Psychologists prefer to learn about behavior through direct observation or experience. This approach reflects what is called empiricism. Psychologists are well-known for creating experiments, conducting interviews and using surveys, and carrying out case studies. The common feature of these approaches is that psychologists wait until observations are made before they draw any conclusions about the behaviors they are interested in.

Scientists often maintain that empiricism fosters healthy skepticism. By this they mean that they will not regard something as being true until they have made the observations themselves. Such an approach means that science can be self-correcting in the sense that when erroneous conclusions are drawn, others can test the original ideas to see if they are correct.

Empiricism is one of the hallmarks of any scientific endeavor. Other disciplines employ different approaches to gaining knowledge. For example, many philosophers use the *a priori* method rather than the empirical method. In the *a priori* method, one uses strictly rational, logical arguments to derive knowledge. Geometric proofs are an example of the use of the *a priori* method.

In everyday life, people accept ideas as being true or false based on authority or on intuition. In many cases, people hold beliefs because individuals who are experts have made pronouncements on some topic. For example, in religious matters, many people rely on the advice and guidance of their religious leaders in deciding on the correct way to lead their lives. Further, we often believe things because they seem intuitively obvious. Relying on authority and intuition may be very useful in some aspects of our lives, like those involving questions of morality.

Scientists prefer the empirical method in their work, however, because the topics of science lend themselves to observation and **measurement**. When something cannot be observed or measured, scientists are likely to con-clude that it is outside the realm of science, even though it may be vitally important in some other realm.

### Further Reading

Carruthers, Peter. *Human Knowledge and Human Nature: A New Introduction to an Ancient Debate.* Oxford, Eng.: Oxford University Press, 1992.

Grossmann, Reinhardt. *The Fourth Way: A Theory of Knowledge.* Bloomington: Indiana University Press, 1990.

# Encounter group

Group of individuals who engage in intensive and psychotherapeutic verbal and nonverbal interaction, with the general intention of increasing awareness of self and sensitivity to others, and improving interpersonal skills.

Encounter groups are formed, usually under the guidance and **leadership** of a psychologists or therapist, to provide an environment for intensive interaction. In general, because the therapy takes place in a group setting, one of the goals of the encounter group is to improve the participants' interpersonal skills. A typical encounter group may consist of fewer that ten persons, one of whom is a trained specialist, or leader. The role of the leader is primarily to develop and maintain an atmosphere of psychological safety conducive to the free and honest expression of the ideas of group members. The leader remains, as much as possible, outside the actual discussion itself. Encounter group members are encouraged to fully examine and explore their reactions to, and feelings about, statements made, and issues raised, in the group. Proponents of the encounter group form of **psychotherapy** tend to believe that the behavior of an individual is shaped to a very large degree by responsive **adaptation** to the attitudes of other individuals, and that encounter groups enable individuals to discover and modify behavior that is perceived as inappropriate. The effectiveness of encounter groups is a matter of some dispute, and there is evidence which suggests that certain behavioral and attitudinal changes accomplished inside the group may not endure outside the group. Although early versions of encounter groups may have existed near the beginning of the 20th century, the encounter group technique as it is currently practiced is derived from **sensitivity training** procedures introduced shortly after World War II. Both the encounter group and sensitivity training techniques are now generally included in a wider array of techniques, some of which are controversial in the field of psychology, that were popularized beginning in the 1960s. These techniques are collectively referred to as the **human potential movement**.

This encounter group for overeaters encourages members to express themselves freely and honestly. *(Photo by Carolyn A. McKeone. Photo Researchers, Inc. Reproduced with permission.)*

## Further Reading

Appelbaum, Stephen. *Out in Inner Space.* Garden City, NY: Anchor Press/Doubleday, 1970.

## Endocrine glands

Ductless glands which secrete chemical substances called hormones into the bloodstream which control the internal environment not only of each cell and organ, but of the entire body.

The endocrine glands—the pineal, pituitary, thyroid, parathyroids, thymus, adrenals, pancreas and gonads (ovaries or testes)—comprise the endocrine system. The **hypothalamus**, the gland in the **brain** which serves as the command center, operates the endocrine system through the pituitary, a pea-sized gland located under it, which directs the work of all the other glands. The thyroid, a gland in the neck, regulates the body's metabolism. The parathyroids, which are attached to the thyroid, control the amount of calcium and phosphate in the bloodstream. The adrenal glands, located near the kid-

neys, produce adrenaline which arouses the body to respond to **stress** and emergencies and other **hormones** active in carbohydrate metabolism. The pancreas secretes insulin which regulates the level of sugar in the bloodstream. The gonads regulate sexual development, ovulation, and growth of sex organs.

## Further Reading

*The Endocrine System: Miraculous Messengers.* New York: Torstar Books, 1985.

## Environment

The combination of physical, social, and cultural conditions that influence an individual's development and behavior.

The relative importance of **heredity** and environment in shaping human lives—nature versus nurture—has long been a topic of debate taken up by thinkers as diverse as **John Locke**, **Charles Darwin**, and **Sigmund Freud**, and forms part of current policy debates in areas

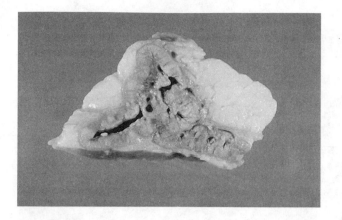

**Cross-section of a human adrenal gland, one of the endocrine glands.** *(Photo by Martin M. Rotker. Phototake NYC. Reproduced with permission.)*

such as crime and education. Traditionally, this controversy pits those who believe that human nature and **intelligence** are biologically determined (eugenicists) against those who contend that, given a positive and enriching environment, most individuals have the potential for high levels of human development (euthenists). It is agreed that such human characteristics as sex, height, skin and hair color, and, to a certain extent, **temperament**, are genetically determined at conception. However, there is disagreement over the extent to which other aspects of human development—including behavior, **personality**, and intelligence—are influenced by such environmental factors as nutrition, emotional climate of the home, and quality of stimulation and parental feedback. In addition to the immediate **family**, many experts consider the social class and culture in which a child is raised as important environmental factors in determining his or her development.

Intelligence testing and race has resurfaced as a volatile topic in the nature/nurture debate, since African-Americans as a group score 10 to 15 points lower on standard IQ tests than whites. Some experts claim that this disparity demonstrates the differences in inherited **ability** among the two races, while others attribute the gap to environmental influences. In 1994, Richard Herrnstein and Charles Murray published *The Bell Curve*, in which they asserted that low-income blacks have innately lower cognitive abilities than whites (based on the gap in IQ scores), a situation that cannot be significantly remedied through government social and educational programs. Many social scientists, however, consider environmental and genetic factors to be so closely intertwined as to make it impossible to clearly separate them. Thus, the contrasting positions of eugenicists and euthenists are actually at opposite ends of a continuum, with most observers of human

behavior taking a middle position that emphasizes the interaction between biological predispositions and life experiences.

Social learning theorists refer to another layer of complexity in the relationship between environment and human behavior: the self-generated environment. This concept refers to the fact that a certain behavior or behaviors may produce environmental conditions that can affect future behavior. People who behave in an abrasive manner, for example, help create a hostile social environment, which in turn leads to further **hostility** on their part. Similarly, the behavior of friendly persons will tend to generate a supportive environment that reinforces and perpetuates their original behavior. Thus, a group of persons who find themselves in the same "potential environment" may experience different "actual environments" as a result of their contrasting behaviors.

Since the 1960s, environmental psychologists have studied the relationship between human behavior and the physical environment, including noise, pollution, and architectural design. Like ethologists, who study animal behavior in their natural habitat, environmental psychologists maintain a holistic view of human behavior that leads them to study it in its natural setting rather than in a laboratory, or at least to supplement laboratory experiments with field research. Environmental psychologists study such topics as the ways in which the architectural design of a psychiatric hospital affects its patients; the effects of aircraft noise on children at a school near an airport; and overcrowding in a college dormitory.

Environment psychology is basically an applied field geared toward solving specific problems rather than a theoretical area of study. Like **social learning theory**, it is heavily concerned with the reciprocal relationship between behavior and environment, including the ways in which people cope with their physical surroundings by altering them. One exception to this orientation is a position known as **determinism**, which has influenced much research into the effects of architecture on behavior. The determinist approach emphasizes the **adaptation** of people to their surroundings, and considers behavior largely as a function of those surroundings, with little reciprocity involved.

*See also* Eugenics; Jensen, Arthur

## Further Reading

Altman, Irwin. *The Environment and Social Behavior: Privacy, Personal Space, Territory, Crowding.* Monterey, CA: Brooks/Cole, 1975.

Gray, Jeffrey Alan. *The Psychology of Fear and Stress.* 2nd ed. New York: Cambridge University Press, 1988.

# Epilepsy

A condition affecting people regardless of age, sex, or race, where a pattern of recurring malfunctioning of the brain is present.

Epilepsy, from the Greek word for seizure, is a recurrent demonstration of a **brain** malfunction. The outward signs of epilepsy may range from only a slight smacking of the lips or staring into space to a generalized convulsion. It is a condition that can affect anyone of any age, sex, or race.

The number of people with epilepsy is not known. Some authorities say that up to 0.5% of the population are epileptic, but others believe this estimate is too low. Many cases of epilepsy, particularly those with very subtle symptoms, are not reported. The most serious form of epilepsy is not considered an inherited condition, though parents with epilepsy are more prone to have children with the disease. On the other hand, an epileptic child may have parents who show no sign of the condition, though they will have some abnormal brain waves.

Though the cause of epilepsy remains unknown, the manner in which the condition is demonstrated indicates the area of the brain that is affected. Jacksonian seizures, for example, which are localized twitching of muscles, originate in the frontal lobe of the brain in the motor cortex. A localized numbness or tingling indicates an origin in the parietal lobe on the side of the brain in the sensory cortex.

The recurrent symptoms, then, are the result of localized, excessive activity of brain cells or neurons. These can be seen on the standard brain test called the electroencephalogram (EEG). For this test electrodes are applied to specific areas of the head to pick up the electrical waves generated by the brain. If the patient experiences an epileptic episode while wired to the EEG, the abnormal brain waves can easily be seen and the determination made as to their origin in the brain. Usually the patient does not experience a seizure and no abnormalities are found.

Grand mal seizures are those that are most characteristic of epilepsy. Immediately prior to the seizure, the patient may have some indication that a seizure is imminent. This feeling is called an aura. Very soon after experiencing the aura the patient will lapse into unconsciousness and experience clonic seizures, which are generalized muscle contractions that may distort the body position. Thrashing movements of the limbs shortly ensue and are caused by opposing sets of muscles alternating in contractions (hence, the other name for grand mal seizures: tonic-clonic seizures). The patient may also

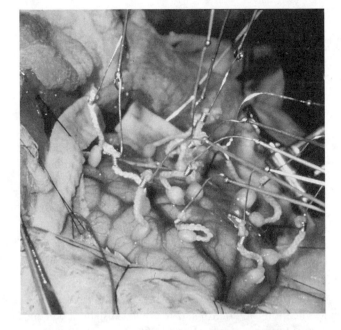

This patient's brain is exposed during surgery in order for surgeons to remove the mass responsible of his epilepsy. *(Custom Medical Stock Photo. Reproduced with permission.)*

lose bladder control. When the seizures cease, usually after three to five minutes, the patient may remain unconscious for up to half an hour. Upon waking, he or she may not remember having had a seizure and may be confused for a time.

In contrast to the drama of the grand mal seizure, the petit mal may seem inconsequential. The patient interrupts whatever he or she is doing and for up to about 30 seconds may show subtle outward signs such as blinking eyes, staring into space, or pausing in conversation. After the seizure previous activities are resumed. Petit mal seizures are associated with **heredity**, and they never occur in people over the age of 20 years. Oddly, though the seizures may occur several times a day, they do so usually when the patient is quiet and not during periods of activity. After **puberty** these seizures may disappear or they may be replaced by the grand mal type of seizure.

A serious form of seizure, *status epilepticus*, indicates a state in which grand mal seizures occur in rapid succession with no period of recovery between them. This can be a life-threatening event because the patient has difficulty breathing and may experience a dangerous rise in blood pressure. This form of seizure is very rare, but it can be brought on if someone abruptly stops taking medication prescribed for the epilepsy. It may also occur during alcohol withdrawal.

A number of drugs are available for the treatment of epilepsy. The oldest is phenobarbital, which has the unfortunate side effect of being addictive. Other commonly used drugs include phenytoin, carbamazepine, and sodium valproate. All have the possibility of causing such undesirable side effects as drowsiness, nausea, or dizziness. Several new drugs are being studied to determine their efficacy and safety.

The epileptic patient needs to be protected from self-injury during an attack. Usually for the patient having a petit mal seizure, little needs to be done. Occasionally these individuals may lose their balance and need to be helped to the ground to avoid hitting their heads, but otherwise need little attention. The individual in a grand mal seizure should not be restrained, but may need some help to avoid striking his limbs or head on the floor or nearby obstruction. If possible, the patient should be rolled onto his side. This will maintain an open airway for breathing by allowing the tongue to fall to one side.

Epilepsy can be a recurrent, lifelong condition. Medication can control seizures in a substantial percentage of patients, perhaps up to 85% of those with grand mal manifestations. Some patients will experience seizures even with maximum dosages of medication, and these individuals need to wear an identification bracelet to let others know of their condition.

### Further Reading
Glanz, J. "Do Chaos-Control Techniques Offer Hope for Epilepsy?" *Science* 265, (August 26, 1994): 1174.

### Further Information
American Epilepsy Foundation. 638 Prospect Avenue, Hartford, CT 06105–2498, (203) 232–4825.
Epilepsy Foundation of America. 4351 Garden City Drive, Landover, MD 20785, (800) 332–1000.

# Equilibrium sense

One of two proprioceptive sensory systems that provide us with input about the positions of our own bodies.

The equilibrium sense, generally associated with balance, provides feedback about the positions and movements of our heads and bodies in space. The other system—the kinesthetic sense—tells us about the orientation of different parts of our bodies in relation to each other. While the kinesthetic information needed by the **brain** comes from joints and muscle fibers throughout the body, the receptors for equilibrium are located in the semicircular canals and vestibular sacs of the inner ear. (The equilibrium sense is also called the vestibular sense, and the relevant parts of the inner ear are sometimes called the vestibular system or apparatus).

The semicircular canals are three pretzel-like curved tubes arranged at angles roughly perpendicular to each other, with the two vestibular sacs located at their base. Both the canals and sacs contain fluid and tiny hair cells, which act as receptors. When a person's head moves, the fluid disturbs the hair cells, which stimulate a branch of the auditory **nerve**, signaling the brain to make adjustments in the eyes and body. A movement at any given angle will have its primary effect on one of the three canals. Overstimulation from extreme movements will produce dizziness and nausea. Our sense of body position when we are at rest is provided by the vestibular sacs, which contain small crystals called otoliths (literally, "ear stones") that exert pressure on the hair cells. In their normal position, the otoliths inform our brains that we are standing or sitting upright. When the head is tilted, the position of the otoliths changes, and the signal sent to the brain changes accordingly. The neural connections of the vestibular system lead to the cerebellum, the eye muscles, and a part of the **autonomic nervous system** involved in digestion (which accounts for the link between dizziness and nausea).

### Further Reading
Burke, Shirley R. *Human Anatomy and Physiology in Health and Disease.* New York: Delmar, 1992.
Martini, Frederic. *Fundamentals of Anatomy and Physiology.* Englewood Cliffs, NJ: Prentice-Hall, 1995.

# Erik Erikson

**1902-1979**
German-born American psychoanalyst best known for his work with children and adolescents.

Erik Erikson was born in Frankfurt, Germany, to Danish parents. As a youth, he was a student and teacher of art. While teaching at a private school in Vienna, he became acquainted with **Anna Freud**, the daughter of **Sigmund Freud**. Erikson underwent **psychoanalysis**, and the experience made him decide to become an analyst himself. He was trained in psychoanalysis at the Vienna Psychoanalytic Institute and also studied the Montessori method of education, which focused on **child development**. Following Erikson's graduation from the Vienna Psychoanalytic Institute in 1933, the Nazis had just come to power in Germany, and he emigrated with his wife, first to Denmark and then to the United States, where he became the first child psychoanalyst in Boston. Erikson held positions at Massachusetts General Hospital, the Judge Baker Guidance Center, and at Harvard's Medical School and Psychological Clinic, establishing a solid reputation as an outstanding clinician. In 1936, Erikson accepted a position at Yale University, where he worked at the Institute of Human Relations and taught at the Medical School. After spending a year observing children on a Sioux reservation in South Dakota, he joined the faculty of the University of California at Berkeley, where he was affiliated with the Institute of Child Welfare, and opened a private practice as well. While in California, Erikson also studied children of the Yurok Native American tribe. After publishing the book for which he is best known, *Childhood and Society,* in 1950, he left Berkeley to join the staff of the Austen Riggs Center, a prominent psychiatric treatment facility in Stockbridge, Massachusetts, where he worked with emotionally troubled young people. In the 1960s, Erikson returned to Harvard as a professor of human development and remained at the university until his retirement in 1970.

Much of Erikson's work is concerned with the formation of individual identity, the creative operation of **consciousness** in a well-adjusted **personality**, and societal influences on child development. He differs from more traditional Freudians by assigning a significantly greater importance to development after the first few years of life, and by arguing that the **ego** plays a highly positive role in that development. Erikson is also noted for the illumination of his concept of the adolescent "identity crisis," a term which he coined. Erikson's theory of personality covers the entire human lifespan, which he divides into eight distinct stages, each with its own tasks and crisis. In **infancy**, the basic conflict is between trust and mistrust. A sense of trust is established according to the quality of the infant's relationship with its care-givers. Achievement of trust is considered especially important for development in the following stages. The crisis in early **childhood**, the next stage, is between the child's need for *autonomy* and the sense of doubt and shame brought on by learning to deal with rules and social demands for self-control, including physical control such as toilet training. Successfully negotiated, this stage leads to the emergence of independence and will power. Later in the preschool period comes the third stage, when the child begins to actively explore his or her **environment**. At this stage, there is a crisis over *initiative* and a possible sense of **guilt** about asserting control over his or her own activities. A sense of purpose, leading to the **ability** to pursue goals in spite of risks and possible failure, emerges with the resolution of this conflict. During the fourth stage, the early school years, the social context expands to include the school environment, where skills and mastery of tasks become a primary focus of **attention**. A conflict arises between *industry*, or the ability to work, and feelings of inferiority, and the former must triumph in order for the development of competence.

**Erik Erikson** *(Archive Photos, Inc. Reproduced with permission.)*

The goals of the first four stages—trust, autonomy, initiative, and industry—create the foundation for the successful negotiation of the fifth stage, in which the adolescent must form a stable identity and achieve a sense of self. While social issues such as "fitting in with the group" are important at this point, Erikson emphasizes the importance of achieving an individual identity based on self-knowledge and continuity of experience. Failure to resolve the conflicts of this stage results in identity or role confusion and affects the experiences of the three adult stages which follow. In young adulthood, the primary issue is *intimacy*, or the ability to love. In middle adulthood, it is *generativity*, or the ability to be productive, whether in work, parenting, or other activities, rather than stagnating. The key quality at this stage is the ability to care for others. Finally, at maturity, the challenge is to achieve a sense of *integrity* and wisdom with which to overcome despair over physical disintegration and death.

Erikson's mapping of the life cycle has had a profound impact on **developmental psychology**, especially in the area of adolescent behavior and in the shift to a life-span perspective among students of human development. He won both the Pulitzer Prize and the National Book Award for his writings, which include the psychobiographies *Young Man Luther* (1958) and *Gandhi's Truth* (1969). Erikson is also the author of *Insight and Responsibility* (1964) and *Identity, Youth, and Crisis* (1968).

*See also* Adolescence

## Further Reading
Coles, Robert. *Erik H. Erikson: The Growth of His Work.* Boston: Little, Brown & Co., 1970.

# Ethics

Personal rules for behavior.

Ethics are rules for behavior, based on beliefs about how things should be. Ethical statements involve: 1) assumptions about humans and their capacities; 2) logical rules extending from these assumptions; and 3) notions of what is good and desirable.

Ethical systems (sets of rules for acceptable behavior) concern the "shoulds" and "should nots" of life, the principles and values on which human relations are based.

The assessment of whether a behavior is ethical is divided into four categories, or domains: consequences, actions, **character**, and motive. In the domain of consequences, a behavior is determined to be "right" or "wrong" based on the results of the action, whereas the domain of actions looks only at the act itself. The domain of character looks at whether a person's overall character is ethical; a person who is deemed as "virtuous" has consistently ethical behavior. The motive domain evaluates a person's intentions, regardless of the consequences. It considers whether the person intended to do good, even if the result was bad. A behavior may be deemed "ethical" according to one domain of assessment, but appear "unethical" according to another. For example, a poor person steals a small amount of food to feed her starving child from a wealthy, well-fed person who does not even notice that the food is missing. This act would be considered ethical in the domain of consequences, since the child can be fed, and motive, since the person is caring for her child, but unethical in the domain of actions, because stealing in itself is wrong. The poor person's general behavior would have to be evaluated to determine whether she is ethical in the domain of character.

Ethics can also be divided into two main schools, absolutism and relativism. Absolutists believe that ethical rules are fixed standards (for example, stealing is always wrong, no matter what the circumstances). Relativists, on the other hand, believe that all ethics are subject to context (for example, stealing may be wrong in certain circumstances but not in others). Few people are actually pure absolutists or pure relativists, but rather fall somewhere along the spectrum between the two extremes, tending towards one or the other. Most who tend towards absolutism will allow for special circumstances and bend the rules on occasion, while those who tend towards relativism will admit to some universal standards that form a "bottom line" of behavior.

In order to develop ethical maturity, people must have moral awareness and moral agency (or autonomy). Moral awareness is the **ability** to recognize the ethical element of a given situation. For some, eating beef is simply an act of appetite and habit, with no thought given to its ethical implications. For others, whether to eat beef is a complicated moral question involving the ethics of land use (grazing cattle vs. growing food crops), conservation (the destruction of rainforests to increase grazing grounds), and the global economy (the transformation of underdeveloped countries into cattle farms for Western industrialized nations). Moral agency or autonomy means the freedom to choose between alternative behaviors. A person cannot develop ethical maturity without being able to choose from alternatives. Without moral awareness and moral agency, ethics become meaningless because behaviors are simply automatic, or forced.

The question of moral agency becomes complicated by the tendency to equate ethical behavior with obedience. Because humans first learn ethics as small children from adult authority figures, our initial understanding of ethics is "obeying." When we do what adults want us to, we are told we are "good." If we disobey, we are "bad." Some people never outgrow this, continuing throughout life to believe that being "good" means obeying external authorities. These people have never developed a sense of moral agency, even though they are capable of making choices. A prime example of this dilemma is the numerous soldiers and citizens who carried out or assisted in the torture and murder of millions of Jews, Russians, gays, and others in the Holocaust of World War II. Do their claims that they were "just following orders" exempt them from ethical responsibility? Likewise, in situations of oppression where people have been traumatized into blind obedience to their oppressors, are the oppressed ethically responsible for their actions, or do they lack moral agency? These are difficult questions with no clear answers, but they do illuminate the essential character of freedom to choose in the development of ethical maturity.

Ethical maturity involves accepting full responsibility for one's ethical choices and their consequences. An ethically mature person obeys her or his own, inner authority (or **conscience**), rather than an outside authority figure. Moving from the infantile state of externally determined obedience to the mature state of self-determination is a long and difficult process, however. In her 1994 book, psychologist Elizabeth McGrath presents nine stages of ethical development.

- Stage 1 = The person sees the world in polar terms of we-right-good versus they-wrong-bad. Right answers for everything are known to an authority whose role is to mediate or teach them.

- Stage 2 = The person perceives diversity of opinion and uncertainty and accounts for these as confusion engendered by poorly qualified authorities or as exercises designed to encourage individuals to find their own system.

- Stage 3 = The person accepts diversity and uncertainty as legitimate, but only as temporary conditions in areas for which the authority has not yet found an answer. The perceived uncertainty on the part of the so-called experts makes the person anxious. Therefore, this stage does not last long.

In Stages 1-3, ethical choices are based completely on obedience to external authorities. A person in these stages of ethical development is rigid in their beliefs and defensive when challenged, because there is no internal sense of confidence. The person's ethics are not grounded in any self-determined understanding of right and wrong, but rather in the dictates of outside authorities. When the infallibility of those authorities comes into question, the anxiety produced either pushes the person on to Stage 4, or back to the unquestioning stance of Stage 1. Some people never progress beyond the first three stages of ethical development.

The biggest shift in ethical understanding comes between Stages 3 and 4, if the person chooses to progress rather than regress. At this point, blind obedience to absolute, externally determined codes of behavior is thrown off and replaced with extreme relativism. As the person matures further, this extreme relativism is gradually modified. In McGrath's words:

- Stage 4 = The person perceives that legitimate uncertainty and diversity of opinion are extensive and concludes that all people have a right to their own opinions. The person rejects ethical authorities in favor of a thoroughgoing relativism in which anyone's opinion, including the individual's, is as good, true, or reliable as anyone else's.

- Stage 5 = The person perceives all knowledge and values, including those of formerly recognized ethical authorities, as contextual and relativistic and relegates dualistic right-wrong functions to a subordinate status by placing them in context.

In other words, Stage 4 reasoning makes "right" and "wrong" meaningless with a completely relativistic, anything-goes ethical stance. In Stage 5, however, "right"

and "wrong" return, not as absolutes as in the first three stages, but as contextual concepts.

The next steps in ethical maturity involve taking responsibility for one's own ethical choices, leading eventually to a solid, well-reasoned, ethical self-determination.

- Stage 6 = The person recognizes that he or she must orient himself or herself in a relativistic world through a personal commitment, as distinct from unquestioned or unconsidered commitment to simple belief in certainty.

- Stage 7 = The person makes an initial, limited commitment.

- Stage 8 = The person experiences the initial implications of commitment and explores the subjective issues of responsibility.

- Stage 9 = The person assumes responsibility for his or her beliefs and realizes that commitment is an ongoing, unfolding activity.

The ethically mature person understands that ethical maturity is not a final achievement but a lifelong process of growth and development.

Ethics are acquired from the day of our **birth** until the day of our death. At first, ethics are absorbed through **parent-child relationships** and the **imitation** of adult behavior. Children should interact with warm, caring, ethically mature adults during their first years of life to promote positive ethical development. Parents and teachers have a strong impact on children through the tenor of their relationships with children and with each other. Adults most often try to promote ethical behavior in children by establishing rules and codes of behavior through rewards and punishments. However, experts have found that this is much less effective than **modeling** and personal interaction.

Ethics are also acquired through labeling and sexual roles. People most often live up to the labels they are given, especially children. If a child is labeled "delinquent," she or he will incorporate that label and behave accordingly. If, on the other hand, a child is labeled "well-behaved," he or she will fulfill that expectation. Sexual roles also confer labels; "masculine" and "feminine" carry distinct expectations in nearly every culture, which children learn to conform to or rebel against early on. To become ethically mature, a person must struggle past assigned labels and roles to develop a freely chosen sense of identity, from which will grow the ethical code.

Two other important sources of ethical development are the practice of ethical behaviors and social interaction. Adults can help promote positive ethical development in children by creating opportunities for the children to make age-appropriate ethical choices and experience the consequences of those choices. It is also important to create a safe, supportive social **environment** so that children can learn to value others and identify with their community. **Empathy** is an essential element in positive ethical behavior; unless a person identifies with others and values them, she or he will have no qualms about causing others **pain** or suffering.

Finally, to reach full ethical maturity, a person must create his or her own ethical systems, born out of a sense of connection with all humans and other forms of life. Children must be given the opportunity to ground themselves in a sense of safety and community, out of which they can develop a responsible code of ethics that will carry them creatively through life.

*See also* Moral development

Dianne K. Daeg de Mott

### Further Reading

McGrath, Elizabeth Z. *The Art of Ethics: A Psychology of Ethical Beliefs*. Chicago: Loyola University Press, 1994.

Messerly, John G. *An Introduction to Ethical Theories*. Lanham, MD: University Press of America, 1995.

Pojman, Louis P. *Ethics: Discovering Right and Wrong*. Belmont, CA: Wadsworth Publishing, 1990.

Terkel, Susan Neiburg. *Ethics*. New York: Lodestar Books, 1992.

**Participating in traditional activities helps this little girl develop a sense of ethnic identity.** *(Corbis/Nik Wheeler. Reproduced with permission.)*

# Ethnic identity

An individual's feeling of belonging to a particular ethnic group.

The adjective *ethnic* is derived from the Greek noun *ethnos*, which means *race, people, nation,* and *tribe*. Although the modern term has a narrower connotation, denoting primarily *people,* vestiges of the older, more inclusive meaning still remain, particularly in types of discourse where the concepts of race and nationality are used interchangeably. Matters get even more complicated when the concept of *identity* is introduced, because, strictly speaking, a person's identity is a sum of essential attributes, and ethnicity, as researchers have asserted, is not necessarily an essential attribute of personal identity.

As a person matures, his or her **perception** of ethnicity undergoes a profound transformation. This transformation is concomitant with **cognitive development**. For example, as Frances Aboud and Anna-Beth Doyle explain (Aboud and Doyle, 1983), in the stage of cognitive development which **Jean Piaget** named *pre-operational* (between the ages of 2 and 7), children show a strong tendency to identify with a group perceived as their own,

while rejecting those seen as different. With the onset of the operation phase, children, who are now capable of rational thought, generally grow more tolerant toward "others," also showing **empathy** and understanding toward children who are viewed as different. This finding shows that the development of ethnic **consciousness**, although related to cognitive development, does not mirror the child's intellectual growth. However, with cognitive maturation, ethnicity, which is initially experienced as an image, or a set of physical attributes, becomes a mental construct which includes language, customs, cultural facts, and general knowledge about one's own ethnic group. Thus, to a four-year-old Mexican American child, ethnic identity is formed on the basis of his or her recognition of certain physical **traits** (Bernal, Knight, Ocampo, Garza, Cota, 1993). Later, as the person becomes aware of ethnicity as an idea, ethnic identity is experienced as an inner quality, or, as Aboud and Skerry note in a study that compared ethnic self-perception in kindergarten, second grade, and university students (Aboud and Skerry, 1983), internal attributes replace external attributes as the determinants of ethnic identity.

A strong sense of ethnic identity can influence a person's **self-esteem**, and it can also lead to dangerous, potentially violent, delusions, such as the idea of the "superiority" of a particular race (e.g., the Nazi myth of an "Aryan" race) or an ethnic group justifying genocide. For some people ethnic identity is a barely acknowledged fact of their life, while for some, it influences how they dress, speak, where they attend school, what they eat, and who they marry.

Zoran Minderovic

**Further Reading**

Aboud, Frances E., and Anna-Beth Doyle. "The Early Development of Ethnic Identity and Attitudes." In *Ethnic Identity: Formation and Transmission among Hispanics and Other Minorities*, edited by Martha Bernal and George P. Knight. Albany: State University of New York Press, (1993): 47-59.

Aboud, Frances E., and Shelagh A. Skerry. "Self and Ethnic Concepts in Relation to Ethnic Constancy." *Canadian Journal of Behavioural Science* 15, no. 1, (1983): 14-26.

Alba, Richard D. *Ethnic Identity: The Transformation of White America*. New Haven: Yale University Press, 1990.

Bernal, Martha E., George P. Knight, Katheryn A. Ocampo, Camille A. Garza, and Marya K. Cota. *Ethnic Identity: Formation and Transmission among Hispanics and Other Minorities*. Albany: State University of New York Press, 1993.

Erikson, Erik. *Identity, Youth and Crisis*. New York: W.W. Norton, 1968.

———. *Identity and the Life Cycle*. New York: W.W. Norton, 1980.

Hall, Thomas D., Christopher Bartalos, Elizabeth Mannebach, and Thomas Perkowitz. "Varieties of Ethnic Conflict in Global Perspective: A Review Essay." *Social Science Quarterly* 77, no. 2, (June 1966): 445-52.

Ocampo, Katheryn A., Martha E. Bernal, and George P. Knight. "Gender, Race, and Ethnicity: The Sequencing of Social Constancies." In *Ethnic Identity: Formation and Transmission among Hispanics and Other Minorities*, edited by Martha Bernal and George P. Knight. Albany: State University of New York Press, 1993, pp. 11-30.

# Ethnocentrism

An attitude of superiority about the ethnic group with which one is identified.

Ethnocentrism is a general belief that the ethnic group with which an individual is identified is superior to all other ethnic groups. Consequently, the individual persistently uses membership in the ethnic group as a primary criterion in the formation of relationships with others, and in evaluating or making judgments concerning other individuals. The term sociocentrism is sometimes used as a synonym of the term ethnocentrism, although sociocentrism is defined more narrowly. Sociocentrism involves the smaller social group rather than the larger ethnic group of the individual. Ethnic groups consist of individuals who are bound together, often closely, by a shared cultural structure and sense of **ethnic identity**. The central and defining feature of an ethnic group may be racial, religious, geopolitical, linguistic, traditional, tribal, or some combination of these or other characteristics. An ethnic group may be a majority or a minority of a population, and may be relatively dominant or powerless in a society. In varying degrees, ethnocentrism is an attribute of ethnic groups, past and present, throughout the world. The ethnocentric view that other ethnic groups and their members are inferior may be expressed in a number of ways: for example, through prejudice, paternalism, contempt, or hate crimes or other acts of **violence**.

**Further Reading**

Forbes, H. D. *Nationalism, Ethnocentrism, and Personality*. Chicago: University of Chicago Press, 1985.

# Ethology

The study of animal behavior as observed in the natural environment and in the context of evolutionary adaptation.

The pioneering work of **Konrad Lorenz** and Niko Tinbergen in the 1930s established a theoretical foundation for ethology, which has had an effect on such wide-ranging disciplines as genetics, anthropology, and political science in addition to psychology. Ethologists believe that an animal must be studied on its own terms rather than primarily in relation to human beings, with a focus on its **normal** behavior and **environment**. They study animal behavior from the dual perspective of both "proximate explanations" (which concern the individual lifetime of an animal) and "ultimate explanations" (which concern an animal's phylogenetic past). Proximate explanations answer questions about how a specific behavior occurs; ultimate explanations answer questions about why a behavior occurs.

Much of the field work performed by ethologists is based on the notion that an animal's behavior is generally adapted to its environment in much the same way as its physical characteristics. From the ethologist's point of view, a laboratory environment constrains animal behavior too much to provide a true understanding of its full range of functions and activities. However, the field work of ethologists consists of more than mere passive observation of animals in their natural habitats. In order to make observations about the behavior of an animal in its environment, ethologists often modify that environment. In a now-classic experiment, Lorenz managed to substitute himself for a mother goose, whose goslings then proceeded to follow him in single file wherever he went. In another well-known experiment, Tinbergen conducted a study of ground-nesting black-headed gulls to explain why a mother gull removes all traces of eggshell from its nest after a chick hatches. He hypothesized that the eggshell might be removed to prevent injuries, disease, or the attention of predatory birds. By placing pieces of shell in exposed locations away from the gulls' nests, Tinbergen found that the white interior of the shells were visible from the air and did indeed attract predators.

The ethologist's method of studying an animal begins with the creation of an ethogram, an objective description of its behavior patterns, including hunting, eating, sleeping, fighting, and nest-building. Four types of questions are raised about each activity: the cause of the behavior, development (within the lifetime of the individual animal), evolution (within the lifetime of the species), and adaptive function (how it helps the animal's species survive). Then, the researcher may turn to existing data on related species in various habitats and/or conduct independent research with reference to the animal's natural environment. Experiments may be conducted within the environment itself, or by investigating the effects of removing the animal from that environment. Laboratory studies may also be done, but these will usually be in relation to some aspect of the animal's own habitat.

Early theories of ethology focused on instinctive behaviors called fixed action patterns (FAPs), unlearned actions activated by "innate releasing mechanisms" that were thought to occur in response to specific stimuli. For example, submissive behavior could be regarded as a stimulus triggering an end to **aggression** on the part of a dominant animal. More recently, the focus of ethological theory has shifted to include an increasing awareness of behaviors that cannot be attributed to innate genetic processes, and learning has come to play a greater role in explanations of animal behavior. One example is the changing attitude toward the key concept of **imprinting**, first used by Lorenz to describe a nonreversible behavioral response acquired early in life, normally released by a specific triggering stimulus or situation. The differences between imprinting and ordinary learning include the fact that imprinting can take place only during a limited "critical period," what is imprinted cannot be forgotten, and imprinting does not occur in response to a reward. Imprinting was initially regarded as totally innate, but subsequent research has found that **conditioning** plays a role in this process.

Initially, ethology encompassed broad areas of behavioral study. More recently it has emphasized detailed study of particular behaviors. An emerging subfield, molecular ethology, focuses on how behaviors are affected by a single gene. Additional subdisciplines derived from classical ethology include **sociobiology**, which also involves gene study, and behavioral ecology, which relates behavior to the ecological conditions in which it occurs.

*See also* Adaptation; Comparative psychology

**Further Reading**

Moynihan, Martin. *The New World Primates: Adaptive Radiation and the Evolution of Social Behavior, Languages, and Intelligence*. Princeton, NJ: Princeton University Press, 1976.

# Etiology

The study and investigation into the root causes of a psychological disorder so that it might be resolved.

Psychological etiology refers to the scientific investigation into the origins of a disorder that cannot be explained biologically. Etiology is complicated by the fact that most disorders have more than one cause. Early etiological theories were the Freudian and post-Freudian psychoanalytic beliefs. **Sigmund Freud** attributed mental or neurotic disorders to deep-seated or hidden psychic motivations. The **unconscious** played the primary role in Freud's approach. According to Freud, the person in conflict was unaware of the cause because it was too deeply embedded in an inaccessible part of the mind. Freud postulated that the occurrence of previous traumas, unacceptable feelings, or wanton drives enacted a defense mechanism that enabled this burial into the unconscious. As a means of survival, a person might push such unsavory thoughts and memories as far from the conscious mind as possible.

**Childhood**, according to Freud, was the time when many repressed motivations and **defense mechanisms** began to thrive. Without control over their own lives, children have no way to resolve such emotions that include frustration, insecurity, or **guilt**. These emotions essentially build up while the child's **personality** is developing into adulthood. Every **psychological disorder** from **sexual dysfunction** to anxiety might be explained after talking about the repressed feelings a person has harbored since childhood.

## The change in theory

A new trend in determining the causes of psychological disorders began to thrive after World War II. Some of the psychologists who proposed this new etiology had studied under Freud but ultimately looked further to explain the nature and causes of psychological disorders. **Carl Jung**, for example, believed that a person's need for spirituality lead to dissatisfaction if it were not met. The inability to thus define oneself spiritually contributed to the rise of psychological or neurotic disorders. For **Alfred Adler**, feelings of inferiority captured the focus of conflict. Others, including Harry Stack Sullivan, **Karen Horney**, and Erick Fromm, used Freud's theory as a basis for their thought but emphasized instead the importance of social, cultural, and environmental factors in uncovering the causes for psychological problems.

Another type of etiology that emerged after Freud is called behavioral etiology. This focuses on learned behaviors as causes of mental disorders. **Ivan Pavlov** and **B. F. Skinner** are two famous behavioral psychologists. Behaviorists argue that the mind can be "trained" to respond to stimuli in various ways. A **conditioned response** is one which is learned when a stimulus produces a response, and that response is somehow reinforced. A young girl, for example, is told she is cute for screeching at the sight of a spider. She learns that this screech produces a favorable response from onlookers. Over time, this learned behavior may develop into a truly paralyzing **fear** of spiders. Behaviorists believe that just as a person can be conditioned to respond to a stimulus in a particular way, that same person can be conditioned to respond differently. In other words, more appropriate behavior can be learned, which is the basis for behavioral therapy.

With modern approaches to therapy, including the existential and cognitive approach, psychology has moved away from depicting mental illnesses as emerging from one root cause. For example, clinical psychologists generally search for a complexity of issues that stem from emotional, psychosexual, social, cultural, or existential causes. The cognitive approach, such as that developed by **Aaron Beck**, attempts to readapt behavioral responses through a rational process that demands an honesty and discipline to undo fears and anxieties. Cognitive therapies might even have a positive role in treating **schizophrenia** without medication.

While psychologists have focused on the mind itself as the location where psychological impairment might begin, medical doctors and researchers have continued to understand the biology that might influence mental disorders. Many of these studies have resulted in the refinement of prescription medications that alter a person's biochemistry to prevent or control various illnesses such as **depression** or schizophrenia. Neuropathology, or damage to **brain** tissue, can also serve as a biological cause of psychological disorders. Genetic research has been conducted to determine causes of certain disorders

at the level of DNA. Researchers have been working for decades to isolate a gene that contains the "program" for schizophrenia. In fact, reports of fully recovered schizophrenics treated without medication continued to rise by 2000. Psychological intervention seems to be just as effective as medical treatment for schizophrenic episodes.

Crucial to the treatment of any disorder is an understanding of its possible causes. Psychologists need to determine the etiology of a disorder before they can modify behavior.

*See also* Behaviorism; Cognitive therapy

Jane Spear

### Further Reading
Benner, David G., and Hill, Peter C., ed. *Baker Encyclopedia of Psychology & Counseling*. Grand Rapids, MI: Baker Books, 1999.

Corsini, Ray, ed. *Encyclopedia of Psychology, Second Edition*. New York: John Wiley & Sons 1994.

McGuire, Patrick A. *New Hope for People with Schizophrenia*. APA Monitor on Psychology, February 2, 2000.

### Further Information
American Psychological Association. 750 First Street, N.E., Washington, D.C., USA. 20002-4242, 202-336-5500, 800-374-2721.

# Eugenics

The systematic attempt to increase desirable genetic traits and to decrease undesirable genetic traits in a population.

As **Charles Darwin**'s ideas on evolutionary theory gained acceptance in the late 1800s, the public's faith in science as a source for social remedies increased in popularity, and scientists have looked for ways to "improve" humanity. British scientist **Francis Galton** introduced the ideas that led to a scientific approach to eugenics, including the concept of "positive eugenics" in which he encouraged the healthiest and most intelligent to marry one another and procreate. Although Galton's theories did not gain widespread acceptance in England, in the United States his ideas were interpreted in programs of "negative eugenics," designed to keep certain people from bearing children. Negative eugenics included such extreme measures as castration and sterilization as well as the **institutionalization** of people considered "defective" or "undesirable."

Racial, social, and moral issues were key factors in the American eugenics movement. Its victims included individuals diagnosed with **mental retardation**, psychiatric symptoms, **epilepsy**, or deafness, and people considered to be of low moral stature—unwed mothers, thieves, and prostitutes, for such behaviors were thought to be genetically based. A number of states enacted miscegenation laws that prohibited marriage between people of different races because it was believed that mixing the genes of different races would allow undesirable **traits** to proliferate in the dominant population. In an attempt to keep the "unfit" from procreating, legislators passed compulsory sterilization laws. Indiana was the first state to pass such legislation in 1907; by 1932, thirty states had similar laws. Prior to these statutes, however, compulsory sterilization had been an accepted practice in parts of the Midwest, and by the end of the eugenics movement, approximately 20,000 people had been sterilized.

In one particularly noteworthy case, the state of Virginia had ordered that Carrie Buck, an allegedly retarded women, be sterilized against her will. Later, Buck sued the state in a case that ultimately went to the Supreme Court. With a single dissenting vote, the Court upheld the existing sterilization laws, with Chief Justice Oliver Wendell Holmes handing down the opinion that it would be better to sterilize a feebleminded woman than to allow her to bear children who would ultimately become thieves and murderers. Recent investigations have revealed that Carrie Buck was completely **normal** intellectually, as was a daughter—conceived before the sterilization in a case of rape—who, before her death at the age of eight, performed quite satisfactorily in school. The daughter, Vivian Dobbs, had been diagnosed as retarded at six months of age during a cursory examination by a social worker.

In some cases, mental retardation was diagnosed on the basis of **intelligence** test scores. One prominent psychologist, Henry H. Goddard (1866-1957) actively campaigned to keep mentally retarded individuals from having children, and segregated students living at the New Jersey Vineland Training School for Feeble-Minded Girls and Boys by sex so that they could not procreate. Goddard also worked to keep "defective" immigrants from entering the United States. In one instance, he used **Alfred Binet**'s intelligence test to assess 35 Jews, 22 Hungarians, 50 Italians, and 45 Russians at Ellis Island in New York as they entered the country, and concluded that on average, over 80 percent of the immigrants scored so low as to be reflective of mental retardation. In this case, low test scores are not surprising given that the immigrants were tested in a language foreign to them (English), were probably intimidated by the testing situation, and were unfamiliar with American culture. Subsequent immigration laws included provisions relating to the intelligence quotients of potential immigrants.

Many of the tenets of the American eugenics movement were initially promulgated by the American Breeder's Association. While reputable scientific research did not support many of the ideas of the eugenicists, they did attempt to invoke science as the foundation for their ideas. The "research" employed was often regarded as low quality by the top scientists of the day, and its "findings" were considered flawed. In fact, Goddard's discredited research involving the famous lineage of the **Kallikak family** is now regarded as an example of poorly conceived and biased science.

American eugenics laws were widely supported up until World War II, when evidence of atrocities committed at Nazi death camps were publicized. The eugenics movement can be seen as more a socially than a scientifically based enterprise; only when the malignant implications of eugenics became clear did the American public withdraw its support.

*See also* Heredity; Jukes family; Nature-nurture controversy

### Further Reading
Bajema, Carl Jay, ed. *Eugenics: Then and Now.* Stroudsburg, PA: Dowden, Hutchinson & Ross, 1976.
Darwin, Leonard. *What Is Eugenics?* London: Watts, 1928.
East, Edward Murray. *Mankind at the Crossroads.* New York: C. Scribner's Sons, 1923.
Goddard, Henry Herbert. *The Kallikak Family: A Study in the Heredity of Feeble-Mindedness.* New York: Macmillan, 1927.
Packard, Vance Oakley. *The People Shapers.* Boston: Little, Brown, 1977.

# Existential psychology

A system in psychology focused on the belief that the essence of humans is their existence.

Existential psychology is an approach to psychology and **psychotherapy** that is based on several premises, including: understanding that a "whole" person is more than the sum of his or her parts; understanding people by examining their interpersonal relationships, understanding that people have many levels of self-awareness that can be neither ignored nor put into an abstract context, understanding that people have free will and are participants rather than observers in their own lives, and understanding that people's lives have purpose, values, and meaning. Therapists who practice existential psychology treat their clients by submerging themselves in the client's world. For the therapist, therapy is a process in which they, too, are participating.

This is a process that seeks meaning within the whole of the person's existence, including the client's personal history.

An important distinction exists between the concept of existentialism and existential phenomenology, even if the two are often linked to one another. According to a leading existential psychologists, Swiss Psychiatrist Ludwig Binswanger, "...while the existential therapist enters into the phenomena present before and with him or her, existentialism does not confine itself to states of withness. It includes the existence of the whole being." In other words, existential therapists are concerned with the whole of their clients as they can experience with them, whereas existential phenomenology studies the whole being—that which can be experienced as well as that which cannot. Binswanger formulated his belief around three different aspects of human existence. These included the *Umwelt*, or "world around," meaning the biological drive natural to humans; *Mitselt,* or "with world," the social and interpersonal human relationships; and the *Eigenwelt,* or "own world," the subjective, phenomenological world of the self.

## History of the movement

Danish philosopher Soren Kierkegaard (1813–55) is commonly referred to as the "Father of Existentialism." Kiekegaard stated, "I exist, therefore I think," in contrast to philosopher **Rene Descartes**'s famous words, "I think, therefore I am." This simple statement influenced an entire group of European philosophers and psychologists, changing their approach to treatment. Kiekegaard's philosophy was not as readily accepted in the United States. **Rollo May** (1909–94), the American psychologist who would become one of the existential movement's biggest proponents, attributed the introduction of the existentialist idea in the United States to the famed psychologist and philosopher, **William James**. James was an advocate of the principle of free will, a crucial component in existential thought. Throughout the 1920s and 1930s, existentialism was being quietly introduced, primarily in university classrooms. May himself was introduced to the idea through Paul Tillich at the Union Theological Seminary in New York where he was studying to be a Congregationalist minister. Noted professionals such as **Viktor Frankl** (1905–97) were beginning to introduce existentialism to the world through their writings and lectures. Frankl had survived internment at the Nazi death camp Theresienstadt and wrote personally of the events that shaped his beliefs. It was not until May and fellow psychologists **Abraham Maslow** and Herman Feifel participated in the **American Psychological Association (APA)** Symposium on Existential Psychology and Psychotherapy on Septem-

ber 5, 1959, that the idea of existential psychology and its terms began to reach the forefront of psychological thought and practice.

After the symposium, the term existentialism had become one of the "buzz" words of psychology in the 1960s. May described the existential approach to psychotherapy by stating that the task of therapy was to understand the patient fully as that patient truly exists. Such therapy would require a commitment on the part of the patients to fully understand the lives they were living, or the lives in which they were *existing*.

In addition to its significance as a major system of psychological practice, existentialism represented an awareness that emerged following World War II, particularly with the Baby Boomer generation. No longer were such philosophical concepts as existentialism left to the private halls of universities. For example, May's book *Love and Will* remained on U.S. lists of bestsellers for over four months, indicating that a new age of people from various educational backgrounds were ready to look into themselves as only a few had done in the preceding decades. Self-help books also lined bookstore shelves, an indication of the willingness of people to explore deep into their own existence.

Jane Spear

### Further Reading

Benner, David G., and Hill, Peter C., eds. *Baker Encyclopedia of Psychology & Counseling* Grand Rapids, MI: Baker Books, 1999.

Frankl, Viktor. *Man's Search for Meaning.* (Original publication date: 1963) Harcover: Beacon Press, May 2000. Mass Market Paperback, 1990.

May, Rollo. *Love and Will.* New York: W.W. Norton & Co., 1969.

May, Rollo. *The Discovery of Being: Writings in Existential Psychology.* (Reprint) New York: W.W. Norton & Co., 1994.

### Further Information

Rollo May Center for Humanistic Studies, Saybrook Graduate School & Research Center. 450 Pacific, 3rd floor, San Francisco, California, USA. 94133, 800-825-4480.

Viktor Frankl Institut. Langwiesgasse 6, A-1140, Vienna, Austria. (+43-1)914-2683.

# Experimenter bias

See **Experimental design**

# Experimental design

*Careful and detailed plan of an experiment.*

In simple psychological experiments, one characteristic—the independent variable—is manipulated by the experimenter to enable the study of its effects on another characteristic—the **dependent variable**. In many experiments, the **independent variable** is a characteristic that can either be present or absent. In these cases, one group of subjects represent the experiment group, where the independent variable characteristic exists. The other group of subjects represent the **control group**, where the independent variable is absent.

The validity of psychological research relies on sound procedures in which the experimental manipulation of an independent variable can be seen as the sole reason for the differences in behavior in two groups. Research has shown, however, that an experimenter can unknowingly affect the outcome of a study by influencing the behavior of the research participants.

When the goal of an experiment is more complicated, the experimenter must design a test that will test the effects of more than one variable. These are called multivariate experiments, and their design requires sophisticated understanding of statistics and careful planning of the variable manipulations.

When the actual experiment is conducted, subjects are selected according to specifications of the independent and dependent variables. People who participate as research subjects often want to be helpful as possible and can be very sensitive to the subtle cues on the part of the experimenter. As a result, the person may use a small smile or a frown by the experimenter as a cue for future behavior. The subject may be as unaware of this condition, known as experimenter bias, as the experimenter.

Experimenter bias is not limited to research with people. Studies have shown that animals (e.g., laboratory rats) may act differently depending on the expectations of the experimenter. For example, when experimenters expected rats to learn a maze-running task quickly, the rats tended to do so; on the other hand, animals expected not to learn quickly showed slower learning. This difference in learning resulted even when the animals were actually very similar; the experimenter's expectations seemed to play a causal role in producing the differences.

Some of the studies that have examined experimenter bias have been criticized because those studies may have had methodological flaws. Nonetheless, most researchers agree that they need to control for the experimenter bias. Some strategies for reducing such bias include automation of research procedures. In this way, an experimenter cannot provide cues to the participant because the procedure is mechanical. Computer-directed experiments can be very useful in reducing this bias.

Another means of eliminating experimenter bias if to create a double-blind procedure in which neither the subject nor the experimenter knows which condition the subject is in. In this way, the experimenter is not able to influence the subject to act in a particular way because the researcher does not know what to expect from that subject.

The results of experiments can also be influenced by characteristics of an experimenter, such as sex, race, euthanasic or other personal factors. As such, a subject might act in an unnatural way not because of any behavior on the part of the experimenter, but because of the subject's own biases.

## Further Reading

Christensen, Larry B. *Experimental Methodology.* 5th ed. Boston: Allyn and Bacon, 1991.
Elmes, David G. *Research Methods in Psychology.* 4th ed. St. Paul: West Publishing Company, 1992.
Martin, David W. *Doing Psychology Experiments.* 2nd ed. Monterey, CA: Brooks/Cole, 1985.

# Experimental group

*A group of subjects in a research experiment that receives an experimental treatment.*

Psychologists conduct experiments in order to isolate causes and effects. Ultimately, explaining human behavior consists of identifying the factors that have a causal influence on how we think or act. The most effective way to investigate causation is through experimentation. Different aspects of an experiment are best explained by providing an example. Suppose a researcher wants to find out if subliminal, auditory self-help tapes have any therapeutic benefits. These cassette tapes are available by mail order from a number of companies. They purport to help people change all sorts of bad habits, such as over-eating or smoking. Most tapes consist of music, ocean waves, and the occasional bird cry. According to the manufacturers, however, there are subliminal (i.e., undetectable) messages embedded in the tapes that have an unconscious influence on the listeners' motivations. Consequently, someone wishing to stop smoking could listen to such a tape on a regular basis, with the expectation that smoking frequency would decline after a few weeks.

To test these products, a research psychologist would conduct a controlled experiment. Research participants would be recruited, and perhaps even paid to participate in the study. Most smokers report difficulty in quitting, even when motivated to do so, thus finding interested volunteers would not be too difficult. Half the participants would be assigned to the "experimental group," and the other half to the "control group." Subjects in the experimental group would be provided with subliminal tapes designed to assist in smoking cessation. Those in the control condition would receive identical tapes, except that the control tapes would contain no subliminal messages. This condition is sometimes referred to as the "placebo" condition. The purpose of randomly assigning subjects to the experimental and control conditions is to try to insure that the two groups are roughly equivalent with respect to characteristics that could affect their reactions to the tapes. For example, we would not want the groups to differ in terms of the composition of heavy versus light smokers. Nor would we want highly motivated individuals in one group, and relatively indifferent participants in the other. Random assignment makes it unlikely that groups differ much from one another on such factors. Establishing the equivalence of groups beforehand is important because the researchers are predicting that people in the experimental group will either stop smoking, or will smoke less after receiving the treatment compared to the **control group** (assuming that the treatment works). A difference in cessation rates between the two groups will be interpreted as evidence of the efficacy of the tapes. If the groups differed from one another beforehand (say in terms of **motivation**), it would be impossible to attribute subsequently observed differences to the treatment.

Some additional factors would also need to be controlled. Expectancy effects can affect peoples' behaviors, independently of whatever treatment they might be receiving. Participants in the experimental group, for example, might expect their smoking to decline because of their faith in the tapes and the knowledge about the subliminal messages contained on them. They could become more self-conscious about their smoking habits, and consequently smoke less. If such a change were to occur, it could be a result of the subjects' beliefs and expectations about the treatment, rather than the treatment itself. To protect against this possibility, subjects are not informed of which group they are members. Because the subliminal tapes are indistinguishable from the placebo tapes, participants would have no way of knowing to which condition they were assigned. The subjects are said to be "blind" with respect to which treatment, if any, they are receiving. Sometimes the researchers' expectations can also influence participants' behavior. If the researcher has high hopes for the success of the treatment, he or she might inadvertently communicate this enthusiasm by means of facial expressions, posture, or tone of voice.

These social cues could alter the motivations of the participants. If the researcher knows which subjects are in the placebo condition and which ones are in the experimental condition, they could unwittingly treat the two groups differently. To protect against this, a double-blind study is conducted. The tapes would be coded in such a way that the person actually administering the tapes and the instructions to the users is kept in the dark about which subjects are receiving which tapes. This would guard against subjects in different conditions getting differential treatment from the research staff.

The experiment described above is relatively simple, but it contains the essential properties of any true experiment—random assignment of subjects to conditions, and the use of a control group. More complex experimental designs may consist of several different conditions or treatments, along with relatively elaborate controls. Controlled experiments are a powerful means of discovering cause-effect relationships, but other research techniques are also valuable. Sometimes experimentation is impossible because of practical or ethical constraints. For example, questions about the effects of homelessness, neglect, or malnutrition cannot be investigated by experimental means. The careful use of alternative methods can help answer some of these difficult yet important questions.

Timothy E. Moore

**Further Reading**
Graziano, A., & Raulin, M. L. *Research Methods: A process of inquiry.* Boston: Allyn & Bacon, 2000.

# Experimental psychology

The scientific investigation of basic behavioral processes including sensation, emotion, and motivation, as well as such cognitive processes as perception, memory, learning, problem-solving, and language.

Experimental psychologists work to understand the underlying causes of behavior by studying humans and animals. Animals are studied within and outside laboratory settings for a variety of reasons. A researcher may wish to learn more about a particular species, to study how different species are interrelated, to investigate the evolutionary significance of certain behaviors, or to learn more about human behavior.

Experimental psychology flourished in the second half of the nineteenth century with the work of such figures as G. T. Fechner (1801-1887), whose *Elements of*

*Psychology* (1860) is considered the first study in the field, and **Wilhelm Wundt** (1832-1920), who established the first psychological laboratory in 1879. Others, including **Hermann Ebbinghaus** and E.B. Titchener (1867-1927), used laboratory methods to investigate such areas as sensation, **memory**, **reaction time**, and rudimentary levels of learning. While controlled laboratory studies continue to make major contributions to the field of psychology, experimental methods have also been used in such diverse areas as **child development**, clinical diagnosis, and social problems. Thus, the concept of experimentation can no longer be limited to the laboratory, and "experimental psychology" is now defined by method and by the kinds of processes being investigated, rather than its setting.

An experiment in any setting tests a hypothesis, a tentative explanation for an observed phenomenon or a prediction about the outcome of a specific event based on theoretical assumptions. All experiments consist of an **independent variable**, which is manipulated by the researcher, and a **dependent variable**, whose outcome will be linked to the independent variable. For example, in an experiment to test the sleep-inducing properties of the hormone melatonin, the administration of the hormone would be the independent variable, and the resulting amount of **sleep** would be the dependent variable.

In simplest terms, the effects of the independent variable are determined by comparing two groups which are as similar to each other as possible, with the exception that only one group has been exposed to the independent variable being tested. That group is called the **experimental group**; the other group, which provides a baseline for **measurement**, is called the **control group**.

Although ideally the experimental and control groups will be as similar as possible, in practice, most psychological research is complicated by a variety of factors. For example, some random variables—differences in both the subjects themselves and in the testing conditions—are unavoidable and have the potential to disrupt the experiment. In addition, many experiments include more than one group of subjects, and establishing a true control group is not possible. One method of offsetting these problems is to randomly assign subjects to each group, thus distributing the effect of uncontrollable variables as evenly as possible.

The subjects' attitudes toward the experimental situation is another condition that may influence the results. This phenomenon is best demonstrated by what is referred to as the **placebo effect**. Subjects in experiments that test medical and psychological treatments often show improvement solely because they believe the treatment has been administered. Thus, the administration of a placebo (a supposed treatment that in fact contains no active ingredient) to a control group can disclose to the experimenter whether improvement in the subjects' conditions has been caused by the treatment itself or only by the subjects' belief that their condition will improve. Interference may come from an additional variable, experimenter bias, the unintentional effect of the experimenter's attitudes, behavior, or personal interests on the results of an experiment. The experimenter may, for example, read instructions to two groups of research subjects differently, or unintentionally allow one group slightly more or less time to complete an experiment. A particularly powerful type of experimenter bias is the **self-fulfilling prophecy**, whereas the researcher's expectations influence the results. In a well-known example, when laboratory assistants working with two groups of randomly selected rats were told that one group was brighter than the other, they treated the rats in such a way that the supposedly "brighter" group learned to negotiate a maze faster than the other group. Subtle differences in the assistants' handling of the "brighter" group had produced the results they were conditioned to expect.

In experiments utilizing a placebo, experimenter bias may be prevented by a double-blind design, in which not only the subjects but also the persons administering the experiment are unaware of which is the control group and what results are expected. In general, experimenters can minimize bias by making a vigilant attempt to recognize it when it appears, as well as resisting the temptation to intentionally influence the outcome of any experiment. The results of experiments are generally presented in a report or article that follows a standard format of introduction, method, results, and conclusion.

Experimental research can also be conducted through quasi-experiments, studies which lack the control of a true experiment because one or more of its requirements cannot be met, such as the deliberate use of an independent variable or the random assignment of subjects to different groups. Studies of the effects of drugs on pregnant women, for instance, are based on data about women who have already been pregnant and either taken or not taken drugs. Thus, the researcher has no control over the assignment of subjects or the choices with which they are presented, but he or she can still measure differences between the two populations and obtain significant findings. These findings gain validity when they are based on data obtained from large numbers of subjects and when their results can be replicated a number of times. Such studies provide a basis for investigations that would otherwise be impossible.

*See also* Experimental design; Research methodology

**Further Reading**
D'Amato, M. R. *Experimental Psychology: Methodology, Psychophysics, and Learning.* New York: McGraw-Hill, 1970

Kantowitz, Barry H. *Experimental Psychology: Understanding Psychological Research.* 5th ed. St. Paul: West Publishing Company, 1994.

# Extinction

The elimination of a conditioned response by withholding reinforcement.

In classical/respondent **conditioning**, the learned response disappears when the association between conditioned and unconditioned stimuli is eliminated. For example, when a **conditioned stimulus** (a light) is presented with an unconditioned stimulus (meat), a dog may be trained to salivate in response to the conditioned stimulus. If the unconditioned stimulus does not appear at least some of the time, however, its association with the conditioned stimulus will be lost, and extinction of the dog's learned or **conditioned response** will occur. As a result, the dog will stop salivating in response to the light.

In **operant conditioning**, the experimental subject acquires a conditioned response by learning that its actions will bring about specific consequences, either positive or negative. When the link between this operant response and its consequences is not reinforced, extinction of the response occurs. Thus, a rat that has learned that pressing a lever in its cage will produce a food pellet will gradually stop pressing the lever if the food pellets fail to appear.

Just as behavioral therapies use **reinforcement** to foster desirable behaviors, they may achieve the extinction of undesirable ones by removing various forms of reinforcement. For example, rowdy or otherwise inappropriate behavior by children is often "rewarded" by **attention** from both adults and peers. Sending a child to "time out" short circuits this process and can eliminate the undesirable behavior by removing the reward. Although it works slowly, extinction is a popular technique for modifying behavior in children.

**Further Reading**
Craighead, W. Edward. *Behavior Modification: Principles, Issues, and Applications.* Boston: Houghton Mifflin, 1976.

Skinner, B.F. *About Behaviorism.* New York: Knopf, 1974.

# Extroversion

A term used to characterize people who are typically outgoing, friendly, and open toward others.

Extroverts are people who are often leaders, work well in groups, and prefer being with others to being alone. Other **personality traits** often associated with extroversion include optimism, risk taking, and love of excitement and change. People who are extroverts prefer having company and tend to have many friends.

Extroversion is generally defined in comparison to its opposite, **introversion**, which is used to describe people who are quieter, more reserved and sensitive, and more comfortable in solitary pursuits. The two tendencies can be regarded as opposite ends of a continuum, with most people falling somewhere in between. Nevertheless, many people have traits that clearly place them closer to one end than to the other. Both extroversion and introversion in some people are thought to be the result of inborn tendencies—called **temperament**—that are shaped by environmental factors. The psychologist **Hans Eysenck** has suggested that the temperamental foundation involves the ease with which the cerebral cortex becomes aroused. Eysenck notes that in introverts some parts of the **brain** are very sensitive to arousal and are easily overstimulated, causing them to prefer quiet surroundings and calm situations. The extrovert, on the other hand, can tolerate a higher level of cortical arousal and thus seeks out social interaction and exciting situations for stimulation.

Tendencies toward extroversion or introversion often lead people to develop and cultivate contrasting strengths, sometimes referred to in terms of contrasting types of **intelligence**. Extroverts more readily develop *inter*personal intelligence, which has to do with making friends easily, demonstrating **leadership** ability, and working effectively with others in groups. In introverts the more highly developed traits are more likely to be those associated with *intra*personal intelligence, such as the deeper awareness of one's feelings and the ability to enjoy extended periods of solitude. All people have both types of intelligence, but in many people one is stronger than the other, depending on whether the person is an introvert or an extrovert.

**Further Reading**
Eysenck, Hans J., and Michael Eysenck. *Personality and Individual Differences.* New York: Plenum Press, 1985.

Campbell, Joseph, ed. *The Portable [Carl] Jung.* New York: Viking, 1971.

# Hans Juergen Eysenck

**1916-1997**
German-born British psychologist whose unorthodox views generated controversy.

Hans Eysenck's obituary in the *New York Times* called him "one of the most distinguished, prolific, and maddeningly perverse psychologists of his generation." This accurately sums up a long career that Eysenck claimed he entered almost by accident. As a **personality** and behavior theorist, he popularized the terms "introvert" and "extrovert," and he created a **personality inventory** test based on his many years of research in London. He published more than 80 books and 1,600 journal articles. Yet he also generated enormous controversy during his career. He argued that **psychotherapy** had little if any value; that smoking did not cause lung cancer, and, most contentious, that there was a correlation between race and I.Q. scores. While he made many enemies in many circles, he also had many supporters who claimed that his ideas had been taken out of context.

Born in Berlin on March 4, 1916, Hans Juergen Eysenck was the son of Eduard Anton and Ruth Werner Eysenck. Both his parents were actors; his mother appeared in silent films. They divorced in 1918 and young Hans was primarily raised by his grandmother. He attended school primarily in Berlin and had planned to go to the University there when he graduated high school in 1934. When he found out that acceptance into the University of Berlin was contingent on joining the Nazi party, he found this unacceptable and left Germany. He studied literature and history at the University of Dijon in France and later at University College of Exeter in England. He moved to London and had planned to study physics there, but he did not qualify for admission into the program. When he tried to register as a science student, he was told that he could only take psychology. Initially disenchanted with the subject, he soon warmed to it, particularly statistical analysis and research. He received his bachelor's degree in 1938 and his Ph.D. in 1940.

## Begins career in behavior research

Turned down for British military service because he was still a German citizen, Eysenck was later allowed to join Britain's civil defense program. In 1942, he took a position as a research psychologist at the Mill Hill Emergency Hospital outside London. Many of the staff were from London's Maudsley Hospital, a psychiatric training institution that had been closed because of the war. When it re-opened in 1946, Eysenck took a position there as a senior research psychologist. He became director of the psychology department there a year later. In 1950 the University of London established its Institute of Psychiatry at Maudsley, and Eysenck established its psychology department. He also became a professor of psychology at the University.

Personality was what most intrigued Eysenck, and he conducted expensive research on different personality types. He was influenced in part by scientists such as **Ivan Pavlov**, famous for his experiments with conditioned **reflexes**. But he also placed considerable importance on statistical research. Genetics, too, played a role in Eysenck's research. He came up with a series of personality "dimensions" to explain different behaviors. These include **neurosis**, introversion-extroversion, and **psychosis**. He used his theories and his statistical research to explain in part what made shy people shy, for example, or what made people engage in criminal behavior. He also developed the Maudsley Personality Inventory (used widely in Britain), a test that determined a person's basic personality type.

## Invites controversy on several fronts

Along with the research results that were lauded by both his colleagues and the public at large, however, he made numerous conclusions that for many called into question his abilities as a serious scientist. As early as the 1950s, Eysenck was claiming that psychotherapy had no beneficial effect on people. He believed that **behavior therapy** yielded much better results because it dealt with the present rather than some deep dark past. Although in later years he did grow somewhat more accepting of certain types of psychotherapy, he remained for the most part skeptical of its true worth.

His theories on smoking and lung cancer were hardly popular (except, perhaps, with tobacco companies). He believed that certain personality types were susceptible both to taking up smoking and to the diseases it could cause.

By far his most controversial views were those on race and **intelligence**. The American psychologist **Arthur Jensen** claimed in the late 1960s that race was a factor in I.Q. scores, with blacks scoring about 15 points lower on the tests. Eysenck came to Jensen's aid and said that the difference in scores was based on genetic as well as physiological factors. Not surprisingly, the negative publicity generated by a statement like this was so strong that when he was visiting the University of California at Berkeley in 1971, he had to be escorted about the campus by armed bodyguards. Eysenck claimed that his conclusions were purely scientific and were not based on **racism**. His detractors were invariably surprised when they found out he had voluntarily left Nazi Germany.

Over the next several years Eysenck continued to conduct research, as well as keeping up his usual output of books and articles. Even after he retired from the University in 1988 he continued to write. His second wife, Sybil Rostal Eysenck, had been a psychology student. Because of this connection, the Eysencks often collaborated on different projects. The Eysencks, who married in 1950, had four children. (Eysenck's first to Margaret Davies produced a son.)

In 1996, Eysenck was diagnosed with a **brain** tumor. He continued to work as much as he could, up until almost the time of his death. Death came on September 4, 1997, at a hospice in London.

*See also* Intelligence quotient

George A. Milite

**Further Reading**

*Current Biography 1972*. New York, H.W. Wilson Co., 1972.

Gibson, H. J. *Hans Eysenck: The Man and His Work*. London, Peter Owen, 1981.

# F

# Familial retardation

Also called sociocultural or cultural-familial retardation, mild mental retardation attributed to environmental causes and generally involving some degree of psychosocial disadvantage.

The majority of persons suffering from **mental retardation** fall into the category of familial retardation rather than that of clinical retardation, which usually has neurological or other organic causes. Persons with familial retardation typically have IQs ranging from 55-69 and show no signs of physical **disability**. Environmental causes thought to contribute to familial retardation include the quality of the mother's prenatal care, maternal and child nutrition, **family** size, the spacing of births within a family, disease, and health risks from environmental toxins such as lead. The 1994 publication of *The Bell Curve*, an analysis, by Richard J. Herrnstein and Charles Murray, of the relative importance of **heredity** and **environment** in determining IQ scores, and the 1995 release of the most in-depth study to date on retardation among school children both renewed public interest in familial retardation and its causes.

Familial retardation is usually not detected until a child enters school and has academic difficulties, at which point the teacher recommends psychological evaluation. Unlike the parents of clinically retarded children, who generally seek out help for their youngsters, the parents of those with familial retardation may take offense when their children are labeled mentally retarded and deny that there is a problem, especially since their children are often able to function competently in their daily lives outside school. Some studies have shown that educators are more likely to classify poor and/or minority children as mentally retarded, while labeling white middle-class children with comparable IQ scores as learning disabled. Other critics have pointed out that familial retardation may be diagnosed in children who are simply unprepared to cope with the demands of school because of cultural and linguistic isolation.

Familial retardation may be reduced by nutritional, health, and educational intervention at an early age. In a study conducted in the 1970s, educators selected mother-child pairs from among a group of women with IQs under 75 living in the poorest section of Milwaukee, Wisconsin, while establishing a **control group** of mothers in the same neighborhood with IQs over 100. For the first five years of the children's lives, the targeted group of mothers and their children received instruction in problem-solving and language skills, as well as counseling to motivate them to learn and succeed. The mothers and children in the control group received no form of environmental enrichment. At the age of five, the children in the target group had IQ scores averaging 26 points higher than those of the children in the control group. At the age of nine, their average IQ was 106 (slightly above the universal **norm** of 100), while that of the other children was only 79. (Later results, however, were somewhat disappointing, as the mothers' **motivation** to continue the program became difficult to maintain over the long term.)

In 1995, an Atlanta study conducted jointly by the Centers for Disease Control and Prevention and Emory University found important new evidence linking mild retardation to social and educational deprivation. It was found that 8.4 out of every 1,000 10-year-olds were mildly retarded (defined as an IQ of 50-70), while 3.6 of every 1,000 suffered severe retardation due to such conditions as cerebral palsy or **Down syndrome**. The incidence of mild retardation was 2.6 higher in blacks than whites, although this difference was halved when socioeconomic factors were taken into account. Children of all races were four times as likely to be mildly retarded if their mothers had not finished high school. The incidence of mental retardation was also slightly higher for children of teenage mothers. The Atlanta study also confirmed earlier claims that teachers are more likely to seek IQ testing for minority children from poor families.

Based on the findings of this survey, the federal government launched a pilot program to improve health and education for disadvantaged mothers and children, with special emphasis on providing a more intellectually stimulating home environment for at-risk youngsters through reading programs and other activities.

As adults, socioculturally retarded individuals live in a variety of settings, including their parental homes, group homes, and their own independent residences. Very few are institutionalized. Most make a satisfactory adjustment to adult life in their communities, although their adjustment in early adulthood is likely to be more difficult than that of the average person. Often they must learn from their own life experiences lessons that others learned (or at least were introduced to) at home. Eventually, however, most become responsible and self-supporting members of their communities with the ability to meet adult responsibilities and commitments.

### Further Reading

Fraser, Steven. *The Bell Curve Wars: Race, Intelligence, and the Future of America*. New York: Basic Books, 1995.

Herrnstein, Richard J., and Charles Murray. *The Bell Curve: Intelligence and Class Structure in American Life*. New York: Free Press, 1994.

## Family size

*The size of a family has a significant effect on the interrelationships among its members and can play a major role in the formation of a child's personality.*

**Family** size is a significant factor in **child development**, but must be considered as only one part of a larger picture, however. Other factors, such as the parents' **personality traits**, and the gender and spacing of the children, contribute significantly to the formation of a child's personality. Children of large families have a greater opportunity to learn cooperation at an early age than children of smaller families as they must learn to get along with siblings. They also take on more responsibility, both for themselves and often for younger brothers and sisters. In addition, children in large families must cope with the emotional crises of sibling rivalry, from which they may learn important lessons that will aid them later in life. This factor, however, may also be a disadvantage; either the older child who was "dethroned" from a privileged position or the younger child who is in the eldest child's shadow may suffer feelings of inferiority. Children in large families tend to adopt specific roles in order to attain a measure of uniqueness and thus gain parental **attention**.

Children in small families receive a greater amount of individual attention and tend to be comfortable around adults at an early age. They may also be overprotected, however, which can result in dependence, lack of initiative, and **fear** of risk, and the increased parental attention may also take the form of excessive scrutiny and pressure to live up to other people's expectations. Researchers have found that only children are often loners and have the lowest need for **affiliation**. They tend to have high IQs and are successful academically. However, only children have also been found to have more psychological problems than children from larger families.

## Family therapy

*The joint treatment of two or more members of the same family in order to change unhealthy patterns of communication and interaction.*

Family therapy is generally initiated because of psychological or emotional problems experienced by a single family member, often a child or adolescent. These problems are treated as symptomatic of dysfunction within the family system as a whole. The therapist focuses on the interaction between family members, analyzing the role played by each member in maintaining the system. Family therapy can be especially helpful for dealing with problems that develop in response to a particular event or situation, such as **divorce** or remarriage, or the **birth** of a new sibling. It can also be an effective means to draw individuals who feel threatened by individual therapy into a therapeutic setting.

Family therapy has a variety of origins. It is related to the long-standing emphasis of **psychoanalysis** and other psychodynamic approaches on the central role that early family relationships play in the formation of **personality** and the manifestation of psychological disorders. Family therapy also grew out of the realization that progress made by patients staying in treatment centers was often reversed when they returned to their families. As a result, a number of therapists became dissatisfied treating clients individually with no opportunity to actively address the harmful family relationships that were often the source of their clients' problems.

Family therapy, either alone or in conjunction with other types of treatment, has been effective in the treatment of children suffering from a variety of problems, including anxiety, enuresis (bed-wetting), and **eating disorders**, and also in working with victims of **child abuse**. In addition to alleviating the child's initial complaint and improving communication within the family unit, family therapy can also help reduce **stress** and conflict by helping families improve their coping skills.

There are a number of approaches to family therapy. Perhaps the best known is structural family therapy, founded by **Salvador Minuchin**. A short-term method that focuses on the present rather than the past, this school of therapy views a family's behavior patterns and rituals as central to the problems of its individual members. Poor communication skills play a key role in perpetuating destructive interactions within families, such as the formation of alliances among some family members against others. The goals of structural family therapy include strengthening parental **leadership**, clarifying boundaries, enhancing coping skills, and freeing family members from their entrenched positions within the family structure. Minuchin divided families' styles of interacting into two basic types—enmeshed and disengaged, considering behavior at either extreme as pathological, with most families falling somewhere on a continuum between the two. Minuchin believed that the functioning of family systems prevented individuals from becoming healthier emotionally, because the family system relied on its troubled member to play a particular role in order to function in its accustomed way. This stability is disrupted if an individual changes significantly.

Psychodynamically oriented family therapy emphasizes **unconscious** processes (such as the projection of unacceptable personality **traits** onto another family member) and unresolved conflicts in the parents' families of origin. The lasting effects of such traumatic experiences as parental divorce and child abuse are explored. This type of therapy focuses more on family history and less on symptoms, resulting in a lengthier therapeutic process. Therapists who employ an object relations approach emphasize the importance of having the parents in a family work out conflicts with their own parents. Some practitioners include grandparents in their work with families in order to better understand intergenerational dynamics and deeply rooted behavior patterns. Ivan Boszormenyi-Nagy, a well-known proponent of this orientation, would only treat families when members of three generations could participate in therapy sessions.

Behavioral family therapy views interactions within the family as a set of behaviors that are either rewarded or punished. The behavioral therapist educates family members to respond to each others' behavior with positive or negative **reinforcement**. A child might be discouraged from repeating a negative behavior, for example, by losing some privileges or receiving a " time-out." Positive behavior might be rewarded with the use of an incentive chart on which points or stickers are accrued and eventually exchanged for a reward. Behavioral approaches sometimes involve the drawing up of behavioral "contracts" by family members, as well as the establishment of rules and reinforcement procedures.

Several other family therapy approaches, including that of **Virginia Satir**, are primarily concerned with communication. Satir's system combines the teaching of family communication skills, the promotion of **self-esteem**, and the removal of obstacles to the emotional growth so that family members can have full access to their innate resources.

## Further Reading

Boyd-Franklin, Nancy. *Black Families in Therapy*. New York: Guilford Press, 1989.

Minuchin, Salvador. *Family Therapy Techniques*. Cambridge: Harvard University Press, 1981.

Nichols, Michael P., and Richard C. Schwartz. *Family Therapy: Concepts and Methods*. Boston: Allyn and Bacon, 1991.

Satir, Virginia. *Conjoint Family Therapy*. Palo Alto, CA: Science and Behavior Books, 1983.

Walters, Marianne, et. al. *The Invisible Web: Gender Patterns in Family Relationships*. New York: Guilford Press, 1988.

## Further Information

American Assocation for Marriage and Family Therapy. 1717 K Street N.W., Suite 407, Washington, DC 20006, (202) 452–0109.

American Family Therapy Association. 2020 Pennsylvania Avenue, N.W., Suite 273, Washington, DC 20006, (202) 994–2776.

# Family

Two or more people related to each other by genetics, adoption, marriage, or in some interpretations, by mutual agreement.

Family is broadly defined as any two people who are related to each other through a genetic connection, **adoption**, marriage, or by mutual agreement. Family members share emotional and economic bonds. The term *nuclear family* is used to refer to family members who live together and share emotional, economic, and social responsibilities. The nuclear family is often comprised of a married couple who are parents to their biological or adopted children; all members live together in one household. This type of nuclear family is increasingly referred to by social scientists as an *intact family*, signifying that the family had not been through a **divorce**, separation, or death of a member.

In addition to the nuclear family, other complex and diverse combinations of individuals lead to what social

**Traditional family sitting down to dinner at the turn of the twentieth century.** *(The Library of Congress. Reproduced by permission.)*

scientists call blended or nontraditional families. When a family has experienced divorce or death leaving one parent to be primarily responsible for raising the children, they become a *single-parent family.* (The terms *broken family* and *broken home* are no longer widely used because of their negative connotations.)

Following the end of one marriage, one or both of the ex-spouses may enter a new marriage. Through this process of remarriage, stepfamilies are formed. The second spouse becomes a stepparent to the children from the first marriage. In the family formed by the second marriage, the children from each spouse's first marriage become step-siblings. Children born or adopted by the couple of the second marriage are half-siblings to the children from the first marriage, since they share one parent in common.

In some cases, a stepparent will legally adopt his or her spouse's children from a previous marriage. The biological father or mother must either be absent with no legal claim to custody, or must grant permission for the stepparent to adopt.

In situations where a single parent lives with someone outside of marriage, that person may be referred to as a co-parent. Co-parent is also the name given to the partner in a homosexual relationship who shares the household and parenting responsibilities with a child's legal adoptive or biological parent.

The home which was owned by the family prior to a divorce or separation is referred to as the *family home* in many state laws. In court settlements of divorce and child custody issues, the sale of the family home may be prohibited as long as the minor children are still living there with the custodial parent. The sale of the home may be permitted (or required to pay the noncustodial parent his or her share of its value) if the custodial parent moves or remarries, or when the children leave home to establish their own residences.

The term *extended family* traditionally meant the biological relatives of a nuclear family; i.e., the parents, sisters, and brothers of both members of a married couple. It was sometimes used to refer to the people living in the household beyond the parents and children. As family relationships and configurations have become more complex due to divorce and remarriage, extended family has come to refer to all the biological, adoptive, step-, and half-relatives.

## FATHER-CHILD HOUSEHOLD

In June 1997, the U.S. Census Bureau reported that the number of single fathers with children under 18 grew from 400,000 in 1970 to 1.7 million in 1995. That same year, government data shows that 2.5 million children lived with just their fathers—48% of whom were divorced, 28% were never married, 18% were married but not living with their wives, and 5% were widowed.

For children living with their father only:
- Median family income was $23,155 (1994).
- Percent that were classified as poor: 26%.
- Six out of ten lived with at least one sibling.
- Percent of fathers with high school diplomas: 76%.
- Percent of fathers with a bachelor's degree or more: 12%.
- Percent with a father who was working: 79%.
- Five out of 10 lived in rental housing.

For children living with both parents:
- Median family income was $46,195 (1994).
- Percent that were classified as poor: 11%.
- More than eight out of ten lived with at least one sibling.
- Percent with at least one parent with a high school diploma: 86%.
- Percent with at least one parent with a bachelor's degree or more: 29%.
- Percent with at least one parent working: 85%.
- Less than 3 out of 10 lived in rental housing.

Government agencies and other statistics-gathering organizations use the term *head of household* to refer to the person who contributes more than half of the necessary support of the family members (other than the spouse); in common usage, the head of household is the person who provides primary financial support for the family.

### Further Reading

Bernardes, Jon. *Family Studies: An Introduction.* New York: Routledge, 1997.

Elkind, David. *Ties That Stress: The New Family Imbalance.* Cambridge, MA: Harvard University Press, 1994.

Eshleman, J. Ross. *The Family: An Introduction.* 7th ed. Boston: Allyn and Bacon, 1994.

Kephart, William M. and Davor Jedlicka. *The Family, Society, and the Individual.* 7th ed. New York: HarperCollins, 1991.

Ohio Cooperative Extension Service. *Changing Families, Challenges and Opportunities.* Columbus, OH: Ohio Cooperative Extension Service: The Ohio State University, 1988. (Four sound cassettes, covering the subjects of latchkey families, single-parent families, strengthening step-families, and two-income families.)

Strong, Bryan and Christine DeVault. *The Marriage and Family Experience.* 4th ed. St. Paul: West Publishing Co., 1989.

White, James M. *Dynamics of Family Development: A Theoretical Perspective.* New York: Guilford Press, 1991.

### Further Information

Family Service Association of America (FSA), formerly the Family Welfare Association of America). 11600 West Lake Park Drive, Milwaukee, WI 53244, (414) 359–1040, (800) 221–3726.

Step Family Foundation (SFF). 333 West End Avenue, New York, NY 10023, (212) 877–3244 (Disseminates information on step families, provides counseling and training service, and publishes informational materials.)

# Fantasy

A set of mental images that generally have no basis in reality.

A fantasy is inspired by **imagination** characterized by mental images that do not necessarily have any relationship to reality. In **psychoanalysis**, fantasy is regarded as a **defense mechanism**. For example, after being reprimanded by a supervisor, a worker may fantasize about taking over the company and firing the supervisor. Similarly, a child may fantasize about running away from home in retaliation against her parents for punishing her.

Vivid fantasies are often a part of **childhood**, diminishing as a child grows older. In the majority of individuals, fantasy is not a cause for concern; as long as the fantasizer is aware that the fantasy is not real, the formation of these mental images may be considered **normal**. When the line between fantasy and reality becomes blurred, however, it is possible that some form of **mental illness** is present. When the individual regards his fantasy as reality, it has become an **hallucination**. In such situations, the hallucination may be a symptom of **schizophrenia**, and professional evaluation by a psychologist or psychiatrist is required.

### Further Reading

Klinger, Eric. *Daydreaming: Using Waking Fantasy and Imagery for Self-Knowledge and Creativity.* Los Angeles, CA: J. P. Tarcher, 1990.

"What Your Fantasies Reveal About You." *American Health* (April 1995): 68+.

# Fear

An intense emotional state caused by specific external stimuli and associated with avoidance, self defense, and escape.

Fear is one of the primary emotions, together with joy, **anger**, and grief. Fear generally refers to feelings elicited by tangible, realistic dangers, as opposed to anxiety, which often arises out of proportion to the actual threat or danger involved. Fear may be provoked by exposure to traumatic situations, observations of other people exhibiting fear, or the receipt of frightening information. Repeated or prolonged exposure to fear can lead to disorders such as combat fatigue, which is characterized by long-term anxiety and other emotional disturbances.

Fear is accompanied by a series of physiological changes produced by the **autonomic nervous system** and adrenal glands, including increased heart rate, rapid breathing, tenseness or trembling of muscles, increased sweating, and dryness of the mouth. Blood is diverted from other parts of the body to the areas where energy is most needed, either to run from danger or to forcibly protect oneself, a reaction known as the "fight or flight" response. This sudden diversion of excess blood from the cerebral cortex of the **brain** may also cause fainting, which in animals may actually serve an adaptive function to protect them from predators. In the 1880s, **William James** concluded that the physiological changes associated with fear actually constitute the **emotion** itself (e.g., "we are afraid because we tremble"), a view that has been challenged by cognitive psychologists since the 1950s.

Fears first appear in human infants at about seven months of age. Young children generally have more fears than older persons and their fears are experienced more intensely. Within families, studies have shown that middle children as a group experience fewer fears than older or younger siblings. Researchers have disagreed about the extent to which fear is innate or learned, with behaviorists arguing that it is largely learned. Animals have been conditioned to fear previously neutral stimuli through various methods including association, the exposure to paired neutral and fear-producing stimuli to the point where the neutral stimuli become associated with fear, even when presented alone. Certain innate fears such as fear of loud noises, **pain**, and injury appear to be universal. Species-specific innate fears have also been documented, including a fear of hawk-like shapes in certain animals and a fear of snakes in humans and other primates.

When a person confronts real dangers, fear can be an important means of self-preservation. However, many people are plagued by chronic and unrealistic fears, including phobias and obsessions, that cause much unnecessary distress and can severely reduce their ability to function normally in society. While it is possible to reduce pathological fears through drug treatment, the results are temporary and drugs do not address the root cause of the problem. **Mental health** professionals offer various types of psychological treatment that either attempt to deal with the underlying cause of the fear through a psychodynamic approach or address the fear directly through behavioral therapy. Behavioral techniques include **desensitization** (gradually increasing exposure to the feared object), flooding (sudden, intensive exposure to the feared object or stimulus), and **modeling** (observing another person being exposed to the feared object without being harmed).

### Further Reading
Bemis, Judith. *Embracing the Fear: Learning to Manage Anxiety and Panic Attacks.* St. Paul, MN: Hazelden, 1994.
Forgione, Albert G. *Fear: Learning to Cope.* New York: Van Nostrand Reinhold, 1977.
Nardo, Don. *Anxiety and Phobias.* New York: Chelsea House, 1991.

# Gustav Theodor Fechner

**1801-1887**
German experimental psychologist who founded psychophysics and formulated Fechner's law, a landmark in the emergence of psychology as an experimental science.

Gustav Theodor Fechner was born on April 19, 1801, at Gross-Särchen, Lower Lusatia. He earned his degree in biological science in 1822 at the University of Leipzig and taught there until his death on Nov. 18, 1887. Having developed an interest in mathematics and physics, he was appointed professor of physics in 1834.

About 1839 Fechner had a breakdown, having injured his eyes while experimenting on afterimages by gazing at the sun. His response was to isolate himself from the world for three years. During this period there was an increase in his interest in philosophy. Fechner believed that everything is endowed with a soul; nothing is without a material basis; mind and matter are the same essence, but seen from different sides. Moreover, he believed that, by means of psychophysical experiments in psychology, the foregoing assertions were demonstrated and proved. He authored many books and monographs on such diverse subjects as medicine, esthetics, and **experimental psychology**, affixing the pseudonym Dr. Mises to some of them.

The ultimate philosophic problem which concerned Fechner, and to which his **psychophysics** was a solution, was the perennial mind-body problem. His solution has been called the identity hypothesis: mind and body are not regarded as a real dualism, but are different sides of

**Gustav Fechner** *(The Library of Congress. Reproduced with permission.)*

one reality. They are separated in the form of sensation and stimulus; that is, what appears from a subjective viewpoint as the mind, appears from an external or objective viewpoint as the body. In the expression of the equation of Fechner's law (sensation intensity = C log stimulus intensity), it becomes evident that the dualism is not real. While this law has been criticized as illogical, and for not having universal applicability, it has been useful in research on **hearing** and **vision**.

Fechner's most significant contribution was made in his *Elemente der Psychophysik* (1860), a text of the "exact science of the functional relations, or relations of dependency, between body and mind," and in his *Revision der Hauptpunkte der Psychophysik* (1882). Upon these works mainly rests Fechner's fame as a psychologist, for in them he conceived, developed, and established new methods of mental **measurement**, and hence the beginning of quantitative experimental psychology. The three methods of measurement were the method of just-noticeable differences, the method of constant stimuli, and the method of average error. According to the authorities, the method of constant stimuli, called also the method of right and wrong cases, has become the most important of the three methods. It was further developed by G. E. Müller and F. M. Urban.

**William James**, who did not care for quantitative analysis or the statistical approach in psychology, dismisses the psychophysic law as an "idol of the den," the psychological outcome of which is nothing. However, the verdict of other appraisers is kinder, for they honor Fechner as the founder of experimental psychology.

**Further Reading**
Brett, George Sidney. *History of psychology.* vol. 3. 1921.
Hall, G. Stanley. *Founders of modern psychology.* 1912.
Klemm, O. *History of psychology.* 1911. trans. 1914.
Ribot, T. *German psychology of today: the empirical school.* trans. 1886.

## Feral children

Lost or abandoned human children raised in extreme social isolation, either surviving in the wild through their own efforts or "adopted" by animals.

The study of children reared in complete or nearly complete isolation from human contact can provide important information to psychologists studying various aspects of **socialization**. After their return to human society, feral children often continue to be seriously retarded, raising the question of whether or not such children manifested abnormalities before their removal from society. Interest in wild or feral children dates back to Carl Linnaeus's 1758 classification of *loco ferus*—"feral" or "wolf" men, characterized as four-footed, nonspeaking, and hairy.

The most famous case of a human being surviving in total isolation for an extended period of time is that of Victor, the "wild boy of Aveyron," discovered in 1799. Lost or abandoned in **childhood**, he had apparently survived on his own in the wild up to the age of approximately 11. **Philippe Pinel**, the renowned director of the asylum at Bicêtre, France, declared Victor an incurable idiot, but Jean-Marc-Gaspard Itard, a physician and teacher of the deaf, undertook to educate him. Although he remained almost totally unable to speak, Victor showed great improvements in socialization and cognitive **ability** in the course of several years spent working with Itard. In 1807, Itard published *Rapports sur le sauvage de l'Aveyron (Reports on the Wild Boy of Aveyron)*, a classic work on human educability, detailing his work with Victor between the years 1801-05.

Unlike Victor, the young man named Kaspar Hauser who appeared in Nuremberg, Germany, in 1828 had apparently been locked up in isolation for an extended period, but without being totally deprived of human care. A 17-year-old with the mentality of a child of three, Hauser was reeducated over the next five years, regaining many of the faculties that had been stunted by extreme social and **sensory deprivation**, to the point where he could communicate verbally although his speech was substandard. After an earlier assassination attempt, Hauser was murdered in 1833, presumably by someone who sought to prevent his origins from becoming known.

Despite the persistence and popularity of stories about children reared by animals throughout history, well-documented cases of such children are very rare, and in most of these cases the documentation begins with the discovery of the child, so that virtually nothing is known about the time actually spent in the company of animals. In the best-known modern case of zoanthropy (humans living among animals), however, researchers did have some opportunities to observe the behavior of two children—the so-called Wolf Children of Midnapore—while they were in the company of wolves, actually removing them from the embrace of a pair of wolf cubs in order to take them back to society. Kamala and Amala, two young girls, were observed living with wolves in India in 1920, when Kamala was approximately eight years of age, and Amala about one and a half. Not only did they exhibit the physical behavior of wolves—running on all fours, eating raw meat, and staying active at night—they displayed physiological adaptations to their feral life, including modifications of the jaw resulting from chewing on bones. Taken to an orphanage run by J.A.L. Singh, the girls were cared for and exposed to human society. Amala, the younger one, died within two years, but Kamala achieved a modicum of socialization over the nine remaining years she lived.

The study of feral children has engaged some of the central philosophical and scientific controversies about human nature, including the nature/nurture debate as well as questions about which human activities require social instruction, whether or not there is a **critical period** for language acquisition, and to what extent can education compensate for delayed development and limited **intelligence**. Itard's pioneering work with the "wild boy of Aveyron" has had a profound impact on both education of the disabled and early childhood education. In 1909, the renowned Italian educator and physician **Maria Montessori** (1870-1952) wrote that she considered her own achievements a "summing up" of previous progress, giving Itard a prominent place among those whose work she saw herself as continuing.

*See also* Nature-nurture controversy

### Further Reading

Candland, Douglas Keith. *Feral Children and Clever Animals: Reflections on Human Nature.* New York: Oxford University Press, 1993.

Singh, Joseph. *Wolf Children and Feral Man.* Hamden, CT: Archon Books, 1966.

# Leon Festinger

**1919-1989**

American psychologist who developed the concept of cognitive dissonance.

Many people know that cigarettes cause cancer and other diseases, but nonetheless continue to smoke. This is an example of what Leon Festinger called cognitive dissonance—the idea that when conflict arises in one's belief system, the resulting tension must be eliminated. People going through **cognitive dissonance** will find some rationale for whatever is causing the conflict, or they may choose to ignore the event in question altogether. Festinger believed that people want balance in their lives and that cognitive dissonance was a way to bring back a lost sense of balance.

Festinger was born in New York City, on May 8, 1919, to Alex Festinger and Sara Solomon. Interested in science at a young age, he decided to pursue a career in psychology. He received his bachelor's degree from City College of New York and went on to Iowa State University for his master's degree and his Ph.D. (which he received in 1942). For the next several years he made his living teaching at different universities until he went to Stanford in 1955.

### Introduces theory of cognitive dissonance

At Stanford, Festinger began to fully develop the idea he called cognitive dissonance. The original idea stemmed from his observation that people generally liked consistency in their daily lives. For example, some individuals always sit in the same seat on the train or bus when they commute to work, or always eat lunch in the same restaurant. Cognitive dissonance is a part of this need for consistence. Essentially, Festinger explained, all people hold certain beliefs, and when they are asked to do something that runs counter to their beliefs, conflict arises. Cognitive dissonance comes into play when people try to reconcile the conflicting behaviors or ideas.

Festinger's research resulted in a number of interesting findings. One was that the level of cognitive dissonance would decrease as the incentive to comply with the conflict situation was increased. The reason was simple: where an incentive was involved, people felt less conflict. Festinger and his associates conducted a simple experiment to prove this point. College students were asked to perform a series of repetitive menial tasks for a specified period of time. As they finished, they were instructed that they had to inform the next group of students that the tasks had been enjoyable and interesting. Later, the subjects were asked to describe their true feelings about the task. Half the group was offered a $1 bill; the rest were offered a $20 bill. Subjects were asked afterward whether they really did find the tasks enjoyable. Interestingly, the students who had been paid one dollar stated that they actually did find the tasks enjoyable. There was little or no dissonance among the students who had been paid the $20, since, after all, they were well rewarded for their participation. The other students, however, had to justify having spent time doing useless tasks and getting only a dollar as a reward. They were the ones who were in a state of cognitive dissonance. By convincing themselves that the tasks they performed were not all that boring, they could rationalize having gone through what was essentially a waste of their time.

Cognitive dissonance soon became an important and much-discussed theory. Over the years it has generated considerable research, in part because it is one of a number of theories based on the idea that consistency of thought is a strong motivating factor in people.

### Continues research at the New School

Festinger continued his work at Stanford until 1968 when he returned to New York City to assume the Else and Hans Staudinger professorship at the New School for Social Research. He continued his research on cognitive dissonance as well as other behavioral issues. He was also active in professional organizations including the National Academy of Sciences and the American Academy of Arts and Sciences. He continued to work until his death on February 11, 1989, from liver cancer. He was survived by his wife Trudy and four children.

George A. Milite

**Further Reading**
Festinger, Leon. *The human legacy.* New York: Columbia University Press, 1983.
Festinger, Leon. *A theory of cognitive dissonance.* Stanford, CA: Stanford University Press, 1962.

# Fetal alcohol effect (FAE) and syndrome (FAS)

*The adverse and chronic effects of maternal alcohol abuse during pregnancy on her infant.*

The effects of heavy maternal alcohol use during pregnancy were first described as fetal alcohol syndrome (FAS) in the United States in 1973. An estimated one to three babies of every thousand births in the United States

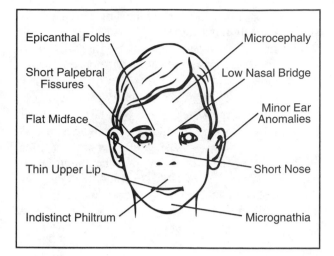

**Facial features of fetal alcohol syndrome.**

has FAS, making FAS the leading cause of **mental retardation**. It is also one of the few preventable causes of mental retardation and other **birth** defects. The U.S. Public Health Service estimates that between two and five of every thousand babies born in the United States exhibits one or more effects from fetal alcohol exposure. Although the precise amount of alcohol that must be consumed to cause damage is not known, it is believed that both heavy, consistent alcohol consumption and occasional binge drinking can produce FAS. In April 1997, the Centers for Disease Control and Prevention released the results of a study it had conducted in 1995. In a survey of 1,313 pregnant women, 3.5% said they "drank frequently" during pregnancy. (The agency defined "frequently" for the survey as having seven or more drinks per week, or binging on five or more drinks once within the previous month.)

Why some fetuses are affected and others are not is not completely understood. However, researchers believe that a combination of genetic and environmental factors work together to determine whether maternal alcohol consumption will affect the development of the fetus. Research has suggested that the genetic makeup of members of some racial and ethnic groups makes them less able to physically break down alcohol in the liver, and as a result, they are more susceptible to alcohol's adverse effects. When alcohol passes from the mother's bloodstream across the placenta to the developing fetus, the developing organs are unable to process it and thus are vulnerable to damage or arrested growth.

Women who drink heavily during pregnancy have a significantly higher risk of spontaneous **abortion** (known as miscarriage); their risk of miscarriage or stillbirth is at least twice that of nondrinkers. For the woman who carries the fetus to term (or near-term), researchers speculate that, in addition to genetic factors, her nutritional status and general health will affect her ability to tolerate alcohol. Due to these and other factors, an estimated 40% of women who drink heavily during pregnancy will give birth to an infant with FAS; all women who drink large amounts of alcohol during pregnancy risk giving birth to an infant with fetal alcohol effects (FAE). FAE describes the condition where the visible physical effects of alcohol are less pronounced than with FAS, but where the learning and psychosocial characteristics are still pronounced. Both FAS and FAE produce lifelong effects that can be managed and treated but not cured.

FAS encompasses a range of physical and mental birth defects:

- Prenatal growth retardation (low birth weight, length, and head circumference); may have difficulty **bonding** with caregiver

- Low Apgar scores at birth

- Postnatal growth retardation (failure to gain weight and develop normally); may show signs of **developmental delay**, such as delayed walking, poor coordination, delayed **language development**, and problems with toilet training. FAE/FAS toddlers may be prone to irritability and temper tantrums.

- Intellectual and **attention** deficiencies

- Behavioral problems; may exhibit antisocial behaviors, such as arson, shoplifting, lying, defiance of authority, and destructiveness. FAS/FAE adolescents often become involved in inappropriate or unsafe sexual situations, brought about by physical maturity and emotional immaturity.

- Skull or **brain** malformations.

Distinctive facial features may include:

- Small head (microcephaly)

- Small eyes with folds in the skin near the nose (epicanthal folds) and short horizontal eye openings (palpebral fissures)

- Underdevelopment of the upper lip with flat philtrum (ridges extending vertically between the upper lip and nose)

- Small jaw (micrognathia).

FAS/FAE is a lifelong condition that, depending on its severity, will limit the individual's ability to function productively in the world. Early diagnosis and intervention with support and education services are the keys to success in social and vocational settings.

### Further Reading

Blume, Sheila B. *What You Can Do to Prevent Fetal Alcohol Syndrome: A Professional's Guide.* Minneapolis: Johnson Institute, 1992.

Dorris, Michael. *The Broken Cord.* New York: Harper and Row, 1989.

*Fetal Alcohol Syndrome (FAS) and Effects: What's the Difference?* Evanston, IL: Altschul Group, 1989. (For information: 1-800-421-2363) (One 24-minute videocassette.)

McCuen, Gary E., ed. *Born Hooked: Poisoned in the Womb.* 2nd ed. Hudson, WI: G.E. McCuen Publications, 1994.

"More Women Report Alcohol Use in Pregnancy." *New York Times,* (April 25, 1997): A13.

Nevitt, Amy. *Fetal Alcohol Syndrome.* New York: Rosen Publishing Group, 1996.

Steinmetz, George. "The Preventable Tragedy, Fetal Alcohol Syndrome." *National Geographic Magazine,* vol. 11, no 2, (February 1992): 36-39.

Stratton, Kathleen, Cynthia Howe, and Frederick Battaglia. *Fetal Alcohol Syndrome: Diagnosis, Epidemiology, Prevention, and Treatment.* Washington, D.C.: National Academy Press, 1997.

# Figure-ground perception

The ability to differentiate visually between an object and its background.

A person's **ability** to separate an object from its surrounding visual field is referred to as figure-ground perception. The object that a person focuses on is called the figure; everything else is referred to as background, or simply ground.

Psychologists have created different kinds of stimuli in order to study how people separate figure from ground. In some cases, these stimuli involve simple ambiguous figures like the famous face-vase figure that can be interpreted as two faces looking at one another or a goblet, depending on what aspect a person focuses on. In other situations, complex stimuli can be used to demonstrate figure-ground relationships. For example, the 3-D Magic Eye pictures involve relaxing the muscles of the eyes to see a three-dimensional figure-ground picture. Until a viewer positions the eyes appropriately, the stimulus is invisible; when the eye muscles are appropriately relaxed, the three-dimensional figure emerges. Easily distracted children are often unable to focus on one object as they ignore or block out the background.

The interpretations that people derive from these stimuli are real, even though the objects are ambiguous or are nonexistent. A good example of this involves illusory or subjective contours. In the illustration, people will see an entire square, complete with borders (contours), even though the borders do not really exist.

Psychologists have also demonstrated figure-ground principles with auditory stimuli. For example, some people have claimed that there are satanic or otherwise harmful lyrics embedded backwards in some rock music. In most cases, when people first listen to the music backwards, they hear absolutely nothing that resembles speech. When somebody tells them to listen for particular words or phrases, however, people report **hearing** satanic words. As with illusory contours, the words are not really there until someone's **attention** is focused appropriately on a particular set of sounds.

### Further Reading

Dance, Sandy. *Picture Interpretation: A Symbolic Approach.* River Edge, NJ: World Scientific, 1995.

Pavel, Monique. *Fundamentals of Pattern Recognition 2nd ed.* New York: M. Dekker, 1993.

## Fine motor skills

Skills involving control of the fingers, hands, and arms.

Fine motor skill involves deliberate and controlled movements requiring both muscle development and maturation of the **central nervous system**. Although newborn infants can move their hands and arms, these motions are **reflexes** that a baby cannot consciously start or stop. The development of fine motor skills is crucial to an infant's **ability** to experience and learn about the world and thus plays a central role in the development of **intelligence**. Like **gross motor skills**, fine motor skills develop in an orderly progression, but at an uneven pace characterized by both rapid spurts and, at times, frustrating but harmless delays. In most cases, difficulty with certain fine motor skills is temporary and does not indicate a serious problem. However, medical help should be sought if a child is significantly behind his peers in multiple aspects of fine motor development or if he regresses, losing previously acquired skills.

### Infancy

The hands of a newborn infant are closed most of the time and, like the rest of her body, she has little control over them. If her palm is touched, she will make a very tight fist, but this is an **unconscious** reflex action called the Darwinian reflex, and it disappears within two to three months. Similarly, the infant will grasp at an object placed in her hand, but without any awareness that she is doing so. At some point her hand muscles will relax, and she will drop the object, equally unaware that she has let it fall. Babies may begin flailing at objects that interest them by two weeks of age but cannot grasp them. By eight weeks, they begin to discover and **play**

with their hands, at first solely by **touch**, and then, at about three months, by sight as well. At this age, however, the deliberate grasp remains largely undeveloped.

**Hand-eye coordination** begins to develop between the ages of 2 and 4 months, inaugurating a period of trial-and-error practice at sighting objects and grabbing at them. At four or five months, most infants can grasp an object that is within reach, looking only at the object and not at their hands. Referred to as "top-level reaching," this achievement is considered an important milestone in fine motor development. At the age of six months, infants can typically hold on to a small block briefly, and many have started banging objects. Although their grasp is still clumsy, they have acquired a fascination with grabbing small objects and trying to put them in their mouths. At first, babies will indiscriminately try to grasp things that cannot be grasped, such as pictures in a book, as well as those that can, such as a rattle or ball. During the latter half of the first year, they begin exploring and testing objects before grabbing, touching them with an entire hand and, eventually, poking them with an index finger.

One of the most significant fine motor accomplishments is the pincer grip, which typically appears between the ages of 12 and 15 months. Initially, an infant can only hold an object, such as a rattle, in his palm, wrapping his fingers (including the thumb) around it from one side, an awkward position called the palmar grasp, which makes it difficult to hold on to and manipulate the object. By the age of eight to ten months, a finger grasp begins, but objects can only be gripped with all four fingers pushing against the thumb, which still makes it awkward to grab small objects. The development of the pincer grip—the ability to hold objects between the thumb and index finger—gives the infant a more sophisticated ability to grasp and manipulate objects, and also to deliberately drop them. By about the age of one, an infant can drop an object into a receptacle, compare objects held in both hands, stack objects, and nest them within each other.

### Toddlerhood

Toddlers develop the ability to manipulate objects with increasing sophistication, including using their fingers to twist dials, pull strings, push levers, turn book pages, and use crayons to produce crude scribbles. Dominance of either the right or left hand usually emerges during this period as well. Toddlers also add a new dimension to touching and manipulating objects by simultaneously being able to name them. Instead of only random scribbles, their drawings include patterns, such as circles. Their play with blocks is more elaborate and purposeful than that of infants, and they can stack as many as six blocks. They are also able to fold a sheet of paper in half (with supervision), string large beads, manipulate snap toys, play with clay, unwrap small objects, and pound pegs.

### Preschool

The more delicate tasks facing preschool children, such as handling silverware or tying shoelaces, represent more of a challenge than most of the gross motor activities learned during this period of development. The central nervous system is still in the process of maturing sufficiently for complex messages from the **brain** to get to the child's fingers. In addition, small muscles tire more easily than large ones, and the short, stubby fingers of preschoolers make delicate or complicated tasks more difficult. Finally, gross motor skills call for energy, which is boundless in preschoolers, while fine motor skills require patience, which is in shorter supply. Thus, there is considerable variation in fine motor development among this age group.

By the age of three, many children have good control of a pencil. Three-year-olds can often draw a circle, although their attempts at drawing people are still very primitive. It is common for four-year-olds to be able to use scissors, copy geometric shapes and letters, button large buttons, and form clay shapes with two or three parts. Some can print their own names in capital letters. A human figure drawn by a four-year-old is typically a head atop two legs with one arm radiating from each leg.

### School age

By the age of five, most children have clearly advanced beyond the fine motor skill development of the preschool age. They can draw recognizably human figures with facial features and legs connected to a distinct trunk. Besides drawing, five-year-olds can also cut, paste, and trace shapes. They can fasten visible buttons (as opposed to those at the back of clothing), and many can tie bows, including shoelace bows. Their right- or left- **handedness** is well established, and they use the preferred hand for writing and drawing.

### Encouraging fine motor development

Encouraging gross motor skills requires a safe, open play space, peers to interact with, and some adult supervision. Nurturing the development of fine motor skills is considerably more complicated. Helping a child succeed in fine motor tasks requires planning, time, and a variety of play materials. Fine motor development can be encouraged by activities that youngsters enjoy, including

This six-month-old has mastered the fine motor skills necessary for picking up an object and guiding it to her mouth. *(Patrick Donehue. Photo Researchers, Inc. Reproduced with permission.)*

crafts, puzzles, and playing with building blocks. Helping parents with everyday domestic activities, such as baking, can be fun for the child in addition to developing fine motor skills. For example, stirring batter provides a good workout for the hand and arm muscles, and cutting and spooning out cookie dough requires hand-eye coordination. Even a computer keyboard and mouse can provide practice in finger, hand, and hand-eye coordination. Because the development of fine motor skills plays a crucial role in school readiness and **cognitive development**, it is considered an important part of the preschool curriculum. The Montessori schools, in particular, were early leaders in emphasizing the significance of fine motor tasks and the use of learning aids such as pegboards and puzzles in early **childhood** education. The development of fine motor skills in children of low-income parents, who often lack the time or knowledge required to foster these abilities, is a key ingredient in the success of programs such as Head Start.

*See also* Gross motor skills

**Further Reading**

Eckert, Helen M. *Motor Development.* 3rd ed. Indianapolis, IN: Benchmark Press, 1987.

Lerch, Harold A., and Christine B. Stopka. *Developmental Motor Activities for All Children: From Theory to Practice.* Dubuque, IA: Brown and Benchmark, 1992.

Thomas, Jerry R., ed. *Motor Development in Childhood and Adolescence.* Minneapolis: Burgess Publishing Co., 1984.

# Fixation

An intense psychological association with a past event or series of events that triggers certain feelings or behaviors in a person when confronted with similar events or series of events.

**Sigmund Freud** theorized that the developmental stages of **infancy** and early **childhood** chart our lives in ways that are difficult to change. He believed that most adult neuroses could be attributed to a fixation developed during one of these stages of early life. Freud was especially concerned about how these stages were related to sexual development in later life, and in this he was, and continues to be, quite controversial. In his time, it was considered by many to be outlandish that an infant sucking on her mother's breast was experiencing sexual gratification, yet Freud classified it as such and composed a theory of psychosexual development.

Freud's theory of psychosexual development suggests that children pass through several stages in their earliest years. These stages are the oral stage, the anal stage, the phallic stage, the latency stage, and genital stage. During each stage, children learn to gratify themselves (Freud would say sexually) via distinct patterns of behavior. During the oral stage, for instance, children learn that the highest level of physical gratification occurs through oral stimulation. (They feed by sucking, they routinely place objects in their mouths, etc.) It was Freud's view that during any one of these stages a person could become fixated—that is, they could be so gratified or, on the other hand, so unfulfilled, that they are marked for life by this fixation. Someone who has a fixation at the oral stage of development, for instance, might suck his or her thumb, eat or drink excessively, chew pencils, or smoke cigarettes. Adults fixated during this period of development are also thought to be inclined toward clinging, dependent relationships. Those fixated during the anal phase of psychosexual development are typically thought of as being overly controlling and obsessed with neatness or cleanliness.

Freud also considered regression closely linked to fixation. In his famous *Introductory Lectures on Psycho-Analysis,* he spoke of human development as a journey into new territory, much like an early migration of primitive peoples into new territory. He states that as people migrated into new, unexplored territory, certain members of the party might stop along the way at a place that offered them the prospect of a good life. These stopping points would be analogous to the fixations people develop in early life, attaching themselves to a period of safety and security before the entire journey of life is fully accomplished.

**Further Reading**

Freud, Sigmund. *Introductory Lectures on Psycho-Analysis.* New York: W.W. Norton & Co., 1966.

# John Hurley Flavell

### 1928-
American developmental and cognitive psychologist known for his studies of role-taking in children.

John Hurley Flavell is a founder of social cognitive **developmental psychology**. His research on "role-taking," the cognitive skills that children require in order to understand and accept the roles of others, was a major contribution to developmental psychology. Flavell was one of the first psychologists to study the ways in which children think about their thinking processes and the human mind. He is the author of more than 120 books and articles and was an advisory editor of the journal *Cognitive Psychology.* In 1984, Flavell received the Distinguished Scientific Contribution Award of the **American Psychological Association (APA)**. He is the Anne T. and Robert M. Bass Professor in the School of Humanities and Sciences at Stanford University.

Flavell was born in 1928 in Rockland, Massachusetts, the son of Paul I. and Anne O'Brien Flavell. His father was a civil engineer who was unemployed for a long period during the Great Depression. Thus, Flavell and his two sisters experienced economic hardship during **childhood**. After graduating from high school in 1945, Flavell joined the Army for two years. He then attended Northeastern University in Boston and graduated in 1951. Because of financial considerations, Flavell chose to enter the psychology graduate program at Clark University in Worcester, Massachusetts, rather than Harvard University. He earned his M.A. degree the following year and his Ph.D. in 1955. Flavell's training at Clark stressed **psychoanalysis** and the developmental psychology of Heinz Werner. In 1954, Flavell married Eleanor R. Wood, who would share his research interests throughout much of his career. The couple have two children.

## Introduces Piaget into American psychology

Flavell's first position was as a clinical psychologist at a Veterans Administration Hospital in Colorado. However he left there a year later to accept a position at the University of Rochester in New York, first as a clinical associate and then as an assistant professor of psychology. He was promoted to associate professor in 1960. Although Flavell first undertook to write a book on theories of developmental psychology, he soon switched to a major study of the work of **Jean Piaget**, publishing *The Developmental Psychology of Jean Piaget* in 1963. This was the first major work in English on the research and theories of Piaget and marked the start of the modern science of **cognitive development**. That same year, Flavell traveled to Paris for additional studies at the Sorbonne.

Flavell's research at Rochester focused on children's understanding of the roles of others and on children's communication skills and developing **memory** skills. He first evaluated the skills needed for role-taking, the understanding of what another person sees, knows, needs, and intends to do. He found that children whose parents talk to them often about emotions and feelings develop these skills at an earlier age. In 1965, he moved to the Institute of Child Development at the University of Minnesota as a professor of psychology. There he continued his work on the cognitive development of children. While researching the development of memory skills in children, Flavell found that children need to understand the concept of memory before they can develop skills for utilizing and improving memory. He called this knowledge "metamemory."

Flavell was president of the APA's Division of Developmental Psychology in 1970. In 1976, he became a professor of psychology at Stanford University. There he continued his involvement with professional organizations. He served as president of the Society for Research in Child Development from 1979 to 1981. In 1986 Flavell was presented with the G. Stanley Hall Award of the APA.

## Studies metacognition in children

Since his arrival at Stanford, Flavell and his long-time research associates, his wife, Ellie Flavell, and Frances L. Greene, have studied preschoolers at the Bing Nursery School on the Stanford campus. They have also studied elementary-school and college students. In recent years, Flavell has researched and developed his theory of "metacognition" or "metaconsciousness," which is a child's understanding about the workings of the human mind and her own thought processes. In 1995, the Flavells and Greene published *Young Children's Knowledge about Thinking*. In their research, they have found that preschoolers understand that thinking is a human, mental activity and that it can involve things that are in the past or in the present, real or imaginary. They distinguish thinking from other activities such as talking, feeling, seeing, or knowing. However preschoolers greatly underestimate the amount that they and others think, and they have difficulty perceiving that other people think. In other words, Flavell has found that, although preschoolers know that rocks do not think, they also don't believe that their parents think all that much.

Throughout his career, Flavell's books have received critical acclaim for both their scholarship and their lively and entertaining prose. Flavell is on the editorial board of the *Journal of Cognition and Development* and continues to teach and advise students.

Margaret Alic

### Further Reading

Coombs, Karen. "John Flavell: 'The Development of Children's Knowledge About the Mind'." *The Bing Times* (June 1994). http://www.stanford.edu/dept/bingschool/rsrchart/flavell1.htm.

Flavell, John H. *Cognitive Development*. Englewood Cliffs, NJ: Prentice-Hall, 1977. 3rd ed. with Patricia A. Miller and Scott A. Miller, 1993.

Flavell, John H., Frances L. Green, and Eleanor R. Flavell. "Development of Children's Awareness of Their Own Thoughts." *Journal of Cognition and Development* 1 (2000): 97.

"Preschoolers Don't Think Much About Thinking." *Stanford News* (1 January 1994). http://www.stanford.edu/dept/news/relaged/940101Arc4532.html.

Rai, Deepa. "Interview with Professor John Flavell." *The Bing Times* (December 1995). http://www.stanford.edu/dept/bingschool/rsrchart/flavell2.htm.

# Forensic psychology

The application of psychology to lawmaking, law enforcement, the examination of witnesses, and the treatment of the criminal; also known as legal psychology.

Forensic psychologists often work within the judicial system in such diverse areas as determining an inmate's readiness for parole; evaluation of **rehabilitation** programs; criminal competency; tort liability and damages; eyewitness testimony and evidence; jury selection; and police training. Forensic psychology may also be employed in other areas of jurisprudence, including patent and trademark disputes, **divorce** and custody cases, product liability, and taxation.

Forensic psychologists advise their clients in several ways, including diagnostic appraisals, which may be used to determine the competency of the client to stand trial, and contributing to defense strategy. They are also called upon to render clinically based opinions on a wide variety of issues arising from their diagnoses, such as the best interests of a child in a custody case, or the readiness of a prisoner for parole. Finally, forensic psychologists advise on the prognosis and treatment of the individuals under evaluation. In most cases, they obtain a "forensic history," which includes hospital records, police reports, witness statements, and provide relevant research. Besides submitting reports on their findings, they are sometimes required to testify in court.

In a typical criminal case, the forensic psychologist may be hired by a defense attorney to evaluate the defendant. (A case will commonly entail the services of a psychologist, for example, if an **insanity defense** is being considered.) The psychologist is briefed on the circumstances of the crime and examines records detailing the defendant's previous criminal record and any history of mental or emotional problems and treatment. In pretrial preparations, the psychologist may administer **personality** and **intelligence** tests to the defendant. Afterwards, the psychologist reports the evaluation findings to the attorney and may be asked to testify at pretrial hearings, the trial itself, or the sentencing.

The most common type of civil case in which a psychologist may be consulted are lawsuits to recover damages for injuries resulting from car accidents. The first task is to become familiarized with the case, which includes an examination of the client's medical records relating to the accident, as well as his or her previous medical history and any records that indicate the client's level of functioning at work or in other settings prior to the accident. The psychologist must then evaluate the plaintiff's emotional or cognitive problems, being careful to distinguish those problems caused by the accident from any preexisting ones.

Forensic psychologists are regularly consulted in child custody cases. In many situations it is the court itself that hires a psychologist to evaluate both parents, children, and other relevant **family** members. These evaluations may involve visits to the home of each parent, which provide additional information on the relationship between parent and child and on a child's possi-ble future **environment**. Such interviews, by their relatively informal nature, serve to facilitate communication with the child.

In addition to providing expert consultation on a contractual basis, forensic psychologists are also employed by community **mental health** centers, police departments, and prisons. They may train police officers to handle diverse situations like domestic abuse, suicide threats, and hostage crises, and how to control crowds. Those who work in prisons provide clinical services to inmates. In addition to the applied work performed by forensic psychologists in these and other settings, some members of the field specialize solely in research, investigating areas such as eyewitness and expert testimony, jury selection, and the jury decision process.

Regardless of specialty, forensic psychologists must be familiar with relevant case law, respect issues of confidentiality, and continually keep apprised of new research in the field. Joint Ph.D.-J.D. programs have been in existence since the early 1970s. It is also possible to earn a Ph.D. in psychology with a specialization in forensic or correctional psychology, and the curricula of graduate programs in psychology include a growing number of law-related courses.

Organizations for forensic psychologists include the American Association for Correctional Psychology and the American Psychology-Law Society. Forensic Psychology has had its own division in the **American Psychological Association** since 1980 (Division 4). The American Board of Forensic Psychology has provided referrals to qualified professionals in the field since its establishment in 1978 as well as promoting the discipline of forensic psychology to the general public. The Board certifies practitioners who have amassed at least 1,000 hours of experience within a five-year period. Applicants must also submit a work sample and undergo a three-hour examination administered by their peers.

## Further Reading

Cooke, Gerald, ed. *The Role of the Forensic Psychologist.* Springfield, IL: Thomas, 1980.

*Criminal Justice and Behavior.* Volume 1-, March 1974- .

*Law and Human Behavior.* Volume 1-, 1977- .

Lipsitt, Paul D. and Dennis Sales. *New Directions in Psycholegal Research.* New York: Van Nostrand Reinhold, 1980.

Schwitzgebel, Robert L., and R. Kirkland Schwitzgebel. *Law and Psychological Practice.* New York: Wiley, 1980.

## Further Information

American Association for Correctional Psychology (Formerly: American Association of Correctional Psychologists). West Virginia University, College of Graduate Studies Institute, Morgantown, West Virginia 25112, (304) 766–1929.

American Psychology-Law Society. University of Massachusetts Medical Center, Department of Psychology, 55 Lake Avenue N., Worcester, Massachusetts 01655, (508) 856–3625.

# Forgetting curve

The general, predictable pattern of the process of forgetting learned information.

Psychologists have been interested in the processes of learning and forgetting since the early days of the discipline. The researcher who pioneered this field, **Hermann Ebbinghaus** (1850-1909), invented the nonsense syllable in order to be able to assess "pure" learning, that is, learning free of meaning, and the rate at which we forget. He served as his own subject and learned an incredible number of lists of nonsense syllables. He used material with little or no meaning because he was aware that learning new information is influenced by what we already know. He decided to create learning situations that were free of prior knowledge.

The way that we forget is highly predictable, following what psychologists call the forgetting curve. When we acquire knowledge, much of our forgetting occurs right away. Ebbinghaus discovered that a significant amount of information was forgotten within twenty minutes of learning; over half of the nonsense material he learned was forgotten within an hour. Although he forgot within a day almost two thirds of the material he learned, retention of the material did not decline much beyond that period. In other words, if information is retained for a day, the knowledge was there to stay.

Ebbinghaus's forgetting curve is actually much more dramatic than a forgetting curve would be for meaningful material. When the learner is able to connect new information with old information, he still might forget what was learned, but the amount and speed of forgetting is likely to be less than what Ebbinghaus experienced.

*See also* Ebbinghaus, Hermann

# Viktor E. Frankl

**1905-1997**
Jewish psychiatrist and author who developed the discipline of logotherapy.

Born March 26, 1905, in Vienna, Austria-Hungary (present-day Austria); died September 2, 1997, in Vi-

**Viktor Frankl** *(DIZ Munchen GmbH. Reproduced with permission.)*

enna, Austria, of heart failure. Viktor E. Frankl, a Jewish psychiatrist and author, drew on his experiences as a survivor of the Holocaust (Nazi Germany's campaign to exterminate the Jewish population of Europe during World War II) to develop the discipline of logotherapy, a form of **psychotherapy** that, by stressing the need to find meaning even in the most tragic circumstances, offered solace to millions of readers of his classic work, *Man's Search for Meaning: An Introduction to Logotherapy.*

Frankl grew up in Vienna, the birthplace of modern psychiatry and home of the renowned psychiatrists **Sigmund Freud** and **Alfred Adler**. A brilliant student, Frankl became interested in psychiatry in his teens. At age 16 he began writing to Freud, and on one occasion sent him a short paper, which Freud regarded so highly that he passed it on to the *International Journal of Psychoanalysis,* where it was published three years later. Frankl earned a medical degree from the University of Vienna in 1930 and was put in charge of a Vienna hospital ward for the treatment of females who had attempted suicide. When Germany seized control of Austria eight years later, the Nazis made Frankl head of the Rothschild Hospital, the only Jewish hospital that was allowed to remain open in Vienna.

After taking power in Austria, the Nazis began removing the Jews of Vienna to the death camps that had been set up in Eastern Europe. Frankl was deported to the Theresienstadt camp near Prague in January 1942, one month after marrying Mathilde Grosser. He was later sent to the Auschwitz camp in Poland, where the camp doctor, Josef Mengele, was supervising the division of the incoming prisoners into two lines. Those in the line moving left were to go to the gas chambers, while those in the line moving right were to be spared. Frankl was directed to join the line moving left, but managed to save his life by slipping into the other line without being noticed. Other members of his family were not so fortunate, however, and by war's end Frankl had lost his pregnant wife, his parents, and a brother.

Before the war Frankl had begun to develop a theory that psychological health depends on finding meaning in one's life. The death camps, he wrote, confirmed his initial insights in a fashion he could never have anticipated. In the camps one lost everything, he once commented as quoted by Holcomb B. Noble in the *New York Times,* except "the last of the human freedoms, to choose one's attitude in any given set of circumstances, to choose one's own way." Prisoners who allowed themselves to be overwhelmed by despair, who gave up their freedom to choose, often descended into paralytic apathy and **depression**. The key to helping such people was to show them how they could find meaning even in the face of unimaginable horror. Meaning might consist of holding onto pleasant memories, or helping other prisoners turn away from **suicide**. Every prisoner had a moral choice to make: to surrender one's inner self to the Nazis, or to find the meaning in one's life that would give one the strength to go on.

On returning to Vienna after Germany's defeat in 1945, Frankl, who had secretly been keeping a record of his observations in the camps on scraps of paper taken from the Nazis, published a book in German setting out his ideas on logotherapy (a term derived from the Greek word for "meaning"). This was translated into English in 1959, and in a revised and enlarged edition appeared as *Man's Search for Meaning: An Introduction to Logotherapy* in 1963. By the time of his death, Frankl's book had been translated into 24 languages and reprinted 73 times and had long been used as a standard text in high school and university courses in psychology, philosophy, and theology. According to the *Los Angeles Times,* Frankl's theory of a psychotherapy that emphasized "the will to meaning" was described as "the Third Vienna School of Psychotherapy," the first being Freud's, which emphasized "the will to pleasure," and the second being Adler's, which emphasized "the will to power." It exerted an important influence on psychiatrists of varying theoretical perspectives, who often recommended Frankl's book to despairing patients who could find no value in their lives.

In 1947, after confirming that his first wife had died in the camps, Frankl married Eleonore Schwindt, who survived him, as did a daughter, Dr. Gabrielle Frankl-Vesely. Frankl's postwar career was spent as a professor of neurology and psychiatry in Vienna, where he taught until he was 85. He was also chief of neurology at the Vienna Polyclinic Hospital for 25 years. Frankl received numerous honorary doctorates, wrote over 30 books, became the first non-American to be awarded the **American Psychiatric Association**'s prestigious Oskar Pfister Prize, and was a visiting professor at Harvard, Stanford, and other universities. His hobbies included mountain climbing, and at 67 he obtained his pilot's license.

Frankl's message that "man is capable of defying and braving even the worst conditions conceivable," as quoted in the *Chicago Tribune,* resonated with people around the world. In a 1991 survey of general-interest readers conducted by the Library of Congress and the Book of the Month Club, *Man's Search for Meaning* was ranked among the ten books that had most influenced the respondents. For them, and for millions of others, Frankl's writings were an inspiration and a reminder that it is "essential to keep practicing the art of living," as quoted by Noble, even when life seems most hopeless.

Howard Baker

## Further Reading

*Chicago Tribune*, http://www.chicago.tribune.com (September 4, 1997)

*Los Angeles Times*, http://www.latimes.com (September 4, 1997)

*New York Times*, http://www.nytimes.com (September 4, 1997)

*Times (London)*, http://www.the-times.co.uk (September 30, 1997).

"Viktor E(mil)Frankl," *Contemporary Authors*, http://galenet.gale.com (November 10, 1997)

*Washington Post*, September 4, 1997, p. B06.

# Waldo David Frank

### 1889-1967
American author and activist whose ideology influenced many intellectuals.

Once considered among the most influential of twentieth-century intellectuals, Waldo Frank is now largely forgotten. This is not for lack of writings; Frank

local paper. Upon graduation, he wrote some pieces for the *New York Times*, traveled through Europe for a year, and tried unsuccessfully to launch a literary magazine.

In his novels Frank tended to advocate social and political reform. His novels include *Unwelcome Man* (1917), *City Block* (1922), and *The Death and Birth of David Markand* (1934). Frank, who described himself as a "naturalistic mystic," was an admirer of Freud, and in many of his works he injected his own understanding of **psychoanalysis**. Thus, although not a psychoanalyst himself, he was able to help popularize analysis through his works. Books on politics by Frank include *The Rediscovery of America* (1929), *America Hispania* (1931), *Birth of the World* (1951), and *The Prophetic Island: A Portrait of Cuba* (1961).

Frank had one son with Naumburg and two children with his second wife, Alma Magoon (whom he married in 1927). By the time he died in January 1967, he was largely forgotten in the United States, although his works and theories flourished in other countries, especially in South America.

George A. Milite

**Further Reading**
*Current Biography, 1940*. New York: H.W. Wilson Co., 1940.

**Waldo Frank** *(AP/Wide World Photos. Reproduced with permission.)*

wrote 14 novels, 18 volumes of social history, and numerous articles for literary and political magazines. During the 1920s, Frank was part of an artistic circle that included such artists as Alfred Stieglitz, Van Wyck Brooks, Countee Cullen, and Jean Toomer. His first wife (1916-1924) was Margaret Naumburg, who pioneered **art therapy**. He was particularly admired in Spain, France, and Latin America, where his writings are still well known.

Waldo David Frank was born in Long Branch, New Jersey, on August 25, 1889. His parents, Julius and Helen Rosenberg Frank, provided their son with a comfortable existence in which his intellectual curiosity was stimulated. A voracious reader, he was expelled from his high school in his senior year for refusing to take a required course on Shakespeare because he felt that he knew more about Shakespeare than the teacher did. At around the same time he completed his first novel, which was never published.

After a year in boarding school in Switzerland, Frank enrolled at Yale University, where he graduated with a combined bachelor's and master's degree in 1911. During his years at Yale, Frank became attracted to radical ideas and contributed to socialist journals such as *The Liberator* and *New Masses*. He also wrote a drama column for the

# Free association

One of the basic techniques of classic psychoanalysis in which the patient says everything that comes to mind without editing or censoring.

The use of free association was pioneered by **Sigmund Freud**, the founder of **psychoanalysis**, after he became dissatisfied with the hypnosis-based "cathartic" treatment of hysterical symptoms practiced by his colleague **Josef Breuer** (1842-1925), through which patients were able to recall traumatic experiences while under **hypnosis** and express the original emotions that had been repressed and forgotten. Freud found the limitations of hypnosis unsatisfactory and began the task of finding another similarly cathartic treatment method. By the late 1890s, he had worked out the essential components of his system of psychoanalysis, including the use of free association as a method of exploring the **unconscious**, identifying repressed memories and the reasons for their repression, and enabling patients to know themselves more fully. The patient, relaxed on a couch in his office, was directed to engage in a free association of ideas that could yield useful insights and to reveal frankly whatever came to mind. Freud, seated behind the patient, would listen to and interpret these associations.

For free association to be effective, it is important for the patient to share his or her thoughts freely without regard to whether they are logical, consistent, or socially appropriate. Even thoughts that seem trivial, bizarre, or embarrassing should be reported without hesitation. Initially, free association can be difficult, because people are accustomed to editing their thoughts, presenting them in a logical, linear fashion, and leaving out potentially embarrassing material. However, the technique becomes more comfortable with practice and with encouragement by the therapist. The more closely the patient can replicate his or her stream of **consciousness**, the more likely it is that defenses will be lowered and repressed material brought to light. Besides the content of the thoughts themselves, the connections between them may also offer important information to the therapist.

### Further Reading
Freud, Sigmund. *An Outline of Psychoanalysis*. New York: W.W. Norton, 1989.

## Free-recall learning

The presentation of material to the learner with the subsequent task of recalling as much as possible about the material without any cues.

A typical experiment involving the use of words as stimuli may include unrelated or related words, single or multiple presentations of the words, and single or multiple tests involving **memory**. In a free-recall test, the learner organizes the information by memory, and the process of recall often reveals the mental processes that the learner uses. For example, words positioned at the beginning and the end of a list are most likely to be remembered, a phenomenon called the serial position effect. Further, any unusual stimuli have a greater chance of being recalled, a phenomenon called the von Restorff effect.

Learners tend to organize related material in ways that enhance recall. One process, clustering, involves placing words that are associated with one another in one "location" in memory. The advantage of clustering is that recall is easier because the person can search one mental "location" and find several stimuli. The disadvantage of this strategy is that people may erroneously think that certain stimuli occurred because they are associated with the clustered items. Such falsely remembered words are referred to as intrusions.

As a rule, an individual can remember an average of about seven stimuli in a typical free recall task. This generally translates into a total of five to nine items. Psychologists refer to the "magic number seven, plus or minus two," as the amount that people can remember without engaging in **rehearsal** or other memory-enhancing tactics. Researchers have discovered that people can recall about seven items, but the "items" are not limited to words. If given a list of book titles, for example, a learner might be able to recall about seven titles, even though each title consists of multiple words. The critical element is the number of meaningful units, not simply the number of words. If the learners have to recall the stimuli in the same order in which they were presented, the results are less successful than if the learners can retrieve the stimuli in their own preferred order.

## Frequency (auditory)

Technical definition of the range of sounds audible to humans.

Humans can detect sound waves with frequencies that vary from approximately 20 to 20,000 Hz. Probably of greatest interest to psychologists are the frequencies around 500-2,000 Hz, the range in which sounds important to speech typically occur. Humans are most responsive to sounds between 1,000 and 5,000 Hz, and are not likely to hear very low or very high frequencies unless they are fairly intense. For example, the average person is approximately 100 times more sensitive to a sound at 3,000 Hz than to one at 100 Hz. People can best differentiate between two similar pitches when they are between 1,000 and 5,000 Hz.

The relationship between frequency and pitch is predictable but not always simple. That is, as frequency increases, pitch becomes higher. At the same time, if the frequency is doubled, the resulting sound does not have a pitch twice as high. In fact, if one listens to a sound at a given frequency, then a second sound at twice the frequency, the pitch would have increased by one octave in pitch. Each doubling of frequencies involves a one-octave change, for example, the Middle C note on a piano has a frequency of 261.2; the C note one octave higher is 522.4, a change of 261.2 Hz. The next C note on the piano has a frequency of 1046.4 Hz, or a change of 523.2 Hz.

When an individual hears a complex sound consisting of many different wavelengths, such as a human voice, music, and most sounds in nature, the ear separates the sound into its different frequencies. This separation begins in the inner ear, specifically the basilar membrane within the cochlea. The basilar membrane is a strip of tissue that is wide at one end and narrow at the other. When the ear responds to a low frequency sound, the entire length of the basilar membrane vibrates; for a high frequency sound, the movement of the membrane is more restricted to locations nearer the narrow end. Thus, a person can hear the different frequencies (and their associated pitches) as separate sounds.

The **ability** to hear declines with age, although the loss is greatest for high frequency sounds. At age 70, for example, sensitivity to sounds at 1,000 Hz is maintained, whereas sensitivity to sounds at 8,000 Hz is markedly diminished. As many as 75 percent of people over 70 years of age have experienced some deterioration in their **hearing**.

# Frequency distribution

Systematic representation of data, arranged so that the observed frequency of occurrence of data falling within certain ranges, classes, or categories, is shown.

When data is presented in a frequency distribution, the objective is to show the number of times a particular value or range of values occurs. Common forms of presentation of frequency distribution include the frequency polygon, the bar graph, and the frequency curve, which associate a number (the frequency) with each range, class, or category of data. A grouped frequency distribution is a kind of frequency distribution in which groups of ranges, classes, or categories are presented. Grouped frequency distributions are generally used when the number of different ranges, classes, or categories is large. A cumulative frequency distribution is a representation in which each successive division includes all of the items in previous divisions (so that, for example, the last division includes all of the data in the entire distribution). A probability distribution is similar to a frequency distribution, except that in a probability distribution the observed probability of occurrence is associated with each range, class, or category. The sum of the probabilities in a probability distribution is one, while the sum of the frequencies in a frequency distribution is the total number of data items.

## Further Reading

Berman, Simeon M. *Mathematical Statistics: An Introduction Based on the Normal Distribution*. Scranton, PA: Intext Educational Publishers, 1971.

Peavy, J. Virgil. *Descriptive Statistics: Measures of Central Tendency and Dispersion*. Atlanta, GA: U.S. Dept. of Health and Human Services/Public Health Service, Centers for Disease Control, 1981.

# Anna Freud

### 1895-1982
Austrian psychoanalyst and pioneer in the field of child psychoanalysis; daughter of psychoanalyst Sigmund Freud.

A seminal figure in the field of child **psychoanalysis** and development, Anna Freud was born in Vienna, Austria, the youngest child of **Sigmund Freud**. She was educated at private schools in Vienna, and at age 19 began two years of study to become a teacher. As the youngest of six children, she became her father's lifelong traveling companion and student. When Freud was 23 years old, she underwent psychoanalysis, with her father as analyst. Despite the fact that psychoanalysis at that time—and until around the mid-1920s—was less formal than it has become, it was nonetheless unusual for a child to become the patient, or analysand, of a parent.

Anna Freud's own interest was in children and their development. Influenced by her father's psychoanalytic theories, she believed that children experience a series of stages of **normal** psychological development. She also felt strongly that, in order to work with children, psycho-

**Anna Freud** *(AP/Wide World Photos. Reproduced with permission.)*

analysts need a thorough understanding of these stages, knowledge she believed was best acquired through direct observation of children. With Dorothy Burlingham, Freud founded a nursery school for poor children in Vienna, becoming an international leader in treating children's mental illnesses. Freud turned her attention to the study of the **ego**, especially in **adolescence**, publishing *The Ego and the Mechanisms of Defense* (1936) in honor of her father's 80th birthday.

After the Nazis took control in Austria in 1938, the Freuds emigrated to London, England, where Sigmund Freud died a year later. In 1947, Freud and Burlingham established the Hampstead Child Therapy Course and Clinic in London, which provided training opportunities for individuals interested in the psychological and **emotional development** of children. From the 1950s until her death, psychoanalysts, child psychologists, and teachers worldwide sought opportunities to hear Freud lecture, and to benefit from the insights she developed from a lifetime of working with children. Freud's other writings include *The Psychoanalytical Treatment of Children* (1946), *Normality and Pathology in Childhood* (1965), and the seven-volume *Writings of Anna Freud* (1973).

### Further Reading

Coles, Robert. *Anna Freud: The Dream of Psychoanalysis.* Reading, MA: Addison-Wesley Publishing Company, Inc., 1992.

**Sigmund Freud** *(The Library of Congress. Reproduced by permission.)*

## Sigmund Freud

### 1856-1939
Austrian neurologist and the founder of psychoanalysis.

Sigmund Freud was born in Moravia. When he was three years old, his family moved to Vienna, the city where he was to live until the last year of his life. At the age of 17, Freud entered the University of Vienna's medical school, where he pursued a variety of research interests. Although primarily interested in physiological research, Freud was forced to enter into clinical practice due to the difficulty of obtaining a university appointment—aggravated, in his case, by anti-Semitic attitudes and policies. After additional independent research and clinical work at the General Hospital of Vienna, Freud entered private practice, specializing in the treatment of patients with neurological and hysterical disorders.

During this period, Freud learned about his colleague **Josef Breuer**'s "cathartic" treatment of hysterical symptoms, which disappeared when a patient recalled traumatic experiences while under **hypnosis** and was able to express original emotions that had been repressed and forgotten. Pursuing this idea further, Freud spent several months in France studying **Jean-Martin Charcot**'s method of treating hysteria by hypnosis. Upon his return to Vienna, Freud began the task of finding a similar method of treatment that did not require hypnosis, whose limitations he found unsatisfactory. In addition to learning by observing the symptoms and experiences of his patients, Freud also engaged in a rigorous self-analysis based on his own **dreams**. In 1895, he and Breuer published *Studies on Hysteria*, a landmark text in the history of **psychoanalysis**, and in 1900 Freud's own groundbreaking work, *The Interpretation of Dreams*, appeared.

By this time, Freud had worked out the essential components of his system of psychoanalysis, including the use of **free association** and **catharsis** as a method of exploring the **unconscious**, identifying repressed memories and the reasons for their repression, and enabling patients to know themselves more fully. The patient, relaxed on a couch in his office, was directed to engage in a free association of ideas that could yield useful insights, and was asked to reveal frankly whatever came to mind. Through both his work with patients and his own self-analysis, Freud came to believe that mental disorders which have no apparent physiological cause are symbolic reactions to psychological shocks, usually of a sexual nature, and that the memories associated with these shocks, although they have been repressed into the unconscious, indirectly affect the content not only of dreams but of conscious activity.

Freud published *The Psychopathology of Everyday Life* in 1904 and three more works the following year, including *Three Essays on the Theory of Sexuality*, which set forth his ideas about the development of the human sex **instinct**, or *libido*, including his theory of **childhood-sexuality** and the **Oedipus complex**. While recognition from the scientific community and the general public was slow in coming, by the early 1900s Freud had attracted a circle of followers, including **Carl Jung**, **Alfred Adler**, and **Otto Rank** (1884-1939), who held weekly discussion meetings at his home and later became known as the Vienna Psychological Society. Although Jung and Adler were eventually to break with Freud, forming their own theories and schools of analysis, their early support helped establish psychoanalysis as a movement of international importance. In 1909, Freud was invited to speak at Clark University in Worcester, Massachusetts, by its president, the distinguished psychologist **G. Stanley Hall** (1844-1924), and was awarded an honorary doctorate. After World War I, Freud gained increasing fame as psychoanalysis became fashionable in intellectual circles and was popularized by the media.

Freud contended that the human **personality** is governed by forces called "instincts" or "drives." Later, he came to believe in the existence of a death instinct, or death wish (Thanatos), directed either outward as **aggression** or inward as self-destructive behavior (noted mainly as repetition compulsions). He constructed a comprehensive theory on the structure of the **psyche**, which he viewed as divided into three parts. The **id**, corresponding to the unconscious, is concerned with the satisfaction of primitive desires and with self-preservation. It operates according to the **pleasure principle** and outside the realm of social rules or moral dictates. The **ego**, associated with reason, controls the forces of the id to bring it into line with the reality principle and make **socialization** possible, and channels the forces of the id into acceptable activities. The critical, moral **superego**—or conscience—developed in early childhood, monitors and censors the ego, turning external values into internalized, self-imposed rules with which to inhibit the id. Freud viewed individual behavior as the result of the interaction among these three components of the psyche.

At the core of Freud's psychological structure is the repression of unfulfilled instinctual demands. An unconscious process, repression is accomplished through a series of **defense mechanisms**. Those most commonly named by Freud include denial (failure to perceive the source of anxiety); rationalization (justification of an action by an acceptable motive); displacement (directing repressed feelings toward an acceptable substitute); projection (attributing one's own unacceptable impulse to others); and sublimation (transforming an unacceptable instinctual demand into a socially acceptable activity).

Freud continued modifying his theories in the 1920s and changed a number of his fundamental views, including his theories of **motivation** and anxiety. In 1923, he developed cancer of the jaw (he had been a heavy cigar smoker throughout his life) and underwent numerous operations for this disease over the next 16 years. Life in Vienna became increasingly precarious for Freud with the rise of Nazism in the 1930s, and he emigrated to London in 1938, only to die of his illness the following year. Many of the concepts and theories Freud introduced—such as the role of the unconscious, the effect of childhood experiences on adult behavior, and the operation of defense mechanisms—continue to be a source of both controversy and inspiration. His books include *Totem and Taboo* (1913), *General Introduction to Psychoanalysis* (1916), *The Ego and the Id* (1923), and *Civilization and Its Discontents* (1930).

*See also* Consciousness; Memory; Psychosexual stages

### Further Reading
Fromm, Erich. *Sigmund Freud's Mission.* New York: Grove Press, 1959.
Gay, Peter. *Freud: A Life for Our Time.* New York: Norton, 1988.

# Friendship

Companions or peers with whom one has common interests, emotional bonds, and social relationships.

Research has shown that people who have friends tend to have better physical health and report a better sense of psychological well-being than those with weak or no network of friends. Although some people may know a lot of people, they have a more select group of friends and an even smaller number of "best" friends.

Friends provide support in three main ways: emotional, cognitive guidance, and tangible help. Friends give each other emotional support by demonstrating care and affection. They also provide guidance during times of decision-making. Friends give help by meeting practical needs, such as loaning a car, cooking a meal, or taking care of a dog while a friend's on vacation. Psychologists have hypothesized that friends are actually coping mechanisms; by providing companionship and resources, friends alleviate **stress** in a person's life.

There are cultural differences in the way friends are viewed across the world. In cultures that value familial network, such as the Asian culture, the function and role of a friend are often found within the **family** structure, and friendships are not given the same weight of importance as in another culture. There are also varying definitions as to what constitutes a friend. Someone might call another person "friend" because they have mutual interests and activities, while another person considers a friend someone he shares similar attitudes, values, and beliefs.

# Erich Fromm

### 1900-1980
German-born American psychoanalyst, social philosopher, and scholar whose writings have attracted the interest of a large general audience.

Erich Fromm was born in Frankfurt, Germany, and studied sociology and psychology at the universities of Frankfurt and Heidelberg, where he received his Ph.D. in 1922. Fromm was trained in **psychoanalysis** at the University of Munich and at the Psychoanalytic Institute of Berlin. In 1925, he began his practice and was associated with the influential Institute for Social Research in Frankfurt. Although Fromm began his professional career as a disciple of **Sigmund Freud**, he soon began to differ with the Freudian emphasis on **unconscious** drives and neglect of the effects of social and economic forces on **personality**. The theories he developed integrate psychology with cultural analysis and Marxist historical materialism. Fromm argued that each socioeconomic class fosters a particular character, governed by ideas that justify and maintain it and that the ultimate purpose of social character is to orient the individual toward those tasks that will assure the perpetuation of the socioeconomic system.

Fromm consistently advocated the primacy of personal relationships and devotion to the common good over subservience to a mechanistic superstate in his work. He believed that humanity had a dual relationship with nature, which they belong to but also transcend. According to Fromm, the unique character of human existence gives rise to five basic needs. First, human beings, having lost their original oneness with nature, need relatedness in order to overcome their essential isolation. They also need to transcend their own nature, as well as the passivity and randomness of existence, which can be accomplished either positively—by loving and creat-

**Erich Fromm** *(The Library of Congress. Reproduced with permission.)*

ing—or negatively, through hatred and destruction. The individual also requires a sense of rootedness, or belonging, in order to gain a feeling of security, and needs a sense of identity as well. The remaining need is for orientation, or a means of facing one's existential situation by finding meaning and value in existence. Orientation can be achieved either through **assimilation** (relating to things) or **socialization** (relating to people).

Fromm identified several character orientations found in Western society. The *receptive character* can only take and not give; the *hoarding character*, threatened by the outside world, can not share; the *exploitative character* satisfies desires through force and deviousness; and the *marketing character*—created by the impersonal nature of modern society—sees itself as a cog in a machine, or as a commodity to be bought or sold. Contrasting with these negative orientations is the *productive character*, capable of loving and realizing its full potential, and devoted to the common good of humanity. Fromm later described two additional character types: the *necrophilouscharacter*, attracted to death, and the *biophilous character*, drawn to life.

Fromm emigrated to the United States in 1934, following the rise of Nazism in Germany. In America,

Fromm became increasingly controversial in orthodox Freudian circles. He served on the faculties of, and lectured at, several universities in the United States, including Columbia University and Yale University, and in Mexico. In 1941, Fromm wrote *Escape from Freedom*, an analysis of totalitarianism that would become a classic in political philosophy and intellectual history as well as in psychology. According to Fromm, the "escape" from freedom experienced upon reaching adulthood and gaining independence from one's parents leads to a profound sense of loneliness and isolation, which the individual attempts to escape by establishing some type of bond with society. In Fromm's view, totalitarianism offered the individual a refuge from individual isolation through social **conformity** and submission to authority. Among his other important books in the areas of psychology, **ethics**, religion, and history are *Man for Himself* (1947), *Psychoanalysis and Religion* (1950), *The Forgotten Language* (1951), *The Sane Society* (1955), *The Art of Loving* (1956), *Beyond the Chains of Illusion* (1962), *The Heart of Man* (1964), *You Shall Be As Gods* (1966), *The Revolution of Hope* (1968), *Social Character in a Mexican Village* (1970), *The Anatomy of Human Destructiveness* (1973), and *To Have or To Be* (1976).

Fromm's work has had a deep and lasting influence on Western thought. One central thesis that appears in much of his writing is that **alienation** is the most serious and fundamental problem of Western civilization. In his view, Western culture must be transformed—through the application of psychoanalytic principles to social issues—into societies that recognize the primacy of human beings as responsible, sovereign individuals and that are conducive to the attainment of individual freedom, which he sees as the ultimate goal of humanity's existence.

### Further Reading

Funk, Rainer. *Erich Fromm: The Courage to be Human*. New York: Human Sciences Press, 1989.

# Fugue

An episode during which an individual leaves his usual surroundings unexpectedly and forgets essential details about himself and his life.

## Causes and symptoms

Fugues are classified as a **dissociative disorder**, a syndrome in which an individual experiences a disruption in **memory**, **consciousness**, and/or identity. This may last anywhere from less than a day to several months, and is sometimes, but not always, brought on by severe **stress** or trauma. Dissociative fugue (formerly termed psychogenic fugue) is usually triggered by traumatic and stressful events, such as wartime battle, abuse, **rape**, accidents, natural disasters, and extreme **violence**, although fugue states may not occur immediately.

Individuals experiencing a fugue exhibit the following symptoms:

- Sudden and unplanned travel away from home together with an inability to recall past events about one's life.
- Confusion or loss of memory about one's identity (**amnesia**). In some cases, an individual may assume a new identity to compensate for the loss.
- Extreme distress and impaired functioning in day-to-day life as a result of the fugue episodes.

If the amnesia of fugue occurs without an episode of unexpected travel (fleeing), dissociative amnesia is usually diagnosed.

## Diagnosis

Patients who experience fugue states should undergo a thorough physical examination and patient history to rule out an organic cause for the illness (e.g., **epilepsy** or other seizure disorder). If no organic cause is found, a psychologist or other mental healthcare professional will conduct a patient interview and administer one or more psychological assessments (also called clinical inventories, scales, or tests). These assessments may include the Dissociative Experiences Scale (DES or DES-II), Structured Clinical Interview for DSM-IV Dissociative Disorders (SCID-D), and the Dissociate Disorders Interview Schedule (DDIS).

The use and abuse of certain medications and illegal drugs can also prompt fugue-like episodes. For example, alcohol-dependent patients frequently report alcohol-induced "blackouts" that mimic the memory loss of the fugue state and sometimes involve unplanned travel.

## Treatment

Dissociative fugue is relatively rare, with a prevalence rate of 0.2% in the general population. The length of a fugue episode is thought to be related to the severity of the stressor or trauma that caused it. The majority of cases appear as single episodes with no recurrence. In some cases, the individual will not remember events that occurred during the fugue state. In other cases, amnesia related to the traumatic event that triggered the fugue may persist to some degree after the fugue episode has concluded.

Treatment for dissociative fugue should focus on helping the patient come to terms with the traumatic event or stressor that caused the disorder. This can be accomplished through various kinds of interactive therapies that explore the trauma and work on building the patient's coping mechanisms to prevent further recurrence. Some therapists use **cognitive therapy**, which focuses on changing maladaptive thought patterns. It is based on the principal that maladaptive behavior (in this case, the fugue episode itself) is triggered by inappropriate or irrational thinking patterns. A cognitive therapist will attempt to change these thought patterns (also known as cognitive distortions) by examining the rationality and validity of the assumptions behind them with the patient. In the case of a dissociative fugue brought on by abuse, this may involve therapeutic work that uncovers and invalidates negative self-concepts the patient has (e.g., "I am a bad person, therefore I brought on the abuse myself").

In some cases, hypnotherapy, or **hypnosis**, may be useful in helping the patient recover lost memories of trauma. Creative therapies (i.e., **art therapy**, **music therapy**) are also constructive in allowing patients to express and explore thoughts and emotions in "safe" ways. They also empower the patient by encouraging self-discovery and a sense of control.

Medication may be a useful adjunct, or complementary, treatment for some of the symptoms that the patient may be experiencing in relation to the dissociative episode. In some cases, antidepressant or anti-anxiety medication may be prescribed.

**Group therapy**, either therapist/counselor-led or in self-help format, can be helpful in providing an on-going support network for the patient. It also provides the patient with opportunities to gain self-confidence and interact with peers in a positive way. **Family therapy** sessions may also be part of the treatment regime, both in exploring the trauma that caused the fugue episode and in educating the rest of the family about the dissociative disorder and the causes behind it.

*See also* Dissociation/Dissociative disorders

Paula Ford-Martin

### Further Reading
American Psychiatric Association. *Diagnostic and statistical manual of mental disorders,* 4th ed. Washington, DC: American Psychiatric Press, Inc., 1994.

### Further Information
National Alliance for the Mentally Ill (NAMI). 200 North Glebe Road, Suite 1015, Arlington, VA, USA. 22203-3754, (800)950-6264. http://www.nami.org.

# Functional disorder

A psychological disorder for which no organic cause can be found.

Disorders traditionally classified as neuroses (including a variety of anxiety and **mood** disorders as well as psychosomatic illnesses) are generally regarded as functional disorders. While conditions classified as psychotic are usually believed to have biological origins, neurotic conditions are generally believed to be caused by developmental, psychosocial, or **personality** factors. **Psychotic disorders** not associated with damage to **brain** tissue from a head injury, infection, or similar causes are also considered functional disorders.

Many **mental health** professionals are uncomfortable with the term "functional disorder" for a variety of reasons. First, its meaning is often distorted. While the term is essentially a designation of what a disorder is *not* (i.e., organic), it tends to be interpreted as making positive statements about what the disorder *is* (i.e., induced by environmental or psychosocial factors) when, in fact, such causes may not have been scientifically proven. In addition, "functional" as a classification continually becomes outdated as new discoveries are made about the origins of certain disorders. **Schizophrenia**, for example, would be considered an *organic* disorder if a biochemical cause for the disease—which some researchers believe exists—could be verified. By comparison, the current system of classifying disorders in the *Diagnostic and Statistical Manual of Mental Disorders*, which is organized by the mental faculty or area of behavior that is impaired, is much less likely to become outdated due to new research. A further objection to the term functional disorder is that it implies an artificial separation of the mind and body, as a number of disorders have both organic and functional components.

# Functional fixedness

A limitation in perception.

In solving problems, humans try to focus on the best strategy to reach the goal. Sometimes problems are more difficult to solve than they need to be because the available solutions are not clear or obvious. That is, humans form mental sets, ways of viewing the potential solutions, that actually hinder progress.

When people develop functional fixedness, they recognize tools only for their obvious function. For example, an object is regarded as having only one fixed function. The problem-solver cannot alter his or her mental set to see that the tool may have multiple uses.

A common theatrical situation involves a group of people who want to enter a locked room when they have no key. A solution often arises when somebody thinks to insert a credit card between the door and the door jamb, releasing the lock. In real life, if one needs to get into a locked room, a useful implement might be present that would help solve your problem. Unfortunately, the person may not recognize that it will help because he or she is a victim of functional fixedness.

In many cases, people are quite adept at avoiding functional fixedness, as when using a nail clipper as a screwdriver or the heel of a shoe as a nutcracker.

# Functionalism

A psychological approach, popular in the early part of the twentieth century, that focused on how consciousness functions to help human beings adapt to their environment.

The goal of the first psychologists was to determine the structure of **consciousness** just as chemists had found the structure of chemicals. Thus, the school of psychology associated with this approach earned the name structuralism. This perspective began in Germany in the laboratory of **Wilhelm Wundt** (1832-1920).

Before long, however, psychologists suggested that psychology should not concern itself with the structure of consciousness because, they argued, consciousness was always changing so it had no basic structure. Instead, they suggested that psychology should focus on the function or purpose of consciousness and how it leads to adaptive behavior. This approach to psychology was consistent with **Charles Darwin**'s theory of evolution, which exerted a significant impact on the character of psychology. The school of functionalism developed and flourished in the United States, which quickly surpassed Germany as the primary location of scientific psychology.

In 1892, George Trumbull Ladd (1842-1921), one of the early presidents of the **American Psychological Association**, had declared that objective psychology should not replace the subjective psychology of the structuralists. By 1900, however, most psychologists agreed with a later president, Joseph Jastrow, that psychology was the science of mental content, not of structure. At that point, structuralism still had some adherents, but it was fast becoming a minor part of psychology.

The early functionalists included the pre-eminent psychologist and philosopher **William James**. James promoted the idea that the mind and consciousness itself would not exist if it did not serve some practical, adaptive purpose. It had evolved because it presented advantages. Along with this idea, James maintained that psychology should be practical and should be developed to make a difference in people's lives.

One of the difficulties that concerned the functionalists was how to reconcile the objective, scientific nature of psychology with its focus on consciousness, which by its nature is not directly observable. Although psychologists like William James accepted the reality of consciousness and the role of the will in people's lives, even he was unable to resolve the issue of scientific acceptance of consciousness and will within functionalism.

Other functionalists, like **John Dewey**, developed ideas that moved ever farther from the realm that structuralism had created. Dewey, for example, used James's ideas as the basis for his writings, but asserted that consciousness and the will were not relevant concepts for scientific psychology. Instead, the behavior is the critical issue and should be considered in the context in which it occurs. For example, a stimulus might be important in one circumstance, but irrelevant in another. A person's response to that stimulus depends on the value of that stimulus in the current situation. Thus, practical and adaptive responses characterize behavior, not some unseen force like consciousness.

This dilemma of how to deal with a phenomenon as subjective as consciousness within the context of an objective psychology ultimately led to the abandonment of functionalism in favor of **behaviorism**, which rejected everything dealing with consciousness. By 1912, very few psychologists regarded psychology as the study of mental content—the focus was on behavior instead. As it turned out, the school of functionalism provided a temporary framework for the replacement of structuralism, but was itself supplanted by the school of behaviorism.

Interestingly, functionalism drew criticism from both the structuralists and from the behaviorists. The structuralists accused the functionalists of failing to define the concepts that were important to functionalism. Further, the structuralists declared that the functionalists were simply not studying psychology at all; psychology to a structuralist involved mental content and nothing else. Finally, the functionalists drew criticism for applying psychology; the structuralists opposed applications in the name of psychology.

On the other hand, behaviorists were uncomfortable with the functionalists' acceptance of consciousness and sought to make psychology the study of behavior. Eventually, the behavioral approach gained ascendance and reigned for the next half century.

Functionalism was important in the development of psychology because it broadened the scope of psychological research and application. Because of the wider perspective, psychologists accepted the validity of research with animals, with children, and with people having psychiatric disabilities. Further, functionalists introduced a wide variety of research techniques that were beyond the boundaries of structural psychology, like physiological measures, mental tests, and questionnaires. The functionalist legacy endures in psychology today.

Some historians have suggested that functional psychology was consistent with the progressivism that characterized American psychology at the end of the nineteenth century: more people were moving to and living in urban areas, science seemed to hold all the answers for creating a Utopian society, educational reform was underway, and many societal changes faced America. It is not surprising that psychologists began to consider the role that psychology could play in developing a better society.

## Further Reading

Biro, J.I., and Robert W. Shahan, eds. *Mind, Brain, and Function: Essays in the Philosophy of Mind.* Norman: University of Oklahoma Press, 1982.

Leahey, T. H. *A History of Modern Psychology.* 2nd ed. Englewood Cliffs, NJ: Prentice-Hall, 1994.

Putnam, Hilary. *Representation and Reality.* Cambridge, MA: MIT Press, 1988.

Schultz, D. P., and S. E. Schultz. *A History of Modern Psychology.* 6th ed. Fort Worth, TX: Harcourt Brace College Publishers, 1996.

# Galen

**130-200**
Physician to Roman emperors and early author of works on anatomy and physiology.

Galen, the last and most influential of the great ancient medical practitioners, was born in Pergamum, Asia Minor. His father, the architect Nicon, is supposed to have prepared Galen for a career in medicine following the instructions given him in a dream by the god of medicine, Asclepius. Accordingly, Galen studied philosophy, mathematics, and logic in his youth and then began his medical training at age sixteen at the medical school of Pergamum attached to the local shrine of Asclepius. At age twenty, Galen embarked on extensive travels, broadening his medical knowledge with studies at Smyrna, Corinth, and Alexandria. At Alexandria, the preeminent research and teaching center of the time, Galen was able to study skeletons (although not actual bodies).

Returning to Pergamum at age twenty-eight, Galen became physician to the gladiators, which gave him great opportunities for observations about human anatomy and physiology. In 161 A.D., Galen moved to Rome and quickly established a successful practice after curing several eminent people, including the philosopher Eudemus. Galen also conducted public lectures and demonstrations, began writing some of his major works on anatomy and physiology, and frequently engaged in polemics with fellow physicians. In 174 A.D., Galen was summoned to treat Marcus Aurelius and became the emperor's personal physician.

Galen once again returned to Pergamum in 166 A.D., perhaps to escape the quarreling, perhaps to avoid an outbreak of plague in Rome. After a few years, Galen was summoned back to Rome by Marcus Aurelius. He became physician to two subsequent emperors, Commodus and Septimius Severvs, and seems to have stayed in Rome for the rest of his career, probably dying there in about 200 A.D.

**Galen** *(Archive Photos, Inc. Reproduced with permission.)*

Galen was an astonishingly prolific writer, producing hundreds of works, of which about 120 have survived. His most important contributions were in anatomy. Galen expertly dissected and accurately observed all kinds of animals, but sometimes mistakenly—because human dissection was forbidden—applied what he saw to the human body. Nevertheless, his descriptions of bones and muscle were notable; he was the first to observe that muscles work in contracting pairs. He described the heart valves and the structural differences between arteries and veins. He used experiments to demonstrate paralysis resulting from spinal cord severing, control of the larynx through the laryngeal **nerve**, and passage of urine from kidneys to bladder. An excellent clinician, Galen pioneered diagnostic use of the pulse rate and described cardiac arrhythmias. Galen also collected therapeutic plants in his extensive travels and explained their uses.

In his observations about the heart and blood vessels, however, Galen made critical errors that remained virtually unchallenged for 1,400 years. He correctly recognized that blood passes from the right to the left side of the heart, but decided this was accomplished through minute pores in the septum, rather than through the pulmonary circulation. Like Erasistratus, Galen believed that blood formed in the liver and was circulated from there throughout the body in the veins. He did show that arteries contain blood, but thought they also contained and distributed *pneuma*, a vital spirit. In a related idea, Galen believed that the **brain** generated and transmitted another vital spirit through the (hollow) nerves to the muscles, allowing movement and sensation.

After Galen, experimental physiology and anatomical research ceased for many centuries. Galen's teachings became the ultimate medical authority, approved by the newly ascendant Christian church because of Galen's belief in a divine purpose for all things, even the structure and functioning of the human body. The medical world moved on from Galenism only with the appearance of Andreas Vesalius 's work on anatomy in 1543 and William Harvey's work on blood circulation in 1628.

# Sir Francis Galton

### 1822-1911
English scientist, explorer, and principal figure in the early history of eugenics.

Born in Birmingham, England, Francis Galton was descended from founders of the Quaker religion. He learned to read before the age of three and became competent in Latin and mathematics by age five. Nevertheless, Galton's formal education was unsuccessful. A rebellious student, he left school at the age of 16 to receive medical training at hospitals in Birmingham and London. Entering Cambridge University two years later, Galton failed to attain the high academic ranking he sought, and this precipitated a mental breakdown, although he did eventually earn his degree.

After several years of living on an inheritance from his father who died in 1845, Galton led a two-year expedition to the interior of southwest Africa, winning a gold medal from the Royal Geographical Society for a highly detailed map he produced from data obtained on this

**Sir Francis Galton** *(The Library of Congress. Reproduced by permission.)*

trip. He also became a fellow of both the Royal Geographical Society and the Royal Society. During the next ten years, Galton was preoccupied with geographical and meteorological studies. Among his other achievements, Galton created the world's first weather maps.

The 1859 publication of *On the Origin of Species* by Galton's cousin, **Charles Darwin**, turned Galton's attention to the subject of **heredity**. Theorizing that the operating principles of Darwin's theory of evolution provided the potential for the positive biological transformation of humankind, Galton began to study the inheritance of intellectual characteristics among human beings. Based on quantitative studies of prominent individuals and their family trees, he concluded that intellectual **ability** is inherited in much the same way as physical **traits**, and he later published his findings in *Hereditary Genius* (1869).

Galton's belief in the hereditary nature of **intelligence** led him to the idea that society should encourage superior individuals to procreate, while those with lesser mental abilities should be discouraged from doing so, a concept for which he coined the term " eugenics," denoting the scientific attempt to genetically improve the human species through selective parenthood. It is interesting to note that Galton's approach to **eugenics** was to encourage the "best specimens" to procreate. This differed from the American approach referred to as "negative eugenics," where the "worst specimens" were prevented from procreating.

Galton carried out further research to distinguish between the effects of heredity and those of **environment**. He polled members of the Royal Society about their lives, using a new research tool of his own devising that was to have a long life as an information-gathering device: the questionnaire. Eventually, Galton modified his original theories to recognize the effects of education and other environmental factors on mental ability, although he continued to regard heredity as the preeminent influence.

Galton made significant contributions in many areas. His strong interest in individual psychological differences led him to pioneer intelligence testing, inventing the word-association test. He also was the first known investigator to study **twins** who had been separated from each other as a means of offering insight into the **nature-nurture controversy**. In his late sixties, Galton discovered the analytical device known as the "regression line" for studying the correlations between sets of data. In 1909, he was knighted in recognition of his manifold accomplishments in such diverse fields as geography, meteorology, biology, statistics, psychology, and even criminology (he had developed a system for classifying fingerprints). While many of Galton's specific conclusions and research methods turned out to have been flawed, his work provided a foundation for the study of individual differences by both psychologists and educators. Among Galton's many publications are *Tropical South Africa* (1853), *The Art of Travel* (1855), *Hereditary Genius* (1869), *English Men of Science: Their Nature and Nurture* (1874), *Inquiries into Human Faculty and Its Development* (1883), and *Memories of My Life* (1908).

### Further Reading

Forrest, D.W. *Francis Galton: The Life and Work of a Victorian Genius.* London: Elek, 1974.

Pearson, Karl. *The Life, Letters and Labours of Francis Galton.* Cambridge, England: Cambridge University Press, 1914-30.

# Gambling, pathological

Preoccupation with gambling and uncontrollable impulse to gamble, regardless of the problems caused in daily life.

The Commission on the Review of the National Policy Toward Gambling reported that 61% of the U.S. population engaged in some form of gambling. The group also estimated that there were 1.1 million compulsive gamblers in the United States. While for many people gambling is a form of harmless recreation, for others it is an uncontrollable and all-consuming pursuit, often eclipsing everything else in their life. Some gamblers borrow or steal money when their funds run out; some lose their jobs and homes; and in almost all cases, their relationships with **family** and friends are aversely affected.

Pathological gambling is defined as a pattern of repeated gambling and preoccupation with gambling. The term was not included in the **American Psychiatric Association**'s *Diagnostic and Statistical Manual of Mental Disorders* until 1980. Since then psychologists have proposed several theories as to why people gamble. For some, they state, it is a form of risk taking, which may be an inherent **personality** trait. For many others, it is the lure of a possible financial payoff. Psychologists are still unsure, however, why some gamblers become pathological gamblers. Some psychiatrists have proposed the "disease model," stating that, like alcoholism, gambling is a disease or a sickness of the mind. Behaviorists, on the other hand, see it as a learned, **conditioned response**. Because gamblers are reinforced intermittently—winning one hand and losing the next—they are motivated to keep playing until they receive a positive **reinforcement**. Various research studies have shown that any behavior that is tied to partial schedules of reinforcement are extremely difficult to stop.

Pathological gambling often begins in **adolescence** in males, and somewhat later in females. Individuals with this disorder often experience a progression in their gambling, becoming increasingly preoccupied with gambling, increasing the amounts wagered, and often continuing to gamble despite attempts to stop or control the behavior.

Unfortunately, pathological gambling is often difficult to treat, but there are several treatment options. Perhaps the most widely practiced treatment is **group therapy**, such as is found in Gambler's Anonymous. **Pain** aversion therapy has also been used, in which a electric shock is associated with gambling. In another therapy called paradoxical intention, the therapist orders the client to gamble according to a strict schedule, whether the gambler wants to or not.

*See also* Impulse control disorders

# Gangs

A group of people recognized as a distinct entity and involved in antisocial, rebellious, or illegal activities.

A gang is a group of people whose members recognize themselves as a distinct entity and are recognized as such by their community. Their involvement in antisocial, rebellious, and illegal activities draws a negative response from the community and from law enforcement officials. Other characteristics of gangs include a recognized leader; formal membership with initiation requirements and rules for its members; its own territory, or turf; standard clothing or tattoos; private slang; and a group name. In a document published by Boys and Girls Clubs of America, the U.S. Department of Justice has divided gangs into several types. Territorial ("turf" or "hood") gangs are concerned with controlling a specific geographical area. Organized, or corporate, gangs are mainly involved in illegal activities such as drug dealing. Scavenger gangs are more loosely organized than the other two types and are identified primarily by common group behavior.

Since the 1980s, gang activities have become an increasing cause for concern in many areas of the United States. It is estimated that hundreds of thousands of people—perhaps upwards of a million—belong to thousands of gangs in major urban centers, suburbs, small cities, and even in rural areas. A study conducted at the University of Southern California found gang activity in 94% of the country's major cities and over 1,000 cities altogether. The number of gang members in Los Angeles County alone was estimated at 130,000 in 1991. In the same year there were an estimated 50 gangs in New York City, 125 in Chicago, and 225 in Dallas. Today's gangs are more involved in serious criminal activities than their predecessors. Gang-related **violence** has risen sharply, involving ever-younger perpetrators who are increasingly ready to use deadly force to perpetuate rivalries or carry out drug activities. In addition, the scope of gang activities has increased, often involving links to drug suppliers or customers in distant locations.

Gangs are found among virtually all ethnic groups. Mexican American gangs, whose members are sometimes referred to as *cholos*, have long been active in the Southwest and are now spreading to other parts of the country. Today these groups include not only the traditional Mexican American membership but also new immigrants from Central American countries such as El Salvador. The most visible Hispanic gangs on the East Coast have traditionally been the Puerto Rican gangs in New York City, originally formed by the children of immigrants who came to this country in the 1940s and 1950s. African American gang affiliations often center around the Crips and Bloods, Los Angeles gangs that are bitter rivals, or the Vice Lords and Folk Nation, which are Chicago gangs. Chinese gangs, which began in New York in the 1960s and 1970s, prey on the Asian community, extorting money in return for protection. With the wave of immigration from Southeast Asia following the Vietnam war, Vietnamese and Cambodian gangs have formed, also terrorizing their own communities.

The most visible white gangs are the skinheads (named for their close-shaven heads), who typically embrace a racist, anti-Semitic, and anti-gay philosophy, often involving neo-Nazi symbolism and beliefs. There are thought to be between 3,000 and 4,000 skinheads in the United States, including such groups as the Aryan Youth Movement, Blitz Krieg, and White Power. Skinhead activities have included painting racial slurs on buildings, damaging synagogues and the homes of Jews and blacks, and sometimes fatal assaults on members of minority groups. The white Spur Posse, a gang of white high school athletes in California, received media attention in the late 1990s for sexually molesting teenage girls.

A variety of factors have been cited as causes for involvement in gangs. Social problems associated with gang activity include poverty, **racism**, and the disintegration of the nuclear **family**. Some critics claim that gangs are glamorized in the media and by the entertainment industry. On a personal level, adolescents whose families are not meeting their emotional needs turn to gangs as substitute families where they can find acceptance, intimacy, and approval. Gangs can also provide the sense of identity that young people crave as they confront the dislocations of **adolescence**. Teenagers also join gangs because of social pressure from friends. Others feel physically unsafe in their neighborhoods if they do not join a gang. For some people, the connection to a gang is through family members who belong—sometimes even several generations of a single family. Yet another incentive for joining is money from the gangs' lucrative drug trade. Drug profits can be so exorbitant as to dwarf the income from any legitimate job: teenagers in one suburban high school in the early 1990s were handling $28,000 a week in drug money, with individual profit averaging $5,000.

The basic unit in gangs, whatever their origin or larger structure, is a clique of members who are about the same age (these groups are also called posses or sets). A gang may consist entirely of such a clique, or it may be allied with similar groups as part of a larger gang. The Crips and Bloods consist of many sets, with names such as the Playboy Gangster Crips, the Bounty Hunters, and the Piru Bloods. It is to their clique or set that members feel the greatest loyalty. These neighborhood groups have leaders, who may command as many as 200 followers. In groups affiliated with larger gangs, these local leaders are accountable to chiefs higher up in the gang hierarchy. At the top is the kingpin, who has the ultimate say in how the gang conducts its financial operations and oversees its members.

The lowest level on which a young person may be associated with a gang is as a lookout—the person who watches for the police during drug deals or other criminal activities. Lookouts, who are commonly between seven and twelve years old, can be paid as much as three hundred dollars a week. At the next level are "wannabes," older children or preteens who identify themselves with a gang although they are still too young for membership. They may wear clothing resembling that of the gang they aspire to and try to ingratiate themselves with its members. Sometimes they cause trouble in or out of school as a way of drawing the gang's attention. Once wannabes are being considered for entrance into a gang they undergo some form of initiation. Often it includes the commission of a specified crime as a way of "proving themselves." In addition, gangs generally practice certain initiation rituals, such as "walking the line," in which initiates have to pass between two lines of members who beat them. In other cases, initiation brutalities follow a less orderly course, with a succession of gang members randomly perpetrating surprise beatings that initiates have to withstand without attempting to defend themselves. Other rituals, such as cutting initiates and mixing their blood with that of older members, are also practiced.

Gangs adopt certain dress codes by which members show their unity and make their gang **affiliation** visible both to members of other gangs and to the community at large. Gang members are usually identifiable by both the style and color of their clothing. Latino gangs traditionally wore khaki pants, white T-shirts, and plain cotton jackets, but today black pants and jackets are favored, often worn with black L.A. Raiders caps. The Crips are strongly associated with the color blue, typically wearing blue jackets, running shoes with blue stripes and laces, and blue bandannas, either tied around their heads or hanging prominently from a back pocket. (The color of the rival Bloods is red.) Two rival African American gangs in Chicago wear hats tilted in different directions to signal their affiliation. With the increased use of deadly force by today's gang members, gang clothing codes can be very dangerous: nonmembers have been killed for accidentally wandering onto gang turf wearing the colors of a rival group. In addition to their clothing, gang members express solidarity by adopting street names and using secret symbols and codes, often in graffiti spray-painted in public places.

Although most gang members are male, women do join gangs—either mixed-gender or all-female gangs (which are sometimes satellites of male gangs and sometimes independent of them). Traditionally they have played a subservient role in mixed gangs, assisting the males in their activities and forming romantic attach-

**Members of the Crips gang in Los Angeles.** *(Photo by Daniel Laini. Corbis/Daniel Laini. Reproduced with permission.)*

ments within the gang, but generally not engaging in criminal activities more serious than shoplifting or fighting girls from other gangs. To be initiated into a mixed-sex gang, female members have often been required to have sex with multiple gang members. Today girl gang members are more apt than in the past to participate in serious violence, such as drive-by shootings, armed robbery, and "wildings," savage group attacks on innocent victims in public places, often involving sexual assault.

Perhaps the most troubling feature of gang activity in the 1980s and 1990s is its increased level of violence, which often victimizes not only gang members themselves but also innocent bystanders who unwittingly find themselves in its path. Thousands of people with no gang connections have been killed because they were in the wrong place at the wrong time. Most gang-related killings are linked to fights over turf (including drug turf), "respect" (perceived threats to a gang member's status), or revenge. In Los Angeles County, the number of gang-related slayings soared from 212 in 1984 to 803 in 1992. Nationwide, the total number of teenagers murdered every year has risen 55% since 1988, an increase thought to be closely linked to the growth of gang activity. In 1991 over 2,000 people were injured or killed in drive-by shootings, 90% of which are thought to be committed by gang members. A major factor that has raised the level of gang violence is easy access to such weapons as automatic rifles, rapid-fire pistols, and submachine guns.

A common feature of membership in gangs is the difficulty encountered by people who want to quit. They are virtually always punished in some way, ranging from ritualized beatings (mirroring the initiation ceremony) to murder. Sometimes the member's entire family is terrorized. Many persons—and sometimes even their families—have had to relocate to another city in order to safely end gang affiliations. In some cities, there are organizations (some staffed by ex-gang members) that help people who want to leave gangs.

## Further Reading

Greenberg, Keith Elliot. *Out of the Gang*. Minneapolis, MN: Lerner Publications, 1992.

Gardner, Sandra. *Street Gangs in America*. New York: Franklin Watts, 1992.

Knox, Mike. *Gangsta in the House: Understanding Gang Culture*. Troy, MI: Momentum Books, 1995.

Monti, Daniel. *Wannabe: Gangs in Suburbs and Schools*. Cambridge, MA: Blackwell, 1994.

Oliver, Marilyn Tower. *Gangs: Trouble in the Streets*. Springfield, NJ: Enslow Publishers, 1995.

Webb, Margot. *Coping with Street Gangs*. New York: Rosen Publishing Group, 1992.

## Further Information

National Youth Gang Information Center. 4301 Fairfax Dr., Suite 730, Arlington, VA 22203, (800) 446–4264.

# Howard Earl Gardner

### 1943-

American psychologist, educator, and creator of theory of multiple intelligence.

Howard Earl Gardner was born and raised in Scranton, Pennsylvania. His parents, Ralph and Hilde (maiden name Weilheimer), were refugees from Nazi Germany. Gardner was a good student who greatly enjoyed playing the piano. In fact, he became an accomplished pianist as a child and considered becoming a professional pianist. While Gardner did not pursue becoming a professional pianist, he did teach piano from 1958 to 1969. The arts and teaching are interests he has pursued throughout his career.

Gardner received his B.A. *summa cum laude* in social relations from Harvard College in 1965 and his Ph.D. in psychology from Harvard University in 1971. At Harvard he studied with the renowned developmental psychologists **Jerome Bruner** and **Erik Erikson**, and the philosopher Nelson Goodman. He had thought he would research children and their artistic abilities but became fascinated with neuropsychology after attending a lecture on the subject given by Norman Geschwind, a well-known neuropsychologist. Indeed, Gardner went on to do a postdoctoral fellowship under Geschwind at the Boston Veterans Hospital where he worked for 20 years.

His research has focused for the most part on the nature of human **intelligence**, the nature of and development of abilities in the arts and how they relate to and reflect intelligence, and on educational processes. For numerous years, Gardner conducted research in symbol-using capac-

ities in **normal** and gifted children, and in adults who had experienced **brain** damage. Through his efforts to bring these two areas of work together, he developed his theory of multiple types of intelligence, which he introduced in *Frames of Mind* (1983). Drawing on research in neuropsychology, he proposes that there are seven distinct types of intelligence, each based in a different area of the brain. Thus intelligence is not one general factor that underlies different abilities—the predominant belief upon which most intelligence tests had been based.

In the mid-1980s Gardner started to become involved in efforts to reform schools in the United States. He started to teach at the Harvard Graduate School of Education in 1986. He is now Co-Director of Harvard Project Zero, which he joined in the mid-1980s. Project Zero is a research group that studies human **cognition**, focusing on the arts in particular. Among other things, he and his colleagues have worked on designing performance-based tests and using the theory of multiple types of intelligence to create more individualized teaching and testing methods. Most recently, Gardner has become involved in carrying out long-term case studies of successful leaders and creators. One aspect of this work investigates the relationship between a person's production of exemplary work and his or her personal values.

Gardner is currently the John H. and Elisabeth A. Hobbs Professor in Cognition and Education at the Harvard Graduate School of Education. In addition he is Adjunct Professor of Psychology at Harvard University, and Adjunct Professor of Neurology at the Boston University School of Medicine.

Gardner has written more than 400 research articles and twenty books. In *The Mind's New Science* (1985) Gardner discussed how cognitive science has the potential to understand **creativity**. Two later books, *The Unschooled Mind* (1991) and *Multiple Intelligences: The Theory in Practice* (1993) spell out how his perspectives can be put into practice in education. Gardner's work has been highly influential. His books have been translated into 20 languages. In addition, he has been given honors by numerous psychological and educational organizations.

Gardner is married to Ellen Winner. He was divorced from the well-respected developmental psychologist, educator, and author Judith (Krieger) Gardner, who passed away in 1994. Gardner has four children.

*See also* Culture-fair test; Emotional intelligence

Marie Doorey

## Further Reading

Cohen, D. "Howard Gardner." In *Psychologists on Psychology, 2nd Ed*. London and New York: Routledge, 1995. Pp. 97-105.

Nucci, L.P. "Gardner, Howard Earl." In *Biographical dictionary of psychology*. London and New York: Routledge, 1997.

*Obituary in The Boston Globe*, Judith Gardner. November 29, 1994.

Harvard Website *Short biography of Howard Gardner* http://www.pz.harvard.edu/Pls/HG.htm

**Further Information**
Harvard University Graduate School of Education. Larsen Hall, Cambridge, MA, USA. 02138.

# Gender bias

Differences in the treatment of males and females.

Gender bias, and its corollary, gender equity, describe the comparison of opportunities and treatment available to males with those available to females. Today, gender bias is observed and discussed in societies and cultures worldwide. Parents and teachers of young people are especially concerned with unequal treatment of boys and girls, particularly the effect these differences have on **child development**. Economic development professionals have observed that, from subsistence to advanced economies, women are assigned different workloads, have different responsibilities for child and family welfare, and receive different rewards for performance.

In the United States, the Education Amendments of 1972 were passed by the U.S. Congress. These included Title IX, introduced by Representative Edith Green of Oregon, requiring educational institutions that receive federal funds to provide equal opportunities in all activities for girls and boys. Title IX applies to all schools, public and private, that receive money from the federal government, from kindergarten through higher education.

However, in 1992 a study published by the American Association of University Women (AAUW) revealed that enforcement of this law has been lax nationwide. The AAUW's report, "How Schools Shortchange Girls," which compiled results from hundreds of research studies and articles on gender bias at every educational level, concluded that schools continue to perpetuate subtle discrimination against girls, stereotyping them as studious and well-behaved, while more aggressive students, usually the boys, may receive more **attention** from the teacher. Additionally, a 1989 study of books used in high school literature classes found that 90 percent of the most frequently assigned books were written by males; a year later, an evaluation of school textbooks specifically written to comply with gender-equity guidelines in California revealed lingering bias toward males in both language usage and in accounts of historical milestones.

Female students are affected by gender bias in many subtle but significant ways. Girls have lower expectations for their success in math and science; are more likely to attribute academic success to luck rather than to **ability**, and are more likely to equate academic failure to lack of ability (boys are more likely to attribute failure to lack of effort). Boys are more likely that girls to challenge the teacher when they do not agree with an answer. Generally, girls earn higher grades than boys, but boys outperform girls on standardized tests. Boys with higher SAT scores are more likely than girls with equal or better grades to be awarded academic scholarships.

The ramifications of gender bias are not limited to the educational arena. Researchers have shown that in most cultures the lack of decision-making **power** among females regarding sexual and economic matters contributes to population growth and confines women to subservient roles to men—usually their fathers, and later, their husbands. Although women make up 45 percent of the workforce in the United States, 60 percent of professional women are in traditionally female occupations such as nursing and teaching.

Gender stereotypes defining appropriate activities and behavior for men and women are prevalent in every culture, even though they may differ slightly from culture to culture. Awareness of the existence of these biases will help to overcome their negative effects.

**Further Reading**
Childs, Ruth Axman. *Gender Bias and Fairness*. Washington, DC: ERIC Clearinghouse on Texts, Measurement, and Evaluation, 1990.

Gay, Kathleen. *Rights and Respect: What You Need to Know About Gender Bias*. Brookfield, CT: Millbrook Press, 1995.

Walker, Michael. "Gender Bias: Is Your Daughter's School Prepping Her for Failure?" *Better Homes and Gardens* (April 1993): 40+.

# Gender constancy

A child's realization that gender is fixed and does not change over time.

The concept of gender constancy, influenced by the **cognitive development** theory of **Jean Piaget**, was introduced by **Lawrence Kohlberg** (1927-1987). Addressing the formation of **gender identity** in terms of cognitive development, Kohlberg advanced the idea that the development of **sex roles** depends in large part on a child's understanding that gender remains constant throughout a person's lifetime. Children realize that they are male or female and are aware of the gender of others by the age of three. However, at these ages they still do not understand that people cannot change genders the way they can change their clothes, names, or behavior. Kohlberg theorized that children do not learn to behave in gender-appropriate ways until they understand that gender is permanent, which occurs at about the age of seven. At this point they start **modeling** the behavior of members of their own sex. Although it has been supported by some research studies, Kohlberg's theory has also been criticized on the grounds that children do show certain types of gender-associated behavior, such as toy and playmate selection, by the ages of two or three. This points to the fact that there are others factors, such as parental **reinforcement**, that influence the adoption of sex-typed behavior.

# Gender identity

The sense of identification with either the male or female sex, as manifested in appearance, behavior, and other aspects of a person's life.

Influenced by a combination of biological and sociological factors, gender identity emerges by the age of two or three and is reinforced at **puberty**. Once established, it is generally fixed for life.

Aside from **sex differences**, other biological contrasts between males and females are already evident in **childhood**. Girls mature faster than boys, are physically healthier, and are more advanced in developing oral and written linguistic skills. Boys are generally more advanced at envisioning and manipulating objects in space. They are more aggressive and more physically active, preferring noisy, boisterous forms of **play** that require larger groups and more space than the play of girls the same age. In spite of conscious attempts to reduce sex role stereotyping in recent decades, boys and girls are still treated differently by adults from the time they are born. The way adults play with infants has been found to differ based on gender—girls are treated more gently and approached more verbally than boys. As children grow older, many parents, teachers, and other authority figures still tend to encourage independence, **competition**, and exploration more in boys and expressivity, nurturance, and obedience in girls.

A major step in the formation of gender identity occurs at about the age of three when children first become aware of anatomical differences between the sexes, usu-

ally through observation of siblings or peers. The awareness of physical difference is followed by awareness of the cultural differences between males and females and identification with the parent of the same sex, whose behavior the child begins to imitate. The most famous 20th-century theory about the acquisition of gender identity at this stage of life is the **Oedipus complex** formulated by **Sigmund Freud** (1856-1939). Like its female counterpart, which Freud termed the Electra complex, the Oedipus complex revolves around a child's wish to possess the parent of the opposite sex, while simultaneously wishing to eliminate the parent of the same sex, who is perceived as a rival.

In the Oedipus complex, the young boy develops incestuous desires toward his mother, while regarding his father as a rival for her affections. Fearing that the father will cut off his penis in retaliation—a phenomenon Freud called castration anxiety—the boy represses his forbidden desires and finally comes to identify with the father, internalizing his values and characteristics, which form the basis for the child's **superego**. In the female version of this theory, the young girl's discovery of sexual difference results in penis envy, which parallels castration anxiety in boys. The girl blames her mother for depriving her of a penis, and desires her father because he possesses one. As in the Oedipus complex, the girl eventually represses her incestuous desires and identifies with the same-sex parent (in this case, the mother).

The Oedipus complex has been widely criticized, especially by feminist critics who reject its assumption that "anatomy is destiny." One respected feminist theory is that of Nancy Chodorow, for whom the central factor in gender identity acquisition is the mother's role as primary caregiver, which leads to a greater sense of interrelatedness in girls, who identify with the mother and go on to reproduce the same patterns of mothering in their own adult lives, while boys, needing to identify with the parent of the opposite sex, acquire a defining sense of separateness and independence early in life. This "reproduction of mothering," being both biologically and sociologically determined, is at least theoretically open to the possibility of change if patterns of parenting can be altered.

The formation of gender identity has been approached in different terms by **Lawrence Kohlberg** (1927-1987), who formulated the concept of **gender constancy**, the awareness that gender remains fixed throughout a person's lifetime. Kohlberg noted that while children are aware of their own gender and the gender of others by the age of three, they do not really begin assuming appropriate gender-based behavior until the age of about seven, when they first understand that gender is permanent—that they cannot change gender the way they can change their clothes or their behavior.

Kohlberg believed that children do not start systematically imitating the behavior of members of their own sex until that point.

While most people follow a predictable pattern in the acquisition of gender identity, some develop a gender identity inconsistent with their biological sex, a condition variously known as gender confusion, **gender identity disorder**, or **transgender**, which affects about 1 in 20,000 males and 1 in 50,000 females. Researchers have found that both early **socialization** and hormonal factors may play a role in the development of gender identity disorder. People with gender identity disorder usually feel from their earliest years that they are trapped in the wrong body and begin to show signs of gender confusion between the ages of two and four. They prefer playmates of the opposite sex at an age when most children prefer to spend time in the company of same-sex peers. They also show a preference for the clothing and typical activities of the opposite sex; transsexual males may show interest in dresses and makeup. Females with gender identity disorder are bored by ordinary female pastimes and prefer the rougher types of activity typically associated with males, such as contact sports.

Both male and female transsexuals believe and repeatedly insist that they actually are members of the opposite sex. They desire to live as members of the opposite sex, sometimes manifesting this desire by cross-dressing, either privately or in public. In some cases, adult transsexuals (both male and female) have their primary and secondary sexual characteristics altered through a sex change operation, consisting of surgery followed by hormone treatments.

## Further Reading

Chodorow, Nancy. *The Reproduction of Mothering: Psycho-analysis and the Sociology of Gender.* Berkeley: University of Berkeley Press, 1978.
Diamant, Louis, and Richard D. McAnulty, eds. *The Psychology of Sexual Orientation, Behavior, and Identity: A Handbook.* Westport, CT: Greenwood Press, 1995.
Golombok, Susan, and Robyn Fivush. *Gender Development.* Cambridge: Cambridge University Press, 1994.

# Gender identity disorder

A condition, sometimes called transsexualism, in which an individual develops a gender identity inconsistent with their anatomical and genetic sex.

Researchers have suggested that both early **socialization** and prenatal **hormones** may play an important role in the development of transsexuality. It is estimated that about 1 in 20,000 males and 1 in 50,000 females are transsexuals. **Gender identity** disorder generally begin to manifest between the ages of two and four, in which a child displays a preference for the clothing and typical activities of the opposite sex and also prefer playmates of the opposite sex. Young boys like to play house (assuming a female role), draw pictures of girls, and play with dolls. Girls with gender identity disorder prefer short hairstyles and boys' clothing, have negative feelings about maturing physically as they approach **adolescence**, and show little interest in typically female pastimes, preferring the traditionally rougher male modes of play, including contact sports. Cross-gender behavior carries a greater social stigma for boys than girls; girls with gender identity disorder experience less overall social rejection, at least until adolescence. Approximately five times more boys than girls are referred to therapists for the disorder.

Most children outgrow gender identity disorder with time and the influence of their parents and peers. Adolescents with gender identity disorder are prone to low **self-esteem**, social isolation, and distress, and are especially vulnerable to **depression** and **suicide**. Preoccupied with cross-gender wishes, they fail to develop both romantic relationships with the opposite sex and peer relationships with members of their own sex, and their relationships with their parents may suffer as well. Approximately 75 percent of boys with gender identity disorder display a homosexual or bisexual orientation by late adolescence or early adulthood, although without a continuation of the disorder. Most of the remaining 25 percent become heterosexual, also without a continuation of the disorder, and those individuals in whom gender identity disorder persists into adulthood may develop either a homosexual or heterosexual orientation.

The major symptom of gender identity disorder in adults is the desire to live as a member of the opposite sex by adopting its social role, behavior, and physical appearance. Some transsexuals become obsessed with activities that reduce gender-related **stress**, including cross-dressing (dressing as a member of the opposite sex), which may be practiced either privately or in public. (*Transvestism* is a condition in which individuals cross-dress primarily for sexual arousal.) Both male and female transsexuals may elect to alter their primary and secondary sexual characteristics by undergoing surgery to make their genitals as much like those of the opposite sex as possible. Sex-change surgery was pioneered in Europe in the early 1930s and had gained international notoriety after the procedure was performed on a former American soldier named George (Christine) Jorgenson in Denmark in 1952.

Public awareness of transsexualism has increased through the publicity surrounding such prominent figures as British travel writer Jan Morris (who wrote about her experiences in her book *Conundrum*) and American tennis star Renee Richards. As of the mid-1970s, it was estimated that more than 2,500 Americans had undergone sex-change operations, and in Europe 1 in 30,000 males and 1 in 100,000 females sought sex-change surgery. The operation itself is accompanied by hormone treatments that aid in acquiring the secondary sex characteristics of the desired sex. While a number of individuals have gone on to lead happy, productive lives following sex-change operations, others fail to make the transition and continue to suffer from gender identity disorder.

*See also* Gender identity; Sex roles; Transgender

## Further Reading

Morrison, James. *DSM-IV Made Easy: The Clinician's Guide to Diagnosis.* New York: The Guilford Press, 1995

# General adaptation syndrome

A profound physiological reaction of an organism to severe stress, consisting of three stages.

The first stage of the general **adaptation** syndrome is alarm reaction, and includes the shock phase and the countershock phase. In the shock phase, there are significant changes in several organic systems. For example, body temperature and blood pressure are lowered, and muscle tone is decreased. In the countershock phase, there is a defensive response to these changes, including an increased production of adrenocortical **hormones**. The second is resistance, during which the affected systems recover toward their **normal** levels of functioning. The third stage is exhaustion, and is reached if the defenses of the organism are unable to withstand the **stress**. In the exhaustion stage, the shock phase of the alarm reaction is essentially repeated, resulting in death.

## Further Reading

Selye, Hans. *The Stress of Life.* New York: McGraw-Hill, 1978.

# Genital stage

See **Psychosexual stages**

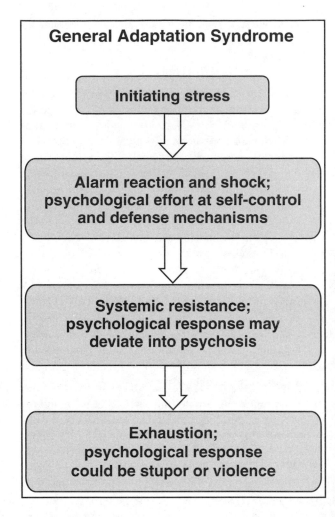

## General Adaptation Syndrome

Initiating stress

Alarm reaction and shock; psychological effort at self-control and defense mechanisms

Systemic resistance; psychological response may deviate into psychosis

Exhaustion; psychological response could be stupor or violence

# Genius

A state of intellectual or creative giftedness.

There are differences in intellectual attainment among people. Some people make strides in learning and **creativity** that are well beyond what would normally be expected and are called geniuses. Although definitions of genius, or **giftedness**, are inevitably culture-bound and subjective, psychologists are trying to determine what factors might contribute to its emergence.

In a 1981 study, William Fowler surveyed decades of scientific inquiry into the making of genius. He found that in one important study, 87% of the gifted children studied had been given substantial, intensive training by their parents at home, focusing on speech, reading, and mathematics—all highly structured avenues. The parents of these gifted children had ambitious and sometimes very specific plans for their children. The parents were nearly all from the professional class, allowing them the time and the money to devote such resources to the intellectual development of their children.

Psychologists have examined various home-tutoring techniques and have found that there appears to be no single kind of stimulation that might turn a **normal** child into a gifted child. All methods seem to work, provided they center on language or math. It has even been suggested that the method matters little because the child is responding to the quantity of **attention** rather than to the content of what is being taught.

When a person reaches school age, it becomes possible to measure his or her **intelligence** more reliably. Intelligence tests are the subject of intense debate among psychologists, educators, and the general public. Most standardized tests measure logical-mathematical, linguistic, and spatial intelligence. However, the idea of multiple intelligences was formulated by psychologist **Howard Gardner**, who defined six components of intelligence: linguistic, logical-mathematical, spatial, musical, bodily-kinesthetic, and personal. Today, many people regard intelligence as comprising different types of skills and talents. Most school systems, however, continue to measure intelligence, and giftedness, according to test results measuring logical-mathematical, linguistic, and spatial intelligence. Gifted people are often identified by their unusually high scores on traditional intelligence tests.

## Further Reading

Allman, Arthur. "The Anatomy of a Genius." *U.S. News and World Report,* (October 25, 1993).

Begley, Sharon. "The Puzzle of Genius." *Newsweek,* (June 28, 1993).

Gottfried, Allen W., et al. *Gifted IQ: Early Developmental Aspects.* New York: Plenum Press, 1994.

Howe, Michael J.A. *The Origins of Exceptional Abilities.* Cambridge, MA: Basil Blackwell, 1990.

# Arnold Gesell

### 1880-1961

American psychologist and pediatrician whose principal area of study was the mental and physical development of normal individuals from birth through adolescence.

Arnold Gesell was born in Alma, Wisconsin, and received his bachelor's degree from the University of Wisconsin. In 1906, he earned his Ph.D. from Clark University, where he was motivated to specialize in **child development** by studying with the prominent American psychologist **G. Stanley Hall** (1844-1924). Gesell received his M.D. from Yale University in 1915. After briefly holding a

**Arnold Gesell** *(UPI/Corbis-Bettmann. Reproduced with permission.)*

position at the Los Angeles State Normal School, he was appointed an assistant professor of at Yale University, where he established the Clinic of Child Development and served as its director from 1911 to 1948. He was later a consultant with the Gesell Institute of Child Development. Gesell's early work involved the study of **mental retardation** in children, but he soon became convinced that an understanding of normal development is necessary for the understanding of abnormal development.

Gesell was among the first to implement a quantitative study of human development from **birth** through **adolescence**, focusing his research on the extensive study of a small number of children. He began with preschool children and later extended his work to ages 5 to 10 and 10 to 16. From his findings, Gesell concluded that mental and physical development in infants, children, and adolescents are comparable and parallel orderly processes. In his clinic, he trained researchers to collect data and produced reports that had a widespread influence on both parents and educators. The results of his research were utilized in creating the Gesell Development Schedules, which can be used with children between four weeks and six years of age. The test measures responses to standardized materials and situations both qualitatively and quantitatively. Areas emphasized include motor and **language development**, adaptive behavior, and personal-social behavior. The results of the test are expressed first as developmental age (DA), which is then converted into developmental quotient (DQ), representing "the portion of normal development that is present at any age." A separate developmental quotient may be obtained for each of the functions on which the scale is built.

In the 1940s and 1950s, Gesell was widely regarded as the nation's foremost authority on child rearing and development, and developmental quotients based on his development schedules were widely used as an assessment of children's **intelligence**. He wrote several best-selling books, including *Infant and Child in the Culture of Today* (1943) and *The Child from Five to Ten* (1946), both co-authored with Frances L. Ilg. Gesell argued, in widely read publications, that the best way to raise children requires reasonable guidance, rather than permissiveness or rigidity. His influence was also felt through the many child psychologists and pediatricians he helped educate. Eventually, the preeminence of Gesell's ideas gave way to theories that stressed the importance of environmental rather than internal elements in child development, as the ideas of **Jerome S. Bruner** and **Jean Piaget** gained prominence. Gesell was criticized for basing his work too rigidly on observation of a small number of research subjects who were all children of white, middle-class parents in a single New England city. He was also faulted for allowing too little leeway for individual and cultural differences in growth patterns.

Although the developmental quotient is no longer accepted as a valid measure of intellectual **ability**, Gesell remains an important pioneer in child development, and is recognized for his advances in the methodology of observing and measuring behavior. He also inaugurated the use of photography and observation through one-way mirrors as research tools. Gesell was also a prolific author, whose other books include *An Atlas of Infant Behavior* (1934) and *Youth: The Years from Ten to Sixteen* (1956).

*See also* Infancy

**Further Reading**
Ames, Louise Bates. *Arnold Gesell: Themes of His Work*. New York: Human Sciences Press, 1989.

# Gestalt principles of organization

Principles of perceptual organization proposed by the early 20th-century German psychologists of the Gestalt school.

The psychologists in Germany who proposed the Gestalt principles of organization developed theories and research focusing on the effects of holistic patterns or configurations (the rough meaning of the German term *Gestalt* ) on **perception**. Much of their work emphasized the concept that the whole affects the way in which parts are perceived: "the whole is more than the sum of its parts."

The Gestalt principles of organization involve observations about the ways in which we group together various stimuli to arrive at perceptions of patterns and shapes. For example, at the most basic level the principle of proximity leads us to group together objects that are close to each other spatially. We also have a powerful tendency to group together mentally items that are similar to each other in terms of their appearance, texture, or other properties. Other qualities that govern our perceptions are continuity and closure: if part of an object (or person) is blocked from view, we assume that it is a continuous whole and automatically "fill in" the missing part or parts.

The attribute of simplicity also affects perception. People will interpret something they see in a manner that provides the simplest possible explanation. For example, if all other things are equal and one has a choice of perceiving a drawing as either two- or three-dimensional, it will be perceived as two-dimensional. However, if its features make it more complex to interpret in two dimensions than in three, one will automatically perceive it as three-dimensional. A final influence on perception, called "common fate," has to do with movement. Visual stimuli (such as a flock of birds or a marching band) that are moving in the same direction and at the same speed are perceived as belonging together.

**Further Reading**
Köhler, Wolfgang. *The Task of Gestalt Psychology.* Princeton, NJ: Princeton University Press, 1972.

# Gestalt psychology

The school of psychology that emphasizes the study of experience and behavior as wholes rather than independently functioning, disparate parts.

The Gestaltists were at odds with the popular school of psychology of the day, known as structuralism, whose proponents believed that the mind consists of units or elements and could be understood by mapping and studying them in combination. The Gestalt psychologists believed that mental experience was dependent not on a simple combination of elements but on the organization and patterning of experience and of one's perceptions. Thus, they held that behavior must be studied in all its complexity rather than separated into discrete components, and that **perception**, learning, and other cognitive functions should be seen as structured wholes.

The Gestalt school of psychology was founded in the early twentieth century by the German psychologist **Max Wertheimer** and his younger colleagues, **Kurt Koffka** and **Wolfgang Köhler**. The association between the three men began in 1910 with early studies of perception that ultimately led to the wide-ranging Gestalt view of the whole as more than the sum of its parts. Investigating the phenomenon of "apparent perception"— on which motion pictures are based—they discovered that when two lights were flashed in succession under specific conditions, an illusion of continuous motion was produced. The subject perceived a single light which appeared to move from the position of the first light to the position of the second light. This and other experiments led the Gestaltists to conclude that the mind imposes its own patterns of organization on the stimuli it receives rather than merely recording them, and that the significance of the mental "wholes" thus formed transcends that of their component parts. In a series of lectures in 1913, Wertheimer outlined a new psychological approach based on the belief that mental operations consist mainly of these organic "wholes" rather than the chains of associated sensations and impressions emphasized by **Wilhelm Wundt** (1832-1920) and other psychological researchers of the day.

In the same year Köhler began six years of experimental animal research on the Canary Islands during which he made many discoveries that applied Gestalt theories to animal learning and perception. One of his most famous experiments was with chickens which he trained to peck grains from either the lighter or darker of two sheets of paper. When the chickens trained to prefer the light color were presented with a choice between that color and a new sheet that was still lighter, a majority switched to the new sheet. Similarly, chickens trained to prefer the darker color, when presented with a parallel choice, chose a new, darker color. These results, Köhler maintained, proved that what the chickens had learned was an association with a *relationship*, rather than with a specific color. This finding, which contradicted contemporary behaviorist theories, became known as the Gestalt *law of transposition*, because the test subjects had transposed their original experience to a new set of circumstances.

Although its founders conceived of Gestalt theory as a way to understand **motivation**, learning, and other cognitive processes, much early Gestalt research was concentrated in the area of perception. In the dozen years following the first studies in apparent motion, additional

rules of perception were discovered. Among the most well-known are laws involving *proximity* (objects that are closer together are more likely to be seen as belonging together); *similarity* (similar elements are perceived as belonging together); *continuity* (sensations that seem to create a continuous form are perceived as belonging together); *closure* (the tendency that makes people mentally fill in missing areas to create a whole); *texture* (the tendency to group together items with a similar texture); *simplicity* (grouping items together in the simplest way possible); and *common fate* (grouping together sets of objects moving in the same direction at the same speed).

Another well-known Gestalt concept illustrating the significance of the whole involves the interdependence of figure and ground. The Gestaltists introduced the idea that perception occurs in "fields" consisting of a figure (which receives most of the viewer's **attention**) and a ground (the background). Neither figure nor ground can exist without the **contrast** they provide for each other: thus, they form an inseparable whole that can only be understood as part of a dynamic process greater than the sum of its individual parts. (The phenomenon of figure and ground is most often illustrated by the Rubin vase, which can be perceived as either two dark profiles on a white background, or a white vase on a dark background.) Köhler's work with primates during this period yielded important findings—transferable to humans—on learning and problem solving that contributed further to the body of Gestalt theory. His experiments emphasized "insight learning," through which the test subject finds a solution to a problem by suddenly "seeing it whole" rather than through random trial and error attempts, or reward-driven **conditioning**. Hence, Köhler offered a basis for viewing learning as the result of higher-level thinking involving the creative reorganization of data to produce new ways of envisioning a problem.

In 1921, Köhler was appointed to the most prestigious position in German psychology—directorship of the Psychological Institute at the University of Berlin. Under his **leadership**, it became a center for Gestalt studies, which remained a major force in German psychology until the mid-1930s, when Nazi pressure led to Köhler's resignation and emigration to the United States. Articles and books published in English by Kurt Koffka had also popularized Gestalt psychology in the United States beginning in 1922, and both Koffka and Köhler received invitations to lecture in America throughout the 1920s. By the early 1930s, however, the Gestalt school had become subordinated to the reigning enthusiasm for **behaviorism**, a movement antithetical to its principles.

While the Gestaltists were at odds with many popular psychological views of their time, including those held in introspective psychology, they did maintain the value of an unstructured form of introspection known as "phenomenology." Phenomenological investigation explored questions regarding personal perception of motion, size, and color and provided additional feedback regarding perception and its importance in psychological experiences. This information influenced later perception-centered theories involving problem solving, **memory**, and learning.

*See also* Gestalt principles of organization

## Further Reading

Köhler, Wolfgang. *The Task of Gestalt Psychology.* Princeton, NJ: Princeton University Press, 1972.

McConville, Mark. *Adolescence: Psychotherapy and the Emergent Self.* San Francisco, CA: Jossey-Bass Publishers, 1995.

# Eleanor J. Gibson

## 1910-

Experimental psychologist noted for her work in the field of perceptual development in children and infants.

Gibson was born Eleanor Jack in Peoria, Illinois, into a successful Presbyterian family on December 7, 1910. Her parents were William A. and Isabel (Grier) Jack. She married fellow psychologist James J. Gibson on September 17, 1932. They had two children, James J. and Jean Grier.

Due to prevailing attitudes discouraging females—even gifted ones—from pursuing an education, young Eleanor was careful not to demonstrate her scholarly capabilities while at school. However, once ensconced in the nurturing atmosphere of Smith College, at Cornell University, where she completed her undergraduate degree in 1931, (and in 1933 her D.Sc.), she excelled in scientific subjects and chose to study psychology, no doubt encouraged by such eminent teachers as **Kurt Koffka**, **Fritz Heider**, and **James Gibson**, who would later become her husband.

Exceptionally brilliant, Jack was able to complete all her graduate training except the thesis in one year at Yale University. Her strength of **character**, confidence in her own research and remarkable insight regarding observation enabled her to overcome many difficulties and carve out a successful career. She was awarded her Ph.D. from Yale in 1938 and taught at Cornell University until her retirement in 1980.

Jack's early career was hampered by many factors. Firstly, she began in the period of the Great Depression.

It was particularly difficult for women to progress under these conditions. Gender discrimination was still the norm, and **Robert Yerkes** initially rejected her for postgraduate studies at Yale on this basis. She was also wrongfully accused of incompetence at one point, and the director of the laboratory later published her work as his own. On another occasion, her research animals were summarily removed from the laboratory. However, her personal strength and enthusiasm for her work enabled her to overcome these setbacks, and made no notable reverses to her distinguished career.

In 1932, after her marriage to James Gibson, Eleanor Gibson became his assistant. She and her husband had similar views regarding rigorous attention to detail when conducting research. In 1942, she went with her husband to Fort Worth, and then on to Santa Ana, California. During this time, her principal role was as wife and mother. However, before long, **boredom** would prompt her return to research.

In 1949, Gibson again accompanied her husband to Cornell as an unpaid research associate. It was here that she developed her theory of **avoidance learning**, based on studies of children. At this time, she and her husband were awarded a large Air Force grant, which enabled her to begin her work on perceptual learning. In 1955, Gibson's first theory of perceptual learning, which was formulated in collaboration with her husband, appeared. Two years later, they again published the results of joint research, on invariants under transformation. These papers later formed the basis for James Gibson's ecological theory.

Gibson's original goal was to become a comparative psychologist, and although at the time she did not have access to her own laboratory and was not able to pursue her chosen field of research with children, she is acknowledged to have single-handedly developed the field. She began work on the "Visual Cliff," her best-known work, with Richard Walk in the mid–1950's. They discovered that baby animals avoided a simulated cliff constructed by suspending a piece of glass above the floor.

In 1975 Gibson was able to establish her own infant study laboratory. This enabled her to devote her research to ecological psychology, perhaps even more so after her husband's death in 1979. She has pursued her work on perceptual development, more recently concentrating on the concept of affordance. Gibson is also an active member of the International Society for Ecological Psychology.

Gibson has been the recipient of many awards during her career, among them an award from the **American Psychological Association** for distinguished scientific contribution in 1968; in 1983 the national medal for science; in 1992 a lifetime achievement award.

Apart from her work at Cornell, Gibson also taught at many other universities, including the University of Pennsylvania in 1984; visiting professor of psychology, Emory University, 1988–90; distinguished visiting professor at the University of California, Davis, 1978; visiting professor at Massachusetts Institute of Technology; and the Institute of Child Development at the University of Minnesota (1980).

Gibson's major published work is possibly *An Odyssey in Learning and Perception*, (1991), which consolidates much of her lifetime's work. She also wrote *Principles of Perceptual Learning and Development*, in 1967, for which she received the Century Award.

Gibson retired in 1980 and is Professor Emeritus at Cornell University. Although now advanced in age, Professor Gibson continues to work at the Middlebury University in Vermont.

Patricia Skinner

**Further Reading**
Gibson, Eleanor J. *An Odyssey in Learning and Perception* Cambridge, Massachusetts: The MIT Press, 1991

## James Jerome Gibson

### 1904-1979
American psychologist known for his work on visual perception.

James Jerome Gibson proposed a theory of **vision** that was a first of its kind; he suggested that visual **perception** was the direct detection of environmental invariances, and that visual perception did not require inference or information processing.

Gibson was born in 1904 in McConnelsville, Ohio. He started his undergraduate career at Northwestern University. He transferred to Princeton University, where he earned his B.A. in 1925 and his Ph.D. in 1928. His dissertation research focused on **memory** and learning. During his career he taught psychology at Smith College between 1928 and 1949 and then went on to teach at Cornell between 1949 and 1972. At Smith, Gibson met **Kurt Koffka**, a proponent of **Gestalt psychology**. Koffka's influence shaped Gibson's future research and practice.

Gibson served in World War II and during his time in the service he directed the U.S. Air Force Research Unit in Aviation Psychology. In the Army, Gibson developed tests used to screen potential pilots. In doing so, he made the observation that more information could be drawn from moving pictures, such as film, than static ones. This observation sparked his interest in visual perception.

After the war, Gibson returned to Smith for a brief period before moving to Cornell. Gibson married **Eleanor Jack Gibson**, who became a major psychologist in her own right. Together they had two sons. In 1950 Gibson published *The Perception of the Visual World* which outlined his ground breaking theory of visual perception. In this publication, Gibson asserted that texture gradients on the ground are linked to similar gradients found on the retina in the eye. These complementary gradients allow humans to have **depth perception**. He further suggested that a new branch of science, called ecological optics, was needed to study perceptions in more detail. His next book, *The Senses Considered as Perceptual Systems*, outlined this new discipline in detail.

Gibson's theory was that of direct perception, which means that humans directly perceive their environment through stimulation of the retina. Traditionally, and especially by Gestalt psychologists, perception was believed to be indirect. According to this theory, humans do not directly perceive their environment. It is only through sensory stimulation over time that we learn what is in our environments, and that we perceive much more than mere sensory input.

Although Gibson's theory was met with much criticism, it did help advance the study of perception. Through his theory of ecological optics, the study of perception shifted from laboratory-created situations to real environmental tests. His ideas also pushed further research into the areas of vision and perception. Gibson died in 1979.

Catherine Dybiec Holm

**Further Reading**
Sheehy et al, eds. *Biographical dictionary of psychology* New York: Routledge, 1997.

## Giftedness

Above-average intellectual or creative ability, or talent in a particular area, such as music, art, or athletics.

Intellectual giftedness is generally indicated by an IQ of at least 125 or 130. People who are extremely creative are also considered gifted, although their giftedness can be hard to identify by academic performance or standardized tests. Giftedness has been defined not only in terms of specific talents and academic abilities, but also by general intellectual characteristics (including curiosity, **motivation**, **ability** to see relationships, and long **attention** span) and **personality traits** such as **leadership** ability, independence, and intuitiveness. In general, gifted people are creative, innovative thinkers who are able to envision multiple approaches to a problem and devise innovative and unusual solutions to it.

In the early days of **intelligence** testing it was widely thought that a person's mental abilities were genetically determined and varied little throughout the life span, but it is now believed that nurture plays a significant role in giftedness. Researchers comparing the behavior of parents of gifted and average children have found significant differences in childrearing practices. The parents of gifted children spend more time reading to them and encouraging creative types of **play** and are more involved with their schooling. They are also more likely to actively encourage **language development** and expose their children to cultural resources outside the home, including those not restricted specifically to children, such as art and natural history museums. The involvement of fathers in a child's academic progress has been found to have a positive effect on both boys and girls in elementary school in terms of both grades and achievement test scores. Within the **family**, grandparents can also play a positive role as mentors, listeners, and role models. A disproportionately large percentage of high-achieving women have reported that at least one grandparent played a significant role in their lives during **childhood**. (The anthropologist **Margaret Mead** named her paternal grandmother as the person with the single greatest influence on her life.) Even within a single family, giftedness can be influenced by such environmental factors as **birth** order, gender, differences in treatment by parents, and other unique aspects of a particular child's experiences.

Standardized intelligence tests—most often the Stanford-Binet or Wechsler tests—almost always play a role in assessing giftedness, even though such tests have been criticized on a variety of grounds, including an overly narrow definition of intelligence, possible racial and cultural bias, and the risk of unreliability due to variations in testing conditions. Critics have questioned the correlation of IQ scores with achievement later in life, pointing out that standardized tests don't measure many of the personal qualities that contribute to professional success, such as independence, motivation, persistence, and interpersonal skills. In addition, the **creativity** and intuition that are hallmarks of giftedness may actually lower a person's scores on tests that ask for a single solution to a problem rather than rewarding the ability to envision multiple solutions, a trait—called **divergent** **thinking** by psychologists and educators—that often characterizes giftedness.

### Further Reading

Sternberg, Robert J. and Janet E. Davidson, eds. *Conceptions of Giftedness*. London: Cambridge University Press, 1986.

# Gross motor skills

The abilities required in order to control the large muscles of the body for walking, running, sitting, crawling, and other activities.

Motor skills are deliberate and controlled movements requiring both muscle development and maturation of the **central nervous system**. In addition, the skeletal system must be strong enough to support the movement and weight involved in any new activity. Once these conditions are met, children learn new physical skills by practicing them until each skill is mastered.

Gross motor skills, like **fine motor skills** —which involve control of the fingers and hands—develop in an orderly sequence. Although norms for motor development have been charted in great detail by researchers and clinicians over the past 50 years, its pace varies considerably from one child to the next. The more complex the skills, the greater the possible variation in **normal** children. The normal age for learning to walk has a range of several months, while the age range for turning one's head, a simpler skill that occurs much earlier, is considerably narrower. In addition to variations among children, an individual child's rate of progress varies as well, often including rapid spurts of development and frustrating periods of delay. Although rapid motor development in early **childhood** is often a good predictor of coordination and athletic **ability** later in life, there is no proven correlation between a child's rate of motor development and his **intelligence**. In most cases, a delay in mastering a specific motor skill is temporary and does not indicate a serious problem. However, medical help should be sought if a child is significantly behind his peers in motor development or if he regresses, losing previously acquired skills.

## Infancy and toddlerhood

The sequence of gross motor development is determined by two developmental principles that also govern physical growth. The cephalo-caudal pattern, or head-to-toe development, refers to the way the upper parts of the body, beginning with the head, develop before the lower ones. Thus, infants can lift their heads and shoulders before they can sit up, which, in turn, precedes standing and walking. The other pattern of both development and maturation is proximo-distal, or trunk to extremities. One of the first things an infant achieves is head control. Although they are born with virtually no head or neck control, most infants can lift their heads to a 45-degree angle by the age of four to six weeks, and they can lift both their heads and chests at an average age of eight weeks. Most infants can turn their heads to both sides within 16 to 20 weeks and lift their heads while lying on their backs within 24 to 28 weeks. By about 36 to 42 weeks, or 9 to 10 months, most infants can sit up unassisted for substantial periods of time with both hands free for playing.

One of the major tasks in gross motor development is locomotion, or the ability to move from one place to another. An infant progresses gradually from rolling (8 to 10 weeks) to creeping on her stomach and dragging her legs behind her (6 to 9 months) to actual crawling (7 months to a year). While the infant is learning these temporary means of locomotion, she is gradually becoming able to support increasing amounts of weight while in a standing position. In the second half year of life, babies begin pulling themselves up on furniture and other stationary objects. By the ages of 28 to 54 weeks, on average, they begin "cruising," or navigating a room in an upright position by holding on to the furniture to keep their balance. Eventually, they are able to walk while holding on to an adult with both hands, and then with only one. They usually take their first uncertain steps alone between the ages of 36 and 64 weeks and are competent walkers by the ages of 52 to 78 weeks. By the age of two years, children have begun to develop a variety of gross motor skills. They can run fairly well and negotiate stairs holding on to a banister with one hand and putting both feet on each step before going on to the next one. Most infants this age climb (some very actively) and have a rudimentary ability to kick and throw a ball.

## Preschool

During a child's first two years, most parents consider gross motor skills a very high priority; a child's first steps are the most universally celebrated developmental milestone. By the time a child is a preschooler, however, many parents shift the majority of their attention to the child's **cognitive development** in preparation for school. In addition, gross motor activity at these ages requires increasing amounts of space, equipment, and supervision. However, gross motor skills remain very important to a child's development, and maintaining a youngster's instinctive love of physical activity can make an important contribution to future fitness and health.

By the age of three, children walk with good posture and without watching their feet. They can also walk backwards and run with enough control for sudden stops or changes of direction. They can hop, stand on one foot, and negotiate the rungs of a jungle gym. They can walk up stairs alternating feet but usually still walk down putting both feet on each step. Other achievements include riding a tricycle and throwing a ball, although they have trouble catching it because they hold their arms out in front of their bodies no matter what direction the ball comes from. Four-year-olds can typically balance or hop on one foot, jump forward and backward over objects, and climb and descend stairs alternating feet. They can bounce and catch balls and throw accurately. Some four-year-olds can also skip. Children this age have gained an increased degree of self-consciousness about their motor activities that leads to increased feelings of pride and success when they master a new skill. However, it can also create feelings of inadequacy when they think they have failed. This concern with success can also lead them to try daring activities beyond their abilities, so they need to be monitored especially carefully.

## School-age

School-age children, who are not going through the rapid, unsettling growth spurts of early childhood or **adolescence**, are quite skilled at controlling their bodies and are generally good at a wide variety of physical activities, although the ability varies on the level of maturation and the physique of a child. Motor skills are mostly equal in boys and girls at this stage, except that boys have more forearm strength and girls have greater flexibility. Five-year-olds can skip, jump rope, catch a bounced ball, walk on their tiptoes, balance on one foot for over eight seconds, and engage in beginning acrobatics. Many can even ride a small two-wheeler bicycle. Eight- and nine-year-olds typically can ride a bicycle, swim, roller-skate, ice-skate, jump rope, scale fences, use a saw, hammer, and garden tools, and play a variety of sports. However, many of the sports prized by adults, often scaled down for play by children, require higher levels of distance judgment and **hand-eye coordination**, as well as quicker reaction times, than are reasonable for middle childhood. Games that are well suited to the motor skills of elementary school-age children include kick ball, dodge ball, and team relay races.

In adolescence, children develop increasing coordination and motor ability. They also gain greater physical strength and prolonged endurance. Adolescents are able to develop better distance judgment and hand-eye coordination than their younger counterparts. With practice, they can master the skills necessary for adult sports.

**Further Reading**

Eckert, Helen M. *Motor Development*. 3rd ed. Indianapolis, IN: Benchmark Press, 1987.

Hoppert, Rita. *Rings, Swings, and Climbing Things*. Chicago: Contemporary Books, 1985.

Lerch, Harold A., and Christine B. Stopka. *Developmental Motor Activities for All Children: From Theory to Practice*. Dubuque, IA: Brown and Benchmark, 1992.

Thomas, Jerry R., ed. *Motor Development in Childhood and Adolescence*. Minneapolis, MN: Burgess Publishing Co., 1984.

# Group therapy

The simultaneous treatment of several clients who meet regularly under the guidance of a therapist to obtain relief from particular symptoms or to pursue personal change.

Group therapy has numerous advantages over individual therapy. The therapist's knowledge about the clients offers an added dimension through the opportunity of observing them interact with each other. Clients are helped by listening to others discuss their problems (including problems more severe than theirs) and by realizing that they are not alone. They also gain hope by watching the progress of other members and experience the satisfaction of being helpful to others. Groups give the individual client the chance to model positive behavior they observe in others. Besides learning from each other, the trust and cohesiveness developed within the group can bolster each member's self-confidence and interpersonal skills. Group therapy gives clients an opportunity to test these new skills in a safe **environment**. In addition, the group experience may be therapeutic by offering the clients a chance to reenact or revise the way in which they relate to their primary families. Finally, group therapy is cost-effective, reducing the use of the therapist's total time.

The average group has six to twelve clients who meet at least once a week. All matters discussed by the group remain confidential. The therapist's functions include facilitating member participation and interaction, focusing conversation, mediating conflicts among members, offering emotional support when needed, facilitat-

**Group therapy sessions often take place in a home-like environment to make members feel more comfortable.** *(Will & Deni McIntyre. Photo Researchers, Inc. Reproduced with permission.)*

ing the establishment of group rules, and ensuring that the rules are followed.

Nevertheless, there are also some possible disadvantages to group therapy. Some clients may be less comfortable speaking openly in a group setting than in individual therapy, and some group feedback may actually be harmful to members. In addition, the process of group interaction itself may become a focal point of discussion, consuming a disproportionate amount of time compared with that spent on the actual problems from which its members are seeking relief. There are many different types of therapy groups, and a wide variety of approaches are used in them. Some groups are organized around a specific problem (such as alcohol dependence) or a type of client (such as single parents), or with the goal of acquiring a particular skill (such as assertiveness training). Groups can be open or closed to accepting new members after the initial session, and their meetings may be either time-limited or open-ended sessions.

Group therapy first came into widespread practice following World War II and employs numerous methods of **psychotherapy**, including psychodynamic, behavioral, and phenomenological. In **Fritz Perls**'s application of his Gestalt approach to group work, the therapist tends to work with one group member at a time. Other approaches, such as J.L. Moreno's psychodrama (role playing) method, stresses the interaction among group members. Psychodrama calls for the group to act out scenes relevant to the situation of a particular member under the therapist's guidance. Influenced by Moreno's approach, new action-based methods were introduced in the 1960s, including encounter groups, **sensitivity training**, marathon groups, and transactional analysis, whose foremost spokesperson was Eric Berne. Marathon groups, which can last for extended periods of time, are geared toward wearing down the members' defenses to allow for more intense interaction. In addition to the **adaptation** of individual psychotherapeutic methods for groups, the popularity of group therapy has also grown out of the development of methods initially intended for groups, including Kurt Lewin's work with T-groups at the National Training Laboratories in Bethel, Maine, during the 1940s and similar work by researchers at the Tavistock Institute in London.

Group therapy is practiced in a variety of settings, including both inpatient and outpatient facilities, and is used to treat anxiety, **mood**, and **personality** disorders as well as psychoses. Since the 1980s, techniques borrowed from group therapy have been widely used by a profusion of **self-help groups** consisting of people who share a specific problem or situation ranging from single parenthood and overeating to drug addiction, **child abuse**, and cancer. The primary difference of these groups from traditional group therapy sessions is the absence of facilitation by a **mental health** professional.

### Further Reading

Friedman, William H. *Practical Group Therapy: A Guide for Clinicians.* San Francisco: Jossey-Bass, 1989.

Helmering, Doris Wild. *Group Therapy—Who Needs It?* Millbrae, CA: Celestial Arts, 1976.

# Guilt

An emotional state produced by thoughts that we have not lived up to our ideal self and could have done otherwise.

Guilt is both a cognitive and an emotional experience that occurs when a person realizes that he or she has violated a moral standard and is responsible for that violation. A guilty **conscience** results from thoughts that we have not lived up to our ideal self. Guilt feelings may also inhibit us from falling short of our ideal again in the future. Individual guilt is an inner reflection on personal wrongdoing, while collective guilt is a shared state resulting from group—such as corporate, national, or community—wrongdoing.

## STAGES OF GUILT DEVELOPMENT

The researcher M. L. Hoffman has proposed the following stages of guilt development:

*Infancy*—Because infants have no clear sense of separate identity or the effect of their behavior on others, it would be impossible for them to feel true guilt over hurting another.

*Early childhood*—Young children understand themselves as physically separate from others, but do not yet have a deep understanding of others' inner states; therefore, they feel guilt over hurting another person physically, but not over doing emotional damage.

*Middle childhood*—With the increased understanding of others' inner states, children develop a sense of guilt over inflicting emotional pain on others or failing to act on another's behalf.

*Adolescence to adulthood*—Cognitive development now allows the young adult to perceive abstract, universal concepts of identity and suffering and, therefore, to feel a sense of guilt over more general harm, such as world hunger, poverty, oppression, etc.

Guilt serves as both an indicator and inhibitor of wrongdoing. Healthy guilt is an appropriate response to harming another and is resolved through atonement, such as making amends, apologizing, or accepting **punishment**. Unhealthy guilt, sometimes called neurotic or debilitating guilt, is a pervasive sense of responsibility for others' pain that is not resolved, despite efforts to atone. Healthy guilt inspires a person to behave in the best interests of him- or herself and others and make amends when any wrong is done. Unhealthy guilt stifles a person's natural expression of self and prohibits intimacy with others.

Unhealthy guilt can be instilled when a child is continually barraged with shaming statements that criticize the child's self, rather than focusing on the specific harmful behavior. A statement such as, "It is wrong to take someone else's things without permission—please return my book," creates an appropriate awareness in the child of healthy guilt for doing wrong. Saying, "Give me my book back! I can't trust you with anything!" shames the child, declaring that he or she is by nature untrustworthy and will never be better than a thief, regardless of future behavior. Consequently, the child sees his or her identity as defective, and may feel powerless to atone for any wrongdoings. This identity can be carried into adulthood, creating a sense of debilitating guilt.

An important difference between shame and guilt is that in the former, a person does not feel he could have avoided the action; in guilt, he feels responsible. Guilt can be used to manipulate someone into behaving in a certain way. This is known as a "guilt trip." Provoking another's sense of guilt in order to obtain something that he or she might not otherwise have offered is a manipulation of internal motivations. If a woman tells her husband that she is going out for the evening with her girlfriends, and her husband responds, "Go ahead and go to the movie, dear . . . don't worry about me . . . I'll be fine here all by myself in this big old house all evening with nothing to do . . . ," the wife will be made to feel guilty for her husband's loneliness. If the guilt trip is heavy, the wife may decide to stay home with the husband, even though she really wants to go to the movie.

It is appropriate to let people know when they have unnecessarily or intentionally hurt others, or have ignored their responsibilities to others. This will instill fair guilt that will help a person be less hurtful in the future.

Although conclusive studies have yet to be conducted, it is likely that the sense of guilt changes along with a person's cognitive and social development. These stages have yet to be thoroughly documented and are still open to critique.

Guilt can be deactivated, the conscience "turned off." Some people never seem to develop a healthy sense of guilt in the first place, through a failure to develop **empathy** or a lack of appropriate limits, while others choose to turn theirs off. Guilt can be deactivated in two different ways:

1) The person convinces him- or herself that the act was not a violation of what is right.

2) The person reasons that he or she has no control over the events of life and is therefore not responsible for the outcome. With no sense of personal responsibility, there can be no sense of guilt.

When guilt is reduced, internal limits on behavior disappear and people can act without remorse.

*See also* Moral development; Self-conscious emotions

Dianne K. Daeg de Mott

## Further Reading

Greenspan, P.S. *Practical Guilt: Moral Dilemmas, Emotions, and Social Norms.* New York/Oxford: Oxford University Press, 1995.

Hoffman, M. L. "Development of Prosocial Motivation: Empathy and Guilt." In *The Development of Prosocial Behavior*, edited by N. Eisenberg, pp. 218-31. New York: Academic Press, 1982.

Kurtines, William M., and Jacob L. Gewirtz, eds. *Moral Development: An Introduction.* Boston: Allyn and Bacon, 1995.

Middleton-Moz, Jane. *Shame and Guilt: Masters of Disguise.* Deerfield Beach, FL: Health Communications, 1990.

Wechsler, Harlan J. *What's So Bad About Guilt? Learning to Live With It Since We Can't Live Without It.* New York: Simon and Schuster, 1990.

# Edwin Ray Guthrie

**1886-1959**
American psychologist primarily noted for his work in evolving a single simple theory of learning.

Edwin Guthrie, born Jan. 9, 1886, in Lincoln, Nebraska, was one of five children. His mother was a schoolteacher, and his father a store manager. He received a bachelor's and a master's degree from the University of Nebraska, specializing in mathematics, philosophy, and psychology. He entered the University of Pennsylvania as a Harrison fellow, receiving his doctorate in 1912. His educational training and background reflect his analytical frame of reference in his psychological writings.

descriptive psychology and physiological concepts as sources of action, Guthrie added an objective theory of learning.

In the latter part of the 1920s Guthrie concerned himself with such topics as fusion on nonmusical intervals, **measurement** of **introversion** and **extroversion**, and purpose and mechanism in psychology. He seemed more inclined toward the exploration of learning in the 1930s and thereafter.

Much honored, Guthrie was elected president of the **American Psychological Association**. During World War II he was a lieutenant in the U.S. Army, serving as a consultant to the overseas branch of the general staff of the War Department and Office of War Information. He was made dean of the graduate school at the University of Washington in 1943.

Guthrie was considered a behaviorist. **Behaviorism** was a school of psychology which felt that psychology as a science must be predicated on a study of what is observable. Behaviorists excluded self-observation as a **scientific method** of investigation and preferred experimentation. They examined the concept of association and its limits in explaining how learning takes place. Guthrie's interpretations in his writings are based on the theory of learning: "A combination of stimuli which has accompanied a movement will on its recurrence tend to be followed by that movement."

In his theory Guthrie avoids mention of drives, successive repetitions, rewards, or **punishment**. He refers to stimuli and movement in combination. There is one type of learning; the same principle which applies for learning in one instance also applies for learning in all instances. The difference seen in learning does not arise from there being different kinds of learning but rather from different kinds of situations.

*See also* Learning theory

## Further Reading

Hilgard, Ernest R. *Theories of learning*. 1948. 3rd ed. 1966.

Bugelski, Bergen Richard. *The psychology of learning*. 1956.

**Edwin Ray Guthrie** *(Archives of the History of American Psychology. Reproduced with permission.)*

Guthrie taught high school mathematics for five years in Lincoln and Philadelphia. In 1914 he joined the University of Washington as an instructor in the department of philosophy, changing to the department of psychology five years later. During his rise to full professor in 1928, he developed his **learning theory** in association with Stevenson Smith, who was then department chairman of psychology at Washington.

Guthrie married Helen MacDonald of Berkeley, Calif., in June 1920. They traveled widely, and in France Guthrie met **Pierre Janet**, whose *Principles of Psychotherapy* he translated with his wife. Janet's writing had a great influence on Guthrie's thinking. To Janet's

# H

## Jay Haley

**1923-**

American psychologist known for his work in family therapy.

Jay Haley is an American psychologist recognized as one of the founders of **family therapy**. Haley was a cofounder of the Family Therapy Institute in Washington, D.C., and he created the publication *Family Process*. His contributions to the field of therapy include the development of strategic and humanistic processes.

Haley was born on July 19, 1923, in Midwest, Wyoming, to Andrew J. and Mary (Sneddon) Haley. On December 25, 1950, Haley married the musician Elizabeth Kuehn. They had three children: Kathleen, Andrew, and Gregory; and were later divorced in 1971. Haley received his B.A. from the University of California, Los Angeles, in 1948. He later earned a B.L.S. from the University of California, Berkeley, in 1951 and an M.A. from Stanford University in 1953.

Haley's career reflected his interest in family therapy, particularly in later years. He first served as a research associate between 1953 and 1962 in the Project for Study of Communication, Veterans Administration and Stanford University, Palo Alto, California. Between 1962 and 1967 Haley was director of family experimentation at the Mental Research Institute in Palo Alto. He served as the director of family research between 1967 and 1974 at the Philadelphia Child Guidance Clinic. Beginning in 1974, Haley was appointed as director of the Family Therapy Institute, Chevy Chase, Maryland, where he serves currently.

Haley published a number of works relating to family therapy. These include *Techniques of Family Therapy* (with Lynn Hoffman) in 1967, *Leaving Home* in 1981, and *Reflections on Therapy* in 1982. Other therapy-related works include *Uncommon Therapy* in 1972 and *Strategies of Psychotherapy* in 1963. He also wrote *The Power Tactics of Jesus Christ: And Other Essays* in 1969 and edited *Changing Families* (1971) and *Advanced Techniques of Hypnosis and Therapy* (1967). Haley received the Lifetime Achievement Award from the Milton H. Erickson Foundation.

Catherine Dybiec Holm

### Further Reading

Haley, Jay and D.R. Grove. *Conversations on Therapy: Popular Problems and Uncommon Solutions*. New York: W.W. Norton & Co., 1993.

Haley, Jay. *Learning and Teaching Therapy*. New York: Guilford Press, 1996.

Haley, Jay. *Leaving Home: The Therapy of Disturbed Young People*. New York: Taylor & Francis, 1997.

Haley, Jay. *Problem-Solving Therapy*. San Francisco: Jossey-Bass Publishers, 1991.

Haley, Jay. *Strategies of Psychotherapy*. New York: Triangle Press/W.W. Norton & Co., 1990.

## Halfway house

A live-in treatment facility for individuals who have completed inpatient, or hospital-based psychiatric treatment, but who are not prepared to make a full transition to independent living.

Halfway houses are typically staffed by therapists, counselors, social workers, other mental healthcare professionals, or lay-people with a background in the treatment area. Time spent both in and away from the house is highly structured. Residents are allowed to leave the facility for work and school, but are assigned housekeeping or other tasks that contribute to the house and its residents during their residential time. Attendance at on-site **group therapy** or support group meetings is usually required.

The average length of stay in a halfway house ranges from three months to a year. Both co-ed and gender specific halfway residences are in operation in the United States. Many halfway houses are converted apartment buildings or large private residences, and are often located in residential areas.

## Applications

A period of residence in a halfway house is often recommended when a controlled social **environment** is critical for the patient's continued recovery (e.g., with individuals leaving inpatient alcohol and/or drug **rehabilitation** facilities), or in cases of long-term **mental illness** (e.g., **schizophrenia**) where vocational rehabilitation (job training) and development of life skills is required.

As its name implies, the halfway house is a transitional treatment setting halfway between the intensive structured setting of an inpatient facility and independent living. The halfway house is designed to put theories and new behaviors discussed and experimented with during treatment into actual practice. Patients can interact with peers and develop healthy social relationships in a safe environment. Ideally, the new life skills and coping techniques they acquire will become habit before the patient is released and reintegrated into the community.

Halfway houses geared towards individuals without chronic mental illnesses also exist. Halfway residences for battered and abused women are in operation, and these facilities frequently provide access to **mental health** counseling and support groups for their residents as well as job training to prepare them for financial independence. And in some states, halfway houses are used as a transitory residence for low-risk prisoners in order to keep prison populations down and facilitate the transition from prison life back into society.

## Origins

In late 18th-century England, halfway houses were created to house, rehabilitate, and care for child criminals who were arrested for minor crimes such as theft. In 1896, Maud Ballington Booth, the co-founder of Volunteers of America and an advocate for prison reform, opened the first privately owned U.S. halfway house. Hope Hall No. 1, which was located in New York, met with great success, and Hope Hall No. 2 in Chicago soon followed. The halls were designed to reintroduce released convicts to the community, get them jobs, and nurse them back to health after serving their sentences in the disease-ridden prisons of the time. By 1902, over 3000 prisoners had passed through the doors of Hope Halls 1 and 2. The facilities declined in popularity after states began to adopt parole policies, but experienced a resurgence in popularity after World War II. Volunteers of America still operates Hope Hall facilities in conjunction with state correctional facilities today.

## Admission requirements

Individuals who are considered to be at risk for harming themselves or others and those who have a history of fleeing treatment facilities are not suitable candidates for halfway house residency. Halfway houses usually require residents to be self-sufficient (e.g., hygiene and other basic self-care skills), and to be free of any severe physical impairment that would require ongoing medical care. Other requirements may exist for admittance into specific halfway house programs.

Paula Ford-Martin

## Further Reading

Flannery, Mary and Mark Glickman. *Fountain House: Portraits of Lives Reclaimed from Mental Illness.* Center City, MN: Hazeldon Information & Educational Services, 1996.

## Further Information

National Institute of Mental Health (NIMH). 6001 Executive Boulevard, Rm. 8184, MSC 9663, Bethesda, MD, USA. 20892-9663, fax: 301-443-4279, 301-443-4513. Email: nimhinfo@nih.gov. http://www.nimh.nih.gov.

# Granville Stanley Hall

### 1844-1924
American psychologist.

Granville Stanley Hall played a decisive role in the organization of American psychology. He invited **Sigmund Freud** and **Carl Jung** to America, thus contributing to the diffusion of **psychoanalysis**. Above all, he gave a crucial impetus to the study of the child and the life cycle (his last psychological book dealt with senescence, the process of becoming old). Hall stressed the social relevance of empirical developmental research, and authored the first major treatise on **adolescence**. His theories and methods have since been superseded, but the lifespan, stage-based perspective typical of this thinking became a central component of modern psychology.

Hall was born in 1844 in rural Massachusetts, the son of educated farmers. He studied at Williams College and at the Union Theological Seminary; in 1878 he received a Ph.D. from Harvard University for a thesis on the role of muscular sensations in space **perception**. He then studied with **Wilhelm Wundt** and Hermann Ludwig Ferdinand von Helmholtz in Germany. He joined

**Granville Stanley Hall** (The Library of Congress. Reproduced with permission.)

Johns Hopkins University in 1884, set up one of the first psychology laboratories in the U.S., and established the *American Journal of Psychology* to promote **experimental psychology**. In 1889, he became the first president of Clark University, which awarded many of the early American doctorates in psychology. He led a popular child-study and educational reform movement, which he supported through his journal *Pedagogical Seminary*. He inspired and was the first president of the **American Psychological Association**. Hall died in 1924.

Hall studied **childhood** by means of questionnaires (a method he pioneered) on topics such as children's **play**, lies, fears, **anger**, language, and art. He distributed them among teachers, thus amassing huge amounts of data. The backbone of Hall's thinking was the concept of recapitulation, according to which individual development repeats the history of the species. As supposedly apparent in children's games, childhood reflected primitive humanity. The following, "juvenile" stage corresponded to an age when humans were well adjusted to their **environment** and displayed tribal inclinations; it was therefore suited to the formation of groups adapted to the child's "social instinct." Adolescence was a "new birth" that brought forth ancestral passions, an age of "storm and stress" characterized by conflicting moods

and dispositions, a capacity for religious conversion, and an unlimited creative potential. Hall claimed that it was essential to channel these energies (especially sexual), and that it was "the apical stage of human development" and the starting point "for the super anthropoid that man is to become." His idealized and lyrical depiction of adolescence synthesized common nineteenth-century ideas about youth into a evolutionary framework and, while conveying nostalgia for a lost closeness to nature, provided an increasingly urban and industrialized society with a confident image of its own future.

**Further Reading**

Hall, G. S. *Adolescence: Its Psychology and its Relations to Physiology, Anthropology, Sociology, Sex, Crime, Religion and Education.* 2 vols., New York: Appleton, 1908.

———. *Life and Confessions of a Psychologist.* New York: Appleton, 1923.

Ross, D. G. *Stanley Hall: The Psychologist as Prophet.* Chicago: University of Chicago Press, 1972.

# Hallucinations

Compelling perceptual experiences which may be visual, tactile, olfactory, or auditory, but which lack a physical stimulus.

Although hallucinations are false perceptions, they carry the force of reality and are a definitive sign of **mental illness**. Hallucinations may be caused by organic deterioration or functional disorders, and can occur in **normal** people while asleep or awake, or as a result of **sensory deprivation**. Generally not positive experiences, hallucinations are often described as frightening and distressing. A person under a hallucinatory state may be either alert and intelligent or incoherent, depending on the type and degree of the disturbance.

One psychological condition commonly characterized by hallucinations is **schizophrenia**. In schizophrenia, the hallucinations are usually auditory, involving one or more voices. The voices may issue commands, comment on or seem to narrate the person's actions, or sound like an overheard conversation, and can be analyzed for greater insight into the patient's emotional state. Auditory hallucinations can also occur in severe **depression** and **mania**; seriously depressed persons may hear voices making derogatory remarks about them or threatening them with bodily harm. Visual hallucinations, on the other hand, are more likely to characterize organic neurological disturbances, such as **epilepsy**, and may occur prior to an epileptic seizure. Hallucinations involving the senses of **smell** and **touch** are less frequent than visual or auditory ones; however, tactile hallucinations have proven useful in the study and diagnosis of schizophrenia. Together with fearfulness and agitation, hallucinations are also a component of **delirium** tremens, which can afflict persons suffering from alcohol dependence.

Hallucinations can also be induced by ingesting drugs that alter the chemistry of the **brain**. (The technical name used for drug-induced hallucinations is hallucinosis.) The most widely known **hallucinogens**, or mind-altering drugs, are LSD, psilocybin, peyote, and mescaline, which act on the brain to produce perceptual, sensory, and cognitive experiences that are not occurring in reality. Effects vary from user to user and also individually from one experience to the next. Hallucinations produced by LSD are usually visual in nature. On an LSD "trip," for example, hallucinations can last eight to ten hours while those produced by mescaline average six to eight hours. Two illegal drugs manufactured to produce psychoactive effects, PCP (phencyclidine) and MDMA (Ecstasy), are not true hallucinogens, but both produce hallucinations of **body image** as well as psychoses. A person may also experience hallucinations while attempting to withdraw from a drug, such as "pink elephants" and other visual hallucinations from alcohol withdrawal. Withdrawal symptoms from cocaine are associated with the hallucinatory tactile sensation of something crawling under one's skin, often termed "the cocaine bug."

Other causes of hallucinations are **hypnosis**, lack of **sleep**, **stress**, illness, and fatigue, which can produce a rare and unique hallucination known as "the doppelganger." A person who has this experience sees his or her mirror image facing him or her three or four feet away, appearing as a transparent projection on a glassy surface. The hypnagogic hallucinations that occur in the zone between sleep and waking are both visual and auditory, and are strikingly detailed to those who can remember them. Sensory deprivation in subjects of laboratory experiments over a period of time has also been shown to produce hallucinations, as has electrical stimulation of the brain. Experiences called pseudohallucinations involve the **perception** of vivid images without the sense that they are actually located in external space—the perceiver recognizes that they are not real. Associated with isolation and emotional distress, they include such examples as shipwrecked sailors visualizing rescue boats or travelers stranded in the desert visualizing an oasis. Pseudohallucinations do not have the same psychiatric significance as true hallucinations.

People suffering from hallucinations may try to conceal them from others because of their negative connotations, and may receive more drastic forms of treatment or inadequate prognoses because of them. In contrast to mainstream cultural opinion, however, users of hallucinogens in the United States view hallucinations as positive and potentially enlightening, and in other cultures they are regarded for their healing faculties. In the Moche culture of coastal Peru, for example, traditional healers may ingest mescaline as part of a healing ritual in the belief that the hallucinations produced by it offer insight into the patient's condition and thus aid in the healing process.

## Further Reading

Andrews, Barbara. *Dreams and Waking Visions: A Journal.* New York: St. Martin's Press, 1989.

Guiley, Rosemary. *The Encyclopedia of Dreams: Symbols and Interpretations.* New York: Crossroad, 1993.

# Hallucinogens

*Substances that cause hallucination—perception of things or feelings that have no foundation in reality—when ingested.*

Hallucinogens, or psychedelics, are substances that alter users' thought processes or moods to the extent that they perceive objects or experience sensations that in fact have no basis in reality. Many natural and some synthetic substances have the **ability** to bring about **hallucinations**. In fact, because of the ready market for such chemicals, they are manufactured in illegal chemical laboratories for sale as hallucinogens. LSD (lysergic acid diethylamide) and many so-called designer drugs have no useful clinical function.

Hallucinogens have long been a component in the religious rites of various cultures, both in the New and Old Worlds. Among the oldest are substances from mushrooms or cactus that have been in use in Native American rites since before recorded history. Hallucinogenic mushrooms have been used for centuries in rites of medicine men to foresee the future or communicate with the gods. The mushroom is consumed by eating it or by drinking a beverage in which the mushroom has been boiled. The effects are similar to those experienced by an LSD user—enhancement of colors and sounds, introspective interludes, **perception** of nonexistent or absent objects or persons, and sometimes terrifying, ominous visions.

Another ancient, natural hallucinogenic substance is derived from the Mexican peyote cactus. The flowering head of the cactus contains a potent alkaloid called mescaline. Hallucinogenic substances can be found in a number of other plant species.

In the 1960s, hallucinogens were discovered and embraced by the hippie movement, which incorporated drugs into its culture. In addition, artists, poets, and writers of the time believed that the use of hallucinogens enhanced their creative prowess.

Use of LSD, the most widely known hallucinogen, declined after large numbers of users experienced serious, sometimes fatal, effects during the 1960s. In the United States, LSD was classified as a Schedule I drug according to the Controlled Substance Act of 1970. That designation is reserved for those drugs considered unsafe, medically useless, and with a high potential for abuse.

LSD made a comeback in the 1990s, becoming the most abused drug of people under 20 years of age. Its low cost ($1 to $5 per "hit"), ready availability, and a renewed interest in 1960s culture are blamed for the resurgence. A 1993 survey reported that 13% of 18- to 25-year-olds had used hallucinogens, in most cases LSD, at least once.

Drugs such as LSD are often differentiated from less potent psychedelics, which have the primary effect of inducing euphoria, relaxation, stimulation, relief from **pain**, or relief from anxiety. This group of drugs is exemplified by **marijuana**, which is available worldwide and constitutes one of the primary money crops in the United States. Opiates such as heroin or morphine, phencyclidine (PCP), and certain tranquilizers such as diazepam (Valium) also belong to this category.

LSD was first synthesized in 1938 by Dr. Albert Hofmann, a Swiss chemist who was seeking a headache remedy. Years later, he accidentally ingested a small, unknown quantity, and shortly afterward he was forced to stop his work and go home. Hofmann lay in a darkened room and later recorded in his diary that he was in a dazed condition and experienced "an uninterrupted stream of fantastic images of extraordinary plasticity and vividness…accompanied by an intense kaleidoscope-like play of colors."

Three days later, Hofmann purposely took another dose of LSD to verify that his previous experience was the result of taking the drug. He ingested what he thought was a small dose (250 micrograms), but which is actually about five times the amount needed to induce pronounced hallucinations in an adult male. His second hallucinatory experience was even more intense, and his journal describes the symptoms of LSD toxicity: a metallic **taste**, difficulty in breathing, dry and constricted throat, cramps, paralysis, and visual disturbances.

LSD is one of the most potent hallucinogens known, and no therapeutic benefits have been discovered. The usual dose for an adult is 50-100 micrograms. (A microgram is a millionth of a gram.) Higher doses will produce more intense effects and lower doses will produce milder effects. The so-called "acid trip" can be induced by swallowing the drug, smoking it (usually with marijuana), injecting it, or rubbing it on the skin. Taken by mouth, the drug will take about 30 minutes to have any effect and up to an hour for its full effect to be felt, which will last 2 to 4 hours.

The physiological effects of LSD include blurred **vision**, dilation of the pupils of the eye, muscle weakness and twitching, and an increase in heart rate, blood pressure, and body temperature. The user may also salivate excessively and shed tears, and the hair on the back of his arms may stand erect. Pregnant women who use LSD or other hallucinogens may have a miscarriage, because these drugs cause the muscles of the uterus to contract. Such a reaction in pregnancy would expel the fetus.

To the observer, the user usually will appear quiet and introspective. Most of the time the user will be unwilling or unable to interact with others, to carry on a conversation, or engage in intimacies. At times even moderate doses of LSD will have profoundly disturbing effects on an individual. Although the physiological effects will seem uniform, the psychological impact of the drug can be terrifying. The distortions in reality, exaggeration of perception and other effects can be horrifying, especially if the user is unaware that he has been given the drug. This constitutes what is called the "bad trip."

Among the psychological effects reported by LSD users is depersonalization, the separation from one's body, yet with the knowledge that the separated mind is observing the passing scene. A confused **body image** (the user cannot tell where his own body ends and the surroundings begin) also is common. A distorted perception of reality is also common. For example, the user's perception of colors, distance, shapes, and sizes is inconsistent and unreliable. In addition, the user may perceive absent objects and forms without substance. He may also taste colors or **smell** sounds, a mixing of the senses called synesthesia. Sounds, colors, and taste are all greatly enhanced, though they may constitute an unrealistic and constantly changing tableau.

The user often talks incessantly on a variety of subjects, often uttering meaningless phrases. But he may also become silent and immobile for long periods of time as he listens to music or contemplates a flower or his thumb. **Mood** swings are frequent, with sudden alternations between total euphoria and complete despair.

Some users will exhibit symptoms of **paranoia**. They become suspicious of persons around them and tend to withdraw from others. Feelings of anxiety can also surface when the user is removed from a quiet environment and exposed to everyday stimuli. Activities such as standing in line with other people or walking down a city sidewalk may seem impossible to handle. Users have been known to jump off buildings or walk in front of moving trucks.

How LSD and other hallucinogens produce these bizarre effects remains unknown. The drug attaches to certain chemical binding sites widely spread through the **brain**, but what ensues thereafter has yet to be described. A person who takes LSD steadily with the doses close together can develop a tolerance to the drug. That is, the amount of drug that once produced a pronounced "high" no longer is effective. A larger dose is required to achieve the same effect. However, if the individual keeps increasing his drug intake he will soon pass over the threshold into the area of toxicity.

Discontinuing LSD or the other hallucinogens, especially after having used them for an extended period of time, is not easy. The residual effects of the drugs produce toxic symptoms and "flashbacks," which are similar to an LSD "trip."

Currently, the most common form of LSD administration is by licking the back of a stamp torn from a perforated sheet of homemade stamps. The drug is coated on the back of the sheet of stamps or is deposited as a colored dot on the paper. Removing one stamp, the user places it on his tongue and allows the LSD to dissolve in his saliva. Because a tiny amount can produce strong effects, overdoses are common.

Teens often experiment with LSD or other hallucinogens in reaction to poor **family** relationships and psychological problems. Others are prompted by curiosity, **peer pressure**, and the desire to escape from feelings of isolation or despair. Typical physical signs of hallucinogen use include rapid breathing, muscle twitching, chills and shaking, upset stomach, enlarged pupils, confusion, and poor coordination.

### Further Reading

Robbins, Paul R. *Hallucinogens*. Springfield, NJ: Enslow, 1996.
Fernandes, B. "The Long, Strange Trip Back." *World Press Review* 40, September 1993, pp. 38-39.
Monroe, Judy. "Designer Drugs: CAT & LSD." *Current Health* 21, September 1994, p. 13.
"The Negative Side of Nostalgia." *Medical Update* 17, July 1993, p. 3.
Porush, D. "Finding God in the Three-Pound Universe: The Neuroscience of Transcendence." *Omni* 16, October 1993, pp. 60-62.

# Halo effect

A type of bias where one characteristic of a person or one factor in a situation affects the evaluation of the person's other traits.

Halo effect is a phenomenon that occurs when one is influenced by a person's strengths, weaknesses, physical appearance, behavior, or any other single factor. The halo effect is most often apparent in situations where one person is responsible for evaluating or assessing another in some way. Examples of such situations include assessment of applicants for jobs, scholarships, or awards; designating job or committee assignments based on perceived capabilities or past performance; and in evaluating academic, job, or athletic performance. The halo effect can undermine an individual's effort to be objective in making judgments because all people respond to others in a variety of ways, making true objectivity nearly impossible. However, the halo effect causes one characteristic or quality of an individual to override all others.

To counteract the halo effect, decision makers can break the evaluation process into specific steps, evaluating only one characteristic at a time, but human judgments can never be free of complex influences.

# Handedness

A person's preference for one hand when performing manual tasks.

The term handedness describes a characteristic form of specialization whereby a person by preference uses one hand for clearly identified activities, such as writing. For example, a person who uses his or her right hand for activities requiring skill and coordination (e.g., writing, drawing, cutting) is defined as right-handed. Roughly 90% of humans are right-handed. Because left-handed people who are forced to write with their right hand sometimes develop the **ability** to write with both hands, the term ambidexterity is often used in everyday parlance to denote balanced handedness.

An often misunderstood phenomenon, handedness is a result of the human brain's unique development. While the human mind is intuitively understood as a single entity, research in **brain** physiology and anatomy has demonstrated that various areas of the brain control different mental aptitudes, and that the physiological structure of the brain affects our mental functions. The brain's fundamental structure is dual (there are two cerebral hemispheres), and this duality is an essential quality of the human body. Generally speaking, each hemisphere is connected to sensory receptors on the opposite side of the body. In other words, the right hand is controlled by the left hemisphere of the cerebral cortex. When scientists started studying the brain's anatomy, they learned that the two hemispheres are not identical. In fact, the French physician and anthropologist **Pierre Broca** (1824-1880) and the German neurologist and psychiatrist **Carl**

**Wernicke** (1848-1905) produced empirical evidence that important language centers were located in the left hemisphere. Since Broca's findings were based on right-handed subjects, and since right-handedness is predominant in humans, psychologists felt prompted to develop the notion of the left hemisphere as the dominant part of the brain. Furthermore, Broca formulated a general rule stating that the language hemisphere is always opposite of a person's preferred side. In other words, the left hemisphere always controls a right-handed person's language abilities. According to Broca rule's, left-handedness would indicate a hemispheric switch. Handedness research, however, uncovered a far more complex situation. While Broca's rule works for right-handers, left-handed people present a rather puzzling picture. Namely, researchers have discovered that only about two out of 10 left-handers follow Broca's rule. In other words, most left-handed people violate Broca's rule by having their language center in the left hemisphere. Furthermore, the idea of clearly defined cerebral dominance seems compromised by the fact that some 70% of left-handed people have bilateral hemispheric control of language.

While hemispheric dominance can be observed in animals, only humans have a clearly defined type of dominance. In other words, while animals may be right or left "pawed," only humans are predominantly right-handed. The American developmental psychologist **Arnold Gesell** (1880-1961), known for his pioneering work in scientific observation of child behavior, noted that as early as the age of four weeks infants display signs of handedness. At that age, according to Gesell, right-handed children assume a "fencing" position, right arm and hand extended; by the age of one, right-handedness is clearly established, the child using the right hand for a variety of operations, and the left for holding and gripping. Predominant right-handedness in humans has led researchers to define right-handedness as genetically coded. If left-handedness also had a genetic basis, was it possible to establish inheritance patterns? However, empirical studies, even studies of identical **twins**, have failed to establish left-handedness as a genetic trait. For example, a person with two left-handed parents has only a 35% chance of being left-handed.

In the past, left-handedness was associated with mental deficiency, as well as emotional and behavioral problems, which led to the popular belief, strengthened by folklore, that left-handed people were somehow flawed. In addition, left-handedness has also been associated with immunological problems and a shorter life span. While not devoid of any foundation, these ideas are based on inconclusive, and sometimes even deceptive, evidence. For example, statistics may indicate a shorter life-span for left-handers, but what statistics omit is the fact that higher mortality should probably be attributed to accidents in an often dangerous right-hand world.

An even greater challenge than right-handed scissors and can openers is what psychologist Stanley Coren calls "handism," the belief that right-handedness is "better" than left-handedness. The idea that left-handers need to conform to a dominant standard has traditionally been translated into punitive educational practices whereby left-handed children were physically forced to write with their right hand. While there is a growing awareness among educators and parents that left-handedness should not be suppressed, the left-handed child is still exposed to a variety of pressures, some subtle, some crude, to conform. These pressures are reinforced by a tradition of maligning left-handed people. Major religious traditions, such as Christianity, Buddhism, and Islam, have described left-handedness in negative terms. Current language is also a rich repository of recorded animosity toward left-handers. For example, the word left evolved from the Anglo-Saxon *lyft*, which means weak. The Latin word sinister, meaning left and unfavorable, is still used to denote something evil, and gauche, the French word for left, generally indicates awkwardness. The numerous expressions which imply that left is the opposite of good include a left-handed compliment.

Zoran Minderovic

**Further Reading**

Coren, Stanley. *The Left-Hander Syndrome: The Causes and Consequences of Left-Handedness*. New York: Vintage Books, 1993.
Temple, Christine. *The Brain*. London: Penguin Books, 1993.

# Hand-eye coordination

The ability to coordinate vision with fine motor skills.

Hand-eye coordination begins developing in **infancy**. Although it is an instinctive developmental achievement that cannot be taught, parents can hasten its progress by providing their children with stimulating toys and other objects that will encourage them to practice reaching out for things and grasping them.

Until the age of eight weeks, infants are too nearsighted to see objects at distances farther than about eight inches from their faces, and they have not yet discovered their hands, which are kept fisted throughout this period. By the age of two to two-and-a-half months, the eyes focus much better, and babies can follow a mov-

**Sports like volleyball help improve hand-eye coordination.** *(Photo by Robert J. Huffman. Field Mark Publications. Reproduced with permission.)*

ing object with their gaze, even turning their heads to keep sight of it longer. However, when a child this age drops an object, she will try to find it by feeling rather than looking for it, and although she plays with her hands, she does it without looking at them.

By three months, most infants will have made an important hand-eye connection; they can deliberately bring their hands into their field of **vision**. By now they are watching their hands when they **play** with them. They also swipe at objects within their view, a repetitive activity that provides practice in estimating distance and controlling the hands. Attempts to grab onto things (which usually fail) consist of a series of tries, with the child looking at the object and then at his hand, moving his hand closer to it, and then re-sighting the object and trying again.

At the age of four or five months, hand-eye coordination is developed sufficiently for an infant to manipulate toys, and she will begin to seek them out. By the age of six months, she can focus on objects at a distance and consistently follow them with her eyes. At this point, the infant can sight an object and reach for it without repeatedly looking at her hand. She senses where her hand is and can lead it straight to the object, keeping her eyes on the object the entire time. By the final months of her first year, an infant can shift her gaze between objects held in both hands and compare them to each other.

## Toddlerhood

The toddler stage brings further progress in hand-eye coordination, resulting in the control necessary to manipulate objects with increasing sophistication. The **ability** to sight and grasp objects accurately improves dramatically with the acquisition of the "pincer grasp." This ability to grasp objects between the thumb and forefinger develops between the ages of 12 and 15 months. Around the same time, children begin stacking objects on top of each other. Most can stack two blocks by the age of 15 months and three by the age of 18 months. At this age they also begin emptying, gathering, and nesting objects, or placing one inside another. Toddlers can also draw horizontal and vertical pencil lines and circular scribbles, twist dials, push levers, pull strings, pound pegs, string large beads, put a key in a lock, and turn book pages. Eventually, they are able to stack as many as six blocks, unwrap small objects, manipulate snap toys, and play with clay. Between the ages of 15 and 23 months there is significant improvement in feeding skills, such as using a spoon and a cup.

## Preschool years

During the preschool period, hand-eye coordination progresses to the point of near independence at self-care activities. A four-year-old is learning to handle eating utensils well and button even small buttons. Four-year-olds can also handle a pencil competently, copy geometric shapes and letters, and use scissors. By the age of five, a child's hand-eye coordination appears quite advanced, although it will still continue to be fine-tuned for several more years. He approaches, grasps, and releases objects with precision and accuracy. He may use the same toys as preschoolers, but he manipulates them with greater skill and purpose and can complete a familiar jigsaw puzzles with lightning speed. An important milestone in hand-eye progress at this stage is the child's ability to tie his own shoelaces. At the age of six, a child's visual orientation changes somewhat. Children of this age and older shift their gaze more frequently than younger children. They also have a tendency to follow the progress of an object rather than looking directly at it, a fact that has been linked to the practice of some six-year-olds using their fingers to mark their places when they are reading. Even when absorbed in tasks, they look away frequently, although their hands remain active.

## School-aged children

Hand-eye coordination improves through middle **childhood**, with advances in speed, timing, and coordination. By the age of nine, the eyes and hands are well differentiated, that is, each can be used independently of the other, and improved finger differentiation is evident as well. Nine-year-olds can use carpentry and garden tools with reasonable skill and complete simple sewing projects.

*See also* Fine motor skills

### Further Reading

Eckert, Helen M. *Motor Development.* 3rd ed. Indianapolis, IN: Benchmark Press, 1987.

Lerch, Harold A., and Christine B. Stopka. *Developmental Motor Activities for All Children: From Theory to Practice.* Dubuque, IA: Brown and Benchmark, 1992.

# Harry F. Harlow

### 1905-1981

American psychologist whose major contributions to psychology arose from his work with rhesus monkeys.

Experimental and comparative psychologist **Harry Harlow** is best known for his work on the importance of maternal contact in the growth and social development of infants. Working with infant monkeys and surrogate mothers made of terrycloth or wire, Harlow concluded that extended social deprivation in the early years of life can severely disrupt later social and sexual behavior. Harlow also conducted important studies involving the behavior of prisoners of war during the Korean War, as well as work concerning problem-solving and learning among primates.

Harlow was born in 1905 in Fairfield, Iowa. Following his education at Stanford, where he earned his bachelor's degree and a Ph.D. in 1930, he began a long academic career at the University of Wisconsin. His teaching career spanned 44 years, beginning in 1930. He also served as director of the university's Regional Primate Center from 1961-71. In his work with primates, Harlow developed what he called a "uniprocess learning theory," which describes how primates learn through a succession of incorrect responses to stimuli.

When Harry Harlow began his famous studies of **attachment** behaviors in rhesus monkeys, he was able to pit two competing theories of the development of affiliative behaviors against each other. Drive-reduction approaches were based on the premise that bonds between mothers and children were nurtured by the fact that mothers provided food and warmth to meet the infant's biological needs. Attachment theorists, on the other hand, felt that the provision of security through contact and proximity were the driving factors in the development of attachment.

Harlow devised a series of ingenious studies in which infant rhesus monkeys were raised in cages without their natural mothers, but with two surrogate objects instead. One surrogate "mother" was a wire form that the monkey could approach to receive food. Another form offered no food, but was wrapped in terry cloth so the infant could cling to a softer and more cuddly surface. What happened when a large, threatening mechanical spider was introduced into the cage? The infant monkeys ran to the terry cloth surrogates, demonstrating that contact comfort was more important than just meeting basic hunger needs for the establishment of a relationship from which the infant might derive security.

In a series of related experiments, Harlow studied the effects of maternal and contact comfort deprivation across the monkey's lifespan, uncovering unexpectedly harmful effects of such deprivation on the monkeys' own childrearing abilities at maturity. Later, Harlow's student, Stephen Suomi, and his colleagues demonstrated that these longstanding effects could be improved by introducing a nurturant "foster grandmother."

Harlow's conclusions about maternal **bonding** and deprivation, based on his work with monkeys and first presented in the early 1960s, later became controversial, but are still considered important developments in the area of **child psychology**.

Harlow served for many years as editor of the *Journal of Comparative and Physiological Psychology*. In 1960, he received the Distinguished Scientific Contributions Award from the **American Psychological Association**, and in 1967, he was awarded the National Medal of Science.

Doreen Arcus, Ph.D.

**Further Reading**
Harlow, Harry. *Learning to Love*. New York: Aronson, 1974.

# Health psychology

A subfield of psychology devoted to health maintenance, including research on the relationship between mental and physical health, guidance in improving individual health through lifestyle changes, and analysis and improvement of the health care system.

Health psychology is a diverse area with a variety of emphases. Medical psychology focuses on the clinical treatment of patients with physical illnesses, offering practical advice people can use in order to improve their health. While there is special emphasis on psychosomatic disorders—those that have traditionally been most closely related to psychological factors—the current trend is toward a holistic perspective that considers all physical health inseparable from a patient's emotional state. As part of this trend, psychologists and pediatricians have joined forces in the growing area of pediatric psychology, collaborating to meet the health and developmental needs of children and their families. Another focal point is **rehabilitation** psychology, which teams **mental health** professionals with health care providers who care for patients with physical disabilities and chronic conditions, often in institutional settings.

Another province of health psychology is the study of "health behavior"—how people take care of or neglect their health, either in a preventative context or when they are ill. This area includes such concerns as drug abuse, utilization of health care resources, and adjustment to chronic illness. Health psychology also addresses the health care system itself, including analysis of the outreach, diagnostic, and prescription processes, provider-patient interaction, and the training of health care personnel.

*See also* Applied psychology

# Hearing

The ability to perceive sound.

The ear, the receptive organ for hearing, has three major parts: the outer, middle, and inner ear. The pinna or outer ear—the part of the ear attached to the head, funnels sound waves through the outer ear. The sound waves pass down the auditory canal to the middle ear, where they strike the tympanic membrane, or eardrum, causing it to vibrate. These vibrations are picked up by three small bones (ossicles) in the middle ear named for their shapes: the malleus (hammer), incus (anvil), and stapes (stirrup). The stirrup is attached to a thin membrane called the oval window, which is much smaller than the eardrum and consequently receives more pressure.

As the oval window vibrates from the increased pressure, the fluid in the coiled, tubular cochlea (inner ear) begins to vibrate the membrane of the cochlea (basilar membrane) which, in turn, bends fine, hairlike cells on its surface. These auditory receptors generate miniature electrical forces which trigger **nerve** impulses that then travel via the auditory nerve, first to the **thalamus** and then to the primary auditory cortex in the temporal lobe of the **brain**. Here, transformed into auditory but meaningless sensations, the impulses are relayed to association areas of the brain which convert them into meaningful sounds by examining the activity patterns of the neurons, or nerve cells, to determine sound frequencies. Although the ear changes sound waves into neural impulses, it is the brain that actually "hears," or perceives the sound as meaningful.

The auditory system contains about 25,000 cochlear neurons that can process a wide range of sounds. The sounds we hear are determined by two characteristics of sound waves: their amplitude (the difference in air pressure between the peak and baseline of a wave) and their frequency (the number of waves that pass by a given point every second). Loudness of sound is influenced by a complex relationship between the wavelength and amplitude of the wave; the greater the amplitude, the faster the neurons fire impulses to the brain, and the louder the sound that is heard. Loudness of sound is usually expressed in decibels (dB). A whisper is about 30 dB, normal conversation is about 60 dB, and a subway train is about 90 dB. Sounds above 120 dB are generally painful

| DECIBEL RATINGS AND HAZARDOUS LEVEL OF NOISE | |
|---|---|
| **Decibel level** | **Example of sounds** |
| 30 | Soft whisper |
| 35 | Noise may prevent the listener from falling asleep |
| 40 | Quiet office noise level |
| 50 | Quiet conversation |
| 60 | Average television, sewing machine, lively conversation |
| 70 | Busy traffic, noisy restaurant |
| 80 | Heavy city traffic, factory noise, alarm clock |
| 90 | Cocktail party, lawn mower |
| 100 | Pneumatic drill |
| 120 | Sandblasting, thunder |
| 140 | Jet airplane |
| 180 | Rocket launching pad |

Above 110 decibels, hearing may become painful.
Above 120 decibels is considered deafening.
Above 135, hearing will become extremely painful and hearing loss may result if exposure is prolonged.
Above 180, hearing loss is almost certain with any exposure.

to the human ear. The loudest rock band on record was measured at 160 dB.

Pitch (how high or low a tone sounds) is a function of frequency. Sounds with high frequencies are heard as having a high pitch; those with low frequencies are heard as low-pitched. The normal frequency range of human hearing is 20 to 20,000 Hz. Frequencies of some commonly heard sounds include the human voice (120 to approximately 1,100 Hz), middle C on the piano (256 Hz), and the highest note on the piano (4,100 Hz). Differences in frequency are discerned, or coded, by the human ear in two ways, frequency matching and place. The lowest sound frequencies are coded by frequency matching, duplicating the frequency with the firing rate of auditory nerve fibers. Frequencies in the low to moderate range are coded both by frequency matching and by the place on the basilar membrane where the sound wave peaks. High frequencies are coded solely by the placement of the wave peak

Loss of hearing can result from conductive or sensorineural deafness or damage to auditory areas of the brain. In conductive hearing loss, the sound waves are unable to reach the inner ear due to disease or obstruction of the auditory conductive system (the external auditory canal; the eardrum, or tympanic membrane; or structures and spaces in the middle ear). Sensorineural hearing loss refers to two different but related types of impairment,

both affecting the inner ear. Sensory hearing loss involves damage, degeneration, or developmental failure of the hair cells in the cochlea's organ of Corti, while neural loss involves the auditory nerve or other parts of the cochlea. Sensorineural hearing loss occurs as a result of disease, **birth** defects, **aging**, or continual exposure to loud sounds. Damage to the auditory areas of the brain through severe head injury, tumors, or strokes can also prevent either the **perception** or the interpretation of sound.

### Further Reading
Davis, Lennard J. *Enforcing Normalcy: Disability, Deafness, and the Body.* New York: Verso, 1995.

## Donald O. Hebb
### 1904-1985
Canadian psychologist who studied the effects of brain development on intelligence.

The difference between the way a young **brain** and an older brain processes information was the focus of Donald Hebb's research during a career that spanned nearly half a century. Hebb was fascinated by the way people learned and the way they retained information. His research opened many doors in the field of behavioral science and made him one of the most influential behaviorists in twentieth-century psychology.

Donald Olding Hebb was born in Cheser, Nova Scotia, on July 22, 1904. Both his parents were physicians, but science was not Hebb's initial interest. As a youth he wanted to become a novelist; he had given up this desire by the time he received his bachelor's degree from Dalhousie University in 1925. He spent the next few years pursuing several occupations including teaching and farming. He finally decided to enter a master's program at McGill University, focusing on psychology. He graduated in 1932 and went to the University of Chicago to study under Professor Karl S. Lashley. When Lashley relocated to Harvard, Hebb followed. He received his doctorate in 1936.

In 1937, Hebb was appointed a research fellow at the Montreal Neurological Institute, where he became involved in studies of the brain. His particular interest was, in simplest terms, the concept of "nature versus nurture." Hebb wanted to find out how much of a role the brain played in behavior. Research had shown that adults could often function quite well even after a significant part of the brain had been damaged; similar damage in infants, however, produced retardation. Hebb reasoned that, for adults, external stimulation might play a more prominent role in how the brain functioned. Over the next several years, first at Montreal, then at Queen's University, and then at the Yerkes Primate Labs, Hebb conducted experiments on animals and humans. His research showed that lack of external stimulation resulted in diminished ability to solve problems and to concentrate. Some subjects even reported **hallucinations**. In practical application, Hebb's research explained in part why airline pilots and long-distance truck drivers sometimes hallucinated.

In 1947 Hebb became professor of psychology at McGill, where he remained until he retired in 1972. He became an emeritus professor four years later. Hebb was a long-time member of both the Canadian and the American Psychological Assocations. He was the first non-U.S. citizen to serve as APA president (1960). He won the APA Distinguished Scientific Contribution Award in 1961. The Donald O. Hebb. Award, of which he was the first recipient in 1980, honors Canadians who have made a lasting contribution to the sciences. Hebb died in Nova Scotia in 1985.

*See also* Cognitive development; Nature-nuture controversy

George A. Milite

## Further Reading

*McGraw-Hill modern scientists and engineers.* New York: McGraw-Hill, 1980.
Restak, Richard M. *The mind.* New York: Bantam, 1988.

# Fritz Heider

### 1896-1988
Austrian-American psychologist who developed concept of attribution theory.

How we interpret our own behavior, as well as that of others, formed the basis for Fritz Heider's work during a career that lasted more than 60 years. Heider explored the nature of interpersonal relations, and his work culminated in the 1958 book *The Psychology of Interpersonal Relations.* Heider espoused the concept of what he called "common-sense" or "naïve" psychology. He believed that people attribute the behavior of others to their own perceptions; and that those perceptions could be determined either by specific situations or by long-held beliefs. The concept may not seem complicated, but it opened important doors to the question of how people relate to each other and why.

Heider, the younger of two sons, was born in Vienna on February 18, 1896, to Moriz and Eugenie von Halaczy Heider. He was an avid reader and a good student, and he entered the University of Graz (Austria). He received his Ph.D. in 1920, and spent the next several years traveling through Europe. Part of this time was spent as a student at the Psychological Institute of Berlin. Pre-World War II Berlin was one of the most intellectually stimulating cities in Europe, and he was privileged to study with outstanding scholars.

## Begins research on interpersonal behavior

In 1930, Heider accepted an offer to conduct research at the Clarke School for the Deaf in Northampton, Massachutsetts, and to be an assistant professor at Smith College. Heider's decision to come to the United States proved auspicious for two reasons. In addition to the work he was to do—first at Smith, and later at the University of Kansas—Heider met Grace Moore, who was doing research of her own at Clarke. They married in December 1930; in his autobiography, *The Life of a Psychologist* (1983), Heider credits his wife for her invaluable contribution to his work. The Heiders had three sons during their years in Northampton.

Beginning at Smith, Heider began to do the research that led to his theories on interpersonal relations. He continued his work when he moved to Lawrence, Kansas, in 1947 to take a professorship at the University of Kansas. It has been said that Heider approached psychology the way a physicist would approach scientific theory. He was extremely methodical and meticulous in his research, which could often be frustrating, but he carefully developed the ideas that he ultimately outlined in *The Psychology of Interpersonal Relations.*

In its simplest terms, **attribution theory** explains the means people use to attribute the behavior of others. Sometimes, behavior is attributed to disposition; in other words, we might decide that altruism is what makes a particular person donate money to a charity. Other times, behavior can be attributed to situations; in this model, the donor gives money to charity because of social pressure. Heider believed that people generally tended to give more attribution than they should to **personality**, and, conversely, less than they should to situations. In other words, personality is not as consistent an indicator of behavior as people tend to believe.

### Allows publication of notebooks

Heider received numerous awards for his research, including the **American Psychological Association**'s Distinguished Scientific Contribution Award in 1965. Although Heider ostensibly retired in the 1960s, he continued to do research as an emeritus professor. He worked on his memoirs, which became his autobiography. More important, however, were series of notebooks Heider had kept during his career, in which he explained and diagramed many of his theories, listed references, and discussed many of the questions he had tried to answer through his research. A former student of Heider's, Marijana Benesh-Weiner, offered to edit and compile the notes. Working with Heider, she put the notes into a six-volume set published by Springer-Verlag under the title, *Fritz Heider: The Notebooks.* The first volume was published in 1987; Benesh-Weiner completed editing the final volume shortly after Heider, aged 91, died at his home in Lawrence, Kansas, on January 2, 1988.

*See also* Attribution theory

George A. Milite

### Further Reading
Harvey, John H. "Fritz Heider." *American Psychologist,* (March 1989): 570-571.
Heider, Fritz. *The Life of a Psychologist: An Autobiography.* Lawrence, KS, University of Kansas Press, 1983.

# Hermann von Helmholtz

**1821-1894**
German scientist who conducted breakthrough research on the nervous system.

Hermann Helmholtz was one of the few scientists to master two disciplines: medicine and physics. He conducted breakthrough research on the **nervous system**, as well as the functions of the eye and ear. In physics, he is recognized (along with two other scientists) as the author of the concept of conservation of energy.

Helmholtz was born into a poor but scholarly **family**; his father was an instructor of philosophy and literature at a gymnasium in his hometown of Potsdam, Germany. At home, his father taught him Latin, Greek, French, Italian, Hebrew, and Arabic, as well as the philosophical ideas of Immanuel Kant and J. G. Fichte (who was a friend of the family). With this background, Helmholtz entered school with a wide scope of knowledge. Though he expressed an interest in the sciences, his father could not afford to send him to a university; instead, he was persuaded to study medicine, an area that would provide him with government aid. In return, Helmholtz was expected to use his medical skills for the good of the government—particularly in army hospitals.

Helmholtz entered the Friedrich Wilhelm Institute in Berlin in 1898, receiving his M.D. four years later. Upon graduation he was immediately assigned to military duty, practicing as a surgeon for the Prussian army. After several years of active duty he was discharged, free to pursue a career in academia. In 1848 he secured a position as lecturer at the Berlin Academy of Arts. Just a year later he was offered a professorship at the University of Konigsberg, teaching physiology. Over the next 22 years he moved to the universities at Bonn and Heidelberg, and it was during this time that he conducted his major works in the field of medicine.

Helmholtz began to study the human eye, a task that was all the more difficult for the lack of precise medical equipment. In order to better understand the function of the eye he invented the ophthalmoscope, a device used to observe the retina. Invented in 1851, the ophthalmoscope—in a slightly modified form—is still used by modern eye specialists. Helmholtz also designed a device used to measure the curvature of the eye called an ophthalmometer. Using these devices he advanced the theory of three-color **vision** first proposed by Thomas Young. This theory, now called the Young-Helmholtz theory, helps ophthalmologists to understand the nature of color blindness and other afflictions.

Intrigued by the inner workings of the sense organs, Helmholtz went on to study the human ear. Being an expert pianist, he was particularly concerned with the way the ear distinguished pitch and tone. He suggested that the inner ear is structured in such a way as to cause resonations at certain frequencies. This allowed the ear to discern similar tones, overtones, and timbres, such as an identical note played by two different instruments.

**Hermann von Helmhotz** *(The Library of Congress. Reproduced by permission.)*

In 1852 Helmholtz conducted what was probably his most important work as a physician: the **measurement** of the speed of a **nerve** impulse. It had been assumed that such a measurement could never be obtained by science, since the speed was far too great for instruments to catch. Some physicians even used this as proof that living organisms were powered by an innate "vital force" rather than energy. Helmholtz disproved this by stimulating a frog's nerve first near a muscle and then farther away; when the stimulus was farther from the muscle, it contracted just a little slower. After a few simple calculations Helmholtz announced the impulse velocity within the nervous system to be about one-tenth the speed of sound.

After completing much of the work on sensory physiology that had interested him, Helmholtz found himself bored with medicine. In 1868 he decided to return to his first love—physical science. However, it was not until 1870 that he was offered the physics chair at the University of Berlin and only after it had been turned down by Gustav Kirchhoff. By that time, Helmholtz had already completed his groundbreaking research on energetics.

The concept of conservation of energy was introduced by Julius Mayer in 1842, but Helmholtz was un-aware of Mayer's work. Helmholtz conducted his own research on energy, basing his theories upon his previous experience with muscles. It could be observed that animal heat was generated by muscle action, as well as chemical reactions within a working muscle. Helmholtz believed that this energy was derived from food and that food got its energy from the Sun. He proposed that energy could not be created spontaneously, nor could it vanish—it was either used or released as heat. This explanation was much clearer and more detailed than the one offered by Mayer, and Helmholtz is often considered the true originator of the concept of conservation of energy.

Helmholtz had been a sickly child; even throughout his adult life he was plagued by migraine headaches and dizzy spells. In 1894, shortly after a lecture tour of the United States, he fainted and fell, suffering a concussion. He never completely recovered, dying of complications several months later.

# Heredity

The process by which the genetic code of parents is passed on to their children.

There are certain **traits** that parents pass on to their children, including eye color, hair color, height, and other physical characteristics. The coding for these traits are contained inside DNA molecules that are present within all human cells. Since the discovery of DNA by James Watson (1928- ) in the 1950s, the science of genetics has focused on the study of DNA and the ways in which physical traits are passed on from generation to generation. Within genetics, a special branch of DNA science—called quantitative, or biometrical, genetics—has emerged, which studies the heritability of such traits as **intelligence**, behavior, and **personality**. This branch focuses on the effects of polygenes in the creation of certain phenotypes. Polygenes, as the name implies, refer to the interaction of several genes; and phenotypes are certain variable characteristics of behavior or personality. Quantitative geneticists, therefore, study the effects of groups of genes on the development of personality and other abstract variables. They rarely, it should be noted, are able to pinpoint a behavior's genesis to a specific gene. Specific genes have been found to cause a small number of diseases, however, such as Huntington's disease and other degenerative disorders.

In studying personality traits and intelligence, the latest research in quantitative genetics suggests that the heritability rate for many characteristics hovers around 50 percent. In 1988 a study of **twins** reared apart revealed the heritability of 11 common **character** traits. The findings, published in the *Journal of Personality and Social Psychology,* reported that social potency is 61% influenced by genes; traditionalism, 60%; **stress** reaction, 55%; absorption (having a vivid **imagination**), 55%; **alienation**, 55%; well-being, 54%; harm avoidance (avoiding dangerous activities), 51%; **aggression**, 48%; achievement, 46%; control, 43%; and social closeness, 33 percent.

Other recent studies have compiled lists of traits most influenced by heredity. Physical characteristics that are most genetically determined include height, weight, tone of voice, tooth decay, athletic **ability**, and age of death, among others. Intellectual capabilities include **memory**, IQ scores, age of language acquisition, reading disabilities, and **mental retardation**. Emotional characteristics found to be most influenced by heredity were **shyness**, **extroversion**, neuroses, **schizophrenia**, anxiety, and alcohol dependence. It is important to note that these are tendencies and not absolutes. Many children of alcoholics, for instance, do not become alcoholics themselves. Many social and cultural factors intervene as humans develop, and the child of an alcoholic, who may be genetically vulnerable to acquiring the disease, may avoid drinking from witnessing the devastation caused by the disease. (For a fuller discussion of the role of **environment**, see Nature-Nurture Controversy.)

Recent work has shown that genes can both be influenced by the environment and can even influence the environments in which we find ourselves. A 1990 study found that animals raised in environments requiring significant motor activity actually developed new structures in the **brain** that were significantly different from the brain structures of animals raised in environments lacking motor stimuli. Observations from such experiments have revealed that complex environments actually "turn on" sets of genes that control other genes, whose job it is to build new cerebral structures. Therefore, living in an environment that provides challenges can genetically alter a person's makeup. Additionally, a genetic predisposition to **introversion** can cause people to isolate themselves, thus changing their environment and, in the process, altering their development of social skills. This, then, contributes further to their genetic predisposition to introversion.

There also appears to be universal, inherited behavior patterns in humans. Common behaviors across diverse cultures include the patterns of protest among infants and small children at being separated from their mothers. A study conducted in 1976 found that separation protests emerge, peak, and then disappear in nearly identical ways across five widely diverse cultures. Other studies have found universal facial expressions for common emotions, even among pre-literate hunter-gatherer

cultures that have had no exposure to media. It used to be thought that the human smile was learned through observation and **imitation**, but a 1975 study found that children who had been blind from **birth** began smiling at the same age as sighted children. Many of these behaviors are thought to be instinctual. Aside from the infant/developmental behaviors already mentioned, other inherited behavior patterns in humans include sex, aggression, **fear**, and curiosity/exploration.

### Further Reading

Beal, Eileen. "Charting the Future? Researching Heredity Quotient in African American Families." *American Visions* (October-November 1994): 44.

Berkowitz, Ari. "Our Genes, Ourselves?" *BioScience* (January 1996): 42.

Metzler, Kristan. "The Apple Doesn't Fall Far in Families Linked to Crime." *Insight on the News* (29 August 1994): 17.

Tellegen, A. "Personality Similarity in Twins Reared Apart and Together." *Journal of Personality and Social Psychology* 54 (1988): 1031.

# Heterosexuality

Sexual attraction to members of the opposite sex.

The sex drive, or sexual desire, is an unlearned, powerful drive that humans share with other animal species. Heterosexuals experience sexual desire in relation to members of the opposite sex. This contrasts with homosexuals, where the object of sexual desire is a member of one's own sex. Most researchers believe that children begin to notice physical differences between males and females by about age two. As children grow, they learn about **sex roles** and **sex differences** by observing their parents and other adults, including teachers, child care providers, and from **play** experiences and the attitudes and behavior of peers. **Gender identity** becomes firmly established, that is, the young boy understands that he is a boy, and thinks of himself as a boy.

Sex researcher **Alfred Kinsey** (1894-1956), who founded the Institute for Sex Research at Indiana University in 1942, believed that sexual orientation in humans is complex, ranging from exclusively homosexual to exclusively heterosexual, with most people's sexual desires falling somewhere between the two. In fact, some individuals practice **bisexuality**, that is, they engage in sexual relations with both members of their own sex and members of the opposite sex. Kinsey's controversial study, popularly known as the "Kinsey Report," was published in 1948 under the title *Sexual Behavior in the Human Male*. His theory caused heated public discussion, since sexual behavior was considered a taboo subject for public discussion and study. In fact, until the late 1960s, any sexual behavior outside of exclusively heterosexual was considered either a **mental illness** or perversion. Although **homosexuality** continues to be prohibited by law in many locales, it is no longer listed as a mental disorder by the **American Psychiatric Association**.

Although much research into underlying causes of sexual orientation has been done, little conclusion evidence has emerged about why one individual is heterosexual and another homosexual. Researchers have studied biological and genetic determinants, hormone levels, and environmental factors. It seems from evidence available in the mid-1990s that environmental and biological factors combine in the complex process of human development to establish sexual orientation.

*See also* Sexuality

## Further Reading

Fisher, Seymour. *Sexual Images of the Self: the Psychology of Erotic Sensations and Illusions*. Hillsdale, NJ: L. Erlbaum Associates, 1989.

Levand, Rhonda. *Sexual Evolution*. Berkeley, CA: Celestial Arts, 1991.

# Heuristics

A methodical procedure for discovering solutions to problems.

The principal feature of heuristics is the formulation of a hypothetical solution to a problem at the beginning of an investigation of the problem. This working hypothesis serves to direct the course of the investigation, and is modified and refined as relevant facts are discovered and analyzed. During the course of the investigation, the heuristic method reduces the range, and increases the plausibility, of possible solutions of the problem. Unlike an algorithm, however, which is a methodical procedure that necessarily produces the solution of a problem, heuristics does not necessarily lead to the solution of a problem. Heuristics has been fundamental in the acquisition of scientific knowledge, and, in fact, is an essential component of many forms of complex human behavior.

# Ernest R. Hilgard

**1904-**
American psychologist who conducted pioneering work in hypnotism.

Ernest Hilgard distinguished himself through his studies of the role of **hypnosis** in human behavior and response. Hypnotism, often regarded as nothing more than a stage trick by pseudo-psychics, is in fact an important psychological tool; it can be used to alter behavior (smoking cessation, for example), and to relieve **pain**. Much of Hilgard's research and writing on the topic was done with his wife, Josephine R. Hilgard (1906-1989).

Born in Belleville, Illinois, on July 25, 1904, Ernest Ropiequit Hilgard was the son of a physician, and he showed an early interest in science. Interestingly, it was engineering, not psychology, that originally attracted Hilgard; he received a bachelor's degree in chemical engineering from the University of Illinois in 1924. He decided that he wanted to study psychology, and he went to Yale, where he was awarded his Ph.D. in 1930. His initial area of interest was conditioned responses. He did extensive research with the human eye lid; as part of this research he developed a photographic technique for examining the responses. His work demonstrated the relation between voluntary and involuntary responses, and won him the Warren Medal in Experimental Psychology in 1940.

## Begins work on hypnosis

Later, Hilgard became intrigued by the mechanism behind hypnosis. In part, this was not an unusual move: his work on voluntary and involuntary responses focused on the control factor, as does hypnosis. The popular stereotype of hypnosis, in which a person falls into a trance-like state after staring at a moving watch and then involuntarily being made to bark like a dog, is hardly all there is to the process. Nor is hypnotism some mystical power that channels evil forces. It is true that, under certain hypnotic conditions, patients can be given suggestions that they will follow—moving a limb, for example, or holding it rigid. But to treat hypnotism as nothing more than showmanship misses the point. Hypnosis is a tool that, used under the right circumstances, can be useful and even beneficial.

Hilgard, working with his wife and other colleagues, began experimenting and collecting data on hypnosis as a means of, among other things, treating pain. One of the interesting aspects of Hilgard's research into hypnosis is the concept of what he calls the "hidden observer." Ostensibly, a person undergoing hypnosis to manage pain, for example, feels no conscious pain. That does not mean the pain is not there, however; nor does it mean that the patient's subconscious is not registering the pain. In one experiment conducted by the Hilgards, subjects were hypnotized and told they would feel no pain or discomfort when an arm was placed in ice water, or when a tourniquet was tied at the elbow to restrict blood flow to the arm. The subjects reported no pain or discomfort during these procedures. When their "hidden observers" were tapped into, however (usually by a prearranged sign or suggestion from the experimenter), there were reports of pain and discomfort (although not necessarily as severe as would be expected). In subjects particularly susceptible to hypnotic suggestion—those who could be rendered hypnotically deaf or blind, for example—the "hidden observer" could recall "heard" or "seen" objects.

### Wins praise for writings

In addition to his important work as a researcher, Hilgard was also a noted author. He wrote a number of books and papers on the specific areas he studied, and his authorship was distinguished by an ability to make complex issues understandable. This was evident not only in his first book (written with Donald G. Marquis in 1940), *Conditioning and Learning,* but throughout his distinguished career, perhaps most notably in his textbooks for introductory psychology courses such as *Introduction to Psychology* (first edition 1953) with Rita and Richard Atkinson.

After teaching at Yale for three years, Hilgard accepted a position at Stanford in 1933 . He headed the psychology department at Stanford from 1942 to 1951 and served as dean of the graduate division from 1951 to 1955. He became a professor emeritus in 1969 but continued on as head of the laboratory of Hypnosis Research. Among Hilgard's awards over the years are the **American Psychological Association**'s Distinguished Scientific Contribution Award (1969) and the American Psychological Foundation's Gold Career Award (1978). His memberships include the National Academy of Sciences, the American Academy of Arts and Sciences, and the National Academy of Education.

George A. Milite

### Further Reading

Bower, Gordon H. and Ernest R. Hilgard. *Theories of Learning,* 5th ed. Englewood Cliffs, NJ, Prentice-Hall, 1981.
Hilgard, Ernest R. and Josephine R. Hilgard. *Hypnosis in the Relief of Pain.* Los Altos, CA: W. Kaufmann, 1983.
*McGraw-Hill Modern Scientists and Engineers.* New York: McGraw-Hill, 1980.

## Robert Aubrey Hinde

**1923-**
British biologist, ethologist, psychologist, and author who has played an important role in integrating ethology with other fields.

Robert Aubrey Hinde has played an important role in integrating **ethology** (the scientific study of typical behavior patterns in animals) with other fields, such as psychology. He was born in 1923 in Norwich, England. The youngest of four children, Hinde's father, Ernest Bertram, was a doctor, and his mother Isabella (maiden name Taylor) was a nurse. He got much of his early education at an English boarding school called Oundle that emphasized natural history.

After serving as a pilot in the Royal Air Force during World War II, he entered St. John's College at Cambridge, where he received his bachelor's degree with first class honors in 1948. He received his Ph.D. from Oxford University in 1950. At Oxford he was influenced by the eminent ecologist David Lack and Nikolaas Tinbergen, a Dutch-born British zoologist who won the Nobel Prize for Medicine in 1973.

After receiving his degree, Hinde became curator of the Ornithological Field Station of the Department of Zoology, University of Cambridge (now it is a sub-department of Animal Behaviour). In this early research on birds Hinde focused on such behaviors as those involved in courtship and conflicts in **motivation**. During the 1950s, spurred in part by research in **imprinting** (an ethological term for rapid learning that only takes place in a certain developmental period that is very resistant to change and effects later social interaction), and an interdisciplinary conference led by psychoanalyst **John Bowlby**, Hinde became interested in human and primate development. In the late 1950s Hinde established a group of rhesus monkeys at the field station to look at the consequences of short-term separation between mother and infant.

Hinde's research with non-human primates in the 1960s and 1970s led to his interest in the nature and dynamics of relationships between people, and eventually to relationships between **family** members and between peers. Hinde's interest in how psychology and ethology are related lead him to write *Animal Behaviour: A Synthesis of Ethology and Comparative Psychology* (1966), a groundbreaking scholarly work that helped integrate research in psychology and ethology.

Some of Hinde's numerous books include *Biological Bases of Human Social Behaviour* (1974) and *Individuals, Relationships and Culture* (1987). His book, *Towards Understanding Relationships* (1979), classifies the chief dimensions of interpersonal relationships, and shows how his categories of behavior relate to the major theories of interpersonal dynamics. In the 1980s, Hinde and his wife Joan Stevenson-Hinde researched preschool children's family and school relationships, and how they affected **personality** development. In 1997 he published *Relationships: A Dialectical Perspective.*

He also has had an interest in how cross-cultural psychological characteristics have been adaptive biologically. In this respect he has looked at sexual relationships, mother-child relationships, and, more recently, religious systems as well as international wars. His most recent book is *Why Gods Persist* (1999).

Hinde was married to Hester Cecily Cotts in 1968. They had four children before divorcing three years later. He married his current wife, Joan Stevenson-Hinde, in 1971. They had two children. He is currently Professor Emeritus in the Department of Zoology, University of Cambridge, U.K.

Marie Doorey

## Further Reading

Cambridge University Website. *Hinde's Page*
http://www.zoo.cam.ac.uk/zoostaff/hinde.htm.
Corsini, R.J., editor. "Hinde, Robert A, (1923- )" In *Encyclopedia of psychology, 2nd Ed., V. 4*. New York: John Wiley & Sons, 1994.
Hinde, Robert A. *Curriculum Vitae.* (courtesy of Robert Hinde), 2000.
Timberlake, W. "Hinde, Robert Aubrey." In *Biographical dictionary of psychology*. London and New York: Routledge, 1997.

## Further Information

St. John's College University of Cambridge. Department of Zoology, Downing Street, Cambridge, U.K. CB2 3EJ.

# Histrionic personality disorder

A maladaptive or inflexible pattern of behavior characterized by emotional instability, excitability, over-reactivity, and self-dramatization.

Individuals with histrionic personality disorder tend to seek **attention** by exaggerating events, even if insignificant, and are immature, self-centered and often vain. They react emotionally to the slightest provocation. Histrionic personality disorder is classified by psychologists with the group of **personality disorders** characterized by overly dramatic, emotional, impulsive or erratic reactions. People with histrionic personality disorder seek stimulation and novelty and easily become bored with routine situations and relationships. Their low tolerance for inactivity leads to hedonistic or impulsive actions. They tend to be preoccupied with their appearance and attractiveness, and their demeanor is often charming and seductive, even if this behavior is inap-

propriate. These individuals pursue a fast-paced social and romantic lifestyle, although their relationships usually are shallow and fleeting. They also tend to be dependent on others.

The use of the term "histrionic" by professional in psychology is relatively recent and replaces the term "hysterical," which has been dropped due to its negative and sexist associations. Women are more likely than men to be diagnosed with histrionic personality disorder, although this may at least partly reflect gender and cultural biases that cause this pattern of behavior to be less easily recognized in men. Individuals with histrionic personality disorder can benefit from psychodynamic therapy or **group therapy**. The latter can help by enabling these individuals to learn how they relate to others and try out new ways of relating. The goals for individuals who undergo therapy should include gaining more control over emotional reactions and understanding how their overly dramatic behavior undermines their relationships or careers. Medication is ineffective in treating histrionic personality disorder, although it might be prescribed for accompanying symptoms, such as anxiety or **depression**.

## Further Reading

Morrison, James. *DSM-IV Made Easy: The Clinician's Guide to Diagnosis*. New York: The Guilford Press, 1995.

# Holtzman inkblot technique

A projective test used for the assessment of personality characteristics

The Holtzman inkblot technique was developed in an attempt to minimize certain statistical difficulties that arise in the analysis of Rorschach results. In the Holtzman inkblot, the subject responds to each of a series of 45 ambiguous inkblots. These responses are scored to describe and to classify the **personality** of the subject. The main difference between the Holtzman inkblot and the Rorschach inkblot technique is that in the Holtzman technique, the subject is permitted to make only one response per inkblot. The empirical validity of the Holtzman inkblot technique, and other **projective techniques**, is disputed by some authorities.

*See also* Rorschach technique

## Further Reading

Holtzman, Wayne. *Inkblot Perception and Personality.* Austin: University of Texas Press, 1961.

# Homosexuality

Enduring emotional, romantic, or sexual attraction to individuals of one's own gender.

For most of history, open discussions about homosexuality—sexual attraction to people of one's own gender—have been taboo. Men and women with a homosexual orientation are referred to as gay, while the term lesbian refers to women only. Homosexuality was classified as a mental disorder until 1973, when the **American Psychiatric Association** removed "homosexuality" from the *Diagnostic and Statistical Manual of Mental Disorders*. Two decades later, bias and discrimination against gays and lesbians still exists, but sexual orientation is discussed more openly.

There are no reliable statistics on the number of people who are homosexual. The American researcher **Alfred C. Kinsey** conducted extensive surveys on sexual behavior in the 1950s, and estimated that about 4% of men and 3% of women were exclusively homosexual; however, his research found that 37% of men and 28% of women had had some sexual experience with a person of their own gender. Most researchers in the 1990s estimate the percentage of the population with homosexual orientation at about 5%, while recognizing that the estimate is based on projections, not hard statistics.

The four components of human **sexuality** are biological sex, **gender identity** (the psychological sense of being male or female), sexual orientation, and social sex role (adherence to cultural norms for feminine and masculine behavior). Sexual orientation refers to enduring emotional, romantic, sexual, or affectionate feelings of attraction to individuals of a particular gender. Sexual orientation may or may not be reflected by the individual in his or her behavior, because feelings of attraction may be repressed or ignored for any number of reasons.

Three sexual orientations are commonly recognized: homosexual, attraction to individuals of one's own gender; heterosexual, attraction to individuals of the opposite gender; bisexual, attractions to members of either gender.

Through history, various theories have been proposed regarding the source and development of sexual orientation. Many scientists believe that sexual orientation is shaped for most people at an early age through complex interactions of biological, psychological, and social factors. In most cases, sexual orientation emerges for most people in early **adolescence** without any prior sexual experience. Many reports have been recorded by people recounting efforts to change their sexual orientation from homosexual to heterosexual with no success. For these reasons, psychologists believe that sexual orientation is

not a conscious choice that can be voluntarily changed. In addition, scientific research over 30 years confirms that homosexual orientation is not associated with emotional or social problems. Based on research conducted in the 1960s, psychologists, psychiatrists, and other **mental health** professionals concluded that homosexuality is not an illness, mental disorder, or emotional problem.

The process of identity development for lesbians and gay men, usually called "coming out," has been found to be strongly related to psychological adjustment. Being able to discuss one's sexual orientation is a sign of positive mental health and strong **self-esteem** for a gay man or lesbian. But even for those gays and lesbians who have adjusted psychologically to their sexual orientation, false stereotypes and prejudice make the process of "coming out" challenging. Lesbian and gay people must risk rejection by **family**, friends, co-workers, and religious institutions when they share their sexual orientation.

In addition, **violence** and discrimination are real threats. In a 1989 national survey, almost half of the gay and lesbian people surveyed reported being the target of some form of discrimination or violence during their lifetime. Legal protection from discrimination and violence for gay and lesbian people is important. Some states categorize violence against an individual on the basis of her or his sexual orientation as a "hate crime" with more stringent **punishment**. Eight U.S. states have laws against discrimination on the basis of sexual orientation.

There is no scientific evidence to support the idea that sexual orientation can be changed through therapy. Some well-meaning parents have sought therapy to help their child change his or her sexual orientation, especially when the admission of homosexuality seems to be causing the child great emotional **pain**. In fact, there have been reports of cases where such therapy was successful; however, several factors in these reports cause psychologists to question the results. First, none of these cases have been reported on by objective mental health researchers; rather, many of the reports about sexual orientation being changed through therapy have been generated by organizations who are ideologically opposed to homosexual orientation. In addition, the reports have not allowed for a realistic follow-up period. In 1990, the **American Psychological Association** stated that scientific evidence does not support conversion therapy; in fact, the evidence reveals that it can actually be psychologically damaging to attempt conversion. Sexual orientation is a complex component of one's **personality** not limited to sexual behavior. Altering sexual orientation is to attempt to alter a key aspect of the individual's identity.

Like people of other sexual orientations, a percentage of gays and lesbians seek counseling. They may see a therapist for any of the reasons many people seek help—coping with grief, anxiety, or other mental health or relationship difficulties. In addition, they may seek psychological help in adjusting to their sexual orientation and in dealing with prejudice, discrimination, and rejection. Families who are adjusting to the news that one of their members is homosexual may also seek counseling to help with the complex feelings and prejudices that such news may elicit.

Since sexual orientation emerges in adolescence—already a stage of challenging emotional, social, and physical development—families of adolescent gays and lesbians should learn as much as they can about sexual orientation. Educational materials and support and discussion groups exist for both adolescents and their family members.

*See also* Bisexuality

## Further Reading

Bass, Ellen, and Kate Kaufman. *Free Your Mind: The Book for Gay, Lesbian, and Bisexual Youth—and Their Allies.* New York: HarperPerennial, 1996.

Dynes, Wayne R., et al. *Encyclopedia of Homosexuality.* New York: Garland, 1990.

Garnets, L. D., et al. "Issues in Psychotherapy with Lesbians and Gay Men." *American Psychologist* 46:9, pp. 964-72.

Garnets, L. D. and D. C. Kimmel. *Psychological Perspectives on Lesbians and Gay Male Experiences.* New York: Columbia University Press, 1993.

Gonsiorek, J.C., and J.D. Weinrich. *Homosexuality: Research Implications For Public Policy.* New York: Sage Publications, 1991.

Goodchilds, J. D., *Psychological Perspectives on Human Diversity in America.* Washington, DC: American Psychological Association, 1993.

Michale, Robert T., et al. *Sex in America: A Definitive Survey.* Boston: Little, Brown, 1994.

Miller, Deborah A., and Alex Waigandt. *Coping with Your Sexual Orientation.* New York: Rosen, 1990. [For adolescents]

Rafkin, Louise, ed. *Different Daughters: A Book by Mothers of Lesbians.* Garden City, NY: Doubleday, 1989.

Schulenburg, Joy. *The Complete Guide to Gay Parenting.* Garden City, NY: Doubleday, 1985.

## Further Information

American Psychological Association. Office of Public Affairs, 750 First St., N.E., Washington, DC 20002-4242, (202) 336–5700. Email: public.affairs@apa.org.

Federation of Parents and Friend of Lesbians and Gays. P.O. Box 27605, Washington, DC 20038, (202) 638–4200.

National Federation of Parents and Friends of Gays. 8020 Eastern Avenue NW, Washington, DC 20004, (202) 726–3223.

National Gay and Lesbian Task Force. 1734 14th Street, NW, Washington, DC 20009, (202) 332–6483.

National Institute of Mental Health. 5600 Fishers Lane, Room 7C02, Rockville, MD 20857, (301) 443–4513.

Parents and Friends of Lesbians and Gays. 1012 14th Street, NW, Suite 700, Washington, DC 20005, (202) 638–4200.

Sex Information and Education Counsel of the United States. 130 W. 42nd Street, Suite 2500, New York, NY 10036.

# Evelyn Hooker

### 1907-1996
American psychologist who helped change stereotypes about homosexuals.

Evelyn Hooker's groundbreaking work on **homosexuality** paved the way for greater acceptance of a group of people who had for years been labeled "abnormal." Modern society still finds many ways to discriminate against gay men and lesbians, but before Hooker's study many viewed homosexuality as a bona fide mental disorder. Hooker's research proved that, aside from their sexual preference, there was no demonstrable psychological difference between heterosexuals and homosexuals.

Evelyn (Gentry) Hooker was born on her grandmother's farm in North Platte, Nebraska, on September 2, 1907. Next door to the farm was the home of the Western showman "Buffalo Bill" Cody. The sixth of nine children, young Evelyn was inspired by her mother to pursue learning. Education for a number of years was a series of one-room schoolhouses as the family moved from farm to farm trying to eke out a living. When she was of high school age, the family moved to Sterling, Colorado, where she attended a large and surprisingly progressive high school.

Hooker originally planned to go to a teacher's college, but her instructors, recognizing her potential, convinced her to go instead to the University of Colorado, where she enrolled in 1924. She took a course with the psychologist Karl Muenzinger and decided to major in psychology. Quickly distinguishing herself, she was offered an instructorship in her senior year. This gave her an opportunity not only to teach but to receive a master's degree. She wanted to stay on at Colorado for her Ph.D., but Muenzinger convinced her that going to another college would broaden her education. She chose Johns Hopkins in Baltimore and received her Ph.D. in 1932.

### Influenced by European experiences

Hooker took a position teaching in a women's college outside of Baltimore. Stricken with tuberculosis in 1934, she was obliged to spend the next two years in a sanitarium in California. She began teaching part-time and in 1937 was awarded a fellowship to study at the Institute for Psychotherapy in Berlin. Her training went on outside the institute as well. She lived with a Jewish family and saw firsthand what the rise of the Nazis had meant to their lives. She also visited the Soviet Union. What she saw in the two dictatorships left a lasting impression on her.

Upon her return to the U.S. she took a position as a research associate at the University of California at Los Angeles (UCLA). She quickly earned a reputation as a brilliant teacher, and she continued to do research. In 1941 she married Donn Caldwell, a writer. The marriage ended in 1947, and she married Edward Niles Hooker, an English professor at UCLA. While both of these events were significant in Hooker's life, there was another event that proved critical for her career.

Sam From, who took a course taught by Hooker in the 1940s, was a homosexual. After he took Hooker's course the two became friends, and he posed a question to her: Why not conduct research on homosexuals to determine whether homosexuality was some sort of disease or disorder—or, as he believed, non-relevant to a person's psychological makeup. Hooker was intrigued, in part because her experiences in Europe had left her with a heightened disdain for social injustice.

Hooker applied for a grant from the National Institute of Mental Health to study two groups of men: heterosexuals and nonclinical (i.e., not patients) homosexuals. Despite the fact that this was during one of the most conservative periods in American political history (the notorious McCarthy Era during the 1950s), she was awarded the grant.

### Experiments dispel beliefs about homosexuals

Hooker's experiments were quite simple. She assembled groups of homosexual and heterosexual males and administered a series of standard psychological tests to them. The test results were then presented to a panel of experts on the assessments. No one on the panel could determine which subjects were heterosexual and which were homosexual; moreover, they gave the homosexual subjects high marks on emotional adjustment and **personality** development.

Hooker presented her results in a series of papers in the 1950s, the most important of which was a 1957 paper published in the *Journal of Projective Techniques* entitled, "The Adjustment of the Male Overt Homosexual." She continued her research throughout the 1960s, and in 1967, was appointed head of a study group on homosexual issues for the **National Institute of Mental Health**. One of the biggest breakthroughs came about in 1973, when the **American Psychiatric Association** removed

homosexuality from its diagnostic handbook—in effect saying that homosexuality was no longer recognized as a form of **mental illness**.

Hooker retired from UCLA in 1970 and continued in private practice for several years. In 1991 she was awarded the **American Psychological Association**'s Award for Distinguished Contribution to Psychology in the Public Interest. She died at her home in Santa Monica, California, on November 18, 1996.

*See also* Homosexuality

George A. Milite

### Further Reading

"Evelyn Hooker." *American Psychologist* 47 (1992): 499-501.
Hooker, Evelyn. "A Preliminary Analysis of Group Behavior of Homosexuals." *Journal of Psychology* 42 (1956): 217-25.
Hooker, Evelyn. "The Adjustment of the Male Overt Homosexual." *Journal of Projective Techniques* 21 (1957): 18-31.

# Hormones

Biochemical agents that transmit messages between components of living organisms.

Hormones are biochemical messengers that regulate physiological events in living organisms. More than 100 hormones have been identified in humans. Hormones are secreted by endocrine (ductless) glands such as the **hypothalamus**, the pituitary gland, the pineal gland, the thyroid, the parathyroid, the thymus, the adrenals, the pancreas, the ovaries, and the testes. Hormones are secreted directly into the blood stream, where they travel to target tissues and modulate digestion, growth, maturation, reproduction, and homeostasis. Hormones do not fall into any one chemical category, but most are either protein molecules or steroid molecules. These biological managers keep the body systems functioning over the long term and help maintain health. The study of hormones is called endocrinology.

### Hypothalamus

Most hormones are released into the bloodstream by a single gland. Testosterone is an exception, because it is secreted by both the adrenal glands and by the testes. The major site that keeps track of hormone levels is the hypothalamus. A number of hormones are secreted by the hypothalamus, and they stimulate or inhibit the secretion of hormones at other sites. When the hypothalamus detects high levels of a hormone, it reacts to inhibit further production. When low levels of a hormone are detected, the hypothalamus reacts to stimulate hormone production or secretion. The body handles the hormone estrogen differently. Each month, the Graafian follicle in the ovary releases increasing amounts of estrogen into the bloodstream as the egg develops. When estrogen levels rise to a certain point, the pituitary gland secretes luteinizing hormone (LH), which triggers the egg's release into the oviduct.

The major hormones secreted by the hypothalamus are corticotropin releasing hormone (CRH), thyrotropin releasing hormone (TRH), follicle stimulating hormone releasing hormone (FSHRH), luteinizing hormone releasing hormone (LHRH), and growth hormone releasing hormone (GHRH). CRH targets the adrenal glands. It triggers the adrenals to release adrenocorticotropic hormone (ACTH). ACTH functions to synthesize and release corticosteroids. TRH targets the thyroid where it functions to synthesize and release the thyroid hormones T3 and T4. FSH targets the ovaries and the testes where it enables the maturation of the ovum and of spermatozoa. LHRH also targets the ovaries and the testes, helping to promote ovulation and increase progesterone synthesis and release. GHRH targets the anterior pituitary to release growth hormone to most body tissues, increase protein synthesis, and increase blood glucose.

The hypothalamus also secretes other important hormones such as prolactin inhibiting hormone (PIH), prolactin releasing hormone (PRH), and melanocyte inhibiting hormone (MIH). PIH targets the anterior pituitary to inhibit milk production at the mammary gland, and PRH has the opposite effect. MIH targets skin pigment cells (melanocytes) to regulate pigmentation.

## Pituitary gland

The pituitary has long been called the master gland because of the vast extent of its activity. It lies deep in the **brain** just behind the nose, and is divided into anterior and posterior regions. Both anti-diuretic hormone (ADH) and oxytocin are synthesized in the hypothalamus before moving to the posterior pituitary prior to secretion. ADH targets the collecting tubules of the kidneys, increasing their permeability to and retention of water. Lack of ADH leads to a condition called diabetes insipidus characterized by excessive urination. Oxytocin targets the uterus and the mammary glands in the breasts. Oxytocin also triggers labor contractions prior to **birth** and functions in the ejection of milk. The drug pitocin is a synthetic form of oxytocin and is used medically to induce labor.

The anterior pituitary (AP) secretes a number of hormones, including growth hormone (GH), ACTH, TSH, prolactin, LH, and FSH. GH controls cellular growth, protein synthesis, and elevation of blood glucose concentration. ACTH controls secretion of some hormones by the adrenal cortex (mainly cortisol). TSH controls thyroid hormone secretion in the thyroid. In males, prolactin enhances testosterone production; in females, it initiates and maintains LH to promote milk secretion from the mammary glands. In females, FSH initiates ova development and induces ovarian estrogen secretion. In males, FSH stimulates sperm production in the testes. LH stimulates ovulation and formation of the corpus luteum, which produces progesterone in females, whereas LH stimulates interstitial cells in males to produce testosterone.

## Thyroid gland

The thyroid lies under the larynx and synthesizes two hormones, thyroxine and tri-iodothyronine. This gland takes up iodine from the blood and has the highest iodine level in the body. The iodine is incorporated into the thyroid hormones. Thyroxine has four iodine atoms and is called T4. Tri-iodothyronine has three iodine atoms and is called T3. Both T3 and T4 function to increase the metabolic rate of several cells and tissues. The brain, testes, lungs, and spleen are not affected by thyroid hormones, however. T3 and T4 indirectly increase blood glucose levels as well as the insulin-promoted uptake of glucose by fat cells. Their release is modulated by TRH-RH from the hypothalamus. When temperature drops, a metabolic increase is triggered by TSH. Chronic **stress** seems to reduce TSH secretion which, in turn, decreases T3 and T4 output.

Depressed T3 and T4 production is the trademark of hypothyroidism. If it occurs in young children, this decreased activity can cause physical and **mental retardation**. In adults, it creates sluggishness—mentally and physically—and is characterized further by weight gain, poor hair growth, and a swollen neck. Excessive T3 and T4 cause sweating, nervousness, weight loss, and fatigue. The thyroid also secretes calcitonin, which serves to reduce blood calcium levels. Calcitonin's role is particularly significant in children whose bones are still forming.

## Parathyroid glands

The parathyroid glands are attached to the bottom of the thyroid gland. They secrete the polypeptide parathyroid hormone (PTH), which plays a crucial role in monitoring blood calcium and phosphate levels. Calcium is a critical element for the human body. Even though the majority of calcium is in bone, it is also used by muscles, including cardiac muscle, for contractions, and by nerves in the release of neurotransmitters. Calcium is a powerful messenger in the immune response of inflammation and blood clotting. Both PTH and calcitonin regulate calcium levels in the kidneys, the gut, bone, and blood.

PTH deficiency can be due to autoimmune diseases or to inherited parathyroid gland problems. Low PTH capabilities cause depressed blood calcium levels and neuromuscular problems. Very low PTH can lead to tetany or muscle spasms. Excess PTH can lead to weakened bones because it causes too much calcium to be drawn from the bones and to be excreted in the urine. Abnormalities of bone mineral deposits can lead to a number of conditions, including osteoporosis and rickets. Osteoporosis can be due to dietary insufficiencies of calcium, phosphate, or vitamin C. The end result is a loss of bone mass. Rickets is usually caused by a vitamin D deficiency and results in lower rates of bone formation in children. These examples show the importance of a balanced, nutritious diet for healthy development.

## Adrenal glands

The two adrenal glands sit one on top of each kidney. Both adrenals have two distinct regions. The outer region (the medulla) produces adrenaline and noradrenaline and is under the control of the sympathetic **nervous system**. The inner region (the cortex) produces a number of steroid hormones. The cortical steroid hormones are derived from cholesterol and include mineralocorticoids (mainly aldosterone), glucocorticoids (mainly cortisol), and gonadocorticoids. Aldosterone and cortisol are the major human steroids in the cortex. However, testosterone and estrogen are secreted by adults (both male and female) at very low levels.

Aldosterone plays an important role in regulating body fluids. It increases blood levels of sodium and water and lowers blood potassium levels. Cortisol secretion is stimulated by physical trauma, exposure to cold temperatures, burns, heavy exercise, and anxiety. Cortisol targets the liver, skeletal muscle, and adipose tissue, and its overall effect is to provide amino acids and glucose to meet synthesis and energy requirements for metabolism and during periods of stress. Because of its anti-inflammatory action, cortisol is used clinically to reduce swelling. Excessive cortisol secretion leads to Cushing's syndrome, which is characterized by weak bones, **obesity**, and a tendency to bruise. Cortisol deficiency can lead to Addison's disease, which has the symptoms of fatigue, low blood sodium levels, low blood pressure, and excess skin pigmentation.

The adrenal medullary hormones are epinephrine (adrenaline) and nor-epinephrine (nor-adrenaline). Both of these hormones serve to supplement and prolong the "fight or flight" response initiated in the nervous system. This response includes increased heart rate, peripheral blood vessel constriction, sweating, spleen contraction, glycogen conversion to glucose, dilation of bronchial tubes, decreased digestive activity, and low urine output.

## Pancreas

The pancreas secretes the hormones insulin, glucagon, and somatostatin, also known as growth hormone inhibiting hormone (GHIH). Insulin and glucagon have reciprocal roles. Insulin promotes the storage of glucose, fatty acids, and amino acids, while glucagon stimulates mobilization of these constituents from storage into the blood. Insulin release is triggered by high blood glucose levels. It lowers blood sugar levels and inhibits the release of glucose by the liver in order to keep blood levels down. Insulin excess can cause hypoglycemia leading to convulsions or **coma**, and insufficient levels of insulin can cause diabetes mellitus, which can be fatal if left untreated. Diabetes mellitus is the most common endocrine disorder.

Glucagon secretion is stimulated by decreased blood glucose levels, infection, cortisol, exercise, and large protein meals. Among other activities, it facilitates glucose release into the blood. Excess glucagon can result from tumors of the pancreatic alpha cells, and a mild diabetes seems to result. Some cases of uncontrolled diabetes are also characterized by high glucagon levels, suggesting that low blood insulin levels are not necessarily the only cause in diabetes cases.

## Female hormones

The female reproductive hormones arise from the hypothalamus, the anterior pituitary, and the ovaries. Although detectable amounts of the steroid hormone estrogen are present during fetal development, at **puberty** estrogen levels rise to initiate secondary sexual characteristics. Gonadotropin releasing hormone (GRH) is released by the hypothalamus to stimulate pituitary release of LH and FSH, which propagate egg development in the ovaries. Eggs (ova) exist at various stages of development, with the maturation of one ovum taking about 28 days. The ova are contained within follicles that are support organs for ova maturation. About 450 of a female's 150,000 germ cells mature to leave the ovary. The hormones secreted by the ovary include estrogen, progesterone, and small amounts of testosterone.

As an ovum matures, rising estrogen levels stimulate additional LH and FSH release from the pituitary. Prior to ovulation, estrogen levels drop, and LH and FSH surge to cause the ovum to be released into the fallopian tube. The cells of the burst follicle begin to secrete progesterone and some estrogen. These hormones trigger thickening of the uterine lining, the endometrium, to prepare it for implantation should fertilization occur. The high progesterone and estrogen levels prevent LH and FSH from further secretion—thus hindering another ovum from developing. If fertilization does not occur, eight days after ovulation the endometrium deteriorates, resulting in menstruation. The falling estrogen and progesterone levels that follow trigger LH and FSH, starting the cycle all over again.

In addition to its major roles in the menstrual cycle, estrogen has a protective effect on bone loss, which can lead to osteoporosis.

Hormones related to pregnancy include human chorionic gonadotrophin (HCG), estrogen, human chorionic somatomammotrophin (HCS), and relaxin. HCG is released by the early embryo to signal implantation. Estrogen and HCS are secreted by the placenta. As birth nears, relaxin is secreted by the ovaries to relax the pelvic area in preparation for labor.

### Male hormones

Male reproductive hormones come from the hypothalamus, the anterior pituitary, and the testes. As in females, GRH is released from the hypothalamus, which stimulates LH and FSH release from the pituitary. Testosterone levels are quite low until puberty. At puberty, rising levels of testosterone stimulate male reproductive development including secondary characteristics. LH stimulates testosterone release from the testes. FSH promotes early spermatogenesis. The male also secretes prostaglandins. These substances promote uterine contractions which help propel sperm towards an egg during sexual intercourse. Prostaglandins are produced in the seminal vesicles, and are not classified as hormones by all authorities.

### Further Reading

Little, M. *The Endocrine System*. New York: Chelsea House Publishers, 1990.

Parker, M., ed. *Steroid Hormone Action*. New York: IRL Press, 1993.

# Karen Horney

### 1885-1952

German-born American psychoanalyst who was among the leading theorists of psychoanalysis in the United States, and cofounder of the American Institute of Psychoanalysis.

**Karen Horney** *(Corbis-Bettmann. Reproduced with permission.)*

Karen Horney was born in Hamburg, Germany, and educated at the University of Berlin and the University of Freiberg. She emigrated to the United States in 1932, after having taught for two years at the Berlin Institute of Psychoanalysis. From 1932-34, she was assistant director of the Chicago Institute for Psychoanalysis; she then left for New York City. In 1935, she was elected to the New York Psychoanalytic Society. Horney believed that **personality** is significantly affected by the **unconscious** mind, but she also theorized that both interpersonal relationships and societal factors were key factors contributing to mental development. She became increasingly outspoken in her disagreements with the theories developed by **Sigmund Freud** on the nature of neuroses and personality. Where Freud advanced a biological basis for neuroses, Horney believed that the **environment** of **childhood** played a key role in **personality development**. She felt strongly that negative experiences in early childhood could trigger anxiety in adulthood. In 1936, Horney published her first book, *The Neurotic Personality of Our Time*, a highly readable work. This was followed in 1939 by *New Ways in Psychoanalysis*, and *Self Analysis* in 1942.

In 1942, Horney cofounded the American Institute for Psychoanalysis. She is best known for broadening the perspective of psychoanalysis to consider childhood, environment, and interpersonal relationship. In 1955, three years after her death, the Karen Horney Clinic was established in New York City in her honor. The Clinic provides psychoanalysis and training for analysts.

**Further Reading**

Rolka, Gail Meyer. *100 Women Who Shaped World History.* San Francisco: Bluewood Books, 1994.

Sayers, Janet. *Mothers of Psychoanalysis.* New York: W.W. Norton, 1991.

# Hostility

A persistent feeling of anger or resentment combined with a strong desire to express it or retaliate.

Hostility is a strong impulse inspired by feelings of **anger** or resentment. Though hostile impulses are **normal**, and everyone has them from time to time (for example, when frustrated, offended, or deprived of something), a hostile person feels those impulses regularly. She or he is always ready to take offense or feel frustrated in some way. This is often described as "having a chip on one's shoulder." Hostility can play a part in anxiety attacks, **depression**, compulsions, and **paranoia**. On a larger scale, hostility leads to violent crime, invasions, wars, and other acts of **aggression**.

**Further Reading**

Lerner, Harriet Goldhor. *The Dance of Anger: A Woman's Guide to Changing the Patterns of Intimate Relationships.* New York: Perennial Library, Harper & Row, 1989.

Williams, Redford, M.D., and Virginia Williams, Ph.D. *Anger Kills: Seventeen Strategies for Controlling the Hostility that Can Harm Your Health.* New York: HarperPerennial, 1993.

# Howes, Ethel Dench Puffer

See **Puffer, Ethel Dench**

# Clark Leonard Hull

### 1884-1952
American psychologist who was a primary representative of the neobehaviorist school.

Clark L. Hull was born in a country farmhouse near Akron, New York, on May 24, 1884. He attended high school for a year in West Saginaw, Michigan, and the acad-

**Clark Hull** *(Archives of the History of American Psychology. Reproduced with permission.)*

emy of Alma College. His education was interrupted by bouts of typhoid fever and poliomyelitis, giving him pause to consider possible vocational choices; he decided upon psychology. He then matriculated at the University of Michigan, took his bachelor's degree, and went on to the University of Wisconsin, receiving his doctorate in 1918. Staying on at Wisconsin to teach, Hull was at first torn between two schools of psychological thought which prevailed at the time: early **behaviorism** and **Gestalt psychology**. He was not long in deciding in favor of the former.

After an experimental project on the influence of tobacco smoking on mental and motor efficiency, Hull was offered the opportunity to teach a course in psychological tests and measurements. Gladly accepting it, he changed the name to "aptitude testing" and worked hard at developing it as a sound basis for vocational guidance. The material which he collected in this course was gathered into a book, *Aptitude Testing* (1928). Next, with the help of a grant from the National Research Council, he built a machine that automatically prepared the correlations he needed in his test-construction work.

In 1929 Hull became a research professor of psychology at the Institute of Psychology at Yale University, later incorporated into the Institute of Human Relations. He came to certain definite conclusions about psychology, and in 1930 he stated that psychology is a true natural science, that its primary laws are expressible quantitatively by means of ordinary equations, and that quantitative laws even for the behavior of groups as a whole could be derived from the same primary equations.

The next 10 years were filled with projects dealing not only with aptitude testing but with learning experiments, behavior theory, and **hypnosis**. As a representative of behaviorism, Hull fell into that school's neobehaviorist period of the 1930s and early 1940s. His basic motivational concept was the "drive." His quantitative system, based on stimulus-response **reinforcement** theory and using the concepts "drive reduction" and "intervening variables," was highly esteemed by psychologists during the 1940s for its objectivity.

Hull was probably the first psychologist to approach hypnosis with the quantitative methodology customarily used in **experimental psychology**. This combination of experimental methods and the phenomena provided by hypnosis yielded many appropriate topics for experimental problems by his students. *Hypnosis and Suggestibility,* the first extensive systematic investigation of hypnosis with experimental methods, was published in 1933, incorporating the earlier, and better, part of the hypnosis program that Hull had carried out at the University of Wisconsin.

In 1940 Hull published, jointly with C. I. Hovland, R. T. Ross, M. Hall, D. T. Perkins, and F. B. Fitch, *Mathematico-Deductive Theory of Rote Learning.* Three years later his *Principles of Behavior* was published, followed by a revision of his theories in *Essentials of Behavior* (1951). Hull expressed **learning theory** in terms of quantification, by means of equations which he had derived from a method of scaling originally devised by L. L. Thurstone. In his last book, *A Behavior System* (1952), Hull applied his principles to the behavior of single organisms. His system stands as an important landmark in the history of theoretical psychology. He died in New Haven, Connecticut, on May 10, 1952.

### Further Reading

Beach, Frank A. *Biographical memoirs.* The National Academy of Sciences, vol. 33. 1959

Boring, Edwin G., et al., eds. *A history of psychology in autobiography.* vol. 4, 1952.

Marx, Melvin H. and William A. Hillix. *Systems and theories in psychology.* 1963.

# Humanistic psychology

A theoretical and therapeutic approach that emphasizes people's uniqueness and their power to control their own destinies.

Humanistic psychology evolved in the 1960s as a reaction to psychodynamic psychology and **behaviorism**. Humanists objected to the pessimistic view of human nature advocated by psychodynamic psychologists who saw the selfish pursuit of pleasure as the root of all human behavior. They also felt that the behaviorists' beliefs that all human behavior is the product of environmental influences reduced people to the status of machines and did not adequately explain the human experience. Humanists faulted both psychodynamic psychologists and behaviorists for viewing human behavior as governed by factors beyond personal control. In contrast, humanists emphasize people's innate potential, and the ability of people to determine their own destinies. The ultimate goal for the humanistic psychologist, therefore, is to help people realize their full potential and live up to their abilities.

## Theories and therapeutic applications

Two particular theoretical approaches have come to characterize humanistic psychology. The "person-centered" approach to therapy advocated by **Carl Rogers** is based on his belief that trusting one's experiences and believing in one's self are the most important elements of self-fulfillment. In person-centered therapy, abnormal behavior is considered to be the result of a person's failure to trust experience, resulting in a distorted or inaccurate view of the self. There is an incongruity between the person's current view of himself and his "ideal" self. Person-centered therapists attempt to help people gain self-understanding and self-acceptance by conveying **empathy**, warmth, and the unconditional belief that no matter what the client says or does, the client is still a worthwhile person.

The second influential theory of humanistic psychology was developed by **Abraham Maslow**. Maslow believed that people are innately good and naturally driven to develop their potential or to achieve "self-actualization." He believed, however, that people were driven by a hierarchy of needs that must be fulfilled in a particular sequence in order for **self-actualization** to occur. First, physiological and safety needs must be met. Then people need to feel a sense of belonging. Once this is achieved, people work on their **self-esteem** needs and then finally self-actualization. Maslow believed that psychological problems result from a difficulty in fulfilling the self-esteem needs, which therefore block self-actualization. Therapy, then, is aimed at correcting people's inaccurate views of themselves, improving their self-esteem, and enabling them to continue on the path toward self-actualization.

## Research

Humanistic psychologists have tended to focus on client care rather than research, although some empirical investigation have been undertaken. Studies of the relationship between the therapist and the client have shown that Rogers's ideals were important to successful outcomes, making his theory very influential in the world of counseling. In fact, empathy, warmth, and acceptance are now commonly referred to as the "core conditions" or "common factors" of counseling and are used by therapists of all psychological perspectives to encourage people to feel and act differently. Research into Maslow's theory has yielded mixed results. The primary importance of physiological and safety needs has been supported by research, however, it has not been clearly demonstrated that fulfillment of these needs is necessary before people can begin to self-actualize. In one important study, for example, subjects were placed in stressful situations that threatened their physiological and safety needs. Shortly thereafter, the researchers measured the **creativity** of the participants' answers on a test. Since creativity is an aspect of self-actualization, it was predicted that creativity would be compromised as a result of the **stress**, however, the opposite result was found; the subjects actually became more creative in reaction to the challenge to their survival needs.

One of the main reasons for the lack of research on humanistic psychology is because of its philosophical and theoretical roots. Humanists stress acceptance of people, instead of critically examining their behavior. Rather than seeking to uncover the common mechanisms underlying human behavior, humanists emphasize human uniqueness and the "phenomenological perspective"—the view that people are best understood by examining their specific, unique experiences and aspirations. This personalized view has recently become very popular outside the field of scientific psychology. In fact, the "Personal Power" system sold on television by Anthony Robbins is largely based on the humanistic belief that you are responsible for creating the life you live.

Timothy Moore

## Further Reading

Capuzzi, D. and D. Gross. *Counseling and Psychotherapy: Theories and Interventions.* New Jersey: Prentice Hall, 1999.

"The Humanistic Psychologist." *Journal of the Division of Humanistic Psychology.* American Psychological Association.

# Human potential movement

A movement that focused on helping normal persons achieve their full potential through an eclectic combination of therapeutic methods and disciplines. The movement's values include tolerance, a basic optimism about human nature, the necessity of honest interpersonal communication, the importance of living life to the fullest in the "here and now," and a spirit of experimentation and openness to new experiences.

**William James**, an early proponent of human potential and altered states of **consciousness**, is considered a forerunner of the human potential movement. However, modern interest in human potential can be traced most directly to the humanistic psychological approach of such figures as **Carl Rogers** and **Abraham Maslow** in the 1950s. **Humanistic psychology** was sometimes referred to as the Third Force because it presented an alternative to the prevailing psychoanalytic and behaviorist methods. Rejecting the view of behavior as determined by **childhood** events or conditioned responses to external stimuli, humanistic practitioners emphasized the individual's power to grow and change in the present and embraced the goal of self-fulfillment through the removal of obstacles.

Maslow, together with Rogers, **Rollo May**, and Charlotte Buhler, founded the American Association of Humanistic Psychology. Subscribing to a positive, optimistic view of human nature, he popularized the concept of **self-actualization**, based on his study of exceptionally successful, rather than exceptionally troubled, people. Selecting a group of "self-actualized" figures from history, including Abraham Lincoln (1809-1865), Albert Einstein (1879-1955), and Eleanor Roosevelt (1884-1962), Maslow constructed a list of their characteristics, some of which later became trademark values of the human potential movement (acceptance of themselves and others, spontaneity, identification with humanity, democratic values, **creativity**). In Maslow's widely popularized hierarchy of **motivation**, the basic human needs were arranged at the bottom of a pyramid, with self-actualization at the highest level. Another of Maslow's ideas was the concept of the "peak experience," a transcendent moment of self-actualization characterized by feelings of joy, wholeness, and fulfillment.

The philosophy of Carl Rogers's **client-centered therapy** (which had been developed by 1940 but peaked in popularity in the 1950s) resembled Maslow's ideas in its view of human impulses as basically positive and in its respect for the inner resources and innate potential of each client. Another strong influence on the development of the human potential movement was the **sensitivity training** inaugurated by Gestalt psychologist **Kurt Lewin** (1890-1947) in his T-groups at the National Training Laboratories in the late 1940s and 1950s. Under the influence of such figures as Maslow and Rogers, sensitivity training—which had initially been used to train professionals in business, industry, and other fields—evolved into the encounter groups of the 1960s and 1970s. Encounter groups used the basic T-group techniques but shifted their emphasis toward personal growth, stressing such factors as self-expression and intense emotional experience.

At the center of the human potential movement was the growth center, for which the model was the Esalen Institute at Big Sur in California. Independent of any university or other institution, Esalen offered workshops by psychologists and authors on many topics of interest to humanists. Its founder, Michael Murphy, envisioned it as a place where humanistic psychology could be integrated with Eastern philosophies. In the mid-1960s its roster of presenters included philosopher Alan Watts (1915-1973), historian Arnold Toynbee (1889-1975), theologian Paul Tillich (1886-1965), and chemist Linus Pauling (1901-1994). Maslow became affiliated with Esalen in 1966. By the early 1970s there were an estimated 150 to 200 growth centers modeled after Esalen throughout the United States.

California's status as the hub of the human potential movement was further enhanced when Carl Rogers moved to La Jolla in 1964, writing and lecturing at the Western Behavioral Science Institute and later at the Center for Studies of the Person. Central tenets of his therapeutic approach were expanded into areas such as philosophy and educational reform that transcended the boundaries of psychology, and the phrases "person-centered approach" and "a way of being" began to replace "client-centered approach." Rogers also became a leader in the **encounter group** movement, adapting the principles of client-centered therapy to a group model. These included the belief that individuals can solve their own problems and reach their full potential in a supportive, permissive environment. Rogers's model called for the group leader to act as a non-authoritarian facilitator, creating a non-threatening atmosphere conducive to open and honest sharing among group members.

Besides encounter groups and a variety of non-traditional therapies (including Gestalt therapy, psychodrama, transactional analysis, primal scream therapy, and Morita therapy), the human potential movement also embraced a number of disciplines and practices (both Eastern and Western) involving healing, self-improvement, and self-awareness, including Zen Buddhism, astrology, art, dance, and various systems of body movement and manipulation. While the flashier and most eccentric aspects of the human potential movement have largely been relegated to fads of the 1960s and 1970s, such as primal scream therapy and EST (Erhard Seminars Training), it endures in other forms. The American Society of Humanistic Psychologists is still an active, well-organized group. Journals in the field include the *Journal of Humanistic Psychology, Journal of Creative Behavior, Journal of Transpersonal Psychology,* and others. Beyond this, the legacy of the human potential movement can be seen in the continuing popularity of self-improvement workshops and books and even in the recent proliferation of 12-step groups, as well as in the many ways its values and principles continue to influence the professional work of therapists with a variety of orientations.

## Further Reading

Maslow, Abraham. *Toward a Psychology of Being*. Princeton: Van Nostrand, 1962.

Rogers, Carl. *On Becoming a Person*. Boston: Houghton Mifflin, 1961.

Severin, F., ed. *Humanistic Viewpoints in Psychology*. New York: McGraw-Hill, 1965.

# David Hume

### 1711-1776

Scottish philosopher who developed a philosophy of "mitigated skepticism," which remains a viable alternative to the systems of rationalism, empiricism, and idealism.

If one was to judge a philosopher by a gauge of relevance—the quantity of issues and arguments raised by him that remain central to contemporary thought—David Hume would be rated among the most important figures in philosophy. Ironically, his philosophical writings went unnoticed during his lifetime, and the considerable fame he achieved derived from his work as an essayist and historian. Immanuel Kant's acknowledgment that Hume roused him from his "dogmatic slumbers" stimulated interest in Hume's thought.

With respect to Hume's life there is no better source than the succinct autobiography, *My Own Life,* written four months before his death. He was born on April 26, 1711, on the family estate, Ninewells, near Edinburgh. According to Hume, the "ruling passion" of his life was literature, and thus his story contains "little more than the History of my writings." As a second son, he was not entitled to a large inheritance, and he failed in two family-sponsored careers in law and business because of his "unsurmountable aversion to everything but the pursuits of Philosophy and general learning." Until he was past 40, Hume was employed only twice. He spent a year in England as a tutor to a mentally ill nobleman, and from 1745 to 1747 Hume was an officer and aide-de-camp to Gen. James Sinclair and attended him on an expedition to the coast of France and military embassies in Vienna and Turin.

## Major works

During an earlier stay in France (1734-1737) Hume had written his major philosophic work, *A Treatise of Human Nature*. The first two volumes were published in 1739 and the third appeared in the following year. The critical reception of the work was singularly unfortunate. In Hume's own words, the *Treatise* "fell dead born from the press." Book I of the *Treatise* was recast as *An Enquiry concerning Human Understanding* and published in 1748. The third volume with minor revisions appeared in 1751 as *An Enquiry concerning the Principles of Morals*. The second volume of the *Treatise* was republished as Part 2 of *Four Dissertations* in 1757. Two sections of this work dealing with liberty and necessity had been incorporated in the first *Enquiry*. Hume's other important work, *Dialogues concerning Natural Religion,* was substantially complete by the mid-1750s, but because of its controversial nature it was published posthumously.

During his lifetime Hume's reputation derived from the publication of his *Political Discourses* (1751) and six-volume *History of England* (1754-1762). When he went to France in 1763 as secretary to the English ambassador, Hume discovered that he was a literary celebrity and a revered figure among the *philosophes*. He led a very happy and active social life even after his retirement to Edinburgh in 1769. He died there on Aug. 25, 1776. He specified in his will that the gravestone be marked only with his name and dates, "leaving it to Posterity to add the rest."

## "Mitigated skepticism"

Skepticism is concerned with the truthfulness of human perceptions and ideas. On the level of **perception**, Hume was the first thinker to consistently point out the disastrous implications of the "representative theory of perception," which he had inherited from both his rationalist and empiricist predecessors. According to this view, when I say that I perceive something such as an elephant, what I actually mean is that I have in my mind a mental idea or image or impression. Such a datum is an internal, mental, subjective *representation* of something that I assume to be an external, physical, objective fact. But there are, at least, two difficulties inherent in ascribing any truth to such perceptions. If truth is understood as the conformity or adequacy between the image and the object, then it is impossible to establish that there is a true world of objects since the only evidence I have of an external world consists of internal images. Further, it is impossible to judge how faithfully mental impressions or ideas represent physical objects.

Hume is aware, however, that this sort of skepticism with regard to the senses does violence to common sense. He suggests that a position of complete skepti-

**David Hume** *(The Library of Congress. Reproduced with permission.)*

cism is neither serious nor useful. Academic skepticism (the name derives from a late branch of Plato's school) states that one can never know the truth or falsity of any statement (except, of course, this one). It is, however, a self-refuting theory and is confounded by life itself because "we make inferences on the basis of our impressions whether they be true or false, real or imaginary." Total skepticism is unlivable since "nature is always too strong for principle." Hume therefore advances what he calls "mitigated skepticism." In addition to the exercise of caution in reasoning, this approach attempts to limit philosophical inquiries to topics that are adapted to the capacities of human **intelligence**. It thus excludes all metaphysical questions concerning the origin of either mind or object as being incapable of demonstration.

## Theory of knowledge

Even though an ultimate explanation of both the subject or object of knowledge is impossible, Hume provides a description of how man senses and understands. He emphasizes the utility of knowledge as opposed to its correctness and suggests that experience begins with feeling rather than thought. He uses the term "perception" in its traditional sense—that is, whatever can be present to the mind from the senses, passions, thought, or reflection. Nonetheless he distinguishes between impressions which are felt and ideas which are thought. In this he stresses the difference between feeling a toothache and thinking about such a **pain**, which had been obscured by both rationalists and empiricists. Both impressions and ideas are subdivided further into simple and complex; for example, the idea of heat is simple, while the idea of combustion is complex.

## Theory of ideas

Hume accepts the Cartesian doctrine of the distinct idea—conceivability subject only to the principle of contradiction—as both the unit of reasoning and the criterion of truth. For Hume, since truth is posterior to fact, the ideas of reason only express what the mind thinks about reality. Distinct ideas, or imaginative concepts, are pure antinomies apart from experience as every factual proposition is equally valid a priori. But Hume does acknowledge that such propositions are not equally meaningful either to thought or action. On the level of ideas, Hume offers a conceptual correlative to the exemption of sensation as a form of **cognition** by his recognition that the meaning of ideas is more important than their truth. What separates meaningful propositions from mere concepts is the subjective impression of belief.

Belief, or the vivacity with which the mind conceives certain ideas and associations, results from the reciprocal relationship between experience and **imagination**. The cumulative experience of the past and present—for example, the relational factors of constancy, conjunction, and resemblance—gives a bias to the imagination. But it is man's imaginative anticipations of the future that give meaning to his experience. Neither the relational elements of experience nor the propensive function of the imagination, from the viewpoint of the criterion of truth, possesses the slightest rational justification. Hence the interplay between the criterion of truth and the logic of the imagination explains both Hume's skepticism and his conception of sensation and intellection.

The most celebrated example of this argument is Hume's analysis of the causal relation. Every statement which points beyond what is immediately available to the senses and **memory** rests on an assumption and/or extension of the cause and effect relation. Let us examine two cases: I see lightning and hear thunder; I see a rabbit and then a fox. The question is why I am right in concluding that lightning causes thunder but wrong in believing that rabbits cause foxes. Experience, in both instances, reveals an A that is followed by B, and repeated experiences show that A is always followed by B. While the constant conjunction of A and B might eliminate the rabbit-fox hypothesis, it is of no help in explain-

ing causality because there are all sorts of objects, such as tables and chairs, which are similarly conjoined but not supposed to be causally related. Thus experience reveals only that constant conjunction and priority are sufficient but not necessary conditions for establishing a causal connection. And it is necessity, understood as that which cannot be otherwise than it is, which makes a relation causal in the propositional form of "If A then B *must* appear and if no A then no B."

But if necessary connection explains causality, what explains necessity? Experience yields only a particular instance and tells us nothing about the past or the future. Nor is there any necessity discoverable in repeated experiences. That the Sun will rise tomorrow because it has in the past is an assumption that the past necessarily causes the future which is, of course, the connection that is to be demonstrated. If experience cannot account for necessity, then reason fares no better. I can always imagine the opposite of any matter of fact without contradiction. If someone tells me that Caesar died of old age or that thunder is uncaused or that the Sun will not rise tomorrow, I will not believe him, but there is nothing logically incorrect about such statements since for every probability "there exists an equal and opposite possibility." Thus there is no justifiable knowledge of causal connections in nature, although this is not a denial that there are real causes. Man's supposed knowledge results from repeated associations of A and B to the point where the imagination makes its customary transition from one object to its usual attendant, that is, "an object followed by another, and whose appearance always conveys the thought to that other."

## Further Reading

Burton, John H. *Life and correspondence of David Hume.* 1846. repr. 1967.

Chappell, V.C., ed. *Hume.* 1966.

Flew, Antony. *Hume's philosophy of belief.* 1961.

Glathe, Alfred B. *Hume's theory of the passions and of morals.* 1950.

Hendel, Charles W. *Studies in the philosophy of David Hume.* 1963.

Mossner, Ernest C. *The life of David Hume.* 1954.

Passmore, John A. *Hume's intentions.* 1952.

Pears, D.F., ed. *David Hume: a symposium.* 1963.

Sesonske, Alexander and Noel Fleming, eds. *Human understanding: studies in the philosophy of David Hume.* 1965.

Zabeeh, Farhang. *Hume, precursor of modern empiricism.* 1960.

# Humor

The mental faculty of discovering, expressing, or appreciating the ludicrous or absurdly incongruous.

**Sigmund Freud** considered humor an outlet for discharging pent up psychic energy and diminishing the importance of potentially damaging events. Since the 1970s, research on humor has shifted from a Freudian focus to an emphasis on its cognitive dimensions, including investigations involving **information-processing theory**. Humor has been found to depend on the disparity between expectations and perceptions, generally termed "incongruity." Not all incongruity, however, is humorous; for humor to be evoked, the incongruous must somehow be meaningful or appropriate, and must be at least partially resolved. Research has shown the importance of humor both in social interaction and human development. Developmental psychologists consider humor a form of **play** characterized by the manipulation of images, symbols, and ideas. Based on this definition, humor can first be detected in infants at about 18 months of age with the acquisition of the **ability** to manipulate symbols. Some researchers believe that humor can be considered present in infants as young as four months old if the criterion used is the ability to perceive incongruities in a playful light and resolve them in some manner. Most research thus far has focused on responsiveness to humor rather than on its instigation, production, or behavioral consequences.

Humor serves a number of social functions. It can serve as a coping strategy, to cement allegiances, or to test the status of relationships. One of the main signs of a healthy **ego** is the ability to laugh at one's own foibles and mistakes. Humor can be used to lend social acceptability to forbidden feelings or attitudes, a phenomenon at least as old as the Renaissance fool or Court Jester who was given license to voice unpleasant truths and mock those in positions of authority. Research has also led to the view that humor is a way of countering anxiety by reasserting mastery over a situation. Feelings of helplessness have been found to characterize both anxiety and **depression**. (One of the signs of depression is the inability to appreciate or use humor.) Humor gives people an opportunity to stand outside the dire aspects of a situation, however briefly, and assert a measure of control through the ability to laugh at their predicament. This dynamic, which drives the phenomenon known as "gallows humor," is expressed in the following witticism about two contrasting cities: "In Berlin, the situation is serious but not hopeless; in Vienna, the situation is hopeless but not serious."

## Further Reading

Dix, Albert S. *Humor: the Bright Side of Pain.* New York, NY: Carlton Press, 1989.

Green, Lila. *Making Sense of Humor: How to Add Joy to Your Life.* Glen Rock, NJ: Knowledge, Ideas, and Trends, 1994.

# Hypnosis

*A temporary narrowing of conscious awareness.*

Practiced since ancient times, hypnosis or hypnotism remains difficult to define accurately and completely. Although the word hypnosis comes from the Greek word *hypnos,* for **sleep**, hypnosis is actually an intense state of concentration.

There are three degrees of hypnosis. Under light hypnosis, the subject becomes sleepy and follows simple directions; under deep hypnosis, the person experiences dulling of sensory **perception**, similar to that of anesthesia. Under deep hypnosis, the subject can move about, open his or her eyes, and can even undergo medical procedures with no additional anesthetic. Magicians and illusionists use deep hypnosis to make a subject behave in unusual ways, such as to suspend the subject's body between two chairs in a posture that is completely stiff. The magician suggests that the subject's body become stiff and rigid, and the result is muscle tension powerful enough to support the body completely. Many researchers contend that the key factor in hypnosis is the subject's willingness to cooperate with the hypnotist, combined with the subject's belief that hypnosis works. People who are easily hypnotized are described as "suggestible"; in fact, if the subject expects to be successfully hypnotized, it is much more likely that he or she will.

Hypnotic induction is the process by which hypnosis is accomplished. In most situations, an individual performs the induction on a willing subject. Classical hypnotic induction involves a series of steps. First, sensory input to the subject is restricted, and the subject is instructed to stop moving. Second, the subject's focus of **attention** is narrowed. This may be accomplished by asking him or her to focus on a specific point of light or a spot on the wall. Finally, the hypnotist begins a pattern of monotonous repetition. The hypnotist may repeatedly tell the subject to relax, to breathe slowly and deeply, and to focus attention on a fixed point. It is estimated that about 70 percent of all people can be hypnotized at some level. Within that group, an estimated 30 percent are in the low range, 60 percent in the middle, and 10 percent are highly hypnotizable using the classical approach to hypnotic induction. The claim that a person could be hypnotized against his or her will is controversial in the scientific community. Many scientists feel that an unwilling subject would be difficult to hypnotize, and most scientists raise ethical questions about any attempts to do so.

While in an hypnotic trance, some subjects are able to recall forgotten experiences. This can be useful in treating **amnesia** or milder forms of **memory** loss. Inter-

| MYTHS ABOUT HYPNOSIS | |
|---|---|
| **Myth** | **Scientific response** |
| Hypnosis places the subject in someone else's control. | Magicians and other entertainers use the illusion of power to control their subjects' behavior. In reality, people who act silly or respond to instructions to do foolish things do so because they want to. The hypnotist creates a setting where the subject will follow suggestions—but the subject must be willing to cooperate. |
| A subject can become "stuck" in a trance. | Subjects can come out of a hypnotic state any time they wish. The subject has control of the process of hypnosis, with the hypnotist simply guiding him or her. |
| The hypnotist can plant a suggestion in the subject's mind—even for something to be done in the future. | It is impossible for anyone to be implanted with suggestions to do anything against his or her will. |
| Hypnosis may be used to improve accuracy of the subject's memory. | Memories recovered under hypnosis are no more reliable than others. |

estingly, many subjects do not recall anything that happened while they were in the hypnotic trance; the hypnotist may direct the person to perform some act or engage in a specific behavior after the trance state has ended. This is termed *post-hypnotic trance* or *post-hypnotic suggestion,* and it is successful in only a small percentage of people who are able to be hypnotized. The post-hypnotic suggestion only works for behaviors that the subject is willing and able to perform; an unscrupulous hypnotist could not enlist an unwilling subject in criminal activity, for example, by post-hypnotic suggestion. Ending the trance is usually accomplished by a preset signal given by the hypnotist. On occasion, the subject may wake from the trance without the signal being given. It is unusual for a hypnotist to have difficulty ending the induced trance. Some people are able to hypnotize themselves in a process called autohypnosis or self-hypnosis.

Doctors also employ hypnosis as a method of **pain** management for chronic headaches, backaches, severe burns, and during childbirth. In cancer treatment, hypnosis is used to control the side effects of chemotherapy and as a self-healing adjunct to chemotherapy. Hypnosis is also used for autoimmune diseases, **sleep disorders**, and skin ailments, including warts and rashes. Some surgeons use hypnosis in the operating room, not only to reduce the amount of anesthesia patients need, but also to lessen anxiety and postoperative swelling and bleeding. A patient in an hypnotic trance can remain immobile for extended periods of time, avoiding aggravation of the injury. Victims under a state of shock are also more responsive to hypnotic induction. Dentists use hypnosis to complete dental work on a relaxed patient without the need for anesthesia. Some

psychotherapists employ hypnotic induction to treat phobias, **sexual dysfunction**, **stress**, **eating disorders**, self-destructive habits (such as smoking and other addictions) and to improve progress on positive behavioral changes. Hypnosis is a primary tool to gain access to memories, a controversial issue in the **mental health** field. In working with children, psychotherapists use hypnosis for enuresis, thumb-sucking, behavioral problems and improving academic performance, among others. Psychiatrists and psychologists may also use hypnosis to learn more about the human mind, and to help patients understand their own emotional and **personality** development. This application of hypnosis is termed *hypnotherapy*. In law enforcement, victims of and witnesses to crimes are sometimes hypnotized to help them remember important clues.

Patients who are responsive to being hypnotized must, first of all, be willing participants in the hypnosis process. One psychiatrist, Dr. Herbert Spiegel, developed the Hypnotic Induction Profile (HIP) to determine whether an individual is a good prospect for hypnosis. When the subject rolls his or her eyes back into the head, Dr. Spiegel suggests that person is likely to be successfully hypnotized if a great deal of white is visible on the eyeball. Other qualities included in Dr. Spiegel's profile include a trusting personality, preference for emotional rather than rational thinking, high **empathy** for others, and an intense capacity for concentration. Other researchers have studied the hypnotic situation and theorize that creating a setting where the subject is more likely to believe that hypnosis will work is a key to successful hypnosis. These scientists contend that the situation, combined with the subject's **motiva-**

tion, has greater influence than any personality trait or physical characteristic.

A number of professional organizations offer training and advanced training in hypnosis. Among these are the American Society of Clinical Hypnosis, the American Board of Medical Hypnosis, the American Board of Psychological Hypnosis, the American Board of Hypnosis in Dentistry and the American Hypnosis Board for Clinical Social Work. The **American Psychiatric Association**, the **American Psychological Association**, and the American Dental Association have all endorsed the technique. Mental health professionals have used hypnosis to treat sexual dysfunction, eating disorders, smoking and other addictions, enuresis and thumb-sucking.

## Further Reading

Hammond, D. Corydon. *Hypnotic Suggestions and Metaphors.* New York: W.W. Norton & Company, 1990.

Manfred, Erica. "The New Uses of Hypnosis." *Cosmopolitan* (February 1996): 104+.

Rossi, E. L.*The Psychobiology of Mind-Body Healing: New Concepts of Therapeutic Hypnosis.* New York: W.W. Norton & Company, 1993.

## Further Information

American Society of Clinical Hypnosis. 2200 East Devon Avenue, Suite 291, Des Plaines, Illinois 60018, (847) 297–3317.

Society for Clinical and Experimental Hypnosis. 3905 Vincennes Road, Suite 304, Indianapolis, Indiana 46268, (800) 214–1738.

## Hypochondria

A mental disorder characterized by an excessive and habitual preoccupation with personal health and a tendency to interpret insignificant or imaginary conditions as evidence of serious disease; also called hypochondriasis.

Typically, hypochondriacs not only falsely believe that they have a serious disease (often, but not exclusively, of the heart or another internal organ), they persist in this belief even after being assured that they do not have the disease by a physician (or, usually, by many physicians). Hypochondriacs seem to have an increased sensitivity to internal sensations. It is also thought that serious **childhood** illness or experience with disease in a family member or friend may be associated with hypochondria, and that psychological **stress** in early adulthood related to disease or death may precipitate or worsen this condition.

## Further Reading

Baur, Susan. *Hypochondria.* Berkeley: University of California Press, 1988.

## Hypothalamus

A section of the forebrain, connected to other parts of the forebrain and midbrain, that is involved in many complex behaviors.

The hypothalamus, which together with the **thalamus** makes up the section of the forebrain called the diencephalon, is involved in such aspects of behavior as **motivation**, **emotion**, eating, drinking, and **sexuality**. Lying under the thalamus, the hypothalamus weighs only a fraction of an ounce and is a little larger than the tip of the thumb. It is connected to the **autonomic nervous system**, and controls the entire endocrine system using the pituitary gland to direct the work of all the other **endocrine glands**. If a particular section of the hypothalamus is destroyed, an overwhelming urge to eat results; damage to another section of a male's hypothalamus can reduce the sex drive. Yet another part of the hypothalamus, the suprachiasmatic nuclei (SCN), is the site of a person's "internal clock" that regulates biological rhythms according to a cycle of roughly 24 hours. From the SCN, signals reach areas of the hindbrain that regulate **sleep** and wakefulness. With neurons firing on a 24- or 25-hour cycle, it determines the periods of greatest alertness—whether one is "morning person" or a "night person." Pathways from the SCN to the eyes connect its circadian rhythms to external cycles of light and dark.

Different roles have been identified for various sections of the hypothalamus in interpreting and acting on hunger signals. The ventromedial nucleus, whose neurons detect blood levels of glucose, signals when it is time to stop eating. Rats in whom this part of the hypothalamus has been destroyed will eat extremely large quantities of food, enough to triple their body weight. Similarly, the lateral hypothalamus signals when it is time to begin eating. Yet another area, the paraventricular nucleus, appears to motivate the desire for particular types of foods, depending on which neurotransmitters are acting on it at a particular time.

*See also* Brain

## Hypothesis testing

The method psychologists employ to prove or disprove the validity of their hypotheses.

When psychologists engage in research, they generate specific questions called hypotheses. Research hypotheses are informed speculations about the likely re-

| HYPOTHESIS TESTING | | |
|---|---|---|
| | You conclude that the two groups differ so you reject the Null Hypothesis. | You conclude that the two groups do not differ so you fail to reject the Null Hypothesis. |
| Two groups really do differ | You correctly rejected the Null Hypothesis. You made a good decision. | You made a Type II error. You should have said there is a difference, but you made a mistake and said there wasn't. |
| Two groups really do not differ | You made a Type I error. You said that the groups are different, but you made a mistake. | You correctly failed to reject the Null Hypothesis. You said that the groups are not different, and you were right. |

sults of a project. In a typical research design, researchers might want to know whether people in two groups differ in their behavior. For example, psychologists have asked whether the amount that we can remember increases if we can find a way to organize related information. The hypothesis here might be that the organization of related information increases the amount that a person can remember in a learning task.

The researcher knows that such a strategy might have no effect, however. Learning may not change or it may actually worsen. In research, psychologists set up their projects to find out which of two conclusions is more likely, the research hypothesis (i.e., whether organizing related information helps **memory**) or its complement (i.e., whether organizing related information does not help memory). The possibility that organizing related information will make no difference is called the Null Hypothesis, because it speculates that there may be no change in learning. (The word "null" means "nothing" or "none.") The other possibility, that organizing related information helps to learn, is called the Research Hypothesis or the Alternate Hypothesis. To see which hypothesis is true, people will be randomly assigned to one of two groups that differ in the way they are told to learn. Then the memory of the people in the two groups is compared.

As a rule, psychologists attempt to rule out the Null Hypothesis and to accept the Research Hypothesis because their research typically tries to focus on changes from one situation to the next, not failure to change. In hypothesis testing, psychologists are aware that they may make erroneous conclusions. For example, they might reject the Null Hypothesis and conclude that performance of people in two groups is different, that is, that one group remembers more than the other because they organize the information differently. In reality, one group might have gotten lucky and if the study were performed a second time, the result might be different. In hypothesis testing, this mistaken conclusion is called a Type I error.

Sometimes researchers erroneously conclude that the difference in the way the two groups learn is not important. That is, they fail to reject the Null Hypothesis when they should. This kind of error is called a Type II error. The table below indicates the relationship among errors and correct decisions.

Unfortunately, when researchers conduct a single experiment, they may be making an error without realizing it. This is why other researchers may try to replicate the research of others in order to spot any errors that previous researchers may have made.

*See also* Scientific method

# Identity/Identity formation

*A person's mental representation of who he or she is.*

Components of identity include a sense of personal continuity and of uniqueness from other people. In addition to carving out a personal identity based on the need for uniqueness, people also acquire a social identity based on their membership in various groups—familial, ethnic, occupational, and others. These group identities, in addition to satisfying the need for **affiliation**, help people define themselves in the eyes of both others and themselves.

Identity formation has been most extensively described by **Erik Erikson** in his theory of developmental stages, which extends from **birth** through adulthood. According to Erikson, identity formation, while beginning in **childhood**, gains prominence during **adolescence**. Faced with physical growth, sexual maturation, and impending career choices, adolescents must accomplish the task of integrating their prior experiences and characteristics into a stable identity. Erikson coined the phrase identity crisis to describe the temporary instability and confusion adolescents experience as they struggle with alternatives and choices. To cope with the uncertainties of this stage, adolescents may overidentify with heroes and mentors, fall in love, and bond together in **cliques**, excluding others on the basis of real or imagined differences.

According to Erikson, successful resolution of this crisis depends on one's progress through previous developmental stages, centering on fundamental issues of trust, autonomy, and initiative. By the age of 21, about half of all adolescents are thought to have resolved their identity crises and are ready to move on to the adult challenges of love and work. Others, however, are unable to achieve an integrated adult identity, either because they have failed to resolve the identity crisis or because they have experienced no crisis. J. E. Marcia identified four common ways in which adolescents deal with the chal-

Developing a special talent, like playing the violin, can give young people a sense of identity. *(Photo by Clayton Wolt. North Dakota Tourism. Reproduced with permission.)*

lenge of identity formation. Those who experience, confront, and resolve the identity crisis are referred to as "identity-achieved." Others, termed "identity-foreclosed," make commitments (often conventional ones, identical or similar to those of their parents) without questioning them or investigating alternatives. Those who are "identity-diffused" shrink from making defining choices about their futures and remain arrested, unable to make whole-hearted commitments to careers, values, or another person. In contrast, those in the "moratorium" group, while unable to make such commitments, are struggling to do so and experience an ongoing though unresolved crisis as they try to "find themselves."

Although the phrase "identity crisis" was initially popularized in connection with adolescence, it is not limited to this time frame: Erikson himself initially formulated the concept in connection with World War II veterans. A variety of changes that affect one's work, status, or interpersonal relationships can bring on a crisis that forces one to redefine oneself in terms of values, priorities, and chosen activities or lifestyle. In *Passages*, Gail Sheehy proposed that there are actually "predictable crises of adult life" that generally challenge people's conceptions of themselves and result either in personal growth or stagnation.

*See also* Personality development; Self-concept

### Further Reading
Erikson, Erik H. *Childhood and Society.* New York: W. W. Norton, 1950.
Josselson, Ruthellen. *Finding Herself: Pathways to Identity Development in Women.* San Francisco: Jossey-Bass, 1987.
Sheehy, Gail. *Passages: Predictable Crises of Adult Life.* New York: E.P. Dutton, 1976.

# Id

In psychoanalytic theory, the most primitive, unconscious element of human personality.

**Sigmund Freud** believed that human **personality** consisted of three components: the id, the **ego**, and the **superego**. The id is the part of the personality that includes such basic biological impulses or drives as eating, drinking, eliminating wastes, avoiding **pain**, attaining sexual pleasure, and **aggression**. The id operates on the "pleasure principle," seeking to satisfy these basic urges immediately with no regard to consequences. Only when tempered through interaction with the ego (reality) and superego (**conscience**) does the id conform to what is considered socially acceptable behavior.

According to Freud, anxiety is caused by the conflict between the id's powerful impulses and the modifying forces of the ego and superego. The more id-driven impulses are stifled through physical reality or societal norms, the greater the level of anxiety. People express their anxiety in various ways, including nervousness,

displaced aggression, and serious anxiety disorders. Healthy personalities are those that have learned to balance the id, ego and superego forces.

### Further Reading
Atkinson, Rita L.; Richard C. Atkinson; Edward E. Smith; and Ernest R. Hilgard. *Introduction to Psychology.* 9th ed. San Diego: Harcourt Brace Jovanovich, 1987.
Zimbardo, Philip G. *Psychology and Life.* 12th ed. Glenview, IL: Scott, Foresman, 1988.

# Imagination

A complex cognitive process of forming a mental scene that includes elements which are not, at the moment, being perceived by the senses.

Imagination involves the synthetic combining of aspects of memories or experiences into a mental construction that differs from past or present perceived reality, and may anticipate future reality. Generally regarded as one of the "higher mental functions," it is not thought to be present in animals. Imagination may be fantastic, fanciful, wishful, or problem-solving, and may differ from reality to a slight or great extent. Imagination is generally considered to be a foundation of artistic expression, and, within limits, to be a healthy, creative, higher mental function.

Observers as diverse as Plato and Samuel Taylor Coleridge have noted two contrasting types of imagination. One is largely imitative and concerned with mentally reconstructing past events or images. Among the imitative types of imagination is eidetic imagery, which consists of rich and vividly recalled images and is especially characteristic of children up to the age of six. Afterimages, such as the green image that appears after looking at the color red, are a type of imitative image and are produced by sense receptors. A synesthetic image is produced by the conjunction of two senses such as occurs when **hearing** a certain piece of music elicits a visual image with which it is associated in the mind of the listener. Hypnagogic images are unusually clear images produced in the state between **sleep** and waking. **Hallucinations** are vivid, detailed images produced in the absence of external stimuli and generally confused with real images. **Dreams** are images occurring in a sleeping state that are usually not confused with reality once the sleeper awakes.

In contrast to imitative images, creative imagination is associated with thought and involves the restructuring, rather than merely the retention, of sensory impressions. It was this faculty that Coleridge called "imagination" as opposed to "fancy," his name for imitative imagining. One common form of creative imagination is **daydreaming**. At one time, daydreaming and fantasies were regarded as compensatory activities that had the function of "letting off steam," but recent research has cast doubt on that theory. Creative imagination is the basis for achievements in the realms of both art and science, and students of behavior have analyzed the creative process in hopes of being able to encourage greater **creativity** through various types of training. New discoveries about the specialized functions of the right- and left-brain hemispheres have revealed that the **right-brain hemisphere** is the center for much of the mental functioning commonly regarded as creative: it is the side associated with intuitive leaps of insight and the **ability** to synthesize existing elements into new wholes. These findings have been applied by educators seeking to enhance individual creativity in areas including writing and drawing.

After falling into neglect as an area of inquiry during the period when **behaviorism** was preeminent, **mental imagery** has become a significant topic of study for cognitive psychologists. Researchers have found that imagery plays a significant role in **emotion**, **motivation**, sexual behavior, and many aspects of **cognition**, including learning, language acquisition, **memory**, problem-solving, and **perception**. Mental imagery has also been found to be a useful technique in clinical work. In addition to Gestalt therapy, which has traditionally involved the use of images, a number of image-based therapies have emerged in the United States and elsewhere. Mental images have also been used as a diagnostic tool to reveal feelings and attitudes not accessible through verbalization.

## Further Reading

Bronowski, Jacob. *The Origins of Knowledge and Imagination.* New Haven, CT: Yale University Press, 1978.

# Imitation

*The act of mimicking or copying; also called modeling or social learning.*

Unlike behaviorist models of learning through various forms of **conditioning**, imitation occurs naturally without outside stimulus or reward. In a child's early years, an enormous amount of learning is done through imitation of parents, peers, and **modeling** based on other stimuli, such as television. Imitative learning occurs in primates, both human and nonhuman, but has not conclusively been proved to exist in other species.

The foremost researcher in the area of imitative learning is **Albert Bandura**, whose work has focused on how modeling—especially the modeling of aggressive behavior—affects the thoughts, feelings, and behavior of children. Bandura's research revealed that imitation may result in the acquisition of new responses as well as the facilitation or inhibition of existing ones. While modeling will occur in situations where neither the observer nor the model is rewarded for performing a particular action, Bandura found that **punishment** and reward can have an effect on the modeling situation. A child will more readily imitate a model who is being rewarded for an act than one who is being punished. Thus, the child can learn without actually being rewarded or punished himself—a concept known as vicarious learning. Similarly, Bandura has shown that when a model is exposed to stimuli intended to have a conditioning effect, a person who simply observes this process, even without participating in it directly, will tend to become conditioned by the stimuli as well.

## Further Reading

Meinhold, Patricia. *Child Psychology: Development and Behavior Analysis.* Dubuque, IA: Kendall/Hunt Publishing Co., 1993.

Owens, Karen. *The World of the Child.* New York: Holt, Rinehart, and Winston, 1987.

Papalia, Diane E. *A Child's World: Infancy through Adolescence.* 5th ed. New York: McGraw-Hill, 1990.

# Imprinting

*A type of learning characteristic of fowls that occurs only during a critical period of development soon after birth.*

Imprinting is the process that prompts ducklings to form an **attachment** to their mothers—or whatever other moving object that appears—within the first two days of life. Ethologists, scientists who study the behavior of animals in their natural **environment**, noted the process of imprinting as they observed newly hatched ducklings. They discovered that if a duckling were introduced to another moving object, alive or not, during a **critical period** after **birth**, the duckling would follow that object as if it were the mother. Humans and even wooden decoys successfully served as maternal substitutes after as little as ten minutes of imprinting. It has been discovered that once the process takes place, the ducklings will follow the substitute, even through adverse circumstances, in preference to a live duck. Imprinting does not take place anytime after the first two days of life because by that time, it is believed, ducklings develop a **fear** of strange objects. There is little evidence that imprinting occurs in humans or most other animals. It has been noted to some

Konrad Lorenz and his famous ducks. The ducks followed him as if he were their mother because of a process called imprinting. *(Photo Researchers, Inc. Reproduced with permission.)*

extent in dogs, sheep, and guinea pigs. The discovery and study of imprinting have prompted continued examination of the relative roles of **instinct** and acquired behavior in the process of learning.

### Further Reading

Bower, Gordon H., and Ernest R. Hilgard. *Theories of Learning*. Englewood Cliffs, NJ: Prentice-Hall, 1981.

## Impulse control disorders

A psychological disorder characterized by the repeated inability to refrain from performing a particular action that is harmful either to oneself or others.

Impulse control disorders are thought to have both neurological and environmental causes and are known to be exacerbated by **stress**. Some **mental health** professionals regard several of these disorders, such as compulsive gambling or shopping, as addictions. In impulse control disorder, the impulse action is typically preceded by feelings of tension and excitement and followed by a sense of relief and gratification, often—but not always—accompanied by **guilt** or remorse.

Researchers have discovered a link between the control of impulses and the **neurotransmitter** serotonin, a chemical agent secreted by **nerve** cells in the **brain**. Selective serotonin reuptake inhibitors (SSRIs), medications such as Prozac that are used to treat **depression** and other disorders, have been effective in the treatment of impulse control disorders. The **American Psychiatric Association** describes several impulse control disorders: **pyromania**, trichotillomania (compulsive hair-pulling), **intermittent explosive disorder**, **kleptomania**, patho-

logical gambling, and other impulse-control disorders not otherwise specified.

A condition not listed by the American Psychiatric Association that some experts consider an impulse-control disorder is repetitive self-mutilation, in which people intentionally harm themselves by cutting, burning, or scratching their bodies. Other forms of repetitive self-mutilation include sticking oneself with needles, punching or slapping the face, and swallowing harmful substances. Self-mutilation tends to occur in persons who have suffered traumas early in life, such as **sexual abuse** or the death of a parent, and often has its onset at times of unusual stress. In many cases, the triggering event is a perceived rejection by a parent or romantic interest. Characteristics commonly seen in persons with this disorder include **perfectionism**, dissatisfaction with one's physical appearance, and difficulty controlling and expressing emotions. It is often seen in conjunction with **schizophrenia**, post-traumatic stress syndrome, and various **personality** disorders. Usual onset is late **childhood** or early **adolescence**; it is more frequent in females than in males.

Those who consider self-mutilation an impulse control disorder do so because, like the other conditions that fall into this category, it is a habitual, harmful activity. Victims often claim that it is accompanied by feelings of excitement, and that it reduces or relieves negative feelings such as tension, **anger**, anxiety, depression, and loneliness. They also describe it as addictive. Self-mutilating behavior may occur in episodes, with periods of remission, or may be continuous over a number of years. Repetitive self-mutilation often worsens over time, resulting in increasingly serious forms of injury that may culminate in **suicide**.

Treatment includes both **psychotherapy** and medication. The SSRI Clomipramine (Anafranil), often used to treat **obsessive-compulsive disorder**, has also been found effective in treating repetitive self-mutilation. Behavioral therapy can teach sufferers certain techniques they can use to block the impulse to harm themselves, such as spending more time in public places (because self-mutilating behavior is almost always practiced secretly), using music to alter the mental state that leads to self-mutilation, and wearing protective garments to prevent or lessen injury. In-depth psychodynamic therapy can help persons with the disorder express the feelings that lead them to harm themselves.

### Further Reading

Koziol, Leonard F., Chris E. Stout, and Douglas H. Ruben, eds. *Handbook of Childhood Impulse Disorders and ADHD: Theory and Practice*. Springfield, IL: C.C. Thomas, 1993.

Stein, D.J., ed. *Impulsivity and Aggression*. Chichester, NY: Wiley, 1995.

# Incest

Prohibited sexual relations between members of a close kinship group, such as between parents and children or between brothers and sisters. The term is often expanded to include not only actual intercourse but other sexual acts as well.

While the incest taboo is nearly universal and exists in nearly all societies, notions of kinship vary greatly from culture to culture. Thus, some cultures would consider sexual relations between first cousins incest, while others would not. The same premise holds true for intercourse between a stepfather and stepdaughter. The very rare exceptions to incest, such as those found in ancient Egyptian and Incan societies, usually involve mandatory incestuous unions within royal families, which may have been motivated by economic or theocratic considerations.

In classical psychoanalytic theory, the psychosexual development of children between the ages of three and five is characterized by incestuous desires toward the parent of the opposite sex. **Sigmund Freud** called these desires in males the **Oedipus complex**, referring to the inadvertent incest between the title character and his mother in the classical Greek tragedy, *Oedipus Rex*. Freud asserted that young boys form a sexual **attachment** to their mothers, accompanied by resentment and **hostility** toward their fathers, whom they regard as rivals for their mother's **attention**. The **fear** of retaliation by the father, which takes the form of castration anxiety, leads the boy to renounce his forbidden desires and begin to identify with his father, thus assuming his proper **gender identity** together with a **superego** composed of his father's moral values. Freud posited roughly the same condition, in reverse, for girls, which he called the Electra complex. While largely recognizing the widespread existence of incestuous desires (which many claim is indirectly demonstrated by the very universality of the incest taboo), contemporary psychologists differ widely with respect to the developmental and other importance they attribute to these desires.

Among the various types of incest, sexual relations between brother and sister and between father and daughter are thought to occur more frequently than mother-son incest, which is believed to be rare. The phenomenon of covert incest has been noted between mother and son, however, in which the mother acts toward her son in a sexual manner without actually seducing him. Usually, other members of the **family** are aware of the incestuous relationship, and it will govern the psychodynamics of the entire family structure. According to contemporary reports by incest survivors, most child **sexual abuse** is committed by male relatives. Fathers who abuse their daughters tend to have a history of psychological problems and emotional deprivation, and will often implement an incestuous relationship with more than one daughter. In many cases, the mother is aware of the abuse and either feels powerless to stop it or colludes with the father for reasons of her own.

Contrary to popular assumptions and stereotypes, incest occurs at all levels of society, is likely to happen in middle and upper-class families as in poor families, and takes place in families that appear outwardly happy, respectable, and well adjusted. Adults who have been incest victims in **childhood** are prone to **depression**, **sexual dysfunction**, and abusive behavior. Incest involving an adult victim is extremely rare. Although there has been increasing public awareness of this problem in recent years, it is believed that most cases of incest remain unreported due to the stigma involved and the powerlessness of dependent children ensnared in incestuous relationships. Over the years, many (more or less speculative) theories have been advanced regarding the origin, nature, structure, function, and interpretation of the incest taboo, but none has been generally accepted as completely definitive. One practical function of the taboo is that the prohibition of incest decreases the incidence of **birth** defects and recessive genetic disorders.

## Further Reading
Maisch, Herbert. *Incest*. New York: Stein and Day, 1972.

# Independent variable

The variable the experimenter manipulates.

In experimental research, psychologists create two or more groups that are as similar as possible except for a single change that the psychologist makes from one group to the next. That single element that varies across groups is called the independent variable. In more complex research, the experimenter may include more than one independent variable.

In one experiment dealing with eyewitness testimony and jury decisions, researchers exposed the eyewitnesses to staged crimes and then had them "testify" what they observed. One group of participants saw the staged crime under good lighting conditions; a second group had a less favorable viewing condition, and the third group had only a poor view of the scene. The independent variable was the viewing condition which had three levels, or different variations: good, moderate, and poor visibility. The researchers investigated whether the "jurors" accepted the testimony as believable and the degree of confidence of the eyewitnesses in their own testimony. The degree to which the jurors accepted the testimony and the stated degree of confidence by the witnesses themselves were dependent variables. The results revealed that the jurors were more likely to believe witnesses who had seen the crime in the best lighting.

The researchers concluded that the independent variable (e.g., the amount of light available for viewing the crime) had affected one **dependent variable** (e.g., the jurors' acceptance of the testimony). At the same time, the independent variable did not affect the confidence of the eyewitnesses concerning their own testimony.

**Further Reading**

Lindsay, R. C.; G. L. Wells; and C. M. Rumple. "Can People Detect Eyewitness Identification Accuracy Within and Across Situations?" *Journal of Applied Psychology* 67 (1981): 79-89.

# Inductive reasoning

Way of thinking that uses comparisons to reach conclusions.

When a child uses inductive thinking or reasoning, he or she engages in the evaluation and comparison of facts to reach a conclusion. Inductive reasoning progresses from observations of individual cases to the development of a generality. (Inductive reasoning, or induction, is often confused with deductive thinking; in the latter, general principles or conditions are applied to specific instances or situations.) If a child puts his or her hand into a bag of candy and withdraws three pieces, all of which are red, he or she may conclude that all the candy is red. Inductive reasoning, or induction, is the process by which a general conclusion is reached from evaluating specific observations or situations.

# Industrial psychology

The subfield of applied psychology in which practical problems in the workplace are addressed through the application of psychological principles.

Some industrial psychologists, also called personnel or organizational psychologists, may be employed by companies to administer tests which measure employee aptitudes or skills in hiring and placement programs. Others work for consulting firms which offer their services to companies on a contractual basis to solve specif-

ic problems. The projects which they work on may include facilitating interpersonal relationships within a company by training management personnel in human relations skills, analyzing and recommending changes in employee training programs, or conducting research to determine what influences consumers to purchase particular products. A distinguishing characteristic of industrial psychology is that the focus of research and other work is to solve specific practical problems.

*See also* Applied psychology; Vocational Aptitude Test

# Infancy

Very early childhood, generally referring to the period up to age two. During this important formative period, children begin to develop habits and behavior patterns, and acquire many basic skills, including speech.

Compared to the young of other mammals, human infants are precocious in some ways—notably sensory development—and relatively helpless in others, such as physical strength and mobility. At **birth**, the average American infant weighs approximately 7.5 pounds (3.37 kg), although a baby born 28 weeks after conception may weigh as little as two pounds (0.9 kg). The average length of an American newborn is about 21 inches (53 cm).

Infants are born with several **reflexes** that are activated by particular stimuli, such as the grasping reflex when a finger is placed in the palm of a baby's hand. Other reflexes include rooting (turning the mouth toward the breast or bottle) and sucking. Many early reflexes—such as reaching and performing a step-like motion—disappear, only to reappear later. While the most important senses in human adults are **vision** and **hearing**, infants acquire much of their information about the world through **touch**. At birth, a baby's eyes and the pathways between the eyes and the **brain** are not fully developed; the eyesight of a newborn is estimated at 20-600 (an object viewed from 20 feet [609 cm] away appears as a distance of 600 feet [182 m] by an adult with 20-20 vision). The senses of newborns are particularly well adapted for **bonding** with their caregivers. Infants can see large objects close up and are especially interested in faces, and their hearing is most acute in the range of human speech.

In the first year, the shape and proportion of an infant's body are better suited to crawling on all fours than to walking erect. During the first three months of life, infants also lack the lower body strength and muscular control to support their weight standing upright. The urge to stand and walk upright is very strong, however, and babies work hard to accomplish this task. By seven to eight months, infants can usually stand holding on to a playpen or other object; at 10 or 11 months they can walk with assistance, and by 13 months they can usually take a few steps unaided.

As infants are developing physically, they are also developing cognitively in their **ability** to perform such mental processes as thinking, knowing, and remembering. The theory of **childhood cognitive development** developed by the Swiss psychology **Jean Piaget** describes four stages of increasingly complex and abstract thought that occur between birth and **adolescence**, each qualitatively different from but dependent upon the stages before it. The first, or sensorimotor, stage, (birth to approximately two years), is a time of nonverbal, experimental basic learning when infants gradually gain mastery of their own bodies and external objects. By sucking, shaking, banging, hitting, and other physical acts, children at this age learn about the properties of objects and how to manipulate them. The main goal at this stage is to achieve what Piaget termed "object constancy," or permanence: the sense that objects exist even when they are not visible and that they are independent of the infant's own actions. This sense forms the basis for the **perception** of a stable universe. The sensorimotor stage is followed by the preoperational stage (ages two to six), which involves the association of objects with words.

Infants are born with different temperaments. There are "easy babies," who are cheerful and seldom fuss; difficult babies, who are often irritable; and timid babies, who are wary when approaching new situations. Most people believe that **temperament** is inborn, although there is little hard evidence to prove it. Temperament's interaction with a variety of environmental factors, including parental expectations, determines the course of an individual's development. The most important aspect of an infant's **socialization** is forming secure attachments, primarily to parents or other principal caregivers. **Attachment** problems may have a negative effect on a child's **normal** development. Initially, infants will respond positively to all contact with adults, even though they recognize familiar faces and prefer their mother or other primary caregiver. By the age of three months, babies will begin to smile in response to outside stimuli, maintain eye contact, and vocalize, as distinguished from crying. Eventually, they will advance to what Piaget called the "secondary level" of concentration, at which they are aware of social changes in addition to objects and events. During this period, infants enjoy social contact and will fuss when left alone. They are able to distinguish their parents from other people, will smile and vocalize at familiar people, and will cry

when those individuals are absent. At the age of six or seven months, when infants develop a conception of object permanence, an especially strong bond begins to form with the primary caregiver, usually the mother. This is accompanied by **separation anxiety** (distress at being separated from the primary caregiver) and **stranger anxiety** (**shyness** or **fear** in the presence of strangers). Such behaviors are an integral part of normal cognitive development and displays a healthy attachment to the primary caregiver.

During the second year of life, the infant's focus of socialization extends beyond the primary caregiver to the **family** unit as a whole and includes gaining some control over emotions and accepting discipline. In Erik Erikson's eight-stage theory of **personality**, the most important task in the first 18 months of an infant's life is establishing a basic sense of trust in the world, accomplished initially by the attachment formed with the primary caregivers. Sometime after his or her first birthday, an infant begins developing a tremendous need for autonomy, inevitably accompanied by a sense of doubt and shame brought on by learning to follow rules and social demands for self-control, including physical control (such as toilet training). The conflict between autonomy and doubt occupies much of a child's second year and continues into the third. Successfully negotiated, this stage leads to the emergence of independence and will power, and a sense of self-awareness—which appears to depend upon a combination of cognitive development, socialization, and linguistic skills—slowly develops during the second year of life.

## Further Reading

Owens, Karen. *The World of the Child.* New York: Holt, Rinehart, and Winston, 1987.

Papalia, Diane E. *A Child's World: Infancy through Adolescence.* 5th ed. New York: McGraw-Hill, 1990.

# Inferiority complex

A psychological condition that exists when a person's feelings of inadequacy are so intense that daily living is impaired.

The term "inferiority complex" was coined in the 1920s by French psychologist **Alfred Adler**, a one-time follower of **Sigmund Freud** who became disenchanted with Freud's emphasis on the influence of **unconscious** factors as motivators in human behavior. While Adler subscribed to the notion that underlying motivations play a part in directing **personality**, he introduced the notion of "ego psychology" in an effort to give equal importance to the role of conscious factors in determining behavior. According to Adler, all humans experience feelings of inferiority as children and spend the rest of their lives trying to compensate for those feelings. As people replace the dependence of **childhood** with the independence of adulthood, the feelings of inferiority persist in varying intensity in different people. For some people, the sense of inferiority serves as a positive motivating factor, as they strive to improve themselves in an effort to neutralize the negative feelings of inferiority. Some, however, become dominated—and, as a result, crippled—by an overwhelming sense of inadequacy. These people, whose thoughts are so overtaken by these feelings that they cannot function normally, are said to have an inferiority complex. The opposite of inferiority complex, a superiority complex, can also result from the inevitable early feelings of inferiority, Adler believed. This results when a person overcompensates and places too much emphasis on striving for perfection.

## Further Reading

Clark, John, ed. *The Mind: Into the Inner World*. New York: Torstar Books, 1986.

Hergenhahn, B.R. *An Introduction to Theories of Personality*. Englewood Cliffs, NJ: Prentice-Hall, 1980.

Zimbardo, Philip G. *Psychology and Life*. Glenview, IL: Scott, Foresman, 1988.

# Information-processing theory

A leading orientation in experimental psychology that focuses on how people select, process, and internalize information and how they use it to make decisions and guide their behavior.

The information-processing theory is associated with the development of high-speed computers in the 1950s. Researchers—most notably Herbert Simon and his colleagues—demonstrated that computers could be used to simulate human **intelligence**. This development led to the realization that computer-oriented information-processing models could provide new insight into how the human mind receives, stores, retrieves, and uses information. The information-processing theory was one of several developments that ended the decades-long dominance of **behaviorism** in American psychology. It focused on innate mental capacities, rather than on conditioned, externally observable behavior. By enabling experimental psychologists to test theories about complex mental processes through computer simulation, information-processing models helped reestablish internal thought processes as a legitimate area of scientific inquiry.

The information-processing theory of human **cognition** encompasses several basic stages. Information received from external or internal stimuli is inputted through the senses and transformed by a variety of mental operations (including representation by symbols). It receives **attention** through the perceptual processes and is stored in either short-term or long-term **memory**, where it interacts with previously stored information to generate a response, or output. These stages may take place in a number of different arrangements. The simplest is the serial model, in which the stages occur in succession like a chain reaction, with the output of each stage becoming the input of the succeeding one. However, stages can also occur simultaneously, a phenomenon known as parallel processing. Serial and parallel processing can also be combined in what are known as hybrid models. Another important characteristic of information-processing models is resource allocation—the way in which energy is distributed in the system. This refers to the fact that the efficiency of each stage in the process may depend on whether certain other stages are operating at the same time.

One of the many areas investigated through the use of information-processing models is human error. Errors that occur during the early stages of processing, such as misunderstandings, are called mistakes, as distinguished from slips, which occur during the selection or execution of responses. The increased understanding of error provided by information-processing models has been useful in eliminating a variety of technical and industrial problems by isolating and addressing their causes. Those problems classified as mistakes often involve the size of an information load and the way it is handled, while slips are commonly remedied by redesigning instruments and equipment so they can be used more efficiently.

Another area that has been investigated using information-processing theory is reaction time—the amount of time needed to respond to a stimulus in a particular situation. **Reaction time** is an important feature in the design of automobiles and many other products. Factors influencing reaction time include complexity of the decision required before action can be taken; stimulus-response compatibility (the physical convenience of the reaction); expectancy (it takes longer to respond to an unexpected stimulus); and the relative importance of speed and accuracy in the required response.

## Further Reading

Johnson-Laird, Philip N. *The Computer and the Mind: An Introduction to Cognitive Science*. Cambridge, MA: Harvard University Press, 1988.

Lindsay, Peter H. *Human Information Processing: An Introduction to Psychology*. San Diego: Academic Press, 1977.

Newell, A., and H. A. Simon. *Human Problem Solving*. Englewood Cliffs, NJ: Prentice-Hall, 1972.

# Bärbel Inhelder

**1913-1997**
Swiss psychologist and educator.

Bärbel Inhelder is permanently linked to **Jean Piaget** as a remarkable instance of scientific collaboration. Inhelder started working with Piaget in the early 1930s; by the 1940s, as she recalled, Piaget told her he needed her "to counter his tendency toward becoming a totally abstract thinker." Piaget never lost sight of his epistemological goals, while Inhelder was much more of a psychologist.

Inhelder was born in 1913 in the German-speaking Swiss city of St. Gall, the only child of cultured parents. In 1932, she moved to Geneva to study at Edouard Claparède's Rosseau Institute. At Piaget's suggestion, she examined children's comprehension of conservation of quantities. The book they published together on the subject in 1941 was the first of many other collaborations. In her dissertation, using conservation tests as diagnostic tools, Inhelder confirmed Piaget's claim that the sequence of developmental stages is invariant, and showed how mentally retarded children were fixated at a certain stage. In exemplary Piagetian fashion, she did not focus on test results alone, but on how subjects arrived at their answers; this allowed her to determine their general cognitive skills as well. In 1943, after finishing her dissertation, Inhelder settled in Geneva for good; she became a professor at Geneva University in 1948, and retired in 1983. She died in 1997.

In the 1950s, after investigating children's conceptions of geometry and probability with Piaget, Inhelder devised a series of clever situations to study the development of **inductive reasoning**. In one of them, subjects were asked to discover the factors (length, thickness, and so forth) that make metal rods more or less flexible. This work led to the definition of the developmental stage of "formal operations," characterized by the capacity for hypothetico-deductive thinking. This study resulted in two influential books, *The Growth of Logical Thinking from Childhood to Adolescence* (1958) and *The Early Growth of Logic in the Child* (1969). In both, Inhelder conducted the psychological research, while Piaget elaborated logical models for describing mental structures. Inhelder's later work with Piaget and others dealt with **mental imagery** and **memory** (both shown to depend on the subject's developmental level), the effects of training on **cognitive development**, and the impact of malnutrition on early intellectual development. Since the 1970s, Inhelder analyzed problem-solving behavior in children and adolescents, with the goal of understanding their strategies and implicit theories.

Inhelder was the first to use Piagetian tests as a diagnostic tool; today, most test batteries include Piagetian items. She also created several of the most widely replicated experiments of developmental research. By the nature of her thinking, which was more focused than Piaget's on the specifically psychological processes of cognitive development, as well as by her close personal contacts with American researches, Inhelder played a crucial role in turning the Piagetian approach into a mainstream paradigm of cognitive **developmental psychology**.

## Further Reading

Inhelder, B. "Autobiography," in G. Lindzey, ed. *A History of Psychology in Autobiography*, vol. 8. Stanford: Stanford University Press, 1989.

———. *The Diagnosis of Reasoning in the Mentally Retarded* [1943]. Trans. W. B. Stephens et al. New York: J. Day, 1968.

# Insanity defense

A defense in which a person can be found not guilty, or not responsible, for a crime because, at the time of the crime, the accused was unable to differentiate between right and wrong, based on the fact that the accused suffers from mental illness or mental defect.

The insanity defense allows a mentally ill person to avoid being imprisoned for a crime on the assumption that he or she was not capable of distinguishing right from wrong. Often, the sentence will substitute psychiatric treatment in place of jail time. The idea that some people with **mental illness** should not be held responsible for crimes they commit dates back to the Roman Empire, if not earlier. The "not guilty by reason of insanity" (NGRI) verdict rests in part on two assumptions: that some mentally ill people cannot be deterred by the threat of **punishment**, and that treatment for the defendant is more likely to protect society than a jail term without treatment.

It is important to note that "insanity" is a legal term, not a psychological one, and experts disagree whether it has valid psychological meaning. Critics of NGRI have claimed that too many sane defendants use NGRI to escape justice; that the state of psychological knowledge encourages expensive "dueling expert" contests that juries are unlikely to understand; and that, in practice, the defense unfairly excludes some defendants. Research on NGRI fails to support most of these claims; but some serious problems may exist with NGRI.

## Insanity defense statistics

One problem with discussing NGRI is that there are, strictly speaking, 51 types of insanity defense in the United States—one for each set of state laws, and one for federal law. Some states allow an NGRI defense either when defendants lack awareness that what they did was wrong (called *mens rea,* or literally "guilty mind") or lack the **ability** to resist committing the crime (*actus rea,* "guilty act"), while other states only recognize *mens rea* defenses.

Successful NGRI defenses are rare. While rates vary from state to state, on average less than one defendant in 100—0.85 percent— actually raises the insanity defense nationwide. Interestingly, states with higher rates of NGRI defenses tend to have lower success rates for NGRI defenses; the percentage of all defendants found NGRI is fairly constant, at around 0.26 percent.

In some studies, as many as 70 percent of NGRI defendants withdrew their plea when a state-appointed expert found them to be legally sane. In most of the rest, the state didn't contest the NGRI claim, the defendant was declared incompetent to stand trial, or charges were dropped. High-profile NGRI cases involving rich defendants with teams of experts may grab headlines and inflame the debate, but they are very rare.

## Problems with NGRI

Some problems, however, have emerged with NGRI. Regulation concerning who can testify as to the sanity of a defendant is very inconsistent from state to state. According to one national survey, only about 60 percent of states required an expert witness in NGRI determinations be a psychiatrist or psychologist; less than 20 percent required additional certification of some sort; and only 12 percent required a test. So the quality of expert witnesses may vary from state to state.

The quality of post-NGRI psychiatric treatment may be another problem. Treatment varies from state to state in both duration and, some say, quality; some defendants spend more time in mental institutions than they would have spent in jail had they been convicted, some less. NGRI defendants tend to spend more time in institutions than patients with similar diagnoses who were not accused of a crime, which undercuts somewhat the argument that treatment, not punishment, is the goal.

In terms of preventing repeat offenses, psychiatric treatment seems to help. Some studies suggest high post-treatment arrest rates, but these arrests tended to be for less serious crimes. At least one study indicated that average time to arrest of these patients after release is no higher than for the general population.

Mock jury studies indicate that jurors do carefully consider and discuss many factors in an insanity defense, but may be ignoring the local legal definitions of insanity. Mock juries tended to render the most NGRI verdicts when the defendant showed a lack of both ability to understand and ability to resist committing the crime, even though no state requires both and some consider ability to resist to be irrelevant. In addition, personal feelings about the legitimacy of the insanity defense may influence jurors' decisions.

One of the most devastating arguments against NGRI is that it may unfairly exclude many defendants. Studies suggest high rates of psychiatric illness in the general prison population. Many mentally ill defendants never get a chance to plead NGRI; some obviously psychotic defendants fight to prevent their attorneys from mounting an insanity defense for them.

The unwillingness of many states to accept an *actus rea* defense bothers some experts. Biochemical studies indicate that some people have biochemical abnormalities that may make them unable to control their impulses. If this is true, these people cannot voluntarily conform to the law, and therefore they have grounds for NGRI. On the other hand, a huge proportion of the prison population may suffer from varying degrees of such a mental defect—and finding them all NGRI would probably be dangerous to society as well as not viable.

## Guilty but mentally ill

As an alternative to NGRI, some states have added a third possible verdict to the usual trio of guilty, not guilty, and NGRI—the verdict of "guilty but mentally ill" (GBMI). In theory, this recognizes when a defendant's mental illness played an important role in a crime without entirely causing it. The state incarcerates the defendant for the crime, but also treats him or her for the mental illness.

Unfortunately, states with GBMI verdicts have sometimes neglected to provide for treatment; therefore many of these defendants are jailed without treatment, exactly as if they had been found guilty. Another dilemma with the GBMI verdict may be an "easy out" for jurors. If a jury finds the defendant guilty, they may not spend time worrying about whether he or she may be sane; because they find the defendant mentally ill, they may not address the fact that the defendant should actually be found NGRI. Hence, the insanity defense "problem" will not yield to easy solutions.

Kenneth B. Chiacchia

## Further Reading

Berman, Mitchell E. and Emil F. Coccaro. "Neurobiologic correlates to violence: relevance to criminal responsibility." *Behavioral Sciences and the Law* 16: 303-318 (1998).

Brewer, Steve and John Makeig. "Mental hospital loses trust of legal system." *Houston Chronicle* (Nov. 15, 1999): A, 1:5.

Caplan, Lincoln. "Annals of law: the insanity defense." *The New Yorker* (July 2, 1984): 45-78.

Lymburner, Jocelyn A. and Ronald Roesch. "The insanity defense: five years of research (1993-1997)." *International Journal of Law and Psychiatry* 22(3-4): 213-240 (1999).

"Real help for inmates." *Denver Post* (Nov. 14, 1999): G4:1.

Shroeder, William A. "Time to abolish the insanity defense." *St. Louis Post-Dispatch* (Jan. 26, 2000): C.13.

Tolson, Mike. "Is mentally ill death row inmate sane enough to die?" *Houston Chronicle* (Nov. 14, 1999): A, 1:1.

# Insomnia

See **Sleep disorders**

# Instinct

The inborn tendency of every member of a certain species to behave in the same way given the same situation or set of stimuli.

Behavior is considered instinctive only if it occurs in the same form in all members of a species. Instincts must be unlearned and characteristic of a specific species. Animals provide the best examples of instinctive behavior. Birds naturally build nests without being taught and feed and protect their young in the exact same ways. Other animals, such as squirrels or dogs, behave in manners characteristic of only squirrels or dogs. Ethologists, scientists who study animals in their natural environments, devote much of their efforts to the observation of instinctive behavior.

Throughout history, theorists have speculated on the role of instinct in determining human behavior. While it has been widely accepted that animal behavior is governed largely by innate, **unconscious** tendencies, the presence and power of instincts in humans have been a source of controversy. Early Christian theorists believed that only animals were guided by instincts, asserting that the absence of instinct-governed behavior and the presence of a moral code provided the major distinction between humans and animals. Instinct assumed a more prominent place in behavior theory in later years. In the late 1800s, **William James** proposed that human behavior is determined largely by instinct, and that people have even more instinctual urges than less complex animals. James believed that certain biological instincts are shared with animals, while human social instincts like sympathy, love, and modesty also provide powerful behavioral forces.

**Sigmund Freud** considered instincts to be basic building blocks of human behavior and play a central role in his drive theory, which postulates that human behavior is motivated by the desire to reduce the tension caused by unfulfilled instinctive urges or drives. For instance, people eat when they are hungry because unsatiated hunger causes tension, which is reduced by eating. For Freud, the life instinct (Eros) and its components motivate people to stay alive and reproduce. The death instinct (Thanatos) represents the negative forces of nature. Another theorist, **William McDougall**, described instincts simply as "inherited dispositions."

The debate continues today over the role of instinct in human behavior, as the balance between learned behavior and innate urges remains a subject ripe for continued research and discussion. It is useful to note a nonscientific use of the term instinct. In casual conversation, a person may use instinct to mean "natural" or "automatic—in describing a baseball player's instinct for batting, for example. This use of the term would not meet the scientist's criteria for instinct.

*See also* Drive reduction theory

## Further Reading

Atkinson, Rita L.; Richard C. Atkinson; Edward E. Smith; and Ernest R. Hilgard. *Introduction to Psychology.* 9th ed. San Diego: Harcourt Brace Jovanovich, 1987.

Zimbardo, Philip G. *Psychology and Life.* 12th ed. Glenview, IL: Scott, Foresman, 1988.

# Institutionalization

Placing emotionally disturbed or psychotic people in a therapeutic facility.

Our views of mental institutions are often colored by media's portrayal of them, such as in the movies *One Flew Over the Cuckoo's Nest* and *Girl, Interrupted*. With an emphasis on care and treatment, the best institutions offer emotionally disturbed people a better chance at life. They can learn new skills, improve behavioral and psychological problems, and develop healthier **self-esteem**.

People with mild emotional or behavior problems often benefit from a short stay at an institution and benefit from a therapy protocol that minimizes the fact of institutionalization. However, severely disturbed people require a longer stay and a highly controlled **environment**.

Psychologists differ widely on the long-term effects of institutionalization. A shortage of research funds means that little solid evidence exists to support one side or the other. Although many improvements have been made in the quality of mental institutions, some civil-rights and patients'-rights groups claim that incidences of neglect or below-standard care still exist. Of particular concern is the lack of proper staff training. Detractors of institutions also point out that patients are often sedated without given any other form of treatment. They assert that institutions do more harm than good.

Some concerns have also been raised regarding the institutionalization of children. In 1990, the American Public Welfare Association estimated that 65,000 children were living in group homes, residential treatment centers, or psychiatric hospitals. Institutionalization for emotionally disturbed children and adolescents is usually not meant to provide long-term treatment. The average stay ranges from several months to two years.

During the 1980s, the federal government began a program of "deinstitutionalizing" the mentally ill. Some returned to their families. Others found themselves in hospitals or community health centers. Today, it is not uncommon to see emotionally disturbed or psychotic people living on the streets, along with other homeless people. Local communities have been reluctant to provide alternatives to mental institutions, refusing to allow **mental health** clinics, half-way houses, or group homes to be established in their neighborhoods.

# Instrumental behavior

Behavior exhibited by persons in response to certain stimuli.

Instrumental behavior is a concept that grew out of the **behavior therapy** movement, originating in the 1950s with the work of **H.J. Eysenck.** Behavior therapy asserts that neuroses are not the symptoms of underlying disorders (as **Sigmund Freud** theorized), but are in fact disorders in and of themselves. Further, these disorders are learned responses to traumatic experiences in much the same way that animals can be demonstrated to learn a response to instrumental, or operant, **conditioning.**

In the classic behaviorist experiments of **Ivan Pavlov** and **B.F. Skinner,** it was shown that animals could be trained to respond in a learned way to external stimuli. Humans also respond in a similar manner. If, for instance, a child has a difficult, painful relationship with his older brother, who is athletic and popular, he may develop a **fear** or hatred of all popular, athletic males that

will stay with him throughout life—even after the original stimuli for the reaction (his older brother) is absent. This behavior is referred to as instrumental behavior.

In treating a patient to eliminate instrumental behaviors, behavioral therapists rely on several fairly well-tested techniques. Perhaps the most popular is counter-conditioning, a process in which a therapist links the stimuli to a different instrumental behavior, or **conditioned response.** Other methods include flooding and **modeling.** In flooding, a therapist will attempt to expose a patient to an overload of the anxiety-producing stimuli in order to lessen its effect. In modeling, the patient is exposed to someone who has successfully dealt with a similar anxiety-producing stimuli.

# Intelligence

An abstract concept whose definition continually evolves and often depends upon current social values as much as scientific ideas. Modern definitions refer to a variety of mental capabilities, including the ability to reason, plan, solve problems, think abstractly, comprehend complex ideas, learn quickly, and learn from experience as well as the potential to do so.

Several theories about intelligence emerged in the 20th century and with them debate about the nature of intelligence, whether it is hereditary, environmental or both. As methods developed to assess intelligence, theorizing occurred about the measurability of intelligence, its accuracy and this field known as psychometrics. As the 20th century drew to a close, publication of *The Bell Curve* by Richard J. Herrnstein and Charles Murray in 1994 stirred the controversy. Their findings pointed to links between social class, race, and IQ scores, despite questions by many about the validity of IQ tests as a **measurement** of intelligence or a predictor of achievement and success.

Part of the problem regarding intelligence stems from the fact that nobody has adequately defined what intelligence really means. In everyday life, we have a general understanding that some people are "smart," but when we try to define "smart" precisely, we often have difficulty because a person can be gifted in one area and average or below in another. To explain this phenomenon, some psychologists have developed theories to include multiple components of intelligence.

**Charles Darwin**'s younger cousin, Sir **Francis Galton,** inspired by the *Origin of the Species,* developed a forerunner of 20th-century testing in the 1860s when he set out to prove that intelligence was inherited. He used quantitative studies of prominent individuals and their families.

British psychologist and statistician **Charles Spearman** in 1904 introduced a central concept of intelligence psychometrics, pointing out that people who perform well on one type of intelligence test tend to do well on others also. This general mental **ability** that carried over from one type of cognitive testing to another, Spearman named g—for general intelligence. Spearman concluded that g consisted mainly of the ability to infer relationships based on one's experiences. Spearman's work led to the idea that intelligence is focused on a single, main component.

French psychologists **Alfred Binet** and Theodore Simon followed in 1905, introducing the concept of **mental age** to match chronological age in children with average ability. In bright children, mental age would exceed chronological age; in slower learners, mental age would fall below chronological age. Simon and Binet's test was introduced into the United States in a modified form in 1916 by Stanford psychologist **Lewis Terman**, and with it the concept of the **intelligence quotient** (I.Q.), the mental age divided by chronological age and multiplied by 100.

With the adoption of widespread testing using the Stanford-Binet and two versions created for the Army in World War I, the concept of the intelligence test departed from Binet and Simon's initial view. Intelligence became associated with a fixed, innate, hereditary value. That is, one's intelligence, as revealed by IQ tests, was locked at a certain level because of what was seen as its hereditary basis. Although a number of well-known and respected psychologists objected to this characterization of intelligence, it gained popularity, especially among the public.

At this time, people placed great faith in the role of science in improving society; intelligence tests were seen as a specific application of science that could be used beneficially. Unfortunately, because of the nature of the tests and because of many people's willingness to accept test results uncritically, people of racial minorities and certain ethnic groups were deemed to be genetically inferior with regard to intelligence compared to the majority.

Some early psychologists thought that measuring the speed of sensory processes and reaction times might indicate an individual's intelligence. This approach provided no useful results. Subsequently, tests reflecting white American culture and its values provided the benchmark for assessing intelligence. Although such tests indicate the degree of academic success that an individual is likely to experience, many have questioned the link to the abstract notion of intelligence, which extends beyond academic areas.

Immigration laws restricted entry into the United States of "inferior" groups, based on the results of early intelligence testing, according to some scholars. This claim seems to have some merit, although many psychologists objected to the conclusions that resulted from mass intelligence testing. In large part, the immigration laws seemed to reflect the attitudes of Americans in general regarding certain groups of people.

In the 1940s, a different view of intelligence emerged. Rejecting Spearman's emphasis on g, American psychologist L.L. Thurstone suggested that intelligence consists of specific abilities. He identified seven primary intellectual abilities: word fluency, verbal comprehension, spatial ability, perceptual speed, numerical ability, **inductive reasoning**, and **memory**.

Taking Thurstone's concept even further, J.P. Guilford developed the theory that intelligence consists of as many as five different operations or processes (evaluation, convergent production, divergent production, memory, and **cognition**), five different types of content (visual, auditory, symbolic, semantic, and behavioral) and six different products (units, classes, relations, systems, transformation, and implications). Each of these different components was seen as independent; the result being an intelligence theory that consisted of 150 different elements.

In the past few decades, psychologists have expanded the notion of what constitutes intelligence. Newer definitions of intelligence encompass more diverse aspects of thought and reasoning. For example, psychologist **Robert Sternberg** developed a three-part theory of intelligence that states that behaviors must be viewed within the context of a particular culture (i.e., in some cultures, a given behavior might be highly regarded whereas in another, the same behavior is given low regard); that a person's experiences impact the expression of intelligence; and that certain cognitive processes control all intelligent behavior. When all these aspects of intelligence are viewed together, the importance of how people use their intelligence becomes more important than the question of "how much" intelligence a person has. Sternberg has suggested that current intelligence tests focus too much on what a person has already learned rather than on how well a person acquires new skills or knowledge. Another multifaceted approach to intelligence is **Howard Gardner**'s proposal that people have eight intelligences: logical-mathematical, linguistic, musical, spatial, bodily-kinesthetic, interpersonal, intrapersonal and the naturalistic.

Daniel Goleman has written about an **emotional intelligence** of how people manage their feelings, interact and communicate, combining the interpersonal and intrapersonal of Gardner's eight intelligences.

One feature that characterizes the newly developing concept of intelligence is that it has broader meaning than a single underlying trait (e.g., Spearman's g). Sternberg and Gardner's emergent ideas suggest that any simple attempt at defining intelligence is inadequate given the wide variety of skills, abilities, and potential that people manifest.

Some of the same controversies that surfaced in the early years of intelligence testing have recurred repeatedly throughout this century. They include the question of the relative effects of **environment** versus **heredity**, the degree to which intelligence can change, the extent of cultural bias in tests, and even whether intelligence tests provide any useful information at all.

The current approach to intelligence involves how people use the information they possess, not merely the knowledge they have acquired. Intelligence is not a concrete and objective entity, though psychologists have looked for different ways to assess it. The particular definition of intelligence that has currency at any given time reflects the social values of the time as much as the scientific ideas.

The approach to intelligence testing, however, remains closely tied to Charles Spearman's ideas, despite new waves of thinking. Tests of intelligence tend to mirror the values of our culture, linking them to academic skills such as verbal and mathematical ability, although performance-oriented tests exist.

*See also* Culture-fair test; Stanford-Binet intelligence scales; Wechsler Intelligence Scales

### Further Reading

Gardner, Howard. *Intelligence Reframed: Multiple intelligences for the 21st Century.* New York: Basic Books, 1999.

Gould, S.J. *The Mismeasure of Man.* New York: W.W. Norton, 1996.

Khalka, Jean Ed. *What Is Intelligence?* Cambridge: Cambridge University Press, 1994.

# Intelligence quotient

A measurement of intelligence based on standardized test scores.

Although intelligence quotient (IQ) tests are still widely used in the United States, there has been increasing doubt voiced about their ability to measure the mental capacities that determine success in life. IQ testing has also been criticized for being biased with regard to race and gender. In modern times, the first scientist to test mental ability was **Alfred Binet**, a French psychologist who devised an intelligence test for children in 1905, based on the idea that intelligence could be expressed in terms of age. Binet created the concept of "mental age," according to which the test performance of a child of average intelligence would match his or her age, while a gifted child's performance would be on par with that of an older child, and a slow learner's abilities would be equal to those of a younger child. Binet's test was introduced to the United States in a modified form in 1916 by **Lewis Terman**. The scoring system of the new test, devised by German psychologist William Stern, consisted of dividing a child's **mental age** by his or her chronological age and multiplying the quotient by 100 to arrive at an "intelligence quotient" (which would equal 100 in a person of average ability).

The **Wechsler Intelligence Scales**, developed in 1949 by **David Wechsler**, addressed an issue that still provokes criticism of IQ tests today: the fact that there are different types of intelligence. The Wechsler scales replaced the single mental-age score with a verbal scale and a performance scale for nonverbal skills to address each test taker's individual combination of strengths and weaknesses. The Stanford-Binet and Wechsler tests (in updated versions) remain the most widely administered IQ tests in the United States. Average performance at each age level is still assigned a score of 100, but today's scores are calculated solely by comparison with the performance of others in the same age group rather than test takers of various ages. Among the general population, scores cluster around 100 and gradually decrease in either direction, in a pattern known as the **normal** distribution (or "bell") curve.

Although IQ scores are good predictors of academic achievement in elementary and secondary school, the correspondence between IQ and academic performance is less consistent at higher levels of education, and many have questioned the ability of IQ tests to predict success later in life. The tests don't measure many of the qualities necessary for achievement in the world of work, such as persistence, self-confidence, **motivation**, and interpersonal skills, or the ability to set priorities and to allocate one's time and effort efficiently. In addition, the **creativity** and intuition responsible for great achievements in both science and the arts are not reflected by IQ tests. For example, creativity often involves the ability to envision multiple solutions to a problem (a trait educators call **divergent thinking** ); in contrast, IQ tests require the choice of a single answer or solution to a problem, a type of task that could penalize highly creative people.

## GENDER DIFFERENCES IN MATH

In the late 1970s, political scientists Sheila Tobias and others called attention to the trend for girls to avoid and feel anxiety about math, a fact she attributed to social conditioning. Girls historically were discouraged from pursuing mathematics by teachers, peers, and parents.

In the early 1990s, two studies suggested that there might be differences in how boys and girls approach mathematics problems. One study, conducted by researchers at Johns Hopkins University, examined differences in mathematical reasoning using the School and College Ability Test (SCAT). The SCAT includes 50 pairs of quantities to compare, and the test-takers must decide whether one is larger than the other or whether the two are equal, or whether there is not enough information. Groups of students in second through sixth grade who had been identified as "high ability" (97th percentile or above on either the verbal or quantitative sections of the California Achievement Test) participated in the study. The boys scored higher than the girls overall, and the average difference between male and female scores was the same for all grade levels included in the study. Another study by Australian researchers at the University of New South Wales and La Trobe University gave 10th-graders 36 algebraic word problems and asked them to group the problems according to the following criteria: whether there was sufficient information to solve the problem; insufficient information; or irrele-

vant information along with sufficient information. (There were 12 problems in each category.) Students were grouped into ability groups according to prior test scores. Boys and girls performed equally well in identifying problems containing sufficient information, but boys were more able than girls to detect problems that had irrelevant information, or those that had missing information. Next, the researchers asked the students to solve the problems. Girls performed as well as boys in solving problems that had sufficient information, but no irrelevant information. On the problems that contained irrelevant information, girls did not perform as well as boys. The researchers offered tentative conclusions that perhaps girls are less able to differentiate between relevant and irrelevant information, and thus allow irrelevant information to confuse their problem-solving process. The researchers hypothesized that this tendency to consider all information relevant may reflect girls' assumption that test designers would not give facts that were unnecessary to reaching a solution.

Some researchers have argued that offering all-girl math classes is an effective way to improve girls' achievement by allowing them to develop their problem-solving skills in an environment that fosters concentration. Others feel this deprives girls of the opportunity to learn from and compete with boys, who are often among the strongest math students.

---

The value of IQ tests has also been called into question by recent theories that define intelligence in ways that transcend the boundaries of tests chiefly designed to measure abstract reasoning and verbal comprehension. For example, Robert Steinberg's triarchical model addresses not only internal thought processes but also how they operate in relation to past experience and to the external environment. Harvard University psychologist **Howard Gardner** has posited a theory of multiple intelligences that includes seven different types of intelligence: linguistic and logical-mathematical (the types measured by IQ tests); spatial; interpersonal (ability to deal with other people); intrapersonal (insight into oneself); musical; and bodily-kinesthetic (athletic ability).

Critics have also questioned whether IQ tests are a fair or valid way of assessing intelligence in members of ethnic and cultural minorities. Early in the 20th century, IQ tests were used to screen foreign immigrants to the United States; roughly 80% of Eastern European immigrants tested during the World War I era were declared

"feeble-minded," even though the tests discriminated against them in terms of language skills and cultural knowledge of the United States. The relationship between IQ and race became an inflammatory issue with the publication of the article "How Much Can We Boost IQ and Scholastic Achievement?" by educational psychologist **Arthur Jensen** in *the Harvard Educational Review* in 1969. Flying in the face of prevailing belief in the effects of environmental factors on intelligence, Jensen argued that the effectiveness of the government social programs of the 1960's War on Poverty had been limited because the children they had been intended to help had relatively low IQs, a situation that could not be remedied by government intervention. Jensen was widely censured for his views, and standardized testing underwent a period of criticism within the educational establishment, as the National Education Association called for a moratorium on testing and major school systems attempted to limit or even abandon publicly administered standardized tests. Another milestone in the public controversy over testing was the 1981 publication of Stephen Jay Gould's best-selling *The Mismeasure of*

*Man,* which critiqued IQ tests as well as the entire concept of measurable intelligence.

Many still claim that IQ tests are unfair to members of minority groups because they are based on the vocabulary, customs, and values of the mainstream, or dominant, culture. Some observers have cited cultural bias in testing to explain the fact that, on average, African-Americans and Hispanic-Americans score 12-15 points lower than European-Americans on IQ tests. (Asian-Americans, however, score an average of four to six points higher than European-Americans.) A new round of controversy was ignited with the 1994 publication of *The Bell Curve* by Richard Herrnstein and Charles Murray, who explore the relationship between IQ, race, and pervasive social problems such as unemployment, crime, and illegitimacy. Given the proliferation of recent theories about the nature of intelligence, many psychologists have disagreed with Herrnstein and Murray's central assumptions that intelligence is measurable by IQ tests, that it is genetically based, and that a person's IQ essentially remains unchanged over time. From a sociopolitical viewpoint, the book's critics have taken issue with *The Bell Curve*'s use of arguments about the genetic nature of intelligence to cast doubt on the power of government to remedy many of the nation's most pressing social problems.

Yet another topic for debate has arisen with the discovery that IQ scores in the world's developed countries—especially scores related to mazes and puzzles—have risen dramatically since the introduction of IQ tests early in the century. Scores in the United States have risen an average of 24 points since 1918, scores in Britain have climbed 27 points since 1942, and comparable figures have been reported throughout Western Europe, as well in Canada, Japan, Israel, Australia, and other parts of the developed world. This phenomenon—named the Flynn effect for the New Zealand researcher who first noticed it—raises important questions about intelligence testing. It has implications for the debate over the relative importance of **heredity** and environment in determining IQ, since experts agree that such a large difference in test scores in so short a time cannot be explained by genetic changes.

A variety of environmental factors have been cited as possible explanations for the Flynn effect, including expanded opportunities for formal education that have given children throughout the world more and earlier exposure to some types of questions they are likely to encounter on an IQ test (although IQ gains in areas such as mathematics and vocabulary, which are most directly linked to formal schooling, have been more modest than those in nonverbal areas). For children in the United States in the 1970s and 1980s, exposure to printed texts and electronic technology—from cereal boxes to video games—has been cited as an explanation for improved familiarity with the types of maze and puzzle questions that have generated the greatest score changes. Improved mastery of spatial relations has also been linked to video games. Other environmental factors mentioned in connection with the Flynn effect include improved nutrition and changes in parenting styles.

## Further Reading

Bridge, R. Gary. *The Determinants of Educational Outcomes: The Impact of Families, Peers, Teachers, and Schools.* Cambridge, MA: Ballinger Publishing Co., 1979.

Eysenck, H. J. *The Intelligence Controversy.* New York: Wiley, 1981.

Fraser, Steven. *The Bell Curve Wars: Race, Intelligence, and the Future of America.* New York: Basic Books, 1995.

Herrnstein, Richard J., and Charles Murray. *The Bell Curve: Intelligence and Class Structure in American Life.* New York: Free Press, 1994.

Kline, Paul. *Intelligence: The Psychometric View.* London: Routledge, 1991.

Sternberg, R. J. *Beyond IQ: A Triarchic Theory of Human Intelligence.* Cambridge, Eng.: Cambridge University Press, 1985.

# Interdisciplinary treatment

Patient care plan that involves healthcare professionals from a wide variety of areas.

Holistic healthcare, the concept that the body is not just a collection of separate and distinct parts but rather an assemblage of interrelated components that form a unified whole, is at the root of interdisciplinary treatment. The holistic viewpoint is that **mental health** is related to and interdependent on physical well-being, and vice-versa. An interdisciplinary treatment team has the ability to pool their knowledge and expertise towards the recovery of the whole individual, not just his or her disease.

The members and make-up of the interdisciplinary team are tailored to the patient and his or her physical, emotional, and functional needs. Team members may include, but are not limited to, physicians (from a variety of medical specialties), nurse practitioners, surgeons, psychologists, psychiatrists, social workers, school counselors, nutritionists, physical therapists, vocational counselors, occupational therapists, and creative therapists (i.e., art therapists, music therapists).

## Origins and applications

Interdisciplinary treatment was first introduced to mental healthcare in the United States in the late 1940s by Dr. William Menninger and colleagues. Menninger, who was then chief of Army neuropsychiatry and president and co-founder of the renowned Menninger Clinic, would become the 75th President of the **American Psychological Association (APA)** in 1949, providing him the opportunity to promote the benefits of treatment teams to a wide audience of healthcare professionals.

Today, mental healthcare professionals are becoming involved in a wider spectrum of what have been traditionally considered physical ailments. Psychologists have become an essential part of the treatment team in oncology (cancer medicine), geriatric medicine, cardiology (heart and circulatory medicine), pediatric medicine, and other specialties. Likewise, cross-disciplinary teams have become more common in mental healthcare. Individuals suffering from a disease such as **schizophrenia**, for example, may be treated by a team consisting of a psychiatrist, a psychologist, a neurologist, a vocational counselor, a family therapist, an art therapist, and a social worker.

Some patients may require ancillary services and after-care support such as vocational **rehabilitation** (job training or retraining), independent living skills training, social skills training, and housing assistance. For these individuals, specialists outside of traditional medical disciplines may be integrated into the interdisciplinary team.

Interdisciplinary teams are becoming more commonplace in clinical settings that involve healthcare research, also. A program for teen pregnancy prevention started at the University of Minnesota in 1997 is staffed with a team of psychologists, sociologists, physicians, nutritionists, nurses, biostatisticians, epidemiologists, and others who can provide effective strategies, and translate their results into meaningful research data that can improve quality of care.

Hospice care, a treatment setting for terminally ill patients, is another example of interdisciplinary treatment at work. Hospice patients, who are often coping with chronic **pain** and with emotional and spiritual issues related to the end of life, require care that focuses on both physical symptom relief and emotional well-being. Their interdisciplinary care may consist of one or more physicians, a psychologist, a family therapist, and other healthcare professionals. In addition, bereavement care for the patient's family is often worked into the overall interdisciplinary treatment plan.

One of the challenges of an interdisciplinary treatment approach is harmonizing the varying methods and philosophies of different professionals into a cohesive care plan that works toward a unified treatment goal. One approach is for the interdisciplinary team to perform the intake interview (or initial assessment) of the patient in a group setting to ensure unity in their treatment approach, and then follow up with regularly scheduled meetings to create the treatment plan and adjust it as necessary as they follow the patient's progress.

However, the logistics of such a plan are often difficult, given the patient care load of many healthcare providers. What is more common is the appointment of a case manager, who is responsible for coordinating delivery of treatment and following the patient's progress, to organize and inform the treatment team. The manager provides the patient with a "point person" to approach with any problems or concerns. They also have responsibility for scheduling therapies and treatments in the correct sequence for maximum benefit to the patient, and for coordinating aftercare services such as housing assistance and networking the patient with support groups. Case managers are often licensed social workers, but can also be laypeople.

Paula Ford-Martin

### Further Reading
Satcher, David. *Mental Health: A Report of the Surgeon General.* Washington, D.C.: Government Printing Office, 1999. [available online at www.surgeongeneral.gov]

### Further Information
American Psychological Association (APA). 750 First Street, NE, Washington, D.C., USA. 20002-4242, 202-336-5500, 800-374-2721. Email: public.affairs@apa.org. http://www.apa.org.

# Interest inventory

A test that determines a person's preferences for specific fields or activities.

An interest inventory is a testing instrument designed for the purpose of measuring and evaluating the level of an individual's interest in, or preference for, a variety of activities; also known as interest test. Testing methods include direct observation of behavior, **ability** tests, and self-reporting inventories of interest in educational, social, recreational, and vocational activities. The activities usually represented in interest inventories are variously related to occupational areas, and these instruments and their results are often used in vocational guidance.

The first widely used interest inventory was the Strong Vocational Interest Blank, developed in 1927 by E.K. Strong. The original test was designed for men only; a version for women was developed in 1933. In 1974 the Strong test was merged into the Strong-Campbell Interest

Inventory, which was further revised in 1981. The test contains 325 activities, subjects, etc. Takers of this test are asked whether they like, dislike, or are indifferent to 325 items representing a wide variety of school subjects, occupations, activities, and types of people. They are also asked to choose their favorite among pairs of activities and indicate which of 14 selected characteristics apply to them. The Strong-Campbell test is scored according to 162 separate occupational scales as well as 23 scales that group together various types of occupations ("basic interest scales"). Examinees are also scored on six "general occupational themes" derived from J.L. Holland's interest classification scheme (realistic, investigative, artistic, social, enterprising, and conventional).

The other most commonly administered interest inventory is the Kuder Preference Record, originally developed in 1939. The Kuder Preference Record contains 168 items, each of which lists three broad choices concerning occupational interests, from which the individual selects the one that is most preferred. The test is scored on 10 interest scales consisting of items having a high degree of correlation with each other. A typical score profile will have high and low scores on one or more of the scales and average scores on the rest.

Other interest inventories include the Guilford-Zimmerman Interest Inventory, the G-S-Z Interest Survey, the California Occupational Preference Survey, the Jackson Vocational Interest Survey, and the Ohio Vocational Interest Survey. There are also inventories designed especially for children, for the disabled, and for those interested in the skilled trades.

Interest inventories are widely used in vocational counseling, both with adolescents and adults. Since these tests measure only interest and not ability, their value as predictors of occupational success, while significant, is limited. They are especially useful in helping high school and college students become familiar with career options and aware of their vocational interests. Interest inventories are also used in employee selection and classification.

# Intermittent explosive disorder

Uncontrollable episodes of aggression, where the person loses control and assaults others or destroys property.

Persons with this disorder experience episodes of aggressive or violent behavior that result in assault of a per-

son or animal or the destruction of property. These intense episodes occur spontaneously, not in response to provocation or threat, and individuals often express regret as soon as the episode ends. Usually he or she does not exhibit aggressive tendencies between episodes. This disorder can appear at any age, but is more common in **adolescence** through the 20s, and is more common in males. This disorder is believed to be rare, and reliable statistics on the frequency of occurrence are not available.

*See also* Impulse control disorders.

# Introversion

A commonly used term for people who are quiet, reserved, thoughtful, and self-reliant and who tend to prefer solitary work and leisure activities.

Individuals who are quiet, reserved, thoughtful, and self-reliant are often referred to as "introverts." They are likely to prefer solitary work and leisure activities. In comparison with extroverts, who draw most of their energy from social interaction and respond to external stimuli immediately and directly, introverts tend to mull things over before formulating a reaction, and their energy is regenerated by time spent alone.

**Carl Jung** was the first psychologist to use the terms *introversion* and *extroversion*, which literally **mean** "inward turning" and "outward turning." More recently, researchers in the field of **personality**, most notably **Hans Eysenck**, have popularized these terms. Eysenck claims a biological basis for introversion and **extroversion**, rooted in differences in sensitivity to physical and emotional stimulation. Eysenck claims that introverts are more sensitive to cortical arousal and thus more likely to be overwhelmed by external stimuli while extroverts, who are less sensitive to arousal, are more likely to actually seek out additional stimuli. Eysenck also created a system of personality types combining introversion and extroversion with degrees of emotionality and stability to arrive at four types corresponding to the classical four temperaments first delineated by Hippocrates. These types (together with Eysenck's formulations) are melancholic (emotional and introverted); phlegmatic (stable and introverted); choleric (stable and extroverted); and sanguine (emotional and extroverted).

Introversion is observable even in early **childhood**. An introverted child is able to entertain herself alone for extended periods of time, while extroverts need company most of the time. When it comes to socializing, introverts are likely to focus their **attention** on only one or a few best friends rather than a larger social group. Introverts like to "look before they leap," observing situations before they are ready to participate, and thinking things over before they speak. They are independent, introspective thinkers, turning inward to formulate their own ideas about things. They are more likely than extroverts to act differently in public than they do at home because they feel less at ease among strangers. They prefer to concentrate on a single activity at a time and dislike interruptions. On an emotional level, they are likely to become absorbed by their own emotions and pay less attention to those of the people around them. They may also be more reluctant than extroverts to talk about their feelings.

The personality **traits** that characterize introversion overlap at several points with those often seen in gifted people, such as independence of thought, the ability to spend extended periods of time absorbed in solitary pursuits, and heightened sensitivity to social interactions. The association between introversion and **giftedness** has been reinforced by the findings of Dr. Linda Silverman at Denver University's Gifted Child Development Cen-

ter, who found that an unusually high percentage of introverted children are gifted.

Although introversion and extroversion are observable, documented personality tendencies, people generally do not conform completely to either description. This fact is reflected, for example, in the **Myers-Briggs Type Indicator**, which treats introversion and extroversion as two ends of a continuum, with most people falling somewhere in between. Some scores come out very close to either end, while others are virtually at the half-way mark. However, it is possible for Myers-Briggs test results to change over time as people change.

*See also* Self-conscious emotions; Shyness; Temperament

### Further Reading

Campbell, Joseph, ed. *The Portable [Carl] Jung.* New York: Viking, 1971.
Eysenck, Hans J. and Michael Eysenck. *Personality and Individual Differences.* New York: Plenum Press, 1985.
Shapiro, Kenneth Joel. *The Experience of Introversion.* Durham, NC: Duke University. Press, 1975.

# J

## William James

**1842-1910**

American philosopher and psychologist who was the principal figure in the establishment and development of functionalism.

William James was born in New York City to a wealthy, educated family that included the future novelist, Henry James, his younger brother. The family traveled extensively in Europe and America in James's youth. James studied chemistry, physiology, and medicine at Harvard College, but was unable to settle on a career, his indecision intensified by physical ailments and **depression**. In 1872, at the invitation of Harvard's president, Charles Eliot, James began teaching physiology at Harvard and achieved a reputation as a committed and inspiring instructor. Throughout the 1870s, his interest in psychology—initially sparked by an article by the German physiologist **Wilhelm Wundt** (1832-1920)—grew. In 1875, James taught the first psychology course offered at an American university and in the same year received funding for the first psychological laboratory in the United States.

James began writing *The Principles of Psychology* in 1878 and published it in 1890. It had been intended as a textbook, but the original version, over 1,000 pages in length, was unsuitable for this purpose (James wrote an abridged version shortly afterwards). Nevertheless, the original text became a seminal work in the field, lauded for James's influential ideas and accessible writing style. James believed that psychology should be seen as closely linked to physiology and other biological sciences. He was among the earliest to argue that mental activity should be understood as dynamic functional processes rather than discrete structural states. The overall name generally associated with this outlook is **functionalism**, and it contrasts with the structural division of **consciousness** into separate elements that was the practice among early German psychologists, including Wundt, whose ideas James eventual-

**William James (right) with his brother Henry.**

ly came to reject. Influenced by **Charles Darwin**'s theories of evolution in *On the Origin of Species*, the functionalist view held that the true goal of psychology was the study of how consciousness functions to aid human beings in adapting to their **environment**.

Probably the most well-known individual topic treated in *Principles of Psychology* is the concept of thought as an unbroken but constantly changing stream, which added the phrase "stream of consciousness" to the English language. Following in the footsteps of the Greek philosopher Heraclitus, James argues that the exact same sensation or idea can never occur twice, and that all experiences are molded by the ones that precede them. He also emphasized the continuous quality of consciousness, even when interrupted by such phenomena as seizures or **sleep**. In contrast, scientific attempts to "break up" or "freeze" consciousness in order to study its disparate elements, such as those of Wundt or Edward Titchener (1867-1927), seemed misguided to James. Also treated prominently in *Principles of Psychology* is the importance and power of habits, as a force either to resist or cultivate, depending on the circumstances.

An especially influential part of James's book is the chapter on **emotion**, which expresses a principle that became known as the James-Lange Theory because the Danish physiologist Carl Lange published similar views at about the same time as James. The theory states that physical responses to stimuli precede emotional ones. In other words, James posited that emotions actually result from rather than cause physical changes. Based on this conclusion, James argued that a person's emotional state could be improved by changing his or her physical activities or attitudes.

Related to this observation about emotion were James's theories of the human will, which were also central to *Principles of Psychology* and contained the germ of his later philosophy of pragmatism. His emphasis on the will had its roots in his personal life: while in his twenties, an essay on free will by the French philosopher Charles-Bernard Renouvier (1815-1903) had inspired him to overcome his emotional problems. James rejected the idea of human beings responding passively to outside influences without power over their circumstances. Having himself triumphed by a strenuous exertion of the will, he recommended this course for others as well, defining an act of will as one characterized by focusing one's **attention** strongly on the object to be attained.

James served as president of the **American Psychological Association** in 1894 and 1904. He applied some of his psychological theories to his other studies, including education and religion. In 1909, the year before his death, James traveled to Clark University to meet **Sigmund Freud**, the founder of **psychoanalysis**, during the latter's only visit to the United States. In addition to *Principles of Psychology* and his other books, James had a great impact on psychology in America through his teaching. The work of his student **G. Stanley Hall** (1844-1924) provided a link between James's psychological theories and the functionalist school of psychology that flourished during the 1920s. James's

other books include *The Will to Believe and Other Essays* (1897), *The Varieties of Religious Experience* (1902), *Pragmatism* (1907), *A Pluralistic Universe* (1909), *The Meaning of Truth* (1909), and *Essays in Radical Empiricism* (1912).

Toward the end of his career, James concentrated his work in the area of philosophy and maintained few ties to the field of psychology.

### Further Reading
Perry, Ralph B. *The Thought and Character of William James.* Cambridge, MA: Harvard University Press, 1948.

## Pierre Marie Félix Janet

### 1859-1947
French psychologist particularly well-known for his work on psychopathology and psychotherapy.

Born in Paris on May 28, 1859, Pierre Janet spent his **childhood** and youth in that city. His bent for natural sciences led him to pursue studies in physiology at the Sorbonne at the same time that he was studying philosophy, for which he received a master's degree in 1882. Janet then left Paris for Le Havre and for seven years taught philosophy there in the lycée.

Janet, however, wanted to study medicine and at the hospital of Le Havre began to do research in **hypnosis**, using the well-known medium Léonie. Through these studies, the first of this sort, Janet came into contact with **Jean Martin Charcot**, but after reading Charcot and Hippolyte Bernheim he thought these investigators did not sufficiently take into consideration the psychological factors involved in neurotic phenomena. This forced Janet to undertake a deep psychological study of the neuroses, in particular of hysterical **neurosis**.

In his doctoral thesis in 1889 entitled "L'Automatisme psychologique" (Psychological Automatism), Janet devised an inventory of the manifestations of automatic activities, thinking that it would help him in studying the "elementary forms of sensibility and conscience." At the age of 30 he returned to Paris, and Charcot appointed him director of the laboratory of pathological psychology at the Salpêtrière hospital. Janet completed his medical studies, and in 1893 he published his medical dissertation entitled "The Mental State of Hysterics."

Janet was by **temperament** a naturalist, and during all his life he improved his herbarium. He had the same acquisitive attitude toward mental patients, from whom he collected thousands of precise and detailed observations.

**Pierre-Marie-Félix Janet** *(Corbis-Bettmann. Reproduced with permission.)*

However, in his books he attempted to give a more theoretical and depth interpretation of a few particular cases. From 1902 until 1934 he taught at the Collège de France.

Janet's works are numerous, and many of his writings have been translated into English. Among his books one can cite *Névroses et idées fixes* (1902); *Les Obsessions et la psychasténie* (1903); *The Major Symptoms of Hysteria* (1907, symposium undertaken in the United States); *Les Médications psychologiques* (1919); *De l'angoisse à l'extase* (1926); *Les Débuts de l'intelligence* (1935); and *L'Intelligence avant le langage* (1936).

Janet characterized his dynamic psychology as being a psychology of conduct, accepting the schema of a psychology of behavior while integrating in his schema conscious processes acting as regulators of action. Janet's work has often been compared to the work of Freud, and his influence has been great in both North and South America.

Well after Janet had retired, he continued to teach and to give conferences, manifesting a great vitality until the time of his death on Feb. 23, 1947.

### Further Reading
Murchison, Carl, et al. *A history of psychology in autobiography.* 4 vols. 1930-1952.

Wolman, Benjamin B., ed. *Historical roots of contemporary psychology.* 1968.

## Jealousy

An envious emotional attitude primarily directed by an individual toward someone perceived as a rival for the affections of a loved one or for something one desires, such as a job, promotion, or award.

Jealousy is a combination of emotional reactions, including **fear**, **anger**, and anxiety. Studies have shown that men and women tend to feel jealous for different reasons; for instance, physical attractiveness in a perceived rival is more likely to incite jealousy in a woman than in a man. Everyone occasionally experiences **normal** jealousy; caring about anyone or anything means that one will become uncomfortable and anxious at the prospect of losing the desired person or object to another. An unhealthy degree of apathy would be required for an individual never to experience jealousy.

The opposite extreme is pathological jealousy, also called morbid jealousy, which differs significantly from normal jealousy in its degree of intensity. Stronger and more long-lasting than normal jealousy, it is generally characterized by serious feelings of insecurity and inadequacy, as well as suspiciousness or **paranoia**. Whereas healthy individuals recover from jealousy fairly rapidly, either by realizing that it is unfounded or through some other coping mechanism, pathologically jealous people become obsessed by their fears and constantly look for signs that their suspicions are true, to the point where they may find it difficult to function normally. Excessive jealousy is unhealthy and destructive in all relationships. By making people behave in ways that will alienate others, jealousy becomes a **self-fulfilling prophecy**, depriving its victims of the affection or success they are so anxious to protect. Individuals suffering from morbid jealousy are prone to severe anxiety, **depression**, difficulty in controlling anger, and may engage in self-destructive behavior or elicit suicidal tendencies.

### Further Reading
White, Gregory. *Jealousy.* New York: Guilford Press, 1989.

## Arthur R. Jensen

**1923-**
American educational psychologist whose work has concentrated in the study of human intelligence.

**Arthur R. Jensen** *(AP/Wide World Photos. Reproduced with permission.)*

Arthur Jensen was born in San Diego, California, and attended the University of California at Berkeley, San Diego State College, and Columbia University. He completed a clinical internship at the University of Maryland's Psychiatric Institute in 1956, after which he won a two-year postdoctoral research fellowship with the Institute of Psychiatry at the University of London, where he worked with **Hans J. Eysenck**, a prominent psychologist known for his evolutionary approach to human behavior. Eysenck's work in **personality** theory, **measurement**, and **intelligence**—areas that were to become Jensen's specialty—challenged humanistic, psychodynamic approaches that stressed the importance of social factors in human behavior. In 1958, Jensen joined the faculty at the University of California at Berkeley, serving as a professor of **educational psychology**, and also served as a research psychologist at the Institute of Human Learning. After early work in the area of verbal learning, Jensen turned to the study of individual differences in human learning and intelligence.

Jensen claimed, on the basis of his research, that general cognitive **ability** is essentially an inherited trait, determined predominantly by genetic factors rather than by environmental conditions. He also contended that while associative learning, or memorizing ability, is equally distributed among the races, conceptual learning, or synthesizing ability, occurs with significantly greater frequency in whites than in blacks. He suggested that from the data, one might conclude that on average, white Americans are more intelligent than African-Americans. Jensen suggested that the difference in average performance between whites and blacks on intelligence tests might be the result of innate differences rather than contrasts in parental upbringing, formal schooling, or other environmental factors. Jensen further surmised from the data that federal educational programs such as Head Start could only raise the IQs of disadvantage children by only a few points and are therefore not worthy of funding. The relative influence of **heredity** and **environment** on intelligence tests had been an area of debate since their inception in the 1920s, and the prevailing view of Jensen's contemporaries was that environmental factors in the home and school play the decisive role.

In 1969, Jensen published his views in a long article entitled "How Much Can We Boost IQ and Scholastic Achievement?" in the *Harvard Education Review,* which rekindled the age-old debate of the relative importance of genetics in determining intellectual ability. Jensen's work was often misquoted by the media and was popularly denounced on college campuses. The belief in a genetic basis for individual and racial differences in intelligence and scholastic performance came to be known as "jensenism." Although Jensen's work in human intelligence has received a mixed reception from professionals in the field, his prolific publications have engaged the serious attention of many researchers and educators in the years since. Jensen's books include *Genetics and Education* (1973), *Educability and Group Differences* (1973), *Bias in Mental Testing* (1979), and *Straight Talk about Mental Tests* (1980).

*See also* Nature-nurture controversy

**Further Reading**
Jensen, Arthur. "How Much Can We Boost IQ and Scholastic Achievement?" *Harvard Education Review* 39 (Winter/Summer 1969): 1-123; 449-83.

# Virginia E. Johnson

**1925-**
Researcher in human sexuality who co-wrote with her then-husband, William H. Masters, *Human Sexual Response* in 1966.

In collaboration with Dr. **William Howell Masters**, psychologist and sex therapist Virginia E. Johnson pioneered the study of human **sexuality** under laboratory conditions. She and Masters published the results of their study as a book entitled *Human Sexual Response* in 1966, causing an immediate sensation. As part of her work at the Reproductive Biology Research Foundation in St. Louis and later at the Masters and Johnson Institute, she counseled many clients and taught sex therapy to many professional practitioners.

Johnson was born Virginia Eshelman on February 11, 1925, in Springfield, Missouri, to Hershel Eshelman, a farmer, and Edna (Evans) Eshelman. The elder of two children, she began school in Palo Alto, California, where her family had moved in 1930. When they returned to Missouri three years later, she was ahead of her school peers and skipped several grades. She studied piano and voice, and read extensively. She entered Drury College in Springfield in 1941. After her freshman year, she was hired to work in the state insurance office, a job she held for four years. Her mother, a republican state committeewoman, introduced her to many elected officials, and Johnson often sang for them at meetings. These performances led to a job as a country music singer for radio station KWTO in Springfield, where her stage name was Virginia Gibson. She studied at the University of Missouri and later at the Kansas City Conservatory of Music. In 1947, she became a business writer for the St. Louis *Daily Record.* She also worked briefly on the marketing staff of KMOX- TV, leaving that position in 1951.

In the early 1940s she married a Missouri politician, but the marriage lasted only two days. Her marriage to an attorney many years her senior also ended in **divorce**. On June 13, 1950, she married George V. Johnson, an engineering student and leader of a dance band. She sang with the band until the **birth** of her two children, Scott Forstall and Lisa Evans. In 1956, the Johnsons divorced.

## Chosen by William Howell Masters as research associate

In 1956, contemplating a return to college for a degree in sociology, Johnson applied for a job at the Washington University employment office. William Howell Masters, associate professor of clinical obstetrics and gynecology, had requested an assistant to interview volunteers for a research project. He personally chose Johnson, who fitted the need for an outgoing, intelligent, mature woman who was preferably a mother. Johnson began work on January 2, 1957, as a research associate, but soon advanced to research instructor.

Gathering scientific data by means of electroencephalography, electrocardiography, and the use of color monitors, Masters and Johnson measured and analyzed 694 volunteers. They were careful to protect the privacy

**Virginia Johnson, left, with coworker William Masters.**
*(UPI/Corbis-Bettmann. Reproduced with permission.)*

of their subjects, who were photographed in various modes of sexual stimulation. In addition to a description of the four stages of sexual arousal, other valuable information was gained from the photographs, including evidence of the failure of some contraceptives, the discovery of a vaginal secretion in some women that prevents conception, and the observation that sexual enjoyment need not decrease with age. In 1964, Masters and Johnson created the non-profit Reproductive Biology Research Foundation in St. Louis and began treating couples for sexual problems. Originally listed as a research associate, Johnson became assistant director of the Foundation in 1969 and co-director in 1973.

In 1966, Masters and Johnson released their book *Human Sexual Response,* in which they detailed the results of their studies. Although the book was written in dry, clinical terms and intended for medical professionals, its titillating subject matter made it front-page news and a runaway best seller, with over 300,000 volumes distributed by 1970. While some reviewers accused the team of dehumanizing and scientizing sex, overall professional and critical response was positive.

## Develops sex therapy institute

At Johnson's suggestion, the two researchers went on the lecture circuit to discuss their findings and appeared on such television programs as NBC's *Today* show and ABC's *Stage '67.* Their book and their public appearances heightened public interest in sex therapy, and a long list of clients developed. Couples referred to their clinic would spend two weeks in intensive therapy and have periodic follow-ups for five years. In a second book, *Human Sexual Inadequacy,* published in 1970,

Masters and Johnson discuss the possibility that sex problems are more cultural than physiological or psychological. In 1975, they wrote *The Pleasure Bond: A New Look at Sexuality and Commitment,* which differs from previous volumes in that it was written for the average reader. This book describes total commitment and fidelity to the partner as the basis for an enduring sexual bond. To expand counseling, Masters and Johnson trained dual-sex therapy teams and conducted regular workshops for college teachers, marriage counselors, and other professionals.

After the release of this second book, Masters divorced his first wife and married Johnson on January 7, 1971, in Fayetteville, Arkansas. They continued their work at the Reproductive Biology Research Foundation, and in 1973 founded the Masters and Johnson Institute. Johnson was co-director of the institute, running the everyday business, and Masters concentrated on scientific work. Johnson, who never received a college degree, was widely recognized along with Masters for her contributions to human sexuality research. Together they received several awards, including the Sex Education and Therapists Award in 1978 and Biomedical Research Award of the World Sexology Association in 1979.

In 1981, the team sold their lab and moved to another location in St. Louis, where they had a staff of 25 and a long waiting list of clients. Their book *Homosexuality in Perspective,* released shortly before the move, documents their research on gay and lesbian sexual practice and homosexual sexual problems and their work with "gender-confused" individuals who sought a "cure" for their **homosexuality**. One of their most controversial conclusions from their 10-year study of 84 men and women was their conviction that homosexuality is primarily not physical, emotional, or genetic, but a learned behavior. Some reviewers hailed the team's claims of success in "converting" homosexuals. Others, however, observed that the handpicked individuals who participated in the study were not a representative sample; moreover, they challenged the team's assumption that heterosexual performance alone was an accurate indicator of a changed sexual preference.

The institute had many associates who assisted in research and writing. Robert Kolodny, an M.D. interested in sexually transmitted diseases, coauthored the book *Crisis: Heterosexual Behavior in the Age of AIDS* with Masters and Johnson in 1988. The book, commented Stephen Fried in *Vanity Fair,* "was politically incorrect in the extreme": it predicted a large-scale outbreak of the virus in the heterosexual community and, in a chapter meant to document how little was known of the AIDS virus, suggested that it might be possible to catch it from a toilet seat. Several prominent members of the medical community questioned the study, and many accused the authors of sowing hysteria. Adverse publicity hurt the team, who were distressed because they felt the medical community had turned against them. The number of therapy clients at the institute declined.

The board of the institute was quietly dissolved and William Young, Johnson's son-in-law, became acting director. Johnson went into semi-retirement. On February 19, 1992, Young announced that after 21 years of marriage, Masters and Johnson were filing for divorce because of differences about goals relating to work and retirement. Following the divorce, Johnson took most of the institute's records with her and is continuing her work independently.

## Further Reading

Duberman, Martin Bauml. Review of "Homosexuality in perspective." *New Republic.* (June 16, 1979): 24–31.

Fried, Stephen. "The new sexperts." *Vanity Fair.* (December 1992): 132.

Masters, William Howell and Robert Kolodny. *Masters and Johnson on sex and human loving.* Little, Brown, 1986.

"Repairing the conjugal bed." *Time.* (March 25, 1970.)

Robinson, Paul. *The modernization of sex: Havelock Ellis, Albert Kinsey, William Masters, and Virginia Johnson.* Cornell University Press, 1988.

# Jukes family

Pseudonym for the family involved in a psychological study of antisocial behavior.

One of the goals of 19th-century American scientists was to determine why some people engaged in undesirable or **antisocial behavior**. A **family** from Ulster County in upstate New York provided a great deal of material for speculation about the origins of such behavior. The family was referred to as the Jukes family (the actual family name was kept anonymous).

One of the initial researchers of the Jukes family was Elisha Harris (1824-1884), a New York City physician. He identified a family that, for six generations, had included large numbers of paupers, criminals, and vagrants. He traced the family to a woman he referred to as "Margaret, mother of criminals." Margaret and her two sisters produced 600 descendants over an 85-year period, many of whom lived on the fringes of society. For example, in one generation that produced 14 children, nine served a total of 50 years in state prison, and the other five were frequently jailed for petty crimes or spent time in poorhouses.

After Harris's discovery, Richard Dugale (1841-1883) studied the family history intensively. He concluded that the repeated appearance of undesirable behaviors could be traced to environmental rather than hereditary factors. Dugale advocated for decent housing and education for people from damaging environments.

After Dugale's death, some of his contemporaries reinterpreted his research in light of hereditarian influences. Instead of advancing the idea that **environment** influenced the behavior of the Jukes, the notion that antisocial behavior was passed from one generation to the next like any other biological trait was favored. Proponents of this idea included the widely respected physician and author Oliver Wendell Holmes (1809-1894). Holmes's son later became a United States Supreme Court Justice and issued a famous ruling that allowed legal, involuntary sterilization of people deemed to be genetically "unfit."

Later research has revealed that the original settlers in Ulster County, like the Jukes, included people who could not adapt to the urban life in 19th-century New York City and moved north, living an itinerant life of trapping and hunting. (The name "Jukes" came from the slang term "to juke," which described the behavior of chickens who did not deposit their eggs in nests, but rather laid them in any convenient spot.) When the area became more densely populated, such individuals lost most of their hunting and trapping land and their way of life. They were looked down upon by later settlers, who preferred to live in houses within a community. The earlier inhabitants, including the Jukes, were forced to live a marginal existence, which foreshadowed their troubles with society.

*See also* Kallikak family; Nature-nurture controversy

# Carl Jung

### 1875-1961
Swiss psychiatrist and founder of analytic psychology.

Carl Jung was born in Switzerland, the son of a Swiss Reform pastor. Having decided to become a psychiatrist, he enrolled in medical school at the University of Basel, from which he received his degree in 1900. Serving as an assistant at the University of Zurich Psychiatric Clinic, Jung worked under psychiatrist Eugen Bleuler (1857-1939), a psychiatrist renowned for his work on **schizophrenia**. Jung also traveled to France to study with the well-known psychiatrist **Pierre Janet** (1859-1947) as well. In 1905, he was appointed to a fac-

**Carl Jung** *(The Library of Congress. Reproduced with permission.)*

ulty position in psychiatry at the University of Zurich and became a senior physician at its clinic. Eventually, a growing private practice forced him to resign his university position. Jung's early published studies on schizophrenia established his reputation, and he also won recognition for developing a **word association test**.

Jung had read **Sigmund Freud**'s *The Interpretation of Dreams* shortly after its publication in 1900 and entered into a correspondence with its author. The two men met in 1907 and began a close association that was to last for over six years. In 1909, they both traveled to the United States to participate in the 20th-anniversary commemoration at Clark University in Worcester, Massachusetts, at the invitation of American psychologist, **G. Stanley Hall** (1844-1924). Jung became part of a weekly discussion group that met at Freud's house and included, among others, **Alfred Adler** and **Otto Rank** (1884-1939). This group evolved into the Vienna Psychoanalytic Society, and Jung became its first president in 1911. Jung had begun to develop concepts about **psychoanalysis** and the nature of the **unconscious** that differed from those of Freud, however, especially Freud's insistence on the sexual basis of **neurosis**. After the publication of Jung's *Psychology of the Unconscious* in 1912, the disagreement between the two men grew, and their relationship ended in

1914. At this period, Jung underwent a period of personal turmoil and, like Freud at a similar juncture in his own life, undertook a thorough self-analysis based on his **dreams**. Jung also explored myths and symbols, an interest he was to investigate further in the 1920s with trips to Africa and the southwestern United States to study the myths and religions of non-Western cultures.

Jung developed his own system of psychoanalysis, which he called analytical psychology, that reflected his interest in symbolism, mythology, and spirituality. A major premise of analytical psychology is that the individual **personality**, or **psyche**, functions on three levels. The *ego* operates at the conscious level, while the *personal unconscious* includes experiences that have been repressed, forgotten, or kept from **consciousness** in some other way. It is also the site of complexes—groups of feelings, thoughts, and memories, usually organized around a significant person (such as a parent) or object (such as money). At the deepest and most powerful level, Jung posited the existence of a racial or *collective unconscious*, which gathers together the experiences of previous generations and even animal ancestors, preserving traces of humanity's evolutionary development over time. The collective unconscious is a repository of shared images and symbols, called *archetypes*, that emerge in dreams, myths, and other forms. These include such common themes as **birth**, rebirth, death, the hero, the earth mother, and the demon. Certain archetypes form separate systems within the personality, including the *persona*, or public image; the *anima* and *animus*, or gender characteristics; the *shadow*, or animal instincts; and the *self*, which strives for unity and wholeness. In Jung's view, a thorough analysis of both the personal and collective unconscious is necessary to fully understand the individual personality.

Perhaps Jung's best-known contribution is his theory that individuals can be categorized according to general attitudinal type as either introverted (inward-looking) or extroverted (outward-looking). The psychic wholeness, or individuation, for which human beings strive depends on reconciling these tendencies as well as the four functional aspects of the mind that are split into opposing pairs: sensing versus intuiting as ways of knowing, and thinking versus feeling as ways of evaluating. If any of these personality characteristics is overly dominant in the conscious mind, its opposite will be exaggerated in the unconscious. These pairs of functions have been widely adapted in vocational and other types of testing.

From 1932 to 1942, Jung was a professor at the Federal Polytechnical University of Zurich. Although his health forced him to resign, he continued writing about analytical psychology for the rest of his life and promot-

ing the attainment of psychic wholeness through personal transformation and self-discovery. Jung's work has been influential in disciplines other than psychology, and his own writing includes works on religion, the arts, literature, and occult topics including alchemy, astrology, yoga, fortune telling, and flying saucers. Jung's autobiography, *Memories, Dreams, Reflections,* was published in 1961, the year of his death. Institutes of analytical psychology have been established throughout the world, although its international center remains the C.J. Jung Institute in Zurich, founded in 1948. Jung was a prolific writer; his collected works fill 19 volumes, but many of his writings were not published in English until after 1965. Shortly before his death, Jung completed work on *Man and His Symbols,* which has served as a popular introduction to his ideas on symbols and dreams.

*See also* Archetype; Character; Extroversion; Introversion

### Further Reading

Fordham, Frieda. *An Introduction to Jung's Psychology.* New York: Penguin Books, 1966.

## Just noticeable difference

Scientific calculation of the average detectable difference between two measurable qualities, such as weight, brightness of light, loudness of sound.

When we try to compare two different objects to see if they are the same or different on some dimension (e.g., weight), the difference between the two that is barely big enough to be noticed is called the just noticeable difference (JND). Just noticeable differences have been studied for many dimensions (e.g., brightness of lights, loudness of sounds, weight, line length, and others).

The human sensory system does not respond identically to the same stimuli on different occasions. As a result, if an individual attempted to identify whether two objects were of the same or different weight he or she might detect a difference on one occasion but will fail to notice it on another occasion. Psychologists calculate the just noticeable difference as an average detectable difference across a large number of trials. The JND does not stay the same when the magnitude of the stimuli change. In assessing heaviness, for example, the difference between two stimuli of 10 and 11 grams could be detected, but we would not be able to detect the difference between 100 and 101 grams. As the magnitude of the stimuli grow, we need a larger actual difference for detection. The percentage of change remains constant in general. To detect the difference in heaviness, one stimulus would have to be approximately 2 percent heavier than the other; otherwise, we will not be able to spot the difference.

Psychologists refer to the percentages that describe the JND as Weber fractions, named after Ernst Weber (1795-1878), a German physiologist whose pioneering research on sensation had a great impact on psychological studies. For example, humans require a 4.8% change in loudness to detect a change; a 7.9% change in brightness is necessary. These values will differ from one person to the next, and from one occasion to the next. However, they do represent generally accurate values.

**Further Reading**

Nietzel, Michael T. *Introduction to Clinical Psychology.* 3rd ed. Englewood Cliffs, NJ: Prentice Hall, 1991.

# Juvenile delinquency

Chronic antisocial behavior by persons 18 years of age or younger that is beyond parental control and is often subjected to legal and punitive action.

According to the Federal Bureau of Investigation (FBI) and the Centers for Disease Control (CDC), the arrest rate of American juveniles (persons 18 years of age or younger) committing violent crimes increased from 137 percent in 1965 to 430 percent in 1990. While teenagers are the population most likely to commit crimes, their delinquency is related to the overall incidence of crime in society: teen crime increases as adult crime does. The majority of violent teenage crime is committed by males. While the same delinquency rates are attributed to both whites and nonwhites, nonwhites have a higher arrest rate.

In spite of the emotional turbulence associated with **adolescence**, most teenagers find legal, nonviolent ways to express feelings of **anger** and frustration and to establish **self-esteem**. Nonetheless, some teenagers turn to criminal activity for these purposes and as a reaction to **peer pressure**. A number of factors have been linked to the rise in teen crime, including **family violence**. Parents who physically or verbally abuse each other or their children are much more likely to raise children who will commit crimes. In a study conducted in 1989, for example, 80 out of 95 incarcerated juvenile delinquents had witnessed or been victims of severe family violence. A similar incidence of abuse was found in a study of teenage murderers.

The growing poverty rate in the U.S., particularly among children, has also been attributed to juvenile delinquency. In the late 1980s, the National Education Association predicted that 40 percent of secondary school students will live below the poverty line. The anger and frustration of low-income youths excluded from the "good life" depicted in the mass media, coupled with the lack of visible opportunities to carve out productive paths for themselves, lead many to crime, much of it drug-related. A dramatic link has been found between drug use and criminal activity: people who abuse illegal drugs, such as cocaine and heroin, have been found to commit six times as many crimes as non-drug users.

For many poor inner-city youths, juvenile delinquency begins with participation in the drug trade. Children as young as 9 or 10 are paid as much as $100 a day to serve as lookouts while drug deals are taking place. Next, they become runners and may eventually graduate to being dealers. The introduction of crack cocaine, one of the most powerfully addictive drugs in existence, in the mid-1980s, has contributed to drug-related delinquency. The neglected children of crack-addicted parents are especially likely to be pulled into the drug culture themselves.

The wealth gained from the drug trade has further escalated levels of juvenile delinquency by fueling the rise of violent street **gangs**. Many gangs are highly organized operations with formal hierarchies and strict codes of dress and behavior. With millions of dollars in drug money behind them, they are expanding from major urban areas to smaller communities. Teens, both poor and middle-class, join gangs for status, respect, and a feeling of belonging denied them in other areas of their lives. Some are pressured into joining to avoid harassment from gang members. Once in a gang, teens are much more likely to be involved in violent acts.

The juvenile justice system has been criticized as outdated and ineffective in dealing with the volume and nature of today's teen crime. A teenager must be either 16 or 18 years of age (depending on the state) to be tried as an adult in criminal court, regardless of the crime committed. Child offenders under the age of 13 are considered juvenile delinquents and can only be tried in family court, no matter what type of crime they have committed. Unless the offender has already committed two serious crimes, the maximum **punishment** is 18 months in a youth facility. Teenagers between the ages of 13 and 16 are classified as "juvenile offenders." They are rarely photographed or fingerprinted, even in cases involving **rape** or murder, and usually receive lenient sentences. Most are confined for period of less than four months.

Of approximately 2 million juveniles arrested each year, an estimated 50 percent are released immediately. Those whose cases are tried in court are often given suspended sentences or put on probation. Of those who are sentenced to prison, most return to criminal activity upon their release, and many **fear** that these young offenders come out of prisons even more violent. In addition, the unmanageable caseloads of probation officers in many cities makes it impossible to keep track of juveniles adequately. Thus, those teens who turn to crime face little in the way of a deterrent, a situation that has caused many authorities to place a large share of the blame for teen crime on the failure of the juvenile justice system.

Alternative community-based programs for all but the most violent teens have had some success in reducing juvenile crime. These include group homes which offer counseling and education; wilderness programs such as Outward Bound; crisis counseling programs that provide emergency aid to teenagers and their families; and placement in a foster home, when a stable home **environment** is lacking.

## Further Reading

Binder, Arnold. *Juvenile Delinquency: Historical, Cultural, Legal Perspectives*. New York: Macmillan, 1988.

Grinney, Ellen Heath. *Delinquency and Criminal Behavior*. New York: Chelsea House Publishers, 1992.

Trojanowicz, Robert C. *Juvenile Delinquency: Concepts and Control*. New York: Prentice Hall, 1983.

# Jerome Kagan

**1929-**
American psychologist who has studied the role of physiology in psychological development.

Jerome Kagan is one of the major developmental biologists of the twentieth century. He has been a pioneer in re-introducing physiology as a determinate of psychological characteristics. The Daniel and Amy Starch Professor of Psychology at Harvard University, Kagan has won numerous awards, including the Hofheimer Prize of the **American Psychiatric Association** (1963) and the G. Stanley Hall Award of the **American Psychological Association (APA)** in 1994. He has served on numerous committees of the National Academy of Sciences, as well as the President's Science Advisory Committee and the Social Science Research Council.

Kagan was born in Newark, New Jersey in 1929, the son of Joseph and Myrtle (Liebermann) Kagan. His father was a businessman. Kagan graduated from Rutgers University in New Jersey in 1950 with a B.S. degree. In 1951 he married Cele Katzman; the couple have one daughter. Kagan earned his master's degree from Harvard University and his Ph.D. from Yale University in 1954 and spent one year as an instructor in psychology at Ohio State University. Following two years as a psychologist at the U.S. Army Hospital at West Point, Kagan joined the Fels Research Institute in Yellow Springs, Ohio, as a research associate. In 1959, he became chairman of the Department of Psychology there.

Since the late 1920s, scientists at Fels had been studying middle-class children from **infancy** through **adolescence** in order to better understand human development. At that time, most psychologists believed that personal characteristics were determined by environmental factors rather than by inheritance. Kagan's early research at Fels focused on the degree to which individual **personality traits** carried through from in-

fancy and **childhood** to adolescence and beyond. On re-examining some of the Fels subjects as adults, Kagan and Howard Moss did not find strong support for the maintenance of behavioral characteristics such as **aggression**, dominance, competitiveness, and dependence. However, they found that a small group who had been very fearful as toddlers had retained aspects of this "behavioral inhibition" as adults. In 1962, Kagan and Moss published their landmark book *Birth to Maturity*.

## Questions environmental determinism

In 1964, Kagan moved to Harvard University. After spending a year doing fieldwork in a small native Guatemalan village, he began to examine the influence of biological factors on development and developmental variation in children. Kagan discovered that the development of **memory** skills, the understanding of symbolism, a sense of morality, and self-awareness arise in a particular order during the first two years of life. He concluded that children are very adaptable and that their biology promotes a regular developmental progression even under unfavorable circumstances. In 1984 he published *The Nature of the Child*, which he revised in 1994. In this book, Kagan argued that biology and **environment** both were important factors in development, and he questioned the widespread belief that adult personality was determined by childhood experience alone.

Since 1979, Kagan and his coworkers have studied inhibited versus uninhibited temperaments among infants and children, particularly in response to unfamiliar situations. A **temperament** is a relatively stable, emotional or behavioral trait that first appears during childhood. They found that about 20% of healthy four-month-old infants reacted to stimulation with thrashing and distress. About two-thirds of these infants became inhibited children who exhibited strong physiological responses to **stress**. He has concluded that there are biological differences in the excitability of individual neurochemical systems. He suggests that children with very excitable systems tend to be timid, anxious, and inhibited, and those with less excitable systems tend to the opposite. These two types of individuals correspond to the "melancholic" and "sanguine" temperaments, first described by the ancient Greek physician Hippocrates. Likewise, they correspond to the introvert and the extrovert described by **Carl Jung**. In the second century A.D., the Roman physician **Galen** argued that these temperaments were determined by a combination of biological inheritance and environmental factors. Kagan's research suggests that Galen was correct. Kagan published *Unstable Ideas: Temperament, Cognition, and Self* in 1989.

## Questions continuity of development and parental influences

In his book *Three Seductive Ideas* (1998), Kagan argued against "infant determinism," the widespread belief that experiences and parenting during the first three years of a child's life are the most important determinants of adult personality. To Kagan, this assumption is unproven, and perhaps unprovable. He also argued against the common belief that development is a continuous process from infancy to adulthood. Rather, he believes that it is discontinuous process.

Kagan's many writings include *Understanding Children: Behavior, Motives, and Thought* (1971), *Growth of the Child* (1978), *The Second Year: The Emergence of Self-Awareness* (1981), and a number of cross-cultural studies of **child development**. He has coauthored numerous editions of a widely used introductory psychology text. In 1982, he was awarded the Wilbur Lucius Cross Medal from Yale University. He also is a recipient of the APA's Distinguished Scientist Award. Kagan is on the editorial board of the journals *Child Development* and *Developmental Psychology*, and is active in numerous professional organizations.

Margaret Alic

### Further Reading
"Galen's prophecy: temperament and human nature" (book review). *The Economist (U.S.)* 332 (23 July 1994): 85-6.
Hulbert, Ann. "Parents, peers, and the rearing of children: the influence of anxiety." *The New Republic* 7 December 1998.
Kagan, Jerome. *Galen's prophecy: temperament in human nature.* New York: Basic Books, 1994.
Kagan, Jerome. "A parent's influence is peerless." *Harvard Education Letter* November/December 1998.
http://www.edletter.org/past/issues/1998-nd/parents.shtml (March/April 2000).

# Kallikak family

Pseudonym for a family involved in a psychological study of the hereditary aspects of intelligence.

The history of **intelligence** testing in the United States has been troublesome from the beginning. Although psychologists attempted to conduct legitimate research and apply psychological knowledge to the study of intelligence, some of the early work was quite unscientific and led to dubious results.

One case involved the descendants of an anonymous man referred to as Martin Kallikak. This man produced two different lines of descent, one with a supposedly "feebleminded" bar maid with whom he had had sexual relations and one with his wife, reputed to be an honest Quaker woman. The offsprings from the two women generated two lineages that could not have been more different. The pseudonym "Kallikak" was taken from two Greek words: *kallos,* meaning beauty (referring to the descendants of the Quaker woman) and *kakos,* meaning bad (referring to the descendants of the bar maid).

The psychologist Henry Goddard (1866-1957) investigated these two groups over a two-year period. According to psychology historian David Hothersall, Goddard discovered that the inferior branch of Martin Kallikak's **family** included "46 **normal** people, 143 who were definitely feebleminded, 36 illegitimate births, 33 sexually immoral people, 3 epileptics, and 24 alcoholics. These people were horse thieves, paupers, convicts, prostitutes, criminals, and keepers of houses of ill repute. On the other hand, Quaker side of the family included only 3 somewhat mentally "degenerate people, 2 alcoholics, 1 sexually loose person, and no illegitimate births or epileptics."

These patterns of behavior were believed to be the results of **heredity**, rather than **environment**, even though the two environments were radically different. Goddard also believed that intelligence was determined by heredity, just like the inclination toward prostitution, theft, and poverty.

Goddard was also a supporter of the **eugenics** movement in the United States. One of the solutions that he proposed for controlling the creation of the "defective classes" was sterilization, which he advocated as being as simple as having a tooth extracted. Later in his career, Goddard retracted some of his earlier conclusions and maintained that, although intelligence had a hereditary basis, morons (at that time a technical term) might beget other morons, but they could be educated and made useful to society.

*See also* Jukes family; Nature-nurture controversy

**Further Reading**

Goddard, Henry Herbert. *The Kallikak Family: A Study in the Heredity of Feeble-Mindedness.* New York: Macmillan, 1927.

Gould, S. J. *The Mismeasure of Man.* New York: W. W. Norton, 1981.

# George Alexander Kelly

### 1905-1967

American psychologist best known for developing the psychology of personal constructs.

George Alexander Kelly, originator of personal construct theory of **personality**, was born on farm near Perth Kansas. He was the only child of Elfleda Merriam Kelly and Theodore Vincent Kelly. Kelly's father trained for the Presbyterian ministry but gave that up and moved to the farm soon after wedding Kelly's mother. When Kelly was four, his **family** moved to Eastern Colorado to make a claim on land given to settlers for free by the U. S. government. Because no water could be located beneath the land, the family moved back to the Kansas farm.

Kelly's early schooling was, by his own words, "rather irregular." He attended various grade schools and was also schooled at home, an obligation his parents took seriously as they were themselves relatively well educated. After age 13 he was sent away to school and attended four different high schools. When he was 16 he transferred to Friends University academy in Wichita, Kansas. There he took a mix of college and academy courses. He then transferred to Park College, Missouri, where he graduated in 1926 with a bachelor's degree in mathematics and physics. During these years he became involved in his college debate team, and was seen as an excellent speaker.

He had planned on going into engineering after college, but his success at debating, and the fact that it provoked his interest in social issues, made him wonder about the real value of an engineering career. Thus, the following fall he entered the educational sociology program of the University of Kansas with minors in sociology and labor relations. In the fall of 1927, with his master's thesis (a study of how Kansas City workers distributed their leisure time activities) incomplete, he moved to Minneapolis. He had sent out many applications for teaching jobs with no success. There he taught three nights a week, one night each for three different schools. He enrolled in the University of Minnesota in biometrics and sociology but was forced to leave after a few weeks, when the school found out he had to been able to pay his fees. He finished his master's thesis in 1927.

In the winter of 1927 Kelly got a job at Sheldon Junior College in Sheldon, Iowa, teaching psychology and speech, and coaching drama. He spent one and a half years there. He then spent a summer at the University of Minnesota, and some months in Wichita, Kansas as an aeronautical engineer for an aircraft company. He then went to the University of Edinburgh, Scotland as an exchange student, where he received his Bachelor's in Education in 1930. He then enrolled in the University of Iowa and received his Ph.D. in psychology in 1931. His doctoral dissertation was on common factors in reading and speech disabilities.

He married Gladys Thompson just two days after attaining his Ph.D. In 1931, Kelly accepted a faculty position at Fort Hays Kansas State College (now called Fort Hays State University) where he was to remain for 12 years. He had wanted to pursue work in **physiological psychology** but found little opportunity to do so. So he turned his **attention** to an area he felt needed some work—providing clinical psychological services to adults and school-aged children on the university's campus. These services included counseling (vocational and academic), academic skill development, **psychotherapy**, and speech therapy.

Eventually, there was a demand for these services beyond campus, and Kelly developed a program for a clinic that traveled to schools in rural Kansas, there providing diagnostic formulations and treatment recommendations for students, typically twelve per day. At this time the United States was in the grips of a severe economic **depression** and the Midwest had experienced a major drought. Economic devastation was commonplace and many families were distressed. Kelly and his crew of four to five undergraduate and graduate students found people who had serious problems in their daily living. The need for these services was so strong and publicly recognized that the state legislature funded the traveling clinic directly through a legislative act.

He found that Freudian approaches to psychological problems worked to help some of the people he saw, but that his own formulations also worked if they were relevant to the person's problem and provided the person with a different way of looking at the problem. In these constructions one can see the seeds of Kelly's *constructive alternativism*. In his view, different people have alternative ways of looking at the world, and each view can capture some element of truth. None are right or wrong, all views are constructed by the individuals and reflect reality for them. In a way, people construct their own reality.

Shortly after World War II started, Kelly entered the U. S. Navy in the aviation psychology division, where he and fellow psychologists worked on ways of choosing the best naval air cadets. After the war ended Kelly taught at the University of Maryland for a year before being appointed a professorship at Ohio State University in 1945. In 1946 he became director of the **clinical psychology** program where he remained until 1965. Kelly served as president of both the Consulting (1954-1955) and Clinical (1956-1957) divisions of the American Psychological Association. In 1965 he took the position of Distinguished Professorial Chair in Theoretical Psychology at Brandeis University, which he held until his sudden death in 1967.

Kelly's personal construct theory of personality is perhaps his most significant contribution to psychology. It is a broad theory based on the idea that people are like scientists who go around testing personal theories, or *personal constructs,* about the world and how it works, and about themselves. Behavior is seen as an experiment. Individuals use these constructs in an attempt to anticipate events and exert control over their lives. He believed that people tend to have certain main personal constructs about large areas of life that guide their behavior. These constructs or concepts can be revised in the face of conflicting information, or they can become stable and internalized as basic personality tendencies. Kelly laid out the theory in his 1955 two-volume book entitled *The Psychology of Personal Constructs.* Kelly also developed the Role Construct Repertory Test, a method of assessing how an individual sees his or her world or *personal-role constructs.* In addition, Kelly experimented with fixed-role therapy, in which a client would "try on" various roles.

Personal construct theory was internationally recognized as a unique theoretical contribution to psychology. Indeed, his work has enjoyed more popularity in Britain than anywhere else. Hundreds of scholarly papers have been published that have personal constructs as their theme. Personal construct methods and ideas have been used to study numerous and varied topics, such as relationship development and breakdown, vocational decision making, psychopathology, education, and cognitive complexity. Since his death in 1967, interest in Kelly's work has grown, and its influence has become even stronger. Since 1975, biennial International Congresses on Personal Construct Psychology have been held, and on alternate years regional conferences are held. *The International Journal of Personal Construct Psychology* was founded in 1988, changing its title and focus in 1994 to the *Journal of Constructivist Psychology.*

Marie Doorey

## Further Reading
Fransella, Fay. *George Kelly* London: Sage Publications, 1995.

Kelly, George A. *The Psychology of Personal Constructs.* London: Routledge, 1991 (originally published in 1955).

Neimeyer, Robert A. "Kelly, George Alexander," In *2000 Encyclopedia of Psychology, V.4.* Alan E. Kazdin, ed. Washington, DC: American Psychological Association & New York: Oxford University Press, Inc., 2000.

Peyser, C.S. "Kelly, George A." In *Encyclopedia of Psychology, 2nd Ed., V. 4.* R.J. Corsini, Editor. NY: John Wiley & Sons, 1994.

# Kinesthetic sense

The ability to know accurately the positions and movements of one's skeletal joints.

Kinesthesis refers to sensory input that occurs within the body. Postural and movement information are communicated via sensory systems by tension and compression of muscles in the body. Even when the body remains stationary, the kinesthetic sense can monitor its position. Humans possess three specialized types of neurons responsive to **touch** and stretching that help keep track of body movement and position. The first class, called Pacinian corpuscles, lies in the deep subcutaneous fatty tissue and responds to pressure. The second class of neurons surrounds the internal organs, and the third class is associated with muscles, tendons, and joints. These neurons work in concert with one another and with cortical neurons as the body moves.

The **ability** to assess the weight of an object is another function of kinesthesia. When an individual picks up an object, the tension in his/her muscles generates signals that are used to adjust posture. This sense does not operate in isolation from other senses. For example, the size-weight illusion results in a mismatch between how heavy an object looks and how heavy the muscles "think" it should be. In general, larger objects are judged as being heavier than smaller objects of the same weight.

The kinesthetic sense does not mediate equilibrium, or sense of balance. Balance involves different sensory pathways and originates in large part within the inner ear.

## Further Reading
Bartenieff, Irmgard. *Body Movement: Coping with the Environment.* New York: Gordon and Breach Science Publishers, 1980.

*Moving Parts* (videorecording). Princeton, NJ: Films for the Humanities, 1985.

# Alfred Charles Kinsey

## 1894-1956
American entomologist and sex researcher who pioneered the study of human sexuality.

Alfred Charles Kinsey was a well-known entomologist, specializing in the study of gall wasps, when his increasing interest in human **sexuality** led him in a entirely new scientific direction. Appalled by the lack of reliable scientific information on human sexual practices and problems, Kinsey began conducting extensive interviews, first with his students and then with larger populations. Kinsey's landmark studies, which emphasized both the variety of human sexual activities and the prevalence of practices that were condemned by society, led to a new openness in attitudes toward sex. His work was part of trend in which laws were liberalized and sex education for children became commonplace. Kinsey's research revived interest in the science of "sexology."

Born in 1894, in Hoboken, New Jersey, Kinsey was the son of a domineering father, Alfred Seguine Kinsey, and a devoutly religious mother, Sarah Anne (Charles) Kinsey. In 1904, the family, including a younger brother and sister, moved to the more fashionable town of South Orange, New Jersey. **Childhood** illnesses and a misdiagnosis of heart disease kept Kinsey out of sports, but his life-long interests in classical music and field biology developed at an early age. He became an avid outdoorsman, was active in the Boy Scouts, and spent summers as a camp counselor. Although he dreamed of becoming a biologist—his high school yearbook predicted that he would become "the second Darwin"—his father, who had worked his way up from shop boy to shop instructor at the Stevens Institute of Technology in Hoboken, demanded that Kinsey study engineering at Stevens.

## Breaks with father to become an entomologist

Almost overnight, Kinsey went from high school valedictorian to a mediocre student at a technical college. After two years at Stevens, Kinsey announced to his father that he was transferring to Bowdoin College in Brunswick, Maine. Financing his education with his summer earnings and aid from a wealthy South Orange widow, Kinsey became the star biology student at Bowdoin, while maintaining his involvement with the local church and the YMCA. Graduating *magna cum laude* in 1916, Kinsey received a fellowship to Harvard University. He began studying gall wasps at the Bussey Institute under William Morton Wheeler. These tiny insects, that form galls, or growths, on roses and oaks, were the per-

**Alfred Kinsey** *(The Library of Congress. Reproduced by permission.)*

fect subject for Kinsey's unwavering attention to detail and his love of collecting large samples in the wild. While at Harvard, Kinsey found time to write a botanical work, *Edible Wild Plants of Eastern North America*, although the book was not published until 1942. After earning his doctor of science in 1919, a Sheldon Travelling Fellowship enabled Kinsey to tramp across the country for a year, collecting gall wasps.

Settling into the life of a college professor at Indiana University in Bloomington, Kinsey married Clara Brachen McMillen in 1921. She was a chemistry student who shared his love of music and the outdoors. Over the next few years, the couple had four children, although the oldest died of diabetes before the age of four. The publication of Kinsey's texts, *An Introduction to Biology* (1926) and *Field and Laboratory Manual in Biology* (1927), provided the family with financial security. His books on gall wasps, published in the 1930s, established him as both the leading expert on these insects and an important theorist in genetics.

## Studies on human sexuality bring fame and notoriety

Kinsey's interests were starting to turn from wasps to people. Disturbed by the lack of scientific knowledge concerning human sexuality, as well as the profound ignorance of his students concerning sexual matters, in 1938 Kinsey began teaching a course on marriage. The Indiana students, anxious for accurate information, flocked to the course and Kinsey turned them into his initial subjects. First with questionnaires and later with private interviews, Kinsey obtained detailed sexual histories of his students and counseled them on the most intimate matters. Soon, using his own funds to expand his research, Kinsey was interviewing large numbers of subjects in Chicago, analyzing data, and training collaborators. With funding from the National Research Council's Committee on the Research in Problems of Sex and the Rockefeller Foundation, he founded the Institute for Sex Research at Indiana University. In 1984 it was renamed the Kinsey Institute for Research in Sex, Gender, and Reproduction.

With the publication of his best-selling book, *Sexual Behavior in the Human Male* in 1948, Kinsey became an icon of popular culture. In language reminiscent of his high school yearbook, the popular press referred to Kinsey as the successor to Darwin. "The Kinsey Report," as it became known, used straightforward and accurate language to report the findings from thousands of interviews: most males, especially teenagers, masturbated frequently without going insane; premarital and extramarital sex were common; and one-third of all men reported having had at least one homosexual experience. Predictably, Kinsey's book was attacked by religious and conservative groups. With the publication of *Sexual Behavior in the Human Female* in 1953, the outcry increased and the Rockefeller Foundation withdrew their support. Kinsey's studies on women's sexuality included frank and detailed discussions of female sexual response and orgasm and further reports of frequent masturbation and premarital and extramarital sex. Kinsey was accused of undermining the morals of America.

Unable to obtain funding for a new large-scale study of sex offenders, Kinsey traveled to Europe and England in 1955. There he lectured and studied sexual attitudes. Despite increasingly poor health, he completed his 7,935th interview in Chicago in the spring of 1956. Ill with pneumonia and a heart condition, Kinsey fell and bruised himself in his garden. The bruise produced a fatal embolism, and he died in a Bloomington hospital in August, 1956, at the age of 62. Although both **Alfred Kinsey** and "The Kinsey Report" remain controversial, and later researchers have raised serious questions about Kinsey's methodologies, his work had a profound impact on sexual attitudes and beliefs.

Margaret Alic

## Further Reading

Christenson, Cornelia V. *Kinsey: A Biography.* Bloomington: Indiana University Press, 1971.

Epstein, Joseph. "The secret life of Alfred Kinsey." *Commentary* 195 (January 1998): 35-39.

Gathorne-Hardy, Jonathan. *Alfred C. Kinsey: Sex the Measure of all Things.* Bloomington: Indiana University Press, 2000.

Jones, James H. *Alfred C. Kinsey: A Public/Private Life.* New York: W. W. Norton & Co., 1997.

Pomeroy, Wardell Baxter. *Dr. Kinsey and the Institute for Sex Research.* New York: Harper & Row, 1972.

# Kleptomania

One of the impulse control disorders, characterized by an overwhelming impulse to steal.

Persons with this disorder, popularly referred to as kleptomaniacs, experience a recurring urge to steal that they are unable to resist. They do not steal for the value of the item, for its use, or because they cannot afford the purchase. The individual knows that it is wrong to steal. Stolen items are often thrown or given away, secretly returned to the store from which they were taken, or hidden.

Persons with this disorder describe a feeling of tension prior to committing the theft, and a feeling of relief or pleasure while stealing the item.

Kleptomania is a rare disorder. It can begin at any age, and is reported to be more common among females. Kleptomania is different from deliberate theft or shoplifting, which is much more common; it is estimated that less than 5 percent of individuals who shoplift exhibit symptoms of kleptomania. Shoplifting often involves two or more individuals working together; among adolescents, peers sometimes challenge or dare each other to commit an act of shoplifting. Individuals with kleptomania are not influenced by peers, nor are they motivated by a need for the item stolen. This disorder may persist despite arrests for shoplifting; the individual is apparently not deterred by the consequences of stealing, but may feel guilty afterwards.

## Further Reading

Morrison, James. *DSM-IV Made Easy: The Clinician's Guide to Diagnosis.* New York: The Guilford Press, 1995.

# Kurt Koffka

**1886-1941**
German-American experimental psychologist and a founder of the Gestalt movement.

Working with **Max Wertheimer** and **Wolfgang Köhler**, Kurt Koffka helped establish the theories of **Gestalt psychology**. It was Koffka who promoted this new psychology in Europe and introduced it to the United States. He was responsible for systematizing Gestalt psychology into a coherent body of theories. He extended Gestalt theories to **developmental psychology**, and his ideas about **perception**, interpretation, and learning influenced American educational theories and policies.

The son of Emil Koffka, a lawyer and royal councilor of law, and Luise Levi (or Levy), Koffka was born in Berlin, Germany, in 1886. His early education was in the hands of an English-speaking governess, and his mother's brother, a biologist, fostered his early interests in philosophy and science. After attending the Wilhelms Gymnasium and passing his exams, Koffka studied at the University of Berlin with the philosopher Alois Riehl. In 1904-1905, Koffka studied at the University of Edinburgh in Scotland, improving his English and becoming acquainted with British scientists and scholars. Upon returning to Berlin, he changed his studies from philosophy to psychology.

Koffka's first published research, an examination of his own color blindness, was carried out in the physiology laboratory of Wilibald Nagel. Koffka completed his doctoral research at Berlin, on the perception of musical and visual rhythms, under Carl Stumpf, one of the major experimental psychologists of the time.

## Cofounds Gestalt psychology

Koffka moved to the University of Freiburg in 1909, as assistant to the physiologist Johannes von Kries, a professor on the medical faculty. Shortly thereafter, he became an assistant to Oswald Külpe and Karl Marbe at the University of Würzburg, a major center of **experimental psychology**. That same year, Koffka married Mira Klein, who had been an experimental subject for his doctoral research. It was Koffka's next move, in 1910, that was to prove the most fateful for his career. Koffka and Köhler both went to work as assistants to Friedrich Schumann at the Psychological Institute in Frankfurt am Main. They shared a laboratory with Wertheimer, who was studying the perception of motion. Soon, Wertheimer, Koffka, and Köhler were establishing the theoretical and experimental basis of Gestalt psychology. Their new approach rejected the mechanistic psychology of the nineteenth century, which had attempted to reduce experience and perception into smaller components or sensations. Instead, they favored a holistic approach to perception. Wertheimer had studied with the phenomenologist Christian von Ehrenfels, and the three scientists tried to combine this philosophy with experimental methods. Koffka left to take a position as lecturer at the

**Kurt Koffka** *(Archives of the History of American Psychology. Reproduced with permission.)*

University of Giessen in 1911, where he continued his experimental research on visual perception and began new studies on **memory** and thinking. However he maintained his close association with Wertheimer and Köhler.

In 1914, Koffka began studying **hearing** impairments in brain-damaged patients, with Robert Sommer, the director of the Psychiatric Clinic at Giessen. During the First World War, he also worked for the military on localization of sound. Koffka was promoted to a professorship in experimental psychology in 1918, a position that increased his teaching responsibilities but not his salary. In 1921, when he became director of the Psychology Institute at Giessen, he was forced to raise his own funds to set up his new laboratory. Nevertheless, Koffka and his students published numerous experimental studies over the next few years, including 18 publications in the Gestalt journal founded and edited by Wertheimer, Köhler, and Koffka.

## Applies Gestalt principles to child development

Koffka's major work extending Gestalt theory to developmental psychology was published in 1921. He maintained that infants first perceive and respond holistically. Only later are they able to perceive the individual sensations that comprise the whole. Soon, Koffka was being invited to lecture in the United States, where his ideas were well received by psychologists. In 1922, he published his first English-language paper, on Gestalt theories of perception, in *Psychological Bulletin*. Robert Ogden, the editor of the *Bulletin*, translated Koffka's work on developmental psychology, and it was published in 1924 as *The Growth of the Mind: An Introduction to Child Psychology*. Translated into numerous languages, this work had a major influence on theories of learning and development. In 1923, Koffka divorced his wife and married Elisabeth Ahlgrimm, who had just finished her Ph.D. at Giessen. However, they were divorced in the same year and he remarried his first wife.

Gestalt psychology was strongly opposed by the traditional psychologists of German academia, and Koffka, as the public advocate for Gestalt, encountered many obstacles to advancement in Germany. Therefore, he spent 1924-1925 as a visiting professor at Cornell University and 1926-1927 at the University of Wisconsin. In 1927, Koffka was offered a five-year appointment as the William Allan Neilson Research Professor at Smith College in Northampton, Massachusetts. The non-teaching position included an equipped and funded laboratory staffed with assistants. He continued his research on visual perception, and his results were published in the four-volume *Smith College Studies in Psychology* (1930-1933), as well as in the German Gestalt journal that he continued to edit. Koffka remained a professor of psychology at Smith until his death. In 1928, he was divorced again and he remarried his second wife, Ahlgrimm.

Koffka undertook a research expedition to Uzbekistan in 1932, with funding from the Soviet Union. However an attack of relapsing fever, an infection transmitted by lice and ticks, forced him to return home. On the way back, he began writing his classic contribution to psychology, *Principles of Gestalt Psychology*, published in 1935. Drawing on his lifetime of experiments, he extended Gestalt theory to many areas of psychology, including memory and learning. In his later lectures and writings, Koffka applied Gestalt principles to a wide range of political, ethical, social, and artistic subjects. In 1939, as a visiting professor at Oxford, he worked with brain-damaged patients at the Military Hospital for Head Injuries. There, he developed the widely adopted evaluation methods for such patients. Although heart disease began to restrict his activities, Koffka continued teaching at Smith until a few days before his death in 1941 from coronary thrombosis.

*See also* Gestalt principles of organization

Margaret Alic

## Further Reading

Garraty, John A. and Mark C. Carnes. "Koffka, Kurt." In *American National Biography,* edited by John A. Garraty and Mark C. Carnes, vol. 12, pp. 861-63. New York: Oxford University Press, 1999.

Henle, Mary. "Koffka, Kurt." In *Thinkers of the Twentieth Century: A Biographical, Bibliographical and Critical Dictionary,* edited by Elizabeth Devine, Michael Held, James Vinson, and George Walsh, pp. 298. Detroit: Gale Research, 1983.

Wesley, Frank. "Koffka, Kurt." In *Biographical Dictionary of Psychology,* edited by Noel Sheehy, Antony J. Chapman, and Wendy A. Conroy, pp. 329-30. London: Routledge, 1997.

# Lawrence Kohlberg

### 1927-1987
American psychologist whose work centered in the area of the development of moral reasoning.

Lawrence Kohlberg was born in Bronxville, New York, and received his B.A. (1948) and Ph.D. (1958) from the University of Chicago. He served as an assistant professor at Yale University from 1959 to 1961 and was a fellow of the Center of Advanced Study of Behavioral Science in 1962. Kohlberg began teaching at the University of Chicago in 1963, where he remained until his 1967 appointment to the faculty of Harvard University, where he has served as professor of education and **social psychology**. Kohlberg is best known for his work in the development of moral reasoning in children and adolescents. Seeking to expand on Jean Piaget's work in **cognitive development** and to determine whether there are universal stages in **moral development** as well, Kohlberg conducted a long-term study in which he recorded the responses of boys aged seven through **adolescence** to hypothetical dilemmas requiring a moral choice. (The most famous sample question is whether the husband of a critically ill woman is justified in stealing a drug that could save her life if the pharmacist is charging much more than he can afford to pay.) Based on the results of his study, Kohlberg concluded that children and adults progress through six stages in the development of moral reasoning. He also concluded that moral development is directly related to cognitive development, with older children able to base their responses on increasingly broad and abstract ethical standards.

In evaluating his research, Kohlberg was primarily interested not in the children's responses themselves, but in the reasoning behind them. Based on their thought processes, he discerned a gradual evolution from self-interest to principled behavior and developed a chronological scheme of moral development consisting of three levels, each made up of two separate stages. Each stage involves increasingly complex thought patterns, and as children arrive at a given stage they tend to consider the bases for previous judgments as invalid. Children from the ages of seven through ten act on the *preconventional* level, at which they defer to adults and obey rules based on the immediate consequences of their actions. The behavior of children at this level is essentially premoral. At Stage 1, they obey rules in order to avoid **punishment**, while at Stage 2 their behavior is mostly motivated by the desire to obtain rewards. Starting at around age ten, children enter the *conventional* level, where their behavior is guided by the opinions of other people and the desire to conform. At Stage 3, the emphasis is on being a "good boy" or "good girl" in order to win approval and avoid disapproval, while at Stage 4 the concept of doing one's duty and upholding the social order becomes predominant. At this stage, respecting and obeying authority (of parents, teachers, God) is an end in itself, without reference to higher principles. By the age of 13, most moral questions are resolved on the conventional level.

During adolescence, children move beyond this level and become capable of *postconventional* morality, which requires the ability to formulate abstract moral principles, which are then obeyed to avoid self-condemnation rather than the censure of others. At Stage 5, adolescents are guided by a "social contract" orientation toward the welfare of the community, the rights of others, and existing laws. At Stage 6, their actions are guided by ethical standards that transcend the actual laws of their society and are based on such abstract concepts as freedom, dignity, and justice. However, Kohlberg's scheme does not imply that all adolescents negotiate the passage to postconventional morality. Progress through the different stages depends upon the type of thinking that a child or adolescent is capable of at a given point, and also on the negotiation of previous stages. Kohlberg points out that many people never pass beyond the conventional level, and that the most clearly principled response at Stage 6 was expressed by fewer than 10 percent of adolescents over the age of 16. (In relation to the dilemma of the stolen drug, such a response would clearly articulate the existence of a moral law that transcends society's laws about stealing, and the sanctity of human life over financial gain.)

Kohlberg's system is closely related to Piaget's theories, both in its emphasis on cognitive development and in its designation of a chronological series of stages, each dependent on the preceding ones. It also has important implications for the **nature-nurture controversy**, as it stresses the role of innate rather than environmental factors in moral development. According to

Kohlberg, progress from one level or stage to the next involves an internal cognitive reorganization that is more complex than a mere acquisition of precepts from peers, parents, and other authorities. Kohlberg's most famous book is *The Philosophy of Moral Development: Moral Stages and the Idea of Justice,* the first volume in a series entitled *Essays on Moral Development.* The second volume, *The Psychology of Moral Development,* was published in 1984.

*See also* Cognitive development

**Further Reading**
Alper, Joseph. "The Roots of Morality," *Science 85,* (March 1985): 70.
Kohlberg, Lawrence. *Child Psychology and Childhood Education: A Cognitive-Developmental View.* New York: Longman, 1987.
Power, F. Clark. *Lawrence Kohlberg's Approach to Moral Education.* New York: Columbia University Press, 1989.

# Kohs block test

Intelligence test.

The Kohs block test, or Kohs block design test, is a cognitive test for children or adults with a **mental age** between 3 and 19. It is mainly used to test persons with language or **hearing** handicaps but also given to disadvantaged and non-English-speaking children. The child is shown 17 cards with a variety of colored designs and asked to reproduce them using a set of colored blocks. Performance is based not just on the accuracy of the drawings but also on the examiner's observation of the child's behavior during the test, including such factors as **attention** level, self-criticism, and adaptive behavior (such as self-help, communication, and social skills). The Kohs block test is sometimes included in other tests, such as the Merrill-Palmer and Arthur Performance scales.

**Further Reading**
McCullough, Virginia. *Testing and Your Child: What You Should Know About 150 of the Most Common Medical, Educational, and Psychological Tests.* New York: Plume, 1992.
Walsh, W. Bruce, and Nancy E. Betz. *Tests and Assessment.* 2nd ed. Englewood Cliffs, NJ: Prentice Hall, 1990.

# Wolfgang Köhler

**1887-1967**
German psychologist and principal figure in the development of Gestalt psychology.

Wolfgang Köhler was born in Revel, Estonia, and grew up in Wolfenbüttel, Germany. He studied at the universities of Bonn and Tübingen, and at the Friedrich Wilhelm University of Berlin, where he received his Ph.D. in 1909, writing a dissertation on psychoacoustics under the direction of Carl Stumpf (1848-1936). In 1910, Köhler began a long professional association with **Max Wertheimer** (1880-1943) when he and **Kurt Koffka** (1886-1941), both assistants to Friedrich Schumann at the University of Frankfurt, served as research subjects for an experiment of Wertheimer's involving **perception** of moving pictures. Within the next ten years, the three men were to found the Gestalt movement in psychology. In reaction to the prevailing behavioristic methods of **Wilhelm Wundt** (1832-1920) and others, the Gestalt psychologists held that behavior must be studied in all its complexity rather than separated into discrete components. Köhler's early work convinced him that perception, learning, and other cognitive functions should be seen as structured wholes.

Unlike Koffka and Wertheimer, Köhler concentrated on animal research. Beginning in 1913, he spent more than six years as director of the anthropoid research facility of the Prussian Academy of Sciences on the island of Tenerife, where he made many discoveries applying Gestalt theories to animal learning and perception. His observations and conclusions from this period contributed to a radical revision of **learning theory**. One of his most famous experiments centered on chickens which he trained to peck grains from either the lighter or darker of two sheets of paper. When the chickens who had been trained to prefer the light color were presented with a choice between that color and a new sheet that was still lighter, a majority switched to the new sheet. Similarly, chickens trained to prefer the darker color, when presented with a parallel choice, chose a new, darker color. These results, Köhler maintained, showed that what the chickens had learned was an association with a *relationship*, rather than with a specific color. This finding, which flew in the face of behaviorist theories deemphasizing the importance of relationships, became known as the Gestalt *law of transposition*, because the test subjects had transposed their original experience to a new set of circumstances.

Köhler also conducted a series of experiments in which chimpanzees were confronted with the problem of obtaining bananas that were hung just out of reach by using "tools"—bamboo poles and stacked boxes. The chimpanzees varied in their **ability** to arrive at the correct combination of actions needed to solve the problem. Often, a test subject would suddenly find a solution at a seemingly random point. This research led Köhler to the concept of learning by a sudden leap of the **imagination,**

**Wolfgang Köhler** *(Archives of the History of American Psychology. Reproduced with permission.)*

or "insight," in which a relationship that had not been seen before was suddenly perceived, a formulation in conflict with the trial-and-error theory of learning resulting from Edward Thorndike's puzzle box experiments. Based on this work, Köhler published *The Mentality of Apes* in 1917, demonstrating that Gestalt theory could be applied to animal behavior.

Köhler returned to Germany after World War I, and in 1921 was appointed to the most prestigious position in German psychology, director of the Psychological Institute at the University of Berlin. For the next 14 years he made the Institute a center for Gestalt studies and was a noted spokesman for the movement. In 1935, however, Köhler resigned due to conflicts with the Nazis, and emigrated to the United States, where he served on the faculties of Swarthmore and Dartmouth Colleges. In 1959, he was appointed president of the American Psychological Association. There has been some speculation that he was a spy during World War I, a thesis explored by his biographer, Ronald Ley. Köhler's books include *Gestalt Psychology* (1929), *The Place of Value in a World of Facts* (1938), and *Dynamics in Psychology* (1940).

*See also* Behaviorism; Cognitive development; Gestalt psychology

**Further Reading**
Ley, Ronald. *A Whisper of Espionage.* Garden City Park, NY: Avery Publishing Group, 1990.
Petermann, Bruno. *The Gestalt Theory and the Problem of Configuration.* London: K. Paul, 1932.

# Emil Kraepelin

**1856-1926**
German experimental psychiatrist who classified types of **mental illness** and studied their neurological bases.

Emil Kraepelin was a pioneer in the development of psychiatry as a scientific discipline. He was convinced that all mental illness had an organic cause, and he was one of the first scientists to emphasize **brain** pathology in mental illness. A renowned clinical and experimental psychiatrist, Kraepelin developed our modern classification system for mental disease. After analyzing thousands of case studies, he introduced and defined the terms "dementia praecox" (**schizophrenia**), "manic-depressive psychosis," and "paranoia." As a founder of psychopharmacology, Kraepelin's experimental work focused on the effects of intoxicants on the **central nervous system**, on the nature of **sleep**, and on the effects of fatigue on the body.

Kraepelin, the son of a civil servant, was born in 1856 in Neustrelitz, in the Mecklenburg district of Germany. He was first introduced to biology by his brother Karl, 10 years older and, later, the director of the Zoological Museum of Hamburg. Kraepelin began his medical studies at 18, in Leipzig and Wurzburg, Germany. At Leipzig, he studied psychology with **Wilhelm Wundt** and wrote a prize-winning essay, "The Influence of Acute Illness in the Causation of Mental Disorders." He received his M.D. in 1878.

## Publishes first edition of his psychiatry compendium

In 1879, Kraepelin went to work with Bernhard von Gudden at the University of Munich, where he completed his thesis, *The Place of Psychology in Psychiatry.* Returning to the University of Leipzig in 1882, he worked in W. Erb's neurology clinic and in Wundt's psychopharmacology laboratory. His major work, *Compendium der Psychiatrie,* was first published in 1883. In it, he argued that psychiatry was a branch of medical science and should be investigated by observation and experimentation like the other natural sciences. He called for research into the physical causes of mental illness and es-

tablished the foundations of the modern classification system for mental disorders. Kraepelin proposed that by studying case histories and identifying specific disorders, the progression of mental illness could be predicted, after taking into account individual differences in **personality** and patient age at the onset of disease. In 1884 he became senior physician in Leubus and the following year he was appointed director of the Treatment and Nursing Institute in Dresden. In 1886, at the age of 30, Kraepelin was named professor of psychiatry at the University of Dorpat. Four years later, he became department head at the University of Heidelberg, where he remained until 1904.

Following the experimental protocols he had learned in Wundt's laboratory, Kraepelin examined the effects of alcohol, morphine, and other drugs on human subjects. Applying Wundt's association experiments to psychiatric problems, Kraepelin found that the associations made by psychotic patients were similar to those made by fatigued or intoxicated subjects. In both cases, the associations tended to be superficial and based on habit rather than on meaningful relationships. Kraepelin also made a study of primitive peoples, and he examined the frequency of insanity and paralysis in tropical regions. His research on mental illness led him to speak out for social reforms. He crusaded against the use of alcohol and against capital **punishment**, and he spoke out for indeterminate criminal sentences. He developed a museum depicting the barbarous treatment that was prevalent in asylums for the insane.

## Studies pathologies of mental disorders

In 1904, Kraepelin was named director of the new psychiatric clinic in Munich and professor of psychiatry at the university there. Under his direction, the Munich Clinic became a renowned center for teaching and research in psychiatry. The training of his postgraduate students combined clinical observations with laboratory investigations. Kraepelin rejected the psychoanalytical theories that placed innate **sexuality** or early sexual experiences at the root of mental illness. Likewise, he rejected as unscientific the philosophical speculations that were at the center of much of early twentieth-century psychology. Kraepelin's research was based on the painstaking collection of clinical data. He was particularly interested in the neuropathology of mental illness, and many important scientists, including Alois Alzheimer, conducted their histological studies of diseased tissues at his clinic.

When Italy declared war on Germany in 1916, Kraepelin's vacation home on the shores of Lake Maggiore was confiscated, although following the armistice his property was returned. However, during the economic crisis in postwar Germany, he lost four of his children as well as his personal property. Kraepelin wrote poetry throughout his life, and his poems were published posthumously.

Kraepelin retired from teaching at the age of 66 and devoted his remaining years to establishing the German Institute for Psychiatric Research, which became a Kaiser Wilhelm Institute within the University of Munich. Built with financial assistance from the Rockefeller Foundation, the Institute was dedicated two years after Kraepelin's death in Munich in 1926. The final edition of *Compendium der Psychiatrie* appeared in 1927. Its four volumes held 10 times more information than the first edition of 1883. Comparisons of the nine editions reveal phenomenal progress in the science of psychiatry over the 44-year period. Part of the *Compendium* was published in English as *Manic-Depressive Insanity and Paranoia*. Considerable amount of Kraepelin's classification system remains in use today.

Margaret Alic

## Further Reading

Talbott, John H. *A Biographical History of Medicine: Excerpts and Essays on the Men and Their Work*. New York: Grune & Stratton, 1970.

Zusne, Leonard. *Biographical Dictionary of Psychology*. Westport, CT: Greenwood Press, 1984.

# Christine Ladd-Franklin

**1847-1930**

American psychologist, logician, and an internationally recognized authority on the theory of color vision.

Born in Windsor, Connecticut, Christine Ladd-Franklin spent her early childhood in New York City. Her father was a prominent merchant and her mother was a feminist. Following her mother's death when Ladd-Franklin was 13, she moved to Portsmouth, New Hampshire, to live with her paternal grandmother. Ladd-Franklin attended the Wesleyan Academy in Wilbraham, Massachusetts for two years, taking classes with boys preparing to enter Harvard University, and was the valedictorian of her graduating class in 1865. After graduating from Vassar College in 1869 with a primary interest in mathematics and science, she taught in secondary schools in Pennsylvania, New York, and Massachusetts for more than a decade and also published numerous articles on mathematics during this period. In 1878, she applied for admission to Johns Hopkins University for advanced study in mathematics. Because of her extraordinary intellectual **ability**, Ladd-Franklin was awarded the stipend of a fellow, although not the actual title because women were not permitted to pursue graduate study at the time. Despite completing requirements for the doctorate in 1882, she was denied the degree until 1926.

At the completion of her fellowship in 1882, Ladd-Franklin married Fabian Franklin, a mathematics professor at Johns Hopkins University, and gave birth to two children, one of whom died in infancy. Atypical for married women of the time, and without a formal academic affiliation, she continued to publish scholarly papers, several of which appeared in the *American Journal of Mathematics*. After hearing Charles S. Peirce (1839-1914) lecture at Johns Hopkins, Ladd-Franklin became interested in symbolic logic and wrote a paper, "The Algebra of Logic," that was published in 1883 in a book of

**Christine Ladd-Franklin** *(Archives of the History of American Psychology. Reproduced with permission.)*

essays by Peirce and his students. In her paper, praised as a landmark achievement by Harvard philosopher Josiah Royce (1815-1916), Ladd-Franklin reduced all syllogisms to a single formula, in which the three parts form an "inconsistent triad."

Ladd-Franklin's mathematical interests ultimately led her to make important contributions to the field of psychology. In 1886, she became interested in the geometrical relationship between binocular **vision** and points in space and published a paper on this topic in the first volume of the *American Journal of Psychology* the following year. During the 1891-92 academic year, Ladd-Franklin took advantage of her husband's sabbatical leave from Johns Hopkins and traveled to Europe to conduct research in **color vision** in the laboratories of Georg Müller (1850-1934) in Göttingen, and **Hermann von Helmholtz** (1821-1894) in Berlin, where she also attended lectures by Arthur König. In contrast to the prevailing three-color and opponent-color explanations of color vision, Ladd-Franklin developed an evolutionary theory that posited three stages in the development of color vision. Presenting her work at the International Congress of Psychology in London in 1892, she argued that black-white vision was the most primitive stage, since it occurs under the greatest variety of conditions, including under very low illumination and at the extreme edges of the visual field. The color white, she theorized, later became differentiated into blue and yellow, with yellow ultimately differentiated into red-green vision. Ladd-Franklin's theory was well-received and remained influential for some years, and its emphasis on evolution is still valid today.

After returning to the United States, Ladd-Franklin taught, lectured, and pursued research. She continued publishing and presented papers at meetings of both the American Philosophical Association and the American Psychological Association, as well as at international congresses. She lectured in philosophy and logic at Johns Hopkins between 1904 and 1909, and served as an associate editor in those fields for Baldwin's *Dictionary of Philosophy and Psychology.* Moving to New York City with her husband in 1910 when he became an associate editor of the *New York Evening Post,* Ladd-Franklin began lecturing at Columbia University. She published an influential paper on the visual phenomenon known as "blue arcs" in 1926, when she was in her late seventies, and in 1929, a year before her death, a collection of her papers on vision was published under the title *Colour and Colour Theories.* In her writings and active correspondence with colleagues, Ladd-Franklin challenged the mores of the day, championing the cause of women in matters of equal rights, access to education and the professions, and the right to vote.

**Further Reading**

Scarborough, Elizabeth, and Laurel Furumoto. *Untold Lives: The First Generation of American Women Psychologists.* New York: Columbia University Press, 1987, pp. 109-129.

# Ronald David Laing

**1927-1989**

Scottish existential psychiatrist who argued that insanity could be a creative and adaptive response to the world.

Ronald David Laing, or R.D., as he was invariably known, developed the theory that **mental illness** was an escape mechanism that allowed individuals to free themselves from intolerable circumstances. As a revolutionary thinker, he questioned the controls that were imposed on the individual by **family**, state, and society. Rejecting a physiological basis for diseases such as **schizophrenia**, Laing argued that madness was a response to insanity in the **environment**. A very prolific writer, during the 1960s and 1970s Laing became a hero of the counterculture and the "New Left."

Born in Glasgow, Scotland, in 1927, Laing was the only child of a working-class Lowland couple, D. P. M. and Amelia Laing. A precocious boy, he was physically abused by his father and he rebelled against his mother's fascist anti-Semitic outlook. Musically talented, Laing might have become a professional pianist had his father allowed it. Instead, he read his way alphabetically through his local public library. Interested in the human mind since **childhood**, after grammar school Laing entered Glasgow University to study medicine and psychiatry.

After earning his M.D. degree in 1951 and serving a six-month internship in neurology and neurosurgery, Laing was drafted into the British army as a psychiatrist. There he made friends among his patients rather than among his fellow servicemen. It was during this period that he began to view **psychosis** as a potentially positive and justifiable state. After his two years of service, Laing began working at the Gartnaval Royal Mental Hospital and teaching in the Department of Psychological Medicine at Glasgow University. There he began working on his first book, *The Divided Self: A Study of Sanity and Madness,* completed in 1957 but not published until 1960. In 1956, he moved to the Tavistock Clinic and the Tavistock Institute of Human Relations in London, to study Freudian **psychoanalysis** and continue his clinical research.

## Develops a radical view of schizophrenia

Laing's view of schizophrenia as an alternative way of perceiving the world created a storm of controversy. Traditional psychotherapists objected to his existentialism; but for many readers, *The Divided Self* expressed their own **alienation** from modern society. In *The Self and Others: Further Studies in Sanity and Madness* (1961), which he revised in 1969 as *Self and Others,* and in *Sanity, Madness, and the Family: Families of Schizophrenics* with Aaron Esterson (1964), Laing continued his examination of the origins of schizophrenia. In *Interpersonal Perception* (1966), with Herbert Phillipson and A. Russell Lee, Laing described his theories and research methodologies. With David G. Cooper, he coauthored a study of the untranslated work of the existential-

used on schizophrenics. In 1967, while continuing his private psychoanalytical practice, Laing founded the Institute of Phenomenological Studies in London.

In *The Politics of the Family* (1969), Laing began to apply the theory of sets and mapping used in other social sciences to the social and psychological structure of families. The work was revised in 1971. In *Knots* (1970), a book of poetry, he examined interpersonal relationships and communication. Following a year of meditation studies with Hindu and Buddhist masters in Ceylon and India, Laing undertook a lecture tour of U. S. colleges, raising funds for the Philadelphia Association.

Laing practiced various forms of yoga and was a vegetarian who preferred to go barefoot. He published *The Facts of Life: An Essay in Feelings, Facts, and Fantasy* in 1976. Laing had five children with his first wife who remained in Glasgow, and two children with his second wife, Jutta, in London. *Conversations with Children*, published in 1978, was a transcription of conversations between his two youngest children. He published *The Voice of Experience* in 1982, followed by his autobiography in 1985.

In all, Laing was the author of fifteen books, including several works of poetry. He was a fellow of the Royal Society of Medicine and was on the editorial boards of the journals *Review of Existential Psychology and Psychiatry* and *Existential Psychiatry*. Laing died of a heart attack in St. Tropez, France, in 1989.

*See also* Existential psychology

Margaret Alic

**R.D. Laing** *(Photo by Jerry Bauer. Reproduced with permission.)*

ist Jean-Paul Sartre, *Reason and Violence: A Decade of Sartre's Philosophy, 1950-1960* (1964).

## Founds communities for patients and therapists

At the Langham Clinic for **Psychotherapy** in London, Laing practiced Jungian psychoanalysis from 1962 until 1965, when his use of psychedelic drugs, both personally and as treatments for his patients, caused controversy. "The Bird of Paradise," an extended prose poem included in his 1967 work, *The Politics of Experience*, was his description of a hallucinogenic experience. The book became a bestseller on college campuses. In 1965, he co-founded an egalitarian community of patients and physicians at Kingsley Hall in London's East End. Although the clinic was closed after five years, amidst rumors of outrageous behavior, offshoots continued to flourish in the London area. Laing's dream was that these communities could provide a safe haven for individuals to experience their madness and heal themselves. To this end, he founded the Philadelphia Association to support such communities. At the least, he believed that his methods were superior to the chemical and electrical shock treatments and lobotomies, which were commonly

### Further Reading

Burston, Daniel. *The Wing of Madness: The Life and Work of R. D. Laing.* Cambridge, MA: Harvard University Press, 1996.

Cohen, David. *Psychologists on Psychology.* New York: Taplinger, 1977.

Collier, Andrew. *R. D. Laing: The Philosophy and Politics of Psychotherapy.* New York: Pantheon, 1977.

Evans, Richard I. *R. D. Laing: The Man and His Ideas.* New York: E. P. Dutton, 1976.

Laing, Adrian C. *R. D. Laing: A Biography.* Chester Springs, PA: P. Owen, 1994.

Laing, R. D. *Wisdom, Madness, and Folly: The Making of a Psychiatrist.* New York: McGraw-Hill, 1985.

# Language delay

Term used to describe a problem in acquiring a first language in childhood on a normal schedule.

The milestones of child **language development**—the onset of babbling, first words, first sentences—are quite variable across individuals in a culture, despite the universal similarity in the general ages of their development. In one study of 32 normally developing children at 13 months, the average number of words reported by parents was 12, but the range was 0 to 45. The two-word-sentence stage was reached anywhere from 16 to 28 months in the same sample. In addition, differing styles of language development are now recognized.

Some children fit the classic pattern of first speaking one word "sentences," such as "truck," then joining two words "truck fall," and then three, "my truck fall." But other children speak in long unintelligible babbles that mimic adult speech cadence and rhythm, so the listeners think they are just missing some important pronouncement. The first is called a *referential* style, because it also correlates with attention to names for objects and event descriptions. The second, with less clearly demarked sentence parts, is called *expressive* style. Such a child is quite imitative, has a good rote **memory**, and often is engaged in language for social purposes—songs, routines, greetings, and so forth. The expressive child seems to be slightly slower at cracking the linguistic code than the referential child, but the long term differences between the two styles seem insignificant. Given this range of individual pace and style, how can one tell if a child is really delayed in language development, and what are some of the causes?

## Monolingual vs. bilingual

A child growing up with two or more languages is often slower to talk than a monolingual child. This is not surprising given the amount of analysis and code-cracking necessary to organize two systems simultaneously, but the life-long advantage of knowing two native languages is usually considered an appropriate balance to the cost of a potential delay. Bilingualism in children and adults is the **norm** throughout the world: monolinguals are the exception. The learning of each language proceeds in the bilingual child in much the same way as it does in the monolingual child. Some mixing may be observed, in which the child uses words or inflections from the two languages in one utterance. Some report that the bilingual child initially resists learning words for the same thing in the two languages: for instance, a child who learned Spanish and English together learned *leche* but then would not say *milk*, a French/English bilingual used *bird* but refused to use *oiseau*.

## Language delay and hearing loss

Children with a **hearing** loss, either from **birth** or acquired during the first year or two of life, generally have a serious delay in spoken language development, despite very early diagnosis and fitting with appropriate hearing aids. However, in the unusual case that sign language is the medium of communication in the **family** rather than speech, such a child shows no delay in learning to use that language. Hearing development is always one of the first things checked if a pediatrician or parent suspects a language delay. The deaf child exposed only to speech will usually begin to babble in "canonical syllables" (baba, gaga) at a slightly later point than the hearing child, and recent work suggests that the babbling is neither as varied nor as sustained as in hearing children. However, there is often a long delay until the first words, sometimes not until age two years or older.

Depending on the severity of the hearing loss, the stages of early language development are also quite delayed. It is not unusual for the profoundly deaf child (greater than 90 decibel loss in both ears) at age four or five years to only have two-word spoken sentences. It is only on entering specialized training programs for oral language development that the profoundly deaf child begins to acquire more spoken language, so that the usual preschool language gains are often made in the grade school years for such children. Many deaf children learning English have pronounced difficulties in articulation and speech quality, especially if they are profoundly deaf, though there is great individual variation. A child who has hearing for the first few years of life has an enormous advantage in speech quality and oral language learning than a child who is deaf from birth or within the first year.

Apart from speech difficulties, deaf children learning English often show considerable difficulty with the inflectional morphology and syntax of the language that marks their writing as well as their speech. The ramifications of this delayed language are significant also for learning to read, and to read proficiently. The average reading age of deaf high school students is often only at the fourth grade level.

For these reasons, many educators of the deaf now urge early compensatory programs in signed languages, because the deaf child shows no handicap in learning a visually based language. Deaf children born to signing parents begin to "babble" in sign at the same point in **infancy** that hearing infants babble speech, and proceed from there to learn a fully expressive language. However, only 10% of deaf children are born to deaf parents, so hearing parents must show a commitment and willingness to learn sign language, too. Furthermore, command of at least written English is still a necessity for such children to be able to function in the larger community.

## Language delay and mental retardation

**Mental retardation** can also affect the age at which children learn to talk. A mentally retarded child is defined as one who falls in the lower end of the range of **intelligence**, usually with an IQ (**intelligence quotient**) lower than 80 on some **standardized test**. There are many causes of mental retardation, including identified genetic syndromes such as **Down syndrome**, Williams syndrome, or fragile X syndrome. There are also cases of retardation caused by insults to the fetus during pregnancy due to alcohol, drug abuse, or toxicity, and disorders of the developing **nervous system** such as hydrocephalus. Finally, there are environmental causes following birth such as lead poisoning, anoxia, or meningitis. Any of these is likely to slow down the child's rate of development in general, and thus to have effects on language development. However, most children with very low IQs nevertheless develop some language, suggesting it is a relatively "buffered" system that can survive a good deal of insult to the developing **brain**.

For example, in cases of hydrocephalus it has been noted that children who are otherwise quite impaired intellectually can have impressive conversational language skills. Sometimes called the "chatterbox syndrome," this linguistic sophistication belies their poor **ability** to deal with the world. In an extreme case, a young man with a tested IQ in the retarded range has an apparent gift for acquiring foreign languages, and can learn a new one with very little exposure. For example, he can do fair translations at a rapid pace from written langages as diverse as Danish, Dutch, Hindi, Polish, French, Spanish, and Greek. He is in fact a savant in the area of language, and delights in comparing linguistic systems, though he cannot live independently.

Adults should not consider retarded children to be a uniform class; different patterns can arise with different syndromes. For example in hydrocephalic children and in Williams syndrome, language skills may be preserved to a degree that is discrepant from their general intellectual level. In other groups, including Down syndrome, there may be more delay in language than in other mental abilities.

Most retarded children babble during the first year and develop their first words within a **normal** time span, but are then slow to develop sentences or a varied vocabulary. Vocabulary size is one of the primary components of standardized tests of verbal intelligence, and it grows slowly in retarded children. Nevertheless, the process of vocabulary development seems quite similar: retarded children also learn words from context and by incidental learning, not just by direct instruction.

Grammatical development, though slow, does not seem particularly deviant, in that the morphology comes in the same way, and in the same order, as it does for normal IQ children. The child's conversation may be marked by more repetition and routines than creative uses, however. By the early teens, the difference in the variety of forms used in a sample of conversation may be more striking in some groups. There may be important differences among types of retarded children in their grammatical proficiency. As of the 1990s, these differences are just beginning to be uncovered. The Down syndrome adolescent with an IQ of around 50 points does not seem to progress beyond the grammatical level of the normally intelligent child at three years, with short sentences that are quite restricted in variety and complexity. Children with Down syndrome are also particularly delayed in speech development. This is due in part to the facial abnormalities that characterize this syndrome, including a relatively large tongue, and also is linked to the higher risk they appear to suffer from ear infections and hearing loss. Speech therapy can be a considerable aid in making such a child's speech more intelligible. Despite the delay, children with Down syndrome are often quite sociable and interested in language for conversation.

## Language delay and blindness

Children who are blind from birth sometimes have other neurological problems, which makes it difficult to assess the effect of blindness itself on cognitive and linguistic development. However, in the cases where blindness seems to be the only condition affecting the child, some initial language delays are noted. On average, blind children seem to be delayed about eight months in the onset of words. In general, though, detailed longitudinal studies have revealed that the blind child learns language in much the same way as the sighted child, with perhaps more reliance on routines and formulas in conversation. Linguists are interested in the process by which blind children learn to use words such as see and look given their lack of experience with sight, but these words were found to come in quite normally, with the appropriately changed meaning of "touch" and "explore tactilely."

Jill De Villiers Ph.D.

### Further Reading
Landau, B., and L. Gleitman. *Language and Experience: Evidence from the Blind Child.* Cambridge, Mass: Harvard University Press, 1985.
Nelson, K. "Individual Differences in Language Development: Implications for Development and Language." *Developmental Psychology* 17, 1981, pp. 170-87.

# Language development

The process by which children acquire their first language in early childhood.

Human infants are acutely attuned to the human voice, and prefer it above all other sounds. In fact, they prefer the higher pitch ranges characteristic of female voices. They are also attentive to the human face, particularly the eyes, which they stare at even more if the face is talking. These preferences are present at **birth**, and some research indicates that babies even listen to their mother's voice during the last few months of pregnancy. Babies who were read to by their mothers while in the womb showed the **ability** to pick out her voice from among other female voices.

## Infancy

Since the early 1970s, it has been known that babies can detect very subtle differences between English *phonemes* (the functional units of speech sound). For example, they can detect the difference between "pa" and "ba," or between "da" and "ga." Of course, they do not attach meaning to the differences for 12 months or more. The original technique of investigating this capacity capitalized on babies' innate ability to suck on a nipple. The nipple is linked to a device that delivers sound contingent on the baby's sucking. Babies introduced to this device suck vigorously to hear the sound, even when it is a repetitive "ba ba ba ba." Because babies also get bored with repetition, they stop sucking hard after a few minutes. At that point the researcher can change the sound in subtle ways, and see if the baby shows renewed interest. For example, it might be a different example of "ba," perhaps one with a bit more breathiness. Or, it could **play** a sound that would fall into a new phoneme class for adults, like "pa." Babies ignore the first kind of change, just as adults would, but they suck with new vigor for the new phoneme.

Babies have finely tuned **perception** when it comes to speech sounds, and, more importantly, they seem to classify many sounds the same way adult speakers would, a phenomenon known as *categorical perception* . These sounds that they perceive as indivisible categories are generally those that form the basis for many speech systems in the world's languages, rather than those that are used only rarely, like "th." Infants come into the world already predisposed to make certain distinctions and classifications: apparently they are not driven to make them by language exposure.

### Babbling

At the beginning of **infancy**, vegetative noises and crying predominate. Observers note that by the age of four months, the baby's repertoire has expanded in more interesting ways. By this point babies are smiling at caregivers and in doing so they engage in a cooing noise that is irresistible to most parents. When the baby is being fed or changed, she will frequently lock gazes with her caregiver and coo in a pleasant way, often making noises that sound like "hi," and gurgles. It is common for the caregiver to respond by echoing these noises, thereby creating an elaborate interchange that can last many minutes. This may not happen universally, however, as not all cultures take the baby's vocalization so seriously. The nature of the sounds made at this stage is not fully speech-like, though there are open mouth noises like vowels, and an occasional "closure" akin to a consonant, but without the full properties that normally make a syllable out of the two.

At some point between four and 10 months, the infant begins producing more speech-like syllables, with a full resonant vowel and an appropriate "closure" of the stream of sound, approaching a true consonant. This stage is called "canonical babbling."

At about six to eight months, the range of vocalizations grows dramatically, and babies can spend hours practicing the sounds they can make with their mouths. Not all of these are human phonemes, and not all of them are found in the language around them. Research has shown that Japanese and American infants sound alike at this stage, and even congenitally deaf infants babble, though less frequently. These facts suggest that the infant is "exercising" her speech organs, but is not being guided very much, if at all, by what she has heard.

By age 10 or 12 months, however, the range of sounds being produced has somewhat narrowed, and now babies' babbling in different cultures begin to take on sound characteristics of the language that surrounds them. The babbling at this stage often consists of reduplicated syllables like "bababa" or "dadada" or "mamama." It is no accident that most of the world's languages have chosen, as names for parents, some variant of "papa," "mama," "dada," "nana." These coincide with articulations that baby can make most easily at the end of the first year.

## Toddlerhood

The first words make their appearance any time between nine and 15 months or so, depending on the child's precocity and the parent's enthusiasm in noticing. That is, the baby begins making sounds that occur fairly

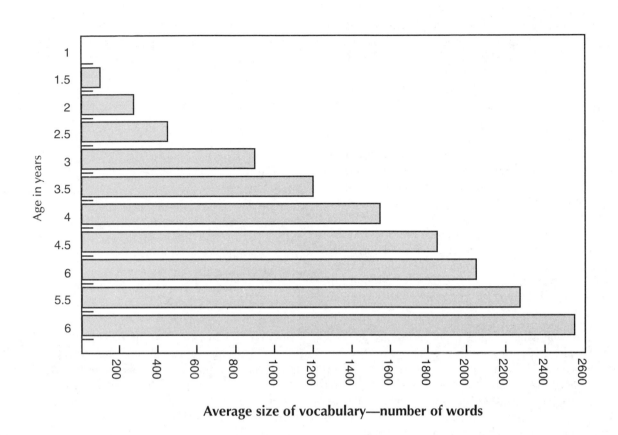

Age in years

1
1.5
2
2.5
3
3.5
4
4.5
6
5.5
6

200  400  600  800  1000  1200  1400  1600  1800  2000  2200  2400  2600

**Average size of vocabulary—number of words**

**Average vocabulary growth of children from ages 1 to 7.**

reliably in some situations AND are at least a vague approximation to an adult-sounding word.

What the baby "means" by these sounds is questionable at first. But before long, the baby uses the sounds to draw a caregiver's attention, and persists until she gets it, or uses a sound to demand an object, and persists until it is given to her. At this point the first words are being used communicatively as well. There is a fairly protracted period for most babies in which their first words come and go, as if there is a "word of the week" that replaces those gone before. One of the characteristics about these first words is that they may be situation-specific, such as the case of a child who says "car" only when looking down on the roofs of cars from her balcony. But after several months of slow growth, there is an explosion of new words, often called the "word spurt." This usually coincides with an interest in what things are called, e.g., the child asking some variant of "What's that?" Vocabulary climbs precipitously from then on—an estimated nine new words a day from ages 2 to 18 years. These developments are noted in all the cultures that have been studied to date.

The nature of the child's first 50 words is quite similar across cultures: the child often names foods, pets, animals, family members, toys, vehicles and clothing that

the child can manipulate. Most of what is named can either move or be moved by the child: she generally omits words for furniture, geographical features, buildings, weather and so forth. Children vary in that some develop an early vocabulary almost exclusively of "thing" words and actions, whereas others develop a social language: words for social routines, and expressions of love, and greetings. Researchers differ as to whether these are seen as different styles inherent in the child or whether their social **environment** encourages them in different ways. Researchers agree that the child learns most effectively from social and interactive routines with an accomplished talker (who may be an older child), and not, at least at the start, from passive observations of adults talking, or from radio or TV shows. Experiments and observations show that children pick up words at this stage most rapidly when the caregiver uses them to name or comment on what the child is already focused on.

*Word meanings*

The meanings of the child's first words are not necessarily the same as those of the adults around her. For instance, children may "overgeneralize" their first words to refer to items beyond their usual scope of application. A child might call all men "Daddy," or all animals "doggie," or all round objects "ball." Others have pointed out that "undergeneralization" also occurs, though it is less likely to be noticed. For instance, a child might call only her own striped ball "ball," and stay silent about all the rest, or refer to the family dog and others of the same type as "doggie" but not name any others. The child may also use a word to refer to a wide variety of objects that hold no single property in common. A child who learned "moon" for the full moon later used it for street lamps, house lights (lights in common), doorknobs and the dial on the dishwasher (shape in common), and toenail clippings on a rug (related shape). Put into a class, these objects share nothing in common except a shifting form of resemblance to the original moon. It has been argued that children's first word meanings have only a family resemblance rather than a common thread. In fact, there are philosophers who argue that such is the nature of many adult words as well.

It has long been recognized that words are inherently ambiguous even when an object is being pointed at: does the word refer to the object, or its color, shape, texture, function, shadow? Recent work on word learning has also drawn attention to the biases the child brings to word learning. One such bias is the *Whole-Object assumption,* that is, children assume a new word refers to the object itself rather than a property. However, a competing constraint is *mutual exclusivity* : if a child already knows a word for an object, a new word is assumed to mean something else; a new object if it is available; or a part, texture, or shape of a known one. Researchers are divided at present on the extent to which these biases are learned, or inherent.

Young children also frequently name objects at an intermediate level of abstraction known as the *basic object* level. That is, they will use the word *dog*, rather than the more specific *collie* or the more general, *animal*, or *flower* rather than *dandelion* or *plant*. This coincides with the naming practices of most parents, and seems to be the level of greatest utility for the two-year old.

## Preschool years: the two-year-old

### Grammar: the two-word utterance

The first sentence is the transition that separates humans from other creatures. Most toddlers produce their first spontaneous two-word sentence at 18 to 24 months, usually once they have acquired between 50 and 500 words. Before their first sentence, they often achieve the effect of complex expressions by stringing together their simple words:

*Book*

*Mine*

*Read*

Then their first sentence puts these words under a single intonational envelope, with no pause. Their first sentences are not profound, but they represent a major advance in the expression of meaning. The listener is also freed of some of the burden of interpretation and does not need to guess so much from context.

For children learning English, their first sentences are *telegraphic*, that is, content words predominate, primarily the nouns and verbs necessary in the situation. Words that have grammatical functions, but do not themselves make reference, such as articles, prepositions and auxiliary verbs, do not occur very often. The true character of this grammar is hotly debated. The fact that the function words and inflections appear variably for a protracted period of months leads some researchers to argue that the child really knows the grammar but has some kind of production limit that precludes saying extra words. On the other side, some researchers argue that the forms that do appear may be imitations, or particular learned fragments, and that the full grammar is not yet present. Tests of comprehension or judgment that might decide between these alternatives are very hard to undertake with two-year-old children, though the little work that does exist suggests children are sensitive to the items they omit in their own speech.

At the start, the child combines the single words into two-word strings that usually preserve the common order of parents' sentences in English. At the time the English-speaking child is producing many two-word utterances, comprehension tests show he can also distinguish between sentences that contrast in word order and hence meaning:

*The dog licks the cat.*

*The cat licks the dog.*

Researchers using innovative techniques with preverbal infants have claimed infants understand basic word order contrasts before they learn to produce them. Infants who saw a choice of two brief movies along with spoken sentences preferred to look at the movie of the event that was congruent with the spoken sentence, where the only contrast was in word order.

### Semantic relations

Most studies on early child language conclude that the child at the two-word stage is concerned with the expression of a small set of semantic relationships. The cross-linguistic study of children includes languages as remotely related as French, Samoan, Luo (spoken in Kenya), German, Finnish, and Cakchiquel (a Mayan language spoken in Guatemala). Two-year-old children learning all these languages expressed only a narrow range of the possible meanings that the adult language could express. All over the world, children apparently talk about the same meanings—or ideas—in their first sentences, despite the variety of forms in those languages. For example, the children refer to possession (Mommy dish, my coat), action-object sequences (hit ball, drop fork), attribute of an object (big truck, wet pants) or an object's location (cup shelf, teddy bed).

Debate has raged over how significant this finding of universal semantic relations is for the study of grammatical development. On the one hand, it might mean that building a grammar based on meaningful relations is a universal first step for language learning. On the other hand, there is the larger problem of how the child builds a grammar that resembles the adult's, because for true linguistic competence, the child needs to build a theory out of the right components: subjects, objects, noun phrases, verb phrases, and the rest. These abstract categories do not translate easily into semantic relations, if at all. To succeed at analyzing or parsing adult sentences into their true grammatical parts, the child must go beyond general meaning. The alternative interpretation of the findings about the first sentences is that children all over the world are constrained by their **cognitive development** to talk about the same ideas and that their doing so need not mean that their grammars are based solely on semantic relations. So the semantic analysis of children's early sentences offers fascinating data on the meanings children express at that age, but it is less clear that these semantic notions are the components out of which children's grammars are constructed. A weaker hypothesis about the role of semantics in the learning of grammar is that perhaps children exploit the correlation between certain grammatical notions, like subject, and certain semantic notions, like agent, to begin parsing adult sentences. The child could then proceed to analyze sentences by knowing already:

a. the meaning of the individual words

b. the conceptual structure of the event, namely that dog is the agent; bit is the action.

Some have proposed that the child may have some further, possibly innate, "hypotheses" that guide his code-cracking:

c. actions are usually verbs

d. things are usually nouns

e. agents are usually subjects.

Semantic notions then become vital bootstraps for the learning of grammar.

## Preschool years: the three-year-old

### Shades of meaning

What is missing from the two-word stage are all the modulations of meaning, the fine tunings, which add immeasurably to the subtlety of what we can express. Consider the shades of meaning in the following sentences:

*He played*

*He's playing*

*He was playing*

*He has played*

*He had played*

*He will play*

*He will have played*

Not all languages make these distinctions explicitly, and some languages make distinctions that English does not. In the next stage of development of English, the extra little function words and inflections that modulate the meaning of the major syntactic relations make their appearance, though it is years until they are fully mastered. For English, it is common to measure the stage of language development by counting and then averaging the morphemes (words and inflections) in a child's set of utterances, and refer to that as the mean length of utterance (MLU). The inflections are surprisingly variable in children's utterances, sometimes present and sometimes absent even within the same stretch of conversation. According to psychologist R. Brown, "All these, like an intricate sort of ivy, begin to grow up between and among the major constituent blocks, the nouns and verbs, to which stage I is largely limited."

A classic error noticed in the acquisition of English inflections is the overgeneralization of plurals and past tenses. In each case, when the regular inflection begins to be mastered, it is overgeneralized to irregular forms, resulting in errors like *foots, sheeps, goed* and *eated*. In the case of the past tense, children usually begin by correctly using a few irregular forms like *fell* and *broke*, perhaps because these forms are frequent in the input and the child learns them by rote. At first they may not be fully analyzed as past tenses of the corresponding verbs *fall* and *break*. But when the child begins to produce regular past tense endings, the irregulars are sometimes also regularized (e.g. *falled* and *breaked*). Two kinds of overgeneralizations occur: one in which the -ed ending is attached to the root form of the irregular verb (e.g. *sing - singed*) and the other in which the ending is attached to the irregular past form (e.g. *broke -broked*).

### Cross-linguistic work

An understanding of how children acquire grammatical morphemes is now thought to require a broader perspective than that obtained from studying English alone. A large research initiative has gathered data from children acquiring other languages, especially languages very different from English. Researchers have studied children acquiring Luo, Samoan, Kaluli, Hungarian, Sesotho and many others in an effort to understand the process of language acquisition in universal terms. One finding is that the telegraphic speech style of English children is not universal—in more heavily inflected languages like Italian, even the youngest speakers do not strip their sentences to the bare stems of nouns and verbs.

One of the purposes of the cross-linguistic work is to try to disentangle some of the variables that are confounded in a single language. For example: English-speaking children acquire the hypothetical (if…then statements) rather late, around four years of age, but the hypothetical form is complex in English grammar. It requires an ability to imagine an unreal situation. Cross-linguistic studies provide a way to tease these variables apart, for Russian has a very simple hypothetical form, though its meaning is as complex as the English version. Research shows that Russian children do not use this simple form until after they are about four years of age. Most morphemes vary along multiple dimensions: phonological, semantic and grammatical. The full program of research may reach fruition only when the massive matrix of possibilities across the world's languages can be entered into a computer, complete with detailed longitudinal data from children learning those languages.

### Auxiliaries

Children's first sentences lack any auxiliaries or tense markers:

*Me go home*

*Daddy have tea*

and they also lack auxiliary-inversion for questions at this stage:

*I ride train?*

*Sit chair?*

They also lack a system for assigning nominative case to the subject, that is, adult sentences mark the subject as nominative:

Adult: *I want that book*

but children at this stage frequently use the accusative case:

Child: *Me want that book*

These facts lead some to conclude that young children's sentences lack the full syntactic structures typical of adult sentences, and undergo a radical restructuring as they develop. Others argue that the limitation is not so much at the level of knowledge of grammar, but merely performance limits, so preserving the continuity of form at an abstract level between child and adult.

In addition to learning the basic word order and inflectional system of the language, a child must learn how to produce sentences of different kinds: not just simple active declarative, but also negatives, questions, imperatives, passives and so forth. In English there are word order changes and auxiliary changes for these sentence modalities.

One type of question is called a yes/no question, for the simple reason that it requires a *yes* or a *no* answer. A second kind of question is called the Wh-question, so-called because it usually begins with the sequence Wh in English (in French, they are Qu-questions). Wh-questions do not require a simple yes or no response: instead they ask for information about one of the constituents in the sentence. *What, who, when, where, why,* and *how* all stand in for possible phrases in the sentence—the subject, or object, or a prepositional phrase. Discourse permits us to respond elliptically with only the missing constituent if we choose:

*What is he buying?*

*Coffee.*

*Where is she going?*

*To the store.*

*How is she getting there?*

*By bike.*

The structure of such questions is similar to that of yes/no questions because the auxiliary and subject are inverted, so that transformation is involved in both. In addition, the Wh-word is in initial position, though it stands for constituents in varied sentence positions. Linguistic evidence suggests that the Wh-word originated at another site in the structure and was moved there by a grammatical rule, called, appropriately, Wh-movement. Children's responses to such questions reveal the sophisticated nature of their grammatical knowledge.

Negation also involves the auxiliary component in the sentence, because for simple sentence negation, the negative is attached to the first member of the auxiliary, and may be contracted:

*She isn't coming home.*

*He won't be having any.*

How do children acquire these rules of English? When auxiliaries do emerge, it seems that they come in first in declarative sentences. Before children master the placement of the auxiliary, they ask questions using rising intonation. They may also pick up a few routine forms of yes/no questions, particularly in households that demand politeness from young children, as in:

May I have one?

When auxiliaries do begin to appear in initial position, what has the child learned? One of the claims made by modern linguistic theory is that the rules of natural languages are "structure dependent," that is, they always refer to structural units, constituents such as "noun phrase" or "auxiliary verb," not to other arbitrary units such as "the fifth word" or "the first word beginning with 'f'." The case of auxiliary inversion provides a nice illustration, used by **Noam Chomsky** to make this point. The child could hear sentence pairings such as:

*The man is here,*

*Is the man here?*

*The boy can swim.*

*Can the boy swim?*

*The dog will bite.*

*Will the dog bite?*

and draw the conclusion that to make a question, you take the *third* word and move it to the front. Of course, that hypothesis would soon be disconfirmed by a pair such as:

*The tall man will come.*

*Will the tall man come?*

not: *Man the tall will come?*

More likely, the child might form the rule "move the first word like *can, will, is,* etc. up to the front," which would fit all of the above and hundreds of other such sentences. However, that is not a structure-dependent rule, because it makes no reference to the grammatical role that word plays in the sentence. The only disconfirmation would come from the occasions when a subject relative clause *appears before the auxiliary:*

*The man who is the teacher will be coming tomorrow.*

*Will the man who is the teacher be coming tomorrow?*

but our earlier, structure-independent rule would produce:

*Is the man who the teacher will be coming tomorrow?*

The child who formulated the almost-adequate rule would fail in such circumstances, but no child has been observed to make the mistake. Hence even from the inadequate data that children receive, they formulate a complex, structure-dependent rule.

### Wh-questions

Wh-questions appear among the child's first utterances, often in a routine form such as "Whazzat?" The forms are routines because they are invariant in form, but more varied productions are not slow to emerge in children's grammar. The first, stereotyped forms may be tied to particular functions or contexts, but genuine interrogatives are varied not only in form but in use.

Just as in yes/no questions, the auxiliary must be in front of the subject noun phrase in a Wh-question, and children seem to have more difficulty with auxiliary-inversion in Wh-questions than in yes/no questions. At the same time children can say:

*Can he come?*

they might say:

*Why he can come?*

failing to invert the auxiliary in the Wh-question.

What else does the child have to learn in Wh-questions? One factor concerns the link between the Wh-word and the "missing constituent." Certain of the Wh-words enter children's speech earlier than others, and there is some consistency across studies in that order: *What, who,* and *where* tend to emerge before *why* and *how,* with *when* coming later. Some have explained the order in terms of semantics, or rather concreteness, of the ideas contained in these words, since *when* and *how* depend upon cognitive developments of time and causality whereas *what* and *who* do not. The question *why* seems to be late for this reason: it is only through discourse that a child can determine the meaning of *why,* which may be the reason some young children ask it endlessly. It is also a question that rarely elicits a one-word answer, so it may be a way to keep the conversation going when you can't say much yourself yet!

### Creativity

A feature that is markedly evident in young children is their **creativity** with language. Children, like adults, continually produce sentences they have not heard before, and one can more easily recognize that novelty in children because sometimes the ideas are rather strange. For example, after hearing many "tag questions" such as "That's nice, isn't it?" and "You're a good girl, aren't you?" and "You can open that, can't you?" a three-year-old figured out how to make her own tags, and used the rules to say, "Goosebumps are hairy legs, aren't they?" and "He's a punk rocker, isn't he?," which were definitely not sentences she had heard. In addition, the creative use is revealed because children overextend rules to exceptional cases. For example, a child may say "My porridge is getting middle-sizeder" as he struggles through a huge bowl of oatmeal. It can also occur because children do not yet have the vocabulary for certain subtleties of expression. But the way that children fill these "lexical gaps" uses the same principles as adults who do the same thing. For example, an adult might use an "innovative verb" such as "I weekended in New York," and a child might similarly say, "I broomed her!" after pursuing a sibling with a broom. However, a child who said "You have to scale it first" as she put a bag on a scale was creating an innovation for which there is already an existing word—namely, weigh. The creativity of children's linguistic innovations has been emphasized because it demonstrates that children do not just imitate what they hear, but extract general rules and principles that allow them to form new expressions.

## Later preschool years

### Joining sentences

Once the child has mastered the fundamentals of sentence construction, what is left to learn? Actually, language would be very dull to listen to or read if we could just produce simple sentences with one verb at a time. Perhaps the first response of a novice to the field of child language is that the sentences children speak are short and not very complicated for a long period. Certainly when one measures the mean length of utterance of children younger than age four, it tends not to be very impressive, ranging from 1.0 to 4.0 morphemes per utterance. Yet by age four, the MLU (mean length of utterance) loses much of its usefulness as a measure, because children's utterances, like those of an adult, fluctuate in length dramatically depending on the circumstances of the conversation. Even before age four, there are rare, but significant, occurrences of surprising complexity, showing that the child is in command of a considerable amount of grammar when needed. The first sentences involving more than one "proposition" are simple coordinations, for instance two sentences joined by *and*. Later other conjunctions come in, such as *so, but, after,* or *because.* But embeddings are not much later: there is evidence of embedded structures even in the primitive talk of two-year-olds.

There are different kinds of embedded structures. One kind are *relative clauses*, clauses that are used to further specify a noun phrase:

*The man* who took the job *is coming to dinner.*

Here is a sample sentence from a child at 2;10 (2 years, 10 months), said in reference to playground equipment:

*I'm going on the one* that you're sitting on.

or the slightly aberrant:

*Where's a hammer* we nailed those nails in?

On the other hand are *complement* constructions, which can be considered the equivalent further specification of the verb phrase:

*The doctor decided* to perform the operation.

Again, a child at age 2;11 was observed to say:

*I don't like* Nicky share a banana.

*I'm going downstairs* to see what Nicky's watching.

Both kinds of embedding are means of packing information into a single sentence that would require multiple sentences (probably with lots of pointing) to convey the equivalent ideas. When children reach the stage at which they can control these and similar structures, they become capable of expressing a much wider variety of ideas and thoughts not dependent on the immediate environment for support, and an important further step is taken in being ready for literacy.

Researchers have used innovative procedures to elicit relative clause structures from children as young as two by arranging the situation to call for specification of a referent. In one procedure, for example, the child, the experimenter, and a confederate are playing with two identical toy bears. The experimenter makes one bear ride a bike. Then the confederate is blindfolded, and the child alone watches the experimenter make that same bear do another action, say jump. Then the blindfold is removed from the confederate and the child has to help him guess which bear did something. Children of two and three can say:

*Pick the one that rode the bike.*

If the literature on comprehension of relative clauses is considered, it appears that children below age five are in very poor control of relative clause sentences. The typical comprehension task uses an "act-out" procedure in which several small animals are provided to the child and he is asked to act out whatever the experimenter says. After a couple of simple warm-ups, e.g.,

Show me:

*The lion hit the kangaroo.*

*The dog jumped.*

the child would be asked to act out relative clause structures in which there are no clues to meaning from the words alone, i.e., the syntax carries all the meaning:

*The lion that hit the dog bit the turtle.*

*The cat that the dog pushed licked the mouse.*

When preschoolers are given such a task, their performance is usually fairly poor, suggesting that they continue to have difficulty reconstructing the speaker's meaning from complex structures: a problem perhaps in processing rather than grammar per se.

Similarly, even five- and six-year-olds continue to have trouble figuring out who did what to whom for sentences containing various kinds of complements:

*Fred told Harry to wash the car.*

*Fred promised Harry to wash the car.*

*Fred told Harry that he washed the car.*

*Fred told Harry after he washed the car.*

The various "complement-taking" verbs in English fall into several distinct patterns, as do the complements themselves, so there is room for lots of confusion.

Finally, there are aspects of the pronoun system that may take several years to get straight. Pronouns in English have to have an "antecedent" (noun which is referred to by the pronoun) outside the sentence in which the pronoun occurs: you can't say, for example:

*John hit him.*

and mean John hit himself. Reflexives like "himself," on the other hand, have to be in the same clause as their antecedent; you can't say:

*John was wondering why Fred hit himself.*

and have it mean that Fred hit John. Children's control over antecedents, particularly of pronouns, is still being acquired after age four or five when complex sentences are involved.

## Later word learning

The child's vocabulary grows enormously in the age period two to five years, and vocabulary size is frequently used by researchers as an index of the child's development. In addition to learning many new nouns and verbs, the child must organize vocabulary, for example, into hierarchies: that Rover is also a dog, a corgi, an animal, a living thing and so on. The child also learns about opposites and relatedness—all necessary forms of connection among words in the "inner lexicon." The child also becomes better able to learn words from linguistic context alone, rapidly homing in on the meaning after only a few scattered exposures. This is a surprisingly effective process, though hardly fail-safe: after being told that screens were to stop flies from bringing germs into the house, one child concluded that germs were "things flies play with."

### Discourse and reference

Researchers have been acutely aware that the child's language learning does not take place in a vacuum or a laboratory—it is enmeshed in the social relationships and circumstances of the child. The child uses language for communication with peers, siblings, parents, and increasingly, relative strangers. All of these individuals make special demands on the child in terms of their different status, knowledge, requirements of politeness, clarity or formality, to which the child must adjust and adapt, and the preschool child is only beginning this process of language **socialization**. Even four-year-olds adjust their style, pitch and sentence length when talking to younger children or infants rather than peers or older people, and in other cultures they master formal devices that acknowledge the status or group membership of different people. However, it is recognized that the three-year-old is rather poor at predicting what others know or think, and therefore will be rather egocentric in expressing himself. Especially when communicating across a barrier or over a telephone, the child of this age might be unable to supply the right kind of information to a listener. However, other researchers show that children become increasingly adept at "repairing" their own communicative breakdowns as they get older.

### Narrative and literacy

The difficulty that children have with predicting what others already know or believe shows itself also in their attempts to produce narratives, that is, extended sentences that convey a story. Retelling a story is considerably easier than constructing one about witnessed events, but may need considerable "scaffolding" by a patient listener who structures it by asking leading questions. Skill in producing a coherent narrative is one of the culminating achievements of language acquisition, but it is acquired late and varies widely according to opportunity for practice and experience with stories. In part, this is because creating a narrative is a cultural event: different cultures have different rules for how stories are structured, which must be learned. At first, children tend to focus just on the actions, with little attention to the motives, or reasons, or consequences of those actions, and little overarching structure that might explain the events. Young children also fail to use the linguistic devices that maintain cohesion among referents, so they may switch from talking about one character to another and call them all "he," to the bewilderment of the listener. Reading and writing in the grade school years depend on this ability and nurture it further, and one of the best predictors of reading readiness is how much children were read to in the first few years. As children begin to read and write, there are further gains in their vocabulary (and new ways to acquire it) and new syntactic forms emerge that are relatively rare in speaking but play important roles in text, such as stage-setting and maintaining cohesion. Mastery of these devices requires a sensitivity to the reader's needs, and it is a lifelong developmental process.

Jill De Villiers Ph.D.

## Further Reading

Berko-Gleason, J. *The Development of Language*. New York: Macmillan, 1993.

de Villiers, P., and J. de Villiers. *Early Language*. The Developing Child series. Cambridge, Mass.: Harvard University Press, 1979.

Fletcher, P., and B. MacWhinney. *The Handbook of Child Language*. Cambridge, Mass.: Blackwell Publishers, 1995.

Goodluck, H. *Language Acquisition: A Linguistic Introduction*. Cambridge, Mass.: Blackwell Publishers, 1991.

Pinker, S. *The Language Instinct*. New York: Morrow, 1994.

# Language disorder

Problem with any function of language and communication.

In adults, much of what is known about the organization of language functions in the **brain** has come from the study of patients with focal brain lesions. It has been known for hundreds of years that a left-hemisphere injury to the brain is more likely to cause language disturbance—**aphasia**—than a right hemisphere injury, especially but not exclusively in right-handed persons. For about a hundred years, certain areas in the adult left hemisphere—Broca's area in the posterior frontal lobe, and Wernicke's area in the temporal lobe—have been identified as centrally involved in language functions. However, researchers in the field of adult aphasia are divided over the exact role these brain areas play in language processing and production. Damage to Broca's area results in marked problems with language fluency; with shortened sentences, impaired flow of speech, poor control of rhythm and intonation (known as prosody); and a telegraphic style, with missing inflections and function words. In contrast, the speech of Wernicke's aphasics is fluent and often rapid, but with relatively empty content and many neologisms (invented words) and word substitutions. It was initially believed that the two areas were responsible for output (Broca's) versus input (Wernicke's), but research does not confirm such a simple split.

Other theories ask whether the two areas might be differentially involved in syntax versus semantics, or phonology versus the lexicon, but the picture is not clear. Some have argued that adult aphasic patients, once they are stable after their injury or stroke, employ many compensatory devices that conceal or disguise the central character of their language difficulties. It then becomes more difficult to assess what is missing or disturbed because the difficulties are overlaid by new strategies, and perhaps new areas of the brain taking over functions for the damaged areas.

Infants and young children who suffer focal brain lesions in advance of acquiring language provide valuable information to neuroscientists who want to know how "plastic" the developing brain is with respect to language functions. For instance, is the left hemisphere uniquely equipped for language, or could the right hemisphere do as well? What if Broca's or Wernicke's areas were damaged before language was acquired? Thirty years ago a review of literature on children who had incurred brain lesions suggested that, unlike the case of adults, recovery from language disruption after left-brain damage was rapid and without lasting effect. Researchers concluded that the two hemispheres of the brain were equipotential for language until around **puberty**, and that this allowed young brain-damaged children to compensate with their undamaged right hemisphere.

However, several studies suggested that left-brain damage caused greater disruption to language than right-sided damage even in the youngest subjects. Children known to be using only their right hemisphere for language (because they had undergone removal of the left hemisphere for congenital abnormalities) demonstrated subtle syntactic deficits on careful linguistic testing, but the deficits failed to show in ordinary conversational analysis. Almost all of these studies were retrospective, that is, they looked at the performance of children at an older age who had suffered an early lesion. Furthermore, the technology for scanning the brain and locating the lesion site, then carefully matching the subjects, was much less developed.

With the invention of new technologies including CT scans and Magnetic Resonance Imaging (MRI), several studies have been conducted to look prospectively at the **language development** of children with focal, defined lesions specifically in the traditional language areas. There is surprising concordance among the studies in their results: all of them find initial (but variable) delays in the onset of lexical, syntactic, and morphological development followed by remarkably similar progress after about age two to three years. Lasting deficits have not been noticed in these children. Surprisingly, there are also no dramatic effects of laterality: lesions to either side of the brain seem to produce virtually the same effects. However, most of the data comes from conversational analysis or relatively unstructured testing, and these children have not been followed until school age.

Until those detailed studies are extended, it is difficult to reconcile the differing results of the retrospective and prospective studies. Nevertheless, the findings suggest remarkable plasticity and robustness of language in spite of brain lesions that would devastate an adult's system.

Jill De Villiers Ph.D.

**Further Reading**

Byers Brown, B., and M. Edwards. *Developmental Disorders of Language.* San Diego: Singular Publishing, 1989.

Miller, J. *Research on Child Language Disorders: A Decade of Progress.* Austin, TX: Pro-ed, 1991.

## Karl Spencer Lashley

### 1890-1958

American neuropsychologist who demonstrated relationships between animal behavior and the size and location of brain injuries, summarizing his findings in terms of the concepts of equipotentiality and mass action.

Karl Spencer Lashley was born at Davis, West Virginia, on June 7, 1890. Even as a child he was interested in animals, an interest which continued throughout his adult life. His mother, Maggie Lashley, encouraged him in intellectual pursuits. After studying at the University of West Virginia and then taking a master's degree in bacteriology at the University of Pittsburgh, Lashley did doctoral and postdoctoral research at Johns Hopkins University. While at Hopkins, he was influenced by the zoologist H. S. Jennings, the psychiatrist **Adolf Meyer**, and the psychologist John B. Watson, the father of **behaviorism**.

Lashley was at once an experimental researcher and a psychological theoretician. His investigations were published in the leading journals and proceedings of major scientific societies. After several joint studies with Jennings, Lashley published his own thesis, "Inheritance in the Asexual Reproduction of Hydra." He collaborated with Watson in studying behavior in seabirds, acknowledging Watson's behavioristic approach the rest of his life.

Collaborating with Shepherd Ivory Franz, Lashley produced several papers on the effects of cerebral destruction upon retention and habit formation in rats. This was the beginning of his preoccupation with one of the persistent problems in psychology, that of cerebral localization. Earlier researchers Gall, Broca, Fritsch and Hitzig, Ferrier, and Munk were all believers in exact

**Karl S. Lashley** *(UPI/Corbis-Bettmann. Reproduced with permission.)*

cerebral localization, whereas Flourens, Goltz, and Franz doubted it. The culmination of his localization experiments was *Brain Mechanisms and Intelligence: A Quantitative Study of Injuries to the Brain* (1929), his longest, most significant monograph. In it he summarized his concepts of equipotentiality and mass action and marshaled the experimental evidence to support them. Thus he accounted for the absence of precise and persistent localization of function in the cortex. Lashley's experiments denied the simple similarity and correspondence, previously assumed, between associationistic connectionism and the neuronal theory of the **brain** as a mass of neurons connected by synapses.

In addition to his researches Lashley taught as professor of psychology at the universities of Minnesota and Chicago and at Harvard University. He held various honorary positions and lectureships, was on the editorial boards of numerous scientific journals, served as member of and adviser to governmental committees, and was elected to many scientific and philosophical societies. He died on August 7, 1958, in Poitiers, France.

**Further Reading**

Beach, Frank A. *Karl Spencer Lashley.* 1961.

Beach, Frank A., ed. *The neuropsychology of Lashley.* 1960.

# Law of effect

A principle associated with learning and behavior which states that behaviors that lead to satisfying outcomes are more likely to be repeated than behaviors that lead to unwanted outcomes.

Psychologists have been interested in the factors that are important in behavior change and control since psychology emerged as a discipline. One of the first principles associated with learning and behavior was the Law of Effect, which states that behaviors that lead to satisfying outcomes are likely to be repeated, whereas behaviors that lead to undesired outcomes are less likely to recur.

This principle, which most learning theorists accept as valid, was developed by Edward Lee Thorndike, who provided the basis for the field of **operant conditioning**. Prior to Thorndike, many psychologists interested in animal behavior attributed learning to reasoning on the animal's part. Thorndike instead theorized that animals learn by trial and error. When something works to the animal's satisfaction, the animal draws a connection or association between the behavior and positive outcome. This association forms the basis for later behavior. When the animal makes an error, on the other hand, no association is formed between the behavior that led to the error and a positive outcome, so the ineffective behavior is less likely to recur.

Initially, Thorndike drew parallels between positive outcomes, which would be termed **reinforcement**s by the behaviorists, and negative outcomes, which would be referred to as punishments. Later, however, he asserted that **punishment** was ineffective in removing the connection between the behavior and the result. Instead, he suggested that, following a punishment, behavior was likely to be less predictable.

Thorndike also developed his Law of Exercise, which states that responses that occur in a given situation become more strongly associated with that situation. He suggested that these two laws could account for all behavior. As such, psychologists had no need to refer to abstract thought in defining the way that behavior is learned. Everything is associated with the effects of reward and punishment, according to Thorndike.

## Further Reading

Clifford, G. J. *Edward L. Thorndike: The Sane Positivist.* Middletown, PA: Wesleyan University Press, 1984.

Mackintosh, N. J. *Conditioning and Associative Learning.* New York: Oxford University Press, 1983.

# Arnold Allan Lazarus

1932-
South African clinical psychologist who developed a comprehensive psychotherapy called multimodal therapy.

As a graduate student in psychology, **Arnold Lazarus** first developed a therapy based on behavioral psychology. He expanded this into cognitive **behavior therapy**, and later into a multi-faceted **psychotherapy** known as multimodal therapy. In recent years, Lazarus has written popular psychology books. Lazarus has held numerous professional positions and won many honors, including the Distinguished Service Award of the American Board of Professional Psychology in 1982 and the Distinguished Psychologist Award of the Division of Psychotherapy of the **American Psychological Association (APA)** in 1992. In 1996 he became the first recipient of the Psyche Award of the Nicholas and Dorothy Cummings Foundation. Lazarus is a professor emeritus in the Graduate School of Applied and Professional Psychology at Rutgers University in Piscataway, New Jersey and continues in private practice.

Lazarus was born in Johannesburg, South Africa, in 1932, the son of Benjamin and Rachel (Mosselson) Lazarus. Educated at the University of Witwatersrand in Johannesburg, he earned his B.A. with honors in 1956, his M.A. in 1957, and his Ph.D. in **clinical psychology** in 1960. In 1956, he married Daphne Ann Kessel; they have a son and a daughter.

## Develops behavior therapy

In 1958, while still a graduate student, Lazarus published a paper in the *South African Medical Journal* describing a new form of psychotherapy that he called behavior therapy. He began his private practice in psychotherapy in Johannesburg in 1959 and, in 1960, he became vice-president of the Transvaal Workers Educational Association. In 1963, Lazarus spent a year as a visiting assistant professor of psychology at Stanford University, and then returned to the University of Witwatersrand as a lecturer in psychiatry at the medical school. In 1966, he returned to the United States as director of the Behavior Therapy Institute in Sausalito, California. That year he published *Behavior Therapy Techniques* with **Joseph Wolpe**. The following year, he moved to Temple University Medical School in Philadelphia as professor of behavioral science. He was a visiting professor of psychology and director of clinical training at Yale University in 1970.

Lazarus was the first psychologist to apply **desensitization** techniques for treating phobias in **group thera-**

py sessions. With Arnold Abramovitz, he was the first to use emotive imagery in treating children. He studied treatments for alcoholism and was one of the first to apply **learning theory** to the treatment of **depression**. By the 1960s, it was clear to Lazarus that the therapy movement he had initiated, utilizing the stimulus-response mechanisms of behaviorist psychology, was too limited for effective psychotherapy. His 1971 book, *Behavior Therapy and Beyond*, laid the foundations for what became known as cognitive-behavior therapy.

## Replaces behavior therapy with multimodal therapy

In 1972, Lazarus received his diploma in clinical psychology from the American Board of Professional Psychology and returned to private practice in Princeton, New Jersey. He also became professor and chairman of the psychology department at Rutgers University in New Brunswick, New Jersey. He joined the Rutgers Graduate School of Applied and Professional Psychology in 1974. As Lazarus examined long-term results in patients who had undergone **cognitive behavior therapy**, he found some inadequacies. For patients with anxiety and panic disorders, obsessive-compulsive problems, depression, and **family** and marital difficulties, the relapse rate following therapy remained very high. He therefore developed a multimodal therapy, which involves examining and treating seven different but interrelated modalities, or psychological parameters. These modalities are behavior, physiology, **cognition**, interpersonal relationships, sensation, imagery, and **affect**. Thus, multimodal therapy involves a complete assessment of the individual and treatments designed specifically for that individual. Lazarus developed his approach, in part, by questioning clients about the factors that had helped them in their therapy. In 1976, Lazarus founded the Multimodal Therapy Institute in Kingston, New Jersey, and he continues to direct that Institute. He established additional Multimodal Therapy Institutes in New York, Virginia, Pennsylvania, Illinois, Texas, and Ohio. His book *Multimodal Behavior Therapy* was published in 1976.

## Joins the self-help movement

In 1975, Lazarus published his first popular self-help book, *I Can If I Want To*, with his colleague Allen Fay. His 1977 book, *In the Mind's Eye: The Power of Imagery for Personal Enrichment*, described the use of **mental imagery** for personal growth. His recent popular psychology writings include several books written with his son, the psychologist Clifford Neil Lazarus. Their 1993 book with Allen Fay, *Don't Believe It for a Minute!: Forty Toxic Ideas That Are Driving You Crazy*,

encouraged people to stop repeating the same mistakes. They argued that misconceptions, such as "life should be fair," lead to depression, anxiety, and feelings of **guilt**.

During his career, Lazarus has treated thousands of clients, as individuals, couples, families, and groups. He is a diplomate of the International Academy of Behavioral Medicine, Counseling, and Psychotherapy, and he was elected to the National Academy of Practice in Psychology in 1982. Lazarus is the author or editor of fifteen books and more than 200 articles and book chapters and has made video and sound recordings. He has served on the editorial boards of numerous psychology journals. Lazarus has been a fellow of the APA since 1972 and has been on the board of Psychologists for Social Responsibility since 1982. He is a recipient of the Distinguished Career Award from the American Board of Medical Psychotherapists and a fellow of the Academy of Clinical Psychology.

Margaret Alic

## Further Reading

Dryden, Windy. *A Dialogue with Arnold Lazarus: "It Depends."* Philadelphia: Open University Press, 1991.

Labriola, Tony. *Multimodal Therapy with Dr. Arnold Lazarus.* Needham Heights, MA: Allyn & Bacon, 1998. Video-recording.

Lazarus, Arnold A. *Marital Myths.* San Luis Obispo, CA: Impact Publishers, 1985.

Lazarus, Arnold A. *Relaxation Exercises.* Guilford, CT: Audio-Forum, 1986. Sound cassettes.

Lazarus, Arnold A. *Brief but Comprehensive Psychotherapy: The Multimodal Way.* New York: Springer, 1997.

Lazarus, Arnold A. and Clifford N. Lazarus. *The 60-Second Shrink: 101 Strategies for Staying Sane in a Crazy World.* San Luis Obispo, CA: Impact Publishers, 1997.

Zilbergeld, Bernie and Arnold A. Lazarus. *Mind Power: Getting What You Want Through Mental Training.* Boston: Little, Brown, 1987.

# Leadership

The ability to take initiative in planning, organizing, and managing group activities and projects.

In any group of people, there are those who step forward to organize people and events to achieve a specific result. In organized activities, leaders can be designated and, in informal contexts, such as a party, they may emerge naturally. What makes certain people into leaders is open to debate. Luella Cole and Irma Nelson Hall have written that leadership "seems to consist of a clus-

**Martin Luther King, Jr. walking arm-in-arm with marchers, leads a march on Washington, D.C.** *(National Archives and Records Administration. Reproduced with permission.)*

A study by T. Sharpe, M. Brown, and K. Crider measured the effects of consistent positive **reinforcement**, favoring skills such as leadership, sportsmanship, and **conflict resolution**, on two urban elementary physical education classes. The researchers found that the focus on positive skills caused a significant increase in leadership and conflict-resolution behavior. These results seem to support the idea, discussed by Maynard, that leadership behavior can be non-competitive (different individuals exercising leadership in different areas) and also conducive to group cohesion.

Zoran Minderovic

### Further Reading

Edwards, Cynthia A. "Leadership in Groups of School-Age Girls." *Developmental Psychology* 30, no. 6, (November 1994): 920-27.

Sharpe, T., M. Browne, and K. Crider. "The Effects of A Sportsmanship Curriculum Intervention on Generalized Positive Social Behavior of Urban Elementary School Students." *Journal of Applied Behavior Analysis* 28, (1995): 401-16.

ter of **traits**, a few inborn but most of them acquired or at least developed by contact with the environment." Psychologists have also defined leadership as a mentality, as opposed to aptitude, the assumption being that mentalities can be acquired. Leaders can be "idea generators" or "social facilitators." Leaders have their own leadership style, and that style may not transfer from one situation to another.

Child psychologists who study girls, and particularly educators and parents advocating equal-opportunity education for girls, have remarked that girls with leadership potential often have to struggle with various prejudices, which also include the notion that leadership is a "male" characteristic. In a study of 304 fourth-, fifth-, and six-graders enrolled in 16 Girl Scout troops, Cynthia A. Edwards found that in an all-female group, leaders consistently display characteristic qualities such as organizational skills and independent thinking. Significantly, election to leadership posts was based on perceived managerial skills, while "feminine" qualities, such as empathic behavior, were generally not taken into account. However, in examining the research on mixed (male-female) groups, Edwards has found studies that show "that the presence of male group members, even in the minority, suppresses the verbal expression and leadership behavior of female group members." The fact that leadership behavior can be suppressed would seem to strengthen the argument that leadership is, indeed, a learned behavior.

# Learned helplessness

An apathetic attitude stemming from the conviction that one's actions do not have the power to affect one's situation.

The concept of learned helplessness was developed in the 1960s and 1970s by Martin Seligman (1942- ) at the University of Pennsylvania. He found that animals receiving electric shocks, which they had no **ability** to prevent or avoid, were unable to act in subsequent situations where avoidance or escape was possible. Extending the ramifications of these findings to humans, Seligman and his colleagues found that human **motivation** to initiate responses is also undermined by a lack of control over one's surroundings. Further research has shown that learned helplessness disrupts **normal** development and learning and leads to emotional disturbances, especially **depression**.

Learned helplessness in humans can begin very early in life if infants see no correlation between actions and their outcome. Institutionalized infants, as well as those suffering from maternal deprivation or inadequate mothering, are especially at risk for learned helplessness due to the lack of adult responses to their actions. It is also possible for mothers who feel helpless to pass this quality on to their children. Learned helplessness in children, as in adults, can lead to anxiety or depression, and it can be especially damaging very early in life, for the sense of mastery over one's **environment** is an important foundation for future **emotional development**. Learned helplessness can also hamper education: a child who fails repeatedly in school will eventually stop trying, convinced that there is nothing he or she can do to succeed.

In the course of studying learned helplessness in humans, Seligman found that it tends to be associated with certain ways of thinking about events that form what he termed a person's "explanatory style." The three major components of explanatory style associated with learned helplessness are permanence, pervasiveness, and personalization. Permanence refers to the belief that negative events and/or their causes are permanent, even when evidence, logic, and past experience indicate that they are probably temporary ("Amy hates me and will never be my friend again" vs. "Amy is angry with me today"; "I'll never be good at math"). Pervasiveness refers to the tendency to generalize so that negative features of one situation are thought to extend to others as well ("I'm stupid" vs. "I failed a math test" or "nobody likes me" vs. "Janet didn't invite me to her party"). Personalization, the third component of explanatory style, refers to whether one tends to attribute negative events to one's own flaws or to outside circumstances or other people. While it is important to take responsibility for one's mistakes, persons suffering from learned helplessness tend to blame themselves for everything, a tendency associated with low **self-esteem** and depression. The other elements of explanatory style—permanence and pervasiveness—can be used as gauges to assess whether the degree of self-blame over a particular event or situation is realistic and appropriate.

Seligman believes it is possible to change people's explanatory styles to replace learned helplessness with "learned optimism." To combat (or even prevent) learned helplessness in both adults and children, he has successfully used techniques similar to those used in **cognitive therapy** with persons suffering from depression. These include identifying negative interpretations of events, evaluating their accuracy, generating more accurate interpretations, and decatastrophizing (countering the tendency to imagine the worst possible consequences for an event). He has also devised exercises to help children overcome negative explanatory style (one that tends toward permanent, pervasive, and personalized responses to negative situations). Other resources for promoting learned optimism in children include teaching them to dispute their own negative thoughts and promoting their problem-solving and social skills.

Seligman claims that parents can also promote learned optimism in children who are too young for the types of techniques outlined above by applauding and encouraging their mastery of new situations and letting them have as much control as possible in everyday activities such as dressing and eating. In addition, parents influence the degree of optimism in their youngsters through their own attitudes toward life and their explanatory styles, which can be transmitted even to very young children.

### Further Reading

Seligman, Martin. *Helplessness: On Development, Depression, and Death.* New York: W.H. Freeman, 1975.
———. *Learned Optimism.* New York: A.A. Knopf, 1991.
———. *The Optimistic Child.* New York: HarperCollins, 1995.

# Learning curve

The timeline of learning.

When a person is introduced to new information or a new skill, it may take several learning sessions to acquire that knowledge or skill. Psychologists refer to this acquisition process as the learning curve. In general, this term refers to the time it takes an individual to develop knowledge or a new skill.

Behavioral psychologists have noted that the degree, or strength, of learning reflects three factors. First, the degree of learning is associated with the number of reinforcements received during the acquisition of the behavior. In animal research, these reinforcements may be food pellets; in human research, the **reinforcement** may simply be knowledge about the number of correct and incorrect answers. In general, as the reinforcement increases, so does the performance level.

Second, there is a maximal level of performance associated with any behavior. This maximum is called the asymptote. Once this asymptote is reached, no further improvement in performance is possible.

Third, the greatest increase in the acquisition of the behavior will occur in the initial phases of learning. As the performance of the behavior approaches the asymptote, there is increasingly less room for further improvement.

Psychologists often use graphs to depict learning curves. The amount of practice at a task appears on the horizontal axis; the strength or accuracy of a response is recorded on the vertical axis. For a single individual, the tendency is to improve over time or practice, although an improvement may be temporarily followed by a decline in performance.

When a large number of individuals are tested and their average performance plotted, the learning curve gives the appearance of a gradual, smooth improvement over time. In the hypothetical learning curve in the accompanying graph, phase one reflects a period of familiarization with the task in which little learning takes place. In the second phase, there is a great deal of learning over a short period of time. In the final phase, the degree of learning is approaching asymptote, that is, the maximum. Any further change in performance will be minimal.

### Further Reading

Teplitz, Charles J. *The Learning Curve Deskbook: A Reference Guide to Theory, Calculations, and Applications.* New York: Quorum Books, 1991.

# Learning disability

A disorder that causes problems in speaking, listening, reading, writing, or mathematical ability.

A learning **disability**, or specific developmental disorder, is a disorder that inhibits or interferes with the skills of learning, including speaking, listening, reading, writing, or mathematical **ability**. Legally, a learning disabled child is one whose level of academic achievement is two or more years below the standard for his age and IQ level. It is estimated that 5-20% of school-age children in the United States, mostly boys, suffer from learning disabilities (currently, most sources place this figure at 20%). Often, learning disabilities appear together with other disorders, such as **attention deficit/hyperactivity disorder** (ADHD). They are thought to be caused by irregularities in the functioning of certain parts of the **brain**. Evidence suggests that these irregularities are often inherited (a person is more likely to develop a learning disability if other **family** members have them). However, learning disabilities are also associated with certain conditions occurring during fetal development or **birth**, including maternal use of alcohol, drugs, and tobacco, exposure to infection, injury during birth, low birth weight, and **sensory deprivation**.

Aside from underachievement, other warning signs that a person may have a learning disability include overall lack of organization, forgetfulness, and taking unusually long amounts of time to complete assignments. In the classroom, the child's teacher may observe one or more of the following characteristics: difficulty paying attention, unusual sloppiness and disorganization, social withdrawal, difficulty working independently, and trouble switching from one activity to another. In addition to the preceding signs, which relate directly to school and schoolwork, certain general behavioral and emotional features often accompany learning disabilities. These include impulsiveness, restlessness, distractibility, poor physical coordination, low tolerance for frustration, low self-esteem, **daydreaming**, inattentiveness, and **anger** or sadness.

## Types of learning disabilities

Learning disabilities are associated with brain dysfunctions that **affect** a number of basic skills. Perhaps the most fundamental is sensory-perceptual ability—the capacity to take in and process information through the senses. Difficulties involving **vision**, **hearing**, and **touch** will have an adverse effect on learning. Although learning is usually considered a mental rather than a physical pursuit, it involves motor skills, and it can also be impaired by problems with motor development. Other basic skills fundamental to learning include **memory**, attention, and language abilities.

The three most common academic skill areas affected by learning disabilities are reading, writing, and arithmetic. Some sources estimate that between 60-80% of children diagnosed with learning disabilities have reading as their only or main problem area. Learning disabilities involving reading have traditionally been known as **dyslexia**; currently the preferred term is **developmental reading disorder**. A wide array of problems is associated with reading disorders, including difficulty identifying groups of letters, problems relating letters to sounds, reversals and other errors involving letter position, chaotic spelling, trouble with syllabication, failure to recognize words, hesitant oral reading, and word-by-word rather than contextual reading. Writing disabilities, known as dysgraphia, include problems with letter formation and writing layout on the page, repetitions and omissions, punctuation and capitalization errors, "mirror writing," and a variety of spelling problems. Children with dysgraphia typically labor at written work much longer than their classmates, only to produce large, uneven writing that would be appropriate for a much younger child. Learning abilities involving math skills, generally referred to as dyscalcula (or dyscalculia), usually become apparent later than reading and writing problems—often at about the age of eight. Children with dyscalcula may have trouble counting, reading and writing numbers, understanding basic math concepts, mastering calculations, and measuring. This type of disability may also involve problems with nonverbal learning, including spatial organization.

## Treatment

The principal forms of treatment for learning disabilities are remedial education and **psychotherapy**. Either may be provided alone, the two may be provided simultaneously, or one may follow the other. Schools are required by law to provide specialized instruction for

This eight-year old boy with a learning disability that causes him to write some of these numbers backwards. *(Ellen B. Senisi. Photo Researchers, Inc. Reproduced with permission.)*

children with learning disabilities. Remediation may take place privately with a tutor or in a school resource center. A remediator works with the child individually, often devising strategies to circumvent the barriers caused by the disability. A child with dyscalcula, for example, may be shown a "shortcut" or "trick" that involves memorizing a spatial pattern or design and then superimposing it on calculations of a specific type, such as double-digit multiplication problems. The most important aspect of remediation is finding new ways to solve old problems. In this respect, remediation diverges from ordinary tutoring methods that use drill and repetition, which are ineffective in dealing with learning disabilities. The earlier remediation is begun, the more effective it will be. At the same time that they are receiving remedial help, children with learning disabilities spend as much time as possible in the regular classroom.

While remediation addresses the obstacles created by the learning disability itself, psychotherapy deals with the emotional and behavioral problems associated with the condition. The difficulties caused by learning disabilities are bound to affect a child's emotional state and behavior. The inability to succeed at tasks that pose no unusual problems for one's peers creates a variety of unpleasant feelings, including shame, doubt, embarrassment, frustration, anger, confusion, **fear**, and sadness. These feelings pose several dangers if they are allowed to persist over time. First, they may aggravate the disability: excessive **stress** can interfere with the performance of many tasks, especially those that are difficult to begin with. In addition, other, previously developed abilities may suffer as well, further eroding the child's self-confidence. Finally, destructive emotional and behavioral patterns that begin in response to a learning disability may become entrenched and extend to other areas of a child's life. Both psychoanalytic and behaviorally oriented methods are used in therapy for children with learning disabilities.

The sensitivity developed over the past two decades to the needs of students with learning disabilities has extended to adults as well in some sectors. Some learning disabled adults have been accommodated by special measures such as extra time on projects at work. They may also be assigned tasks that does not require a lot of written communication. For example, a learning disabled person might take customer service phone calls, rather than reading and processing customer comment cards.

Because there is no "cure" for learning disability, it will continue to affect the lives of learning-disabled people, and the strategies they may have learned to succeed in school must also be applied in their vocation.

**Further Reading**

Tuttle, Cheryl Gerson, and Gerald A. Tuttle, eds. *Challenging Voices: Writings By, For, and About People with Learning Disabilities.* Los Angeles: Lowell House, 1995.
Wong, Y.L., ed. *Learning About Learning Disabilities.* San Diego: Academic Press, 1991.

**Further Information**

Association for Children and Adults with Learning Disabilities. 4900 Girard Rd., Pittsburgh, PA 15227–1444, (412) 881–2253.
National Center for Learning Disabilities. 99 Park Ave., New York, NY 10016, (212) 687–7211.

# Learning theory

Theory about how people learn and modify pre-existing thoughts and behavior.

Psychologists have suggested a variety of theories to explain the process of learning. During the first half of the 20th century, American psychologists approached the concept of learning primarily in terms of behaviorist principles that focused on the automatic formation of associations between stimuli and responses. One form of associative learning— classical conditioning—is based on the pairing of two stimuli. Through an association with an unconditioned stimulus (such as meat offered to a dog), a **conditioned stimulus** (such as a bell) eventually elicits a **conditioned response** (salivation), even when the unconditioned stimulus is absent. Principles of **classical conditioning** include the **extinction** of the response if the conditioned and unconditioned stimuli cease to be paired, and the generalization of the response to stimuli that are similar but not identical to the original ones. In **operant conditioning**, a response is learned because it leads to a particular consequence (**reinforcement**), and it is strengthened each time it is reinforced. Positive reinforcement strengthens a response if it is presented afterwards, while negative reinforcement strengthens it by being withheld. Once a response has been learned, it may be sustained by partial reinforcement, which is provided only after selective responses.

In **contrast** to theories of classical and **operant conditioning**, which describe learning in terms of observable behavior, intervening variable theories introduce such elements as **memory**, **motivation**, and **cognition**. **Edward Tolman** demonstrated in the 1920s that learning can in-

volve knowledge without observable performance. The performance of rats who negotiated the same maze on consecutive days with no reward improved drastically after the introduction of a goal box with food, leading to the conclusion that they had developed "cognitive maps" of the maze earlier, even in the absence of a reward, although this "latent learning" had not been reflected in their observable behavior. Even earlier, **Wolfgang Köhler**, a founder of the Gestalt school of psychology, had argued for the place of cognition in learning. Based on experiments conducted on the island of Tenerife during World War I, Köhler concluded that insight played a role in problem-solving by chimpanzees. Rather than simply stumbling on solutions through trial and error, the animals he observed seemed to demonstrate a holistic understanding of problems, such as getting hold of fruit that was placed out of reach, by arriving at solutions in a sudden moment of revelation or insight.

The drive-reduction theory of Clark L. Hull and Kenneth W. Spence, which became influential in the 1930s, introduced motivation as an intervening variable in the form of homeostasis, the tendency to maintain equilibrium by adjusting physiological responses. An imbalance creates needs, which in turn create drives. Actions can be seen as attempts to reduce these drives by meeting the associated needs. According to drive-reduction theory, the association of stimulus and response in classical and operant conditioning only results in learning if accompanied by drive reduction.

In recent decades, cognitive theories such as those of social learning theorist **Albert Bandura** have been influential. Bandura is particularly known for his work on observational learning, also referred to as **modeling** or **imitation**. It is common knowledge that children learn by watching their parents, other adults, and their peers. According to Bandura, the extent to which children and adults learn behaviors through imitation is influenced not only by the observed activity itself but also by its consequences. Behavior that is rewarded is more readily imitated than behavior that is punished. Bandura coined the term "vicarious conditioning" for learning based on the observed consequences of others' actions, listing the following requirements for this type of learning: attention to the behavior; retention of what is seen; ability to reproduce the behavior; and motivation. Cognitive approaches such as Bandura's have led to an enhanced understanding of how conditioning works, while conditioning principles have helped researchers better understand certain facets of cognition.

Computers play an important role in current research on learning, both in the areas of computer-assisted learning and in the attempt to further understand the neurological processes involved in learning through the development of computer-based neural networks that can simulate various forms of learning.

## Further Reading

Bower, G. H., and E. Hilgard. *Theories of Learning.* 5th ed. Englewood Cliffs, NJ: Prentice-Hall, 1981.

Grippin, Pauline. *Learning Theory and Learning Outcomes: The Connection.* Lanham, MD: University Press of America, 1984.

Norman, D.A. *Learning and Memory.* San Francisco: Freeman, 1982.

# Learning-to-learn

*The phenomenon of greater improvement in speed of learning as one's experience with learning increases.*

When people try to learn a new behavior, the first attempts are often not very successful. After a time, however, they seem to get the idea of the behavior and the pace of learning increases. This phenomenon of greater improvement in speed of learning is called learning-to-learn (LTL). There are two general reasons for the existence of LTL. First, negative transfer diminishes. When people have learned to do something, they have often developed schemas or learning sets, that is, ways to approach those tasks. When a new behavior is required, old approaches that may be irrelevant or that may get in the way must be discarded. Learning becomes easier when irrelevant or distracting behaviors disappear. Second, there may be positive transfer of previous knowledge that might be usefully applied to the situation.

Learning-to-learn is most obvious in tasks that are somewhat complicated or varied. LTL occurs when the learner realizes how the various components of an overall behavior fit together. When learners must deal with a lot of information, they can develop the required higher order principles that allow them to develop a general perspective on the behavior. As a result, subsequent learning fits together because it fits in more naturally with the person's overall perspective. When the behavior to be learned is simple, no such perspective is needed, so LTL is less relevant.

# Left-brain hemisphere

*The hemisphere of the brain that specializes in spoken and written language, logic, number skills, and scientific concepts.*

The left-brain hemisphere neurologically controls the right side of the body and is connected to the **right-brain hemisphere** by an extensive bundle of over a million **nerve** fibers called the corpus callosum. Scientific study of the **brain** hemispheres dates back to the 1800s. In the 1860s, French physician Paul Broca (1824-1880) observed speech dysfunction in patients with lesions on the left frontal lobes of their brains. Initially, the discovery of specialized functioning of the right and left sides of the brain led to the assumption that all higher reasoning **ability** resided in the left-brain hemisphere, which was thus regarded as dominant overall. The right-brain hemisphere was thought to possess only lower-level capabilities and was considered subordinate to the left-brain hemisphere.

Interest in the functions of the brain hemispheres was revived in the 1960s, with Roger Sperry's studies of patients who had the corpus callosum severed to control epileptic seizures. It was discovered that each hemisphere of the brain specialized in performing certain types of functions, a phenomenon now known as *lateralization* . While the left-brain hemisphere performs functions involving logic and language more efficiently, the right-brain hemisphere is more adept in the areas of music, art, and spatial relations. Each hemisphere processes information differently; the left-brain hemisphere is thought to function in a logical and sequential way; the right appears to synthesize material simultaneously. These differences can also be investigated in **normal** patients (in whom the hemispheres are connected) by temporarily disabling a single brain hemisphere with sodium amytal, a fast-acting barbiturate, and by other means.

Lateralization varies considerably among individuals. Two factors known to affect it are **handedness** and gender. In one experiment, almost all right-handed persons were unable to speak when their left-brain hemispheres were disabled. In contrast, the incidence decreased to 20 to 40 percent among left-handed people, indicating that only this percentage had their speech centers located in the left-brain hemisphere. Other left-handed subjects appear to use both hemispheres for speech. In general, each gender is known to excel at certain lateralized functions: women are more adept in language-based skills, perceptual fluency tasks (such as identifying matching terms rapidly), and arithmetic calculations. Men are generally more proficient in envisioning and manipulating objects in space. It has also been found that brain function in males is more lateralized than in females. Men who have had one brain hemisphere disabled are more debilitated than similarly affected women. In particular, men display more language difficulties than women when the left hemisphere is damaged. However, it is also known that the sexes are more dependent on different areas of each hemisphere, so the assessment of function after damage also depends on where the damage is localized. In addition, conclusions about lateralization and gender are complicated by the fact that those functions at which members of a particular gender appear to be more adept are often those they are likely to have done more of (such as men manipulating tools), raising the question of environmental as opposed to biological factors.

When the left-brain hemisphere is damaged, the result is often severe aphasia—difficulty using or understanding spoken or written language. Damage localized in the left temporal cortex can cause Wernicke's **aphasia**, which disturbs the ability to comprehend language. A different condition, called Broca's aphasia, results from damage to the left frontal cortex and interferes with a person's ability to produce language. Persons affected with this disorder experience halting speech, and they often have difficulty recalling even the most familiar words.

Additional methods for studying brain hemispheres include autopsies of cadavers that reveal the location of brain lesions, observation of dysfunction in living patients with known brain lesions, and electrical stimulation of various areas of the brain. **Biofeedback** instruments have also contributed to the body of knowledge about brain hemispheres; when wired to a research subject, they show a higher electrical discharge from whichever hemisphere is active at a given point in time, while recording alpha rhythms from an inactive hemisphere. Researchers have also made use of the discovery that the eyes will typically move away from the more active hemisphere and toward the side of the body controlled by that hemisphere.

*See also* Brain

# Kurt Lewin

**1890-1947**
American social psychologist who carried out researches that are fundamental to the study of the dynamics and the manipulation of human behavior. He is the originator of field theory.

Kurt Lewin was born in Mogilno, Prussia, on September 9, 1899. He studied at the universities of Freiburg and Munich and completed his doctorate at the University of Berlin in 1914. He taught in Berlin from 1921 until the advent of Hitler to **power** in 1933, when he emigrated to the United States. He was visiting professor at Stanford and at Cornell before receiving an appointment as professor of **child psychology** in the Child Welfare Research Station of the State University of Iowa in 1935.

In 1945 he left Iowa to start the Research Center for Group Dynamics at the Massachusetts Institute of Technology. He also served as visiting professor at the University of California, Berkeley, and at Harvard.

At Iowa, Lewin and his associates conducted notable research on the effect of democratic, autocratic, and laissez-faire methods of **leadership** upon the other members of groups. Largely on the basis of controlled experiments with groups of children, Lewin maintained that contrary to popular belief the democratic leader has no less power than the autocratic leader and that the characters and personalities of those who are led are rapidly and profoundly affected by a change in social atmosphere. In effecting such changes on human behavior patterns, Lewin argued, the democratic group that has long-range planning surpasses both the autocratic and laissez-faire groups in creative initiative and sociality. As a general rule, he contended, the more democratic the procedures are, the less resistance there is to change.

The central factors to be considered if one wishes to transform a nondemocratic group into a democratic one are ideology, the **character** of its members, and the locus of coercive physical power within the group. Although coercive physical power is thus not the *only* factor to be considered, Lewin warns against the naive belief in the goodness of human nature, which overlooks the fact that ideology itself cannot be changed by teaching and moral suasion alone. It can be done only by a change in the distribution of coercive physical power. But he also warns that democratic behavior cannot be learned by autocratic methods. The members of the group must at least *feel* that the procedures are "democratic."

Lewin was a Gestalt psychologist, and that approach materially influenced him when he originated field theory. Strictly speaking, field theory is an approach to the study of human behavior, not a theory with content which can be used for explanatory, predictive, or control purposes. His work in this area has been judged as the single most influential element in modern **social psychology**, leading to large amounts of research and opening new fields of inquiry. According to Lewin, field theory (which is a complex concept) is best characterized as a method, a method of analyzing causal relations and building scientific constructs. It is an approach which maintains that to represent and interpret faithfully the complexity of concrete reality requires continual crossing of the traditional boundaries of the social sciences, rather than a progressive narrowing of **attention** to a limited number of variables. The theory, which requires an interdisciplinary approach to the understanding of concrete reality, has also been termed dynamic theory and topological psychology. It holds that events are determined by forces acting on them in an immediate field rather than by forces acting at

**Kurt Lewin** *(The Library of Congress. Reproduced with permission.)*

a distance. In the last analysis, it is a theory about theory building, or a metatheory.

Lewin believed that a social scientist has an obligation to use his resources to solve social problems. He helped found the Commission on Community Interrelations of the American Jewish Congress and the National Training Laboratories. Shortly after his death on February 12, 1947, the Research Center for Group Dynamics was moved to the University of Michigan, where it became one of two divisions of the Institute for Social Research and continued to exercise an important influence.

*See also* Gestalt psychology

**Further Reading**

Leeper, Robert W. *Lewin's topological and vector psychology: a digest and a critique.* 1943.

Marrow, Alfred Jay, *The practical theorist: the life and work of Kurt Lewin,* New York: Teachers College Press, 1977.

## Libido

In Freudian psychology, a term designating psychic or sexual energy.

The term libido, which **Sigmund Freud** used as early as 1894 and as late as the 1930s, underwent changes as he expanded, developed, and revised his theories of **sexuality, personality** development, and **motivation**. In Freud's early works, it is associated specifically with sexuality. Libido is central to the theory of psychosexual development outlined in *Three Essays on the Theory of Sexuality* (1905). It is the energy that is repeatedly redirected to different erogenous zones throughout the stages of pregenital sexuality (oral, anal, phallic) that take place between **birth** and the age of about five years. After the latency period, the libido reemerges in its mature manifestation at the genital stage that begins in **adolescence**. During all these permutations, the libido also shifts from being primarily autoerotic and narcissistic to being directed at a love object.

When Freud reformulated his theory of motivation around 1920, he defined libido more broadly in terms of opposed life and death instincts (Eros and Thanatos). Libido in this context is the source of the life instincts that motivate not only sexuality and other basic drives but also more complex human activities such as the creation of art.

**Further Reading**

Freud, Sigmund. *New Introductory Lectures on Psychoanalysis.* New York: W. W. Norton, 1933.

Hall, Calvin S. *A Primer of Freudian Psychology.* New York: Harper and Row, 1982.

## Lie detection

A procedure (or machine) designed to distinguish truth-tellers from liars.

Because emotional states are often accompanied by physiological arousal, researchers have often wondered if physiological measurements could be used to detect what a person is thinking or feeling. If you feel guilty for telling a lie, are there physiological cues that will betray you? The assumption that there are such cues forms the basic rationale behind the polygraph test. It is assumed that a guilty person will have increased autonomic arousal in response to certain key questions, compared to the arousal levels of an innocent person. In a conventional polygraph examination, GSR, blood pressure, and heart rate are monitored. GSR refers to galvanic skin response. Sweating causes a brief drop in the electrical resistance of the skin. This resistance (the GSR) can be measured by means of electrodes attached to the hand. An arm band is used to measure blood pressure and pulse rate. Thus the polygraph does not measure lying directly, it measures the physiological responses that are

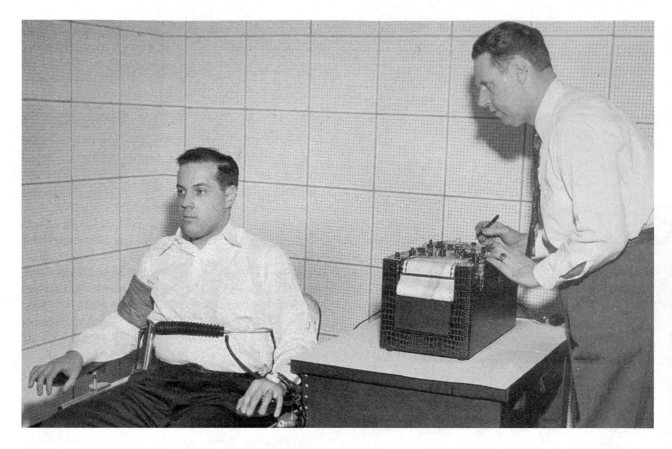

**An early lie detector in use.** *(Archive Photos. Reproduced with permission.)*

assumed to accompany lying. Does it work? Can the polygraph help us distinguish between truth-tellers and liars? Some psychologists maintain that it is both reliable and valid, however this is a minority view. Most researchers dispute its usefulness—largely because no physiological pattern of activity is a foolproof reflection of deceit. There is a real danger that innocent people could be misidentified as liars, simply because of high anxiety triggered by a potentially incriminating question (e.g., "Did you steal the car?"). Alternatively, accomplished liars may be able to lie without flinching.

Consider what could happen if a polygraph test were administered to 1000 employees of a large department store, the owners of which are worried about employee theft. Let us assume that the test is 90% accurate (a generous assumption). Most people do not steal from their employers, so let us also assume that only 10% of the 1000 employees are thieves. Of the 100 thieves, the test will correctly identify 90% of them, assuming that all 100 lie when administered the test. These 90 liars could then be fired, and the costs of employee theft would be reduced. But what about the honest people who have not stolen anything? Of the 900 people who

told the truth, 90% of them will be correctly identified as truth-tellers, but the other 10% will be misidentified as liars. Ten percent of 900 is 90. In other words, the test misidentifies 90 truth-tellers as liars, along with the original 90 who really did lie. At the end of the day, the store owners have 180 people classified as liars, but only half of them actually lied. If all 180 are fired, fully half of them have been wrongfully dismissed. For obvious reasons, the preceding scenario would be totally unacceptable. Most courts in the United States and Canada do not admit polygraph evidence in trials, and there are legal prohibitions against using lie detectors to screen job applicants or randomly test employees.

In criminal investigations, the polygraph test can sometimes be very helpful. If the police have information about a crime that would only be known to the perpetrator, the polygraph may reveal "guilty knowledge." Suppose a mugging victim was wearing a red sweater and was robbed on the corner of 5th and Main. A series of questions can be prepared, such as: "Was the victim wearing a green sweater?", "A yellow sweater?", "A rain coat?", etc. An innocent person would have no knowledge of what the victim was wearing, thus patterns of physiological arousal would be similar across all questions. Similarly, questions about the location of the crime scene would not be expected to show increased arousal on the key question (e.g., "5th & Main?" versus "3rd & Oak?"). An accused who answers "I don't know" to all questions, but who shows arousal only to the key questions may be indicating to the police that further investigation of that particular suspect is warranted.

Timothy E. Moore

## Further Reading
Iacono, W., and D. Lykken. "The scientific status of research on polygraph techniques: The case against polygraph tests." In D. Faigman et al. (eds.). *Modern scientific evidence: The law and science of expert testimony.* St. Paul, MN: West, 1997.

Saxe, L. "Detection of deception: Polygraph and integrity tests." *Current directions in psychological science,* 3, (1994): 69-73.

# Localization (brain function)

Refers to the concept that different areas of the brain control different aspects of behavior.

Theories of localization first gained scientific credence in the 1860s with Paul Broca's discovery that damage to a specific part of the brain—the left frontal lobe—was associated with speech impairment. Other discoveries followed: in 1874, **Carl Wernicke** identified the part of the **brain** responsible for receptive speech (the upper rear part of the left temporal lobe, known as Wernicke's area), and in 1870 Gustav Fritsch and J. L. Hitzig found that stimulating different parts of the cerebral cortex produced movement in different areas of the body. By the beginning of the twentieth century, detailed maps were available showing the functions of the different areas of the brain.

Not all researchers have agreed with theories of localization, however. An influential conflicting view is the equipotential theory, which asserts that all areas of the brain are equally active in overall mental functioning. According to this theory, the effects of damage to the brain are determined by the extent rather than the location of the damage. Early exponents of this view—including Goldstein and Lashley—believed that basic motor and sensory functions are localized, but that higher mental functions are not. There is still controversy between adherents of the localization and equipotential theories of brain function. Some experts advocate a com-

bination of the two theories, while others search for new alternatives, such as that proposed by J. Hughlings Jackson in 1973. Jackson claimed that the most basic skills were localized but that most complex mental functions combined these so extensively that the whole brain was actually involved in most types of behavior.

## Further Reading
Corballis, Michael C. *The Lopsided Ape: Evolution of the Generative Mind.* New York: Oxford University Press, 1991.

Edwards, Betty. *Drawing on the Right Side of the Brain.* Los Angeles: J. P. Tarcher, 1979.

Hampden-Turner, Charles. *Maps of the Mind.* New York: Collier Books, 1981.

# Localization (sensory)

The ability of animals and humans to determine the origin of a sensory input.

One of the highly developed abilities that humans and other animals possess is the ability to determine where a sensory input originates.

The capacity to localize a sound, for example, depends on two general mechanisms. The first is relevant for low frequency (i.e., low pitch) sounds and involves the fact that sound coming from a given source arrives at our ears at slightly different times. The second mechanisms applies to high frequency (i.e., high pitch) sounds; if such a sound comes from one side, one ear hears it more loudly than the other and we can detect location based on differences in the loudness of the sound at each ear.

Low frequency sounds that come from the noise-making source will enter the nearer ear first; these sound waves will then bend around our head and arrive at the far ear a short time later. If the sound is almost directly in front of us, the sound arrives at one ear an extremely short time ahead of its arrival at the other ear. Humans can detect differences of perhaps 10 millionths of a second in arrival time. If the sound comes from the side, the difference in time of arrival at the two ears is longer. In either case, our **brain** executes quick computations to inform us about the location of the sound. Other animals, like nocturnal owls, have shown greater sensitivity to differences in time of arrival.

The second mechanism involves intensity differences in sound waves traveling to the ears. High frequency sound waves do not bend around the head like low frequency waves. Instead, high frequency sound waves tend to reflect off the surface of the head. As a consequence, a sound coming from one side of the head will show greater intensity in one ear; that is, it will be slightly louder in one ear. The brain uses this intensity difference to tell us where a sound originates.

In general, we locate sounds below about 1500 Hz (i.e., 1500 cycles per second) by analyzing differences in time of arrival at each ear; above 1500 Hz, we use intensity differences. Sounds that are right around 1500 Hz are hardest to localize. Further, we are likely to confuse sounds that are directly in front of us, above us, and behind us because their positions are such that we cannot use time of arrival and intensity differences.

Finally, sometimes we ignore the cues for sound localization if logic tells us that the sound should be coming from another direction. For example, when we listen to somebody on a stage, we may hear the sounds they produce from a loudspeaker that is above us. Nonetheless, we localize the sound as coming from the person on the stage because it seems more logical. Psychologists refer to this phenomenon as "visual capture."

## Further Reading

Corballis, Michael C. *The Lopsided Ape: Evolution of the Generative Mind*. New York: Oxford University Press, 1991.

Hampden-Turner, Charles. *Maps of the Mind*. New York: Collier Books, 1981

# John Locke

### 1632-1704
English philosopher and political theorist who attempted to center philosophy on an analysis of the extent and capabilities of the human mind.

John Locke was born on August 29, 1632, in Wrington, in Somerset, where his mother's family resided. She died during his infancy, and Locke was raised by his father, who was an attorney in the small town of Pensford near Bristol. John was tutored at home because of his always-delicate health and the outbreak of civil war in 1642. When he was 14, he entered Westminster School, where he remained for six years. He then went to Christ Church, Oxford. In 1658 he was elected a senior student at his college. In this capacity he taught Greek and moral philosophy. Under conditions at the time he would have had to be ordained to retain his fellowship. Instead he changed to another faculty, medicine, and eventually received a license to practice. During the same period Locke made the acquaintance of Robert Boyle, the distinguished scientist and one of the founders of the Royal Society, and, under Boyle's direction, took up study of natural science. Finally, in 1668, Locke was made a fellow of the Royal Society.

In 1665, Locke traveled to the Continent as secretary to the English ambassador to the Brandenburg court. Upon his return to England he chanced to medically attend Lord Ashley, First Earl of Shaftesbury, and later lord chancellor of England. Their friendship and lifelong association drew Locke into political affairs. He attended Shaftesbury as physician and adviser, and in this latter capacity Locke drafted *The Fundamental Constitutions of Carolina* and served as secretary to the Board of Trade. In 1676 Locke went to France for his health. An inheritance from his father made him financially independent, and he remained in Montpellier for three years.

Locke rejoined Shaftesbury's service, and when the latter fled to Holland, the philosopher followed. He remained in exile from 1683 to 1689, and during these years he was deprived of his studentship by express order of Charles III. Most of his important writings were composed during this period. After the Glorious Revolution of 1689 Locke returned to England and later served with distinction as a commissioner of trade until 1700. He spent his retirement at Oates in Essex as the guest of the Mashams. Lady Masham was the daughter of Ralph Cudworth, the philosopher. Locke died there on October 28, 1704.

## Major works

Locke, by virtue of his **temperament** and **mode** of existence, was a man of great circumspection. None of his major writings was published until he was nearly 60. In 1690 he brought out his major works: *Two Treatises* and the *Essay Concerning Human Understanding* . But the four books of the *Essay* were the culmination of 20 years of intellectual labor. He relates that, together with a few friends, probably in 1670, a discussion arose concerning the basis of morality and religion. The conclusion was that they were unable to resolve the question until an investigation had been made to see "what objects our understandings were or were not fitted to deal with." Thus the aim of this work is "to inquire into the origin, certainty, and extent of human knowledge, together with the grounds of belief, opinion, and assent."

The procedure employed is what he called the "historical, plain method," which consists of observations derived from external sensations and the internal processes of reflection or introspection. This psychological definition of experience as sensation and reflection shifted the focus of philosophy from an analysis of reality to an exploration of the mind. The new perspective was Locke's major contribution, and it dominated European thought for at least two centuries. But if knowledge consists entirely of experience, then the objects of **cognition** are ideas. The term "idea" was ambiguously defined by Locke as "whatsoever is the object of the understanding when a man thinks." This broad use means that sensations, memories, imaginings, and feelings as well as concepts are ideas insofar as they are mental. The danger of Locke's epistemology is the inherent skepticism contained in a technique which describes what is "in" the mind. For if everything is an idea, then it is difficult to distinguish between true and false, real and imaginary, impressed sensations and expressed concepts. Thus Locke, and the subsequent history of philosophy, had to wrestle with the dilemma that a psychological description of the origin of ideas seriously undermines the extent of their objective validity.

Nonetheless the intention of the *Essay* was positive in that Locke wished to establish the dependence of all human knowledge upon everyday experience or sensation. The alternative theory of innate ideas is vigorously attacked. Although it is not historically certain whether anyone seriously maintained such a doctrine, Locke's general criticism lends indirect support to an experiential view of knowledge. Innatism can be understood in a naive way to mean that there are ideas of which we are fully conscious at **birth** or which are universally acknowledged, so that the mind possesses a disposition to think in terms of certain ideas. The first position is refuted by observation of children, and the second by the fact that there are no acknowledged universal ideas to which everyone agrees. The sophisticated version falls into contradiction by maintaining that we are conscious of an **unconscious** disposition.

## Theory of knowledge

Having refuted the a priori, or nonexperiential, account of knowledge, Locke devotes the first two books of the *Essay* to developing a deceptively simple empirical theory of knowledge. Knowing originates in external and internal sources of sensation and reflection. The objects or ideas present to **consciousness** are divided into simple and complex. Simple ideas are primitive sense data, which the mind passively receives and cannot alter, delivered by one sense (seeing blue), by several senses (eating an orange as a synthesis of **taste**, **touch**, and **smell**), by reflection (hunger), or by a combination of sensation and reflection (pleasure and **pain**). The objective orientation of simple ideas follows from the fact that we cannot add or subtract from their appearance or conception in the mind. In relation to simple ideas, at least, the mind is passive, a "blank" or "white" tablet upon which sensations are impressed. Complex ideas are formed by actively combining, comparing, or abstracting simple ideas to yield "modes, substances, and relations." Modes are class concepts or ideas that do not exist independently, such as beauty. Substance is a complex idea

**John Locke** *(Rutgers University Library. Reproduced with permission.)*

of the unity of substrate of the simple qualities we perceive. And relations are the powers in objects capable of causing minds to make comparisons, for example, identity and cause and effect. The difficulty is that complex ideas do not relate to perceivable existents, but hopefully, complex ideas do express elements or characteristics of the real world.

Locke is faced with an acute dilemma. If the immediate object of knowledge is an idea, then man possesses only a derivative knowledge of the physical world. To know the real world adequately requires a complex idea which expresses the relation between the qualities that we perceive subjectively and the unperceived existent. The substance which unites the common perceived qualities of figure, bulk, and color into this one existing brown table is, in Locke's terms, an "I don't know what." His honesty almost brought Locke to a modern relational definition of substance instead of the traditional notion of a thing characterized by its properties. But the conclusion drawn in the *Essay* is that knowledge is relational; that is, it consists in the perception "of the agreement or disagreement among ideas." For if Locke had argued that knowledge expresses an adequation between the complex idea in the mind and the real object, then man would have the **power** to go beyond ideas to the object itself. But this is impossible, since every object is, by definition, an idea, and thus ironically, experiential knowledge is not about real objects but only about the perceived relations of ideas.

The third book of the *Essay* deals with words, and it is a pioneer contribution to the philosophy of language. Locke is a consistent nominalist in that for him language is an arbitrary convention and words are things which "stand for nothing but the ideas in the mind of the man that has them." Each man's understanding can be confirmed by other minds insofar as they share the same linguistic conventions, although one of the singular abuses of language results from the fact that we learn names or words before understanding their use.

The purpose of Locke's analysis is to account for generalization, abstraction, and universals in terms of language. Generalizations are the result of drawing, or abstracting, what is common to many. In this sense, generalizations and universals are inventions of the mind which concern only signs. But they have a foundation in the similitude of things. And those class concepts which have a fixed meaning and definition can be understood as essences, but they are only nominal and not real. The difference between our knowledge and reality is like that between seeing the exterior of Big Ben and understanding how the clock works.

The final section of the *Essay* deals with the extent, types, and divisions of knowledge. This work seems to have been written earlier than the others, and many of its conclusions are qualified by preceding material. The agreement or disagreement of ideas, which constitutes knowledge, consists of identity and diversity, perceived relations, coexistence or real existence known by way of intuition, and demonstration or sensation of a given existent.

In this view the actual extent of man's knowledge is less than his ideas because he does not know the real connections between simple ideas, or primary and secondary qualities. Also, an intuitive knowledge of existence is limited to the self, and the only demonstrable existence is that of God as an eternal, omnipotent being. With the exception of the self and God, all knowledge of existing things is dependent upon sensation, whose cognitive status is "a little bit better than probability." The poverty of real knowledge is compensated to some extent by human judgment, which presumes things to be true without actually perceiving the connections. And, according to Locke's commonsense attitude, the severe restrictions placed upon knowledge merely reflect that man's mental capacity is suitable for his nature and condition.

**Further Reading**

Yolton, John W., ed. *An essay concerning human understanding.* 2 vols. 1961. rev. ed. 1965.

Laslett, Peter, ed. *Two treatises of government.* 1960.
Cranston, Maurice. *John Locke: a biography.* 1957.
Yolton, John W. *John Locke and the way of ideas.* 1956.
Kendall, Willmoore. *John Locke and the doctrine of majority rule.* 1959.
Martin, Charles B. and D.M. Armstrong, eds. *Locke and Berkeley: a collection of critical essays.* 1968.
Yolton, John W. *John Locke: problems and perspectives: a collection of new essays.* 1969.

# Locus of control

A personality orientation characterized either by the belief that one can control events by one's own efforts (internal locus of control) or that the future is determined by forces outside one's control (external locus of control).

If a person with an internal locus of control does badly on a test, she is likely to blame either her own lack of ability or preparation for the test. By comparison, a person with an external locus of control will tend to explain a low grade by saying that the test was too hard or that the teacher graded unfairly. The concept of locus of control was developed by psychologist **Julian Rotter**, who devised the Internal-External Locus of Control Scale (I-E) to assess this dimension of **personality**. Studies have found that this test is a valid predictor of behavior typically associated with locus of control.

Links have been found between locus of control and behavior patterns in a number of different areas. People with an internal locus of control are inclined to take responsibility for their actions, are not easily influenced by the opinions of others, and tend to do better at tasks when they can work at their own pace. By comparison, people with an external locus of control tend to blame outside circumstances for their mistakes and credit their successes to luck rather than to their own efforts. They are readily influenced by the opinions of others and are more likely to pay attention to the status of the opinion-holder, while people with an internal locus of control pay more attention to the content of the opinion regardless of who holds it. Some researchers have claimed that "internals" tend to be more intelligent and more success-oriented than "externals." In the elementary grades, children with an internal locus of control have been found to earn higher grades, although there are conflicting reports about whether there is a relationship between college grades and locus of control. There is also a relationship between a child's locus of control and his or her ability to delay gratification (to forgo an immediate pleasure or desire in order to be rewarded with a more substantial one later). In middle **childhood**, children with an internal locus of control are relatively successful in the **delay of gratification**, while children with an external locus of control are likely to make less of an effort to exert self-control in the present because they doubt their ability to influence events in the future.

Although people can be classified comparatively as "internals" or "externals," chronological development within each individual generally proceeds in the direction of an internal locus control. As infants and children grow older they feel increasingly competent to control events in their lives. Consequently, they move from being more externally focused to a more internal locus.

**Further Reading**

Bem, Allen P. *Personality Theories.* Boston: Allyn and Bacon, 1994.

Burger, Jerry M. *Personality.* Pacific Grove, CA: Brooks/Cole Publishing Company, 1993.

# Logical thinking

The ability to understand and to incorporate the rules of basic logical inference in everyday activities.

Regarded as a universal human trait, the ability to think logically, following the rules of logical inference, has traditionally been defined as a higher cognitive skill. The field of cognitive **child psychology** was dominated for more than half a century by the Swiss philosopher and psychologist **Jean Piaget**, whose studies are considered fundamental. Piaget identified four stages of **cognitive development**. During the *sensory-motor stage* (ages 0-2), the child learns to experience the world physically and attains a rudimentary grasp of symbols. In the *preoperational stage* (ages 2-7), symbols are used, but thought is still "preoperational," which means that the child does not understand that a logical, or mathematical, operation can be reversed. The *concrete operations stage* (ages 6 or 7-11) ushers in logical thinking; children, for instance, understand principles such as cause and effect. The *formal operations stage* (12-adulthood), introduces abstract thinking (i.e., thought operations that do not need to relate to concrete concepts and phenomena).

Logical thinking, in Piaget's developmental scheme, is operational, which means that it does not appear before the concrete operations stage. While students of child **cognition** generally agree with Piaget's developmental milestones, subsequent research in the area has led researchers to question the idea that some logical thinking cannot appear in the preoperational stage. For example, Olivier Houdè and Camilo Charron tested a

group of 72 children between the ages of five and eight, giving them various tasks related to classes of objects, and found that children who could not perform extensional logic tasks were nevertheless able to practice intensional logic. (Intension defines the properties of a class, while extension determines who or what can be a member of a particular class; if the intension of a class is "red objects," the extension will include any particular object that happens to be red.) However, Piaget knew that preoperational children could practice intensional logic, but, in his view, incomplete logical thought was, by definition, pre-logical. For example, children who understand the meaning (intensionality) of a "red objects" class may decide not to include certain red objects—for reasons that the experimenter would define as illogical (e.g.: "it's too little").

Houdè and Charron have identified an "operational proto-logic" in children whom Piaget would define as pre-logical. Instead of arbitrarily promoting purely intensional thinking to the rank of full-fledged (extensional and intensional) logical thought, Houdè and Charron decided to investigate the mental processes underlying seemingly illogical behavior. In a series of experiments involving children aged five to eight, a group straddling the pre-operational/operational boundary, the two researchers focused on the intensional logicians who failed the extensional logic (inclusion). Clearly, the act of not including some red object in the "red objects" class was, in a strictly Piagetian sense, illogical, or, more precisely, illogical behavior, but was that behavior determined by irrational thinking? To their surprise, they found, particularly in a modified form of the "partition" experiment (Piaget and Garcia, 1987), that, when shown the drawing of a circle (B) divided into two by a line (the two sub-classes being A and A'), A' may be ignored as a subclass of B, not because of illogical thinking, but because A is more compelling from the point of view of **perception**. According to Pascual-Leone (Pascual-Leone, 1988), there is a misleading scheme underlying the perception of B, and a subclass is excluded. According to Houdè and Charron, the child understands the intensional logic, or meaning, of the "red objects" class, but stumbles at the extensional, or inclusion, level because of perceptual factors. Thus, the undeniable Piagetian shift, around the age of seven years, from non-inclusive to inclusive behavior does not indicate a quantum leap from pre-logical to logical thinking, but, rather, reflects the presence of an inhibiting mechanism, whereby the confusing effect of perception on cognition is neutralized. Thus, as Houdè and Charron have remarked, a non-inclusive six-year-old may have an inefficient inhibiting mechanism. These findings, although suggesting a continuum model of cognitive development, as opposed to the Piagetian idea of a quantum leap from pre-logical to logical thinking, does not, in fact question the foundations of Piaget's essentially developmental theory of cognition. Piaget himself, in his search for the origins of logical thinking, studied very young children, ever mindful of the relevance of other mental, and non-mental, factors and processes to the emergence of logical thought. Finally, Piaget's work was the foundation from which emerged the insight, corroborated by empirical observation, that the very young child is already a logician.

Philosophers specializing in the study of **childhood** have found that the logical repertoire of young children is not limited to intensional logic. Many utterances made by children, particularly statements involving the concepts of possibility and necessity, exhibit a grasp, albeit rudimentary, of modal logic, i.e., the branch of logic which formulates rules for propositions about possibility and necessity (Matthews, 1980). The fact that the discourse of young children fits easily into the formal context of modal logic, which is related to intensional logic, indicates that the children's logical aptitude may yield new surprises. Building on the rich legacy of Piaget's work, researchers have significantly expanded the field of cognitive development, gaining critical insights which will further elucidate the human paradigm. The crucial relevance of Piagetian and post-Piagetian studies for the inquiry concerning logical thinking in children lies in the fact that these studies have shed light on the important role played by non-logical, and non-mental, factors in the formation of logical thought.

Zoran Minderovic

### Further Reading

Inhelder, Bärbel, and Jean Piaget. *The Early Growth of Logic in the Child: Classification and Seriation*. London: Routledge and Kegan Paul, 1964.

Matthews, Gareth B. *Philosophy and the Young Child*. Cambridge: Harvard University Press, 1980.

Pascal-Leone, J. "Organismic Processes for Neo-Piagetian Theories: A Dialectical Causal Account of Cognitive Development." In *The Neo-Piagetian Theories of Cognitive Development: Toward an Integration*. A. Demetriou, ed. Amsterdam: North-Holland, 1988.

## Longitudinal study

Research method used to study changes over time.

Researchers in such fields as **developmental psychology** use longitudinal studies to study changes in in-

dividual or group behavior over an extended period of time by repeatedly monitoring the same subjects. In longitudinal research, results are recorded for the same group of subjects, referred to as a cohort, throughout the course of the study.

An example of a longitudinal study might be an examination of the effects of preschool attendance on later school performance. The researchers would select two groups of children—one comprised of children who attend preschool, and the other comprised of children who had no preschool experience prior to attending kindergarten. These children would be evaluated at different points during their school career. The longitudinal study allows the researcher to focus on these children as they mature and record developmental patterns across time. A disadvantage of the longitudinal study is that researchers must be engaged in the study over a period of years and risk losing some of their research subjects, who may discontinue their participation for any number of reasons. Another disadvantage of the longitudinal study reflects the fact that some of the changes or behaviors observed during the study may be the effects of the assessment process itself. In addition to the longitudinal study, some researchers may employ the **cross-sectional study** method. In this method, the subjects, or cohort, are drawn from different groups and are studied at the same point in time.

## Konrad Lorenz

### 1903-1989
Austrian behaviorist and early leader in the field of ethology.

Konrad Lorenz played a lead role in forging the field of **ethology**, the comparative study of animal behavior, and helped regain the stature of observation as a recognized and respected **scientific method**. Along the way, his observations—particularly of greylag geese —led to important discoveries in animal behavior. Perhaps his most influential determination was that behavior, like physical **traits**, evolves by natural selection. In one of his many books, *On Aggression,* he wrote, "Historians will have to face the fact that natural selection determined the evolution of cultures in the same manner as it did that of species." In 1973, he and two other ethologists jointly accepted the Nobel Prize for physiology or medicine for their behavioral research. Born on November 7, 1903, in Vienna, Austria, Lorenz was the younger of two sons born to Adolf Lorenz and his wife and assistant, Emma Lecher. His father was an orthopedic surgeon whose new hip-joint operation brought him renown on both sides of the Atlantic Ocean. The young Konrad Lorenz received his schooling in Vienna at a private elementary school and at the Schottengymnasium, one of the city's best secondary schools. But his love of animals began outside of school, primarily at the family's summer home in Altenberg, Austria. Lorenz's parents indulged his interests, allowing him to have many pets as a youth. His interests became more grounded in science when he read about Charles Darwin's evolutionary theory at the age of 10.

Although Lorenz had an apparent interest in animals, his father insisted he study medicine. In 1922, Lorenz began premedical training at Columbia University in New York but returned early to Austria to continue the program at the University of Vienna. Despite his medical studies, Lorenz found time to informally study animals. He also kept a detailed diary of the activities of his pet bird Jock, a jackdaw. In 1927, his career as an animal behaviorist was launched when an ornithological journal printed his jackdaw diary. During the following year, he received an M.D. degree from the University of Vienna and became an assistant to a professor at the anatomical institute there. Lorenz recalled that period in his 1982 book *The Foundations of Ethology:* "When studying at the university under the Viennese anatomist, Ferdinand Hochstetter, and after I had become thoroughly conversant with the methodology and procedure of phylogenetic (evolutionary) comparison, it became immediately clear that the methods employed in comparative morphology were just as applicable to the behavior of the many species of fish and birds I knew so thoroughly, thanks to the early onset of my love for animals." His interests led him to study zoology at the University of Vienna, and in 1933, Lorenz earned his Ph.D. in that field.

## Spends "goose summers" in Altenberg

Lorenz then turned to animal behavior research for several years. It was during this time, 1935–38, that Lorenz developed the theories for which he is best known. He spent what he called his "goose summers" at the Altenberg home, concentrating on the behavior of greylag geese and confirming many hypotheses that he had formed while observing his pet birds. In his later book *The Year of the Greylag Goose,* Lorenz explains that he studied greylag geese for "many reasons, but the most important is that greylag geese exhibit a family existence that is analogous in many significant ways to human family life." While working with the geese, Lorenz developed the concept of **imprinting**. Imprinting occurs in many species, most noticeably in geese and ducks, when—within a short, genetically set time frame—an animal will accept a foster mother in the place of its biological moth-

**Konrad Lorenz** *(UPI/Corbis-Bettmann. Reproduced with permission.)*

er, even if that foster mother is a different species. Lorenz raised goslings which, deprived of their parents and confronted instead with Lorenz, accepted him and attached themselves to him as they normally would to their mother. Lorenz has often been photographed in Altenberg walking down a path or rowing across the water with a string of goslings following, single-file, behind him. He similarly found that mallard ducks would imprint on him, but only when he quacked and presented a shortened version of himself by squatting. While he enjoyed his close contact with animals, it did present some awkward situations. On one occasion, while walking his ducklings, which were hidden in the tall grass behind him, he stopped quacking for a minute and looked up from his squatted position to see a group of tourists quizzically watching from beyond the fence.

In addition he and Nikolaas Tinbergen, future Nobel Prize cowinner, developed the concept of the innate releasing mechanism. Lorenz found that animals have instinctive behavior patterns, or fixed-action patterns, that remain dormant until a specific event triggers the animal to exhibit this behavior for the first time. The fixed-action pattern is a specific, ordered series of behaviors, such as the fighting and surrender postures used by many animals. He emphasized that these fixed-action patterns are not learned but are genetically programmed. The stimulus is called the "releaser," and the **nervous system** structure that responds to the stimulus and prompts the instinctive behavior is the innate releasing mechanism.

In *The Foundations of Ethology,* Lorenz explained that animals have an "innate schoolmarm" that reinforces useful behavior and checks harmful behavior through a feedback apparatus. "Whenever a modification of an organ, as well as of a behavior pattern, proves to be adaptive to a particular environmental circumstance, this also proves incontrovertibly that information about this circumstance must have been 'fed into' the organism." This information can take one of two routes: learning, or genetic programming.

Lorenz later devised a hydraulic model to explain an animal's **motivation** to perform fixed-action patterns. In this model, he explained that energy for a specific action accumulates either until a stimulus occurs or until so much energy has built up that the animal displays the fixed-action pattern spontaneously. He witnessed the spontaneous performance of a fixed-action pattern first when, as a boy, he watched his pet starling suddenly fly off its perch to the ceiling of the room, snap at the air in the same way it would snap at an insect, then return to beat the "insect" on the perch, and finally swallow.

These exciting years for Lorenz did not go without controversy. He wrote a paper, "Disorders Caused by the Domestication of Species-Specific Behavior," which some critics felt contained a strong Nazi flavor in its word choice. While Lorenz repeatedly condemned Nazi ideology, many still believed the paper reflected a pro-Nazi stance; he had to weather many criticisms.

### Tells of his life with animals

While the research continued, Lorenz accepted an appointment in 1937 as lecturer in comparative anatomy and animal psychology at the University of Vienna. In 1940, he became professor of psychology at the University of Konigsberg in Germany but a year later answered the call to serve in the German Army. In 1944, Lorenz was captured by the Russians and sent to a prison camp. It was not until 1948 that he was released. Upon his return, Lorenz went back to the University of Vienna before accepting a small stipend from the Max Planck Society for the Advancement of Science to resume his studies at Altenberg. By 1952, Lorenz had published a popular book *King Solomon's Ring,* an account of animal behavior presented in easily understood terminology. Included in the book are many of his often-humorous experiences with his study subjects. The book also includes a collection of his illustrations. As he writes in the book: "Without supernatural assistance, our fellow creatures can tell us the most beautiful stories and that means *true* stories, because the truth about nature is always far more beautiful even than what our great poets sing of it, and they are the only real magicians that exist."

Lorenz writes that he was prompted to pen *King Solomon's Ring* by an occasion when his assistant and friend Dr. Alfred Seitz and he were working on a film about the greylag geese. Seitz was trying to call in some ducklings and accidentally used the language of the geese. When he realized his error, Seitz apologized to the ducklings before switching to their quacking. Lorenz recalls in the book, "it was at that very moment that the thought of writing a book first crossed my mind. There was nobody to appreciate the joke, Alfred being far too preoccupied with his work. I wanted to tell it to somebody and so it occurred to me to tell it to everybody."

In 1955, with the increased support of the Max Planck society, Lorenz, ethologist Gustav Kramer, and physiologist Erich von Holst established and then codirected the Institute for Behavioral Physiology in Seewiesen, Bavaria, near Munich. During the ensuing years at Seewiesen, Lorenz again drew attention, this time for the analogies he drew between human and animal behavior—which many scientists felt were improper—and his continuing work on **instinct**. The latter work gave further support to ethologists who believed that the innate behavior patterns found in animals evolved through natural selection, just as anatomical and physiological characters evolved. This drew arguments from many animal psychologists who contended that all behavior is learned.

Following the deaths of codirectors von Holst and Kramer, Lorenz became the sole director of the Seewiesen institute in 1961. In 1966, Lorenz again faced some controversy with his book *On Aggression*. In the book, Lorenz describes **aggression** as "the fighting instinct in beast and man which is directed against members of same species." He writes that this instinct aids the survival of both the individual and the species, in the latter case by giving the stronger males the better mating opportunities and territories. The book goes on to state that animals—particularly animals that can inflict severe damage to one another with sharp canines or horns—will use rank, territory, or evolved instinctual behavior patterns to avoid actual **violence** and fatalities. Lorenz says only humans purposefully kill each other—a fact that he attributes to the development of artificial weapons outpacing the human evolution of killing inhibitions. Critics say the book's conclusions encourage the acceptance of violence in human behavior. *On Aggression* is an example of Lorenz's shift in the 1960s from solely animal behavior to include human social behavior.

## Accepts nobel prize for behavioral research

In 1973, Lorenz, Tinbergen, and Karl Frisch, who studied bee communication, jointly accepted the Nobel Prize for their behavioral research. In the same year, Lorenz retired from his position as director of the Seewiesen institute. He then returned to Altenberg where he continued writing and began directing the department of animal sociology at the Austrian Academy of Science. In addition, the Max Planck Society for the Promotion of Science set up a research station for him at his ancestral home in Altenberg. In 1978, Lorenz gave a more personal view of his work with his picturebook *The Year of the Greylag Goose*. As he begins the volume: "This is not a scientific book. It would be true to say that it grew out of the pleasure I take in my observations of living animals, but that is nothing unusual, since all my academic works have also originated in the same pleasure. The only way a scientist can make novel, unexpected discoveries is through observation free of any preconceived notions."

In 1927, the same year his career-launching diary was published, Lorenz married childhood friend Margarethe "Gretl" Gebhardt, a gynecologist. They had two daughters, Agnes and Dagmar, and a son, Thomas. Lorenz was 85 years old when he died February 27, 1989 of kidney failure at his home in Altenburg, Austria.

*See also* Imprinting

Leslie Mertz

### Further Reading

Evans, Richard I., *Konrad Lorenz: The Man and His Ideas*, Harcourt, 1975.
Nisbett, Alec, *Konrad Lorenz*, Harcourt, 1976.
Nisbett, Alec, *Nobel Prize Winners*, Wilson, 1987, pp. 645–47.
Nisbett, Alec, *Time*, (March 13, 1989): B6.
Nisbett, Alec, *Washington Post*, (March 1, 1989).

# Loss and grief

Loss, a state of being without, is usually accompanied by grief, which is an emotional state of intense sadness and a reaction to the disruption of attachment.

There are many kinds of loss and each has its own kind of grief. People lose loved ones like spouses, partners, children, family members, and friends. Even pet losses can cause grief. Job or property loss can be painful. Mourning is the conventional cultural behavior for those experiencing a loss. Grief reactions are those personal reactions to a loss, independent of expected cultural standards.

## The emotional process of grieving

Everyone's grief is personalized, although most people share many of the same feelings. There is no order or schedule to grieving. The process may take a few days or years. Grieving that goes on and on, such a chronic grieving resulting in severe **depression**, or being stuck in a certain phase of the process, like denial, is considered to indicate pathological grief, and may require intervention by a trained professional. Other signs of pathological grief include extreme **guilt** feelings, irrational feelings of responsibility for the loss, and excessive despondency.

How people cope with life in general often indicates how they will deal with loss. Some coping behaviors are: avoidance of painful stimuli, or triggers, (such as photographs, favorite restaurants, clothing that smells like the loved one); distraction, such as keeping busy with work; "filling up" the empty space with drugs or food or alcohol; obsessing or thinking a lot about the details of the death; impulsive behavior like moving or quitting work; praying; intellectualizing or thinking about the loss without being emotional; and attaching to other people. While these coping skills may help a person feel better until they are able to reconstruct their lives without the object of the loss.

Most psychologists identify the stages of grief and suggest that the typical emotional process of most people is as follows.

Initially, a person may feel numbness, shock, and/or disbelief. A sudden change in reality occurs when someone dies. Even if the death was expected, in the case of an extended illness, and there was anticipatory grief, or grieving before the event happened, there can still be disbelief that the person is actually gone. There may be a sense of being distant or paralyzed. Some psychologists say that this is a way of protecting oneself from being overwhelmed. People's reactions vary widely and while one person may feel listless and introverted, withdrawn and reflective, another person may burst out crying and be unable to accept that their loved one is gone. Some denial is acute, while others are more subconscious, like "accidentally" setting that person's place at the table, or hearing the deceased's car in the garage. Most people pass through the denial stage fairly quickly and accept that the deceased is not coming back.

Once the death has been accepted as real, the process of healing begins. Now a person can enter into the emotions of grief. People who have survived a loss may be preoccupied with thoughts about the deceased. A person may feel angry about their loss, or guilty that

**Columbine High School students in Colorado grieving for their lost classmates.** *(Photo by David Zalubowski. AP/Wide World Photos. Reproduced with permission.)*

move past grief. In the final stages of grieving, a people re-establish themselves, let go of the deceased or reconciles with the loss, and begin to live in the present as opposed to the past or the transition of grief process.

## Physical symptoms of grief

Sighing, sobbing, crying, and weeping are common and **normal** physical signs of grief. Some psychological studies show that these forms of feeling are necessary physical release of **stress** and sadness mechanisms. Stress and sadness that are not relieved arise in other physical effects like, not being able to pay attention to present experience, lack of concentration, poor **memory**, disrupted **sleep** patterns like insomnia, little or no appetite, abusing drugs or alcohol, and/or thoughts of suicide.

Psychologists and medical doctors have identified some common physical symptoms of grieving which include: tightness in the throat, a choking or suffocating feeling, shortness of breath, sighing, empty stomach feeling, lack of muscular **power**, tension, **pain**, and absent mindedness. These are physiological and/or biochemical reactions. Grief can have major physical health consequences. There can be (especially among older people) compromised immune function, increased hospitalization or surgeries, and/or increased mortality rates.

## Different kinds of losses

All loss can be painful and different kinds of losses bring up particular issues. For instance, a child's death brings up grief about the loss of what the future might have brought and a feeling of the loss of innocence. Parents may also feel like major parts of themselves are gone and feel overwhelmingly guilty for surviving their child.

Losing someone to suicide or a drug overdose can be confusing and shocking. Survivors often feel guilty, shameful, helpless, and angry. Multiple losses are also more complex. People who have lost a group of friends or a number of family members, or who have witnessed a mass loss, may feel strong urges of wanting to go too, or guilt for being a survivor. Others, like people who have lost many loved ones to AIDS or old-age, must contend with separate issues of becoming desensitized to loss, or feeling completely isolated.

## Therapies and tasks of grieving

Millions of people work through grief without therapy, but it can be invaluable to have psychological counseling during times of major stress. Understanding friends and family can be essential in these times. Support groups may also prove beneficial.

they've survived the deceased. For some people there are unresolved issues, or regrets, that come up, like having had a disagreement as last words, or having kept a secret. Some people get depressed, feel hopeless, and believe that they cannot go on. Others experience anxiety. The risk of suicide is a real concern in some situations. Some people re-evaluate their own lives as a result of the loss.

As a person processes through his or her emotions and deals with the changes brought on by the loss, he/she begins to reorganize, re-build, and re-invest energy into different attachments. Loss of a loved one may change a person's entire social support framework. A person may have to acquire new skills to move on. For instance, married women who were financially dependent upon husbands may have to become financially educated. Partners who relied on the deceased for emotional support must find that support elsewhere. Children who have lost parents must look to other role models. Although loss leaves permanent marks on someone's life, most people do

Grieving is an important process in which people learn to accept their losses. Althought some people grief rather easily and naturally, not allowing oneself to grieve can lead to unresolved grief. There are many forms of unresolved grief, like not grieving at all, blocked grief, delayed or conflicted grief, unanticipated grief that comes up later, and/or chronic grief. The symptoms of unresolved grief are numerous, including but not limited to: over-activity, having the symptoms of the deceased, psychosomatic (imagined and possibly created) illnesses, drastic changes in social network, **hostility** towards people connected with the death, self-sabotage, severe depression, suicidal tendencies, over-identification with the deceased, and/or phobias about illness or death. Unresolved grief can come about because of guilt, the new loss awakening an old loss, multiple losses, an inability to cope, or resistance to the process of mourning. Any unresolved grief holds up growth in life and can lead to serious mental or physical problems.

Psychologists have many specialized ways of dealing with grief. Sometimes they suggest that a client write a letter to the deceased, or they may use **psychoanalysis** in order to aid in the detachment process. Traditional cultural and/or religious customs may help, too. For psychologists the core of their job in helping someone grieve is: reaching out, being a physical presence, being empathic and providing emotional support, giving permission to grieve, making sure the griever doesn't isolate him or herself, and assessing the grief so as to help the process along.

Dealing with grief or helping someone deal with grief-work involves taking the steps of the grief stages. Accepting and facing the reality of loss, functioning in a healthy way like eating right and sleeping well, working through the pain of memories and missing someone, dealing with all the emotions that arise, coping with social and life changes brought on by the loss, detaching from the deceased, accepting support, re-investing energy, letting go, and making a new identity for oneself which includes having lost someone and being a survivor.

Lara Lynn Lane

## Further Reading

Leick, Nini and Marianne Davidsen-Nielsen. *Healing pain: attachment, loss and grief therapy.* London and NY: Tavistock Routledge, 1991.

Deits, Bob. *Life after loss: a personal guide to dealing with death, divorce, job change and relocation.* Tucson, Arizona: Fisher Books, 1992.

Bowlby, John. *Attachment and loss.* New York: Basic Books, 1980.

Kubler-Ross, Elizabeth. *On death and dying.* New York: Macmillan, (1969)1971.

Kastenbaum, Robert J. *Death, society, and human experience.* New York, Oxford, Singapore, Sydney: Maxwell Macmillan International Publishing Group, 1991.

Kato, Pamela M. and Traci Mann. "A synthesis of psychological interventions for the bereaved." *Clinical Psychology Review,* vol. 19, no. 3, 275-296, 1999.

Rando, Therese A. *Grief, dying, and death: clinical interventions for caregivers.* Illinois: Research Press Company, 1984.

## Further Information

National Mental Health Association. 1021 Prince Street, Alexandria, VA, USA. 22314, 800-969-6642. http://www.nmha.org.

Grief Recovery Institute. 8306 Wilshire Blvd., Beverly Hills, CA, USA. 90211, 800-445-4808.

Self Help & Psychology Magazine. http://shpm.com/articles/loss/griefcontinuum.html.

The Grief Continuum: Three Stages of Grief Work. http://shpm.com/articles/loss/griefcontinuum.html.

# Aleksandr Romanovich Luria

Russian psychologist who conducted groundbreaking work on brain function.

### 1902-1977

Aleksander Luria's research on **normal** versus abnormal **brain** function was critically important in the understanding of how to approach brain injuries. Through his work, much was learned about the impact of head injuries, brain tumors, and the effects of **mental retardation**. He also studied brain activity among children in an attempt to understand how to minimize abnormal behavior.

Luria was born in Kazan, Russia, on July 16, 1902, where he attended local schools. He went on to the University of Kazan and the Moscow Medical Institute. He received both an M.D. and a doctorate in education. Initially he worked with the educational psychologist Lev Vygotsky at Moscow University. Luria researched the role speech plays in how children develop their conceptual thought processes. Upon Vigotsky's death in 1934, Luria continued this research. In particular, he was interested in finding out how different functions, such as speech, were controlled in normal and abnormal brains.

**Memory** fascinated Luria—both what people did and did not remember. One of his earliest subjects, a newspaper reporter identified as S., was sent to Luria because of what seemed to be a nearly perfect memory. Over the course of many years Luria conducted experiments on S., trying to pinpoint precisely what it was that accounted for this exceptional memory. He concluded that S's brain was able to process information in a unique way, using **perception** as well as memory. Luria wrote about his experiments with S. in *The Mind of a Mnemonist*.

During the Second World war Luria's research and experimentation were put into action, as he developed new ways to treat soldiers suffering from head wounds. Specifically, his research into speech and the brain helped him to treat soldiers whose injuries had robbed them of the ability to speak. He developed new programs for **rehabilitation** over the next three decades. Another famous patient of Luria's was the physicist Lev Landau. Landau had been severely injured in an automobile crash, and other doctors pronounced him dead and rescuscitated him four times. Thanks to the work of Luria and his assistants, Landau was revived and able to restore much of his normal brain function.

Luria also continued his work with children. His research led him to the conclusion that retarded children could make the most progress in an **environment** that focused on their specific handicap, and he advocated the creation of special schools for this function.

Luria was recognized in his own country with the Order of Lenin, and he received several other awards from the Soviet Union and other countries. Fluent in English, he made several trips to the United States to lecture. He was a member of the National Academy of Sciences of the United States, the American Academy of Arts and Sciences, and the American Academy of Education.

He was married in 1933 to Lana Lipchina; the couple had one daughter. Luria continued his work into the 1970s; he died on August 16, 1977.

George A. Milite

## Further Reading

Luria, Aleksandr R. *The Mind of a Mnemonist: A Little Book about a Vast Memory.* New York: Basic Books, 1968.

# Eleanor Emmons Maccoby

1917-
American psychologist and educator.

Most widely known for her work in the psychology of **sex differences**, Eleanor Maccoby has achieved a distinguished career as an educator as well. She spent eight years in the 1950s as a lecturer and research associate in social relations at Harvard University. Later, she joined the faculty at Stanford University and eventually became chairman of the psychology department.

Eleanor Emmons was born May 15, 1916, in Tacoma, Washington, to Harry Eugene and Viva May Emmons. She married Nathan Maccoby in 1938, received her bachelor's degree from the University of Washington in 1939, and then traveled to Washington, D.C., where she spent the years during World War II working for a government agency. Returning to her studies at the University of Michigan, Maccoby earned her master's degree in 1949 and her Ph.D. in 1950. She spent the next eight years at Harvard University in Cambridge, Massachusetts, before moving to Stanford University in California, where she served as a professor and chairman of the psychology department from 1973-76.

Although Eleanor Maccoby's interests lay primarily in studying the social factors that influence human development, she also considered the interweaving contributions of other factors, such as biological and cognitive processes. In fact, for her doctoral dissertation, which she completed under the guidance of B.F. Skinner, she conducted experiments in learning and **reinforcement**.

After finishing her doctoral work, Maccoby joined Robert Sears, then a professor of social relations at Harvard, in a large-scale study investigating whether certain parental practices were related to children's **personality** characteristics. This study resulted in an influential book, *Patterns of Child Rearing.* Maccoby's work led her to believe that identification was an important mod-

erating variable in the development of personality. This notion was supported in her work in parent-child **socialization** and also in studies of children's identification with film characters.

Maccoby's interest in children and research never flagged. Even while deeply involved in this socialization project, she conducted studies on the effects of television on children, identifying the kinds of activities that were displaced when families acquired televisions, and other studies of the influence of neighborhood cohesion on delinquency rates in low-income areas. She found that neighborhoods in low-income, "at risk" areas had lower rates of **juvenile delinquency** when they were relatively tightly knit and, simply put, people looked out for one another and one another's children.

After moving to Stanford, Maccoby added studies of developmental changes in **attention** to her areas of study. She and her colleagues demonstrated that as they grew, children improved first in the **ability** to attend to a single message in the presence of distractions, and then in the ability to divide attention between simultaneously competing stimuli.

It was also at Stanford that Maccoby began a long association with Carol Nagy Jacklin that would result in the work for which she is most well known. Jacklin and Maccoby studied differences and similarities in boys and girls, using a thorough review of available literature as well as original research. Their 1974 book, *The Psychology of Sex Differences,* represented an unparalleled synthesis of research in the area of sex differences in development, and, given the political climate of the 1970s, stimulated much discussion. Maccoby and Jacklin were simultaneously criticized for being too biological, not biological enough, giving too much credence to socialization pressures, and not giving enough credence to social forces.

Interestingly, however, Maccoby and Jacklin offered a third possibility for forces that shape differences between the sexes that reflected Maccoby's earlier interests in **cognition** and identification. They argued that, in addition to being influenced by their biology and the social **environment** around them, children engaged in "self-socialization." The authors suggested that in this proactive process, children themselves draw inferences from the roles and behaviors in which they see men and women, boys and girls engaging. Depending on their developmental level, children then use these inferences to guide their own behavior.

Maccoby's published works reflect her abiding interest in the socialdevelopment of children and differences between the sexes. Maccoby has received many honors and awards during her career. They include the Gores Award for excellence in teaching from Stanford (1981); a research award from the American Educational Research Association (1984); an award recognizing her research from the Society for Research in **Child Development** (1987); and the Distinguished Scientific Contribution Award from the American Psychological Association (1988). She was elected to the National Academy of Sciences in 1993.

Doreen Arcus Ph.D.

## Further Reading
Maccoby, E. "Eleanor E. Maccoby." In *A History of Psychology in Autobiography*. G. Lindzey, ed. Stanford, CA: Stanford University Press, 1989.

———. *Social Development: Psychological Growth and the Parent-Child Relationship*. New York: Harcourt, Brace and Jovanovich, 1980.

Maccoby, E., and C.N. Jacklin. *Psychology of Sex Differences*. Stanford: Stanford Univesity Press, 1974.

Maccoby, E., and R.H. Mnookin. *Dividing the Child: Social and Legal Dilemmas of Custody*. Cambridge, MA: Harvard University Press, 1992.

# Mania

A description of the condition opposite depression in manic-depressive psychosis, or bipolar disorder. It is characterized by a mood of elation without apparent reason.

Most episodes of mania—elation without reasonable cause or justification—are followed in short order by **depression**; together they represent the opposites described as **bipolar disorder**. Manic episodes are characterized by intense feelings of energy and enthusiasm, uncharacteristic self-confidence, continuous talking, and little need for **sleep**. People experiencing a manic period tend to make grandiose plans and maintain inflated beliefs about their own personal abilities. While manic people appear to be joyful and celebratory, their **mood** corresponds little to conditions they are experiencing in reality. Expressions of **hostility** and irritability also are common during manic episodes.

## Further Reading
Duke, Patty. *Call Me Anna*. New York: Bantam, 1987.

Jamison, Kay. *Touched with Fire: Manic-Depressive Illness and the Artistic Temperament*. New York: Free Press, 1993

# Manic depression

See **Bipolar disorder**

# Marijuana

The common name of a small number of varieties of Cannabis sativa, or Indian hemp plant, which contain tetrahydrocannabinol (THC), a psychoactive drug.

Cannabis, in the form of marijuana, hashish (a dried resinous material that seeps from cannabis leaves and is more potent than marijuana), or other cannabinoids, is probably the most often used illegal substance in the world. In the United States, marijuana use became widespread among young people in the 1960s. By 1979, 68 percent of young adults between the ages of 18 and 25 had experimented with it at least once, and it was reported that as of the same year the total number of people in the U.S. who had tried the drug was 50 million. In the late 1980s, it was estimated that about 50 to 60 percent of people between the ages of 21 and 29 had tried marijuana at least once.

Marijuana and hashish are usually smoked, but may also be ingested orally, and are sometimes added to food or beverages. The psychoactive substance of cannabis is tetrahydrocannabinol, or THC, especially delta-9-tetrahydrocannabinol. Delta-9-THC can be synthesized, is known to **affect** the **central nervous system**, and has been legally used to treat side-effects of chemotherapy and weight loss in persons affected with AIDS. Other legal therapeutic uses of marijuana include the treatment of glaucoma and **epilepsy**.

The effects of cannabis use vary from individual to individual, depending on the physical and psychological condition of the user, the amount of THC consumed, and

**A chemical present in marijuana has been shown to destroy brain cells in rats.** *(Photo by Tom McHugh. National Audubon Society Collection/Photo Researchers, Inc. Reproduced by permission.)*

many other factors. Technically, marijuana is classified as a hallucinogen, but its effects are usually much milder than those of other drugs in this category, such as LSD, mescaline, and psilocybin. When it is inhaled through a marijuana cigarette, THC reaches its highest concentration in the blood within a half hour, and is absorbed by the **brain** and other organs, and can affect **consciousness** for several hours. THC can remain stored in body fat for several weeks. Marijuana users commonly experience feelings of euphoria, self-confidence, reduced inhibition, relaxation, and a floating sensation. Feelings of giddiness and mild feelings of **paranoia** are also common. Physiological effects include increases in pulse and heart rates, reddened eyes, dryness of the mouth, and an increased appetite. The initial euphoric feelings after ingesting marijuana are generally followed by sleepiness. Although marijuana has been known to produce psychological dependence, there is little tendency to become physically dependent on it, and withdrawal from the drug does not pose medical problems. Recently, receptors for THC have been discovered in the brain, together with a naturally-occurring substance—anandamide—that binds the chemical to its receptors and may be a **neurotransmitter**.

Documented negative effects of marijuana use include impairment in **perception**, sensory motor coordination, short-term **memory**, and panic attacks, and is also linked to impairment of the immune system, lowered testosterone levels in males, and chromosome damage. If taken by pregnant women, marijuana affects the developing fetus. Long-term marijuana smokers display similar respiratory dysfunctions as tobacco smokers In research on rats, THC has been found to destroy cells in the hippocampus, a part of the brain that is important in the formation of new memories. Psychologically, chronic use of marijuana has been associated with a loss of ambition known as amotivational syndrome. Authorities differ with respect to the physical and psychological risks of short-term and long-term use/abuse of cannabis. Current penalties for the illegal possession of marijuana, hashish, or other form of cannabis can be extremely severe.

*See also* Drugs/Drug abuse

**Further Reading**
Grinspoon, Lester. *Marijuana Reconsidered.* Oakland, CA: Quick American Archives, 1994.

# Marriage counseling

A clinical specialty of family and marital therapy.

There are many different approaches to marriage counseling, which may be used alone or combined with other methods by the therapist. Among the oldest is the psychodynamic approach, which attributes problems within a marriage to the unresolved conflicts and needs of each spouse. Each client's personal history and underlying motivations are central to this mode of therapy. Therapists using this approach apply the principles of **psychoanalysis** in their treatment; they may either treat both marriage partners individually, or treat one spouse in collaboration with another therapist who treats the other.

Marriage counseling that follows a systems approach stresses the interaction between partners as the origin of marital difficulties, rather than their actions or **personality**. Behavior and communication patterns are analyzed as well as the interlocking roles portrayed by the couple or members of the **family**. Family members may be conditioned to consistently **play** "the strong one" or "the weak one," or such other roles as "scapegoat," "caretaker," or "clown." Although initially it may seem that only one member of a family system is troubled, on closer inspection his or her difficulties are often found to be symptomatic of an unhealthy pattern in which all the members play an active part. Systems theory is actually an umbrella term for a range of therapies, and systems-oriented counseling may take a variety of forms, including both short- and long-term therapy.

A popular individual treatment approach also used in marriage counseling is Rogerian or **client-centered therapy**, also referred to as humanistic therapy. Here, the emphasis is on communication and the open sharing of feelings. Through specially formulated exercises, couples work on improving their speaking and listening skills and enhancing their capacity for emotional honesty. Another widely employed mode of marriage counseling is based on a behavioral approach, in which marital problems are treated as dysfunctional behaviors that can be observed and modified. Couples are made aware of destructive behavior patterns, often by systematically recording their behavior until certain patterns emerge. The therapist then coaches them in various modifying strategies with the goal of achieving positive, mutually reinforcing interactions. Behavior-oriented therapy also focuses on improving a couple's problem-solving and conflict-resolution skills.

Marriage counselors may conduct therapy sessions with both spouses, treating one as the primary client and the other one only occasionally, while another therapist treats the other spouse. An increasing number of therapists counsel couples in pairs, with married therapists sometimes working together as a team. Theoretically, the relationship between the co-therapists is supposed to serve as a model for their clients. Marriage counseling in groups, which is becoming increasingly common, offers clients some of the same advantages that **group therapy** offers individuals. Sex counseling, which had previously been part of marital therapy, emerged as an independent field following the pioneering work of **William Masters** and **Virginia Johnson** in the 1950s and 1960s. Couples seeking treatment for **sexual dysfunction** have the option of working with a sex therapist.

Marriage counseling is usually practiced by licensed individuals with specialized training in psychology, psychiatry, and counseling, or by persons without such training, including members of the clergy. The first marriage counseling centers were established in the 1930s, and the American Association of Marriage and Family Therapy (formally the American Association of Marriage Counselors) was founded in 1942.

## Further Reading

Brammer, Lawrence M. *Therapeutic Psychology: Fundamentals of Counseling and Psychotherapy.* 5th ed. Englewood Cliffs, NJ: Prentice Hall, 1989.

Ronch, Judah L, William van Ornum, and Nicholas C. Stilwell, eds. *The Counseling Sourcebook: A Practical Reference on Contemporary Issues.* New York: Crossroad, 1994.

# Maslow's Hierarchy of Needs

See **Maslow, Abraham**

# Abraham Maslow

**1908-1970**
American psychologist.

A central figure in **humanistic psychology** and in the **human potential movement**, Abraham Maslow is known especially for his theory of **motivation**. He was born and raised in Brooklyn, New York, and received his Ph.D. in psychology from the University of Wisconsin in 1934. Maslow then began medical studies, which he discontinued within a year, after which he was offered a postdoctoral research fellowship to work with **Edward Thorndike** at Columbia University. After moving to New York, Maslow met many prominent European psy-

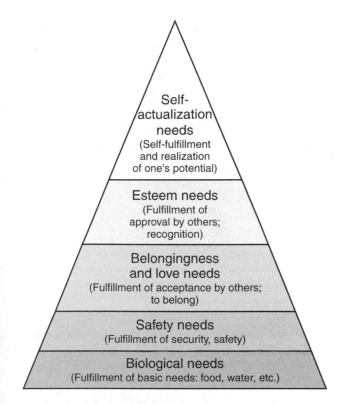

Self-
actualization
needs
(Self-fulfillment
and realization
of one's potential)

Esteem needs
(Fulfillment of
approval by others;
recognition)

Belongingness
and love needs
(Fulfillment of acceptance by others;
to belong)

Safety needs
(Fulfillment of security, safety)

Biological needs
(Fulfillment of basic needs: food, water, etc.)

**Maslow's hierarchy of needs.**

**Abraham Maslow** (UPI/Corbis-Bettmann. Reproduced with permission.)

chologists and social scientists who had fled Nazi Germany. Several of these emigrés became his mentors, including psychoanalysts **Alfred Adler**, **Erich Fromm**, and **Karen Horney** and Gestalt psychologists **Max Wertheimer** (1880-1943) and **Kurt Koffka** (1886-1941). In 1937 Maslow began teaching at the newly opened Brooklyn College. At the urging of anthropologist Ruth Benedict (1887-1948), whom Maslow had met at Columbia, he spent the summer of 1938 doing field work on a Blackfoot Indian reservation in Alberta, Canada, with financial support from the Social Science Research Council. In 1951 Maslow became the head of the psychology department at Brandeis University, where he remained until a year before his death in 1970.

During the 1940s, Maslow began to work out his theory of human motivation, which was eventually published in *Motivation and Human Personality* in 1954. Rejecting the **determinism** of both the psychoanalytic and behaviorist approaches, Maslow took an optimistic approach to human behavior that emphasized developing one's full potential. Instead of basing his psychological model on people with mental and emotional problems, he used as his point of reference a collection of exceptionally dynamic and successful historical and contemporary figures whom he considered "self-actualizers," including Thomas Jefferson (1743-1826), Abraham Lin-

coln (1809-1865), Jane Addams (1860-1935), Albert Einstein (1879-1955), and Eleanor Roosevelt (1884-1962). In addition to drawing up a list of the common **traits** of self-actualized individuals, Maslow placed **self-actualization** at the peak of his hierarchy of human motivations, the concept for which he is best known today.

This hierarchy is generally portrayed as a pyramid with five levels, ranging from the most basic needs at the bottom to the most complex and sophisticated at the top. From bottom to top, the levels are biological needs (food, water, shelter); safety; belongingness and love; the need to be esteemed by others; and self-actualization, the need to realize one's full potential. According to Maslow, the needs at each level must be met before one can move on to the next level. With so many other issues to concern them, the vast majority of people never grapple with self-actualization; Maslow considered fewer than one percent of the population to be self-actualized individuals. However, he believed that all human beings still possessed an innate (if unmet) need to reach this state.

During the 1950s and 1960s, Maslow became associated with the movement known as humanistic psychology, which he also referred to as the Third Force because it offered an alternative to the prevailing schools of **psychoanalysis** and **behaviorism** in both theory and therapeutic practice. Like Maslow, colleagues such as **Carl Rogers** and **Rollo May** rejected the idea that human behavior was determined by **childhood** events or **conditioning** and stressed instead the individual's **power** to grow and change in the present. They believed that the goal of **psychotherapy** was to remove the obstacles that prevented their clients from self-actualizing.

As humanistic psychology gave birth to the human potential movement of the 1960s, Maslow became one of its central figures, lecturing at the Esalen Institute at Big Sur, California, which offered workshops by psychologists, social scientists, philosophers, and other intellectual figures. During these years, he also popularized the concept of the peak experience, an unusual moment of extreme joy, serenity, beauty, or wonder that he believed was closely related to self-actualization. In 1967 and 1968, Maslow served as president of the American Psychological Association. In 1969, he moved to Menlo Park, California, where he died of a heart attack a year later. In his lifetime Maslow published over 100 articles in magazines and professional journals. His other books include *Toward a Psychology of Being* (1962), *Religions, Values, and Peak Experiences* (1964), *Eupsychian Management* (1965), *The Psychology of Science* (1966), and a posthumous collection of papers entitled *The Farther Reaches of Human Nature* (1971).

**Further Reading**

Hoffman, Edward. *The Right to be Human: A Biography of Abraham Maslow.* Los Angeles: Tarcher, 1988.

# Masochism

See **Paraphilias**

# William Masters

### 1915-
American physician and researcher who, in collaboration with Virginia Johnson, pioneered in the physiological study of human sexual function.

William Masters was born in Cleveland, Ohio, grew up in Kansas City, and did his undergraduate work at Hamilton College. He received his M.D. degree in 1943 from the University of Rochester School of Medicine, where he assisted in the laboratory research of George Washington Corner, who was studying and comparing the reproductive systems of animals and humans. Masters's interest in the study of

**William Masters, right, with coworker Virginia Johnson.**
*(UPI/Corbis-Bettmann. Reproduced with permission.)*

**sexuality** was reinforced when he learned of the research done by **Alfred Kinsey** (1894-1956) at the University of Indiana, where he had interviewed men and women about their sexual experiences. Masters completed his internship and residency at St. Louis Hospital and Barnes Hospital, choosing obstetrics and gynecology as a speciality. He also did an internship in pathology at the Washington University School of Medicine.

In 1947, Masters was appointed to the faculty of Washington University, where he conducted research in areas including hormone-replacement therapy for postmenopausal women. In 1954, he began researching the physiology of sex by collecting data about sexual stimulation in a laboratory situation. His work, which took place at Washington University, was supported by a grant from the United States Institute of Health. By 1956, **Virginia Johnson**, a sociology student, was assisting Masters interview and screen research volunteers. Over an 11-year period, Masters studied 382 women and 312 men ranging in age from 18 to 89, recording their sexual responses using electrocardiographs and electroencephalographs.

Masters established the Reproductive Biology Research Foundation in 1964. Two years later, Masters and Johnson published the results of their long-term laboratory investigation of the physiology of human sexual activity in *Human Sexual Response.* This book is generally considered to be the first major scientific analysis of the subject, and was produced to provide physicians and psychologists with factual information useful in the treatment of **sexual dysfunction**. Despite the book's promotion solely as a serious research work, it won wide popular acclaim, and its authors were soon in demand as speakers and lecturers.

Since 1959, Masters and Johnson had been applying their studies to counseling sexually dysfunctional couples, working together as a team so that each member of a couple would have a therapist of the same sex to relate to. Having found sexual functioning susceptible to **conditioning**, much like other human and animal behaviors, they used learning strategies based on the theories of **Ivan Pavlov**, **B. F. Skinner**, Wolpe, and others. Following the principles of **operant conditioning** and **desensitization**, they helped their patients "unlearn" blocks involving arousal and/or orgasm. Masters and Johnson were married in 1971 and became co-directors of the Masters and Johnson Institute in 1973. In their 1979 work, *Homosexuality in Perspective*, Masters and Johnson detailed the results of studies based on the responses of homosexuals and lesbians, whose sexual preferences they claimed to be able to change.

Masters retired from private practice in gynecology in 1981, although he and his wife continued to operate the Masters and Johnson Institute, which moved to a new location that year. In 1988, they co-authored the book *Crisis: Heterosexual Behavior in the Age of AIDS* with Robert Kolodny, attracting criticism within the medical community—including that of then Attorney General C. Everett Koop—for their prediction that the AIDS epidemic would spread to the heterosexual population. Masters and Johnson were divorced in 1992, ending their work together at the Institute. Their other books include *Human Sexual Inadequacy* (1970), *The Pleasure Bond* (1974), *Human Sexuality* (1988), and *Heterosexuality* (1994).

**Further Reading**
Robinson, Paul. *The Modernization of Sex.* New York: Harper & Row, 1976.

# Masturbation

See **Autoeroticism**

# Rollo May

**1909-1994**
American existential psychoanalyst who popularized a humanistic, spiritually based psychology.

Rollo May was one of the most influential American psychologists of the twentieth century. He helped to introduce European existential **psychoanalysis** to an American audience. He was a founder of **humanistic** **psychology**, with its focus on the individual, as opposed to the behaviorist psychology and Freudian psychoanalysis that was prevalent in the 1940s and 1950s. May's writings were both practical and spiritual and they promoted the **power** and worth of the individual. As such, they contributed to the development of the **human potential movement**. May maintained that widespread **alienation** and anxiety were a result of breakdown and upheaval in culture and society, rather than the result of individual psychological problems. Among May's many honors were the annual award of the New York Society of Clinical Psychologists in 1954 and a 1971 gold medal from the American Psychological Association.

Born in Ada, Ohio, in 1909, as Reece May, he was the second of six children of Earl Tittle May and Matie Boughton. His father, a field secretary for the Young Men's Christian Association, moved the **family** to Michigan when May was still a child. Although initially he was a reticent student, at Michigan State College of Agriculture and Applied Science (now Michigan State University) in East Lansing, he co-founded a magazine that was critical of the state legislature. The flap that followed caused him to transfer to Oberlin College, a small liberal arts school in Ohio. An English major, with a minor in Greek literature and history, May graduated in 1930 and spent the next three years teaching English in Salonika, Greece. During that period, he attended seminars in Vienna, Austria, with the famous psychoanalyst **Alfred Adler**.

## Studies for the ministry

In 1933 May entered the Union Theological Seminary in New York City. His studies were interrupted for two years when his parents divorced. He returned to Michigan to help with his younger siblings and worked as a student adviser at Michigan State. In 1938, he earned his divinity degree from Union, studying with the existentialist theologian Paul Tillich. May married Florence De Frees in 1938, and eventually they had a son and twin daughters. After two years as a minister at a Congregational Church in New Jersey, May decided that his true interests lay in psychology. In 1939, he published *The Art of Counseling: How to Gain and Give Mental Health*, and two years later his second book, *Springs of Creative Living: A Study of Human Nature and God*, was published.

In 1942, May was stricken with tuberculosis. After eighteen months in a sanitarium in upstate New York, he decided that his attitudes and his personal will were more important to his recovery than the treatments. He entered the graduate psychology program at Columbia University in New York City, receiving his Ph.D. in **clinical psychology** in 1949 with the highest honors. In the decades that followed, May's dissertation, *The Meaning* *of Anxiety*, published in 1950, and revised in 1977, had a major influence on the development of humanistic psychology. He argued that culture was in an "age of anxiety" and, furthermore, that channeling his own high anxiety was a major factor in overcoming his tuberculosis.

By 1948, May had become an assistant professor of psychiatry at the William Alanson White Institute of Psychiatry, Psychoanalysis, and Psychology in New York City. In 1958, he became the training and supervisory psychoanalyst there. He remained at the Institute until his retirement in 1974. He also served as an adjunct professor of clinical psychology at New York University and as a lecturer in **psychotherapy** at the New School for Social Research from 1955 until 1976. May held visiting professorships at Harvard, Princeton, and Yale Universities, and at Brooklyn College. In 1973, he became a Regents' Professor at the University of California at Santa Cruz. May maintained a private psychoanalysis practice in New York City and, following his retirement from academia, in Tiburon, California.

### Writings influence the activists of the 1960s

May was a prolific and influential author whose books often were aimed at the general reader. His major works included *Existential Psychology* in 1961, *Psychology and the Human Dilemma* in 1967, *The Courage to Create* in 1975, *Freedom and Destiny* in 1981, and *The Cry for Myth* in 1991. *Love and Will*, published in 1969, won the Ralph Waldo Emerson Award of Phi Beta Kappa and became a guidebook for political and social activists. In 1972, *Power and Innocence: A Search for the Sources of Violence* won the Dr. Martin Luther King, Jr. Award from the New York Society of Clinical Psychologists. In May's later writings, the "age of anxiety" became the "age of despair." To reach a larger audience, May made a number of sound recordings.

May and his first wife were divorced in 1969 and in 1971 he married Ingrid Schöll. That marriage ended in 1978. In 1989, May married Georgia Lee Miller Johnson. May was a member of numerous professional organizations and his honorary degrees included L.H.D.s from Kingfisher College of the University of Oklahoma, St. Regis College, St. Vincent College, Michigan State University, Rockford College, Ohio Northern University, and Oberlin College. He died of congestive heart failure at his home in Tiburon, California, in 1994.

Margaret Alic

### Further Reading

Crompton, Samuel Willard. "May, Rollo." In *American National Biography*, edited by John A. Garraty and Mark C. Carnes. Vol. 14. New York: Oxford University Press, 1999.

May, Rollo. *Man's Search for Himself.* New York: Norton, 1953.

Reeves, Clement. *The Psychology of Rollo May; with Reflections and Commentary by Rollo May.* San Francisco: Jossey-Bass Publishers, 1977.

Serlin, Ilene A. "Rollo May." *Tikkun* 10 (January-February, 1995): 65.

# William McDougall

**1871-1938**

British experimental psychologist who developed a theory of human instincts and studied psychic phenomena.

William McDougall was an experimental psychologist and theorist of wide-ranging interests. Above all, he believed in a holistic psychology that utilized every available tool for understanding the human **psyche**. He was the first to formulate a theory of human instinctual behavior, and he influenced the development of the new field of **social psychology**.

Born in 1871, in Lancashire, England, the second son of Rebekah Smalley and Isaac Shimwell McDougall, a wealthy Scottish industrialist, McDougall was educated at a local private school and then at the Realgynmnasium in Weimar, Germany. Although his father wanted him to study law or work in the family businesses, his mother supported his desire to become a scientist.

### Studies medicine and psychology

At 15, McDougall entered the university in Manchester, earning degrees in biology and geology. A scholarship took him to St. John's College of Cambridge University, where he received his B.A. in natural science in 1894. It was at Cambridge that McDougall became interested in the melding of biology and the social sciences. Another scholarship enabled him to study medicine at St. Thomas Hospital in London. He earned his medical degree in 1898, with specialties in physiology and neurology. He was awarded the Grainger Testimonial Prize for his research on muscle contractions. However, the work of **William James** inspired McDougall to pursue psychology.

In 1898, McDougall became a fellow of St. John's College, as a result of his proposal for a neurophysiological study of the mind-body problem. In 1899 he accompanied the Cambridge Anthropological Expedition to the Torres Straits near New Guinea as the attending physician. His studies from the expedition, *The Pagan Tribes of Borneo*, with Charles Hose, were published in 1912.

**William McDougall** *(Archives of the History of American Psychology. Reproduced with permission.)*

### Introduces experimental psychology in England

In 1900, McDougall married Annie Aurelia Hickmore and the couple eventually had three sons and two daughters. They spent their first year together in Göttingen, Germany, where McDougall studied **experimental psychology** with G. E. Müller. McDougall then became a lecturer at University College, London. His first publications, "On the Seat of the Psycho-Physical Processes" and "New Observations in Support of Thomas Young's Theory of Light- and Color-Vision, I-III" appeared in 1901. These were followed by papers on the physiology of **attention** and on the senses. In London, he also began working with **Francis Galton** and **Charles Spearman** on mental testing and **eugenics**, the theory that genetics could be used to improve the human race. McDougall co-founded the British Psychological Society in 1901. He also co-founded the *British Journal of Psychology.*

In 1904, McDougall moved to Oxford University as the Wilde Reader in Mental Philosophy, a post he held until 1920. He was the first experimental psychologist at Oxford. The first of McDougall's textbooks, *Physiological Psychology*, was published in 1905. One of his most successful texts, *An Introduction to Social Psychology*, first

published in 1908, was also his most influential. In it, McDougall introduced his controversial theory of instincts, arguing that all human behavior, including social relationships, could be explained by the many instincts which were related to primary emotions. For example, fleeing was an **instinct** related to the **emotion** of **fear**. In later writings, instincts became "propensities" and he argued that the purpose of an instinct was to move one toward a goal. He called this "purposive" or "hormic" psychology.

### Pursues paranormal psychology

In 1911, McDougall published *Body and Mind* in which he argued for the scientific existence of the human soul and discussed psychic research. His interest in paranormal psychology, including mental telepathy and clairvoyance, was increasing. In 1912, he was named a fellow of Corpus Christi College at Oxford. That same year, he became a fellow of the Royal Society of London. He served as vice-president of the Psychiatric Section of the Royal Society of Medicine from 1914 until 1918, when he became president. In 1920 he became president of the British Society for Psychical Research.

With the onset of World War I, McDougall joined the French army as an ambulance driver. Between 1915 and 1919, he served as a major in the British Army Medical Corps where he worked with victims of shell shock (**post-traumatic stress disorder**). This work led, in 1926, to his *Outline of Abnormal Psychology.*

### Moves to Harvard University

McDougall moved to the United States in 1920, accepting the William James Chair of Psychology at Harvard University. *Outline of Psychology*, published in 1923, is considered to be one of his most important books. However McDougall was not well-received at Harvard, due to the racist nature of his views on eugenics and his opposition to **behaviorism**. His debate with John B. Watson was published in 1928 as *The Battle of Behaviorism*. His interest in psychic phenomena also was controversial. McDougall became president of the American Society for Psychical Research and investigated the medium known as "Margery" (Mina S. Crandon), whom he eventually decided was a fraud. In 1925, he co-founded the Boston Society for Psychical Research.

In 1927, McDougall became chairman of the Psychology Department at Duke University in North Carolina. There he supported the establishment of the **Parapsychology** Laboratory and in the last year of his life he co-edited the *Journal of Parapsychology*. McDougall also continued experiments in which he attempted to prove that white rats could inherit acquired **traits**. He wrote critiques of dynamic, Gestalt, and Freudian psychologies, exemplified by his 1935 book, *Psychoanalysis and Social Psychology*. He also wrote books on a variety of social issues, including world peace. In all, McDougall wrote more than 20 books and 167 articles. He held an honorary doctorate from the University of Manchester and was named an honorary fellow of St. John's College, Cambridge, in 1938. McDougall died of cancer in Durham, North Carolina, in 1938. In 1957, the Parapsychology Laboratory at Duke established the McDougall Award for Distinguished Work in Parapsychology.

*See also* Parapsychology

Margaret Alic

## Further Reading

Nordby, Vernon J. and Calvin S. Hall. *A Guide to Psychologists and Their Concepts.* San Francisco: W. H. Freeman and Company, 1974.

McCurdy, Harold G. "McDougall, William." In *Thinkers of the Twentieth Century,* edited by Elizabeth Devine, Michael Held, James Vinson, and George Walsh., 373-75. Detroit: Gale Research Company, 1983.

McDougall, William. *The Riddle of Life: A Survey of Theories.* London: Methuen, 1938.

Van Over, Raymond and Laura Oteri, eds. *William McDougall: Explorer of the Mind: Studies in Psychical Research.* New York: Garrett, 1967.

# Margaret Mead

## 1901-1978
American anthropologist whose work emphasized the relationship between culture and personality formation.

Margaret Mead was born in Philadelphia to a family of educators. In her youth, her main influences were her mother and maternal grandmother, both of whom had raised families and also pursued careers. Mead's formal education before entering college was sporadic, and she was mainly educated at home by her grandmother. An unhappy year at DePauw University turned Mead against coeducation, and she subsequently transferred to Barnard College. She first concentrated in English and psychology but became interested in anthropology under the influence of Columbia University anthropologists Franz Boas (1858-1942) and Ruth Benedict (1887-1948). Boas was urgently organizing ethnographic investigations of primitive cultures throughout the world before eventual contact with modern society, and he convinced Mead that she could make a contribution to this

burgeoning field. After receiving her M.A. in psychology in 1924, she conducted her first field work in American Samoa, where she observed adolescent girls to determine if the turmoil associated with **adolescence** in the West is universal. Living with her research subjects in a Samoan village, Mead was the first American to use the participant-observer method developed by British anthropologist Bronislaw Malinowski (1884-1942). Upon her return to the United States, she received her Ph.D. in anthropology in 1929 and published *Coming of Age in Samoa* (1928), in which she presented a portrait of Samoan culture as free from the *sturm und drang* of the teen years in Western societies because preparation for adulthood is a continuous process that begins early in life rather than a series of stages, which create a more stressful transition process.

Mead did extensive field work throughout the 1920s and 1930s. After her initial trip, she was always joined by a collaborator. These included her second husband, New Zealand psychologist Reo Fortune, and her third husband, the British anthropologist Gregory Bateson, whom she married in 1935. Mead and Bateson conducted two years of intensive field work together in Bali, pursuing their different research interests. They pioneered the use of film as a resource for anthropological research, shooting some 22,000 feet of film as well as thousands of still photographs. Besides the Balinese, groups studied by Mead included the Manus people of the Admiralty Islands, and the Arapesh, Mundugumor, Tchambuli, and Iatmul of New Guinea. A tireless investigator, she made many repeat visits to her research sites; over a 47-year period, she observed the Manus people seven times. Having studied seven different Pacific cultures as well as the Omaha tribe of North America, Mead became convinced of the importance of culture as a determinant of **personality**, following in the footsteps of **Alfred Adler** in the field of psychology and Ruth Benedict in anthropology. Mead detailed her theories of **character** formation and culture in *Sex and Temperament in Three Primitive Societies* (1935) and expanded further on the role of culture in gender formation in her 1949 work, *Male and Female: A Study of the Sexes in a Changing World.* (Although Mead's stature as an anthropologist is unquestioned, there has been some speculation that her subjects may have systematically lied to her during her investigations.)In contrast to Sigmund Freud's dictum, "anatomy is destiny," Mead found gender roles to be culturally determined rather than innate, noting that behavior regarded as masculine in one culture could be considered feminine in another.

Mead's professional skills were enlisted by the United States government during World War II to analyze the cultural characteristics of its wartime adversaries, the

**Margaret Mead (sitting) with Manus children during 1928 visit to Admiralty Islands.** *(UPI/Bettmann. Reproduced with permisison.)*

Germans and Japanese, and facilitate relations with its allies, especially the British. From 1926 to 1964, Mead was associated with the American Museum of Natural History in New York City as a curator of ethnology, eventually attaining the status of curator emeritus. She became an adjunct professor at Columbia in 1954 and also held a number of visiting professorships elsewhere. Mead was also the chairperson of the Social Sciences division of Fordham University beginning in 1968. She served as president of the World Federation of Mental Health (1956-57), the American Anthropological Association (1960), and the American Association for the Advancement of Science (1975). Beginning in the 1960s, Mead's influence expanded to include a wider audience, as she agreed to write a monthly column for *Redbook* magazine, in which she discussed topics she had concentrated on for much of her career—child-rearing practices and the family. In turn, she used her readers' letters to learn more about the concerns of American women. Mead was posthumously awarded the Presidential Medal of Freedom. Her other books include *Growing Up in New Guinea* (1930), *Balinese Character* (with Gregory Bateson, 1942), *Soviet Attitudes Toward Authority* (1951), *Childhood in Contemporary Societies* (1955),

*Anthropology: A Human Science* (1964), *Blackberry Winter* (1972), an autobiographical account of her early life, and *Letters from the Field, 1925-1975* (1977).

*See also* Child development; Conditioning; Sexuality

**Further Reading**

Bateson, Mary Catherine. *With a Daughter's Eye: A Memoir of Margaret Mead and Gregory Bateson.* New York: William Morrow, 1984.

Foerstel, Lenora, and Angela Gilliam, eds. *Confronting the Margaret Mead Legacy: Scholarship, Empire, and the South Pacific.* Philadelphia: Temple University Press, 1992.

Holmes, Lowell D. *Quest for the Real Samoa: The Mead/Freeman Controversy and Beyond.* South Hadley, MA: Bergin & Garvey, 1987.

Rice, Edward. *Margaret Mead: A Portrait.* New York: Harper & Row, 1979.

# Mean

The sum of the values of the points in a data set divided by the number of points.

**HEIGHTS IN CENTIMETERS OF FIFTEEN CHILDREN ARE:**

124, 137, 144, 136, 157, 129, 130, 131, 125, 128, 133, 133, 129

Sum equals 1995; divide by 15 to get the mean of **133.**

In statistics, the mean refers to the value that results when all the scores in a data set are added together and the total is divided by the number of scores in the data set. In the example, the mean for a set of fifteen data points is calculated. The mean balances the scores on either side of it. Also called the arithmetic mean or average, the mean is one of the measures of central tendency; the others being the **median** and the **mode**.

**Further Reading**

Peavy, J. Virgil. *Descriptive Statistics: Measures of Central Tendency and Dispersion.* Atlanta, GA: U.S. Dept. of Health and Human Services/Public Health Service, Centers for Disease Control, 1981.

# Measurement

The assessment of a trait or feature against a standard scale.

Psychologists rely heavily on measurements for very different purposes, ranging from clinical diagnoses based on test scores to the effects of an **independent variable** on a **dependent variable** in an experiment. Several different issues arise when considering measurement. One consideration is whether the measurement shows reliability and validity. Reliability refers to consistency: if the results of a test or measurement are reliable, a person should receive a similar score if tested on different occasions. Validity refers to whether the measurement will be useful for the purposes for which it is intended.

The **Scholastic Assessment Test** (SAT) is reasonably reliable, for example, because many students obtain nearly the same score if they take the test more than once. If the test score is valid, it should be useful for predicting how well a student will perform in college. Research suggests that the SAT is a sufficient but not perfect predictor of how well students will perform in their first year in college; thus, it shows some

validity. However, a test can be reliable without being valid. If a person wanted to make a prediction about an individual's **personality** based on an SAT score, they would not succeed very well because the SAT is not a valid test for that purpose, even though it would still be reliable.

Another dimension of measurement involves what is called the scale of measurement. There are four different scales of measurement: nominal, ordinal, interval, and ratio. Nominal scales involve simple categorization but does not make use of the notion of comparisons like larger, bigger, and better. Ordinal scales involve ranking different elements in some dimension. Interval scales are used to assess by how much two measurements differ, and ratio scales can determine the difference between measurements and by how much. One advantage of more complex scales of measurement is that they can be applied to more sophisticated research. More complex scales also lend themselves to more useful statistical tests that give researchers more confidence in the results of their work.

# Median

The middle value in a group of measurements.

In statistics, the median represents the middle value in a group of measurements. It is a commonly used indicator of what **measurement** is typical or **normal** for a group. The median is joined by the **mean** and the **mode** to create a grouping called measures of central tendency. Although the mean is used more frequently than the median, the median is still an important measure of central tendency because it is not affected by the presence or a score that is extremely high or extremely low relative to the other numbers in the group.

*See also* Mode

**Further Reading**

Peavy, J. Virgil. *Descriptive Statistics: Measures of Central Tendency and Dispersion.* Atlanta, GA: U.S. Dept. of Health and Human Services/Public Health Service, Centers for Disease Control, 1981.

125-128-129-129-129-130-130-131-133

The median is **129.**

# Media psychology

Area of psychology that researches the complex ways in which media influence attitudes, behavior, and feelings.

According to reports the average American household has the television on for about seven hours a day. It is also reported that young people are increasingly turning to the Internet as a form of escape and information-gathering. The movie industry spends billions of dollars on new films every year. Advertising currently has more outlets, like television, billboards, magazines, radio, the Internet, and even movies, than it has ever had in history. And while reading is taking a backseat to newer technological forms of media, newspapers are still a primary source for news about the world. On a planet filled with information and entertainment, in a time when our social evolution seems bound to media, it is more important than ever to study its effects.

## What does psychology have to do with media?

In academic discussions of mass media, psychology has long provided concepts, techniques, and theories of its function. All media can be described in simple terms, like someone saying a movie was funny or sad, or saying an article was very polished, or describing the Internet as chaotic. But when the theories of a discipline are added to an analysis of something, those theories give the subject matter a framework, or a theoretical perspective. Psychology, for example, brings cognitive theories to media studies. Such theories look at the interactions between receivers and the media.

What psychologists have discovered about media and people is varied, and the research has really just begun. Some psychologists explore the messages we see and hear and the effects those messages have on people. For instance, psychology has been studying the way women are portrayed on television. Women on television are generally very, very thin. Some psychologists have done research that suggests that the thin women on television make a **stereotype** that dictates that women should be thin, and if real-life women have different body sizes they do not feel good about themselves. Sometimes it is what we do not see and hear in the media that makes or enforces a stereotype. For instance, have you ever seen a sitcom that centers around an Asian-American **family**? Not seeing Asian-Americans on television keeps such people invisible in the mainstream of society. Since the media has become a source of shared cultural experience that people use to understand the world around them, it is important to explore what we are getting from the media.

## Processing information

There are different theories on how we understand what we see and hear. The *culturalist approach* suggests that the meaning or interpretation of media is subjective or individualized. Since **perception** involves all the senses and also giving meaning to all information a person takes in, different people can get different meanings from the same media. The **memory** has patterns of organization, also called *scripts* or *schemata*, which contain strings of associations that are activated by new experiences. New fragments of information are added to the existing scripts whenever we experience something new. For instance, when you go to see a movie about slavery, your memory brings up the script you have about that topic. All relevant information is added to what you are seeing in the movie. You may even think you see things in the movie that are not there, but exist in your perception because your script is running while you experience the film.

Perception is also affected by our belief systems, attitudes, and needs. For instance, if you are someone who is a passivist, that is, a person who does not condone **violence** at any time, you may watch a movie about war and take away the message that the movie was showing what a tragedy violence can be. If someone who is patriotic or fascinated by weaponry watches the same movie, they may think the movie was glorifying war and showing off some of the best guns ever made. In this way, it is said that there exists *selective perception*, or, "the principle of least effort." It is easier to perceive messages that go along with what you expect or believe. Every receiver of information has their own *frame of reference*, or place they are coming from when they receive new media.

Psychologists also study how media acts as a social tool. People joining book clubs, or a bunch of kids going to the movies together and then talking about what they saw, friends asking each other if they'd seen the latest episode of the hottest new show on T.V., or families watching television together are instances of meanings being created socially. Groups of people discussing media might be called "interpretive communities," of "reference groups." You may use different scripts, or frames of reference, depending on the social group you are with because our interpretive communites also influence our perception.

*See also* Television and aggression

Lara Lynn Lane

## Further Reading

*Perspectives on Psychology and the Media* Washington, D.C.: APA, 1997.

*Psychology and the Media: A Second Look* Washington, D.C.: APA, 1999.

*A Cognitive Psychology of Mass Communication* Harris, Richard Jackson, Lawrence Erlbaum Associates, Publishers, 1994.

Becker, Samuel L. "Constructing the World in Your Head: How Mass Media Influences the Way People Process Information," *ETC.: A Review of General Semantics,* vol. 44, no. 4, (Winter 1987): 373-382.

Buck, Ross. "Nonverbal Communication: Spontaneous and Symbolic Aspects," *American Behavioral Scientist,* vol. 31, no. 3, (Jan/Feb 1988).

Comstock, George and Stuart Fischoff. "The Field and the Discipline." *American Behavioral Scientist,* vol.35, no.2, (Nov/Dec 1991).

McIlwrath, Robert, et. al. "Television Addiction: Theories and Data Behind the Ubiquitous Metaphor." *American Behavioral Scientist,* vol.35, no.2, (Nov/Dec 1991): 104-121.

Reeces, Byron and Daniel R. Anderson. "Media Studies and Psychology." *Communication Research,* vol.16, no.5, (October 1991): 597-600.

Shapiro, Michael A. and Annie Lang. "Making Television Reality: Unconscious Processes in the Construction of Social Reality." *Communication Research,* vol.18, no.5, (October 1991): 685-705.

# Medical psychology

See **Health psychology**

# Paul J. Meehl

**1920-**
American clinical psychologist and pioneer in the field of learning theory.

## Minnesota professor influenced the world

Paul Everett Meehl, born on January 3, 1920, is a renowned expert in various aspects of **clinical psychology**. He earned his A.B. from the University of Minnesota in 1941, where he remained throughout his entire professional career. In 1945 he was awarded his doctorate from the same institution. His career as a faculty member at Minnesota has included his position as chair of the Department of Psychology from 1951 through 1958. In 2000 Meehl remains actively engaged in research and is the Regents' (Emeritus) Professor. His scholarship led also to a post as a professor in the medical school's Department of Psychiatry, in the Minnesota Center for the Philosophy of Science, and on the faculty of the Department of Philosophy. Among his many roles is his seat on the Advisory Board of *Philosophy, Psychiatry, & Psychology*, published by The Johns Hopkins University Press.

Meehl's pursuits since his early career have reached a broad spectrum of interests and concerns. He has focused on the field of clinical psychology, in particular clinical assessment, and in **personality**, learning, psychometrics, and the philosophy of science. Meehl's exploration into the learning process led to his influence in the field of assessment. Traditionally, using subjective clinical judgment was used to perform psychological assessments. Meehl's work changed this approach. He developed ways to make assessments on an actuarial basis in line with quantitative standards. This approach was instrumental in the eventual computerized evaluation of psychological tests and revolutionized testing forever.

## Respected by colleagues

Meehl's work in testing was as significant among his own colleagues as it was with the general population. For the **American Psychological Association (APA)**, he served as a member of the Committee on Test Standards and as chair for the Special Committee on Certification and Licensure of Psychologists. His professional contributions have represented a continually evolving passion for the scientific treatment of psychological study.

Perhaps Meehl's most significant contribution to his field was the fact that he helped prepare many of the most prominent practicing psychologists in the United States. He has been a leader in **psychotherapy**, behavior genetics, the philosophy of science, and **forensic psychology**, authoring over 160 publications. One of his first major studies was published in *Modern Learning Theory* in 1954. In 1958 Meehl published *What, Then, Is Man?* Active as a Lutheran layman, he co-authored this monograph exploring the relationship between behavioral science and Christian faith. Three of his works published in the 1990s reflected his current area of research. As Meehl himself noted, that work covers three areas; first, the development of testing of taxometric (assigning objects to appropriate classes) statistical procedures for the classification and genetic analysis of mental disorders and personality types, second, cliometric (the use of mathematical and statistical methods, often using computers, in order to analyze historical data) metatheory, and third, philosophical and mathematical contributions to the significance test controversy. His later publications include

*Cliometric Metatheory: The actuarial approach to empirical, history-based philosophy of science* in 1992.

Meehl's impact throughout psychology, philosophy, and medicine was significant enough to earn him numerous awards from his professional associations throughout his career. One of his earliest awards was that for Distinguished Scientific Contributions from the APA in 1958. Meehl was awarded the "Centennial Award" on August 9, 1996, from Division 12 of the APA in honor of 100 years of clinical psychology. This award honored the pioneering work he had done when the study of psychology was only beginning to gain scientific recognition. He has served as a member and Diplomate on the American Board of Professional Psychology (Clinical).

Meehl's major contributions to the field of psychology were his systematic and mathematical methods of research. He pioneered this systematic approach to diagnosis and evaluation. In addition to research, Meehl operated a private practice where he performed psychotherapy using both psychoanalytical and rational approaches.

*See also* Assessment, psychological

Jane Spear

**Further Reading**

American Psychological Association. *Meehl Publications, Professional Information* Available at the American Psychological Association Website at: http://www.apa.org, 2000.

Benner, David G., and Hill, Peter C., ed. *Baker Encyclopedia of Psychology & Counseling* Grand Rapids, MI: Baker Books, 1999.

# Melancholia

Melancholia is both an outdated term for depression itself and, currently, a clinically defined characteristic of major depression listed in the Diagnostic and Statistical Manual of Mental Disorders.

The term "melancholia" is derived from the Greek words *melas*, meaning black, and *chole*, meaning bile, and is a vestige of the ancient belief that a person's health and **temperament** are determined by the relative proportions of the four cardinal humors, or body fluids, which are blood, phlegm, choler (yellow bile), and melancholy (black bile). The central feature of melancholic **depression** is persistent and unremitting sadness. Persons suffering from this disorder are unable to enjoy normally pleasurable experiences, even brief ones, and they exhibit a greatly reduced sensitivity to pleasurable stimuli.

Melancholic depression is characterized by other features as well. The quality of the depressed **mood** is unique, differing from the sadness that an emotionally healthy person would feel even in response to a very painful event, such as the death of a loved one. The depression tends to be worse in the morning and associated with early morning awakening (at least two hours before the normal waking time). There is often a marked change in the affected person's physical movements, which can become either agitated or slowed down. Many persons suffering from melancholic depression show significant weight loss, with or without anorexic behavior. A final feature is the presence of intense and inappropriate **guilt** feelings.

A person is officially classified as suffering from depression with melancholic features when the persistent feelings of unhappiness are accompanied by at least three of the other symptoms listed above. Individuals with melancholic depression generally respond to antidepressant medications or electroconvulsive therapy. Depression with melancholic features occurs equally in both men and women but more often in older persons and more frequently in hospital inpatients than outpatients. Organic conditions associated with melancholic depression include hyperadrenocorticism, reduced **rapid eye movement (REM)** latency, and dexamethasone nonsuppression.

**Further Reading**

Ostow, Mortimer. *The Psychology of Melancholy.* New York: Harper & Row, 1970.

# Memory improvement

See **Memory; Mnemonic strategies**

# Memory

The ability to store and later recall previously learned facts and experiences.

The brain's capacity to remember remains one of the least understood areas of science. What is understood is that memory is a process that occurs constantly and in varying stages. The memory process occurs in three stages: encoding, storage, and retrieval. Conditions present during each of these stages affect the quality of the memory, and breakdowns at any of these points can cause memory failure.

## Stages of Memory

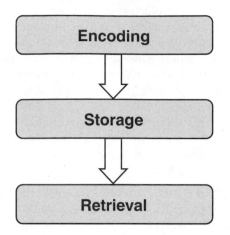

The first stage, encoding, is the reception by the **brain** of some physical input that is changed into a form that the memory accepts. When a person is introduced to someone new, for example, that person's name becomes a part of memory. Before information can be encoded, it first must be recognized and noted by the recipient. During the second stage, storage, learned facts or experiences are retained in either short-term or long-term memory. In the third, or retrieval, stage, memory allows the previously learned facts or experiences to be recalled. Each of these stages play an important role in both short-term and long-term memory, although it is believed they work differently depending on which memory is used.

As the term implies, short-term memory is used for items that need recall over short periods of time, sometimes as little as seconds. It is believed that short-term memories are encoded either visually or acoustically. Visual encoding is primary for recalling faces, places, and other visual experiences, while acoustic encoding is most important for verbal material. After looking up a number in a telephone book, for example, most people repeat the number to themselves several times before dialing the number. Rather than visualizing the written form of the numbers, the sound of the words becomes the means for recall. Experiments have demonstrated the importance of acoustic coding in the ability to recall lists of words or letters as well. When subjects were asked to recall a sequence of letters, those who made errors replaced the correct letter with a similarly sounding letter, for example "D" instead of "T."

Adequate operation of short-term memory is crucial when performing such everyday activities as reading or conversing. However, the capacity of short-term memory is quite limited. Studies have shown consistently that there is room in short-term memory for an average of seven items, plus or minus two (known as magic number seven). In experiments in which subjects are asked to recall a series of unrelated numbers or words, for example, some are able to recall nine and others only five, but most will recall seven words. As the list of things to be remembered increases, new items can displace previous items in the current list. Memory uses a process called "chunking" to increase the capacity of short-term memory. While most people still can use only seven "slots" of memory, facts or information can be grouped in meaningful ways to form a chunk of memory. These chunks of related items then act as one item within short-term memory.

Long-term memory contains information that has been stored for longer periods of time, ranging from a few minutes to a lifetime. When translating information for long-term memory, the brain uses meaning as a primary method for encoding. When attempting to recall a list of unrelated words, for instance, subjects often try to link the words in a sentence. The more the meaning of the information is elaborated, the more it will be recalled. Voices, odors, and tastes also are stored in long-term memory, which indicates that other means of encoding besides meaning, are also used. Items are regularly transferred back and forth from short-term to long-term memory. For example, rehearsing facts can transfer short-term memory into long-term. The chunking process in long-term memory can increase the capacity of short-term memory when various chunks of information are called upon to be used.

The breakdown in the retrieval of information from either memory can be the result of various factors, including interference, decay, or storage problems. In addition, researchers believe it is unlikely that all experiences or facts are stored in memory and thus are available for retrieval. Emotional factors, including anxiety, also contribute to memory failure in certain situations. **Test anxiety**, for example, may cause a student to forget factual information despite how well it has been learned. **Amnesia**, a partial or total loss of memory, may be caused by stroke, injury to the brain, surgery, alcohol dependence, encephalitis, and **electroconvulsive therapy (ECT)**.

Many methods can be used to improve memory. Long-term memory may be improved using mnemonic, or memory-aiding, systems. One, the "method of loci" system, encourages an association between various images and unrelated words. The "key word" method of learning a foreign language links the pronunciation of a new word with a picture that corresponds to the sound of the word. Context is another powerful memory aid that recognizes that people recall more easily facts or events

# FALSE AND RECOVERED MEMORIES

As of the late 1990s, research into recovered memories was characterized by tremendous controversy. A leading researcher in this subject, Elizabeth Loftus, conducted studies on over 20,000 subjects, and pointed to evidence she felt was convincing that memory is both fragile and unreliable. Her work supported, the notion that eyewitness accounts of events are often inaccurate, and that false memories can be created through suggestion in approximately 25% of the population. Loftus's work calls into question the validity of memories that are recovered under coaching or questioning; such memories have provided the basis for countless lawsuits brought against adults who are accused of molesting children. Her research has shown that emotional state—either low points, such as **boredom** or sleepiness or high points, such as **stress** or trauma—decrease the reliability of memory. She has also shown that experiencing violent and traumatic events decreases the accuracy of memory. Loftus theorizes that memory is suggestible and deteriorates over time. In her classic study, known as "Lost in the Shopping Mall," she demonstrated that subjects—children and teenagers—could be induced to remember being lost in a mall at an early age, even though it never actually happened, by simply questioning them about it as if it had happened.

One of the problems with the recovery of repressed memories is the very process of recovery. Many individuals recover memories while in therapy, under **hypnosis**, or in some other situation where the possibility of suggestion is powerful. In the late 1990s, in response to the swelling controversy over recovered memories, the American Medical Association, **American Psychiatric Association**, and American Psychological Association all issued guidelines to help practitioners deal with reports of recovered memories, especially of **sexual abuse** during **childhood**. In general, most physicians, psychiatrists, and psychologists suggest that recovered memories be corroborated through external investigation, and that alternative explanations for the existence of the memories be considered before any legal action be taken based on them.

False memory syndrome is dividing the field of professional **psychotherapy**. Some psychotherapists believe that to question the interpretation of and belief in recovered memories is to undermine the possibility of the existence of repression; others see the challenge to recovered memories as a sign of society's refusal to confront a serious problem with **child abuse** and abuse of women. Others contend that there are no psychoanalytic theories to support forgetting of traumatic events, or their detailed recall after the passage of time.

more easily if they are placed in the same **environment** in which they learned them. For example, a person is more likely to recall specific memories from high school if they go to the school and retrace their paths.

Imposing a meaningful organization on an unrelated group of facts or words also improves memory. The EGBDF notes that represent the lines on a musical staff often are recalled using the sentence, "Every good boy does fine." The sentence has nothing to do with music; rather, it places a meaning on letters that, at first glance, seem random. Another notable mnemonic system, the PQRST method, is helpful in assisting students learn textbook material. The letters correspond to the five steps of the method: preview, question, read, self-recitation and test.

Questions of the reliability and fragility of memory have surrounded the controversy of false and recovered memory that surface under questioning primarily by psychotherapists. As lawsuits based upon recovered memory have been filed against adults accused of molesting children and in at least one case, the death of a childhood friend, recovered memories have come under scrutiny and questions raised about the validity, especially when

memory has been recovered under coaching. Researcher Elizabeth Loftus, who conducted studies on 20,000 subjects, found that false memories could be created through suggestion in 25% of the population; eye witness accounts, she found, are often inaccurate. The emotional state of either low points, such as boredom or sleepiness or high points, such as stress or trauma, decrease the accuracy of memory, Loftus found. She theorizes that memory deteriorates over time and is vulnerable to suggestion. In one study, known as "Lost in the Shopping Mall," Loftus demonstrated that subjects, children and teenagers, could be induced to remember being lost in a mall at an early age by simply questioning them about the experience as if it happened.

In response to increasing controversy over recovered memories, the American Medical Association, American Psychiatric Association and American Psychological Association all issued guidelines to help practitioners deal with reports of recovered memories, especially of sexual abuse during childhood. Before any legal action is taken based on recovered memories, most physicians, psychiatrists, and psychologists suggest that recovered memories receive corroboration through external investigation and an alternative explanation for the existence of the memories be considered. The field of professional psychotherapy is divided on false memory syndrome. To question the interpretation of and belief in recovered memories undermines the possibility of the existence of repression, according to some psychotherapists; others see the challenge to recovered memories as coming from a refusal by society to confront a serious problem with child abuse and abuse of women. Yet others contend there are no psychoanalytic theories to support forgetting traumatic events or support their detailed recall after the passage of time.

*See also* Mnemonic strategies; Serial learning; Serial position function

## Further Reading

Bartlett, Frederic C. *Remembering: A Study in Experimental and Social Psychology* New York: Cambridge University Press,1995.

Damasio, Antonio. *Descartes' Error: Emotion, Reason, and the Human Brain..* New York: G.P. Putnam, 1994.

Loftus, Elizabeth F. and Ketcham, Katherine. *The Myth of Repressed Memory: False Memories and Allegations of Sexual Abuse.* New York: St. Martin's Press, 1994.

Rubin, David C. *Remembering Our Past: Studies in Autobiographical Memory.* Cambridge University Press, 1996.

Schacter, Daniel L. *Searching for Memory: The Brain, the Mind, and the Past.* New York: Basic Books, 1996.

# Mental age

A scale used to correlate intelligence to the typical changes that occur as a child matures.

French psychologist and educator **Alfred Binet** theorized that a child who appears to have limited mental abilities is able to perform on a level characteristic of younger children; conversely, a child who appears to be gifted is able to perform on the level of older children. In 1905 Binet, in collaboration with Thèophile Simon, developed a scale on which mental age could be compared to the chronological age. Thus, a bright child's mental age is higher than his or her chronological age.

In 1916, **Lewis Terman**, a psychologist at Stanford University, devised an **intelligence** test based on Binet's work (referred to today as the Stanford-Binet Intelligence Scale) and was administered to assess American school children. Terman maintained the concept of mental age in devising his formula for calculating the **intelligence quotient** (IQ). The formula is IQ = mental age/chronological age multiplied by 100. Thus if the child's mental age equals her chronological age, her IQ will equal 100.

# Mental health

Personal well-being, characterized by self-acceptance and feelings of emotional security.

After decades of concentrating on **mental illness** and emotional disorders, many psychologists during the 1950s turned their focus toward the promotion of mental health. Attempts to prevent mental illness joined the emphasis on treatment methods, and promotion of "self-help" in many cases replaced the dependence on professionals and drug therapies. American psychologist **Gordon Allport** (1897-1967) viewed the difference between an emotionally healthy person and a neurotic one as the difference in outlook between the past and the future. Healthy people motivate themselves toward the future; unhealthy ones dwell on events in the past that have caused their current condition. Allport also considered these qualities characteristic of mentally healthy individuals: capacity for self-extension; capacity for warm human interactions; demonstrated emotional security and self-acceptance; realistic perceptions of one's own talents and abilities; sense of humor, and a unifying philosophy of life such as religion.

In the United States, the Community Mental Health Centers Act of 1963 attempted to localize and individualize the promotion of personal well-being. Community mental health centers were established for outpatient treatment, emergency service, and short-term hospitalizations. Professional therapists and paraprofessionals consulted with schools, courts, and other local agencies to devise and maintain prevention programs, particularly for young people. Halfway houses enabled formerly ill patients to make an easier transition back to everyday life. Youth centers provided an available source of counseling for jobs and personal problems. Hot lines became staffed 24 hours a day in attempts to prevent suicide and **child abuse**.

Aided in large part by these community mental health centers, mental health professionals have strived to reduce the severity of existing disorders through the use of traditional therapies, the duration of disorders that do occur, and the incidence of new mental illness cases. In addition, attempts have been to decrease the stigma attached to mental illness by making mental health services more commonly available. Self-help strategies have also played an important role in the mental health arena. People with particular anxieties are encouraged to reduce them through training. For example, people afraid to speak in public are encouraged to take classes to help them cope with their anxiety and overcome it so that it does not interfere with their personal or professional lives. The proliferation of self-help support groups are also outgrowths of the efforts to personalize, rather than institutionalize, mental health care. People who participate in such groups not only learn to cope with the stresses that erode their well-being, they also receive the social support thought to be equally important in building strong mental health.

### Further Reading

Hergenhahn, B.R. *An Introduction to Theories of Personality.* Englewood Cliffs, NJ: Prentice-Hall, 1980.

Zimbardo, Philip G. *Psychology and Life.* Glenview, IL: Scott, Foresman, 1988.

---

# Mental hospitals

Institutions for the mentally ill, formerly called asylums, and now called psychiatric institutions.

Beginning in the Middle Ages, mental hospitals were basically prisons. By the end of the eighteenth century, the term asylum was used, and some reforms were being implemented when the notion was introduced that psychological disturbances, like physical ailments, could be viewed as diseases requiring treatment rather than crimes calling for imprisonment. By the late 1800s, reactions against conditions in mental hospitals led to a reform movement in the care and treatment of people with mental disorders. The Mental Health Act of 1946 and the Community Mental Health Centers Act of 1963 allotted federal funds for the establishment of community treatment centers, which provide a variety of services—including short-term and partial hospitalization—in an effort toward the deinstitutionalization of mental patients. As of the late 1990s, institutions for the treatment of mental disorders are called psychiatric institutions. These institutions—along with mental health centers and halfway houses—form a system for treatment of mental disorders at all levels of severity.

### Further Reading

Wyer, Robert S., Jr., ed. *Knowledge and Memory: The Real Story.* Hillsdale, NJ: Lawrence Erlbaum, 1995.

Hartmann, Ernest. *Boundaries in the Mind: A New Psychology of Personality Difference.* New York: Basic Books, 1991.

*See also* Institutionalization

---

# Mental illness

The term used to describe a disorder or condition that negatively affect cognition (thought), behavior, and/or affect (mood) to such a point where it causes a significant amount of distress and functional impairment for a prolonged period of time.

**Many mental hospitals are modernizing their treatment methods, including this one with patients participating in dance therapy.** *(Photo Researchers, Inc. Reproduced with permission.)*

## Overview

Mental illness is a serious public health problem. According to the World Health Organization and the Harvard School of Public Health, mental illness accounts for nearly 11 percent of total worldwide disease burden. (Disease burden is determined by the calculation of DALYs, or disability-adjusted life years. The DALY statistic measures lost years of healthy life from death or **disability** due to a disease.) In countries that are considered "established market economies" (i.e., United States, Great Britain), mental illness is second only to heart disease as the most disabling disease category. Unipolar major **depression** was determined to be the second leading source of disease burden (after ischemic heart disease) in established market economies, and the fourth leading cause of disease burden worldwide.

In its *Diagnostic and Statistical Manual of Mental Disorders, Fourth Edition (DSM-IV)*, a reference standard for **mental health** professionals, the **American Psychiatric Association** distinguishes 16 different subtypes (or categories) of mental illness. These include:

- *Disorders usually first diagnosed in infancy childhood, or adolescence.* These include learning and developmental disorders, **mental retardation**, and attention-deficit hyperactivity disorder.

- *Delirium, dementia, amnestia, and other cognitive disorders.* These include **dementia** related to **Alzheimer's disease**, head injury, and **central nervous system** infection; and substance-induced delirium.

- *Mental disorders due to a general medical condition.* Medical/mental conditions that are not classified in other areas of the DSM-IV are found in this category.

- *Substance-related disorders.* Disorders related to alcohol and drug use, abuse, dependence, and withdrawal are included in this category.

- *Schizophrenia and other psychotic disorders.* These include the schizoid disorders (**schizophrenia**, schizophreniform, and schizoaffective disorder), delusional disorder, and psychotic disorders.

- *Mood disorders.* Depressive disorders (major, dysthymic) and bipolar disorders are classified as **mood** disorders.

- *Anxiety disorders.* This classification includes panic disorder, agoraphobia, social **phobia, obsessive-compulsive disorder**, posttraumatic **stress** disorder, and generalized anxiety disorders, all disorders in which a certain situation or place triggers excessive **fear** and/or panic symptoms (i.e., dizziness, racing heart).

- *Somatoform disorders.* Somatoform disorders involve clinically significant physical symptoms that cannot be explained by a medical condition. Somatization disorder, conversion disorder, **pain** disorder, hypochondriasis, and body dysmorphic disorder.

- *Factitious disorders.* These are disorders in which the individual creates and complains of symptoms of a non-existent illness in order to assume the role of a patient (or sick role).

- *Dissociative disorders.* These disorders involve a change in **memory**, identity, and/or **consciousness**. They include dissociative **amnesia**, dissociative **fugue**, **dissociative identity disorder**, and depersonalization disorder.

- *Sexual and gender identity disorders.* Disorders of sexual desire, arousal, performance, and pain are included here, as is **gender identity** disorder. It should be noted that the inclusion of **gender identity disorder** as a mental illness in the DSM-IV has been a point of some contention among mental health professionals.

- *Eating disorders.* **Anorexia** and **bulimia** are both eating disorders.

- *Sleep disorders.* Insomnia, **narcolepsy**, hypersomnia, and parasomnias (**nightmares** and sleepwalking) are all considered **sleep** disorders.

- *Impulse-control disorders not elsewhere classified.* Includes **kleptomania** and pyromania.

- *Adjustment disorders.* **Adjustment disorders** involve an excessive emotional or behavioral reaction to a stressful event.

- *Personality disorders.* These are maladjustments of **personality**, including paranoid, schizoid, schizotypal, antisocial, borderline, histrionic, narcissistic, avoidant, dependent, and obsessive-compulsive personality disorder (not to be confused with the anxiety disorder OCD).

## Causes and symptoms

The causes of mental illness are not completely understood, but organic, genetic (hereditary), familial, traumatic life events, and social factors all may play a part in triggering mental illness. Frequently, it is a combination and interrelationship of several of these factors. For example, schizophrenia is caused by genetically determined abnormalities in the structure and chemistry of the **brain**, but the course and severity of the disease can be influenced by social factors such as environmental stress and the absence of a **family** or peer support system.

In some cases, mental illness is primarily a byproduct of a disease or general medical condition. For example, central **nervous system** infections that can occur in advanced AIDS can cause dementia. Depending on their location and severity, neurological conditions such as traumatic brain injury, tumor, or infarct (areas of tissue death as a result of loss of blood supply) can also cause various symptoms of mental illness.

Individuals dealing with traumatic life events (e.g., death of a close friend, experiencing a natural disaster, witnessing a brutal crime) may experience psychological distress and difficulty dealing with day-to-day tasks. Because these mental health problems tend to be of a temporary nature, they aren't termed mental illness. It is important to remember that prompt and proper treatment of these issues in the form of counseling or other psychological interventions is critical, as they have the potential to progress into a long-term mental disorder or illness.

## Diagnosis and treatment

Patients with symptoms of mental illness should undergo a thorough physical examination and patient history to rule out an organic or structural cause for the illness. If a neurological cause for the disorder is suspected, further diagnostic tests (e.g., CT scan, MRI, PET scan, neuropsychological assessments) are typically required. If a disorder with no organic cause is suspected, a psychologist or other mental healthcare professional will conduct a patient interview and administer one or more psychological assessments (also called clinical inventories, scales, or tests).

Counseling is typically a front-line treatment for mental illness. A number of counseling or talk therapy approaches exist, including **psychotherapy**, **cognitive therapy**, behavioral therapy, and **group therapy**. These are sometimes used in conjunction with alternative therapy approaches such as art or **music therapy** that use the creative process to promote patient self-discovery and awareness. A number of mental healthcare professionals are involved in the treatment of mental illness, including licensed counselors and therapists, social workers, nurses, psychologists, and psychiatrists.

Psychoactive medication is prescribed for symptom relief in patients with organic and non-organic mental illness. For mental illnesses that are considered biological in nature, such as **bipolar disorder** or schizophrenia, pharmaceutical therapy is considered a primary treatment approach. In other cases, such as in personality disorder or dissociative disorder, psychoactive medications are usually considered a secondary, or companion treatment to psychotherapy.

Many individuals suffering from mental illness choose to treat their illness through regular attendance in **self-help groups**, where they can seek advice and counsel from others in similar circumstances. Some of the most popular self-help organizations (i.e., Alcoholics Anonymous), are as, if not more, effective than traditional doctor/patient therapy for many individuals.

In some cases, effectively treating mental illness requires hospitalization of the patient. This hospitalization, also known as inpatient treatment, is usually employed in situations where a controlled therapeutic environment is critical for the patient's recovery (e.g., **rehabilitation** treatment for alcoholism or other drug addictions), or when there is a risk that the patient may harm himself (suicide) or others. One popular variation of the inpatient treatment program, known as milieu therapy, focuses on providing the patient with opportunities to gain self-confidence and interact with peers in a positive way. Activities that encourage self-discovery and empowerment such as art, music, dance, and writing are important components of this approach.

## Further Reading

American Psychiatric Association. *Diagnostic and Statistical Manual of Mental Disorders* 4th ed. Washington, DC: American Psychiatric Press, Inc., 1994.

World Health Organization, World Bank, and Harvard University. Murray CL, Lopez AD, eds. *The Global Burden of Disease: A comprehensive assessment of mortality and disability from diseases, injuries, and risk factors in 1990 and projected to 2020*. Cambridge, MA: Harvard University Press, 1996.

Satcher, David. *Mental Health: A Report of the Surgeon General*. Washington, DC: Government Printing Office, 1999. [available online at www.surgeongeneral.gov]

## Further Information

National Institute of Mental Health (NIMH). 6001 Executive Boulevard, Rm. 8184, MSC 9663, Bethesda, MD, USA. 20892-9663, fax: 301-443-4279, 301-443-4513. Email: nimhinfo@nih.gov. http://www.nimh.nih.gov.

# Mental imagery

A picture created by the imagination with no visual stimulus required.

Mental images are created by the **brain** from memories, **imagination**, or a combination of both. In the 1990s, scientists were gaining knowledge of how the brain forms these visual pictures without input from the eyes. According to researchers at Harvard University, the brain may generate these mental pictures in the area of the brain responsible for **vision**. Stephen Kosslyn, a psychologist, used positron emission tomography (PET) technology to examine the flow of blood in the brains of twelve men. The men were asked to close their eyes and imagine total darkness. Subsequently, they were asked to imagine a series of different items. The tests seem to indicate that the primary visual cortex, the area of the brain that interprets vision, was activated when creating the imagined images.

*See also* Daydreaming; Dreams; Fantasy

Paula Ford-Martin

## Further Reading

Bower, Bruce. "Brain Scans Set Sights on Mind's Eye." *Science News* (December 2, 1995): 372.

# Mental retardation

Below-average intellectual abilities that are present before the age of 18 and interfere with developmental processes and with the ability to function normally in daily life (adaptive behavior).

The term mental retardation is commonly used to refer to people with an **intelligence** quotient (IQ) below 70. An IQ of 80-130 is considered the **normal** range, and 100 is considered average. According to the definition in the American Psychiatric Association's *Diagnostic and Statistical Manual* (DSM-IV), a mentally retarded person is significantly limited in at least two of the following areas: self-care, communication, home living, social/interpersonal skills, self-direction, use of community resources, functional academic skills, work, leisure, health, and safety. Mental retardation affects roughly 1% of the American population. According to the U.S. Department of Education, about 11% of school-aged children were enrolled in **special education** programs for students with mental retardation.

There are four categories of mental retardation: mild, moderate, severe, and profound. The roughly 80% of retarded persons who are classified as mildly retarded have an IQ between 50 or 55 and 70. Mild retardation, which may not be detected in early **childhood**, usually involves little sensorimotor impairment. Persons in this category can be educated up to a sixth-grade level. With adequate vocational guidance, they can live and work productively in the community as adults, either independently or with some degree of supervision.

About 10% of retarded persons are classified as moderately retarded, with IQs generally between 35 and 50. Although they usually do not progress beyond the second-grade level academically, as adults they can take care of themselves within supervised settings and perform unskilled or semiskilled work.

Persons with severe retardation, who account for 3-4% of the retarded population, have serious language and motor impairment. They usually do not speak in early childhood but can learn communication and basic self-care during the school years. Their language skills may be limited to the most basic functional words necessary to meet their daily needs. As adults, they live either with their families, in group homes, or, when necessary, in facilities that can provide skilled medical or nursing care.

Profound retardation, which accounts for 1-2% of the retarded population, is usually associated with a neurological condition. It is characterized by severe sensorimotor difficulties beginning in early childhood and serious long-term limitations on both communication and the **ability** to care for oneself. Some profoundly retarded individuals are never able to speak or to be toilet trained. Most need constant care throughout their lives.

In addition to the categories of mild, moderate, severe, and profound retardation, separate categories are sometimes used to designate those retarded persons who can benefit from some degree of academic training. Those designated "educable mentally retarded" (EMR) can handle academic work at a third- to sixth-grade level, and usually have IQs that fall between 50 and 75. The "trainable mentally retarded" (TMR) have IQs of between 30 and 50 and can progress as far as second-grade level work. It is important to note that IQ scores are not foolproof ways of detecting the abilities and potential of mentally retarded children. Some children with lower IQs ultimately prove to be more capable of leading independent, productive lives than others who score higher. Factors such as emotional support, medical **attention**, and vocational training can **play** as great a role as IQ in determining the future of a retarded child.

## Causes of mental retardation

There are many different causes of mental retardation, both biological and environmental. In about 5% of cases, retardation is transmitted genetically, usually through chromosomal abnormalities, such as **Down syndrome** or fragile X syndrome. Down syndrome occurs when there is an extra chromosome in the 21st pair of chromosomes (known as trisomy 21). People with Down syndrome have 47 chromosomes instead of the normal 46. The disorder occurs in one out of every 600-700 births worldwide. Women over 35 are at greater risk of bearing a child with Down syndrome than younger women, and Down syndrome births are over 20 times more likely in women over 45 than in those under the age of 30. Children and adults with Down syndrome demonstrate both mental and motor retardation. Most are severely retarded, with IQs between 20 and 49, and prone to a number of physical problems, including poor **vision**, **hearing** and heart defects, and low resistance to respiratory infections. Individuals with Down syndrome (formerly called mongoloidism) also have distinctive physical features, including upward-slanting, almond-shaped eyes and a short, stocky build with a short neck and a smaller than average skull, which is usually flat in back.

Besides Down syndrome, the chromosomal condition that most commonly causes mental retardation is fragile X syndrome, in which a segment of the chromosome that determines gender is abnormal. Fragile X syndrome primarily affects males, in whom the incidence of the condition is 1 in 1,000, as opposed to 1 in 2,500 for females. Males with fragile X syndrome tend to have long, thin faces with prominent ears and jaws, and they often have characteristics of **autism**. Some researchers suspect that as many as 15% of people diagnosed with autism actually have fragile X syndrome. About 20% of genetically caused mental retardation results from single gene mutations, including Tay-Sachs disease, phenylketonuria (PKU), and metachromatic leukodystrophy.

Mental retardation may be caused by problems that occur during pregnancy and **birth**, including maternal nutritional deficiencies, toxemia, infections such as rubella, maternal phenylketonuria (even if the fetus doesn't have the condition), use of drugs or alcohol, maternal injury during pregnancy, extreme prematurity, low birth weight, perinatal injury, or lack of oxygen at birth. Retardation can also be the result of medical conditions and injuries that occur after birth, including metabolic disorders, severe childhood malnutrition, prolonged high fever, near drowning, lead poisoning, severe mental disorders such as autism, and infections such as meningitis that affect the **brain**. Environmental factors influencing mental retardation include deprivation of physical or emotional nurturance and stimulation. Altogether, there are hundreds of possible causes of, or factors contributing to, mental retardation.

Mentally retarded people are more prone to both physical and mental disorders than the general population. Some of the conditions that cause mental retardation may also be characterized by seizures, hearing problems, congenital heart defects, and other symptoms. Mental disorders are much more common among the mentally retarded than among the general population: an estimated one million Americans have some degree of mental retardation as well as a mental disorder of some kind. The most severely retarded appear to be most at risk for mental disorders, and the more severe the retardation the more serious the disorder. Diagnosis and treatment of these disorders can be especially difficult due to communication problems. In addition, **mental illness** in the retarded may also be caused by the stresses, frustrations, and loneliness they encounter in daily life. **Depression**, for example, is a common disorder of the mentally retarded, and one that often goes undiagnosed. In spite of their limited intellectual capabilities, retarded children realize that they are different and that other people are often uncomfortable around them. Professional counseling, along with parental love and attention, can help a retarded child maintain a positive self-image, which is crucial to the ability to function effectively with **family**, peers, and in the larger community.

## Preventive measures

Some types of mental retardation can be prevented through genetic counseling to determine the risk of a couple having a retarded baby. Other prenatal preventative measures include ensuring that a pregnant mother has adequate nutrition and immunization against infectious diseases; monitoring to screen for fetal abnormalities that are associated with mental retardation; and reduced use of drugs and alcohol by women during pregnancy. Following the birth of a child, the chances of retardation can be reduced by maintaining good nutrition for both the nursing mother and the young child; avoiding environmental hazards such as lead; and providing the child with emotional, intellectual, and social stimulation.

Another important preventative measure is early detection of certain metabolic and nutritional conditions that result in mental retardation following a period of degeneration. Screening for certain disorders is mandatory in most states. Hypothyroidism, which affects 1 in 4,000 infants born in the United States, can be prevented if a thyroid hormone is administered by the first month of an infant's life. However, if the condition goes untreated, it will cause impaired mental development in 20% of af-

fected children by the age of three months, and in 50% by the age of six months. Phenylketonuria (PKU) prevents an infant from metabolizing the amino acid phenylalanine. Reducing the amount of this substance in an infant's diet can prevent retardation. Infants with galactosemia lack the enzyme needed to convert the sugar galactose to glucose. Avoiding milk and certain other dairy products prevents galactose from accumulating in the blood and eventually interfering with the child's normal mental development. However, none of the preceding measures can be taken if the conditions involved are not detected, and most are undetectable without screening.

The symptoms of mental retardation are usually evident by a child's first or second year. In the case of Down syndrome, which involves distinctive physical characteristics, a diagnosis can usually be made shortly after birth. Mentally retarded children lag behind their peers in developmental milestones such as sitting up, smiling, walking, and talking. They often demonstrate lower than normal levels of interest in their **environment** and responsiveness to others, and they are slower than other children in reacting to visual or auditory stimulation. By the time a child reaches the age of two or three, retardation can be determined using physical and psychological tests. Testing is important at this age if a child shows signs of possible retardation because alternate causes, such as impaired hearing, may be found and treated.

There is no cure for mental retardation once it has occurred. Treatment programs are geared toward helping retarded children reach their own full potential, not toward helping them catch up with their peers who aren't retarded. Nevertheless, this type of habilitative intervention can prepare most retarded people to lead fulfilling and productive lives as active members of their communities. All states are required by law to offer early intervention programs for mentally retarded children from the time they are born. The sooner the diagnosis of mental retardation is made, the more the child can be helped. With mentally retarded infants, the treatment emphasis is on sensorimotor development, which can be stimulated by exercises and special types of play. It is required that special education programs be available for retarded children starting at three years of age. These programs concentrate on essential self-care, such as feeding, dressing, and toilet training. There is also specialized help available for language and communication difficulties and physical disabilities. As children grow older, training in daily living skills, as well as academic subjects, is offered.

Counseling and therapy are another important type of treatment for the mentally retarded. Retarded children as a group are prone to behavioral problems caused by short attention spans, low tolerance for frustration, and poor impulse control. **Behavior therapy** with a **mental health** professional can help combat negative behavior patterns and replace them with more functional ones. A counselor or therapist can also help retarded children cope with the low **self-esteem** that often results from the realization that they are different from other children, including siblings. Counseling can also be valuable for the family of a retarded child to help parents cope with painful feelings about the child's condition, and with the extra time and patience needed for the care and education of a special-needs child. Siblings may need to talk about the pressures they face, such as accepting the extra time and attention their parents must devote to a retarded brother or sister. Sometimes parents have trouble **bonding** with an infant who is retarded and need professional help and reassurance to establish a close and loving relationship.

Current social and health care policies encourage keeping mentally retarded persons in their own homes or in informal group home settings rather than institutions. The variety of social and mental health services available to the mentally retarded, including pre-vocational and vocational training, are geared toward making this possible.

## Further Reading
Beirne-Smith, Mary, et al., eds. *Mental Retardation.* New York: Merrill, 1994.

Drew, Clifford J. *Retardation: A Life Cycle Approach.* Columbus: Merrill, 1988.

Grossman, Herbert J., et al, eds. *AMA Handbook on Mental Retardation.* Chicago: American Medical Association, 1987.

Matson, Johnny L., and James A. Mulick, eds. *Handbook of Mental Retardation.* New York: Pergamon Press, 1991.

## Further Information
American Association on Mental Deficiency (AAMD). 1719 Kalorama Rd. NW, Washington, DC 20009, (202) 387–1968.

Association for Retarded Citizens (ARC). P.O. Box 6109, Arlington, TX 76005, (817) 640-0204.

National Down Syndrome Congress. 1800 Dempster, Park Ridge, IL 60068–1146, (708) 823–7550.

# Merrill-Palmer scales of mental tests

Intelligence test.

The Merrill-Palmer scales of mental tests are **intelligence** test for children aged 18 months to four years, which can be used to supplement or substitute for the Stanford-Binet test. Its 19 subtests cover language skills, motor skills, manual dexterity, and matching **ability**. They require both oral responses and tasks involving a variety of materials including pegboards, formboards, cubes, Kohs design blocks, buttons, scissors, sticks, and strings. The following comprise about half of the Merrill-Palmer scales: the Color Matching Test; Buttoning Test; Stick and String, and Scissors tests; Language Test; Picture Formboards 1, 2, and 3; Nested Cubes; Copying Test; Pyramid Test; and Little Pink Tower Test. The remaining Merrill-Palmer subtests are the Wallin Pegboards A and B; Mare-Foal Formboard; Seguin-Goddard Formboard; Pintner-Manikin Test; Decroly Matching Game; Woodworth-Wells Association Test; and the Kohs Block Design Test. Resistance to the testing situation is taken into account in scoring. The test is accompanied by a detailed list of factors that can influence a child's willingness to cooperate, and refused or omitted items are considered when arriving at the total score, which may then be converted and reported in a variety of ways, including **mental age** and percentile ranking.

## Further Reading
Cohen, Libby G., and Loraine J. Spenciner. *Assessment of Young Children.* New York: Longman, 1994.

McCullough, Virginia. *Testing and Your Child: What You Should Know About 150 of the Most Common Medical, Educational, and Psychological Tests.* New York: Plume, 1992.

Wortham, Sue Clark. *Tests and Measurement in Early Childhood Education.* Columbus: Merrill Publishing Co., 1990.

# Franz Anton Mesmer

**1734-1815**
German physician whose theories and practices led to modern-day hypnotism.

The word "mesmerize" means to hold one's **attention** as though that person were in a trance. Such was the popularity of Franz Mesmer, whose unorthodox methods of treating illness were highly popular with his patients. Those methods were criticized and ultimately dismissed by his contemporaries, and he lived out his days in obscurity. Yet his initial fame was the result of his successes with patients. Mesmer did not know the concept of psychosomatic illness, but he did recognize the role the mind played in disease. His practices evolved into **hypnosis**, which today is recognized by many as a valid and highly effective means of treating certain conditions.

The son of a forester, Mesmer was born on May 23, 1734, in Iznang, in the German province of Swabia. He did not begin college until he was 25, and when he first enrolled at the University of Vienna he planned to study law. He soon changed his mind and instead worked toward a medical degree, which he received in 1766. It was in his doctoral dissertation that he described his theory of "animal gravitation," in which health in humans is affected by the gravitational pull of the various planets. Mesmer also believed that there was a specific though unidentifiable fluid-like substance occurring in nature that channeled this gravity.

## Begins "animal magnetism" studies

Mesmer concluded that people did not need to rely on planetary gravitational pull; rather, they could manipulate their health through the use of any magnetic force. Today, some advocates of alternative medicine make use of magnets, which, worn or passed over the body, are said to restore balance or harmony and thus thwart disease. Most scientists consider this to be nothing more than quackery, and eighteenth-century Austrians were equally skeptical. Nonetheless, Mesmer attracted a considerable following and his practice became quite lucrative.

By 1775, Mesmer had revised his animal gravitation theory, renaming it "animal magnetism." He believed that magnets were not necessary after all; the passing of hands over the body were enough to create the necessary magnetic forces.

Other physicians were especially harsh toward Mesmer and his practices, and they actually tried to bring him up on charges of fraud. In addition, while there were patients who had been "cured" by Mesmer, there were many who had not been, and with the encouragement of the established medical profession they began to threaten legal action. Mesmer finally left Vienna in 1778, settling in Paris. There he found many French patients who were willing to engage in "Mesmerism." In addition to the magnetic forces, Mesmer also developed techniques to put people in trancelike states he called "crises." Mesmer believed that these crises, whose side effects included convulsion, actually acted as a means of forcing the body fluid back to its proper flow.

## Methods challenged in France

Mesmer remained popular in France for several years, but the medical establishment there was no more welcoming than the Austrian doctors had been. The controversy eventually reached King Louis XVI, who in 1784 appointed a group of scientists to examine Mesmer's methods and present their conclusions. The commission included some of the leading scientific minds of the day, including Antoine Lavoisier and Dr. Joseph Guillotin. Also on the commission was an American, Benjamin Franklin. The commission, perhaps not surprisingly, concluded that Mesmer's techniques could not be backed up with scientific evidence. Mesmer's following

**Franz A. Mesmer** *(Corbis-Bettmann. Reproduced with permission.)*

dropped off quickly after that pronouncement, and he left Paris in 1785. He stayed briefly in Versailles, then went to Switzerland, and finally returned to his native Germany.

It is interesting to note that although other scientists and physicians found fault with Mesmer's methods and theories, they did not discount the idea of mind-over matter treatment of illness. Franklin, in particular, believed that some diseases were more in the mind than in the body; he acknowledged that in those cases the power of suggestion could be enough to "cure" the disease. Also, Mesmer truly believed in his treatment, and his earnestness was no doubt the reason it took so much to discredit him. A common quack would have been discovered years earlier.

Mesmer spent his remaining years quietly. He died in Meersburg, Germany on March 5, 1815.

George A. Milite

## Further Reading

Asimov, Isaac. *Asimov's Biographical Encyclopedia of Science and Technology.*. Garden City, NY: Doubleday & Company, 1982.
Daintith, John, et al. *Biographical Encyclopedia of Scientists.* Philadelphia: Institute of Physics Publishing, 1994.

Mackay, Charles. *Extraordinary popular delusions and the madness of crowds*. New York: Farrar, Straus and Giroux, 1932.

# Metapsychology

Umbrella term used to describe the attempt to establish general principles to explain all psychological phenomena.

Metapsychology describes the effort to construct or to postulate a systematic and comprehensive set of general principles encompassing all of psychology, specifically including elements that are theoretical in addition to elements that are considered to have been empirically demonstrated; also known as nomothetic psychology. In classical Freudian psychoanalytical theory, the term metapsychology is used in reference to the analysis of the dynamic (instinctive), topological (association with **id**, **ego**, or **superego**), and economic (allocation of psychic energy) aspects of mental processes. The term metapsychology is sometimes used as a synonym of the term **parapsychology**. Parapsychology is a field of study that involves the investigation of paranormal phenomena, such as extrasensory **perception**, precognition, telepathy, clairvoyance, and telekinesis, that are (presumably) not explainable in terms of scientifically established principles or natural laws.

# Adolf Meyer

### 1866-1950
Swiss-born American psychiatrist who developed the concept of psychobiology.

Adolph Meyer was born in Niederweningen, Switzerland, and received an extensive medical education in neurology in Zurich, obtaining his M.D. in 1892. He emigrated to the United States in the same year. Beginning in 1893, Meyer worked for several hospitals, including a state hospital in Kankakee, Illinois, as a pathologist, and the New York State Hospital Service Pathological Institute, where he was involved with the training of psychiatrists. Meyer later joined the faculty of Cornell Medical College in New York City, where he served as professor of psychiatry. In 1909 G. Stanley Hall (1844-1924), a prominent psychologist and former student of **William James**, invited Meyer to Clark College in Worcester, Massachusetts, on the occasion of the college's twentieth anniversary, where he met with **Sigmund Freud** and **Carl Jung**.

**Adolf Meyer** *(AP/Wide World Photos. Reproduced with permission.)*

In following year Meyer was appointed professor of psychiatry at Johns Hopkins University and director of its Henry Phipps Psychiatric Clinic, which became an internationally renowned training center for psychiatrists.

Meyer became so influential in his adopted country that he was known as "the dean of American psychiatry," and his work has had a wide influence on psychiatric theory and practice. In Meyer's view, the diagnosis and treatment of a mental disorder must include a thorough understanding of the patient as a whole person. This approach, which would today be termed "holistic," involved studying the patient from various perspectives—medical, biographical, educational, and even artistic. It was this goal that led him to introduce the use of the individual case history, bringing together in one place information about a patient's physical condition, past history, **family** life, work situation, and other facts that could be relevant to treatment. Meyer also pioneered in promoting visits to the patient's family in order for the psychiatrist to understand the **environment** in which the patient lived, and to which he or she would return when treatment was completed.

Meyer believed that the constituent elements of human existence are actively interrelated, from the lowest biochemical level to the highest cognitive level. Arguing that psychological factors may be as important as neuropathology in causing **mental illness**, Meyer advocated integrating the studies of human psychology and biology into a single system that he called psychobiology. The goal of psychobiological therapy was the successful integration of different aspects of the patient's **personality**. Steps involved in this **psychotherapy** included analyzing the psychological, sociological, and biological factors relevant to the patient's illness; working with the patient on a conscious level, staying close to the original complaint; and utilizing a combination of treatment methods satisfactory to both psychiatrist and patient.

Through therapy that addressed both short-term and long-term problems, Meyer's goal was to help the patient adjust as well as possible to life and change. Part of the therapy process consisted of aiding the patient in modifying unhealthy adjustments to his or her situation through guidance, suggestion, and reeducation, which Meyer called "habit training." His emphasis on habits extended to include **schizophrenia**, which he viewed as caused by harmful habits acquired over a long period of time, in combination with biological factors, including **heredity**. **Neurosis**, Meyer believed, differed from **psychosis** in that only a part of the personality was involved. He viewed neurotic patients as suffering from unrealistic expectations and the inability to accept themselves as they were.

Meyer, together with **Clifford Beers**, was also a founder of the mental hygiene movement (and the one who suggested its name). The goal of this movement was to educate the public about mental illness and achieve more humane treatment of institutionalized patients. Meyer contributed significantly to the medical literature on psychiatry. His papers were collected and published in *Collected Papers* (1950-1952).

# Middle years

*While there is no exact consensus as to the age range of this period of life, it generally refers to the ages between approximately 40 and 60, with the lower limit sometimes placed as low as age 35 and the upper one as high as 65 years of age.*

In Erik Erikson's influential scheme of human development, middle age is the period in which an individual is presented with the developmental task of choosing between **ego** stagnation (self-interest) and generativity, the capacity to care for others and make a positive contribution to society by being productive in work, parenting, or other activities. **Carl Jung** characterized the mid-

dle years as a time for self-realization and the exploration of spiritual and social values once the practical tasks of finding an occupation and establishing a **family** have been accomplished.

For many people, middle age is a stable period in which they are settled in a long-term love relationship, have committed themselves to a career, and have established a family and a permanent home. The middle years can also be a time of exploration and radical change, sometimes fueled by the much-publicized "midlife crisis." For some individuals, failure to achieve goals set earlier in life or reassessment of those goals may produce discontent or even despair, resulting in major lifestyle changes, both professional and personal. It is important to note that personal and professional growth at midlife may also be indicative of an individual's socioeconomic status: the poor generally have less flexibility and fewer opportunities to make sweeping changes in their lives at this stage.

The **ability** to realize one's full potential in middle age is also closely related to developmental experiences earlier in life. Unresolved issues of **childhood** and **adolescence** are often felt keenly during this period, and the greatest number of **psychotherapy** clients are thought to be of middle aged. In addition, coping with **aging** parents and their eventual deaths compels middle-aged individuals to acknowledge their own mortality, resulting in a restructuring of priorities. Professionally, people may change careers, return to school, or enter into business for themselves, voluntarily decreasing their earning potential or accepting a lower measure of financial security in order to pursue their dreams while they still have a chance. Some women who have stayed home to raise children often reenter the job market at midlife, a challenge that can involve major personal reassessments and lifestyle changes.

Women in midlife are confronted with the approaching end of their childbearing years and begin experiencing symptoms of menopause. Men commonly become concerned about their levels of sexual prowess and activity in middle age. Affluent, well-educated men are especially prone to engaging in extramarital affairs at this time, often with younger women. Both sexes also face the disengagement of their children, first through the detachment of adolescence, and then when the children finally leave the family home.

## Further Reading
Anderson, Clifford. *The Stages of Life: A Groundbreaking Discovery: the Steps to Psychological Maturity.* New York: Atlantic Monthly Press, 1995.
Berger, Kathleen Stassen. *The Developing Person Through the Life Span.* 2nd ed. New York: Worth Publishers, 1988.

Inglehart, Marita Rosc. *Reactions to Critical Life Events: A Social Psychological Analysis.* New York: Praeger, 1991.

Zimbardo, Philip G. *The Psychology of Attitude Change and Social Influence.* Philadelphia: Temple University Press, 1991.

# Milgram's obedience experiment

A controversial experiment on conformity and obedience conducted in the early 1960s.

**Stanley Milgram** (1933-1984), an American experimental psychologist at Yale University, conducted a series of experiments on **conformity** and obedience to authority. In these experiments, Milgram recruited subjects—ordinary citizens—through newspaper advertisements offering four dollars for one hour's participation in a "study of memory." When the subject arrived at the experimental laboratory, he or she was assigned the role of "teacher," and asked to read a series of word pairs to another subject, or learner. The teacher-subject then would test the learner's **ability** to recall the pairs by reading back the first word in each pair. Whenever the learner made a mistake, the teacher-subject was instructed to administer **punishment** in the form of electric shock. This instruction, by an authority figure or employer to administer **pain** to a human being, is at the heart of the controversy.

The teacher-subject watched as the learner was strapped into a chair and an electrode was attached to the learner's wrist. The teacher was encouraged by the experimenters to continue to administer the shocks. Milgram found that the 65 percent of the teacher-subjects would continue to do what they were told, even though the learners could be heard pleading and screaming, and concluded that most people will follow the instructions of an authority figure as long as they considered the authority as legitimate. Many psychologists and others questioned the **ethics** of conducting such experiments, where participants were encouraged, in the name of scientific experimentation, to inflict pain on others. Another aspect of the controversy surrounding Milgram's work focused on the implications of his findings for the future of societies and their authority figures.

## Further Reading

Milgram, Stanley. "Behavior Study of Obedience." *Journal of Abnormal Psychology,* 1963.

_____. "Some Conditions of Obedience and Disobedience to Authority," *Human Relations,* 1965.

_____. "Issues in the Study of Authority: A Reply to Baumrind," *American Psychologist,* 1964.

# Stanley Milgram

**1933-1984**
American experimental social psychologist known for his innovative experimental techniques.

Stanley Milgram carried out influential and controversial experiments that demonstrated that blind obedience to authority could override moral **conscience**. His early studies on **conformity** were the first experiments to compare behavioral differences between people from different parts of the world. Milgram also examined the effects of television **violence**, studied whether New York City subway riders would give up their seats if asked to do so, and made award-winning documentary films.

Milgram, born in 1933 in the Bronx, New York, was the son of Eastern European Jewish immigrants, Samuel Milgram, a baker, and Adele Israel. Growing up in the Bronx, with an older sister and a younger brother, Milgram attended James Monroe High School and graduated from Queens College in 1954. He had a majored in political science and planned to enter the School of International Affairs at Columbia University to prepare for the Foreign Service. Instead, he enrolled in Harvard University's new interdisciplinary Department of Social Relations. There, **Gordon Allport** became his mentor and a series of fellowships enabled him to earn his Ph.D. in **social psychology** in 1960.

At Harvard, Milgram became Solomon E. Asch's teaching assistant. Asch was applying **Gestalt psychology** to social relations and designing experiments to examine conformity. For his doctoral research, Milgram spent a year in Norway and a year in France, exploring the cultural differences in conformity. He found that pressure for conformity was greater for Norwegians than for the French. After returning from France, Milgram worked with Asch at the Institute for Advanced Study in Princeton, New Jersey.

Moving to Yale University in 1960, as an assistant professor of psychology, Milgram began his experiments on obedience, with funding from the National Science Foundation. Much to his surprise, he found that 65% of his subjects would inflict what they believed to be painful electric shocks on others, simply because they were told to do so.

Milgram married Alexandra "Sasha" Menkin, a psychiatric social worker, in 1961 and the couple eventually had a daughter and a son. Returning to the Department of

Social Relations at Harvard in 1963 as an assistant professor of social psychology, Milgram used his "lost-letter technique" to study people's inclinations to help others when it wasn't required. These experiments examined whether subjects would re-mail lost letters. Milgram also addressed the "small-world problem," determining that any two individuals in the United States could reach each other via an average of five acquaintances.

In 1967, Milgram moved to the Graduate Center of the City University of New York as professor and chairman of the social psychology program. In 1970 he published "The Experience of Living in Cities," which had a major influence on the new field of urban psychology. He also examined how residents of New York and Paris perceived the geographies of their cities. One of Milgram's most unique social experiments, designed to study the effects of television violence, involved an episode of the CBS program "Medical Center," with subjects viewing one of three endings. He found that viewers watching a violent ending were no more likely than others to commit an antisocial act when given the opportunity. He also performed experiments with "cyranoids," intermediaries who communicated with someone using words from a third person. He found, for example, that listeners never suspected that an 11-year-old cyranoid's words were actually those of a 50-year-old professor. In 1980, in the midst of these experiments, Milgram suffered the first of a series of massive heart attacks. He died of his fifth heart attack in New York City in 1984, at the age of 51.

Margaret Alic

### Further Reading
Milgram, Stanley. *Obedience to Authority: an Experimental View.* New York: Harper & Row, 1974.
Milgram, Stanley. *The Individual in a Social World: Essays and Experiments.* Reading, MA: Addison-Wesley, 1977.

# Military psychology

The psychological study of military organization, military life, and combat.

Military psychology, when defined broadly, can include a vast array of activities in psychological research, assessment, and treatment. Military psychologists may be either soldiers or civilians. The field can encompass every aspect of the human mind that interests the military., but researchers focus on the psychology of military organization, military life, and the psychology of combat.

## The psychology of military organization

Military psychologists are intimately involved in testing recruits for **intelligence** and aptitude for military specializations, and helping to find more effective ways of training them. A critical subset of such testing focuses on identifying and optimally training officers and other leaders—a task that many practitioners admit is as much art as science.

A whole field of study revolves around what military psychologists call group cohesion—the difficult-to-quantify spirit of camaraderie, mutual trust, and confidence soldiers have in their unit. Studies have linked high group cohesion to soldiers performing better both as a team and individually; soldiers in units with good group cohesion are less likely to suffer psychological **disability** after combat.

Another military psychology subspecialty identifies people who might prove emotionally unstable in military life; in the nuclear era, this type of testing is especially crucial. In addition, military personnel who are privy to classified information are screened for psychological conditions that might make them a security risk.

One of the most controversial areas in military psychology concerns the integration of nontraditional groups into the often-conservative military society. Through World War II and Korea, military psychologists helped confirm that African Americans could be integrated into white units successfully. Today, military psychologists are trying to find ways to ease the introduction of women into front-line units; some psychologists consider acceptance of gay troops as a future goal.

## The psychology of military life

Military life places unique stresses on individuals and their families. Aside from the possibility of being wounded or killed in combat, military service often involves long hours of work, extended absences from home, and frequent transfer across the globe.

Some military psychologists research the sources of marital discord among military families; interestingly enough, some studies suggest that military life doesn't destabilize families, but it can bring already unstable families to the breaking point. In some respects, clinical military psychology is not very different from civilian **family** practice, since military psychologists may treat both soldiers and their civilian spouses and children.

The military has traditionally taken a harsh stance with soldiers who risk their own and their comrades' lives by abusing alcohol; but the macho culture has often worked at cross-purpose to that stance. In Vietnam, abuse of other drugs also became far more prevalent among American soldiers. While harsh punishments can still occur, soldiers are now offered treatment for substance abuse as well.

## The psychology of combat

Most soldiers never experience combat; but for those who do, a lifetime of learning about the rules of society and morality must be suppressed in the interests of survival. Military psychologists must help soldiers act effectively in combat—and suffer a minimum of emotional fallout afterward.

One facet of the psychology of combat is integrating humans with increasingly sophisticated weapons systems. Military psychologists are researching what display formats can help soldiers make split-second sense out of complex computer-screen images that carry life-or-death importance. Others focus on the effects of harsh environmental effects such as weather on soldiers' performance. Virtual reality has become an important focus for more effective combat training.

Military psychologists also study the emotional aspects of combat. Early military psychologists suspected that combat **stress** reaction (CRS)—a progressive psychological breakdown in response to combat—was a matter of psychological "weakness." Today, most agree that any human being will break down if exposed for long enough to enough death, **fear**, and **violence**.

Modern treatment for CSR stresses short-term desensitizing therapy and a quick return to combat. While this may seem harsh and self-serving on the part of the military, wartime studies indicate that soldiers with CSR who are treated in this fashion are less likely to suffer from post-traumatic stress disorder than those pulled to rear-echelon units for treatment.

Some soldiers who have experienced battle—as well as some victims of disasters or violent crime—suffer from a lingering version of CSR called **post-traumatic stress disorder (PTSD)**. A person with PTSD may chronically re-experience traumatic events, in **nightmares** or even in waking **hallucinations**. Other PTSD sufferers "close up," refusing to confront their emotional trauma but expressing it in substance abuse, **depression**, or chronic unemployment. PTSD has proved possible but difficult to treat successfully—hence the military's focus on preventing PTSD through proper CSR treatment.

One somewhat controversial school of thought holds that the inhibition against killing is so strong that the emotional cost of killing—rather than fear of death or loss of comrades—is the most defining aspect of CSR and PTSD. Adherents believe that increasingly realistic weapons training conditions soldiers to kill reflexively—a desired outcome for the military, but one that can contribute to emo-

tional problems among combat veterans in the absence of psychological support that recognizes this problem.

## The ethics of military psychology

As both therapists with a duty to their patients and subordinates with a duty to the military command structure, military psychologists must sometimes carry out a tricky ethical balancing act. Patient confidentiality is a particular problem, since commanders have the right to examine their subordinates' medical files when making decisions in assignments, promotion, and **punishment**.

Military psychologists have been sanctioned by the American Psychological Association for following legal military orders that violated APA ethical rules; they have also been disciplined by the military for following APA rules that violate military regulations. Both the military and the APA are working to establish clear guidelines to help military psychologists avoid the trap of the "company doctor."

*See also* Television and aggression

Kenneth B. Chiacchia

### Further Reading

Cronin, Christopher (ed.) *Military Psychology: An Introduction* Simon and Schuster, 1998.

Grossman, Dave *On Killing: The Psychological Cost of Learning to Kill in War and Society* Little, Brown & Company, 1996.

Jeffrey, Timothy B., Robert J. Rankin, and Louise K. Jeffrey "In Service of Two Masters: The Ethical-Legal Dilemma Faced by Military Psychologists." *Professional Psychology: Research and Practice* 23(2): 91-95 (1992).

Schwartz, T. P., and Robert M. Marsh. "The American Soldier Studies of WWII: A 50th Anniversary Commemorative." *Journal of Political and Military Sociology* 27(1): 21-37 (1999).

Oei, Tian P. S., Bernard Lim, and Brian Hennessy. "Psychological Dysfunction in Battle: Combat Stress Reactions and Posttraumatic Stress Disorder." *Clinical Psychology Review* 10: 355-388 (1990).

Page, Gary D. "Clinical Psychology in the Military: Developments and Issues." *Clinical Psychology Review* 16(5): 383-396 (1996).

Van Breda, Adrian D. "Developing Resilience to Routine Separations: An Occupational Social Work Intervention." *Families in Society* 80(6): 597-605 (1999).

# Minimal brain dysfunction

A term often used either in connection (or interchangeably) with hyperactivity and/or attention deficit disorder.

Minimal **brain** dysfunction was formally defined in 1966 by Samuel Clements as a combination of average or above average **intelligence** with certain mild to severe learning or behavioral disabilities characterizing deviant functioning of the **central nervous system**. It can involve impairments in visual or auditory **perception**, conceptualization, language, and **memory**, and difficulty controlling **attention**, impulses, and motor function. Minimal brain dysfunction is thought to be associated with minor damage to the brain stem, the part of the brain that controls arousal. A likely cause of this type of damage is oxygen deprivation during childbirth. While such damage does not affect intelligence, it does have an effect on motor activity and attention span. Minimal brain disorder usually does not become apparent until a child reaches school age.

Minimal brain dysfunction has also been linked to **heredity**; poor nutrition; exposure to toxic substances; and illness *in utero*. Other symptoms that may be associated with the disorder include poor or inaccurate **body image**, immaturity, difficulties with coordination, both hypoactivity and hyperactivity, difficulty with writing or calculating, speech and communication problems, and cognitive difficulties. Secondary problems can include social, affective, and **personality** disturbances.

# Minnesota Multiphasic Personality Inventory

Gathers information on personality, attitudes, and mental health.

The Minnesota Multiphasic **Personality** Inventory is a test used to gather information on personality, attitudes, and **mental health** of persons aged 16 or older and to aid in clinical diagnosis. It consists of 556 true-false questions, with different formats available for individual and group use. The MMPI is untimed and can take anywhere from 45 minutes to 2 hours to complete. This is normally done in a single session, but can be extended to a second session if necessary. Specific conditions or syndromes that the test can help identify include hypochondriasis, **depression**, hysteria, **paranoia**, and **schizophrenia**. Raw scores based on deviations from standard responses are entered on personality profile forms to obtain the individual results. There is also a validity scale to thwart attempts to "fake" the test. Because the MMPI is a complex test whose results can sometimes be ambiguous (and/or skewed by various factors), professionals tend to be cautious in interpreting it, often preferring broad descriptions to specific psychiatric diagnoses, unless these are supported by further testing and observable behavior. A sixth-grade reading level is required in order to take the test. However, a tape-recorded version is available for those with limited literacy, visual impairments, or other problems.

## Further Reading

Aylward, Elizabeth H. *Understanding Children's Testing: Psychological Testing.* Austin, TX: Pro-Ed, 1991.

Blau, Theodore H. *The Psychological Examination of the Child.* New York: J. Wiley & Sons, 1991.

Knoff, Howard M. *The Assessment of Child and Adolescent Personality.* New York: Guilford Press, 1986.

McCullough, Virginia. *Testing and Your Child: What You Should Know About 150 of the Most Common Medical, Educational, and Psychological Tests.* New York: Plume, 1992.

O'Neill, Audrey Myerson. *Clinical Inference: How to Draw Meaningful Conclusions from Psychological Tests.* Brandon, VT: Clinical Psychology Publishing Co., 1993.

Walsh, W. Bruce, and Nancy E. Betz. *Tests and Assessment.* 2nd ed. Englewood Cliffs, NJ: Prentice Hall, 1990.

Wodrich, David L., and Sally A. Kush. *Children's Psychological Testing: A Guide for Nonpsychologists.* 2nd ed. Baltimore, MD: Brookes Publishing Co., 1990.

# Salvador Minuchin

**1921-**
Argentinian physician, one of the founders of family therapy and of structural family therapy.

The eldest of three children born to the children of Russian-Jewish immigrants, Salvador Minuchin was born and raised in a closely knit small Jewish community in rural Argentina. His father had been a prosperous businessman until the Great Depression forced his family into poverty. In high school he decided he would help juvenile delinquents after hearing his psychology teacher discuss the philosopher Rousseau's ideas that delinquents are victims of society.

At age 18 he entered the university as a medical student. In 1944, as a student, he became active in the leftist political movement opposing the dictator Juan Peron who had taken control of Argentina's universities. He was jailed for three months. Upon graduation in 1946 he began a residency in pediatrics and took a subspecialty in psychiatry. In 1948, as Minuchin was opening a pediatric practice, the state of Israel was created and immediately plunged into war. He moved to Israel and joined its army where he treated young Jewish soldiers who had survived the holocaust.

In 1950 he came to the Untied States to study psychiatry. He worked with psychotic children at Bellevue

Hospital in New York City as a part-time psychiatric resident. Minuchin also worked at the Jewish Board of Guardians where he lived in its institutional housing with 20 disturbed children. His training there was psychoanalytic, which did not seem compatible with his work with the children.

In 1951 Minuchin married Patricia Pittluck, a psychologist, and emigrated to Israel. There he co-directed five residential institutions for disturbed children . Most of them were orphans of the holocaust and Jewish children from Asia and the Middle East. Here he first began to work therapeutically with groups instead of individuals. Between 1954 and 1958, Minuchin trained at the William Alanson White Institute of **Psychoanalysis** in New York City. He went there because the Institute supported the ideas of Harry Stack Sullivan, who created interpersonal psychiatry and stressed the importance of interpersonal interaction. As he was training there, he began practicing **family therapy** at the Wiltwyck School for Boys, a school for troubled young people, or juvenile delinquents. Slowly, he began to feel that he needed to see a client's family. He felt that seeing them alone, as per psychoanalysis, was not an effective treatment technique.

Minuchin and a number of other professionals there began working as a team to develop approaches to family therapy. These youths and their families tended not be very introspective, so Minuchin and his team focused on communication and behavior, and developed a therapy form in which the therapist is very active, making suggestions and directing activities, for instance.

In 1965, Minuchin and his family (he now had two children) moved to Philadelphia, where he became, at the same time, director of psychiatry at Children's Hospital of Philadelphia, director of the Philadelphia Child Guidance Clinic, and professor of child psychiatry at the University of Pennsylvania School of Medicine. During this time he began working therapeutically with children with psychosomatic illnesses. (Illnesses in which no physical basis for an illness can be found so the illness is attributed to psychological factors.) Research with these children and families indicated that family therapy could help these patients improve, and indicated maladaptive family patterns were partly to blame for these illnesses.

During the 1960s and 1970s, Minuchin became interested in the larger social world in which families are embedded. Thus he and his group started looking at communities and social service agencies, among other societal agents. In one project he and his colleagues, under an intensive program, trained minorities from the community to be family therapists.

During the 1960s, Minuchin and his colleagues, as well as a number of other groups, struggled to understand family dynamics. He explored what other family therapists and colleagues in the social sciences were doing, and drew on those that seemed to work. He found Gregory Bateson's systems theory (a system is comprised of interdependent parts that mutually effect each other) to go a long way in explaining family dynamics. Minuchin also drew on the ideas of **Nathan Ackerman**, a child analyst who began to look at the interpersonal aspects of the family unit, and the ways individual behavior relates to that unit. Minuchin believes these are perspectives that are complementary.

Very basically, structural family therapy uses short-term methods to alter the coalitions and alliances of family members, and by doing so, alter how they experience one another. Faulty family organization is responsible for causing family maladjustment.

In 1975, Minuchin retired from his position as director of the Philadelphia Clinic. He was Director Emeritus of the Clinic from 1975 through 1981. In 1981, Minuchin established Family Studies, Inc., in New York City, an organization to teach family therapists. Minuchin left the University of Pennsylvania, Philadelphia in 1983, when he joined New York University School of Medicine as a Research Professor. His wife is also a Research Professor there. He retired in 1996 and currently lives in Boston.

Minuchin has contributed to numerous professional journals and coauthored numerous books, many of which explore the effects of poverty and socials systems on families.

Marie Doorey

## Further Reading

*Allyn & Bacon Family Therapy Website* http://www.abacon. com/famtherapy/

Foley, V. "Family Therapy." In Corsini, R.J., ed. In *Encyclopedia of Psychology, 1st Ed., V. 2* New York: John Wiley & Sons, 1984.

Goleman, Daniel. "Family Therapist Takes on Agencies." *New York Times*, (May 19, 1987).

Minuchin, Salvador, and Nichols, Michael . *Family Healing: Tales of Hope and Renewal from Family Therapy.* New York: The Free Press, 1993.

*Writers Directory 2000, 15th Ed.* Detroit, MI: Gale Group, 2000.

## Further Information

New York University School of Medicine Department of Psychiatry. 550 First Avenue, New York, NY, USA. 10016.

# Mnemonic strategies

Any technique used for the purpose of either assisting in the memorizing of specific material or improving the function of memory in general.

The basic coding procedure common to most mnemonic strategies is to mentally associate, in some manner, items of new or unfamiliar information with various interconnected parts of a familiar, known whole. Mnemonic devices range from the very simple to the remarkably complex. An example of a very simple mnemonic device is the use of the acronymic word HOMES to remember the names of the Great Lakes (Huron, Ontario, Michigan, Erie, and Superior). An example of a remarkably complex mnemonic device is the ancient Greek and Roman system of topical mnemonics, in which a large imaginary house, or even a town full of large imaginary houses, is intricately subdivided into thousands of quadrates, or **memory** places, each of which is available to be associated with an item of material to be remembered. The difficulties encountered in the application of mnemonic strategies appear to increase as the amount of information to be mastered increases, and involve issues such as ambiguity, confusion, and complexity.

There are several commonly employed mnemonic devices. For example, the *method of loci* is a system where objects to be remembered are imagined to be arranged in geographical locations, or locations in a building, the map or layout of which is well-known. The learner uses this map or layout to remember unordered items, such as a shopping list, by placing the grocery items on the map, and recalling them later in a well-known order. In this way, no items will be forgotten or missed.

---

**MNEMONIC DEVICE FOR THE FIVE GREAT LAKES**

THIS MNEMONIC DEVICE CAN HELP THE LEARNER REMEMBER THE NAMES OF THE FIVE U.S. GREAT LAKES.

H - Huron

O - Ontario

M - Michigan

E - Erie

S - Superior

---

## Further Reading

Higbee, Kenneth. *Your Memory: How It Works and How to Improve It.* New York: Paragon House, 1993.

Maguire, Jack. *Your Guide to a Better Memory.* New York: Berkley Books, 1995.

Sandstrom, Robert. *The Ultimate Memory Book: Remember Anything Quickly and Easily.* Granada Hills, CA: Stepping Stone Books, 1990.

# Mode

One of the measures of central tendency in statistics.

In statistics, the mode is a descriptive number that indicates the most frequently occurring score or scores in a group of numbers. Along with the **mean** and the **median**, the mode constitutes the grouping of descriptive statistics known as measures of central tendency. Although the mode is the easiest of the measures of central tendency to determine, it is the least used because it gives only a crude estimate of typical scores.

*See also* Median; Mean

## Further Reading

Peavy, J. Virgil. *Descriptive Statistics: Measures of Central Tendency and Dispersion.* Atlanta, GA: U.S. Dept. of Health and Human Services/Public Health Service, Centers for Disease Control, 1981.

---

**EXAMPLE**

124-125-128-129-129-**130-130-130-130**-131-133-133-133

The mode is **130.**

---

# Modeling

The process of learning by watching others; a therapeutic technique used to effect behavioral change.

The use of modeling in **psychotherapy** was influenced by the research of social learning theorist **Albert Bandura**, who studied observational learning in children, particularly in relation to **aggression**. Bandura pioneered the concept of vicarious **conditioning**, by which one learns not only from the observed behavior of others but also from whether that behavior is rewarded or punished. Bandura concluded that certain conditions determine whether or not people learn from observed behavior. They must pay attention and retain what they have observed, and they must be capable of and motivated to reproduce the behavior. The effects of observed behavior are also stronger if the model has characteristics similar to those of the observer or is particularly attractive or powerful (the principle behind celebrity endorsements). Bandura maintained that television offered a major source of modeling, educating thousands of people to drink certain sodas or use brand name soaps. Likewise, **violence** and death modeled on television influenced behaviors, according to some social learning who cite the assassination attempt on President Ronald Reagan. John Hinckley made the attempt after watching *Taxi Driver* 15 times. Four girls testified in court that they watched *Born Innocent* before raping a California girl with a bottle, similar to a scene in the movie. Other theorists counter that television provides a release, rather than a modeling for aggressive behavior. In one study, researchers found that juvenile boys who watched aggressive television shows were less likely to exhibit violence than juvenile boys who did not.

Critics of modeling as an explanation for violent behavior maintain that the theory does not allow for differences in genetics, brain functioning and learning differences. Critics of the Bandura's findings on aggression maintain that the methods employed led to the outcome, including high frustration levels of children because they were not allowed to touch the toys.

As a therapeutic technique for changing one's behavior, modeling has been especially effective in the treatment of phobias. As with systematic **desensitization**, an individual is exposed to the feared object or situation in progressively anxiety-provoking forms. However, this series of confrontations, instead of being imagined or experienced directly, is first modeled by another person. In symbolic modeling, the person receiving treatment has also had relaxation training, and his or her task is to watch the series of modeled situations (live or on film) while remaining relaxed. As soon as a situation or action provokes anxiety, it is discontinued and the observer returns to a state of relaxation. In another effective technique, "live modeling with participation," the observer actively imitates the behavior of a live model in a series of confrontations with a feared object or situation. For example, persons being treated to overcome **fear** of snakes watch and imitate a model. They gradually progress from touching a snake with a gloved hand to retrieving a loose snake bare-handed and letting it crawl on their bodies.

In individual therapy sessions, the therapist may model anxiety-producing behaviors while the client, remaining relaxed, first watches and then imitates them. In therapy involving social skills and assertiveness training, this technique may take the form of behavioral **rehearsal**, in which the therapist models and then helps the client practice new, more socially adaptive behaviors.

Beyond phobias, modeling has wide application in therapy. Therapists use the modeling technique to illustrate healthy behaviors that clients can learn by example and practice in session. With children, the therapist models a variety of responses to difficult situations. In the situation of dealing with a classroom bully, the therapist models alternate responses in the context of a role **play**, where the therapist acts as the child initially and the child assumes the role of the bully. Then roles reverse. The child practices the behavior and responses modeled while the therapist portrays the bully. In couples' therapy, modeling is used to teach listening and communications skills. With quarreling couples, the therapist models responses to facilitate resolution rather than spiral the discussion downward into name-calling. Modeling has also been used effectively in **anger** management and in abuse cases.

Schools offer one of the largest arenas for modeling where teachers first demonstrate the behavior they seek, be it classroom decorum or how to work a long division problem. Bandura maintains that self-efficacy may be influenced by modeling. A behavior modeled increases the student's belief about what is possible, enhancing the student's **ability** to accomplish the task set forth.

*See also* Imitation

**Further Reading**
Bandura, Albert. *Self-Efficacy: The Exercise of Control.* New York: W. H. Freeman, 1997.
Decker, Phillip J. and Nathan, Barry R. *Behavior Modeling Training: Principles and Application.* New York: Praeger, 1985.

## Maria Montessori

**1870-1952**
Innovative Italian educator.

Maria Montessori is best known for the progressive method of education that bears her name. She earned her medical degree from the University of Rome in 1894, the first Italian woman to do so. A psychiatrist by training, Montessorri worked with deprived and retarded children at the Orthophrenic School in Rome starting in 1899. Her observations of the educational challenges facing these children lead to the formulation of her theories of **cognitive development** and early **childhood** education.

As she observed the progress of pupils previously considered to be uneducable, Montessori pondered the poor performance of **normal** children in regular schools. These schools, she concluded, were unable to address the individual educational needs of children and therefore stifled, rather than encouraged, learning. She described children in standard classrooms as butterflies mounted on pins, wings motionless with useless knowledge. To see whether her ideas could be adapted to the education of normal children, Montessori opened her own school in 1907, the Casa dei Bambini, for 3-7-year-olds living in the tenements of Rome.

Montessori believed that children learn what they are ready to learn, and that there may be considerable differences among children in what phase they might be going through and to what materials they might be receptive at any given time. Therefore, Montessori individualized her educational method. Children were free to work at their own pace and to choose what they would like to do and where they would like to do it without **competition** with others. The materials in Montessori's classrooms reflected her value in self selected and pursued activity, training of the senses through the manipulation of physical objects, and individualized cognitive growth facilitated by items that allowed the child to monitor and correct his or her own errors—boards in which pegs of various shapes were to be fitted into corresponding holes, lacing boards, and sandpaper alphabets so that children could feel the letters as they worked with them while beginning to read and write, for example. While other schools at the beginning of the 20th century emphasized rote learning and "toeing the line," self absorption in discovery and mastery tasks was the trademark of Montessori classrooms. Still, her classrooms combined this seemingly playful self direction with Montessori self discipline and respect for authority. Continued effort and progress was sustained by the satisfaction and enjoyment children received from mastering tasks and from engaging in activities they themselves have chosen. Montessori believed that these methods would lead to maximal independence for each child from dressing him or herself to organizing his or her day.

Interestingly, Montessori's educational approach also reflected the Darwinian notion that the development of each individual is a microcosm of the development of the entire species, or that "Ontogeny recapitulates phylogeny." She therefore advocated that even young children be taught to grow plants and tend animals so that, like their agrarian ancestors, they would ultimately achieve the highest level of civilization.

In 1922 Montessori became the government inspector of schools in Italy. She left Italy in 1934, traveled, and

**Maria Montessori** *(The Library of Congress. Reproduced with permission.)*

eventually moved to the Netherlands where she died in 1952. Maria Montessori left behind a rich legacy. Her educational approach to young and special needs children quickly became a popular progressive alternative to traditional classrooms. Today Montessori schools are common in many communities, and even traditional approaches to education embrace many of Montessori's ideas.

Doreen Arcus Ph.D.

## Further Reading

Britton, L. *Montessori Play and Learn*. New York: Crown, 1992.

Hainstock, E.G. *Teaching Montessori in the Home: The Preschool Years*. New York: NAL-Dutto, 1976.

Hainstock, E.G. *Teaching Montessori in the Home: The School Years*. New York: NAL-Dutton, 1989.

Montessori, M. *The Montessori Method*. 1939

Montessori, M. *The Secret of Childhood*. New York: Ballantine, 1982.

Montessori, M. *Spontaneous Activity in Education*. Cambridge, MA: Robert Bentley, 1964.

## Further Information

American Montessori Society. 150 Fifth Avenue, Suite 203, New York, NY 10011, (212) 924–3209.

# Mood

Loosely defined and subjectively experienced general emotional condition.

A mood, while relatively pervasive, is typically neither highly intense nor sustained over an extended period of time. Examples of mood include happiness, sadness, contemplativeness, and irritability. The definitions of phrases to describe moods—such as good mood and bad mood—are imprecise. In addition, the range of what is regarded as a **normal** or appropriate mood varies considerably from individual to individual and from culture to culture.

**Further Reading**

Kuiken, Don, ed. *Mood and Memory.* Newbury Park, CA: Sage Publications, 1991.

*See also* Affect; Emotion

# Moral development

The formation of a system of underlying assumptions about standards and principles that govern moral decisions.

Moral development involves the formation of a system of values on which to base decisions concerning "right" and "wrong, " or "good" and "bad." Values are underlying assumptions about standards that govern moral decisions.

Although morality has been a topic of discussion since the beginning of human civilization, the scientific study of moral development did not begin in earnest until the late 1950s. **Lawrence Kohlberg** (1927-1987), an American psychologist building upon Jean Piaget's work in cognitive reasoning, posited six stages of moral development in his 1958 doctoral thesis. Since that time, morality and moral development have become acceptable subjects of scientific research. Prior to Kohlberg's work, the prevailing positivist view claimed that science should be"value-free"—that morality had no place in scientific studies. By choosing to study moral development scientifically, Kohlberg broke through the positivist boundary and established morality as a legitimate subject of scientific research.

There are several approaches to the study of moral development, which are categorized in a variety of ways. Briefly, the social learning theory approach claims that humans develop morality by learning the rules of acceptable behavior from their external **environment** (an essentially behaviorist approach). Psychoanalytic theory proposes instead that morality develops through humans' conflict between their instinctual drives and the demands of society. **Cognitive development** theories view morality as an outgrowth of **cognition**, or reasoning, whereas **personality** theories are holistic in their approach, taking into account all the factors that contribute to human development.

The differences between these approaches rest on two questions: 1) where do humans begin on their moral journey; and 2) where do we end up? In other words, how moral are infants at **birth**? And how is "moral maturity" defined? What is the ideal morality to which we aspire? The contrasting philosophies at the heart of the answers to these questions determine the essential perspective of each moral development theory. Those who believe infants are born with no moral sense tend towards social learning or behaviorist theories (as all morality must therefore be learned from the external environment). Others who believe humans are innately aggressive and completely self-oriented are more likely to accept psychoanalytic theories (where morality is the learned management of socially destructive internal drives). Those who believe it is our reasoning abilities that separate us from the rest of creation will find cognitive development theories the most attractive, while those who view humans as holistic beings who are born with a full range of potentialities will most likely be drawn to personality theories.

What constitutes "mature morality" is a subject of great controversy. Each society develops its own set of norms and standards for acceptable behavior, leading many to say that morality is entirely culturally conditioned. Does this mean there are no universal truths, no cross-cultural standards for human behavior? The debate over this question fuels the critiques of many moral development theories. Kohlberg's six stages of moral development, for example, have been criticized for elevating Western, urban, intellectual (upper class) understandings of morality, while discrediting rural, tribal, working class, or Eastern moral understandings. (See Kohlberg's theory of moral reasoning. ) Feminists have pointed out potential sexist elements in moral development theories devised by male researchers using male subjects only (such as Kohlberg's early work). Because women's experience in the world is different from men's (in every culture), it would stand to reason that women's moral development might differ from men's, perhaps in significant ways.

Definitions of what is or is not moral are currently in a state of upheaval within individual societies as well as, at least, in the Western world. Controversies rage over the morality of warfare (especially nuclear), ecological conservation, genetic research and manipulation, alternative fertility and childbearing methods, **abortion**, **sexuality**, **pornography**, drug use, euthanasia, **racism**, sexism, and human rights issues, among others. Determining the limits of moral behavior becomes increasingly difficult as human capabilities, choices, and responsibilities proliferate with advances in technology and scientific knowledge. For example, prenatal testing techniques that determine birth defects in utero force parents to make new moral choices about whether to birth a child. Other examples of recently created moral questions abound in modern-day society.

Therefore, the study of moral development is lively today. The rise in crime, drug and alcohol abuse, gang violence, teen parenthood, and suicide in recent years in Western society has also caused a rise in concern over morality and moral development. Parents and teachers want to know how to raise moral children, and they turn to moral development theorists to find the answers. Freudian personality theories became more widely known to the Western public in the 1960s and were understood to imply that repression of a child's natural drives would lead to neuroses. Many parents and teachers were therefore afraid to discipline their children, and permissiveness became the rule. Cognitive development theories did little to change things, as they focus on reasoning and disregard behavior. (After a great deal of criticism in this regard, Kohlberg and other cognitive development theorists did begin to include moral actions in their discussions and education programs, but their emphasis is still on reasoning alone.) Behaviorist theories, with their complete denial of free will in moral decision-making, are unattractive to many and require such precise, dedicated, **behavior modification** techniques to succeed that few people are able to apply them in real-life situations.

The continuing breakdown of society, however, is beginning to persuade people that permissiveness is not the answer and another approach must be found. Schools are returning to"character education" programs, popular in the 1920s and 1930s, where certain "virtues" such as honesty, fairness, and loyalty, are taught to students along with the regular academic subjects. Unfortunately, there is little or no agreement as to which "virtues" are important and what exactly each "virtue" means. For example, when a student expresses dislike of another student, is she or he practicing the virtue of "fairness" or, rather, being insensitive to another's feelings? If a student refuses to salute the flag, is he or she betraying the virtue of "loyalty" or, rather, being loyal to some higher moral precept? These complex questions plague "character education" programs today, and their effectiveness remains in dispute.

Another approach to moral education that became popular in the 1960s and 1970s is known as "values clar-

## STAGES OF MORAL DEVELOPMENT

**Childhood** is often divided into five approximate stages of moral development:

- Stage 1 = infancy—the child's only sense of right and wrong is what feels good or bad;

- Stage 2 = toddler years—the child learns "right" and "wrong" from what she or he is told by others;

- Stage 3 = preschool years—the child begins to internalize family values as his or her own, and begins to perceive the consequences of his or her behavior;

- Stage 4 = ages 7-10 years—the child begins to question the infallibility of parents, teachers, and other adults, and develops a strong sense of "should" and "should not";

- Stage 5 = preteen and teenage years—peers, rather than adults, become of ultimate importance to the child, who begins to try on different values systems to see which fits best; teens also become more aware of and concerned with the larger society, and begin to reason more abstractly about "right" and "wrong."

ification" or "values modification." The purpose of these programs is to guide students to establish (or discern) their own system of values on which to base their moral decisions. Students are also taught that others may have different values systems, and that they must be tolerant of those differences. The advantages of this approach are that it promotes self-investigation and awareness and the development of internal moral motivations (which are more reliable than external motivations), and prevents fanaticism, authoritarianism, and moral coercion. The disadvantage is that it encourages moral relativism, the belief that "anything goes." Pushed to its extreme, it creates social chaos because no one can be held to any universal (or societal) moral standard. "Values clarification" is generally seen today to be a valuable *component* of moral education, but incomplete on its own.

Lawrence Kohlberg devised a moral education program in the 1960s based on his cognitive development theory. Called the Just Community program, it utilizes age-appropriate (or stage-appropriate) discussions of moral dilemmas, democratic rule-making, and the creation of a community context where students and teachers can *act* on their moral decisions. Just Community programs have been established in schools, prisons, and other institutions with a fair amount of success. Exposure to moral questions and the opportunity to practice moral behavior in a supportive community appear to foster deeper moral reasoning and more constructive behavior.

Overall, democratic **family** and school systems are much more likely to promote the development of internal self-controls and moral growth than are authoritarian or permissive systems. Permissive systems fail to instill *any* controls, while authoritarian systems instill only **fear** of **punishment**, which is not an effective deterrent unless there is a real chance of being caught (punishment can even become a reward for immoral behavior when it is the only **attention** a person ever gets). True moral behavior involves a number of internal processes that are best developed through warm, caring parenting with clear and consistent expectations, emphasis on the **reinforcement** of positive behaviors (rather than the punishment of negative ones), **modeling** of moral behavior by adults, and creation of opportunities for the child to practice moral reasoning and actions.

As previously stated, there is disagreement as to the exact motivations involved in moral behavior. Whatever the motivations, however, the internal processes remain the same.

The Four Component model describes them as follows:

1) moral sensitivity = **empathy** (identifying with another's experience) and cognition of the effect of various possible actions on others;

2) moral judgment = choosing which action is the most moral;

3) moral **motivation** = deciding to behave in the moral way, as opposed to other options; and

4) implementation = carrying out the chosen moral action.

According to personal (social) goal theory, moral (or prosocial) behavior is motivated by the desire to satisfy a variety of personal and social goals, some of which are self-oriented (selfish), and some of which are other-oriented (altruistic). The four major internal motivations for moral behavior as presented by personal (social) goal theorists are: 1) empathy; 2) the belief that people are valuable in and of themselves and therefore should be helped; 3) the desire to fulfill moral rules; and 4) self-interest. In social domain theory, moral reasoning is said to develop within particular social "domains": 1) moral (e.g., welfare, justice, rights); 2) social-conventional (social rules for the orderly function of society); and 3) personal (pure self-interest, exempt from social or moral rules).

Most people in fact have more than one moral "voice" and shift among them depending on the situation. In one context, a person may respond out of empathy and place care for one person over concern for social rules. In a different context, that same person might instead insist on following social rules for the good of society, even though someone may suffer because of it. People also show a lack of consistent morality by sometimes choosing to act in a way that they know is not moral, while continuing to consider themselves "moral" people. This discrepancy between moral judgment (perceiving an act as morally right or wrong) and moral choice (deciding whether to act in the morally "right" way) can be explained in a number of ways, any one of which may be true in a given situation:

• weakness of will (the person is overwhelmed by desire);

• weakness of **conscience** (**guilt** feelings are not strong enough to overcome tempation); or

• limited/flexible morality (some latitude allowed in moral behavior while still maintaining a "moral" identity).

The Moral Balance model proposes that most humans operate out of a limited or flexible morality. Rather than expecting moral perfection from ourselves or others, we set certain limits beyond which we cannot go. Within those limits, however, there is some flexibility in moral decision-making. Actions such as taking coins left in the change-box of a public telephone may be deemed acceptable (though not perfectly moral), while stealing money from an open, unattended cash register is not. Many factors are involved in the determination of moral acceptability from situation to situation, and the limits on moral behavior are often slippery. If given proper encouragement and the opportunity to practice a coherent inner sense of morality, however, most people will develop a balanced morality to guide their day-to-day interactions with their world.

Dianne K. Daeg de Mott

## Further Reading

Crittenden, Paul. *Learning to be Moral: Philosophical Thoughts About Moral Development.* Atlantic Highlands, NJ: Humanities Press International, 1990.

Gilligan, Carol. *In a Different Voice: Psychological Theory and Women's Development.* Cambridge: Harvard University Press, 1982.

Kohlberg, Lawrence. *Essays on Moral Development, I: The Philosophy of Moral Development: Moral Stages and the Idea of Justice.* San Francisco: Harper & Row, 1981.

———. *Essays on Moral Development, II: The Psychology of Moral Development.* San Francisco: Harper & Row, 1984.

———. *Child Psychology and Childhood Education: A Cognitive-Developmental View.* New York: Longman, 1987.

Kurtines, William M., and Jacob L. Gewirtz, eds. *Moral Development: An Introduction.* Boston: Allyn and Bacon, 1995.

Power, F. C., Ann Higgins, and Lawrence Kohlberg. *Lawrence Kohlberg's Approach to Moral Education: A Study of Three Democratic High Schools*. New York: Columbia University Press, 1989.

Schulman, Michael, and Eva Mekler. *Bringing Up a Moral Child: A New Approach for Teaching Your Child to Be Kind, Just, and Responsible*, rev. ed. New York: Main Street Books/Doubleday, 1994.

### Further Information

Developmental Studies Center. 2000 Embarcadero, Suite 305, Oakland, CA 94606-5300, (510) 533–0213, (800) 666–7270.

Center for the Advancement of Ethics and Character. Boston University School of Education, 605 Commonwealth Ave., Room 356, Boston, MA 02215, (617) 353–3262, fax: (617) 353–3924.

Educators for Social Responsibility (ESR). 23 Garden St., Cambridge, MA 02138, (800) 370–2515.

The Heartwood Institute. 425 N. Craig St., Suite 302, Pittsburgh, PA 15213, (800) 432–7810.

# Christiana Drummond Morgan

**1897-1967**
American clinician who co-created the Thematic Apperception Test (TAT).

Christiana Drummond Morgan grew up living the life of a debutante and may well have become no more than a society figure. Because she came of age at a time of social upheaval throughout the world, and because her life crossed paths with many influential scientists and intellectuals, she was able to expand her talents and make important contributions to behavioral therapy. Her unorthodox romance with the behaviorist **Henry Murray** no doubt opened many doors for her, and she served as an inspiration for much of Murray's work as well. Yet the affair also kept her, in large part, in Murray's shadow. Combined with often precarious health, as well as the skepticism male psychologists harbored toward female psychologists, it is not merely a platitude to say that she possessed a store of untapped potential.

Born in Boston on October 6, 1897, Morgan was the second of three daughters of William and Isabella Coolidge Councilman. William Councilman was a physician who served as a professor at Harvard Medical School. Young Christiana and her sisters were raised like many well-to-do girls and attended private schools. In 1917 she met William Morgan, a Harvard student; they became engaged shortly before he went to fight in the First World War. She went to New York, where she enrolled in a nursing program and received a nurse's aide certificate. When the war ended, William Morgan returned, and the two were married in 1919. A year later **Christiana Morgan** gave **birth** to a son, Thomas.

## Embarks on research career

The **family** moved to New York, where Morgan studied at the Art Students League from 1921 to 1924. Around this time the Morgans became increasingly close to Henry Murray and his wife. Henry Murray and Christiana Morgan were quickly drawn to each other but were reluctant to begin an affair. Both allowed themselves to be analyzed in Switzerland by the psychiatrist and former Freud disciple **Carl Jung**, who encouraged the affair as a way for both to unlock their **unconscious**. Although both Morgan and Murray remained married to their respective spouses, (her husband died in 1934; Murray's wife in 1964), the two were together until Morgan's death. In the 1930s Murray and Morgan were part of the group that created the Harvard Psychological Clinic; later, Morgan was named a Radcliffe Research Fellow, a title she held for the rest of her career.

## Co-creates Thematic Apperception Test

Morgan's analysis with Jung led to a series of "visions" experienced in a semi-hypnotic state. Jung encouraged her to draw these visions, which he used in his ongoing research into the unconscious mind. Morgan's visions eventually became less psychologically provocative to Jung, but her experience set the stage for what she and Murray would develop together in the 1930s in Cambridge, Massachusetts—the **Thematic Apperception Test** (TAT).

The TAT was a series of pictures (the test today consists of 31 pictures), each depicting some sort of interpersonal problem between people. Subjects are asked to create a short narrative story to go along with each picture. Different pictures can be used for men, women, and children. The idea behind the TAT is that as a person composes a story to accompany each picture, he or she will unconsciously reveal information that would not otherwise be shared. Based on this information, a trained psychologist can determine some of the dynamics of the individual's **personality**. Morgan and Murray first published their description of TAT in 1935. Initially, the TAT was known as the Morgan-Murray Thematic Apperception Test. Later, Murray was given primary credit for the test, along with "the staff of the Harvard Psychological Clinic." Why Morgan's credit was downplayed has been the source of speculation, but apparently she did not question this move.

For the next three decades, Morgan continued her work at Harvard, although she was plagued by a number of health problems. Her blood pressure was so dangerously high that she was obliged to undergo an operation called a radical sympathectomy, which severs the body's sympathetic **nervous system** from the spinal cord. (This operation, which can have severe side effects, is no longer performed today.) In later years, she succumbed to alcoholism. All the while her stormy relationship with Murray continued. By now Murray was recognized as an important figure in behavioral psychology. His interest in her seemed to wax and wane—and even though she was aware of what was happening, her emotional attachment was too strong for her to break off the relationship. In the mid-1960s Murray became infatuated with a younger woman, although he did not break off his relationship with Morgan. The strain appeared to be too much for Morgan, now 69. On March 14, 1967, during a trip with Murray to the Virgin islands, Morgan drowned herself.

George A. Milite

**Further Reading**

Douglas, Claire. *Translate This Darkness: The Life of Christiana Morgan.* New York: Simon and Schuster, 1993.

# Motivation

The drive that produces goal-directed behavior.

The study of motivation is concerned with the influences that govern the initiation, direction, intensity, and persistence of behavior. Three categories of motives have been recognized by many researchers: primary or biological (hunger and the regulation of food intake); stimulus-seeking (internal needs for cognitive, physical, and emotional stimulation, or intrinsic and extrinsic rewards); and learned (motives acquired through reward and **punishment**, or by observation of others).

**Instinct** theories, which were popular early in the twentieth century, take a biological approach to motivation. Ethologists study instinctual animal behavior to find patterns that are unlearned, uniform in expression, and universal in a species. Similarly, instinct theory in humans emphasizes the inborn, automatic, involuntary, and unlearned processes which control and direct human behavior. Scientific development of the instinct theory consisted largely of drawing up lists of instincts. In 1908, **William McDougall** (1871-1938) postulated 18 human instincts; within 20 years, the list of instincts had grown to 10,000. Although instinct theory has since been abandoned, its evolutionary perspective has been adopted by sociobiologists considering a wide range of human behavior, from **aggression** to interpersonal attraction, from the standpoint of natural selection and the survival of humans as a species.

Drive-reduction theory, which is biologically-oriented but also encompasses learning, centers on the concept of *homeostasis,* or equilibrium. According to this theory, humans are constantly striving to maintain homeostasis by adjusting themselves to change. Any imbalance creates a need and a resulting drive—a state of arousal that prompts action to restore the sense of balance and thereby reduce the drive. The drive called thirst, for example, prompts us to drink, after which the thirst is reduced. In drive-reduction theory, motivation is seen not just as a result of biological instincts, but rather as a combination of learning and biology. The *primary drives,* such as hunger and thirst, are basic physiological needs that are unlearned. However, there is also a system of learned drives known as *secondary-drives* that are not biological (such as the desire for money) but that prompt action in much the same way as the primary drives.

Another biologically-oriented theory of motivation is arousal theory, which posits that each person is driven to achieve his or her optimum level of arousal, acting in ways that will increase this level when it is too low and decrease it when it is too high. Peak performance of tasks is usually associated with moderate levels of arousal. Researchers have found that difficult tasks (at which people might "freeze" from nervousness) are best accomplished at moderate arousal levels, while easier ones can be successfully completed at higher levels.

Psychologically-oriented theories of motivation emphasize external environmental factors and the role of thoughts and expectations in motivation. Incentive theory argues that motivation results from environmental stimuli in the form of positive and negative incentives, and the value these incentives hold at a given time. Food, for example, would be a stronger incentive when a person is hungry. Cognitive theories emphasize the importance of mental processes in goal-directed behavior. Many theorists have agreed, for example, that people are more strongly motivated when they project a positive outcome to their actions. Achievement-oriented individuals learn at an early age to strive for excellence, maintain optimistic expectations, and to not be readily discouraged by failure. Conversely, individuals who consistently fear failure have been found to set goals that are too high or too low and become easily discouraged by obstacles. The concept of **learned helplessness** centers on how behavior is affected by the degree of control that is possible in a given situation.

American psychologist **Abraham Maslow** developed a five-level hierarchy of needs, or motives, that influence human behavior. The "lower" physiological and biological urges at the bottom of the hierarchy must be at least partially satisfied before people will be motivated by those urges closer to the top. The levels in Maslow's system are as follows: 1) *biological* (food, water, oxygen, **sleep**); 2) *safety* ; 3) *belongingness and love* (participating in affectionate sexual and non-sexual relationships, belonging to social groups); 4) *esteem* (being respected as an individual); and 5) self-actualization(becoming all that one is capable of being).

In addition to individual motivations themselves, conflicts between different motivations exert a strong influence on human behavior. Four basic types of conflict have been identified: 1) *approach-approach* conflicts, in which a person must choose between two desirable activities that cannot both be pursued; 2) *avoidance-avoidance* conflicts, in which neither choice in a situation is considered acceptable and one must choose the lesser of two evils; 3) *approach-avoidance* conflicts, where one event or activity has both positive and negative features; and 4) *multiple approach-avoidance* conflicts involving two or more alternatives, all of which have both positive and negative features.

*See also* Cognitive development; Environment; Ethology

## Further Reading
Hoffman, Edward. *The Right to be Human: A Biography of Abraham Maslow.* Los Angeles: Tarcher, 1988.

## Multiple personality

See **Dissociative identity disorder**

## Henry Alexander Murray Jr.

**1893-1988**
American biochemist, physician, and clinical and experimental psychologist who developed an integrated theory of **personality**.

Henry Alexander Murray, Jr. developed "personology," the integrated study of the individual from physiological, psychoanalytical, and social viewpoints. His background in medicine, biology, Freudian and Jungian **psychoanalysis**, and clinical and **experimental psychology**, as well as his work in anthropology, sociology, and

**Henry Murray** *(Archives of the History of American Psychology. Reproduced with permission.)*

literature, enabled him to develop an interdisciplinary approach to psychology. His concepts of **motivation**, particularly the need to achieve, had a major influence on theories of psychology. In 1961, Murray earned the Distinguished Scientific Contribution Award of the American Psychological Association, followed by the Gold Medal Award of the American Psychological Foundation in 1969.

Murray, born in New York City in 1893, was the second of three children of Henry Alexander Murray, Sr., and Fannie Morris Babcock. His father was a poor Scottish immigrant who became a wealthy investor. His mother, a New York socialite, was the daughter of the founder of the Guaranty Trust Company. Murray was educated at the Craegie School and, later, at Groton Academy. He entered Harvard University in 1911.

### Becomes a physician and researcher

Although Murray's Harvard major was history, he entered the Columbia College of Physicians and Surgeons in New York in 1915, earning his M.D. in 1919. In 1916, he married Josephine Rantoul, the daughter of a prominent Boston family and herself a graduate of Radcliffe College. The Murrays had one daughter.

At Columbia, George Draper stimulated Murray's interests in psychological factors affecting illness, and he stayed on at Columbia to earn an M.A. in biology in 1920. Returning to Harvard, Murray went to work with L.J. Henderson, applying the Henderson-Hasselbach equation to the acidity of the blood. Between 1919 and 1923, Murray published 10 papers on his physiological research.

Following two years as a surgical intern at Presbyterian Hospital in New York, Murray was awarded a research fellowship at the Rockefeller Institute for Medical Research in New York. He studied the development of chicken embryos, publishing 10 papers in that field, while simultaneously working towards his Ph.D. in biochemistry from Cambridge University in England.

## Discovers psychoanalysis and "depth psychology"

In 1925, Murray first met the Swiss psychiatrist **Carl Jung**, and the two became lifelong friends. With his discovery of the writings of Herman Melville, the author of *Moby Dick*, Murray began to develop his theory of personality, using Melville as a case study. Although never published, Murray's biography of Melville had a major influence on the scholarship of the day, and Murray's published articles and book chapters introduced the application of Jung's "depth psychology" to literary criticism. At about this time, Murray began his relationship with **Christiana Morgan**, who remained his lover and coworker until her suicide in 1967.

After earning his Ph.D. in 1927, Murray became an instructor at Harvard under Morton Prince, a psychopathologist who had founded the Harvard Psychological Clinic. Following Prince's death in 1929, Murray became director of the clinic, despite the fact that he had never taken a psychology course. Together with the neuropsychiatrist Stanley Cobb, Murray moved the focus of the clinic from experimental research in **hypnosis** and multiple personality to Freudian and Jungian psychoanalysis. He also introduced these subjects into the Harvard curriculum. Murray pursued his study of personality or "personology." At a time when American experimental psychologists studied rat behavior, Murray and his interdisciplinary research team studied single individuals on a variety of levels. With his staff, Murray published *Explorations in Personality: A Clinical Study of Fifty Men of College Age* in 1938. For decades, this remained the principle text for personality theory. With Morgan, Murray developed the **Thematic Apperception Test**, in which the subject is asked to tell stories about a series of pictures. This test remains an important tool in **clinical psychology**. Murray became an assistant professor at Harvard in 1929, associate professor in 1937, and professor of clinical psychology in 1948.

Murray served in the Army from 1943 until 1948, selecting personnel for the Office of Strategic Services (which later became the Central **Intelligence** Agency) and training agents in the United States and abroad. He was awarded the Legion of Merit by the War Department in 1946.

## Further develops his theory of "personology"

After his discharge from the Army as a lieutenant colonel, Murray joined **Gordon Allport** in the new Department of Social Relations at Harvard. There his research interests broadened further. With Clyde Kluckhohn, he began studying personality in society and investigated personality from the viewpoint of the dyadic interaction—the idea that a relationship between two people could be viewed as a single system with equal input from both partners. He also studied the role of mythology in personality and in society. Murray was best known, however, for his development of a human motivational system of social needs. He described behavior as a function of the interaction of individual needs, such as a need for achievement or a need for **affiliation**, and the "press" of the **environment**.

Interestingly, Ted Kaczynski, the serial bomber who killed and injured several people with mail bombs, was a participant in one of Murray's psychological experiments when he was a Harvard undergraduate. The study had to do with identifying men who would not break under pressure.

Murray held numerous honorary doctorates and was a member of the American Academy of Arts and Sciences. He retired in 1962 as a professor emeritus, the same year that his wife died. In 1969 he married Caroline Chandler Fish and became step-father to her five children. Murray died in Cambridge, Massachusetts, in 1988, at the age of 95. In his **memory**, Radcliffe College established the Henry A. Murray Research Center for the Study of Lives.

Margaret Alic

## Further Reading
Douglas, Claire. *Translate This Darkness: The Life of Christiana Morgan, the Veiled Woman in Jung's Circle.* Princeton, NJ: Princeton University Press, 1997.

Nordby, Vernon J. and Calvin S. Hall. *A Guide to Psychologists and Their Concepts.* San Francisco: W.H. Freeman and Company, 1974.

Robinson, Forrest G. *Love's Story Told: A Life of Henry A. Murray.* Cambridge, MA: Harvard University Press, 1992.

Schneidman, Edwin S., ed. *Endeavors in Psychology: Selections from the Personology of Henry A. Murray.* New York: Harper & Row, 1981.

# Music therapy

*A technique of complementary medicine that uses music prescribed in a skilled manner by trained therapists.*

## General effects of music therapy

Music has been used throughout human history to express and affect human **emotion**. The health benefits of music to patients in Veterans Administration hospitals following World War II became apparent, leading to its use as a complementary healing practice. Musicians were hired to work in hospitals. Degrees in music therapy became available in the late 1940s, and in 1950, the first professional association of music therapists was formed in the United States. The National Association of Music Therapy merged with the American Association of Music Therapy in 1998 to become the American Music Therapy Association.

Music can be beneficial for anyone. Although it can be used therapeutically for people who have physical, emotional, social, or cognitive deficits, even those who are healthy can use music to relax, reduce **stress**, improve **mood**, or to accompany exercise. There are no potentially harmful or toxic effects. Music therapists help their patients achieve a number of goals through music, including improvement of communication, academic strengths, **attention** span, and motor skills. They may also assist with behavioral therapy and **pain** management.

Depending on the type and style of sound, music can either sharpen mental acuity or assist in relaxation. **Memory** and learning can be enhanced, and this used with good results in children with learning disabilities. This effect may also be partially due to increased concentration that many people have while listening to music. Better productivity is another outcome of an improved **ability** to concentrate. The term "Mozart effect" was coined after a study showed that college students performed better on math problems when listening to classical music.

## How music therapy is used

Music is used to form a relationship with the patient. The music therapist sets goals on an individual basis, depending on the reasons for treatment, and selects specific activities and exercises to help the patient progress. Ob-

jectives may include development of communication, cognitive, motor, emotional, and social skills. Some of the techniques used to achieve this are singing, listening, instrumental music, composition, creative movement, guided imagery, and other methods as appropriate. Other disciplines may be integrated as well, such as dance, art, and psychology. Patients may develop musical abilities as a result of therapy, but this is not a major concern. The primary aim is to improve the patient's ability to function.

Learning to play an instrument is an excellent musical activity to develop motor skills in individuals with developmental delays, **brain** injuries, or other motor impairment. It is also an exercise in impulse control and group cooperation. Creative movement is another activity that can help to improve coordination, as well as strength, balance, and gait. Improvisation facilitates the nonverbal expression of emotion. It encourages **socialization** and communication about feelings as well. Singing develops articulation, rhythm, and breath control. Remembering lyrics and melody is an exercise in sequencing for stroke victims and others who may be intellectually impaired. Composition of words and music is one avenue available to assist the patient in working through fears and negative feelings. Listening is an excellent way to practice attending and remembering. It may also make the patient aware of memories and emotions that need to be acknowledged and perhaps talked about. Singing and discussion is a similar method, which is used with some patient populations to encourage dialogue. Guided Imagery and Music (GIM) is a very popular technique developed by music therapist Helen Bonny. Listening to music is used as a path to invoke emotions, pictures, and symbols from the patient. This is a bridge to the exploration and expression of feelings.

Music therapy is particularly effective with children. The sensory stimulation and playful nature of music can help to develop a child's ability to express emotion, communicate, and develop rhythmic movement. There is also some evidence to show that speech and language skills can be improved through the stimulation of both hemispheres of the brain. Just as with adults, appropriately selected music can decrease stress, anxiety, and pain. Music therapy in a hospital environment with those who are sick, preparing for surgery, or recovering postoperatively is appropriate and beneficial. Children can also experience improved **self-esteem** through musical activities that allow them to succeed.

The geriatric population can be particularly prone to anxiety and **depression**, particularly in nursing home residents. Chronic diseases causing pain are also not uncommon in this setting. Music is an excellent outlet to provide enjoyment, relaxation, relief from pain, and an opportunity to socialize and reminisce about music that has had special importance to the individual. It can have a striking effect on patients with **Alzheimer's disease**, even sometimes allowing them to focus and become responsive for a time. Music has also been observed to decrease the agitation that is so common with this disease. One study shows that elderly people who play a musical instrument are more physically and emotionally fit as they age than their nonmusical peers.

Music can be an effective tool for the mentally or emotionally ill. **Autism** is one disorder that has been particularly researched. Music therapy has enabled some autistic children to relate to others and have improved learning skills. Substance abuse, **schizophrenia**, **paranoia**, and disorders of **personality**, anxiety, and affect are all conditions that may be benefited by music therapy. In these groups, participation and social interaction are promoted through music. Reality orientation is improved. Patients are helped to develop coping skills, reduce stress, and express their feelings.

Pain, anxiety, and depression are major concerns with patients who are terminally ill. Music can provide some relief from pain, through release of endorphins and promotion of relaxation. It can also provide an opportunity for the patient to reminisce and talk about the fears that are associated with death and dying. Music may help regulate the rapid breathing of a patient who is anxious, and soothe the mind. The Chalice of Repose project, headquartered at St. Patrick Hospital in Missoula, Montana, is one organization that attends and nurtures dying patients through the use of music, in a practice they called music-thanatology by developer Therese Schroeder-Sheker. Practitioners in this program work to relieve suffering through music prescribed for the individual patient.

Judith Turner

**Further Reading**
Campbell, Don. *The Mozart Effect* Avon Books, 1997
Cassileth, Barrie. *The Alternative Medicine Handbook* W. W. Norton & Co., Inc., 1998
Woodham, Anne and David Peters. *Encyclopedia of Healing Therapies* DK Publishing, Inc., 1997

**Further Information**
American Music Therapy Association, Inc. 8455 Colesville Road, Suite 1000, Silver Spring, Maryland, USA. 20910, (301) 589-3300. http://www.musictherapy.org/.

# Myers-Briggs Type Indicator

A personality test that categorizes people according to stated preferences in thinking and perceiving.

The Myers-Briggs Type Indicator (MBTI) assigns people to one of sixteen different categories or types, based on their answers to 126 questions, such as: "How easy or difficult do you find it to present yourself, consistently, over a long period as a person who is patient?" There are 4 different subscales of the test, which purport to measure different **personality** tendencies. Extraversion-introversion (E-I) distinguishes between people who are sociable and outgoing, versus those who are more inward looking. Sensing-intuition (S-I) sorts people according to their attention to practical realities as opposed to relying on their **imagination**. Thinking-feeling (T-F) shows the difference between relying on logic versus intuition when making decisions. Finally, judging-perceiving (J-P) refers to one's tendency to analyze and categorize one's experiences, as opposed to responding spontaneously. Sixteen different types emerge from the combination of the above four pairs of **traits**.

The MBTI is probably the most popular self-insight psychological test in use today, with at least a million people per year completing it. It is widely used in business, industry, educational settings, and government because of its assumed **ability** to capture people's interests, needs, and values. MBTI profiles are often used in career counseling or as a basis for matching work partners or for selecting tasks that are best suited for one's MBTI type.

With any psychological test, its utility is dependent on its reliability and validity. A reliable test is one that produces consistent results over time. For example, IQ tests have high reliability, inasmuch as your IQ as measured today will not be appreciably different a year from now. The MBTI's reliability is only fair. One study showed that fewer than half of the respondents retained their initial types over a 5-week period. Consequently, we should be careful about making career decisions based on a classification system that is unstable. People change over time as a result of experience. The MBTI may capture a person's current state, but that state should probably not be treated as a fixed typology. Does the MBTI assist in career counseling? Is the test diagnostic of successful performance in particular occupations? These questions pertain to validity—the ability of the test to predict future performance. There have been no long-term studies showing that successful or unsuccessful careers can be predicted from MBTI profiles. Nor is there any evidence that on-the-job performance is related to MBTI scores. Thus, there is a discrepancy between the MBTI's popularity and its proven scientific worth. From the point of view of the test-taker, the MBTI provides positive feedback in the form of unique attributes that are both vague and complimentary, and thus could appeal to large numbers of people. It is possible that the MBTI could be useful as a vehicle for guiding discussions about work-related problems, but its utility for career counseling has not been established.

Timothy Moore

**Further Reading**

Pittenger, D. "The utility of the Myers-Briggs Type Indicator." *Review of Educational Research*, 63, (1993) 467-488.

# N

# Narcissism

Excessive preoccupation with self and lack of empathy for others.

Narcissism is the **personality** trait that features an exaggerated sense of the person's own importance and abilities. People with this trait believe themselves to be uniquely gifted and commonly engage in fantasies of fabulous success, **power**, or fame. Arrogant and egotistical, narcissistics are often snobs, defining themselves by their **ability** to associate with (or purchase the services of) the "best" people. They expect special treatment and concessions from others. Paradoxically, these individuals are generally insecure and have low **self-esteem**. They require considerable admiration from others and find it difficult to cope with criticism. Adversity or criticism may cause the narcissistic person to either counterattack in **anger** or withdraw socially. Because narcissistic individuals cannot cope with setbacks or failure, they often avoid risks and situations in which defeat is a possibility.

Another common characteristic of narcissistic individuals is envy and the expectation that others are envious as well. The self-aggrandizement and self-absorption of narcissistic individuals is accompanied by a pronounced lack of interest in and **empathy** for others. They expect people to be devoted to them but have no impulse to reciprocate, being unable to identify with the feelings of others or anticipate their needs. Narcissistic people often enter into relationships based on what other people can do for them.

During **adolescence**, when the individual is making the transition from **childhood** to adulthood, many demonstrate aspects of narcissism. These **traits**, related to the adolescent's need to develop his or her own sense of self, do not necessarily develop into the disorder that psychologists have studied for decades, known as narcissistic personality disorder. In 1898, Havelock Ellis (1859-1939) was the first psychologist to address narcissism in a published work. **Sigmund Freud** claimed that sexual perversion is linked to the narcissistic substitution of the self for one's mother as the primary love object in **infancy**. In 1933, psychoanalyst **Wilhelm Reich** (1897-1957) described the "phallic-narcissistic" personality type in terms that foreshadow the present-day definition: self-assured, arrogant, and disdainful. In 1969, Theodore Milton specified five criteria for narcissistic personality disorder in the third edition of the *Diagnostic and Statistical Manual of Mental Disorders (DSM-III)*: (1) inflated self-image; (2) exploitative; (3) cognitive expansiveness; (4) insouciant **temperament**; and (5) deficient social **conscience**.

The person with narcissistic personality disorder experiences a powerful need to be admired and seems consumed with his or her own interests and feelings. Individuals with this disorder have little or no empathy for others and an inflated sense of their own importance and of the significance of their achievements. It is common for persons with this disorder to compare themselves to famous people of achievement and to express surprise when others do not share or voice the same **perception**. They feel entitled to great praise, attention, and deferential treatment by others, and have difficulty understanding or acknowledging the needs of others. They envy others and imagine that others are envious of them. The person with narcissistic personality disorder has no patience with others, and quickly strays from situations where he or she is not the center of attention and conversation. According to *DSM-IV*, narcissistic personality disorder affects less than 1% of the general population. Of those, between half and three-fourths are male.

Secondary features of narcissistic personality disorder include feelings of shame or humiliation, **depression**, and **mania**. Narcissistic personality disorder has also been linked to **anorexia** nervosa, substance-related disorders (especially cocaine abuse), and other **personality disorders**.

**Further Reading**

Masterson, James F. *The Emerging Self: A Developmental, Self, and Object Relations Approach to the Treatment of the Closet Narcissistic Disorder.* New York: Brunner/Mazel, 1993.

Sandler, Joseph, Ethel Spector Person, and Peter Fonagy, eds. *Freud's "On Narcissism—an Introduction."* New Haven, CT: Yale University Press, 1991.

Westen, Drew. *Self and Society: Narcissism, Collectivism, and the Development of Morals.* New York: Cambridge University Press, 1985.

# Narcolepsy

A sleep disorder whose primary symptom is irresistible attacks of sleepiness during the daytime.

Narcolepsy, which usually begins in **adolescence** or early adulthood, affects about one in every 1,000 persons and is equally common in males and females. The **sleep** attacks, which can occur anywhere from six to 20 times a day, usually last about 10 to 20 minutes but can persist for as long as two to three hours. Narcolepsy is diagnosed if sleep attacks occur every day for at least three months (although most people treated for the disorder suffer from it for a much longer period of time—often years—before seeking help). In addition to the sleep attacks, persons suffering from narcolepsy often display several other characteristic symptoms. The most debilitating of these is cataplexy, a sudden loss of muscle tone that can affect a part or all of the body. Cataplectic attacks range from a sagging jaw or drooping head to a total collapse that causes the person to fall to the ground. Affecting about 70% of narcoleptics, they are usually triggered by strong emotions, ranging from **fear** and **anger** to excitement and amusement (laughter often provokes cataplectic attacks). Respiration is not affected, and full **consciousness** is maintained throughout the episode. Usually the attacks only last a few seconds, after which normal muscle strength returns. Other symptoms of narcolepsy include vivid dreamlike imagery while waking or falling asleep, episodes of sleep paralysis (in which the person wakes but is temporarily unable to move), and automatic behavior (sleepwalking-type actions which are performed without the person's conscious knowledge).

The cause of narcolepsy is not known, but sleep researchers believe it comes from a malfunction of the mechanism in the **brain** that regulates sleeping and waking, especially the regulation of REM (rapid eye movement) sleep, the part of the sleep cycle associated with dreaming. It is also known that there is a hereditary component to narcolepsy: having a narcoleptic parent dramatically increases one's chances of developing the disorder, from the normal 1 in 1,000 to 1 in 20. In recent research, a genetic marker has been found in the blood of over 95% of narcolepsy sufferers who were tested for it. Narcolepsy may also develop as a consequence of brain damage caused by injury or disease.

Narcolepsy is a chronic illness that lasts throughout a person's lifetime and has no known cure. Napping during the daytime can reduce the number of sleep attacks by lessening sleepiness. For those severely affected by the disorder, stimulants such as methylphenidate (Ritalin) and Dexedrine have been prescribed to ward off sleep attacks. Cataplexy—thought to be a partial intrusion of REM sleep into the waking state—has been treated with medications known to suppress REM sleep, such as tricyclic **antidepressants**. Doctors have had good results with another medication, the experimental drug gamma-hydroxybutyrate, prescribed for narcoleptics to improve the quality of their nighttime sleep, which is usually fitful and fragmented. The resulting improvement of nighttime sleep has had marked success in the reduction (and in some cases complete remission) of symptoms, including both daytime sleep attacks and cataplexy. To avoid the potential danger and embarrassment of cataleptic episodes, some persons with narcolepsy try to control the emotions that trigger them, even avoiding situations that are likely to bring on these emotions.

Narcolepsy has a crippling effect on the lives of those afflicted with it, causing disruption, embarrassment, and, potentially, danger in their everyday lives and interfering with both work and family life. **Self-help groups** sponsored by the American Narcolepsy Association (and a similar group in Canada) offer support to narcoleptics and their families. These organizations also work to help raise public awareness about the disorder.

**Further Reading**

Dement, William C. *The Sleepwatchers.* Stanford: Stanford Alumni Association, 1992.

Dotto, Lydia. *Losing Sleep: How Your Sleeping Habits Affect Your Life.* New York: William Morrow, 1990.

Ince, Susan. *Sleep Disturbances.* Boston: Harvard Medical School, Health Publications Groups, 1995.

**Further Information**

American Narcolepsy Association. 425 California Street, Suite 201, San Francisco, CA 94104, (415) 788–4793.

# Narcotic drugs

A category of addictive drugs that reduce the perception of pain and induce euphoria.

A narcotic is a depressant that produces a stuporous state in the person who takes it. Narcotics, while often inducing a state of euphoria or feeling of extreme well being, are powerfully addictive. The body quickly builds a tolerance to narcotics, so that greater doses are required to achieve the same effect. Because of their addictive qualities, most countries have strict laws regarding the production and distribution of narcotics.

Historically, the term narcotic was used to refer to the drugs known as opiates. Opium, morphine, codeine, and heroin are the most important opiate alkaloids—compounds extracted from the milky latex contained in the unripe seedpods of the opium poppy. Opium, the first of the opiates to be widely used, was a common folk medicine for centuries, often leading to addiction for the user. The invention of the hypodermic needle during the mid-19th century allowed opiates to be delivered directly into the blood stream, thereby dramatically increasing their effect. By the late 20th century, the legal definition of a narcotic drug had been expanded to include such non-opiate addictive drugs as cocaine and cannabis.

Narcotic drugs decrease the user's **perception** of **pain** and alter his or her reaction to pain. For this reason, narcotics—primarily codeine and morphine—are prescribed legitimately as pain killers. In a medical setting, they are referred to as narcotic analgesics. For pain relief, scientists have developed opioids, which are synthetic drugs with morphine-like properties. Some common synthetic opioids include meperidine (trade name Demerol) and methadone, a drug often used to treat heroin addiction. The use of methadone as a treatment for addiction is controversial, however, since methadone itself is addicting.

Scientists have attempted to develop ways to use the pain-killing properties of narcotics while counteracting their addictive qualitites. Such investigations have led to the discovery of narcotic receptors in the **brain**, and of the body's own natural pain-killing substances, called endorphins. Narcotics behave like endorphins and act on, or bind to, the receptors to produce their associated effects. Substances known as narcotic or opioid antagonists are drugs that block the actions of narcotics and are used to reverse the side effects of narcotic abuse or an overdose. A new class of drugs, a mixture of opioids and opioid antagonists, has been developed so that patients can be relieved of pain without the addictive or other unpleasant side effects associated with narcotics.

Narcotic drugs are among those substances used illegally, or abused, by adolescents. Some estimate that as many as 90% of adult drug addicts began a pattern of substance abuse during **adolescence**.

## Further Reading

Sanberg, Paul R. *Prescription Narcotics: The Addictive Painkillers.* New York: Chelsea House, 1986.

Traub, James. *The Billion-Dollar Connection: The International Drug Trade.* New York: J. Messner, 1982.

Willette, Robert E., and Gene Barnett, eds. *Narcotic Antagonists: Naltrexone Pharmacochemistry and Sustained-Release Preparations.* DHHS Publications No. ADM 81-102 490 1, NIDA Research Monograph No. 28. Rockville, MD: U.S. Department of Health and Human Services, Public Health Service, 1981.

# National Association of School Psychologists

Organization of school psychologists and related professionals, with members in the United States and 25 other countries.

The National Association of School Psychologists (NASP) has over 21,000 members from the United States and abroad. Founded in 1969, NASP is dedicated to serving the **mental health** and educational needs of school age children and adolescents. Members are school psychologists or professionals in related fields. The association encourages professional development and provides publications, meetings, workshops, and seminars for its members, and maintains a resource library and a placement service for school psychologists. In addition, NASP plays an activist role on behalf of school-age children, issuing position statements and resolutions to its membership, the general public, and government officials at all levels on such issues as **violence** in media and toys; legislative priorities; advocacy for appropriate educational services for all children; corporal **punishment**; and **racism**, prejudice, and discrimination.

NASP operates a national certification program for school psychologists. In addition, NASP is approved by the American Psychological Association and the National Board of Certified Counselors to provide continuing education for psychologists and National Certified Counselors. This allows participants in NASP's convention workshops and regional workshops to apply these sessions to their state's requirements for renewal of professional licenses.

## Further Reading

National Association of School Psychologists. 4340 East-West Highway, Suite 402, Bethesda, MD 20814-4411, (301) 657–0270. www.naspweb.org.

# National Institute of Mental Health

A component of the U.S. Department of Health and Human Services, with a mission to increase knowledge and understanding in all aspects of mental health, and to develop effective strategies to promote mental health and to prevent or treat mental illness.

The National Institute of **Mental Health** conducts and supports research in a very broad array of areas of mental health and illness. The Institute also collects and analyzes a vast amount of scientific data, widely distributes those data and analyses, and provides technical assistance to numerous federal, state, local, and private agencies and organizations. The National Institute of Mental Health consists of nine principal divisions and offices, and oversees the administration of a hospital.

# Natural selection

See **Darwin, Charles**

# Nature-nurture controversy

Colloquial term for the two views of human development, one emphasizing heredity and the other environment.

The nature-nurture controversy is an age-old dispute among behavioral psychologists, philosophers, theologians, and theorists of **consciousness** as to the source of the creation of human personality: Does it develop primarily from biology (nature), or from the environments in which we are raised (nurture)? People have been pondering the role of nature and environment since the time of Hippocrates (c. 460-c. 377 B.C. ). He, for instance, linked human behavior to four bodily fluids, or humors: yellow bile, blood, black bile, and phlegm. Hippocrates classified personalities into four types related to these four humors: choleric (yellow bile), or hot-tempered; sanguine (blood), or confident; melancholic (black bile), or moody; and phlegmatic, or slow to take action.

Unlike Hippocrates, the philosopher **John Locke** (1632-1704), whose ideas were a precursor to **behaviorism**, believed that behaviors were externally determined. Similarly, the philosopher Jean-Jacques Rousseau (1712–1778) theorized that people were born essentially good, and that positive aspects of the environmental contribute to the development of behavior. Locke believed that people were born essentially blank, like a blackboard, and who they "became" was entirely the result of their experiences.

The first scientist of the modern era to seriously consider the genetic and environmental effects in **personality development** was Sir **Francis Galton**, a wealthy British scientist. He dabbled in the arts and sciences but became primarily interested in what we today call genetics after his cousin, **Charles Darwin**, published *The Origin of the Species* in 1859. He was fascinated by the idea of genetic pre-programming and sought to uncover the ways in which humans are predestined. Many of his experiments were eccentric and ill-conceived, but his contributions to the field are still considered vital. His studies, curiously, led to the development of the science of fingerprinting and to the concept of the **word association test**. He also coined the term "eugenics" and believed that science would one day be able to direct, with absolute precision, the development patterns of human evolution. Taking the other position in this early debate was **John Watson**, the eminent behaviorist who once made the outlandish claim—which he later modified—that he could turn babies into any kind of specialist he wanted.

Over the years, much research has been done in the nature/nurture controversy, and today nearly everyone agrees that both nature and nurture **play** crucial roles in human development. This outlook has come to be known as interactionism and is the dominant system of belief among biologists, psychologists, and philosophers nearly everywhere.

Much of the research in the late 20th century has focused on twins who were separated at birth. In studying such pairs, psychologists can be relatively certain that any behavior the twins share has a genetic component, and those behaviors that are different have environmental causes. There are many famous cases of twins separated at birth being reunited later in life to find that they have many things in common. One of the most striking studies of twins, reported in a 1995 *New Yorker* article, was conducted by Thomas Bouchard, a professor of psychology at the University of Minnesota and founder of the Center for Twin and Adoptive Research. The twins, Daphne Goodship and Barbara Herbert, had been separated at birth and sent to economically different areas of London. The article's author, Lawrence Wright writes, "When they finally met, at King's Cross Station in May of 1979, each was wearing a beige dress and a brown velvet jacket. . . . Both had the eccentric habit of pushing up their noses, which they called 'squidging.' Both had fallen

# GENES AND BEHAVIOR

Is a child's athletic **ability** inherited, or simply a product of training? If one parent hasschizophrenia, will his child acquire the disease? The genetic foundations of behavior are studied by behavior genetics, an interdisciplinary science which draws on the resources of several scientific disciplines, including genetics, physiology, and psychology. Because of the nature of heredity, behavior geneticists are unable to assess the role played by genetic factors in an *individual's* behavior: their estimates by definition apply to *groups*. There are 23 pairs of chromosomes in each human cell (a total of 46 chromosomes-each with approximately 20,000 genes). Genes from both members of a pair act in concert to produce a particular trait. What makes **heredity** complex and extremely difficult to measure is the fact that human sperm and eggs, which are produced by cell division,have 23 unpaired chromosomes. This means that one half of a person's genes comes from the mother, and the other half from the father, and that each individual, with the exception of his orher identical twin, has a unique genetic profile.

Scientists are working on the Human Genome Project recently finished mapping anestimated 100,000 genes in the human DNA. They have been able to identify genes responsiblefor a variety of diseases, including Huntington's disease, **Down syndrome**, cystic fibrosis,Tay-Sachs disease, and a number of cancers. Genetic information about a particular disease constitutes a crucial milestone in the search for a cure. For example, phenylketonuria (PKIU) is a disease caused by a recessive gene from each parent; PKU's genetic basis is clearly understood. A child with PKU is unable to metabolize phenylalanine, an amino acid found in proteins. Thephenylalanine build-up afflicts the **central nervous system**, causing severe **brain** damage. Because the genetic processes underlying PKU are known, scientists have been able to develop a screening test, and thus can quickly diagnose the afflicted children shortly after **birth**. When diagnosed early, PKU can be successfully controlled by diet.

While genetic research can determine the heritability of a some diseases, the genetic foundations of behavior are much more difficult to identify. From a genetic point of view,physical **traits**, such as the color of a person's hair, have a much higher heritability than behavior. In fact, behavior genetics assumes that the genetic bases of an *individual's* behavior simply cannot be determined. Consequently, researchers have focused their efforts on the behavior of groups, particularly families. However, even controlled studies of families have failed to establish conclusive links between genetics and behavior, or between genetics and particular psychological traits and aptitudes. In theory, these links probably exist; in practice, however, researchers have been unable to isolate traits that are unmodified by environmental factors. For example, musical aptitude seems to recur in certainfamilies. While it is tempting to assume that this aptitude is an inherited genetic trait, it would bea mistake to ignore the **environment**. What is colloquially known as "talent" is probably a combination of genetic and other, highly variable, factors.

More reliable information about genetics and behavior can be gleaned from twin studies.When compared to fraternal (dizygotic) **twins**, identical (monozygotic) twins display remarkable behavioral similarities. (Unlike fraternal twins, who develop from two separate eggs, identical twins originate from a single divided fertilized egg.) However, even studies of identical twins reared in different families are inconclusive, because, as scientists have discovered, in many cases, the different environments often turn out to be quite comparable, thus invalidating the hypothesis that the twins' behavioral similarities are entirely genetically determined. Conversely,studies of identical twins raised in the same environment have shown that identical twins can develop markedly different personalities. Thus, while certain types of behavior can be traced to certain genetic characteristics, there is no genetic blueprint for an individual's **personality**.

Twin studies have also attempted to elucidate the genetic basis of **intelligence**, which,according to many psychologists, is not one trait, but a cluster of distinct traits. Generally, these studies indicate that identical twins reared in different families show a high correlation in IQ scores. No one questions the genetic basis of intelligence, but scientists still do not know how intelligence is inherited and what specific aspects of intelligence can be linked to genetic factors.

down the stairs at the age of fifteen and had weak ankles as a result. At sixteen, each had met at a local dance the man she was going to marry. The twins suffered miscarriages with their first children, then proceeded to have two boys followed by a girl. And both laughed more than anyone they knew. . . . Neither had ever voted, except once, when she was employed as a polling clerk."

Twin researchers, buoyed by stunning accounts like this, have been boldly asserting that nature determines who we are to a far greater degree than nurture. But twin research has its critics. One commonly pointed out flaw in twin research is that twins often mythologize, i.e., imagine or manufacture stories about, their shared characteristics. Also in dispute is how "different" the environments really are. Because **adoption** agencies screen applicants, families generally have certain shared socioeconomic characteristics. In addition, little research has beenconducted on "disconfirming evidence," that is, to ask the question, "Are there twins who show no remarkable similarities?" The nature-nurture controversy is far from settled.

*See also* Jukes family; Kallikak family

## Further Reading

Bouchard, Thomas. "Genes, Personality, and Environment." *Science* (17 June 1994): 1700.

Cohen, Jack, and Ian Stewart. "Our Genes Aren't Us."*Discover* (April 1994).

Cowley, Geoffrey. "It's Time to Rethink Nature and Nurture." *Newsweek* (27 March 1995): 52-53.

Gallagher, Winifred. "How We Become What We Are." *Atlantic Monthly* (September 1994): 39-55.

Wright, Lawrence. "Double Mystery." *NewYorker* (7 August 1995): 45-62.

# Margaret Naumburg

**1890-1983**
American educator; founder of the Walden School and pioneer in art therapy.

Margaret Naumburg was not a psychologist, but her work as an educator and as a therapist influenced twentieth century ideas about **creativity** and **mental illness**. Her work with children and with the mentally ill was widely studied by psychologists and psychiatrists. She was able to achieve all this despite her lack of training as a scientist.

Naumburg was born in New York on May 14, 1890. She attended Barnard College (graduating in 1911) and continued with graduate studies at Columbia University. Later, she studied in Europe; while in Rome, she studied briefly with the educational innovator **Maria Montessori**. Part of Montessori's educational philosophy was that children learn more effectively when they are allowed to explore ideas on their own rather than have information merely fed to them.

Naumburg, impressed by Montessori's theories, returned to the United States and in 1915 opened the Walden School in New York City. The school began with two teachers and 10 students, and the educational focus was on letting children develop their own ideas and interests. In this way, believed Naumburg, children would not merely acquire knowledge but learn how to use that knowledge to their best advantage.

In 1916 Naumburg married the writer **Waldo Frank**. Through him she became acquainted with a literary and intellectual circle that included such artists Alfred Stieglitz, Van Wyck Brooks, Countee Cullen, and Jean Toomer. The couple, who had a son, divorced in 1924, but Naumburg continued her involvement in the artistic community. In the 1930s she began to develop **art therapy** programs for psychiatric patients. Naumburg believed that art gave emotionally ill people an opportunity to express themselves and reach into their **unconscious**; this in turn would give therapists a better idea of how to help them.

Naumburg continued her work with art therapy, writing several books on her theories. She remained active in the art therapy movement in New York until she moved to Massachusetts in 1975. She died at her home in Needham, Massachusetts, on February 26, 1983.

George A. Milite

## Further Reading

Naumburg, Margaret. *Child And the World: Dialogues in Modern Education*. New York, Harcourt Brace, 1928.

Naumburg, Margaret. *Schizophrenic Art: Its Meaning in Psychotherapy*. New York, Grune & Stratton, 1950.

# Near-death experience

Intense, pleasant, and sometimes profound experiences that people report when they have "come back" from states close to death.

Tales of near-death experiences (NDEs) are not unusual. Out-of-body experiences, the sensation of moving through a tunnel toward a light, the review of the events of one's life, and pleasurable glimpses of other worlds are relatively consistent features of people's "near death" reports. In fact, research suggests that almost one fifth of Americans report having almost died, and a large proportion of them have recounted experiences like the ones mentioned above. The reported events are very vivid, seem completely real, and can sometimes transform people's lives. How to explain these experiences is the subject of debate. Throughout history people have interpreted them as journeys toward the divine. The out-of-body experience was the soul or spirit leaving the body, the tunnel was the passageway, the life review was the time of judgement, and the light at the end of the tunnel was heaven (or the equivalent).

It appears that, rather than any spiritual journey or other world phenomenon, NDEs may be best understood by examining human physiology, neurochemistry, and psychology. At this time, there is strong research evidence to indicate that many of the symptoms of NDEs may be caused by anoxia, or a lack of oxygen to the **brain**. In the human visual system, for example, neurons (brain cells) deprived of oxygen will start to fire out of control. Since the majority of the cells in our visual cortex (the portion of the brain where visual information is processed) respond to stimulation in the central visual field, the result is a white spot in the center with fewer cells firing out of control in the periphery. As oxygen deprivation continues, the white spot grows and the sensation of moving through a tunnel toward a white light is produced. Similarly, it is possible that the life review process is a result of depriving the temporal lobes of oxygen. When the temporal lobes of the brain, an area largely involved in **memory** production, are deprived of oxygen, neurotransmitters are released and massive electrical activity ensues. In laboratory research, when people's temporal lobes are stimulated with electrodes, many subjects experience the reliving of memories, out of body experiences, and even the sensation of moving through a tunnel toward a light. Oxygen deprivation can also affect the limbic system, which contains the seat of emotions in the brain. The intensely pleasurable feelings of love and well-being that accompany moving toward the light may therefore be a consequence of increased activity in the limbic system.

According to some people, the similarities among people's accounts of NDEs provide powerful evidence for the existence of an afterlife. These similarities however, can also be interpreted as evidence in support of the involvement of human physiology, neurochemistry, and psychology. The visual cortex, temporal lobes, and limbic system are structurally and functionally common to everyone. Consequently neurological activity associated with **stress** or oxygen deprivation may be similar across many different individuals.

Timothy Moore

## Further Reading
Blackmore, S. "Near-death experiences: In or out of the body?" *Skeptical Inquirer,* 16, (1991): 34-45.

# Necrophilia

See **Paraphilias**

# Negativism

A tendency to resist complying with directions or suggestions.

Negativism is a behavior characterized by the tendency to resist direction from others, and the refusal to comply with requests. Negativism appears and wanes at various stages of a person's development. Active negativism, that is, behavior characterized by doing the opposite of what is being asked, is commonly encountered with young children. For example, a parent may ask a toddler to come away from the playground to return home; on **hearing** these instructions, the toddler demonstrates active negativism by running away.

Studies have revealed that negativism develops during the first year of life, and resurfaces during toddlerhood and again during **adolescence**. Negativism is used by adolescents as a way to assert their autonomy from their parents and to control their own behavior. When negativism does not diminish, it becomes a characteristic of the individual's **personality**. Negativism is an aspect of one of the essential features of **oppositional-defiant disorder**, characterized by a pattern of behavior that is defiant, negativistic, and hostile toward authority figures.

## Further Reading
Baker, Lynne Rudder. *Explaining Attitudes: A Practical Approach to the Mind.* New York: Cambridge University Press, 1995.

Eagly, Alice Hendrickson. *The Psychology of Attitudes.* Fort Worth, TX: Harcourt Brace Jovanovich, 1993.

Wenar, Charles. "On Negativism." *Human Development* 25, January-February 1982, pp. 1-23.

# Neocortex

The exterior covering of the cerebral hemispheres of the brain.

The neocortex, the exterior covering of the cerebral hemispheres of the **brain**, is approximately 2 millimeters thick and consists of six thin layers of cells. The cortex is convoluted, furrowed, and, if stretched out, would measure 1.5 square feet. In terms of function, the cortex is divided into four lobes distinguished by the lateral and central fissures: the frontal lobe; parietal lobe (which controls sense of **touch** and body position); temporal lobe (which controls speech, **hearing** and **vision**); and occipital lobe, which also controls vision.

*See also* Brain

## Further Reading
Hoffman, Edward. *The Right to be Human: A Biography of Abraham Maslow.* Los Angeles: Tarcher, 1988.

# Nerve

The common name for neuron, the basic fiber, or bundles of fibers, that transmit information to and from the muscles, glands, organs, spinal cord, and brain.

Nerves form the network of connections that receive signals, known as sensory input, from the **environment** and within the body and transmit the body's responses, or instructions for action, to the muscles, organs, and glands. The **central nervous system**, comprised of the **brain** and spinal cord, sends information throughout the body over the network of nerves known collectively as the peripheral **nervous system**. The nerves of the peripheral nervous system are in pairs, with one usually leading to the left side and the other to the right side of the body. There are 12 nerve pairs, called cranial nerves, that connect directly to the brain and control such functions as **vision** and **hearing**. Thirty-one nerve pairs are connected directly to the spinal cord, branching out to the rest of the body.

The peripheral nervous system may be further subdivided into the **autonomic nervous system**, which regulates involuntary functions such as breathing, digestion, beating of the heart, and the somatic nervous system, which controls voluntary functions, such as walking, picking up a pencil, and reading this page. The cells of the central nervous system do not have the ability to regenerate, and are not replaced directly if they are damaged.

*See also* Neuron

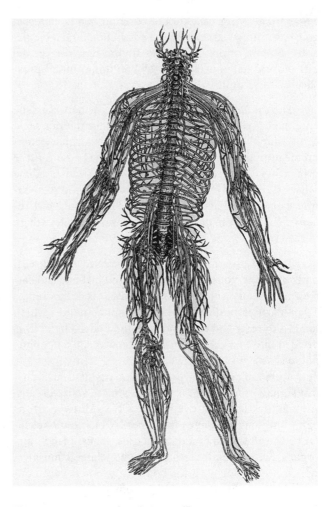

**The nervous system in a human.** *(Bettmann Archive/Newsphotos, Inc. Reproduced with permission.)*

# Nervous system

An electrochemical conducting network that transmits messages from the brain through the nerves to locations throughout the body.

The nervous system is responsible for the **perception** of external and internal conditions and the body's response to them. It has two major divisions: the central and peripheral nervous systems. The **central nervous system** (CNS), consisting of the **brain** and the spinal cord, is that part of the nervous system that is encased in bone; the brain is located in the cranial cavity of the skull, and the spinal cord in the spinal column, or backbone. Both are protected by cerebrospinal fluid and a series of three membranes called meninges. The CNS receives information from the skin and muscles and sends out motor commands as well.

The brain functions as the center of instinctive, emotional, and cognitive processes. It is composed of three primary divisions, the forebrain, midbrain, and hindbrain, and divided into the left and right hemispheres. The first division, the forebrain, is the largest and most complicated of the brain structures and is responsible for most types of complex mental activity and behavior. The forebrain consists of two main divisions: the diencephalon and the cerebrum. The **thalamus** and **hypothalamus** make up the diencephalon. The parts of the cerebrum—the larger part of the forebrain—include the corpus callosum, striatum, septum, hippocampus, and amygdala, all covered by the cerebral cortex.

The midbrain, or mesencephalon, is the small area near the lower middle of the brain. Portions of the midbrain have been shown to control smooth and reflexive movements and it is important in the regulation of **attention, sleep,** and arousal. The hindbrain (rhombencephalon), which is basically a continuation of the spinal cord, is the part of the brain that receives incoming messages first. Lying beneath the cerebral hemispheres, it consists of three structures: the cerebellum, the medulla, and the pons, which control such vital functions of the **autonomic nervous system** as breathing, blood pressure, and heart rate.

The spinal cord is a long bundle of neural tissue continuous with the brain that occupies the interior canal of the spinal column and functions as the primary communication link between the brain and the body. It is the origin of 31 bilateral pairs of spinal nerves which radiate outward from the central nervous system through openings between adjacent vertebrae. The spinal cord receives signals from the peripheral senses and relays them to the brain.

The peripheral nervous system (PNS) includes all parts of the nervous system not covered by bone and carries out sensory and motor functions. It is composed of 12 pairs of cranial and 31 pairs of spinal nerves which lead to the left and right sides of the body. The PNS is divided into two subsystems: the somatic and autonomic nervous systems. The somatic nervous system senses and acts upon the external world. Its sensory neurons transmit signals from receptor cells located in sense organs, such as the skin and eye, to the CNS. Motor neurons carry outgoing messages from the CNS to neuromuscular cells ( effectors) found in muscles, joints, glands, and organs, which facilitate action. The skeletal muscles, which are responsible for bodily movement, are controlled by the somatic nervous system.

The autonomic nervous system (ANS) relays messages between the CNS and the heart, lungs, and other glands and organs. These messages increase or decrease their activity in accordance with demands placed on the body. The ANS affects activities that are basically outside of conscious control, such as respiration and digestion. The autonomic nervous system is further subdivided into two branches. The sympathetic system speeds up muscles and mobilizes the body for action. This is the system responsible for the reaction to danger known as the "fight or flight" response. In contrast, the parasympathetic system, which slows down muscles, regulates bodily functions to conserve energy. For example, it is this system that slows heart rate and blood flow after a large meal is eaten to conserve energy for digestion. Disorders of the autonomic nervous system involve reactions such as fainting, uncontrollable sweating, and **sexual dysfunction**.

The nervous system is composed of two types of cells: neurons, which transmit information through electrochemical impulses, and glial cells, which hold the neurons together and help them communicate with each other. There are three kinds of neurons. *Receptor* neurons register stimulation from the **environment** (such as cells in the eye responding to light or skin cells responding to pressure). When they are stimulated, they send signals to the brain, which are then converted into various types of information. *Motor,* or effector neurons transmit messages from the brain and spinal cord that provide for muscular contraction, which results in movement. Finally, *interneurons* transmit signals between different parts of the nervous system. Most neurons are composed of five parts: the *cell body*, which contains the nucleus; dendrites, short fibers that usually receive signals from other neurons; the *axon*, a long fiber leading away from the cell body that transmits signals to other neurons, muscles, or glands; the *myelin sheath*, a fatty substance that insulates the axon; and synapses , minute gaps through which signals are transmitted between neurons. The many axon and **dendrite** fibers radiating from neurons permit each one to be in contact with many thousands of other neurons.

Communication at the synapses between neurons relies on chemicals called neurotransmitters. More than 50 different neurotransmitters have been identified, and more are constantly being discovered. Recently, it was found that the gases nitric oxide and carbon monoxide are neurotransmitters. Different transmitters predominate in different parts of the nervous system, and a particular **neurotransmitter** may perform different functions in different locations. Researchers have proposed that almost all drugs work through interaction with neurotransmitters. Important neurotransmitters include acetylcholine (ACh), which is used by motor neurons in the spinal cord; the catecholamines (including norepinephrine and dopamine), which are important in the arousal of the sympathetic nervous system; serotonin, which affects body temperature, sensory perception, and the onset of sleep; and a group of transmitters called endorphins, which are involved in the relief of **pain**.

Among the major functions of the central nervous system is that of the *reflex arc,* which provides immediate, involuntary reaction to potentially harmful stimulireactions commonly referred to as **reflexes** (such as drawing one's hand back from a hot stove). The reflex arc is a circuit of neurons by which signals travel from a sensory receptor to a motor **neuron**, rapidly turning sensory input into action. The complexity of the nervous system makes it a challenge to study—millions of neurons may lie beneath a single square centimeter of brain surface, each synapsing with as many as 600 other neurons, and many different parts of the brain may be involved in a single task.

## Further Reading
*The Mind and Beyond.* Alexandria, VA: Time-Life Books, 1991.

# Neuron

Technical term for nerve cell.

Neurons are the basic working unit of the **nervous system**, sending, receiving, and storing signals through a unique blend of electricity and chemistry. The human **brain** has more than 100 billion neurons.

Neurons that receive information and transmit it to the spinal cord or brain are classified as *afferent* or *sensory;* those that carry information from the brain or spinal cord to the muscles or glands are classified as *efferent* or *motor.* The third type of neuron connects the vast network of neurons and may be referred to as *interneuron,association neuron,internuncial neuron, connector neuron,* and *adjustor neuron.*

Although neurons come in many sizes and shapes, they all have certain features in common. Each neuron has a *cell body* where the components necessary to keep the neuron alive are centered. Additionally, each neuron has two types of fiber. The *axon* is a large tentacle and is often quite long. (For example, the axons connecting the toes with the spinal cord are more than a meter in length.) The function of the axon is to conduct **nerve** impulses to other neurons or to muscles and glands. The signals transmitted by the axon are received by other neurons through the second type of fiber, the dendrites. The dendrites are usually relatively short and have many branches to receive stimulation from other neurons. In many cases, the axon (but not the cell body or the dendrites) has a white, fatty covering called the *myelin sheath.* This covering is believed to increase the speed with which nerve impulses are sent down the axon.

An unstimulated neuron has a negative electrical charge. The introduction of a stimulus makes the charge a little less negative until a critical point—the threshold—is reached. Then the membrane surrounding the neuron changes, opening channels briefly to allowing positively charged sodium *ions* to enter the cell. Thus, the inside of the neuron becomes positive in charge for a millisecond (thousandth of a second) or so. This brief change in electrical charge is the nerve impulse, or spike, after which the neuron is restored to its original resting charge.

This weak electrical impulse travels down the axon to the **synapse**. The synapse or *synaptic gap* forms the connection between neurons, and is actually a place where the neurons almost **touch**, but are separated by a gap no wider than a few billionths of an inch. At the synapses, information is passed from one neuron to another by chemicals known as neurotransmitters. The **neurotransmitter** then combines with specialized receptor molecules of the receiving cell.

Neurotransmitters either excite the receiving cell (that is, increase its tendency to fire nerve impulses) or inhibit it (decrease its tendency to fire impulses), and often both actions are required to accomplish the desired response. For example, the neurons controlling the muscles that pull your arm down (the triceps) must be inhibited when you are trying to reach up to your nose (biceps excited); if they are not, you will have difficulty bending your arm.

Physiological psychologists are interested in the involvement of the nervous system in behavior and experience. The chemistry and operation of the nervous system is a key component in the complex human puzzle. A number of chemical substances act as neurotransmitters at synapses in the nervous system and at the junction between nerves and muscles. These include acetylcholine, dopamine, epinephrine (adrenalin), and neuropeptides (enkephalins, endorphins, etc.). A decrease in acetylocholine has been noted in **Alzheimer's disease** which causes deterioration of the thought processes; shortage of dopamine has been linked to **Parkinson's disease**, whereas elevated dopamine has been observed in schizophrenics.

Drugs that affect behavior and experience—the *psychoactive drugs* —generally work on the nervous system by influencing the flow of information across synapses. For instance, they may interfere with one or several of the stages in synaptic transmission, or they may have actions like the natural neurotransmitters and excite or inhibit receiving cells. This is also true of the drugs which are used in the treatment of certain psychological disorders.

# Neurosis

A term generally used to describe a nonpsychotic mental illness that triggers feelings of distress and anxiety and impairs functioning.

## Origins

The word neurosis means "nerve disorder," and was first coined in the late eighteenth century by William Cullen, a Scottish physician. Cullen's concept of neurosis encompassed those nervous disorders and symptoms that do not have a clear organic cause. **Sigmund Freud** later used the term *anxiety neurosis* to describe **mental illness** or distress with extreme anxiety as a defining feature.

There is a difference of opinion over the clinical use of the term neurosis today. It is not generally used as a diagnostic category by American psychologists and psychiatrists any longer, and was removed from the Ameri-

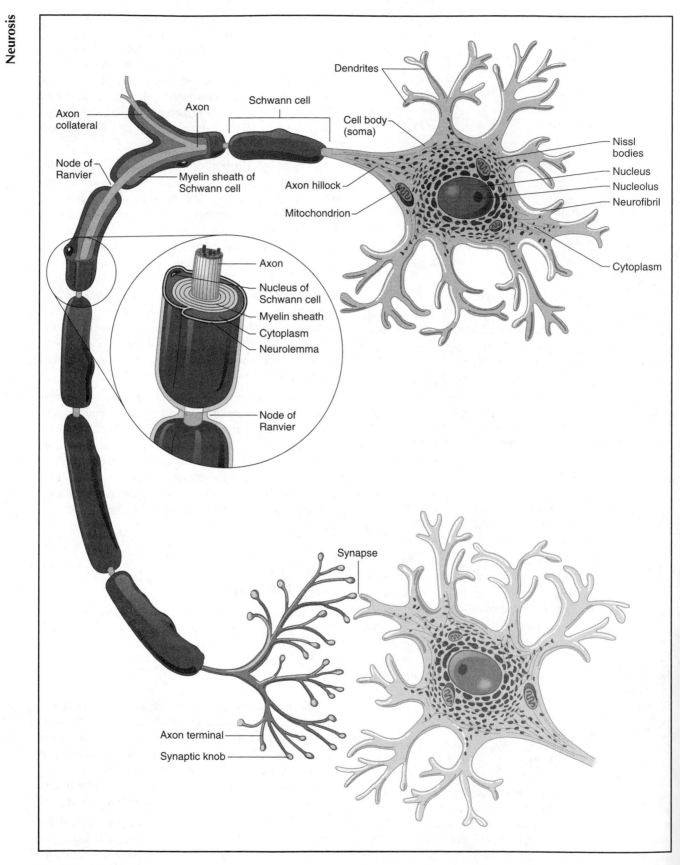

Axon collateral

Axon

Schwann cell

Dendrites

Cell body (soma)

Nissl bodies

Nucleus

Nucleolus

Neurofibril

Node of Ranvier

Myelin sheath of Schwann cell

Axon hillock

Mitochondrion

Cytoplasm

Axon

Nucleus of Schwann cell

Myelin sheath

Cytoplasm

Neurolemma

Node of Ranvier

Synapse

Axon terminal

Synaptic knob

**The features of a typical neuron.** *(Hans & Cassidy. Gale Group. Reproduced with permission.)*

can Psychiatric Association's *Diagnostic and Statistical Manual of Mental Disorders* in 1980 with the publication of the third edition (it last appeared as a diagnostic category in *DSM-II*). Some professionals use the term to describe anxious symptoms and associated behavior, or to describe the range of mental illnesses outside of the **psychotic disorders** (e.g., **schizophrenia**, delusional disorder). Others, particularly psychoanalysts (psychiatrists who follow a psychoanalytical model of treatment, as popularized by Freud and **Carl Jung**), use the term to describe the internal process itself (called an **unconscious** conflict) that triggers the anxiety characteristic of the neurosis.

## Categories

The neurotic disorders are distinct from psychotic disorders in that the individual with neurotic symptoms has a firm grip on reality, and the psychotic patient does not. There are several major traditional categories of psychological neuroses. These include:

- *Anxiety neurosis.* Mental illness defined by excessive anxiety and worry, sometimes involving panic attacks and manifesting itself in physical symptoms such as tremor, chest pain, sweating, and nausea.
- *Depressive neurosis.* A mental illness characterized by a profound feeling of sadness or despair and a lack of interest in things that were once pleasurable.
- *Obsessive-compulsive neurosis.* The persistent and distressing recurrence of intrusive thoughts or images (obsessions) and repetitive behaviors or mental acts (compulsions).
- *Somatization (formerly called hysterical neurosis).* The presence of real and significant physical symptoms that cannot be explained by a medical condition, but are instead a manifestation of anxiety or other mental distress.
- *Post-traumatic stress disorder (also called war or combat neurosis).* Severe **stress** and functional **disability** caused by witnessing a traumatic event such as war combat or any other event that involved death or serious injury.
- *Compensation neurosis.* Not a true neurosis, but a form of malingering, or feigning psychological symptoms for monetary or other personal gain.

## Causes

In 1996, a specific human gene and its corresponding alleles (two components of a gene which are responsible for encoding the gene) were linked to neuroticism. The identified gene and its allele pair help to control the amount of *serotonin* (a **central nervous system neurotransmitter**) released into the body through the produc-

tion of a protein known as a transporter. This transporter protein, which helps to carry the serotonin across the synaptic space (the gap between **nerve** cells) to stimulate nerve cells, also assists the cell in reabsorbing the serotonin (a process known as "reuptake").

In the case of the "neurosis gene," one possible version of its corresponding alleles (called *s* for their short length) was found to produce an insufficient amount of this transporter protein, and the other (named *l* for long), a significantly large amount. If the amount of transporter protein produced is inadequate, an excessive amount of serotonin must remain in the synaptic gap while the protein "catches up" with reuptake, and the serotonin will continue to stimulate surrounding nerve cells, resulting in neurosis or neurotic symptoms. A corresponding study of 500 patients showed that patients who were assessed as having neurotic **personality** traits usually possessed the shorter allele pair (or a combination of one short and one long) that produced insufficient transporter protein.

This finding is consistent with a study published the same year that found that women in 37 different countries scored consistently higher on measurements of neuroticism than men. The fact that such high scores were found across a variety of socioeconomic classes and cultures but specific to one gender seems to support a genetic basis for the disorder. However, a 1998 study of over 9,500 United Kingdom residents found that those with a lower standard of living had a higher prevalence of neurotic disorders. It is possible that genetic factors predispose an individual to anxiety and neurosis, and outside factors such as socioeconomic status trigger the symptoms.

## Diagnosis

Patients with symptoms of mental illness should undergo a thorough physical examination and detailed patient history to rule out organic causes (such as **brain** tumor or head injury). If a neurotic disorder is suspected, a psychologist or psychiatrist will usually conduct an interview with the patient and administer clinical assessments (also called scales, inventories, or tests), to evaluate mental status. Tests which may be administered for the diagnosis and assessment of neurosis include the Neuroticism Extraversion and Openness (NEO-R) scale, the Sixteen Personality Factor Questionnaire (16PF), and the Social Maladjustment Schedule.

## Treatment

Neurosis should be treated by a counselor, therapist, psychologist, psychiatrist, or other mental healthcare professional. Treatment for a neurotic disorder depends on the presenting symptoms and the level of discomfort they are causing the patient. Modes of treatment are similar to that of other mental disorders, and can include **psychotherapy**, cognitive-behavioral therapy, creative therapies (e.g., art or **music therapy**), **psychoactive drugs**, and relaxation exercises.

Paula Ford-Martin

**Further Reading**

Fenichel, Otto M. *The Psychoanalytic Theory of Neurosis: 50th Anniversary Edition.* New York: W.W. Norton & Son. 1995.

American Psychiatric Association. *Diagnostic and Statistical Manual of Mental Disorders* 4th ed. Washington, DC: American Psychiatric Press, Inc., 1994.

**Further Information**

Anxiety Disorders Association of America (ADAA). 11900 Parklawn Drive, Suite 100, Rockville, MD, USA. 20852, fax: 301-231-7392, 301-231-9350. Email: AnxDis@adaa.org. http://www.adaa.org.

# Neurotransmitter

Chemical substances or molecules which aid in message transmission between neurons.

Communication at the synapses between neurons relies on chemicals called neurotransmitters. Secreted from a part of one **neuron** (the axon) into the synaptic gap between two others, neurotransmitters diffuse across this space and combine with specific proteins on the surface of the receiving cell, triggering an electrochemical response in the target cell. Afterward, neurotransmitters are either destroyed or reabsorbed back into the neuron for storage and reuse. The release of neurotransmitters by a neuron has three main functions: 1) exciting a second neuron, thus causing it to depolarize; 2) inhibiting a second neuron, which prevents it from depolarizing; and 3) stimulating a muscle fiber to contract.

More than 50 different neurotransmitters have been identified, and more are constantly being discovered. Researchers have proposed that almost all drugs work through interaction with neurotransmitters. Important neurotransmitters include acetylcholine (ACh), which is used by motor neurons in the spinal cord; the catecholamines (including norepinephrine and dopamine), which are important in the arousal of the sympathetic **nervous system**; serotonin, which affects body tempera-

ture, sensory **perception**, and the onset of **sleep**; and a group of transmitters called endorphins, which are involved in the relief of **pain**. In recent years, it has been recognized that biochemical imbalances in the **brain** play an important role in **mental illness**. Low levels of norepinephrine characterize some varieties of **depression**, for example, and an imbalance of dopamine is considered a factor in **schizophrenia**.

# Nightmares

A frightening dream that occurs during REM (rapid eye movement) sleep.

Nightmares—frightening dreams—are experienced by most everyone at one time or another. Nightmares are thought to be caused by a **central nervous system** response, and are related to other parasomnias such as sleepwalking.

In children, nightmares begin between the ages of 18 months and three years and increase in frequency and intensity around the ages of four and five years. Children this age have an exceptionally vivid **fantasy** life that carries over into their **sleep**. Their nightmares are typically characterized by feelings of danger and helplessness and often involve fleeing from monsters or wild animals. It is not unusual for a **normal** child this age to have nightmares as often as once or twice a week. The increase in nightmares among preschoolers reflects not only their capacity for vivid fantasy but also the fact that as they become increasingly active, their daily lives hold more opportunities for frightening experiences, and growing interaction with peers and siblings produces added potential for conflict and tension. **Separation anxiety** and exposure to frightening programs on television are additional sources of emotional turbulence.

The American Psychiatric Association's *Diagnostic and Statistical Manual (DSM-IV)* recognizes an anxiety disorder characterized by persistent, severe nightmares (nightmare disorder, formerly dream anxiety disorder). Generally, nightmare disorder is found only in children who have experienced severe psychological **stress**.

Adults also occasionally experience nightmares. The average college student has between four and eight nightmares per year, and this figure generally drops to one or two in adults. Adults who experience excessive nightmares may be dealing with other issues, and may benefit from professional counseling.

# Night terrors

Also referred to as pavor nocturnus, a childhood sleep disorder featuring behavior that appears to be intense fear.

Night terrors, known medically as *pavor nocturnus,* are episodes that apparently occur during the non-dreaming stages of **sleep** in some children. Episodes of night terrors are most common in the preschool and early school years. Night terrors usually occur within an hour or two after the child has fallen asleep, and generally do not recur with any frequency or regularity. Many children experience only one episode of night terrors, and few experience more than three or four such episodes over the whole course of **childhood**. A parent or caregiver witnessing an episode of night terrors, which usually lasts from ten to thirty minutes, will find the behavior unsettling. The child sits up abruptly in bed, appears to be extremely upset, cries out or screams, breathes heavily, and perspires. He or she might also thrash about, kicking, and his or her eyes may bulge out, seemingly in **fear** of something. The child does not wake during the episode, although his or her eyes will be open, and he or she will be unresponsive to any offers of comfort. The child falls back to sleep, and will have no **memory** of the occurrence. Night terrors have not been shown to have any link to **personality** or emotional disorders, although they may be related to a specific feeling of fear that the child has experienced, such as being startled by someone leaping at him or her from behind a chair, or the sight of someone fainting or having an accident.

## Further Reading

Beaudet, Denise. *Encountering the Monster: Pathways in Children's Dreams.* New York: CrossroadContinuum, 1990.

Lansky, Vicki. *Getting Your Child to Sleep—and Back to Sleep: Tips for Parents of Infants, Toddlers, and Preschoolers.* Deephaven, MN: Book Peddlers, 1991.

Thorpy, Michael. *The Encyclopedia of Sleep and Sleep Disorders.* New York: Facts of File, 1990.

## Further Information

Association of Sleep Disorders Centers (ASDC). 602 Second Street, SW, Rochester, MN 55902 (Professional organization of specialists in sleep disorders; publishes the journal *Sleep.*)

# Normal distribution

The common pattern of numbers in which the majority of the measurements tend to cluster near the mean of distribution.

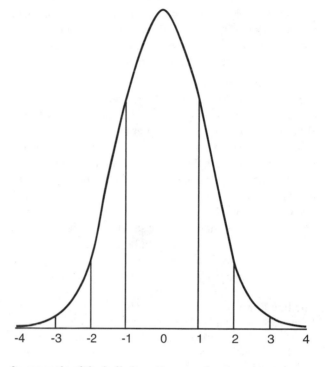

An example of the bell-shaped curve of a normal distribution.

Psychological research involves **measurement** of behavior. This measurement results in numbers that differ from one another individually but that are predictable as a group. One of the common patterns of numbers involves most of the measurements being clustered together near the **mean** of the distribution, with fewer cases occurring as they deviate farther from the mean. When a **frequency distribution** is drawn in pictorial form, the resulting pattern produces the bell-shaped curve that scientists call a **normal** distribution.

When measurements produce a normal distribution, certain things are predictable. First, the mean, **median**, and **mode** are all equal. Second, a scientist can predict how far from the mean most scores are likely to fall. Thus, it is possible to determine which scores are more likely to occur and the proportion of score likely to be above or below any given score.

Many behavioral measurements result in normal distributions. For example, scores on **intelligence** tests are likely to be normally distributed. The mean is about 100 and a typical person is likely to score within about 15 points of the mean, that is, between 85 and 115. If the psychologist knows the mean and the typical deviation from the mean (called the standard deviation), the researcher can determine what proportion of scores is likely to fall in any given range. For instance, in the range between one standard deviation below the mean (about 85 for IQ scores) and one deviation above the mean (about

115 for IQ scores), one expects to find the scores of about two thirds of all test takers. Further, only about two and a half percent of test takers will score higher than two standard deviations above the mean (about 130).

Although psychologists rely on the fact that many measurements are normally distributed, there are certain cases where scores are unlikely to be normally distributed. Whenever scores cannot be higher than some upper value or smaller than some lower value, a non-normal distribution may occur. For example, salaries are not normally distributed because there is a lower value (i.e., nobody can make less than zero dollars), but there is no upper value. Consequently, there will be some high salaries that will not be balanced by corresponding, lower salaries. It is important to know whether scores are normally distributed because it makes a difference in the kind of statistical tests that are appropriate for analyzing and interpreting the numbers.

### Further Reading

Berman, Simeon M. *Mathematical Statistics: An Introduction Based on the Normal Distribution.* Scranton, PA: Intext Educational Publishers, 1971.

Martin, David W. *Doing Psychology Experiments.* 2nd ed. Monterey, CA: Brooks/Cole, 1985.

## Norm

A measure of central tendency in statistics, describing a value's frequency.

In testing, norms are figures describing the frequency with which particular scores appear. They provide information about whether a score is above or below average and about what percentage of the persons tested received that score. Norms may apply to tests of mental **ability** or achievement, such as IQ tests or SATs. They are also used in **personality** assessment to measure variables such as anxiety, introversion-extroversion, and **paranoia**. The term "norm" may also refer to social norms, unwritten social rules that define acceptable and unacceptable behavior in a variety of situations.

*See also* Mean; Median; Mode

## Normal

Represents the characteristics that are typical for—that is, exhibited by—most members of a particular group.

For statistical purposes, normal means whatever is average for a given group of people ("the norm"). Therefore, the term normal does include those group members who deviate significantly from the measures of central tendency (the **mean**, the **median**, or the **mode**) of a given distribution.

The term normal is fundamentally statistical and quantitative. In testing and measuring, for example, normal can be defined as a central cluster of scores in relation to a larger grouping. In **intelligence** testing normal is also defined by the average, or mean, which is established as an IQ score of around 100.

However, in many contexts normal is a subjective term that is very difficult to define. In the absence of fixed standards, normal and abnormal are often defined in terms of each other. However, rather than a simple pairing of opposites, they are generally thought of as points on a continuum of social adjustment, with normal people possessing certain positive **traits** to a greater degree, while abnormal people are characterized by deficiencies in these traits. Some of the traits that help define psychological normalcy are efficient **perception** of reality; self-knowledge; self-control; **ability** to form affectionate relationships; **self-esteem**; and productivity. The notion of defining normalcy in terms of social adjustment has its detractors, who argue that such a definition places too much emphasis on **conformity** and too little on such traits as individuality and **creativity**.

### Further Reading

Martin, David W. *Doing Psychology Experiments.* 2nd ed. Monterey, CA: Brooks/Cole, 1985.

Berman, Simeon M. *Mathematical Statistics: An Introduction Based on the Normal Distribution.* Scranton, PA: Intext Educational Publishers, 1971.

# Obesity

A condition of having an excessive accumulation of fat in the body, resulting in a body weight that is at least 20 percent above normal when measured against standard tables of optimal weight ranges according to age, sex, height, and body type.

Individuals who are 20 percent overweight are considered *slightly* obese. Those who are 40 percent above standard weight are *moderately* obese, while those 50 percent above it are *morbidly* obese. Persons who exceed desired weight levels by 100 pounds (45 kg) or more are *hyperobese*. Obesity is a serious health problem in the United States. Studies suggests that between 10 and 20 percent of Americans are slightly to moderately obese. Obesity places **stress** on the body's organs, and is associated with joint problems, high blood pressure, indigestion, dizzy spells, rashes, menstrual disorders, and premature **aging**. Generally, when compared to persons of normal weight, obese individuals suffer more severely from many diseases, including degenerative diseases of the heart and arteries, and a shorter life expectancy. Obesity can also cause complications during childbirth and surgery.

Obesity may be familial, as the body weight of children appears to be linked to that of their parents. Children of obese parents have been found to be 13 times more likely than other children to be obese, suggesting a genetic predisposition to body fat accumulation. Recent animal research suggests the existence of a "fat gene," and the tendency toward a body type with an unusually high number of fat cells—termed *endomorphic*— appears to be inherited. However, the generational transmission of obesity may be as cultural as it is genetic, as early feeding patterns may produce unhealthy eating habits.

Some cases of obesity have a purely physiological cause, such as glandular malfunction or a disorder of the **hypothalamus**. Individuals with a low production of the hormone thyroxin tend to metabolize food slowly, which results in excess unburned calories. When more calories are consumed than the body can metabolize, excess calories are stored in the body as fat, or adipose tissue. Some persons with hypoglycemia have a specific metabolic problem with carbohydrates that can also lead to the storage of unburned calories as fat.

In the great majority of cases, however, obesity is caused by overeating. Overeating itself often combines physical and psychological components. People may eat compulsively to overcome **fear** or social maladjustment, express defiance, or avoid intimate relationships. However, researchers have also suggested physical correlates for overeating, including deficits in the **neurotransmitter** serotonin that increase cravings for carbohydrates, and possibly a higher "set point" for body weight that makes obese persons feel hungry more often than thinner people. This raised set point could result from both genetics and early nutritional habits. Lack of exercise and sedentary living also contribute to obesity.

The most effective treatment of obesity includes both the reduction of surplus body fat and the elimination of causative factors, and is best accomplished under medical supervision. An appropriate weight loss plan includes exercise (which burns calories without slowing metabolism), reduced food intake, **behavior modification** to change food-related attitudes and behavior, and **psychotherapy** if there are underlying psychological causes for overeating. Other possible treatment measures include hormone therapy, appetite-suppressant drugs, and surgical intervention to alter satiety signals by reducing the size of the stomach and intestines.

Behavior modification has been especially successful and widely used in the treatment of obesity. Treatment techniques include stimulus control (removing environmental cues that play a role in inappropriate eating), eating management (slowing the pace of eating to allow satiation to catch up with it), contingency management (applying a system of positive **reinforcement** and punishments), and self-monitoring of daily dietary intake and factors associated with it. Despite all of the available treatments, the difficulty of reversing obesity in adults makes

| OBESITY IN ADOLESCENT YOUTHS (AGES 6 TO 17) IN THE UNITED STATES | |
| --- | --- |
| Prevalence of overweight | Doubled since 1965 |
| Number who are overweight | 4.7 million |
| Percent who are overweight | 11 percent |
| Related disorders | Elevated blood cholesterol; high blood pressure; increased adult mortality |
| Social consequences | Excluded from peer groups, discriminated against by adults, experience psychological stress, poor body image, and low self-esteem. |

*Source: Centers for Disease Control, U.S. Department of Health and Human Services.*

preventative treatment an important factor during **childhood**. Today, an increasing percentage of children in the United States are overweight. Recent studies have shown that metabolic rates of children are lower when they watch television than when they are at rest. Unhealthy eating patterns and behaviors associated with obesity can be addressed by programs in nutrition, exercise, and stress management involving both children and families.

# Obsessive-compulsive disorder

Mental illness characterized by the recurrence of intrusive, anxiety-producing thoughts (obsessions) accompanied by repeated attempts to suppress these thoughts through the performance of certain irrational, often ritualistic, behaviors (compulsions).

Obsessive-compulsive disorder (OCD) is classified as a **mental illness**, and is characterized by the recurrence of intrusive, anxiety-producing thoughts (obsessions). The person with obsessive-compulsive disorder repeatedly and consistently tries to suppress these thoughts through the performance of certain irrational, often ritualistic, behaviors (compulsions).

## Symptoms

Although there are marked similarities between cases, no two people experience this anxiety disorder in exactly the same way. In one common form of obsessive-compulsive disorder, an exaggerated **fear** of contamination (the obsession) leads to washing one's hands so much that they become raw (the compulsion). Other common manifestations of OCD involve sorting, checking, and counting compulsions. Checking compulsions

seem to be more common among men, whereas washing is more common among women. Another type of OCD is trichotillomania, the compulsion to pull hair. The compulsive behavior is usually not related in any logical way to the obsessive fear, or else it is clearly excessive (as in the case of hand-washing).

Everyone engages in these types of behavior to a certain extent—counting steps as we walk up them, double-checking to make sure we've turned off the oven or locked the door—but in a person with OCD, such behaviors are so greatly exaggerated that they interfere with relationships and day-to-day functioning at school or work. A child with a counting compulsion, for example, might not be able to listen to what the teacher is saying because he or she is too busy counting the syllables of the teacher's words as they are spoken.

These are some of the signs that a child might be suffering from OCD:

• *Avoidance of scissors or other sharp objects*. A child might be obsessed with fears of hurting herself or others.

• *Chronic lateness or the appearance of dawdling*. A child could be performing checking rituals (e.g., repeatedly making sure all her school supplies are in her bookbag).

• *Daydreaming or preoccupation*. A child might actually be counting or balancing things mentally.

• *Inordinate amounts of time spent in the bathroom*. A child could be involved in a hand-washing ritual.

• *Late schoolwork*. A child might be repeatedly checking her work.

• *Papers with holes erased in them*. This might also indicate a checking ritual.

• *Secretive and defensive behavior*. People with OCD will go to extreme lengths in order not to reveal or give up their compulsions.

Although people with OCD realize that their thought processes are irrational, they are unable to control their compulsions, and they become painfully embarrassed when a bizarre behavior is discovered. Usually certain behaviors called rituals are repeated in response to an obsession. Rituals only temporarily reduce discomfort or anxiety caused by an obsession, and thus they must be repeated frequently. However, the fear that something terrible will happen if a ritual is discontinued often locks OCD sufferers into a life ruled by what appears to be **superstition**.

## Causes

**Sigmund Freud** attributed obsessive-compulsive disorder to traumatic toilet training and, although not supported by any empirical evidence, this theory was widely accepted for many years. Current research, however, indicates that OCD is neurobiological in origin, and researchers have found physical differences between the brains of OCD sufferers and those without the disorder. Specifically, neurons in the brains of OCD patients appear to be overly sensitive to *serotonin*, the chemical which transmits signals in the **brain**. A recent study at the National Institute of **Mental Health** suggests a link between **childhood** streptococcal infections and the onset of OCD. Other research indicates that a predisposition for OCD is probably inherited. It is possible that physical or mental stresses can precipitate the onset of OCD in people with a predisposition towards it. **Puberty** also appears to trigger the disorder in some people.

## Prevalence

Once considered rare, OCD is now believed to affect between 5 and 6 million Americans (2-3% of the population), which makes it almost as common as asthma or diabetes mellitus. Among mental disorders, OCD is the fourth most prevalent (after phobias, substance abuse, and **depression** ). In more than one-third of cases, onset of OCD occurs in childhood or **adolescence**. Although the disorder occurs equally among adults of both genders, among children it is three times more common in boys than girls.

## Treatment

Fewer than one in five OCD sufferers receive professional help; the typical OCD patient suffers for seven years before seeking treatment. Many times, OCD is diagnosed when a patient sees a professional for another problem, often depression. Major depression affects close to one-third of patients with obsessive-compulsive disorder.

In recent years, a new family of antidepressant medications called *selective serotonin reuptake inhibitors* (SSRIs) has revolutionized the treatment of obsessive-compulsive disorder. These drugs include clomipramine (Anafranil), fluoxetine (Prozac), fluvoxamine (Luvox), and sertraline (Zoloft). They work by altering the level of serotonin available to transmit signals in the brain. Thanks to these medications, the overwhelming majority of OCD sufferers (75-90%) can be successfully treated.

In addition to medication, an extreme type of **behavior therapy** is sometimes used in patients with OCD. In *exposure-response prevention* therapy, a patient slowly gives up his or her compulsive behaviors with the help of a therapist. Someone with a hand-washing compulsion, for example, would have to touch something perceived as unclean and then refrain from washing his/her hands. The resulting extreme anxiety eventually diminishes when the patient realizes that nothing terrible is going to happen.

### Further Reading

Rapoport, Judith L. *The Boy Who Couldn't Stop Washing: The Experience and Treatment of Obsessive-Compulsive Disorder*. New York: E.P. Dutton, 1989.

### Further Information

The Obsessive-Compulsive Foundation Inc. P.O. Box 70, Milford, CT 06460–0070, (203) 878–5669, (800) NEWS-4-OCD.

Obsessive Compulsive Anonymous (OCA). P.O. Box 215, New Hyde Park, NY 11040, (516) 741–4901.

The Obsessive Compulsive Information Center. Dean Foundation for Health, Research and Education, 8000 Excelsior Drive, Suite 302, Madison, WI 53717-1914, (608) 836–8070. http://www.fairlite.com/ocd.

# Occupational therapist

A professional who promotes health, enhances development, and increases independent functioning in people through activities involving work, play, and self-care.

Occupational therapists help persons with both physical and emotional problems as well as learning difficulties. Although occupational therapy was initially associated with reintegrating veterans of First and Second World Wars into the work force, the term "occupation" used in the context of this profession actually refers to any activity with which persons occupy their time. Occupational therapists focus on helping people master the everyday activities of life and work.

Occupational therapists undergo a rigorous training program. Four-year undergraduate programs, offered by many institutions, include courses in anatomy, psychology, and the theory and practice of occupational therapy. In addition, occupational therapists must complete six to nine months of clinical training. After graduation, most take a national examination to qualify as a Registered Occupational Therapist (R.O.T.). Occupational therapists work in various settings, including hospitals, nursing homes, **rehabilitation** centers, schools, day care centers, and patients' homes.

Occupational therapists work with people who have mental and emotional problems. Their goal is to help clients cope with daily life, which may include teaching skills in self-care, cooking, shopping, and budgeting. They may help people suffering from **depression**, anxiety, or **obsessive-compulsive disorder** plan their day in order to function more effectively.

### Further Reading

Breines, Estelle. *Occupational Therapy Activities from Clay to Computers: Theory and Practice.* Philadelphia: F.A. Davis Company, 1995.

### Further Information

The American Occupational Therapy Association. 1383 Piccard Drive, P.O. Box 1725, Rockville, MD 20850.

# Oedipus complex

The theory that children are torn between feelings of love for one parent while feeling a sense of competition with the other; first put forth by Sigmund Freud as one possible cause of neuroses in later life.

**Sigmund Freud** first suggested the existence of what he would later call the Oedipus complex in *The Interpretation of Dreams* (1900). In this work, he describes a subconscious feelings in children of intense **competition** and even hatred toward the parent of the same sex, and feelings of romantic love toward the parent of the opposite sex. He felt that if these conflicting feelings were not successfully resolved, they would contribute to neuroses in later life. The name "Oedipus" refers to *Oedipus Rex,* the classic Greek play by Sophocles, which tells the story of Oedipus, who is abandoned at birth by his parents, King Lauis and Queen Jocasta. He later comes back and, as foretold by prophecy, kills his father and marries his mother before finding out his true identity. Freud saw in the play an archetypal dynamic being played out, and so coopted the character's name for his description.

In traditional Freudian psychoanalytical theory, the term Electra complex was used when these **unconscious** wishes were attributed to a young girl and centered around sexual involvement with her father and jealous rivalry with her mother. Like Oedipus, Electra is a figure in Greek mythology who participated in the killing of her parent (in Electra's case, her mother). Contemporary psychology no longer distinguishes this complex by gender, and the Electra complex is included in the definition of the Oedipus complex.

Modern interpretations of Freudian theories are often critical, and his Oedipus theory has been no exception. Many current psychologists think of it as too simplistic, and the authors of the *Oxford Companion to the Mind* (1987) state, "Freud's formula . . . gives a one-sided and too simple an account of the complex interactions of the family." It would be fair to say that this is the current view of Freud's Oedipal notions. Yet, looking to Freud's *Introductory Lectures on Psychoanalysis* (1920), Freud writes, "I do not wish to assert that the Oedipus complex exhausts the relation of children to their parents: it can easily be far more complicated. The Oedipus complex can, moreover, be developed to a greater or lesser strength, it can even be reversed; but it is a regular and very important factor in a child's mental life."

### Further Reading

Montrelay, Michele. "Why Did You Tell Me I Love Mommy and That's Why I'm Frightened When I Love You." *American Imago* (Summer 1994): 213.

Sophocles. *Oedipus Rex.* Cambridge, England: Cambridge University Press, 1982.

Tabin, Johanna. *On the Way to Self.* New York: Columbia University Press, 1985.

# Operant conditioning

Approach to human learning based on the premise that human intelligence and will operate on the environment rather than merely respond to the environment's stimuli.

Operant conditioning is an elaboration of **classical conditioning**. Operant conditioning holds that human learning is more complex than the model developed by **Ivan Pavlov** (1849-1936) and involves human **intelligence** and will operating (thus its name) on its **environment** rather than being a slave to stimuli.

The Pavlovian model of classical conditioning was revolutionary in its time but eventually came to be seen as limited in its application to most human behavior, which is far more complex than a series of automatic re-

| | POSITIVE | NEGATIVE |
|---|---|---|
| **REINFORCEMENT** | | |
| The frequency of a behavior is increased because of the behavior of the subject. | When a person receives reinforcement after engaging in some behavior, the person is likely to repeat that behavior. | When a person experiences a negative state and does something to eliminate the undesired state, the person is likely to repeat that behavior. |
| **PUNISHMENT** | | |
| The frequency of a behavior is decreased because of the behavior of the subject. | When a person engages in a behavior and something negative is applied as a result, that behavior is less likely to be repeated. | When a person engages in a behavior and something positive is taken away, that behavior is less likely to be repeated. |

sponses to various stimuli. B.F. Skinner (1904-1990) elaborated on this concept by introducing the idea of consequences into the behaviorist formula of human learning. Pavlov's classical conditioning explained behavior strictly in terms of stimuli, demonstrating a causal relationship between stimuli and behavior. In Pavlov's model, humans responded to stimuli in specific, predictable ways. According to Skinner, however, behavior is seen as far more complex, allowing for the introduction of choice and free will. According to operant conditioning, the likelihood that a behavior will be repeated depends to a great degree on the amount of pleasure (or **pain**) that behavior has caused or brought about in the past. Skinner also added to the vocabulary of **behaviorism** the concepts of negative and positive reinforcer and of **punishment**.

According to the Skinner model of operant conditioning humans learn behaviors based on a trial and error process whereby they remember what behaviors elicited positive, or pleasurable, responses and which elicited negative ones. He derived these theories from observing the behaviors of rats and pigeons isolated in what have come to be known as Skinner boxes. Inside the boxes, rats that had been deprived of food were presented with a lever that, when pushed, would drop a pellet of food into the cage. Of course, the rat wouldn't know this, and so the first time it hit the lever, it was a purely accidental, the result of what Skinner called random trial and error behavior. Eventually, however, the rat would "learn" that hitting the lever resulted in the appearance of food and it would continue doing so. Receiving the food, then, in the language of operant conditioning, is considered the reinforcer while hitting the lever becomes the operant, the way the organism operates on its environment.

Skinner's model of operant conditioning broke down reinforcements into four kinds to study the effects these various "schedules of reinforcement" would have

on behavior. These schedules are: fixed interval, variable interval, fixed ration, and variable ration. In a fixed interval schedule experiment, the lever in the rat's box would only provide food at a specific rate, regardless of how often the rat pulled the lever. In other words, food would be provided every 60 seconds. Eventually, the rat adapts to this schedule, pushing the lever with greater frequency approximately every 60 seconds. In variable interval experiments, the lever becomes active at random intervals. Rats presented with this problem adapt by pressing the lever less frequently but at more regular intervals. An experiment using a fixed ratio schedule uses a lever that becomes active only after the rat pulls it a specific number of times, and in a variable ration experiment the number of pulls between activity is random. Behavior of the rats adapts to these conditions and is adjusted to provide the most rewards.

The real-world ramifications of operant conditioning experiments are easy to imagine, and many of the experiments described would probably sound very familiar to parents who use such systems of rewards and punishments on a daily basis with their children regardless of whether they have ever heard of B.F. Skinner. His model has been used by learning theorists of various sorts to describe all kinds of human behaviors. Since the 1960s, however, behaviorism has taken a back seat to cognitive theories of learning, although few dispute the elementary tenets of operant conditioning and their use in the acquisition of rudimentary adaptive behaviors.

## Further Reading

Blackman, Derek E. *Operant Conditioning: An Experimental Analysis of Behaviour.* London: Methuen, 1974.

Mackintosh, Nicholas John. *Conditioning and Associative Learning.* New York: Oxford University Press, 1983.

Smith, Terry L. *Behavior and Its Causes: Philosophical Foundations of Operant Psychology.* Boston: Kluwer Academic Publishers, 1994.

# Oppositional-defiant disorder

A form of antisocial behavior disorder characterized by opposition to authority figures such as parents and teachers, and by excessive anger and hostility.

Depending on the population, 2-6% of children have oppositional-defiant disorder. Oppositional-defiant disorder is similar to **conduct disorder**, without the more severe behavior components of **aggression**, property destruction, deceit, and theft. Oppositional-defiant children often go on to develop conduct disorder. Many children, especially during transitional periods such as preschool and **adolescence**, exhibit transient oppositional behavior towards parents and peers that will decline as they mature. If oppositional behavior is initiated during adolescence in particular it is probably part of the child's process of individuation, and should not be mistaken for a disorder. Children with oppositional-defiant disorder (1) are oppositional much more frequently than other children of their age and (2) increase their oppositional behaviors rather than decrease them with age. Disobedience and **hostility** usually appear first in the home **environment**, and may or may not ever emerge in school settings. Oppositional-defiant disorder is more common in families where there is marital discord, where a parent has a history of an antisocial, **mood**, or **attention** disorder, and where child rearing practices are either harsh (punishing), inconsistent (a succession of different caregivers), or neglectful.

## Criteria for diagnosis

According to the *Diagnostic and Statistical Manual of Mental Disorders (DSM-IV),* oppositional-defiant disorder is diagnosed when (1) there is a pattern of defiant, disobedient, and hostile behavior towards authority figures lasting for at least six months, including frequent occurrence of at least four of the following behaviors; (2) the child exhibits the behaviors more frequently than other individuals of the same age or developmental level.

The child with oppositional-defiant disorder will:

- often lose his or her temper
- often argue with adults
- defy or refuse to comply with requests or rules
- deliberately do things that annoy other people
- blame others for his or her own mistakes
- be touchy or easily annoyed
- be angry and resentful
- be spiteful or vindictive.

Care should be taken to distinguish oppositional-defiant behavior that results from other problems, such as mood or **psychotic disorders**, attention deficit/hyperactivity disorder, **mental retardation**, and language disorders.

*See also* Antisocial behavior; Conduct disorder

## Further Reading

Bernstein, Neil I. *Treating the Unmanageable Adolescent: A Guide to Oppositional Defiant and Conduct Disorders.* Northvale, NJ: Jason Aronson, 1997.

Price, Jerome A. *Power and Compassion: Working with Difficult Adolescents and Abused Parents.* New York: Guilford Press, 1996.

Wenning, Kenneth. *Winning Cooperation from Your Child!: A Comprehensive Method to Stop Defiant and Aggressive Behavior in Children.* Northvale, NJ: J. Aronson, 1996.

# Organic disorder

Disorder caused by a known pathological condition.

In general, any disorder that is caused by a known pathological condition of an organic structure may be categorized as an organic disorder, or more specifically, as an organic mental disorder, or a **psychological disorder**. An example is **delirium**, a disorder that is caused by a known physical dysfunction of the **brain**. Most psychologists and psychiatrists now believe that virtually all serious, or psychotic, mental disorders will eventually be proven to have an organic cause. Consequently, many psychologists and psychiatrists prefer not to use the term organic mental disorder because the term implies that those disorders which have not yet been shown to have an organic cause do not have an organic cause, and that functional disorders (a term that has often been contrasted with the term organic disorders) have no organic causal component.

# Organizational psychology

See **Industrial psychology**

# Arthur Otis

**1886-1964**

American psychologist whose most enduring work was done in the field of group intelligence testing.

Arthur Otis was born in Denver, Colorado, and educated at Stanford University. He served on the faculty of

Stanford University, and held various consulting and research positions at several U.S. government agencies. He was also an editor of tests in mathematics for an educational publishing company. Otis introduced and developed the Otis Group Intelligence Scale, which is considered to be the earliest scientifically reliable instrument for the intelligence testing of subjects in groups. First published in 1918, the Otis Group Intelligence Scale consisted of verbal and nonverbal items and became very widely used, especially in schools. The test was substantially revised by Roger Lennon, and continues to be used. Otis' books include: *Statistical Method in Educational Measurement* (1925), *Modern School Arithmetic* (1929), and *Primary Arithmetic Through Experience* (1939).

*See also* Intelligence quotient

# Overachiever

A person whose performance disproportionately exceeds ability; academically, a student, whose academic achievement disproportionately exceeds his or her performance on standardized intelligence tests.

The terms "overachiever" and "underachiever," most often applied to school and academia, both refer to gaps between academic performance and IQ test scores. Generally, these terms are not used by either educators or psychologists. However, clinical psychologist Marilyn Sorenson in her book, *Breaking the Chain of Low Self-Esteem,* maintains that people with low **self-esteem** often find themselves driven to overachieve to build self-worth. Overachievers increasingly take on new projects and drive themselves to perfection, often becoming known as "workaholics." Overachievement may occur in one area of a person's life without pervading the entire life. The fear of failure drives underachievers, according to Sorenson. Gripped by their fears of failure and humiliation, underachievers fail to realize their skill or talent potential. While often viewed with a negative connotation, overachievement has come to be valued in a number of corporations, competing to remain at the top of their field. Sometimes the term is used in informal communication to describe a person intent on gathering tangible or recognized symbols of accomplishment, such as educational degrees, awards, and honorary positions.

*See also* Perfectionism

### Further Reading
Sorensen, Marilyn J. *Breaking the Chain of Low Self-Esteem.* Sherwood, OR: Wolf Pub., 1998.

# Overactive children

See **Attention deficit/hyperactivity disorder (ADHD)**

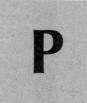

# Pain

*Physical suffering resulting from some sort of injury or disease, experienced through the central nervous system.*

Pain is a complex phenomenon that scientists are still struggling to understand. Its purpose is to alert the body of damage or danger to its system, yet scientists do not fully understand the level and intensity of pain sometimes experienced by people. Long-lasting, severe pain does not serve the same purpose as acute pain, which triggers an immediate physical response. Pain that persists without diminishing over long periods of time is known as chronic pain. It is estimated that almost one-third of all Americans suffer from some form of chronic pain. Of these, 70 million have back pain, 36 million have arthritis, 20 million suffer from migraine headaches, and at least 800,000 Americans suffer severe pain associated with the growth of cancerous tumors. An additional kind of pain is psychological pain. Recent research has shown that the chemicals produced by anxiety are similar to those that are released in response to physical injury.

Pain signals travel through the body along billions of special **nerve** cells reserved specifically for transmitting pain messages. These cells are known as nociceptors. The chemical neurotransmitters carrying the message include prostaglandins, bradykinin—the most painful substance known to humans—and a chemical known as P, which stands for pain. Prostaglandins are manufactured from fatty acids in nearly every tissue in the body. Analgesic pain relievers, such as aspirin and ibuprofen, work by inhibiting prostaglandin production.

After an injury, cells near the trauma site release these chemicals into the **central nervous system**. In the spinal cord, they are carried by the dorsal horn, and it is at this point that the body pulls away from the source of the pain. When the signal reaches the **brain**, it is first processed by the **thalamus** and then passed to the cerebral cortex. Here, the brain fully processes the information, locates its source in the body, and begins sending signals to relieve the pain.

As they travel, the pain messages are sorted according to severity. Recent research has discovered that the body has two distinct pathways for transmitting pain messages. The epicritic system is used to transmit messages of sudden, intense pain, such as that caused by cuts or burns. The neurons that transmit such messages are called A fibers, and they are built to transmit messages quickly. The protopathic system is used to transmit less severe messages of pain, such as the kind one might experience from over-strenuous exercise. The C fibers of the protopathic system do not send messages as quickly as A fibers.

In 1965, Ronald Melzack and Patrick Wall, leading pain researchers at the Massachusetts Institute of Technology, proposed what has come to be known as the gate theory of pain. This theory holds that the **nervous system** has the capacity to process only limited amounts of information at a time. For example, if the body is overwhelmed by multiple messages, the nervous system will "shut down" certain messages. This would explain why rubbing an injury often lessens its pain. The rubbing, in essence, competes with the injury for space in the nervous system.

One application of the gate theory is the use of small bursts of electricity to help manage pain. Experiments were first conducted on animals, whose brains were stimulated electronically at certain points, shutting down their capacity to feel pain. The animals were then operated on using no anesthetic. This method has been adapted for humans as well and has led to the development of a pain relief method known as transcutaneous electrical nerve stimulation, or TENS. In this technique, pain sufferers are jolted with tiny bits of electricity at strategic points. As predicted by the gate theory, the nerve endings at the point of the shock are overwhelmed and divert some of the space in the central nervous system to processing it, thereby relieving the original pain.

Chronic pain, on the other hand, presents its own set of problems. Treating chronic pain is difficult because by its very nature, such pain damages the central nervous system, making it weaker and more susceptible to pain. This residue of pain is called pain **memory**. Problems also arise when nerve cells are damaged by chemotherapy, diabetes, shingles, and other diseases. And in the case of arthritis and other inflammatory diseases, the body's threshold for pain is lowered, thus causing increased pain from "less" stimuli.

Treatments for pain vary widely. For mild pain, the most common form of treatment is aspirin, a medication discovered in the 19th century and derived from salicin, a chemical found in the bark of the willow tree. Today, there are several aspirin-like drugs on the market for the relief of minor, inflammatory pain, including ibuprofen and acetaminophen. For more severe pain, opiates—derived from the opium poppy, a common flowering plant—are often used. Opiates work by attaching themselves, on the molecular level, to nerve cells normally used to transmit pain messages. (The place on the nerve cells where the opiates reside are called opiate receptors). Opiates work very well in relieving pain, but are quite dangerous and can become addictive.

In the 1970s, scientists began looking for natural opiate-like substances, and found that the body does indeed produce its own painkillers, which has come to be called opioids. The two most common opioids are endorphins and enkephalins. These chemicals attach themselves to the opiate receptors in nerve cells just as opiates do. It has been found that the body can be stimulated to release these chemicals by TENS and by acupuncture, a Chinese method of placing tiny needles at specific points in the body to relieve pain. Other methods for treating pain include hypnotism, massage, and **biofeedback**.

**Further Reading**

Arnold, Caroline. *Pain: What Is It? How Do We Deal With It?* New York: William Morrow and Company, 1986.

Atkinson, Jim. "Nerve Center." *Texas Monthly* (June 1994): 54.

Bower, Bruce. "Brain Changes Linked to Phantom-Limb Pain." *Science News* (10 June 1995).

Chase, Marilyn. "When Treating Pain, All Roads Lead to the Brain." *Wall Street Journal* (17 October 1994): B1.

Strobel, Gabrielle. "Pain Message Travels via Diffuse Signal." *Science News* (27 November 1993).

"Tips for Coping with Chronic Agony." *USA. Today Magazine* (October 1993): 3.

# Paired-associate learning

Strategy used by psychologists to study learning.

Paired-associate (PA) learning was invented by Mary Whiton Calkins in 1894 and involves the pairing of two items (usually words)—a stimulus and a response. For example, words such as *calendar* (stimulus) and *shoe* (response) may be paired, and when the learner is prompted with the stimulus, he responds with the appropriate word (*shoe*).

The study of PA learning has been important for a number of reasons. Psychologists view it as representative of the kind of learning that people engage in every day. For example, when learning a new word, a person must pair the word itself with the concept it represents. This is the essence of PA learning. Another reason is that it allows researchers to study the associations between stimuli and responses. Although this stimulus-response approach has lost some of its importance in contemporary psychology, researchers—especially behaviorists—have been interested in how stimulus-response links are formed and broken.

Psychological research has revealed that when people learn paired associates, they engage in two separate mental processes. The first is the learning of the response; the second is the formation of a bond between the two words. This second process seems to produce a one-way association in many circumstances. That is, a learner is much more likely to remember the response word if given the stimulus; people have a harder time remembering the stimulus if presented with the response word.

This pattern holds true when the response has never been used as a stimulus. On the other hand, if a particular word (e.g., *cloud* ) has been used both as a stimulus and as a response (e.g., *cloud-pen* and *bag-cloud* ), the learner gets accustomed to using the word in two ways. In later testing, the subject is likely to remember the word pair correctly when presented with either word. Based on research such as this, psychologists have concluded that learners remember the word pair as a unit, not as a stimulus that simply leads to a response.

**Further Reading**

Deese, J., and S.H. Hulse. *The Psychology of Learning.* 3rd ed. New York: McGrawHill, 1967.

# Panic/Panic disorders

An acute feeling of intense fear, accentuated by increased heart rate, shortness of breath, sweating, and mild convulsions.

Feelings of **fear** and panic are common to all species, and humans are certainly no exception. Psycho-

Paranoia

logically speaking, however, panic can be an obtrusive, life-altering phenomena for many people who suffer panic attacks. Such attacks occur commonly in people suffering from various phobias. People suffering from agoraphobia, for instance, can expect to suffer panic attacks when out in public. While panic attacks are generally short-lived, their recurrence and the severity of the physical symptoms that accompany them can lead people to fear them so intensely that they develop a more severe condition known as anxiety disorder.

Panic attacks usually originate as realistic responses to fearful or stressful experiences, usually in **childhood**. In more mature persons, however, memories of fearful events are put in perspective, and people generally do not feel the same fear they felt as a child when confronting a similar situation as an adult. Often, however, certain people will be susceptible to a variety of subconscious triggers. For instance, a person may experience intense fear every time he or she goes to the mall, not because of the mall, per se, but perhaps because they once had a very fearful experience, like being lost from a parent, in a mall. Panic attacks can also be caused by internal reactions. For example, increased heart rate can remind a person of an early panic experience, and every time his or her heart rate increases, the person experiences another panic attack.

Psychiatrists have documented the physical manifestations of panic, and are fairly certain that there is a genetic component to panic attacks. Neurologically, recent psychiatric research has identified a **brain** circuit called the flight/fight system, or FFS. This neurologic area, when stimulated in animals, produces features of tremendous fear and panic. Research in this area is still very new, and with each finding there are controversies and conflicting views. Brain imaging technology should help psychiatrists better understand the neurology of panic attacks, but they are still largely a mystery.

**Further Reading**

Chase, Marilyn. "Psychiatry Finds Answers to Mystery of Panic Attacks." *Wall Street Journal* (12 June 1995): B1.
Segal, Mariah. "Panic Disorder: The Heart That Goes Thump in the Night—and Day." *FDA Consumer* (April 1992): 22.
Seymour, Lesley Jane. "Fear of Almost Everything." *Mademoiselle* (September 1993): 252.
"What Triggers Panic Attacks?" *USA. Today Magazine* (October 1992): 2.

# Paranoia

A pervasive feeling of distrust of others.

Paranoia is an ever-present feeling of suspicion that others cannot be trusted. Such feelings are not based on fact or reality; insecurity and low **self-esteem** often exaggerate these emotions. Typically, paranoia is not seen in children, but in most cases it begins to develop in late **adolescence** and early adulthood. Most people experience feelings of paranoia, usually in response to a threatening situation or in connection with feelings of insecurity based on real circumstances. These feelings are related to the mild anxiety people experience at some points during their lives.

The fourth edition of Diagnostic and Statistical Manual of Mental Disorders *(DSM-IV)* includes diagnostic criteria for the more serious condition, paranoid **personality** disorder. According to the *DSM-IV*, individuals afflicted with this disorder assume, with little concrete evidence to support the assumption, that others plan to exploit, harm, or deceive him or her; and continually analyzes the motivations of friends, **family**, and others to confirm his or her doubts about their trustworthiness; expects friends and family to abandon him or her in times of trouble or **stress**; avoids revealing personal information because of **fear** that it will be used against him or her; interprets remarks and actions as having hidden, demeaning, and threatening connotations; and is unwilling to forgive an insult. The behavior of an individual with paranoid personality disorder may compel others to react with **anger** or **hostility**. This tends to reinforce the individual's suspiciousness and feelings that friends and associates are "against" him or her.

In the 1990s, the term "everyday paranoia" (EP) came into usage among psychologists to describe the intense anxiety that was becoming prevalent in society. Everyday paranoia is sparked by fear of losing one's job, feelings of inadequacy when confronting a new interpersonal or romantic relationship, or insecurity in a marriage or other long-term relationship. Low self-esteem and feelings of insecurity contribute to a person's susceptibility to feelings of everyday paranoia. Stressful situations—economic insecurity, **divorce**, a move, a job change—can also reinforce a person's paranoia. Almost everyone experiences feelings of suspicion or insecurity—and in fact, paranoia can be a mechanism for coping with misfortune or personal problems. Rather than view the situation as "bad luck" or personal failure or incompetence, paranoia places the responsibility for the problem on some "enemy."

The term paranoia is used erroneously at times to define special life circumstances. Members of minority groups and new immigrants may exhibit guarded behavior due to unfamiliarity with their new **environment** and lack of knowledge of language and cultural norms. This display of suspicion of authority figures and lack of trust in outsiders is based on a real lack of understanding of the person's surroundings, and does not represent an abnormal reaction. In addition, the term "political paranoia" is used to describe attitudes shared by members of groups on the fringes of society who suspect that government agencies are conspiring to control the lives of citizens by imposing new values, or suspect that other dominant groups are persecuting them. The growth of paramilitary organizations in the United States in recent years appears to be indicative of such feelings of political paranoia among a small percentage of citizens.

## Further Reading
*Diagnostic and Statistical Manual of Mental Disorders.* 4th ed. Washington, DC: American Psychiatric Association, 1994.
Goodwin, Jan. "Paranoia." *Cosmopolitan* (August 1994):184+.
Kelly, Michael. "The Road to Paranoia." *The New Yorker* (June 19, 1995): 60+.

# Paraphilia

Sexual feelings or behaviors that may involve sexual partners that are not human, not consenting, or that involve suffering by one or both partners.

To diagnose an individual with a paraphilia, the psychologist or other diagnostician must confirm recurrent, intense, sexually arousing feelings, fantasies, or behaviors over a period of at least six months. According to the Diagnostic and Statistical Manual of Mental Disorders *(DSM-IV)*, it is not uncommon for an individual to have more than one paraphilia.

## Bestiality

Bestiality is a term that describes sexual feelings or behaviors involving animals. Termed zoophilia by the fourth edition of Diagnostic and Statistical Manual of Mental Disorders *(DSM-IV)*, this is a relatively uncommon disorder. The disorder does not specify an animal or category of animals; the person with zoophilia may focus sexual feelings on domesticated animals, such as dogs, or farm animals, such as sheep or goats.

## Exhibitionism

Exhibitionism is the exposure of genitals to a nonconsenting stranger. In some cases, the individual may also engage in **autoeroticism** while exposing himself. Generally, no additional contact with the observer is sought; the individual is stimulated sexually by gaining the **attention** of and startling the observer.

## Masochism (Sexual)

Masochism is a term applied to a specific sexual disorder but which also has a broader usage. The sexual disorder involves pleasure and excitement produced by **pain**, either inflicted by others or by oneself. It usually begins in **childhood** or **adolescence** and is chronic. Masochism is the only paraphilia in which any noticeable number of women participate—about 5 percent of masochists are female. The term comes from the name of a nineteenth century Austrian writer, Leopold von Sacher-Masoch, whose novels often included characters who were obsessed with the combination of sex and pain.

In the broader sense, masochism refers to any experience of receiving pleasure or satisfaction from suffering pain. The psychoanalytic view is that masochism is **aggression** turned inward, onto the self, when a person feels too guilty or afraid to express it outwardly.

## Pedophilia

**Pedophilia** involves sexual activity with a child, generally under age 13. The Diagnostic and Statistical Manual of Mental Disorders describes a criterion that the individual with pedophilia be over 16 years of age and be at least five years older than the child. Individuals with this disorder may be attracted to either males or females or both, although incidents of pedophilic activity are almost twice as likely to be repeated by those individuals attracted to males. Individuals with this disorder develop procedures and strategies for gaining access to and trust of children.

## Sadomasochism

Sadomasochism applies to deviant sexual behavior in which an individual achieves gratification either by experiencing pain (masochism) or inflicting it on another (sadism).

In psychoanalytic theory, sadism is related to the **fear** of castration, while the behaviorist explanation of sadomasochism is that its constituent feelings are physiologically similar to sexual arousal. Separate but parallel descriptions are given for sexual sadism and sexual masochism in the Diagnostic and Statistical Manual of Mental Disorders *(DSM-IV)* . The clinical diagnostic criteria for both are recurrence of the behavior over a period of at least six months, and significant distress or impairment of the **ability** to function as a result of the behavior or associated urges or fantasies. Either type of behavior may be limited to fantasies (sometimes while one is engaged in outwardly nondeviant sex) or acted out with a consenting partner, a non-consenting partner, or in the case of masochism, alone. Sadomasochism occurs in both males and females, and in both heterosexual and homosexual relationships.

Sadistic activities, which may express dominance or inflict pain and /or humiliation on the other person, include restraint, blindfolding, whipping, burning, **rape**, stabbing, strangulation, and even death. Masochists may seek to be the object of some of these acts as well as other types of humiliation, including forced cross-dressing. A particularly dangerous and fatal masochistic practice is hypoxyphilia, which consists of deliberately cutting off one's oxygen supply through mechanical or chemical means. Both sadistic and masochistic fantasies usually begin in childhood, and the disorders usually manifest in early adulthood. When associated with **antisocial personality disorder**, it may result in serious injury to others or death.

### Voyeurism

Voyeurism is a paraphilia in which a person finds sexual excitement in watching unsuspecting people who are nude, undressing, or having sex. Voyeurs are almost always male, and the victims are usually strangers. A voyeur may fantasize about having sex with the victim but almost never actually pursues this. The voyeur may return to watch the same stranger repeatedly, but there is rarely physical contact.

Voyeurs are popularly known as "peeping Toms," based on the eleventh-century legend of Lady Godiva. According to the story, Tom was a tailor who "peeped" at Lady Godiva as she rode naked through the streets of Coventry, England, in a sacrificial act to get her husband to lower taxes. Tom was struck with blindness for not looking away like everyone else did.

### Incidence and treatment

Psychologists estimate that a greater percentage of people experience sexual deviance than is officially reported. This is because many people who carry out sexual deviations do not consider their activities to be deviant. For instance, sadomasochists have group meetings, workshops, and large gatherings and have become something of a subculture. They do not typically think of themselves as needing therapy or treatment.

People who seek treatment for paraphilias often do so because they have been cited for illegal activity or because they are afraid they may do something illegal and be caught for it. Many different treatments have been tried with paraphilias, from medication to **group therapy**, to eliminate the behavior. Psychologists report low success rates, especially among criminally charged child molesters. **Behavior modification** is most likely to suc-

ceed when a combination of therapy, aversion technique (using electric shock or visualization to change pleasure experience), and medication is employed.

*See also* Pedophilia

### Further Reading

Baumeister, Roy F. *Escaping the Self: Alcoholism, Spirituality, Masochism, and Other Flights from the Burden of Self-hood.* New York: Basic Books, 1991.
Caplan, Paula J. *The Myth of Women's Masochism.* Toronto: University of Toronto Press, 1993.
Carnes, Patrick. *Out of the Shadows: Understanding Sexual Addiction.* 2nd ed. Center City, MN: Hazelden Educational Materials, 1992.

# Parapsychology

Meaning "beside psychology," term used to describe the study of paranormal, or psi, phenomena, the most significant being extra-sensory perception (ESP) and psychokinesis (PK).

The study of paranormal activities and phenomena has been riddled with controversy since its conception. It is claimed that some people, utilizing senses beyond the ordinary, exhibit powers that cannot be explained by traditional science. Skeptics of the paranormal point to the fact that in over a century since the first serious studies of the paranormal began, usually dated to the opening of the Society for Psychical Research in London in 1882, no replicable demonstration of any such powers has ever been conducted. Yet many people continue to believe in the existence of the paranormal.

The most studied and debated paranormal phenomena are ESP and psychokinesis. ESP is an acronym for extra-sensory **perception** and encompasses clairvoyance, the ability to perceive something without the use of the senses, and telepathy, the ability to communicate with another person without the use of the senses. (Parapsychologists currently refer to telepathy as "anomalous processes of information or energy transfer.")

Clairvoyance was the first paranormal phenomena to be seriously considered by scientists, probably because devising tests to prove or disprove its existence was easy. In the late 1920s, many such tests were devised by J.B. Rhine, a psychology professor who had left Harvard University to help found the Parapsychology Laboratory at Duke University. Rhine's tests often produced positive results for clairvoyance, and at the time his work was seriously regarded. In recent decades, however, much of Rhine's work has been discredited as being biased, careless, and, in some cases, utterly fraudulent.

Recent studies have proven more reputable but far from conclusive. One such study revealed statistically significant telepathic abilities among 100 men and 140 women tested in Scotland over six years in the mid-1980s. In the tests, "senders" focused on images or video clips and attempted to send those impressions to a "receiver" in a sensory-isolated room. The researchers reported that one in three sessions led to a "hit," meaning that the receiver reported visualizing images similar to those being sent. A hit is expected to occur by chance in one in four instances. On the other hand, the Central Intelligence Agency of the United States discounted the existence of ESP after conducting its own experiments in "remote viewing." The agency concluded that there were not enough evidence for its existence.

Psychokinesis (PK) is the ability to manipulate physical objects with the mind. Probably the most infamous purveyor of psychokinetic powers was the Israeli psychic and entertainer Uri Geller, who became an international celebrity by bending spoons, supposedly with his mind. During his career, he would never demonstrate his spoon bending ability in a controlled **environment**, and he was on several occasions shown to be faking. Another form of PK is known as spontaneous PK, in which a physical action occurs in response to psychological trauma. There are personal accounts, for instance, of clocks and watches stopping at the moment of a loved one's death. J.B. Rhine was one of the first to conduct experiments in PK, primarily with the use of dice. He tested a subject's ability to influence the outcome of a toss and found that many people demonstrated a slight ability, beyond chance, of "controlling" the dice.

There are other phenomena studies by parapsychologists, including hauntings, UFOs, near-death and after-death experiences, out-of-body experiences, psychic healing, and many others. All of these share the curious nature of ESP and PK in that, anecdotally speaking, occurrences are widespread, believed by members of many cultures, and discussed throughout history. Yet none have been scientifically demonstrated or reproduced. Despite the lack of proof, many people firmly believe in the paranormal, as evidenced by personal testimony, the popularity of television shows such as "The X-Files," and by the huge profits generated by psychic phone lines and other occult enterprises. One of the reasons the scientific community is skeptical about paranormal phenomena is that there is no apparent basis in physical laws for such phenomena. In every other scientific discipline, it is possible to speculate reasonably that events occur as they do because they follow a recognized natural law, such as gravity or conservation of energy. Parapsychologists have failed to develop adequate theoretical reasons for the existence of the phenomena they purport to demonstrate.

Nevertheless, it seems that most people are open to the possibility of the paranormal despite the lack of evidence.

## Further Reading

Blackmore, Susan. "Psi in Psychology." *Skeptical Inquirer* (Summer 1994): 351.

Bower, B. "CIA Studies Fan Debate Over Psi Abilities." *Science News* (9 December 1995): 390.

————. "Scientists Peer into the Mind's Psi." *Science News* (29 January 1994): 68.

Irwin, H.J. *An Introduction to Parapsychology.* Jefferson, NC: McFarland & Co., 1989.

Jaroff, Leon. "Weird Science: Catering to Viewers' Growing Appetite for Paranormal . . ." *Time* (15 May 1995): 75.

Yam, Philip. "A Skeptically Inquiring Mind." *Scientific American* (July 1995): 34.

# Parent-child relationships

The relationship, over the full extent of a child's development, between parent and child.

Of the many different relationships we form over the course of the life span, the relationship between parent and child is among the most important. Not surprisingly, students of **child development** have devoted considerable **attention** to the parent-child relationship, in order to understand how it develops and functions over the lifespan. Among the many questions researchers examine are those concerning normative changes in the parent-child relationship over the course of development (e.g., How does the parent-child relationship change during adolescence?), the impact of variations in the parent-child relationship on the child's behavior and functioning (e.g., Which types of discipline are most effective during the preschool years?), and the effects of the parent-child relationship on the parent (e.g., How are adults affected by parenthood?).

### Infancy

A baby cries, a parent feeds her; a baby snuggles, a parent hugs her. Day after day, night after night, mothers and fathers feed, burp, wash, change, dress, and hold their babies. Out of these interactions, feelings and expectations grow. The baby feels distressed and hungry, then satisfied; the parent feels tenderness, joy, annoyance, exhaustion, pleasure. Gradually, the baby begins to expect that her parent will care for her when she cries. Gradually, parents respond to and even anticipate their baby's needs. These elements form the basis for a developing relationship, a combination of behaviors, interactions, feelings, and expectations that are unique to a particular parent and a particular child.

By the end of the first year, most infants who are cared for in families develop an **attachment** relationship, usually with the primary caretaker. This relationship is central to the child's development.

Developmental psychologists have studied attachment in **infancy** mainly by watching how infants react when they are separated from, and then reunited with, their caregiver (usually one of the infant's parents). An experimental laboratory procedure called the **Strange Situation** is the most common assessment. Researchers have been particularly interested in understanding individual differences in the quality of attachment is inferred from behavior in the Strange Situation. The majority of children develop a *secure attachment*: when reunited with their caregiver after a temporary absence of several minutes, they greet her in two distinctive ways. If distressed, they want to be picked up and find comfort in her arms; if content, they smile, talk to her, or show her a toy. In contrast, some children with an *insecure attachment* want to be picked up, but they are not comforted; they kick or push away. Others seem indifferent to the caregiver's return, and ignore her when she returns.

The quality of the infant's attachment seems to be predictive of aspects of later development. Youngsters who emerge from infancy with a secure attachment stand a better chance of developing happy, competent relationships with others. The attachment relationship not only forms the emotional basis for the continued development of the parent-child relationship, but can serve as a foundation upon which subsequent social relationships are built.

Researchers disagree about the origins of a secure attachment relationship. One account focuses on the way caregivers behave toward their infants. According to this view, the key element is the caregiver's sensitivity in responding to the infant's signals. Secure infants have mothers who sensitively read their infant's cues and respond appropriately to their needs.

Another perspective emphasizes the **temperament** of the infants. A secure attachment is more easily formed between a caregiver and an infant with an easier disposition, or temperament, than between a caregiver and an infant who is characteristically negative, fearful, or not especially sociable. In this respect, security of attachment may reflect what the infant is like rather than how the caregiver behaves. Most likely, the early parent-child relationship is the product both of what the infant *and* caregiver bring to it.

## Toddlerhood

When children move from infancy into toddlerhood, the parent-child relationship begins to change its focus. During infancy, the primary function of the parent-child relationship is nurturance and predictability, and much of the relationship revolves around the day-to-day demands of caregiving: feeding, sleeping, toileting, bathing. The attachment relationship develops out of these day-to-day interactions.

As youngsters begin to talk and become more mobile during the second and third years of life, however, parents usually attempt to shape their child's social behavior. In essence, parents become teachers as well as nurturers, providers of guidance as well as affection. The process of socialization—preparing the youngster to function as a member of a social group—implicit during most of the first two years of life, becomes explicit as the child moves toward his or her third birthday.

**Socialization** has been an important focus of research in child development for well over 60 years. Initially, researchers focused on particular child-rearing practices—including types of discipline and approaches to toilet training and weaning —in an effort to link specific parenting practices to aspects of the child's development. Findings from this research were inconsistent and not especially informative. Over time, such efforts gave way to research that emphasized the overall emotional climate of the parent-child relationship, instead of discrete parenting practices.

A number of studies conducted during the past 30 years have pointed to two overarching dimensions of the parent-child relationship that appear to be systematically linked to the child's psychological development: how responsive the parents are, and how demanding they are. Responsive parents are warm and accepting toward their children, enjoying them and trying to see things from their perspective. In contrast, parents who are low in responsiveness tend to be aloof, rejecting, or critical. They show little pleasure in their children and are often insensitive to their emotional needs. Demanding parents maintain consistent standards for their child's behavior. In contrast, parents who are insufficiently demanding are too lenient; they exercise minimal control, provide little guidance, and often yield to their child's demands. Children's healthy psychological development is facilitated when the parents are both responsive and moderately demanding.

During toddlerhood, children often begin to assert their desire for autonomy by challenging their parents. Sometimes, the child's newfound assertiveness during the "terrible twos" can put a strain on the parent-child relationship. It is important that parents recognize that this behavior is normal for the toddler, and that the healthy development of independence is facilitated by a parent-child relationship that provides support and structure for the child's developing sense of autonomy. In many regards, the security of the initial attachment between in-

**Involving children in leisure activities, like fishing, can build stronger parent-child relationships.** *(Photo by Susan D. Rock. Reproduced with permission.)*

fant and parent provides the child with the emotional wherewithal to begin exploring the world outside the parent-child relationship.

## Preschool

Many researchers study the ways in which responsiveness and demandingness interact to form a general tone, or climate, in the household. Using this sort of approach, experts have identified four main parenting styles that typically emerge during the preschool years: authoritative, authoritarian, indulgent, and disengaged. Although no parent is absolutely consistent across situations and over time, parents do seem to follow some general tendencies in their approach to childrearing, and it is possible to describe a parent-child relationship in terms of the prevailing style of parenting employed. These descriptions can be used to provide guidelines for both professionals and parents interested in understanding how variations in the parent-child relationship **affect** the child's development.

*Authoritative* parents are both responsive and demanding; they are firm, but they discipline with love and affection, rather than **power**, and they are likely to explain rules and expectations to their children instead of simply asserting them. *Authoritarian* parents are also highly demanding, but they are not less responsive; authoritarian parents tend to be strict disciplinarians, frequently relying on physical **punishment** and the withdrawal of affection to shape their child's behavior. *Indulgent* parents are responsive, but not especially demanding; they have few expectations of their children and impose little discipline. *Disengaged* parents are neither responsive nor demanding. They may be neglectful or unaware of the child's needs for affection and discipline.

What makes a parent more likely to use one style as opposed to another? Ultimately, the parenting style a parent employs is shaped by many factors: the parent's developmental history, education, and **personality**, the child's behavior, and the immediate and broader context of the parent's life. Thus, the parent's behavior vis-à-vis the child is influenced by such things as work, marriage, **family** finances, and other factors likely to affect the parent's behavior and psychological well-being. In addition, systematic comparisons of parenting practices among families living in different circumstances teach us that parents in different cultures, from different social classes, and from different ethnic groups rear their children differently.

Nevertheless, research has shown that aspects of children's behavior and psychological development are linked to the style of parenting with which they have been raised. Generally speaking, preschoolers with authoritative parents tend to be curious about new situations, focused and skilled at **play**, self-reliant, self-controlled, and cheerful. Children who are routinely treated in an authoritarian way tend to be moody, unhappy, fearful, withdrawn, unspontaneous, and irritable. Children of permissive parents tend to be low in both social responsibility and independence, but they are usually more cheerful than the conflicted and irritable children of authoritarian parents. Finally, children whose parents are disengaged tend to have a higher proportion of psychological difficulties than other youngsters.

### School age

During the elementary school years, the child becomes increasingly interested in peers, but this should not be taken as a sign of disinterest in the parent-child relationship. Rather, with the natural broadening of psychosocial and cognitive abilities, the child's social world expands to include more people and settings beyond the home **environment**. The parent-child relationship continues to remain the most important influence on the child's development. Generally speaking, children whose parents are both responsive and demanding continue to thrive psychologically and socially during the middle **childhood** years.

The parenting styles that first become apparent during the preschool years continue to influence development across middle childhood. Over the course of childhood, parents' styles tend to remain the same, and their effects on the child quite similar. Children of authoritative parents tend to be socially competent, responsible, successful in school, and high in **self-esteem**. The authoritarian style, with its **perfectionism**, rigidity, and harsh discipline, continues to affect children adversely, with these youngsters generally rated lower than their peers in appropriate social assertiveness, cognitive ability, competence, and self-esteem, but higher in **aggression**. Children of permissive parents also tend to be more aggressive than their peers, but also more impulsive, less self-reliant, and less responsible. Children raised in disengaged homes continue to have the most difficulty, and show more behavior problems.

The natural tendency is to think of the parent-child relationship as a one-way street, with the parent influencing the child. But in actuality the relationship is reciprocal and bi-directional. During the school years especially, the parent-child relationship is influenced not only by the child's parents but by the child. In most families, patterns of interaction between parent and child are well established by the elementary school years. Overly harsh parenting, for example, often leads to aggressive behavior in children, leading children to join antisocial peer groups, further heightening their aggressiveness. This, in turn, may provoke harsher parenting, leading to further aggressiveness in the child, and so on. Authoritative parenting, in contrast, helps children develop self-reliance and **social competence**, which, of course, makes it easier for parents to rear their child in an authoritative, reasoned fashion. Continued authoritativeness on the part of the parent contributes to increased competence in the child, and so on. Rather than trying to solve the "which came first" puzzle—the parenting or the child's characteristics—it is more useful to think of parenting as a process and the parent-child relationship as one part of an intricate social system.

Much research has examined how the child's development is affected by such factors as **divorce**, remarriage, and parental (especially, maternal) employment. As a rule, these studies show that the quality of the parent-child relationship is a more important influence on the child's psychological development than changes in the structure or composition of the household. Generally speaking, parenting that is responsive and demanding is associated with healthier child development regardless of the parent's marital status or employment situation. If changes in the parent's marital status or work life disrupt the parent-child relationship, however, short-term effects on the child's behavior are likely to be seen. One goal of professionals who work with families under **stress** is to help them re-establish healthy patterns of parent-child interaction.

### Adolescence

Early **adolescence** marks an important turning point in the parent-child relationship. As the child enters adolescence, the biological, cognitive, and emotional changes of the period spark transformations in the parent-child relationship. In many families, the transition into adolescence coincides with the parent's transition into mid-life, and this, too, may introduce additional challenges into the family system that spill over into the parent-child relationship.

Early adolescence is a time during which the child's urges for independence may challenge parents' authority, as the young adolescent strives to establish a sense of emotional autonomy, or *individuation*. And much like toddlerhood, many parents find early adolescence to be a difficult period requiring a fair amount of **adaptation**. But, as is also the case with toddlerhood, research shows that most families are able to cope with these adaptational demands successfully. Adolescents fare best, and their family relationships are happiest, in households in which parents are both supportive and are accepting of the child's needs for more psychological independence.

Although the significance of peer relationships grows during adolescence, the parent-child relationship maintains its importance for the psychological development of the child. As in previous eras, authoritative parenting—parenting that combines warmth and firmness—seems to have the most positive impact on the youngster's development. Research shows that over time, adolescents who have been reared authoritatively continue to show more success in school, better psychological development, and fewer behavior problems than their counterparts from other types of homes. Youngsters whose parents are disengaged continue to show the most difficulty.

It is widely assumed that conflict between parents and children is an inherent feature of family life in adolescence, but systematic research on the so-called "generation gap" indicates that the phenomenon has been exaggerated in the popular media. Early adolescence may be a time of heightened bickering and somewhat diminished closeness in the parent-child relationship, but most disagreements between parents and young teenagers are over fairly mundane matters, and most teenagers and parents agree on the essentials. Nevertheless, the increased frequency with which these squabbles occur may take its toll on parents' **mental health**, especially on the mothers'. This period appears to be temporary, however, and most parents and adolescents are able to establish a comfortable working relationship by the beginning of high school. Indeed, by late adolescence most children report feeling as close to their parents as they did during elementary school.

## Adults

Many adults maintain an active relationship with their parents. As adults, they can now relate to each other as equals, although the feeling of one being the parent and the other a "child" (even though the child is now an adult) endures in some relationships. Increasingly, adult children are sandwiched between the demands of caring for their own children and their **aging** parents, who may need more assistance as they get older and physically weaker. In some families, the adult children take care of their parents, much in the same way that their parents took care of them when they were younger. This situation has brought both stress and joy as parents and adult children struggle to redefine their relationship.

Laurence Steinberg Ph.D.

### Further Reading
Bornstein, M., ed. *Handbook of Parenting*. Hillsdale, NJ: Erlbaum, 1995.

## Parkinson's disease

*A relatively common degenerative disorder of the central nervous system.*

Parkinson's disease is a degenerative disorder of the **central nervous system** named for James Parkinson (1755-1824), the physician who first described it in 1817. This disorder is also called paralysis agitans, shaking palsy, or parkinsonism.

Typically, the symptoms of Parkinson's disease begin to appear in late middle life, and the course of the disease is slowly progressive over 20 years or more. In its advanced stages, Parkinson's disease is characterized by poorly articulated speech, difficulty in chewing and swallowing, loss of motor coordination, a general tendency toward exhaustion, and especially by stooped posture, positioning the arms in front of the body when walking, caution and slowness of movement, rigidity of facial expression, and tremor of the hands. Mental **ability** and the senses are not directly affected by this disease. Parkinson's disease is believed to be caused by a deficiency of dopamine in the basal ganglia of the **brain**.

### Further Reading
McGoon, Dwight. *The Parkinson's Handbook.* New York: Norton, 1990.

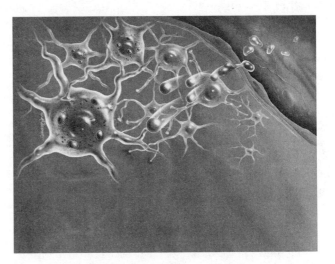

**Parkinson's disease seen at cellular level. Scientists believe that nerve cells in the brain fail to get enough dopamine.** *(Teri J. McDermott. Custom Medical Stock Photo. Reproduced with permission.)*

# Passive-aggressive personality

A pattern of behavior formerly classified as a personality disorder.

Formerly listed among the **personality** disorders in the American Psychiatric Association's Diagnostic and Statistical Manual of Mental Disorders, the passive-aggressive personality type has been described by a number of psychologists and psychiatrists, including **Karen Horney**, Karl Menninger, and **Wilhelm Reich** (1897-1957). Its main distinguishing feature is indirect resistance to the demands or expectations of others through stubbornness, forgetfulness, inefficiency, procrastination, and other covert means. Rather than refusing outright to perform a task, the passive-aggressive person will do it badly or procrastinate until the deadline for its completion has passed. Passive-aggressive people, at one time called "ill-tempered depressives," are also generally moody, discontented, and critical of others, and they tend to see themselves as victims, feeling that they are singled out for bad luck and ill treatment by others. In their interpersonal relationships, they are unable to find a healthy balance between dependence and assertiveness.

Passive **aggression** also refers more generally to a type of behavior not limited to a certain personality type and characterized by the covert expression of aggressive feelings one is unable or unwilling to express directly. Passive aggression may be expressed in a variety of ways, including tardiness for an event or job about which one has negative feelings or poor performance of a task one resents.

## Further Reading

Cicchetti, Dante, and Donald J. Cohen (eds.) *Developmental Psychopathology*. New York: J. Wiley, 1995.
Eysenck, Michael W. *Individual Differences: Normal and Abnormal*. Hillsdale, NJ: L. Erlbaum Associates, 1994.

# Ivan Pavlov

### 1849-1936
Russian physiologist and Nobel laureate best known for his development of the concept of the conditioned reflex, or conditioned response.

Ivan Pavlov was born into an impoverished **family** in the rural village of Ryazan, Russia. He won a government scholarship to the University of St. Petersburg and studied medicine at the Imperial Medical Academy, receiving his degree in 1883. In 1890, Pavlov was appointed to a professorship at the St. Petersburg Military Academy and a few years later joined the faculty of the University of St. Petersburg. He organized the Institute of Experimental Medicine in 1895, which was to be his research laboratory for the next 40 years.

In the 1890s, Pavlov investigated the workings of the digestive system—focusing on digestive secretions—using special surgically created openings in the digestive tracts of dogs, a project strongly influenced by the work of an earlier physiologist, Ivan Sechenov (1829-1905). As a result of this research, Pavlov was awarded the Nobel Prize for Physiology and Medicine in 1904. During his investigations in this area, Pavlov observed that normal, healthy dogs would salivate upon seeing their keeper, apparently in anticipation of being fed. This led him, through a systematic series of experiments, to formulate the principles of the **conditioned response**, which he believed could be applied to humans as well as to animals. According to Pavlov's system, an *unconditioned stimulus*, such as offering food to a dog, produced a response, or *unconditioned reflex*, that required no training (salivation). In contrast, a normally neutral act, such as ringing a bell, became a **conditioned stimulus** when associated with the offering of food and eventually would produce salivation also, but as a *conditioned reflex*. According to Pavlov, the conditioned reflex was a physiological phenomenon caused by the creation of new reflexive pathways created in the cortex of the **brain** by the **conditioning** process. In further studies of the cortex, Pavlov posited the presence of two important processes that accompany conditioning: *excitation*, which leads to the acquisition of conditioned responses, and *inhibition*, which suppresses them. He eventually came to believe that cortical inhibition was an important factor in the **sleep** process.

Pavlov continued working with conditioned **reflexes** throughout the early decades of the twentieth century, generating several addition principles through further experimentation. The principle of *timing* dictated that the neutral stimulus must precede the unconditioned reflex in order to become a conditioned stimulus. (In other words, a buzzer would have to go off before food was offered to a dog in order for the dog to associate the food and buzzer with each other). The concept of **extinction** referred to the fact that a conditioned response could be "unlearned" if the neutral stimulus (buzzer) was repeatedly used without **reinforcement** (food). *Generalization* was the name given to the observation that a stimulus similar to the conditioned stimulus would still produce a response as the dog generalized from its original experience to a similar one, but the response would be less pronounced in proportion to the difference between the stimuli. Finally, testing the limits of the dogs' ability to differentiate among stimuli led, unexpectedly, to *experi-*

Ivan Pavlov (right of center) with his staff and one of his laboratory dogs. *(The Bettmann Archive. Reproduced with permission.)*

*mental neuroses*, similar to mental breakdowns in humans, when the subjects were forced to confront conflicting or ambiguous stimuli for any length of time. Observing the ways in which neurotic symptoms differed among test subjects led Pavlov between 1916 and 1936 to formulate a theory of four different types of **temperament** linked to physiological differences based on differences in excitatory and inhibitory activity. Attempting to extend the implications of this theory to human psychopathology, Pavlov helped establish the Soviet Union's continuing tradition of organically-based psychiatric treatment.

Pavlov, who died of pneumonia in 1936, tried to apply his ideas to psychiatry, and was influential enough to be considered one of the founders of Russian psychiatry, and he remains a dominant figure in Russian psychology. Although he never considered himself a psychologist, Pavlov's ultimate belief in conditioning as the fundamental unit of learning in humans and animals provided one of the cornerstones of the behaviorist school of psychology in the United States. It is ironic that, although Pavlov was a staunch critic of communism, in the late 1920s Joseph Stalin (1879-1953) chose Pavlov's

work as the basis for a new Soviet psychology. Pavlov's books include *Lectures on the Work of the Principal Digestive Glands* (1897), *Lectures on Conditioned Reflexes* (1928), and *Conditioned Reflexes and Psychiatry* (1941).

*See also* Behaviorism

**Further Reading**

Babkin, Boris P. *Pavlov: A Biography.* Chicago: University of Chicago Press, 1949.

# Pedophilia

The recurrent, intense presence of sexual urges and fantasies of at least six months' duration, involving sexual activity with prepubescent children.

## Assessment

Pedophilia is a subcategory of a larger group of sexual disorders commonly classified as paraphilias. These are defined as recurrent, intense, aphrodisiac fantasies, sexual urges, or behaviors, over a period of at least six months, which involve non-human objects, the suffering or humiliation of oneself or one's partner, or children or other non-consenting partners. If these recurrent fantasies, urges, and behaviors involve sexual activities with prepubescent children (generally age 13 or younger), the main diagnostic criterion for pedophilia is met.

Pedophilia encompasses simple voyeurism of nude children, observing children at various stages of undress or assisting them to undress, sexual fondling, exposing oneself, performing oral sex on children and/or requesting them to return oral sex, or mutual masturbation. In most cases (except those involving **incest**), pedophiles do not require sexual penetration, and do not force their attentions on a child. They instead rely on guile, persuasion, and **friendship**, often displaying great tenderness and affection toward the child of their desire. Once a person has engaged in sexual activity with a child, he or she is then additionally labeled a "child molester." Thus, child molestation is subsumed in the overall condition of pedophilia.

A psychological profile of pedophilia escapes development because perpetrators appear to constitute a heterogenous group. However, some common characteristics prevail among both pedophiles and child molesters. The great majority of pedophiles are male, and they may be heterosexual, homosexual, or bisexual in orientation. Preference for children as sex partners may not be exclusive, and more often than not, pedophiles have no gender preference in prepubescent children. However, by a margin greater than two to one, most victims are girls. Moreover, the pedophile is usually a relative, friend, or neighbor of the child's **family**. Alcohol is associated with almost 50 percent of molestation cases, but is not necessarily correlated with pedophilia in general. Pedophilia tends to be a chronic condition, and recidivism is high.

The motives for engaging in sexual activity with children are rather divergent among pedophiles, but one theme recurs: the pedophile tends to justify his/her conduct. Pedophiles often indicate to authorities that the child solicited sexual contact or activity, and also claim that the child derives as much sexual pleasure from the activity as the perpetrator. Pedophiles also excuse their behavior as non-harmful, non-violent, non-forced, even "educational" for the child. They often tend not to see themselves as abusers, molesters, or sexually deviant. This quality of being into denial as to the true harm that they may cause belies the fact that clearly, most pedophiles act for their own gratification and not that of the child. In fact, more often than not, they describe their urges as compulsive, non-controllable and overwhelming.

The pedophilic disposition may not manifest until later in life, but more often than not, manifests in **adolescence**. By definition, it requires a minimum of five years' age between the perpetrator and the child in order to be classified as pedophilia. The disorder is more common in those who have been sexually abused in their own childhoods. In that subcategory of persons, the perpetrators choose victims in accordance with their own ages at the time of their experiences.

Pedophiles describe themselves as introverted, shy, sensitive, and depressed. Objective **personality** test results tend to confirm these subjective assessments, with the addition **traits** of emotional immaturity and a **fear** of being able to function in mature adult heterosexual relationships. A common characteristic of pedophiles is a moralistic sexual attitude or sexual repression.

Accurate diagnostic studies of prevalence among populations are unreliable for two reasons. First, the tendency may remain latent and undiagnosible unless the person voluntarily seeks counseling or help. Often the condition is masked by feigned responses to diagnostic criteria. Second, there is even among professionals a wide variance in definitional criteria and identification of this disorder.

There are two major professional tools employed to assess and diagnose pedophilia. The first is through phallometric testing (also referred to as penile plethysmographic assessment, or PPG), which measures changes in penile blood volume occurring simultaneously with the presentation of varying erotic stimuli. There has been some criticism of the reliability of this test because physiological changes are easier to measure than interpret. Second, arousal also may be a function of general arousability rather than of specific stimuli. To address this, researchers have developed a second diagnostic tool as a central arousability system intended to work adjunctly with PPG. The contingent negative variation (CNV) system measures **brain** waves as putative indices of sexual desire under conditions of sexual stimulation relevant to pedophilic arousal.

## Treatment

Behavioral treatment of pedophilia does not affect recidivism, nor apparently does incarceration. The condition remains chronic, and for this reason, societal interest in incarceration prevails over what is generally seen as equivocal behavior treatment.

Although most practitioners believe that the **etiology** of pedophilia is psychologically oriented, a report published in the *Journal of Neuro Psychiatry and Clinical Neuroscience* suggested that bilateral anterior temporal disease, affecting more right than left temporal lobe, could increase sexual interest. The authors' study was limited to two adult professional patients with late-life homosexual pedophilia. Therefore, further observation and research is necessary to assess diagnostic and treatment implications for all neurologically based paraphilias.

In late 1999, Israeli researchers published a report on the discovery of the drug triptorelin as an effective treatment for males sex offenders in general. The drug regulates the production of testosterone. Of interest is that it can be injected once a month, compared to other similar anti-androgen drugs, which must be administered more often and have more serious side effects.

### Current trends

The effective diagnosis and treatment of pedophilia is threatened by three key developments going into the new century. The 1994 (Fourth) edition of the professional therapists' bible, the *Diagnostic and Statistical Manual of Mental Disorders (DSM-IV)*, adds another (controversial) criterion for diagnosing pedophilia. It includes, in its diagnostic definitional criteria, that the fantasies, urges, or behaviors "…cause clinically significant distress or impairment in social, occupational, or other important areas of functioning." This latest definitional criterion has met with considerable resistance, due to the fact that so many pedophiles deny that their conduct is harmful. The denial serves to assuage any **guilt**, and therefore may significantly mask or otherwise repress any distress or impairment on the part of the perpetrator.

Secondly, there has been marked pervasiveness and proliferation of child pornographic materials on the Internet and international websites. In a 1998 Interpol raid (the latest data available), a total of 500,000 child pornographic images were found on computers in the United States alone. According to one study, as much as 45 percent of child **pornography** on the Internet comes from Japan, where child pornography is not an offense. The second largest concentration of child pornographic sites come from Russia. The United Nations Educational, Scientific, and Cultural Organization (UNESCO), in cooperation with the Interpol, continue to police global websites and shut down operations.

Another area of controversy was the late 1998 American Psychological Association's publication of a study entitled, "A MetaAnalytic Examination of Assumed Properties of Child **Sexual Abuse** Using College Samples." The study's authors advised practitioners not to assume that sexual activity between non-related adults and children was harmful. The study, which was limited to interviews with college students, further posited that if the involved child/victim consented to the sexual activity, little or no harm was done to the child's adult life or personality. Most of the research in the study had not been subjected to peer review. The study caused an im-

mediate reaction in professional, family, and media entities. On July 12, 1999, the U.S. House of Representatives voted a shut-out 355-0 to condemn the study. As Representative Dave Weldon (R-Fla.) stated to the press, "Children are not capable of giving consent to sexual encounters with adults."

*See also* Paraphilias

Lauri R. Harding

### Further Reading
"A New Treatment for Pedophilia." *Harvard Mental Health Letter*, (October 1999): 7.

D'Agnostino, Joseph. "Pro-Child Advocates Challenge Study Legitimizing Pedophilia." *American Spectator*, (November 1999): 66.

Gahr, Evan. "Psyched Out in Left Field." *American Spectator*, (November 1999): 66.

Ivey, Gavin; and Peta Simpson. "The Psychological Life of Paedophiles: A Phenomenological Study." *South African Journal of Psychology*, (March 1998): 15.

Martin, Ann-Louise. "Paedophilia Online, Off Limits!" *UNESCO Sources*, (February 1999): 21.

Murray, John B. "Psychological Profile of Pedophiles and Child Molesters." *Journal of Psychology Interdisciplinary & Applied*, (March 2000): 211.

Repique, RJR. "Assessment & Treatment of Persons with Pedophilia." *Journal of Psychosocial Nursing and Mental Health Services*, (December 1999).

Tavris, Carol. "The Uproar Over Sexual Abuse Research and Its Findings." *Society*, (May/June 2000): 15.

# Peer acceptance

The degree to which a child or adolescent is socially accepted by peers; the level of peer popularity.

Peer acceptance is measured by the quality rather than the quantity of a child or adolescent's relationships. While the number of friends varies among children and over time as a child develops, peer acceptance is often established as early as preschool. Factors such as physical attractiveness, cultural **traits**, and disabilities **affect** the level of peer acceptance, with a child's degree of **social competence** being the best predictor of peer acceptance. Children who are peer-accepted or popular have fewer problems in middle and high school, and teens who are peer-accepted have fewer emotional and social adjustment problems as adults. Peer-accepted children may be shy or assertive, but they often have well-developed communication skills. Peer-accepted children tend to:

- Correctly interpret other children's body language and tone of voice. Well-liked children can distinguish subtleties in emotions. For example, they can distinguish between **anger** directed toward them versus toward a parent.

- Directly respond to the statements and gestures of other children. Well-liked children will say other children's names, establish eye contact, and use **touch** to get **attention**.

- Give reasons for their own statements and gestures (actions). For example, well-liked children will explain why they want to do something the other child does not want to do.

- Cooperate with, show tact towards, and compromise with other children, demonstrating the willingness to subordinate the self by modifying behavior and opinions in the interests of others. For example, when joining a new group where a conversation is already in progress, well-liked children will listen first, establishing a tentative presence in the group before speaking (even if it is to change the subject).

These skills are crucial in initiating and maintaining relationships, and in resolving conflicts. By **contrast**, rejected children tend either towards aggressive, **antisocial behavior**, or withdrawn, depressive behavior. They also don't listen well, tend not to offer reasons for their behavior, don't positively reinforce their peers, and have trouble cooperating. Antisocial children will interrupt people, dominate other children, and either verbally or physically attack them. Depressive or withdrawn children may be excessively reserved, submissive, anxious, and inhibited. Competitiveness or dominance by itself is not necessarily indicative of low peer acceptance. In fact, popular children tend to have the characteristics of both competitiveness and friendliness.

Although biological predisposition may be a factor in a child's social competence and level of peer acceptance, environmental factors are also extremely important. Some of the factors contributing to peer acceptance include (1) during **infancy**, the quality of **attachment** between mother or primary caregiver and child; (2) during **childhood**, the quantity and quality of opportunities for interaction with different types of peers in different environments (in the **family**, at school, church, camp, activity centers, in sports, or in the neighborhood); (3) the type of parenting style. A highly nurturant but moderately controlling "authoritative" parenting style is associated with the highest levels of social competence. By contrast, a low nurturant, highly controlling "authoritarian" parenting style is associated with children's aggressiveness, while the high nurturant but low-controlling "permissive" style is associated with failure to take responsibility for behavior.

Children learn to relate to peers by engaging in peer relationships. Often a vicious circle develops where a rejected child is given fewer and fewer opportunities by his peers to relate and thereby learn new skills. Lack of opportunity to participate normally in peer interaction is especially problematic for children who differ in some obvious way, either culturally, racially, or through some mental or physical **disability**. Issues of peer acceptance should be addressed as early as possible in order to prevent loss of self-confidence and **self-esteem**.

In addition to providing direct social skills training or counseling for the child with peer acceptance problems, parents and teachers can create opportunities for non-threatening social interaction to occur. Though children should never be forced to **play** together (this can create the rejection it is intended to remedy), popular and less-popular preschoolers can be encouraged to interact with one another. For example, a less sociable child may be encouraged to answer and ask questions of others. Older children should be provided opportunities to interact in smaller groups and in one-on-one situations, where it may be easier to try out new behaviors and make up for social mistakes. Shy or withdrawn children can be encouraged to develop outside interests that will place them in structured contact with others. In school, peer helping programs and collaborative learning provide opportunities for popular and less-popular children to work together. Ideally, collaboration should highlight the less-popular students' strengths, such as special interests and talents, rather than weaknesses. At any age, the smallest positive change in behavior should be reinforced with attention and praise.

## Further Reading

Asher, S. R., and J. D. Coie, eds. *Peer Rejection in Childhood.* New York: Cambridge University Press, 1990.

Goleman, Daniel. *Emotional Intelligence.* New York: Bantam Books, 1995.

Ramsey, P.G. *Making Friends in School: Promoting Peer Relationships in Early Childhood.* New York: Teacher's College Press, 1991.

Selman, R. *The Growth of Interpersonal Understanding.* New York: Academic Press, 1980.

# Peer mediation

A process by which students act as mediators to resolve disputes among themselves. A form of conflict resolution used to address student disagreements and low-level disciplinary problems in schools.

Peer mediation is a form of **conflict resolution** based on integrative negotiation and mediation. Disputing parties converse with the goal of finding a mutually satisfying solution to their disagreement, and a neutral third party facilitates the resolution process. The salient feature of peer mediation as opposed to traditional discipline measures and other forms of conflict resolution is that, outside of the initial training and ongoing support services for students, the mediation process is entirely carried out by students and for students. Due to the rise of **violence** in schools, the sharp increase in serious crime committed by youths, and the increasing awareness of the need for social skills instruction in education, peer mediation programs exploded in the 1980s. In 1984, when the National Association for Mediation in Education (NAME) was formed, there were about 50 mediation programs in school districts nationwide. Eleven years later NAME reported over 5,000 programs across the country. Peer mediation programs that have gained national stature include the early Educators for Social Responsibility program, San Francisco's Community Board program, New York's School Mediators Alternative Resolution Team (SMART), and New Mexico's Center for Dispute Resolution.

### Purposes of peer mediation

In accordance with the principles of conflict resolution, peer mediation programs start with the assumption that conflict is a natural part of life that should neither be avoided nor allowed to escalate into verbal or physical violence. Equally important is the idea that children and adolescents need a venue in which they are allowed to practically apply the conflict resolution skills they are taught. Peer mediation programs vary widely in their scope and function within a school or system. In some schools, mediation is offered as an alternative to traditional disciplinary measures for low-level disruptive behavior. For example, students who swear at each other or initiate fights might agree to participate in mediation rather than being referred to the playground supervisor or principal. In other schools, mediation takes place in addition to disciplinary measures. In either case, peer mediation is intended to prevent the escalation of conflict. Serious violations of rules or violent attacks are not usually addressed through mediation.

Although peer mediation is primarily carried out by students, at least a few staff members and teachers are actively involved in training and facilitation. Ideally, peer mediation will encourage a culture of open communication and peaceful solutions to conflict. According to the NAME, five of the most common purposes of a school mediation program are:

1. to increase communication among students, teachers, administrators, and parents.

## PEER MEDIATION PROCESS

The process varies, but most programs use the following general format:

I. Introduction—The mediator introduces him or herself and explains the rules. The mediator tries to make the disputants feel comfortable.

II. Identifying the Problem—The mediator listens to each party describe the problem and writes down an agreed-upon "agenda" that includes all the elements of a dispute.

III. Identifying Facts and Feelings—The disputants tell their sides of the story to each other. The goal is to "surface" all of the underlying facts and feelings pertaining to the problem. The mediator asks many questions with the goal of helping to refocus the problem by viewing it differently.

IV. Generating Options—The mediator asks both parties to brainstorm how they might solve the problem. The mediator writes down all the solutions, marking the ones that are mutually agreed upon. If none are forthcoming, participants return to previous steps. Sometimes, individual sessions with each disputant and the mediator are necessary.

V. Agreement—The mediator writes a contract using the solutions to which both parties agree, and everyone signs it.

VI. Follow-Up—After a period of time the former disputants will report back to the mediator on whether the contract is being upheld by both parties.

2. to reduce school violence, vandalism, and suspensions.

3. to encourage children, adolescents, and teens to resolve their own disputes by developing listening, critical thinking, and problem-solving skills.

4. to teach peaceful resolution of differences, a skill needed to live in a multicultural world.

5. to motivate students' interest in conflict resolution, justice, and the American legal system, and encourage active citizenship.

### Training of peer mediators

Programs vary in whether they train all the students in the school to act as mediators, or only as a "cadre" of selected students. The cadre approach may be used initially with the intention of expanding later. Mediators either volunteer or are nominated by teachers or other students;

often, students who are "troublemakers" turn out to be the best mediators. Many programs have a required conflict resolution course sometime during the middle school years. Training is done by teachers, counseling staff, or outside consultants, and ranges from the semester-long course (15-20 hours of training), to a two-day workshop for middle or high school students, to a three-hour workshop for elementary students. Through discussion and role play, students learn conflict resolution skills such as active listening, cooperation in achieving a goal, acceptance of differences, problem-solving, **anger** management, and methods of maintaining neutrality as a mediator. They also practice the structured mediation process they will be following in actual dispute resolution.

### The mediation session

Elementary mediators usually work in teams, visiting designated school areas and responding to signs of antagonism between students as they arise. They will approach the disputants, ask if they need help, and take them aside for mediation, if the students agree. Middle and high school programs may employ resident mediators in the cafeteria or public areas, using a more formal procedure for students to refer themselves or others for mediation. There is usually a separate mediation room or rooms set up to facilitate private communication among the disputants and the mediator.

It is essential that disputants voluntarily agree to participate in mediation, and ground rules for the process prohibit name-calling or interrupting someone who is talking.

### Success of peer mediation programs

It is difficult to measure the success of peer mediation programs. Almost all teachers and administrators report that their programs are extremely successful, and that they perceive a more positive climate and see less destructive behavior in the school. When measuring success in reaching or maintaining agreement between disputants, rates vary between 58-93%. A few studies show reductions in suspension rates, suspension rates for fighting, or incidence of fighting by as much as 50%. Even elementary students learn and retain the knowledge of conflict resolution techniques, and those who participate in mediation, either as mediators or as disputants, benefit from the experience. The NAME found that peer mediation programs reduce the amount of teacher and administrator time spent on discipline, reduce violence and crime in schools, and increase the **self-esteem** and academic achievement of students trained as mediators.

One critical factor in the success of peer mediation programs is the active support of the school principal, and in some cases of the local community. A comprehensive planning process is necessary to outline goals and administrative accountability for each phase of the program. Provision for the ongoing support of the peer mediators is especially important. At minimum, a weekly meeting should be held for the students to debrief, engage in guided reflection, and receive continued training.

One of the reasons for the success of peer mediation is the fact that it is student run. Children and adolescents build a culture of positive **peer pressure** within which they can begin to establish independence from adult guidance. When given the opportunity, they are capable of using their own judgment to creatively solve disputes, and often their solutions are less punitive than those of adults. Research shows that children's solutions to conflict are more aggressive when adults are present. As children grow older they rely increasingly on their peers as models and measures of correct behavior. The potential judgment of peers during the mediation process may have a higher degree of moral significance to a teen than would the same judgment coming from an adult. In peer mediation, students have the opportunity to conform to positive social standards without sacrificing their identification with the peer group.

*See also* Conflict resolution

### Further Reading

Ferrara, Judith M. *Peer Mediation: Finding a Way to Care.* York, ME: Stenhouse Publishing, 1996.

Robertson, Gwendolyn. *School-Based Peer Mediation Programs: A Natural Extension of Developmental Guidance Programs.* Gorham, ME: University of Southern Maine, 1991.

Sorenson, Don L. *Conflict Resolution and Mediation for Peer Helpers.* Minneapolis, MN: Educational Media Corporation, 1992.

Wolowiec, Jack, ed. *Everybody Wins: Mediation in the Schools,* Chicago: American Bar Association, 1994.

### Further Information

American Bar Association. Special Committee on Dispute Resolution, 1800 M Street, NW, Washington, DC 20036.

Educators for Social Responsibility. 475 Riverside Drive, Room 450, New York, NY 10115.

National Association for Mediation in Education (NAME). 205 Hampshire House, Box 33635, University of Massachusetts, Amherst, MA 01003–3635, (413) 545–2462.

School Initiatives Program. Community Board Center for Policy and Training, 149 Ninth Street, San Francisco, CA 94103.

School Mediation Associates. 702 Green Street #8, Cambridge, MA 02139.

# Peer pressure

*The influence of the social group on an individual.*

Peers are the individuals with whom a child or adolescent identifies, who are usually but not always of the same age-group. Peer pressure occurs when the individual experiences implicit or explicit persuasion, sometimes amounting to coercion, to adopt similar values, beliefs, and goals, or to participate in the same activities as those in the peer group.

Although it is usually conceived of as primarily a negative influence acting on adolescents or teens, peer pressure can be a positive influence as well, and it can act on children at any age, depending on their level of contact with others. The influence of peer pressure is usually addressed in relation to the relative influence of the **family** on an individual. Some characteristics that peer groups offer and which families may be lacking are: (1) a strong belief structure; (2) a clear system of rules; and (3) communication and discussion about taboo subjects such as drugs, sex, and religion.

Peer pressure is strongly associated with level of academic success, drug and substance use, and gender role **conformity**. The level of peer influence increases with age, and resistance to peer influence often declines as the child gains independence from the family or caretakers, yet has not fully formed an autonomous identity. One study in particular confirms other research findings that the values of the peer group with whom the high schooler spends the most time are a stronger factor in the student's level of academic success than the values, attitudes, and support provided by the family. Compared to others who started high school with the same grades, students whose families were not especially supportive but who spent time with an academically oriented peer group were successful, while those students whose families stressed academics but who spent time with peers whose orientation was not academic performed less well.

The peer pressure study contradicts prevailing ideas about the influence of families on the success of racial and cultural minorities such as Asians and African Americans. While some Asian families were not especially involved in their children's education, the students, who found little social support of any type, tended to band together in academic study groups. Conversely, African American students, whose families tended to be highly involved in and supportive of education, were subjected to intense peer pressure not to perform academically. According to the study, the African American peer groups associated the activities of studying and spending time at the library with "white" behavior, and adopted the idea that the student who gets good grades, participates in school activities, or speaks Standard English is betraying his racial heritage and community. Consequently, gifted students "dumb-down" as they make the choice between academics and "fitting in." Research suggests that this type of peer pressure contributes to a decline in the grades of African American students (especially males) as early as the first through fourth grades.

Peer pressure similarly compels students of all ethnic backgrounds to engage in other at-risk behaviors such as cigarette smoking, truancy, drug use, sexual activity, fighting, theft, and daredevil stunts. Again, peer group values and attitudes influence, more strongly than do family values, the level of teenage alcohol use. Regardless of the parenting style, peer pressure also influences the degree to which children, especially girls, conform to expected gender roles. Up until about grade six, girls' performance in science and math are on par with that of boys, but during **adolescence** girls' test scores and level of expressed interest declines. The tendency is to abandon **competition** with boys in favor of placing more emphasis on relationships and on physical appearance.

Ideally the child, adolescent, or teen should make decisions based on a combination of values internalized from the family, values derived from thinking independently, and values derived from friends and other role models. In order to achieve this balance, rather than attempting to minimize peer influence, families and schools must provide strong alternative beliefs, patterns of behavior, and encourage formation of peer groups that engage in positive academic, athletic, artistic, and social activities.

Hallie Bourne

## Further Reading

Bernard, B. *The Case for Peers.* Portland, OR: Northwest Regional Educational Laboratory, 1990.

Feller, Robyn M. *Everything You Need to Know About Peer Pressure.* New York: Rosen Publishing Group, 1995.

Juvonen, Jaana, and Kathryn R. Wentzel, eds. *Social Motivation: Understanding Children's School Adjustment.* New York: Cambridge University Press, 1996.

Myrick, R.D. and D.L. Sorenson. *Peer Helping: A Practical Guide.* Minneapolis, MN: Educational Media Corporation, 1988.

# Wilder Graves Penfield

## 1891-1976

American-born Canadian neurosurgeon who diagnosed the cause of epilepsy and perfected a surgical cure.

**Wilder G. Penfield and his wife.** *(The Library of Congress. Reproduced with permission.)*

Wilder Graves Penfield was born in Spokane, Washington, on January 26, 1891. He was one of three children born to Charles Samuel and Jean (Jefferson) Penfield. His father was a physician and died when Penfield was very young. To support herself and her **family**, Penfield's mother became a writer and Bible teacher. Penfield spent his early years at the Galahad School in Hudson, Wisconsin, where his mother worked as a housekeeper.

Upon graduation in 1909, Penfield was accepted at Princeton University. He was active in extra-curricular activities and became president of his class. He was so good at football, that upon graduation in 1913, he was hired as a coach. After graduation from Princeton with a degree in literature, Penfield held a Rhodes scholarship and a Beit Memorial Research fellowship at Oxford University, where he studied with Sir William Osler and Sir Charles Scott Sherrington. He married Helen Katherine Kermott in 1917 and eventually raised four children. Penfield received his medical degree from Johns Hopkins University in Baltimore in 1918. He worked in

Sherrington's research laboratory at Oxford from 1919 to 1921.

Penfield returned to the United States in 1918 to receive training in general surgery and neurosurgery in New York City. In 1924 he founded the Laboratory of Neurocytology at Presbyterian Hospital, Columbia University, and worked there as associate attending surgeon from 1921 to 1928. In 1928 he was appointed neurosurgeon to the Royal Victoria Hospital and the Montreal General Hospital. It was here that he perfected his surgical operation for severe **epilepsy**. He had learned, perfected, and adapted the many techniques used in this operation from visits to Europe he had made while at Montreal.

The results of one of these operations in 1931 gave Penfield the idea to write a general textbook regarding neurosurgery. Instead of writing it all himself, he decided to ask other specialists in this field to contribute to the book. The resulting book, *Cytology and Cellular Pathology of the Nervous System* (1932), turned into a three volume discussion of neurology. The collaboration that had produced the book gave Penfield the idea to create an institute furthered by the same cooperative techniques. He established the Montreal Neurological Institute on this idea and became its first director in 1934, holding this post until 1960. He was a professor of neurology and neurosurgery at McGill University from 1933 to 1954.

Penfield became a naturalized Canadian citizen in 1934 and served as a colonel in the Royal Canadian Army Medical Corps from 1945 to 1946. He headed many wartime projects including investigating motion sickness, decompression sickness, and air transportation of persons with head injuries. Penfield's wartime experiences supplied two books; *Manual of Military Neurosurgery* (1941) and *Epilepsy and Cerebral Localization* (1941).

After the war he continued his studies on epilepsy by undertaking a study of the removal of **brain** scars resulting from birth injuries. He was a fellow of the Royal Society of London and of the Royal Society of Canada and received the Order of Merit from Queen Elizabeth (1953). He also received numerous scientific awards and lectureships. He helped found the Vanier Institute of the Family and served as its first president (1965-1968).

After his retirement from the Montreal Neurological Institute in 1960, Penfield set out on what he called his "second career" of writing and lecturing around the world. Not one to take to retirement easily, Penfield said "…rest is not what the brain needs. Rest destroys the brain." He traveled abroad many times during this period and even lectured in China and Russia.

Penfield published *The Difficult Art of Giving, The Epic of Alan Gregg* (1967), a biography of the Rockefeller Foundation and the director who had approved the $1.2 million grant for the founding of the Montreal Neurological Institute, during this period. *Second Thoughts; Science, the Arts and the Spirit* (1970) and *The Mystery of the Mind: A Critical Study of Conscience and the Human Brain* (1975) were also published as he lectured around the world. Penfield finished his final work, the autobiographical *No Man Alone: A Surgeons Story,* just three weeks before his death from abdominal cancer in Montreal's Royal Victoria Hospital on April 5, 1976. This work was published posthumously in 1977 and was a fitting tribute to a man who was remembered by his friends and colleagues as one who always thought of his discoveries as just "exciting beginnings."

## Medical research

Penfield chose epilepsy as his special interest and approached the study of brain function through an intensive study of people suffering from this condition. In choosing this approach, he was influenced by Sherrington and by John Hughlings Jackson, a British neurologist who viewed epilepsy as "an experiment of nature," which may reveal the functional organization of the human brain. To this study Penfield brought the modern techniques of neurosurgery—which allow the surgeon to study the exposed brain of the conscious patient under local anesthesia—while using electrical methods for stimulating and recording from the cortex and from deeper structures. The patient is able to cooperate fully in describing the results of cortical stimulation. By this surgical method it is possible in some patients to localize and remove a brain lesion responsible for epileptic attacks. Penfield used this approach primarily for the treatment of focal epilepsy. His pioneer work yielded impressive results, and his techniques for the surgical treatment of epilepsy became standard procedure in neurosurgery.

## Writings and theories

Penfield's *The Cerebral Cortex of Man* (1950) summarizes the results of mapping the principal motor and sensory areas of the cortex, including the delineation of a new "supplementary motor area" and a "second sensory area." The results of temporal lobe stimulation are described in *Epilepsy and the Functional Anatomy of the Human Brain* (1954), and his remarkable observations on temporal lobe epilepsy are also recorded there. Penfield also defined four areas of the cortex concerned with human speech function and described them in *Speech and Brain-Mechanisms.*

Penfield was convinced that the brain of man—including all cortical areas—is controlled and "organized" through a group of subcortical centers. These centers lie within the upper brainstem and include the **thalamus**. For this functionally important area he coined the term "centrencephalon," and his view may be described as a "centrencephalic" theory of cerebral organization. In his view **consciousness**, self-awareness, depends upon the integrating action of this subcortical system, which in some way, as yet unknown, unites the brain into a single functioning organ. There is much evidence for such a theory, and Penfield developed it in his Sherrington Lectures, *The Excitable Cortex in Conscious Man* (1958).

### Further Reading

*Current Biography Yearbook.* New York: H.W. Wilson Co., 1968. *Current Biography Yearbook.* New York: H.W. Wilson Co., 1976.
Fulton, John F. and Leonard G. Wilson, eds. *Selected readings in the history of physiology.* 1930. 2nd ed. 1966.
Granit, Ragnar. *Charles Scott Sherrington: an appraisal.* 1967.
Obituary. *New York Times.* April 6, 1976.
Penfield, Wilder Graves. *No man alone: a surgeon's story.* 1977.
Penfield, Wilder Graves. *McGraw-Hill modern men of science.* 1966.

## Perception

The area of psychology associated with the functioning of sensory systems and how information from the external world is interpreted.

Psychologists have identified two general ways in which humans perceive their **environment**. One involves what is called "top-down" processing. In this **mode**, what is perceived depends on such factors as expectations and knowledge. That is, sensory events are interpreted based on a combination of what occurs in the external world and on existing thoughts, experience, and expectations. When a perception is based on what is expected, it is called a perceptual set, a predisposition to experience an event in a particular way. One example of such a predisposition involves **hearing** potentially disturbing words or phrases when rock music is played backwards. Although most people will not detect such words or phrases when they first listen to the backward sounds (when they do not have a perceptual set), these same people will hear them quite clearly if they are then told what to listen for. Psychologists regard this process as involving a perceptual set because perception of the distressing message does not occur until the individual is primed to hear it.

**Motivation** can also influence the way an event is perceived. At sporting events, the same episode can be interpreted in exactly opposite ways by fans of two different teams. In this instance, people are interpreting the episode with what they regard as an open mind, but their subjectivity colors their perceptions. The alternate approach is "bottom-up" processing that relies less on what is already known or expected and more on the nature of the external stimulus. If there are no preconceived notions of what to expect, cues present in the stimulus are used to a greater extent. One part of this process is called feature analysis, which involves taking the elementary cues in a situation and attempting to put them together to create a meaningful stimulus. When children listen to an initially unfamiliar set of sounds, like the "Pledge of Allegiance," they often hear words and phrases that adults (who use top-down processing) do not hear. Thus, the phrase "one nation indivisible," may be heard by a child as "one naked individual." The child has heard the correct number of syllables, some key sounds, and the rhythm of the phrase, but too many features are unclear, resulting in an inaccurate perception. In general, many psychologists have concluded that perceptual abilities rely both on external stimuli and on expectation and knowledge.

Much of the research in perception has involved **vision** for two general reasons. First, psychologists recognize that these this sense dominates much of human perception and, second, it is easier to study than audition ( hearing) or the minor senses like **taste**, **smell**, **touch**, and balance. Other perceptual research has investigated the way people pay attention to the world around them and learn to ignore information that is irrelevant to their needs at any given moment.

Within the realm of vision, several areas have especially captured the attention of psychologists: **depth perception**, form perception, perceptual constancy, and perceptual organization. When a visual scene contains information that includes conflicting information about depth, form, and organization, the result is a visual illusion, commonly referred to as an optical illusion. Such illusions can occur when there is too little information available to generate an accurate interpretation of the stimulus; when experience leads to the formulation of a specific interpretation; or when the sensory systems process information in a consistent, but inaccurate, fashion. Illusions are completely normal, unlike delusions that may reflect abnormal psychological processes.

Another aspect of perception that psychologists have studied intensively is attention. Often, people can selectively attend to different aspects of their world and tune others out. In a loud, crowded room, for example, a person can understand a single speaker by turning his or her attention to the location of the speaker and concentrating on the frequency (pitch) of the speaker's voice; the individual can also use the meaning of the conversation to help in concentration and to ignore irrelevant speech. In some cases, however, we seem incapable of

ignoring information. One common example is the "cocktail party phenomenon." If something is holding our attention but an individual within earshot speaks our name, our attention is quickly diverted to that individual. When we perceive a stimulus that is important to us (like our name), our attention switches. One famous example that involves an inability to ignore information is the Stroop effect. If words are printed in colored ink, it is normally an easy task to name the color of the ink. If the words are color names, however, (e.g., "RED") that appear in a different ink color (e.g., the word "RED" in green ink), we have difficulty naming the ink color because we tend to read the word instead of paying attention to the ink color. This process seems entirely automatic in proficient readers.

Research on the perceptual capabilities of young children is more difficult because of insufficient communication skills. At birth, infants can see objects clearly only when those objects are about eight inches (20 cm) from the eye, but distance vision improves within the first month. Infants also exhibit depth perception and appear to have some **color vision**. Similarly, infants can detect speech sounds shortly after birth and can locate the origin of sounds in the environment, as is smell and taste. Within a few days following birth, breast-fed babies can differentiate their own mother's milk from that of another mother, and also prefer odors that adults like and respond more negatively to the types of odors adults do not like.

## Further Reading

Chapman, Elwood N. *Attitude: Your Most Priceless Possession.* 2nd ed. Los Altos, CA: Crisp Publications, 1990.
Eiser, J. Richard. *Social Psychology: Attitudes, Cognition, and Social Behaviour.* New York: Cambridge University Press, 1986.

# Perfectionism

The tendency to set unrealistically high standards for performance of oneself and others, along with the inability to accept mistakes or imperfections in matters of personal appearance, care of the home, or work; may be accompanied by an obsession with completeness, purity, or goodness.

Perfectionism is a psychological orientation which, depending on the severity, may have biological and/or environmental causes. To an educated observer, a perfectionist orientation is usually evident by the preschool years, though it may not cause problems until the college years. The perfectionist orientation has two components: impossibly high standards, and the behaviors intended to help achieve the standards and avoid mistakes. The high standards interfere with performance, and perfectionist behavior becomes an obstacle instead of a means to achieving the goal. For example, when a five-year-old who is learning to write repeatedly erases his lines because they are not exactly straight, he is exhibiting a perfectionistic tendency.

Due to obsessive effort and high standards of performance combined with natural gifts, perfectionists may be athletic, musical, academic, or social achievers, but they may equally as often be underachievers. Perfectionists engage in dichotomous thinking, believing that there is only one right outcome and one way to achieve that outcome. Dichotomous thinking causes indecisiveness, since according to the individual's **perception** a decision, once made, will be either entirely right or entirely wrong. Due to their exacting precision, they take an excessive amount of time to perform tasks. Even small tasks become overwhelming, which leads to frustration, procrastination, and further anxiety caused by time constraints.

Perfectionists also pay selective **attention** to their own achievements, criticizing themselves for mistakes or failures, and downplaying their successes. Overwhelmed by anxiety about their future performance, they are unable to enjoy successes.

Perfectionist anxiety can cause headaches, digestive problems, muscle tension, and heart and vascular problems. Anxiety can also cause "blanking" or temporary **memory** losses before events such as musical performances or academic exams. Perfectionists also hesitate to try new activities for **fear** of being a beginner at an activity, even for a short period of time. Negative effects of perfectionism are felt especially when an individual is a perfectionist in all areas of life, rather than in one realm, such as an artistic or scientific pursuit, which might allow room for mistakes in other areas of life.

In extreme forms perfectionism may contribute to **depression** or be diagnosed as obsessive-compulsive **personality** disorder (which should be distinguished from the more serious **obsessive-compulsive disorder**). The more common syndromes of **anorexia** nervosa and **bulimia** can be considered an extreme form of perfectionism directed towards the body and its appearance. The irrational distortions of perception that can arise from abnormally high standards of "performance" (i.e., thinness) are evident in the anorexic's perception of her or himself as fat.

Perfectionist behavior functions essentially to control events. Conditions that place the person in a position of vulnerability and/or that require the person to take extra responsibility for events can contribute to perfectionism. First-born children, children with excessively critical parents, and children who have lost a parent or sibling all may be predisposed towards perfectionism.

## Further Reading

Adderholdt-Elliott, M.R. *Perfectionism: What's Bad About Being Too Good*. Minneapolis: Free Spirit, 1987.

Mallinger, A.E. and J. DeWyze. *Too Perfect: When Being in Control Gets Out of Control*. NY: Random House, 1993.

Manes, S. *Be a Perfect Person in Just Three Days*. New York: Bantam/Skylark Books, 1987.

Zadra, D. *Mistakes Are Great*. Mankato, MN: Creative Education, 1986.

# Frederick S. Perls

### 1893-1970
German-American psychotherapist who co-founded Gestalt therapy.

Frederick S. Perls, known to his friends and colleagues as Fritz, was the co-founder with his wife Laura (1905-1990) of the Gestalt school of **psychotherapy**. Trained as a Freudian, Perls felt that Freud's ideas had limitations, in part because they focused on past experiences. One of the key elements of Gestalt therapy is its focus on what Perls called the "here and now." During the 1960s, Gestalt therapy gained a reputation as yet another of the "feel-good" therapeutic techniques then so common. Today, Gestalt is recognized as one of several standard approaches (often part of what is called an "eclectic" approach) to modern therapy.

Perls was born in Berlin in 1893 into a middle class **family**. He was a bright student, but his interest in science did not emerge until after he enrolled in college in 1913. Before that he had been interested in the theater. He toyed briefly with the idea of studying law but settled on medicine.

The First World War interrupted his college years. He served until the war ended in 1918, then continued his medical studies. He received his M.D. in 1921 By this time he had decided that he wanted to focus on psychiatry. Perls was an admirer and follower of **Sigmund Freud** and his psychoanalytic techniques. At the same time, he was becoming more and more intrigued by **Gestalt psychology**.

The English language has no equivalent word for "Gestalt," but it is commonly translated as "pattern" or "form." Gestalt psychology states, in simplest terms, that the whole is greater than the sum of its parts. In other words, in order to understand the various components of a particular issue or event, one must understand the event itself and put the components in perspective. In the

1920s and 1930s, Perls began to move away from the classic Freudian model and create a more holistic approach to therapy. In the meantime, he continued his education in psychotherapy in Berlin, Vienna, and Frankfurt. While studying in Frankfurt, he met his future wife; they married in 1930 and later had two children.

## Formulates concept of Gestalt therapy

Germany in the 1920s and early 1930s was a magnet for avant-garde intellectuals, and both Fritz and Laura Perls met many. Unfortunately, the rise of Hitler quickly changed the course of German intellectual life. The Perls family left Germany in 1934, settling in Johannesburg, South Africa. Over the next several years, Fritz and Laura Perls developed the ideas that would become Gestalt psychotherapy. Perls wrote his first book, *Ego, Hunger, and Aggression,* while in South Africa. It generated limited interest; it was republished in England in 1946 but still attracted less interest than Perls had hoped.

It should be understood that Perls did not abandon Freud's teachings in developing Gestalt therapy. Rather, he modified some of Freud's theories to create what he called a more holistic approach. In particular, he focused on present influences and experience, unlike strict Freudians, who relied on analyzing a patient's past experiences going back to early **childhood**.

In 1946, the Perls family moved briefly to Canada and then the United States. Fritz and Laura Perls continued their work on Gestalt therapy, and Fritz Perls co-wrote a book with Paul Goodman and Robert Hefferline. The book, *Gestalt Therapy,* was published in 1951. It was initially not taken seriously by the Gestalt psychology movement. In the ensuing years, however, it attracted a greater following. Meanwhile, Perls spent his time lecturing and opening institutes where he could train Gestalt therapists. Among the schools he founded was the New York Institute for Gestalt Therapy, which was run by Laura Perls.

## Joins Esalen Institute

In 1964, Perls became resident psychiatrist at the Esalen Institute in Big Sur, California. There he organized and conducted "dream workshops," in which participants would discuss their **dreams** and engage in role-playing exercises based on the characters (and sometimes objects) in their dreams. In the ensuing years he continued to open new institutes around the country and conduct Gestalt workshops. By this time Perls sported a long white beard and a flowing white mane—resembling to some a member of the counterculture that was to define the 1960s.

Perls later moved to an island off the coast of Vancouver, British Columbia, where in 1970 he started a training community for Gestalt therapists. In March 1970, shortly after conducting a workshop in Lexington, Massachusetts, Perls underwent surgery in Chicago. He suffered heart failure and died there on March 10 at the age of 76.

George A. Milite

## Further Reading

Perls, Frederick S. *Ego, hunger, and aggression: a revision of Freud's theory and method.* London: Allen and Unwin, 1947.
Perls, Frederick S., Paul Goodman, and Robert Hefferline. *Gestalt therapy: excitement and growth in the human personality.* New York: Julian Press, 1951.

# Personality

The unique pattern of psychological and behavioral characteristics by which each person can be distinguished from other people.

Personality is fundamental to the study of psychology. The major systems evolved by psychiatrists and psychologists since **Sigmund Freud** to explain human mental and behavioral processes can be considered theories of personality. These theories generally provide ways of describing personal characteristics and behavior, establish an overall framework for organizing a wide range of information, and address such issues as individual differences, **personality development** from **birth** through adulthood, and the causes, nature, and treatment of psychological disorders.

## Type theory of personality

Perhaps the earliest known theory of personality is that of the Greek physician Hippocrates (c. 400 B.C.), who characterized human behavior in terms of four temperaments, each associated with a different bodily fluid, or "humor." The sanguine, or optimistic, type was associated with blood; the phlegmatic type (slow and lethargic) with phlegm; the melancholic type (sad, depressed) with black bile; and the choleric (angry) type with yellow bile. Individual personality was determined by the amount of each of the four humors. Hippocrates' system remained influential in Western Europe throughout the medieval and Renaissance periods. Abundant references to the four humors can be found in the plays of Shakespeare, and the terms with which Hippocrates labeled the four personality types are still in common use today. The theory of temperaments is among a variety of systems that deal with human personality by dividing it into types. A widely popularized (but scientifically dubious) modern typology of personality was developed in the 1940s by **William Sheldon**, an American psychologist. Sheldon classified personality into three categories based on body types: the endomorph (heavy and easy-going), mesomorph (muscular and aggressive), and ectomorph (thin and intellectual or artistic).

## Trait theory of personality

A major weakness of Sheldon's morphological classification system and other type theories in general is the element of oversimplification inherent in placing individuals into a single category, which ignores the fact that every personality represents a unique combination of qualities. Systems that address personality as a combination of qualities or dimensions are called trait theories. Well-known trait theorist **Gordon Allport** (1897-1967) extensively investigated the ways in which **traits** combine to form normal personalities, cataloguing over 18,000 separate traits over a period of 30 years. He proposed that each person has about seven central traits that dominate his or her behavior. Allport's attempt to make trait analysis more manageable and useful by simplifying it was expanded by subsequent researchers, who found ways to group traits into clusters through a process known as factor analysis. Raymond B. Cattell reduced Allport's extensive list to 16 fundamental groups of inter-related characteristics, and **Hans Eysenck** claimed that personality could be described based on three fundamental factors: psychoticism (such antisocial traits as cruelty and rejection of social customs), introversion-extroversion, and emotionality-stability (also called neuroticism). Eysenck also formulated a quadrant based on intersecting emotional-stable and introverted-extroverted axes.

## Psychodynamic theory of personality

Twentieth-century views on personality have been heavily influenced by the psychodynamic approach of Sigmund Freud . Freud proposed a three-part personality structure consisting of the **id** (concerned with the gratification of basic instincts), the **ego** (which mediates between the demands of the id and the constraints of society), and the **superego** (through which parental and social values are internalized). In contrast to type or trait theories of personality, the dynamic model proposed by Freud involved an ongoing element of conflict, and it was these conflicts that Freud saw as the primary determinant of personality. His psychoanalytic method was designed to help patients resolve their conflicts by ex-

ploring **unconscious** thoughts, motivations, and conflicts through the use of **free association** and other techniques. Another distinctive feature of Freudian **psychoanalysis** is its emphasis on the importance of **childhood** experiences in personality formation. Other psychodynamic models were later developed by colleagues and followers of Freud, including **Carl Jung**, **Alfred Adler**, and **Otto Rank** (1884-1939), as well as other neo-Freudians such as **Erich Fromm**, **Karen Horney**, Harry Stack Sullivan (1892-1949), and **Erik Erikson**.

## Phenomenological theory of personality

Another major view of personality developed during the twentieth century is the phenomenological approach, which emphasizes people's self- perceptions and their drive for **self-actualization** as determinants of personality. This optimistic orientation holds that people are innately inclined toward goodness, love, and **creativity** and that the primary natural **motivation** is the drive to fulfill one's potential. **Carl Rogers**, the figure whose name is most closely associated with phenomenological theories of personality, viewed authentic experience of one's self as the basic component of growth and well-being. This experience together with one's **self-concept** can become distorted when other people make the positive regard we need dependent on conditions that require the suppression of our true feelings. The **client-centered therapy** developed by Rogers relies on the therapist's continuous demonstration of **empathy** and unconditional positive regard to give clients the self-confidence to express and act on their true feelings and beliefs. Another prominent exponent of the phenomenological approach was **Abraham Maslow**, who placed self-actualization at the top of his hierarchy of human needs. Maslow focused on the need to replace a deficiency orientation, which consists of focusing on what one does not have, with a growth orientation based on satisfaction with one's identity and capabilities.

## Behavioral theory of personality

The behaviorist approach views personality as a pattern of learned behaviors acquired through either classical (Pavlovian) or operant (Skinnerian) **conditioning** and shaped by **reinforcement** in the form of rewards or **punishment**. A relatively recent extension of **behaviorism**, the cognitive-behavioral approach emphasizes the role **cognition** plays in the learning process. Cognitive and social learning theorists focus not only on the outward behaviors people demonstrate but also on their expectations and their thoughts about others, themselves, and their own behavior. For example, one variable in the general theory of personality developed by social learning theorist Julian B. Rotter is internal-external orientation. "Internals" think of themselves as controlling events, while "externals" view events as largely outside their control. Like phenomenological theorists, those who take a social learning approach also emphasize people's perceptions of themselves and their abilities (a concept called "self-efficacy" by **Albert Bandura**). Another characteristic that sets the cognitive-behavioral approach apart from traditional forms of behaviorism is its focus on learning that takes place in social situations through observation and reinforcement, which contrasts with the dependence of classical and **operant conditioning** models on laboratory research.

Aside from theories about personality structure and dynamics, a major area of investigation in the study of personality is how it develops in the course of a person's lifetime. The Freudian approach includes an extensive description of psychosexual development from birth up to adulthood. Erik Erikson outlined eight stages of development spanning the entire human lifetime, from birth to death. In contrast, various other approaches, such as those of Jung, Adler, and Rogers, have rejected the notion of separate developmental stages.

An area of increasing interest is the study of how personality varies across cultures. In order to know whether observations about personality structure and formation reflect universal truths or merely cultural influences, it is necessary to study and compare personality characteristics in different societies. For example, significant differences have been found between personality development in the individualistic cultures of the West and in collectivist societies such as Japan, where children are taught from a young age that fitting in with the group takes precedence over the recognition of individual achievement. Cross-cultural differences may also be observed within a given society by studying the contrasts between its dominant culture and its subcultures (usually ethnic, racial, or religious groups).

### Further Reading

Allport, Gordon W. *Personality and Social Encounter: Selected Essays.* Boston: Beacon Press, 1960.

Eysenck, Hans. *The Structure of Human Personality.* London: Methuen, 1970.

Mischel, Walter. *Introduction to Personality.* 4th ed. New York: Holt, Rinehart, and Winston, 1986.

# Personality development

The development of the beliefs, moods, and behaviors that differentiate among people.

The concept of **personality** refers to the profile of stable beliefs, moods, and behaviors that differentiate among children (and adults) who live in a particular society. The profiles that differentiate children across cultures of different historical times will not be the same because the most adaptive profiles vary with the values of the society and the historical era. An essay on personality development written 300 years ago by a New England Puritan would have listed piety as a major psychological trait but that would not be regarded as an important personality trait in contemporary America.

Contemporary theorists emphasize personality **traits** having to do with individualism, internalized **conscience**, sociability with strangers, the **ability** to control strong **emotion** and impulse, and personal achievement.

An important reason for the immaturity of our understanding of personality development is the heavy reliance on questionnaires that are filled out by parents of children or the responses of older children to questionnaires. Because there is less use of behavioral observations of children, our theories of personality development are not strong.

There are five different hypotheses regarding the early origins of personality (see accompanying table). One assumes that the child's inherited biology, usually called a temperamental bias, is an important basis for the child's later personality. Alexander Thomas and StellaChess suggested there were nine temperamental dimensions along with three synthetic types they called the difficult child, the easy child, and the child who is slow to warm up to unfamiliarity. Longitudinal studies of children suggest that a shy and fearful style of reacting to challenge and novelty predicts, to a modest degree, an adult personality that is passive to challenge and introverted in **mood**.

A second hypothesis regarding personality development comes from Sigmund Freud's suggestion that variation in the sexual and aggressive aims of the **id**, which is biological in nature, combined with **family** experience, leads to the development of the **ego** and **superego**. Freud suggested that differences in parental **socialization** produced variation in anxiety which, in turn, leads to different personalities.

A third set of hypotheses emphasizes direct social experiences with parents. After World War II, Americans and Europeans held the more benevolent idealistic conception of the child that described growth as motivated by affectionate ties to others rather than by the **narcissism** and **hostility** implied by Freud's writings. **John Bowlby** contributed to this new emphasis on the infant's relationships with parents in his books on **attachment**. Bowlby argued that the nature of the infant's relationship to the caretakers and especially the mother created a profile of emotional reactions toward adults that might last indefinitely.

A fourth source of ideas for personality centers on whether or not it is necessary to posit a self that monitors, integrates, and initiates reaction. This idea traces itself to the Judeo-Christian assumption that it is necessary to award children a will so that they could be held responsible for their actions. A second basis is the discovery that children who had the same objective experiences develop different personality profiles because they construct different conceptions about themselves and others from the same experiences. The notion that each child imposes a personal interpretation to their experiences makes the concept of self critical to the child's personality.

An advantage of awarding importance to a concept of self and personality development is that the process of identification with parents and others gains in significance. All children wish to possess the qualities that their culture regards as good. Some of these qualities are the product of identification with each parent.

A final source of hypotheses regarding the origins of personality comes from inferences based on direct observations of a child's behavior. This strategy, which relies on induction, focuses on different characteristics at different ages. Infants differ in irritability, three-year-olds differ in **shyness**, and six-year-olds differ in seriousness of mood. A major problem with this approach is that each class of behavior can have different historical antecedents. Children who prefer to **play** alone rather than with others do so for a variety of reasons. Some might be temperamentally shy and are uneasy with other children while others might prefer solitary activity.

The current categories of child psychopathology influenced the behaviors that are chosen by scientists for study. Fearfulness and **conduct disorder** predominate in clinical referrals to psychiatrists and psychologists. A cluster of behaviors that includes avoidance of unfamiliar events and places, **fear** of dangerous animals, shyness with strangers, sensitivity to **punishment**, and extreme **guilt** is called the internalizing profile. The cluster that includes disobedience toward parent and teachers, **aggression** to peers, excessive dominance of other children, and impulsive decisions is called the externalizing profile. These children are most likely to be at risk for later **juvenile delinquency**. The association between inability of a three-year-old to inhibit socially inappropriate behavior and later **antisocial behavior** is the most reliable predictive relation between a characteristic scene in the young child and later personality trait.

## Influences on personality development

The influence comes from a variety of **temperament** but especially ease of arousal, irritability, fearfulness, sociability, and activity level. The experiential contributions to personality include early attachment relations, parental socialization, identification with parents, class, and ethnic groups, experiences with other children, ordinal position in the family, physical attractiveness, and school success or failure, along with a number of unpredictable experiences like **divorce**, early parental death, **mental illness** in the family, and supporting relationships with relatives or teachers.

The most important personality profiles in a particular culture stem from the challenges to which the children of that culture must accommodate. Most children must deal with three classes of external challenges: (1) unfamiliarity, especially unfamiliar people, tasks, and situations; (2) request by legitimate authority or **conformity** to and acceptance of their standards, and (3) domination by or attack by other children. In addition, all children must learn to control two important families of emotions: anxiety, fear, and guilt, on the one hand, and on the other, **anger**, **jealousy**, and resentment.

Of the four important influences on personality—identification, ordinal position, social class, and parental socialization—identification is the most important. By six years of age, children assume that some of the characteristics of their parents belong to them and they experience vicariously the emotion that is appropriate to the parent's experience. A six-year-old girl identified with her mother will experience pride should mother win a prize or be praised by a friend. However, she will experience shame or anxiety if her mother is criticized or is rejected by friends. The process of identification has great relevance to personalty development.

The child's ordinal position in the family has its most important influence on receptivity to accepting or rejecting the requests and ideas of legitimate authority. First-born children in most families are most willing than later-borns to conform to the requests of authority. They are more strongly motivated to achieve in school, more conscientious, and less aggressive.

The child's social class affects the preparation and **motivation** for academic achievement. Children from middle-class families typically obtain higher grades in school than children of working or lower-class families because different value systems and practices are promoted by families from varied social class backgrounds.

The patterns of socialization used by parents also influence the child's personality. Baumrind suggests that parents could be classified as authoritative, authoritarian, or permissive. More competent and mature preschool children usually have authoritative parents who were nurturant but made maturity demands. Moderately self-reliant children who were a bit withdrawn have authoritarian parents who more often relied on coercive discipline. The least mature children have overly permissive parents who are nurturant but lack discipline.

Jerome Kagan Ph.D.

## Further Reading
Ainsworth, M. B. S., M. C. Blehar, E. Waters, and S. Wall. *Patterns of Attachment.* Hillsdale, NJ: L. Erlbaum, 1978.

Bowlby, J. *Attachment.* New York: Basic Books, 1969.

———. *Loss: Sadness and Depression.* New York: Basic Books, 1980.

———. *Separation: Anxiety and Anger.* New York: Basic Books, 1973.

Erikson, E. H. *Childhood and Society.* New York: W. W. Norton, 1963.

Kagan, J. *Birth to Maturity.* New York: Wiley, 1962.

———. *Galen's Prophecy.* New York: Basic Books, 1994.

———. *The Nature of the Child.* rev. ed. New York: Basic Books, 1994.

Rothbart, M. K. "Temperament in Childhood." n G. A. Kohnstamm, J. E. Bates, and M. K. Rothbart, eds. *Temperament in Childhood.* New York: Wiley, 1989, pp. 59-73.

Thomas, A. and S. Chess. *Temperament and Development.* New York: Brunner Mazel, 1977.

## Personality disorders

Long-standing, deeply ingrained patterns of socially maladaptive behavior that are detrimental to those who display them or to others.

**Personality** disorders constitute a separate diagnostic category (Axis II) in the American Psychiatric Association's Diagnostic and Statistical Manual of Mental Disorders (DSM-IV). Unlike the major mental disorders (Axis I), which are characterized by periods of illness and remission, personality disorders are generally ongoing. Often, they first appear in **childhood** or **adolescence** and persist throughout a person's lifetime. Aside from their persistence, the other major characteristic of personality disorders is inflexibility. Persons affected by these disorders have rigid personality **traits** and coping styles that they are unable to adapt to changing situations and that impair their social and/or occupational functioning. A further difference between personality disorders and the major clinical syndromes listed in Axis I of *DSM-IV* is that people with personality disorders generally do not perceive that there is anything wrong with their behavior and are not motivated to change it. Although the *DSM-IV* lists specific descriptions of ten personality disorders, these conditions are often difficult to diagnose. Some characteristics of the various disorders overlap. In other cases, the complexity of human behavior makes it difficult to pinpoint a clear dividing line between pathology and normality in the assessment of personality. There also has been relatively little research done on some of the personality disorders listed in *DSM-IV* .

The most effectively-diagnosed personality disorder is the antisocial personality. The outstanding traits of this disturbance are an inability to feel love, **empathy**, or loyalty towards other people and a lack of **guilt** or remorse for one's actions. Due to the lack of **conscience** that characterizes it, the condition that is currently known as **antisocial personality disorder** was labeled moral insanity in the nineteenth century. More recent names associated with this personality type are psychopath and sociopath. Unable to base their actions on anything except their own immediate desires, persons with this disorder demonstrate a pattern of impulsive, irresponsible, thoughtless, and sometimes criminal behavior. They are often intelligent, articulate individuals with an **ability** to charm and manipulate others; at their most dangerous, they can become violent criminals who are particularly dangerous to society because of their ability to gain the trust of others combined with their lack of conscience or remorse.

There are both biological and psychosocial theories of the origin of antisocial personality disorder. Two of the major components of the antisocial personality—the constant need for thrills and excitement and the lack of anxiety about punishment—may be at least partially explained by research suggesting that antisocial individuals experience chronic underarousal of the central and autonomic nervous systems. In one experiment, anticipation of an electric shock produced a dramatically lower increase of tension in teenagers diagnosed with antisocial personality disorder than in other individuals. In terms of environmental influences, connections have been suggested between the antisocial personality and various patterns of familial interaction, including parental rejection or inconsistency and the retraction of **punishment** when repentance is claimed.

Some personality disorders resemble chronic but milder versions of the mental disorders listed in Axis I of *DSM-IV* . In schizotypal personality disorder, for example, the schizophrenic's **hallucinations** or voices are moderated to the less extreme symptom of an "illusion" that others are present when they are not. Speech patterns, while not incoherent like those of **schizophrenia**, tend to be vague and digressive. Similarly, **avoidant personality** disorder has characteristics that resemble those of social **phobia**, including hypersensitivity to possible rejection and the resulting social withdrawal in spite of a strong need for love and acceptance. The paranoid and schizoid personality disorders are usually manifested primarily in odd or eccentric behavior. The former is characterized mainly by suspiciousness of others, extreme vigilance against anticipated misdeeds, and insistence on personal autonomy. The latter involves emotional coldness and passivity, indifference to the feelings of others, and trouble forming close relationships.

Several personality disorders, including antisocial personality, are associated with extreme and erratic behavior. The most dramatic is the histrionic personality type, which is characterized by persistent attention-getting behavior that includes exaggerated emotional displays (such as tantrums) and overreaction to trivial problems and events. Manipulative suicide attempts may also occur. Narcissistic personality disorder consists primarily of an inflated sense of self-importance coupled with a lack of empathy for others. Individuals with this disorder display an exaggerated sense of their own importance and abilities and tend to fantasize about them. Such persons also have a sense of entitlement, expecting (and taking for granted) special treatment and concessions from others. Paradoxically, individuals with narcissistic personality disorder are generally very insecure and suffer from low **self-esteem**. Another personality disorder that is characterized by erratic behavior is the **borderline personality**. Individuals with this disorder are extremely unstable and inconsistent in their feelings about themselves and others and tend toward impulsive and unpredictable behavior.

Several personality disorders are manifested primarily by anxiety and fearfulness. In addition to the avoidant personality, these include the dependent, compulsive, and **passive-aggressive personality** disorders. Persons with **dependent personality disorder** are extremely passive and tend to subordinate their own needs to those of others. Due to their lack of self-confidence, they avoid asserting themselves and allow others to take responsibility for their lives. Compulsive personality disorder is characterized by behavioral rigidity, excessive emotional restraint, and overly conscientious compliance with rules. Persons with this disorder are overly cautious and indecisive and tend to procrastinate and to become overly upset by deviations from rules and routines. Passive-aggressive personality disorder involves covert **aggression** expressed by a refusal to meet the expectations of others in such areas as adequate job performance, which may be sabotaged through procrastination, forgetfulness, and inefficiency. This disorder is also characterized by irritability, volatility, and a tendency to blame others for one's problems.

**Further Reading**

Beck, Aaron. *Cognitive Therapy of Personality Disorders.* Guilford Press, 1990.
Millon, T. *Disorders of Personality.* New York: Wiley, 1981.

# Personality inventory

A method of personality assessment based on a questionnaire asking a person to report feelings or reactions in certain situations.

**Personality** inventories, also called objective tests, are standardized and can be administered to a number of people at the same time. A psychologist need not be present when the test is given, and the answers can usually be scored by a computer. Scores are obtained by comparison with norms for each category on the test. A personality inventory may measure one factor, such as anxiety level, or it may measure a number of different personality **traits** at the same time, such as the Sixteen Personality Factor Questionnaire (16 PF).

The personality inventory used most often for diagnosing psychological disorders is the **Minnesota Multiphasic Personality Inventory**, generally referred to as the MMPI. It consists of 550 statements that the test taker has to mark as "true," "false," or "cannot say." Answers are scored according to how they correspond with those given by persons with various psychological disorders, including **depression**, hysteria, **paranoia**, psychopathic deviancy, and **schizophrenia**. The MMPI was originally developed (and is still used) for the diagnosis of these and other serious psychological problems. However enough responses have been collected from people with less severe problems to allow for reliable scoring of responses from these persons as well. Many people with no severe disorder are now given the MMPI as an assessment tool when they begin **psychotherapy**, with scoring geared toward personality attributes rather than clinical disorders.

The California Psychological Inventory (CPI), based on less extreme measures of personality than the MMPI, assesses traits, including dominance, responsibility, self-acceptance, and **socialization**. In addition, some parts of the test specifically measure traits relevant to academic achievement. Another inventory designed to measure a spectrum of personality variables in **normal** populations is the Personality Research Form (PRF), whose **measurement** scales include **affiliation**, autonomy, change, endurance, and exhibition. The Neuroticism **Extroversion** Openness Personality Inventory, Revised (NEO-PI-R) also measures common dimensions of personality such as sensitivity and extroversion, but it differs from other tests in its inclusion of both "private" and "public" versions. The questions in the private version are answered like those in other personality inventories, but the public version consists of having another person acquainted with the test taker answer questions about him or her. Significant discrepancies between the two versions can be an important source of information for those interpreting the test.

**Further Reading**

Cronbach, L.J. *Essentials of Psychological Testing.* New York: Harper and Row, 1970.

Sundberg, N. *The Assessment of Persons.* Englewood Cliffs, NJ: Prentice-Hall, 1977.

# Pervasive developmental disorder (PDD)

*A group of conditions involving serious impairment in several areas of development, including physical, behavioral, cognitive, social, and language development.*

The incidence of pervasive development disorders (PDDs) in the general population is estimated at 1%. These disorders are thought to be genetically based, and there is no evidence linking them to environmental factors. Many children who are diagnosed with PDDs today would have been labeled psychotic or schizophrenic in the past. The most serious form of pervasive developmental disorder is **autism**, a congenital condition characterized by severely impaired social interaction, communication, and abstract thought, and often manifested by stereotyped and repetitive behavior patterns.

In addition to autism, several other conditions are considered pervasive developmental disorders by the **American Psychiatric Association**. Rett's disorder is characterized by physical, mental, and social impairment that appears between the ages of five months and four years in children whose development has been normal up to that point. Occurring only in girls, it involves impairment of coordination, repetitive movements, a slowing of head growth, and severe or profound **mental retardation**, as well as impaired social and communication skills. **Childhood** disintegrative disorder is marked by the deteri-

This autistic child is encouraged to interact with the guinea pig in an effort to improve his social interaction. *(Photo by Helen B. Senisi. Photo Researchers, Inc. Reproduced with permission.)*

oration of previously acquired physical, social, and communication skills after at least two years of normal development. It first appears between the ages of two and 10, usually at three or four years of age, and many of its symptoms resemble those of autism. Other names for this disorder are Heller's syndrome, **dementia** infantilis, and disintegrative **psychosis**. It sometimes appears in conjunction with a medical condition such as Schilder's disease, but usually no organic cause can be found.

Asperger's disorder includes many of the same social and behavioral impairments as autism, except for difficulties with language. Children with this disorder lack normal tools of social interaction, such as the **ability** to meet someone else's gaze, use appropriate body language and gestures, or react to another person's thoughts and feelings. Behavioral impairments include the repetitive, stereotyped motions and rigid adherence to routines that are characteristic of autism. Like childhood disintegrative disorder, Asperger's disorder is thought to be more common in males than females.

Research based on autopsies and magnetic resonance imaging (MRI) of live patients shows that PDDs are connected with specific abnormalities in the **brain**. These conditions are usually evident in early childhood and often cause some degree of mental retardation. They are not curable, but there are a variety of treatments that can alleviate specific symptoms and help children function better in daily life. Drugs like Prozac, Zoloft, and Luvox, all selective serotonin reuptake inhibitors (SSRIs), can reduce **aggression** and repetitive thoughts and improve social interaction. **Attention** problems and hyperactivity respond to psychostimulants, such as Ritalin, Dexedrine, and Cylert, which can make children more responsive to other types of intervention. **Behavior therapy** has helped children with PDDs minimize negative behavior, such as repetitive activities and persistent preoccupations, and **group therapy** has helped improve social skills.

Education is an important component in the treatment of PDDs. **Special education** programs that address all types of developmental problems—social, linguistic, and behavioral—are mandated by federal law and available to children from the ages of four or five. Even those children with PDDs who can be enrolled in regular classes can benefit from supplemental special instruction programs. Speech, language, and occupational therapy can help children with PDDs, including autism, function at the highest level possible. In many cases, appropriate education and therapy from the earliest age can save these children from **institutionalization**.

**Further Reading**

Haskell, Simon H. *The Education of Children with Motor and Neurological Disabilities*. New York: Nichols, 1989.

Lewis, Vicky. *Development and Handicap*. New York: B. Blackwell, 1987.

# Phallic stage

See **Psychosexual stages**

# Philosophical psychology

The area of study where psychology and philosophy intersect, focusing on metaphysical and speculative problems in the study of mental processes.

One of the central questions in philosophical psychology has been the relationship between the mind and body, a perennial area of inquiry throughout the history of philosophy. Other topics considered in this discipline include **memory**, **perception**, and **consciousness**; the nature of the self; the existence of free will; the relationship between thought and **emotion**; and so-called irrational phenomena, such as self-deception.

The study of the mind and mental processes was traditionally the province of philosophers, but philosophy and psychology began to diverge with the advent of **experimental psychology** as practiced by such figures as **Gustav Fechner** (1801-1887) and **Wilhelm Wundt** (1832-1920) in the nineteenth century. In the twentieth century, the separation of the two disciplines became standard in American universities, resulting in the establishment of professional associations and journals devoted to psychology and its practitioners. This schism was further entrenched with the rise of **behaviorism**, which advocated behavior as the sole focus of psychology and rejected introspective inquiry and the study of consciousness. In 1925, the prominent American behaviorist **John Watson** predicted the demise of philosophy as a field of inquiry altogether.

In the 1950s, however, psychologists and philosophers increasingly found themselves once again on common ground. The "cognitive revolution" shifted the focus of psychology back to mental processes and such topics as language acquisition and mental representation. In turn, philosophy has demonstrated a growing interest in the empirical side of psychology; philosophers have studied the clinical foundations of **psychoanalysis** as well as topics such as **behavior modification**. Representative journals in philosophical psychology include *Philosophy of Science, Mind, British Journal of Psychology*, and *The Philosophical Review*.

**Further Reading**

Russell, Bertrand. *The Analysis of Mind*. New York: Macmillan, 1921.

Strawson, Peter. *Individuals: An Essay in Descriptive Metaphysics*. Garden City, NY: Doubleday, 1959.

# Phobia

An excessive, unrealistic fear of a specific object, situation, or activity that causes a person to avoid that object, situation, or activity.

Unlike generalized anxiety, phobias involve specific, identifiable but usually irrational fears. Phobias are common occurrences among a large segment of the population. People with phobias recognize that their fears are irrational, yet avoid the source to spare themselves of the resulting anxiety. Phobias are classified as disorders only when they interfere substantially with a person's daily life.

Psychologists have identified three categories of phobic disorders. The first, simple phobia, is defined in Diagnostic and Statistical Manual of Mental Disorders as a persistent, irrational **fear** of, and compelling desire to avoid, an object or a situation other than being alone, or in public places away from home (agoraphobia) or of humiliation or embarrassment in certain social situations (social phobia). Simple phobia causes considerable distress when confronted because the person realizes that the fear is excessive and irrational. Such phobias are not indicative of other mental disorders. Almost any object or situation can be the cause of a simple phobia. Common phobias include fear of snakes (ophidiophobia), enclosed places (claustrophobia), and spiders (arachnophobia). Fear of heights, doctors and dentists, loud noises, storms, and the sight of blood also are experienced by large numbers of people. Animal phobias, the most common type of simple phobia, usually develop in early **childhood**. Most people do not seek treatment for simple phobias; they simply avoid the object or situation.

The second category of phobic disorders are social phobias. People with social phobias avoid social situations because they are afraid of embarrassing themselves. Fear of public speaking, fear of using public toilets, and fear of eating in public are common social phobias. Most social phobias develop over a period of time, beginning in **adolescence** or the early 20s, and rarely over the age of 30.

Agoraphobia, the third category of phobic disorders, is the most disabling and the most difficult to treat. Agoraphobia can be defined as the fear of being alone, or the fear of being in public places in unfamiliar settings. Some agoraphobics fear open spaces, like large bodies of water or open fields without fences. Most agoraphobics fear more than one situation, which contributes to the disabling nature of the disorder. The list of fears is long and extensive: public transportation, bridges, tunnels, crowded theaters, or simply being home alone. Agoraphobia rarely begins before age 18 or after 35. Sometimes it appears to be precipitated by major illness or **stress**.

Like other anxiety disorders, phobias can be treated with drugs, **behavior therapy** or both. **Drug therapy** usually includes minor tranquilizers like Librium or Valium, taken before a situation in which a phobia is likely to be introduced. Behavior therapy attempts to reduce a patient's anxiety through exposure to the phobia. For example, patients are guided step-by-step from imaginary confrontation of the phobia (visualizing a snake, for example) to actually experiencing it (holding a real snake). Gradual desensitization is most successful in treating simple phobias.

**Further Reading**

Atkinson, Rita L.; Richard C. Atkinson; Edward E. Smith; and Ernest R. Hilgard. *Introduction to Psychology*. 9th ed. San Diego: Harcourt Brace Jovanovich, 1987.

Goodwin, Donald W. *Anxiety*. New York: Oxford University Press, 1986.

Zimbardo, Philip G. *Psychology and Life*. 12th ed. Glenview, IL: Scott, Foresman, 1988.

# Phrenology

An approach, primarily of historical interest, to describing the thinking process based on the belief that different mental capacities are controlled by specific locations in the brain.

Although people recognize the **brain** as the center of mental processes, this contemporary view has not always been accepted. Philosophers and scientists have proposed different ideas throughout history about the process of thinking that have since been rejected as inaccurate. One such rejected approach was phrenology. Phrenologists believed that our different mental capacities were controlled by specific locations in the brain. Although scientists today recognize the general validity of this belief, the problem was that the phrenologists developed ideas that did not really describe the way the brain functions.

German scientist Franz Joseph Gall (1758-1828), a recognized expert on anatomy, proposed the initial ideas on phrenology. He proposed that some areas of the brain were highly developed in certain individuals, which lead to specific behaviors. For instance, he claimed that pickpockets were acquisitive (i.e., possessed the desire to own things) because of excess development of an area on the side of the head. One of Gall's contemporaries, Johann Spurzheim (1776-1832) identified 35 different mental faculties and suggested the location in the brain that related to each one. Each trait was claimed to lead to a certain behavior; the inclination toward that behavior could be detected by assessing the bumps on a person's skull. Scientists now recognize that the shape of the skull does not relate to the shape of the brain.

From the start, phrenology was controversial. For instance, the Roman Catholic church pressured the Austrian government to prevent Gall from lecturing in an area that the Church regarded as materialistic and atheistic. This tactic apparently served to increase the interest in phrenology. Although Gall developed his ideas with a serious scientific perspective, Spurzheim was more of an entrepreneur. He coined the term phrenology (which Gall never accepted), popularized it, and brought it to the United States. Spurzheim's goal was to reform education, religion, and penology using principles of phrenology. He died shortly after arriving in America, however. Spurzheim's work was continued by the British phrenologist George Combe (1788-1858), whose book on phrenology, *Constitution of Man,* was quite popular. According to psychology historian David Hothersall, Combe was highly respected by scientists in the United States. He was elected to the National Academy of Sciences. Interestingly, at one point he was asked to justify slavery on the grounds that people of African descent had "inferior" skulls. Combe refused, noting that educated slaves were the intellectual equals of white people. Similarly, Combe rejected the second-class status of women, asserting that they were not intellectually or emotionally inferior to men.

Two enterprising brothers, Orson and Lorenzo Fowler, marketed phrenology as a means by which people could improve themselves. Unlike Gall, who believed that **heredity** dictated one's strengths and weaknesses, the Fowlers preached the environmental message that people could improve themselves by practice and could overcome weaknesses by virtue of their will. They wrote extensively for popular audiences and published a journal of phrenology that existed from the 1840s to 1911. They also set up a clinic in New York where clients could be tested; they toured the United States, giving advice wherever they went; and they emphasized the practical vision of phrenology, minimizing the scientific aspects of their field.

Meanwhile, scientists and philosophers quickly dismissed phrenological ideas. Leading biologists and

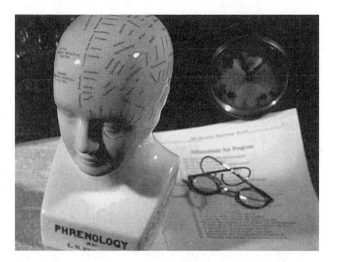

**Bust showing the traits that phrenologists assigned to the different parts of the skull.** *(Brooks/Brown. Photo Researchers, Inc. Reproduced with permission.)*

physicians of the day showed that the specific locations deemed important by the phrenologists were not associated with specific mental processes. Similarly, careful research in the area revealed that phrenologists were susceptible to biased observations in cases in which the research supported phrenological claims. During the 19th century, at the height of phrenology's popularity among the general public, scientists regarded the field with disdain and characterized it as a discipline dressed up to look like science. Nonetheless, phrenology exerted a positive influence on the fields of physiology and, later, biology, and sparked research on the relationship between the brain and behavior.

**Further Reading**
Cooter, Roger. *The Cultural Meaning of Popular Science.* Cambridge, Eng.: Cambridge University Press, 1984.
Hothersall, David. *History of Psychology.* 2nd ed. New York: McGraw-Hill, 1990.

# Physiological psychology

The area of experimental psychology concerned specifically with how biology shapes behavior and mental processes.

The area of experimental known as physiological psychology has evolved in the 1990s. Increasingly, the field is being referred to as behavioral neuroscience, replacing physiological psychology and biological psychology. Nonetheless, the goals of psychologists in this field remain the same: to utilize basic research to explain behavior in physiological terms, working on the assumption that for every behavioral event there is a corresponding physical event or series of events.

The physiological psychologist (or behavioral neuroscientist) is also concerned with the functioning of the adrenal glands and with the physical processes involved in sensation. Although physiological psychology is concerned with physical organisms, it is distinguished from such life sciences as physiology and biology by its focus on behavior. Researchers may investigate questions such as how the **brain** controls physical movements or regulates eating; the role of sex **hormones** in violent behavior; the effects of drugs on **memory** and **personality**; the physiological basis for **sleep** and dreaming; and the areas of the brain devoted to language functions. Physiological psychology overlaps with the field of neurobiology, which is the study of the **nervous system** and its functions. A related field is psychopharmacology, the study of drugs and behavior.

Another subfield of physiological psychology, psychophysiology, deals with the **measurement** of physiological responses as they relate to behavior. Practical applications include lie detector tests; clinical tests of **vision** and **hearing**; tests of brain activity in individuals with **mental retardation** and neurological and behavioral disorders; and **biofeedback** training.

### Further Reading

Asimov, Isaac. *The Human Brain: Its Capacities and Functions.* New York: Penguin, 1994.

Guiley, Rosemary. *The Encyclopedia of Dreams: Symbols and Interpretations.* New York: Crossroad, 1993.

*Mind and Brain: Readings from Scientific American Magazine.* New York: W.H. Freeman, 1993.

## Jean Piaget

### 1896-1980
French psychologist, philosopher, and naturalist.

Jean Piaget is universally known for his studies of the development of **intelligence** in children. Although he is one of the creators of **child psychology** as it exists today, psychology was for him only a tool of epistemology (the theory of knowledge). He identified his domain as "genetic [i.e., developmental] epistemology." He thus studied the growth of children's capacity to think in abstract, logical terms, and of such categories as time, space, number, causality, and permanency, describing an invariable sequence of stages from **birth** through **adolescence**. A prolific author, he wrote over fifty books and hundreds of articles.

**Jean Piaget** *(Farrell Grehan/Corbis. Reproduced with permission.)*

Piaget was born in 1896 in the French-speaking Swiss city of Neuchâtel, the son of an agnostic medievalist and a religious mother with socialist leanings. After completing a doctoral thesis in natural sciences (1918), and studies in psychology and philosophy in Zurich and Paris, he joined the Rousseau Institute of Geneva in 1921, which was founded by Edouard Claparède as a center for research on **child development** and education. He later taught experimental and **developmental psychology**, sociology, and history and philosophy of sciences, mainly at the University of Geneva. Piaget died in 1980. His interdisciplinary International Center for Genetic Epistemology (established in 1955) closed in 1984.

As an adolescent, Piaget published numerous papers on the classification of mollusks. During World War I, he was active in socialist and Christian student groups, and sketched a theory of organic, psychological, and social phenomena aimed at providing a scientific basis for postwar reconstruction. Much of his later thinking built directly on his youthful speculations and values, but its empirical impetus derived from his own reaction against the metaphysical and mystical tendencies of his adolescence.

Piaget devised a "clinical method" that combined standard intelligence tests and open-ended conversations with school-age children. In his first five books, he studied children's language, reasoning, conceptions of the world, theories of causality, and moral judgment. He found that children are at first "egocentric" (incapable of taking another person's point of view) and attached to concrete appearances, but that they gradually move away from egocentrism and become capable of abstract thinking. Piaget's observations of his own children led to *The Origins of Intelligence* (1952) and *The Construction of Reality* (1954), where he describes how basic forms of intentionality, and of the categories of object, space, causality, and time evolve between the onset of the newborn's reflex activities and the emergence of language at about 18 months; *Play, Dreams, and Imitation* (1951), deals with the development of mental representation up to the age of six. In these three classics, Piaget expounded the notion of intelligence as a form of **adaptation** to the external world. Starting in the 1940s, Piaget and **Bärbel Inhelder** studied the development of logical and formal thought in various fields (conceptions of movement, speed, time, space, geometry, chance, and probability). One of his major works, *Introduction to Genetic Epistemology* (1950), remains untranslated.

Piaget and his collaborators created many original and ingenious problem-solving situations that became paradigms for research all of the world. In one famous experiment, children sat facing a scale model of three mountains and were asked to choose from a series of pictures the one that represents the mountains as seen by a doll sitting at other positions. Younger subjects systematically identified the doll's viewpoint with their own. Studies of "conservation" provide further notable examples: the child is presented with two identical balls of clay; the shape of one is modified, and the child is asked whether the amount, weight, or volume of clay has changed. Other situations involve manipulating blocks or pouring identical quantities of liquid in differently shaped containers.

Most of the research Piaget inspired is disconnected from the theoretical goals of genetic epistemology. His work had some direct impact on mathematical and moral education, and reinforced the belief that instruction must be adapted to the child's developmental level. But it is Piaget's investigative techniques, formulation of new problems, insightful observations, and emphasis on the development of cognitive capacities that form some of the bases of contemporary child psychology.

## Further Reading

Boden, M. *Jean Piaget*. Penguin Books, 1979.
Gruber, H., and J. Voneche, eds. *The Essential Piaget*. New York: Basic Books, 1977.
Piaget, J. *Genetic Epistemology*. Trans. E. Duckworth. New York: Norton, 1970.

Vidal, F. *Piaget Before Piaget*. Cambridge: Harvard University Press, 1994.

# Philippe Pinel

**1745-1826**
French physician and one of the founders of psychiatry.

Philippe Pinel was born near Toulouse, France, the son of a surgeon. After first studying literature and theology, he pursued medical studies at the University of Toulouse, receiving his M.D. in 1773. In 1778, Pinel moved to Paris, where he worked as a publisher, translator of scientific writings, and teacher of mathematics. He also wrote and published articles, a number of them about mental disorders, a topic in which he had become interested due to the illness of a friend. In 1792, Pinel was appointed chief physician and director of the Bicêtre asylum, where he was able to put into practice his ideas on treatment of the mentally ill, who were commonly kept chained in dungeons at the time. Pinel petitioned to the Revolutionary Committee for permission to remove the chains from some of the patients as an experiment, and to allow them to exercise in the open air. When these steps proved to be effective, he was able to change the conditions at the hospital and discontinue the customary methods of treatment, which included bloodletting, purging, and physical abuse.

Rejecting the prevailing popular notion that **mental illness** was caused by demonic possession, Pinel was among the first to believe that mental disorders could be caused by psychological or social **stress**, congenital conditions, or physiological injury. He strongly argued for the humane treatment of mental patients, including a friendly interaction between doctor and patient, and for the maintenance and preservation of detailed case histories for the purpose of treatment and research. In 1795, Pinel was appointed chief physician at Salpêtrière, where he effected reforms similar to those at Bicétre. Pinel remained at Salpêtrière for the remainder of his career. His student, Jean Esquirol, succeeded him and expanded his reform efforts throughout France. The success of Pinel's methods also influenced practices in other countries, including England.

In 1795, Pinel was appointed to the faculty of the newly opened medical school in Paris, where he was professor of medical pathology for the next 20 years. He was elected to the Academy of Science in 1804 and the Academy of Medicine in 1820. Besides his work in hospitals, Pinel also treated patients privately as a consulting physician. Although he is regarded today as a pioneering

**Philippe Pinel** *(The Library of Congress. Reproduced with permission.)*

figure in psychiatry, during his lifetime Pinel was known chiefly for his contributions to internal medicine, especially his authoritative classification of diseases in the textbook *Nosographie philosophique* (1798), in which he divided diseases into five classes—fevers, phlegmasias, hemorrhages, neuroses, and diseases caused by organic lesions. Pinel's extensive contributions to medical research also include data on the development, prognosis, and frequency of occurrence of various illnesses, and experiments measuring the effectiveness of medicines. Pinel established an inoculation clinic at Salpêtrière in 1799, and the first vaccination in Paris was given there in April of the following year.

In addition to transforming psychiatric facilities from prisons into hospitals, Pinel did much to establish psychiatry formally as a separate branch of medicine, publishing numerous articles on the topic which were collected in "Recherches et observations sur le traitement moral des aliénés" (1799) and his book *Traîte medico-philosophique de l'aliénation mentale* (*Medical-Philosophical Treatise on Mental Alienation or Mania*, 1801), which is considered a classic of psychiatry. Pinel's practice of interacting individually with his patients in a humane and understanding manner represented the first known attempt at **psychotherapy**. He also emphasized the importance of physical hygiene and exercise, and pioneered in recommending productive work for mental patients. In addition, Pinel concerned himself with the proper administration of psychiatric facilities, including the training of their personnel.

# Placebo effect

*In research, a scientifically significant response that cannot be explained by physiological variables and is assumed to be psychological in origin.*

Placebos are substances with no known pharmacological value that are given to members of a **control group** in an experiment. In studies determining the effectiveness of a particular drug, for example, the **experimental group** is given the drug being studied and the control group is given a placebo, which is made to look exactly like the actual drug. Neither group, nor the researchers, knows which received the drug and which the placebo. If the members of each group show similar responses, the placebo effect has been produced. For reasons not completely understood, the patients given the placebo have experienced the effects of the drug without actually taking it. In such cases, the drug itself is considered ineffective.

The placebo effect has been noted since ancient times, when animal parts or other naturally occurring substances were given as treatment for various human diseases and ailments. Throughout medical history, patients have recovered from illnesses after healers employed substances or methods that scientifically should have no effect. It is believed that patients' expectations that their condition will improve plays a major role in producing the placebo effect.

The use of placebos in **psychotherapy** is controversial, with some critics contending that it links therapists with "quack" treatments rather than legitimate, scientifically measurable methods. However, most researchers agree that the placebo effect, while not completely understood, plays a major and beneficial role in both physiological and psychological treatment.

## Further Reading

Atkinson, Rita L.; Richard C. Atkinson; Edward E. Smith; and Ernest R. Hilgard. *Introduction to Psychology.* 9th ed. San Diego: Harcourt Brace Jovanovich, 1987.

Zimbardo, Philip G. *Psychology and Life.* 12th ed. Glenview, IL: Scott, Foresman, 1988.

# Play

*Activity that is not required, but is enjoyed.*

While the term "play" may refer to an extremely varied range of activities, certain broad, defining characteristics have been noted. Perhaps the most basic one is that play is something that is not required. Although the enjoyment derived from it may be needed emotionally, no single play activity itself is necessary for survival. Thus, play is referred to as "autotelic"—it is engaged in for its own sake, with the reward inherent in the activity itself. Nevertheless, in spite of its detachment from survival and financial gain, play is engaged in wholeheartedly. During the time allotted to play, it commands a person's entire **attention**.

Play takes place in a realm divorced from ordinary reality and governed by its own rules, which may be more complex and absolute than those of many "serious" activities. It is also bound in terms of both time and space. The period during which one engages in play has time limits: it begins, proceeds, and inevitably ends when one returns to "real life." Play is also set apart in space—a person generally goes somewhere special (even if it is only the "play room" or the "playground") to engage in play. The relationship between play and tension has also been noted. While tension is not absent from play itself, the ultimate result is the reduction of tension and conflict. Based on this feature, play has often been viewed as a "safety valve" for the harmless discharge of tensions and conflicts.

In children, play is a necessary vehicle for **normal** physical, social, and **cognitive development**. The well known early 20th-century American psychologist G. Stanley Hall (1844-1924) viewed the evolution of children's play as recapitulating the evolution of the human species. Individually, play develops in stages that correspond to a child's social and cognitive development. Initially, a child's play is solitary in nature. Next comes parallel play, where children are in each others' company but playing independently. Socially, the final stage is cooperative play, which consists of organized activities characterized by social roles.

**Jean Piaget** formulated a series of developmental stages of play that corresponded to the successive stages in his influential theory of cognitive development in children. The sensorimotor stage (**birth** to approximately two years old), when children are focused on gaining mastery of their own bodies and external objects, is characterized by "practice play" consisting of repeated patterns of movement or sound, such as sucking, shaking, banging, babbling, and, eventually, "peekaboo" games in which objects are made to repeatedly disappear and reappear. As children learn more about the properties of objects and learn how to manipulate them, they begin to monitor the effects of play on their **environment**, and their relationship with that environment becomes increasingly systematic.

The preoperational stage (ages 2-7 years) is marked by the **ability** to master symbolic functions, including the association of objects with words, and the transition from an egocentric focus to an awareness that events have causes outside themselves. At this stage, children begin to engage in make-believe games marked by the use of objects for purposes other than their intended function. Between the ages of 4 and 7, when their thinking is still dominated by intuition rather than logic, children first become interested in games characterized by rules, structure, and social interaction. As they move through the concrete operational stage (ages 7-11), during which categorizing activities and the earliest logical operations occur, the types of rules governing their play and the reasons for following them change. At first, rules are centered on the sensorimotor aspects of play and largely provide structure and repetition. Gradually, they become more focused on the social aspects of play and are connected with acceptance by the group. By the fourth, or formal operations stage (ages 12 and higher), with the gradual emergence of a mature ability to reason, competitive games and games with codes of rules begin to predominate.

While other psychologists have proposed schemes that vary from this one theory, there is general agreement on its broad outlines. Some additional categorizations of children's play that have been proposed include diversive play, composed of aimless activities that serve as a diversion when a child is bored; mimetic play, which is repetitious, structured, and symbolic; and cathartic play, which is therapeutic in nature.

One of the first to use play in therapy with children was Hermine Hug-Hellmuth in 1921, following Freud's work with "Little Hans," a five-year-old boy with a **phobia**. British psychoanalyst Melanie Klein used play as a source to a child's **unconscious** from which she could make interpretations, starting in 1919. Just as adults used **free association** to communicate about their unconscious and talk to communicate about their feelings, theorists reasoned that children communicate through their natural play what they cannot yet verbalize. Play therapy was used by **Anna Freud** to help children develop a closer connection to the therapist. A more structured approach came about in the 1930s with David Levy using play therapy to help children work through and re-enact stressful situations to release them. In keeping with Carl Rogers' non-directive play work in the 1940s, Virginia

**These Columbian girls are engaged in cooperative play, the final stage of playing activities.** *(AP/Wide World Photos. Reproduced with permission.)*

Axline used non-directive play to allow a child to freely be himself or herself, working toward self-realization. By the 1960s, schools had introduced guidance and counseling services. A number of counselors, including Garry Landreth urged in writings that school counselors incorporate play therapy to meet the developmental needs of all children. The International Association for Play Therapy formed in 1982 and now has 3,300 members worldwide. Play therapy has grown in its applications, expanding to include adults and families and into hospitals as well. The therapy usually occurs in a playroom, specially designed for children and furnished with toys and equipment to facilitate children's play.

*See also* Cognitive development

### Further Reading

Dolinar, Kathleen J. *Learning Through Play: Curriculum and Activities for the Inclusive Classroom.* Albany, NY: Delmar, 1994.

Gil, Eliana *Play in Family Therapy.* New York: Guilford Press, 1994.

Landreth, Garry L. *Play Therapy: The Art of the Relationship* Muncie, Indiana: Accelerated Development Inc., 1991.

Moyles, Janet R. *The Excellence of Play.* Philadelphia: Open University Press, 1994.

Hughes, Fergus P. *Children, Play, and Development.* Boston: Allyn and Bacon, 1991.

## Pleasure principle

The theoretical principle that humans make decisions to seek pleasure and minimize pain.

Among other principles, Freudian psychology states that there is a basic human tendency to seek pleasure and avoid **pain**. It arises from the desire for unrestrained expression of both the life **instinct** (Eros) associated with **sexuality** and the death instinct (Thanatos) associated with **aggression** and destructiveness. Freud described the pleasure principle in terms of the need to discharge or reduce tensions—experienced as pain or discomfort—created internally or by external stimuli. The **id**, which operates on the pleasure principle, is the instrument for discharging these tensions. However, it is held in check by the **ego**, operating on the opposed reality principle, which mediates between the primitive desires of the id and the constraints of the external world.

The promptings of the pleasure principle, which are often compared to the demands of a child, seek immediate gratification and are ungoverned by social or moral rules. The reality principle opposes many of these promptings, denying them altogether or postponing gratification either until a socially appropriate time (waiting until a meal to eat) or so that greater pleasure may be achieved in the long run (studying for a degree or training for a sport).

## Further Reading
Freud, Sigmund. *New Introductory Lectures on Psychoanalysis.* New York: W. W. Norton, 1933.
Hall, Calvin S. *A Primer of Freudian Psychology.* New York: Harper and Row, 1982.

# Pornography

Any printed or pictorial material containing representations of sexually obscene behavior, intended to sexually arouse its audience.

There is an obvious and necessary imprecision in this definition of the term pornography, in the sense that what is considered to be sexually obscene behavior, and, for that matter, what might sexually arouse an audience, vary quite widely from time to time, from place to place, and from individual to individual. Nearly all modern societies have laws that prohibit the possession or distribution of at least some forms of pornography, although the statutory suppression and criminalization of sexually obscene material is a relatively recent phenomenon, and is significantly predated by the legal censorship of material that was judged to be sacrilegious or antireligious (religiously obscene) or seditious or treasonous (politically obscene). Generally, laws against pornography have been based on the controversial assumption that exposure to pornography morally corrupts individuals and is a cause of sexual crimes. In the United States, legislation concerning pornography dates from the middle of the 19th century. Since that time, the admittedly elusive legal definition of what constitutes pornography and can be regulated by law has evolved into material that portrays sexual conduct in a patently offensive way and appeals to prurient interest in sex, as judged by an average person applying contemporary community standards, and which, on the whole, does not have serious literary, artistic, political, or scientific value. When necessary, the judgment of whether or not material is pornographic is usually made by a jury. Many authorities have concluded that, because of the constantly

shifting moral connotations of the concept of sexual obscenity, it is not possible to completely and objectively define the term pornography, and that, in the final analysis, pornography is in the eye of the beholder.

## Further Reading
Hunter, Ian. *On Pornography.* New York: St. Martin's Press, 1993.

# Post-traumatic stress disorder (PTSD)

A psychological disorder that develops in response to an extremely traumatic event that threatens a person's safety or life.

Although the term post-traumatic stress disorder is relatively new, the symptoms of PTSD can be recognized in many guises throughout history, from the reactions to the great fire of London that Samuel Pepys (1633-1703) described in the 1600s to the "shell shock" of soldiers in World War I. Some psychologists suspect that the "hysterical" women treated by **Josef Breuer** (1842-1925) and **Sigmund Freud** at the turn of the twentieth century may have been suffering from symptoms of PTSD as a result of childhood **sexual abuse** or battering by their husbands.

Post-traumatic stress disorder has been classified as an anxiety disorder in the American Psychiatric Association's Diagnostic and Statistical Manual of Mental Disorders since 1980. People suffering from PTSD repeatedly re-experience the traumatic event vividly in their thoughts, perceptions, images, or **dreams**. They may be aware that they are recollecting a previous experience, or they may have **hallucinations**, delusions, or dissociative flashbacks that make them feel as though the trauma is actually recurring in the present. Children may engage in repetitive **play** that expresses some aspect of the trauma. A related symptom is the consistent avoidance of people, objects, situations, and other stimuli connected with the event. PTSD sufferers usually experience heightened arousal in the form of agitation, irritability, insomnia, difficulty concentrating, or being easily startled. In contrast, they often "shut down" emotionally and become incapable of expressing certain feelings, especially those associated with affection and intimacy. Children who have been traumatized may stop talking altogether or refuse to discuss the traumatic event that affected them. They may also experience physical symptoms such as headaches or stomach aches.

Events that may lead to post-traumatic stress disorder include natural disasters (earthquakes, floods, hurri-

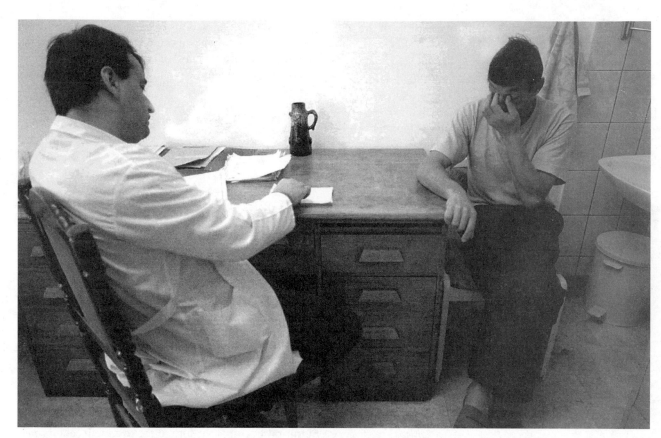

**A Bosnian man with post-traumatic stress disorder talks to a therapist.** *(AP/Wide World Photos. Reproduced with permission.)*

canes) or serious accidents such as automobile or plane crashes. However, PTSD is most likely to be caused by traumas in which death and injury are inflicted by other human beings: war, torture, **rape**, terrorism, and other types of personal assault that violate one's sense of **self-esteem** and personal integrity. (PTSD also tends to be more severe and long-lasting when it results from traumas of this nature.) In addition to the direct experience of traumatic events, PTSD can also be caused by witnessing such events or by learning of serious harm to a **family** member or a close friend. Specific populations in which PTSD has been studied include Vietnam veterans and Holocaust survivors.

Among the disorders listed in the *Diagnostic and Statistical Manual,* the diagnosis for PTSD is unique in its focus on external events rather than internal predispositions or **personality** features. Studies have found that such factors as race, sex, socioeconomic status, and even previous psychiatric history have little to do with the incidence of PTSD. Whether a person develops PTSD is much more closely related to the severity and duration of the traumatic event experienced than to any preexisting characteristics or situations. Physiologically, post-trau-

matic stress disorder is thought to be related to changes in **brain** chemistry and levels of stress-related **hormones**. When a person is subjected to excessive stress levels on a prolonged basis, the adrenal glands—which fuel the "fight-or-flight" reaction by producing adrenaline—may be permanently damaged. One possible result is overfunctioning during subsequent stress, causing hyperarousal symptoms such as insomnia, jumpiness, and irritability. The brain's neurotransmitters, which play a role in transmitting **nerve** impulses from one cell to another, may be depleted by severe stress, leading to **mood** swings, outbursts of temper, and **depression**.

Post-traumatic stress disorder can affect persons of any age and is thought to occur in as many as 30 percent of disaster victims. In men, it is most commonly caused by war; in women, by rape. Symptoms usually begin within one to three months of the trauma, although in some cases they are delayed by months or even years. If left undiagnosed and untreated, PTSD can last for decades. However, over half of all affected persons who receive treatment recover completely within three months. Short-term **psychotherapy** (12 to 20 sessions) has been the single most effective treatment for PTSD. It may be accompanied by medication for specific purposes, but medication alone or for extended periods is not recommended as a course of treatment. Sleeping pills may help survivors cope in the immediate aftermath of a trauma, anti-anxiety medications may temporarily ease emotional distress, and **antidepressants** may reduce **nightmares**, flashbacks, and panic attacks.

The primary goal of psychotherapy is to have the person confront and work through the traumatic experience. **Hypnosis** may be especially valuable in retrieving thoughts and memories that have been blocked. One technique used by therapists is to focus on measures that PTSD sufferers took to save or otherwise assert themselves in the face of traumatic events, thus helping to allay the feelings of powerlessness and loss of control that play a large part in the disorder. Behavioral techniques such as relaxation training and systematic **desensitization** to "triggering" stimuli have also proven helpful. Support groups consisting of other persons who have experienced the same or similar traumas have facilitated the healing process for many persons with PTSD.

*See also* Combat neurosis

## Further Reading

Matsakis, Aphrodite. *I Can't Get Over It: A Handbook for Trauma Survivors*. Oakland, CA: New Harbinger Publications, 1992.

McCann, Lisa. *Psychological Trauma and the Adult Survivor: Theory, Therapy, and Transformation*. New York: Brunner/Mazel, 1990.

Porterfield, Kay Marie. *Straight Talk about Post-Traumatic Stress Disorder: Coping with the Aftermath of Trauma*. New York: Facts on File, 1996.

## Further Information

The International Society for Traumatic Stress Studies. 435 North Michigan Ave., Suite 1717, Chicago, IL 60611, (312) 644–0828.

# Power

One's capacity to act or to influence the behavior of others.

Power may be defined in both personal and interpersonal terms. In the first sense, it refers to one's physical, intellectual, or moral capacity to act. In the second, it denotes the **ability** to influence the behavior of others. Philosophers have often described power as an integral facet of human existence. Psychologist Harry Stack Sullivan (1892-1949) has claimed that power is a more crucial **motivation** than hunger or thirst.

**Rollo May** has written about power in terms of individual human potential, referring to the roots of the word "power" in the Latin word *posse*, which means "to be able." May distinguishes among five levels of intrapsychic power. The most basic level, the power to be, is literally the power to exist, which is threatened if one is denied the basic conditions of human sustenance. The second level, self-affirmation, goes beyond mere survival and involves recognition and esteem by others, while the third, self-assertion, refers to the more strenuous affirmation of one's existence that is required in the face of opposition. The next level of power, **aggression**, develops when one's access to other forms of self-assertion is blocked. In **contrast** to self-assertion, which May views as essentially defensive, aggression involves the active pursuit of power or territory. The endpoint in May's continuum of power is **violence**, which, unlike the other levels, is divorced from reason and verbal persuasion.

Power in its other sense—that of power over others—is a fundamental feature of all relationships, whether each party has a certain degree of power over the other (which is usually the case) or all the power resides with one party. Power may be based on force, acknowledged expertise, the possession of specific information that people want, the ability to reward others, or legitimization (the **perception** that one has the right to exercise it).

Other bases for power include identification with those who wield it and reciprocity (indebtedness to the wielder of power for providing a prior benefit of some sort). May has described various types of interpersonal power, ranging from harmful to beneficial: exploitative (characterized solely by brute force); manipulative (various types of power over another person); competitive (power *against* another); nurturing (power *for* another person); and integrative (power *with* another person).

## Further Reading

May, Rollo. *Power and Innocence: A Search for the Sources of Violence*. New York: W. W. Norton, 1972.

Tillich, Paul. *Love, Power, and Justice: Ontological Analyses and Ethical Applications*. New York: Oxford University Press, 1960.

# Preconscious

In psychoanalytic theory, knowledge, images, emotions, and other mental phenomena that are not present in immediate consciousness but are quickly accessible and can be brought into consciousness easily without the use of special techniques.

**Sigmund Freud** theorized that the human mind was divided into three parts: the conscious, preconscious, and **unconscious**. This schema first appeared in his earliest model of mental functioning, published in his classic work, *The Interpretation of Dreams* (1900). Freud believed that the preconscious functions as an intermediate or transitional level of the mind—between the unconscious and the conscious—through which repressed material passes.

Freud described this arrangement spatially, depicting the unconscious as a large room crowded with thoughts and the conscious area as a smaller reception room, with a doorkeeper between the two rooms selectively admitting thoughts from the unconscious to the **consciousness**. Those thoughts that are restricted to the unconscious area remain repressed, meaning that they are totally invisible to the conscious self, and can be recovered only by **hypnosis**, **free association**, or some other technique. Not all thoughts allowed into the "reception area" necessarily become conscious, however. Rather, they become *available* for consciousness, with one or another becoming conscious at a given time when attention is drawn to it in some way. Thus, the smaller room might more properly be thought of as a preconscious area, in which are gathered all of the thoughts that are not deliberately repressed. Because of their relative closeness to each other, Freud actually grouped the conscious and preconscious systems together in contrast to the unconscious, emphasizing that thoughts in the conscious and preconscious categories do not differ in any essential way and can be distinguished only functionally. A preconscious thought can quickly become conscious by receiving attention, and a conscious thought can slip into the preconscious when attention is withdrawn from it.

### Further Reading

Firestone, Robert. *Psychological Defenses in Everyday Life.* New York: Human Sciences Press, 1989.

Goleman, Daniel. *Vital Lies, Simple Truths: the Psychology of Self-Deception.* New York: Simon and Schuster, 1985.

# Prejudice and discrimination

A positive or negative attitude toward an individual based on his or her membership in a religious, racial, ethnic, political, or other group.

Prejudice has cognitive, affective, and behavioral components. Based on *beliefs*, it can affect one's emotions and *behavior*, sometimes leading to discrimination. Prejudiced beliefs primarily take the form of stereotypes, overall impressions based on the assumption that all members of a group possess similar attributes.

Various theories have been proposed to explain the causes and dynamics of prejudice. In the 1940s, a University of California study on anti-Semitism and other forms of prejudice created a profile of a particular **personality** type—the authoritarian personality—believed to be associated with prejudice. Persons fitting this profile are typically raised by strict, emotionally distant parents who exact rigid adherence to rules and commands. Obedience is ensured through both verbal and physical **punishment**, and independent thought and action are discouraged. As adults, people fitting this personality type define their world in terms of a social hierarchy, deferring to persons of higher status and acting with **hostility** and contempt toward those they regard as inferior. They often discriminate against or overtly persecute those whom they perceive to be of lower status. It has also been suggested that they may also be projecting their own weaknesses and fears onto the groups they denigrate. Other **traits** associated with this personality type include strict obedience to rules and authority, **conformity**, admiration of powerful figures, and inability to tolerate ambiguity. The California study also found that those who are prejudiced against one group are likely to be prejudiced against other groups as well.

Investigators have also studied prejudice as a pattern of learned attitudes and behaviors. People are not born prejudiced: many prejudices are formed against groups with which a person has never had any contact. They acquire prejudiced views by observing and listening to others, particularly one's parents and other elders. Cultural influences such as movies and television may also create or perpetuate stereotypes. The ways in which women, ethnic groups, and racial minorities are represented in the media and by the entertainment industry have been the target of much discussion and criticism. Cognitive theories have proposed that stereotypes are unavoidable because they help people categorize and make sense of a complex and diverse society.

It is a popular belief that prejudices can be overcome by direct contact between people of different backgrounds. However, social psychologists have noted that contact alone cannot eliminate stereotypes and prejudice—in fact, some types of contact can even reinforce prejudiced beliefs. For change to occur, contact between different groups must meet certain conditions: 1) members of the groups should be of equal status. 2) The interaction should move beyond the confines of ritualized interactions (such as those between employer and employee or customer and salesperson) and into personal acquaintance.

**Prejudical attitudes led whites to designate water fountains for "colored" people before the civil rights movement of the 1950s and '60s.** *(The Library of Congress. Reproduced by permission.)*

Exposure to persons who dispel or contradict stereotypes about a particular group can also help a prejudiced person to rethink his views. For example, the growing willingness of gays to be open about their sexual orientation has helped dispel the **stereotype** that all gay men are effeminate. Another important element in overcoming prejudice is the social support of one's community. During the civil rights struggles of the 1950s and 1960s, the lack of community support for desegregation and school busing further increased prejudiced feelings and behavior among some individuals. Finally, cooperative effort is an effective way of reducing prejudice. Working together toward a common goal can bring different groups of people together.

*See also* Racism

### Further Reading

Adorno, Theodor, et al. *The Authoritarian Personality.* New York: Harper and Row, 1950.

Allport, Gordon. *The Nature of Prejudice.* Reading, MA: Addison-Wesley Publishing Co., 1954.

Terkel, Studs. *Race: How Blacks and Whites Think and Feel About the American Obsession.* New York: New Press, 1992.

# Premenstrual syndrome (PMS)

Symptoms that occur several days before the onset, and sometimes during the first day of, menstruation.

Premenstrual syndrome (PMS) exhibits both physiological and psychological symptoms. The primary physiological symptoms are water retention and bloating, slightly enlarged and tender breasts, and food cravings. Psychological symptoms include irritability and **depression**. The full range of symptoms that have been attributed to PMS is extremely broad: as many as 150 have been identified. Because the symptoms are so varied from one woman to another (and even within the same woman at different times) it has been very difficult to arrive at a clinical definition of PMS. In addition, researchers disagree over whether PMS consists solely of symptoms that disappear completely at the onset of menstruation or of the premenstrual intensification of symptoms or conditions that are present, although to a lesser degree, during the rest of the month. Most women with premenstrual syndrome typically suffer from more than one symptom during each menstrual cycle.

Although there is no conclusive evidence that PMS is caused by hormone imbalances, some women have been successfully treated by hormonal therapy, which consists of oral contraceptives and monthly injections of progesterone. Recent research has linked premenstrual syndrome to an inadequate number of progesterone receptors or to the failure of those receptors to function properly, suggesting that PMS may be a disorder of progesterone response rather than progesterone deficiency. Other studies have posited a link between PMS and **brain** opioid (opiate-like) activity, based on alleged similarities between the symptoms of PMS and those of heroin withdrawal. Regular aerobic exercise, which helps stabilize opioid levels in the brain, has been shown to decrease PMS.

The physiological effects of PMS can be reduced through natural means, including **stress** management, dietary changes, acupressure massage, yoga, regular exercise, and adequate rest. Nutritional supplements, such as vitamins A, E, and B-6 have been shown to aid in the treatment of PMS, as have calcium and magnesium. Some physicians prescribe diuretics to treat water retention or tranquilizers for the treatment of irritability and **mood** swings. Recent research has suggested that drugs which increase the brain's serotonin levels, such Prozac, may also be helpful in treating PMS.

Although PMS has received much **attention** from the medical establishment, some women's health experts believe that its severity and significance have been exaggerated, and claim that only a small percentage of women have premenstrual symptoms so disabling that it interferes with work or other aspects of their lives. They also contend that the increased awareness of PMS contributes to a cultural bias that disproportionately attributes a woman's fluctuations in mood to her menstrual cycle, when the moods of both males and females will fluctuate within the course of a month for many reasons—both physiological and environmental—that have nothing to do with menstruation. In a recent investigation into the link between a woman's psychological characteristics and premenstrual syndrome, it was noted that whether or not women report PMS has less to do with the number and severity of their actual symptoms than with their general outlook on life, including levels of **self-esteem** and the **ability** to express feelings and manage stress.

### Further Reading

Dalton, Katharina. *PMS: the Essential Guide to Treatment Options*. London, Eng.: Thorsons, 1994.

*PMS: It's Not in Your Head*. [videorecording] Omaha, NB: Envision Communications, 1993.

# Primal therapy

*A therapeutic technique that claims to cure psychological disorders by encouraging people to feel deeply the pain and trauma they experienced very early in life.*

Primal therapy was pioneered by Dr. Arthur Janov in the late 1960s. Janov describes it as a "natural therapy" based on his hypothesis that most psychological disturbances are disorders of feeling which can be traced back to the traumas of conception and childbirth. The theoretical basis for the therapy is the supposition that prenatal experiences and **birth** trauma form people's primary impressions of life and that they subsequently influence the direction our lives take. The "natural" part of the theory is based on Janov's belief that these early primary experiences imprint on the human **central nervous system**, creating physiological and psychological problems in the future. Primal therapy is designed to enable clients to re-experience those critical moments. By doing so, it is assumed that underlying tensions are released, problems are alleviated, and psychological and physiological well being are restored.

The component of primal therapy with which most people are familiar is "The Primal Scream"—also the title of Janov's first book on primal therapy (New York: Perigee Books, 1970). The book describes how, with primal therapy, clients are encouraged to fully feel their original traumas (namely those of birth and conception) and to scream in response to the intense **pain** these "repressed memories" are thought to elicit. These memories are believed to be so intense that they can only be expressed with loud screaming. The process is best undertaken in a safe and controlled environment—a room with dim lighting, a padded floor, and padded walls.

Using these techniques, Janov claims that primal therapy reduces or eliminates a host of physical and psychological ailments in a relatively short time with lasting results. In fact, Janov reports that ridding the mind of so-called repressed early **childhood** or infant traumas has been scientifically linked to the reduction of many serious medical problems including **stress**, anxiety, **depression**, **sleep** disorders, high blood pressure, cancer, drug and alcohol addiction, sexual difficulties, phobias, obsessions, ulcers, migraines, asthma, and arthritis. Unfortunately, there exists no scientific evidence to support these claims; Janov's assertions of scientific linkage are based on uncontrolled case histories and personal observations.

Truth be known, primal therapy cannot be defended on scientifically established principles. This is not surprising considering its questionable theoretical rationale.

For instance, clinicians at one Canadian **psychotherapy** clinic specializing in primal therapy make the claim that, if a child is conceived through **rape**, the mother's egg and the father's sperm are "imprinted with the specific feeling state about the incident and pass this 'memory' on to the child's every cell." This supposedly causes the child a lifetime of pain and psychological trouble unless he or she learns to express his or her real feelings about the **memory** of this event. Evidence from research on memory and emotions, however, does not support the existence of retrievable memories of **birth trauma**. In short, "cellular" memories of conception are a scientific fiction. Moreover, even if infant memories were retrievable, there is no evidence to suggest that they should have such a disproportionate impact on people's lives. A recent survey of the opinions of 300 clinicians and researchers regarding psychotherapeutic techniques revealed that primal therapy was the technique whose soundness was most often questioned. Likewise, an evaluation of primal therapy commissioned by German courts concluded that primal therapy is not a valid therapeutic technique.

In Dr. Janov's latest book, *The Biology of Love,* primal therapy is discussed in the context of neuroanatomy and neurochemistry. This relationship is, however, scientifically tenuous. For example, although it is accepted among neuroscientists that working yourself into a frenzy and screaming can lead to the subsequent release of endorphins that produce feelings of relaxation and well-being, there is no evidence to support Janov's assertion that this relaxation can be attributable to the release of repressed memories. A far more likely explanation is that the endorphins are released, much like in "runner's high," in response to the strenuous activity involved. Primal therapy remains essentially unaltered from what it was 30 years ago—a creative theory and an interesting approach to therapy, but one lacking scientific substantiation.

Timothy Moore

## Further Reading

Cunningham, J. "Primal therapies—stillborn theories." In Feltham, C. et al., eds. *Controversies in Psychotherapy and Counselling.* London; Sage Publications Ltd., 1999, 25-33.
Janov, A. *The Biology of Love.* Amherst: Prometheus Books, 2000.

# Programmed learning

A method of self-instruction that enlists machines or specially prepared books to teach information.

Originally introduced in the mid-1950s by behaviorist B.F. Skinner, programmed instruction is a system whereby the learner uses specially prepared books or equipment to learn without a teacher. It was intended to free teachers from burdensome drills and repetitive problem-solving inherent in teaching basic academic subjects like spelling, arithmetic, and reading. Skinner based his ideas on the principle of **operant conditioning**, which theorized that learning takes place when a reinforcing stimulus is presented to reward a correct response. In early programmed instruction, students punched answers to simple math problems into a type of keyboard. If the answer was correct, the machine would advance to another problem. Incorrect answers would not advance. Skinner believed such learning could, in fact, be superior to traditional teacher-based instruction because children were rewarded immediately and individually for correct answers rather than waiting for a teacher to correct written answers or respond verbally. Programmed instruction quickly became popular and spawned much educational research and commercial enterprise in the production of programmed instructional materials. It is considered the antecedent of modern computer-assisted learning.

Two types of programmed learning can be compared. Linear programming involves a simple step-by-step procedure. There is a single set of materials and students work from one problem to the next until the end of the program. Branching programming is more complex. Students choose from multiple-choice answers and then are prompted to proceed to another page of the book depending on their answer. If a correct answer is given, students move on to another page with more information to learn and more questions to answer. An incorrect answer leads to comments on why the answer is incorrect and a direction to return to the original question to make another selection.

Just as the programming developed more complexity over the years, so did the teaching machines themselves. Early, simple machines were little more than electronic workbooks. Later machines allowed students to be instructed on more complex material that required more than one-word or one-number responses. In some, students could write their responses and move ahead by comparing their answers to acceptable answers. Programmed-learning books differ from traditional workbooks because they actually teach new information through this step-by-step stimulus-response method rather than simply offering practice material for already-learned skills.

Research has shown that programmed learning often is as successful, and sometimes more successful, than traditional teacher-based learning because it recognizes the different abilities and needs of individual children.

Students who have mastered the material can move ahead more quickly, while those who need more practice are repeatedly exposed to the problems. Programmed learning also allows teachers more time to concentrate on more complex tasks. One criticism of programmed learning centers on the lack of student-teacher interaction. It has been shown that some students thrive more fully with the human **motivation** inherent in more traditional learning situations.

### Further Reading
Bower, Gordon H., and Ernest R. Hilgard. *Theories of Learning.* Englewood Cliffs, NJ: Prentice-Hall, 1981.

## Projective techniques

Unstructured tests used for personality assessment that rely on the subject's interpretation of ambiguous stimuli.

Projective techniques involve asking subjects to interpret or fill in visual stimuli, complete sentences, or report what associations particular words bring to mind. Because of the leeway provided by the tests, subjects project their own personalities onto the stimulus, often revealing personal conflicts, motivations, coping styles, and other characteristics.

The best known projective test is the Rorschach test, created in the 1920s by Swiss psychologist Hermann Rorschach (1884-1922). It consists of a series of 10 cards, each containing a complicated inkblot. Some are in black and white, some in color. Subjects are asked to describe what they see in each card. Test scores are based on several parameters: 1) what part of the blot a person focuses on; 2) what particular details determine the response; 3) the content of the responses (what objects, persons, or situations they involve); and 4) the frequency with which a particular response has been given by previous test takers. A number of different scoring methods have been devised for the Rorschach test, some aimed at providing greater objectivity and validity for this highly impressionistic form of assessment. However, many psychologists still interpret the test freely according to their subjective impressions. Some also take into account the subject's demeanor while taking the test (cooperative, anxious, defensive, etc.).

Another widely used projective test is the **Thematic Apperception Test** (TAT) introduced at Harvard University in 1935 by **Henry Murray**. Test takers look at a series of up to 20 pictures of people in a variety of recognizable settings and construct a story about what is happening in each one. They are asked to describe not only what is happening at the moment shown in the picture but also what events led up to the present situation and what the characters are thinking and feeling. They are encouraged to interpret the pictures as freely and imaginatively as they want and to be completely open and honest in their responses. As with the Rorschach test, the psychologist often interprets the test results subjectively, focusing on any recurring themes in responses to the different pictures. However, scoring methods have also been developed that focus on specific aspects of the subjects' responses, including **aggression**, expression of needs, and perceptions of reality.

Still another type of projective technique is the sentence completion test. Many tests of this type have been developed, some of which investigate particular **personality** features. Others are designed specifically for children or adolescents. Subjects are asked to complete sentences with such open-ended beginnings as "I wish . . ." or "My mother . . ." Although the same sentence beginnings are shown to different test takers, there are no norms for comparing their answers to those of previous subjects. Still other types of projective tests have been developed, including some that ask the subject to create drawings or complete a story.

Compared to the more objective questionnaire-type personality assessments, projective tests are difficult to score, and questions are often raised about their degree of reliability and validity. In most cases, not enough research has been done on such tests to determine scientifically how effective they actually are in assessing personality. Results of the Thematic Apperception Test obtained by different scorers have proven relatively reliable when specific features (such as aggression) are measured. However, the reliability of the Rorschach test, which has also been researched, has generally proven unsatisfactory because test results are dependent on the psychologist's judgment. Different interpretations of the same set of responses may vary significantly. Although newer scoring systems—including one that allows for computer scoring—may yield greater reliability, free interpretation of the test is valuable to clinicians.

In addition to their weaknesses in terms of reliability and validation, projective tests also require more time and skill to administer than more objective testing methods. However, they continue to be employed because of their usefulness in helping psychologists obtain a comprehensive picture of an individual's personality. The results are most useful when combined with information obtained from personal observation, other test scores, and familiarity with a client's previous history. In addition, projective tests make it especially difficult for subjects to skew their answers in a particular direction as they sometimes attempt to do with other types of assessment.

*See also* Holtzman inkblot technique; Rorschach technique

**Further Reading**

Cronbach, L.J. *Essentials of Psychological Testing.* New York: Harper and Row, 1970.

Sundberg, N. *The Assessment of Persons.* Englewood Cliffs, NJ: Prentice-Hall, 1977.

# Psyche

In psychology, an individual's consciousness.

The term psyche actually takes its meaning from ancient myth. In Roman mythology, Psyche represented the human spirit and was portrayed as a beautiful girl with butterfly wings. Psyche was a beautiful mortal desired by Cupid, to the dismay of Cupid's mother Venus. Venus demanded that her son order Psyche to fall in love with the ugliest man in the world. Cupid refused and loved Psyche himself, visiting her only by night and commanding that she not look at him. Eventually, Psyche broke Cupid's rule and lit a lamp to look upon his face. For this disloyalty, Cupid abandoned her and Psyche wandered through the world in search of her lover. Eventually she was reunited with Cupid and made immortal by Jupiter.

The modern day use of the concept of psyche still incorporates the meaning of the human soul or spirit. It can also refer to the mind. Many different branches of science may have an interest in studying matters of the psyche. An online academic journal titled *Psyche* illustrates the wide range of study around the concept of psyche; participants come from the fields of cognitive science, philosophy, psychology, physics, neuroscience, and **artificial intelligence**. The magazine refers to its mission as an "interdisciplinary exploration of the nature of **consciousness** and its relation to the brain." Topics discussed regarding psyche in this diverse forum have included animal consciousness, the visual **brain**, and the triangular circuit of **attention**.

Psychiatrist **Carl Jung** (1875–1961) believed that the psyche was self regulating, and that it became more defined as a person went through the process of "individuation." Jung's theories, which he called analytical psychology, also included recognition and exploration of a "collective unconsciousness."

Catherine Dybiec Holm

# Psychiatry/Psychiatrist

A physician who specializes in the diagnosis and treatment of mental disorders.

Psychiatrists treat patients privately and in hospital settings through a combination of **psychotherapy** and medication. There are about 41,000 practicing psychiatrists in the United States. Their training consists of four years of medical school, followed by one year of internship and at least three years of psychiatric residency. Psychiatrists may receive certification from the American Board of Psychiatry and Neurology (ABPN), which requires two years of clinical experience beyond residency and the successful completion of a written and an oral test. Unlike a medical license, board certification is not legally required in order to practice psychiatry.

Psychiatrists may practice general psychiatry or choose a specialty, such as child psychiatry, geriatric psychiatry, treatment of substance abuse, forensic (legal) psychiatry, emergency psychiatry, **mental retardation**, community psychiatry, or public health. Some focus their research and clinical work primarily on psychoactive medication, in which case they are referred to as psychopharmacologists. Psychiatrists may be called upon to address numerous social issues, including **juvenile delinquency**, family and marital dysfunction, legal competency in criminal and financial matters, and treatment of mental and emotional problems among prison inmates and in the military.

Psychiatrists treat the biological, psychological, and social components of **mental illness** simultaneously. They can investigate whether symptoms of mental disorders have physical causes, such as a hormone imbalance or an adverse reaction to medication, or whether psychological symptoms are contributing to physical conditions, such as cardiovascular problems and high blood pressure. Because they are licensed physicians, psychiatrists, unlike psychologists and psychiatric social workers, can prescribe medication; they are also able to admit patients to the hospital. Other **mental health** professionals who cannot prescribe medication themselves often establish a professional relationship with a psychiatrist.

Psychiatrists may work in private offices, private psychiatric hospitals, community hospitals, state and federal hospitals, or community mental centers. Often, they combine work in several settings. As of 1988, 15 percent of psychiatrists belonged to group practices. In addition to their clinical work, psychiatrists often engage in related professional activities, including teaching, research, and administration. The **American Psychiatric Association**, the oldest medical specialty organization in the United States, supports the profession by offering continuing education and research opportunities, keeping members informed about new research and public policy issues, helping to educate the public about mental health issues, and serving as an advocate for people affected by mental illness.

Traditional psychiatry has been challenged in a variety of ways since the end of World War II. The most widespread and significant change has been the removal of the psychiatric hospital from its central role in the practice of psychiatry. This development resulted from a number of factors: the financial inability of state governments to remedy the deteriorating condition of many institutions; the discovery of new, more effective drugs enabling patients to medicate themselves at home; social activists' charges of abuse and neglect in state mental facilities; and activism by former mental patients protesting involuntary **institutionalization** and treatment. In addition, a growing movement, led by Karl Menninger, sought to replace state **mental hospitals** with community mental health centers. The Community Mental Health Centers Act of 1963 allotted federal funds for the establishment of community treatment centers, which provide a variety of services, including short-term and partial hospitalization. The establishment of these centers has contributed to the growing trend toward the deinstitutionalization of mental patients.

In the 1960s and 1970s radical critics within the profession, such as Thomas Szasz and **R. D. Laing**, challenged basic assumptions about psychiatric treatment and about the medical model of mental illness itself. Sociologists, including Erving Goffman and Thomas Scheff, produced critiques of mental institutions as a form of social control, and the anti-psychiatry ideas of French philosopher Michel Foucault gained currency among American intellectuals. Psychiatry also came under fire from the feminist movement, which saw it as a vehicle for controlling women. Feminist authors Kate Millett and Shulamith Firestone have portrayed **psychoanalysis** as instrumental in suppressing the original feminist movement of the late 19th and early 20th centuries by labeling women's legitimate dissatisfaction and agitation as hysteria and providing an intellectual theory that aided in legitimizing society's continuing subordination of women. Published in 1972, Phyllis Chesler's *Women and Madness* was a landmark in feminist criticism.

Advances in neuroscience, endocrinology, and immunology have had a major effect on the way psychiatry is practiced today. The study of neurotransmitters—chemicals in the **brain** that are related to anxiety, **depression**, and other disorders—have been significant both in the development of new medications and in the way psychiatrists think about **mood**, **personality**, and

behavior. Currently, a major (and highly publicized) issue in psychiatry is the use of Prozac and other specialized serotonin reuptake inhibitors (SSRIs), a new class of **antidepressants** that has fewer side effects than drugs previously used to treat depression. These drugs have become controversial because of their potential use for "cosmetic psychopharmacology," the transformation of mood and personality in persons with no diagnosable mental disorder. Both psychiatrists and others in the medical and mental health professions must confront the issue of using **psychoactive drugs** as "mood brighteners" to make clinically healthy individuals more energetic, assertive, and resilient.

Another contemporary development with wide-ranging implications for psychiatry is the growth of health maintenance organizations (HMOs) and managed care programs, whose cost-containment policies have already had a significant effect on the way psychiatry is practiced. Expensive long-term psychotherapy is discouraged by such organizations, and medication is generally favored over therapy. Recently, concern has been expressed over the practice of promoting cheaper medications over more expensive ones, even when those that cost more offer greater benefits.

### Further Reading

Coles, Robert. *The Mind's Fate: A Psychiatrist Looks at His Profession.* Boston: Little, Brown and Co., 1995.

Kramer, Peter D. *Listening to Prozac: A Psychiatrist Explores Antidepressant Drugs and the Remaking of the Self.* New York: Viking, 1993.

Laing, R. D. *Wisdom, Madness, and Folly: The Making of a Psychiatrist.* New York: McGraw-Hill, 1985.

# Psychoactive drugs

Medications used to treat mental illness and brain disorders.

## Overview and use

The role of psychoactive drugs, also called psychotherapeutic agents or psychotropic drugs, in the treatment of **mental illness** is dependent on the disorder for which they are prescribed. In cases where mental illness is considered biological in nature, such as with a diagnosis of **bipolar disorder** or **schizophrenia**, pharmaceutical therapy with psychotherapeutic drugs is recommended as a primary method of treatment. In other cases, such as in **personality** disorder or dissociative disorder, psychoactive medications are usually considered a secondary, companion treatment (or adjunct) to a type of **psychotherapy**, such as cognitive-behavioral therapy. In these situations, medication is used to provide temporary symptom relief while the patient works on the issues leading to his illness with a therapist or other **mental health** professional.

Psychoactive drugs can be classified into seven major categories. These include:

- *Antianxiety agents.* Drugs used to treat anxiety disorders and symptoms. These include benzodiazepines such as alprazolam (Xanax), lorazepam (Ativan), diazepam (Valium), and chlordiazepoxide (Librium), and other medications including buspirone (BuSpar) and paroxetine (Paxil).

- *Antidepressants.* Prescribed to treat major depressive disorder, dysthymic disorder, and bipolar disorder. Popular **antidepressants** include venlafaxine (Effexor), nefazodone (Serzone), bupropion (Wellbutrin), MAOI inhibitors such as phenelzine (Nardil) and tranylcypromine (Parnate); selective serotonin reuptake inhibitors (SSRIs) such as fluoxetine (Prozac), paroxetine (Paxil), and sertraline (Zoloft); tricyclic antidepressants such as amitriptyline (Elavil), doxepin hydrochloride (Sinequan), desipramine (Norpramin), and perphenazine/amitriptyline combinations (Etrafon).

- *Antimanic agents.* This category includes medications used to treat **mania** associated with bipolar disorder (or manic-depressive disorder) such as divalproex sodium (Depakote) and lithium carbonate (Lithium, Eskalith, Lithobid, Tegrator).

- *Antipanic agents.* Prescribed to treat the panic symptoms that are a defining feature of many anxiety disorders. Medications include clonazepam (Klonopin), paroxetine (Paxil), alprazolam (Xanax), and sertraline (Zoloft).

- *Antipsychotic agents.* Also known as neuroleptic agents, these medications are used to manage **psychosis** related to schizophrenia, delusional disorder, and brief psychotic disorder. They include clozapine (Clozaril), haloperidol (Haldol), loxapine (Loxitane), molindone (Moban), thiothixene (Navane), risperidone (Risperdal), and olanzapine (Zyprexa); also includes phenothiazines such as prochlorperazine (Compazine), trifluoperazine hydrochloride (Stelazine), and chlorpromazine (Thorazine).

- *Obsessive-compulsive disorder medications.* Drugs used to treat OCD include fluvoxamine (Luvox), paroxetine (Paxil), fluoxetine (Prozac), and sertraline (Zoloft).

- *Psychostimulants.* Also known as **central nervous system** stimulants, these medications are used to treat **attention deficit disorders** (ADD and ADHD) and **narcolepsy.** They include methylphenidate hydrochloride (Methylin, Ritalin) and methaamphetamines (Desoxyn, Dexedrine, and DextroStat).

## Side effects

There are a number of side-effects associated with psychotherapeutic agents. These can include, and are not limited to, dry mouth, drowsiness, disorientation, **delirium,** agitation, tremor, irregular heartbeat, headache, insomnia, gastrointestinal distress, nausea, menstrual irregularity, weight gain, weight loss, loss of sex drive, skin rashes, and sweating. Patients should inform their healthcare provider if they experience any of these side effects. In some cases, a dosage adjustment or change of prescription can alleviate any discomfort caused by them. Additional medications may also be prescribed to address severe side effects (e.g., anticholinergic medication may be prescribed for muscle spasms caused by antipsychotic medications).

*Tardive dyskinesia,* a condition characterized by involuntary movements of the mouth and other locations on the body, has been reported in some patients who take antipsychotic medication on a long-term basis. In some cases, the condition is permanent, although discontinuing or changing medication may halt or reverse it in some patients.

*Agranulocytosis,* a potentially serious illness in which the white blood cells that typically fight infection in the body are destroyed, is a possible side effect of clozapine, another antipsychotic. Patients taking this medication should undergo weekly blood tests to monitor their white blood cell counts.

## Precautions

Psychotherapeutic agents can be contraindicated (not recommended for use) in patients with certain medical conditions. They may also interact with other prescription and over-the-counter medications, either magnifying or reducing the intended effects of one or both drugs. In some circumstances, they can trigger serious, even life-threatening, physical side effects. For this reason, individuals who are prescribed psychoactive medication should inform their mental healthcare provider and any other prescribing doctor of all medications they are taking, and of any medical conditions they have not yet disclosed.

Monoamine oxidase inhibitors (MAOIs) such as tranylcypromine (Parnate) and phenelzine (Nardil) block the action of monoamine oxidase (MAO), a chemical agent of the central **nervous system.** Patients who are prescribed MAOIs must eliminate foods high in tyramine (found in aged cheeses, red wines, and meats) from their diets to avoid potentially serious hypotensive side effects.

Patients taking Lithium, an antimanic medication, must carefully monitor their salt intake. Diarrhea, sweating, fever, change in diet, or anything else that lowers the level of sodium in their system can result in a toxic build up of Lithium, which can result in slurred speech, confusion, irregular heart beat, vomiting, blurred **vision**, and possibly death.

Certain psychoactive drugs are lethal in excessive doses, and therefore may not be a viable treatment option for patients at risk for suicide unless they can be dispensed in a controlled manner.

Many psychoactive drugs are contraindicated in pregnancy, particularly in the first trimester. Patients should check with their doctor about the risks associated with psychotherapeutic medications and possible treatment options when planning a pregnancy.

Paula Ford-Martin

**Further Reading**

Medical Economics Company. *The Physicians Desk Reference (PDR)*. 54th edition. Montvale, NJ: Medical Economics Company, 2000.

**Further Information**

National Institute of Mental Health (NIMH). 6001 Executive Boulevard, Rm. 8184, MSC 9663, Bethesda, MD, USA. 20892-9663, fax: (301)443-4279, (301)443-4513. Email: nimhinfo@nih.gov. http://www.nimh.nih.gov.

# Psychoanalysis

A method of treatment for mental, emotional, and behavioral dysfunctions as developed by Sigmund Freud.

Developed in Vienna, Austria, by **Sigmund Freud** (1856-1939), psychoanalysis is based on an approach in which the therapist helps the patient better understand him- or herself through examination of the deep personal feelings, relationships, and events that have shaped motivations and behavior. Freud developed his theories during the end of the 19th and the early part of the 20th centuries in Vienna, Austria, where he was a practicing physician specializing in neurological disorders. Freud's interest originated in his medical practice when he encountered patients who were clearly suffering physical symptoms for which he could find no organic, or biological, cause. Freud's first attempt to get at the psychological cause of these patients' pain was through **hypnosis**, which he studied in Paris in 1885. He found the results to be less than he'd hoped, however, and soon borrowed

from a Viennese contemporary the idea of getting a patient to simply talk about his or her problems. Freud expanded upon this practice, however, by creating the idea of "free association," in which a patient is encouraged to speak in a non-narrative, non-directed manner, with the hope that he or she will eventually reveal/uncover the **unconscious** heart of the problem. This sort of unbridled, undirected self-exploration became one of the signature tenets of psychoanalysis.

Continuing his research of the mind and the unconscious, Freud published *The Interpretation of Dreams* in 1900. In this work he outlined his ideas about the construction of the mind and human **personality**. This book was followed by the now basics of the Freudian canon: *The Psychopathology of Everyday Life* in 1904 and *A Case of Hysteria* and *Three Essays on the Theory of Sexuality,* both in 1905. By the second decade of the 20th century, Freud had become an internationally renowned thinker, and psychoanalysis had emerged as a significant intellectual achievement on par with the work of Albert Einstein in physics and in many ways comparable to the modernist movement in the visual arts. Psychoanalysis was in its prime and it became something of a fad to undergo psychoanalytic treatment among the Western world's elite.

## Psychoanalysis and the development of personality

Freud believed that human personality was constructed of three parts: the **id**, the **ego**, and the **superego**. The id, according to this schema, is comprised largely of instinctual drives—for food and sex, for instance. These drives are essentially unconscious and result in satisfaction when they are fulfilled and frustration and anxiety when they are thwarted. The ego is linked to the id, but is the component that has undergone **socialization** and which recognizes that instant gratification of the id urges is not always possible. The superego acts in many ways like the ego, as a moderator of behavior; but whereas the ego moderates urges based on social constraints, the superego operates as an arbiter of right and wrong. It moderates the id's urges based on a moral code. Having theorized this framework of human personality, Freud used it to demonstrate how instinctual drives are inevitably confounded with strictly social codes (by the ego) and by notions of morality (by the superego). This conflict, psychoanalytic theory supposes, is at the heart of anxiety and neuroses.

In dealing with these conflicts, Freud's psychoanalytic theory suggests that the human mind constructs three forms of adaptive mechanisms: namely, *defense mechanisms,* neurotic symptoms, and *dreams.* Freud believed **dreams** were vivid representations of repressed urges: the id speaking out in wildly incongruous nighttime parables. He considered dreams to have two parts, the manifest content, the narrative that one is able to remember upon waking, and the latent content, the underlying, largely symbolic message. Because Freud believed dreams to represent unfulfilled longings of the id, psychoanalysis deals heavily with dream interpretation.

Psychoanalytic theory also sees various neurotic symptoms as symbolic acts representing the repressed longings of the id. For Freud, a neurotic symptom was what we now consider a psychosomatic disorder, some physical symptom that has a psychological, or in Freud's terms, neurological, origin. Psychoanalytic theory suggests that conditions like blindness, paralysis, and severe headaches can result from unfulfilled longings that the patient is unable to confront on a conscious level. Because of this inability, the patient develops some acceptable symptom, such as headaches, for which he or she can then seek medical **attention**.

The final adaptive mechanism Freud suggested are **defense mechanisms**. Freud identified several defense mechanisms, such as repression, displacement, denial, rationalization, projection, and identification. Each has its own peculiar dynamic but all work to distance a person from a conflict that is too difficult to confront realistically. These conflicts, according to psychoanalytic theory, originate during one of the four developmental stages Freud identified. These stages, and the infantile **sexuality** he identified as occurring within them, are some of the most controversial aspects of psychoanalytic theory. Freud suggested that adult neuroses was a result of and could be traced back to frustrated sexual gratification during these stages, which are: the oral stage, **birth** to one year; the anal stage, 1-3 years; the phallic stage, 3-5 years; and latency, five years to **puberty**. Each of these stages is in turn divided into sub-stages. In each of the major stages, the infant has sexual needs which, because of social mores, are left largely unfulfilled, causing neuroses to originate.

It is during the phallic stage that Freud hypothesized the development of the **Oedipus complex**, easily the most renowned and controversial theoretical construction of the Freudian canon. The Oedipus complex suggests that during the phallic stage, a child begins associating his genitals with sexual pleasure and becomes erotically attracted to the parent of the opposite sex while at the same time developing an intense **jealousy** of the same-sex parent. While Freud's original theory excludes consideration of females, his contemporary, **Carl Jung** (1875-1961), expanded this particular dynamic and theorized an Electra complex for women in which the same psychodrama of erotic attraction and jealousy is played out from the young girl's point of view.

### Freud's critics

From nearly the beginning, Freud and his construction of psychoanalytic theory have faced intense criticism. His most famous dissenter is Jung, his former disciple. Jung split with Freud in 1913 over a variety of issues, including, but certainly not limited to, Freud's emphasis on infantile sexuality. Jung had a different view of the construction of human personality, for instance, and had different ideas about how dreams should be interpreted and viewed as part of psychoanalysis. **Alfred Adler**, another disciple of Freud, broke with the master over infantile sexuality, positing a view that infants and children are driven primarily by a need for self-affirmation rather than sexual gratification. In modern times, Freud has been the target of criticism from many corners. Feminists especially criticize his understanding of "hysteria" and his theory of Oedipal conflict.

Freudian psychoanalysis focuses on uncovering unconscious motivations and breaking down defenses. Many therapists feel that psychoanalysis is the most effective technique to identify and deal with internal conflicts and feelings that contribute to dysfunctional behavior. Through psychoanalysis, the patient increases his understanding of himself and his internal conflicts so that they will no longer exert as much influence on mental and emotional health.

### Further Reading

Hall, Calvin S. *A Primer of Freudian Psychology.* New York: Harper and Row, 1982.

Menninger, K. and P.S. Holzman. *Theory of Psychoanalytic Technique.* New York: Basic Book, 1973.

Mitchell, Juliet. *Psychoanalysis and Feminism.* New York: Vintage Book, 1975.

# Psychodrama

See **Role playing/psychodrama**

# Psychological Abstracts

Monthly journal published by the American Psychological Association.

Founded in 1927, *Psychological Abstracts* contains nonevaluative summary abstracts of literature in the field of psychology and related disciplines, which are grouped into 22 major classification categories. It includes summaries of technical reports as well as journal articles and books. Each edition is collected into a cumulative volume every six months, with an index listing both the volume's contents and the national and international journals in which the abstracted literature appear. These journals are cited within the volume by codes listed in each monthly issue. A table of contents near the beginning of each issue guides readers to broad general areas that they may wish to investigate, while the subject indexes in the cumulative volumes refers them to articles on a particular topic.

In addition to research articles, *Psychological Abstracts* features theoretical discussions and reviews of other investigations, and alsocontains an author index for readers who would like to follow up their research by studying additional articles or books by a given author.

*PsycLIT®,* the CD-ROM version of *Psychological Abstracts,* became available in 1993, and is used by many academic and large public libraries. *PsycLIT®,* a two-CD set which is updated quarterly, includes over 670,000 records. *PsycLIT®* indexes and abstracts articles dating from 1973 from 1,300 professional journals. The database also indexes and abstracts books and book chapters dating from 1987.

**Further Information**

EBSCO Publishing. 10 Estes Street, Ispwich, MA 01938, (800) 653–2726.

# Psychological disorder

A condition characterized by patterns of thought, emotion, or behavior that are maladaptive, disruptive, or uncomfortable either for the person affected or for others.

While psychological disorders are generally signaled by some form of abnormal behavior or thought process, abnormality can be difficult to define, especially since it varies from culture to culture. Psychologists have several standard approaches to defining abnormality for diagnostic purposes. One is the statistical approach, which evaluates behavior by determining how closely it conforms to or deviates from that of the majority of people. Behavior may also be evaluated by whether it conforms to social rules and cultural norms, an approach that avoids condemning nonconformists as abnormal for behavior that, while unusual, may not violate social standards and may even be valued in their culture. Yet another way to gauge the normality of behavior is by whether it is adaptive or maladaptive—and to what extent it interferes with the conduct of everyday life. In some situations, psychologists may also evaluate normality solely on the basis of whether or not a person is made unhappy or uncomfortable by his or her own behavior.

The official standard for the classification of psychological disorders is the American Psychiatric Association's Diagnostic and Statistical Manual of Mental Disorders, whose most recent edition is also referred to as *DSM-IV.* Its five dimensions, or axes for evaluating behavior and thought patterns, provide a thorough context in which to assess an individual's psychological profile. Axis I lists major mental disorders that may **affect** a patient. Axis II is for assessing of **personality** disorders—lifelong, deeply ingrained patterns of behavior that are destructive to those who display them or to others. Axis III deals with any organic medical problems that may be present. The fourth axis includes any environmental or psychosocial factors affecting a person's condition (such as the loss of a loved one, **sexual abuse**, **divorce**, career changes, poverty, or homelessness). In Axis V, the diagnostician assesses the person's level of functioning within the previous 12 months on a scale of one to 100.

Conditions that would formerly have been described as neurotic are now found in five Axis I classifications: anxiety disorders, somatoform disorders, dissociative disorders, **mood** disorders, and sexual disorders. Anxiety disorders—conditions involving longstanding, intense, or disruptive anxiety—are the most common of psychological disorders among Americans. These include phobias (a strong **fear** of a specific object or situation); generalized anxiety (a diffuse, free-floating anxiety); panic disorder (an acute anxiety attack often accompanied by agoraphobia, or fear of being separated from a safe place); and **obsessive-compulsive disorder** (a repetitive, uncontrollable behavior triggered by persistent, unwanted thoughts).

Somatoform disorders are characterized by psychological problems that take a physical, or somatic, form. A person suffering from a somatoform disorder will show persistent physical symptoms for which no physiological cause can be found. Included among these disorders are hypochondriasis (a strong, unjustified fear of contracting a serious disease); **pain** disorder (severe pain with no apparent physical cause); and somatization disorder (complaints about a variety of physical problems). Another somatoform condition, conversion disorder (formerly called conversion hysteria), is characterized by apparent blindness, deafness, paralysis, or insensitivity to pain with no physiological cause. Conversion disorders, which are most prevalent in **adolescence** or early adulthood, are usually accompanied by some form of severe **stress** and often appear to elicit surprisingly little concern in the patient. Dissociative disorders involve the fragmentation, or dissociation, of personality components that are usually integrated, such as **memory, consciousness**, or even identity itself. These disorders include **amnesia, dissociative identity disorder**, and dissociative **fugue** (in which amnesia is accompanied by assumption of a new identity in a new location).

Mood disorders (also called affective disorders), are characterized by extremes of mood, abnormal mood fluctuations, or inconsistency between mood and the surrounding events or **environment**. The two leading mood disorders are **depression** and **bipolar disorder**. Major depressive disorder is characterized by feelings and behaviors that many people experience at times—sadness, **guilt**, fatigue, loss of appetite—but it is distinguished by their persistence and severity. Major depression may be accompanied by feelings of inadequacy and worthlessness, weight loss or gain, **sleep** disturbances, difficulty concentrating and making decisions, and, in the most severe cases, delusions and suicidal impulses. Depression is a major problem in the United States; one-third of all psychiatric outpatients suffer from depression. The percentage of Americans who will experience at least one major depressive episode during their lives has been estimated at between eight and 12 percent for men and between 20 and 26 percent for women. Bipolar disorder (also known as manic depression) is characterized by the alternation of depression with **mania**, an abnormally active and elated emotional state in which a person becomes overly optimistic, energetic, and convinced of his or her own powers and abilities. Manic episodes can result in impulsive and unwise decisions, and may even pose physical dangers.

The *DSM-IV* list of mental disorders also includes **psychotic disorders**, which are severe conditions characterized by abnormalities in thinking, false beliefs, and other symptoms indicating a highly distorted **perception** of reality and severe interference with the capacity to function normally. Probably the best known of these disorders is **schizophrenia**, which seriously disrupts communication and other **normal** functions, including profound disturbances in thinking, **emotion**, perception, and behavior. About one percent of Americans suffer from schizophrenia. Other mental disorders listed in *DSM-IV* include eating and **sleep disorders**; impulse control and **adjustment disorders**; substance-related disorders; cognitive disorders, such as **delirium**, and **dementia**; and disorders usually diagnosed in **infancy, childhood**, or adolescence, such as hyperactivity, **mental retardation**, and **autism**. **Personality disorders**, which are listed in Axis II of *DSM-IV*, include narcissistic, dependent, avoidant, and antisocial personality types. This axis also includes developmental disorders in children.

# Psychological testing

See **Assessment, psychological**

# Psychology/Psychologist

The science which studies behavior and mental processes.

As psychology has grown and changed throughout its history, it has been defined in numerous ways. As early as 400 B.C., the ancient Greeks philosophized about the relationship of **personality** characteristics to physiological **traits**. Since then, philosophers have proposed theories to explain human behavior. In the late 1800s the emergence of **scientific method** gave the study of psychology a new focus. In 1879, the first psychological laboratory was opened in Leipzig, Germany, by **Wilhelm Wundt** (1832-1920), and soon afterwards the first experimental studies of **memory** were published. Wundt was instrumental in establishing psychology as the study of conscious experience, which he viewed as made up of elemental sensations. In addition to the type of psychology practiced by Wundt—which became known as structuralism—other early schools of psychology were **functionalism**, which led to the development of **behaviorism**, and **Gestalt psychology**. The American Psychological Association was founded in 1892 with the goals of encouraging research, enhancing professional competence, and disseminating knowledge about the field.

With the ascendance of the Viennese psychologist **Sigmund Freud** and his method of **psychoanalysis** early in the twentieth century, emphasis shifted from conscious experience to **unconscious** processes investigated by means of **free association** and other techniques. According to Freud, behavior and mental processes were the result of mostly unconscious struggles within each person between the drive to satisfy basic instincts, such as sex or **aggression**, and the limits imposed by society. At the same time that Freud's views were gaining popularity in Europe, an American psychology professor, John B. Watson, was pioneering the behavioral approach, which focuses on observing and measuring external behaviors rather than the internal workings of the mind. B.F. Skinner, who spent decades studying the effects of reward and **punishment** on behavior, helped maintain the predominance of behaviorism in the United States through the 1950s and 1960s. Since the 1970s, many psychologists have been influenced by the cognitive approach, which is

*Psychology/Psychologist*

concerned with the relationship of mental processes to behavior. **Cognitive psychology** focuses on how people take in, perceive, and store information, and how they process and act on that information.

Additional psychological perspectives include the neurobiological approach, focusing on relating behavior to internal processes within the **brain** and **nervous system**, and the phenomenological approach, which is most concerned with the individual's subjective experience of the world rather than the application of psychological theory to behavior. While all these approaches differ in their explanations of individual behavior, each contributes an important perspective to the psychological image of the total human being. Most psychologists apply the principles of various approaches in studying and understanding human nature.

Along with several approaches to psychology there are also numerous subfields in which these approaches may be applied. Most subfields can be categorized under one of two major areas of psychology referred to as basic and **applied psychology**. Individual psychologists may specialize in one of the subfields in either of these areas. The subfields are often overlapping areas of interest rather than isolated domains. Basic psychology encompasses the subfields concerned with the advancement of psychological theory and research. **Experimental psychology** employs laboratory experiments to study basic behavioral processes shared by different species, including sensation, **perception**, learning, memory, communication, and **motivation**. **Physiological psychology** is concerned with the ways in which biology shapes behavior and mental processes, and **developmental psychology** is concerned with behavioral development over the entire life span. Other subfields include **social psychology**, quantitative psychology, and the psychology of personality.

Applied psychology is the area of psychology concerned with applying psychological research and theory to problems posed by everyday life. It includes **clinical psychology**, the largest single field in psychology. Clinical psychologists—accounting for 40 percent of all psychologists—are involved in **psychotherapy** and psychological testing. Like clinical psychologists, counseling psychologists apply psychological principles to diagnose and treat individual emotional and behavioral problems. Other subfields of applied psychology include **school psychology**, which involves the evaluation and placement of students; **educational psychology**, which investigates the psychological aspects of the learning process; and **industrial psychology** and organizational psychology,whichstudy the relationship between people and their jobs. Community psychologists investigate environmental factors that contribute to mental and emotional disorders; health psychologistsdeal with the psychological aspects of physical illness, investigating the connections between the mind and a person's physical condition; and consumer psychologistsstudy the preferences and buying habits of consumers as well as their reactions to certain advertising.

In response to society's changing needs, new fields of psychology are constantly emerging. One new type of specialization, called environmental psychology, focuses on the relationship between people and their physical surroundings. Its areas of inquiry include such issues as the effects of overcrowding and noise on urban dwellers and the effects of building design. Another relatively new specialty is forensic psychology,involving the application of psychology to law enforcement and the judicial system. Forensic psychologists may help create personality profiles of criminals, formulate principles for jury selection, or study the problems involved in eyewitness testimony. Yet another emerging area is program evaluation, whose practitioners evaluate the effectiveness and cost efficiency of government programs.

Depending on the nature of their work, psychologists may practice in a variety of settings, including colleges and universities, hospitals and community **mental health** centers, schools, and businesses. A growing number of psychologists work in private practice and may also specialize in multiple subfields. Most psychologists earn a Ph.D. degree in the field, which requires completion of a four- to six-year program offered by a university psychology department. The course of study includes a broad overview of the field, as well as specialization in a particular subfield, and completion of a dissertation and an internship. Students who intend to practice only applied psychology rather than conduct research have the option of obtaining a Psy.D. degree, which does not entail writing a dissertation.

*See also* Behavior therapy; Cognitive therapy; Counseling psychology; Developmental psychology; Experimental psychology; Health psychology; Research Methodology

# Psychophysics

The subfield of psychology that deals with the transformation from the physical to the psychological through detection, identification, discrimination, and scaling.

Psychophysics originated with the research of **Gustav Fechner** (1801-1887), who first studied the relationship between incoming physical stimuli and the responses to them. Psychophysicists have generally used two approaches in studying our sensitivity to stimuli around us: measuring the **absolute threshold** or discovering the difference threshold. In studying the absolute threshold using the method of constant stimuli, an experimenter will, for example, produce an extremely faint tone which the listener cannot hear, then gradually increase the intensity until the person can just hear it; on the next trial, the experimenter will play a sound that is clearly heard, then reduce its intensity until the listener can no longer hear it. Thresholds can also be ascertained through the method of constant stimuli. In this approach, stimuli of varying intensity are randomly presented. Although an observer's measured threshold will change depending on methodology, this technique gives an estimate of an individual's sensitivity.

A different psychophysical approach combines the concept of sensory abilities with the decisions and strategies that an observer uses to maximize performance in a difficult task. Rather than try to identify a single point for the threshold, psychophysicists who employ the **signal detection theory** have developed ways to measure an observer's sensitivity to stimuli in ways that go beyond the simple concept of the threshold. Some psychophysical research involves the identification of stimuli. There may be no question as to whether we can detect a stimulus, but sometimes we cannot identify it. For example, people can often detect odors but cannot identify them. Research in this area has centered on determining how much information is needed to allow a person to identify a stimulus. Identification constitutes a relatively small part of psychophysical research, although such research has important practical applications. For example, in the development of useful telephones, researchers had to assess how much "noise" or unwanted sound could accompany speech in a phone conversation so that a listener could understand what was said—that is, identify the spoken words accurately.

A third area of psychophysics involves discrimination of different stimuli, or difference thresholds. No two physical stimuli are absolutely identical, although they may seem to be. The question of interest here is how large must the difference be between two stimuli in order for us to detect it. The amount by which two stimuli must differ in order for us to detect the difference is referred to as the JND, or **just noticeable difference**. Research has indicated that for stimuli of low intensity, we can detect a difference that is small, as the intensity increases, we need a larger difference. Sometimes psychophysicists use **reaction time** as a measure of how different two stimuli are from one another. When two stimuli are very similar, it takes a longer time to decide if they are different, whereas large differences lead to fast reaction times.

## CONCEPTS IN PSYCHOPHYSICS

**Absolute threshold:** as the stimulus strengthens from the undetectable, the point at which the person first detects it.

**Signal detection theory:** theory pertaining to the interaction of the sensory capabilities and the decision-making factors in detecting a stimulus.

**Difference thresholds:** at which point can one differentiate between two stimuli. This point is termed just-noticeable difference.

**Scaling:** using rating scales to assign relative values (for example, rating on a scale of one to ten) to sensory experiences.

The final area of interest to psychophysicists is scaling, the activity of deciding how large or small something is or how much of it is present. Any sensory experience can be scaled. For instance, if the attractiveness of a painting is rated on a scale of one to ten, it is being scaled. If the painting is rated nine, it is considered more attractive than a painting rated eight. This simple example gives the concept underlying scaling, but psychologists have developed more complicated techniques and sophisticated mathematical approaches to scaling.

# Psychosexual stages

Psychoanalytical theory of development based on sexual impulses.

Austrian psychotherapist **Sigmund Freud** described **personality** development during **childhood** in terms of stages based on shifts in the primary location of sexual impulses. During each stage libidinal pleasure is derived from a particular area of the body—called an erogenous zone—and the activities centered in that area. If the problems and conflicts of a particular stage are not adequately resolved, the child—and, later, the adult—may remain fixated at that stage. A **fixation** consists of a conscious or **unconscious** preoccupation with an area of the body (such as the mouth in a compulsive eater), as well as certain personality **traits**. Freud believed that some degree of fixation is present in everyone and that it is an important determinant of personality.

During the three pregenital stages that occur in a child's first five years, **sexuality** is narcissistic: it is di-

**Babies derive pleasure from sucking and mouthing various objects, including their own toes, like this infant. This illustrates the oral stage.** *(Lousasa/Petit. Photo Researchers, Inc. Reproduced with permission.)*

rected toward the child's own body as a source of pleasure rather than outward. In the oral stage, which occupies approximately the first year of life, pleasurable impulses are concentrated in the area of the mouth and lips, the infant's source of nourishment. The child derives pleasure from sucking, mouthing, swallowing, and, later, biting and chewing food. The mouth is also used for exploring. The primary emotional issues at this stage of life are nurturance and dependency. A person who develops an oral fixation—for example, by being weaned too early or too late—is likely to focus on forms of oral gratification such as smoking, drinking, or compulsive eating. Personality traits may include excessive dependency and desire for the approval of others or a drive to acquire possessions that recalls the infant's drive to incorporate food.

The next stage—the anal stage—takes place during the infant's second year. At this point, voluntary control of elimination becomes physically possible and is inculcated through toilet training. This is a child's first major experience with discipline and outside authority and requires the subordination of natural instincts to social demands. Experiences at this stage play a role in determining a person's degree of initiative and attitude toward authority. A child who is harshly disciplined in the course of toilet training may later rebel against authority or become overly fastidious, controlled, or stingy. Conversely, a child who is rewarded and praised for attempts to control elimination is more likely to develop a willingness to "let go" that is associated with generosity and **creativity**.

Between the ages of two and three years, the focus of a child's **attention** and pleasure shifts from the anal to the genital area, initiating what Freud termed the phallic stage. During this period, important changes take place in the child's attitude toward his or her parents. Sexual longings are experienced toward the parent of the opposite sex, accompanied by feelings of rivalry and **hostility** for the same-sex parent. Freud called this situation the **Oedipus complex** for its similarity to the plot of the Greek tragedy *Oedipus Rex,* in which the central character unknowingly kills his father and marries his mother. While the broad outlines of the Oedipal stage are similar for both sexes, it takes a somewhat different course in male and female children. A boy fears that his father will punish him for his feelings toward his mother by removing the locus of these feelings, the penis. This **fear**, which Freud called castration anxiety, causes the boy to abandon his incestuous **attachment** to his mother and begin to identify with his father, imitating him and adopting his values, a process that results in the formation of the boy's **superego**. To describe the experience undergone by girls in the Oedipal stage, Freud used the term "Electra complex," which was derived from the name of a figure in Greek mythology who was strongly attached to her father, Agamemnon, and participated in avenging his death at the hands of her mother, Clytemnestra. Paralleling the castration anxiety felt by boys, girls, according to Freud, experience penis envy. The girl blames her mother for depriving her of a penis and desires her father because he possesses one. Ultimately, the girl, like the boy, represses her incestuous desires and comes to identify with the same-sex parent, the mother, through the development of a superego.

As the phallic stage ends, its conflicts are resolved or repressed, and it is followed by the latency period, during which sexual impulses are dormant. The latency period separates pregenital sexuality from the genital stage, which begins with **adolescence** and lasts through adulthood. In the genital stage, **narcissism** is replaced by focusing sexual energy on a partner of the opposite sex, ultimately resulting in sexual union and extending to feelings such as **friendship**, altruism, and love.

### Further Reading

Freud, Sigmund. *New Introductory Lectures on Psychoanalysis*, Chapter Five. New York: W. W. Norton and Co., 1933.

Hall, Calvin S. *A Primer of Freudian Psychology*. New York: Harper and Row, 1982.

# Psychosis

A symptom of mental illness characterized by a radical change in personality and a distorted or diminished sense of objective reality.

## Characteristics

Psychosis may appear as a symptom of a number of mental disorders, including **mood** and **personality** disorders, **schizophrenia**, delusional disorder, and substance abuse. It is also the defining feature of the **psychotic disorders** (i.e., brief psychotic disorder, shared psychotic disorder, psychotic disorder due to a general medical condition, and substance-induced psychotic disorder).

Patients suffering from psychosis are unable to distinguish the real from the unreal. They experience **hallucinations** and/or delusions that they believe are real, and they typically behave in an inappropriate and confused manner.

## Causes and symptoms

Psychosis may be caused by a number of biological and social factors, depending on the disorder underlying the symptom. Trauma and **stress** can induce a short-term psychosis known as *brief psychotic disorder*. This psychotic episode, which lasts a month or less, can be brought on by the stress of major life-changing events (e.g., death of a close friend or **family** member, natural disaster, traumatic event), and can occur in patients with no prior history of **mental illness**.

Psychosis can also occur as a result of an organic medical condition (known as *psychotic disorder due to a general medical condition*). Neurological conditions (e.g., **epilepsy**, migraines, **Parkinson's disease**, cerebrovascular disease, **dementia**), metabolic imbalances (hypoglycemia), endocrine disorders (hyper- and hypothyroidism), renal disease, electrolyte imbalance, and autoimmune disorders may all trigger psychotic episodes.

Hallucinogenics, PCP, amphetamines, cocaine, **marijuana**, and alcohol may cause a psychotic reaction during use, abuse, or withdrawal. Certain prescription medications such as anesthetics, anticonvulsants, chemotherapeutic agents, and antiparkinsonian medications may also induce psychotic symptoms as a side-effect. In addition, toxic substances like carbon dioxide and carbon monoxide, which may be deliberately or accidentally ingested, have been reported to cause substance-induced psychotic disorder.

Schizophrenia and its related disorders (schizophreniform disorder and schizoaffective disorder), mental illnesses with strong psychotic features, are thought to be caused by abnormalities in the structure and chemistry of the **brain** and influenced by both social and genetic factors. Delusional disorder, another mental illness defined by psychotic episodes, is also thought to have a possible hereditary and neurological base. Abnormalities in the limbic system, the portion of the brain on the inner edge of the cerebral cortex that is believed to regulate emotions, are suspected to cause the delusions that are a feature of psychosis.

Psychosis is characterized by the following symptoms:

- *Delusions*. An unshakable and irrational belief in something untrue. Delusions defy normal reasoning, and remain firm even when overwhelming proof is presented to disprove them.

- *Hallucinations*. Psychosis causes false or distorted sensory experience that appear to be real. Psychotic patients often see, hear, **smell**, **taste**, or feel things that aren't there.

- *Disorganized speech*. Psychotic patients often speak incoherently, using noises instead of words and "talking" in unintelligible speech patterns.

- *Disorganized or catatonic behavior*. Behavior that is completely inappropriate to the situation or **environment**. Catatonic patients have either a complete lack of or inappropriate excess of motor activity. They can be completely rigid and unable to move (vegetative), or in constant motion. Disorganized behavior is unpredictable and inappropriate for a situation (e.g., screaming obscenities in the middle of class).

## Diagnosis

Patients with psychotic symptoms should undergo a thorough physical examination and detailed patient history to rule out organic causes of the psychosis (such as brain tumor). If a psychiatric cause is suspected, a psychologist or psychiatrist will usually conduct an interview with the patient and administer clinical assessments. These assessments may include the Adolescent Behavior Checklist (ABC), Anxiety Disorders Interview Schedule for DSM-IV (ADIS-IV), Psychotic Behavior

Rating Scale (PBRS), and the Chapman Psychosis Proneness Scales.

## Treatment

Psychosis caused by schizophrenia or another mental illness should be treated by a psychiatrist and/or psychologist. Other medical and **mental health** professionals may be part of the treatment team, depending on the severity of the psychosis and the needs of the patient. Medication and/or psychosocial therapy is typically employed to treat the underlying disorder.

Antipsychotic medications commonly prescribed to treat psychosis include risperidone (Risperdal), thioridazine (Mellaril), halperidol (Haldol), chlorpromazine (Thorazine), clozapine (Clozaril), loxapine (Loxitane), molindone hydrochloride (Moban), thiothixene (Navane), and olanzapine (Zyprexa). Possible common side-effects of antipsychotics include dry mouth, drowsiness, muscle stiffness, and hypotension. More serious side effects include tardive dyskinesia (involuntary movements of the body) and neuroleptic malignant syndrome (NMS), a potentially fatal condition characterized by muscle rigidity, altered mental status, and irregular pulse and blood pressure.

Once an acute psychotic episode has subsided, psychosocial therapy and living and vocational skills training may be recommended. Drug maintenance treatment is usually prescribed to prevent further episodes.

## Prognosis

The longer and more severe a psychotic episode, the poorer the prognosis for the patient. However, early diagnosis and long-term follow-up care can improve the outcome for patients with psychotic disorders. Schizophrenia has a 60% treatment success rate.

*See also* Neurosis

Paula Ford-Martin

## Further Reading

American Psychiatric Association. *Diagnostic and Statistical Manual of Mental Disorders* 4th ed. Washington, D.C.: American Psychiatric Press, Inc., 1994.

## Further Information

National Alliance for the Mentally Ill (NAMI). 200 North Glebe Road, Suite 1015, Arlington, VA, USA. 22203-3754, (800)950-6264. http://www.nami.org.

National Institute of Mental Health (NIMH). 6001 Executive Boulevard, Rm. 8184, MSC 9663, Bethesda, MD, USA. 20892-9663, fax: (301)443-4279, (301)443-4513. Email: nimhinfo@nih.gov. http://www.nimh.nih.gov.

# Psychosomatic disorders

Physical illnesses that are believed to be psychologically based; also referred to as psychophysiological disorders.

The American Psychiatric Association's Diagnostic and Statistical Manual of Mental Disorders (*DSM-IV*) classifies psychosomatic illnesses under "Psychological Factors Affecting Physical Conditions." Physicians have been aware that people's mental and emotional states influence their physical well-being since the time of Hippocrates. In the twentieth century, the discoveries of psychologists have shed new light on how the mind and body interact to produce health or illness. **Sigmund Freud** introduced the idea that **unconscious** thoughts can be converted into physical symptoms (**conversion reaction**). The formal study of psychosomatic illnesses began in Europe in the 1920s, and by 1939, the journal *Psychosomatic Medicine* had been founded in the United States. Eventually, sophisticated laboratory experiments replaced clinical observation as the primary method of studying psychosomatic illness. Researchers in the field of psychophysiology measured such responses as blood pressure, heart rate, and skin temperature to determine the physiological effects of human behavior. Animal research have also contributed to the growing body of knowledge about psychosomatic disorders. Three theories have been particularly popular in explaining why certain persons develop psychosomatic disorders and what determines the forms these illnesses take. One theory contends that psychological **stress** affects bodily organs that are constitutionally weak or weakened by stress. Another links specific types of illness with particular types of stress. Still another theory suggests that physiological predispositions combined with psychological stress to produce psychosomatic illness.

The parts of the body most commonly affected by psychosomatic disorders are the gastrointestinal and respiratory systems. Gastrointestinal disorders include gastric and duodenal ulcers, ulcerative colitis, and irritable bowel syndrome. (**Anorexia** nervosa and **bulimia** are sometimes considered psychosomatic disorders, but they also appear under the category of "anxiety disorder—eating disorders" in *DSM-IV.*) Respiratory problems caused or worsened by psychological factors include asthma and hyperventilation syndrome. Cardiovascular complaints include coronary artery disease, hypertension, tachycardia (speeded-up and irregular heart rhythm), and migraine headaches. Psychosomatic disorders also affect the skin (eczema, allergies, and neurodermatitis) and genitourinary system (menstrual disorders and **sexual dysfunction**).

Probably the most well-known psychosomatic connection is that of stress and coronary heart disease. The term "Type A" has been used for over twenty years to describe the aggressive, competitive, impatient, controlling type of person whom researchers have found to be more prone to heart disease than people who are more easygoing and mild-mannered and less hostile and concerned with time. In 1981, a panel appointed by the National Heart, Lung, and Blood Institute found that Type A behavior poses a greater risk of coronary heart disease and myocardial infarction (heart attack) than do cigarette smoking, age, hypertension, or a high serum cholesterol count.

Emotional stress can also affect the immune system, raising the risk to the body from such foreign invaders as bacteria, viruses, and cancer cells. People under stress are more likely to develop infectious diseases, including those stemming from the reactivation of latent herpes viruses. It is known that several of the body's reactions to stress, including the release of cortisol, adrenaline, and other **hormones**, suppress the activity of the immune system. A special field, psychoneuroimmunology, studies how the interaction of psychological and physiological reactions affects the functioning of the immune system.

People suffering from psychosomatic disorders have been helped by treatment of either their physical symptoms, the underlying psychological causes, or both. If the disorder is in an advanced stage (such as in severe asthma attacks, perforated ulcers, or debilitating colitis) symptomatic treatment must be undertaken initially as an emergency measure before the emotional component can be addressed. Psychological approaches range from classic **psychoanalysis**, which addresses a person's early traumas and conflicts, to **behavior therapy** that focuses on changing learned behaviors that create or increase anxiety. Medications such as tranquilizers or **antidepressants** may be effective in relieving symptoms of psychosomatic disorders. **Hypnosis** has successfully been used to treat hyperventilation, ulcers, migraine headaches, and other complaints. Today, psychologists commonly treat psychosomatic ailments with the aid of such relaxation techniques as progressive relaxation, autogenic training, transcendental meditation, and yoga. **Biofeedback** has been used in treating a number of different clinical problems, including tachycardia, hypertension, and both tension and migraine headaches.

### Further Reading

*Mind, Body, Medicine: How to Use Your Mind for Better Health.* Consumer Reports Books, 1993.

# Psychosurgery

Highly controversial medical procedures where areas of the brain are destroyed or disabled through surgery as treatment for mental illness.

Psychosurgery involves severing or otherwise disabling areas of the **brain** to treat a **personality** disorder, behavior disorder or other **mental illness**. The most common form of psychosurgery is the lobotomy, where the nerves connecting the frontal lobes of the brain and the **thalamus** or **hypothalamus** are severed. Performed first in the late 1930s, by the 1940s lobotomies were recommended for patients diagnosed with **schizophrenia**, severe **obsessive-compulsive disorder**, severe **depression**, and uncontrollable aggressive behavior. Other psychosurgeries also involve severing **nerve** connections to the hypothalamus, since it plays a key role in controlling emotions. Psychosurgery has been recommended less frequently as more effective drugs for treatment of psychological disorders have been developed.

### Further Reading

Rodgers, Joann Ellison. *Psychosurgery: Damaging the Brain to Save the Mind.* New York: HarperCollins Publishers, 1992.

Valenstein, Elliott S. *The Psychosurgery Debate: Scientific, Legal, and Ethical Perspectives.* San Francisco: W. H. Freeman, 1980.

# Psychotherapy

The treatment of mental or emotional disorders and adjustment problems through the use of psychological techniques rather than through physical or biological means.

**Psychoanalysis**, the first modern form of psychotherapy, was called the "talking cure," and the many varieties of therapy practiced today are still characterized by their common dependence on a verbal exchange between the counselor or therapist and the person seeking help. The therapeutic interaction is characterized by mutual trust, with the goal of helping individuals change destructive or unhealthy behaviors, thoughts, and emotions. It is common for experienced therapists to combine several different approaches or techniques. The most common approaches are discussed below.

## Psychodynamic approach

Freudian psychoanalysis places emphasis on uncovering **unconscious** motivations and breaking down defenses. Therapy sessions may be scheduled once or even twice a week for a year or more. This type of therapy is appropriate when internal conflicts contribute significantly to a person's problems. (For more information, see entry on Psychoanalysis).

### Behavioral techniques

In contrast to the psychodynamic approach, behavior-oriented therapy is geared toward helping people see their problems as learned behaviors that can be modified, without looking for unconscious motivations or hidden meanings. According to the theory behind this approach, once behavior is changed, feelings will change as well. Probably the best-known type of behavioral therapy is **behavior modification**, which focuses on eliminating undesirable habits by providing positive **reinforcement** for the more desirable behaviors.

Another behavioral technique is systematic **desensitization**, in which people are deliberately and gradually exposed to a feared object or experience to help them overcome their fears. A person who is afraid of dogs may first be given a stuffed toy dog, then be exposed to a real dog seen at a distance, and eventually forced to interact with a dog at close range. Relaxation training is another popular form of **behavior therapy**. Through such techniques as deep breathing, visualization, and progressive muscle relaxation, clients learn to control **fear** and anxiety.

### Cognitive methods

Some behavior-oriented therapy methods are used to alter not only overt behavior, but also the thought patterns that drive it. This type of treatment is known as cognitive-behavior therapy (or just **cognitive therapy**). Its goal is to help people break out of distorted, harmful patterns of thinking and replace them with healthier ones. Common examples of negative thought patterns include magnifying or minimizing the extent of a problem; "all or nothing" thinking (i.e., a person regards himself as either perfect or worthless); overgeneralization (arriving at broad conclusions based on one incident, for example); and personalization (continually seeing oneself as the cause or focus of events).

In cognitive-behavioral therapy, a therapist may talk to the client, pointing out illogical thought patterns, or use a variety of techniques, such as thought substitution, in which a frightening or otherwise negative thought is driven out by substituting a pleasant thought in its place. Clients may also be taught to use positive self-talk, a repetition of positive affirmations. Cognitive therapy is usually provided on a short-term basis (generally 10-20 sessions).

### Family and group therapy

**Family** therapy has proven effective in treating a number of emotional and adjustment problems. While the client's immediate complaint is the initial focus of **attention**, the ultimate goal of **family therapy** is to improve the interaction between all family members and enhance communication and coping skills on a long-term basis (although therapy itself need not cover an extended time period). **Group therapy**, which is often combined with individual therapy, offers the support and companionship of other people experiencing the same problems and issues.

Therapy is terminated when the treatment goals have been met or if the client and/or therapist conclude that it isn't working. It can be effective to phase out treatment by gradually reducing the frequency of therapy sessions. Even after regular therapy has ended, the client may return for periodic follow-up and reassessment sessions.

### Further Reading

Engler, Jack and Daniel Goleman. *The Consumer's Guide to Psychotherapy*. New York: Fireside, 1992.
Kanfer, Frederick H. and Arnold P. Goldstein, eds. *Helping People Change: A Textbook of Methods*. New York: Pergamon Press, 1991.

## Psychotic disorders

A diagnostic term formerly used in a general way to designate the most severe psychological disorders; now used in a much narrower sense in connection with specific symptoms and conditions.

Formerly, all psychological disorders were considered either psychotic or neurotic. Psychotic disorders were those that rendered patients unable to function normally in their daily lives and left them "out of touch with reality." They were associated with impaired **memory**, language, and speech and an inability to think rationally. Neurotic disorders, by comparison, were characterized chiefly by anxiety; any impairment of functioning was primarily social. Psychotic conditions were attributed to physiological causes, neurotic conditions to psychosocial ones. Other distinguishing features associated primarily with psychotic disorders were hospitalization and treatment by biological methods—medication and electroconvulsive therapy. With the development of new types of **psychoactive drugs** in the 1950s and 1960s, medication became a common form of therapy for anxiety, **depression**, and other problems categorized as neurotic.

"Psychotic" and "neurotic" are no longer employed as major categories in the American Psychiatric Association's Diagnostic and Statistical Manual of Mental Disorders *(DSM-IV)* . Instead, disorders that formerly belonged to either one category or the other appear side by side in Axis I of the manual under the heading "Clinical Syndromes." The term "psychotic" still appears in *DSM-IV,* most prominently in the categorization "Schizophrenia and Other Psychotic Disorders." The disorders in this section have as their defining feature symptoms considered psychotic, which in this context can refer to delusions, **hallucinations**, and other positive symptoms of **schizophrenia**, such as confused speech and catatonia. In other parts of *DSM-IV,* "psychotic" is also used to describe aspects of a disorder even when they are not its defining feature, as in "Major Depressive Disorder with Psychotic Features."

## Further Reading

Hales, Dianne, and Robert E. Hales, M.D. *Caring for the Mind: The Comprehensive Guide to Mental Health.* New York: Bantam Books, 1995.

# Puberty

The process of physical growth and sexual maturation that signals the end of childhood and the advent of adolescence. (Also, the period during which this process takes place.)

The word *puberty* is derived from the Latin *pubertas,* which means adulthood. Puberty is initiated by hormonal changes triggered by a part of the **brain** called the **hypothalamus**, which stimulates the pituitary gland, which in turn activates other glands as well. These changes begin about a year before any of their results are visible. Both the male reproductive hormone testosterone and female hormone estrogen are present in children of both sexes. However, their balance changes at puberty, with girls producing relatively more estrogen and boys producing more testosterone.

Most experts suggest that parents begin short and casual discussions about puberty with their children by the age of seven or eight. Offering the child reading materials about puberty can impart information to the young person without the awkwardness that may characterize the parent-child conversations. Parents can then offer their children opportunities to ask questions or to discuss any aspects of puberty and **sexuality** that may arise from their reading.

The first obvious sign of puberty is a growth spurt that typically occurs in girls between the ages of 10 and 14 and in boys between 12 and 16. Between these ages both sexes grow about nine inches. The average girl gains about 38 pounds, and the average boy gains about 42. One reason for the awkwardness of **adolescence** is the fact that this growth spurt proceeds at different rates in different parts of the body. Hands and feet grow faster than arms and legs, which, in turn, lengthen before the torso does, all of which create the impression of gawkiness common to many teenagers. In addition, there can be temporary unevenness of growth on the two sides of the body, and even facial development is disproportionate, as the nose, lips, and ears grow before the head attains its full adult size. The growth spurt at puberty is not solely an external one. Various internal organs increase significantly in size, in some cases with observable consequences. Increases in heart and lung size and in the total volume of blood give adolescents increased strength and endurance for athletics and for recreational activities such as dancing. (During puberty, the heart doubles in size.) Teenagers' ravenous appetites are related to the increased capacity of the digestive system, and the decrease in respiratory problems (including asthma ) is associated with the fact that the lymphoid system, which includes the tonsils and adenoids, actually shrinks in adolescence. Yet another change, the increase in secretions from the sebaceous glands, triggered by the growth hormone androgen, is responsible for acne, which affects about 75% of teenagers. The excess oil from these glands clogs pores, and they become inflamed, causing the reddening and swelling of acne.

Following the beginning of the growth spurt, the sexual organs begin to mature and secondary sex characteristics appear. In girls, the uterus and vagina become larger, and the lining of the vagina thickens. The first visible sign of sexual maturation is often the appearance of a small amount of colorless pubic hair shortly after the growth spurt begins. Over the next three years, the pubic hair becomes thicker, darker, coarser, and curlier and spreads to cover a larger area. Hair also develops under the arms, on the arms and legs (sufficiently so that most girls start shaving), and, to a slight degree, on the face. Around the age of 10 or 11, "breast buds," the first sign of breast development, appear. Full breast development takes about three or four years and is generally not complete until puberty is almost over. The single most dramatic sign of sexual maturation in girls is menarche, the onset of menstruation, which usually occurs after a girl's growth rate has peaked. In virtually all cases it occurs between the ages of 10 and 16, with the average age in the United States being 12.8 years. The first menstrual periods are usually anovulatory, meaning that they happen without ovulation. Periods remain irregular for a while, and for at

# HORMONE SURGE TRIGGERS PUBERTY

A point in **child development** known as adrenarche—the beginning of adrenal androgen activity—may represent the beginning of the process of puberty. Two University of Chicago researchers, Dr. Martha K. McClintock and Dr. Gilbert Herdt, believe that puberty is triggered by dihydroepiandrosterone (DHEA), a hormone produced by the adrenal glands. According to data the two gathered from three separate studies, DHEA levels begin to increase at around the age of six and reach a critical level around age ten. The researchers characterize these hormonal changes as triggering a number of cognitive, emotional, and social changes in around fourth or fifth grade. Students in these grades begin to engage in boy-girl teasing, exhibit a significant increase in abstract reasoning skills, and experience vulnerability to embarrassment. The three studies also gathered data on subjects' (who were mostly in their mid 30s) first recollected feelings of sexual attraction. The **mean** age reported by the subjects was around 10 or 11 . This finding has led the researchers to postulate that sexual development moves along a continuum, beginning with attraction, progressing to desire, and leading to the willingness and readiness to act on the desire. McClintock, quoted in the *New York Times,* noted: "Our culture regards middle **childhood** as a time of hormonal quiescence. Freud called it 'latency.' But actually a great deal of activity is going on."

least a year after menarche young women's fertility levels are very low, and they are prone to spontaneous abortions if they do conceive.

In boys, as in girls, the first outward sign of sexual maturation is often light-colored pubic hair around the time the growth spurt begins. The testes and scrotum begin to grow, and the scrotum darkens, thickens, and becomes pendulous. About a year after the testes begin to increase in size, the penis lengthens and widens, taking several years to reach its full size. Sperm production increases, and ejaculations—the male counterpart to menarche in girls—begin, occurring through nocturnal emission, masturbation, or sexual intercourse. (It takes from one to three years until ejaculations contain enough sperm for a boy to be really fertile.) Boys' pubic hair, like that of girls, gradually becomes thicker and curlier and covers a wider area, and facial hair appears, first in the mustache area above the upper lip and later at the sides of the face and on the chin. As a boy's larynx grows and the vocal cords lengthen, his voice drops (roughly an octave in pitch) and changes in quality. Although girls' voices also become lower, the change is more dramatic (and less controlled) in boys, whose voices occasionally break, producing an embarrassing high-pitched squeak.

The sequence and age range of the developmental changes associated with puberty can vary widely. Although most children begin puberty between the ages of 10 and 12, it can start at any age from 8 to 16. The most obvious determining factor is gender; on average, puberty arrives earlier for girls than boys. **Heredity** also appears to play an important role. Compared to an overall age range of nine to 18 for menarche, the age difference for sisters averages only 13 months and for identical **twins**, less than three months. Body weight is a factor as well: puberty often begins earlier in heavier children of both sexes and later in thinner ones. The onset of menstruation, in particular, appears to be related to amounts of body fat. Girls with little body fat, especially athletes, often start menstruating at a later-than-average age. Over the past 100 years, puberty has tended to begin increasingly early in both sexes (a phenomenon called the *secular trend* ). In 1997, the results of a study led by Dr. Marcia E. Herman-Giddens of University of North Carolina at Chapel Hill School of Public Health provided evidence that the average age of menarche was declining. Instead of occurring between the ages of 12 and 14, as is typical in the late 1990s, girls' first menstrual periods commonly appeared between the ages of 15 and 17 in the 19th century. Puberty in boys usually didn't begin until the ages of 15 or 16 (in the late 18th and early 19th centuries, boy sopranos in their mid-to-late teens still sang in church choirs). Explanations for this pattern have ranged from evolution to better health, especially as a consequence of improved nutrition.

An important aspect of puberty is the development of **body image**. Teenagers are often critical of their bodies during this period, either because they feel they are maturing too early or too late, or because they fail to match the stereotyped ideals of attractiveness for their sex (i.e., tall and muscular for men, fashionably thin for women). Girls who mature early have a hard time initially because they feel self-conscious and isolated, but they adjust well and even gain in status once their peers begin to catch up. Some research even suggests that girls who mature early may ultimately be better off than those who mature late because the turmoil of their early teenage years helps them develop coping skills that stand them in good stead later on. For boys, the relative positions of early and late maturers is reversed. Those who are already tall and athletic in junior high school feel better about themselves than those who remain short and skinny. Researchers have linked late physical maturation in boys to the develop-

## ADOLESCENTS WHO HAVE BECOME SEXUALLY ACTIVE*

| Sexually active by age | All (Number) | All (Percent) | Boys (Number) | Boys (Percent) | Girls (Number) | Girls (Percent) |
|---|---|---|---|---|---|---|
| 13 | 749 | 8.6% | 389 | 14.7% | 350 | 2.7% |
| 14 | 509 | 17.7% | 263 | 24.6% | 246 | 10.8% |
| 15 | 320 | 31.2% | 166 | 35.0% | 154 | 27.3% |
| 16 | 169 | 54.9% | 82 | 63.1% | 87 | 47.1% |
| 17 | 78 | 68.6% | 38 | 72.1% | 40 | 65.8% |

*This table reports data on the number and percent of adolescents who have become sexually active by a certain age. Data were gathered by the National Longitudinal Survey of Youth, 1988-92.

ment of both positive **personalitytraits** (**humor**, perceptiveness, flexibility, **creativity**, and **leadership** skills) and negative ones (restlessness and lack of poise). In most cases, adolescents gradually become more accepting of their bodies in the years following junior high school.

### Further Reading

Bell, Alison, and Lisa Rooney. *Your Body Yourself: A Guide to Your Changing Body.* Chicago: Contemporary Books, 1993.

Bourgeois, Paulette, and Martin Wolfish. *Changes in You and Me: A Book About Puberty, Mostly for Boys.* Kansas City: Andrews and McMeel, 1994.

Children's Television Workshop. *What Kids Want to Know About Sex and Growing Up.* Los Angeles, CA: Pacific Arts Video Publishing, 1992. (One 60-minute videocassette and one 20-page parent's guide.)

Chirinian, Alain. *Boys' Puberty: An Illustrated Manual for Parents and Sons.* New York: Tom Doherty Associates, 1989.

Feldman, Shirley, and Glen R. Elliott, eds. *At the Threshold: The Developing Adolescent.* Cambridge, MA: Harvard University Press, 1990.

Gilbert, Susan. "Early Puberty Onset Seems Prevalent." *New York Times* 146, April 9, 1997, p. B12.

Jukes, Mavis. *It's a Girl Thing: How to Stay Healthy, Safe, and In Charge.* New York: A. Knopf, 1996.

Marano, Hara Estroff. "Puberty May Start at 6 as Hormones Surge." *New York Times* 146, July 1, 1997, p. B9+.

Nathanson, Laura. "Prepuberty Coaching." *Parents Magazine* 72 (March 1997): pp. 110+.

———. *Changes in You and Me: A Book About Puberty, Mostly for Girls.* Kansas City: Andrews and McMeel, 1994.

Steinberg, Laurence, and Ann Levine. *You and Your Adolescent: A Parent's Guide for Ages 10-20.* New York: Harper & Row, 1990.

*What's Happening to Me? A Guide to Puberty.* Los Angeles, CA: LCA, 1986. (Video recording)

# Ethel Dench Puffer

**1872-1950**
American educator and psychologist.

Ethel Dench Puffer was born in Framingham, Massachusetts, the eldest of four daughters. Her family was of native New England stock and highly educated by the standard of the era. After graduating from Smith College in 1891 at the age of 19 and teaching high school for one year in New Hampshire, Puffer returned to Smith as an instructor of mathematics, where she taught for the next three years while developing a keen interest in psychology. In 1895, Puffer traveled to Germany to study aesthetics under Hugo Münsterberg (1863-1916), then a professor of psychology at the University of Freiberg. On the strength of her research, she was awarded a fellowship for graduate study by the Association of Collegiate Alumnae. Enrolling in Radcliffe College in 1897 and working again under Münsterberg at Harvard University, she earned a certificate stating she had completed work equivalent to that of a doctoral candidate for the Harvard Ph.D. Because of the restrictions against granting the Harvard degree to women, however, Puffer was forced to make a special appeal to Radcliffe to grant her the doctoral degree. In 1902, she was one of the first four women to be offered the Radcliffe Ph.D.

Restricted from many research opportunities because of her gender, Puffer returned to teaching psychology at Radcliffe, Wellesley, and Simmons Colleges, and published a book, *The Psychology of Beauty,* in 1905, based on her research in aesthetics. In 1908, her marriage to Benjamin Howes further impacted her career due to cultural norms of the period which did not permit married women to work outside of the home. She continued to write scholarly articles through her forties while raising two children. Puffer's published reflections of the role of women and the conflict between marriage and career in the *Atlantic Monthly* in 1922 brought attention to one of the basic dilemmas confronting educated women of that time.

### Further Reading

Scarborough, Elizabeth and Laurel Furumoto. *Untold Lives: The First Generation of American Women Psychologists* . New York: Columbia University Press, 1987, pp. 70-90.

## Punishment

Penalty imposed on another as a result of unwanted behavior.

Punishment is defined as the administration of aversive stimulus to reduce or eliminate unwanted behavior. It can be either physical or nonphysical. Punishment differs from negative **reinforcement** in that the latter *increases* the frequency of behavior by removing a negative event. Punishment can be as simple as giving electric shocks to lab rats to prevent them from touching a lever or as complex—and controversial—as placing criminals in jail for breaking the law. The use and effectiveness of corporal punishment have also been debated by psychologists, parents, teachers, and religious leaders for many years.

Research studies have found that punishment *is* effective in suppressing or eliminating unwanted behavior. But in order for punishment to be effective it must happen *immediately* after the behavior, be *severe*, and occur *every time* the behavior occurs. Detractors of the use of punishment have pointed out that, outside the laboratory setting, it is almost impossible to consistently administer punishment in this manner.

Even when punishment is administered "properly," psychologists have questioned the value of punishment in truly changing behavior, arguing that the desired outcome is only temporary. As evidenced by increasing crime rates in most major cities, punishment (fines, imprisonment,

social stigma, etc.) does not appear to deter unwanted behavior. In addition, psychologists have identified other "downsides" to using punishment. For instance, people use punishment inappropriately, decreasing its effectiveness. People punish when they are upset or angry. The recipient experiences anxiety, **fear**, rage, or hatred. The use of punishment can lead to more resistance and **aggression** on the part of the one being punished. The punishment can also backfire—instead of serving to punish a child, for example, spanking brings the wanted **attention** of a parent. In addition, corporal punishment defeats its own purpose by **modeling** aggressive or physical behavior, the very behavior it is often attempting to correct.

Most current promoters of punitive discipline in the United States espouse nonphysical forms of control, such as the use of reinforcements, logical consequences, or penalties. With children, **behavior modification** techniques such as time-out have proven very effective in modifying disruptive behaviors such as hitting, grabbing, talking back, or tantrums.

### Further Reading

McCord, Joan, ed. *Coercion and Punishment in Long-Term Perspectives*. Cambridge/New York: Cambridge University Press, 1995.
Straus, Murray, Richard Gelles, and Suzanne Steinmetz. *Behind Closed Doors: Violence in the American Family*. New York: Anchor Press/Doubleday, 1980.

## Pyromania

Irresistible urge to start fires.

Little is known about pyromania. The term comes from the Greek words *pyr* (fire) and *mania* (madness). It is a rare condition, listed under the heading of **impulse control disorders**. Pyromania is not the same as arson (deliberate fire-setting), and not all arsonists (fire-setters) are pyromaniacs. Fires are often started by individuals with this disorder deliberately and with careful planning, rather than by accident. A key feature of this disorder is the presence of repeated association with fire, but with no evidence of a reason or **motivation** for the fire (such as profit or to hide criminal activity). Nearly all pyromaniacs are male. Pyromania may begin in **childhood**, but there is no conclusive data regarding the typical age of onset. Similarly, there is no documented link between fire-setting in childhood and adult pyromania.

*See also* Impulse control disorders

### Further Reading

Morrison, James. *DSM-IV Made Easy: The Clinician's Guide to Diagnosis*. New York: Guilford Press, 1995.

| PUNISHMENT | |
|---|---|
| **Positive punishment** | **Negative punishment** |
| When the subject—a person or animal—engages in a behavior and something negative is applied as a result, the behavior is less likely to be repeated. | When the subject—a person or animal—engages in a behavior and something positive is taken away, that behavior is less likely to be repeated. |

# Q

# Qualitative methods

*Research methods that emphasize detailed, personal descriptions of phenomena.*

Research psychologists can collect two kinds of information: quantitative data and qualitative data. Quantitative data are often represented numerically in the form of means, percentages, or frequency counts. Such data are often referred to as "measurement" data, referring to the fact that we often like to measure the amount or extent of some behavior, trait, or disposition. For example, **shyness**, **test anxiety**, and **depression** can all be appraised by means of paper-and-pencil tests which yield numerical scores representing the extent of shyness, anxiety, etc. that resides in the individual taking the test. A psychologist interested in the relationship between test anxiety and grade point average would collect the appropriate quantitative information on each of these two variables and conduct statistical tests that would reveal the strength (or absence) of the relationship.

The term "qualitative research methods" refers to a variety of ways of collecting information that is less amenable to quantification and statistical manipulation. Qualitative methods differ from quantitative methods largely because their ultimate purpose is different. The goal of qualitative research is to arrive at some general, overall appreciation of a phenomenon—highlighting interesting aspects and perhaps generating specific hypotheses. In contrast, quantitative research is typically designed to test relatively specific predictions. Qualitative research thus provides an initial description of a phenomenon, whereas quantitative research aims to investigate its various details. Some examples of qualitative methods include focus groups, surveys, naturalistic observations, interviews, content analyses of archival material, and case studies. What these approaches share is an emphasis on revealing some general pattern by observing a few particular cases.

Focus groups are commonly used by marketing or advertising agencies to derive information about people's reactions to a particular product or event. A small number of people, often fewer than 10, are asked their opinions. A focus group engaged by the marketing department of a breakfast cereal company, for example, might be asked how appealing the cereal looks, whether the box would make them consider buying it, and how agreeable the cereal's texture and **taste** were. A facilitator would encourage the participants to share their opinions and reactions in the context of a group discussion. The session would be taped and transcribed. Researchers would then use the information to make their product more appealing. Naturalistic observations involve studying individuals in their natural environments. One common variant consists of participant observation research in which the researcher, in order to understand it, becomes part of a particular group. George Kirkham was a criminologist who took a year off from his university position to work as a police patrolman. He then wrote about the changes in his attitudes and values that occurred when he worked in high-crime neighborhood.

There are several drawbacks to qualitative methods of inquiry. Firstly, the results are always subject to personal biases. A person who is interviewed, for example, is stating their version of the truth. Personal perspectives invariably affect what the individual believes and understands. Similarly, the results reported by the researcher conducting a naturalistic observation will be tainted by that researcher's individual interpretation of the events. Further, while case studies are rich sources of information about individuals, it is risky to assume that the information can be generalized to the rest of the population. Moreover, analyzing the data from qualitative research can be difficult, since open-ended questions and naturalistic observation leave room for so much variability between individuals that comparisons are difficult. Finally, although it may be tempting for researchers to infer cause and effect relationships from the results of naturalistic observations, interviews, archival data and case studies, this would be irresponsible. Qualitative methods rarely attempt to control any of the factors that affect situations, so although one factor may appear to have caused an event, its influence cannot be confirmed without conducting more precise investigations. There is thus a tradeoff between flexibility and precision.

The advantages of doing qualitative research are numerous. One of the most important of these is that the flexibility of qualitative data collection methods can provide researchers access to individuals who would be unable or unwilling to respond in more structured formats. For this reason, much research on children is qualitative. Naturalistic observations of children are sometimes undertaken to assess social dynamics. For example, covert videotaping of elementary school playgrounds has revealed that bullying and **aggression** are far more common than most teachers and parents realize, and that bullying is not uncommon among girls. Similarly, comparative psychologists learn a lot about the social, behavioral, and cognitive abilities of animals by studying them in their natural habitats. A further advantage of this type of research is that the validity of the results is not jeopardized by the laboratory **environment**. An animal or child may not act the way they usually would in their natural surroundings if they are studied in a laboratory.

Another important application of qualitative research is in the study of new areas of interest, or topics about which not very much is known. Qualitative research usually yields a lot of information. In contrast with quantitative research, the information gathered by qualitative researchers is usually broadly focused. This means that qualitative methods can yield information about the major factors at play, highlighting areas that might warrant more in-depth quantitative study. Although many researchers believe quantitative methods to be superior to qualitative methods, the two are probably best seen as complementary. Qualitative research can suggest what should be measured and in what way, while controlled quantitative studies may be the most accurate way of doing the actual measuring.

Timothy E. Moore

## Further Reading

Murray, J. "Qualitative methods." *International Review of Psychiatry,* vol 10, no. 4 (1998): 312-316.

Marecek, J. "Qualitative methods and social psychology." *Journal of Social Issues* vol 53, no. 4 (1997): 631-644.

# Race and intelligence

Throughout human history, people have tended to divide each other into groups. Most often, physical characteristics are used to distinguish between groups, and the groups are called races. Some people have long believed that many characteristics about a person could be determined by simply looking at the person's race. **Intelligence** is one trait that has been studied in an attempt to correlate it to racial groups. In fact, at present the best evidence does not strongly support the idea that the people of any race are more or less intelligent than those of any other race. In addition, intelligence testing is an imperfect science. Traditional tests are skewed to favor certain segments of society.

## Genes and intelligence: a clear verdict

Saying that intelligence is partly genetic—programmed in the genes and inherited from one generation to the next—is vastly different than saying that genes underlie any racial differences. To give a classic example, scatter two identical groups of seed on a rich and a barren, dry plot of land. Within the rich plot, genetics will determine any difference in seed growth. But **environment** will cause most of the difference between the two plots.

Studies estimate that genes account for between 30 and 80% of our intelligence. Using meta-analysis—a statistical method that allows researchers to compare data from different experiments—a group of researchers showed that, when all these studies are taken together, genetics appear to determine roughly half of intelligence, environment the other half. Interestingly, the meta-analysis also suggested that pre-birth environmental factors such as the mother's nutrition, which are difficult to measure in any study, might underlie most of the environmental difference.

These results make some common sense. We know that intelligent people tend to have intelligent children—but not always. Some studies have also suggested that in-tensive programs may make a large difference in disadvantaged children's **intelligence quotient** (IQ) scores.

The problem with this split is that unrecognized differences in either genetic inheritance or environment might skew otherwise carefully crafted studies of race and intelligence. This problem will haunt nearly every single study we discuss.

## Race and IQ: not so clear

The question of whether human races possess different intellectual capacities comes, at least in part, from an early twentieth-century observation that African Americans' IQ scores were, on the average, 15 points lower than those of white Americans. Recently, the black/white IQ difference has decreased; today it's closer to 10 points.

It's difficult to see how a five-point change in the IQ difference between black and white Americans could have come about in less than a century if genetics caused the difference entirely. Even more interesting, Americans and western Europeans today score 15 points higher on identical IQ tests than their great-grandparents did. A 15-point difference in IQ is significant (an IQ of 100 is "average," 130 "gifted"); but we clearly aren't more intelligent than our great-grandparents. It seems that environmental factors can and do play havoc with our attempts to measure intelligence.

A number of researchers have undertaken studies to uncover the source of the 10-point IQ difference between the races. One type of study measures the IQs of children of different racial backgrounds who are raised in similar environments. African Americans, on the average, have 70% African and 30% European ancestry. If whites were genetically more intelligent than blacks, we would expect black children with more European ancestry to have higher IQs than those with more African ancestry, even when they're raised in the same family.

Psychologists have used three ways to estimate white ancestry in African Americans. (It is worth noting that there are no "pure" racial groups.) Skin color is an imperfect measure, because not all native African peoples have dark skin. Also, children with lighter skin may be treated differently, even in the same family. Family histories of white ancestry may or may not be accurate. Possibly the best method tests blood groups; different racial groups have different rates of certain blood groups, allowing one to make a statistical estimate of ancestry.

The results of these studies suggest little, if any, intelligence difference between the races. The skin-color studies do tend to show a slight advantage for lighter-skinned children—with all the reservations about children with lighter skin getting different treatment. But family history and blood group studies show no difference in IQ, apart from the skin-color effect.

Another approach to these studies measures the IQs of black children brought up in white families. In one study of black, interracial, and white adopted children raised in white families, the white children showed the highest IQ scores, with interracial children scoring in the middle. But it's not clear whether the white families treated the black children differently; whether the black children had suffered from IQ-reducing environments before they were born; or whether the older average age of **adoption** for the black children in the study prevented a fair comparison.

Another study, of black West Indian (Caribbean) children and English children raised in an orphanage in England, found that the Caribbean children had *higher* IQs than those from England, with mixed-race children scoring in between. But were the black children given more **attention** by orphanage staff? Were particularly intelligent Caribbeans emigrating to England for better economic opportunity?

Finally, a study of black children adopted by white versus black families in America showed that the black children raised by whites had higher IQ scores than those raised by blacks—suggesting an environmental cause. When the studies are taken together, the many caveats involved with the role of genetics and environment make it hard to draw firm conclusions. But the balance of data suggests no racial difference in intelligence.

*See also* Intelligence quotient; Culture-fair test

Kenneth B. Chiacchia

### Further Reading

Devlin, B., Michael Daniels, and Kathryn Roeder. "The Heritability of IQ." *Nature* 388 (1997): 468-71.

Holloway, Marguerite. "Flynn's Effect." *Scientific American* (January 1999).

Jencks, Christopher and Meredith Phillips, eds. *The Black-White Test Score Gap*. Washington, D.C.: Brookings Institution Press, 1998.

McGue, Matt. "The Democracy of the Genes." *Nature* 388 (1997): 417-18.

Plomin, Robert. "Genetics and General Cognitive Ability." *Nature* 402 (supplement) (1999): C25-C29.

Plomin, Robert and Stephen A. Petrill. "Genetics and Intelligence: What's New?" *Intelligence* 24, no. 1 (1997): 53-77.

Wickelgren, Ingrid. "Nurture Helps Mold Able Minds." *Science* 283, no. 5409 (1999): 1832-834.

## Racism

The belief that members of one (or more) races are inferior to members of other races.

Racism is most commonly used to describe the belief that members of one's own race are superior physically, mentally, culturally, and morally to members of other races. Racist beliefs provide the foundation for extending special rights, privileges, and opportunities to the race that is believed to be superior, and to withholding rights, privileges, and opportunities from the races believed to be inferior. No scientific evidence supports racist claims, although racism exists in all countries and cultures. The definition of racism has evolved to describe prejudice against a group of people based on the belief that human groups are unequal genetically, and that members of some racial groups are thus inferior. Sociologists distinguish between *individual racism*, a term describing attitudes and beliefs of individuals, and *institutional racism*, which denotes governmental and organizational policies that restrict minority groups or demean them by the application of stereotypes. While such policies are being corrected to eliminate institutional racism, individual racism nonetheless persists.

Scientists have acknowledged individual differences among ethnic and racial groups, citing the importance of **environment** in **shaping** performance and measurable **ability**. When test results appear to indicate differences in ability and performance that follow racial lines, the effect of environment must be considered in interpreting the results. In addition, tests and other instruments for evaluating ability may be biased to favor knowledge and experiences of one racial or ethnic group over others. Thus, test scores must be analyzed with great caution with regard to patterns of performance and their relationship to race.

By studying genetic patterns in humans, scientists have demonstrated that genetic differences between races are not very significant. As humans migrate from continent to continent and ethnic groups intermingle, racial categories will have less meaning, but prejudice is not likely to disappear.

*See also* Ethnocentrism; Eugenics

## Further Reading

Balibar, Etienne. "Racism and Anti-Racism." *UNESCO Courier* (March 1996): 14+.

Dawes, Kwame. "Clothed Against Naked Racism." *World Press Review* (April 1996): 32+.

Jacquard, Albert. "An Unscientific Notion." *UNESCO Courier* (March 1996): 22+.

Wieviorka, Michel. "The Seeds of Hate: Racism and Nationalism After World War II." *UNESCO Courier* (March 1996): 104+.

# Otto Rank

### 1884-1939

Austrian psychoanalyst and collaborator of Sigmund Freud, who developed theories of will and birth trauma.

Otto Rank was Sigmund Freud's closest collaborator for 20 years. Later, he strongly influenced the development of **psychotherapy** in the United States. He was the first psychoanalyst to examine mother-child relationships, including **separation anxiety**. He also was one of the first to practice a briefer form of psychotherapy, called "active therapy." His work, in contrast to orthodox Freudian psychology, emphasized free will, relationships, and **creativity**. Many of Rank's ideas, including the importance of the **ego**, **consciousness**, and the present, have become mainstays of psychoanalytic theory.

Born in Vienna, Austria, in 1884, Otto Rosenfeld changed his name to Otto Rank as an adolescent. It was one of his first acts of "self-creation." The second son of Simon Rosenfeld, a jeweler, and Karoline Fleischner, the **family** could only afford a higher education for one son. Rank attended trade school, despite recurring bouts of rheumatic fever, and became a locksmith, while his brother studied law. In 1904, Rank suffered a suicidal **depression**, after which he experienced a spiritual rebirth.

## Hired by Freud

Rank was extremely well-read in literature and philosophy. After discovering the works of Freud, he wrote an essay that applied Freud's theory of **dreams** to the creativity of artists. On reading the essay, Freud was so impressed that in 1906 he hired Rank as the secretary of the newly founded Vienna Psychoanalytic Society. Soon, Rank was a member of the "Committee of Seven," Freud's inner circle. Although only 22, Rank was considered to be the resident expert on mythology, literature, and philosophy. With financial support from Freud, Rank earned his Ph.D. from the University of Vienna in 1912, with the first ever dissertation on **psychoanalysis**. Entitled *The Lohengrin Legend*, it was published in 1911. Rank was the first psychoanalyst without a medical degree.

Rank lived with Freud and together they trained psychoanalysts from all over the world. However as Freud's favorite, he engendered the anger and jealousy of other Freud disciples. Rank edited Freud's *The Interpretation of Dreams*, co-edited their psychoanalytic journals, and became director of their publishing house. In 1918 in Poland, while serving in the Austrian army, Rank married Beata "Tola" Mincer, who also joined Freud's circle and became a psychoanalyst. Their only child, a daughter, was born in 1919.

## Breaks with Freud

In *The Trauma of Birth*, published in German in 1924 and in English in 1929, Rank extended Freud's ideas to mother-child relationships. He viewed the child's separation from the mother at birth and weaning as the basis of **neurosis** and argued that the male sex drive was a desire to return to the womb. Rank's therapy involved re-experiencing the trauma of birth. On a trip to the United States in 1924, Rank lectured on his own ideas as well as Freud's. Although Freud originally praised Rank's new work, soon he was attacking him, and they broke off their relationship in 1926. Rank moved his family to Paris and began spending a great deal of time in the United States, lecturing and treating patients. His new "active therapy" stressed a more equal relationship between the patient and therapist, with a focus on terminating the analysis, as opposed to the open-ended and intensive psychoanalysis of Freud. The Freudians labeled Rank as mentally ill, and he was expelled from the American Psychoanalytic Association. To remain in the Association, those who had undergone analysis with Rank were forced to undergo analysis again with a Freudian practitioner.

Rank was a prolific writer. His works included a 700-page survey, *The Incest Theme in Literature and Legend*, first published in 1912. Between 1926 and 1931, he wrote important works on **developmental psychology**, education, and therapeutic methods. The English translation of an expanded version of his early essay on art, *Art and Artist*, appeared in 1932. In sharp contrast to Freudian principles, *Will Therapy* (1936) stressed consciousness, choice, responsibility, and action. Rank argued that neurotics were failed artists who could regain their will through analysis, in a process of self-creation or rebirth.

## Emigrates to the United States

With the rise of Nazi Germany, Rank, a Jew, emigrated to the United States in 1935. Teaching at the Pennsylvania School of Social Work, he adopted the nickname "Huck," after his favorite American book, *The Adventures of Huckleberry Finn*. Rank and his wife separated in 1934. Three months before his death in New York City in 1939, from side effects of the sulfa drug he was taking for a kidney infection, Rank married Estelle Buel.

Rank has never received full credit for his contributions to psychoanalysis and psychotherapy, primarily because of the attacks by Freudians. Although Rank abhorred the Nazis, in 1939 the psychologist **Erich Fromm** labeled Rank's "will therapy" a Nazi-style philosophy. Rank's work was ignored for years, until the 1970s when it was resurrected by the psychologists **Rollo May** and **Carl Rogers**, among others, and by writers such as Anaïs Nin. The *Journal of the Otto Rank Association*, with writings by Rank and his followers, was published biannually from 1966 until 1983. Rank's 1930 work, *Psychology and the Soul*, was finally published in English in 1998.

Margaret Alic

### Further Reading

Lieberman, E. James. *Acts of Will: The Life and Work of Otto Rank: With a New Preface.* Amherst, MA: University of Massachusetts Press, 1993.

Menaker, Esther. *Otto Rank: A Rediscovered Legacy.* New York: Columbia University Press, 1982.

Rudnytsky, Peter L. *The Psychoanalytic Vocation: Rank, Winnicott, and the Legacy of Freud.* New Haven, CT: Yale University Press, 1991.

Taft, Jessie. *Otto Rank: A Biographical Study Based on Notebooks, Letters, Collected Writings, Therapeutic Achievements and Personal Associations.* New York: Julian Press, 1958.

# Rape

*Sexual intercourse forced on a person without the person's consent.*

Rape is essentially an act of **power** and dominance. Although an estimated 15 to 40 percent of American women are victims of rape or attempted rape, men are raped as well. Women are more likely to be raped by someone they know; between 50 and 70 percent of all rapes occur within the context of a romantic relationship, and more than half the time the assault takes place in the victim's home. Rape is one of the most underreported crimes in the United States, due to the victim's fear of embarrassment, humiliation, or retaliation by the rapist. Estimates of the percentage of rapes reported to authorities range from 10 to 50 percent. Because of the difficulty of obtaining a conviction, about two percent of all rapists are convicted, and most serve approximately half of their original sentence.

A survey conducted in 1987 found that 57 percent of women who have been raped develop post-traumatic **stress** disorder. These women may lose their appetite, become easily startled, and suffer from headaches, **sleep** disorders, or fatigue. Many women have difficulty maintaining a normal life following a rape, and may repress the experience for an extended period before they are able to talk about it. Over the past 20 years feminist organizations have fought successfully to change public attitudes toward rape as well as treatment of rape victims. Efforts have been made to increase the sensitivity of police and hospital personnel to rape victims through special training programs. Today, women police officers routinely investigate rape cases. Rape crisis centers in local communities throughout the nation counsel rape victims and perform other services, such as instruction on rape prevention, providing hotline services and legal advice, and supplying hospital emergency room advocates to offer emotional support to victims and assure that they are treated fairly by physicians and the police.

Despite these and other advances in combating rape, it remains a difficult crime to prosecute. Traditionally, rape victims have been questioned about their sexual histories, although most states now place restrictions on the admissibility and usage of such information at trial. In some states, evidence by witnesses or proof of bodily injury to the victim are still required; in other states, a struggle between the woman and her attacker must be proven. Most states require physical evidence of recent sexual intercourse in which the victim most undergo a medical examination within 24 hours of the assault.

In recent years, increased attention has been focused on "date" or "acquaintance" rape, a widespread phenomena that is particularly insidious because women who are victimized in this way are more likely to blame themselves and are less likely to seek help or prosecute their attackers. A 1987 study of acquaintance rape at 32 college campuses sponsored by *Ms.* magazine found that one in four women surveyed were victims of rape or attempted rape, that most rape victims knew their attackers, and over half the assaults were date rapes. Only 27 percent of the women identified themselves as rape victims, and five percent reported the rapes to police. Of the

| RAPE: DOES THE VICTIM KNOW THE OFFENDER? | |
| --- | --- |
| Offender was a stranger | 68,140 |
| Rate per 1,000 persons for cases involving strangers | 0.3 |
| Offender was a nonstranger* | 72,790 |
| Rate per 1,000 persons for cases involving nonstrangers | 0.4 |

*A "nonstranger" offender is someone who is either related to, well-known to, or casually acquainted with the victim. **Source: Statistics on Crime & Punishment, p. 32.**

acquaintance rape victims in the *Ms.* magazine survey, 38 percent were between 14 and 17 years old. Rape can be particularly devastating for adolescents; the damage it inflicts on the victim's sense of personal integrity interferes with the fragile personal identity and sense of **self-esteem** that are being forged during this period. It also upsets the adolescent's need to assert some control over her **environment**. Young rape victims, who are often sexually inactive at the time of the attack, may have their ideas and feelings about sex distorted by the experience. Often, they have daily encounters with their attacker or his friends at school or social events, adding to their sense of shame and humiliation. Most are unlikely to report the rape to parents or other adults, fearing they will be blamed or that their parents may press charges against their own wishes.

**Further Reading**

Brownmiller, Susan. *Against Our Will: Men, Women, and Rape*. Bantam, 1986.

Guernsey, JoAnn B. *The Facts about Rape*. Crestwood, 1990.

Parrot, Andrea. *Coping with Date Rape and Acquaintance Rape*. Rosen Publishers, 1988.

# Rapid eye movement (REM)

The stage of sleep most closely associated with dreaming.

First described in 1953 by Nathaniel Kleitman and Eugene Aserinsky, rapid eye movement (REM) **sleep** is also called active sleep because the EEG ( electroencephalogram) patterns in this stage are similar to the patterns during the awake stage. The four stages of slow-wave, or non-REM, sleep are accompanied by deep breathing, a relatively slow heartbeat, and lowered blood pressure. In contrast, levels of physiological arousal during REM sleep resemble those of the waking state. In some ways, however, people are more deeply asleep during the REM stage than at other times: the major muscle groups go limp in a sort of paralysis, and people are

hardest to waken during REM sleep. The contradictions between the active, "awake" features of REM sleep and its soundness have caused some people to refer to REM sleep as "paradoxical sleep." At **birth** about 50 percent of all sleep is REM sleep, but by the age of 10 this figure drops to 25 percent.

In the course of a night, periods of REM sleep occur every 90 to 100 minutes, becoming longer as the night progresses, in contrast to the deeper stage four sleep, most of which occurs early in the night. About 80 percent of the time, people awakened from REM sleep will say they have been dreaming, while those awakened during other sleep stages rarely report **dreams**. Experiments

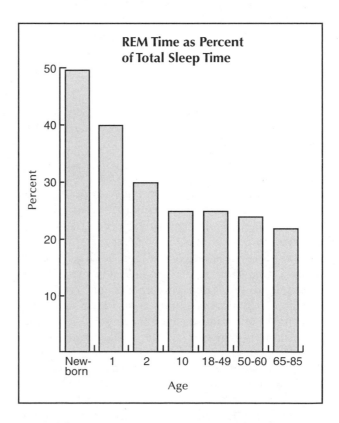

**REM sleep decreases from about 50 percent of a newborn baby's sleep to about 25 percent by age 10.**

have shown that people repeatedly awakened during the REM stage for several nights will compensate by spending twice as much time in REM sleep the first night they are left alone, an observation that has led to much speculation about the role of this type of sleep.

Some researchers have hypothesized that REM sleep strengthens neural connections in the **brain**, a theory supported by the fact that infants and children, whose brains are still developing, require larger amounts of REM sleep than adults. It has also been suggested that REM sleep may be linked to a specific **neurotransmitter**, norepinephrine, which helps maintain alertness when people are awake. In addition, REM sleep has been investigated in connection with learning and **memory** in studies that showed decreased retention of learned skills in persons who were deprived of REM sleep. However, a contrasting (and controversial) theory maintains that the REM stage is a way for the body to "empty" the brain so that its neural networks do not become overloaded.

### Further Reading

Hartmann, Ernest. *The Functions of Sleep*. New Haven, CT: Yale University Press, 1973.
Hobson, J. Allan. *Sleep*. New York: Scientific American Library, 1989.
———. *The Dreaming Brain*. New York: Basic Books, 1988.

# Rating scale

Any instrument designed to assist in the measurement of subjective evaluations of, or reactions to, a person, object, event, statement, or other item of interest.

Several varieties of rating scales have been developed. One common form of rating scale presents the rater with a spectrum of potential responses that includes antithetical elements at each end of a range of intermediate possibilities, on which the rater is expected to indicate the position that most accurately represents the rater's response to the subject in question. Another form of rating scale presents the rater with a list of characteristics or attributes from which the rater is expected to select those which the rater believes apply to the subject in question. Rating scale instruments are used in psychological research primarily to assess qualities for which no objective **measurement** techniques have been developed.

### Further Reading

Bech, Per. *Rating Scales for Psychopathology, Health Status, and Quality of Life*. New York: Springer-Verlag, 1993.

# Rational-emotive behavior therapy

A therapeutic technique that reduces maladaptive behaviors by showing clients that their behavior is caused by irrational thoughts.

Rational-emotive **behavior therapy** (REBT) belongs to a class of therapies termed "cognitive-behavioral" therapies. The defining features of these therapies are an emphasis on achieving measurable goals by manipulating internal and external reinforcers. That is, cognitive-behavioral therapists help clients identify the thoughts and beliefs that might be prolonging their distress or anxiety. The assumption is that attitudes and expectations that we have for ourselves influence how we cope and respond to challenge.

Rational-emotive behavior therapy is the creation of psychologist **Albert Ellis**. Ellis believes that people are born with a predisposition to be either rational or irrational, and that mental disorders are the product of faulty learning. Specifically, REBT conceptualizes psychological disturbances as the products of maladaptive and irrational cognitions (thoughts) that have been learned, and which cause and are in turn caused by emotions and behaviors. It is not only the events in our lives, but also our interpretation of those events that can cause psychological disturbances. This is an optimistic theory, inasmuch as it predicts that, since mental disorders are the result of learning, they can be unlearned. The ultimate goals of REBT are to teach clients to think more rationally, to feel more appropriately, and to behave more adaptively.

As a therapy, REBT is active and sometimes confrontational. Cognitive, emotive, and behavioral methods are used in combination to facilitate client change. Some of the cognitive methods include: disputing irrational beliefs (e.g., pointing out how irrational it would be for a client to believe he/she had to be good at everything in order to consider himself/herself worthwhile); thought stopping (the therapist interrupts the maladaptive thought by yelling "STOP"); reframing (situations are looked at from a more positive angle); and problem solving. The emotive techniques, including role playing, **modeling**, the use of **humor**, and shame-attacking exercises, are all aimed at diffusing the upsetting emotions connected with certain behaviors or situations. Finally, behavioral techniques such as the use of homework assignments, risk-taking exercises, systematic **desensitization** (which involves incremental exposure to the frightening situation while focusing on remaining relaxed), and bibliotherapy (reading about the disorder) are all used to teach clients that they can safely and comfortably substitute adaptive behaviors for the maladaptive ones they have relied on in the past.

REBT uses something called the ABCDE model to help clients understand how their thoughts, feelings, and behaviors are related. The A stands for "activating events," which are related to rational or irrational "beliefs" (B). The beliefs involve "consequences" (C), which, if the belief is irrational, may be emotional disturbances. The D represents the therapist "disputing" the irrational belief and the E stands for the more "effective" way of thinking that marks success with REBT.

Consider, as an example, a student who performs badly on an exam. The poor grade is the activating event. The student's irrational belief is that, because of this bad grade, he or she is neither intelligent nor a worthwhile person. The consequence is depressed **mood** and perhaps feelings of anxiety connected to test-taking. These reactions could, in turn, result in avoidance of classes and tests or withdrawal from academically related activities. In REBT, the therapist would dispute the student's belief that the bad grade represents incompetence or worthlessness. The therapist would help the student to adopt more effective behaviors and beliefs, such as the belief that the poor grade is simply a reflection of course difficulty or the student's inadequate preparation, rather than a measure of the student's worth as a person.

REBT has been extensively researched. Many studies have demonstrated its success in treating various psychological troubles ranging from **depression** to anxiety disorders and even **eating disorders** such as **bulimia**. Additionally, REBT has been shown to work in both individual and group counseling settings. Because REBT teaches clients to monitor and alter their thoughts, feelings and behaviors, it teaches clients to help themselves. This feature is one of its greatest strengths, and is reflected in low relapse rates, compared to drug treatment in the absence of any accompanying therapy. Further advantages of REBT include its rapid symptom reduction and the short duration of therapy; therapeutic goals are frequently achieved within 10 to 20 sessions.

Timothy Moore

## Further Reading
Capuzzi, D., & Gross, D. *Counselling & Psychotherapy: Theories and Interventions.* New Jersey: Prentice Hall, 1999.

Ellis, A. & Blau, S. "Rational emotive behavior therapy." *Directions in Clinical and Counseling Psychology,* 8, 41-56, 1993.

# Reaction time

Generally, in psychological measurement, the interval of time between the presentation of a stimulus to a subject and the beginning of the subject's response to that stimulus.

Several categories of reaction time, such as simple reaction time, have been established and studied in **experimental psychology**. In a simple reaction time experiment, the subject is presented with one simple stimulus, such as a light, and instructed to perform one simple response, such as pressing a button. In a discrimination reaction time experiment, the subject is presented with one of two or more different stimuli, such as a red light and a green light, and instructed to perform a response to only one of the stimuli, such as pressing a button when the red light is presented but not when the green light is presented. In a choice reaction time experiment, the subject is presented with one of two or more different stimuli, such as a red light and a green light, and instructed to perform different responses depending upon which stimulus is presented, such as pressing a red button when the red light is presented and pressing a green button when the green light is presented. There are other types, and many variations of reaction time experiments.

# Readiness test

A test designed to assess the developmental condition of an individual to determine whether or not, or to what extent, the individual could gain from some particular experience.

Readiness tests are commonly used in educational situations, and often include the **measurement** of cognitive, perceptual, emotional, motivational, and other factors involved in the learning process, in an attempt to determine if a student is in a position to benefit from a particular course of instruction. Readiness tests are based on the view, shared by almost all psychologists, that an individual reaches maturity in various areas only by passing through corresponding series of consecutive developmental levels, and that these series of levels are essentially similar in all **normal** individuals.

# Reality therapy

A therapeutic approach in which a therapist helps a client understand the reality of the world around them and how to function accordingly.

Reality therapy was developed by William Glasser, who wrote a book of the same name in the 1960s. This type of counseling suggests that all psychiatric subjects have the same basic underlying problem, namely an inability to fulfill their *essential needs*. Specific problems, like alcoholism or misbehavior in school, are the symptoms and not the problem. Troublesome symptoms occur when a person cannot or will not meet their needs.

## Language of reality therapy

*Essential needs* can be broken down into two categories. One is the need to love and be loved at all times during the course of a lifetime. The other is the need to feel worthwhile to oneself and others. In order to feel worthwhile, one must maintain a satisfactory standard of behavior. In other words, if a person is drinking to avoid facing reality, then he or she is not maintaining a satisfactory standard of behavior and not feeling worthwhile. Everyone has these essential needs but peoples's abilities to fulfill them vary.

The process of fulfilling the essential needs requires, first and foremost, involvement with other people who are in touch with the reality of the world. Without involvement with other people, we try to fulfill the basic needs in unhealthy ways, like overeating or abusing drugs. Not knowing how to fulfill essential needs always leads to **pain**, either physical or emotional, for the client or those around him or her. Reality therapy holds that any time a person comes to therapy, they are lacking a true involvement with a healthy person. A therapist can be the person who becomes healthily involved with a client. Since fulfilling essential needs is part of person's present life, reality therapy does not concern itself with a client's past. Neither does this type of therapy deal with **unconscious** mental processes. In these two ways reality therapy is very different from other forms of psychology like **psychoanalysis**.

Reality therapy tends not to use typical psychology labels, like "neurotic" or "dysfunctional," because these terms tend to **stereotype** people. *Responsibility and irresponsibility* are two terms commonly used in reality therapy. Responsibility refers to the ability to fulfill one's needs and to do so in a way that doesn't interfere with someone else fulfilling their needs. Irresponsible people cannot fulfill their own needs, or they fulfill their needs at the cost of negatively affecting someone else. For example, responsible students do their own homework. Irresponsible students look for someone else to do their work. If a parent does the homework for the child, the parent is also being irresponsible. The student who doesn't do their homework is harming his or her learning process and being a burden on those around them. The parent who does the homework is harming the student by not teaching that child responsibility. Reality therapy holds that we learn responsibility through involvement with another responsible person. We can learn and relearn responsibility at any time in life.

## Procedure

The procedure of reality therapy is basically threefold. First, an involvement must be established between the therapist and the client. This means a firm emotional bond must be established fairly quickly through discussing all aspects of a client's current life. This way the client begins to understand that the therapist cares and also that the therapist is a responsible person who can help clarify the reality of the client's world. It has been suggested that through this involvement a client also develops increased self-worth. Once involvement has been established, the therapist begins rejecting the unrealistic or irresponsible behavior of the client. The therapist points out irresponsible behavior. Irresponsible behavior is never justified, nor is it viewed as caused by anyone but the client. The therapist expects and encourages new behavior that is builds confidence in the client. Finally, the therapist acts as a guide or a teacher of responsible behavior. Clients learn that happiness can only be gained by being responsible. A therapist illuminates a client's hopes, helps a person expand a range of interests, and teaches a client to recognize his or her own needs and use new behaviors to fulfill those needs.

Lara Lynn Lane

## Further Reading
Collins, Perry L. "The historical development of reality therapy." *TCA Journal* vol. 25(2) Fall 1997, 50-57.
Glasser, William, M.D. *Reality Therapy: A New Approach to Psychiatry.* NY: Harper & Row, Publishers, 1965.
Glasser, William. *Reality Therapy in Action.* NY, US: Harpercollins Publishers, 2000.

## Further Information
William Glasser Institute. 22024 Lassen Street, Suite 118, Chatsworth, CA, USA. 91311, fax: 818-700-0555, 800-899-0688. Email: wginst@earthlink.net. www.glasserinst.com.

# Reflective listening

Listening practice used by psychotherapists that requires focus, intent, and very active participation.

Very often in Western culture, listening is considered to be the passive part of a conversation while speaking is seen as active. Reflective listening practices requires focus, intent, and very active participation. The term stems from work done by psychologist **Carl Rogers** who developed **client-centered therapy**. Rogers believed that by listening intently to the client, a therapist could determine best what the client needed. This was unlike **psychoanalysis**, which had more formula-like approaches that were used for all patients. Rogers wrote about *reflection of attitudes,* which asserts that a therapist needs to have empathic understanding with his/her client. Empathic understanding means understanding a person from his or her frame of reference. What a therapist attempts to do is reconstruct what the client is thinking and feeling and to relay this understanding back to the client. By explaining that he or she understands what the client is saying, a therapist is establishing a trust and clarifying the client's expression. For example, a client may make a statement like, "My mother is such a jerk. She's always telling me what to do and won't let me do anything I want to do." The therapist who uses reflective listening might respond by saying, "So you feel frustrated because you're mother treats you like a child instead of an adult." This will allow the client to feel understood and open up even more about his or her feelings about being a teenager. Alternately, a client may feel misunderstood and then try again to explain what he or she is thinking or feeling. This will also allow a therapist to make sure he or she is understanding the client.

By re-stating or reflecting what clients have expressed, the clients then listen to what they have said in a new way. They hear their feelings and thoughts in a different voice and can look at their life through another's eyes. Such therapy also helps a client to feel validated. This type of re-stating what has been heard is also called mirroring. This technique can be used in one-to-one therapy or **group therapy**.

Lara Lynn Lane

**Further Reading**

Baker, Ann C. and Patricia J. Jensen and David A. Kolb. *In Conversation: Transforming Experience into Learning.* Simulation and Gaming, Vol 28(1), March 1997, pp. 6-12.

Gerwood, Joseph B. *Nondirective Counseling Interventions with Schizophrenics.* Psychological Reports, vol. 73, pp.1147-1151. 1993.

Rogers, Carl. *Client-Centered Therapy: Its Current Practice, Implications, and Theory.* Boston: Houghton Mifflin Company, (1951)1965.

Sahakian, William S. *History and Systems of Psychology.* NY and London: Schenkman Publishing Co., 1975.

# Reflexes

Movements or involuntary reponses initiated by an external stimulus which do not require input from the brain.

In a simple reflex, a sensory receptor initiates a **nerve** impulse in an afferent sensory nerve fiber which conducts it to the spinal cord. In the gray matter of the spinal cord, the afferent nerve impulse is fired over the synaptic gap to an efferent motor fiber which passes along the impulse to the appropriate muscle, producing the reflex.

There are other reflexes which involve neural pathways connected to the **brain**. When an ice cube is touched, cold receptors in the skin are stimulated and that afferent information is transmitted to the gray matter of the spinal cord, where it then travels via axons in the white matter to the brain. There, the sensory information is analyzed and movement such as dropping the ice cube (or keeping hold of it) may be initiated. This message is sent down the axons of the white matter to the appropriate motor nerves in the gray matter. This efferent motor information travels to the muscles which initiate the reflex.

# Rehabilitation

A process geared toward helping persons suffering from an injury, disease, or other debilitating condition to reach their highest possible level of self-sufficiency.

Rehabilitation begins once a debilitating condition has been evaluated and treatment is either in progress or completed. Impairments are evaluated for their effects on the individual's psychological, social, and vocational functioning. Depending on the type of **disability** involved, "self-sufficiency" may mean a full-time job, employment in a sheltered workshop, or simply an independent living situation. Rehabilitation involves a combination of medicine, therapy, education, or vocational training. There are special centers for various mental and physical problems that require rehabilitation, including psychiatric disorders, **mental retardation**, alcohol dependence, **brain** and spinal cord injuries, stroke, burns, and other physically disabling conditions.

The goal of medical rehabilitation is the restoration of normal functioning to the greatest degree possible. Specialities involved include physical, occupational, and speech therapy, recreation, psychology, and social work. Medical rehabilitation facilities often include an "activities of daily living" (ADL) department, which offers activities in a simulated apartment setting where patients may learn and practice tasks they will need in everyday living. Also included in the field of medical rehabilitation is a special area called rehabilitation technology (formerly rehabilitation engineering), developed during the 1970s and 1980s, that deals with prosthetics (devices attached to the body) and orthotics (equipment used by disabled people). In addition to the actual engineers who design these products, rehabilitation technology also includes professionals who serve as consultants to manufacturers on the design, production, and marketing of medical devices.

Vocational rehabilitation helps the client achieve a specific goal, which can be either a type of employment (competitive, sheltered, volunteer) or a living situation. Services include prevocational evaluation, work evaluation, work adjustment, job placement, and on-the-job training. Facilities offering vocational rehabilitation include state-supported local units in hospitals, the Veterans Administration, sheltered workshops, insurance companies, and speech and **hearing** clinics. Rehabilitation counseling is a relatively new field whose support personnel offer a variety of services to the disabled, particularly that of coordinating and intergrating the various types of assistance available to a particular client. The rehabilitation counselor also assists in locating job opportunities, interpreting test results, and assisting with personal problems.

Since the 1980s, supported employment (employment of the disabled through programs that provide them with ongoing support services) has become increasingly popular as a means of vocational rehabilitation. Traditionally, the most common form of supported employment has been the sheltered workshop, a nonprofit organization—often receiving government funds—that provides both services and employment to the disabled. Today, sheltered industrial employment mainstreams disabled workers into the regular workplace with jobs modified to meet their needs, especially those of the severely disabled. However, both cutbacks in funding for government support services and affirmative action provisions of the 1973 Rehabilitation Act pertaining to federal contractors led to increasing private sector participation efforts in the 1980s. Some firms became involved in career education, offering internships to disabled students, which sometimes led to permanent employment. Other recent trends include rehabilitation of persons with traumatic brain injuries and severe learning disabilities, and rehabilitation of the homebound and the elderly.

The U. S. Department of Education administers most federal programs for rehabilitation of the disabled, often through its Office of **Special Education** and Reha-

bilitative Services (OSERS). Within OSERS, the Rehabilitation Services Administration (RSA) supervises the state offices of vocational rehabilitation. Organizations involved in rehabilitation efforts include the National Rehabilitation Association, the National Association of Rehabilitation Facilities, and the President's Committee on Employment of People with Disabilities.

## Further Information

American Paralysis Association 24-hour tool-free information and referral hotline. (800) 526–3256.
National Association of Rehabilitation Facilities. P.O. Box 17675, Washington, D.C. 20041, (703) 648–9300.
National Rehabilitation Association. 633 S. Washington St., Alexandria, Virginia 22314, (703) 836–0850.
National Spinal Cord Injury Association . (800) 962–9629.

# Rehearsal

Mental activities associated with committing information to memory.

Rehearsal is a term used by **memory** researchers to refer to mental techniques for helping us remember information. Its technical meaning is not very different from our everyday use of the term. Actors rehearse their lines so that they won't forget them. Similarly, if we want to retain information over time, there are strategies for enhancing future recall. There are two main types of rehearsal. The first is maintenance rehearsal, which involves continuously repeating the to-be-remembered material. This method is effective in maintaining information over the short term. We have all had the experience of looking up a phone number and subsequently forgetting it (or part of it) before we have dialed it. This illustrates the fact that new material will fade from memory relatively quickly unless we make a purposeful effort to remember it. One of the advantages of a touch tone telephone is that the number can be dialed more quickly compared to the old rotary dial phones, thereby reducing the length of time required to keep the number in memory. Maintenance rehearsal typically involves rote repetition, either out loud or covertly. It is effective for maintaining relatively small amounts in memory for brief periods, but is not likely to affect retention in the long term.

In order to retain information for longer periods of time, elaborative rehearsal is more useful. This second main type of rehearsal involves associating new material with information that already exists in long-term memory. There are numerous occasions on which students are required to remember large amounts of relatively complex information—certainly more complex than a phone number. In these situations, reciting the information over and over again is not going to help commit it to memory. Such a strategy would be hopelessly inefficient and ineffective. Instead, elaboration strategies that engage the learner in understanding the material are helpful, both for storing information, and for retrieving it in the future. Elaboration can take a variety of forms. For example the learner can generate personal examples that help illustrate concepts or principles. Enriching the material by concentrating on its meaning not only makes it more understandable, it also helps establish potential pathways for subsequent retrieval. Study groups provide a context for elaborative rehearsal. Discussions or arguments about various topics will enrich the subject matter and add to its meaningfulness. The most effective studying techniques are those that enhance understanding. Trying to explain a concept to a friend is a good way of testing your own grasp of it, and at the same time engages you in a form of elaborative rehearsal.

Timothy Moore

**Further Reading**

Reisberg, D. *Cognition: Exploring the science of the mind.* New York: Norton & Co., 1997.

# Wilhelm Reich

### 1897-1957

Austrian psychoanalyst whose unorthodox ideas contributed to the development of psychoanalytic theory.

Although Wilhelm Reich is remembered primarily for his legal battle with the United States Food and Drug Administration (FDA) over their outlawing of his "orgone energy accumulator," his earlier works were influential in the development of **psychoanalysis**. In *The Function of the Orgasm*, published in German in 1927 and in English in 1942, Reich placed the drive for sexual fulfillment at the center of human psychology and argued that neuroses resulted from sexual repression. In his *Character Analysis*, published in Vienna in 1933 and in the United States in 1949, he described how defensive **character traits** were developed to cope with specific emotions, and he argued that the goal of therapy was to remove these repressive traits. These ideas have become mainstays of psychoanalytic theory.

Born in 1897 in Dobrzcynica, in the region of Galacia that was part of the Austrian Empire, Reich's family soon moved to Jujinetz in Bukovina in the Ukrainian re-

gion of Austria. There his father, Leon Reich, raised cattle on a large estate. Reich was educated at home by tutors until age 14, when he entered the German gymnasium at Czernowitz. At 12, Reich told his father about an affair between his mother, Cecile Roniger, and one of his tutors. After a year of brutal beatings by her husband, Reich's mother committed suicide. Following his father's death in 1914, Reich managed the farm and cared for his younger brother while attending school. After graduating in 1915, he joined the Austro-Hungarian army, becoming an officer on the Italian front.

### Becomes a disciple of Freud

With the end of World War I in 1918, Reich entered medical school at the University of Vienna. There he encountered **Sigmund Freud**, joined the Vienna Psychoanalytic Society, and began practicing psychoanalysis. He earned his M. D. in 1922 and married a fellow medical student and psychoanalyst, Annie Pink. The couple had two daughters. Reich continued to study psychiatry for two more years at the Neurological and Psychiatric Clinic in Vienna. When Freud established the Psychoanalytic Polyclinic in 1922, Reich was his first clinical assistant. In 1928, Reich became vice-director. Between 1924 and 1930, he was also director of the Seminar for Psychoanalytic Theory. During this period, Reich developed his theories of "character analysis" and his controversial theory of "orgastic potency," that defined orgasm as the basis for **mental health**.

In 1928, Reich joined the Communist Party and co-founded the Socialist Society for Sex Consultation and Sexological Research, a clinic that provided workers with sex education and birth control information. Reich's increasing interest in reconciling Marxism and psychoanalysis, culminating with his *Dialectic Materialism and Psychoanalysis*, first published in Moscow in 1929, was a factor in his break with Freud. Freud's rejection left him deeply depressed. He developed tuberculosis, which had killed both his father and his brother, and spent several months in a sanitarium in Switzerland.

### Attacked for unorthodox ideas

Reich moved to Berlin, Germany, in 1930, where he continued to write prolifically and organize "mental hygiene" clinics for workers. In 1933 he published *The Mass Psychology of Fascism*, an attack on Nazism which emphasized the connections between personal and sexual issues and political issues. He found himself expelled from the German Communist Party for his sexual and psychoanalytic views, and from the International Psychoanalytic Association for his political views. His marriage also ended in 1933, and he entered into a marital relationship with Elsa Lindenberg, a dancer and fellow communist. In 1934 Reich began moving across Europe, first to Denmark, then Sweden, and finally settling in Oslo, Norway. During this period, he developed his theory of "muscular armor," the outward bodily attributes that represent character traits; for example, a stubborn person might develop a stiff neck. Reich used physical methods in his therapy to break these patterns, methods that were adopted by other therapies, including bioenergetics and **Gestalt psychology**. He published *The Sexual Revolution* (1936), an indictment of conventional sexual morality, and undertook experiments on energetic particles that he called "bions." Reich believed that he had discovered and could measure a new form of energy, the "orgone," which controlled sexual drive and love.

In Norway, Reich came under attack by both the medical establishment and the press. In 1939, as a Jew living under the growing Nazi threat, he emigrated to the United States. Reich moved his laboratory from Oslo to Long Island and lectured at the New School for Social Research in New York City for the next two years. In 1940, he built his first "orgone energy accumulator," or "orgone box." Reich claimed that this telephone booth-sized machine trapped orgone energy, which could be used to prevent and treat mental and physical illnesses, particularly cancer. He described his research in *The Cancer Biopathy*, published in 1948. In 1944, Reich had a son with the German-born socialist, Ilse Ollendorff, and the following year the family moved to Rangeley, Maine, where Reich founded the Orgone Institute, with research laboratories and a publishing house.

Reich and Ollendorff were divorced in 1954, the same year that the FDA obtained an injunction against his energy accumulator. The injunction made it a crime not only to build or use the orgone box, but to even mention the term "orgone" in print. Reich defied the order. He was found in contempt and, in March, 1957, sentenced to two years in the Lewisburg Federal Penitentiary in Pennsylvania. The following November, he died of a heart attack in the psychiatric wing of the prison. The FDA destroyed his remaining accumulators, as well as many of his books on a variety of subjects. However in recent years, Reich's contributions to psychoanalysis have been re-examined and many of his books have been translated and reprinted.

Margaret Alic

**Further Reading**
Reich, Wilhelm. *Passion of youth: an autobiography, 1897-1922.* Edited by Mary Boyd Higgins and Chester M. Raphael; translations by Philip Schmitz and Jerri Tompkins. New York: Farrar, Straus & Giroux, 1988.
Reich, Wilhelm. *Beyond psychology: letters and journals, 1934-1939.* Edited by Mary Boyd Higgins; translations by Philip Schmitz, Derek Jordan, and Inge Jordan. New York: Farrar, Straus & Giroux, 1994.
Reich, Wilhelm. *American odyssey: letters and journals, 1940-1947.* Edited by Mary Boyd Higgins; translations by Derek Jordan, Inge Jordan, and Philip Schmitz. New York: Farrar, Straus & Giroux, 1999.
Sharaf, Myron. *Fury on earth: a biography of Wilhelm Reich.* New York: St. Martin's Press, 1983.
Wilson, Colin. *The quest for Wilhelm Reich.* Garden City, NY: Doubleday, 1981.

# Reinforcement

In either classical or operant conditioning, a stimulus that increases the probability that a particular behavior will occur.

In **classical** (Pavlovian) **conditioning**, where the response has no effect on whether the stimulus will occur, reinforcement produces an immediate response without any training or conditioning. When meat is offered to a hungry dog, it does not learn to salivate, the behavior occurs spontaneously. Similarly, a negative reinforcer, such as an electric shock, produces an immediate, unconditioned escape response. To produce a classically-conditioned response, the positive or negative reinforcer is paired with a neutral stimulus until the two become associated with each other. Thus, if the sound of a bell accompanies a negative stimulus such as an electric shock, the experimental subject will eventually be conditioned to produce an escape or avoidance response to the sound of the bell alone. Once conditioning has created an association between a certain behavior and a neutral stimulus, such as the bell, this stimulus itself may serve as a reinforcer to condition future behavior. When this happens, the formerly neutral stimulus is called a conditioned reinforcer, as opposed to a naturally positive or negative reinforcer, such as food or an electric shock.

In **operant conditioning** (as developed by **B. F. Skinner**), positive reinforcers are rewards that strengthen a **conditioned response** after it has occurred, such as feeding a hungry pigeon after it has pecked a key. Negative reinforcers are unpleasant stimuli that are removed when the desired response has been obtained. The application of negative reinforcement may be divided into two types: escape and avoidance conditioning. In escape conditioning, the subject learns to escape an unpleasant or aversive stimulus (a dog jumps over a barrier to escape electric shock). In avoidance conditioning, the subject is presented with a warning stimulus, such as a buzzer, just before the aversive stimulus occurs and learns to act on it in order to avoid the unpleasant stimulus altogether.

Reinforcement may be administered according to various schedules. A particular behavior may be reinforced every time it occurs, which is referred to as continuous reinforcement. In many cases, however, behaviors are reinforced only some of the time, which is termed partial or intermittent reinforcement. Reinforcement may also be based on the number of responses or scheduled at particular time intervals. In addition, it may be delivered in regularly or irregularly. These variables combine to produce four basic types of partial reinforcement. In fixed-ratio (FR) schedules, reinforcement is provided following a set number of responses (a factory worker is paid for every garment he assembles). With variable-ratio (VR) schedules, reinforcement is provided after a variable number of responses (a slot machine pays off after varying numbers of attempts). Fixed-interval (FI) schedules provide for reinforcement of the first response made within a given interval since the previous one (contest entrants are not eligible for a prize if they have won one within the past 30 days). Finally, with variable-interval (VI) schedules, first responses are rewarded at varying intervals from the previous one.

*See also* Avoidance learning; Behavior modification; Classical conditioning; Pavlov, Ivan

**Further Reading**
Craighead, W. Edward. *Behavior Modification: Principles, Issues, and Applications.* Boston: Houghton Mifflin, 1976.
Skinner, B.F. *About Behaviorism.* New York:Knopf, 1974.

# Religion and psychology

Psychologists have long studied religion and religious practices. Using principles of traditional psychology, researchers try to understand religious experience, including prayer, **cults**, and mystical experiences. The study of religion and psychology began in the early twentieth century, but faded before it was revived in the 1980s, when the American Psychological Association began to formally investigate aspects of religion in psychology. The only classic text relating to the psychological study of religion, *Varieties of Religious Experience*, was written by **William James** in 1902.

**Sigmund Freud**, who called religion an "illusion," nonetheless studied religion with great interest, and wrote three books and some papers on his studies of how religion impacted human lives. Later psychoanalysts has studied the psychological value of religion. However, only a few psychologists, including **Paul Meehl, Erich Fromm, Abraham Maslow**, and Solomon Asch, deemed belief systems, moral and ethical conduct, and the reasons people abide by a certain religion as significant factors in human behavior.

Psychologist William James studied the intricate influences of religious conversions, mystical experience, saintliness, and prayer on a person's belief system. Twenty-first century psychologists investigate such topics as cults, confession (particularly as it is practiced among Roman Catholics), ritual, faith healing, and explanations for miracles. Modern psychologists actively pursue the interrelationship between religion and psychology and note that just as religion influences human existence, human perceptions also influence the practice of religion.

Psychologists use various methods to study religion. They have used personal revelations, observation through clinical means, participant observation, surveys and interviews, and examinations of religious documents, treatises, and journals. All these methods must be used to help psychologists understand such a complex topic. A concept such as faith is not easily categorized or discussed, despite scientific analysis. Understanding the psychological origins of religion is difficult as well. Modern psychologists tend to focus their study on individual practices rather than the historical nature of religion as a whole. They look for psychological underpinnings of religion on modern people. This also means that an individual's religion and belief system changes as that person ages. As their mental and **emotional development** progresses, so their image of God and religion does also.

There are many areas of interest to psychologists. Psychologists hold special interest in the social dynamics of religions and their organized structures. They study the influence that these bodies have on the lives of their members and the communities in which they exist. Some psychologists analyze the workings of cults and how these social groups differ from more traditional religions. Many psychologists and religious leaders are attempting to integrate theology and psychology through these pursuits.

The ever-growing group of psychologists attempting to define the psychology of religion include the religiously devout as well as atheists and agnostics. In a study published in the June 2000 issue of *Health Psychology* by the American Psychological Association, Michael E. McCullough, of the National Institute of Healthcare Research noted that "the odds of survival for people who scored higher on measures of public and

Research shows that religious people, like this man, tend to report greater happiness than non-religious people. *(Bildarchiv Preussischer Kulturbestiz. Reproduced with permission.)*

private religious involvement were 20 percent higher than those people who scored lower on such measures." The analysis was done of 42 different studies and examined 125,826 people, and shows a correlation between participation in a religion and an increased life expectancy. As McCullough added, "this is a phenomenon that deserves a lot more research attention than it has traditionally received." As a result, religion is likely to become a central area of focus in psychology well into the twenty-first century.

Jane Spear

**Further Reading**

Collins, G. R. *Religion and Philosophy.* Encyclopedia of Psychology, Second Edition. Ray Corsini, Ed. New York: John Wiley & Sons 1994.

Neuhaus, Richard John. *Religion and Psychology.* National Review, Feb. 19, 1988.

**Further Information**

American Psychological Association. 750 First Street, N.E., Washington, D.C., USA. 20002-4242, 202-336-5500, 800-374-2721.

# Research methodology

The wide variety of strategies employed by psychologists to answer research questions.

Psychologists use a wide variety of techniques to answer research questions. The most commonly used techniques include experiments, correlational studies, observational studies, case studies, and archival research. Each approach has its own strengths and weaknesses. Psychologists have developed a diversity of research strategies because a single approach cannot answer all types of questions that psychologists ask.

Psychologists prefer to use experiments whenever possible because this approach allows them to determine whether a stimulus or an event actually causes something to happen. In an experimental approach, researchers randomly assign participants to different conditions. These conditions should be identical except for one variable that the researcher is interested in. For example, psychologists have asked whether people learn more if they study for one long period or several short periods. To study this experimentally, the psychologist would assign people into one of two groups—one group that studies for an extended period of time or to another group that studies for the same total amount of time, but in short segments.

The researcher would make sure that all the participants studied the same material, for the same total time, and were in the same study **environment**; the only thing that would differentiate the two groups is whether the learners studied for short or long segments. Thus, any difference in the amount of learning should be due only to the length of the study periods. (This kind of research has revealed that people learn better with several shorter study periods.) The experimental approach is useful when the research can establish control over the environment; this work is often done in a simple laboratory setting.

A second approach involves the correlational technique. This approach does not include control of the environment by the researcher. Instead, measurements are made as they naturally occur. For example, a group of high school students took two tests that required them to solve analogies and to recognize antonyms. The researchers discovered a correlation between students' abilities to complete analogies correctly and to identify antonyms. In general, students who were good at one task were also good at the other; students weak in one task were weak in the other. In correlational research, no attempt is made to state that one thing causes another, only that one thing is predictable from the other.

Correlational approaches are most useful when the researchers cannot control the environment or when the phenomena they want to study are complex. Instead of trying to simplify the situation, the researchers observe the complex behaviors as they naturally occur. A third approach is called naturalistic observation. This kind of research often is not highly quantitative; that is, observations are likely to be descriptive. The researcher decides on some class of behavior to observe and records the situations in which that behavior occurs and how it develops. A classic example of observational research was done by Jane Goodall in her work with chimpanzees in the wild. She spent years observing their social interactions and how the chimp "society" changed over time.

The previous techniques all involve observing a group of individuals. Sometimes, psychologists are interested in studying a single person in depth. This is called a case study. This approach is common when clinical psychologists work with a person over a long period of time. The final product in a case study is an in-depth description of a great number of different aspects of the individual's life and development. The strength of this approach is that detail is abundant; the weakness is that the psychologist cannot generalize to other people from the single individual being analyzed because that person may differ in important ways from the average person.

Finally, psychologists can use archival information to answer questions. Archival research differs considerably from the other approaches because it does not rely on direct observation or interaction with the people being studied. Rather, psychologists use records or other already existing information. For example, some psychologists were interested in whether the percentage of left-handed people in the population has remained constant throughout history. They obviously could not observe people who have died, so they decided to use existing information about the past. They recorded the percentage of left-handed people in paintings and other such renderings. After poring over paintings, they concluded that the percentage of left-handed people has not changed over the last few centuries. More commonly, archival information comes from **birth** and death records and other official statistics.

*See also* Correlational method; Scientific method

**Further Reading**
Cozby, Paul C. *Methods in Behavioral Science.* Mountain View, CA: Mayfield Publishing Company, 1993.

# Ribonucleic acid (RNA)

A complex organic substance involved in protein synthesis in cells.

RNA consists of a five-carbon sugar (ribose), phosphate, and four nitrogenous bases (adenine, guanine, cytosine, and uracil). In an RNA molecule, the sugar and phosphate combine to form a structure to

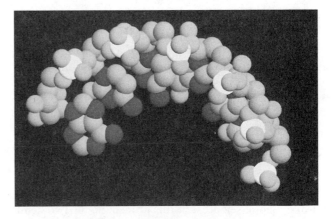

**Computer-generated image of ribonucleic acid.** *(Photo by Ken Eward. National Audubon Society Collection/Photo Researchers, Inc. Reproduced by permission.)*

which the nitrogenous bases are attached. These molecules range in composition from fewer than 100 to several thousand nitrogenous bases, and vary in shape from helical to uncoiled. RNA is the primary agent of protein formation, and processes genetic information from **deoxyribonucleic acid (DNA)** molecules into enzymes necessary for life.

# Right-brain hemisphere

*The hemisphere of the brain that neurologically controls the left side of the body and is thought to control spatial tasks, musical and artistic endeavors, body control and awareness, and creativity and imagination.*

In normal human adults, each hemisphere of the **brain**, working in concert with the other, performs certain types of functions more efficiently than the other. While the **left-brain hemisphere** is dominant in the areas of language and logic, the right-brain hemisphere is the center of nonverbal, intuitive, holistic modes of thinking. Each hemisphere mostly receives perceptions from and controls the activities of the opposite side of the body. Scientists have been aware of the specialized functioning of the hemispheres—also known as lateralization—for over one hundred years, having discovered that language skills are controlled by the left side of the brain in approximately 95 percent of right-handed people and about two thirds of left-handed individuals. In the nineteenth century, however, this discovery led to the assumption that all higher reasoning **ability** resided in the left-brain hemisphere, which was thus regarded as dominant overall. The right brain hemisphere was thought to possess only lower-level capabilities and was considered subordinate to the left.

Research conducted in the 1950s and 1960s established that the two hemispheres of a normally functioning brain—connected by the corpus callosum, a thick cable of nerves—operate in a complementary fashion with both hemispheres involved in higher cognitive functioning. The primary difference between them was found to involve the *mode* rather than the level of thinking. A research group under the direction of Roger Sperry at the California Institute of Technology observed and tested patients who had undergone a surgical procedure in which the corpus callosumwas severed to control epileptic seizures. In this procedure, the two hemispheres of the brain, which normally have a strong tendency to work together, were uncoupled, and each side of the brain remained ignorant of information received by the other. Thus, right-handed people had no trouble writing, which is usually governed by the left-brain hemisphere in righthanders, but were unable to draw, as the left brain was cut off from the spatial capacity of the right. When a special apparatus was used to present the image of a spoon only to a split-brain patient's left hemisphere, the subject could name it readily, but when the same image was presented to the right-brain hemisphere, the subject could not, although they were still aware of what it was.

Research on both split-brain and normal subjects since the 1960s has confirmed that both hemispheres of the brain use high-level cognitive modes. That of the left brain is verbal and analytic, while right brain thought processes are rapid, complex, whole-pattern, spatial, and specialized for visualimagery and musical ability. The right temporal lobe, in particular, governs visual and auditory imagery. People in whom this area is damaged have difficulty recognizing familiar melodies, faces, and pictures, and learning to identify new ones. The right brain hemisphere also appears to have special links to **emotion**. Right-brain damage interferes with both the ability to produce and interpret expressions of emotion. Damage to the front part of the right-brain hemisphere renders people unable to act on or express strong emotions. If the damage is further back in the brain, the person can express emotion but not recognize it in other people or in pictures.

Other general characteristics of right-brain thought processes include the tendency to synthesize rather than analyze, and to relate to things in a concrete rather than a symbolic fashion. Where left-brain thinking tends to represent wholes by abstraction (using one piece of information to represent something larger), the right brain is more likely to interpret data through analogies ó —seeing relationships between wholes. Right-brain functioning is nontemporal, nonrational, holistic, and intuitive, relying on leaps of insight, hunches, or visual images. Discoveries about the right- and left-brain hemispheres have led some researchers and educators to advocate educational reforms that would allow right-brain modes of thought a greater place in the current educational system, which reflects society's overall tendency to reward the verbal, analytical left-brain skills. As split-brain researcher Roger Sperry notes, our educational system "tends to neglect the nonverbal form of intellect. What it comes down to is that modern society discriminates against the right hemisphere." The artistic, creative right brain is relegated to the "minor" subjects of art and music, but the main programs of study do not, as a rule, focus on developing the right-brain skills of **imagination, creativity**, or visualization.

*See also* Brain; Handedness; Split-brain technique

# Carl Rogers

## 1902-1987

American psychologist who developed a nondirective, patient-centered method of psychotherapy known as humanistic psychology.

Carl Rogers was born in Oak Park, Illinois. Raised in a fundamentalist Christian home, Rogers attended the University of Wisconsin and studied for the ministry at Union Theological Seminary before deciding to pursue a doctorate in education and **clinical psychology** at Columbia University. Between 1928 and 1939, Rogers worked as a counselor at the Society for the Prevention of Cruelty to Children in Rochester. In 1940, he was appointed to the faculty of Ohio State University. By this time, he had worked out much of his new client-centered system of therapy, which was set forth in his second book, *Counseling and Psychotherapy*, published in 1942.

Rogers believed that the mental condition of virtually all patients, whom he referred to as clients, can be improved, given an appropriate psychotherapeutic **environment**. Central to this environment is a close personal relationship between client and therapist. Rogers's use of the term "client" rather than "patient" expresses his rejection of the traditionally authoritarian relationship between therapist and client, and his view of them as equals. The client determines the general direction of therapy, while the therapist seeks to increase the client's insightful self-understanding through informal clarifying questions. A hallmark of Rogers's method is the therapist echoing or reflecting the client's remarks, which is supposed to convey a sense of respect as well as a belief in the patient's ability to deal with his or her problems. The concept of an alliance between client and therapist has affinities with the methods of **Carl Jung**. **Otto Rank** (1884-1939) was also an early influence on the development of Rogers's system.

Rogerian therapy is a natural consequence of its creator's belief that a fundamental element of human nature is the drive to fully actualize one's positive potential, a concept based on an essentially positive view of humanity that contrasts with the psychoanalytic view of human beings as driven by antisocial impulses that are suppressed with difficulty and often at great cost. In Rogers's view, the primary task of therapy is to remove the client's obstacles to **self-actualization**. A further **contrast** to **psychoanalysis** lies in the fact that Rogerian therapy emphasizes the current emotions and attitudes of the client rather than early **childhood** experiences.

After leaving Ohio State in 1945, Rogers served on the faculties of the University of Chicago and the Uni-

**Carl Rogers** *(Corbis-Bettmann. Reproduced with permission.)*

versity of Wisconsin. Between 1956 and 1947, he served as president of the American Psychological Association. As Rogers gained increasing acclaim, the popularity of his method grew rapidly. Rogerian therapy was widely practiced in the 1950s and 1960s, when its tenets of antiauthoritarianism and permissiveness gave it a wide appeal to many. Rogers published *Client-Centered Therapy: Its Current Practice, Implications, and Theory* in 1951 and produced numerous of papers in the decade that followed. In 1956, the American Psychological Association awarded him its Distinguished Scientific Contribution Award. In the 1960s, Rogers was attracted to the **human potential movement** that had begun in California, and he adopted some of its principles, including its emphasis on frank and open expression of feelings and its use of **group therapy**. In 1964, he and his wife moved to La Jolla, California, where he continued to write and lecture, and served as a resident fellow at the Western Behavioral Science Institute. *On Becoming a Person*, published in 1961, became his most widely read book. In the last ten years of his life, Rogers became deeply interested in educational reform. Borrowing a central principle from his therapeutic method, he came to believe that teachers (like therapists) should serve as facilitators rather than judges or mere conveyors of facts.

Roger's other books include *Psychotherapy and Personality Change* (1954), *Freedom to Learn: A View of What Education Might Become* (1969), *Carl Rogers on Encounter Groups* (1970), *Carl Rogers on Personal Power* (1977), and *A Way of Being* (1980).

*See also* Client-centered therapy

**Further Reading**
Thorne, Brian. *Carl Rogers*. London: Sage Publications, 1992.

# Role playing/psychodrama

A group therapy approach in which clients act out their problems to gain new insights and achieve emotional catharsis.

Role playing was developed by Jacob Moreno, a Viennese psychologist who contended that people could gain more from acting out their problems than from talking about them. This method requires a protagonist (the client whose problems are being acted out); auxiliary egos (group members who assume the roles of other people in the protagonist's life); an audience (other group members who observe and react to the drama); and a director (the therapist). The protagonist selects an event from his or her life and provides the information necessary for it to be reenacted. Although every detail of the event cannot be reproduced, the reenactment can be effective if it captures the essence of the original experience. The group members who serve as auxiliary egos impersonate significant people from the protagonist's past or present, following the protagonist's instructions as closely as possible. Techniques used in the reenactment may include role reversal, doubling, mirror technique, future projection, and dream work.

The therapist, acting as facilitator and director, assists the protagonist in orchestrating the scene, offers emotional support, enlists the audience's response, and helps the protagonist gain new insights from the experience. Immediately preceding the reenactment is a warmup period designed to prepare all the participants for the experience by motivating them and establishing a safe and trusting atmosphere. After the reenactment, members of the audience discuss their reactions to the reenactment, including ways that it touched on their own experiences. Encouragement and support is offered to the protagonist, as well as suggestions for responding to the problems dealt within the reenactment.

Role playing is sometimes employed in a combination of techniques in other types of therapy, such as Gestalt therapy. The client may role play with the therapist in an individual treatment session or with group members in **group therapy**.

# Rorschach technique

A projective personality assessment based on the subject's reactions to a series of ten inkblot pictures.

Popularly known as the "Inkblot" test, the Rorschach technique, or Rorschach Psychodiagnostic Test is the most widely used projective psychological test. The Rorschach is used to help assess **personality** structure and identify emotional problems. Like other **projective techniques**, it is based on the principle that subjects viewing neutral, ambiguous stimuli will project their own personalities onto them, thereby revealing a variety of **unconscious** conflicts and motivations. Administered to both adolescents and adults, the Rorschach can also be used with children as young as three years old. The test provides information about a person's thought processes, perceptions, motivations, and attitude toward his or her **environment**, and it can detect internal and external pressures and conflicts as well as illogical or psychotic thought patterns.

The Rorschach technique is named for Swiss psychiatrist Hermann Rorschach (1884-1922), who developed it. Rorschach, whose primary interest was in Jungian analysis, began experimenting with inkblots as early as 1911 as a means of determining **introversion** and **extroversion**. The Rorschach technique is administered using 10 cards, each containing a complicated inkblot pattern, five in color and five in black and white. Subjects look at the cards one at a time and describe what each inkblot resembles. After the subject has viewed all 10 cards, the examiner usually goes back over the responses for additional information. The subject may be asked to clarify some responses or to describe which features of each inkblot prompted the responses.

Test scores are based on several factors. One is location, or what part of the blot a person focuses on: the whole blot (W), sections of it (D), or only specific details (Dd). Another is whether the response is based on factors such as form, color, movement, or shading (referred to as determinants). For example, people who tend to see movement in Rorschach blots are thought to be intellectual and introspective; those who see mostly stationary objects or patterns are described as practical and action-oriented. Finally, content refers to which objects, persons, or situations the person sees in the blot (categories include humans, animals, clothing, and nature). Most examiners also assess responses based on the frequency of

**Example of a Rorschach ink blot test.** *(Stan Goldblatt. Photo Researchers, Inc. Reproduced with permission.)*

certain responses as given by previous test takers. Many psychologists interpret the test freely according to their subjective impressions, including their impression of the subject's demeanor while taking the test (cooperative, anxious, defensive, and so forth). Such interpretations, especially when combined with clinical observation and knowledge of a client's personal history, can help a therapist arrive at a more expansive, in-depth understanding of the client's personality.

While the Rorschach technique is still widely used, its popularity has decreased somewhat in recent decades. Unlike objective personality inventories, which can be administered to a group, the Rorschach test must be given individually. A skilled examiner is required, and the test can take several hours to complete and interpret. Like other projective tests, it has been criticized for lack of validity and reliability. Interpretation of responses is highly dependent on an examiner's individual judgment: two different testers may interpret the same responses quite differently. In addition, treatment procedures at **mental health** facilities often require more specific, objective types of personality description than those provided by the Rorschach technique.

Rorschach, who pioneered the test in 1921, did not provide a comprehensive scoring system. In response to complaints about validity, scoring methods have been devised which aim at providing greater objectivity by clearly specifying certain personality variables and relating them to clinical diagnoses. The Exner Comprehensive Rorschach System, released in 1987, is a computer-based scoring system that provides score summaries and lists likely personality and adjustment descriptions for each test taker. To overcome limitations in the Rorschach, Wayne Holtzman and his colleagues developed the Holtzman Inkblot Test that uses 45 inkblots, scores for 22 characteristics and allows for only one response per card.

The Rorschach is generally used as part of a battery of tests and must be administered by a trained psychologist.

*See also* Personality inventory

### Further Reading

Aronow, Edward. *The Rorschach Technique: Perceptual Basics, Content Interpretation, and Applications.* Needham Heights, MA: Allyn and Bacon, 1994.

Lerner, Paul M. *Psychoanalytic Theory and the Rorschach.* Hillsdale, NJ: Analytic Press, 1991.

# Rosenzweig picture frustration study

A projective test administered to assess personality characteristics, in which the subject is shown scenes depicting moderately frustrating situations and asked what the frustrated person depicted would probably do, or how the subject would react in such situations.

The Rosenzweig Picture Frustration test consists of 24 cartoon pictures, each portraying two persons in a frustrating situation. Each picture contains two "speech balloons," a filled one for the "frustrator" or antagonist, and a blank one for the frustrated person, or protagonist. The subject is asked to fill in the blank balloon with his or her response to the situation, and the responses are scored in relation to a number of psychological **defense mechanisms**. For example, responses are scored as to whether, and to what degree, they indicate that the subject exhibits **aggression** toward the source of the frustration, assumes blame or **guilt** as the cause of the frustration, or justifies, minimizes, or denies the frustration. The score is based on a total of nine factors, derived from combinations of three types of aggression (obstacle-dominance, ego-defense, and need-persistence) and three directions of aggression (extraggression, imaggression, and intraggression). However, testers often analyze the subject's responses more informally and intuitively.

Originally developed for adults by Saul Rosenzweig, the test is now available in versions for children and adolescents. The empirical validity of the Rosenzweig Picture Frustration Study and other **projective techniques** is disputed by some authorities.

## Further Reading
Rosenzweig, Saul. *The Rosenzweig Picture Frustration (P-F) Study*. St. Louis: Rana House, 1978.

# Julian B. Rotter

### 1916-
American psychologist best known for his social learning theory of personality.

Julian B. Rotter was born in Brooklyn, New York. His parents were Jewish immigrants, and he was their third son. His father operated a profitable business until it ran into trouble during the Great Depression. The economic downturn greatly affected Rotter and his **family**, and made him realize how strongly people are affected by their environments. In high school, Rotter's interest in psychology began when he read books by eminent psychotherapists **Alfred Adler** and **Sigmund Freud**. He attended Brooklyn College, where he received a bachelor of arts degree in chemistry in 1937. While in college he started going to seminars given by Adler as well as attending meetings of Adler's Society of Individual Psychology.

After graduating, Rotter entered the State University of Iowa. He minored in speech pathology and studied with Wendell Johnson, a linguist whose work focused on meanings in language. Johnson's ideas had a great influence on Rotter in terms of his coming to believe that language should be used very carefully in psychology in terms of how one defines terms and theoretical constructs. One of Rotter's instructors in Iowa was **Kurt Lewin**, the Prussian-born psychologist known primarily for field theory. Rotter received his master of arts in psychology degree in 1938. Rotter then did a one-year internship in **clinical psychology** at Worcester State Hospital in Massachusetts. At that time there were very few internships in clinical psychology available. He met his wife to be, Clara Barnes, at the hospital and they married in 1941. They would have two children.

In 1939, Rotter enrolled in Indiana University's doctoral program in clinical psychology, one of the few schools offering such a program at that time. He received his doctorate in 1941. In doing a predoctoral internship before receiving his Ph.D. in clinical psychology, he was one of the first clinical psychologists to be trained in what is now the standard model. During World War II Rotter entered the United States Army and served as a personnel consultant in the armored force before becoming an aviation psychologist in the Air Force. In 1946 he joined the faculty of Ohio State University and served as director for its clinical psychology training program from 1951 to 1959, and in 1962 to 1963.

Rotter was very active in setting up standards for the training of clinical psychologists. In 1949, Rotter participated in what became known as the Boulder Conference where training requirements were developed for clinical psychologists at the doctoral level. He argued that psychologists should not be trained as psychiatrists (medical doctors who, after receiving their primary training in medicine, then focus on the psychological). Rotter felt clinical psychologists should be trained in academic departments of psychology as scientists and therapists (the scientist-practitioner model), being steeped in the study of general psychology throughout their training.

While at Ohio State, Rotter began work on his **social learning theory** of personality and in 1954 *Social Learning and Clinical Psychology* was published. In this book he laid out the basic tenets of his social learning theory, the main idea of which is that personality is really the interaction between a person and his or her **environment**. Personality does not reside within an individual independent of the environment he or she is in. By the same token, an individual's behaviors are not simple, reflexive responses to an objective environment. Rather, the environment an individual responds to or acts in is dependent on that particular individual's learning experiences and life history. What stimuli people respond to are shaped by their experiences. Two people might experience the same environment in very different ways. For example, Joe might respond to a visit to the doctor with apprehension because his last visit involved getting a painful shot, whereas Sam would not be apprehensive at all because his last visit was pleasant and did not involve any discomfort. To Rotter, personality is a relatively fixed group of dispositions to react to situations in a certain manner. He stressed that most learning takes place in social situations with other people. Rotter's personality theory was the first to comprehensively integrate **cognition**, in the form of expectancy, with learning and **motivation**, in the form of **reinforcement**.

In 1966, Rotter published a monograph entitled *Generalized Expectancies for Interval Versus External Control of Reinforcement*, where he explored people's expectancies as to whether they can influence the reinforcements they receive. At one extreme are people who believe that reinforcements are due to fate or luck. They would be said to have an external **locus of control**. At the other extreme are those who believe that reinforcements are a function of one's behavior. They have an internal locus of control. Rotter also created the Internal-External Locus of Control Scale to measure individual differences in this characteristic. The scale has been widely used, and research on I-E flourished in the 1970s. This dimension of internal versus external locus of control has come to be seen as a relatively stable dimension of personality.

Rotter has served as president of the divisions of Clinical Psychology and Social and Personality Psychology of the American Psychological Association. In 1963, Rotter left Ohio State to become director of the Clinical Psychology Training Program at the University of Connecticut. He retired in 1987 and is currently Professor Emeritus of Clinical Psychology. In 1989, Rotter received the American Psychological Association's Distinguished Scientific Contribution Award. His wife passed away in 1985.

Marie Doorey

## Further Reading

Rotter, Julian B. *Social learning and clinical psychology.* Englewood Cliffs, NJ: Prentice Hall, 1954.

Rotter, Julian B. "Generalized expectancies for interval versus external control of reinforcement." *Psychological Monographs*, 80, (1966): 1-28.

Rotter, Julian B. *The development and applications of social learning theory: Selected papers.* Englewood Cliffs, NJ: Prentice Hall, 1982.

Hock, R.R. *Forty studies that changed psychology.* Englewood Cliffs, NJ: Prentice Hall, 1995.

## Further Information

Department of Psychology, U-20 University of Connecticut. 406 Babbidge Road, Storrs, CT, USA. 06269-1020.

# Benjamin Rush

### 1746-1813
American physician, teacher, and statesman known as the "father of American psychiatry" for his work with the mentally ill.

Benjamin Rush was born near Philadelphia. He attended the College of New Jersey (the future Princeton University), intending to enter the ministry. Finally deciding in favor of medicine, Rush began his medical studies in Philadelphia, serving a six-year apprenticeship to a local physician. He then enrolled in the University of Edinburgh, Scotland, where many American physicians received their training at the time. Rush earned his M.D. degree in 1768, having concentrated in the study of chemistry. Returning to America, he began his own private practice the following year, when he was also appointed to a teaching position at the College of Philadelphia, becoming the first professor of chemistry in North America and authoring the first chemistry text by an American (*Syllabus of a Course of Lectures on Chemistry*). Rush's medical practice grew rapidly. He was known in particular for his strong endorsement of the contemporary practice of treating fevers by bloodletting and purges, as a result of his conviction that fevers resulted from arterial tension which could only be relieved by bloodletting. In severe cases, he recommended that as much as four-fifths of the patient's blood be drained.

Rush played a prominent role in the American Revolution. In 1776, he served as a member of the Continental Congress, and was also a signer of the Declaration of Independence. He also served from 1776 to 1778 as Physician General of the Continental Army. Rush was an enthusiastic supporter of the U.S. Constitution and a member of the Pennsylvania Convention that ratified it.

In 1787, Rush took charge of the treatment of mental patients at the Pennsylvania Hospital, beginning the work that eventually earned him the title "father of American psychiatry." While his treatment methods—which includ-

**Benjamin Rush** *(Reproduced with permission.)*

onment, Rush helped bring **mental health** under the domain of medicine. He also authored the first psychiatry book written by an American, *Medical Inquiries and Observations upon the Diseases of the Mind*, in 1812.

In addition to his contributions to medicine and politics, Rush worked on behalf of many social issues of his day, including the establishment of public schools, education for women, prison reform, and the abolition of slavery and capital **punishment**. He was in the forefront of the struggle against Philadelphia's yellow-fever epidemics of the 1790s. Although he did note the apparent connection between the disease and the presence of mosquitoes, he continued to advocate bloodletting as the primary method of treatment, unfortunately influencing several generations of physicians who treated similar epidemics in the nineteenth century. (He fell ill when he used his treatment method on himself in 1793.) Rush's name is also linked with physicians' rights in relation to freedom of the press. Attacked in the newspapers for his controversial medical and political views, he sued his detractors and was awarded damages by a Pennsylvania court.

In 1789, Rush gave up his chemistry professorship at the University of Pennsylvania in order to begin teaching medicine, which he continued to do for the remainder of his career, serving as a mentor to a generation of medical students. In 1797, he was appointed to the position of treasurer at the United States Mint and held that office until his death in 1813. Rush's other books include *Medical Inquiries and Observations* (1794-98) and *Essays: Literary, Moral and Philosophical* (1798).

### Further Reading

Binger, Carl A. *Revolutionary Doctor: Benjamin Rush.* New York: Norton, 1966.

Weisberger, Bernard A. "The Paradoxical Doctor Benjamin Rush." *American Heritage* 27 (1975): 40-47, 98-99.

ed bloodletting, purging, intimidation, hot and cold baths, and chair restraints—can hardly be considered clinical advances, Rush's view of mental disease represented a major advance in the understanding of that subject. He believed that insanity often has a physical cause, and that mental illnesses, like physical illnesses, may be as treatable. Through his insistence that insanity was a disease requiring treatment rather than a crime calling for impris-

# Satanic ritual abuse

Activities such as cannibalism, animal sacrifice, and child sexual abuse that are assumed to be carried out by organized underground cults.

In 1984, *Newsweek* printed a feature article on an "epidemic" of **child abuse** in day-care settings. During the next 10 years or so, numerous newspaper and magazine articles described criminal trials in which reference was made to **sexual abuse**, torture, and ritual worship of one kind or another. For example, in 1988 Kelly Michaels was charged with sexually abusing children in her care at a nursery school in New Jersey. On the basis of children's testimony, she was convicted of 115 counts of sexual abuse against 20 different children. In Manhattan Beach, California, seven teachers were accused of abusing hundreds of preschool children over a 10-year period. The case was one of the longest and most expensive trials in California history. There have been numerous cases like these in the U.S., Canada, and the U.K. All have involved accusations by children that they had been terrorized, abused, and tortured during strange ceremonies with satanic, ritualistic overtones. Some professional child care workers assumed that the accused perpetrators were members of an organized network of child predators.

What evidence is there to support the belief in an organization of child abusers? One study in Great Britain investigated 84 cases of reported ritualistic abuse involving sexual abuse, murder, bestiality, and torture. In only 3 of the 84 cases was there any material evidence to support the allegations, and none of them entailed witchcraft or Satanism. In the United States, a nationwide study identified more than 12,000 accusations of cult-like, satanic, ritual abuse. None of the allegations were substantiated, and neither the police nor the FBI have ever uncovered any evidence of child-abusing satanic **cults**. In the McMartin Preschool case, none of the accused teachers was ever convicted of a crime. Kelly Michaels was

released from jail when the Appeals Court of New Jersey reversed her conviction.

There is no dispute that children are often abused, and that the consequences can be devastating. Raising questions about the (assumed) existence of organized, satanic, child-abusing cults is not the same as doubting the existence of actual child abuse, nor to question its wrongfulness. If organized ritualistic abuse does not occur, then how can we explain the widespread belief in it? Contributing factors include adults who have been persuaded by their therapists that they were abused as children, children who have been interviewed in aggressive and manipulative ways by investigators who believe the worst, and uncritical and sensationalized media accounts of satanic sexual abuse.

Timothy Moore

## Further Reading

Bottoms, B.L., and S.L. Davis. "The Creation of Satanic Ritual Abuse." *Journal of Social and Clinical Psychology* 16 (1997): 112-32.

Nathan, D., and M. Snedeker. *Satan's Silence: Ritual Abuse and the Making of a Modern American Witch Hunt*. New York: Basic Books, 1995.

# Virginia M. Satir

**1916-1988**
American family therapist who championed the worth of the individual person.

Although Virginia Satir devoted her career to **family therapy**, she believed strongly in focusing on the self-worth of individuals. The family unit might be critically important, she felt, but the **self-esteem** of each member of the family had to come from within each person. Because of her studies, her experience based on working with thousands of families, and her instinctive understanding of family issues, she earned a reputation as a pioneer and leader in the field of family therapy.

The oldest of five children, Satir was born on a farm in Nellsville, Wisconsin, on June 26, 1916, to Oscar and Minnie Happe Pagenkopf. She displayed what would be a lifelong desire for knowledge at an early age; she was reading by the age of three, and through her **childhood** she read voraciously, often saying that she would like to be a detective and unravel mysteries when she grew up. As one of five children whose parents had large families (her parents came from families of 13 and seven children), she was able to observe the family dynamic long before she had thought of becoming a therapist.

Satir received her early education in a one-room school, but by the time she was of high school age the family had moved to Milwaukee. She excelled in high school and upon graduation enrolled in Milwaukee State Teachers College (now part of the University of Wisconsin). She worked her way through school and graduated in 1936 with a bachelor of arts degree in education.

## Embarks on social work career

For the first few years after she graduated, Satir was a schoolteacher. Because she felt she would learn more about people by being exposed to a variety of individuals and communities, she traveled to different cities to teach, including Ann Arbor, Michigan; Shreveport, Louisiana; St. Louis, Missouri; and Miami, Florida. She then decided to pursue a career in social work; in 1937 she enrolled at Northwestern University in Chicago, taking classes in the summer and teaching school the rest of the year. After three summers, she enrolled full time at the University of Chicago, completing her coursework by 1943 and her thesis in 1948.

Being a graduate student was a difficult but ultimately rewarding experience for Satir. During the 1940s, there was still a stigma against women in graduate programs, even in an ostensibly more liberal discipline such as social work. Satire later said that these experiences made her stronger and more determined to keep going.

## Begins family therapy training programs

After receiving her master's degree, Satir went into private practice. She met with an entire family instead of an individual for the first time in 1951, and it convinced her that therapy that included the family was more effective than working with the individual alone. She lived out her lifelong dream of unraveling the mysteries of family dynamics. Through the 1950s, she continued to focus on working with families. After her second marriage (she had previously married Gordon Rodgers) to Norman Satir ended in 1957, she moved to California, and with two other therapists founded the Mental Health Research Institute (MHRI). In 1962, MHRI obtained a grant from the **National Institute of Mental Health** to begin what would be the first formal family therapy training program. Satir published her first book, *Conjoint Family Therapy*, in 1964. She traveled extensively throughout the 1960s and 1970s, conducting workshops and seminars.

Recognizing the importance of networking for therapists, Satir founded the International Human Resources Learning Network (IHRLN) in 1970 and the Avanta Network (now known as Avanta, the Virginia Satir Network) in 1977. During these years, she received recognition for her important work. She received a Distinguished Service Award from the American Association for Marriage and Family Therapy, and the University of Wisconsin awarded her an honorary doctorate in 1973.

Satir continued her work into the 1980s. She established the Satir Family Camps program through Avanta, which allows families and their therapists to spend one or two weeks in selected wilderness settings. She continued to travel and conduct training programs and seminars. In the summer of 1988, she was diagnosed with pancreatic cancer. She stayed active through the summer but the cancer spread, and she died at her home in Menlo Park, California, on September 10, 1988.

George A. Milite

### Further Reading
Satir, Virginia. *Conjoint Family Therapy: A Guide to Theory and Techniques*. Palo Alto, CA: Science and Behavior Books, 1964.
Satir, Virginia. *Peoplemaking*. Palo Alto, CA: Science and Behavior Books, 1972.

# Savant syndrome

A condition characterized by a combination of below normal intelligence and extraordinary mental abilities in one or a few narrow areas.

Persons who display savant syndrome have traditionally been called idiot savants, a term that many currently avoid because of its negative connotations. Alternate terms include retarded savant and autistic savant, the latter referring to the fact that savant syndrome is often associated with **autism**. It is difficult to arrive at an exact figure for the incidence of savant syndrome. A 1977 study found the incidence among the institutionalized mentally handicapped in the United States to be 0.06 percent of the population, or one in roughly 2,000. Most savants are males.

Savant skills occur in a number of different areas. Savants with musical abilities demonstrate an excellent ear for music from an early age, often including perfect pitch. They are able to reproduce melodies and even entire compositions with great accuracy and often show considerable performing talent, including both technical and interpretive skills. Others show unusual talent in the visual arts, which may include the **ability** to produce life-like reproductions at a very young age, when most children can turn out only primitive drawings. Some savants demonstrate a computer-like ability to perform difficult mathematical calculations at lightning speeds.

Perhaps the most common area where savants show extraordinary abilities is **memory**. They may memorize historical data, sports statistics, population figures, biographical information, or even telephone directories. One savant with uncommon musical abilities could also provide biographical information about the composer of almost any piece of music, as well as stating the key and opus of the piece. She could describe in detail every musical performance she had heard within a 20-year period and provide biographical information about every member of the local symphony orchestra. One particular type of memorization common to a large proportion of savants is calendar calculating, the ability to say what day of the week a particular date will fall (or has already fallen) on. Some savants can provide this type of information for periods covering hundreds of years.

Savants have been studied by researchers investigating such topics as the nature of human **intelligence** and the relative influence of **heredity** and **environment**.

## Further Reading

Howe, Michael J. A. *Fragments of Genius: The Strange Feats of Idiots Savants*. London: Routledge, 1989.

Obler, L.K., and D. Fein, eds. *The Exceptional Brain: Neuropsychology of Talent and Special Abilities*. New York: Guilford Press, 1988.

Treffert, D.A. *Extraordinary People*. New York: Harper and Row, 1989.

## Further Information

Autism Society of America (formerly National Society for Autistic Children). 8601 Georgia Ave., Suite 503, Silver Spring, MD 20910, (301) 565–0433.

# Scapegoating

*A powerful and destructive phenomenon wherein a person or group of people are blamed for whatever is wrong.*

In ancient times, there were rituals of scapegoating. A tribe or person would literally sacrifice an animal to the gods, or send an animal into the desert declaring that that animal was carrying away the tribe's sins. In today's culture, psychology uses the term to discuss certain forms of victimization. A particular child of an alcoholic **family** can be deemed the scapegoat, for instance, and may be the object of a parent's abuse and the reason for seeking professional help. The child is "innocent," but receives the blame for the problems in the household. Historically, entire groups of people have been scapegoated. In Nazi Germany, Hitler and his army scapegoated the Jewish people. The Nazis declared the Jews to be the reason for their societal ills and further believed that if they eliminated the Jewish people, then their problems would be solved. Currently in America, there is scapegoating of lesbian and gay people. Some heterosexuals, often with strong religious ties, blame lesbian and gay people for the moral decay in America.

Why scapegoating occurs is rather complex. Scapegoating serves the need of the dominant social group to feel better about themselves. It relieves the group's responsibility for their own problems. The scapegoated person or group becomes the focus and the reason for the difficult life condition. It was easier for Hitler to blame the problems of German society on the Jews than it would have been for him to truly understand the complex socio-political changes that were happening at the time. Scapegoating also allows people to feel united when they join together to blame someone else. And when action is taken against the scapegoat, the dominant group can feel that they have accomplished something.

Scapegoating begins with devaluation, or putting someone else down. Then the scapegoated person or group is blamed as the cause of a problem. Once a victim has been blamed, they are then dehumanized so that it is easier to treat them with less compassion. For instance, in some circles, people with HIV/AIDS are often spoken of only as statistics, not as real people who need compassion and care.

In many scapegoating situations, the **anger** and **aggression** of the dominant person or group is displaced, or projected, onto the victim. Really the frustration lies within the person doing the scapegoating. Scapegoating never truly solves any problems, it merely deflects **attention** away from the person or group who most needs help.

Lara Lynn Lane

## Further Reading

Allport, G.W. *The Nature of Prejudice*. Reading, MA: Addison Wesley, 1995.

Gilmore, Norbert, and Margaret A. Somerville. "Stigmatization, Scapegoating, and Discrimination in Sexually Transmitted Diseases: Overcoming 'Them' and 'Us'." *Social Science and Medicine* vol. 39, no. 9 (November 1994): 1339-358.

Hafsi, Mohamed. "Experimental Inquiry into the Psychodynamics of the Relationship between the Group's Dominant Basic Assumption Type and Scapegoating Phenomenon." *Psychologica: An International Journal of Psychology in the Orient* vol. 41, no. 4 (December 1998): 272-84.

Staub, Ervin. "Cultural-Societal Roots of Violence: The Examples of Genocidal Violence and of Contemporary Youth Violence in the U.S." *American Psychologist* vol. 51, no. 2 (February 1996): 117-32.

## Further Information

The Scapegoat Society. Hindleap Corner, Priory Road, Forest Row, East Sussex, England RH18 5JF. http://www.scapegoat.demon.co.uk/.

# Schizophrenia

A mental illness characterized by disordered thinking, delusions, hallucinations, emotional disturbance, and withdrawal from reality.

Some experts view schizophrenia as a group of related illnesses with similar characteristics. The condition affects between one-half and one percent of the world's population, occurring with equal frequency in males and females (although the onset of symptoms is usually earlier in males). Between 1 and 2% of Americans are thought to be afflicted with schizophrenia—at least 2.5 million at any given time, with an estimated 100,000 to 200,000 new cases every year. Although the name "schizophrenia," coined in 1911 by Swiss psychologist Eugene Bleuler (1857-1939), is associated with the idea of a "split" mind, the disorder is different from a "split personality" (**dissociative identity disorder**), with which it is frequently confused. Schizophrenia is commonly thought to disproportionately affect people in the lowest socioeconomic groups, although some claim that socially disadvantaged persons with schizophrenia are only more visible than their more privileged counterparts, not more numerous. In the United States, schizophrenics occupy more hospital beds than patients suffering from cancer, heart disease, or diabetes. At any given time, they account for up to half the beds in long-term care facilities. With the aid of antipsychotic medication to control delusions and **hallucinations**, about 70% of schizophrenics are able to function adequately in society.

## Causes of schizophrenia

While the exact cause of schizophrenia is not known, it is believed to be caused by a combination of physiological and environmental factors. Studies have shown that there is clearly a hereditary component to the disorder. **Family** members of schizophrenics are ten times more prone to schizophrenia than the general population, and identical **twins** of schizophrenics have a 46% likelihood of having the illness themselves. Relatives of schizophrenics also tend to have milder psychological disorders with some of the same symptoms as schizophrenia, such as suspicion, communication problems, and eccentric behavior.

In the years following World War II, many doctors blamed schizophrenia on bad parenting. In recent years, however, advanced neurological research has strengthened the case for a physiological basis for the disease. It has been discovered that the brains of schizophrenics have certain features in common, including smaller volume, reduced blood flow to certain areas, and enlargement of the ventricles (cavities filled with fluid that are found at the brain's center). Over the past decade much **attention** has focused on the connection between schizophrenia and neurotransmitters, the chemicals that transmit **nerve** impulses within the **brain**. One such chemical—dopamine—has been found to **play** an especially important role in the disease. Additional research has concentrated on how and when the brain abnormalities that characterize the disorder develop. Some are believed to originate prenatally for a variety of reasons, including trauma, viral infections, malnutrition during pregnancy, or a difference in Rh blood factor between the fetus and the mother. Environmental factors associated with schizophrenia include **birth** complications, viral infections during **infancy**, and head injuries in **childhood**. While the notion of child rearing practices causing schizophrenia has been largely discredited, there is evidence that certain family dynamics do contribute to the likelihood of relapse in persons who already have shown symptoms of the disease.

## Types of schizophrenia

Schizophrenia is generally divided into four types. The most prevalent, found in some 40% of affected persons, is paranoid schizophrenia, characterized by delusions and hallucinations centering on persecution, and by feelings of **jealousy** and grandiosity. Other possible symptoms include argumentativeness, **anger**, and **violence**. Catatonic schizophrenia is known primarily for its catatonic state, in which persons retain fixed and sometimes bizarre positions for extended periods of time without moving or speaking. However, catatonic schizophrenics may also experience periods of restless movement. In disorganized, or hebephrenic, schizophrenia, the patient is incoherent, with flat or inappropriate emotions, disorganized behavior, and bizarre, stereotyped movements and grimaces. Catatonic and disorganized schizophrenia affect far fewer people than paranoid schizophrenia. Most schizophrenics not diagnosed as paranoid schizophrenics fall into the large category of undifferentiated schizophrenia (the fourth type), which consists of variations of the disorder that do not correspond to the criteria of the other three types. Generally, symptoms of any type of schizophrenia must be present for at least six months before a diagnosis can be made. Over the long term, about one-third of patients experience recovery or remission.

The initial symptoms of schizophrenia usually occur between the ages of 16 and 30, with some variation depending on the type. (The average age of hospital admission for the disease is between 28 and 34.) Disorganized schizophrenia tends to begin early, usually in **adolescence** or young adulthood, while paranoid schizophrenia tends to start later, usually after the age of 25 or 30. The onset of acute symptoms is referred to as the first psychotic break, or break from reality. In general, the earlier the onset of symptoms, the more severe the illness will be. Before the disease becomes full-blown, schizophrenics may go through a period called the prodromal stage, lasting about a year, when they experience behavioral changes that precede and are less dramatic than those of the acute stage. These may include social withdrawal, trouble concentrating or sleeping, neglect of personal grooming and hygiene, and eccentric behavior.

The prodromal stage is followed by the acute phase of the disease, which is characterized by "positive" symptoms and requires medical intervention. During this stage, three-fourths of schizophrenics experience delusions—illogical and bizarre beliefs that are held despite objections. A typical delusion might be a belief that the afflicted person is under the control of a sinister force located in the sewer system that dictates his every move and thought. Hallucinations are another common symptom of acute schizophrenia. These may be auditory (**hearing** voices) or tactile (feeling as though worms are crawling over one's skin). The acute phase of schizophrenia is also characterized by incoherent thinking, rambling or discontinuous speech, use of nonsense words, and odd physical behavior, including grimacing, pacing, and unusual postures. Persons in the grip of acute schizophrenia may also become violent, although often this violence is directed at themselves—it is estimated that 15-20% of schizophrenics commit suicide out of despair over their condition or because the voices they hear "tell" them to do so, and up to 35% attempt to take their own lives or seriously consider doing so. In addi-

tion, between 25 and 50% of people with schizophrenia abuse drugs or alcohol. As the positive symptoms of the acute phase subside, they may give way to the negative symptoms of what is called residual schizophrenia. These include flat or inappropriate emotions, an inability to experience pleasure (anhedonia), lack of **motivation**, reduced attention span, lack of interest in one's surroundings, and social withdrawal.

Researchers have found correlations between childhood behavior and the onset of schizophrenia in adulthood. A 30-year longitudinal research project studied over 4,000 people born within a single week in 1946 in order to document any unusual developmental patterns observed in those children who later became schizophrenic. It was found that a disproportionate number of them learned to sit, stand, and walk late. They were also twice as likely as their peers to have speech disorders at the age of six and to have played alone when they were young. Home movies have enabled other researchers to collect information about the childhood characteristics of adult schizophrenics. One study found that the routine physical movements of these children tended to be slightly abnormal in ways that most parents wouldn't suspect were associated with a major **mental illness** and that the children also tended to show **fear** and anger to an unusual degree.

## Treatment

Schizophrenia has historically been very difficult to treat, usually requiring hospitalization during its acute stage. In recent decades, antipsychotic drugs have become the most important component of treatment. They can control delusions and hallucinations, improve thought coherence, and, if taken on a long-term maintenance basis, prevent relapses. However, antipsychotic drugs do not work for all schizophrenics, and their use has been complicated by side effects, such as akathisia (motor restlessness), dystonia (rigidity of the neck muscles), and tardive dyskinesia (uncontrollable repeated movements of the tongue and the muscles of the face and neck). In addition, many schizophrenics resist taking medication, some because of the side effects, others because they may feel better and mistakenly decide they don't need the drugs anymore, or because being dependent on medication to function makes them feel bad about themselves. The tendency of schizophrenics to discontinue medication is very harmful. Each time a schizophrenic goes off medication, the symptoms of the disease return with greater severity, and the effectiveness of the drugs is reduced.

Until recently, the drugs most often prescribed for schizophrenia have been neuroleptics such as Haldol,

Prolixin, Thorazine, and Mellaril. A major breakthrough in the treatment of schizophrenia occurred in 1990 with the introduction of the drug clozapine to the U.S. market. Clozapine, which affects the neurotransmitters in the brain (specifically serotonin and dopamine), has been dramatically successful in relieving both positive and negative symptoms of schizophrenia, especially in patients in whom other medications have not been effective. However, even clozapine doesn't work for all patients. In addition, about 1% of those who take it develop agranulocytosis, a potentially fatal blood disease, within the first year of use, and all patients on clozapine must be monitored regularly for this side effect. (Clozapine was first developed decades ago but could not be introduced until it became possible to screen for this disorder.) The screening itself is expensive, creating another problem for those using the drug. Risperidone, a new, safer medication that offers benefits similar to those of clozapine, was introduced in 1994 and is now the most frequently prescribed antipsychotic medication in the United States. Olanzapine, another in the new generation of schizophrenia drugs, received FDA approval in the fall of 1996, and more medications are under development. Electroconvulsive therapy (ECT, also called electric shock treatments) has been utilized to relieve symptoms of catatonia and **depression** in schizophrenics, especially in cases where medication is not effective.

Although medication is the most important part of treatment, **psychotherapy** can also play an important role in helping schizophrenics manage anxiety and deal with interpersonal relationships, and treatment for the disorder usually consists of a combination of medication, therapy, and various types of **rehabilitation**. **Family therapy** has worked well for many patients, educating both patients and their families about the nature of schizophrenia and helping them in their cooperative effort to cope with the disorder.

### Further Reading

Atkinson, Jacqueline M. *Schizophrenia: A Guide to What It Is and What Can Be Done to Help.* San Bernardino, CA: R. Reginald Borgo Press, 1989.

Hoffer, Abram, and Humphry Osmond. *How to Live with Schizophrenia.* New York: Carol Publishing Group, 1992.

Lidz, Theodore. *The Origin and Treatment of Schizophrenic Disorders.* International Universities Press, 1990.

Walsh, Maryellen. *Schizophrenia: Straight Talk for Families and Friends.* New York: William Morrow, 1985.

### Further Information

American Schizophrenia Association. 900 North Federal Highway, Suite 330, Boca Raton, FL 33432, (407) 393–6167.

National Alliance for Research on Schizophrenia and Depression. 60 Cutter Mill Rd., Suite 200, Great Neck, NY 11202, (516) 829–0091.

Schizophrenics Anonymous. 1209 California Rd., Eastchester, NY 10709, (914) 337–2252.

# Scholastic Assessment Test

*A test that measures verbal and mathematical abilities and achievement in specific subject areas.*

In March 1994, the test formerly known as the Scholastic Aptitude Test became the Scholastic Assessment Test (SAT). The name change reflects the test's objectives more accurately, that is, to measure a student's scholastic **ability** and achievement rather than his or her aptitude. The format of the SAT remains basically the same, however; it is a series of tests, given to groups of students. The tests measure verbal and mathematical abilities and achievement in a variety of subject areas. It is offered on Saturday mornings seven months of the year at locations across the United States. Over 2,000 colleges and universities use the test scores as part of the college admissions process. The SAT scores provide an indicator of the student's ability to do college-level work. Intended as an objective standard for comparing the abilities of students from widely different cultural backgrounds and types of schools, the test can also help students, their parents, and guidance counselors make decisions in the college application process.

The two major components of the test are SAT I: Reasoning Test, and SAT II: Subject Tests (formerly called **Achievement Tests**). All SAT test-takers complete SAT I, a three-hour multiple-choice test. The Test of Standard Written English, which prior to 1994 comprised a half-hour section of SAT I, has been eliminated. The new SAT I has three verbal reasoning and three mathematical reasoning sections. However, not all of these are half-hour sections. For both the verbal and mathematical components, two sections take 30 minutes, and the third takes only 15. This brings the total test time to 2.5 hours. The remaining half hour is devoted to an experimental section called Equating, which can be either a math or a verbal section. This section is not counted in the student's score, but the test-taker does not know which one is the Equating section while taking the test.

The Verbal Reasoning sections in the SAT I no longer contains antonym questions, and a greater emphasis has been placed on reading comprehension (called Critical Reading), which, in some cases, requires the student to answer questions on two different text passages instead of just one. As before, the Verbal Reasoning sections also include sentence completion and analogy questions.

The Mathematical Reasoning sections consist of multiple-choice questions covering arithmetic, algebra, and geometry; quantitative comparison (which are also multiple choice); and a section of problems requiring students to calculate their own answers (multiple-choice answers are not provided). Students are allowed (and encouraged) to use calculators for the math sections.

SAT II includes a variety of tests in subjects such as English, foreign languages, math, history and social studies, psychology, and the sciences. SAT I and II cannot be taken on the same day. Raw SAT scores are calculated based on the number of correct answers minus a fraction of a point for each wrong answer. Subtracting points for wrong answers compensates for guesses made by the test-taker, and is called the "guessing penalty." The raw score is converted using a scale ranging from 200 to 800, with separate scores provided for the verbal and math sections, and for each subject test in SAT II. Scores are reported about six weeks after the test date to students and their high schools, and to the colleges of their choice. Students may take the SAT more than once, and many do, hoping to improve upon their initial scores.

The SAT has been criticized on grounds of cultural and **gender bias**, charges that the revised version has attempted to rectify. The widespread use of test preparation courses and services for the SAT has also generated controversy, with detractors arguing that the test is unfair to economically disadvantaged students, who have limited access to coaching.

## Further Reading

Bartl, Lisa. *10-Minute Guide to Upping Your SAT Scores.* New York: Alpha Books/ARCO, 1996.
Carris, Joan Davenport. *SAT Success.* 5th ed. Princeton, NJ: Peterson's, 1996.
*Inside the SAT.* New York: Princeton Review Publications, 1995. (A multimedia format including laser optical disc, reference manual, and practice test.)
*Introducing the New SAT: The College Board's Official Guide.* New York: College Entrance Examination Boards, 1993.

# School phobia/School refusal

Reluctance or refusal to attend school.

School **phobia** is an imprecise, general term used to describe a situation in which a child is reluctant to go to school. According to the American Academy of Child and Adolescent Psychiatry, refusal to go to school is most common in the period from preschool through second grade. In most cases, school phobia is a symptom of an educational, social, or emotional problem the child is experiencing.

The child with school phobia develops a pattern of predictable behavior. At first, the child may begin the day complaining that he is too sick to go to school, with a headache, sore throat, stomachache, or other symptom. After the parent agrees that the child may stay home from school, he begins to feel better, although his symptoms often do not completely disappear. By the next morning, the symptoms are back in full intensity. When the child repeats this pattern, or simply refuses to go to school without complaining of any symptoms of illness on a chronic and consistent basis, school phobia is considered to have evolved into school refusal (or school refusal syndrome).

School refusal is a diagnostic criterion for **separation anxiety** disorder, a mental condition characterized by abnormally high anxiety concerning possible or actual separation from parents or other individuals to whom the child is attached. When school refusal is related to separation anxiety disorder, it is likely that the child will also display aversion to other activities (after-school clubs and sports, birthday parties, summer camp) that involve being away from the person to whom the child is attached. In addition, he may cling to the person, and refuse to allow her out of his sight for even short periods of time. Children experiencing separation anxiety disorder and school refusal may express feelings of **fear** when left alone in a room.

Refusal to go to school may begin as a result of any of the following stresses: **birth** of a sibling; death of a **family** member, close friend, or pet; change in school, such as a new teacher; loss of a friend due to a move or change in school; or a change in family, such as **divorce** or remarriage. It may also follow summer vacation or holiday break, when the young child has spent more time with his primary caregiver.

Almost every child will display behavior to avoid going to school—for academic or social reasons—at some point during his school career. In these cases, the situation the child is trying to avoid is usually temporary—an argument with a friend, the threat of a bully, or the consequences of a missed homework assignment, for example. When the avoidance of school becomes a chronic pattern, the child may develop serious social and academic problems. A professional counselor or child psychiatrist working with the child's teacher and other school personnel can all support the family in overcoming a child's refusal to go to school.

Returning the child to school is the highest priority so that disruption to the child's educational and **emotional development** is minimized. Depending on the severity of the fears that produced the symptom of school refusal, ongoing counseling or psychiatric treatment may be necessary for a length of time, even after the child is successfully back in school.

**Further Reading**

Kahn, Jack. *Unwillingly to School.* New York: Pergamon Press, 1981.

# School psychology

One of the human service fields of psychology whose aim is to help students, teachers, parents, and others understand each other.

Developed in 1896 at the University of Pennsylvania in a clinic that studied and treated children considered morally or mentally defective, the field of school psychology today includes 30,000 psychologists, most of whom work in educational systems throughout the United States.

School psychologists, in various roles within the school systems they serve, focus on the development and adjustment of the child in his or her school setting. School psychologists minimally are required to have completed two years of training after earning a bachelor's degree; those who have earned their Ph.Ds. may hold administrative or supervisory positions and are often involved in training teachers and psychologists. School psychologists play a key role in the development of school policies and procedures.

School psychologists administer and interpret tests and assist teachers with classroom-related problems and learning difficulties. School psychologists play a key role in addressing behavior issues in the classroom, and in working with parents and teachers to develop strategies to deal with behavior problems.

In some cases, the school psychologist provides teachers and parents with information about students' progress and potential, while advising them how to help students increase their achievement. They also promote communication between parents, teachers, administrators, and other psychologists in the school system.

*See also* National Association of School Psychologists.

# Scientific method

An approach to research that relies on observation and data collection, hypothesis testing, and the falsifiability of ideas.

The scientific method involves a wide array of approaches and is better seen as an overall perspective rather than a single, specific method. The scientific method that has been adopted was initially based on the concept of positivism, which involved the search for general descriptive laws that could be used to predict natural phenomena. Once predictions were possible, scientists could attempt to control the occurrence of those phenomena. Subsequently, scientists developed underlying explanations and theories. In the case of psychology, the goal would be to describe, to predict, then to control behavior, with knowledge based on underlying theory.

Although the positivist approach to science has undergone change and scientists are continually redefining the philosophy of science, the premises on which it was based continue to be the mainstream of current research. One of the prime requisites of a scientific approach is falsifiability; that is, a theory is seen as scientific if it makes predictions that can be demonstrated as true or false. Another critical element of the scientific method is that it relies on **empiricism**, that is, observation and data collection.

Research often involves the hypothetico-inductive method. The scientist starts with a hypothesis based on observation, insight, or theory. A hypothesis is a tentative statement of belief based on the expert judgment of the researcher. This hypothesis must be subject to falsification; that is, the research needs to be set up in such a way that the scientist is able to conclude logically either that the hypothesis is correct or incorrect. In many cases, a research project may allow the scientist to accept or reject a hypothesis and will lead to more research questions.

Psychologists employ a diversity of scientific approaches. These include controlled experiments that allow the researcher to determine cause and effect relationships; correlation methods that reveal predictable relations among variables; case studies involving in-depth study of single individuals; archival approaches that make novel use of records, documents, and other existing information; and surveys and questionnaires about opinions and attitudes.

Because the scientific method deals with the approach to research rather than the content of the research, disciplines are not regarded as scientific because of their content, but rather because of their reliance on data and observation, **hypothesis testing**, and the falsifiability of their ideas. Thus, scientific research legitimately includes the study of attitudes, **intelligence**, and other complicated human behaviors. Although the tools that psychologists use to measure human behavior may not lead to the same degree of precision as those in some other sciences, it is not the precision that determines the scientific status of a discipline, but rather the means by which ideas are generated and tested.

*See also* Research method.

# Security objects

*A soft, clingable object that provides the child with security and comfort in mildly or moderately fearful situations.*

Security objects are items, usually soft and easily held or carried, that offer a young child comfort. Security objects are also referred to as **attachment** objects, inanimate attachment agents, nonsocial attachments, comfort habits, transitional objects, not-me possessions, substitute objects, cuddlies, treasured possessions, soothers, pacifiers, special soft objects, Linus phenomenon, and security blankets.

## Early history

In the 1940s, attachment to a special object was regarded as a **childhood** fetish reflecting pathology in the relationship between the mother and her child (Wulff, 1946). D. W. Winnicott (1953), however, regarded the object as necessary for **normal** development: it was a "transitional" experience, intermediate between the infant's **ability** to distinguish the inner subjective world from outside reality. John Bowlby considered transitional objects to be a "substitute" for the absent mother, and he deemed the child's attachment to them normal and even desirable.

Nevertheless, throughout the 1970s, but progressively less in the 1980s and 1990s, a stigma remained attached to children who hugged a blanket in times of **stress**. The popular—but now generally discredited—stereotype was that these children, being overly anxious and insecure, were better off without their blanket. As a result, the blanket was often taken away from the child, sometimes forcibly, just when it could have been beneficial. Although some disagreement and inconsistency persist in the research literature, there is no justification for such drastic actions. Evidence does not support ascribing psychopathology to children just because they demonstrate an attachment to a security object. Blanket-attached children appear to be neither more nor less maladjusted or insecure than other children.

## Theoretical underpinnings

Three current theories pertain to nonsocial attachment. Psychoanalytic theory surmises that it is created as a

necessary transition between the child's outside and inside worlds once the child has formed a sufficient relationship with the mother. It helps augment feelings of personal control and continuity of the self. Ethological theory argues that the comfort object substitutes for the mother and should form only if attachment to the mother is secure. Social learning theory states that the physical characteristics of the object (softness, warmth, fuzziness, etc.) can be rewarding per se. Furthermore, if the mother's nuturing and distress-reducing presence is associated with the inanimate object, attachment behaviors toward the object may ensue. Because the child is able to control a security object more readily than the mother, attachment to it should begin to develop relatively independently of the mother.

It is not, however, clear from any of these theories why some children engage in comfort habits while others do not. Child-rearing practices are frequently cited as contributing factors, especially children's sleeping arrangements and parental behavior at bedtime, but evidence has largely been inconclusive. Cultural and socioeconomic factors have received stronger support, although, again, the exact mechanisms underlying the differential acquisition of nonsocial attachments remain unclear. A mother's sensitivity to her children's security needs may be relevant, but the quality of the mother-child relationship seems not to be. However, preliminary evidence suggests that the security of a child's attachment to the mother does predict how a security object will be used in novel situations.

One problem in evaluating attachments to objects is the lack of uniformity in definitions and criteria. Divergent theoretical positions as well as cultural backgrounds have brought forth a variety of interpretations. Another complication involves the unreliability of adults' recollections about former treasured possessions. In studies attempting to link older children's or adults' current behaviors with their previous relationships to a special object, they—or their parents—are requested to recall details. However, such retrospective reports may misrepresent actual events. When college students and their mothers were questioned, 24% of the pairs disagreed totally about whether there had been a childhood attachment, and an additional 19% disagreed on what the object was (Mahalski, 1982). In a follow-up study one year later, 18% of the students contradicted their earlier statements about having had a security object! Clearly, mothers' concurrent reports and investigators' direct observations are necessary to generate reliable information about security objects.

## Cultural issues

Despite current theoretical assertions that attachment to transitional objects is normal and almost universal, it should be pointed out that this attachment is culture-specific. For instance, in the United States, 60% of children have at least a mild degree of attachment to a soft, inanimate object some time during their life, and 32% exhibit strong attachment (Passman and Halonen, 1979). The incidence of attachments to soft objects in the Netherlands, New Zealand, and Sweden is comparable to that in the United States. Korean children have substantially fewer attachments to blankets (18%) than do American children, but Korean-born children living in the United States display an intermediate percentage (34%). Only 5% of rural Italian children have transitional objects, compared to 31% of urban Romans and 62% of foreign children living in Rome. However, just 16% of Londoners' children have a special security object.

## Developmental trends

In a cross-sectional investigation surveying the mothers of almost 700 children in the United States through their first 63 months of life, R. H. Passman and J. S. Halonen (1979) examined children's attachments to various classes of objects. The percentage of children who are not attached to any object remains relatively stable throughout the first three years, averaging around 40%, with a low of 28% at three months of age. From 33 months, it rises consistently to a high of 84% at 63 months. The number of children having at least a slight attachment to a favorite *hard* toy (like blocks or a toy truck) remains steady and low through the first four years, averaging approximately 14%, but then drops swiftly toward 0% through 63 months. Attachment to a pacifier peaks early at three months, with 66% reported as having at least some attachment. Pacifier usage declines quickly through the first 18 months, after which attachments are extremely unusual (averaging under 3%) through 63 months. Attachment to blankets begins at a later age than it does to pacifiers. Mild attachment to a blanket is rare at 3 months (8%), but increases somewhat through 15 months (22%), peaks rapidly at 18 months (60%), stays near this level through 39 months (57%), tapers off to 40% at 48 months, and falls suddenly to 16% through 63 months. Simultaneous attachment to both a pacifier and a blanket is infrequent; it rises from 4% at 3 months to 12% at 9 months, remains at a relative plateau through 21 months, then drops sharply, averaging about 1% thereafter. Passman and Halonen also investigated children's intense attachments to these objects and found similar patterns with respect to age. At three months, 16% are strongly attached to pacifiers. Strong attachment to blankets peaks at 18 and 24 months (32%), stays near this high level through 39 months, and diminishes steadily to 8% through 63 months. Generally in the United States, attachments to various objects are now regarded as conventional throughout the first five years of life.

## Advantages of having security objects

Being attached to a security object can be beneficial to a child. Left in an unfamiliar playroom with a supportive agent (mother or transitional object), children played, explored, and refrained from crying more so than did children who had their favorite hard toy or who had no supportive agent available (Passman & Weisberg, 1975). Thus, children's attachment to a special soft object is something qualitatively different from their relationship with a noncuddly toy. The blanket provided comfort as well as the mother did—but only if the children were attached to it; nonattached children entering the room with their blanket adapted relatively poorly, with greater dismay. The security blanket, therefore, is aptly named; it indeed provides security to those attached to it.

Because security objects may serve as a substitute for the mother in her absence, they can be employed practically by parents, teachers, doctors, babysitters, and other professionals. Besides facilitating separation from the mother or father, the attachment object can promote interactions with strangers. At bedtime, it can soothe and facilitate **sleep**. A study by G. J. Ybarra, R. H. Passman, and C. Eisenberg found that during a routine third-year pediatric examination, the security object enhanced rapport with the examining nurse. Children attached to a blanket who were allowed access to it were rated as less distressed and experienced less physiological stress—as evidenced by heart rate and systolic blood pressure—than children undergoing the medical evaluation without their security object. The comfort provided by a blanket in novel situations has even been shown to enhance children's learning (Passman, 1977).

## Alternatives to blankets

A variety of soft objects besides the blanket (e.g., diapers, pillow cases, sheepskins, soft toys, stuffed animals, dolls, napkins, handkerchiefs) may also provide security. Furthermore, research has shown that representations of the mother (e.g., films, videotapes, photographs, audiotapes of her) can also help children's adjustment. Although most children are thought to respond to their special object through touching or sucking, merely seeing (or **hearing**) it seems sufficient. Even an object as tactile as the security blanket does not have to be touched; visual contact alone evokes its soothing effects. For children too young for an attachment to a blanket, the pacifier seems to share many of the same functional characteristics (although its origins may be different).

## Limitations

The positive effects of an attachment to an object have restrictions. If the situation is particularly arousing or threatening, the attachment object can be less effective in providing security than the child's mother.

Richard H. Passman Ph.D.

## Further Reading

Greenberg, Mark T., Dante Cicchetti, and E. Mark Cummings, eds. *Attachment in the Preschool Years: Theory, Research, and Intervention.* Chicago: University of Chicago Press, 1990.

Adams, R. E., and R. H. Passman. "Effects of Visual and Auditory Aspects of Mothers and Strangers on the Play and Exploration of Children." *Developmental Psychology* 15, 1979, pp. 269-74.

Haslam, N. "Temperament and the Transitional Object." *Child Psychiatry and Human Development* 22, 1992, pp. 237-47.

Hong, K. M., and B. D. Townes. "Infants' Attachment to Inanimate Objects: A Cross-Cultural Study." *Journal of the American Academy of Child Psychiatry* 15, 1976, pp. 49-61.

Mahalski, P. "The Reliability of Memories for Attachment to Special, Soft Objects During Childhood." *Journal of the American Academy of Child Psychiatry* 21, 1982, pp. 465-67.

Mahalski, P. A., P. A. Silva, and G. F. S. Spears. "Children's Attachment to Soft Objects at Bedtime, Child Rearing, and Child Development." *Journal of the American Academy of Child Psychiatry* 24, 1985, pp.442-46.

Passman, R. H. "Arousal-Reducing Properties of Attachment Objects: Testing the Functional Limits of the Security Blanket Relative to the Mother." *Developmental Psychology* 12, 1976, pp. 468-69.

———. "Providing Attachment Objects to Facilitate Learning and Reduce Distress: Effects of Mothers and Security Blankets." *Developmental Psychology* 13, 1977, pp. 25-28.

———. "Attachments to Inanimate Objects: Are Children Who Have Security Blankets Insecure?" *Journal of Consulting and Clinical Psychology* 55, 1987, pp. 825-30.

Passman, R. H., and R. E. Adams. "Preferences for Mothers and Security Blankets and Their Effectiveness as Reinforcers for Young Children's Behavior." *Journal of Child Psychology and Psychiatry* 23, 1982, pp. 223-36.

Passman, R. H., and J. S. Halonen. "A Developmental Survey of Young Children's Attachments to Inanimate Objects." *Journal of Genetic Psychology* 134, 1979, pp. 165-78.

Passman, R. H., and L. A. Lautmann. "Fathers', Mothers', and Security Blankets' Effects on the Responsiveness of Young Children during Projective Testing." *Journal of Consulting and Clinical Psychology* 50, 1982, pp. 310-12.

Passman, R. H., and P. Weisberg. "Mothers and Blankets as Agents for Promoting Play and Exploration by Young Children in a Novel Environment: The Effects of Social and Nonsocial Attachment Objects." *Developmental Psychology* 11, 1975, pp. 170-77.

Van Ijzendoorn, M. H., F. A. Goosens, L. W. C. Tavecchio, M. M. Vergeer, and F. O. A. Hubbard. "Attachments to Soft Objects: Its Relationship with Attachment to the Mother and with Thumbsucking." *Child Psychiatry and Human Development* 14, 1983, pp. 97-105.

Winnicott, D. W. "Transitional Objects and Transitional Phenomena: A Study of the First Not-Me Possession." *International Journal of Psycho-analysis* 34, 1953, pp. 89-97.

Wulff, M. "Fetishism and Object Choice in Early Childhood." *Psychoanalytic Quarterly* 15, 1946, pp. 450-71.

# Self-actualization

A prominent term in humanistic psychology that refers to the basic human need for self-fulfillment.

The term self-actualization was used most extensively by **Abraham Maslow**, who placed it at the apex of his hierarchy of human motives, which is conceived as a pyramid ascending from the most basic biological needs, such as hunger and thirst, to increasingly complex ones, such as belongingness and **self-esteem**. The needs at each level must be at least partially satisfied before those at the next can be addressed. Thus, while Maslow considered self-actualization to be the highest **motivation** possible and the essence of **mental health**, he recognized that most people are too preoccupied with more basic needs to seek it actively.

To arrive at a detailed description of self-actualization, Maslow studied historical figures—including Thomas Jefferson (1743-1826), Jane Addams (1860-1935), Albert Einstein (1879-1955), Eleanor Roosevelt (1884-1962), and Martin Luther King, Jr. (1929-1968)—whom he believed had made extraordinary use of their potential and looked for common characteristics. He found that self-actualizers were creative, spontaneous, and able to tolerate uncertainty. Other common qualities included a good sense of **humor**, concern for the welfare of humanity, deep appreciation of the basic experiences of life, and a tendency to establish close personal relationships with a few people. Maslow also formulated a list of behaviors that he believed could lead to self-actualization. These included such directives as: experience life with the full absorption and concentration of a child; try something new; listen to your own feelings rather than the voices of others; be honest; be willing to risk unpopularity by disagreeing with others; assume responsibility; work hard at whatever you do; and identify and be willing to give up your defenses.

**Carl Rogers** also emphasized the importance of self-actualization in his client-centered therapeutic

**Abraham Maslow studied strong historical figures, like Eleanor Roosevelt, in his studies on self-actualization.** *(The Library of Congress. Reproduced with permission.)*

approach and theoretical writings. Like Maslow, he used the term to designate a universal and innate tendency toward growth and fulfillment that governs the human **personality**. Rogers believed that self-actualization is closely related to each individual's perceived reality and self-concept—the way one thinks of oneself. According to Rogers, one's **self-concept** can become distorted by the need for approval by others, which can lead to **alienation** from one's true beliefs and desires and suppression of one's self-actualizing tendency. Rogers' **client-centered therapy** is based on the idea that people will instinctively choose the path to self-actualization on their own once it becomes clear to them.

The Personal Orientation Inventory, a test designed to measure self-actualization, is based on Maslow's writings and consists of 12 scales, including time competence, inner directedness, spontaneity, self-acceptance, and capacity for intimate contact.

## Further Reading

Maslow, Abraham. *Toward a Psychology of Being*. Princeton: Van Nostrand, 1968.

———. *Motivation and Personality*. 2d ed. New York: Harper and Row, 1970.

Rogers, Carl. *On Becoming a Person: A Therapist's View of Psychotherapy*. Boston: Houghton Mifflin, 1970.

# Self-concept

*The way in which one perceives oneself.*

Self-concept—the way in which one perceives oneself—can be divided into categories, such as personal self-concept (facts or one's own opinions about oneself, such as "I have brown eyes" or "I am attractive"); social self-concept (one's perceptions about how one is regarded by others: "people think I have a great sense of humor"); and self-ideals (what or how one would like to be: "I want to be a lawyer" or "I wish I were thinner").

While a number of philosophers and psychologists have addressed the idea that behavior is influenced by the way people see themselves, investigation into the importance of self-concept is most closely associated with the writings and therapeutic practices of **Carl Rogers**. The self—and one's awareness of it—lie at the heart of Rogers' **client-centered therapy** and the philosophy behind it. According to Rogers, one's self-concept influences how one regards both oneself and one's **environment**. The self-concept of a mentally healthy person is consistent with his or her thoughts, experiences, and behavior. However, people may maintain a self-concept that is at odds with their true feelings to win the approval of others and "fit in," either socially or professionally. This involves repressing their true feelings and impulses, which eventually causes them to become alienated from themselves, distorting their own experience of the world and limiting their potential for **self-actualization**, or fulfillment. The gulf between a person's self-concept and his or her actual experiences (which Rogers called incongruence) is a chronic source of anxiety and can even result in mental disorders. According to Rogers, a strong self-concept is flexible and allows a person to confront new experiences and ideas without feeling threatened.

Social psychologists have pointed out that self-concept also plays an important role in social perception—the process by which we form impressions of others. Attribution—how we explain the causes of our own and other people's behavior—is particularly influenced by our own self-concept. Social **learning theory** is also concerned with the ways in which we view ourselves, especially in terms of our perceived impact on our environment. In the first major theory of social learning, Julian B. Rotter claimed that the expected outcome of an action and the value we place on that outcome determine much of our behavior. For example, people whose positive self-concept leads them to believe they will succeed at a task are likely to behave in ways that ultimately lead to success, while those who expect failure are much more likely to bring it about through their own actions. In a general theory of **personality** he developed subsequently with two colleagues, Rotter designated variables based on the ways that individuals habitually think about their experiences. One of the most important was I-E, which distinguished "internals," who think of themselves as controlling events, from "externals," who view events as largely outside their control. Internal-external orientation has been found to affect a variety of behaviors and attitudes.

## Further Reading

Rogers, Carl. *Client-Centered Therapy*. Boston: Beacon Press, 1952.

Rogers, Carl, and B. Stevens. *Person to Person: The Problem of Being Human*. New York: Pocket Books, 1967.

Rotter, Julian B., June Chance, and Jerry Phares. *Applications of a Social Learning Theory of Personality*. New York: Holt, Rinehart, and Winston, 1972.

# Self-conscious emotions

Emotions such as guilt, pride, shame, and hubris.

Succeeding or failing to meet the standards, rules, and goals of one's group or society determines how well an individual forms relationships with other members of the group. Living up to one's own internalized set of standards—or failing to live up to them—is the basis of complex emotions. The so-called self-conscious emotions, such as **guilt**, pride, shame, and hubris, require a fairly sophisticated level of intellectual development. To feel them, individuals must have a sense of self as well as a set of standards. They must also have notions of what constitutes success and failure, and the capacity to evaluate their own behavior.

Self-conscious emotions are difficult to study. For one thing, there are no clear elicitors of these emotions. Joy registers predictably on a person's face at the approach of a friend, and caution appears at the approach of a stranger. But what situation is guaranteed to elicit pride or shame, guilt or embarrassment? These emotions are so dependent on a person's own experience, expectations, and culture, that it is difficult to design uniform experiments.

Some psychoanalysts, notably **Sigmund Freud** and **Erik Erikson**, argued that there must be some universal elicitors of shame, such as failure at toilet training or exposure of the backside. But the idea of an automatic noncognitive elicitor does not make much sense. Cognitive processes are likely to be the elicitors of these complex emotions. It is the way people think or what they think about that becomes the elicitor of pride, shame, guilt, or embarrassment. There may be a one-to-one correspondence between certain thoughts and certain emo-

tions; however, in the case of self-conscious emotions, the elicitor is a cognitive event. This does not mean that the earlier primary emotions are elicited by noncognitive events. Cognitive factors may play a role in eliciting any **emotion**, but the nature of the cognitive events is much less articulated and differentiated in the primary than in the self-conscious emotions.

Those who study self-conscious emotions have begun to determine the role of the self in such emotions, and in particular the age at which the notion of self emerges in **childhood**.

Recently, models of these emotions are beginning to emerge. These models provide testable distinctions between often-confused emotions, such as guilt and shame. Moreover, nonverbal tools for studying these emotions in children are being developed. As a result, models exist to explain when and how self-conscious emotions develop.

The self-conscious emotions depend on the development of a number of cognitive skills. First, individuals must absorb a set of standards, rules, and goals. Second, they must have a sense of self. And finally, they must be able to evaluate the self with regard to those standards, rules, and goals and then make a determination of success or failure.

As a first step in self-evaluation, a person has to decide whether a particular event is the result of his or her own action. If, for example, an object breaks while you are using it, you might blame yourself for breaking it, or you might decide the object was faulty. If you place the blame on yourself, you are making an internal attribution. If you decide the object was defective, then you are making an external attribution. If you don't blame yourself, chances are you will give the matter no more thought. But if you do blame yourself, you are likely to go on to the next step of evaluation. Whether a person is inclined to make an internal or an external attribution depends on the situation and on the individual's own characteristics. Some people are likely to blame themselves no matter what happens.

Psychologists still do not entirely understand how people decide what constitutes success and failure after they have assumed responsibility for an event. This aspect of self-evaluation is particularly important because the same standards, rules, and goals can result in radically different feelings, depending on whether success or failure is attributed to oneself. Sometimes people assess their actions in ways that do not conform to the evaluation that others might give them. Many factors are involved in producing inaccurate or unique evaluations. These include early failures in the self system, leading to narcissistic disorders, harsh **socialization** experiences, and high levels of reward for success or **punishment** for failure. The evaluation of one's own behavior in terms of success and failure plays a very important role in **shaping** an individual's goals and new plans.

In a final evaluation step, an individual determines whether success or failure is global or specific. Global attributions come about when a person is inclined to focus on the total self. Some individuals, some of the time, attribute the success or failure of a particular action to the total self: they use such self-evaluative phrases as "I am bad (or good)." On such occasions, the focus is not on the behavior, but on the self, both as object and as subject. Using such global attribution results in thinking of nothing else but the self. During these times, especially when the global evaluation is negative, a person becomes confused and speechless. The individual is unable to act and is driven away from action, wanting to hide or disappear.

In some situations, individuals make specific attributions focusing on specific actions. Thus, it is not the total self that has done something wrong or good; instead, a particular behavior is judged. At such times, individuals will use such evaluative phrases as, "What I did was wrong, and I must not do it again." Notice that the individual's focus here is not on the totality of the self, but on the specific behavior of the self in a specific situation.

The tendency to make global or specific attributions may be a **personality** style. Global attributions for negative events are generally uncorrelated with global attributions for positive events. It is only when positive or negative events are taken into account that relatively stable and consistent attributional patterns are observed. Some individuals are likely to be stable in their global and specific evaluations under most conditions of success or failure. Such factors are thought to have important consequences for a variety of fixed personality patterns. For example, Beck (1979) and others have found that depressed individuals are likely to make stable, negative, global attributions, whereas nondepressed individuals are less likely to be stable in their global attributions.

### Shame and guilt

An important determinant of whether shame or guilt follows failure to live up to a standard is whether a person believes he could have avoided the violating act. If not, shame is likely. If the person feels he could have done otherwise, guilt is likely to occur.

Shame or guilt occurs when an individual judges his or her actions as a failure in regard to his or her standards, rules, and goals and then makes a global attribution. The person wishes to hide, disappear, or die (Lewis, 1992; Nathanson, 1987). It is a highly negative and painful state that also disrupts ongoing behavior and causes confusion in thought and an inability to speak. The body of the shamed person seems to shrink, as if to disappear from the eye of the self or others. Because of the intensity of this emotional state, and the global attack on the self system, all that individuals can do when presented with such a state is to attempt to rid themselves of it. Its global nature, however, makes it very difficult to dissipate.

The **power** of shame drives people to employ strategies to rid themselves of this feeling. These strategies may generate behavior that is generally considered abnormal. Some people readjust their notions of success and failure, at least as they apply to their own actions. The narcissistic personality, for example, perceives its actions to be successful while others perceive them as failure. The narcissist is characterized by an exaggerated sense of his or her own accomplishments and is likely to appear hubristic. But underlying the bombast is an attempt to avoid the exaggerated shame the narcissist may really feel. In contrast to the narcissist, a depressed person may be acutely aware of shame and feel helpless, hopeless, and worthless.

Shame and guilt are not produced by any specific situation, but rather by an individual's interpretation of an event. Even more important is the observation that shame is not necessarily related to whether the event is public or private. Although many theorists hold that shame is a public failure, this need not be so. Failure attributed to the self can be public or private, and can center around moral as well as social action.

Guilt is produced when an individual evaluates his or her behavior as a failure, but focuses on the specific features of the self that led to the failure. A guilty person is likely to feel responsible and try to repair the failure. Guilty individuals are pained by their evaluation of failure. Guilt is often associated with a corrective action that the individual can take (but does not necessarily take) to repair the failure and prevent it from happening again (Barrett, 1995; Tangney, 1990). In guilt, the self is differentiated from the object.

### Hubris and pride

Self-consciousness is not entirely a negative feeling. Self-evaluation can also lead to positive and even overly positive emotions. Hubris, defined as exaggerated pride or self-confidence, is an example of the latter. Hubris is the emotion elicited when success with regard to one's standards, rules, and goals is applied to a person's entire self. People inclined to be hubristic evaluate their actions positively and then say to themselves: "I have succeeded. I am a success." Often, hubris is considered an undesirable trait to be avoided.

Hubris is difficult to sustain because of its globality. The feeling is generated by a nonspecific action. Because such a feeling is alluring, yet transient, people prone to hubris ultimately derive little satisfaction from the emotion. Consequently, they seek out and invent situations likely to repeat this emotional state. According to Morrison (1989), this can be done either by altering their standards, rules, and goals, or by reevaluating what constitutes success.

An individual who considers himself or herself globally successful may be viewed with disdain by others. Often the hubristic person is described as "puffed up" or, in extreme cases, grandiose or narcissistic. The hubristic person may be perceived as insolent or contemptuous. Hubristic people have difficulty in interpersonal relations, since their hubris likely makes them insensitive to the wishes, needs, and desires of others, leading to interpersonal conflict. Moreover, given the contemptuousness associated with hubris, other people are likely to be shamed by the nature of the actions of the hubristic person. Narcissists often derive pleasure in shaming others by claiming their superiority.

If hubris is the global emotion that follows a positive assessment of an action, then pride is the specific emotion. A person experiencing pride feels joyful at the successful outcome of a particular action, thought, or feeling. Here the focus of pleasure is specific and related to a particular behavior. In pride, the self and object are separated, as in guilt, and unlike shame and hubris, where subject and object are fused. Heckhausen (1984, 1987) and Stipek et al. (1992) have made a particularly apt comparison between pride and achievement **motivation**, where succeeding at a particular goal motivates activity. Because the positive state engendered by pride is associated with a particular action, individuals are able to reproduce the emotion: pride's specific focus allows for action.

### Shyness and embarrassment

In addition to the emotions already discussed, two others bear mention—embarrassment and **shyness**, which are frequently confused. Some consider shyness to be sheepishness, bashfulness, uneasiness, or psychological discomfort in social situations. According to this definition, shyness is related to **fear** and is a nonevaluative emotion precipitated by an individual's discomfort with others. Such a description fits Buss's (1980) notion of shyness as an emotional response elicited by experiences of novelty or conspicuousness. For Buss (1980), shyness and fear are closely related and represent fear of others. One way of distinguishing shyness from shame, with which it is sometimes confused, is that it appears much earlier in childhood than either shame or guilt.

This approach to shyness seems reasonable because it fits with other notions relating the self to others, or

what we might call the "social self." Eysenck (1954) has characterized people as social or asocial by genetic disposition, and recently Kagan, Reznick, and Snidman (1988) have pointed out the physiological responses of children they call "inhibited." Inhibited children are withdrawn, are uncomfortable in social situations, and appear fearful. Shyness may be a dispositional factor not related to self-evaluation. Rather, it may simply be the discomfort of being in the company of other social objects; in other words, it is the opposite of sociability.

If shyness does not seem to rely on self-evaluation, embarrassment often does. It is important, however, to distinguish among types of embarrassment. Sometimes, the self-consciousness of shyness can lead a person to become embarrassed (Buss, 1980). In certain situations of exposure, people become embarrassed, but this is not related to negative evaluation. Perhaps the best example of this is the case of a compliment. A speaker might feel embarrassed after a particularly flattering introduction. Surprisingly, praise, rather than the displeasure resulting from negative evaluation, elicits such embarrassment.

Another example of this type of embarrassment can be seen in people's reactions to public display. When people observe someone looking at them, they are apt to become self-conscious, look away, and **touch** or adjust their bodies. Women being observed often adjust or touch their hair. Men may adjust their clothes or change their body posture. In few cases do the observed people look sad; if anything, they appear pleased by the **attention**. The combination of a briefly averted gaze and nervous touching characterizes the first type of embarrassment.

A related example of embarrassment from exposure can be seen in the work of Lewis et al. (1991) which demonstrates that embarrassment can be elicited just by exposure. In their experiment, a professor, announcing that he is going to randomly point to a student, and shows that pointing is random and does not reflect a judgment about the person, closes his eyes and points. The pointing invariably elicits embarrassment in the student selected, even though the student has done nothing, good or bad, to deserve attention.

In each of these examples, there is no negative evaluation of the self in regard to standards, rules, and goals. Nevertheless, work with children has shown that a sense of self is a prerequisite for feeling embarrassment (Lewis et al., 1989). In these situations, it is difficult to imagine embarrassment as related to shame. Since praise cannot readily lead to an evaluation of failure, it is likely that embarrassment resulting from compliments, from being looked at, and from being pointed to, has more to do with the exposure of the self than with evaluation. Situations other than praise come to mind, in which a negative evaluation is inferred (perhaps incorrectly). Take, for example, walking into a crowded meeting room before the speaker has started to talk. It is possible to arrive on time only to find people already seated. When walking into the room, eyes turn toward you, and you may experience embarrassment. One could say that there is a negative self-evaluation: "I should have been earlier, I should not have made noise." However, the experience of embarrassment in this case may not be elicited by negative self-evaluation, but simply by public exposure.

In contrast, a second type of embarrassment is closely related to shame and is therefore dependent on self-evaluation. For Izard (1977) and Tomkins (1963), embarrassment is distinguished from shame by the intensity of the latter. Whereas shame appears to be strong and disruptive, embarrassment is clearly less intense and does not involve disruption of thought and language. Furthermore, people who are embarrassed do not assume the posture of someone wishing to hide, disappear, or die. In fact, their bodies reflect an ambivalent approach and avoidance posture. An embarrassed person alternatively looks at people and then looks away, smiling all the while. In contrast, the shamed person rarely smiles while averting his or her gaze. Thus, from a behavioral point of view, shame and embarrassment appear to be different.

The difference in intensity can probably be attributed to the nature of the failed standard, rule, or goal. Some standards are more or less associated with the core of self; for one person, failure at driving a car is less important than failing to help someone. Failures associated with less important and less central standards, rules, and goals result in embarrassment rather than shame.

The study of self-conscious emotions has only recently begun. The model outlined here offers an opportunity to consider and to define carefully some of the self-conscious emotions. Unless we develop a more accurate taxonomy, we will be unable to proceed in our study of these emotions. Given the renewed interest in emotional life, it is now appropriate to consider these more complex emotions rather than the primary ones. Moreover, as others have pointed out, these self-conscious emotions are intimately connected with other emotions, such as **anger** and sadness. Finally, given the place of self-evaluation in adult life, it seems clear that the self-conscious evaluative emotions are likely to stand in the center of our emotional life.

Michael Lewis

### Further Reading

Barrett, K. "A Functionalist Approach to Shame and Guilt." In J. Tangney and K. Fischer (Eds.). *Self-Conscious Emotions*. New York: Guilford, 1995, pp. 25-63.

Beck, A.T. *Cognitive Therapy and the Emotional Disorders*. New York: Times Mirror, 1979.

Buss, A.H. *Self Consciousness and Social Anxiety*. San Francisco: W.H. Freeman, 1980.

Dweck, C.S., and E.L. Leggett. "A Social Cognitive Approach to Motivation and Personality." *Psychological Review* 95, (1988): 256-73.

Edelman, R.J., and S.E. Hampson. "The Recognition of Embarrassment." *Personality and Social Psychology Bulletin* 7, (1981): 109-116.

Ferguson, T.J., and H. Stegge. "Children's Understanding of Guilt and Shame." *Child Development* 62, (1991): 827-39.

Eysenck, H.J. *The Psychology of Politics*. London, England: Routledge & Kegan Paul, 1954.

Heckhausen, H. "Emotional Components of Action: Their Ontogeny as Reflected in Achievement Behavior." In D. Glitz and J.F. Wohlwill (Eds.). *Curiosity, Imagination and Play: On the Development of Spontaneous Cognitive and Motivational Processes*. Hillsdale, NJ: Erlbaum, 1987, pp. 326-48.

Izard, C. *Human Emotions*. New York: Plenum Press, 1977.

Kagan, J., and N. Snidman. "Biological Bases of Childhood Shyness." *Science* 240, (1988): 167-71.

Lewis, M., M.W. Sullivan, and P. Barone. "Changes in Embarrassment as a Function of Age, Sex, and Situation." *British Journal of Developmental Psychology* 9, (1991): 485-92.

Lewis, M., M.W. Sullivan, C. Stanger, and M. Weiss. "Self-Development and Self-Conscious Emotions." *Child Development* 60, (1989): 146-56.

Lewis, M. *Shame, the Exposed Self*. New York: The Free Press, 1992.

Morrison, A.P. *Shame: The Underside of Narcissism*. Hillsdale, NJ: Analytic Press, 1989.

Nathanson, D.L., ed. *The Many Faces of Shame*. New York: Gilford Press, 1987.

Stipek, D.J. and S. McClintic. "Self-Evaluation in Young Children." *Monographs of the Society for Research in Child Development* 57 (Serial No. 226), 1992.

Tangney, J.P., "Assessing Individual Differences in Proneness to Shame and Guilt: Development of the Self-Conscious Affect and Attribution Inventory." *Journal of Personality and Social Psychology* 59, (1990): 102-111.

Tangney, J.P., and K.W. Fischer, eds. *Self-Conscious Emotions: Shame, Guilt and Pride*. New York: Guilford, 1995.

Tomkins, S.S. *Affect, Imagery, and Consciousness: Volume 2: The Negative Affects*. New York: Springer, 1963.

# Self-esteem

Considered an important component of emotional health, self-esteem encompasses both self-confidence and self-acceptance.

Psychologists who write about self-esteem generally discuss it in terms of two key components: the feeling of being loved and accepted by others and a sense of competence and mastery in performing tasks and solving problems independently.

Much research has been conducted in the area of developing self-esteem in children. Martin Seligman claims that in order for children to feel good about themselves, they must feel that they are able to do things well. He claims that trying to shield children from feelings of sadness, frustration, and anxiety when they fail robs them of the **motivation** to persist in difficult tasks until they succeed. It is precisely such success in the face of difficulties that can truly make them feel good about themselves. Seligman believes that this attempt to cushion children against unpleasant emotions is in large part responsible for an increase in the prevalence of **depression** since the 1950s, an increase that he associates with a conditioned sense of helplessness.

Self-esteem comes from different sources for children at different stages of development. The development of self-esteem in young children is heavily influenced by parental attitudes and behavior. Supportive parental behavior, including the encouragement and praise of mastery, as well as the child's internalization of the parents' own attitudes toward success and failure, are the most powerful factors in the development of self-esteem in early **childhood**. Later, older children's experiences outside the home—in school and with peers—become increasingly important in determining their self-esteem. Schools can influence their students' self-esteem through the attitudes they foster toward **competition** and diversity and their recognition of achievement in academics, sports, and the arts. By middle childhood, friendships have assumed a pivotal role in a child's life. Studies have shown that school-age youngsters spend more time with their friends than they spend doing homework, watching television, or playing alone. In addition, the amount of time they interact with their parents is greatly reduced from when they were younger. At this stage, social acceptance by a child's peer group plays a major role in developing and maintaining self-esteem.

The physical and emotional changes that take place in **adolescence**, especially early adolescence, present new challenges to a child's self-esteem. Boys whose growth spurt comes late compare themselves with peers who have matured early and seem more athletic, masculine, and confident. In contrast, early physical maturation can be embarrassing for girls, who feel gawky and self-conscious in their newly developed bodies. Fitting in with their peers becomes more important than ever to their self-esteem, and, in later adolescence, relationships with the opposite sex can become a major source of confidence or insecurity.

**Further Reading**

Seligman, Martin E.P. *The Optimistic Child.* Boston: Houghton Mifflin Co., 1995.

# Self-fulfilling prophecy

An initial expectation that is confirmed by the behavior it elicits.

One's beliefs about other people determine how one acts towards them, and thus play a role in determining the behavior that results. Experiments have demonstrated this process in a variety of settings. In one of the best-known examples, teachers were told (falsely) that certain students in their class were "bloomers" on the verge of dramatic intellectual development. When the students were tested eight months later, the "special" students outperformed their peers, fulfilling the prediction that had been made about them. During the intervening period, the teachers had apparently behaved in ways that facilitated the students' intellectual development, perhaps by giving them increased **attention** and support and setting higher goals for them.

In another experiment, a group of men became acquainted with a group of women by telephone after seeing what they thought were pictures of their "partners." The supposedly attractive women were considered more interesting and intelligent. Researchers concluded that the men's own behavior had been more engaging toward those women whom they thought were attractive, drawing livelier responses than the men who thought their partners were unattractive.

Racial and ethnic stereotypes can become self-fulfilling prophecies if members of disadvantaged groups are discouraged from setting ambitious goals because of other people's low expectations. The term self-fulfilling prophecy can also refer to the effect that people's beliefs about themselves have on their own behavior. Those who expect to succeed at a task, for example, tend to be more successful than those who believe they will fail.

**Further Reading**

Halloran, James D. *Attitude Formation and Change.* Westport, CT: Greenwood Press, 1976.

Harvey, Terri L., Ann L. Orbuch, and John H. Weber, eds. *Attributions, Accounts, and Close Relationships.* New York: Springer-Verlag, 1992.

Weary, Gifford. *Attribution.* New York: Springer-Verlag, 1989.

Wyer, R. S., and T. K. Srull, eds. *Handbook of Social Cognition.* 2d ed. Hillsdale, NJ: Erlbaum Associates, 1994.

# Self-help groups

Groups that support communities of peers with a similar interest or illness.

Since the advent of managed health care and the cost-controls that have accompanied it, self-help groups have grown in popularity. Individuals who are offered limited **mental health** coverage through their healthcare plan often find self-help a positive and economical way to gain emotional support.

## Overview

Twelve-step groups, one of the most popular types of self-help organizations, have been active in the United States since the founding of Alcoholics Anonymous (AA) in 1935. AA and other 12-step programs are based on the spiritual premise that turning one's life and will over to "a higher power" (i.e., God, another spiritual entity, or the group itself) for guidance and self-evaluation is the key to recovery. Outside of AA and its sister organizations (Narcotics Anonymous, or NA; Cocaine Anonymous, or CA), a number of 12-step programs have sprung up to treat a range of mental disorders, such as Gambler's Anonymous (GA), Schizophrenics Anonymous (SA), and Overeaters Anonymous (OA).

Self-help organizations also provide support for individuals who are ill or have health issues. Support exists for people dealing with weight management, HIV, multiple sclerosis, muscular dystrophy, cancer, and incontinence, and for the families of individuals who suffer from these conditions. Self-help has moved beyond what are considered "problem" conditions to assist people who share interests or circumstances, including support groups for women who breast-feed (LaLeche league), singles, older adults, and new parents.

**Family** self-help groups are also available. Al-Anon, an organization for friends and family of alcoholics, is a companion organization to AA, as is Alateen, a program for teenagers who have been affected by alcoholics. Support groups for caregivers of individuals with life-threatening illnesses, such as cancer, often meet at treatment centers and hospitals that specialize or treat the illness in question.

A growing trend in self-help is the creation of online support communities. Chat-rooms, bulletin boards, and electronic mailing lists all provide convenient, around-the-clock access to peer support. Many large-scale consumer healthcare web sites provide forums for discussion on countless diseases and disorders, and major online commercial services such as America Online (AOL) provide sites for healthcare and patient support. In some cases, these groups may be moderated by a healthcare professional, although many are exclusively peer organized and populated. Some long-established self-help groups such as the LaLeche league now hold some of their meetings online, often out of their own web site.

## Benefits

The accessibility of self-help groups is one of their most attractive features. Since no dues or fees are required, except for small voluntary contributions to cover meeting expenses, organizations such as AA are the most cost-effective treatment option available. In addition, meetings are usually easy to locate through local hospitals, healthcare centers, churches, and other community organizations. For AA and sister organizations, where daily attendance is encouraged if possible, the number of meetings held each week often number in the hundreds in large metropolitan areas. And with the proliferation of new online support communities and rapid growth of access to the Internet, self-help groups are becoming as accessible to individuals in rural areas as they are to those in large cities. Online self-help also offers the added benefit of anonymity and breaks down any barriers of age discrepancies, physical disabilities, race and culture differences, or other possible inhibiting factors in a face-to-face encounter.

Participation in self-help groups provides an essential sense of community and belonging. For individuals suffering from mental and organic illnesses, who may be lacking emotional support and **empathy** from their friends and family, this **environment** is a critical part of recovery. In addition to relieving emotional isolation, self-help groups tend to empower an individual and promote **self-esteem**. For example, AA encourages sponsorship (building a mentor relationship with another member), speaking at meetings, and other positive interactions with peers.

Introspection is another essential feature of many self-help groups, particularly in organizations that follow a 12-step program of recovery. For example, the fourth step of AA is for members to make "a searching and fearless moral inventory" of themselves, and the tenth step mandates that members continue "to take personal inventory" and admit wrongdoings. Such introspection may be beneficial to individuals who are having difficulties coming to terms with the thoughts and emotions that may be guiding their behavior. In this respect, a 12-step program may resemble **cognitive therapy** to a degree, in that recognition of maladaptive thoughts can ideally lead to a change in negative behavior.

## Results

Several major studies have shown that 12-step programs can be just as, if not more, effective in treating alcohol- and drug-dependent patients as a regime of cognitive-behavioral therapy or **psychotherapy**. Further, if an inpatient is started on a 12-step program while in a traditional treatment or therapy, setting and the program is encouraged by the patient's healthcare provider, then the patient is more likely to remain in the 12-step program after traditional treatment has ended.

*See also* Alcohol abuse and dependence; Drugs/ Drug abuse

Paula Ford-Martin

## Further Reading

American Self-Help Clearinghouse. *Self-Help Sourcebook Online.* http://mentalhelp.net/selfhelp/

## Further Information

Alcoholics Anonymous World Services, Inc. General Service Office. P.O. Box 459, Grand Central Station, New York, NY, USA. 10163, fax: 212-870-3003, 212-870-3400. http://www.alcoholics-anonymous.org.
National Self-Help Clearinghouse. Graduate School and University Center of The City University of New York, 365 5th Avenue, Suite 3300, New York, NY, USA. 10016, 212-817-1822. Email: info@selfhelpweb.org. www.self-helpweb.org.

## Semantic memory

The part of long-term memory dealing with words, their symbols, and meanings.

Semantic **memory** allows humans to communicate with language. In semantic memory, the **brain** stores information about words, what they look like and represent, and how they are used in an organized way. It is unusual for a person to forget the meaning of the word "dictionary," or to be unable to conjure up a visual image of a refrigerator when the word is heard or read. Semantic memory contrasts with episodic memory, where memories are dependent upon a relationship in time. An example of an episodic memory is "I played in a piano recital at the end of my senior year in high school."

The "tip of the tongue" phenomenon provides some insight into the way information is stored in semantic memory. Most people have experienced this situation where they are trying to recall a person's name. As the person searches through his or her memory for the name Stern, for example, he or she will recall other similar names—Stone, Stein—but not Douglas or Zimmer. Semantic memory appears to categorize information that has similar meaning (in this case, surnames), that begins with the same letter, and has the same number of syllables.

Words and other memories that are stored in semantic memory contribute to episodic memory and the two work together to function as an effective long-term memory system.

## Further Reading

Bolles, Edmund Blair. *Remembering and Forgetting: Inquiries Into the Nature of Memory.* New York: Walker and Co., 1988.

## Sensitivity training

A group experience that gives people new insight into how they relate to others.

Sensitivity training began in the 1940s and 1950s with experimental studies of groups carried out by psychologist **Kurt Lewin** at the National Training Laboratories in Maine. Although the groups (called training or T-groups) were originally intended only to provide research data, their members requested a more active role in the project. The researchers agreed, and T-group experiments also became learning experiences for their subjects. The techniques employed by Lewin and his colleagues, collectively known as sensitivity training, were widely adopted for use in a variety of settings. Initially, they were used to train individuals in business, industry, the military, the ministry, education, and other professions. In the 1960s and 1970s, sensitivity training was adopted by the **human potential movement**, which introduced the "encounter group." Although encounter groups apply the basic T-group techniques, they emphasize personal growth, stressing such factors as self-expression and intense emotional experience.

Encounter groups generally consist of between 12 and 20 people and a facilitator who meet in an intensive weekend session or in a number of sessions over a period of weeks or months. The group members work on reducing defensiveness and achieving a maximum of openness and honesty. Initially, participants tend to resist expressing their feelings fully, but eventually become more open in discussing both their lives outside the group and the interactions within the group itself. Gradually, a climate of trust develops among the group members, and they increasingly abandon the defenses and facades habitually used in dealing with other people. Although the increased self-awareness resulting from sensitivity training is presumed to change a person's behavior in daily life, studies of encounter-group participants have raised doubts as to whether their training experiences actually effect long-lasting behavioral changes. In addition, the usefulness of encounter groups is limited to psychologically healthy individuals, as the intense and honest nature of the group discussions may prove harmful to persons with emotional disorders.

*See also* Group therapy

**Further Reading**

Kanfer, Frederick H., and Arnold P. Goldstein, eds. *Helping People Change: A Textbook of Methods,* 4th ed. New York: Pergamon Press, 1991.

Zimbardo, Philip G. *The Psychology of Attitude Change and Social Influence.* Philadelphia: Temple University Press, 1991.

# Sensory deprivation

An experimental procedure involving prolonged reduction of sensory stimuli.

Sensory deprivation experiments of the 1950s have shown that human beings need environmental stimulation to function normally. In a classic early experiment, college students lay on a cot in a small, empty cubicle nearly 24 hours a day, leaving only to eat and use the bathroom. They wore translucent goggles that let in light but prevented them from seeing any shapes or patterns, and they were fitted with cotton gloves and cardboard cuffs to restrict the sense of **touch**. The continuous hum of an air conditioner and U-shaped pillows placed around their heads blocked out auditory stimulation.

Initially, the subjects slept, but eventually they became bored, restless, and moody. They became disoriented and had difficulty concentrating, and their performance on problem-solving tests progressively deteriorated the longer they were isolated in the cubicle. Some experienced auditory or visual **hallucinations**. Although they were paid a generous sum for each day they participated in the experiment, most subjects refused to continue past the second or third day. After they left the isolation chamber, the perceptions of many were temporarily distorted, and their brain-wave patterns, which had slowed down during the experiment, took several hours to return to **normal**. The intensity of the discomfort these volunteers experienced helps explain why solitary confinement is often regarded as the most severe form of **punishment** in prisons.

The deterioration in both physical and psychological functioning that occurs with sensory deprivation has been linked to the need of human beings for an optimal level of arousal. Too much or too little arousal can produce **stress** and impair a person's mental and physical abilities. Thus, appropriate degrees of sensory deprivation may actually have a therapeutic effect when arousal levels are too high. A form of sensory deprivation known as REST (restricted environmental stimulation), which consists of floating for several hours in a dark, soundproof tank of water heated to body temperature, has been used to treat drug and smoking addictions, lower back **pain**, and other conditions associated with excessive stress.

**Further Reading**

Lilly, John Cunningham. *The Deep Self: Profound Relaxation and the Tank Isolation Technique.* New York: Simon and Schuster, 1977.

Solomon, Philip. *Sensory Deprivation: A Symposium Held at Harvard Medical School.* Cambridge, MA: Harvard University Press, 1961.

# Separation anxiety

Distress reaction to the absence of the parent or caregiver.

Separation anxiety emerges according to a developmental timetable during the second half year in human infants. This development reflects advancing cognitive maturation, rather than the onset of problem behaviors.

As illustrated in the accompanying figure, infants from cultures as diverse as Kalahari bushmen, Israeli kibbutzim, and Guatemalan Indians display quite similar patterns in their response to maternal separation, which peaks at the end of the first year and gradually becomes less frequent and less intense throughout later **infancy** and the preschool years. This fact has been interpreted to **mean** that the one-year-old is alerted by the absence of the parent and tries to understand that discrete event. If it fails, **fear** is created and the child cries.

Cultural practices have an impact on separation anxiety. Infants who remain in constant contact with their mothers may show an earlier onset of separation anxiety, and possibly more intense and longer periods of reactivity. For example, Japanese infants who are tested in **Mary Ainsworth**'s Strange Situation show more intense reactions to the separation, presumably as a result of cultural norms prescribing constant contact between mother and infant for the first several years of life.

Like separation anxiety, researchers who observe infant emotions and behavior in the first month or two of life generally agree that no specific fear reaction is present at this early stage. Rather, infants become distressed due to unpleasant stimulation involving **pain**, discomfort, or hunger.

Typically researchers have found that by five to six months, if a stranger stares in silence at an infant, the infant will often return the look and after about 30 seconds begin to cry. Bronson has termed this distress reaction to a stranger's sober face "wariness." Because of the gradual building up of tension in the infant, Bronson interprets the emotional distress as a reaction to the failure to assimilate the unfamiliar face to a more familar schema. In another words, the older infant can distinguish between familiar and unfamiliar faces, tries to understand the distinction, and becomes upset if the new face does not match the now familiar pattern.

A few months later, infants may react immediately to strangers, especially if approached suddenly or picked up by the stranger. This fear reaction, which can be readily elicited in most infants between seven and twelve months, has been called stranger distress or **stranger anxiety**.

The context and qualitative aspects of the stranger's approach are critical in determining how an infant might respond. If the stranger approaches slowly when the caregiver is nearby, smiling and speaking softly, offering a toy, the infant will often show interest or joy, and distress is unlikely. Also, the degree of distress shown by an infant to the silent intrusion of the stranger varies greatly from baby to baby, a finding that many believe to be rooted in the **temperament** of the infant. Finally, if the infant finds the stranger's approach to be ambiguous, the caregiver's reaction will often influence the infant's response. Should the parent smile and warmly greet the new person, the older infant will often use these emotional reactions as cues for how to respond.

Stranger distress was originally described by Rene Spitz as an **emotion** that suddenly appears in all infants at about 8 months. While we now understand how important a role context and **cognition** play in determining this response, there is nevertheless evidence suggesting a precise timetable for its emergence across different cultures, including Uganda, Hopi Indian, and the United States. A genetic basis has also been shown by twin research, with identical **twins** showing more similar onset of stranger distress than fraternal twins. Rather than indicating emotional difficulties, the emergence of a fear of strangers in the second half of the first year is an indicator of **cognitive development**. For example, EEG and heart rate patterns in human infants both show a major developmental shift at this time in response to the presentation of threatening stimuli.

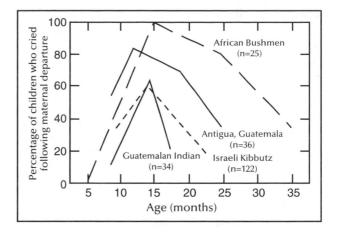

**Children who cried during separation (in percent). These graphs show the course of separation distress in children of the African Bushmen, the Guatemalan Indians, lower-class families from Antigua, Guatemala, and infants from an Israeli kibbutz.**

As infants acquire more experience in dealing with unfamiliar persons at **family** outings, visits to the home, or in day care, they no longer become distressed at the sight of a stranger. Young children show a wide variety of responses depending on the situation, their past experiences, and their level of sociability. Parents will want to encourage their child's natural curiosity and friendliness, while at the same time teaching them that they should always rely on parental guidance and approval in dealing with strangers.

The study of these two common fears of infancy underscores the important links between emotion and cognition. Discrepancy theories originating in the work of Hebb and Jean Piaget provide an account of the steps in the development of this basic emotional system in infancy and demonstrate its dependence on perceptual and cognitive development. In addition, the importance of context and meaning have been clearly shown in the work of **Jerome Kagan**, Alan Sroufe, and others to be the hallmark of the mature fear response, as distinct from the general distress of early infancy.

While stranger distress and separation anxiety are **normal** for one-year-old infants, should a parent become concerned if they persist into the toddler or preschool years? The key to answering this question depends upon the nature of the child's response, its intensity, and persistence over time. For example, it is commonplace for young preschoolers to show some distress at separation from their parents during the first week or two of daycare in a new setting. Typically this settling in period does not last too long. If a preschooler persists in showing excessive separation anxiety even after several weeks at a new preschool and this interferes with the child's participation with peers and teachers, parents should consult with the teacher and other child care professionals. **Childhood** anxieties of this sort are generally quite responsive to treatment, and this may be a better option than waiting for the problem to resolve itself.

*See also* Strange situation; Stranger anxiety

Peter LaFreniere

# Serial learning

*Recalling patterns of facts or stimuli in the order in which they were presented.*

In some research on **memory** for words, the learner is exposed to stimuli to be remembered and later recalls those stimuli in the same order in which they initially appeared. This procedure is called serial learning. In general, when people must recall stimuli in a particular order, they remember less material than when allowed to engage in free recall, which imposes no constraints on the order or recall.

**Hermann Ebbinghaus** is credited with conducting the first studies of verbal memory involving serial learning. Most serial learning studies use a procedure called serial anticipation, where one stimulus is presented at a time and the learner uses that word as a cue for the next word. The second word then serves as a cue for the third, and so on. One of the most consistent findings in research involving single words or nonsense syllables involves the **serial position function** or effect: learners show greatest recall for stimuli at the beginning of the list, and good but somewhat less recall for items appearing at the end of the list. Stimuli in the middle of the list fare least well. When learners must remember single words or nonsense syllables in free recall, the greatest recall usually occurs at the end of the list, with good but lower recall at the beginning. If the words to be learned are meaningfully related, such as those in a sentence, people tend to remember them by using serial anticipation, even when they are allowed to use free recall. The first seven items in a list are often the easiest to learn. This fact is consistent with the research that indicates that, regardless of the type of learning, humans can remember "the magic number seven" items without relying on **rehearsal** or other **mnemonic strategies**.

Serial learning occurs when students attempt to learn school-related material. For example, when trying to remember the names of the American presidents, students typically begin with Washington, Adams, and Jefferson, and continue with their serial anticipation, using each president as a cue for the next one. Somewhere in the middle of the list, though, students fail to remember names, then, toward the end of the presidents, performance improves as the students retrieve the names of more recent presidents. Quite often, people show similar patterns when attempting to memorize poems, prayers, or a short text such as the Declaration of Independence. These behaviors conform with the serial position effect that is typical for most serial learning studies.

*See also* Free-recall learning.

# Serial position function

*The predictable patterns of memory and forgetting of lists of stimuli.*

When a person attempts to recall a set of stimuli that exceeds about seven items, there is a high likelihood that he or she will forget some of them. The generally accepted limit to **memory** for material that is not rehearsed is referred to as "the magic number seven" (plus or minus two items). Most studies in this area have employed lists of words or nonsense syllables, but the research results hold true for a wide range of stimuli.

As a rule, if free recall is engaged, the words that are best remembered are those from the end of the list, and they are also likely to be the first to be recalled. This tendency for the best memory for recently presented items is referred to as the recency effect. (The tendency for retrieving words from the beginning of a list is called the primacy effect.) Recall will be poorest for items in the middle of the list, unless a stimulus has special characteristics and stands out.

When a learner must use serial recall, or recall of the stimuli in their order of presentation, the items appearing first and last on the list still show an advantage over those in the middle, but the items at the beginning of the list are recalled more often than items at the end of the list, a reversal of the pattern in free recall.

The serial position effect occurs due to three factors: distinctiveness, constraints of short-term memory, and inhibition. First, the primacy and recency effects occur because items at the beginning and the end of the list are distinct or isolated from the other stimuli due to their positions. Second, short-term memory involves keeping some information in active, working memory; this information is likely to be the most recently presented stimuli. Third, inhibition hampers memory. Words in a list tend to interfere with one another. When they are at the beginning or at the end of the list, they are not surrounded by as many words that could interfere with them; words in the middle, on the other hand, must compete for space in working memory with more words around them.

*See also* Free-recall learning.

**Further Reading**
Squire, Larry R. *Memory and Brain.* New York: Oxford University Press, 1989.

# Sex differences

Physical and mental differences between men and women.

The most basic question of sex differences is whether the differences between the sexes are a result of our sex chromosomes, and genetic in nature, or did humans learn them from our social and cultural environments? This argument, usually referred to as the **nature-nurture controversy**, is one that is common in psychological work. Most psychologists attribute our differences to a combination of nature and nurture factors. However, psychologists must be careful in their study of sex differences. After all, men and women are much more similar to each other than they are different. In the past, too, many more apparent differences—either mental or physical—between the sexes were assumed to be inherent before they were proven untrue.

There are many issues to consider when considering general differences between the men and women. The modern study of sex differences can fuel stereotypes and lead to greater misunderstanding between the sexes. Also, research is discussed in terms of statistics, which does not speak of specific people. For instance, some men may be very nurturing even though, as a group, statistics show that men tend to be less nurturing than women. Another issue is that animals, such as mice and rats and even primates, are often used to study biological sex differences, and this information does not always translate to human beings. And lastly, throughout history, psychological exploration, like many of the sciences, has focused on male subjects and male theorizing. While this work is important, there is a great deal of work yet to be accomplished in studying the psychology of women.

In the time of ancient Greece and Rome, many philosophers theorized that women were incomplete men. These theories seem to have influenced the early psychologists as well. The functional psychologists of the late 19th century, who put forth very academic studies of the sexes, made sweeping generalizations, such as women are more nurturing because they have babies. In part this information may have been true, but generalizations lead to stereotypes and stereotypes can be wrong and mistaken as truth, which can aid in developing self-fulfilling prophesies. For example, if it is widely believed, or stereotyped, that girls are not as good in math as boys, then some girls might not even try to be good at math, or teachers may not make the same effort to teach math to girls.

In the beginning of the twentieth century, psychoanalytic psychology was studying psychosexual differences and making connections between sexual organs and behaviors. By the mid-20th century, **Abraham Maslow** espoused a humanistic theory of **personality** which pointed to more similarity between the sexes than differences. By the late 20th century, psychologists and medical scientists made even greater progress in the study of the sexes through the work of sexology, endocrinology, neurophysiology, psychology, genetics, evolutionary theory, and **sociobiology**. Today, sex differences and similarities can be examined from many different aspects.

## The biological process of sexual differentiation

There is a genetic sex differentiation at conception. Every human being starts out as 46 chromosomes arranged in 23 pairs. Twenty-two of the pairs determine hereditary characteristics, like eye color and disease potential, the 23rd pair are the sex chromosomes. This chromosome alone is completely different in males and females. If the chromosome pair is an "XX", then the embryo will be female, but if it is an "XY", it will be male. If there is a "Y" chromosome present, then the embryonic gonadal (sex glands) become a penis. If there is no "Y" chromosome present, the human embryo is automatically female. In extremely rare cases, there are embryos that have different combinations of chromosomes, which are called hermaphrodites because they are technically both sexes.

After the embryonic development of the sex glands, **hormones**, which are powerful chemical substances, are secreted into the blood stream and reach every cell of the embryo. These hormones form a defined reproductive tract in females and tell a male's reproductive tract not to form. The hormones also force the development of external genitalia (sex organs on the outside of the body). Finally, the hormones travel to the **brain** and cause differences between males and females to occur there. For example, in a female brain there are lifelong cycles or patterns of hormone release.

Sexism

## The social process of sexual differentiation

Biological organisms are modified once they are born. Every individual is born into an existing social context, so if it is time on the planet when females are, according to the social structure, supposed to be nurturing, then girls will be taught to be that way from a very early age. Behavior that fits that structure will be rewarded and reinforced, and behavior that goes against that **norm** will be discouraged. Throughout human history opposing principles have been ascribed male/female labels. The sun, for instance, has been thought of as male energy, while the more passive moon is seen as female. Mythology has reinforced human behavior, because people make up mythology. Likewise, if most literature is written by males and those males portray women in a certain way, such as being content with less political **power**, then the literature is reinforcing that **stereotype**.

Most sex differences are a combination of biological and social processes. Differences in **ability**, for instance, do seem to exist according to research. Men tend to be physically larger and more muscular than women, while women have proven to be constitutionally stronger, that is, less prone to certain diseases and having longer life spans. Men perform better on some cognitive tests, like visualizing 3D objects. Women tend to have greater verbal abilities. These differences are biological, but are accentuated by cultural environmental influences. Differences in achievement studies show that there is not a great difference in **motivation**, but motivation is activated under different conditions for males and females. These differences are socially reinforced. In looking at differences in **aggression** (nonaccidental behavior that causes harm), studies repeatedly show that men are more aggressive than women. This may be due to evolutionary processes. If women were busy having babies and nursing babies, then men had to go and hunt and ward off enemies, forcing men into a more aggressive role. It is possible that this information has come down genetically to modern men. Yet, studies also show that learning by example is one way that behavior evolves. If a father is physically aggressive with his **family**, sons tend to be that way also. In addition to evolutional and learned behaviors, there are physiological reasons, such as hormones and brain design, which can account for greater levels of aggression found in men.

There are many factors that account for our differences, and there are many similarities among us, too. In exploring sex differences, it is important to look at the questions from many angles.

Lara Lynn Lane

## Further Reading
Solheim, Bruce Olav. *On top of the world*. Westport, CT: Greenwood Press, 2000.

Classen, Constance. *The color of angels*. London: Routledge, 1998.

Lips, Hilary M., and Nina Lee Colwill. *The psychology of sex differences*. Englewood Cliffs, NJ: Prentice-Hall, Inc., 1978.

Christen, Yves. Trans. by Nicholas Davidson. *Sex differences: modern biology and the unisex fallacy*. New Brunswick, USA. and London: Transaction Publishers, 1991.

Sayers, Janet. *Sexual contradictions: psychology, psychoanalysis, and feminism*. London and New York: Tavistock Publications, 1986.

Wright, Elizabeth, ed. *Feminism and psychoanalysis: a critical dictionary*. Oxford, England and Cambridge, MA: Basil Blackwell, Ltd., 1992.

# Sexism

See **Gender bias**

# Sex roles

Sets of attributes, including attitudes, personality traits, abilities, interests, and behaviors that are defined as appropriate for each sex.

Men and women are different not only in anatomy, but also in terms of how they behave and in the interests they express. Certain behavioral differences are believed to be biologically determined. For example, the male sex hormone testosterone is believed to be the reason why males are considered more aggressive than females. However, many nonanatomical differences appear to be based on sex roles that are learned by every individual. In other words, people are born male or female but are taught how to be masculine or feminine.

Roles are sets of norms that define how people in a given social position ought to behave. For example, people who have a particular occupation are subjected to a set of expectations concerning the work performed and the style in which it is accomplished. While one might anticipate a mechanic's soiled appearance, such an appearance would be considered unsanitary and unprofessional for a dentist. In contrast to specific roles based on occupations (e.g., teacher, firefighter) or **family** relationships (e.g., mother, son), sex roles are diffuse because they pertain to virtually all people and apply to all parts of one's daily life. It is therefore important to understand

**A little girl practices a typically feminine sex role, caring for an infant.** *(Vanessa Vick. Photo Researchers, Inc. Reproduced with permission.)*

how each of us learns his or her own sex role and the significance it has on our daily lives.

A sex-role concept is a set of shared expectations that people hold about the characteristics suitable for individuals on the basis of their gender. The notion of these roles being shared implies that most people endorse the expected behaviors as appropriate for men and for women. We all have beliefs about what males or females do and are supposed to do. In your family, whose job is it to send greeting cards to friends, buy gifts, remember a niece's birthday, organize parties, prepare food, and keep in touch with extended family members? You are probably thinking of a woman because the above activities are considered part of the woman's role in most cultures.

There is no direct relationship between biological sex and the various social aspects of sex roles. Accordingly, some psychologists have recommended that the term sex be used to designate biological maleness/femaleness as opposed to the term gender role, which refers to basic notions of masculinity and femininity. Much of what we consider masculine and feminine is learned as a result of **socialization** experiences. It is not a biological necessity that women tend to be the ones

who remember birthdays and send greeting cards. Rather it is simply a cultural expectation that gets passed on from generation to generation.

## Sex-role stereotypes

Sex-role beliefs become sex-role stereotypes when individuals employ those sets of behaviors as rules to be applied to all males and females. In western society, for example, women have traditionally been regarded as more delicate and compassionate than men. Stereotypes for femininity include expectations to be domestic, warm, pretty, emotional, dependent, physically weak, and passive. By contrast, men are thought of as being more competitive and less emotional than women. Masculinity stereotypes can be described by words such as unemotional, physically strong, independent, active, and aggressive. These implicit or explicit expectations are taught from a very early age. For instance, it is not uncommon to see family and friends **play** more roughly with baby boys than with baby girls. In terms of career expectations, until fairly recently women have traditionally been associated with homemaking and a relatively narrow range of occupations such as nursing or teaching, while men have been expected to hold a wide variety of jobs outside the home in business, politics, and industry.

Although certain common beliefs regarding the way each sex should behave are present across societies, substantial variations exist between cultures when examining sex roles and their accompanying stereotypes. For example, after studying the behaviors of men and women in three cultures in New Guinea, **Margaret Mead** found that each culture had its own sex roles and stereotypes. Interestingly, few of them corresponded to the stereotypes expressed in industrialized nations. This finding provides some support for sex roles as cultural constructions. The diverse characteristics associated with sex roles are not biologically determined, but rather culturally transmitted.

Stereotyping itself is a **normal** cognitive process. In fact, this act of forming general impressions is of great help in allowing us to categorize the tremendous amount of information we continually experience. However, the excessive use of masculine and feminine labels can place undue restrictions on people's behaviors and attitudes. Certain beliefs about sex-appropriate behaviors can determine the types of experiences to which we are exposed during the course of our lifetime. For example, some grade school teachers may form quick assumptions about a student's scholastic abilities largely on the basis his or her sex. As a result, a boy may be encouraged in math class while little effort is given to refining his talent for writing poetry. At more advanced levels, males may be more encouraged than females to enroll in mathematics, science, and engineering courses.

## Sex-role socialization

From **infancy** to adulthood, people receive informal but potent impressions of the role they are expected to play in society. As infants, little girls may be cuddled and handled in a more delicate manner than little boys. As children mature, family members continue to cultivate masculinity and femininity by encouraging a child to act in ways and develop interests the family members feel are appropriate for the child's sex, while at the same time discouraging any conduct considered inappropriate. For example, parents may reward a daughter's interest in sewing and housekeeping with praise and encouragement while actively discouraging a son who shows similar interest. Once a child is of school age, his or her peers generally provide additional information about what is considered acceptable or unacceptable within one's own sex role.

In the 1960s, social learning theorists such as Walter Mischel and **Albert Bandura** emphasized the role of both direct **reinforcement** and **modeling** in **shaping**

children's sex-role behavior and attitudes. Boys and girls learn new sex roles by observing and imitating their parents or some other person important to them of the same sex. For instance, little girls copy their mother's grooming activities by putting on makeup and dressing up in her jewelry while young boys imitate their father's behaviors by pretending to shave or work in the garage. Furthermore, parents seem to reinforce sex-typed activities in their children by either rewarding (e.g., a smile or laughter) their son for playing with trucks and their daughter for playing with dolls. They may also respond negatively (e.g., a frown or removal of the toy) when the form of play does not meet sex-role expectations. Another explanation for sex-role development is found in a cognitive developmental theory proposed by **Lawrence Kohlberg**. It is based on the view that children play an active role in the reinforcement of appropriate sex roles. Once children become aware of their gender label, they come to value behaviors, objects, and attitudes associated with their sex. Each child becomes highly motivated to learn about how members of his or her own sex act and then behaves in the way that is considered appropriate for that gender.

Sex-role development has been an area of extensive research over the past several decades. The first step in this process consists of acquiring **gender identity**. This is the point at which the child is able to label herself or himself accurately and can categorize others appropriately as male or female. For example, a two-year old child who is shown pictures of a same-sex child and an opposite sex child and is asked "which one is you?" will correctly choose the same-sex picture. By age four, most children understand that they will remain the same sex throughout their life, a concept known as gender stability. A child's **ability** to recognize that someone remains male or female despite a change of clothing or altered hair length demonstrates the development of true **gender constancy** that is not typically achieved until about the age of five or six.

Since the 1960s, sex roles in North America have become increasingly flexible. Whereas "masculinity" and "femininity" had long been considered to be opposite ends of the same continuum, (meaning a person could be one or the other but not both), psychologists today conceive of masculinity and femininity as two separate dimensions. Therefore, a person can be both compassionate and independent, both gentle and assertive. Many people no longer regard fearfulness or tenderness as unmanly emotions nor is it considered unfeminine if a woman is assertive. Men and women can also hold jobs that were once considered inappropriate for their sex. For instance, most women work outside their homes and are, in increasing numbers, entering professions traditionally considered to be almost exclusively male occupations such as medicine, engineering, and politics.

Timothy Moore

**Further Reading**

Jacobs, J. A., ed. *Gender inequality at work*. Thousand Oaks, CA: Sage, 1995.

Leaper, D., ed. *Childhood gender segregation: Causes and consequences*. San Francisco: Jossey-Bass, 1994.

Macoby, E. *The two sexes: Growing up apart, coming together* Cambridge: Harvard University Press, 1998.

# Sex therapies

*Various psychological treatments for the correction of sexual dysfunction which cannot be identified by a biological inadequacy.*

### Changing attitudes towards sex

Sex therapy, the treatment of sexual disorders, has evolved from early studies on sexual behavior made over 50 years ago. During these 50 years, the approach to sex therapy has changed immensely. When **William Masters** and **Virginia Johnson** published *Human Sexual Inadequacy* in 1970, the sexual revolution, born in the 1960s, was not yet in full force. Due in part to the development of the oral contraceptive known as "the pill" and the rise in the politics of feminism, society began to take a different, more open view of **sexuality**. For many, the sexual morals of the Victorian age and strict religious backgrounds had lingered even into the years after World War II. Traditionally, women were afraid to admit an interest in or even pleasure from sex. Men were permitted even less freedom to discuss sexual problems such as impotence. The rise in sex therapy addressed those issues as they had never been addressed before, in the privacy of a doctor's office.

In addition to shifting attitudes about sex, developments in medicine allowed more people to experience a satisfying sex life. By the 1990s, medications were developed that addressed the biological nature of sexual dysfunctions. Before these developments, if a man or a woman had trouble functioning sexually, the cause was often considered merely "psychological" and not a medical matter. Such medical treatments as penile implants, the prescription drug Viagra, and surgery or hormone replacement therapy for women can now be used to solve sexual disorders. If medical treatment does not solve a patient's disorder, sexual pleasure becomes a key issue for therapists.

### Masters and Johnson out, postmoderns in

Masters and Johnson were pioneers in sex therapy. Their research focused on three basic ideas: first, on encouraging couples to engage in completely new experiences; second, on persuading couples to perform in a previously prohibitive way that would hopefully dissolve their sexual conflicts; and third, on allowing couples to openly discuss such taboo subjects as premature ejaculation. By the 1990s, however, other researchers began noting that this form of therapy was not as useful with the coming of what is termed the "postmodern" age. In this new era, a different approach to sex therapy was deemed necessary.

Love and intimacy in the postmodern era affords the luxury of modern medicine and biology. Once medical factors are ruled out, a more ominous issue arises, that of *desire disorders*. Postmodern sex therapies consider many complex problems when approaching **sexual dysfunction**. According to current research, sexual disorders might have a host of underlying causes. These causes might even make sexual dysfunction desirable to the person suffering from such problems. For example, if a couple is having problems with intimacy, trust, or control in their relationship, creating sexual problems might be a way of avoiding dealing directly with the real issues. Low **self-esteem**, unresolved **family** or parental conflicts, or using energy for performance at work instead of for sex are all examples of problems that a couple must address before any promising sex therapy can begin.

### Benefits

If medical issues have been ruled out, once a person resolves whatever problem is causing a difficulty with intimacy, loving sexual relationships will be able to proceed. In an age of mobility with computers and email replacing interpersonal contact, avoiding intimacy is rather easy. Such technological "advances" as relying on automatic teller machines to hand out money, using computer keyboards to order products and services, and even machines to check out groceries all eliminate the opportunity for conversation or to release tension through personal contact. When people are allowed, or even expected, to become self-absorbed, sexual desire becomes even less necessary. In this age of over-achievers and cyberspace millionaires, living a life of all work and no **play** is considered a virtue. With so many issues at hand, a qualified sex therapist is often needed to help a person reach to the core of his or her problems. Most experts agree, sex therapies that address people and their personal histories, and not only problems that are manifested at the time of therapy, are those that have the best chance for success.

Jane Spear

**Further Reading**

Gochros, Harvey L. *Sexual Distress.* The Encyclopedia of Social Work, 19th edition. Edwards, Richard L., Ed.-in-Chief. Washington, D.C.: NASW Press, 1995.

Hight, T. L. *Sex Therapy.* The Baker Encyclopedia of Psychology. Grand Rapids, MI: Baker Books, 1999.

Packer, Jennifer. *Get Rid of the Fears That Keep You from True Intimacy.* Knight Ridder/Tribune, The Dallas Morning News, June 6, 2000.

**Further Information**

American Psychological Association. 750 First Street, N.E., Washington, D.C., USA. 20002-4242, 202-336-5500, 800-374-2721.

# Sexual abuse

Any sexual act or sexual exposure that is not consensual or that occurs between a child and an older individual.

Sexual abuse includes any sexual act or experience which is forced upon a person or which occurs as a result of coercion. In general, any sexual experience or exposure that occurs between a child and an older child, an adolescent, or an adult, for the gratification of the older individual, is considered to be sexual abuse. Sexual abuse includes **rape**, **incest**, inappropriate touching, exhibitionism, and physical or verbal harassment. Exposing children to pornographic material or using children in the production of **pornography** also constitutes sexual abuse.

Since many or even most cases of sexual abuse are not reported to the authorities, it has been difficult to determine the extent of sexual abuse in our society. The victims of sexual abuse can be males or females of any age, from infants to the elderly. The perpetrators of sexual abuse are predominantly male, but include some females, and come from all socioeconomic classes and racial and ethnic groups. They may be educated professionals, working people, or unemployed. They may or may not be under the influence of alcohol or drugs. Many abusers were themselves abused as children. Although the abuser may be a stranger to the victim, most often it is a **family** member, friend or acquaintance, or a caregiver. In recent years, an increased public awareness of sexual abuse has resulted in more abuse reports and prosecutions, as well as increasing the development of recovery programs for victims and treatment programs for abusers. Furthermore, there have been major initiatives aimed at preventing the sexual abuse of both children and adults. Unfortunately, in a few cases this heightened awareness of the problem of sexual abuse has resulted in false accusations, overzealous prosecution of innocent people, or manipulation of victims by unqualified therapists.

Victims of sexual abuse often feel guilty and believe that they are at fault for the abuse. Sexual assault on an adult often involves **violence** or the threat of violence. Although violence may be involved in the sexual abuse of children, most often the coercion is based upon the inherent **power** that the adult has over the child. An infant or very young child has no defense against an abuser. Although an older child may be bribed or threatened, the child usually has been taught to acquiesce to adult demands. The abuser usually insists that the child keep "their secret," and the shame and **guilt** felt by the child reinforces the need for secrecy.

## Historical perspectives

The definition of sexual abuse varies among cultures and has changed over time. Feminist movements have promoted broader definitions of what constitutes sexual abuse. Although most societies view sex between children and adults as inappropriate, mores concerning appropriate ages and age differences for sexual partners vary. Even today, there are individuals and organizations that promote sex between children and adults and argue for the elimination of laws against incest and statutory rape.

The early work of psychoanalyst **Sigmund Freud** suggested that, for many of his patients, repressed memories of **childhood** incest lay at the root of neuroses. However, many of Freud's colleagues argued that the early sexual encounters described by patients in **psychoanalysis** were actually memories of childhood sexual fantasies. Freud himself later adopted this position, although his colleague, Sandor Ferenczi, confirmed the involvement of childhood sexual abuse in many psychological disorders. As a result of Freud's influence, reports of sexual abuse often were discounted as the products of a child's **imagination**. When the evidence of abuse was undeniable, the child was viewed as having allowed or encouraged the abuse. To some extent, these attitudes survive today.

In the 1940s and 1950s, **Alfred Kinsey** and his coworkers first documented the extent of childhood sexual abuse. However, they did not view these early sexual experiences as particularly significant. It was not until the women's movement of the 1970s that the extent and significance of sexual abuse began to be appreciated.

## Immediate effects of sexual abuse

The victim's initial response to sexual abuse is usually horror and disbelief. This may be followed by a false sense of calm, brought on by **fear**. Many victims report that they mentally leave their bodies, to dissociate themselves from the physical event. This passivity may be misinterpreted as consent by both the abuser and the victim. Sexual abuse may or may not result in physical injury.

Following the experience, the victim of sexual abuse may be confused, frightened, furious, resentful, and depressed. These emotions can continue for a very long time. Child victims may become withdrawn, may regress to earlier developmental stages, or may display precocious sexualized behavior. Non-abusive parents of abused children, as well as the innocent partners of adult victims, may experience many of these same emotions. This is called "secondary victimization."

Many victims of sexual abuse blame themselves. They may be overwhelmed by guilt and shame. Some victims repress all memories of the experience or rationalize it in a way that makes it seem insignificant.

## Long-term effects of sexual abuse

Victims of sexual abuse may develop many of the symptoms of post-traumatic **stress** disorders. For children, the guilt, fear, shame, and **anger** brought on by sexual abuse, if untreated, can last into adulthood. Long-term effects of sexual abuse can include chronic anxiety, low **self-esteem**, and problems with intimacy and **sexuality**. Victims may become severely depressed, even suicidal, or develop psychotic symptoms. They may suffer from alcohol or drug abuse or **eating disorders**. Many victims experience marital and family difficulties. In severe cases, a victim's efforts to dissociate from the experience can lead to the development of multiple **personality** disorder.

Many factors influence the effects of sexual abuse on the victim. These include the type of abuse, the age of the victim, the frequency of abuse, and the relationship of the victim to the abuser. Children who are victimized by a trusted adult experience the betrayal of this trust. Victims who obtain support from family, friends, and trained professionals following the abuse are less likely to experience long-term effects. In general, abused children who have been coerced into maintaining secrecy suffer from the most serious long-term effects.

## Recovery from sexual abuse

Recovery from sexual abuse occurs in recognizable stages. These stages are analogous to those of the grieving or mourning process. Often, the first stage is a denial, which may involve the suppression or even total repression of memories of the abuse. In therapy or **self-help groups**, adults who were sexually abused as children may begin to recover these memories. However, in a few cases, overzealous counselors and therapists have elicited memories of childhood sexual abuse from patients who apparently were never abused. In the popular press, this has become known as "false **memory** syndrome."

Once the abuse is recognized, the victim may try to excuse it, rationalize it, or minimize it by suggesting that it was not really significant. Eventually, recovering victims come to accept that the abuse had major consequences in their lives and that it was not their fault. The later stages of recovery include anger, sadness, and finally, acceptance. Many law enforcement agencies provide support services to victims of sexual abuse. Trained therapists and self-help groups, including 12-step programs, may be indispensable for the recovery process. Individuals who have recovered from the effects of sexual abuse often are referred to as survivors.

## The sexual offender

Many sexual offenders abuse multiple victims. The perpetrators of sexual abuse are usually angry individuals who are driven by a need to dominate or control others. They may be psychotic or have **personality disorders**. Some sexual abuse is perpetrated by pedophiles who are sexually attracted to prepubescent children. Other sexual abuse appears to be situational. For example, incest may occur only when the parent is intoxicated or under stress.

Most sexual offenders deny that the abuse occurred. If they do admit to it, they usually blame it on the victim or the circumstances. They also may blame alcohol or drugs. A limited number of treatment programs are available for sexual offenders, both inside and outside of prisons. Recidivism is usually high for chronic sexual abusers.

Margaret Alic

### Further Reading

Adams, Caren, and Jennifer Fay. *No More Secrets: Protecting Your Child from Sexual Assault.* San Luis Obispo, CA: Impact Publishers, 1981.

Adams, Caren, and Jennifer Fay. *Helping Your Child Recover from Sexual Abuse.* Seattle: University of Washington Press, 1992.

Bass, Ellen, and Laura Davis. *The Courage to Heal: A Guide for Women Survivors of Child Sexual Abuse.* 3rd ed. New York: HarperPerennial, 1994.

Bass, Ellen, and Louise Thornton, eds. *I Never Told Anyone: Writings by Women Survivors of Child Sexual Abuse.* New York: HarperPerennial, 1991.

Hagans, Kathryn B., and Joyce Case. *When Your Child Has Been Molested: A Parent's Guide to Healing and Recovery.* Lexington, MA: Lexington Books, 1988.

Hunter, Mic. *Abused Boys: The Neglected Victims of Sexual Abuse.* Lexington, MA: Lexington Books, 1990.

Pendergrast, Mark. "Daughters Lost." In *Fathering Daughters: Reflections by Men,* edited by DeWitt Henry and James Alan McPherson. Boston: Beacon Press, 1998.

Westerlund, Elaine. *Women's Sexuality After Childhood Incest.* New York: W. W. Norton & Company, 1992.

**Further Information**

National Coalition Against Sexual Assault. 125 N. Enola Drive, Enola, PA, USA. 17025, fax: 717-728-9781, 717-728-9764. Email: ncasa@redrose.net. http://ncasa.org/main.html.

# Sexual deviations

See **Paraphilias**

# Sexual dysfunction

The persistent or recurrent inability or lack of desire to perform sexually or engage in sexual activity.

Sexual dysfunction involves both somatic and psychic phenomena which contribute to an overall inability or lack of interest in performing sexually. In males, the condition is most associated with erectile dysfunction (ED), formerly referred to as male "impotence." Studies estimate that 10-20 million American males have some degree of ED, which clinically presents as a persistent inability to attain or maintain penile erection sufficient for sexual intercourse.

Female sexual dysfunction falls into four main categories: (1) a low **libido** or aversion to sex; (2) difficulty in attaining sexual arousal; (3) inability to experience or attain orgasm; and (4) **pain** during sexual intercourse. Research in this area indicates that as many as 4 in 10 American women experience some form of sexual dysfunction.

## Assessment

As recently as the mid-twentieth century, sexual dysfunction was considered a psychological condition or disorder. The *Kinsey Reports* and Masters and Johnson's studies tended to isolate "performance anxiety" as the root of most sexual disorders. Later, in the 1970s, Helen Singer Kaplan impressed many colleagues and practitioners with her focus on enhancing sexual desire rather than sexual performance. Her biological approach to **sexuality**, i.e., equating sexual desire with physical appetite, was indeed

helpful in sex therapy. Her approach was further justified by the fact that epidemiological studies during the 1980s showed a disproportionate incidence of treatment-resistant desire disorders in the sex-therapy clinical populations of the United States and Northern Europe. It is clear that the proliferation of erotic material available to the general public (pornographic publications, movies, videos, sex toys, Internet sites, etc.) from the 1970s to the 1990s paralleled the therapeutic effort to enhance sexual desire rather than treat sexual performance.

However, by the 1990s, human sexuality was emerging as a complex bio-psychosocial phenomenon. Contemporary studies view the great majority of sexual dysfunction cases as having somatic or organic rather than psychologic etiologies, or at least as being "comorbid" in origin. This is particularly true in male disorders, where up to 80 percent of ED is the result of physical conditions which interfere with nerves and blood vessels. Most commonly, vascular disease is blamed for decreased blood flow to the penis. Once a physical condition affects the **ability** to maintain penile erection, psychological distress and performance anxiety sets in, complicating the problem. This leads to avoidance of sexual activity and the male may become socially withdrawn or depressed.

It is generally believed that for women, more so than for men, sexual drives and satisfactions are more complex and organized around the entire sexual relationship or sexual partner. Moreover, collateral factors such as birth control, **abortion**, **fear** of sexually-transmitted diseases, and feminism have greatly affected womens' general approach to sexual activity and sexual behavior. Key psychological causes associated with sexual dysfunction range from past **sexual abuse**, to unsatisfactory emotional relationships with sexual partners, to poor self-assessment regarding **body image** or appearance. Another factor to be considered is that half of all women over the age of 60 are without a partner (even though they have forestalled menopause with hormone replacement therapy), and the "use it or lose it" thinking about sexual activity has proven to have some medical basis. (Research suggests that long periods of sexual inactivity may result in loss of elasticity to the vagina in females, and muscle atrophy in the penis of males.) All of these factors may put pressure on both sexes to "perform" or engage in sexual activity more often, even if sexual intercourse results in physical pain. Thus, "remedicalization" of dysfunction from the psychological to the medical arena may not always address the coexisting psychosocial aspects of the condition. Adjunct psychological therapy may be warranted.

## Treatment

The recent emphasis on physical rather than psychological **etiology** in addressing sexual dysfunction correlates with the widespread success of prescription and non-prescription **drug therapy** for ED, such as that found in Viagra (sildenafil citrate), which effectively increases blood flow to the genitals. By 2000, doctors increasingly considered therapeutic doses of testosterone to both male and female patients, as testosterone is known to enhance sexual libido in both sexes.

For women, treatment of sexual dysfunction has been more varied because of the varying causes and presenting symptoms. During 1999, studies were commenced to test the efficacy of Viagra on females who complained of low sexual desire or inability to become sexually aroused. However, initial results published in May 2000 indicated that Viagra proved no more effective than a placebo in the female group. This finding may further support the belief that a synergy between the mind and body provides the best relief for female sexual dysfunction.

Notwithstanding, for both genders, several physical conditions greatly affect sexual functioning. These include diabetes, **obesity**, vascular disease, **stress**, fatigue, and untoward affects of medication. Menopausal and post-menopausal women may experience pain with sexual intercourse caused by decreased lubrication of mucous membranes and tissues. In all of the above, treatment of the underlying medical condition may render the sexual dysfunction as nonexistent or effectively relieved.

Some studies have shown that a decrease in dietary minerals, particularly zinc, may adversely affect libido. Such dietary deficits are related to pituitary hormone production of prolactin, which, at high levels, contributes to sexual dysfunction. It is therefore believed that some persons may be helped by increasing their dietary intake of red meats, dark meat poultry, seafood, leafy greens, and whole grains (all rich in zinc).

Finally, in treating sexual dysfunction, clients and couples are encouraged to refrain from thinking of sexual intercourse as the only or the ultimate goal of sexual activity. Therapists advise couples to frequently engage in non-coital sexual activity, including oral and manual stimulation, and to continue to provide such sexual pleasure even if the male loses his erection. Further, couples are encouraged to make sexual activity a priority and not an incidental happening when they retire at night. This is because testosterone levels are in fact lower in the evening hours, and both persons may be tired. Added to this is the fact that with age, it takes both sexes longer to become sexually stimulated. Partners should also try to incorporate sensual and affectional feelings into their activities, for obvious benefit.

Lauri R. Harding

**Further Reading**
"FDA Approves First Device to Aid Female Version of Impotence." *Jet,* (May 22, 2000): 33.
"It Takes Two: Coping With Erectile Dysfunction." *Harvard Womens Health Watch,* (March 2000): 2.
Dosa, Laszlo. "Careful History Essential in All Patients With ED." *Urology Times,* (May 2000): 19.
Kring, Brunhild. "Psychotherapy of Sexual Dysfunction." *American Journal of Psychotherapy,* (Winter 2000): 97.
Leland, John, Kalb, Claudia, and Nadine Joseph. "The Science of Women and Sex." *Newsweek,* (May 29, 2000): 48.
Miller, TA. "Diagnostic Evaluation of Erectile Dysfunction." *American Family Physician,* (January 2000): 95.
Henderson, C.W. "Lahey Clinic to Study Effects of Viagra on Women." *Women's Health Weekly,* (April 1, 2000): 27.

# Sexuality

The full range of thoughts and actions that describe sexual motivation and behavior.

While sex is not necessary for an individual's survival, without it a species would cease to exist. The determinants of sexual **motivation** and behavior include an individual's physiology, learned behavior, the physical **environment**, and the social environment.

A person's sex is determined at conception by whether one out of the 23 chromosomes in the father's sperm is either X (female) or Y (male). All female eggs contain an X chromosome, so each fertilized egg, or embryo, has a genotype of either XX (female) or XY (male). Reproductive **hormones** produced by the gonads (male testes and female ovaries) determine the development of the reproductive organs and the fetal **brain**, especially the **hypothalamus**. All the human reproductive hormones are found in both sexes but in different amounts. The principal female hormones are estrogens and progesterone (of which the main ones are estradiol and progesterone); the primarily male hormones are androgens (mainly testosterone). In males, levels of testosterone remain fairly constant, regulated by a feedback loop to the brain and pituitary gland, which control hormone secretion. In females, hormone levels fluctuate within each menstrual cycle, rising at ovulation. Reproductive hormones have two types of effects on the body. Organizational effects, which occur primarily before **birth**, are irreversible and permanently govern an individual's response to further hormone secretion. Activational effects govern behavior temporarily while hormone levels are elevated.

Human females are born with about 400,000 immature eggs. Each one is contained in a sac called a follicle. When a girl reaches **puberty**, one or more eggs mature every month, stimulated by the release of a hormone from the pituitary gland. As the egg matures, it secretes the hormone estrogen, causing the uterine lining to thicken in anticipation of the implantation of a fertilized egg. This is followed by ovulation, as the follicle ruptures, releasing the mature egg which travels through the fallopian tube towards the uterus. If the egg is not fertilized by sperm, it disintegrates and the uterine lining leaves the body, a process called menstruation. Women remain fertile until menopause, which normally occurs around the age of fifty. Unlike the production of female eggs, the male production of sperm is not cyclical and men remain fertile throughout their lives, although they may produce fewer sperm as they age. A man produces several billion sperm each year, releasing 300 to 500 million sperm in an average ejaculation.

Unlike that of other species, human sexual behavior is not bound to the female reproductive cycle. Women may engage in or refrain from sexual intercourse at any time during the cycle. Some women have reported increased sexual interest at the time of ovulation, others around the time of menstruation, and still others experience no link at all between their sexual behavior and menstrual cycle. After their initial organizational effects at birth, hormone levels stay low until puberty when activational effects first begin, triggering the reproductive system and generating an interest in sexual behavior. Whether or not sexual activity actually occurs at this point, however, depends on the interaction of physical readiness, social skills, and opportunity. For adults, as for adolescents, sexuality is not governed solely by hormones but also by a repertoire of learned attitudes and behaviors. This learning begins in **childhood** with the development of gender roles and continues throughout the life span, and it depends on attitudes prevalent in a culture at a given time.

The laboratory research conducted by **William Masters** and **Virginia Johnson** in the 1950s and 1960s yielded important information about the human cycle of sexual response. This cycle has four phases for both men and women: initial excitement, a plateau stage, orgasm, and resolution, during which the person returns to a state of relaxation. Males experience a refractory period after orgasm during which they are temporarily insensitive to sexual stimulation.

The same combination of physical, psychological, and social factors that govern sexuality may contribute to **sexual dysfunction**, any condition that inhibits the desire for, or **ability** to have, satisfying sexual experiences. In males, the most common dysfunction is impotence, or the inability to have or maintain an erection sufficient for intercourse. While impotence can have physical origins, including fatigue, diabetes, alcoholism, and the side effects of certain medications, it is usually psychological in nature. In females, a common sexual dysfunction is the inability to reach orgasm, also called arousal disorder, which is also associated with such psychological factors as self-consciousness, lack of self-confidence, **depression**, and dissatisfaction with the nature of the romantic relationship itself.

Although human sexual activity is primarily heterosexual, between 5 and 10 percent of males and 2 to 6 percent of females in the United States are homosexuals, individuals in whom sexual attraction and behavior are directed at members of their own sex. (Persons whose sexual behavior is directed at members of both sexes are known as bisexuals.) Researchers have found evidence of both biological and environmental origins of **homosexuality**. While no significant differences have been found in the levels of hormones that circulate in the blood of homosexuals and heterosexuals, exposure to high levels of certain reproductive hormones during fetal development has been linked to homosexuality. In addition, anatomical differences have been found between the hypothalamus of heterosexual and homosexual men, and studies of **twins** have found distinct evidence of a hereditary component to homosexuality. Environmental influences include early **family** relationships and the **modeling** of behaviors observed in the parent of the opposite sex, as well as social learning throughout the life span.

Sexual preference—the gender to which one is attracted—is only one aspect of human sexual orientation. Also involved is gender role, a general pattern of masculine or feminine behaviors that is strongly influenced by cultural factors. Distinct from this is sex identity, referring to whether individuals consider themselves to be male or female. Transsexualism, a condition in which a person believes he or she is of the wrong sex, occurs in approximately one in 20,000 in men and one in 50,000 in women. Today, these individuals have the option of a sex change operation that allows them to live as a member of the sex with which they identify.

*See also* Gender Identity Disorder; Heterosexuality.

## Further Reading

Fisher, Seymour. *Sexual Images of the Self: The Psychology of Erotic Sensations and Illusions*. Hillsdale, NJ: L. Erlbaum Associates, 1989.

Levand, Rhonda. *Sexual Evolution*. Berkeley, CA: Celestial Arts, 1991.

# David Shakow

### 1901-1981
American psychologist who conducted ground-breaking studies on schizophrenia.

In a career that spanned nearly 50 years, David Shakow conducted research that led to a vastly improved understanding of **schizophrenia**, one of the most complex mental disorders. Shakow's research covered all aspects of the disease, but in particular he focused on the mental deterioration that accompanied its progression. He was a strong advocate for patients of schizophrenia, which helped lessen the stigma that so often accompanies them.

Shakow was born on January 2, 1901 in New York City. Growing up in the lower east side of New York, which he later described as a "most auspicious place to have one's beginnings" because of the strength of the community, was an important influence on him.

## Begins clinical work at Worcester

Shakow went on to Harvard, where he received both his bachelors' and master's degrees in science. He embarked upon a doctorate in psychology, but his dissertation research progressed more slowly than he had anticipated. He was married, and he and his wife Sophie had begun their **family**. Shakow decided that to support his family he needed to take a more practical career approach over the short term, and he accepted a position at the nearby Worcester State Hospital in 1932. It was at Worcester that he began his research into schizophrenia.

Schizophrenia is not a "split personality" disorder as many people mistakenly believed at that time. Rather, it is a disease in which symptoms can range from mild confusion to violent self-destructive outbursts. Those who sufferer from the disease often show marked deterioration in their **ability** to function normally, frequently becoming less aware of their condition. (One of the common difficulties associated with schizophrenic patients is their refusal to take medication to control their symptoms.)

What Shakow tried to ascertain through his research was how much of the loss of **normal** function was the result of deterioration (which is reversible) and deficit (which is not). Among his findings, true deterioration in the schizophrenic occurs at a basic, reflexive level, while deficit occurs at the cognitive and perceptual levels.

Shakow entered the world of psychology at a time when the mentally ill were considered dangerous and un-treatable. Through his work with patients, Shakow made clear that, whatever their condition, they were still human beings and needed to be treated compassionately. He put forth the idea that patients should be allowed to serve as "partners" in those studies in which they participated, not merely experimental subjects.

During his years at Worcester, Shakow began one of the nation's first **clinical psychology** internship programs. He also continued his work on his doctoral dissertation, the focus of which he had shifted as a result of his research on schizophrenia. In 1946, the completed dissertation, *The Nature of Deterioration in Schizophrenia* was not only accepted enthusiastically, it was also recognized as a classic study on the psychology of the disease.

Shakow also chaired a committee of the **American Psychiatric Association** charged with defining the standards of education and training of the developing field of clinical psychology. Results of the committee report set the agenda for the famous Boulder Conference of 1949 that defined clinical psychology as a scientist/practitioner model.

## Continues research at NIMH

Shakow left Worcester that same year, heading to the University of Illinois Medical School as a professor in the psychiatry department. He was named a professor of psychology at the University of Chicago two years later; he held both positions concurrently. After a few years of teaching, Shakow decided that he wanted to devote more time to research and accepted an appointment to the National Institute of Mental Health in 1954. There, he served as the first head of the Laboratory of Psychology in NIMH's Intramural Research Program.

Under Shakow's 12-year tenure, the laboratory developed special sections to study not only schizophrenia, but also **perception, aging, childhood** development, and **personality**. The laboratory published more than 500 articles highlighting its research during those years. Shakow retired from his position in 1966 but stayed on as senior research psychologist. During the 1970s he and his staff continued to do important research on schizophrenia. During these years he was awarded both the Distinguished Scientific Contribution Award and the Distinguished Professional Contribution Award of the American Psychological Association.

Shakow continued his work at NIMH, conducting research, writing articles, and working on his scientific memoirs. In late February 1981, he suffered a heart attack while at work and died a few days later on February 26.

George A. Milite

**Further Reading**
Garmezy, Norman, and Philip S. Holzman. "David Shakow." *American Psychologist.* June 1984, pp. 698-699.
Shakow, David. *Clinical psychology as a science and profession: a forty-year odyssey.* Chicago: Aldine Publishing Co., 1969.
Shakow, David. *Schizophrenia: selected papers.* New York: International Universities Press, 1977.

# Shaping

A gradual, behavior modification technique in which successive approximations to the desired behavior is rewarded.

Shaping, or behavior-shaping, is a variant of operant **conditioning**. Instead of waiting for a subject to exhibit a desired behavior, any behavior leading to the target behavior is rewarded. For example, **B. F. Skinner** (1904-1990) discovered that, in order to train a rat to push a lever, any movement in the direction of the lever had to be rewarded, until finally, the rat was trained to push a lever. Once the target behavior is reached, however, no other behavior is rewarded. In other words, the subject behavior is shaped, or molded, into the desired form.

Although rejected by many orientations within the field of psychology, behavioral techniques, particularly shaping, are widely used as therapeutic tools for the treatment of various disorders, especially those affecting verbal behavior. For example, behavior shaping has been used to treat selective, or elective, mutism, a condition manifested by an otherwise **normal** child's refusal to speak in school.

Therapists have also relied on behavior shaping in treating cases of severe **autism** in children. While autistic children respond to such stimulus objects as toys and musical instruments, it is difficult to elicit speech from them. However, researchers have noted that behavior shaping is more effective when speech *attempts* are reinforced than when speech production is expected. When unsuccessful efforts to produce speech are rewarded, the child feels inspired to make a greater effort, which may lead to actual speech.

While recognizing the effectiveness of behavior shaping in the laboratory and in therapy, experts, particularly psychologists who do not subscribe to **behaviorism**, have questioned the long-term validity of induced behavior change. For example, researchers have noted that people have a tendency to revert to old behavior patterns, particularly when the new behavior is not rewarded any more. In many cases, as Alfie Kohn has written, behavior-shaping techniques used in school, instead of motivating a child to succeed, actually create nothing more than a craving for further rewards.

Zoran Minderovic

**Further Reading**
Nye, Robert D. *The Legacy of B.F. Skinner: Concepts and Perspectives, Controversies and Misunderstandings.* Pacific Grove, CA: Brooks/Cole, 1992.

# William Herbert Sheldon

### 1898-1977
American physician and psychologist who attempted to correlate body type with **personality**.

William Herbert Sheldon developed "constitutional psychology," the study of the relationships between physical attributes and personality **traits**. To describe physical build, Sheldon studied thousands of photographs and developed a rating system for three major components or somatotypes—endomorphy, mesomorphy, and ectomorphy—and three secondary components. Likewise, he developed a rating system for three primary components of **temperament**. He found a correlation between the physical and temperamental ratings. Sheldon was the first to use standardized photography for studying physical traits.

Born in 1898, Sheldon grew up on a farm in Warwick, Rhode Island, as one of three children of William Herbert and Mary Abby (Greene) Sheldon. Educated at local public schools, Sheldon, whose father was a naturalist, worked as an ornithologist while studying at Brown University. After serving in the army as a second lieutenant during World War I, Sheldon received his A.B. degree in 1919. Subsequently, he worked as an oil field scout, a wolf hunter in New Mexico, and a high school teacher before earning his master's degree at the University of Colorado and his Ph.D. in psychology from the University of Chicago in 1925. That year he married Louise Steger, although they later divorced. Sheldon taught psychology at the University of Texas in Austin, at the University of Chicago, and at the University of Wisconsin. In 1933 he earned his M.D. from the University of Chicago. Following an internship, he won a fellowship to study psychiatry with **Carl Jung** in Zurich, Switzerland.

In 1936, Sheldon became a professor of psychology at the University of Chicago. After two years, he moved to Harvard University to collaborate with Smith S. Stevens, an experimental psychologist. After serving in the Army as a lieutenant colonel during the Second World War, in 1945, he married Milancie Hill. The following year, Sheldon became Director of the Constitution Clinic and Laboratory at the Columbia University College of Physicians and Surgeons, and he began examining the relationships between physical attributes and disease. In 1959, he became a clinical professor of medicine at the University of Oregon Medical School in Portland. From 1951 until 1977, he directed the Oregon follow-up studies in constitutional medicine. Concurrently, he held positions as the director of research for the Biological Humanics Foundation of Cambridge, Massachusetts, as a research associate at the Institute of Human Development at the University of California at Berkeley, and as attending chief of research at Rockland State Hospital in Orangeburg, New York. Sheldon became emeritus professor at the University of Oregon in 1970.

Sheldon authored several books in the "Human Constitution Series," as well as two books of essays in which he tried to merge religion with social psychiatry. He believed that the correlations he observed between physique and personality reflected both the rewards based on behavior for a given physical type, and societal expectations based on physical appearance. Sheldon also examined relationships between physique and delinquent behavior and physique and psychopathology. He used three primary components to define psychopathology. In later years, Sheldon replaced his somatotyping scheme with a method called the Trunk Index.

Sheldon's correlations remain unproven and, in 1995, it was revealed that many of the photographs Sheldon studied were obtained by requiring students at universities to be photographed naked and without informed consent as to how the pictures might be used. Sheldon died of heart disease in Cambridge, Massachusetts, in 1977.

Margaret Alic

# Milicent W. Shinn

**1858-1940**
American child psychologist best known for her seminal systematic observational study of a child.

As the first woman to earn a Ph.D. from the University of California, **Milicent Shinn** is credited today for her outstanding early American study, "Notes on the Development of a Child." First published in 1898 as a doctoral dissertation, this work is still hailed as a masterpiece and a classic in its field.

A native Californian, Shinn was born in 1858 to parents who emigrated from the East and established a farming homestead in Niles, California, where she lived her entire life. In 1879, at the age of 25, she became editor of the Overland Monthly, a literary magazine that had fallen on hard times in post-Civil War California. Dividing her time between the **family** ranch and the journal, Shinn cared for her aging parents, ran the ranch with her brother and his wife, and helped care for their daughter, Ruth, who was born in 1890. Inspired by personal interest in her niece, Shinn applied her writer's skills to create a carefully recorded and minutely detailed two-year account of her niece's physical growth and **emotional development**. Delivered as a paper entitled "The First Two Years of the Child" at the World's Columbian Exposition in Chicago in 1893, Shinn's observational study was hailed as the first of its kind in America. Convinced by others that her work represented a significant contribution to **child psychology**, Shinn resigned from the Overland Monthly in 1894 and enrolled as a doctoral candidate at the University of California at Berkeley, completing the degree with the publication of her dissertation in 1898.

Compelling family needs and pressures led Shinn to abandon her scholarly pursuits and return to the family ranch to care for her invalid mother and aging father. By 1913, in her mid-fifties and in ill-health herself, Shinn undertook the education of her younger brother's four children, devoting the rest of her life to her family until her death in 1940.

**Further Reading**
Scarborough, Elizabeth, and Laurel Furumoto. *Untold Lives: The First Generation of American Women Psychologists.* 52-69. New York: Columbia University Press, 1987.

# Shyness

Uneasiness experienced when confronted by new people and situations.

Most people, from social recluses to the rich and famous, probably have experienced feelings of shyness at various times in their lives. Physiological symptoms may include blushing, increased heart rate, sweating, and shaking. Just as these outward manifestations vary in type and intensity from person to person, so do the inner feelings. Anxious thoughts and worries, low **self-esteem**, self-criticism, and concern over a lack of social skills, real or imagined, are common. The causes of shyness are not known. Some researchers believe it results from a genetic predisposition. Others theorize that uncommunicative parents restrict a child's development of the so-

cial skills that compensate for discomfort caused by new experiences and people, resulting in shyness. Variously, it has been considered a symptom of social **phobia** or a simple characteristic of **introversion**.

Psychological research that follows large numbers of children from very early **childhood** to adulthood has found that a tendency to be shy with others is one of the most stable **traits** that is preserved from the first three or four years of life through young adulthood. Learning or improving social skills through self-help courses or formal training in assertiveness and public speaking are some of the methods used to diminish the effects of shyness.

### Further Reading

Izard, C. *Human Emotions*. New York: Plenum Press, 1977.

Kagan, Jerome. *Galen's Prophecy: Temperament in Human Nature.* New York: Basic Books, 1994.

Kagan, J., and N. Snidman. "Biological Bases of Childhood Shyness." *Science* 240, 1988, pp. 167-71.

Tangney, J.P., and K.W. Fischer, eds. *Self-Conscious Emotions: Shame, Guilt and Pride.* New York: Guilford, 1995.

# Sibling rivalry

See **Birth order**

# Signal detection theory

A psychological theory regarding a threshold of sensory detection.

One of the early goals of psychologists was to measure the sensitivity of our sensory systems. This activity led to the development of the idea of a threshold, the least intense amount of stimulation needed for a person to be able to see, hear, feel, or detect the stimulus. Unfortunately, one of the problems with this concept was that even though the level of stimulation remained constant, people were inconsistent in detecting the stimulus. Factors other than the sensitivity of sense receptors influence the signal detection process. There is no single, fixed value below which a person never detects the stimulus and above which the person always detects it. In general, psychologists typically define threshold as that intensity of stimulation that a person can detect some percentage of the time, for example, 50 percent of the time.

An approach to resolving this dilemma is provided by signal detection theory. This approach abandons the idea of a threshold. Instead, the theory involves treating detection of the stimulus as a decision-making process, part of which is determined by the nature of the stimulus, by how sensitive a person is to the stimulus, and by cognitive factors. In other words, a person will be able to detect more intense sounds or lights more easily than less intense stimuli. Further, a more sensitive person requires less stimulus intensity than a less sensitive person would. Finally, when a person is quite uncertain as to whether the stimulus was present, the individual will decide based on what kind of mistake in judgment is worse: to say that no stimulus was present when there actually was one or to say that there was a stimulus when, in reality, there was none.

An example from everyday life illustrates this point. Suppose a person is expecting an important visitor, someone that it would be unfortunate to miss. As time goes on, the person begins to "hear" the visitor and may open the door, only to find that nobody is there. This person is "detecting" a stimulus, or signal, that is not there because it would be worse to miss the person than to check to see if the individual is there, only to find that the visitor has not yet arrived.

In a typical sensory experiment that involves a large number of trials, an observer must try to detect a very faint sound or light that varies in intensity from clearly below normal detection levels to clearly above. The person responds positively (i.e., there is a stimulus) or negatively (i.e., there is no stimulus). There are two possible responses, "Yes" and "No." There are also two different possibilities for the stimulus, either present or absent. The accompanying table describes the combination of an observer's response and whether the stimulus is actually there. The table refers to a task with an auditory stimulus, but it could be modified to involve stimuli for any sense.

Psychologists have established that when stimuli are difficult to detect, cognitive factors are critical in the decision an observer makes. If a person participates in an experiment and receives one dollar for each Hit and there is no penalty for a False Alarm, then it is in the person's best interest to say that the stimulus was present whenever there is uncertainty. On the other hand, if the person loses two dollars for each False Alarm, then it is better for the observer to be cautious in saying that a stimulus occurred. This combination of rewards and penalties for correct and incorrect decisions is referred to as the Payoff Matrix. If the Payoff Matrix changes, then the person's pattern of responses will also change. This alteration in responses is called a criterion shift.

There is always a trade-off between the number of Hits and False Alarms. When a person is very willing to say that the signal was present, that individual will show

| SIGNAL DETECTION THEORY | |
| --- | --- |
| **Status of Stimulus** | **Observer's Decision** |
| Stimulus is present | *Yes, there is a sound.* This is termed a HIT, because the sound is there and the observer detects it. |
| | *No, there is no sound.* This is termed a MISS, because the sound is there, but the observer fails to detect it. |
| Stimulus is absent | *Yes, there is a sound.* This is termed a FALSE ALARM, because the sound is present, but the observer fails to detect it. |
| | *No, there is no sound.* This is termed CORRECT REJECTION, because the sound is not there, and the observer correctly notes its absence. |

more Hits, but will also have more False Alarms. Fewer Hits will be associated with fewer False Alarms. As such, the number of Hits is not a very revealing indicator of how sensitive a person is; if the person claims to have heard the stimulus on every single trial, then the person will have said "Yes" in every instance in which the stimulus was actually there. This is not very impressive, however, because the person will also have said "Yes" on every trial on which there was no stimulus. Psychologists have used mathematical approaches to determine the sensitivity of an individual for any given pattern of Hits and False Alarms; this index of sensitivity is called d' (called d-prime). A large value of d' reflects greater sensitivity.

The basic idea behind signal detection theory is that neurons are constantly sending information to the **brain**, even when no stimuli are present. This is called neural noise. The level of neural noise fluctuates constantly. When a faint stimulus, or signal, occurs, it creates a neural response. The brain must decide whether the neural activity reflects noise alone, or whether there was also a signal.

For very intense signals, there is no problem in deciding if there was a stimulus because the neural effect of the signal far outweighs the neural effect of the noise. Similarly, when there is no signal, the **nervous system** does not respond as it does when an outside signal is present, so decisions are easy. On the other hand, for near-threshold signals, it can be difficult to know whether neural activity results from noise alone or from a signal plus noise. At this point, the observer makes a decision based on the payoff matrix.

**Further Reading**
Goldstein, E.B. *Sensation and Perception*, 3rd ed. Belmont, CA: Wadsworth Publishing Company, 1989.

# Significance level

A method to describe the reliability of test results.

When researchers measure a behavior, they often compare groups to determine whether they differ on that behavior. The ultimate goal is to determine whether the difference would occur if the measurements were administered a second time, or whether the difference is accidental and not likely to recur. The degree of reliability relates to the concept of significance level. The significance level refers to how likely it is that an error (that is, a wrong decision about whether the groups differ from one another) would be made. Psychologists generally accept a 5 percent error rate as reasonable. In order to decide whether differences are reliable, psychologists conduct statistical tests that provide a measure of confidence in their conclusions. This area of statistics is called inferential statistics because psychologists draw inferences, or conclusions, about what would happen if they made similar measurements with a different set of subjects.

If two similar groups are being measured, then they will produce different scores even though the difference is not particularly meaningful. If a researcher measures how much time students in separate mathematics classes take to solve a similar problem, the average for those two classes is likely to differ somewhat, even if the two classes consist of students with comparable abilities

**Further Reading**
Berman, Simeon M. *Mathematical Statistics: An Introduction Based on the Normal Distribution*. Scranton, PA: Intext Educational Publishers, 1971.

Christensen, Larry B. *Experimental Methodology, 5th ed.* Boston: Allyn and Bacon, 1991.

D'Amato, M. R. *Experimental Psychology: Methodology, Psychophysics, and Learning.* New York: McGraw-Hill, 1970

Elmes, David G. *Research Methods in Psychology, 4th ed.* St. Paul: West Publishing Company, 1992.

Kantowitz, Barry H. *Experimental Psychology: Understanding Psychological Research, 5th ed.* St. Paul: West Publishing Company, 1994.

Martin, David W. *Doing Psychology Experiments, 2nd ed.* Monterey, CA: Brooks/Cole, 1985.

# B. F. Skinner

### 1904-1990
American psychologist and advocate of behaviorism.

B. F. (Burrhus Frederic) Skinner was born in Susquehanna, Pennsylvania. As a youth, he showed talent for music and writing, as well as mechanical aptitude. He attended Hamilton College as an English major, with the goal of becoming a professional writer. After graduation, Skinner, discouraged over his literary prospects, became interested in behavioristic psychology after reading the works of **John Watson** and **Ivan Pavlov**. He entered Harvard University as a graduate student in psychology in 1928 and received his degree three years later. Skinner remained at Harvard through 1936, by which time he was a junior fellow of the prestigious Society of Fellows. While at Harvard, he laid the foundation for a new system of behavioral analysis through his research in the field of animal learning, utilizing unique experimental equipment of his own design.

His most successful and well-known apparatus, known as the Skinner Box, was a cage in which a laboratory rat could, by pressing on a bar, activate a mechanism that would drop a food pellet into the cage. Another device recorded each press of the bar, producing a permanent record of experimental results without the presence of a tester. Skinner analyzed the rats' bar-pressing behavior by varying his patterns of **reinforcement** (feeding) to learn their responses to different schedules (including random ones). Using this box to study how rats "operated on" their **environment** led Skinner to formulate the principle of operant conditioning—applicable to a wide range of both human and animal behaviors—through which an experimenter can gradually shape the behavior of a subject by manipulating its responses through reinforcement or lack of it. In **contrast** to Pavlovian, or response, **conditioning**, which depends on an outside stimulus, Skinner's **operant conditioning** depends on the subject's responses themselves. Skinner in-

**B. F. Skinner** *(The Library of Congress. Reproduced with permission.)*

troduced the concept of operant conditioning to the public in his first book, *The Behavior of Organisms* (1938).

Between 1936 and 1948 Skinner held faculty positions at the University of Minnesota and the University of Indiana, after which he returned permanently to Harvard. His ideas eventually became so influential that the American Psychological Association created a separate division of studies related to them (Division 25: "The Experimental Analysis of Behavior"), and four journals of behaviorist research were established. In the 1940s Skinner began training animals to perform complex activities by first teaching them chains of simpler ones. He was quite successful in training laboratory animals to perform apparently remarkable and complex activities. One example of this involved pigeons that learned to play table tennis.

Skinner's observation of the effectiveness of incremental training of animals led him to formulate the principles of programmed instruction for human students, in which the concept of reward, or reinforcement, is fundamental, and complex subjects such as mathematics are broken down into simple components presented in order of increasing difficulty. Presented with a set of relatively simple questions, students receive immediate reinforcement—and thus incentive to continue—by being told that their answers were correct. The **programmed learning** movement became highly influential in the United States and abroad. Although this technique eventually came under criticism by educators advocating more holistic methods of instruction, it remains a valuable teaching tool. Courses and course materials based on it have been developed for many subjects, and at levels of difficulty ranging from kindergarten through graduate school.

Skinner's work was also influential in the clinical treatment of mental and emotional disorders. In the late 1940s he began to develop the **behavior modification** method, in which subjects receive a series of small rewards for desired behavior. Considered a useful technique for psychologists and psychiatrists with deeply disturbed patients, behavior modification has also been widely used by the general population in overcoming **obesity, shyness**, speech defects, addiction to smoking, and other problems. Extending his ideas to the realm of philosophy, Skinner concluded that all behavior was the result of either positive or negative reinforcement, and thus the existence of free will was merely an illusion. To explore the social ramifications of his behaviorist principles, he wrote the novel *Walden Two* (1948), which depicted a utopian society in which all reinforcement was positive. While detractors of this controversial work regarded its **vision** of social control through strict positive reinforcement as totalitarian, the 1967 founding of the Twin Oaks Community in Virginia was inspired by Skinner's ideas. Skinner elaborated further on his ideas about positive social control in his book *Beyond Freedom and Dignity* (1971), which critiques the notion of human autonomy, arguing that many actions ascribed to free will are performed due to necessity.

Skinner has been listed in The 100 Most Important People in the World, and in a 1975 survey he was identified as the best-known scientist in the United States. Skinner's other books include *Science and Human Behavior* (1953) and *Verbal Behavior* (1957).

*See also* Behaviorism

### Further Reading
Carpenter, Finley. *The Skinner Primer: Behind Freedom and Dignity.* New York: Free Press, 1974.
Skinner, B.F. *Particulars of My Life.* New York: Knopf, 1976.
———. *The Shaping of a Behaviorist.* New York: Knopf, 1979.
———. *A Matter of Consequences.* New York: Knopf, 1983.

# Sleep

A state that suspends the voluntary exercise of bodily functions and consciousness.

A healthy adult sleeps an average of 7.5 hours each night and most people (approximately 95 percent) sleep between 6.5 and 8.5 hours. Tracking **brain** waves with the aid of electroencephalographs (EEGs), researchers have identified six stages of sleep (including a pre-sleep stage), each characterized by distinctive brain-wave frequencies. Stage 0 is the prelude to sleep, which is characterized by low amplitude and fast frequency alpha waves in the brain. At this stage, a person becomes relaxed, drowsy, and closes their eyes. Stages 1 through 4 are sometimes characterized as NREM (non-rapid eye movement) sleep. In Stage 1, the eyes begin to roll and rhythmic alpha waves give way to irregular theta waves that are lower in amplitude and slower in frequency as the person loses responsiveness to stimuli, experiences, fleeting thoughts, and images. In Stage 2, electroencephalogram tracings show fast frequency bursts of brain activity called sleep spindles, marked by muscle tension and accompanied by a gradual decline in heart rate, respiration, and temperature. Stages 3 and 4 normally occur 30 to 45 minutes after falling asleep. In Stage 3, there are fewer sleep spindles, but high amplitude and low frequency delta waves appear. When these begin to occur more than 50 percent of the time, the fourth stage of sleep has been entered. Delta waves demarcate the deepest levels of sleep, when heart rate, respiration, temperature, and blood flow to the brain are reduced and growth **hormones** are secreted. A person roused from Stage 4 sleep will be groggy and confused. Altogether, it takes about a half hour to pass through these four stages of sleep.

Rapid eye movement (REM sleep), which makes up approximately 20 percent of sleep time, is interspersed with NREM sleep every 30 to 40 minutes throughout the night. It is during REM sleep that **dreams** are experienced. In this state, the same fast frequency, low-amplitude beta waves that characterize waking states occur, and a person's physiological signs—heart rate, breathing, and blood pressure—also resemble those in a waking state. However, muscle tone decreases to the point of paralysis, with sudden twitches, especially in the face and hands. REM periods may last from 15 minutes at the beginning of a sleep cycle to one hour at the end of it. Most people complete four to six complete sleep cycles each night, with each cycle lasting about 90 minutes. These cycles vary in composition, however; early in the night most of the time is spent in Stage 3 and 4 sleep, with Stage 2 and REM sleep predominating later on. Sleep patterns also vary in the course of a person's life. On the average, an infant sleeps about 16 hours a day, in **contrast** to a 70-year-old who sleeps only about six hours. While REM sleep comprises about half of total sleep at **birth**, it eventually decreases to only 25 percent.

Sleeping patterns also vary greatly among individuals, and even among different cultures (in terms of napping, for example).

Two theories of sleep, the repair and the adaptive theories, attempt to explain why sleep occurs. In the repair theory, sleep serves a biological need, replenishing key areas of the brain or body which are depleted during the day. The adaptive theory suggests that sleep as a function evolved over time because it prevented early humans from wasting energy and exposing themselves to nocturnal predators, thus aiding in survival. REM sleep in particular has been thought to serve special functions. Research subjects whose REM sleep was interrupted made up for the loss by spending extra time in the REM stage on successive nights. It has also been suggested that REM sleep aids the activity of neurons that use the **neurotransmitter** norepinephrine, thus maintaining waking alertness. Persons deprived of REM sleep have shown poorer retention of skills learned during the day, leading to the hypothesis that REM sleep helps in assimilating daytime learning experiences.

As with many other physiological processes, sleep is linked to a 24-hour circadian rhythm and affected by signals such as light and dark. The effects of disrupting the sleep-wake cycle can be seen in jet lag, which is characterized by fatigue, irritability, lack of alertness, and sleeping problems. A person affected by jet lag feels like sleeping at the wrong times of day. It has been found that the body maintains a circadian sleep-wake rhythm even in the absence of external cues like lightness and darkness, although research subjects deprived of such cues eventually adopt a 25-hour "day." The "internal clock" that maintains this pattern is a section of the brain called the supra chiasmatic nucleus (SCN), located in the **hypothalamus**.

Various disorders interfere with sleep. The most common is insomnia, the inability to fall asleep or stay asleep. Nearly one-third of all Americans are affected by some degree of insomnia. Often associated with mental distress, insomnia is treated with medication, **psychotherapy**, relaxation techniques, or a combination of these methods. The medications most commonly prescribed are benzodiazepines (Valium, Halcyon, Restoril) and barbiturates. While they alleviate insomnia in the short run, these drugs interfere with **normal** sleep patterns, and can lead to increased tolerance and dependence. Researchers and clinicians have had success treating insomnia with the hormone melatonin, a naturally occurring substance related to sleep onset and secreted by the pineal gland. Melatonin supplements first became available in American health food stores in 1993 and have become increasingly popular as a sleep aid, although their use has caused some controversy in medical circles.

**Narcolepsy**, a disorder characterized by sudden and uncontrollable occurrences of sleep, afflicts 100,000 people in the United States. This condition is genetically linked, and may be curable in the future. Individuals affected by narcolepsy abruptly enter REM sleep states during the daytime, collapsing and remaining immobile for a period of time after awakening. Napping and stimulants have both been used to treat this condition. Another disorder associated with sleep is sudden infant death syndrome (SIDS), in which a healthy baby stops breathing during sleep, fails to awaken, and suffocates. While the exact cause of SIDS is unknown, researchers are attempting to identify and save at-risk infants by studying the relationship between the disorder and sleeping patterns. In sleep apnea, a person repeatedly stops breathing while asleep but awakes each time. The disrupted sleep that results from these multiple awakenings leaves the sleeper fatigued and sleepy during the daytime. **Night terrors** are non-REM dream experiences from which the sleeper never fully awakes and which he or she does not recall upon awakening. This condition mostly occurs in children and can be treated with **hypnosis** or medication in severe cases.

*See also* Sleep Disorders.

## Sleep disorders

Chronic disturbances in the quantity or quality of sleep that interfere with a person's ability to function normally.

An estimated 15 percent of Americans have chronic **sleep** problems, while about 10 percent have occasional trouble sleeping. Sleep disorders are listed among the clinical syndromes in Axis I of the American Psychiatric Association's Diagnostic and Statistical Manual of Mental Disorders. They may be either primary (unrelated to any other disorder, medical or psychological) or secondary (the result of physical illness, psychological disorders such as **depression**, drug or alcohol use, **stress**, or lifestyle factors, such as jet lag).

The Association for Sleep Disorders Centers has divided sleep problems into four categories. The first and most common is insomnia (Disorders of Initiating and Maintaining Sleep). In insomnia, sleep loss is so severe that it interferes with daytime functioning and well-being. Three types of insomnia have been identified (although a single person can have more than one): sleep-onset insomnia (difficulty falling asleep); sleep-

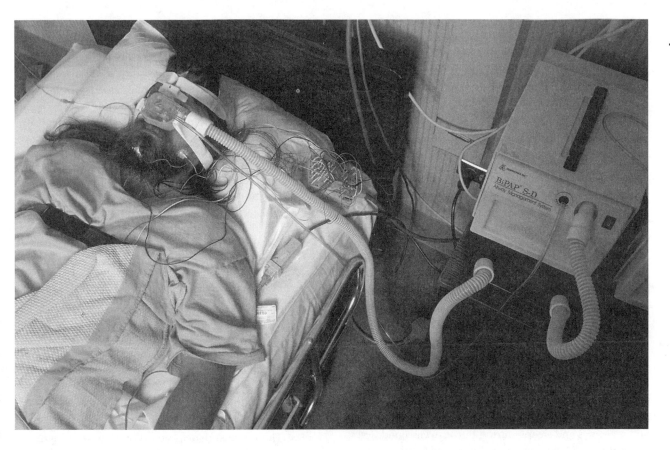

**A patient suffering from acute sleep apnea is hooked up to monitors in preparation for a night's sleep at a Stanford University sleep lab.** *(Photo by Russell D. Curtis. National Audubon Society Collection/ Photo Researchers, Inc. Reproduced by permission.)*

maintenance insomnia (difficulty staying asleep); and terminal insomnia (waking early and not being able to go back to sleep). While insomnia can occur at any stage of life, it becomes increasingly common as people get older.

Some cases of insomnia are thought to be caused by abnormalities in the part of the **brain** that controls sleeping and waking. However, insomnia commonly has a wide variety of non-neurological causes, including stress, physical **pain**, irregular hours, and psychological disorders. Temporary acute insomnia related to a major event or crisis can turn chronic if a person becomes overly anxious about sleep itself and is unable to return to his or her **normal** sleep pattern. Called learned or behavioral insomnia, this problem troubles about 15 percent of people who seek professional help. In about 30 percent of cases, an underlying psychological disorder—often depression—is responsible for insomnia. Disorders that can cause insomnia include anxiety disorders (such as post-traumatic stress disorder), **obsessive-compulsive disorder**, and **schizophrenia**. Normal sleep may be disrupted by a variety of substances, including caffeine, nicotine, alcohol, appetite suppressants, and prescription

medications such as steroids, thyroid medications, and certain antihypertensive drugs.

Many people take medications for insomnia, ranging from over-the-counter preparations (which are basically antihistamines) to prescription drugs including barbiturates and benzodiazepines. The American Sleep Disorders Association recommends benzodiazepines (a class of drugs that includes Valium and Restoril) over barbiturates and other sedatives, although only for limited use to treat temporary insomnia or as a supplement to **psychotherapy** and other treatments for chronic insomnia. Benzodiazepines can lead to tolerance and addiction, and withdrawal can actually worsen insomnia. People who take sleeping pills for two weeks or more and then quit are likely to experience a rebound effect that can disrupt their sleep for a period of up to several weeks.

A variety of behavioral treatments are available for insomnia which, when practiced consistently, can be as effective as medication without side effects or withdrawal symptoms. Different types of relaxation therapy, including progressive muscle relaxation, **hypnosis**, meditation, and **biofeedback**, can be taught through special classes, audiotapes, or individual sessions. **Cognitive therapy** focuses on deflecting anxiety-producing thoughts and behaviors at bedtime. Stimulus control therapy is based on the idea that people with learned insomnia have become conditioned to associate their beds with wakefulness. Persons involved in this type of therapy are not allowed to remain in bed at night if they can not fall asleep; they are instructed to go to another room and engage in a non-stressful activity until they become sleepy. In the morning, they must arise at a set hour no matter how much or little sleep they have had the night before. Finally, sleep restriction therapy consists of limiting one's hours in bed to the average number of hours one has generally been sleeping and then gradually increasing them.

The second category of sleep disorder is hypersomnia, or Disorders of Excessive Somnolence. People affected by any type of hypersomnia report abnormal degrees of sleepiness, either at night or in the daytime. While the most common causes are sleep apnea and **narcolepsy**, hypersomnia may also be caused by physical illness, medications, withdrawal from stimulants, or other psychological disorders. Sleep apnea consists of disrupted breathing which wakens a person repeatedly during the night. Though unaware of the problem while it is occurring, people with sleep apnea are unable to get a good night's sleep and feel tired and sleepy during the day. The condition is generally caused either by a physical obstruction of the upper airway or an impairment of the brain's respiration control centers. Common treatment methods include weight loss (**obesity** is a risk factor for the condition), refraining from sleeping on one's back, and medications that reduce **rapid eye movement (REM)** sleep. A technique called continuous positive airway pressure (CPAP) pushes air into the sleeper's throat all night through a small mask, preventing the airway from collapsing. In addition, a surgical procedure is available that modifies the upper airway to allow for freer breathing.

The other main type of hypersomnia is narcolepsy—sudden attacks of REM sleep during waking hours. Many narcoleptics experience additional symptoms including cataplexy (a sudden loss of muscle tone while in a conscious state), **hallucinations** and other unusual perceptual phenomena, and sleep paralysis, an inability to move for several minutes upon awakening. Between 200,000 and 500,000 Americans are affected by narcolepsy, which is caused by a physiological brain dysfunction that can be inherited or develop after trauma to the brain from disease or injury. Treatments include stimulants to combat daytime sleepiness, tricyclic **antidepressants** to suppress REM sleep, and other medications to control cataplexy.

Disorders of the Sleep-Wake Schedule—the third type of sleep disturbance—are also called circadian rhythm disorders because they interfere with the 24-hour biological clock that regulates many bodily processes. People with these disorders have trouble adhering to the sleep-wake schedule required by their job or **environment**, often due to shift work or jet lag. However, some persons suffer from delayed or advanced sleep onset problems with no external aggravating factor. Exposure to bright lights and chronotherapy, a technique for resetting one's biological clock, have been effective in the treatment of some circadian rhythm disorders.

Parasomnias, the final category of sleep disorder, involve unusual phenomena—nightmares, sleep terrors, and sleepwalking—that occur during sleep or during the period between sleeping and waking. Nightmare and sleep terror disorders are similar in that both occur mainly in children and involve frightening nighttime awakenings (in the case of sleep terrors, the person is awakened from non-REM sleep by feelings of agitation that can last for up to 10 minutes). Both are often outgrown but may be treated with psychotherapy, low-dose benzodiazepines, and, in the case of nightmare disorder, relaxation training. Sleepwalking occurs during the deep non-REM sleep of stages three and four and is also most common in children, who tend to outgrow it after the age of 12. It is also more common among males than females. The greatest danger posed by sleepwalking is injury through falls or other mishaps.

Other features of parasomnias include bruxism (teeth grinding) and enuresis (bedwetting). Both are often stress-related, although enuresis may also be caused by genitourinary disorders, neurological disturbances, or toilet training problems. Bruxism may be relieved through relaxation techniques or the use of a custom-made oral device that discourages grinding or at least prevents tooth damage. Enuresis often responds to the medication imipramine (Tofranil) and various **behavior modification** techniques. A parasomnia only identified within the past decade is REM sleep behavior disorder. Those affected by this condition—usually middle-aged or older men—engage in vigorous and bizarre physical activities during REM sleep in response to **dreams**, which are generally of a violent, intense nature. As their actions may injure themselves or their sleeping partners, this disorder, thought to be neurological in nature, has been treated with hypnosis and medications including clonazepam and carbamazepine.

## Further Reading

Hales, Dianne R. *The Complete Book of Sleep: How Your Nights Affect Your Days*. Reading, MA: Addison-Wesley Longman, 1981.

Lamberg, Lynne. *The American Medical Association Guide to Better Sleep*. New York: Random House, 1984.

# Smell

*The sense that perceives odor by means of the nose and olfactory nerve.*

Olfaction is one of the two chemical senses: smell and **taste**. Both arise from interaction between chemical and receptor cells. In olfaction, the chemical is volatile, or airborne. Breathed in through the nostrils or taken in via the throat by chewing and swallowing, it passes through either the nose or an opening in the palate at the back of the mouth, and moves toward receptor cells located in the lining of the nasal passage. As the chemical moves past the receptor cells, part of it is absorbed into the uppermost surface of the nasal passages called the olfactory epithelium, located at the top of the nasal cavity. There, two one-inch-square patches of tissue covered with mucus dissolve the chemical, stimulating the receptors, which lie under the mucus. The chemical molecules bind to the receptors, triggering impulses that travel to the **brain**. There are thousands of different receptors in the cells of the nasal cavity that can detect as many as 10,000 different odors. Each receptor contains hair-like structures, or cilia, which are probably the initial point of contact with olfactory stimuli. Research suggests that the sensitivity of the olfactory system is related to the number of both receptors and cilia. For example, a dog has 20 times as many receptor cells as a human and over 10 times as many cilia per receptor.

The cribriform plate forms the roof of the nasal cavity. The olfactory **nerve** passes through openings in this bone and ends in the olfactory bulb, a neural structure at the base of the brain. From there, olfactory signals are diffused throughout the brain to areas including the amygdala, hippocampus, pyriform cortex (located at the base of the temporal lobe), and the **hypothalamus**. Olfaction is the only sense that does not involve the **thalamus**. Olfaction messages are especially intensive in the amygdala, a part of the brain responsible for emotions, which may help the unusual **power** of certain smells to trigger emotions and recollections based on memories from the past. Further, a person's reaction to smell is mediated by context. For example, the same smell present in body odor is responsible for the flavor of cheese. In the first case, the smell is perceived as negative, in the second, it is positive. In humans, olfaction intensifies the taste of food, warns of potentially dangerous food, as well as other dangers (such as fire), and triggers associations involving **memory** and **emotion**. Olfaction is an especially important sense in many animals. A predator may use it to detect prey, while prey may use it to avoid predators. It also has a role in the mating process through chemicals called pheromones, which can cause ovulation in females or signal a male that a female is in a sexually receptive state. Although the existence of human pheromones has not been verified, olfaction still plays a role in human sexual attraction, as well as in parenting. Mothers can usually identify their newborn infants by smell, and breast-feeding babies can distinguish between the smell of their mothers and that of other breast-feeding women. Researchers have also found that children are able to recognize their siblings by smell and parents can use smell to distinguish among their own children. However, as people age the sense of smell diminishes, especially for men. By age 80, many men have almost no **ability** to detect odors. The intensity of a particular odor is strongly affected by **adaptation**. Odors may become undetectable after only a brief period of exposure. The sense of smell also plays an important role in the discrimination of flavors, a fact demonstrated by the reduced sense of taste in people with colds. The enjoyment of food actually comes more from odors detected by the olfactory system than from the functioning of the taste system. The olfactory and gustatory (taste) pathways are known to converge in parts of the brain, although it is not known exactly how the two systems work together. While an aversion to certain flavors (such as bitter flavors) is innate, associations with odors are learned.

# Social competence

*Mastering the social, emotional, and cognitive skills and behaviors needed to succeed as a member of society.*

Social competence refers to the social, emotional, and cognitive skills and behaviors that children need for successful social **adaptation**. Despite this simple definition, social competence is an elusive concept, because the skills and behaviors required for healthy social development vary with the age of the child and with the demands of particular situations. A socially competent preschool child behaves in a much different manner than a socially competent adolescent; conversely, the same behaviors (e.g., **aggression**, **shyness**) have different implications for social adaptation depending upon the age of the child and the particulars of the social context.

A child's social competence depends upon a number of factors including the child's social skills, social awareness, and self-confidence. Social skills is a term used to describe the child's knowledge of, and **ability** to use, a variety of social behaviors that are appropriate to a given interpersonal situation and that are pleasing to others in each situation. The capacity to inhibit egocentric, impulsive, or negative social behavior is also a reflection of a child's social skills. The term **emotional intelligence** refers to the child's ability to understand others' emotions, perceive subtle social cues, "read" complex social situations, and demonstrate insight about others' motivations and goals. Children who have a wide repertoire of social skills and who are socially aware and perceptive are likely to be socially competent. Social competence is the broader term used to describe a child's social effectiveness—a child's ability to establish and maintain high quality and mutually satisfying relationships and to avoid negative treatment or victimization from others. In addition to social skills and emotional **intelligence**, factors such as the child's self-confidence or social anxiety can affect his/her social competence. Social competence can also be affected by the social context and the extent to which there is a good match between the child's skills, interests, and abilities and those of the other children in his/her **environment**. For example, a quiet and studious boy may appear socially incompetent in a peer group full of raucous athletes, but may do fine socially if a better peer group "niche" can be found for him, such as a group of peers who share his interests in quiet games or computers.

### Importance of social competence

Whereas parents are the primary source of social and emotional support for children during the first years of life, in later years peers begin to play a significant complementary and unique role in promoting child social-emotional development. Increasingly with age, peers rather than parents become preferred companions, providing important sources of entertainment and support. In the context of peer interactions, young children engage in **fantasy** play that allows them to assume different roles, learn to take another person's perspective, and develop an understanding of the social rules and conventions of their culture. In addition, relationships with peers typically involve more give-and-take than relationships with adults, and thus provide an opportunity for the development of social competencies such as cooperation and negotiation. During **adolescence**, peer relations become particularly important for children. A key developmental task of adolescence is the formation of an identity—a sense of the kind of person you are and the kind of person you want to be. Adolescents "try on" different social roles as they interact with peers, and peers serve as a social "stepping stone" as adolescents move away from their emotional dependence upon their parents and toward autonomous functioning as an adult. In many ways, then, **childhood** peer relations serve as "training grounds" for future interpersonal relations, providing children with opportunities to learn about reciprocity and intimacy. These skills are associated with effective interpersonal relations in adult life, including relations with co-workers and with romantic partners.

When children experience serious difficulties in the domain of peer relations, the development of social competencies may be threatened. Rejection or victimization by peers may become a source of significant **stress** to children, contributing to feelings of loneliness and low **self-esteem**. In addition, peer rejection can escalate in a negative developmental spiral. That is, when children with poor social skills become rejected, they are often excluded from positive interactions with peers—interactions that are critical for the learning of social skills. Rejected children typically have fewer options in terms of play partners and friends than do accepted children. Observations of rejected children have revealed that they spend more time playing alone and interacting in smaller groups than their more popular peers. In addition, the companions of rejected children tend to be younger or more unpopular than the companions of accepted children. Exclusion from a **normal** peer group can deprive rejected children of opportunities to develop adaptive social behaviors. Hence, the social competence deficits of rejected children may increase over time, along with feelings of social anxiety and inadequacy.

### Social competence deficits and peer rejection

Many children experience difficulties getting along with peers at some point during their youth. Sometimes these problems are short-lived and for some children the effects of being left out or teased by classmates are transitory. For other children, however, being ignored or rejected by peers may be a lasting problem that has life-long consequences, such as a dislike for school, poor self-esteem, social withdrawal, and difficulties with adult relationships.

Considerable research has been undertaken to try to understand why some children experience serious and long-lasting difficulties in the area of peer relations. To explore factors leading to peer difficulties, researchers typically employ the sociometric method to identify children who are or are not successful with peers. In this method, children in a classroom or a group are asked to list children who they like most and those who they like least. Children who receive many positive ("like most") nominations and few negative ("like least") nominations are classified as"popular;" those who receive few positive and few negative nominations are designated"neglected," and those who receive few positive and many negative nominations are classified as"rejected."

Evidence compiled from studies using child interviews, direct observations, and teacher ratings all suggest that popular children exhibit high levels of social competence. They are friendly and cooperative and engage readily in conversation. Peers describe them as helpful, nice, understanding, attractive, and good at games. Popular and socially competent children are able to consider others' perspectives, can sustain their **attention** to the play task, and are able to "keep their cool" in situations involving conflict. They are agreeable and have good problem-solving skills. Socially competent children are also sensitive to the nuances of "play etiquette." They enter a group using diplomatic strategies, such as commenting upon the ongoing activity and asking permission to join in. They uphold standards of equity and show good sportsmanship, making them good companions and fun play partners.

Children who have problems making friends, those who are either "neglected" or "rejected" sociometrically, often show deficits in social skills. One of the most common reasons for **friendship** problems is behavior that annoys other children. Children, like adults, do not like behavior that is bossy, self-centered, or disruptive. It is simply not fun to play with someone who doesn't share or doesn't follow the rules. Sometimes children who have learning problems or attention problems can have trouble making friends, because they find it hard to understand and follow the rules of games. Children who get angry easily and lose their temper when things don't go their way can also have a hard time getting along with others. Children who are rejected by peers often have difficulties focusing their attention and controlling their behavior. They may show high rates of noncompliance, interference with others, or aggression (teasing or fighting). Peers often describe rejected classmates as disruptive, short-tempered, unattractive, and likely to brag, to start fights, and to get in trouble with the teacher.

Not all aggressive children are rejected by their peers. Children are particularly likely to become rejected if they show a wide range of conduct problems, including disruptive, hyperactive, and disagreeable behaviors in addition to physical aggression. Socially competent children who are aggressive tend to use aggression in a way that is accepted by peers (e.g., fighting back when provoked), whereas the aggressive acts of rejected children include tantrums, verbal insults, cheating, or tattling. In addition, aggressive children are more likely to be rejected if they are hyperactive, immature, and lacking in positive social skills.

Children can also have friendship problems because they are very shy and feel uncomfortable and unsure of themselves around others. Sometimes children are ignored or teased by classmates because there is something "different" about them that sets them apart from other children. When children are shy in the classroom and ignored by classmates, becoming classified as "neglected," it does not necessarily indicate deficits in social competence. Many neglected children have friendships outside of the classroom setting, and their neglected status is simply a reflection of their quiet attitude and low profile in the classroom. Developmentally, peer neglect is not a very stable classification, and many neglected children develop more confidence as they move into classrooms with more familiar or more compatible peers. However, some shy children are highly anxious socially, and uncomfortable around peers in many situations. Shy, passive children who are actively disliked and rejected by classmates often become teased and victimized. These children often do have deficits in core areas of social competence that have a negative impact on their social development. For example, many are emotionally dependent on adults, and immature in their social behavior. They may be inattentive, moody, depressed, or emotionally volatile, making it difficult for them to sustain positive play interactions with others.

The long-term consequences of sustained peer rejection can be quite serious. Often, deficits in social competence and peer rejection coincide with other emotional and behavioral problems, including attention deficits, aggression, and **depression**. The importance of social competence and satisfying social relations is life-long. Studies of adults have revealed that friendship is a critical source of social support that protects against the negative effects of life stress. People with few friends are at elevated risk for depression and anxiety.

Childhood peer rejection predicts a variety of difficulties in later life, including school problems, **mental health** disorders, and **antisocial behavior**. In fact, in one study, peer rejection proved to be a more sensitive predictor of later mental health problems than school records, achievement, and IQ scores or teacher ratings.

It appears, then, that positive peer relations play an important role in supporting the process of healthy social and **emotional development**. Problematic peer relations are associated with both concurrent and future maladjustment of children, and hence warrant serious attention from parents and professionals working with children. When assessing the possible factors contributing to a child's social difficulties and when planning remedial interventions, it is important to understand developmental processes associated with social competence and peer relations.

## Developmental changes and social competence

The key markers of social competence listed in the previous section are remarkably consistent across the developmental periods of the preschool years, middle childhood, and adolescence. Across these developmental periods, prosocial skills (friendly, cooperative, helpful behaviors) and self-control skills (**anger** management, negotiation skills, problem-solving skills) are key facets of social competence. In addition, however, developmental changes occur in the structure and quality of peer interactions which affect the complexity of skills contributing to social competence. That is, as children grow, their preferences for play change, and the thinking skills and language skills that provide a foundation for social competence also change. Hence, the kinds of interactions that children have with peers change qualitatively and quantitatively with development.

The ways in which children spend their time together, for example, changes with development. During the preschool years, social competence involves the ability to separate from parents and engage with peers in shared play activities, particularly fantasy play. As preschool children are just learning to coordinate their social behavior, their interactions are often short and marked by frequent squabbles, and friendships are less stable than at later developmental stages. In addition, physical rough-and-tumble play is common, particularly among boys.

By grade school, children begin to develop an interest in sports, structured board games, and group games with complex sets of rules. Being able to understand and follow game rules and being able to handle **competition** in appropriate ways (e.g., being a good sport) become important skills for social competence. Children play primarily in same-sex groups of friends, and expect more stability in their friendships. Loyalty and dependability become important qualities of good friends.

During the preadolescent and early adolescent years, communication (including sending notes, calling on the phone, and "hanging out") becomes a major focus for peer interactions. Increasingly, social competence involves the willingness and ability to share thoughts and feelings with one another, especially for girls. When adolescent friends squabble, their conflicts typically center around issues such as gossiping, disclosing secrets, or loyalty and perceived betrayal. It is at this stage that friends and romantic partners consistently rival parents as the primary sources of intimacy and social support.

In addition to developmental changes in the content and focus of peer relations, development brings changes in the structure of peer relations. During the preschool and early grade school years, children are primarily focused on group acceptance and having companions to spend time with and play with. However, during the middle to late grade school years, children begin to distinguish "regular" friends from "best" friends. The establishment of close, best friendships is an important developmental milestone. That is, in addition to gaining acceptance from a group of peers, one of the hallmarks of social competence is the ability to form and maintain satisfying close friendships. Many of the positive characteristics that promote popularity (such as cooperativeness, friendliness, and consideration for others) also assist children in developing and maintaining friendships. Friendships emerge when children share similar activities and interests and, in addition, when they develop a positive and mutual bond between them. Group acceptance and close friendships follow different timetables and serve different developmental functions, with the need for group acceptance emerging during the early grade school years and filling a need for belonging, and the need for close friends emerging in preadolescence to meet newfound needs for affection, alliance, and intimacy outside the **family**. Key features of close friendships are reciprocity and similarity, mutual intimacy, and social support.

A third major shift in the complexity of peer relations involves the changing role of **cliques** and crowds. Grade school children often have little conception of peer groups. For example, when we interviewed fifth graders and asked them about groups at their school, a typical reply was, "what do you mean, reading groups?" In contrast, by eighth grade, children had distinct ideas about groups at their school, responding to our questions with labels such as "the jocks, the brains, the nerds." The recognition of cliques and crowds as organizational structures of the peer group usually emerges during early adolescence. In part, the understanding of cliques reflects a cognitive advance, as children in adolescence are able to use formal operational thinking to consider abstract ideas such as "cliques" and apply them to their thinking about peers. In part, the rise of cliques in the organizational structure of peer groups reflects the structure of American schools, which typically transition from small elementary schools to large middle schools or junior high schools around sixth or seventh grade. The change in the school context has a large impact on the nature of the peer group, as the typical middle school or junior high school peer group involves a very large and diverse set of peers. In the context of this large group, children associate with smaller networks of familiar classmates. Typically, the grouping into friendship networks takes place on the basis of shared interests, activities, and attitudes. Children in the same friendship networks influence each other in matters of dress, behavior, and language, leading to identifiable characteristics of group members that become the basis for group labels (e.g., jocks or brains).

From an emotional standpoint, adolescents are focused on developing a sense of themselves and in sorting out how their identities fit (or do not fit) with the expectations of others and the social niches available to them. As a correlate to identity formation, adolescents become keenly aware of group peer norms and increasingly seek to associate with peers and use peer standards to evaluate their own and other's social behavior. Whereas in grade school peer status referred to one's state of acceptance or rejection from the classroom group, by adolescence one's peer status is complicated by the nature of the various groups toward which one may seek and attain (or be refused) membership status. In other words, in addition to finding friends, adolescents often worry about their placement in the larger social structure of cliques and crowds.

The increased level of social awareness and self-consciousness that accompanies the advanced social reasoning of adolescence and the increased importance that adolescents place on **peer acceptance** may strengthen the impact of perceived peer rejection on emotional adjustment and **self-concept**. Social ostracism or self-imposed isolation my also become a more important determinant of peer rejection during adolescence than at younger ages.

At all ages, the treatment a child receives from peers may influence his or her social adaptation. Once rejected by peers, disliked children may find themselves excluded from peer activities and exposed to ostracism, or more severely to victimization by peers. Peers may develop negatively biased attitudes and expectations for rejected children and treat these children differently (with more counteraggression and **hostility**) than they treat their well-accepted peers. Children who are particularly stressed by the academic demands of school, such as those aggressive-rejected children with attentional deficits or hyperactive behaviors, may be at increased risk for negative interactions with teachers and peers. Over time, teachers tend to become less positive and less contingent in their reactions to these problematic students, decreasing their effectiveness at managing social behavior.

During the preadolescent and later adolescent years, the combination of ostracism from conventional peer groups and the evolution of peer group cliques and crowds can be problematic for rejected children. That is, adolescents who feel pushed out of the conventional peer groups may begin to affiliate with defiant peers. As cliques of deviant peers form in adolescence, these groups may begin to exert a strong influence on children, **shaping** their attitudes and social behaviors and increasing the likelihood of future antisocial and deviant behavior. Particularly in adolescence, youth turn to their peer groups for guidance in matters of dress code, social behavior, social attitudes, and identity formation. In peer networks containing many members who exhibit high rates of aggression, group norms are likely to be accepting of aggression. Hence, although affiliations with deviant peers may provide companionship and support, the "cost" of such affiliations may be great in terms of their negative influence exacerbating antisocial behavior and attitudes. Preadolescent children who form friendships with antisocial peers appear to be at heightened risk for later antisocial behavior, including delinquency, drug use, and school dropout.

## Family contributions to social competence

Because the family is the primary context for social development, there are a number of ways in which family interaction patterns may help or hinder the development of children's social competence. Some researchers have speculated that the origins of social competence can be found in **infancy**, in the quality of the parent-child **attachment** relationship. Studies have shown that babies whose parents are consistent and sensitive in their responses to distress are less irritable, less anxious, and better emotionally regulated. By contrast, parents who are inconsistent and insensitive to their infants' signals are more likely to have anxious, irritable babies who are difficult to soothe. These children may learn both to model their parents' insensitivity and to rely on intrusive, demanding behavior of their own in order to get attention. If they then generalize these socially incompetent behaviors to their peer interactions, peer rejection may result.

As children get older, family interaction styles and the ways in which parents discipline may play a primary role in the development of noncompliant or aggressive behaviors in children. In families where parents are extremely demanding and use inconsistent, harsh, and punitive discipline strategies, family interaction patterns are frequently characterized by escalation and conflict, and children often exhibit behavior problems. When children generalize the aggressive and oppositional behavior that they have learned at home to their interactions with peers, other children often reject them. Indeed, research has revealed that aggressive behavior is the common link between harsh, inconsistent discipline and rejection by peers.

By contrast, parents of popular children are typically more positive and less demanding with their children than parents of unpopular children. In addition, parents of popular children "set a good example" by **modeling** appropriate social interactions, and assist their children by arranging opportunities for peer interaction, carefully supervising these experiences, and providing helpful feedback about **conflict resolution** and making friends.

## Child characteristics and social competence

In addition to family interaction patterns and various aspects of the parent-child relationship, children's own thoughts, feelings, and attitudes may influence their social behavior. Research has revealed that many rejected children make impulsive, inaccurate, and incomplete judgments about how to behave in social situations and are lacking in social problem-solving skills. They may make numerous errors in processing social information, including misinterpretation of other people's motives and behavior, setting social goals for themselves that are unrealistic or inappropriate, and making poor decisions about their own conduct in social situations. For example, aggressive children are more likely to interpret an accidental push or bump from a peer as intentionally hostile, and respond accordingly. Similarly, socially incompetent children are often more interested in "getting even" with peers for injustices than they are in finding positive solutions to social problems, and expect that aggressive, coercive strategies will lead to desired outcomes.

Many children who are rejected by peers have lower self-esteem, feel lonelier, and are more dissatisfied with their social situations than are average or popular children. These feelings can cause them to give up and avoid social situations, which can in turn exacerbate their peer problems. Interestingly, not all rejected children feel badly about their social difficulties. Studies have shown that aggressive-rejected children, who tend to blame outside factors for their peer problems, are less likely to express distress than withdrawn-rejected children, who often attribute their problems to themselves.

## Assessing social competence

There is an important difference between not being "popular" and having friendship problems. Some children are outgoing and have many friends. Other children are quite content with just a good friend or two. Either one of these friendship patterns is fine. Distinguishing "normative" friendship problems from problematic peer relations that signal serious deficits in social competence is an important goal of assessment. There are several key signs that a child's peer difficulties may be more serious and long-lasting rather than temporary. First, the nature of the child's social behavior is important. If children behave aggressively with peers, act bossy and domineering, or are disruptive and impulsive at school, they are more likely to have stable and long-lasting peer difficulties than are children who are simply shy. Children who display aggressive or disruptive behavior often have many discouraging experiences at school, including discipline problems and learning difficulties as well as poor peer relations. School adjustment can be a downhill slide for these children as teachers may get discouraged and peers may get angered by their behaviors. Peers may attempt to "get back" at these children by teasing, which

only increases the frustrations and helplessness experienced by aggressive, disruptive children.

Second, children who are actively disliked, teased, or ostracized by peers are at more risk than children who are simply ignored. It is not necessary for a child to be popular in order to gain the advantages of peer support. When children are ignored by peers and are neither disliked nor liked, teachers and parents can take steps to foster friendship development and peer support. When children are actively disliked by peers and the victims of teasing or ostracism, the task is harder for parents and teachers and the likelihood of the child reestablishing positive peer relations without help is slimmer.

Third, the stability and chronicity of peer problems should be considered. It is not unusual for children to experience short-term social difficulties when they are moving into new peer situations, such as a new school or a new classroom. Peer problems may also emerge if children are distressed about other changes in their lives, such as a reaction to parental conflict or the **birth** of a sibling. When peer problems emerge at a time that corresponds to other family or situational changes, they may serve as signals to let parents and teachers know that the child needs extra support at that time. When peer problems have been stable and have existed for a long time, more extensive intervention focused on improving peer relations may be needed.

There is a variety of methods available for the assessment of social competence. When choosing a particular assessment strategy, it is important to consider the nature of a particular child's problem. Some children have difficulty with all types of social relationships, while others do well in their neighborhoods or in one-on-one friendships but experience problems with the peer group at school. When problems occur in the school setting, teachers and other school personnel who have opportunities to see children interacting in several peer group situations (such as the classroom, playground, and lunchroom) are often the best first step in assessment. Teachers can often provide information about how children treat and are treated by peers, and can also offer opinions about how typical or unusual a child's peer problems are relative to others of the same age. Teacher assessments can include behavioral checklists and rating scales and direct observations of specific social behaviors.

Similarly, parents can also provide information about children's social competence. Parents can help to identify problem behaviors such as aggression, withdrawal, and noncompliance that may interfere with social skills. In addition, parents are usually more aware than teachers of their children's social activities outside of school, such as their participation in sports, clubs, or hobbies.

Because they do not have access to the full range of situations in which children interact, however, teachers and parents may not always be the best source of information on children's peer problems. In some cases, it is most helpful to get information directly from peers themselves. One method of obtaining such information is the use of sociometric ratings and nominations. With these procedures, all of the children in a classroom are asked to rate how much they like to play with or spend time with each of their classmates. In addition, they nominate specific peers with whom they particularly like or dislike, and may be asked to identify peers who exhibit particular behavioral characteristics (e.g., nice, aggressive, shy, etc.). The sociometric method, although cumbersome to administer, identifies children who are popular, rejected, and neglected by their peers more accurately than parent or teacher reports, and provides useful information about the reasons for peer dislike.

A third approach to assessment of social competence involves children's self-reports. Although input from parents, teachers, and peers can provide valuable insight into children's social behavior and their status within the peer group, information regarding children's thoughts, feelings, and perceptions of their social situations can be obtained only by asking the children themselves. Depending upon the age of the child, information about social competence can be obtained through the use of questionnaires and rating scales that measure children's self-perceptions of their peer relations, the use of stories and hypothetical social situations to elicit information about the child's social reasoning, or simply talking with children to determine their perspectives on their social situations.

Because children may have different experiences in different kinds of peer settings and because no one particular method of assessment is entirely reliable or complete, it is desirable to use a variety of sources when attempting to assess children's social competence. Teacher, parent, peer, and self-reports may yield distinct but complementary information, and hence, by gathering multiple perspectives, a more complete picture of a child's social strengths and weaknesses can be obtained.

## Interventions to promote social competence

Different strategies may be needed to help children develop social competencies and establish positive peer relations depending upon the age of the child and the type of peer problem being experienced. Different children have different needs when it comes to helping them get along better with others and making friends. The age of the child, the kinds of behaviors that are part of the problem, the reasons for the friendship problem—all of these may affect the development of the helping strategy.

One strategy involves social skill training. Observations have revealed that children who are well-liked by peers typically show helpful, courteous, and considerate behavior. The purpose of social skill training is to help unpopular children learn to treat their peers in positive ways. The specific skills taught in different programs vary depending upon the age and type of child involved. Commonly taught skills include helping, sharing, and cooperation. Often children are taught how to enter a group, how to be a good group participant, how to be a fair player (e.g., following rules, taking turns), and how to have a conversation with peers. The skills might also include anger management, negotiation, and conflict resolution skills. Problem solving skills (e.g., identifying the problem, considering alternative solutions, choosing a solution and making a plan) are often included in social skill training programs. Sometimes social skill training is done individually with children, but often it is done in a small group. A particular skill concept is discussed, and children may watch a short film or hear a story that illustrates the usefulness of the skill. They then have the opportunity to practice the skill during activities or role-plays with other children in the group. A trained group leader helps guide the children in their use of the skill and provides support and positive feedback to help children become more natural and spontaneous in socially skillful behavior.

Another intervention strategy focuses on helping children who are having trouble getting along with others because of angry, aggressive, or bossy behavior. It can be difficult to suppress aggressive and disruptive behaviors in peer settings for several reasons. For one thing, these behaviors often "work" in the sense that they can be instrumental in achieving desired goals. By complaining loudly, hitting, or otherwise using force or noise, children may be able to get access to a toy they want or they may be able to get peers to stop doing something noxious to them. In this type of situation, an adult's expressed disapproval may suppress the behavior, but the behavior is likely to emerge again in situations where an adult supervisor is not present. Often contracts and point systems are used to suppress aggressive behavior and bossiness; however, positive skill training must be used in conjunction with behavior management in order to provide the child with alternative skills to use in situations requiring negotiations with peers. Often parents are included in programs to help children develop better anger management skills and to help children reduce fighting. Trained counselors, educators, or psychologists work with parents to help them find positive discipline strategies and positive communication skills to promote child anger management and conflict resolution skills.

A third helping strategy focuses on finding a good social "niche" for the child. Large, unstructured peer group settings (such as recess) are particularly difficult situations for many of the children who have peer problems. These children need a more structured, smaller peer interaction setting in which an adult's support is available to guide positive peer interaction. Finding a good social "niche" for some children can be a difficult task, but an important one. Sometimes a teacher can organize cooperative learning groups that help an isolated child make friends in the classroom. Sometimes parents can help by inviting potential friends over to play or getting their child involved in a social activity outside of school that is rewarding (such as scouting, church group, sports groups). Providing positive opportunities for friendship development is important, as it provides children with an appropriate and positive learning environment for the development of social competence.

Janet A. Welsh, Ph.D., Karen L. Bierman, Ph.D.

## Further Reading

Asher, Steven R., et al. *Children's Social Development: Information for Teachers and Parents.* Urbana, IL: ERIC Clearinghouse on Elementary and Early Childhood Education, University of Illinois, 1987.

——— and J. D. Coie. (eds.) *Peer Rejection in Childhood.* Cambridge, Eng.: Cambridge University Press, 1990.

——— and John M. Gottman. (eds.) *The Development of Children's Friendships.* Cambridge, Eng.: Cambridge University Press, 1981.

Berndt, Thomas J., and Gary W. Ladd. (eds.) *Peer Relationships in Child Development.* New York: Wiley, 1989.

Bierman, Karen L. "Improving the Peer Relationships of Rejected Children." In Lahey, B., and A. Kazdin (eds.), *Advances in Clinical Child Psychology.* New York: Plenum, 1989, pp. 53-84.

Bukowski, William M., Andrew Newcomb, and Willard W. Hartup. (eds.) *The Company They Keep: Friendship During Childhood and Adolescence.* New York: Cambridge University Press, 1996.

Cicchetti, Dante, and William M. Bukowski. "Developmental Processes in Peer Relations and Psychopathology." *Development and Psychopathology* 7, 1995, pp. 587-89.

Coie, J. D., and G. K. Koeppl. "Adapting Intervention to the Problems of Aggressive and Disruptive Children." In Asher, S. R., & J. D. Coie. (eds.) *Peer Rejection in Childhood.* New York: Cambridge University Press, l990, pp. 275-308.

Crick, N. R., and K. A. Dodge. "A Review and Reformulation of Social Information-Processing Mechanisms in Children's Social Adjustment." *Psychological Bulletin* 115, 1994, pp. 74-101.

Dodge, K. A., and R. R. Murphy. "The Assessment of Social Competence in Adolescents." *Advances in Child Behavior Analysis and Therapy* 3, 1984, pp. 61-96.

Dodge, K. A. "Problems in Social Relationships." In Mash, E., and R. Barkley (eds.) *Treatment of Childhood Disorders.* New York: Guilford Press, l989, pp. 222-44.

Hartup, Willard W. "Social Relationships and Their Developmental Significance." *American Psychologist* 44, 1989, pp. 120-26.

Olweus, D. "Victimization by Peers: Antecedents and Long-Term Outcomes." In Rubin, Kenneth H., and J.B. Asendorpf (eds.) *Social Withdrawal, Inhibition and Shyness in Childhood.* Hillsdale, NJ: Erlbaum, 1993, pp. 315-344.

Parke, R. D., and G. W. Ladd. *Family-Peer Relationships: Modes of Linkage.* Hillsdale, NJ: Erlbaum, 1992.

Parker, J., and S. R. Asher. "Peer Acceptance and Later Personal Adjustment: Are Low-Accepted Children at Risk?" *Psychological Bulletin* 102, no. 3, 1987, pp. 357-89.

Pepler, Debra J., and Kenneth H. Rubin. (eds.) *The Development and Treatment of Childhood Aggression.* Hillsdale, NJ: L. Erlbaum, 1991.

Rubin, K. H., and S. L Stewart. "Social Withdrawal." In Mash, E.J., and R. A.Barkley. (eds.) *Child Psychopathology.* New York: Guilford, 1996, pp. 277-310.

Schneider, B., K. H. Rubin, and J. E. Ledingham, (eds.) *Children's Peer Relations: Issues in Assessment and Intervention.* New York: Springer-Verlag, 1985.

# Social influence

The influence of others on an individual's behavior.

Human behavior is influenced by other people in countless ways and on a variety of levels. The mere presence of others—as co-actors or spectators—can stimulate or improve one's performance of a task, a process known as social facilitation (and also observed in non-human species). However, the increased level of arousal responsible for this phenomenon can backfire and create social interference, impairing performance on complex, unfamiliar, and difficult tasks.

Overt, deliberate persuasion by other people can cause us to change our opinions and/or behavior. However, a great deal of social influence operates more subtly in the form of norms—acquired social rules that people are generally unaware of until they are violated. For example, every culture has a **norm** for "personal space"—the physical distance maintained between adults. Violation of norms generally makes people uncomfortable, while adherence to them provides security and confidence in a variety of social situations. Norms may be classified as one of two types: descriptive and injunctive. Descriptive norms are simply based on what a majority of people do, while injunctive norms involve a value judgment about what is proper and improper behavior.

Both **conformity** and compliance are attempts to adhere to social norms—conformity occurs in response to unspoken group pressure, as opposed to compliance, which results from a direct request. Research has shown that conformity is influenced by the ambiguity of a situation (people are more apt to go along with the majority when they are uncertain about which course of action to pursue), the size of the majority, and the personal characteristics of the people involved, including their **self-esteem** and their status within the group. A person may conform by acting in accordance with group norms while privately disagreeing with them (public conformity) or by actually changing his or her opinions to coincide with those of the group (private acceptance).

In contrast to compliance, which characterizes behavior toward those who make direct requests but have no authority over us, obedience is elicited in response to a specific demand by an authority figure. The most famous experiment involving obedience was conducted by **Stanley Milgram** in the early 1960s at Yale University. Forty men and women were instructed to administer electric shocks to another person, supposedly as part of an experiment in learning. (In fact, there were actually no shocks administered, and responses were faked by the "victim," who was part of the experiment.) When the scientist in charge directed the subjects to administer increasingly severe shocks, most of them, while uncomfortable, did so in spite of the apparent **pain** and protests of the supposed victim. This experiment—which is often referred to in connection with German obedience to authority during the Nazi era—gained widespread attention as evidence of the extent to which people will forfeit their own judgment, will, and values in order to follow orders by an authority figure (65 percent of the volunteers, when asked to do so, administered the maximum level of shock possible). In variations on this experiment, Milgram found that factors affecting obedience included the reputation of the authority figure and his proximity to the subject (obedience decreased when instructions were issued by phone), as well as the presence of others who disobey (the most powerful factor in reducing the level of obedience).

Another type of social influence that can lead **normal** people to engage in cruel or **antisocial behavior** is participation in a crowd or mob. Being part of a crowd can allow a person's identity to become submerged in a group, a process known as deindividuation. Contributing factors include anonymity, which

Cal Ripkin, who broke the record for consecutive major league baseball games played, waves to his home crowd. The home advantage in sports is due to the social influence of the crowd. *(Archive Photos, Inc. Reproduced with permission.)*

brings with it a reduction of accountability; a high level of arousal; and a shifting of attention from oneself to external events, resulting in reduced self-awareness. The so-called "herd mentality" that results weakens people's normal restraints against impulsive behavior, increases their sensitivity to environmental stimuli, and reduces their abilities to think rationally and **fear** censure by others.

The relatively new field of environmental psychology investigates the ways in which human behavior is affected by proximity to others in urban environments, most notably the effects of noise and overcrowding. Living in high-density environments has been associated with feelings of helplessness resulting from lack of control and predictability in one's social interactions.

### Further Reading
Freedman, J. L., D. O. Sears, and J. M. Carlsmith. *Social Psychology.* 4th ed. Englewood Cliffs, NJ: Prentice-Hall, 1981.
Milgram, Stanley. *Obedience to Authority: An Experimental View.* New York: Harper and Row, 1974.
Paulus, P. B., ed. *Psychology of Group Influence.* 2nd ed. Hillsdale, NJ: Lawrence Erlbaum Associates, 1989.

# Social learning theory

An approach to personality that emphasizes the interaction between personal traits and environment and their mediation by cognitive processes.

Social **learning theory** has its roots in the behaviorist notion of human behavior as being determined by learning, particularly as shaped by **reinforcement** in the form of rewards or **punishment**. Early research in **behaviorism** conducted by **Ivan Pavlov**, **John Watson**, and **B. F. Skinner** used animals in a laboratory. Subsequently, researchers became dissatisfied with the capacity of their findings to fully account for the complexities of human **personality**. Criticism centered particularly on the fact that behaviorism's focus on observable behaviors left out the role played by **cognition**.

The first major theory of social learning, that of Julian B. Rotter, argued that cognition, in the form of expectations, is a crucial factor in social learning. In his influential 1954 book, *Social Learning and Clinical Psychology*, Rotter claimed that behavior is determined by two major types of "expectancy": the expected outcome of a behavior and the value a person places on that outcome. In *Applications of a Social Learning Theory of Personality* (1972), Rotter, in collaboration with June Chance and Jerry Phares, described a general theory of personality with variables based on the ways that different individuals habitually think about their experiences. One of the major variables was I-E, which distinguished "internals," who think of themselves as controlling events, from "externals," who view events as largely outside their control. Correlations have since been found between I-E orientations and a variety of behaviors, ranging from job performance to attitudes toward one's health.

The social learning theories of **Albert Bandura** emphasize the reciprocal relationship among cognition, behavior, and **environment**, for which Bandura coined the term reciprocal **determinism**. Hostile thoughts can result in hostile behavior, for example, which can effect our environment by making others hostile and evoking additional hostile thoughts. Thus, not only does our environment influence our thoughts and behavior—our thoughts and behavior also play a role in determining our environment. Bandura is especially well known for his research on the importance of **imitation** and reinforcement in learning. His work on **modeling** has been influential in the development of new therapeutic approaches, especially the methods used in cognitive-behavior therapy. Bandura also expanded on Rotter's notion of expectancy by arguing that our expectations about the outcome of situations are heavily influenced by whether or not we think we will succeed at the things

we attempt. Bandura introduced the term self-efficacy for this concept, arguing that it has a high degree of influence not only on our expectations but also on our performance itself.

Most recently, Walter Mischel, building on the work of both Rotter and Bandura, has framed the determinants of human behavior in particular situations in terms of "person variables." These include competencies (those things we know we can do); perceptions (how we perceive our environment); expectations (what we expect will be the outcome of our behavior); subject values (our goals and ideals); and self-regulation and plans (our standards for ourselves and plans for reaching our goals).

**Further Reading**

Bandura, Albert. *Social Learning Theory.* Englewood Cliffs, NJ: Prentice-Hall, 1971.
———. *Social Foundations of Thought and Action: A Social Cognitive Theory.* Englewood Cliffs, NJ: Prentice-Hall, 1986.

# Social perception

The processes through which people form impressions of others and interpret information about them.

Researchers have confirmed the conventional wisdom that first impressions are important. Studies show that first impressions are easily formed, difficult to change, and have a long-lasting influence. Rather than absorbing each piece of new information about an individual in a vacuum, it is common for people to invoke a preexisting prototype or schema based on some aspect of the person (for example, "grandmother" or "graduate student"), modifying it with specific information about the particular individual to arrive at an overall first impression. One term for this process is schema-plus-correction. It can be dangerous because it allows people to infer many things from a very limited amount of information, which partially explains why first impressions are often wrong.

If there is no special reason to think negatively about a person, one's first impression of that person will normally be positive, as people tend to give others the benefit of the doubt. However, people are especially attentive to negative factors, and if these are present, they will outweigh the positive ones in generating impressions. One reason first impressions are so indelible is that people have a tendency to interpret new information about a person in a light that will reinforce their first impression. They also tend to remember the first impression, or overall schema, better than any subsequent corrections. Thus if a person whom one thinks of as competent makes a mistake, it will tend to be overlooked and eventually forgotten, and the original impression is the one that will prevail. Conversely, one will tend to forget or undervalue good work performed by someone initially judged to be incompetent. In addition, people often treat each other in ways that tend to elicit behavior that conforms to their impressions of each other.

Besides impression formation, the other key area focused on in the study of social **perception** is attribution, the thought processes we employ in explaining the behavior of other people and our own as well. The most fundamental observation we make about a person's behavior is whether it is due to internal or external causes (Is the behavior determined by the person's own characteristics or by the situation in which it occurs?). We tend to base this decision on a combination of three factors. Consensus refers to whether other people exhibit similar behavior; consistency refers to whether the behavior occurs repeatedly; and distinctiveness is concerned with whether the behavior occurs in other, similar situations.

Certain cognitive biases tend to influence whether people attribute behavior to internal or external causes. When we observe the behavior of others, our knowledge of the external factors influencing that behavior is limited, which often leads us to attribute it to internal factors (a tendency known as the fundamental attribution error). However, we are aware of numerous external factors that **play** a role in our own behavior. This fact, combined with a natural desire to think well of ourselves, produces actor-observer bias, a tendency to attribute our own behavior (especially when inappropriate or unsuccessful) to external factors.

**Further Reading**
Zebrowitz, Leslie. *Social Perception*. Pacific Grove, CA: Brooks/Cole Publishing Co., 1990.

# Social psychology

The study of the psychology of interpersonal relationships.

Social psychology is the study of human interaction, including communication, cooperation, **competition**, **leadership**, and attitude development. Although the first textbooks on the subject of social psychology were published in the early 1900s, much of the foundation for social psychology studied in the 1990s is based on the work of the behavioral psychologists of the 1930s. Behavioral psychologists were among the first to call for

scientific measures and analysis of human behavior, an emphasis on which social psychologists continue to focus. Social psychologists also study the way individuals behave in relationship to others, and, alternatively, how groups act to shape the behavior of individuals.

As do other scientists, social psychologists develop a theory and then design experiments to test it. For example, Leon Feistinger, an American social psychologist, theorized that a person feels uncomfortable when confronted with information that contradicts something he or she already believes. He labeled this uneasiness **cognitive dissonance**. Other social psychologists subsequently conducted research to confirm Feistinger's theory by studying individuals who believed themselves to be failures. The psychologists found that such people avoid success, even when it would be easily achieved, because it would conflict with their firmly held belief that they are unsuccessful.

Social psychologists work in academic settings, teaching and conducting research. They also work with businesses and other organizations to design personnel management programs based on their knowledge of interpersonal relations. Social psychologists also contribute their expertise to market research, government agencies, and educational institutions.

**Further Reading**
Argyle, Michael. *The Social Psychology of Everyday Life*. New York: Routledge, 1992.
Aronson, Elliot. *The Social Animal*. New York: W.H. Freeman, 1995.
Bandura, Albert. *Social Foundations of Thought and Action: A Social and Cognitive Theory*. Englewood Cliffs, NJ: Prentice-Hall, 1986.
Baron, Robert A. *Exploring Social Psychology*. Boston, MA: Allyn and Bacon, 1989.

# Socialization

The process by which a person learns to conform individual behavior and responses to the norms and values of society.

Socialization is a lifelong process that begins during **infancy** in the complex interaction between parent and child. As parents respond to a baby's physical requirements for food and shelter, they are also beginning to teach the baby what to expect from their **environment** and how to communicate their needs. The action-reaction cycle of smiling, cooing, and touching is a child's earliest interaction with "society." It is believed that these early interactions during infancy play a major role

As children are socialized, they learn which behaviors are acceptable and which are unacceptable. Boys are often encouraged to imitate their fathers' activities, as this boy is doing. *(David Frazier. Photo Researchers, Inc. Reproduced with permission.)*

in future social adjustment. Consistent, responsive care helps lead to healthy relationships with others and **normal** personal development. Caretakers who neglect an infant's needs or otherwise stifle early attempts at communication can cause serious damage to the child's future social interactions.

The **family** is the most influential socialization force. Parents, grandparents, and siblings all transmit to infants and young children what they consider to be important values, behavior, skills, and attitudes. Household rules govern behavior, interpersonal behavior serves as a model for interactions with outside people, and socially valued qualities such as generosity and caring are learned through example within the home and in the culture. As children grow and interact more with the environment outside the family home, others begin to play important roles in the socialization process. Friends, institutions such as church and school, the media (particularly television) and co-workers all become important factors in **shaping** a person's attitudes and behavior.

Researchers have theorized that socialization is a complex process that involves both personal and environmental factors. For example, studies of aggressive

tendencies in children have pointed out that certain children are more influenced than others when exposed to television **violence** or aggressive behavior by authority figures in the home. Some blind and deaf children display aggressive behavior such as stamping feet or yelling even though they have never had the opportunity to see or hear such displays of temper. Thus, it has been concluded that genetic factors must also be considered part of the socialization process.

Studies of sex-type models also point to this complex interaction between environmental and genetic factors. While many researchers believe that most of the stereotypical differences between boys and girls are invalid, some do appear significant. For example, boys tend to perform better on tests involving spatial relationships, and girls tend to score better on tests involving verbal skills. There is such an overlap among boys and girls, even on these tests, that it would be impossible to predict the scores of an individual boy or girl. It is believed, however, that perceived differences often **affect** the behavior of one of the most influential socialization forces of children—teachers. Some teachers reinforce the male image of dominance and independence by responding more to boys and demanding more from them in the classroom. Girls are often rewarded for passive, less demanding behavior. Similarly, some parents respond differently to sons and daughters, encouraging stereotypical behavior and traditionally male or female hobbies and careers. Media portrayals of one-dimensional characters can also perpetuate sex role stereotypes.

## Further Reading

Clark, John, ed. *The Mind: Into the Inner World.* New York: Torstar Books, 1986.

Zimbardo, Philip G. *Psychology and Life.* Glenview, IL: Scott, Foresman, 1988.

# Sociobiology

A term coined by the eminent entomologist Edward O. Wilson to define a field of study combining biology and social sciences.

In his 1975 work, *Sociobiology: The New Synthesis,* entomologist Edward O. Wilson first coined the term "sociobiology" to create a new field of study combining biology and social sciences, especially anthropology and sociology. Sociobiologists study the biological nature of human behavior and **personality** according to the tenet that all social behavior has a biological basis.

The field of sociobiology has not been widely accepted by contemporary theorists of personality and culture. The trend of social thought for several decades has been that humans are by and large responsible for their personal behaviors and for the ways they interact with others and with society as a whole. Wilson and other sociobiological theorists consider many human behaviors to be genetically based, including **aggression**, mother-child bond, language, the taboo against **incest**, sexual division of labor, altruism, allegiance, **conformity**, xenophobia, genocide, **ethics**, love, spite, and other emotions.

Traditional social scientists, however, debate sociobiology. Feminists have been particularly critical of the new field's view on gender roles. Feminists believe that gender roles are culturally determined. Sociobiologists see gender roles as basic human **traits** and point out that in almost no culture in the history of the world have women, for example, taken the role of sexual aggressor or exhibited a propensity to collect harems of sexually active men—two human traits that appear in nearly every culture.

Sociobiologists point to the mother-child bond as one of the prime examples of genetically based behavior. According to sociobiologists, the **attachment** a mother feels for her infant is a genetically programmed response to the biological need to continue the human gene pool. While this is almost certainly true to some extent, many psychologists and those in the various fields of social science argue otherwise. They point out that non-genetic mothers in contemporary society, for example, adoptive parents and step-mothers, demonstrate a bond just as deep as those between genetic mothers and their children.

Sociobiologists have also tried to explain the prevalence of gender stereotypes across different cultures. As children approach school age in Western culture, their experiences become more social and less domestic as they spend a great deal of time away from home with people other than their parents. During this time, children start to identify with their same-sex peers and learn stereotypical gender roles whether or not these roles are enforced in the home. Sociobiologists believe the current trend to avoid gender-marking is a wasted effort since gender roles are an intractable part of human nature.

Young boys tend to be aggressive in their **play**, while young girls tend to be reflective, or, to use a term widely applied in sociobiology, coy. This tendency is also seen in other primates and occurs across a variety of human cultures. It is therefore logical to assume that a young boy is naturally predisposed to aggressive behavior while a young girl is naturally predisposed to less violent modes of play. It is also widely held that boys and girls have different intellectual capacities, with boys being more adept at spatial reasoning and girls at verbal. There are reams of **standardized test** score data backing up such assertions, but it is not clear whether such differences are genetically determined.

Sociobiologists do not claim that aggression in males is acceptable. Even though male domination seems to be the predominant form of social organization, organized societies are not in any way obliged to defer to it. Social structures have for thousands of years modified what might be considered "natural" behaviors. Murder is an example. In preliterate societies murder is sanctioned under a variety of conditions. Human sacrifice, for example, used to play a large role in preliterate societies. But as societies develop, these "natural" tendencies are, necessarily, curbed. Instinctive behavior is replaced by social behavior because a culture sees social behavior as more desirable. While sociobiology may predict patterns of behavior in young children, there is no reason to believe that these tendencies cannot or should not be altered.

If there is any stage of life that most exemplifies the ideas of sociobiologists, it is **adolescence**. During this period, **hormones** are changing the body at a pace unmatched during any time in life, and with those changes in physical appearance, behavior also changes. Boys and girls take on social roles during adolescence that are radically different from their roles as children.

Some sociobiologists believe that many of the problems adolescents face in constructing their adult identities have a basis in evolution. There is increasing evidence, for instance, that certain adolescents are genetically predisposed to fall into clinical depressions. Genetic research has shown that many people suffering **depression** share a genetic abnormality that may only "turn on" if confronted with certain overwhelming social problems such as those faced by adolescents. There is also evidence that a predisposition to drugs and alcohol dependency is genetically determined. Recent studies have found links between several biological functions and anti-social and criminal behavior among adolescents. Included in this list are a slowly developing frontal lobe system in the **brain**, a variety of genes, a faulty **autonomic nervous system**, abnormal blood sugar levels, deviant brain waves, and hyperactivity. So, while specific behaviors are not linked to a specific gene or to evolutionary **adaptation**, a propensity to behave in a certain way, in the absence of more socially acceptable alternatives, may have a partial foundation in biology.

### Further Reading

Wilson, Edward. *Sociobiology—the New Synthesis.* Cambridge, MA: Harvard University Press, 1975
de Wal, Frans B.M. "The Biological Basis of Behavior." *The Chronicle of Higher Education,* June 14, 1996, p. B1.
Horgan, John. "The New Social Darwinists." *Scientific American,* October, 1995, p. 174.
————. "Revisiting Old Battlefields." *Scientific American,* April 1994, p. 36.
"Irven DeVore." *Omni* (interview) June 1993, p. 69.
Laying, Anthony. "Why Don't We Act Like the Opposite Sex?" *USA Today,* January 1993, p. 87.

## Somnambulism

Also known as sleepwalking, a common disorder among children that involves getting out of bed and moving about while still asleep.

Somnambulism, or sleepwalking, affects an estimated 15% of children in the early school years. It is similar to pavor nocturnus (**night terrors**) in that it occurs during the non-dreaming stage of **sleep**, usually within an hour or two of going to bed. The sleepwalking child feels an intense need to take action and may appear alert, purposeful, or anxious as he moves about. For many years, people believed that it was dangerous to waken a sleepwalker, but there is no basis for this view. There is, however, little reason to waken a sleepwalking child, and

it may be impossible to do so. Sleepwalking children should be gently guided back to bed, and will usually be cooperative in this effort. Episodes of sleepwalking may be signs of a child's heightened anxiety about something. Parents should give careful consideration to events and environmental changes that may have triggered the onset of sleepwalking. If sleepwalking is common among **family** members, it is more likely that the child may respond to even slight increases in anxiety with sleepwalking behavior.

## Charles Edward Spearman

**1863-1945**
British theoretical and experimental psychologist who pioneered studies of intelligence.

Charles Edward Spearman was an influential psychologist who developed commonly used statistical measures and the statistical method known as factor analysis. His studies on the nature of human abilities led to his "two-factor" theory of **intelligence**. Whereas most psychologists believed that mental abilities were determined by various independent factors, Spearman concluded that general intelligence, "g," was a single factor that was correlated with specific abilities, "s," to varying degrees. Spearman's work became the theoretical justification for intelligence testing. He also formulated eight basic laws of psychology.

Spearman was born in London in 1863, the second son of Alexander Young and Louisa Ann Caroline Amelia (Mainwaring) Spearman. Educated at Leamington College, Spearman joined the army in 1883 and served as a much-decorated infantry officer in Burma and India. However his early interest in philosophy led him to his desire to study psychology and, in 1897, he resigned from the army as a captain and continued his education.

For the next ten years, Spearman studied **experimental psychology** in Germany. After earning his Ph.D. with **Wilhelm Wundt** at the University of Leipzig in 1906, he worked with Oswald Külpe at the University of Würzburg and with Georg Elias Müller at the University of Göttingen. His studies were interrupted for a time by the Boer War, during which Spearman served as deputy-assistant-adjutant-general in Guernsey. Spearman married Fanny Aikman in 1901. The couple had four daughters, as well as a son who was killed in the Second World War.

### Measures intelligence

In 1904, Spearman published "General Intelligence Objectively Determined and Measured" in the *American*

## Publishes laws of psychology

In 1923 Spearman published *The Nature of "Intelligence" and the Principles of Cognition*, in which he set down his principles of psychology. In 1930, in the *Creative Mind*, he applied his laws of psychology to various other fields, including aesthetics.

Spearman was the leader of what became the "London school" of psychology that stressed statistical methods and systematic testing of human abilities. Through Spearman's influence, University College became the center of psychological studies in Britain. He was elected a fellow of the Royal Society in 1924 and was president of the British Psychological Society from 1923 until 1926. In 1925 Spearman served as president of the psychology section of the British Association for the Advancement of Science. He became professor of psychology at University College in 1928 and was awarded an honorary L.L.D. from the University of Wittenberg in 1929. Spearman held honorary memberships in a number of foreign scientific societies.

## Writes a history of psychology

Following his retirement as an emeritus professor in 1931, Spearman traveled extensively and taught in the United States, India, and Egypt. His historical survey, *Psychology Down the Ages* was published in 1937. During the Second World War, he served as honorary advisor on psychology to the school district of Chesterfield. Spearman died in London in 1945. His final work on intelligence, *Human Ability*, written with L. Wynn Jones, was published posthumously in 1950.

Margaret Alic

### Further Reading

Hearnshaw, Leslie. "Spearman, Charles E(dward)." In *Thinkers of the twentieth century: a biographical, bibliographical and critical dictionary,* edited by Elizabeth Devine, Michael Held, James Vinson, and George Walsh. Detroit: Gale Research, 1983.

Spearman, C. "C. Spearman." In *A history of psychology in autobiography,* edited by Carl Allanmore Murchison. New York: Appleton-Century-Crofts, 1967.

**Charles Spearman** *(Archives of the History of American Psychology. Reproduced with permission.)*

*Journal of Psychology*. In this work, the first of its kind, he introduced factor analysis and attempted to determine the factors that were measured by intelligence tests. Using statistical methods, Spearman found that the general intelligence factor "g" was associated with mental processes that were distinct from **memory**, physical abilities, and the senses. He demonstrated that intelligence tests, in addition to measuring "g," also measured specific abilities that he called "s" factors, such as verbal, mathematical, and artistic skills. This became Spearman's "two-factor" theory of intelligence.

Returning to England in 1907, Spearman joined University College, London, as a reader in experimental psychology. In 1911 he became Grote Professor of Mind and Logic. During the First World War, Spearman returned to the army and then, as a civilian, carried out psychological research for the military. Spearman's work on intelligence resulted in *A Measure of "Intelligence" for Use in Schools* (1925) and *The Abilities of Man, their Nature and Measurement* (1927). Spearman's "two-factor" theory was never widely accepted, and by the 1930s it was being replaced by multi-factor theories of intelligence. Nevertheless, his work laid the foundation for statistical "factor analysis" in psychology.

# Special education

Educational instruction or social services designed or modified to assist individuals with disabilities.

Special education refers to a range of services, including social work services and rehabilitative counseling, provided to individuals with disabilities from ages 3-21 through the public school system, including instruction given in the classroom, at home, or in institutions. Special education classes are taught by teachers with professional certification. Some teachers specialize in working with children with learning disabilities or multiple handicaps, and instruction may take place within a regular school or a residential school for students with disabilities.

In 1975, the Education for All Handicapped Children Act (EHCA, PL 94-142) mandated that states provide a "free and appropriate public education" (FAPE) to all students, including those with physical, mental, or behavioral disabilities. This special education must include a comprehensive screening and diagnosis by a multi-disciplinary team and the development of an annual Individualized Education Plan (IEP) for each student, outlining academic and behavioral goals, services to be provided, and methods of evaluation. The student's parents must consent to initial screening and must be invited to participate in all phases of the process. Besides the unprecedented move in guaranteeing free comprehensive services to children with special needs, the act was revolutionary in that it specified that special education take place in the "least restrictive environment" (LRE). In 1991 the Individuals with Disabilities Education Act (IDEA) provided federal assistance to state and local agencies to implement EHCA and made some revisions including: requiring that the **disability** status of the special-needs student be reevaluated every three years; adding the category of learning disabled as a qualifying disability; and further interpreting the LRE clause to require that the special-needs student be educated "to the maximum extent appropriate" with children who are not disabled. Services are available to individuals ages 2-21, and states are required to seek and initiate contact with qualifying individuals.

During the nearly 20 years after the passage of special education laws (1977-94), the rate of enrollment in public special education programs increased by 46%, while total enrollment in public schools declined 2%. In 1994, 12% of students enrolled in public schools or institutions were in special education programs. Much of the increase took place after 1991, when children identified with learning disabilities dominated special education classrooms: in 1994 learning disabled students made up 5% of total enrollment, falling short of just half of all special education students. Children's disabilities are defined under 13 categories: **autism**, blindness, visual impairment, deafness, **hearing** impairment, deaf-blindness, orthopedic (movement) impairments, multiple handicaps (several disabilities), **mental retardation** (also called developmental disability), serious emotional disturbance, speech and language disorders, specific learning disabilities (e.g., **dyslexia** ), and specialized health care needs (e.g., oxygen dependence). Traumatic **brain** injury also qualifies. Of students enrolled in special education programs in 1994, 45% were learning disabled; 19% had speech and language disorders; 10% were mentally retarded; 8% were deaf or hearing impaired; 8% were seriously emotionally disturbed; and 8% had other disabilities

## Screening and evaluation

To qualify for special education, a child must be diagnosed as having a disability and the disability must be found to "adversely affect educational performance" so as to require special services. There is wide variability in the way students are referred and evaluated for special education. For children with severe disabilities, the physician and parents identify and refer the child to special education. Other disabilities or deficits in the child's developing physical and cognitive abilities may be identified by teacher and parent observation or revealed by academic or developmental tests. Most districts have standardized programs to screen large numbers of children between kindergarten and third grade. Other disabilities may be subtle or compensated for, such as dyslexia, and may not be discovered until demands on the student increase in college. After referral, a meeting is held to determine whether the child should be "assessed" or "evaluated" to determine the type of disability he or she may have. Tests will attempt to identify the cognitive (academic), social, or physical tasks which the child has difficulty performing, and why the difficulty exists, i.e., what disability or disabilities are present. Tests may include: reading, writing, spelling, and math tests; psychological or **intelligence** tests; speech and language tests; **vision** and hearing tests; or an examination by a doctor. Parents must consent to all testing, evaluation, and placement, and can appeal most decisions if they disagree with the conclusions.

## Over- and under-referral

There is some concern about over- or under-referral in particular disability categories. Mild disabilities are especially difficult to diagnose. Since special education laws went into effect, the enrollment of students diagnosed with mental retardation and speech and language disorders decreased sharply, while those with learning disabilities increased. The changes reflect a social **consciousness** about the stigma of labeling and fundamental changes in the way people view disabilities. Yet, under-referral of mental retardation in particular may reflect schools' realistic **fear** of litigation. Others are concerned about over referral for mild disabilities (learning and behavioral disorders) as a method of classroom management. Thirty-four states require some method of pre-referral intervention. If a teacher suspects a disability, he or she must consult with a team of teachers and develop alternate methods of effectively addressing the student's problems, through modifications in instruction or classroom **environment**, before the school will consider special education referral.

## Race

There is a concern that minority students are disproportionately represented in special education, mostly with learning disabilities. In 1993, white, learning-disabled students made up 5% of total enrollment in special education. The corresponding percentage of black students (proportionate to their representation in the total population) would be 0.5%, but African American students with learning disabilities make up 6% of total enrollment. There is no consensus on the exact diagnosis of specific learning disabilities, and the same treatment goals and teaching strategies are used for all types of learning disabilities. Often psychologists will continue testing until they "find" a **learning disability** for which a student can receive special instruction. Criticism can be levied from both sides against this practice: white, low-achieving students do not receive special **attention** they need, and black students are segregated and labeled incorrectly.

## Location of services, mainstreaming, and inclusion

Before passage of the EHCA and IDEA, many disabled children were either not provided public education services at all, were in residential settings, or at best in separate day schools. In addition to providing special education in regular public school buildings, the stipulation that special-needs children be educated in the "least restrictive environment" led to the practice of mainstreaming. Mainstreaming is the policy of placing special education students in regular classrooms as much as possible, and using resource rooms where the student receives special tutoring, review, and instruction. In 1993, 40% of children received instruction primarily in regular classrooms, 30% in resource rooms, 24% in separate, special education classrooms, and the remaining 6% in public or private day schools and residential facilities. Students with speech or language impairments (80%) were most likely to be in general education classrooms. Mentally retarded and multiple-handicapped students (7% of each group) were the least likely to be in general education classrooms.

The type of contact special education teachers have with students varies according to district resources and student population. Some teachers, such as visual impairment specialists, may serve a whole region, tutoring a specific student only once a week. Others teach entire special education classes, providing general education teachers with support, ideas, and resources for mainstreamed pupils. Inclusion, sometimes considered the logical goal of mainstreaming, is total integration of special education students and services into the general education classroom, where special education teachers collaborate with general education teachers to teach the entire class. Full inclusion of all special education students would require restructuring of several traditional educational policies. To the extent that it necessitates extensive continuing collaboration between special education teachers, general education teachers, and support paraprofessionals, and requires restructuring of curricula and lessons, full inclusion represents a revolution in educational methods. Research on existing programs suggests that for inclusion to be successful certain attitudes and beliefs must be held and certain resources must be available:

- The general education teacher must believe the special-needs student can succeed
- The school must be committed to accepting responsibility for the learning outcomes of special education students
- Parents must be informed and supportive
- Services and physical accommodations must be adequate for the student's needs
- The principal must understand the needs of special education students
- Enough teacher and staff hours must be devoted to the child's care
- Continuing staff development and technical assistance must be provided
- Evaluation procedures must be clear
- Special education teachers must be part of the entire planning process
- A team approach is used by teachers and other specialists
- A variety of instructional arrangements must be available (team teaching, **ability** grouping, peer tutoring)

## Matriculation and employment

In 1992, 44% of special education students graduated with a diploma, 13% graduated with a certificate (including GED finished by age 21), 22% dropped out, and 21% exited school for other reasons. The highest dropout category was seriously emotionally disturbed students at 35%. The lowest was deaf-blind students, only 4% of whom dropped out. Graduation and employment rates for students with disabilities rose over the two decades after the passage of EHCA and IDEA and other disability legislation such as the Americans with Disabilities Act. Yet depending on the disability, as many as 45-70% of disabled adults were still unemployed in the early 1990s. People with learning disabilities and speech disorders have the lowest rates of unemployment. Because 77% of students take vocational education classes, a comprehensive vocational assessment, including assessment of independent living skills, is necessary. The assessment may take place at a regional center and follow an adult **rehabilitation** model. Assessments should take place several times in the course of a student's school career.

## Gifted and talented

Gifted and talented children are those who demonstrate special abilities, aptitude, or **creativity**. Often they will express themselves primarily in one area such as humanities, sciences, mathematics, art, music, or **leadership**. Gifted and talented students are not usually considered clients of special education. There is no federal mandate or regular funding to support gifted and talented students, although about half of the states have programs for the gifted and talented. As a percentage of total public school enrollment, students in gifted and talented programs range from 1-2% in Idaho, Nevada, Alabama, and Washington to over 10% in Hawaii, Maryland, Michigan, Nebraska, Ohio, Wisconsin, and South Carolina.

In addition to special counseling, grade skipping, taking summer or correspondence courses, or early graduation, there are a variety of adaptations that can be made to serve the needs of gifted students. Adaptations can be made to the content, the process, or the products of learning. Some strategies include:

*Acceleration*—Raising the academic level of assignments and giving the student reading material at a higher level of difficulty.

*Telescoping*—Reducing the time allowed the student to cover given content. For example, a teacher could give the student two successive mathematics chapters to complete in the ordinary time period used to cover one chapter.

*Compacting*—Testing to determine how much of a certain content unit the student knows already and custom designing a curriculum to fill in the gaps. Students can then use the gained time for creative or exploratory activities.

*Independent study*—Allowing the student to choose his or her own focus, plan research, present material, and evaluate the process.

*Tiered assignments*—Preparing assignments at different levels for different students. Asking more complex and higher order questions in assignments for gifted and talented students.

Other tools for pacing the learning of gifted and talented students are portfolios and learning centers. Several commercially prepared curricula that provide structured exploratory and design projects are also available.

## Further Reading

Adelman, H., and L. Taylor. *Learning Problems and Learning Disabilities.* Pacific, CA: Brooks, 1993.

Algozzine, B. et al. *Behaviorally Disordered? Assessment for Identification and Instruction.* Reston, VA: The Council for Exceptional Children, 1991.

Council of Administrators of Special Education. *Student Access: A Resource Guide for Educators, Section 504 of the Rehabilitation Act of 1973.* Albuquerque, NM: Author, 1991.

Cummins, J. *Bilingualism and Special Education: Issues in Assessment and Pedagogy.* Clevedon, England: Multilingual Matters. Co-published in the U.S. by College-Hill Press, San Diego, 1994.

Cook, L., and M. Friend. *Interactions: Collaboration Skills for School Professionals.* White Plains, NY: Longman Publishing, 1992.

Council for Exceptional Children, Department of Public Policy. *The Rights of Children with Disabilities under ADA and Section 504: A Comparison to IDEA.* Reston, VA: Author, 1994.

Giangreco, M. F., et al. *Choosing Options and Accommodations for Children: A Guide to Planning Inclusive Education.* Baltimore: Paul H. Brookes, 1993.

Gutkin, T. B., and C. R. Reynolds, eds. *The Handbook of School Psychology.* 2nd ed. New York: Wiley, 1990.

Hallahan, D., and J. Kaufmann. *Exceptional Children.* Englewood Cliffs, NJ: Prentice Hall, 1991.

Hunt, N., and K. Marshall. *Exceptional Children and Youth.* Boston, MA: Houghton Mifflin Co., 1994.

Levinson, E. M. *Transdisciplinary Vocational Assessment: Issues in School-Based Programs.* Brandon, VT: Clinical Psychology Publishing Co., 1993.

Marder, C., and R. D'Amico. *How Well Are Youth with Disabilities Really Doing? A Comparison of Youth with Disabilities and Youth in General.* Menlo Park, CA: SRI International, 1992.

National Center for Education Statistics. *Products Avaialbe from the National Center for Education Statistics.* Washington, DC: NCES, 1997.

Stoner, G., et al. *Interventions for Achievement and Behavior Problems.* Silver Spring, MD: National Association of School Psychologists, 1991.

U.S. Department of Education. *Eighteenth Annual Report to Congress on the Implementation of the Individuals with Disabilities Act.* Washington, DC: Office of Special Education Programs, 1996.

Wang, M. C., et al. *The Handbook of Special Education: Research and Practice.* Vols 1 & 2. Oxford, England: Pergamon Press, 1987.

## Further Information

American Coalition of Citizens with Disabilities. 1012 Fourteenth Street, NW, Washington, DC 20005.

Association for Children and Adults with Learning Disabilities. 4156 Library Road, Pittsburgh, PA 15234.

National Information Center for Handicapped Children and Youth. 155 Wilson Boulevard, Suite 508, Arlington, VA 22209.

National Center for Education Statistics. 555 New Jersey Ave., NW, Washington, DC 20208-5574. nces.gov.

The Council for Exceptional Children. 1920 Association Drive, Reston, VA 22091, (703) 620–3660.

Learning Disabilities Association of America. 4156 Library Road, Pittsburgh, PA 15234, (412) 341–1515.

# Specific language impairment (SLI)

Describes a condition of markedly delayed language development in the absence of any apparent handicapping conditions.

Many different terms have been used to describe the disorder of **childhood** characterized by markedly delayed **language development** in the absence of any apparent handicapping conditions such as deafness, **autism**, or **mental retardation**. It is sometimes called childhood dysphasia, or developmental **language disorder**. Much research since the 1960s has attempted to identify clinical subtypes of the disorder. These include *verbal auditory agnosia* and *specific language impairment*. Some children have a very precise difficulty in processing speech, called *verbal auditory agnosia*, that may be due to an underlying pathology in the temporal lobes of the **brain**. The most prevalent sub-type of childhood language disorder, *phonosyntactic disorder*, is now commonly termed *specific language impairment* or *SLI*. These children have a disorder specifically affecting inflectional morphology and syntax.

Very little is known about the cause or origin (referred to as *etiology*) of specific language impairment, though evidence is growing that the underlying condition may be a form of brain abnormality, not obvious with existing diagnostic technologies: SLI children do not have clear brain lesions or marked anatomical differences in either brain hemisphere. However, there is some indication of a familial pattern in SLI, with clinicians noting patterns across generations. It is more common in boys than girls. As of the 1990s, research suggests a possible genetic link, though there are still many problems in identifying such a gene. Sometimes the siblings of an affected child show milder forms of the difficulty, complicating the picture. One of the major stumbling blocks is the definition of the disorder, because the population of children

with language impairments is still much more heterogeneous than required to support a search for a gene.

Children with SLI usually begin to talk at roughly the same age as **normal** children but are markedly slower in the progress they make. They seem to have particular problems with inflection and word forms (inflectional morphology), such as leaving off endings as in the past tense verb form. This problem persists much longer than early childhood, often into the grade school years and beyond, where the children encounter renewed difficulties in reading and writing. The SLI child has also been observed to have difficulties learning language "incidentally," that is, in picking up a new word from context, or generalizing a new syntactic form. This is in decided **contrast** to the normal child's case, where incidental learning and generalization are the hallmarks of language acquisition. Children with SLI are not necessarily cognitively impaired, and are not withdrawn or socially aloof like the autistic child.

Some investigators have attributed the SLI child's difficulty to speech sounds (a *phonological* problem), suggesting that inflection and word forms (morphology) such as endings are vulnerable because those items are so fleeting and unstressed in speech. It is not that the child is deaf in general, but that he has a specific difficulty discriminating speech sounds.

Other researchers have argued that this difficulty is not specific to speech but reflects a general perceptual difficulty with the processing of rapidly timed events, of which speech is the most taxing example. The left hemisphere of the brain seems to be specialized for processing rapid acoustic events, so perhaps the SLI child has a unique difficulty with that part of the brain. Yet phonology does not seem to be the whole problem because the child may be quite good at articulation or speech **perception** per se. Instead, it is argued that the child may have a linguistic difficulty with morphology, going beyond the sounds themselves. Cross-linguistic work supports a more refined perspective that suggests certain kinds of inflectional morphology, especially those associated with the verb, may be more likely to be disrupted than others. If so, that would suggest the problem is not just phonological and not just inflectional. Given the centrality of the verb to sentence structure, the difficulty causes pervasive problems.

Whatever the final identification of the linguistic problem, researchers are curious to discover how such a specific disorder could come about: is a language "module" of the brain somehow compromised in these children? The puzzle is that children with very precise lesions of the usual language areas somehow overcome those difficulties more easily than the SLI child who presents no such dramatic brain abnormalities.

The child with SLI becomes increasingly aware of his difficulties with language and may lose spontaneity and avoid conversation as he gets older. Intensive language intervention can allow these children to make considerable gains, with **modeling** of appropriate linguistic forms producing more gains than simply "enriching" the child's language **environment**. Early identification is thus seen as very important for intervention. One procedure for children aged 24 to 36 months asks parents to complete a standardized questionnaire in which they check off the vocabulary the child knows, and write down examples of the child's two-word sentences. If the child has fewer than 50 words and no two-word sentences, that is an indication of risk for language disorder. Estimates of true SLI vary according to the age of identification: some experts argue that as many as 10% of 2-year-olds may have a specific language impairment, but by age 3 or 4, that percentage drops considerably, presumably because some difficulties resolve themselves. The incidence in the general population is estimated at about 1%.

Jill De Villiers, Ph.D.

## Further Reading

Gleason, Jean Berko. *The Development of Language.* (4th ed.) Boston: Allyn and Bacon, 1996.

Peterson, Harold A. *Appraisal and Diagnosis of Speech and Language Disorders.* (3rd ed.) Englewood Cliffs, NJ: Prentice Hall, 1994.

Taylor, Orlando L. *Nature of Communication Disorders in Culturally and Linguistically Diverse Populations.* San Diego: College-Hill Press, 1986.

# Speech-language pathology

Treatment for the improvement or cure of communication disorders, including both speech problems and language disorders.

Formerly referred to as speech therapy, the techniques, strategies, and interventions designed to improve or correct communication disorders are known as speech-language pathology. Both speech disorders, which involve difficulty in producing the sounds of language, and language disorders, which involve difficulty in understanding language or using words in spoken communication, are treated by speech-language pathologists.

In 1993, there were nearly 70,000 speech-language pathologists in the United States certified by the American Speech-Language-Hearing Association (ASHA).

Speech disorders treated by speech-language pathologists include voice disorders (abnormalities in pitch, volume, vocal quality, or resonance or duration of sounds), articulation disorders (problems producing speech sounds), and fluency disorders (impairment in the **normal** rate or rhythm of speech, such as stuttering). Speech-language pathologists participate in the screening, assessment, and treatment of patients.

Persons with isolated speech disorders are often helped by articulation therapy, in which they practice repeating specific sounds, words, phrases, and sentences. For stuttering and other fluency disorders, a popular treatment method is fluency training, which develops coordination between speech and breathing, slows down the rate of speech, and develops the **ability** to prolong syllables. A person may practice saying a single word fluently and then gradually add more words, slowly increasing the amount and difficulty of speech that can be mastered without stuttering. The speaking situations can gradually be made more challenging as well, starting with speaking alone to the pathologist and ending with speaking to a group of people. Delayed auditory feedback (DAF), in which stutterers hear an echo of their own speech sounds, has also been effective in treating stuttering. When a speech problem is caused by serious or multiple disabilities, a neurodevelopmental approach, which inhibits certain **reflexes** to promote normal movement, is often preferred. Other techniques used in speech therapy include the motor-kinesthetic approach and **biofeedback**, which helps people know whether the sounds they are producing are faulty or correct. For people with severe communication disorders, speech pathologists can assist with alternate means of communication, such as manual signing and computer-synthesized speech.

The majority of speech-language pathologists work in educational institutions, many of them in public elementary schools. They are also found at both residential health care facilities and over 300 outpatient clinics that specialize in communication disorders and are often affiliated with hospitals and universities. Professional training programs in speech-language pathology are offered at both the undergraduate and graduate levels. Undergraduate training may include classes in biology, anatomy, psychology, linguistics, education, and **special education**. Most clinicians hold a master's degree in communications sciences and disorders from a program accredited by the ASHA.

## Further Reading

Flower, R.M. *Delivery of Speech-Language Pathology and Audiology Services.* Baltimore, MD: Williams and Wilkins, 1986.

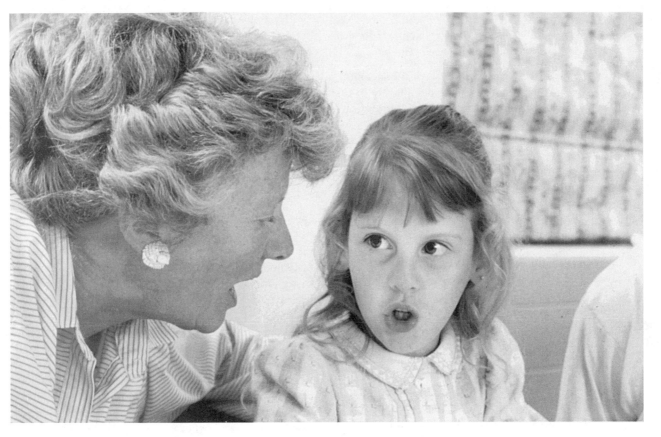

**A school-age girl is repeating phrases in speech therapy.** ( *Photo Researchers, Inc. Reproduced with permission.*)

Hicks, Patricia Larkins. *Opportunities in Speech-Language Pathology Careers.* Lincolnwood, IL: VGM Career Horizons, 1996.

Lass, N.J., L.V. McReynolds, and J.L. Northern. *Handbook on Speech-Language Pathology and Audiology.* Philadelphia: B.C. Decker, 1988.

**Further Information**

American Academy of Private Practice in Speech-Language Pathology and Audiology. 7349 Topanga Canyon Boulevard, Canoga Park, CA 91303.

American Speech-Language-Hearing Association. 10801 Rockville Pike, Rockville, MD 20785, (301) 897–5700.

National Black Association for Speech, Language and Hearing. 3542 Gentry Ridge Court, Silver Spring, MD 20904.

# Speech perception

The ability to hear and understand speech.

Speech perception, the process by which we employ cognitive, motor, and sensory processes to hear and understand speech, is a product of innate preparation ("nature") and sensitivity to experience ("nurture") as demonstrated in infants' abilities to perceive speech. Studies of infants from **birth** have shown that they respond to speech signals in a special way, suggesting a strong innate component to language. Other research has shown the strong effect of **environment** on language acquisition by proving that the language an infant listens to during the first year of life enables the child to begin producing a distinct set of sounds (babbling) specific to the language spoken by its parents.

Since the 1950s, great strides have been made in research on the acoustics of speech (i.e., how sound is produced by the human vocal tract). It has been demonstrated how certain physiologic gestures used during speech produce specific sounds and which speech features are sufficient for the listener to determine the phonetic identity of these sound units. Speech prosody (the pitch, rhythm, tempo, **stress**, and intonation of speech) also plays a critical role in infants' **ability** to perceive language. Two other distinct aspects of perception—segmentation (the ability to break the spoken language signal into the parts that make up words) and normalization (the ability to perceive words spoken by different speakers, at different rates, and in different phonetic contexts as the same)—are also essential components of speech perception demonstrated at an early age by infants.

In addition to the acoustic analysis of the incoming messages of spoken language, two other sources of information are used to understand speech: "bottom-up" and "top-down". In the former, we receive auditory information, convert it into a neural signal and process the phonetic feature information. In the latter, we use stored information about language and the world to make sense of the speech. Perception occurs when both sources of information interact to make only one alternative plausible to the listener who then perceives a specific message.

To understand how bottom-up processing works in the absence of a knowledge base providing top-down information, researchers have studied infant speech perception using two techniques: high-amplitude sucking (HAS) and head-turn (HT). In HAS, infants from 1 to 4 months of age suck on a pacifier connected with a pressure transducer which measures the pressure changes caused by sucking responses when a speech sound is presented. Head turn **conditioning** is used to test infants between 6 months and one year of age. With this technique, a child is trained to turn his or her head when a speech sound, repeated once every second as a background stimulus, is changed to a comparison speech sound. When the head is turned during the presentation of the comparison stimulus, the child is rewarded with a visual stimulus of a toy which makes a sound.

As a result of studies using these techniques, it has been shown that infants at the earliest ages have the ability to discriminate phonetic contrasts (/bat/ and /pat/) and prosodic changes such as intonation contours in speech. However, to understand speech, more than the ability to discriminate between sounds is needed; speech must be perceptually organized into phonetic categories, ignoring some differences and listening to others.

To measure categorical perception, adults were asked to discriminate between a series of sounds varying in equal steps in acoustic dimension from /ra/ to /la/. As predicted by the categorical perception phenomenon, their discrimination improved at the boundary between the two phonetic categories. However, adult listeners could do this only for sounds in their native language. The discovery that categorical perception was language-specific suggested that it might be a learned behavior. This prompted researchers to question if categorical perception was the result of experience with language. If so, young infants could not be expected to show it, while older infants, who had experienced language, might be expected to do so.

Using the sucking technique, this study revealed that at birth, infants' discrimination of /pa/ and /ba/ was categorical not only with the perception of sounds in their native language but also with sounds from foreign languages as if the infants heard all the phonetic distinctions used in all languages. But if this "language-general" speech perception ability of infants later became "language-specific" speech perception in adults, when and by what process did this change occur? To answer this question, researchers began to study the perception of phonetic prototypes (i.e., the "best" members of a phonetic category).

Under the assumption that sound prototypes exist in speech categories, adults were asked to judge the category "goodness" of a sampling of one hundred instances of the vowel /i/ using a scale from 1 to 7. Results indicated evidence of a vowel prototype for /i/, but also showed that phonetic prototypes or "best" vowels differed for speakers of different languages. Further perceptual testing revealed an even more unique occurrence: sounds that were close to a prototype could not be distinguished from the prototype, even though they were physically different. It appeared as if the prototype perceptually assimilated nearby sounds like a magnet, attracting the other sounds in that category. Dubbed the perceptual magnet effect, this theory offered a possible explanation of why adult speakers of a given language can no longer hear certain phonetic distinctions as is the case with Japanese speakers who have difficulty discriminating between /r/ and /l/; the Japanese prototype is something that is acoustically similar to both sounds and results in their **assimilation** by the Japanese prototype.

To discover whether infants are born with all the prototypes of all languages and whether language experience then eliminates those prototypes which are not reinforced, an experiment in which 6-month-old American infants listened to English was performed (Kuhl, 1991). It confirmed the perceptual magnet effect but left the question of the role of language experience unresolved. When a study was conducted (Kuhl, Williams, Lacerda, Stevens & Lindblom, 1992) with listeners from two different languages (English and Swedish) on the same vowel prototypes it was demonstrated that the perceptual magnet effect is strongly affected by exposure to a specific language.

The Native Language Magnet (NLM) theory grew out of the research on the development of speech perception. Simply stated, it explains how infants at birth can hear all of the phonetic distinctions used in the world's languages. However, during the first year of life, prior to the acquisition of word meaning and contrastive phonology, infants begin to perceive speech by forming mental representations or perceptual maps of the speech they hear in their environment. These representations, stored in the **brain**, constitute the beginnings of language-specific speech perception and serve as a blueprint which guides infants' attempts to produce speech. The native language magnet effect works to partition the infant's perceptual space in a way that conforms to phonetic categories in the language that is heard. Sounds in the spoken language that are close to a given magnet or prototype are perceptually pulled into the magnet and thus assimilated, and not discriminated, by the listener. As the perceptual space surrounding a category prototype or magnet shrinks, it takes a very large acoustic difference for the listener to hear that sound. However, a very small acoustic difference in the region of a nonprototype can be heard easily. Thus the developing magnet pulls sounds that were once discriminable toward a single magnet, making them no longer discriminable and changing the infant's perception of speech.

Patricia Kuhl, Ph.D.

### Further Reading
Aitchison, Jean. *The Seeds of Speech: Language Origin and Evolution.* New York: Cambridge University Press, 1996.
Kuhl, Patricia K, Ph.D. "Speech Perception." Introduction to *Communication Sciences and Disorders.* San Diego: Singular Publishing Group, Inc.
———. *Learning and Representation in Speech and Language.* Philadelphia: Current Biology Ltd.

# Speech

## See **Language development**

# Janet Taylor Spence

**1923-**
American clinical, experimental, and social psychologist, known for her studies on motivation and on gender identity.

Janet Taylor Spence has made important contributions to several branches of psychology. Her early work, the Taylor Manifest Anxiety Scale (MAS), became a standard method for relating anxiety to performance. She discovered the importance of intrinsic **motivation** in performance, at a time when most psychologists believed in reward models of learning and performance. Later, Spence turned her **attention** to gender studies and developed a general theory of **gender identity**. The only individual who has served as president of both the American Psychological Association and the American Psychological Society, Spence has been the recipient of numerous awards. She was elected to the American Academy of Arts and Sciences and holds honorary degrees from Oberlin College and Ohio State University.

Born in Toledo, Ohio, in 1923, young Janet was the elder of two daughters of John C. and Helen Hodge Taylor. Both her mother and grandmother were graduates of Vassar College. Helen Taylor also held a master's degree in economics from Columbia. She worked for the League of Women Voters, managed Republican election campaigns, and eventually became director of a social service agency. John Taylor was the business manager of a labor union and an active Socialist. After two years at a girls' high school in Northfield, Massachusetts, Spence enrolled at Oberlin College, a liberal arts school in Ohio. Following graduation in 1945, she entered the graduate **clinical psychology** program at Yale University.

### Measures anxiety and motivation

After a year of working with **intelligence** tests at Yale with Catherine Cox Miles, Janet Taylor took a rotating internship in New York State. Deciding against pursuing clinical psychology, she moved to the University of Iowa to work with **Kenneth Spence**, co-author of the Hull-Spence theory of behavior. For her dissertation, Taylor developed the MAS, which measured individual motivational levels and was used to select subjects for experimental studies. In further research, she studied the relationship between anxiety levels and performance. The MAS is still used in psychology to measure anxiety levels.

After receiving her Ph.D. in 1949, Taylor joined the psychology department of Northwestern University in Evanston, Illinois, as the first woman faculty member. Two years later, she was promoted from instructor to assistant professor and she became an associate professor in 1956. Despite a demanding teaching load, that required her to develop seven different courses, from introductory and **experimental psychology** to statistics, during her first year at Northwestern, she continued her productive research program. Taylor published eighteen papers and co-authored a statistics textbook during her ten years at Northwestern.

### Marries Kenneth Spence

Janet Taylor Spence returned to Iowa City with her new husband in 1959. Since nepotism policies at the university prevented her from working in the same department as her husband, she became a research psychologist at the Veterans Administration Hospital. When Kenneth Spence moved to the psychology department at the University of Texas at Austin, she found a research associate position at a Texas state school for retarded children. In 1965, she obtained a faculty appointment in the Department of **Educational Psychology** at the University of Texas. During this period, Spence studied motivation and **reinforcement**, first with schizophrenics at the Veterans Hospital and then applying her experimental methods to developmental issues in children. She made the remarkable discovery that rewards were not only ineffective, but were counterproductive, as motivators of performance. Instead, Spence demonstrated the importance of intrinsic motivation in individual performance.

With her husband's death in 1967, Spence finally was able to join the psychology department of the University of Texas. Between 1968 and 1972, she served as department chair. In addition to her numerous publications, Spence served on the editorial boards of a number of psychology journals and, from 1973 until 1979, she edited *Contemporary Psychology*. She also has worked with many professional committees, including those of the American Association for the Advancement of Science. Spence was as a Fellow at the Center for Advanced Study in the Behavioral Sciences in 1978 and, in 1979, she became Ashbel Smith Professor of Psychology and Educational Psychology at the University of Texas.

### Undertakes gender research

In the 1970s, Spence began collaborating with Robert Helmreich. Their "Work and **Family** Orientation Questionnaire" examined various factors in achievement motivation; in particular, perseverance, mastery, and competitiveness. They also began examining achievement motivation and behavior. At the same time, Spence and Helmreich began examining gender issues. They developed several indices for measuring gender-related characteristics and attitudes, including the "Attitudes toward Women Scale" and the "Personal Attributes Questionnaire." Their 1978 book, *Masculinity and Femininity: Their Psychological Dimensions, Correlates and Antecedents*, moved the study of gender into the mainstream of psychological research. Spence's theory of gender identity was published in 1985.

Spence, who also became the Alma Cowden Madden Professor of Liberal Arts at the University of Texas, retired in 1997. She lives on Cape Cod in Massachusetts.

Margaret Alic

### Further Reading

Deaux, Kay. "Janet Taylor Spence (1923- )." In *Women in psychology: a bio-bibliographic sourcebook,* edited by Agnes N. O'Connell and Nancy Felipe Russo. New York: Greenwood Press, 1990.

Spence, J. T. "Janet Taylor Spence, 1923-." In *Models of achievement: reflections of eminent women in psychology,* edited by A. N. O'Connell and N. F. Russo. Vol. 2. Hillsdale, NJ: Erlbaum, 1988.

Swann, William B., Judith H. Langlois, and Lucia Albino Gilbert. *Sexism and stereotypes in modern Society: the gender science of Janet Taylor.* Washington, DC: American Psychological Association, 1999.

# Kenneth W. Spence

**1907-1967**
American neobehavioral psychologist known for both theoretical and experimental research on learning.

Kenneth Wartinbee Spence was known for his theoretical and experimental studies of **conditioning** and learning. His analyses and interpretations of the theories of other psychologists also were very influential. Spence was elected to the National Academy of Sciences in 1954 and was a fellow of the American Association for the Advancement of Science and the **American Psychological Association (APA)**.

The son of Mary E. Wartinbee and **William James** Spence, an electrical engineer, Spence was born in Chicago, Illinois, in 1907, but he grew up in Montreal, Quebec, Canada. Spence attended West Hill High School and McGill University in Montreal, earning his bachelor's degree in 1929 and his master's degree the following year. He won the Wales Gold Medal in Mental Sciences from McGill in 1929 and the university's Governor-General's Medal for Research in 1930. Moving to Yale University, Spence studied with the famous primate biologist Robert M. Yerkes and with the behavioral psychologist Clark L. Hull. Spence's early work was concerned with discrimination learning in animals. After receiving his Ph.D. in psychology in 1933, Spence was a National Research Council fellow and research assistant, working with chimpanzees at the Yale Laboratories of Primate Biology in Orange Park., Florida.

### Elaborates on Hull's learning theories

In 1937, Spence became an assistant professor of psychology at the University of Virginia and, a year later, he moved to the State University of Iowa (now the University of Iowa) in Iowa City, as an associate professor. Spence was particularly interested in learning and conditioning. He extended the research and theories of Hull, in an attempt to establish a precise, mathematical formulation to describe the acquisition of learned behavior. He tried to measure simple learned behaviors such as salivating in anticipation of eating. Much of his research focused on classically conditioned, easily measured, eye-blinking behavior in relation to anxiety and other factors. He measured anxiety using the Taylor Manifest Anxiety Scale developed by his graduate student, Janet Taylor, whom he eventually married. Spence believed in "latent learning," that **reinforcement** was not necessary for learning to occur. However, he thought that reinforcement was a strong motivator for performance. Collectively, this work eventually became known as the Hull-Spence theory of conditioning and learning.

## University of Iowa becomes center of theoretical psychology

Spence became a full professor and head of the psychology department at Iowa in 1942. Together with **Kurt Lewin** at the Child Welfare Research Station, and the science philosopher Gustav Bergmann, Spence made the University of Iowa into a major center of theoretical psychology, with the goal of transforming psychology into an advanced natural science. Spence collaborated with Bergmann on logical positivism, the framework for his theories of psychology. In 1956, Spence's Silliman Lectures at Yale University were published as *Behavior Theory and Conditioning* . In 1960, many of his papers were collected as *Behavior Theory and Learning*. Spence also served on the U. S. Air Force Committee on Human Resources and the Army Scientific Advisory Panel.

By the late 1940s, Spence and other neobehaviorists had succeeded in infusing all of American psychology with **behaviorism**. Spence pointed out that American psychologists no longer bothered to identify themselves as behaviorists; rather, it was taken for granted. With the rise of cognitive behavioral approaches, Spence's theories received less attention. However his experimental methods continued to be regarded highly.

Spence married his former graduate student, Janet Taylor Spence, in 1959. In 1964, he moved to the psychology department at the University of Texas in Austin. Over the course of his career, Spence was advisor to some 75 Ph.D. students. His many awards included the Howard Crosby Warren Medal of the Society of Experimental Psychologists in 1953 and the first Distinguished Scientific Contribution Award of the APA in 1956. Spence died of cancer in Austin, Texas, in 1967.

Margaret Alic

### Further Reading

Amsel, A. "Kenneth Wartenbee Spence." *Biographical memoir.* Vol. 66. Washington, DC: National Academy of Sciences, 1995.

Amsel, K. W. S. "Spence, Kenneth Wartenbee." In *Biographical dictionary of psychology,* edited by Noel Sheehy, Antony J. Chapman, and Wendy A. Conroy. London: Routledge, 1997.

Kendler, Howard H., and Janet T. Spence. *Essays in neobehaviorism: a memorial volume to Kenneth W. Spence.* New York: Appleton-Century-Crofts,1971.

# Split-brain technique

Procedure used to study the activities of the two hemispheres of the brain separately, and independent of each other.

Psychologists have demonstrated that even simple human tasks, like thinking of a word when viewing an object, involve separate subtasks within the **brain**. These smaller tasks involve identifying the object, assessing its use, remembering what other objects are related to it, determining how many syllables are in the word associated with the object, and so on.

People do not realize the complexity of seemingly simple tasks because the brain integrates information smoothly and flawlessly almost all the time. One structure in the brain involved in the exchange and integration of information from one part to the next is the corpus callosum, a bundle of about 200 million **nerve** fibers that connect the right and left hemispheres of the brain.

Beginning in the 1940s, neurologists questioned whether the corpus callosum was involved in the development of epileptic seizures. Evidence from monkeys suggested that abnormal neural responses in one hemisphere spread to the other via the corpus callosum, resulting in major seizure activity. As such, it might be beneficial to patients suffering from **epilepsy** to sever the corpus callosum in order to prevent the spread of this abnormal neural activity. After some initial problems with the surgical procedure, neurologists documented the benefit of such surgery, called cerebral commisurotomy. This so-called split-brain surgery resulted in an increase in split-brain research. One of the primary researchers in this area was neurosurgeon Roger Sperry (1913-1994).

Research neurosurgeons discovered that after surgery, patients often experienced a short period during which they could not speak and had difficulty controlling the left side of their bodies. This set of problems, called acute disconnection syndrome, probably reflected the trauma caused by the surgery itself. After the patient recovered from this trauma, his or her everyday behavior appeared unchanged. The two hemispheres of the brain were no longer directly connected, so information from one half of the brain should not have been able to get to the other. Researchers required subtle and sophisticated techniques to be able to differentiate people whose corpus callosum had been cut from those with intact brains.

Such techniques involve using apparatus that can present visual information so that it goes to only one side of the brain. In this case, split-brain patients may not be able to label a picture that stimulates on the right side of the brain; they may have no difficulty when the left side of the brain, which normally controls language production, receives stimulation. At the same time, research in the area has been conflicting. Some work reveals considerable sophistication in language **ability** in the right hemisphere. Although language functions do differ across hemispheres, split-brain research has not completely resolved the issue about the nature and the degree to which the left and right hemispheres differ.

More recent research has suggested that the left hemisphere may be involved in much linguistic behavior because of its strength in dealing with analytical, structured tasks. On the other hand, the right hemisphere may be better in spatial tasks because these tasks require holistic, synthetic functioning—the strength of the right hemisphere.

When the patients were asked to point to pictures of the **normal** faces, they selected the normal face associated with the half of the chimeric face that stimulated the right hemisphere. When forced to respond verbally, the patients showed a preference for the picture that had stimulated the left hemisphere. Although researchers cannot specify the exact differences in the functioning of the two hemispheres, regular differences along visual and linguistic lines have emerged.

Although the research has demonstrated differences in the functioning of the two hemispheres of the brain, everyday behavior may appear completely normal in split-brain patients. This is true because human behavior is very flexible and adaptable. For example, a split-brain patient might turn the head when focusing on an object; thereby stimulating both hemispheres. Further, these patients use cross-cuing in which they invoke as many different modalities, like **vision**, audition, and **touch**, to help them make sense of their world.

*See also* Left-Brain Hemisphere; Psychosurgery; Right-Brain Hemisphere.

### Further Reading
Springer, S. P., and G. Deutsch. *Left Brain, Right Brain.* 2d ed. New York: W. H. Freeman, 1985.

# Benjamin Spock

### 1903-1998
Pediatrician most noted for his authorship of *Baby and Child Care,* which significantly changed predominant attitudes toward the raising of infants and children.

Benjamin McLane Spock was born on May 2, 1903, in New Haven, Connecticut, the oldest child in a large, strict New England **family**. His family was so strict that in his 82nd year he would still be saying "I love to dance in order to liberate myself from my puritanical upbringing." Educated at private preparatory schools, he attended Yale from 1921 to 1925, majoring in English literature. He was a member of the racing crew that represented the United States in the 1924 Olympic Games at Paris, finishing 300 feet ahead of its nearest rival. He began medical school at Yale in 1925, and transferred to Columbia University's College of Physicians and Surgeons in 1927. He had, by this time, married Jane Davenport Cheney, whom he had met after a Yale-Harvard boat race.

Spock had decided well before starting his medical studies that he would "work with children, who have their whole lives ahead of them" and so, upon taking his M.D. degree in 1929 and serving his general internship at the prestigious Presbyterian Hospital, he specialized in pediatrics at a small hospital crowded with children in New York's Hell's Kitchen area. Believing that pediatricians at that time were focusing too much on the physical side of **child development**, he took up a residency in psychiatry as well.

Between 1933 and 1944, Spock practiced pediatric medicine, while at the same time teaching pediatrics at Cornell Medical College and consulting in pediatric psychiatry for the New York City Health Department. On a summer vacation in 1943, he began to write his most famous book, *Baby and Child Care,* and he continued to work on it from 1944 to 1946 while serving as a medical officer in the Navy.

The book sharply broke with the authoritarian tone and rigorous instructions found in earlier generations of baby-care books, most of which said to feed infants on a strict schedule and not to pick them up when they cried. Spock, who spent ten years trying to reconcile his psychoanalytic training with what mothers were telling him about their children, told his readers "You know more than you think you do.... Don't be afraid to trust your own common sense.... Take it easy, trust your own instincts, and follow the directions that your doctor gives you." The response was overwhelming. *Baby and Child Care* rapidly became America's all-time best-seller except for Shakespeare and the Bible; by 1976, it had also eclipsed Shakespeare.

After his discharge from the Navy, Spock became associated with the famous Mayo Clinic (1947-1951) and then became a professor of child development at the University of Pittsburgh (1951-1955) and at Case Western Reserve (1955-1967). His political activism began during this period, growing logically out of his concern for children. A healthy **environment** for growing children, he believed, included a radiation-free atmosphere to breathe and so, in 1962, he became co-chairman of SANE, an organization dedicated to stopping nuclear bomb tests in the Earth's atmosphere. The following year, in which the United States did ratify a nuclear test ban treaty, he campaigned for Medicare, incurring the wrath of the American Medical Association, many of whose members were already suspicious of a colleague who wrote advice columns for the *Ladies Home Journal* and *Redbook* instead of writing technical monographs for the medical journals.

Spock was an early opponent of the Indo-China war; his view on that subject, *Dr. Spock on Vietnam,* appeared in 1968. As the war escalated, so did antiwar protest, in which Spock participated vigorously, marching and demonstrating with militant youths who had not yet been born when he began his medical career. Conservatives accused him of having *created,* in large measure, the youth protest movement of the 1960s. Ignoring his many admonitions to parents in *Baby and Child Care* that they should "set limits," his political opponents accused Spock of teaching "permissiveness," by which they claimed an entire generation of American youth had been raised and ruined. In vain, Spock pointed out that similar student protests were happening in Third World countries where his book enjoyed no circulation and were not happening in Western Europe countries where it sold well.

Because of his own strict personal upbringing and his acute moral sense, Spock may have intended a lot less when he told parents to "relax" than some of them realized. In 1968, he revised *Baby and Child Care* to make his intentions more clear, now cautioning his readers "Don't be afraid that your children will dislike you" if you set those limits and enforce them. Nevertheless, that 1968 edition showed a 50 percent drop in sales, mainly, Spock thought, because of his stand on Vietnam.

On May 20, 1968, along with several other leading war protesters, Spock was put on trial for conspiracy. The charge was that he had counseled young people to resist the draft. In the superheated political atmosphere of the times, he was convicted, but on appeal the verdict was set aside on a technicality. Some indignant readers

**Benjamin Spock** *(The Library of Congress. Reproduced with permission.)*

returned their well-thumbed copies of *Baby and Child Care* in order to prevent further undermining of their children's patriotism. To many other readers, however, the government's indictment of the baby doctor seemed rather like prosecuting Santa Claus.

Two books published in 1970, *Decent and Indecent: Our Personal and Political Behavior* and *A Teenager's Guide to Life and Love,* made it clear that Spock was a good deal more of a traditional moralist than either his friends or his enemies were aware. He had been driven into the antiwar and other reform movements by the same imperious, old-fashioned **conscience** that propelled some of his opponents in exactly the opposite direction.

At the same time, the doctor showed himself capable of growing and changing. His social activism mutated into socialism, and in 1972 he ran for president on the People's Party ticket. He was also capable of admitting a mistake. Badgered for some five years on the lecture platform by feminist objectors to the gender-role stereotypes of fathers and mothers as they appeared in *Baby and Child Care,* he eventually conceded that much of what they had said had been right. In 1976, 30 years after its initial publication, Spock brought out a third version of the famous book, deleting material he himself termed "sexist" and calling for greater sharing by fathers in the parental role. He also yielded 45 percent of subsequent book royalties in the **divorce** settlement that year with his wife, who contended she had done much more of the work on *Baby and Child Care* than he had ever acknowledged. Spock was remarried in the fall of 1976 to Mary Morgan Councille.

Formally retired in 1967, Spock was the kind of person who in spirit never really retires. Contemplating his own death as his health began to fail in the 1980s, he wrote in 1985 (at the age of 82) that he did not want any lugubrious funeral tunes played over him: "My ideal would be the New Orleans black funeral, in which friends snake-dance through the streets to the music of a jazz band." He had chronic bronchitis and suffered a stroke in 1989. His wife, Mary, collaborated with Spock on his autobiography, *Spock on Spock,* which was published in 1989. His book *A Better World for Our Children* was published in 1994 and explored the relationship between child-rearing and politics. According to an article in the *Detroit Free Press,* Spock said "When I look at our society and think of the millions of children exposed every day to its harmful effects, I am near despair." Dr. Spock died at his home in La Jolla, California on March 15, 1998 at the age of 94.

*See also* Child development; Child psychology

### Further Reading

Bloom, Lynn Z. *Doctor Spock: biography of a conservative radical.* 1972.

Maier, Thomas. *Dr. Spock: an American life.* 1998.

Mitford, Jessica. *The trial of Dr. Spock, the Rev. William Sloane Coffin, Jr., Michael Ferber, Mitchell Goodman, and Marcus Raskin.* 1969.

Kellogg, M.A. "Updating Dr. Spock." *Newsweek.* March 3, 1976.

Spock, Benjamin. *Decent and indecent.* 1970.

Spock, Benjamin. *A Teenager's Guide to Life and Love.* 1970.

Spock, Benjamin. "A way to say farewell." *Parade Magazine.* March 10, 1985.

Spock, Benjamin. *Spock on parenting.* 1988.

Spock, Benjamin. *Spock on Spock: a memoir of growing up with the century.* 1989.

Spock, Benjamin. *A better world for our children.* National Press Books, 1994.

# Sports psychology

A developing subfield of psychology concerned with applying psychological theories and research to sports and other recreational activities.

Sports—which involve **emotion**, **competition**, co-operation, achievement, and play—provide a rich area for psychological study. People involved in sports attempt to master very difficult skills, often subjecting themselves to intense physical **stress** as well as social pressure. When psychologists began studying sports in the 1930s and 1940s, they focused on motor performance and the acquisition of motor skills. Sports psychology emerged as a distinct discipline in the 1960s, dominated by theories of **social psychology**. Since then, research has expanded into numerous areas such as imagery training, **hypnosis**, relaxation training, **motivation**, **socialization**, conflict and competition, counseling, and coaching. Specific sports and recreational specialties studied include baseball, basketball, soccer, volleyball, tennis, golf, fencing, dance, and many others.

Three primary areas of sports research are **personality**, motivation, and **social influence**. Personality studies have investigated whether there are specific **traits** that distinguish athletes from non-athletes. Although most of these studies failed to yield significant results, some valid connections were made between success in athletics and positive **mental health**. Research on wrestlers, runners, and oarsmen found lower levels of **depression**, tension, **hostility**, and fatigue among more successful athletes when compared with their peers and with the general population. Individual differences within a sport have also been studied. One instrument devised for this type of investigation is the Sport Competition Anxiety Test (SCAT), developed by Rainer Martens, which measures levels of anxiety in competitive sport. Studies of motivation have focused on optimum arousal levels for athletes. Mostly such studies have corroborated existing research on arousal by relating peak performance to a moderate, optimum arousal level, with performance diminishing if arousal is either increased or decreased from that level. Negative effects of excess arousal include inefficient movement patterns and loss of sensitivity to environmental cues. In successful athletes, the **ability** to control arousal and focus **attention** has proven to be as important as the level of arousal itself. Motivation in sports has also been approached from the angle of **behavior modification**, with attention to such issues as the effects of intrinsic versus extrinsic rewards.

Studies of social influence, which were predominant in the 1960s and 1970s, focused on such issues as the influence of spectators, teammates, and competitors. Sports psychologists have also studied specific types of behavior. For example, the origin and effect of **aggression** in sports have been investigated by researchers testing the concept of sport as a cathartic release of aggression. (It was found that aggressive sports tend to increase rather than diminish hostility and aggression.) The social dynamics of team sports have also been studied. Psychological theories from other subfields, such as social psychology and behavioral psychology, have been applied successfully to the study of sports and recreation. At times, research has yielded findings which are different from those seen in these more traditional areas. Contrary to what a behavioral psychologist might predict, for instance, some studies done on coaching behaviors reveal that effective methods of instruction are not always related to high levels of praise or positive **reinforcement**. The common behavior of coaches, even successful ones, is disproportionately composed of scolding and "hustling," or urging on, rather than providing supportive feedback. Another finding that goes against conventional wisdom is that team cohesiveness in team-oriented sports does not necessarily lead to top performance.

Following the already existing practice in Europe, sports psychologists in North America now work directly with professional athletes and teams to help improve performance. Techniques applied include anxiety management, progressive relaxation, autogenic training, **biofeedback**, hypnosis, and cognitive behavioral therapy. **Mental imagery**, attention control, goal-setting, and work on interpersonal skills are also part of sports psychology programs for athletes. Positive results have been reported in enhancing performance and controlling anxiety.

As the study of sports psychology has grown, it has borrowed less from other specialties, such as **behaviorism**, making its own contributions to the field of psychology. The unique findings in this discipline have contributed to other, more conventional areas of psychology and are recognized as having significant applications to the mental health of the general population. One example can be seen in numerous research reports which have cited the benefits of jogging and other sports in alleviating depression. (Some studies have found that running is equal to **psychotherapy** in its ability to relieve depressive symptoms.) Sports psychology has also gained recognition through the popularity of such books as Thaddeus Kostrubala's *The Joy of Running,* David Kauss's *Peak Performance,* and Timothy Gallwey's "inner game" books. Psychologically-oriented instruction books, such as Vic Braden's *Tennis for the Future,* have also gained wide audiences. Principles developed through sports research, such as attention control training, have also been adapted for use in business and other organizational settings. Coaching and fitness models and other sports psychology concepts have been used in training managers and supervisors. Books on this topic include *Coaching for Improved Work Performance* by Ferdinand Fournies and *Coaching, Learning, and Action* by B.C. Lovin and E. Casstevens.

As medical findings continue to support the role of exercise and fitness in building and maintaining health, people are interested in learning how they can apply re-

Speed skater Eric Heiden. Individual sports, like speed skating, require greater self-motivation in their athletes. *(AP/Wide World Photos. Reproduced by permission.)*

lated information to build skills and enjoy their activities more fully. These individuals become likely subjects, along with athletes, for psychologists seeking to do research or to provide counseling in the area of sports and recreation.

While there is no specific division devoted to sports psychology within the American Psychological Association, those involved in the discipline may join the Academy of Sport Psychology International (ASPI), the American College of Sports Medicine, the International Society of Sports Psychology, or various other organizations. English-language journals in the field include the *Journal of Sport Psychology,* the *International Journal of Sport Psychology,* the *Journal of Sport and Social Issues,* and *Psychology of Motor Behavior and Sport.*

## Further Reading

Bird, Anne Marie. *Psychology and Sport Behavior.* St. Louis: Times Mirror/Mosby College Pub., 1986.

Cratty, Bryant J. *Psychology in Contemporary Sport: Guidelines for Coaches and Athletes.* Englewood Cliffs, NJ: Prentice-Hall, 1983.

LeUnes, Arnold D. *Sport Psychology: An Introduction.* Chicago: Nelson-Hall, 1996.

## Further Information

Academy of Sport Psychology International (ASPI). 6079 Northgate Rd., Columbus, Ohio 43229, (614) 846–2275.

American College of Sports Medicine. P.O. Box 1440, Indianapolis, Indiana 46206-1440, (317) 637–9200.

International Society of Sports Psychology. Department of Kinesiology, University of Illinois at Urbana-Champaign, 906 S. Goodwin Ave., Urbana, Illinois 61801, (217) 333–6563.

# Standard progressive matrices (SPM)

*Assesses intelligence nonverbally in children and adults.*

The **Standard Progressive Matrices (SPM)** is a group or individually administered test that nonverbally assesses **intelligence** in children and adults through abstract reasoning tasks. It is sometimes called Raven's, although the SPM is only one of three tests that together comprise Raven's Progressive Matrices. Appropriate for ages 8-65, the SPM consists of 60 problems (five sets of 12), all of which involve completing a pattern or figure with a part missing by choosing the correct missing piece from among six alternatives. Patterns are arranged in order of increasing difficulty. The test is untimed but generally takes 15-45 minutes and results in a raw score which is then converted to a percentile ranking. The test can be given to hearing- and speech-impaired children, as well as non-English speakers. The Standard Progressive Matrices is usually used as part of a battery of diagnostic tests, often with the Mill Hill Vocabulary Scales. The SPM is part of a series of three tests (Raven's Progressive Matrices) for persons of varying ages and/or abilities, all consisting of the same kind of nonverbal reasoning problems. The SPM is considered an "average"-level test for the general population. The Coloured Progressive Matrices (CPM), which includes the two easiest sets from the SPM and a dozen other questions of similar difficulty, is designed for five- to 11-year-olds, persons with mental or physical handicaps, and non-English speakers. The Advanced Progressive Matrices (APM) is generally for ages 11 to adult or, specifically, for gifted students. It consists of a practice and screening test (Set I) and a 36-problem series for use with persons of above-average intellectual **ability**.

## Further Reading

McCullough, Virginia. *Testing and Your Child: What You Should Know About 150 of the Most Common Medical, Educational, and Psychological Tests.* New York: Plume, 1992.

Shore, Milton F., Patrick J. Brice, and Barbara G. Love. *When Your Child Needs Testing: What Parents, Teachers, and Other Helpers Need to Know about Psychological Testing.* New York: Crossroad, 1992.

Walsh, W. Bruce, and Nancy E. Betz. *Tests and Assessment.* 2nd ed. Englewood Cliffs, NJ: Prentice Hall, 1990.

# Standardized test

*A test administered to a group of subjects under exactly the same experimental conditions and scored in exactly the same way.*

Standardized tests are used in psychology, as well as in everyday life, to measure **intelligence**, aptitude, achievement, **personality**, attitudes and interests. Attempts are made to standardize tests in order to eliminate biases that may result, consciously or unconsciously, from varied administration of the test. Standardized tests are used to produce norms—or statistical standards—that provide a basis for comparisons among individual members of the group of subjects. Tests must be standardized, reliable (give consistent results), and valid (reproducible) before they can be considered useful psychological tools.

Standardized tests are highly controversial both in psychological circles and particularly in education because true standardization is difficult to attain. Certain requirements must be rigidly enforced. For example, subjects must be given exactly the same amount of time to take the test. Directions must be given using precisely the same wording from group to group, with no embellishments, encouragement, or warnings. Scoring must be exact and consistent. Even an unwitting joke spoken by the test administrator that relaxes the subjects or giving a test in a room that is too hot or too cold could be considered violations of standardization specifications. Because of the difficulty of meeting such stringent standards, standardized tests are widely criticized.

Critics of the use of standardized tests for measuring educational achievement or classifying children are critical for other reasons as well. They say the establishment of norms does not give enough specific information about what children know. Rather, they reveal the average level of knowledge. Secondly, critics contend that such tests encourage educators and the public to focus their **attention** on groups rather than on individuals. Improving tests scores to enhance public image or achieve public funding become more of a focus than teaching individual children the skills they need to advance. Another criticism is that the tests, by nature, cannot measure knowledge of complex skills such as problem solving and critical thinking. "Teaching to the test"—drilling students in how to answer fill-in-the-blank or multiple-choice questions—takes precedence over instruction in more practical, less objective skills such as writing or logic.

**Achievement tests**, I.Q. tests, and the **Stanford-Binet intelligence scales** are examples of widely used standardized tests.

### Further Reading

Houts, Paul L., ed. The Myth of Measurability. New York: Hart Publishing Co., 1977.

Wallace, Betty, and William Graves. *Poisoned Apple: The Bell-Curve Crisis and How Our Schools Create Mediocrity and Failure.* New York: St. Martin's Press, 1995.

Zimbardo, Philip G. *Psychology and Life.* Glenview, IL: Scott, Foresman, 1988.

## Stanford-Binet intelligence scales

The oldest and most influential intelligence test, devised in 1916 by Stanford psychologist Lewis Terman.

Consisting of questions and short tasks arranged from easy to difficult, the Stanford-Binet measures a wide variety of verbal and nonverbal skills. Its fifteen tests are divided into the following four cognitive areas: 1) verbal reasoning (vocabulary, comprehension, absurdities, verbal relations); 2) quantitative reasoning (math, number series, equation building); 3) abstract/visual reasoning (pattern analysis, matrices, paper folding and cutting, copying); and 4) short-term **memory** (memory for sentences, digits, and objects, and bead memory). While the child's **attitude and behavior** during the test are noted, they are not used to determine the result, which is arrived at by converting a single raw score for the entire test to a figure indicating "mental age" (the average age of a child achieving that score). A formula is then used to arrive at the **intelligence** quotient, or I.Q. An I.Q. of 100 means that the child's chronological and mental ages match. Traditionally, I.Q. scores of 90-109 are considered average, scores below 70 indicate **mental retardation**. Gifted children achieve scores of 140 or above. Most recently revised in 1986, the Stanford-Binet intelligence test can be used with children from age two, as well as with adults. Although some of its concepts—such as **mental age** and intelligence quotient—are being questioned, the test is still widely used to assess **cognitive development** and often to determine placement in **special education** classes.

*See also* Terman, Lewis; Wechsler Intelligence Scales.

**Abstract and visual reasoning are analyzed in Stanford-Binet intelligence tests. This blindfolded subject is matching shapes by touch.** *(Richard Nowitz. Photo Researchers, Inc. Reproduced with permission.)*

## Statistics in psychology

A branch of mathematics devoted to the collection, compilation, display, and interpretation of numerical data.

Psychologists rely heavily on statistics to help assess the meaning of the measurements they make. Sometimes the measurements involve individuals who complete psychological tests; at other times, the measurements involve statistics that describe general properties of groups of people or animals.

In psychological testing, the psychologist may interpret test results in light of norms, or the typical results, provided from previous testing. In research, psychologists use two kinds of statistics, descriptive and inferential. Descriptive statistics simply give a general picture of the scores in a given group. They include the measures of central tendency and the measures of variability. Central tendency involves different kinds of averages: the **mean**, **median**, and **mode**. Variability involves the standard deviation, which indicates how far scores in a group are likely to be from the average.

Inferential statistics are used to help psychologists draw inferences, or conclusions, from the data obtained from their research. The most common statistical tests include the student's T-test and the Analysis of Variance (or F-test); these statistics help the psychologist assess whether the differences in averages across groups are due to the effects of an **independent variable**. Another widely used inferential statistic is the correlation coefficient, which describes the strength of the relationship between two variables. For example, there is a positive correlation between a student's score on the **Scholastic Assessment Test** (SAT) and his/her grades in the first year of college. Correlations involve patterns that exist in groups; individuals within those groups may not perform in the manner the correlation predicts that they will, but if large numbers of students are tested, general trends may be detected.

**Further Reading**

Anderson, David Ray. *Introduction to Statistics: Concepts and Applications*. St. Paul, MN: West Pub. Co., 1990.

Bluman, Allan G. *Elementary Statistics: A Step-by-Step Approach*. Dubuque, IA: Wm. C. Brown Publishers, 1995.

Freund, John E. *Statistics: A First Course*. Englewood Cliffs, NJ: Prentice Hall, 1995.

# Stereotype

An unvarying view about the physical appearance, personality, or behavior of a particular group of people.

Some people believe and perpetuate stereotypes about particular ethnic groups: Italians are emotionally sensitive, loud, and talk with their hands; Irish people drink too much; Germans are serious and intelligent. While such characteristics may apply to few members of that ethnic group, some people characterize all people in a certain group to share these **traits**. Psychologists have also noted the role stereotypes **play** in human **memory**. When meeting a new person, for example, people sometimes combine their firsthand perceptions of that person—appearance, **personality**, intelligence—with stereotypes they have formed about similar people. Later, when trying to describe or recall that person, the actual characteristics become distorted by the stereotypical features that often have no relation to that person.

Television has been criticized for perpetuating stereotypes, particularly regarding racial groups and women. Studies have shown that early television programs, in particular, were guilty of portraying stereotyped characters. For instance, minorities were more likely than whites to be criminals, and women were often shown in the roles of wife, mother, or sex object. Children proved to be especially vulnerable to the influence of these stereotypes. The civil rights movement of the 1960s and the women's movement of the 1970s prompted the development of "prosocial" programs such as Sesame Street that sought to counter racial, ethnic, and gender stereotypes.

**Further Reading**

Liebert, Robert M.; Joyce N. Sprafkin; and Emily S. Davidson. *The Early Window: Effects of Television on Children and Youth*. New York: Pergamon Press, 1982.

# Robert J. Sternberg

**1949-**
American cognitive psychologist who developed a new model of learning and intelligence.

## From childhood anxiety to a career

Robert J. Sternberg was born in December 1949 in Newark, New Jersey. As a child growing up in Maplewood, New Jersey, Sternberg suffered from a problem common to many children. An otherwise bright student, he suffered such severe anxiety when taking IQ tests that he consistently scored low. His active **brain** was evident when he discovered as a sixth grader re-taking a test among fifth graders that his anxiety was pointless. In seventh grade, his science project was called the "Sternberg Test of Mental Ability." He gave the test to his classmates along with the traditional Stanford-Binet **intelligence** scales that he had discovered in the town library. From this point on, Sternberg devoted his time to researching the processes of testing and learning.

As a student at Yale University, Sternberg spent his summers working for the Psychological Corporation in New York, and the Educational Testing Service in Princeton, New Jersey, alongside writers who wrote **standardized test** materials. While at Yale he studied with Endel Tulving, graduating summa cum laude in 1972 with a BA in psychology. He also received the prestigious Wohlenberg Prize and was named to Phi Beta Kappa. Sternberg received his Ph.D. from Stanford in 1975. While at Stanford he studied with Gordon Bower and received the Sidney Siegel Memorial Award. He also continued to work on investigating the analytical processes people utilize while taking intelligence tests. Along with his work as the IBM Professor of Education and Director of Graduate Studies in the Department of Psychology at Yale, Sternberg has enjoyed a prolific career as a writer and editor. In 1994, he served as president of the **American Psychological Association (APA)** Division 1 (General) and in 1994–95 as president of APA Division 15 (Educational). In all, he is a fellow of nine APA divisions, and has won two APA awards, the Distinguished Scientific Award for an Early Career Contribution to Psychology in 1981, and the McCandless Award. Other awards have come to him from around the world.

According to a profile of Sternberg from the *APA Monitor*, "Sternberg views himself as a generalist dedicated to improving the profession for all psychologists." His book, *Beyond IQ: A Triarchic Theory of Human Intelligence*, however, began to define his studies more closely. Sternberg's compilation of the "componential" theory associated information processing stages with specific brain functions. To that, he added the "experiential" and "contextual," or external, to signify the entirety of cognitive **ability**, re-defining intelligence. Sternberg believes that life, not what is learned in the classroom, determines intelligence. His creative approach to understanding human intelligence as a composition of **creativity**, emotional balance, and cognitive abilities has made him a celebrity not only among his professional colleagues, but with the general public, especially through his books, *The Triangle of Love*, *Love The Way You Want It*, and *Love Is a Story: A New Theory of Relationships*. Sternberg has been determined to keep the integrity of his occupation at the highest level and yet available to those other than seasoned professionals. His writing style is conversational and not prohibitively academic.

His work has also extended into studying learning disabilities in children and understanding exactly what such a designation implies. One book he has published on this subject is *Our Labeled Children* co-authored with Elena L. Grigorenko and published in 1999.

### International collaborations and a "labor of love"

Sternberg's research group is actively connected to groups around the world, including Israel, Tanzania, France, Norway, and Spain. Sternberg describes the various projects of his students as "interrelated" while individually developing a specific focus. For Sternberg himself, the study of love and close relationships often catches his greatest interest. Sternberg states that "here, we are studying issues such as people's conceptions of love, the growth and decline of love over the course of relationships, and the structure of love in different relationships."

Sternberg not only studies love in the research setting. His marriage to Alejandra Campos, also trained in **clinical psychology**, has produced two children, Seth and Sara. Sternberg has observed that his children also have the same **test anxiety** from which he suffered, even though they are "A" students. In an interview with *Psychology Today* in 1986, Sternberg told Robert J. Trotter "it's really important to me that my work has an effect that goes beyond the psychology journals. I really think

it's important to bring intelligence into the real world and the real world into intelligence."

*See also* Intelligence quotient

Jane Spear

### Further Reading
Paul, Annie Murphy. *Sternberg: a wayward path to wisdom.* Psychology Today, May-June 1998.
Sternberg, Robert J. *Successful Intelligence.* New York: Simon & Schuster, 1996.
Trotter, Robert J. *Three heads are better than one.* Psychology Today, August 1986.

# Stimulant drugs

Also called psychostimulants, drugs that produce increased levels of mental and physical energy and alertness and an elevated mood by stimulating the central nervous system.

Stimulants are used for the treatment of certain psychiatric conditions and also used (and abused) for recreational purposes, enhanced levels of energy, and weight loss. They may be prescription or over-the-counter medications, illegal street drugs, or ingredients in commonly ingested substances, such as the caffeine in coffee or the nicotine in cigarettes. Whatever their form, stimulants increase respiration, heart rate, and blood pressure, and their abuse can cause adverse physical effects and endanger a person's health and even his or her life. An overdose of stimulants can result in chest pains, convulsions, paralysis, **coma**, and death.

### Caffeine and nicotine

The most commonly used stimulant (and the most widely consumed drug) in the United States is caffeine. Found in coffee, tea, soft drinks, chocolate, and drugs, including **pain** relievers, diet pills, and cold and allergy medications, caffeine belongs to a family of drugs called methylxanthines. It works by disrupting the action of a **neurotransmitter** called adenosine. Since caffeine is usually consumed in food, it normally enters the body through the gastrointestinal system, passing from the intestines into the blood, which circulates it through the body. It reaches its maximum effect within 30-60 seconds from the time it is consumed, although it remains in the body for several hours. Caffeine is addictive. People who consume it regularly develop a tolerance for it, meaning that they need to ingest progressively greater amounts to continue getting the same effect. (Thus, diet pills containing caffeine lose their effectiveness after a few days, when a tolerance is established.) Caffeine causes physical dependence, producing withdrawal symptoms including anxiety, headaches, and fatigue when its use is discontinued. People who stop using caffeine also experience a craving for it, which is a sign of psychological dependence. It is generally agreed that daily caffeine consumption equal to the amount contained in one cup of coffee or soft drink (under 240 milligrams) is probably harmless, but that consumption over 600 milligrams (the amount in four cups of coffee) can cause anxiety, **sleep** and digestive disorders, a rapid heartbeat, and other health problems. The National College Athletic Association has limited the amount of caffeine that its players can consume.

Besides caffeine, the other stimulant widely ingested is the nicotine consumed in smoking. Both caffeine and nicotine are classified as secondary stimulants because, unlike drugs such as amphetamines and cocaine, they affect the sympathetic **nervous system** more than the **central nervous system**. Also unlike stimulants that are abused for recreational purposes, caffeine and nicotine produce only an increased energy level but not a feeling of intoxication. Nicotine acts mostly as a stimulant in new users, but long-term users claim that it relaxes them. Teenage smoking has been rising steadily throughout the 1990s. A 1995 survey of high school students by the Centers for Disease Control and Prevention found that on average 34.8% of teenagers smoke. Like users of other addictive substances, teen smokers start out thinking they will be able to control their use of cigarettes, but two-thirds of young people who smoke have tried to quit and failed. Nicotine withdrawal symptoms include anxiety, irritability, insomnia, **depression**, headaches, **mood** swings, difficulty concentrating, and changes in appetite.

## Stimulants used for therapeutic purposes

Stimulant drugs have long been used to treat psychological disorders. In the past, psychiatrists used certain stimulants as **antidepressants**, but today this practice is confined primarily to seriously depressed patients who have failed to respond to either **psychotherapy** or to the wide range of other antidepressants that are currently available (and that, unlike stimulants, are not addictive). Today the primary therapeutic use of stimulants is for the treatment of **attention deficit/hyperactivity disorder** (ADHD) in children, and the most widely used drug is Ritalin (methylphenidate). Ritalin works by facilitating the release of the neurotransmitter norepinephrine, which improves alertness, attention span, and the **ability** to focus. Although it is generally considered safe and effective for the treatment of ADHD, there is still controversy surrounding the frequency with which this medication—whose use by children doubled between 1988 and 1994—is prescribed. Side effects include insomnia, appetite loss, and stomach pains. Ritalin may also produce withdrawal symptoms, including headache, irritability, nausea, and abnormal chewing movements and movements of the tongue. Other stimulants used for ADHD (usually when Ritalin doesn't work or produces too many negative side effects) are Dexedrine and Cyclert (pemoline), a stimulant similar to Ritalin. Ritalin and other stimulants have also been prescribed to prevent daytime sleep episodes in persons suffering from severe **narcolepsy**.

## Abuse of illegal stimulants

The primary illegal stimulants used for recreational purposes are amphetamines and cocaine. Street names for various types of amphetamines include speed, uppers, dexies, bennies, ice, L.A. ice, Ecstasy, and crank. Amphetamines produce an effect similar to that of the hormone adrenaline, making its users feel awake, alert, and energetic. Drugs of this type were abused by young people as early as the 1930s, when it was popular to tear the medicated strip out of Benzedrine nasal inhalers and ingest them directly or in coffee. By the 1950s and 1960s amphetamines were widely used by people who needed to keep themselves awake through the night, such as truck drivers and night musicians, or by athletes for extra energy. Many young people used them to stay awake when they needed to cram for tests or complete school assignments. It is estimated that up to half the amphetamines sold by drug companies in the 1960s were sold illegally. After the government imposed controls on the manufacture of these drugs, they began to be produced illegally in home laboratories. Not only are these preparations vulnerable to contamination, they are often diluted by manufacturers and dealers. Many supposed amphetamines sold on the street contain mostly caffeine and other drugs, with a very small percentage of amphetamine or even none at all.

The use of amphetamines declined in the 1980s as cocaine became the drug of choice. However, in the 1990s methamphetamine (traditionally known as speed) has become newly popular, especially among middle-class suburban teenagers, in a crystalline form—known as ice, L.A. ice, or crank—that can either be smoked or snorted like cocaine. Smoking methamphetamine first became fashionable in Hawaii. Use of the drug then became widespread in California, and now it is increasing in other parts of the country. A 1994 survey conducted at the University of Michigan found that more high school seniors had used methamphetamine than cocaine. In 1993 alone, the number of emergency room admissions related to the use of this drug increased by 61%. Crank is much cheaper to produce than cocaine, so its manufacturers realize a larger profit (a pound can be produced for $700 and sold for as much as $225,000). Users like it because it reaches the **brain** almost immediately, and its effects last longer than those of cocaine. It produces feelings of alertness, euphoria, and increased energy. Like other amphetamines, crank also decreases appetite and promotes weight loss, making it attractive to young women, who represent 50% of the teenage market for the drug.

People taking methamphetamine, which remains in the body for as long as four days, quickly establish a tolerance for the drug and require ever greater amounts to experience the same effect. Users can become addicted within four to six months. Side effects of the drug include a dry mouth, sweating, diarrhea, insomnia, anxiety, and blurred **vision**. Severe reactions can include **hallucinations** (called "tweaking"), **paranoia**, and speech disorders, all of which may persist for up to two days after use of the drug. In addition to physical addiction, amphetamines produce a psychological dependency on the euphoric effects produced by these drugs, especially since when they wear off they are followed by a "crash" that produces a depression so severe it can lead to suicide.

A related stimulant, which is derived from methamphetamine, is MDMA, also known as Ecstasy. MDMA combines the characteristics of a stimulant and a psychedelic drug, producing hallucinations and enhanced feelings of sociability and closeness to others. It is less addictive than amphetamines but more dangerous. Persons have died from taking this drug; some had preexisting heart conditions, but others had no known medical problems. MDMA causes brain damage, and its use can lead to the development of panic disorder.

Cocaine is a stimulant made from the leaves of the coca plant. Its street names include coke, snow, toot, blow, stardust, nose candy, and flake. When the pure drug was first extracted from the leaves in the 19th century, its harmful effects—including addiction—weren't known, and early in the 20th century it was legally sold in medicines and soft drinks, including Coca-Cola, which originally contained small amounts of the substance (from which its name is derived). Cocaine use has been illegal since 1914. Until the 1970s it was not widely used, except among some members of the arts community. At first cocaine was largely used in a diluted powder form that was inhaled. Eventually, more potent smokable forms were developed, first "freebase" then "crack," which has been widely used since the 1980s. In 1988, the *National Household Survey on Drug Abuse* reported that 1 in 10 Americans had used cocaine. Of young adults between the ages of 18 and 25, one in four reported having used cocaine at some point. Cocaine also became visible as a substance abused by celebrities, including actor John Belushi (who died of a cocaine-heroin overdose), comedian Richard Pryor (who was badly burned freebasing cocaine), and Washington, D.C. mayor Marion Barry, who was forced to resign from office but was later reelected. In 1991, a government study found that 15% of high school seniors and 21% of college students had tried cocaine, and cocaine use by teenagers continued to increase significantly through the 1990s.

Cocaine produces a physical addiction by affecting the brain's chemistry and a psychological addiction because users become dependent on the confident, euphoric feeling it creates to help them cope with the stresses of daily life. Possible negative reactions to large doses of cocaine use include hallucinations, paranoia, aggressive behavior, and even psychotic "breaks" with reality. Cocaine can cause heart problems, seizures, strokes, and comas. Reactions to withdrawal from the drug are so severe that most users are unable to quit without professional help. Withdrawal symptoms, which may last for weeks, include muscle pains and spasms, shaking, fatigue, and reduced mental function. Both inpatient and outpatient programs are available to treat persons for cocaine addiction.

### Further Reading

Carroll, Marilyn. *Cocaine and Crack. The Drug Library.* Springfield, NJ: Enslow Publishers, 1994.

Chomet, Julian. *Speed and Amphetamines.* New York: Franklin Watts, 1990.

DeBenedette, Valerie. *Caffeine.* The Drug Library. Springfield, NJ: Enslow Publishers, 1996.

Jahanson, C.E. *Cocaine: A New Epidemic.* New York: Main Line Book Co., 1992.

Lukas, Scott E. *Amphetamines: Danger in the Fast Lane.* New York: Chelsea House, 1985.

Salzman, Bernard. *The Handbook of Psychiatric Drugs.* New York: Henry Holt, 1996.

### Further Information

Drug Abuse Clearinghouse. P.O. Box 2345, Rockville, MD 20847–2345, (301) 443–6500, (800) 729–6686.

National Cocaine Hotline. (800) COCAINE.

# Stranger anxiety

Fear of people with whom a child is not familiar.

An infant learns to recognize her parents within the first few months of **birth** by sight, sound, and even **smell**. Up until six months, a baby will usually seem interested in other adults as well, engaging in games such as peek-a-boo. After six months, many babies undergo a period of **fear** and unhappiness around anyone except their parents. The child may burst into tears if an unknown person makes eye contact or shriek if left even momentarily in the care of an unfamiliar person. This stranger anxiety is a **normal** part of a child's **cognitive development**; the baby has learned to differentiate her caretakers from other people and exhibits her strong preference for familiar faces. Stranger anxiety begins around eight or nine months and generally lasts into the child's second year.

Stranger anxiety can be upsetting to friends and relatives, who may feel rebuffed by a suddenly shy child. The baby may reject a babysitter she was previously comfortable with or grow hysterical when relatives visit. It can also be a trying time for the child's parents; the baby may reject the parent who is not the principal caregiver. Furthermore, the child may be particularly upset around people who look different to her—perhaps people with glasses, men with beards, or people of an unfamiliar skin tone. Parents should respect the child's fear as much as possible, and allow her to approach people as she is able. Extra time should be spent with the child when dropping her off at a babysitter or relative's house. The new face should be introduced slowly. If the child does not want to be hugged by or sit with a relative, it is unwise to force her. Generally, the child will outgrow his fear and may become more sociable.

## Further Reading

Greenberg, Mark T., Dante Cicchetti, and E. Mark Cummings. *Attachment in the Preschool Years: Theory, Research, and Intervention.* Chicago: University of Chicago Press, 1990.

Watkins, Kathleen Pullan. *Parent-child Attachment: A Guide to Research.* New York: Garland Publishing, 1987.

Spock, Benjamin. "Mommy, Don't Go!" *Parenting* (10): June-July 1996, pp. 86+.

Sroufe, L. A., and J. Fleeson. "Attachment and the Construction of Relationships." In Hartup, W., and Z. Rubin (Eds.) *Relationships and Development.* Hillsdale, NJ: Erlbaum, 1986, pp. 51-71.

Wingate, Carrie. "Separation Distress." *American Baby* (58): May 1996. pp. 20+.

## Strange Situation

A research technique developed by American psychologist Mary Ainsworth and used in the assessment of attachment.

The Strange Situation procedure, developed by American psychologist **Mary Ainsworth**, is widely used in **child development** research. The goal of the Strange Situation procedure is to provide an **environment** that would arouse in the infant both the **motivation** to explore and the urge to seek security. An observer (often a researcher or therapist) takes a mother and her child (usually around the age of 12 months) to an unfamiliar room containing toys. A series of eight separations and reunions are staged involving mild, but cumulative, **stress** for the infant. Separation in such an unfamiliar setting would also likely activate the child's **attachment** system and allow for a direct test of its functioning. Although no single behavior can be used to assess the quality of the infant's attachment to the caregiver, the pattern of the infant's responses to the changing situation is of interest to psychologists. The validation of the procedure and its scoring method were grounded in the naturalistic observation of the child's exploration, crying, and proximity-seeking in the home.

Ainsworth's research revealed key individual differences among children, demonstrated by the child's reaction to the mother's return. Ainsworth categorized these responses into three major types:

(A) Anxious/avoidant—the child may not be distressed at the mother's departure and may avoid or turn away from her on her return;

(B) Securely attached—the child is distressed by the mother's departure and easily soothed by her on her return;

(C) Anxious/resistant—the child may stay extremely close to the mother during the first few minutes and become highly distressed at her departure. When she returns, the child will simultaneously seek both comfort and distance from the mother. The child's behavior will be characterized by crying and reaching to be held and then attempting to leave once picked up.

Using the Strange Situation procedure, many researchers have studied the development of child attachment to the mother and to other caregivers. However, there continues to be much debate about the origins of the child's reaction in the Strange Situation, and about what factors influence the development of an infant's attachment relationships.

## Further Reading

Ainsworth, M. *Infancy in Uganda: Infant Care and the Growth of Love.* Baltimore: Johns Hopkins University Press, 1967.

Ainsworth, M., M. C. Blehar, E. Waters, and S. Wall. *Patterns of Attachment: A Psychological Study of the Strange Situation.* Hillsdale, NJ: Earlbaum, 1978.

Bowlby, J. *A Secure Base: Parent-Child Attachment and Healthy Human Development.* New York: Basic Books, 1988.

Sroufe, L. A., and J. Fleeson. "Attachment and the Construction of Relationships." In Hartup, W. and Z. Rubin, eds.

*Relationships and Development.* Hillsdale, NJ: Erlbaum, 1986, pp. 51-71.

Ainsworth, M., and S. M. Bell. "Infant Crying and Maternal Responsiveness." In *Child Development*, 1171-90.

Silver, Nan. "The ABCs of Intimacy." *Parents Magazine* 71, June 1996, p. 72+.

Spock, Benjamin. "Mommy, Don't Go!" *Parenting* 10, June-July 1996, pp. 86+.

# Stress

The physiological and psychological responses to situations or events that disturb the equilibrium of an organism.

While there is little consensus among psychologists about the exact definition of stress, it is agreed that stress results when demands placed on an organism cause unusual physical, psychological, or emotional responses. In humans, stress originates from a multitude of sources and causes a wide variety of responses, both positive and negative. Despite its negative connotation, many experts believe some level of stress is essential for well-being and **mental health**.

Stressors—events or situations that cause stress—can range from everyday hassles such as traffic jams to chronic sources such as the threat of nuclear war or overpopulation. Much research has studied how people respond to the stresses of major life changes. The Life Events Scale lists these events as the top ten stressors: death of spouse, **divorce**, marital separation, jail term, death of close **family** member, personal injury or illness, marriage, loss of job through firing, marital reconciliation, and retirement. It is obvious from this list that even good things—marriage, retirement, and marital reconciliation—can cause substantial stress.

When presented with a stressful event or situation, the process of cognitive appraisal determines an individual's response to it. One option—to judge the stressor as irrelevant—would cause little disturbance and thus little stress. For example, a high school student who does not plan to attend college will experience much less stress during the **Scholastic Assessment Test** (SAT) than a student who wants to attend a top university, even though both are in the same situation. Another option is recognizing the stressor as disturbing, yet positive. Retirement or marriage could fit into this category. The judgment that a situation truly is stressful would cause the most disturbance and thus the most stress. For example, few people would consider a serious traffic accident as anything less than stressful. The magnitude of resulting stress from any

**TOP TEN STRESSFUL EVENTS**

Death of spouse
Divorce
Marital separation
Jail term or death of close family member
Personal injury or illness
Marriage
Loss of job due to termination
Marital reconciliation or retirement
Pregnancy
Change in financial state

Source: "What Are the Leading Causes of Stress?" In *Science and Technology Desk Reference.* Edited by The Carnegie Library of Pittsburgh Science and Technology Department. Detroit: Gale Research, Inc. 1993, p. 415. *(Stanley Publishing. Reproduced with permission.)*

situation generally depends upon a person's perceived ability to cope with it. If the stress is predictable—a scheduled dentist appointment, for example—it usually causes less stress. A person's ability to control the stressor also can mitigate its effects. A strong network of social support undermines the magnitude of stress in most situations.

Reactions to stress, then, vary by individual and the perceived threat presented by it. Psychological responses may include cognitive impairment—as in test anxiety, feelings of anxiety, **anger**, apathy, **depression**, and **aggression**. Behavioral responses may include a change in eating or drinking habits. Physiological responses also vary widely. The "fight or flight" response involves a complex pattern of innate responses that occur in reaction to emergency situations. The body prepares to handle the emergency by releasing extra sugar for quick energy; heart rate, blood pressure, and breathing increase; muscles tense; infection-preventing systems activate; and **hormones** are secreted to assist in garnering energy. The **hypothalamus**, often called the stress center of the **brain**, controls these emergency responses to perceived life-threatening situations.

Research has shown that stress is a contributing factor in a majority of disease cases. A relatively new area of behavioral medicine, psychoimmunology, has been developed to study how the body's immune system is affected by psychological causes like stress. While it is widely recognized that heart disease and ulcers may result from excess stress, psychoimmunologists believe many other types of illness also result from impaired immune capabilities due to stress. Cancer, allergies, and arthritis all may result from the body's weakened ability to defend itself because of stress.

Coping with stress is a subject of great interest and is the subject of many popular books and media coverage. One method focuses on eliminating or mitigating the effects of the stressor itself. For example, people who experience extreme stress when they encounter daily traffic jams along their route to work may decide to change their route to avoid the traffic, or change their schedule to less busy hours. Instead of trying to modify their response to the stressor, they attempt to alleviate the problem itself. Generally, this problem-focused strategy is considered the most effective way to battle stress. Another method, dealing with the effects of the stressor, is used most often in cases in which the stress is serious and difficult to change. Major illnesses, deaths, and catastrophes like hurricanes or airplane crashes cannot be changed, so people use emotion-focused methods in their attempts to cope. Examples of emotion-focused coping include exercise, drinking, and seeking support from emotional confidants. **Defense mechanisms** are **unconscious** coping methods that help to bury, but not cure, the stress. **Sigmund Freud** considered repression—pushing the source of stress to the unconscious—one way of coping with stress. Rationalization and denial are other common emotional responses to stress.

**Further Reading**
Tanner, Ogden. *Stress.* New York: Time-Life Books, 1976.

# Stuttering

See **Speech-language pathology**

# Subliminal influence

The effects of stimuli that are so weak the receiver is unaware of their presence.

The term subliminal is derived from the Latin words *sub* (below) and *limen* (threshold). The threshold, in this case, is the threshold of conscious awareness. Can we be influenced by stimuli that are so faint or brief that we are unaware of their presence? In other words, can people be affected by invisible stimuli? This controversial notion has intrigued scientists and the public for decades. A public relations stunt in 1957 triggered widespread concern that consumers were being induced to "eat popcorn" and "drink cola" by means of subliminal messages flashed onto a movie screen. Although there was never any good evidence that this procedure actually worked, the possibility of such "mind control" caused considerable alarm.

Careful laboratory research has explored the extent to which subliminal stimulation can affect our behavior. The best evidence for subliminal **perception** comes from studies on semantic priming. In a priming task, the viewer's task is to decide whether or not a presented letter string (the target) is a word or not. The task is not difficult. If the target is a legitimate word (e.g., DOCTOR), the respondent pushes the "yes" button. If it isn't a word (e.g., TOR-COD), he pushes the "no" button. Of special interest is how long it takes the subject to make his or her decision. Reaction times are faster when the target is preceded by a word whose meaning is similar to the target's meaning (e.g., NURSE). Thus, people will identify the target string DOCTOR as a word more quickly if it is primed with NURSE than they would if it were primed with an unrelated word like TRUCK. This priming effect is a well-established phenomenon. Researchers interested in subliminal perception wondered what would happen if the prime was presented so briefly that the viewer could not recognize it. Would the priming effect still occur? The answer is yes, and this finding is interesting because it shows that the prime initiates cognitive activity in the **brain**, even though the viewer does not feel as if any word recognition took place. Thus, there is a discrepancy between what is perceived and what the viewer is aware of having perceived.

It is important to emphasize that subliminal priming is obtained under extraordinarily artificial conditions, and that the effect is very subtle and brief. It does not show that people's motives, beliefs, or behavior can be significantly altered by secret messages. In fact, two-word subliminal primes do not appear to work. While some researchers have reported subliminal effects of a more profound nature than a mere priming effect, the claims are, at best, controversial and sometimes completely false. For example, in the 1980s subliminal auditory tapes were advertised as being able to produce many desirable effects, including weight loss, **memory** enhancement, and improvement of sexual function. Extensive testing by researchers has shown that these products have no therapeutic utility.

Timothy E. Moore

**Further Reading**
Moore, T. E., "Subliminal Perception: Facts and Fallacies" *Skeptical Inquirer,* 16, 273-281, 1992.

# Suicide/Suicidal behavior

The act of taking one's own life voluntarily and intentionally.

The annual death toll from suicide worldwide is 120,000, and it is the eighth leading cause of death in the United States, accounting for one percent of all deaths. Between 240,000 and 600,000 people in the U.S. and Canada attempt suicide every year, and over 30,000 succeed. The suicide rate is three times higher for men than for women in the United States, although females make three times as many suicide attempts as males. Traditionally, men over 45 and living alone are the demographic group at greatest risk for suicide. However, in the past 30 years, youth suicides have risen alarmingly, tripling for people aged 15 to 24. The suicide rate among persons aged 10 to 24 between 1980 and 1992 rose an average of 177%. Suicide among women has also increased dramatically since 1960, when the ratio of male to female suicides was 4 to 1. Suicide rates vary significantly among different ethnic groups in the United States; Native Americans have the highest rate at 13.6 per 100,000 (although there are sizable variations among tribes), compared with 12.9 for European-Americans, and 5.7 for African-Americans.

Attitudes toward suicide have varied throughout history. The ancient Greeks considered it an offense against the state, which was deprived of contributions by potentially useful citizens. The Romans, by comparison, thought that suicide could be a noble form of death, although they legislated against persons taking their own lives before an impending criminal conviction in order to insure their families' financial inheritance. Early Christianity, which downplayed the importance of life on earth, was not critical of suicide until the fourth century, when St. Augustine condemned it as a sin because it violated the sixth commandment ("Thou shalt not kill"). Eventually, the Roman Catholic Church excommunicated and even denied funeral rites to people who killed themselves. The medieval theologian St. Thomas Aquinas condemned suicide because it usurped God's **power** over life and death, and in The Divine Comedy, the great writer Dante placed suicides in one of the lowest circles of Hell. The view of suicide as a sin prevailed in Western societies for hundreds of years, and many people are still influenced by it, either consciously or unconsciously. Suicide was a felony and attempted suicide a misdemeanor in England until 1961.

One of the greatest influences on 20th-century notions about suicide has been French sociologist Emile Durkheim's 1897 work Le suicide. Analyzing French statistics on suicide, Durkheim concluded that suicide is primarily a function of the strength or weakness of a person's ties to **family**, religion, and community. Persons with weak social ties and those for whom such ties have been disrupted (such as divorced or widowed people) are the most vulnerable to suicide. Durkheim also catego-

rized suicide into four types. Altruistic suicide is actually mandated by society, as in the case of suttee, where an Indian wife commits suicide by throwing herself on her husband's funeral pyre. In egoistic suicide, individuals kill themselves because they lack the social ties that could motivate them to go on living. Anomic suicide occurs following the loss of a spouse, child, job, or other significant connection to the community, and fatalistic suicides are committed by people driven to despair by dire external circumstances from which there appears to be no escape.

Twenty years after the publication of Durkheim's work, **Sigmund Freud** provided the first theory that addressed suicide in terms of one's inner mental and emotional state. In *Mourning and Melancholia* (1917), he proposed that suicide was the result of turning **hostility** toward a loved one back on oneself. In *Man Against Himself* (1936), Karl Menninger extended Freud's contribution to the psychodynamic study of suicide, relating it to other forms of self-destructive behavior such as alcoholism.

Today, many possible contributing factors are associated with suicide. Psychological disorders linked to suicide include **depression, schizophrenia**, and panic disorder. A variety of research studies indicate a possible physiological predisposition to suicide as well. In a study of the Amish of southeastern Pennsylvania—a population whose close-knit community structure and isolation from such influences as drugs and alcohol make suicide extremely infrequent—four families accounted for 73 percent of suicides between 1880 and 1980, suggesting a hereditary tendency toward self-destructive impulses. Separate studies have found a correlation between suicide and levels of the **neurotransmitter** serotonin in the **brain**. **Personality** features associated with suicide include low **self-esteem**, impulsiveness, and what social learning theorists call an "external locus of control"—an orientation toward believing that one's fate is determined by forces beyond one's control.

Social scientists have found that media coverage of suicides can spur imitative behavior. In the 1970s, sociologist David P. Phillips found that increased numbers of people killed themselves following front-page coverage of suicides. He also observed that such articles had a "copycat" effect, primarily in the geographic area where the original suicides took place, and that the more publicity, the greater the effect of the suicide. The issue of whether fictional accounts of suicide in movies or television influence real life behavior is more controversial and harder to document, but evidence has been found to link increases in both attempted and completed suicide to the release of televised movies featuring suicide. Probably the best-known examples of this phenomenon are the 37 deaths by "Russian roulette" linked to the movie *The Deer Hunter.*

Suicide is the third leading cause of death among all adolescents and the second leading cause among college students. The rate of suicide is highest at the beginning of the school year and at the end of each academic term. Teenagers who contemplate or commit suicide are likely to have family problems, such as an alcoholic parent, an unwanted stepparent, or some other ongoing source of conflict. The breakup of romantic relationships is among the most common triggering factors—one study found over a third of suicidal teens were involved in the final stages of a relationship. Teen pregnancy can be another contributing factor. Drug and alcohol problems are closely related to teen suicide—one study found that drinking had preceded about a third of all suicide attempts by teenagers. In another study, almost half of all teens between the ages of 15 and 19 who committed suicide in a particular geographic area were found to have had alcohol in their blood.

Various harmful myths have been perpetuated about suicide. One is that people who talk about killing themselves do not actually do it—in fact, one of the main warning signs of suicide is thinking and talking about it. Another myth is the fatalistic idea that people who want to kill themselves will keep trying until they eventually succeed. For many people, the suicidal urge is related to a temporary crisis that will pass. Of all people who attempt suicide, 90 percent never try again. Yet another myth is the idea that nothing can be done to stop someone who is bent on suicide. Most people who feel suicidal are ambivalent about their intentions. **Mental health** professionals claim that all persons contemplating suicide give at least one warning, and 80 percent provide repeated warnings. If these warnings are heeded, potential suicides can be averted. Common warning signs include giving away prized possessions; changes in eating or sleeping habits; social withdrawal; declining performance at work or in school; and violent or rebellious behavior.

Suicide can be averted when family members or friends recognize these and other warnings and actively seek help for a loved one contemplating suicide. Suicide hotlines staffed by paraprofessional volunteers are an important source of support and assistance to people who are thinking of killing themselves. **Psychotherapy** can help a troubled person build self-esteem, frustration tolerance, and goal orientation. In cases of severe depression, antidepressant medication is an important resource; electroconvulsive therapy is recommended for persons who have not been helped by medication or who are so severely suicidal that it is considered too risky to wait until medication can take effect.

## Further Reading

Biskup, Michael, and Carol Wekesser, eds. *Suicide: Opposing Viewpoints.* San Diego: Greenhaven Press, 1992.

Colt, George Howe. *The Enigma of Suicide.* Fort Worth, TX: Summit Books, 1991.

Francis, Dorothy. *Suicide: A Preventable Tragedy.* New York: E. P. Dutton, 1989.

## Harry Stack Sullivan

### 1892-1949

American psychiatrist who based his approach to mental illness primarily upon interpersonal theory.

Harry Stack Sullivan, born on February 21, 1892, in the farming community of Norwich, New York, was the only surviving child of a poor Irish farmer. His **childhood** was apparently a lonely one, his friends and playmates consisting largely of the farm animals. His mother, who was sickly, was unhappy with the family's poor situation, and is reported to have shown her son little affection. These personal experiences seem to have had a marked effect on Sullivan's professional views in later life.

Sullivan took his medical degree in 1917 at the Chicago College of Medicine and Surgery. In 1919 he began working at St. Elizabeth's Hospital in Washington, D.C., with William Alanson White, an early American psychoanalyst. Clinical research at Sheppard and Enoch Pratt Hospital occupied a portion of Sullivan's life, as did an appointment in the University of Maryland's School of Medicine. In 1936, he helped establish the Washington School of Psychiatry. In later life, he served as professor and head of the department of psychiatry in Georgetown University Medical School, president of the William Alanson White Psychiatric Foundation, editor of *Psychiatry,* and chairman of the Council of Fellows of the Washington School of Psychiatry.

Sullivan's approach to psychiatry emphasized the social factors which contribute to the development of **personality**. He differed from **Sigmund Freud** in viewing the significance of the early parent-child relationship as being not primarily sexual but, rather, as an early quest for security by the child. It is here that one can see Sullivan's own childhood experiences determining the direction of his professional thought.

Characteristic of Sullivan's work was his attempt to integrate multiple disciplines and ideas borrowed from those disciplines. His interests ranged from evolution to communication, from learning to social organization. He emphasized interpersonal relations. He ob-

**Harry Stack Sullivan** *(The Library of Congress. Reproduced with permission.)*

jected to studying **mental illness** in people isolated from society. Personality characteristics were, he felt, determined by the relationship between each individual and the people in his **environment**. He avoided thinking of personality as a unique, individual, unchanging entity and preferred to define it as a manifestation of the interaction between people.

On January 14, 1949, while returning from a meeting of the executive board of the World Federation for **Mental Health**, Sullivan died in Paris. He was buried in Arlington National Cemetery.

### Further Reading

Mullahy, Patrick, ed. *The contributions of Harry Stack Sullivan: a symposium on interpersonal theory in psychiatry and social science.* 1952.

Ellenberger, Henri F. *The discovery of the unconscious: the history and evolution of dynamic Psychiatry.* 1970.

Chapman, A. H. (Arthur Harry). *Harry Stack Sullivan: his life and his work.* New York: Putnam, 1976.

Chatelaine, Kenneth L. *Good me, bad me, not me: Harry Stack Sullivan: an introduction to his thought.* Dubuque, Ia.: Kendall/Hunt Pub. Co., 1992.

Chatelaine, Kenneth L. *Harry Stack Sullivan, the formative years.* Washington, DC: University Press of America, 1981.

# Superego

In psychoanalytic theory, the part of the human personality that represents a person's inner values and morals; also known as conscience.

The superego is one of three basic components of human **personality**, according to **Sigmund Freud**. The **id** is the most primitive, consisting of largely **unconscious** biological impulses. The **ego** uses reality and its consequences to modify the behavior being urged by the id. The superego judges actions as right or wrong based on the person's internal value system.

Freud believed that a child develops the superego by storing up the moral standards learned from experience in society and from parents and other adults. When a parent scolds a child for hitting another child, for example, the child learns that such **aggression** is unacceptable. Stored in that child's superego, or **conscience**, is that moral judgment which will be used in determining future behavior. Another component of the superego is a person's own concept of perfect behavior, which presents a second standard used to govern actions.

The complex interaction among the id, the ego, and the superego is what determines human behavior, according to Freud. A healthy balance between the more instinctual demands of the id and the moral demands of the superego, as negotiated by the ego, results in a "normal" or healthy personality.

### Further Reading

Atkinson, Rita L.; Richard C. Atkinson; Edward E. Smith; and Ernest R. Hilgard. *Introduction to Psychology.* 9th ed. San Diego: Harcourt Brace Jovanovich, 1987.

Zimbardo, Philip G. *Psychology and Life.* 12th ed. Glenview, IL.: Scott, Foresman, 1988.

# Superstition

A belief or attitude that does not correspond to what is generally believed to be true or rational.

The study of psychology generally does not include any emphasis on these seemingly irrational beliefs that motivate behavior. Nevertheless, superstitious actions are common in our society. Avoiding walking under ladders in order to ward off disaster, crossing fingers for good luck, and knocking on wood surfaces to ensure continued prosperity or avoid tragedy are examples of commonplace superstitions that have permeated society since ancient times. **Sigmund Freud** called such superstitions "faulty actions." Some psychologists consider them expressions of inner tensions and anxieties. Others believe intense superstitious feelings indicate some sort of mental disorder. However, there has been no reliable clinical correlation between superstitious beliefs and **mental illness**.

**Further Reading**

Lorie, Peter. *Superstitions.* New York: Simon & Schuster, 1992.
Rachleff, Owen S. *The Secrets of Superstitions: How They Help, How They Hurt.* Garden City, NY: Doubleday, 1976.

# Synapse

The tiny gap through which communication between two neurons takes place.

Every thought, movement, and sensation occurs due to communication between different neurons, which provide information throughout the **nervous system**. Within a single **neuron**, information proceeds through electrical signals, but when information must be transmitted from one neuron to a succeeding neuron, the transmission is chemical.

For two neurons to communicate, chemical messengers, or neurotransmitters, are released into the synaptic cleft (a tiny gap about one thousandth of a millimeter between neurons), at which point they migrate to the next neuron and attach themselves to locations called receptor sites. The result is an initiation of electrical current that moves through that neuron toward the next one. After the **neurotransmitter** exerts its effect, it is either destroyed by other chemicals in the synaptic cleft or is reabsorbed into the original neuron. This action prevents the neurons from becoming overstimulated.

When neurons communicate, the effect can be either stimulation or inhibition of the next neuron. For example, when a person pays **attention** to one conversation and ignore others, the neurons in the **brain** are actively seeking out that information (stimulation) and actively ignoring the rest (inhibition). Neurons come in different shapes and sizes, affecting many other neurons, and can have different numbers of synapses. Some neurons, called Purkinje cells, may have as many as 100,000 synapses.

# Taste

*The chemical sense which perceives or distinguishes flavor.*

Taste, or gustation, is one of the two senses triggered by chemical stimuli (the other is olfaction). A person has approximately 10,000 taste buds. Most are on the tongue, but some are located in the back of the throat. Grouped together in bumps or papillae on the surface of the tongue, the taste buds contain receptors that respond to four basic tastes: sweet, salty, sour, and bitter. (It has also been proposed that monosodium glutamate (MSG) produces a fifth taste, called "umami," that enhances other tastes.) Each receptor responds most strongly to one or two of the four basic tastes and slightly to the others. The receptors that are sensitive to bitter substances are located on the back of the tongue. Beginning at the tip of the tongue and progressing to the rear on each side are overlapping receptors for sweet, salty, and sour tastes. Although the number of basic tastes registered by human taste receptors is extremely limited when compared with the hundreds of odors that can be identified by olfactory

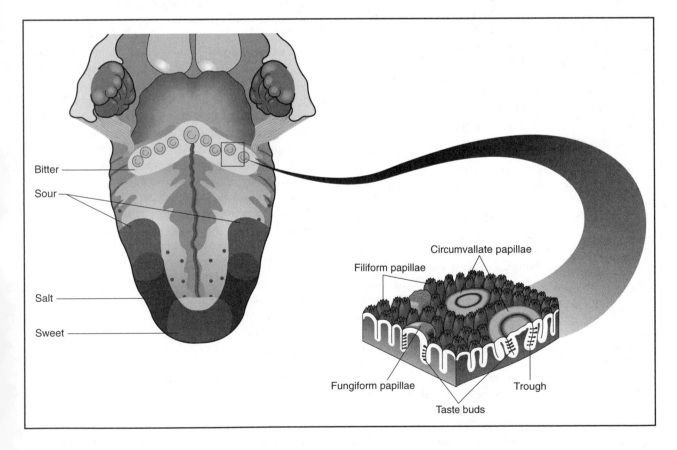

**Taste regions of the tongue (left) and taste bud anatomy (right).** *(Hans & Cassidy. Gale Group. Reproduced with permission.)*

receptors, the taste buds work together to send a unique pattern of impulses to the **brain** for each substance tasted. As any gourmet or wine taster will attest, a wide range of patterns can be created by mixing and blending the four primary tastes in different combinations.

As food is chewed, its chemicals act as the stimuli for taste, breaking down into molecules, mixing with saliva, and infiltrating the areas that contain the receptors. Activation of the taste buds triggers **nerve** impulses that travel to the brain and are there transformed into sensations of taste. Because of their relatively "toxic" **environment**, taste buds live short lives, being replaced about every ten days. The sense of **smell** often works in conjunction with our sense of taste by combining sensations to achieve the **perception** of flavor. In fact, the olfactory sense actually contributes more to the perception of specific flavors than does the sense of taste. This phenomenon is commonly demonstrated in people whose sense of taste becomes dulled by colds. It has also been investigated in laboratory research, including tests in which subjects detected little taste in such strong substances as peppermint, onions, and cinnamon when their noses were congested.

When a person eats, chemical stimuli taken in through chewing and swallowing pass through an opening in the palate at the back of the mouth and move toward receptor cells located at the top of the nasal cavity, where they are converted to olfactory nerve impulses that travel to the brain, just as the impulses from olfactory stimuli taken in through the nose. The olfactory and gustatory pathways are known to converge in various parts of the brain, although it is not known exactly how the two systems work together.

Another way to regard the relationship between taste and smell is as two component parts of a perceptual function identified as the "flavor system," which also includes temperature and tactile receptors. Warm foods seem tastier because warming releases additional aromas from the mouth to the olfactory receptors. Warm foods also seem sweeter, although temperature has no effect on the perception of salty foods. A food's tactile properties (how it feels in one's mouth) influence perception of its flavor, hence distinctions such as that between smooth and crunchy peanut butter. **Pain** receptors are even included among the mouth's nerve endings involved in flavor perception, and may account for some of the appeal of hot and spicy foods. A person's nutritional state can influence perceived tastes, as well as the desire for particular foods: salt deficiency and food deprivation increase the desire for salty foods. The sweet properties of saccharin and aspartame were discovered by accident in laboratory settings, and researchers are now actively working on developing new artificial sweeteners to allow consumption of sweet foods that are low in calories.

# Television and aggression

For many years, behavioral and educational researchers have studied the psychological effects of television programs on viewers, particularly children. Substantial debate over television began as early as the 1960s. The term "TV violence" was coined in 1963 as critics accused programs of promoting antisocial violent and aggressive behavior. More contemporary discussions center on the use of rating systems to label the content of programs and the use of technology to allow parents to censor children's viewing habits.

Although there have been cases of "copy-cat" crimes, where an actual murder or suicide is said to have been triggered by a specific television incident, a direct correlation between what a person sees and does is difficult to prove. Since the 1950s, more than 3,000 studies have been dedicated to tracing more indirect links between actual **violence** and televised violence. Some researchers have employed a laboratory setting where children watched either violent cartoons or more passive children's programming, and then measured the children's aggressiveness. Much research has been done comparing communities without television (such as a town in a remote part of Canada) to similar communities with television. Researchers have also compared crime rates and indicators of violence and **aggression** in communities before and after television became available. Such studies concluded that verbal and physical aggressiveness increased in children exposed to television. One long-term study, carried out by a psychiatrist at the University of Michigan, tracked hundreds of subjects from age eight to age 30, and the ones who watched the most television were the most aggressive, were more likely to be convicted of a serious crime, and were prone to use violence to punish their children.

Other studies have found concomitant effects. People may become more aggressive as well as more fearful of becoming a victim of violence. They may also become desensitized to violence and not react to help someone who is in trouble. Not only does exposure to television violence stimulate **antisocial behavior**, it also seems to block prosocial, altruistic behavior. Other researchers note a difference between the way violence is depicted on television and in movies, and the way violence is portrayed in literature, from fairy tales to Shakespeare, noting that television violence often seems to be without consequences. It is not portrayed as tragic or

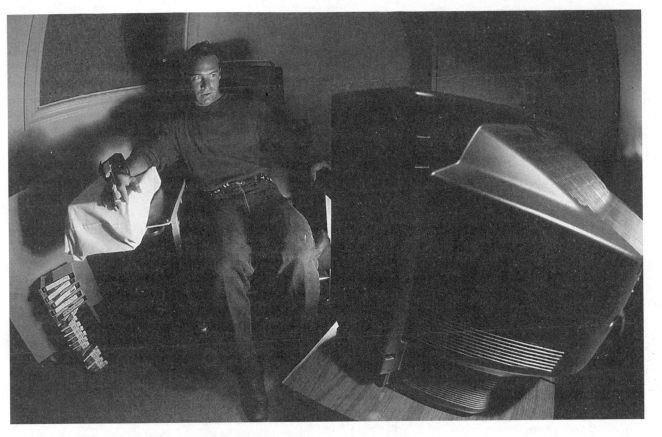

**A test subject is hooked up to machines that monitor his reactions to violent television scenes.** *(Will & Deni McIntyre. Photo Researchers, Inc. Reproduced with permission.)*

symbolic and seems an easy solution to a difficult situation. There is little differentiation between a hero's and a villain's use of violence, and realistic portrayals of injured victims and perpetrators, grieving relatives and friends, as well as other tragic consequences of violence are often not dramatized.

There have been recurring attempts by public interest groups to censor television violence or to persuade television industry executives to agree to censor themselves. Such campaigns run into problems, not only with issues of free speech, but also with accountability, as the television industry claims to be providing what their viewers want and to be reflecting a violent society, rather than creating one. Since television is broadcast indiscriminately, any attempt to regulate what some people watch will impinge on the freedom of others to view what they want. Some recent proposals for federal regulation of television violence, short of direct censorship, resulted in a ratings system, similar to that for movies, which includes warnings, before broadcasts, about the possible ill effects of viewing violence.

Since 1984, all cable companies have been required to offer a lock box that prevents certain programs from being received. These locking devices are becoming more sophisticated, with the advent of the so-called "V-chip"—a computer chip that can be programmed to block out programs with violent content.

A. Woodward

**Further Reading**
Huesmann, L. Rowell, and Leonard D. Eron, eds. *Television and the Aggressive Child: A Cross National Comparison.* Hillsdale, New Jersey: Lawrence Erlbaum Associates, 1986.
Reiss, Albert J. Jr., and Jeffrey A. Roth, eds. *Understanding and Preventing Violence.* Washington, D.C.: National Academy Press, 1993.

# Temperament

An individual's characteristic emotional nature, including energy level, prevailing mood and sensitivity to stimulation.

Individual variations in temperament are most readily observed in newborn babies. Even immediately after birth, some babies are calm while others cry a lot. Some respond favorably to being held while others squirm and protest. Some are soothed by soft music and others do not stop crying long enough to hear it. Because of these immediately observable variations, temperament is often considered a biologically based characteristic.

Hippocrates discussed variations in temperament as early as the 5th century B.C. His hypothesis that there are four basic human temperaments that correspond to various bodily characteristics—choleric, sanguine, melancholic, and phlegmatic— endured for many years before modern theories became accepted. American psychologist **Gordon Allport** (1897-1967), who came to dislike psychoanalytic theory and **behaviorism** because of their emphasis on seeking universal theories to explain all human behavior and disorders, believed temperament was one of three "raw materials" that distinguish individuals from one another and from other living beings. Along with **intelligence** and physique, temperament was genetically determined and unique within each person. Allport wrote that temperament includes a person's susceptibility to emotional stimulation, strength and speed of response, and **mood**. In a **longitudinal study** in New York starting in 1956 with data from more than 100 children that they tracked through **adolescence**, child psychiatrists Stella Chess and Alexander Thomas identified at birth nine different temperament characteristics. These characteristics, which could be observed at widely varying degrees in babies influenced their development: activity level, rhythmicity or regularity in biological functions, tendency to approach or withdraw, adaptability, threshold of responsiveness, intensity or energy level of reactions, quality of mood, distractibility and **attention** span, and persistence. From these nine dimensions emerged three major temperamental types: easy-going children, difficult children, and slow-to-warm-up children. Chess and Thomas also examined the goodness of fit between the individual child and the **environment** of the child.

Assuming that temperamental qualities can be rated on continuous dimensions across individuals, some approaches focus the study of temperament on **traits**. Isabel Myers, with her mother, Katherine Briggs, published the **Myers-Briggs Type Indicator** in 1962, identifying 16 different behavior patterns and drawing upon Carl Jung's four psychological types. The test was widely used by psychologists in individual and couples counseling, as well as in business to provide greater self-understanding. Adults as well as children display temperaments that are individually and uniquely determined by biology. Discussion in this field has centered on the degree to which temperament is inborn nature and the degree to which temperament is nurtured or coaxed along by an infant or child's environment.

While supporting the belief that temperament is biologically based, many **personality** experts also maintain that temperament can develop and change over the course of a person's life in response to personal experiences and environmental conditions. Fussy babies can grow to be placid toddlers. Similarly, passive infants sometimes grow up to be classroom troublemakers. Interaction with parents, siblings, and other social contacts as well as life experiences **affect** an individual's predisposition toward a particular temperament. Doreen Arcus in her study observed infants in their homes for their first year of life. Highly reactive infants were less likely to become timid and inhibited one-year-olds when their mothers were firm and direct in their limit-setting behavior in response to infant transgressions like pulling at plants or getting into the cat food. When mothers were highly permissive and indirect in their discipline, highly reactive infants tended to become fearful and inhibited. Emmy Werner in a study found that temperament could ease difficult circumstances in the environment. An easy, sociable temperament provided a protective buffer for children growing up in difficult circumstances. The environment can nurture changes both positive and negative to reshape an infant's natural tendencies. Natural tendencies can ameliorate or worsen environmental situations. Acknowledging the interactions of both temperament and environment during development should make possible continued progress in understanding of the intricate multiple influences on a human's life and growth. Neither temperament nor biology is destiny.

## Further Reading

Bates, J.E., and Wachs, T.D. *Temperament: Individual Differences at the Interface of Biology and Behavior.* Washington, D.C.: APA Press, 1994.

Carey, W.B., and McDevitt, S.C. *Coping With Children's Temperament: A Guide for Professionals.* New York: Basic Books, 1995.

Chess, Stella, and Thomas, Alexander. *Know Your Child.* Northvale, N.J.: Jason Aronson, 1996.

# Lewis Terman

## 1877-1956
American psychologist whose notable work was concentrated in the areas of intelligence testing and the comprehensive study of intellectually gifted children.

Terman was born in Indiana and attended Indiana University and Clark University. He served on the faculty of Stanford University as professor of education

**Lewis Terman** *(Archives of the History of American Psychology. Reproduced with permission.)*

and as professor of psychology. In 1916, Terman published the first important individual **intelligence** test to be used in the United States, the **Stanford-Binet Intelligence scales**. This test was an American revision and expansion of the Binet-Simon intelligence test, which had been developed in France. Along with the Stanford-Binet, Terman introduced the term **intelligence quotient**, or I.Q., and its formulation. This concept, and the Stanford-Binet test, became very widely used in the **measurement** of intelligence. Terman believed that society has a need to identify academically gifted children and to provide them with appropriate educational opportunities. In 1921, he began a thoroughly exhaustive and very long term study of such children. The results of this study, which are scheduled to be announced in the year 2010, may be found in *Genetic Studies of Genius* (1926). Terman's other books include: *The Measurement of Intelligence* (1916), *Sex and Personality* (1936), and *The Gifted Child Grows Up* (1947).

*See also* Binet, Alfred.

**Further Reading**
Minton, Henry L. *Lewis M. Terman.* New York: New York University Press, 1988.

# Test anxiety

A condition characterized by persistent anxiety in test situations that is severe enough to seriously interfere with performance.

Physical symptoms of test anxiety include a rapid heartbeat, dry mouth, sweating, stomach ache, dizziness, and desire to urinate. The anxiety interferes with concentration and **memory**, making it difficult or impossible to recall previously memorized material and resulting in test performance that does not accurately reflect a person's **intelligence** or the amount of effort spent preparing for the exam. Often, the memorized material is recalled once the test is over and the person leaves the test room.

People with text anxiety are usually conscientious students who work hard and have high expectations of themselves. The condition may begin with inadequate performance on a particular test, which then creates a general **fear** of the testing situation that hampers future performance, creating a vicious cycle of anxiety and low scores. Very creative students may develop test anxiety when unorthodox responses to questions result in low grades that make them question their own abilities and intelligence. Test anxiety can interfere significantly with a person's academic accomplishment and impair confidence and **self-esteem**.

Sometimes teachers are willing to consider alternative testing procedures, such as oral exams instead of written tests. In some cases, test anxiety can be reduced or eliminated by having a person work on test-taking skills, such as strategies for answering different types of questions, and then hone them through practice testing (including timed testing if this is a source of apprehension). Both creating and taking practice tests can help defuse anxiety.

Other techniques that have been used to treat test anxiety include hypnotherapy and **biofeedback**. The beta blocker Inderal, taken on an as-needed basis, has helped some people overcome anxiety in test situations.

**Further Reading**
Erwin, Bette, and Elza Teresa Dinwiddie. *Test Without Trauma: How to Overcome Test Anxiety and Score Higher on Every Test.* New York: Grosset and Dunlap, 1983.

# Thalamus

A collection of cell body clusters located in the middle of the forebrain.

The thalamus is a relatively large collection of cell body clusters shaped like two small footballs. It is involved in receiving sensory information from the eyes and other sense organs, processing that information, and then transmitting it to primary sensory zones in the cerebral cortex. The thalamus also processes **pain** signals from the spinal cord as well as information from different parts of the cerebral hemispheres, and relays it to the cerebellum and the medulla. Together with the **hypothalamus**, the thalamus forms part of the forebrain called the diencephalon.

By registering the sensory properties of food, such as texture and temperature, the thalamus plays a role in appetite. It is also known to be involved in the control of **sleep** and wakefulness. Cognitive researchers have found that the thalamus activates or integrates language functions, plays a role in **memory**, and that a portion of the thalamus, called the pulvinar, helps in refocusing **attention**. Together with the hippocampus and parts of the cortex, it is instrumental in the formation of new memories, which are then thought to be stored in the cerebral cortex.

*See also* Brain.

# Thematic Apperception Test

Assesses personality.

The Thematic Apperception Test is an untimed, individually administered psychological test used for **personality** assessment. Suitable for ages 14-40, it is used to identify dominant drives, emotions, and conflicts, as well as levels of emotional maturity, observational skills, **imagination**, and **creativity**. The subject is shown a series of pictures, one at a time, and asked to make up a story about each one, and his or her responses are evaluated by a trained psychologist. The test is usually given in two sessions, with 10 pictures shown in each one. Sessions are untimed but generally last about an hour. (For children ages 3-10, see Children's Apperception Test.)

## Further Reading

McCullough, Virginia. *Testing and Your Child: What You Should Know About 150 of the Most Common Medical, Educational, and Psychological Tests.* New York: Plume, 1992.

Shore, Milton F., Patrick J. Brice, and Barbara G. Love. *When Your Child Needs Testing: What Parents, Teachers, and Other Helpers Need to Know about Psychological Testing.* New York: Crossroad, 1992.

Walsh, W. Bruce, and Nancy E. Betz. *Tests and Assessment.* 2nd ed. Englewood Cliffs, NJ: Prentice Hall, 1990.

Wodrich, David L., and Sally A. Kush. *Children's Psychological Testing: A Guide for Nonpsychologists.* 2nd ed. Baltimore, MD: Brookes Publishing Co., 1990.

# Edward Thorndike

## 1874-1949

American educational psychologist best known for his experimentally derived theories of learning and his influence on behaviorism.

Edward Thorndike was born in Williamsburg, Massachusetts, and grew up in a succession of New England towns where his father served as a Methodist minister. After receiving his bachelor's degree from Wesleyan University, Thorndike did graduate work in psychology, first at Harvard under the guidance of **William James** and later at Columbia under James McKeen Cattell. His first major research project—undertaken while he was still a graduate student—involved trial-and-error learning, using first chickens and then cats. Observing the behavior of cats attempting to escape from enclosed "puzzle boxes," Thorndike noted that responses that produced satisfaction—escape from the box and subsequent feeding—were "stamped in" and more likely to be repeated in the future, while responses that led to failure, and thus dissatisfaction, tended to be "stamped out." Thorndike termed this observation the **law of effect**, one of two laws of learning he derived from his research. The other law, called the law of exercise, stated that associations that are practiced are stamped in, while others are extinguished. Applied to humans, these laws became an important foundation of both behaviorist psychology and modern **learning theory**. Thorndike based his doctoral dissertation on his research, which he also published in the form of a monograph in 1898. After earning his Ph.D., Thorndike spent a year on the faculty of Case Western Reserve University, after which he was appointed professor of **educational psychology** at Columbia's Teachers' College, where he remained until his retirement. Thorndike made many early and significant contributions to the field of experimental animal psychology, successfully arguing that his findings had relevant implications for human psychology.

Upon his return to New York, Thorndike turned his attention to a new research area—termed "transfer of training"—which was concerned with the effect of performance in one discipline on performance in others. The belief in such a connection had sustained the traditional system of instruction in formal disciplines, such as the classics, through the rationale that achievement in a given field equipped students for success in other areas. Working together with his friend and colleague, Robert Woodworth, Thorndike found that training in specific tasks produced very little improvement in the **ability** to perform different tasks. These findings, published in

**Edward L. Thorndike** *(The Library of Congress. Reproduced with permission.)*

1901, helped undermine the tradition of formal disciplines in favor of educational methods that were more specifically task-oriented.

Continuing to focus on human learning, Thorndike became a pioneer in the application of psychological principles to areas such as the teaching of reading, language acquisition, and mental testing. In 1903, he published *Educational Psychology,* in which he applied the learning principles he had discovered in his animal research to humans. In the following year, Thorndike's *Introduction to the Theory of Mental and Social Measurements* (1904), which provided administrators and users of **intelligence** tests access to statistical data about test results. Thorndike also devised a scale to measure children's handwriting in 1910 and a table showing the frequency of words in English (*The Teacher's Word Book of 30,000 Words,* 1944), which has been useful to researchers who rely on dictionary words. As a teacher of teachers, Thorndike was directly and indirectly responsible for a number of curricular and methodological changes in education throughout the United States. A prolific writer, Thorndike produced over 450 articles and books, including *The Elements of Psychology* (1905), *Animal Intelligence* (1911), *The Measurement of Intelli-*

gence (1926), *The Fundamentals of Learning* (1932), *The Psychology of Wants, Interests, and Attitudes* (1935), and *Human Nature and the Social Order* (1940).

**Further Reading**

Clifford, G. J. *Edward L. Thorndike: The Sane Positivist.* Middletown, CT: Wesleyan University Press, 1984.

## Edward Chace Tolman

**1886-1959**
American psychologist and one of the leaders of the behaviorist movement.

**Edward Tolman** was born on April 14, 1886, in Newton, Massachusetts. After graduation from the Newton public schools in 1907 and from the Massachusetts Institute of Technology in 1911, he did graduate study in psychology at Harvard. At Harvard (1911-1915), Tolman witnessed the initial reaction of the academic world to two new sets of psychological ideas: those of the Gestalt psychologists (**Wolfgang Köhler, Kurt Koffka,** and **Max Wertheimer**) and those of John B. Watson, the behaviorist.

Tolman's later theory of behavior is rooted in these two schools. From **Gestalt psychology** he borrowed the idea of pattern: in Tolman's theory, **perception, motivation,** and **cognition** are regarded as processes in which patterns of stimulation are identified and interpreted and patterns of reactions are planned and executed. From **behaviorism** he borrowed the idea that such mental processes must be objectively defined in terms of behavioral properties that can be objectively recorded. Such objectivity is necessary, he thought, not only in our study of the mental processes of rats, cats, monkeys, and so on, but also in our study of our own mental processes. Whatever is private or subjective in our mental processes is, he claimed, forever protected from scientific scrutiny because by definition such intrinsically private states have no influence on our overt behavior.

In 1918, Tolman went to the University of California at Berkeley, where he began to study maze learning in rats—a research program that made the department of psychology at Berkeley world-famous. In 1932, Tolman published *Purposive Behavior in Animals and Men.* This book presented Tolman's purposive behaviorism and reviewed the new research on rat learning done in his Berkeley laboratory.

From 1932 on, Tolman and his students turned out a constant flood of papers on animal learning. Tolman's

**Edward Chase Tolman** *(Archives of the History of American Psychology. Reproduced with permission.)*

only other book was *Drives toward War* (1942). This book surveyed studies of animal behavior in search of an explanation of the motives that drive men to war and a description of the social controls that would have to be enforced in a warless society. The book also shows the strong impact of **Sigmund Freud** upon Tolman's theory of motivation.

On June 14, 1949, the regents of the University of California handed an ultimatum to the Academic Senate: sign the new special loyalty oath or face dismissal! On that day Tolman became the leader of the nonsigners, those who were fired by the regents for refusing to submit to this naked attack upon academic freedom. After a 10-year court battle, the regents' case was repudiated by the courts: the special loyalty oath was declared unconstitutional, and the nonsigners were reinstated with back pay. On November 19, 1959, Tolman died in Berkeley.

### Further Reading

Tolman, Edward Chace. *Purposive behavior in animals and men.* 1932.

Tolman, Edward Chace. *Collected papers in psychology.* 1951.

Taylor, Charles. *The explanation of behavior.* 1964.

Stewart, George R. *The year of the oath* 1950.

# Touch

*The skin sense that allows us to perceive pressure and related sensations, including temperature and pain.*

The sense of touch is located in the skin, which is composed of three layers: the epidermis, dermis, and hypodermis. Different types of sensory receptors, varying in size, shape, number, and distribution within the skin, are responsible for relaying information about pressure, temperature, and **pain**. The largest touch sensor, the Pacinian corpuscle, is located in the hypodermis, the innermost thick fatty layer of skin, which responds to vibration. Free **nerve** endings—neurons that originate in the spinal cord, enter and remain in the skin—transmit information about temperature and pain from their location at the bottom of the epidermis. Hair receptors in the dermis, which are wrapped around each follicle, respond to the pressure produced when the hairs are bent. All the sensory receptors respond not to continued pressure but rather to changes in pressure, adapting quickly to each new change, so that, for example, the skin is unaware of the continual pressure produced by clothes. Once stimulated by sensation, the receptors trigger nerve impulses which travel to the somatosensory cortex in the parietal lobe of the **brain**, where they are transformed into sensations. Sensitivity to touch varies greatly among different parts of the body. Areas that are highly sensitive, such as the fingers and lips, correspond to a proportionately large area of the sensory cortex.

Sensory receptors encode various types of information about objects with which the skin comes in contact. We can tell how heavy an object is by both the firing rate of individual neurons and by the number of neurons stimulated. (Both the firing rate and the number of neurons are higher with a heavier object.) Changes in the firing rate of neurons tell us whether an object is stationary or vibrating, and the spatial organization of the neurons gives us information about its location.

The temperature of human skin is usually about 89°F (32°C). Objects or surroundings at this level—known as physiological zero—produce no sensation of temperature. Warmth is felt at higher temperatures and coldness at lower ones. Some of the sensory receptors in the skin respond specifically to changes in temperature. These receptors are further specialized, as certain ones sense warmth and increase their firing rates in temperatures of 95 to 115°F (33 to 46°C), while others sense cold. Sensations of warmth and coldness are differentiated on a skin area as small as one square centimeter. Within that area, cold will be felt at about six points and warmth at two. When cold and warm stimuli are touched at the same time, a sensation of extreme heat is felt, a phenomenon known as "paradoxical hotness." Touch and temperature interact in some sensors, producing phenomena such as the fact that warm and cold objects feel heavier than those at moderate temperatures.

With free nerve endings as receptors, pain carries information to the brain about a real or potential injury to the body. Pain from the skin is transmitted through two types of nerve fibers. A-delta fibers relay sharp, pricking types of pain, while C fibers carry dull aches and burning sensations. Pain impulses are relayed to the spinal cord, where they interact with special neurons that transmit signals to the **thalamus** and other areas of the brain. Each **neuron** responds to a number of different pain stimuli. Pain is carried by many types of neurotransmitters, a fact that has made it possible to develop numerous types of pain-relieving medications. Many factors affect how pain is experienced. Pain thresholds vary with the individual and the occasion. Intensely concentrated activity may diminish or even eliminate the **perception** of pain for the duration of the activity. Natural mechanisms, including replacement by input from other senses, can block pain sensations. The brain can also block pain by signals sent through the spinal cord, a process that involves the **neurotransmitter** serotonin and natural painkillers known as endorphins.

# Tourette syndrome

A genetic, neurological disorder characterized by motor and vocal tics and associated behavioral features including obsessions and compulsions and hyperactivity.

Tourette syndrome (TS) affects roughly one in every 2,500 persons. The incidence of the condition is at least three times higher in males than in females. Historically, Tourette syndrome has been a largely misunderstood condition; it has been identified as demonic possession, epilepsy, **schizophrenia**, and other mental disorders, and was formerly thought to be the result of emotional problems due to faulty childrearing. The condition was first identified as a physiological disorder in 1885 by the French neurologist Gilles de la Tourette. Although the causes of Tourette syndrome are still not fully understood, researchers have made substantial progress in understanding and treating the condition.

## Symptoms

Tics—sudden, repetitive, involuntary muscular movements—are the hallmark of Tourette syndrome, appearing in two forms: motor and vocal tics. Motor tics are uncontrollable body movements, such as blinking, grimacing, shrugging, or tossing one's head. Vocal tics, which involve the muscles that produce speech, take the form of uncontrolled speech and involuntary noises, including snorting, hissing, yelping, sniffing, grunting, throat-clearing, and yelling. For a diagnosis of Tourette syndrome to be made, the *Diagnostic and Statistical Manual (DSM-IV)* of the American Psychiatric Association specifies criteria, including multiple motor tics and at least one vocal tic, occurring numerous times every day or almost daily for a period of over one year, with no tic-free period longer than three months, and onset of symptoms before the age of 18. There are two basic types of tics: simple and complex. Simple tics are isolated movements (such as blinking, kicking, or twitching) that involve only one part of the body. Complex tics are more involved and take the form of recognizable actions, such as poking, hitting, biting, and grooming behaviors (such as smoothing one's hair). They also include imitating the actions of others and making involuntary obscene gestures. Complex vocal tics involve recognizable words (or animal sounds) as opposed to simple noises. These may include the repetition of short phrases, such as "Oh, boy," the repetition of a single word, repetition of the words of others (**echolalia**), or involuntary swearing (coprolalia), which is one of the most publicized symptoms of the disorder, although it affects fewer than 10% of people with TS.

Besides tics, there are several types of behavior often associated with Tourette syndrome. At least half the persons affected with TS show symptoms of obsessive-compulsive disorder (OCD), a psychological condition that involves repeated intrusive and senseless thoughts (obsessions) and repetitive behavior (compulsions) intended to stop them. An obsession may be an ordinary but inappropriately intense desire (such as a preoccupation with visiting a certain store) or an outlandish idea, such as a wish to walk across the dinner table or **touch** a stranger. Compulsions are pointless activities that a person with OCD can not help repeating, such as turning lights on and off, counting things over and over, or arranging objects in a certain pattern. OCD symptoms can be extremely debilitating, taking time away from **normal** pursuits, including schoolwork and social activities. The other major behavior disorder associated with Tourette syndrome is **attention deficit/hyperactivity disorder** (ADHD), whose symptoms include hyperactivity, inability to concentrate, and impulse control disorders. Some persons with Tourette syndrome have both OCD and ADHD.

## Causes and onset of Tourette syndrome

Tourette syndrome, once thought to be caused by psychological problems, is now known to be a genetic disorder. About 90% of children with TS have a **family** history of TS or related disorders, such as other conditions involving tics. Some persons are genetic carriers of Tourette syndrome without actually having symptoms themselves (these are almost always females; roughly 99% of males who carry the genetic tendency toward the disorder develop symptoms). The biological basis for Tourette syndrome is an imbalance in the brain's neurotransmitters, chemicals that transport messages between **nerve** cells. The main **neurotransmitter** affected in people with TS is dopamine, which controls movement. Research has shown that two other neurotransmitters, norepinephrine and serotonin, also **play** a role in the condition. In addition, imaging techniques, such as brain scans, have shown abnormalities in the size and functioning of certain parts of the brain in persons affected by TS.

Symptoms of Tourette syndrome usually appear before the age of 18. Children with TS develop their first tics at the age of six or seven, but show other signs of the disorder, including sleep problems, language difficulties, and oppositional behavior, in early **childhood**, often by the age of two or three. TS usually starts with a single tic, often in the head area (most frequently repeated blinking). The initial tics are generally simple motor tics in the head and upper extremities. As the disorder progresses, the tics gradually move downward to include the torso and lower extremities. Vocal tics usually begin at about the age of nine; complex vocal tics such as coprolalia are among the last to appear. Tics in people with TS are suppressed under certain conditions, usually during **sleep** and when an individual is engaged in an activity that requires intense concentration. In some cases, children with TS can even manage to keep their tics under-control voluntarily in situations where they **fear** embarrassment, although this takes an immense effort and afterwards the suppressed tics emerge with even greater force than usual. The symptoms of Tourette syndrome increase through childhood and peak during **adolescence**, after which their intensity usually decreases. An estimated 20-30% of all children with TS outgrow the condition entirely by adulthood.

### Treatment

Although there is no medical cure for Tourette syndrome, medications can relieve many of its symptoms. Currently, the medications of choice for the suppression of tics are antihypertensives, notably Catapres, which reduces tics by 60% in most patients with only minor side effects. Related drugs that have proven effective in tic suppression are Tenex, another antihypertensive, and Klonopin, an antianxiety medication. Another class of drugs, theneuroleptics (including Haldol, Orap, and Prolixin) are even more effective than antihypertensives in suppressing tics, but for most children their advantages are outweighed by side effects, including concentration and **memory** impairment, weight gain, and drowsiness.

In addition to drugs used for the suppression of tics, additional medications are used to treat other behavioral symptoms associated with Tourette syndrome. **Antidepressants**, such as Prozac and Anafranil, are effective in treating obsessive compulsive symptoms, and ADHD is commonly treated with Ritalin or other stimulants. Combining these different types of medications can be a difficult balancing act, and their effects need to be carefully monitored by both parents and physicians. For example, the Ritalin used for ADHD may worsen a child's tics, and tricyclic antidepressants such as Norpramin and Anafranil may have to be considered as an alternative treatment for ADHD symptoms. Another symptom of

Tourette syndrome that is sometimes treated with medication is uncontrolled **aggression**, which may be decreased by Tegretol or lithium carbonate. Although medications are universally considered the first line of treatment for Tourette syndrome, relaxation techniques, including self-hypnosis, can also be very helpful in reducing symptoms of the disorder, which worsen with tension. Physical activity is also an excellent way for children with TS to reduce tension and work off their extra energy.

## Effects on schoolwork

In spite of the variety of possible symptoms associated with Tourette syndrome, about half of all children who have the disorder require only minor adjustments in order to function successfully in school. The rest require special educational programs to accommodate their needs. TS can disrupt a child's schoolwork in a number of different ways. Tics can make it difficult to concentrate or to perform certain tasks. Ironically, the effort required to suppress them can be just as disruptive because it requires so much energy. Tics can also interfere with the normal school experience by impeding the development of social skills if youngsters feel ostracized by their peers because of their unusual behavior. OCD symptoms also interfere with school performance because preoccupation with obsessive thoughts and the time spent performing compulsive actions make it difficult for children to concentrate on and complete theiracademic tasks. Children whose TS symptoms include ADHD have trouble with the organizational and concentration skills and the self-control needed for successful performance in school. Fortunately, medication helps alleviate tics and symptoms of OCD and ADHD in many children, giving them a better chance of succeeding in school. However, about 40% of children with Tourette syndrome often have additional learning disabilities that require attention, including problems with reading, math, handwriting, and spelling. In many children with TS, educational problems peak between the ages of 11 and 13 and then gradually decrease in severity. Parents of children with Tourette syndrome whose symptoms interfere with their ability to learn in a regular classroom **environment** should become familiar with their children's rights to an individualized education program under Public Law 94-142, the 1975 federal law aimed at insuring an adequate education for children with special needs.

## Further Reading

Baton Rouge Tourette's Support Group. *Toughing Out-Tourette's.* Baton Rouge, LA: Baton Rouge Tourette's Support Group,1989.

Buehrens, Adam. *Hi, I'm Adam.* Duarte, CA:Hope Press, 1991. [Juvenile]

Bruun, Ruth Dowling, and Bertel Bruun. *A Mind of Its Own: Tourette's Syndrome, A Story and a Guide.* New York: Oxford University Press,1994.

Comings, David. *Tourette Syndrome and Human Behavior.* Duarte, CA: Hope Press, 1990.

Fowler, Rick. *The Unwelcome Companion: An Insider's View of Tourette Syndrome.* Cashiers, NC: Silver Run Publications,1995.

Haerle, Tracy, ed. *Children with Tourette Syndrome: A Parents' Guide.* Rockville, MD: Woodbine House,1992.

Koplewicz, Harold. *It's Nobody's Fault: New Hope and Help for Difficult Children and Their Parents.* New York: Random House, 1996.

Kurlan, Roger, ed. *Handbook of Tourette's Syndrome and Related Tic and Behavioral Disorders.* New York: M. Dekker,1993.

Seligman, Adam, and John S. Hilkevich, eds. *Don't Think About Monkeys: Extraordinary Stories by People with Tourette Syndrome.* Duarte, Calif.: Hope Press, 1992.

## Further Information

Tourette Syndrome Association, Inc. 42-40 Bell Boulevard, Bayside, NY 11361–2820, (800) 237–0717, (718) 224–2999.

Tourette Syndrome Clinic. City of Hope National Medical Center. 1500 E. Duarte Rd., Duarte, CA 91010, (818) 359–8111.

# Traits

Characteristics that differ from one person to another in a continuous and consistent way.

Traits include such **personality** characteristics as **introversion**, aggressiveness, generosity, nervousness, and **creativity**. Systems that address personality as a combination of qualities or dimensions are called trait theories.

The first comprehensive trait theory was that of **Gordon Allport** (1897-1967). Over a period of thirty years, Allport investigated over 18,000 separate traits, proposing several principles to make this lengthy list manageable for practical purposes. One was the distinction between personal dispositions, which are peculiar to a single individual, and common traits, which can be used for describing and comparing different people. While personal dispositions reflect the individual personality more accurately, one needs to use common traits to make any kind of meaningful assessment of people in relation to each other. Allport also claimed that about seven central traits dominated each individual personality (he described these as the type of characteristic that would appear in a letter of recommendation). Another concept devised by Allport was the cardinal trait—a quality so intense that it governs virtually all of a person's activities (Mother

Theresa's cardinal trait would be humanitarianism, for example, while that of the fictional character Ebenezer Scrooge would be avarice). Secondary traits, in contrast, are those that govern less of a person's behavior and are more specific to certain situations.

Using the statistical technique of factor analysis, Raymond B. Cattell reduced Allport's list of traits to a much smaller number and then proceeded to divide these into clusters that express more basic dimensions of personality (for example, the pairs talkative-silent, open-secretive, and adventurous-cautious can all be grouped under the overall source trait of **extroversion**). Eventually he arrived at 16 fundamental source traits and developed a questionnaire to measure them—the Sixteen Personality Factor Questionnaire (16 PF)—which uses the answers to over 100 yes-or-no questions to arrive at a personality profile.

**Hans Eysenck** has also proposed a factor-analytic trait model of human personality. However, Eysenck's model focuses on the following three dominant dimensions that combine various related traits: psychoticism (characterized by various types of **antisocial behavior**), introversion-extroversion, and emotionality/neuroticism-stability. Eysenck has also combined the introversion-extroversion and emotionality-stability scales into a model containing four quadrants whose groupings of traits correspond roughly to the four types of personality outlined by the physician Hippocrates over 2,000 years ago in ancient Greece—sanguine, choleric, phlegmatic, and melancholic.

Other trait-oriented theories include those of J.P. Guilford and David McClelland. Currently, a number of psychologists interested in a trait approach to personality believe that the following five factors, rather than Eysenck's three, are most useful in assessing personality: extroversion, agreeableness, conscientiousness, neuroticism, and openness to experience. A questionnaire called the NEO **Personality Inventory**, often called "the big five," has been developed to assess these factors.

**Further Reading**
Allport, Gordon W. *Personality and Social Encounter: Selected Essays.* Boston: Beacon Press, 1960.
Eysenck, Hans. *The Structure of Human Personality.* London: Methuen, 1970.

# Transference

The tendency of clients to transfer to the therapist their emotional responses to significant people in their lives.

Transference is the tendency for a client in **psychotherapy**, known as the analysand, to transfer emotional responses to their therapists that reflect feelings the analysand has for other significant people in his or her life. Transference often echoes clients' relationships with their parents or with other persons who played a central role in their **childhood**. They may become excessively dependent on or sexually attracted to the therapist; they may develop feelings of **hostility** or detachment. Whatever form transference takes, it is considered to be at the heart of the therapeutic process. **Sigmund Freud** believed that clients need to relive the central emotional experiences of their lives through transference in order to become convinced of the existence and **power** of their own **unconscious** attachments and motivations. The awareness gained through transference helps clients understand the sources of their behavior and actively aids them in working through and resolving their problems.

Sigmund Freud described the workings of transference using an analogy to chemistry. Likening the clients' symptoms to precipitates resulting from earlier emotional attachments, he compared the therapist to a catalyst and the effects of transference to a higher temperature at which the symptoms could be transformed. According to Freud, the phenomenon of transference is not unique to the psychoanalytic relationship between client and therapist—significant patterns of relationship are commonly re-enacted with "substitutes" other than psychotherapists. **Psychoanalysis**, however, is unique in drawing **attention** to this process and utilizing it for therapeutic purposes.

**Further Reading**
Freud, Sigmund. *New Introductory Lectures on Psychoanalysis.* New York: W. W. Norton, 1933.
Hall, Calvin S. *A Primer of Freudian Psychology.* New York: Harper and Row, 1982.

# Transgender

Condition in which an individual wishes to live as if he or she were of the opposite gender, sometimes seeking surgical procedures to change from one sex to the other.

Transgender, or transsexualism, a condition in which the individual defines him or herself as male or female in opposition to their physical gender, or feels strongly that he or she wants to live as a member of the other gender, is rare. By some estimates, no more than 1 person in 350,000 believes he or she was born the wrong gender.

**650**      GALE ENCYCLOPEDIA OF PSYCHOLOGY, 2ND EDITION

As they progress through **childhood**, their inability to relate to their own **gender identity** increases. Some seek the advice of a physician, and by the time they reach early adulthood, begin to take medical action to alter their gender. Since more males than females are diagnosed as transsexuals, it is more common for males to receive hormone treatment to develop secondary sex characteristics, such as breasts. In some cases, a surgical procedure is performed to alter the male sex organs to physically complete the transformation from one gender to the other.

At the Netherlands Institute for Brain Research in Amsterdam, scientists studied six male-to-female transsexuals and found evidence that a section of the **hypothalamus** that controls sexual function appeared to be more like the type found in women than that found in men. Because human embryos destined to become males differentiate early in the development process, the Netherlands study raises the question of whether the developing embryo could receive mixed hormonal signals to portions of the brain and the developing genitalia. Thus, as of the late 1990s, research seems to indicate that there may be physical reasons for transsexualism.

### Further Reading
Glausiusz, Josie. "Transsexual Brains." *Discover* 17, January 1996, p. 83.
Gorman, Christine. "Trapped in the Body of a Man?" *Time* 146, November 13, 1995, pp. 94+.

# Twins

Two children or animals born at the same birth.

Identical, or monozygotic, twins are of the same sex and are genetically and physically similar because they both come from one ovum, which, after fertilization, divides in two and develops into two separate individuals. Fraternal, or dizygotic, twins occur when the mother produces two eggs in one monthly cycle and both eggs are fertilized. The conceptions may take place on two separate occasions and could involve different fathers. Fraternal twins, who are no more genetically alike than ordinary siblings, may be of the same or different sex and may bear some similarity of appearance. Twin pregnancies occur on the average in one out of every 80 to 100 births. However, the incidence of twins reflects the number of twin babies born per thousand completed pregnancies, and it is a fact that many more twins are conceived than are born.

The causes of identical twinning are not fully understood. Factors affecting the frequency of twin and other multiple births include the mother's race and age, and the number of previous births. The rate of twin births in Japan is 0.7 percent, while the Yoruba of Nigeria have a rate as high as 4 percent. Dizygotic twinning appears to be a sex-linked genetic trait passed on by female relatives in the same **family**. The chances of having fraternal twins are increased about five times if a woman is a fraternal twin, has fraternal twin siblings or fraternal twin relatives on her side of the family, or has already given **birth** to fraternal twins (one in twenty chance). While the rate of identical twin births is stable for all ages of childbearing women, the chance of any mother bearing fraternal twins increases from the age of 15 to 39 and then drops after age 40. For women of all ages, the more children they have had previously, the more likely they are to bear twins. Since the 1960s, fertility drugs have also been linked to the chances of producing twins. The majority of research indicates that fathers' genes have little effect on the chances of producing twins.

There are four types of monozygotic twins, determined by the manner in which the fertilized egg, or zygote, divides and the stage at which this occurs. Two independent embryonic structures may be produced immediately at division, or the zygote may form two inner cell masses, with each developing into an embryo. A late or incomplete division may produce conjoined, or Siamese twins. As the zygote develops, it is encased in membranes, the inner of which is called the amnion, and the outer one the chorion. Among monozygotic twins, either or both of these membranes may be either separate or shared, as may the placenta. Together, the arrangement of these membranes and the placenta occurs in four possible permutations. Among dizygotic twins, each one has separate amnion and chorion membranes, although the placenta may be shared. Ascertaining zygosity, or the genetic make up of twins, can be done by analyzing the placenta(s) to determine if it is a single placenta with a single membrane or a double placenta, which account for one-third of identical twins and all fraternal twins. In the case of same-sex twins with two placentas, a DNA or blood test can determine whether they share the same genes or blood groups.

The scientific study of twins, pioneered by Sir **Francis Galton** in 1876, is one effective means of determining genetic influences on human behavior. The most widely used method of comparison is comparing monozygotic and dizygotic twins for concordance and discordance of **traits**. Concordant traits are those possessed by either both or neither of a pair of twins; discordant traits are possessed by only one of the pair. Monozygotic twins who are discordant for a particular trait can be compared with each other with reference to

These identical twins in San Francisco make an effort to act and dress alike. *(Alison Wright. Photo Researchers, Inc. Reproduced with permission.)*

other traits. This type of study has provided valuable information on the causes of **schizophrenia**.

Another common type of twin research compares monozygotic twins reared together with those reared apart, providing valuable information about the role of **environment** in determining behavior. In general, monozygotic twins reared apart are found to bear more similarities to each other than to their respective adoptive parents or siblings. This finding demonstrates the interaction between the effects of environment and genetic predispositions on an individual's psychological development.

*See also* Nature-Nurture Controversy.

## Type A personality

A collection of traits consisting of competitiveness, urgency, high achievement, and irritability.

In the 1970s, psychologists started investigating possible links between **personality** and health. Initial

research seemed to indicate that persons with a type A Personality were at higher risk for coronary heart disease—a medical condition that consists of a narrowing of the blood vessels that supply blood to the heart. Type A people are achievement oriented, irritable, impatient with delays, and seem to be always in a hurry. The association between heart disease and type A behaviors was evident, even when other risk factors such as smoking, **obesity**, or **family** history were ruled out. In contrast to type As, type B people are less competitive, and more easygoing than their type A counterparts. In a traffic jam, a type A might curse, fume, and change lanes. A type B might relax and listen to the car stereo. While most people do not fall into the extreme ends of the continuum, there are significant numbers of people who do seem to be far more intense and reactive than others.

These initial findings provoked widespread public interest. Checklists in the popular press allowed people to identify their own personality type. But subsequent studies showed that the relationship between type A behavior and heart disease was less clear than the initial study had suggested. In the initial 1974 study, over 3,000 men aged 35 to 59 were interviewed and classified as either type A or type B. Of those who suffered a heart attack during the next nine years, 69% were type As. However, if they survived the first attack, they subsequently lived longer than the type Bs. What could account for this apparent contradiction? It turns out that the description of type A behavior needs to be more carefully refined if we are to learn anything useful about its link with heart disease. Type As are not only reactive, they are also achievement oriented and highly motivated to succeed. They enjoy challenge and like to know how well they are doing. These qualities are likely to cause heart attack victims to change their lifestyles in order to prevent a recurrence.

More recent research has demonstrated that the feature of type A behavior that is particularly "toxic" is **hostility**. Men who are cynical, resentful, chronically angry, and mistrustful are far more likely than non-hostile men to get heart disease. The picture is less clear for women because fewer women have been included in the studies. The physiological explanation of the link between hostility and heart disease continues to be a focus of research.

Timothy Moore

**Further Reading**

Miller, T., et al. A meta-analytic review of research on hostility and physical health. *Psychological Bulletin,* 119, 322-348, 1996.

# U

## Unconscious

*The part of the mind whose contents people resist bringing into awareness.*

**Sigmund Freud** assumed that the human mind was divided into three divisions: the **id**, **ego**, and **super-ego**, which, in turn, had both conscious and unconscious portions. The id, motivated by two biological drives—sex and aggression—operates according to the **pleasure principle**, seeking satisfaction and avoiding **pain**. Guided by the reality principle, the ego's goal is to find safe and socially acceptable ways of satisfying the id's desires without transgressing the limits imposed by the superego. Developing from the ego in **childhood**, the superego, or **conscience**, has as its goal to apply moral values in satisfying one's wishes. Both the ego and superego operate consciously and unconsciously, according to Freud, while the id is entirely unconscious.

In psychoanalytic theory, developed by Freud in the treatment of **normal** and abnormal personalities, the **preconscious** and unconscious minds are the repositories of secret or sexual desires that threaten our **self-esteem**, or ego. Once in the unconscious, these repressed desires and fears give rise to anxiety and **guilt**, which influence conscious behavior and thoughts. Freud attributed the cause of many psychological disorders to the conflict between conscious and unconscious urges. In order to understand abnormal behaviors and eliminate them, he theorized, an expert was required, who, in a trusting relationship with the patient, would employ techniques such as dream analysis and **free association** to retrieve materials buried in the unconscious mind. Thus, the driving forces behind behavior could be understood, and unresolved unconscious conflicts and anxiety could become a source of insight for the patient, eliminating the primary source of abnormal behavior.

*See also* Repression.

## Unconscious motivation

*Motivating impulses that influence behavior without conscious awareness.*

Unconscious motivation plays a prominent role in Sigmund Freud's theories of human behavior. According to Freud and his followers, most human behavior is the result of desires, impulses, and memories that have been repressed into an unconscious state, yet still influence actions. Freud believed that the human mind consists of a tiny, conscious part that is available for direct observation and a much larger subconscious portion that plays an even more important role in determining behavior.

The term "Freudian slip" refers to the manifestation of these unconscious impulses. For example, a person who responds "Bad to meet you" instead of the usual "Glad to meet you" may be revealing true feelings. The substitution of "bad" for "glad" is more than a slip of the tongue; it is an expression of the person's unconscious feelings of **fear** or dislike. Similarly, a talented athlete who plays an uncharacteristically poor game could be acting on an unconscious desire to punish overbearing or inattentive parents. Unknown to the athlete, the substandard performance actually is communicating an important message.

Freud also contended that repressed memories and desires are the origins of most mental disorders. **Psychoanalysis** was developed as a method of assisting patients in bringing their unconscious thoughts to **consciousness**. This increased awareness of the causes for behavior and feelings then would assist the patient in modifying the undesired aspects of behavior.

*See also* Memory; Repression.

### Further Reading
Atkinson, Rita L.; Richard C. Atkinson; Edward E. Smith; and Ernest R. Hilgard. *Introduction to Psychology.* 9th ed. San Diego: Harcourt Brace Jovanovich, 1987.

Clark, David Stafford. *What Freud Really Said.* New York: Schocken Books, 1965.

# Underachiever

Also referred to as a latent achiever, a person whose performance is significantly below that which would be predicted by educators.

Although the term "underachiever" commonly refers to anyone, child or adult, who performs below his or her potential, psychologists typically use the term to refer to a student whose performance in academic studies falls significantly below his scores on standardized tests of aptitude or **ability**. A student may also be considered to be underachieving based on the educator's evaluation of her learning potential in relation to the quality of the work she does on class assignments.

There are many explanations for achievement that falls below evaluated potential. Some problems may be the educational experience itself: bright students may be bored by class assignments, and therefore do not give them much **attention**; or a student's learning style may conflict with the method of instruction used in his school. Underachievers may also have learning disabilities that prevent them from making full use of their capabilities. **Family** factors may also contribute to a pattern of underachievement in a variety of ways. When parents' expectations are low or nonexistent (the family doesn't expect the student to do more than pass), the student may work "just hard enough"—well below his full potential—to get by. When a student's peer group does not value academic achievement, **peer** pressure may be another factor contributing to underachievement.

Parents, educators, and the student can all work together to counter underachievement. First, working with the family and school personnel, the student must understand the factors that contribute to low academic achievement. Factors may include poor time management, self-defeating thought patterns ("I could never get a B in science."), weak writing skills, poor (or no) study **environment** (i.e., homework done while watching television), friends or role models who do not value academic performance, or self-destructive habits like alcohol or drug abuse. Next, the student needs to acknowledge that she could be more successful in school. Parents and teachers can help the student compile a list of strengths, both academic and other, that she can build upon. They can also help direct the student to peer groups (through clubs, sports, or other extracurricular activities) that support academic success. In addition, role models can be presented to the student to help her focus on the possibilities in academic life, rather than the limitations. Finally, where necessary, families can seek counseling and treatment for problems such as alcohol abuse that prevent the student from focusing on school.

## Further Reading
Griffin, Robert S. *Underachievers in Secondary School: Education Off the Mark.* Hillsdale, NJ: Lawrence Erlbaum Associates, 1988.
Holt, John. *How Children Fail.* Revised edition. Reading, MA: Addison-Wesley Publishing Company, 1995.
Lehr, Judy Brown. *At-Risk, Low-Achieving Students in the Classroom.* Washington, D.C.: National Education Association, 1988.
Varma, Ved. *How and Why Children Fail.* Philadelphia: J. Kingsley, 1993.

# V

## Violence

*The use of unjustified physical force with the intention to injure or damage.*

The high incidence of violence in the United States is of great concern to citizens, lawmakers, and law enforcement agencies alike. Between 1960 and 1991, violent crime in the U.S. rose over 370 percent, and over 600,000 Americans are victimized by handgun crimes annually. Violent acts committed by juveniles are of particular concern: the number of American adolescents arrested for homicide has increased by 85 percent between 1987 and 1991, and more juveniles are committing serious crimes at younger ages than ever before. Young African American males are particularly at risk for becoming either perpetrators or victims of violent crime. The Centers for Disease Control (CDC) has identified homicide as the leading cause of death for this demographic group, estimating that one in every 28 black males born in 1987 is likely to be murdered. For white males born in 1987, the ratio is one in 205.

The threat of violence is particularly disturbing because of new variants—including carjackings, drive-by shootings, and workplace killings—that threaten Americans in places or situations formerly considered safe. The CDC has declared workplace violence an epidemic, with the number of homicides in the workplace tripling in the last ten years. Workplace violence may be divided into two types: external and internal. External workplace violence is committed by persons unfamiliar with the employer and employees, occurring at random or as an attempt at making a symbolic statement to society at large. Internal workplace violence is generally committed by an individual involved in either a troubled spousal or personal relationship with a co-worker, or as an attempt to seek revenge against an employer, usually for being released from employment. The rising percentage of layoffs, downsizing, and impersonal management styles in many American corporations have been linked to the increase in workplace violence, nearly one-fourth of which end in the perpetrator's suicide.

One type of violence that has received increased attention in recent years is domestic violence, a crime for which statistics are difficult to compile because it is so heavily underreported—only about one in 270 incidents are thought to be reported to authorities. Estimates of the percentage of women who have been physically abused by a spouse or partner range from 20 percent to as high as 50 percent. According to the FBI, a woman is beaten every 18 seconds in the United States, and almost one-third of American females murdered in 1992 were killed by their husbands or boyfriends. Battering is experienced by women of all ages, races, ethnic groups, and social classes. A chronic pattern of ongoing physical violence and verbal abuse may produce a variant of post-traumatic **stress** disorder referred to as Battered Woman Syndrome, in which the victim experiences **depression**, **guilt**, passivity, **fear**, and low **self-esteem**.

Various explanations have been offered for the high prevalence of violence in the United States, which is by far the most violent nation in the industrialized world. Among the most prominent has been the argument that violence depicted in the mass media—including television, movies, rock and rap music videos, and video games—have contributed to the rise in violence in society. Quantitative studies have found that prime time television programs average 10 violent acts per hour, while children's cartoons average 32 acts of violence per hour. On-screen deaths in feature films such as Robocop and Die Hard range from 80 to 264. It has also been argued that experiencing violence vicariously in these forms is not a significant determinant of violent behavior and that it may even have a beneficial cathartic effect. However, experimental studies have found correlations between the viewing of violence and increased interpersonal **aggression**, both in **childhood** and, later, in **adolescence**. Viewing violence can elicit aggressive

The fence surrounding the Murrah Federal Building in Oklahoma City bears the memories of the victims of the building's 1995 bombing. Violent crime rates in the U.S. have dramatically increased in recent years. *(Pat J. Carter. AP/Wide World Photos. Reproduced with permission.)*

behavior through **modeling**, increasing the viewer's arousal, desensitizing viewers to violence, reducing restraints on aggressive behavior, and distorting views about **conflict resolution**.

Other causal factors that have been linked to violence include the prevalence of **gangs**, the introduction of crack cocaine in the mid-1980s, the increase in single-parent families, and the lack of tighter restrictions on gun ownership. In addition, scientists have found a possible link between violence and **heredity**: studies have shown that males born with an extra Y chromosome (type XYY) are more likely than **normal** to be inmates of prisons or **mental hospitals**. The significance of these findings has been disputed, however, as XYY males in the general population are not more violent than other males. The effects of a genetic predisposition are also tempered by interaction with a variety of environmental factors. Of the men who are genetically predisposed to violence, only a minority will actually commit acts of aggression.

There are a number of more credible predictors of individual violence, most of them psychological. The most reliable indicator is a history of violence: each time

a person commits a violent act, the probability that he or she will commit more violent acts increases. Psychoses, including **schizophrenia**, major affective disorders, and paranoid states are also closely linked to violence, as is erotomania, or romantic obsession. This condition involves an idealized romantic love (often for someone, such as a celebrity, with whom one has no personal relationship) that becomes a **fixation**. Such actions as unsolicited letters and phone calls, and stalking eventually lead to violence, either out of revenge for being rejected or so that the object of the fixation may not become involved with anyone else.

Depression is also associated with violence, often in the form of suicide. Two **personality** disorders related to violence—particularly in the workplace—are **antisocial personality disorder** ("sociopaths") and **borderline personality** disorder (characterized by instability and lack of boundaries in interpersonal relationships). Chemical dependence can lead to violence by interfering with the **ability** to distinguish right from wrong, removing social inhibitions, and inducing **paranoia** and/or aggression. Other possible indicators of violence include neurological impairment, an excessive interest in weapons, a high level of frustration with one's **environment**, and the pathological blaming of others for one's problems.

In recent years, a public health approach to violence has been widely advocated. This orientation stresses outreach to those segments of the population among whom violence is most prevalent in an attempt to alter attitudes and behaviors that contribute to it, and to teach the skills necessary for the nonviolent resolution of conflicts. Teenagers, in particular, as well as their parents, are targeted in these efforts, especially in areas with high crime rates. This approach has been criticized by those who believe that violence should be dealt with by addressing its underlying structural causes—including poverty, racial discrimination, and unemployment—through direct socioeconomic intervention.

# Vision

The process of transforming light energy into neural impulses that can then be interpreted by the brain.

The human eye is sensitive to only a limited range of radiation, consisting of wavelengths between approximately 400 to 750 nanometers (billionths of a meter).

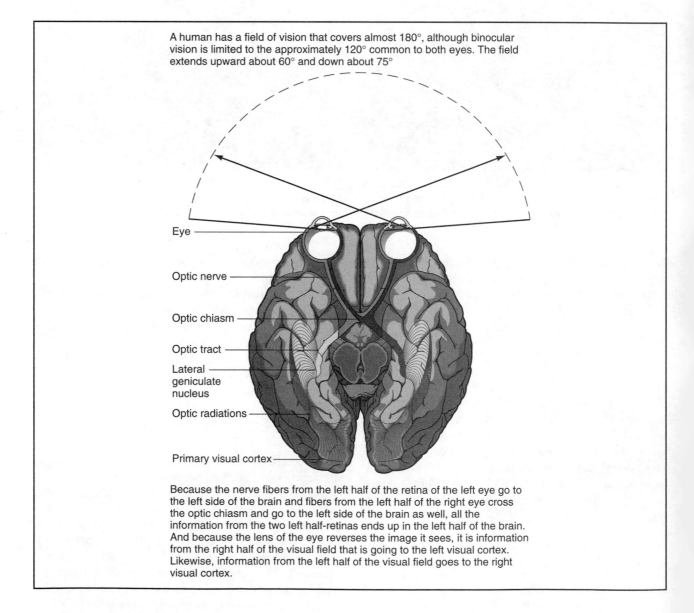

A human has a field of vision that covers almost 180°, although binocular vision is limited to the approximately 120° common to both eyes. The field extends upward about 60° and down about 75°

Eye

Optic nerve

Optic chiasm

Optic tract

Lateral geniculate nucleus

Optic radiations

Primary visual cortex

Because the nerve fibers from the left half of the retina of the left eye go to the left side of the brain and fibers from the left half of the right eye cross the optic chiasm and go to the left side of the brain as well, all the information from the two left half-retinas ends up in the left half of the brain. And because the lens of the eye reverses the image it sees, it is information from the right half of the visual field that is going to the left visual cortex. Likewise, information from the left half of the visual field goes to the right visual cortex.

**How the eye works.** (Hans & Cassidy. Gale Research. Reproduced with permission.)

The full spectrum of visible color is contained within this range, with violet at the low end and red at the high end. Light is converted into neural impulses by the eye, whose spherical shape is maintained by its outermost layer, the sclera. When a beam of light is reflected off an object, it first enters the eye through the cornea, a rounded transparent portion of the sclera that covers the pigmented iris. The iris constricts to control the amount of light entering the pupil, a round opening at the front of the eye. A short distance beyond the pupil, the light passes through the lens, a transparent oval structure whose curved surface bends and focuses the light wave into a narrower beam, which is received by the retina. When the retina receives an image, it is upside down because light rays from the top of the object are focused at the bottom of the retina, and vice versa. This upside-down image must be rearranged by the **brain** so that objects can be seen right side up. In order for the image to be focused properly, light rays from each of its points must converge at a point on the retina, rather than in front of or behind it. Aided by the surrounding muscles, the lens of the eye adjusts its shape to focus images properly on the retina so that objects viewed at different distances can be brought into focus, a process known as accommodation. As people age, this process is impaired because the lens loses flexibility, and it becomes difficult to read or do close work without glasses.

The retina, lining the back of the eye, consists of ten layers of cells containing photoreceptors (rods and cones) that convert the light waves to neural impulses through a photochemical reaction. Aside from the differences in shape suggested by their names, rod and cone cells contain different light-processing chemicals (photopigments), perform different functions, and are distributed differently within the retina. Cone cells, which provide **color vision** and enable us to distinguish details, adapt quickly to light and are most useful in adequate lighting. Rod cells, which can pick up very small amounts of light but are not color-sensitive, are best suited for situations in which lighting is minimal. Because the rod cells are active at night or in dim lighting, it is difficult to distinguish colors under these circumstances. Cones are concentrated in the fovea, an area at the center of the retina, whereas rods are found only outside this area and become more numerous the farther they are from it. Thus, it is more difficult to distinguish colors when viewing objects at the periphery of one's visual field.

The photoreceptor cells of the retina generate an electrical force that triggers impulses in neighboring bipolar and ganglion cells. These impulses flow from the back layer of retinal cells to the front layer containing the fibers of the optic **nerve**, which leaves the eye though a part of the retina known as the optic disk. This area, which contains no receptor cells, creates a blind spot in each eye, whose effects are offset by using both eyes together and also by an illusion the brain creates to fill in this area when one eye is used alone. Branches of the optic nerve cross at a junction in the brain in front of the pituitary gland and underneath the frontal lobes called the optic chiasm and ascend into the brain itself. The nerve fibers extend to a part of the **thalamus** called the lateral geniculate nucleus (LGN), and neurons from the LGN relay their visual input to the primary visual cortex of both the left and right hemispheres of the brain, where the impulses are transformed into simple visual sensations. (Objects in the left visual field are viewed only through the right brain hemisphere, and vice versa.) The primary visual cortex then sends the impulses to neighboring association areas which add meaning or "associations" to them.

## Further Reading
Hubel, David. *Eye, Brain, and Vision.* New York: Scientific American Library, 1987.

# Visual angle

In viewing an object through one eye, the visual angle is the angle formed at the nodal point of the eye by straight lines from opposite edges of the object.

# Vocational Aptitude Test

A predictive test designed to measure an individual's potential for success and satisfaction in any of various occupations and professions.

As a general example, a vocational aptitude test might consist of an instrument that assesses an individual's abilities, **personality** characteristics, and interests, and compares the individual's responses to those persons considered to be successful in their occupations and professions, with a notation of points of similarity and dissimilarity.

Vocational aptitude tests are valuable to both employers and prospective employees in a given occupation. To the prospective employee, the test results offer guidance in choosing a particular career. To the employer, they aid in the process of screening suitable employees. Vocational aptitude tests measure a wider variety of skill areas than scholastic aptitude tests. For example, the Differential Aptitude Test, one of the most widely used vocational tests, measures verbal, numerical, abstract, and mechanical reasoning; spatial relations; clerical speed and accuracy; and language usage.

Vocational aptitude tests have three primary orientations. The interactional perspective stresses the interaction between the individual and the work **environment** as the determining factor in vocational success and satisfaction. The theories of John Holland and the widely used tests based on them are an example of this approach. The central focus for Holland is congruence between an individual's personality type (realistic, investigative, artistic, social, enterprising, or conventional) and his or her vocational environment. Research has indicated that congruent person-environment interactions lead to personal and vocational stability and fulfillment.

Tests based on the person perspective emphasize the individual, rather than the work environment, as the crucial variable in vocational success. Theories associated with this orientation include Osipow's Trait Factor approach, focusing on personal characteristics linking an individual to various vocational groups, and Super's developmental **self-concept** theory, which regards vocational choice as a means of self-expression. Roe's personality theory concentrates on individuals employed in scientific fields and their relative degree of interest in people and things. Finally, the environment perspective views vocational choice and performance as primarily a function of environmental or situational factors.

**Further Reading**
Gale, Barry. *Discover What You're Best At*. New York: Simon & Schuster, 1990.

# Voyeurism

See **Paraphilias**

# W

## Margaret Floy Washburn

**1871-1939**
American psychologist.

Margaret Floy Washburn was the first woman ever to receive a doctorate in psychology and the second woman to be elected to the National Academy of Sciences (1931), the most eminent scientific society in the United States. The only child of Francis Washburn and Elizabeth Floy Davis, Washburn was raised in a middle class home in New York. The women in her **family** were exceptional and attained high levels of academic accomplishment for the era. Educated both in public and private schools, Washburn graduated from Vassar College in 1891 with a keen interest in science and philosophy. She audited graduate courses taught by James McKeen Cattell at Columbia University, but in spite of his full support, she was denied admission to the graduate program due to gender restrictions. Admitted as a degree candidate at Cornell University, she won the Susan Lynn Sage Fellowship in Philosophy and Ethics. In two short years, working with the noted researcher Edward B. Titchener (1886-1927) in **experimental psychology**, Washburn earned her Ph.D., the first woman ever to receive a doctorate in psychology. In 1894, she was elected to membership in the American Psychological Association where she eventually became a council member, establishing policy and serving on many committees.

Because women were not eligible to be hired as regular faculty in psychology or philosophy departments in any major Eastern university at the close of the nineteenth century, Washburn held a series of teaching positions at women's colleges, including Wells College (1894), Sage College at Cornell University (1900) and the University of Cincinnati (1902). Although Edward Titchener had been her mentor at Cornell, he refused to admit her to the Society of Experimental Psychologists he formed in 1904. While this group was expressly designed to help young researchers, he summarily exclud-

**Margaret Floy Washburn** *(Archives of the History of American Psychology. Reproduced with permission.)*

ed all women on the grounds that their presence would inhibit "frank discussion" among the male members. In 1903, Washburn became Assistant Professor of Philosophy at Vassar College, where she was promoted to professor in 1908, eventually becoming professor emeritus in 1937.

Washburn was known primarily for her work in animal psychology. *The Animal Mind,* which she published in 1908, was the first book by an American in this field and remained the standard **comparative psychology** textbook for the next 25 years. (Subsequent editions appeared in 1917, 1926, and 1936.) In *Movement and Men-*

tal Imagery (1916), she presented her motor theory of **consciousness**, in which she attempted to mediate between the structuralist, or "introspective" tradition of **Wilhelm Wundt** (1832-1920) and Titchener, in which she had been schooled, and the opposing behaviorist view. These competing movements had divorced consciousness from behavior, with the structuralists studying only the former, while the behaviorists maintained that psychology should only be concerned with the latter. Washburn's theory reconciled these two perspectives by exploring the ways in which thoughts and perceptions produce motor reaction.

In 1925, Washburn was named one of four coeditors of the American Journal of Psychology. She was elected president of the American Psychological Association in 1921 and elected to the National Academy of Sciences in 1931, the second woman ever to be chosen for that honor. Altogether, Washburn published over 200 articles and reviews, including more than 70 research articles during her 33-year tenure at Vassar. In her writings, she developed her theory of consciousness at greater length and explored such diverse topics as individual differences, **color vision** in animals, aesthetic preferences for colors and sounds, after-images, and psychology of the affective processes.

### Further Reading
Scarborough, Elizabeth, and Laurel Furumoto. *Untold Lives: The First Generation of American Women Psychologists.* New York: Columbia University Press, 1987, pp. 109-29.

# John Broadus Watson

## 1878-1958
American psychologist and founder of behaviorism.

John Broadus Watson is best known as the founder of **behaviorism**, which he defined as an experimental branch of natural science aimed at the prediction and control of behavior. Its model was based on Ivan Pavlov's studies of conditioned reflex: every conduct is a response to a stimulus or to a complex set of stimulus situations. From **birth**, a few stimuli elicit definite reactions. But most behaviors are conditioned; they result from the association of unconditioned stimuli to other stimuli.

Watson was born in 1878 to a poor, rural South Carolina **family**. His mother was a pious Baptist; his father left the family in 1891. After taking a traditional classical curriculum at Furman University, he studied philosophy at the University of Chicago. Disappointed with John Dewey's teaching, he began work in animal psychology, and received his Ph.D. in 1903. Watson was a professor at

Johns Hopkins University from 1908 to 1920, when he was dismissed because of his relationship with a graduate student, Rosalie Rayner. He divorced his wife, married Rosalie, and had a successful career in advertising. In 1957, he was awarded a gold medal by the American Psychological Association (of which he had been the youngest president, in 1915). Watson died in 1958.

Developmental issues were crucial for behaviorism. According to Watson, unhealthy adult personalities resulted from habit systems carried over from **infancy**. Early **childhood** was key, and a detailed knowledge of **child development** was indispensable for designing a behavioral social technology. The significance of childhood and child-study for behaviorism is summed up in Watson's most famous statement: "Give me a dozen healthy infants . . . and my own specified world to bring them up in and I'll guarantee to take any one at random and train him to become any type of specialist I might select . . . regardless of his talents, penchants, tendencies, abilities, vocations, and the race of his ancestors."

By 1917, Watson had focused his research on children. He carried out pioneering observational and experimental work on newborns and infants, produced *Experimental Investigation of Babies* (1919), one of the first psychology films done in the United States, wrote the best-selling manual *Psychological Care of Infant and Child*, and became a popular child-rearing expert. Much of his research was directed at distinguishing unlearned from learned behavior. Observations of hundreds of babies revealed that sneezing, hiccoughing, crying, erection of penis, voiding of urine, defecation, smiling, certain eye movements and motor reactions, feeding responses, grasping, and blinking were unlearned, but that they began to become conditioned a few hours after birth. Crawling, swimming, and **handedness** appeared to be learned. Watson also traced the beginnings of language to unlearned vocal sounds, and found that three forms of emotional ("visceral") response can be elicited at birth by three sets of stimuli: **fear** (by loss of support and loud sounds; Watson did not notice that his **conditioning** fear of fire through burning alone contradicted his view), rage (by hampering of bodily movement), and love (by stroking of the skin, tickling, gentle rocking, patting). Just as there was no innate fear of darkness, there was no instinctive love of the child for the mother; all "visceral habits" were shaped by conditioning. In one of the most controversial experiments of all psychology, Watson conditioned eleven-month-old "little Albert" to fear furry objects; this case was for him proof that complex behavior develops by conditioning out of simple unlearned responses.

Watson considered the ultimate aim of psychology to be the adjustment of individual needs to the needs of society. He encouraged parents to approach childrearing

Cohen, D. *Behaviorism*. [1924, 1930], New York: W.W. Norton, 1970.

———. *Psychological Care of Infant and Child*. New York: W.W. Norton, 1928.

———. *J.B. Watson: The Founder of Behaviorism*. London: Routledge & Kegan Paul, 1979.

**John B. Watson** *(The Library of Congress. Reproduced with permission.)*

as a professional application of behaviorism. *Psychological Care of Infant and Child* (1928) is dedicated "to the first mother who brings up a happy child." Such a child would be an autonomous, fearless, self-reliant, adaptable, problem-solving being, who does not cry unless physically hurt, is absorbed in work and **play**, and has no great attachments to any place or person. Watson warned against the dangers of "too much mother love," and advocated strict routines and a tight control over the child's **environment** and behavior. His disapproval of thumb-sucking, masturbation, and **homosexuality** was not moral, but practical, and he encouraged parents to be honest about sex. He agreed with psychoanalysts on the importance of **sexuality**. Partly because of the premature end to Watson's university career, his views did not have a decisive influence on academic **child psychology**. They contributed, however, to professionalizing child-rearing, and bolstered contemporary arguments, by Fred and **John Dewey** for example, on the determining life-long effects of early development.

## Further Reading

Buckley, K.W. *Mechanical Man. John Broadus Watson and the Beginnings of Behaviorism*. New York: Guilford Press, 1989.

# David Wechsler

### 1896-1981
American experimental and clinical psychologist who developed new types of intelligence tests.

David Wechsler developed the first standardized adult **intelligence** test, the Bellevue-Wechsler Scale, in 1939. Likewise, the Wechsler Intelligence Scale for Children, published in 1949 and revised in 1974, was considered to be the best test available. The concept that intelligence involves the abilities necessary to succeed in life was one of Wechsler's major contributions to psychology. He promoted the idea that intelligence includes **personality traits** and emotional states, as well as mental abilities, and that all of these should be measured to assess intelligent behavior in one's **environment**. Wechsler also promoted the idea that educational, cultural, and socioeconomic factors must be considered when evaluating intelligence. The author of more than 60 books and articles, Wechsler served as president of the American Psychopathology Association in 1959-60 and earned the Distinguished Professional Contribution Award of the American Psychological Association in 1973.

Born in Lespedi, Romania, in 1896, Wechsler was the youngest of seven children of Moses S. Wechsler, a Hebrew scholar, and Leah W. Pascal, a shopkeeper. The **family** moved to New York City in 1902, and Wechsler graduated from the City College of New York in 1916. He earned his master's degree in experimental psychopathology the following year, working with Robert S. Woodworth at Columbia University. His dissertation was published in 1917.

## Recognizes the limitations of intelligence testing

During the First World War, Wechsler worked at Camp Yaphank on Long Island under E. G. Boring, scoring intelligence tests for the army as a civilian volunteer. He continued working with intelligence testing while serving with the army's Psychological Division of the Sanitary Corps at Fort Logan, Texas. These experiences convinced Wechsler of the limitations of available intelligence tests, particular for uneducated or foreign-born adults. After serving in France, Wechsler became an army student at the University of London in 1919, where he studied with Karl Pearson and **Charles Spearman**, who shared his interests in intelligence testing. Wechsler then obtained a two-year fellowship to study in Paris with the physiologist Louis Lapique and the experimental psychologist Henri Piéron. Wechsler's research focused on the psychogalvanic response, the changes in electrical conductivity of the skin that accompany emotional changes.

After spending the summer of 1922 working at the Psychopathic Hospital in Boston, Wechsler returned to New York City, as a psychologist with the Bureau of Child Guidance. There, for the next two years, he administered psychological tests. Concurrently, he completed his Ph.D. dissertation at Columbia under Woodworth. This work, "The Measurement of Emotional Reactions: Researches on the Psychogalvanic Reflex," was published in *Archives of Psychology* in 1925.

During the next seven years, Wechsler had a private clinical practice, as well as working as acting secretary of the Psychological Corporation, which later published his intelligence tests. He also was a psychologist at the Brooklyn Jewish Social Service Bureau. Wechsler continued to look for more broadly based measurements of intelligence. His 1930 article in *The Scientific Monthly* was expanded into his 1935 book, *The Range of Human Capacities*. In this work, Wechsler argued that psychologists had overestimated the range of variations among individuals and that human beings were actually surprisingly similar. He further argued that abilities peaked at a certain age and then began to decline. Wechsler began devising a variety of different types of tests. In 1926, he developed "Tests for Taxi Cab Drivers" for the Yellow Cab Company of Pittsburgh.

## Develops new ways to measure intelligence

In 1932, Wechsler began his long career as chief psychologist at the Bellevue Psychiatric Hospital in New York and, the following year, joined the faculty of the New York University College of Medicine. Although he engaged in a variety of research projects, his major focus continued to be intelligence. At Bellevue, Wechsler tested both children and adults from a wide variety of backgrounds and with numerous problems. Again, he found that traditional testing methods were not suitable. In particular, he concluded that the commonly used Binet tests of intelligence were too narrow in scope and were inappropriate for adults. In addition to his well-known tests for adults and children, Wechsler developed the Army Wechsler (1942), the Wechsler Adult Intelligence Scale in 1955 which he revised in 1981, and the Wechsler Preschool and Primary Scale of Intelligence in 1967.

Wechsler's tests measured abilities in performing tasks as well as mental abilities. He also introduced the deviation quotient, a new calculation that compared individuals with their peer group, rather than calculating a "mental age" as in the Binet tests. The deviation quotient corrected for abilities that changed with age and made it easier to detect abnormalities. In 1939, Wechsler published *The Measurement of Adult Intelligence*.

Wechsler never lost sight of the limitations of his intelligence tests. Although his tests often are interpreted as a clear measure of intelligence, Wechsler himself believed that they were useful only in conjunction with other clinical measurements. To Wechsler, assessments were far superior to mere testing.

Wechsler's first wife, Florence Felske, died in an automobile accident three weeks after their marriage in 1934. In 1939, he married Ruth A. Halpern and the couple had two children. During World War II, Wechsler acted as special consultant to the secretary of war and, beginning in 1948, he was consultant to the Veterans Administration. In 1947, Wechsler participated in a mission to Cyprus to form a **mental health** program for Holocaust survivors. A founder of Hebrew University in Jerusalem, he was Beber Visiting Professor of **Clinical Psychology** there in 1967, the year he retired from his posts at Bellevue and New York University. Wechsler was the recipient of numerous awards, including a special award from the American Association on Mental Deficiency and an honorary doctorate from Hebrew University. Wechsler died in New York City in 1981.

Margaret Alic

### Further Reading

Carson, John. "Wechsler, David." In *American national biography,* edited by John A. Garraty and Mark C. Carnes. Vol 22. New York: Oxford University Press, 1999.

Wechsler, David. *Selected papers of David Wechsler.* With introductory material by Allen J. Edwards. New York: Academic Press, 1974.

## Wechsler Intelligence Scales

A widely used series of intelligence tests developed by clinical psychologist David Wechsler.

The Wechsler **Intelligence** Scales are divided into two sections: verbal and nonverbal (or "performance"), with separate scores for each. Verbal intelligence, the component most often associated with academic success, implies the **ability** to think in abstract terms using either

tracting, counting); sentences (repeating progressively longer sentences); and similarities (responding to questions such as "How are a pen and pencil alike?"). The Performance section includes picture completion; copying geometric designs; using blocks to reproduce designs; working through a maze; and building an "animal house" from a model.

The Wechsler Intelligence Scale for Children (WISC), now in its second revision (WISC-III, 1991), is designed for children and adolescents ages six to sixteen. The WISC differs from the WIPPSI in the following notable ways: geometric designs are replaced by assembly of three-dimensional objects; children arrange groups of pictures to tell simple stories; they are asked to remember and repeat lists of digits; a coding exercise is performed in place of the animal house; and mazes are a subtest. For all of the Wechsler scales (which also include the Wechsler Adult Intelligence Scale, or WAIS), separate verbal and performance scores, as well as a total score, are computed. These are then converted using a scale divided into categories (such as average and superior), and the final score is generally given as one of these categories rather than as a number or percentile ranking.

*See also* Intelligence Quotient, I.Q. test; Stanford-Binet Intelligence Scales.

A test subject performs the block test portion of the Wechsler intelligence scales. *(Will & Deni McIntyre. Photo Researchers, Inc. Reproduced with permission.)*

words or mathematical symbols. Performance intelligence suggests the ability to perceive relationships and fit separate parts together logically into a whole. The inclusion of the performance section in the Wechsler scales is especially helpful in assessing the cognitive ability of children with speech and language disorders or whose first language is not English. The test can be of particular value to school psychologists screening for specific learning disabilities because of the number of specific subtests that make up each section.

The Wechsler Preschool and Primary Scales of Intelligence (WPPSI) have traditionally been geared toward children ages four to six, although the 1989 version of the test (WPPSI-III, 1989) extends the age range down to three years and upward to seven years, three months. The Verbal section covers the following areas: general information (food, money, the body, etc.); vocabulary (definitions of increasing difficulty); comprehension (responses to questions); arithmetic (adding, sub-

# Carl Wernicke

### 1848-1905
German neuroanatomist, pathologist, and psychiatrist who made fundamental discoveries about brain function.

Carl Wernicke was an influential member of the nineteenth-century German school of neuropsychiatry, which viewed all mental illnesses as resulting from defects in **brain** physiology. A practicing clinical neuropsychiatrist, Wernicke also made major discoveries in brain anatomy and pathology. He believed that abnormalities could be localized to specific regions of the cerebral cortex and thus could be used to determine the functions of these regions. Wernicke was one of the first to conceive of brain function as dependent on neural pathways that connected different regions of the brain, with each region contributing a relatively simple sensory-motor activity. At the time, most scientists conceived of the brain as functioning as a single organ. Wernicke also helped demonstrate dominance by either the right or left hemispheres of the cerebrum.

Wernicke was born in 1848 in the German town of Tarnowitz in Upper Silesia, in what is now Tarnowskie

Gory, Poland. He earned his medical degree at the University of Breslau in 1870 and stayed on to work with Heinrich Neumann. Wernicke also spent six months studying with Theodor Meynert in Vienna. He earned his psychiatry qualification in 1875 and moved to Berlin, where he spent three years at the Charité Hospital as assistant to Karl Westphal, before starting a private practice in Berlin. With his mentors, Meynert and Westphal, Wernicke continued the neuropsychiatric tradition begun by Wilhelm Griesinger.

### Describes Wernicke's aphasia

In 1873, Wernicke studied a patient who had suffered a stroke. Although the man was able to speak and his **hearing** was unimpaired, he could barely understand what was said to him. Nor could he understand written words. After he died, Wernicke found a lesion in the rear parietal/temporal region of the patient's left brain hemisphere. Wernicke concluded that this region, which is close to the auditory region of the brain, was involved in speech comprehension. Wernicke named the syndrome sensory **aphasia**, although now it is usually called Wernicke's aphasia. The affected region of the brain is known as Wernicke's area. The syndrome is sometimes called fluent aphasia since the victim is capable of speech; however words may be misused and the speech may be disordered or even without content. For this reason, scientists now believe that Wernicke's area may be involved in semantic processing, and it is sometimes called the receptive language area.

Wernicke published *The Aphasic Symptom Complex* in 1874 when he was 26. In this work, he developed many of his ideas about brain localization, and he related different types of aphasia to specific damaged regions of the brain. In contrast to Wernicke's aphasia, motor aphasia involves damage to the part of the brain known as Broca's area. With this syndrome, a patient understands speech, but cannot speak himself. Wernicke postulated that Broca's area and Wernicke's area were connected, and he predicted that damage to this connection would cause conduction aphasia, a syndrome wherein a patient could both speak and understand language, but would misuse words and could not repeat words. Wernicke's prediction turned out to be correct. Two of Wernicke's early aphasia papers were published in English in 1994.

### Describes Wernicke's encephalopathy

The three volumes of Wernicke's comprehensive work, *Textbook of Brain Disorders*, appeared between 1881 and 1883. In this work, based on careful case studies, Wernicke attempted to relate all known neurological diseases to specific regions of the brain. The volumes included many of Wernicke's original observations on brain anatomy, pathology, and clinical manifestations. Based on his observations, he predicted the symptoms that would result from blockage of the posterior inferior cerebellar artery. Again, his hypothesis was later confirmed. In the second volume, Wernicke described for the first time a syndrome resulting from the ingestion of sulfuric acid, which caused specific mental and motor abnormalities and paralysis of muscles in the eyes. He called this syndrome acute hemorrhagic superior polioencephalitis. It now is called Wernicke's encephalopathy and is known to be caused by a nutritional thiamine deficiency.

In 1885, Wernicke became an associate professor of neurology and psychiatry at the University of Breslau. Five years later, he was awarded the department chair. Wernicke's clinical studies were published as *Grundriss der Psychiatrie in klinischen Vorlesungen* in 1894, with a second edition in 1906, and as *Krankenvorstellungen aus der psychiatrischen Klinik in Breslau*, in the years 1899-1900. Between 1897 and 1903, Wernicke published the three-part *Atlas des Gehirns* on neuroanatomy and pathology. His last work on aphasia appeared in 1903 and was translated into English in 1908.

Wernicke moved to the University of Halle in 1904 as a full professor. The following year, he died in Dörrberg im Geratal, Germany, of injuries suffered in a bicycling accident. Wernicke's research laid the foundation for the Wernicke-Geschwind model of language, which predicted the neural pathways involved in simple language tasks, such as reading a word aloud.

Margaret Alic

### Further Reading

Bynum, William F. "Wernicke, Carl." In *Dictionary of Scientific Biography,* edited by Charles Coulston Gillispie. Vol. 14. New York: Charles Scribner's Sons, 1970.

Lanczik, M., and G. Keil. "Carl Wernicke's Localization Theory and its Significance for the Development of Scientific Psychiatry." *History of Psychiatry* 2 (1991): 171-180.

# Max Wertheimer

### 1880-1943

German psychologist who was the originator of Gestalt psychology, which had a profound influence on the whole science of psychology.

Max Wertheimer was born in Prague on April 15, 1880. At the University in Prague he first studied law and then philosophy; he continued his studies in Berlin

**Max Wertheimer** *(Corbis-Bettmann. Reproduced with permission.)*

and then in Würzburg, where he received his doctorate in 1904. During the following years, his work included research on the psychology of testimony, deriving no doubt from his early interest in law and his abiding interest in the nature of truth; he also carried on research in music, another lifelong interest.

In 1910, Wertheimer performed his now famous experiments on apparent movement, that movement which we see when, under certain conditions, two *stationary* objects are presented in succession at different places (a phenomenon familiar in moving pictures). This was the beginning of Gestalt psychology—a major revolution in psychological thinking.

The phenomena which Wertheimer was investigating could not be explained by the then-prevailing psychology. Psychology was, in 1910, characteristically analytical: in naive **imitation** of the natural sciences, it attempted to reduce every complex phenomenon to simpler ones, the elements which were supposed to make up the whole.

But it was already clear that this analytical procedure could not account for many well-known psychological facts. Some advocates of the older psychology tried to patch it up by adding assumptions to take care of trou-

blesome findings, while leaving the old framework intact. Other scholars, seeing the inadequacy of the customary approach, denied that the problems of psychology could be treated scientifically.

For Wertheimer, neither line of criticism went to the core of the problem. The difficulties of the older psychology went far beyond its failure to explain special laboratory findings. Everything that was vital, meaningful, and essential seemed to be lost in the traditional approach. The trouble, he held, was not in the **scientific method** itself but rather in an assumption generally made about that method—that it must be atomistic.

But science need not only be analytical in this sense. The viewing of complex wholes as "and-sums," to be reduced to accidentally and arbitrarily associated elements, Wertheimer described as an approach "from below," whereas many situations need to be approached "from above." In these cases, what happens in the whole cannot be understood from a knowledge of its components considered piecemeal; rather the behavior of the parts themselves depends on their place in the structured whole, in the context in which they exist.

These are precisely the situations which are most important for psychology, those in which we find meaning, value, order. Thus, apparent movement cannot be understood if one knows only the "stills" by which it is produced; nor can the form of a circle, the peacefulness of a landscape, the sternness of a command, the inevitability of a conclusion be understood from a knowledge of independent elements. Here, whole properties are primary, and the characteristics of parts are derived from the dynamics of their wholes.

Wertheimer became a lecturer in Frankfurt in 1912. Later he went to Berlin and in 1929 returned to Frankfurt as professor. All this time he was developing his ideas and influencing students who themselves became distinguished psychologists. Although he preferred the spoken to the written word as a vehicle for communication, he wrote some notable articles applying the new approach "from above" to the organization of the perceptual field and to the nature of thinking.

Just before the German elections in 1933, Wertheimer heard a speech by Hitler over a neighbor's radio. He decided that he did not want his **family** to live in a country where such a man could run, with likelihood of success, for the highest office in the land; and the next day the family moved to Marienbad, Czechoslovakia. Soon Wertheimer realized that Hitler was not a passing phenomenon, and he accepted an invitation from the New School for Social Research in New York City to join its University in Exile (later the Graduate Faculty of Political and Social Science). He resumed his studies of thinking, completing his major work, *Productive Thinking,* a highly original and penetrating examination of the processes that occur in thinking at its best. In a series of articles, he showed the application of Gestalt thinking to problems of truth, **ethics**, freedom, and democracy. Unfortunately, he did not live to write his projected Gestalt logic.

*See also* Gestalt principles of organization

**Further Reading**
Köhler, Wolfgang. *The task of Gestalt psychology.* 1969.

# Withdrawal behavior

Tendency to avoid either unfamiliar persons, locations, or situations.

Withdrawal behavior is characterized by the tendency to avoid the unfamiliar, either people, places, or situations. Though withdrawal, or avoidance, can be the result of a temperamental tendency toward inhibition to unfamiliar events, anxiety over the anticipation of a critical evaluation, or a conditioned avoidant response, often called a **phobia**, can produce withdrawal. These are three different mechanisms, each of which can mediate withdrawal behavior.

Withdrawal behavior is typically seen in children. The withdrawal or avoidance that is seen in the preschool years is, most of the time, due to a temperamental bias that makes some children uncertain over unfamiliar events. During later **childhood**, withdrawal or avoidance occurs due to very specific events, like lightening, animals, insects, or foods. At this point, withdrawal is usually not the result of a temperamental bias, but more often is due to **conditioning** experiences in which the child had a painful or frightening experience in association with the event he avoids.

A small group of children who appear withdrawn may have serious **mental illness**, including **schizophrenia** or **autism**. However, these are relatively rare illnesses and therefore the average child who appears withdrawn will probably not be afflicted with these problems.

Jerome Kagan

# Joseph Wolpe

**1915-1997**
South African-born American psychiatrist who made significant contributions to behavior therapy.

Joseph Wolpe's groundbreaking work as a behaviorist was grounded in his belief that **behavior therapy** was as much an applied science as any other aspect of medicine. He is probably best known for his work in the areas of **desensitization** and assertiveness training, both of which have become important elements of behavioral therapy.

He was born on April 20, 1915 in Johannesburg, South Africa, to Michael Salmon and Sarah Millner Wolpe. He grew up in South Africa and attended college there, obtaining his M.D. from the University of Witwatersrand. When the Second World War began, he joined the South African army as a medical officer. He worked in a military psychiatric hospital, and witnessed soldiers who were suffering from what would today be called post-traumatic **stress** syndrome. At the time, it was known as "war neurosis," and Wolpe and his colleagues first tried to treat the problem with **drug therapy**. The results were marginally helpful, however, and Wolpe decided to work on finding more effective means for dealing with the problem.

He came up with the concept now known as desensitization. Reasoning that much of our behavior, both good and bad, is learned, there was no reason why it could not be unlearned. Wolpe's initial experiments were with cats. These animals were given mild electric shocks accompanied by specific sounds and visual stimuli. Once the cats knew to equate the unpleasant shock with these images or sounds, the images and sounds created a feeling of **fear**. By gradually exposing the cats to these same sights and sounds—with food being given instead of shocks—the cats gradually "unlearned" their fear.

Those who suffer phobias—whether rational or unfounded—know that exposure to the object of fear can be crippling. Modern desensitization techniques include teaching patients relaxation techniques and gradually rehearsing stressful situations, until the patient is finally able to handle the fear-inducing objects.

Sometimes, as Wolpe found out, the problem may not be fear of the object per se, but a negative association coming from another source. In one instance, Wolpe tried to desensitize a woman to an inordinate fear of insects. The usual methods did not work; then Wolpe found out that the woman's husband, with whom she had not been getting along, was nicknamed for an insect. The key then was to work on the marital problems. Once these had been dealt with, the woman's **phobia** gradually disappeared.

Wolpe's research also led to assertiveness training. As with desensitization, it requires a gradual move into new behaviors. People who have trouble asserting themselves are very much like phobics in that they fear confrontation and conflict, **anger** in others, and rejection.

Assertiveness training gives them the framework to build their confidence, relax in formerly stressful situations, and conquer their fear.

Perhaps Wolpe's most important contribution to psychiatry was that he managed to combine two seemingly disparate disciplines. Many psychologists and psychiatrists felt that methods based in applied science lacked the humanistic touch they felt was so important when dealing with people. What Wolpe did was show that effective, compassionate therapy could be combined with empirical methods in a way that used both to their best advantage. Among his writings, his books *Pyschotheraphy by Reciprocal Inhibition* (1958) and *The Practice of Behavior Therapy* (1969) are considered classics in behavior therapy studies.

After the war, Wolpe worked at the University of Witwatersrand; later, he moved to the U.S., where he initially taught at the University of Virginia. In 1965, he became a professor of psychiatry at Temple University Medical School in Philadelphia, a post that he held until 1988. During this time, he also served as director of the behavior therapy unit at the nearby Eastern Pennsylvania Psychiatric Institute. He served as the second president of the Association for the Advancement of Behavior Therapy, from which he received a lifetime achievement award.

Wolpe retired in 1988 and moved to California. Once he had settled in California, however, his retirement did not last long. He began lecturing at Pepperdine University and continued until a month before his death. He was married twice. His first wife, whom he married in 1948, was Stella Ettman. She died in 1990, and he married Eva Gyarmati in 1996. He had two children and three stepchildren. Lung cancer claimed Wolpe's life on December 4, 1998.

George A. Milite

# Word association test

A procedure for investigating how word meanings are stored in memory.

In a word association test, the researcher presents a series of words to individual respondents. For each word, participants are instructed to respond with the first word (i.e., associate) that comes to mind. Freud believed that such responses provided clues to peoples' personalities (**free association**). Cognitive psychologists, however, use this procedure to investigate how semantic informa-

tion is stored in **memory**. Studies have demonstrated that word associations are almost always based on a word's meaning, as opposed to its physical properties. For example, a typical response to the word KNIFE might be FORK or perhaps SPOON, but not WIFE or LIFE. Over the years, psychologists have collected word association norms that describe the relative frequencies with which various responses are given to different words. These frequencies are then used as a measure of the associative strength between the words. If 90% of a large sample of people give the word DOCTOR as a response to the word NURSE, this percentage (90) is used as an index of the associative connection between DOCTOR and NURSE. Another way of determining the strength of an association is to measure how much time it takes to produce a response in a word association test. High frequency associates are also the ones with the fastest reaction times.

By comparing children's word associations to those of adults, we can learn something about how word meanings are acquired. Five year-olds are likely to respond to the word LONG with a response like GRASS—indicating that words are organized in their memory according to real world situations and personal experience. By age 10, the most common response is SHORT, thereby revealing a growing awareness of linguistic relations and grammatical categories.

*See also* Free association

Timothy E. Moore

# Wilhelm Max Wundt

**1832-1920**
German psychologist and philosopher who founded experimental psychology.

Wilhelm Wundt was born on August 16, 1832, in Baden, in a suburb of Mannheim called Neckarau. As a child, he was tutored by Friedrich Müller. Wundt attended the Gymnasium at Bruschel and at Heidelberg, the University of Tübingen for a year, then Heidelberg for more than three years, receiving a medical degree in 1856. He remained at Heidelberg as a lecturer in physiology from 1857 to 1864, then was appointed assistant professor in physiology. The great physiologist, physicist, and physiological psychologist **Hermann von Helmholtz** came there in 1858, and Wundt was his assistant for a period of time.

**Wilhelm Wundt** *(Corbis-Bettmann. Reproduced with permission.)*

During the period from 1857 to 1874, Wundt evolved from a physiologist to a psychologist. In these years he also wrote *Grundzüge der physiologischen psychologie (Principles of Physiological Psychology).* The two-volume work, published in 1873-1874, stressed the relations between psychology and physiology, and it showed how the methods of natural science could be used in psychology. Six revised editions of this work were published, the last completed in 1911.

As a psychologist, Wundt used the method of investigating conscious processes in their own context by "experiment" and introspection. This technique has been referred to as content psychology, reflecting Wundt's belief that psychology should concern itself with the immediate content of experience unmodified by abstraction or reflection.

In 1874, Wundt left Heidelberg for the chair of inductive philosophy at Zurich, staying there only a year. He accepted the chair of philosophy at the University of Leipzig, and in 1879 he founded the first psychological laboratory in the world. To Leipzig, men came from all over the world to study in Wundt's laboratory. In 1879,

G. Stanley Hall, Wundt's first American student, arrived, followed by many other Americans. From this first laboratory for **experimental psychology**, a steady stream of psychologists returned to their own countries to teach and to continue their researches. Some founded psychological laboratories of their own.

In 1881, Wundt founded *Philosophische Studien* as a vehicle for the new experimental psychology, especially as a publication organ for the products of his psychological laboratory. The contents of *Philosophische Studien* (changed to *Psychologische Studien* in 1903) reveal that the experiments fell mainly into four categories: sensation and **perception**; **reaction time**; time perception and association; and **attention**, **memory**, feeling, and association. Optical phenomena led with 46 articles; audition was second in importance. Sight and **hearing**, which Helmholtz had already carefully studied, were the main themes of Wundt's laboratory. Some of the contributions to the *Studien* were by Wundt himself. Helmholtz is reported to have said of some of Wundt's experiments that they were *schlampig* (sloppy). Comparing Wundt to Helmholtz, who was a careful experimentalist and productive researcher, one must conclude that Wundt's most important contributions were as a systematizer, organizer, and encyclopedist. **William James** considered Wundt "only a rather ordinary man who has worked up certain things uncommonly well."

Wundt's *Grundriss der Psychologie* (1896; *Outline of Psychology*) was a less detailed treatment than his *Principles,* but it contained the new theory of feeling. A popular presentation of his system of psychology was *Einführung in die Psychologie* (1911; *Introduction to Psychology*). His monumental *Völkerpsychologie* (1912; *Folk Psychology*), a natural history of man, attempted to understand man's higher thought processes by studying language, art, mythology, religion, custom, and law. Besides his psychological works he wrote three philosophical texts: *Logic* (1880-1883), *Ethics* (1886), and *System of Philosophy* (1889). Wundt died near Leipzig on August 31, 1920.

**Further Reading**

Brett, George Sidney. *Brett's history of psychology.* R. S. Peters, ed. 1953. 2nd rev. ed. 1965.

Hall, G. Stanley. *Founders of modern psychology.* 1912.

Flugel, J.C. *A hundred years of psychology.* 1933. rev. 1965.

Boring, Edwin G. *A history of experimental psychology.* 1929. 2nd ed. 1950.

Wolman, Benjamin B. *Historical roots of contemporary psychology.* 1968.

*Wundt studies: a centennial collection.* Toronto: C.J. Hogrefe, 1980.

**Y**

# Robert Yerkes

**1876-1956**
American psychologist who made important contributions to the fields of comparative animal psychology, particularly in the areas of animal intelligence and behavior.

Robert Yerkes was born in Pennsylvania, and was educated at Harvard University, where he received his doctorate in psychology in 1902. He served as professor of psychology at Harvard, the University of Minnesota, and Yale University, and as a member of the National Research Council. In 1919, Yerkes founded the Yale Laboratories of Primate Biology and served as its director from 1929 to 1941, when the lab was moved to Orange Park, Florida. A year later, it was renamed the Yerkes Laboratories of Primate Biology. A pioneer in the field of **comparative psychology**, Yerkes studied the **intelligence** and behavior of many forms of animal life, from jellyfish to humans, but he focused most of his attention on primates. Among his findings were the discovery that chimpanzees imitate both each other and human beings, and the observation that orangutans can pile boxes on top of one another to reach food after seeing this demonstrated, thus transferring this experience to other learning problems.

Yerkes also worked on the Yerkes-Dodson Law, which states that for every task there is an optimum level of **motivation**, and that motivation that is too strong can actually interfere with the **ability** to perform a difficult task. Yerkes also pioneered the use of monochromatic light to study **color vision** in animals. In 1911, he developed the first multiple-choice test for animals, designed to test abstraction abilities. A row of nine or fewer boxes were shown to the animal, which had to determine which of the open boxes had food in it and then remember that box in subsequent rounds of testing.

Turning his attention to human testing, Yerkes revised the **Stanford-Binet Intelligence scales** in 1915 to create a widely used point scale for the **measurement** of

**Robert Mearns Yerkes** *(The Library of Congress. Reproduced with permission.)*

human mental ability. He was also a principal figure in the development of human multiple choice testing. During World War I, Yerkes directed a team of 40 psychologists charged with assessing the abilities of army recruits for training, assignment, and discharge purposes. Together they developed the Army Alpha test, a written intelligence test, and Army Beta, a pictorial test for the 40 percent of draftees who were functionally illiterate. By the end of the war, these tests had been used to classify some 1.75 million men. As a result of taking these tests, some 8,000 had been discharged as unfit, while the Alpha test played a role in the selection of two thirds of the 200,000 men who served as commissioned officers during the war.

In addition to its impact on the military, the wartime testing developed by Yerkes and his colleagues had a far-reaching effect on civilian life after the war. Unlike the Stanford Binet scale, which had to be individually administered by a tester, the Alpha and Beta tests were developed to be administered to groups, making them faster, simpler, and far less expensive to use. After the war, this breakthrough in mental measurement led to a dramatic expansion in intelligence testing. Yerkes and several colleagues devised one of several pencil-and-paper tests that were marketed to school administrators throughout the country. The National Research Council, the test's sponsor, described it as deriving from "the application of the army testing methods to school needs." By 1930, it had been administered to seven million schoolchildren. (The Scholastic Aptitude Test was developed by one of Yerkes' colleagues during this same period.) Yerkes' books include: *Introduction to Psychology* (1911), *The Mental Life of Monkeys and Apes* (1916), *The Great Apes* (1929) (coauthored with Ada Yerkes), and *Chimpanzees: A Laboratory Colony* (1943).

# Z

# Edward F. Zigler

**1930-**
Developmental psychologist who has focused on maximizing the potential of children from underprivileged backgrounds, and who has significantly contributed to national programs for children such as the Head Start program.

Edward Frank Zigler was born in 1930 to Louis Zigler and Gertrude (Gleitman) Zigler of Kansas, Missouri. His parents and two older sisters immigrated to the United States from Poland. After attending a vocational high school in Kansas City, Zigler earned his B.S. at the University of Missouri, Kansas City. He went on to obtain his Ph.D. in **developmental psychology** from the University of Texas at Austin in 1958. He then taught for a year at the University of Missouri at Columbia before going to Yale in 1959, where he became director of the Yale University department of **child development** in 1961. Zigler married Bernice Gorelick in 1955 and has one son, Scott.

In 1970, Zigler was appointed by President Nixon to the post of first director of the office of Child Development, which has since been renamed the Administration of Children, Youth and Families. He was also appointed as chief of the U.S. Children's Bureau. While he was the director of the Office of Child Development in Washington, Zigler administered the nation's Head Start Program, which was established by the United States Congress in 1965, and funded by the U.S. Department of Health and Human Services as part of the "war on poverty" legislation of 1964. Its purpose is to provide educational, health, and social services for pregnant mothers, children from **birth** to age five, and their families through the channels of preschool education, medical treatment, and developmental screenings. The Head Start theory is that all of a child's early needs must be met in order for them to reach their full potential later on. Theoretically, the program enables underprivileged children,

or those with severe learning disabilities, to develop and be better prepared to face life later on.

Zigler is frequently called as an expert witness before congressional committees and to comment on social policy issues that concern children and families in the United States. He has also chaired numerous conferences concerned with children. Notably, he was appointed as Honorary Commissioner for the National Commission on the Year of the Child in 1979.

Zigler served on the President's Committee on **Mental Retardation** and was requested by president Ford to chair the Vietnamese Children's Resettlement Advisory Group. In 1980, at President Carter's request, he chaired the fifteenth anniversary Head Start Committee. This committee was charged with planning future policy for this government-run intervention program. As director of the Office of Child Development, Zigler is also credited with conceptualizing and initiating other programs such as Health Start, Home Start, Education for Parenthood, the Child Development Associate Program and the Child and **Family** Resource Program.

In 1993, Zigler was appointed as head of a national committee of distinguished Americans who were charged with looking into the possibilities for legislation to make infant care leave a reality in the United States. The work of this committee culminated in the Family and Medical Leave act of 1993.

Zigler has written 26 books and over five hundred articles about his research and theories. In addition, he is a member of the editorial boards of ten professional journals, Associate Editor of *Children and Youth Services Review,* and consulting editor of the *Merril-Palmer Quarterly.* In August 1999, Zigler published *Personality Development in Individuals with Mental Retardation,* consolidating forty years of his research on the subject.

Zigler has been awarded numerous honors, among them the Harold W. McGraw, Jr., Prize in Education, awards from the Joseph P. Kennedy, Jr., Foundation, the American Psychological Association, the American

Academy of Pediatrics, the National Association for Retarded Citizens, the American Association on Mental Deficiency, the National Academy of Sciences, the American Academy of Child and Adolescent Psychiatry, the National Head Start Association, and the American Orthopsychiatric Association.

Currently Sterling Professor of Psychology at Yale, Zigler is head of the Yale Child Study Facility and also director of the Bush Center in Child Development and Social Policy. His laboratory is notable for the range of basic and applied studies of child development and family functioning studies in which it is engaged.

*See also* Child development

Patricia Skinner

## Further Reading

Sheehy, et al, eds. *Biographical dictionary of psychology.* New York: Routledge, 1997.

# GLOSSARY

## A

**Absolute threshold.** The minimal amount of energy necessary to stimulate the sensory receptors.

**Action potential.** A momentary electrical event occurring through the membrane of a nerve cell fiber in response to a stimulus, forming a nerve impulse.

**Addiction/addictive personality.** A wide spectrum of complex behaviors that arises from dependence on drugs or participation in some other activity.

**Adjustment disorders.** The development of significant emotional or behavioral symptoms in response to an identifiable event that precipitated psychological or social stress.

**Alcoholic psychoses.** Acute reactions to alcohol characterized by alcohol idiosyncratic intoxication, alcohol withdrawal delirium, hallucinations, and irreversible brain damage involving severe memory loss.

**Alexia.** Inability to read; a form of dyslexia.

**Ambivalence.** The concurrent existence of contrasting, opposing, or contradictory feelings, emotions, or attitudes regarding a person, object, or idea.

**Ames room.** Specially constructed space that demonstrates aspects of visual perception.

**Anal stage.** The second stage in Sigmund Freud's theory of psychosexual development characterized by concerns over elimination, usually taking place around two years of age.

**Anonymity.** A condition in which the identity of an individual is not known to others.

**Anorexia.** An eating disorder in which preoccupation with dieting and thinness leads to excessive and dangerous weight loss.

**Anoxia.** Lack of oxygen in the blood supply; also called oxygen starvation.

**Antisocial behavior.** A pattern of behavior that is verbally or physically harmful to other people, animals, or property, including behavior that severely violates social expectations.

**Antisocial personality disorder.** A behavior disorder characterized by disregard for social norms and laws, manipulation, impulsivity, recklessness, and lack of remorse; also known as sociopathy or psychopathy.

**Anxiety/anxiety disorders.** An unpleasant emotional state characterized by apprehension, worry, and fear.

**Apgar score.** The sum of numerical results indicating a newborn infant's overall medical condition.

**Aphasia.** A condition in which a person's previous capacity to understand or express language is impaired.

**Archetype.** Primordial images and symbols found in the collective unconscious that are passed on from generation to generation.

**Arousal.** An increase in the level of an individual's readiness for activity.

**Associationism.** The view that mental processes can be explained in terms of the association of ideas.

**Attention deficit/hyperactivity disorder (ADHD).** Disorder characterized by inattention, impulsivity, and hyperactivity.

**Attribution theory.** A term used to describe how people explain the causes of behavior, both their own and those of others.

**Authoritarian personality.** A personality pattern characterized by rigidity, dependence on authority, conformity to group values, and intolerance of ambiguity.

**Autoeroticism.** Commonly referred to as masturbation, self-stimulation of the genital organs with the intention of producing sexual arousal and orgasm.

**Autohypnosis.** The ability to hypnotize oneself without the aid of another person.

**Autonomic nervous system.** The nervous system responsible for regulating automatic bodily processes, such as breathing and heart rate. It also involves the processes of metabolism, or the storage and expenditure of energy.

**Aversive conditioning.** Also referred to as aversion therapy, a technique that links undesired behavior with physical or psychological discomfort.

**Avoidance learning.** An individual's response to avoid an unpleasant or stressful situation; also known as escape learning.

**Avoidant personality.** Personality disorder characterized by social withdrawal and fear of rejection.

**Axon.** One of two types of short, threadlike fibers that extend from the cell body of a nerve cell, or neuron (the other type are called dendrites), and which sends electrochemical signals.

# B

**Battered child syndrome.** A group of physical and mental symptoms arising from long-term physical violence against a child.

**Bayley Scales of Infant Development.** A comprehensive developmental test for infants and toddlers from two to 30 months of age.

**Behavior modification.** A treatment approach, based on the principles of operant conditioning, that replaces undesirable behaviors with more desirable ones through reinforcements.

**Behavior therapy.** A goal-oriented, therapeutic approach that treats disorders as maladaptive learned responses that can be replaced by healthier ones.

**Behaviorism.** A theory of human development initiated by Edward Thorndike and developed by John Watson and B.F. Skinner, emphasizing the study of measurable and observable behavior.

**Bender-Gestalt test.** Diagnostic assessment test to identify learning disability, neurological disorders, and developmental delay.

**Bestiality.** Sexual feelings or behaviors involving animals; also referred to as zoophilia.

**Binocular depth cues.** Properties of the visual system that facilitate depth perception by the nature of messages that are sent to the brain.

**Bipolar disorder.** A condition traditionally called manic depression in which a person alternates between the two emotional extremes of depression and mania.

**Borderline personality.** Mental illness characterized by erratic and impulsive self-destructive behavior and an intense fear of abandonment.

**Bowen theory.** An approach to family therapy proposed by Murray Bowen in which family members are taught to reestablish their "real" identities.

**Brainstem.** Connector between the brain and the spinal cord.

**Brief reactive psychosis.** An uncommon acute mental disorder precipitated by an event that causes intense psychological stress.

**Broca's aphasia.** Type of aphasia characterized by slow, labored, "telegraphic" speech with propositions and articles missing.

**Bulimia.** Eating disorder marked by episodes of binge eating followed by behaviors to control weight.

**Bystander effect.** The effect of the presence of others on an individual's perception of and response to a situation.

# C

**Castration anxiety.** The fear of losing one's penis. In Freudian terms, this fear causes the boy to abandon his incestuous attachment to his mother and begin to identify with his father.

**Catharsis.** The release of repressed psychic energy.

**Cathexis.** The investment of psychic energy in a person or object connected with the gratification of instincts.

**Central nervous system.** The portion of the nervous system that lies within the brain and spinal cord; it receives impulses from nerve cells throughout the body, regulates bodily functions, and directs behavior.

**Cerebellum.** Located below the cerebrum and behind the brainstem, it controls subconscious activities, such as balance and muscular coordination.

**Cerebral cortex.** Cerebrum's outer layer consisting of nerve cell bodies.

**Cerebral palsy.** A permanent motor disability caused by brain damage associated with birth.

**Cerebrum.** Divided into two hemispheres (left and right), the part of the brain that interprets sensory impulses. The left side functions mainly in speech, logic, writing, and arithmetic. The right side is linked with imagination, art, symbols, and spatial relations.

**Childhood amnesia.** The common inability to recall childhood experiences during the first three to five years of life.

**Classical conditioning.** The process of closely associating a neutral stimulus with one that evokes a reflexive response so that eventually the neutral stimulus alone will evoke the same response.

**Clinical psychology.** The application of psychological principles to diagnosing and treating persons with emotional and behavioral problems.

**Codependence.** A term used to describe a person who is intimately involved with a person who is abusing or addicted to alcohol or another substance.

**Cognition.** A general term for the higher mental processes by which people acquire knowledge, solve problems, and plan for the future.

**Cognitive behavior therapy.** A therapeutic approach based on the principle that maladaptive moods and behavior can be changed by replacing distorted or inappropriate ways of thinking with thought patterns that are healthier and more realistic.

**Cognitive dissonance.** Inconsistency between attitude (or belief) and behavior.

**Cognitive psychology.** An approach to psychology that focuses on the relationship between cognitive or mental processes and behavior.

**Cognitive restructuring.** Process of replacing negative thoughts with alternative thoughts that are positive and calming.

**Collective unconscious.** Consciousness that is shared by all people regardless of generation or culture.

**Combat neurosis.** Mental disturbances related to the stress of military combat.

**Comparative psychology.** A subfield of experimental psychology that focuses on the study of animals for the purpose of comparing the behavior of different species.

**Compensation.** A defense mechanism in which an individual unconsciously develops or overdevelops one area of personality as substitutive behavior to make up for a deficiency or inferiority in another area.

**Concept formation.** Learning process by which items are categorized and related to each other.

**Concrete operational stage.** Third stage of Jean Piaget's theory of cognitive development. At this stage, children begin to develop clearer methods of thinking, although they have difficulty conceiving abstract thought.

**Conditioned response.** Behavior that is learned in response to a particular stimulus.

**Conditioned stimulus.** Stimulus that leads to a learned response.

**Conduct disorder.** Childhood antisocial behavior disorder characterized by aggressive and destructive actions that harm others or property.

**Consciousness.** Awareness of external stimuli and of one's own mental activity.

**Convergent thinking.** The ability to narrow the number of possible solutions to a problem by applying logic and knowledge.

**Conversion reaction.** A psychological disorder characterized by physical symptoms for which no physiological cause can be found.

**Correlational method.** A technique used to measure the likelihood of two behaviors or events relating to each other.

**Counterconditioning.** Weakening or eliminating an undesired response by introducing and strengthening a second response that is incompatible with it.

**Covert conditioning.** A method for changing behavior that involves the client using imagination to target unwanted behavior.

**Cross-cultural psychology.** A subfield of psychology concerned with observing human behavior in contrasting cultures.

**Cross-sectional study.** Research that collects data simultaneously from people of different ages.

**Cybernetics.** The study of artificial intelligence systems and their comparison to human brain functions.

# D

**Deductive reasoning.** Way of thinking that relates ideas to one another in reaching conclusions.

**Defense mechanisms.** Unconscious strategies for avoiding or reducing threatening feelings such as fear and anxiety.

**Delusion.** Beliefs that are in stark contrast to reality, often having to do with persecution or an exaggerated sense of importance or glory.

**Dementia.** A gradual deterioration of mental functioning affecting all areas of cognition, including judgment, language, and memory.

**Dendrites.** Nerve cell fibers that receive signals from other cells.

**Deoxyribonucleic acid (DNA).** An organic substance that encodes and carries genetic information and is the fundamental element of heredity.

**Dependent personality disorder.** Disorder characterized by a lack of self-confidence coupled with excessive dependence on others.

**Dependent variable.** Variable measured in an experiment or study; what the experimenter measures.

**Depression.** An emotional state or mood characterized by one or more of these symptoms: sad mood, low energy, poor concentration, sleep or appetite changes, feelings of worthlessness or hopelessness, and thoughts of suicide.

**Derealization.** Type of dissociation in which a person perceives reality in a grossly distorted way.

**Desensitization.** Behavioral modification technique in which undesired behavior, such as anxiety, is paired with another response that is incompatible with it, such as relaxation.

**Determinism.** A scientific perspective that specifies that events occur in completely predictable ways as a result of natural and physical laws.

**Developmental delay.** Any delay in a person's physical, cognitive, behavioral, emotional, or social development, due to any number of reasons.

**Developmental psychology.** The study of the ways in which people develop physically, emotionally, intellectually, and socially over the course of their lives.

***Diagnostic and Statistical Manual of Mental Disorders (DSM-IV).*** A reference work developed by the American Psychiatric Association and designed to provide guidelines for the diagnosis and classification of mental disorders.

**Diencephalon.** Located above the brainstem, the site of the thalamus and hypothalamus.

**Differential psychology.** The area of psychology concerned with measuring and comparing differences in individual and group behavior.

**Displacement.** A defense mechanism in which an unacceptable impulse, such as aggression, is redirected to something more acceptable, such as participating in a boxing match.

**Dissociative identity disorder.** A disorder in which a person's identity dissociates, or fragments, creating additional, distinct identities that exist independently of each other within the same person; also known as multiple personality disorder.

**Divergent thinking.** The ability to come up with original and unique ideas and to envision multiple solutions to a problem.

**Double bind.** Term used to describe situations in which communication and behavior conflict (for example, using warm, comforting voice while administering physical punishment to a child).

**Draw-a-person test.** A test that measures nonverbal intelligence or to screen for emotional or behavioral disorders.

**Drive reduction theory.** A popular theory of the 1940s and 1950s that attributed behavior to the desire to reduce tension produced by primary (biological) or secondary (acquired) drives.

**Dyslexia.** A reading disability that is not caused by an identifiable physical problem.

# E

**Echolalia.** Repetition of another person's words or phrases.

**Ectomorph.** A body type proposed by William Sheldon, who characterized ectomorphs as thin and intellectual or artistic.

**Effector.** Peripheral tissue at the outer end of an efferent neural path (one leading away from the central nervous system).

**Ego.** In psychoanalytic theory, the part of human personality that combines innate biological impulses (id) or drives with reality to produce appropriate behavior.

**Electroconvulsive therapy (ECT).** Also known as shock therapy, the application of mild electric current to the brain to produce an epileptic-like seizure as a means of treating certain psychological disorders, primarily severe depression.

**Electroencephalograph (EEG).** A device used to record the electrical activity of the brain.

**Emotional intelligence.** The ability to perceive and constructively act on both one's own emotions and the feelings of others.

**Empiricism.** Type of research that is based on direct observation.

**Encounter group.** Group of individuals who engage in intensive and psychotherapeutic interaction, with the general intention of increasing awareness of self and sensitivity to others, and improving interpersonal skills.

**Endocrine glands.** Ductless glands that secrete hormones into the bloodstream.

**Endomorph.** A body type proposed by William Sheldon, who characterized endomorphs as heavy and easy-going.

**Enuresis.** Also known as bedwetting, the inability to control urination during periods of sleep.

**Equilibrium sense.** One of two proprioceptive sensory systems that provide input about the positions of one's body.

**Ethology.** The study of animal behavior as observed in the natural environment and in the context of evolutionary adaptation.

**Etiology.** The study of how and why diseases or disorders originate.

**Eugenics.** The systematic attempt to increase desirable genetic traits and to decrease undesirable ones in a population.

**Experimental design.** Careful and detailed plan of an experiment.

**Experimenter bias.** The subtle and unintentional influence of the experimenter on the subjects in an experiment.

**Exposure-response prevention.** A behavioral treatment technique in which a person is exposed to an anxiety-producing event and kept from responding in an undesirable manner.

**Extinction.** The elimination of a conditioned response by withholding reinforcement.

**Forensic psychology.** The application of psychology to lawmaking, law enforcement, the examination of witnesses, and the treatment of the criminal; also known as legal psychology.

**Forgetting curve.** The general, predictable pattern of the process of forgetting learned information.

**Formal operations stage.** The fourth stage in Jean Piaget's theory of cognitive development characterized by a person's ability to reason about abstract concepts.

**Fragile x syndrome.** A genetic disorder that causes mental retardation.

**Free-recall learning.** The presentation of material to the learner with the subsequent task of recalling as much as possible about the material without any cues.

**Frequency distribution.** Systematic representation of data, arranged so that the observed frequency of occurrence of data falling within certain ranges, classes, or categories is shown.

**Frustration-aggression hypothesis.** Theory that aggression is a response to the frustration of some goal-directed behavior by an outside source.

**Fugue.** A dissociative disorder in which a person has no recollection of events during an amnesic episode.

**Functional disorder.** A psychological disorder for which no organic cause can be found.

**Functionalism.** A psychological approach that focuses on how consciousness functions to help human beings adapt to their environment.

# F

**Failure to thrive.** Failure of an infant, toddler, or child to grow at a normal rate.

**Familial retardation.** Mild mental retardation attributed to environmental causes and generally involving some degree of psychosocial disadvantage.

**Family therapy.** The joint treatment of two or more members of the same family in order to change unhealthy patterns of communication and interaction.

**Fetal alcohol effect (FAE) and Fetal alcohol syndrome (FAS).** The adverse and chronic effects of maternal alcohol abuse during pregnancy on her infant. FAS is the leading cause of mental retardation.

**Figure-ground perception.** The ability to visually differentiate between a sensory stimulation and its background.

# G

**Gender identity disorder.** A condition in which an individual develops a gender identity inconsistent with his or her anatomical and genetic sex.

**General adaptation syndrome.** A profound physiological reaction to severe stress.

**Genital stage.** The fifth and last stage in Sigmund Freud's theory of psychosexual development in which a person's sexual drives are increased and parental attachments are dissolved.

**Gestalt psychology.** A field of psychology that emphasizes the study of experience and behavior as wholes rather than independently functioning, disparate parts.

**Group therapy.** The simultaneous treatment of several clients who meet regularly under the guidance of a therapist to receive support or to pursue personal change.

# H

**Hallucinations.** Perception of things or feelings that have no foundation in reality.

**Hallucinogens.** Substances that cause hallucination when ingested.

**Halo effect.** A type of bias in which one characteristic of a person or one factor in a situation affects the evaluation of the person's other traits.

**Heuristics.** A methodical procedure for discovering solutions to problems.

**Histrionic personality disorder.** A maladaptive or inflexible pattern of behavior characterized by emotional instability, excitability, over-reactivity, and self-dramatization.

**Holtzman inkblot technique.** A projective test used to assess personality characteristics.

**Human potential movement.** A movement that focuses on helping people achieve their full potential through an eclectic combination of therapeutic methods and discipline.

**Humanistic psychology.** A theoretical and therapeutic approach that emphasizes people's uniqueness and their power to control their own destinies.

**Hydrocephalus.** A condition in which fluid collects inside the skull.

**Hypnosis.** A temporary narrowing of conscious awareness.

**Hypochondria.** A disorder characterized by an excessive and habitual preoccupation with personal health and a tendency to interpret insignificant conditions as evidence of serious disease.

**Hypothalamus.** A section of the forebrain that is involved in such aspects of behavior as motivation, emotion, eating, drinking, and sexuality.

# I

**Id.** In psychoanalytic theory, the most primitive, unconscious element of human personality.

**Identification.** A type of defense mechanism in which a person takes on the characteristics of someone else.

**Imprinting.** A type of learning characteristic of fowls that occurs only during a critical period of development soon after birth.

**Impulse control disorders.** A psychological disorder characterized by the repeated inability to refrain from performing a particular action that is harmful either to oneself or others.

**Independent variable.** The variable the experimenter manipulates in an experiment.

**Inductive reasoning.** Way of thinking that uses comparison to reach conclusions.

**Industrial psychology.** A subfield of applied psychology in which practical problems in the workplace are addressed through the application of psychological principles.

**Information-processing theory.** An orientation that focuses on how people select, process, and internalize information and how they use it to make decisions and guide their behavior.

**Instrumental behavior.** Behavior exhibited by persons in response to certain stimuli.

**Intellectualization.** A type of defense mechanism in which a person detaches himself from a painful or anxiety-producing situation by dealing with it solely in intellectual, abstract terms and ignoring its emotional components.

**Interest inventory.** A test that determines a person's preference for specific fields or activities.

**Intermittent explosive disorder.** Uncontrollable episodes of aggression, where the person loses control and assaults others or destroys property.

# J

**Just noticeable difference.** Scientific calculation of the average detectable difference between two measurable qualities.

# K

**Kinesthetic sense.** The ability to know accurately the positions and movements of one's skeletal joints.

**Kleptomania.** Overwhelming impulse to steal.

**Kohlberg's theory.** A theory advanced by Lawrence Kohlberg on the six stages of moral development.

**Kohs block test.** Intelligence test most often used with persons with language or hearing handicaps.

# L

**Language acquisition device.** Notion that some knowledge about language is built into the brain of the human child.

**Latency stage.** The fourth stage in Sigmund Freud's theory of psychosexual development, in which a person's sexuality is dormant and his or her attentions are focused outside the family.

**Law of effect.** Principle that states that behavior that leads to a satisfying outcome is likely to be repeated, while behaviors that lead to undesired outcomes are less likely to be repeated.

**Learned helplessness.** An apathetic attitude stemming from the conviction that one's actions do not have the power to affect one's situation.

**Learning theory.** Theory about how people learn and modify pre-existing thoughts and behavior.

**Learning-to-learn.** The phenomenon of greater improvement in speed of learning as one's experience with learning increases.

**Lobotomy.** The severing of the nerves connecting the frontal lobes of the brain and the thalamus or hypothalamus.

**Locus of control.** A personality orientation characterized either by the belief that one can control events by one's own efforts or that the future is determined by forces outside one's control.

**Longitudinal study.** Research method used to study changes over time.

# M

**Magnetic resonance imaging.** Technique for studying the brain using magnetic fields.

**Mania.** Mood of elation without apparent cause or justification.

**Maslow's hierarchy of needs.** Theory of human motivation developed by Abraham Maslow that emphasizes developing one's full potential. The hierarchy is depicted as a pyramid with five levels, ranging from the most basic needs at the bottom to the most complex and sophisticated at the top.

**Mean.** The sum of the values of the points in a data set divided by the number of points.

**Median.** The middle value in a group of measurements.

**Melancholia.** Outdated term for depression itself and a clinically defined characteristic of major depression.

**Menarche.** The first menstrual period, which occurs at an average age of 12.8 years for girls in the United States.

**Meningitis.** Inflammation of the meninges, most often caused by infection.

**Mental age.** A scale used to correlate intelligence to a child's chronological age.

**Merrill-Palmer scales of mental development.** Tests that measure intelligence for children ages 18 months to four years of age.

**Mesomorph.** A body type proposed by William Sheldon, who characterized mesomorphs as muscular and aggressive.

**Metapsychology.** General term used to describe the attempt to establish principles to explain all psychological phenomena.

**Methylphenidate.** The generic name for the drug Ritalin, the most commonly prescribed medication for treating attention deficit/hyperactivity disorder.

**Midbrain.** Also called mesencephalon, the small area near the lower middle of the brain that controls smooth and reflexive movements and regulates attention, sleep, and arousal.

**Milgram's obedience experiment.** A controversial experiment on conformity and obedience to authority conducted in the early 1960s by Stanley Milgram.

**Minimal brain dysfunction.** Term used in connection with hyperactivity and/or attention deficit disorder.

**Minnesota Multiphasic Personality Inventory.** Test used to gather information on personality, attitudes, and mental health.

**Mnemonic strategies.** Any technique used for the purpose of memorizing or improving the function of memory in general.

**Mode.** The most frequently occurring member of a set of numbers.

**Montessori method.** A progressive system of education for early childhood through adolescence developed by Maria Montessori, emphasizing individualized, self-directed study.

**Muscular dystrophy.** A category of inherited, incurable, and often life-threatening diseases in which the limb and trunk muscles deteriorate.

# N

**Narcissism.** Excessive preoccupation with self and lack of empathy for others.

**Narcolepsy.** A sleep disorder whose primary symptoms is irresistible attacks of sleepiness during the daytime.

**Negativism.** Tendency to resist complying with suggestions or directions.

**Neocortex.** The exterior covering of the cerebral hemispheres of the brain.

**Nervous system.** An electrochemical conducting network that transmits messages from the brain through the nerves to locations throughout the body.

**Neuron.** Technical term for nerve cell, responsible for sending, receiving, and storing signals through a unique blend of electricity and chemistry.

**Neurosis.** Term used to describe conditions involving anxiety or psychological distress.

**Neurosurgery.** Surgery of the nervous system.

**Neurotransmitter.** Chemical substances or molecules that aid in message transmission between neurons.

**Nicotine.** Addictive substance in cigarettes.

**Night terrors.** A childhood sleep disorder featuring behavior that appears to be intense fear.

# O

**Obsessive-compulsive disorder.** Mental illness characterized by the recurrence of intrusive, anxiety-producing thoughts accompanied by repeated attempts to suppress these thoughts through the performance of certain irrational, often ritualistic, behaviors.

**Oedipus complex.** Theory set forth by Sigmund Freud that children are torn between feelings of love for one parent while feeling a sense of competition with the other.

**Operant conditioning.** Approach to human learning based on the premise that human intelligence and will operate on the environment rather than merely respond to the environment's stimuli.

**Opiates.** Addictive narcotic drug derived from opium.

**Oppositional-defiant disorder.** A form of antisocial behavior disorder characterized by opposition to authority figures and by excessive anger and hostility.

**Oral stage.** The first stage in Sigmund Freud's theory of psychosexual development in which a child is primarily concerned with gratification through sucking.

**Organic disorder.** Disorder caused by a known pathological condition.

# P

**Paired-associate learning.** Pairing of two items (usually words) as stimulus and response.

**Panic/panic disorders.** Acute feelings of intense fear, accentuated by increased heart rate, shortness of breath, sweating, and mild convulsions.

**Paralysis agitans.** Another name for Parkinson's disease, a relatively common degenerative disorder of the central nervous system.

**Paranoia.** A pervasive feeling of distrust of others.

**Paraphilia.** Sexual feelings or behaviors that may involve sexual partners that are not human, not consenting, or that involve suffering by one or both partners. Common types of paraphilia are bestiality, exhibitionism, masochism, pedophilia, sadomasochism, and voyeurism.

**Parapsychology.** The study of paranormal phenomena, the most significant being ESP and psychokinesis.

**Parasomnia.** Sleeping disorder that involves unusual phenomena such as nightmares, sleep terrors, and sleepwalking that occur during sleep or during the period between sleeping and waking.

**Passive-aggressive personality.** A pattern of behavior characterized by indirect resistance to the demands or expectations of others, usually by covert means.

**Pedophilia.** Sexual activity with a child, generally under the age of 13.

**Penis envy.** According to psychoanalytic theory, a girl's wish for a penis; she blames her mother for depriving her of a penis and desires her father because he possesses one.

**Perception.** Area of psychology associated with the functioning of sensory systems and how information from the external world is interpreted.

**Perfectionism.** Tendency to set unrealistically high standards for performance of oneself and others, along with the inability to accept mistakes or imperfections.

**Pervasive development disorder.** A group of conditions involving serious impairment in several areas of development, including physical, behavioral, cognitive, social, and language development.

**Phallic stage.** The third stage in Sigmund Freud's theory of psychosexual development in which a child experiences and resolves the Oedipal crisis and assumes his or her sexual identity.

**Phenomenological therapy.** Also called humanistic therapy, an approach emphasizing a close, supportive relationship between the client and the therapist. Two well-known forms of phenomenological therapy are client-centered therapy and Gestalt therapy.

**Phenylketonuria (PKU).** An inherited metabolic disease caused by a defect in the liver enzyme that prevents the conversion of the protein called phenylalanine into a useful form.

**Phobia.** An intense, irrational, persistent fear that interferes with normal functioning.

**Phonation disorders.** Disturbances in speech timbre, intensity, or pitch.

**Placebo effect.** A scientifically significant response that cannot be explained by physiological variables and is assumed to be psychological in origin.

**Positron emission tomography.** Technique for studying the chemistry and activity of the brain and to diagnose abnormalities such as tumors.

**Post-traumatic stress disorder (PTSD).** A psychological disorder that develops in response to an extremely traumatic event that threatens a person's safety or life.

**Preconscious.** According to Sigmund Freud, that part of the human mind that lies between the conscious and the unconscious, which can be accessed and brought into consciousness without the use of special techniques.

**Preoperational stage.** The second stage in Jean Piaget's theory of cognitive development characterized by egocentrism, centration, and irreversibility in thought.

**Primal therapy.** A type of treatment method where early traumas are re-experienced in physical ways.

**Programmed learning.** A method of self-instruction that enlists machines or specially prepared books to teach information.

**Projection.** A type of defense mechanism in which a person assigns to others characteristics or motivations that an individual would prefer not to recognize in himself.

**Projective techniques.** Unstructured tests used in personality assessment that rely on the subject's interpretation of ambiguous stimuli.

**Psychoactive drugs.** Category of drugs that affect mood and behavior.

**Psychoanalysis.** A method of treatment developed by Sigmund Freud that emphasizes thorough examination of a person's unconscious motivations, feelings, and relationships.

**Psychobiology.** Developed by Adolf Meyer, the integration of psychology and biology to treat the whole person.

**Psychokinesis.** The ability to manipulate physical objects with the mind.

**Psycholinguistics.** The psychology of language.

**Psychophysics.** Subfield of psychology that studies the transformation from the physical to the psychological.

**Psychosexual stages.** Stages of development described by Sigmund Freud that focuses on the location of sexual impulses at different ages.

**Psychosis.** A symptom of mental illness characterized by a radical change in personality and a distorted or diminished sense of objective reality.

**Psychosomatic disorders.** Physical illnesses that are believed to be psychologically based.

**Psychostimulants.** Also called stimulants, drugs that produce increased levels of mental and physical energy and alertness and an elevated mood by stimulating the central nervous system.

**Psychosurgery.** Medical procedure in which specific areas of the brain are destroyed or disabled through surgery as treatment for mental illness.

**Psychotherapy.** The treatment of mental or emotional disorders through the use of psychological techniques rather than through physical or biological means.

**Pyromania.** Irresistible urge to start fires.

# R

**Rating scale.** Any instrument designed to assist in the measurement of subjective evaluation.

**Rational-emotive behavior therapy.** A mode of treatment developed by Albert Ellis in which a client is challenged to examine his or her irrational beliefs and taught to think more rationally with the goal of reducing emotional problems.

**Rationalization.** A type of defense mechanism in which a person gives an intellectual reason or rationale for an emotionally motivated action in order to assign socially acceptable motives to one's behavior or to mask disappointment.

**Reaction formation.** A type of defense mechanism in which a person deals with unacceptable feelings by adopting diametrically opposite ones.

**Readiness test.** A test designed to assess the developmental condition of an individual to determine whether he or she would benefit from some particular experience.

**Reflective listening.** A way of responding to a person in order to create empathy. Often used in a therapeutic setting, this technique involves accepting the person as he is and trying to understand the other person's reality.

**Regression.** A type of defense mechanism in which a person reverts to behavior characteristic of an earlier period of life in order to gain access to the sources of gratification experienced during that period.

**Reinforcement.** A stimulus that increases the probability that a particular behavior will occur.

**Reliability (in testing).** Term used in testing to describe tests that produce consistent and reproducible results.

**Repression.** A principal defense mechanism in which a person selectively forgets disturbing material.

**Ribonucleic acid (RNA).** A complex organic substance involved in protein synthesis in cells.

**Rorschach technique.** Popularly known as the "Inkblot Test," a widely used projective psychological test used to assess personality structure and identify emotional problems.

**Rosenzweig picture frustration study.** A projective test consisting of 24 cartoon pictures, each portraying a frustrating situation, used to assess personality characteristics.

# S

**Sadomasochism.** Sexual behavior in which an individual achieves gratification either by experiencing pain or inflicting pain on another person.

**Satanic ritualistic abuse.** Activities such as cannibalism, animal sacrifice, and child sexual abuse that are assumed to be carried out by organized underground cults.

**Savant syndrome.** A condition in which a person has below normal intelligence combined with a special talent or ability in a specific area; also known as autistic savant or idiot savant.

**Scapegoating.** A powerful and destructive phenomenon wherein a person or group of people are blamed for whatever is wrong.

**Schemas.** A term defined by Jean Piaget as the basic units of knowledge that a person uses to organize past experiences and to understand new ones.

**Schizophrenia.** A mental illness characterized by disordered thinking, delusions, hallucinations, emotional disturbance, and withdrawal from reality.

**Scholastic Assessment Test.** Series of tests used to measure verbal and mathematical abilities and achievement in specific subject areas.

**Seasonal affective disorder.** A bipolar disorder associated with lack of light and melatonin excess in the body. It generally corresponds to the seasons and how much light a person experiences.

**Seizures.** A temporary series of uncontrollable muscle spasms brought on by unusual electrical activity in the brain.

**Selective serotonin reuptake inhibitors (SSRIs).** A category of antidepressants, including Prozac, Zoloft, and Paxil.

**Self-actualization.** The final and most complex step in Abraham Maslow's hierarchy of human motives, encompassing the basic need for self-fulfillment.

**Self-conscious emotions.** Emotions such as guilt, pride, shame, and hubris.

**Semantic memory.** The part of long-term memory dealing with words, their symbols, and meanings.

**Sensitivity training.** A group experience that gives people new insight into how they relate to others.

**Sensorimotor stage.** The first stage in Jean Piaget's theory of cognitive development characterized by a child's ability to grasp properties of objects and the concept of object constancy.

**Sensory deprivation.** An experimental procedure involving prolonged reduction of sensory stimuli.

**Serial learning.** Recalling patterns of facts or stimuli in the order in which they were presented.

**Serial position function.** The predictable patterns of memory and forgetting when a person is presented with a list of stimuli.

**Shaping.** A gradual behavior modification technique in which successive approximations to the desired behavior is rewarded.

**Signal detection theory.** A psychological theory regarding a threshold of sensory detection.

**Significance level.** A method to describe the reliability of test results.

**Skinner box.** A specially made cage with levers for releasing food.

**Sleep apnea.** Disrupted breathing that wakens a person repeatedly during the night.

**Social cognitive theory.** Also known as social learning theory.

**Social learning theory.** A theory that posits that people learn behavior by copying "models" and receiving reinforcements.

**Social referencing.** The process by which infants seek out and interpret the emotional responses of their parents to form their own emotional understanding of unfamiliar events, objects, or persons.

**Sociobiology.** A field of study combining biology and social sciences.

**Somnambulism.** Also known as sleepwalking, a disorder that involves getting out of bed and moving about while still asleep.

**Specific language impairment.** A condition of markedly delayed language development in the absence of any apparent handicapping conditions.

**Split-brain technique.** Procedures used to study the activities of the two hemispheres of the brain separately, and independent of each other.

**Stanford-Binet intelligence scales.** A widely used test to measure intelligence.

**Stanford Progressive Matrices (SPM).** A test that assesses intelligence nonverbally in children and adults.

**Strange situation.** A research technique developed by Mary Ainsworth and used in the assessment of attachments.

**Stranger anxiety.** Fear of people with whom a child is not familiar.

**Sublimations.** A type of defense mechanism in which unacceptable impulse is diverted to a more appropriate or socially acceptable form. It differs from displacement in that sublimations are generally associated with the conversion of impulses to scientific, artistic, and other creative or intellectual activities.

**Superego.** In psychoanalytic theory, the part of the human personality that represents a person's inner values and morals; also known as conscience.

**Sympathetic nervous system.** Part of the autonomic nervous system that mobilizes the body for action.

**Synapse.** The tiny gap through which communication between two neurons takes place.

# T

**Tay-Sachs disease.** A genetically transmitted disease of the central nervous system affecting young children.

**Temperament.** An individual's characteristic emotional nature, including energy level, prevailing mood, and sensitivity to stimuli.

**Thalamus.** A collection of cell body clusters located in the middle of the forebrain that process sensory information.

**Thematic apperception test.** A psychological test, in which subjects are shown a series of pictures and asked to make up a story, used to assess personality.

**Tourette syndrome.** A genetic, neurological disorder characterized by motor and vocal tics and associated behavioral features including obsessions and compulsions and hyperactivity.

**Traits.** A stable, relatively permanent characteristic.

**Transference.** The tendency of clients to transfer to the therapist their emotional responses to significant people in their lives.

**Transsexualism.** Condition in which a person defines him or herself as male or female in opposition to physical gender, sometimes seeking surgical procedures to change from one sex to the other.

**Triangulation.** A situation in which two persons deal with the tension between them by using a third person as a buffer.

**Trichotillomania.** Uncontrollable or overwhelming urge to pull out one's own hair.

**Type A personality.** A personality characterized by competitive achievement, time urgency, and aggressiveness or hostility when frustrated.

# U

**Unconditioned response.** Response that is natural and not learned, such as jerking the hand from a hot stove.

**Unconditioned stimulus.** Stimulus that naturally elicits behavior, such as food.

**Unconscious.** The part of the mind whose contents people resist bringing into awareness.

# V

**Validity (in testing).** Term used in testing to describe tests that measure what they are intended to measure.

**Vocational aptitude test.** A predictive test designed to measure an individual's potential for success and satisfaction in any of various occupations and professions.

**Voyeurism.** A sexual disorder in which a person finds sexual excitement in watching unsuspecting people who are nude, undressing, or having sex.

# W

**Wechsler intelligence scales.** Series of intelligence tests encompassing both verbal and nonverbal abilities.

**Wernicke's aphasia.** A type of aphasia in which a person's speech is overflowing with words that do not convey meaning.

# PSYCHOLOGICAL ORGANIZATIONS

**Albert Ellis Institute**
45 E. 65th St.
New York, NY 10021 USA
Phone:(212) 535-0822
Fax: (212) 249-3582
Toll-Free: 800-323-4738
E-Mail: info@rebt.org
URL: http://www.rebt.org

**Alfred Adler Institute (AAI)**
24 E. 21st St., Fl. 8
New York, NY 10010-7200 USA
Phone:(212) 254-1048
Fax: (212) 254-8271

**American Academy of Child and Adolescent Psychiatry (AACAP)**
3615 Wisconsin Ave. NW
Washington, DC 20016-3007 USA
Phone:(202) 966-7300
Fax: (202) 966-2891
Toll-Free: 800-333-7636
E-Mail: executive@aacap.org
URL: http://www.aacap.org

**American Academy of Psychoanalysis (AAP)**
47 E. 19th St.
New York, NY 10003-1323 USA
Phone:(212) 475-7980
Fax: (212) 475-8101
E-Mail: aapny@aol.com
URL: http://www.aapsa.org

**American Anorexia Bulimia Association (AA/BA)**
165 W. 46th St., 1108
New York, NY 10036 USA
Phone:(212) 575-6200
Fax: (212) 278-0698
E-Mail: amanbu@aol.com
URL: http://www.aabainc.org

**American Board of Professional Psychology (ABPP)**
514 E. Capitol Ave.
Jefferson City, MO 65101-3008 USA
Phone:(573) 875-1267
Fax: (573) 443-1199
Toll-Free: 800-255-7792

E-Mail: ambra@abpp.org
URL: http://www.abpp.org

**American Board of Psychological Hypnosis (ABPH)**
c/o Samuel M. Migdole, Ed.D., ABPH
North Shore Counseling Center
23 Broadway
Beverly, MA 01915 USA
Phone:(978) 922-2280
Fax: (978) 927-1758

**American Psychological Association (APA)**
750 First St. NE
Washington, DC 20002-4242 USA
Phone:(202) 336-5500
Fax: (202) 336-5997
Toll-Free: 800-374-2721
E-Mail: executiveoffice@apa.org
URL: http://www.apa.org/

**American Psychological Society (APS)**
1010 Vermont Ave. NW, Ste. 1100
Washington, DC 20005-4907 USA
Phone:(202) 783-2077
Fax: (202) 783-2083
E-Mail: aps@aps.washington.dc.us
URL: http://www.psychological science.org

**American Psychopathological Association (APPA)**
Dept-Psyc University of Maryland
College Park, MD 20742 USA
Phone:(803) 852-4190
Fax: (803) 852-4195

**Anorexia Nervosa and Related Eating Disorders (ANRED)**
PO Box 5102
Eugene, OR 97405 USA
Phone:(541) 344-1144
E-Mail: jarinor@rio.com
URL: http://www.anred.com

**Association for Advancement of Behavior Therapy (AABT)**
305 7th Ave., Ste. 16A

New York, NY 10001-6008 USA
Phone:(212) 647-1890
Fax: (212) 647-1865
Toll-Free: 800-685-AABT
E-Mail: info@aabt.org
URL: http://www.aabt.org/

**Association for Advancement of Psychology (AAP)**
PO Box 38129
Colorado Springs, CO 80937 USA
Phone:(719) 520-0688
Fax: (719) 520-0375
Toll-Free: 800-869-6595

**Association for Child Psychology and Psychiatry (ACPP)**
St. Saviours House
39/41 Union St.
London SE1 1SD, England
Phone:44 171 4037458
Fax: 44 171 4037081
E-Mail: cjackson@acpp.co.uk

**Association for Humanistic Psychology (AHP)**
45 Franklin St., No. 315
San Francisco, CA 94102 USA
Phone:(415) 864-8850
Fax: (415) 864-8853
E-Mail: ahpoffice@aol.com
URL: http://www.ahpweb.org

**Association for the Advancement of Applied Sport Psychology**
c/o Jim Whelan, Ph.D.
Univ. of Memphis
Dept. of Psychology
Memphis, TN 38152-1389 USA
Phone:(901) 678-2147
URL: http://www.aaasponline.org

**Association for the Teaching of Psychology**
c/o British Psychological Society
48 Princess Rd., E
Leicester LE1 7DR, England

**Association for Women in Psychology (AWP)**
PO Box 11474
Portland, OR 97211 USA
URL: http://www.theworks.baka.com/
awp/

**Association of Black Psychologists (ABPsi)**
PO Box 55999
Washington, DC 20040-5999 USA
Phone:(202) 722-0808
Fax: (202) 722-5941
E-Mail: admin@abpsi.org
URL: http://www.abpsi.org

**Association of Psychology Postdoctoral and Internship Centers (APPIC)**
733 15th St. NW, Ste. 719
Washington, DC 20005-2112 USA
Phone:(202) 347-0022
Fax: (202) 347-8480
E-Mail: appic@aol.com
URL: http://www.appic.org

**C. G. Jung Foundation for Analytical Psychology**
28 E. 39th St.
New York, NY 10016 USA
Phone:(212) 697-6430
Fax: (212) 953-3989
E-Mail: cgjungny@aol.com

**Canadian Psychological Association (CPA)**
*Societe Canadienne de Psychologie (SCP)*
151 Slater St., Ste. 205
Ottawa, ON, Canada K1P 5H3
Phone:(613) 237-2144
Fax: (613) 237-1674
E-Mail: cpa@cpa.ca

**Canadian Society for Psychomotor Learning and Sport Psychology**
*Societe Canadienne d'Apprentissage Psychomoteur et de Psychologie du Sport*
Faculty of Kinesiology
University of Calgary
Calgary, AB, Canada T2N 1N4
Phone:(403) 492-2187
Fax: (403) 492-2364
URL: http://www.scapps.org

**Center for the Study of Psychiatry and Psychology**
4628 Chestnut St.
Bethesda, MD 20814 USA
Phone:(301) 652-5580
Fax: (301) 652-5924

**International Association for Child and Adolescent Psychiatry and Allied Professions (IACAPAP)**
PO Box 207900
New Haven, CT 06520-7900 USA
Phone:(203) 785-5759
Fax: (203) 785-7402
E-Mail: donald.cohen@yale.edu

**International Council of Psychologists (ICP)**
Psych Department
Southwest Texas State Univ.
San Marcos, TX 78666-4601 USA
Phone:(512) 245-7605
Fax: (512) 245-3153
E-Mail: jd04@academia.swt.edu

**International Dyslexia Association**
8600 LaSalle Rd.
Baltimore, MD 21286-2044 USA
Phone:(410) 296-0232
Fax: (410) 321-5069
Toll-Free: 800-ABCD-123
E-Mail: info@interdys.org
URL: http://www.interdys.org

**International Society for Comparative Psychology (ISCP)**
PO Box 1897
Lawrence, KS 66044-8897 USA
Phone:(913) 843-1235
Fax: (913) 843-1274
E-Mail: rmmurphey@ucdavis.edu
URL: http://www.psy.tcu.edu/psy/iscp/
iscp.html

**International Society for Developmental Psychobiology (ISDP)**
c/o Dr. Robert Lickliter
Virginia Tech
Blacksburg, VA 24061-0436 USA
Phone:(540) 231-5346
Fax: (540) 231-3652
E-Mail: duckling@vt.edu

**International Society of Political Psychology (ISPP)**
c/o Dana Ward, Exec. Dir.
ISPP Central Office
Pitzer College
1050 N. Mills Ave.
Claremont, CA 91711 USA
Phone:(909) 621-8442
Fax: (909) 621-8481
E-Mail: ispp@pitzer.edu

**International Society of Sports Psychology (ISSP)**
c/o Prof. Glyn C. Roberts
University of Illinois at Urbana - Champaign
Department of Kinesiology
906 S. Goodwin Ave.
Urbana, IL 61801 USA

Phone:(217) 333-2461
Fax: (217) 244-7322

**Jean Piaget Society: Society for the Study of Knowledge and Development (JPSSSKD)**
Human Development
Larsen Hall
Harvard GS Education
Cambridge, MA 02138 USA
Phone:(617) 495-3614
Fax: (617) 495-3626
URL: http://www.piaget.org

**Mental Research Institute (MRI)**
555 Middlefield Rd.
Palo Alto, CA 94301 USA
Phone:(650) 321-3055
Fax: (650) 321-3785
E-Mail: mri@mri.org
URL: http://www.mri.org

**National Association for Sport and Physical Education (NASPE)**
1900 Association Dr.
Reston, VA 20191 USA
Phone:(703) 476-3410
Fax: (703) 476-8316
Toll-Free: 800-213-7193
E-Mail: naspe@aahperd.org

**National Association of School Psychologists (NASP)**
4340 East West Hwy., Ste. 402
Bethesda, MD 20814-4411 USA
Phone:(301) 657-0270
Fax: (301) 657-0275
E-Mail: ahyman@naspweb.org
URL: http://www.naspweb.org

**National Eating Disorder Information Centre (NEDIC)**
College Wing, 1-211
200 Elizabeth St.
Toronto, ON, Canada M5G 2C4
Phone:(416) 340-4156
Fax: (416) 340-3430
E-Mail: mbear@torhosp.toronto.on.ca
URL: http://www.nedic.on.ca

**National Eating Disorders Organization (NEDO)**
6655 S. Yale Ave.
Tulsa, OK 74136 USA
Phone:(918) 481-4044
Fax: (918) 481-4076
URL: http://www.laureate.com

**National Guild of Hypnotists (NGH)**
PO Box 308
Merrimack, NH 03054-0308 USA
Phone:(603) 429-9438
Fax: (603) 424-8066
E-Mail: ngn@ngn.net

**Play Therapy International (PTI)**
11E-900 Greenbank Rd., Ste. 527
Nepean, ON, Canada K2J 4P6
Phone:(613) 634-3125
E-Mail: pti@playtherapy.org
URL: http://www.playtherapy.org/

**Psychology Society (PS)**
100 Beekman St.
New York, NY 10038-1810 USA
Phone:(212) 285-1872

**Society for Pediatric Psychology (SPP)**
c/o Conway Saylor, Ph.D.
Department of Psychiatry
The Citadel
Charleston, SC 29409 USA
Phone:(843) 953-5320
Fax: (843) 953-6797

**Society for Psychophysiological Research (SPR)**
c/o Connie Duncan

1010 Vermont Ave., Ste. 1100
Washington, DC 20005 USA
Phone (202) 393-4810
Fax: (202) 783-2083
E-Mail: spr@aps.washington.dc.us
URL: http://www.sprweb.org/

**Society for Research in the Psychology of Music and Music Education**
c/o Music Dept.
University of Sheffield
Sheffield S10 2TN, England
Phone:44 114 2667234
Fax: 44 114 2668053

**Society for Sex Therapy and Research (SSTAR)**
c/o Dr. P. Schreiner-Engel
Mt. Sinai Medical Ctr.
1176 Fifth Ave., Box 1170
New York, NY 10029 USA
Phone:(212) 241-6758
Fax: (212) 360-6917

**Society for the Advancement of Social Psychology (SASP)**
c/o Francis C. Dane
Department of Psychology
Mercer University
1400 Coleman Ave.
Macon, GA 31207-0001 USA
Phone:(912) 752-2972
Fax: (912) 752-2956
E-Mail: dane_fc@mercer.edu

**Society for the Psychological Study of Lesbian, Gay and Bisexual Issues (SPSLGBI)**
c/o American Psychological Association
750 1st St. NE
Washington, DC 20002-4242 USA
Phone:(202) 336-6037
Fax: (202) 336-6040
Toll-Free: 800-374-2721
URL: http://www.apa.org/divisions/div44

# INDEX

# D

# E

# F

# L

Labor. *See* Birth.
Ladd-Franklin, Christine 363 (ill.), 363–364
Laing, Ronald David 364–365
Lamaze, Fernand 83
Lange, C. G. 218
Language
  aphasia 43
  bilingual education 74
  cognition 131
  communication skills 139
  disorders 139
Language acquisition
  children 118
  cognition 131
  inherent ability 120
Language delay 365–367
Language development 368–376
Language disorder 376–377
  specific language impairment (SLI) 615
Lashley, Karl Spencer 377
Lateralization 385
Law of effect 72, 378, 644
Law of exercise 72, 378, 644
Lazarus, Arnold Allan 378
Leadership 379–380
Learned helplessness 175, 258, 380–381
Learning 433
  concept formation 143
  conditioning 145
  forgetting curve 255
  free-recall 258
  paired-associate learning 469
  programmed learning 511
Learning curve 381–382
  *See also* Forgetting curve.
Learning disability 382–384
  race 613
  testing 73
Learning theory 287, 384–385
Learning, serial 576
Learning-to-learn 385
Left-brain hemisphere 385–386
Left-handed. *See* Handedness.
Legal psychology. *See* Forensic psychology.
Lewin, Kurt 314, 386–387
  sensitivity training 573
Libido 387
Lie detection 387–389
Light
  depression 176
Listening, reflective. *See* Reflective listening.
Lithium 79
Localization (brain function) 389
Localization (sensory) 389
Locke, John 50, 390–392, 391 (ill.)
  tabula rasa theory of childhood 117

Locus of control 58, 392–393
Logical thinking 393–394
Logotherapy 255
Longitudinal study 163, 394
Lorenz, Konrad 21, 91, 394–397, 395 (ill.)
  imprinting 161
Loss and grief 397–399
LSD 292
Luria, Aleksandr Romanovich 399–400

# M

Maccoby, Eleanor Emmons 401–402
Magnesium pemoline 54
Magnetic resonance imaging (MRI) 95
Magnetoencephalography (MEG) 95
Maintenance rehearsal 542
Malinowski, Bronislaw 162
Mania 176, 402
  electroconvulsive therapy (ECT) 209
  hallucinations 290
Manic depression. *See* Bipolar disorder.
Marijuana 292, 402–403
Marketing 152
Marriage counseling 404
Maslow, Abraham 20, 313, 314, 404–406, 405 (ill.), 566 (ill.)
  self-actualization 565
Maslow's hierarchy of needs 405, 441
Masochism 471
Masters, William 344, 406 (ill.), 406–407
Masturbation 15
May, Rollo 233, 314, 407–408
  power 507
Mayer, John 217
McDougall, William 408–410, 409 (ill.)
McGrath, Elizabeth 227
Mead, Margaret 410–411
Mean 411–412
Measurement 412
  mean 411
  median 412
  mode 433
  norm 460
  normal distribution 459
  rating scale 538
Media psychology 413–414
Median 412
Mediation
  peer mediation 482
Medical psychology 297
*Meditations on First Philosophy* 178
Medulla 110
Meehl, Paul J. 414–415
MEG. *See* Magnetoencephalography (MEG).

Melancholia 415
*The Melting Pot* 4
Memory 131, 415–418
  cathexis 106
  Ebbinghaus, Hermann 203
  false memories 417
  free-recall learning 258
  long-term memory 573
  recovered memories 417
  rehearsal 542
  savant syndrome 557
  semantic memory 573
  serial learning 576
  serial position function 576
  stages of 416
  techniques for improving 415, 433
  word association test 669
Memory loss 31
Mental age 334, 335, 418
Mental disorders, classification of 186
Mental health 418–419
Mental hospitals 419
Mental hygiene movement 70, 427
Mental illness 419–421
  causes 422
  neurological classification of 361
  psychosis 523
  psychotherapy 525
  treatment 420, 513, 514
  types of 419, 420
  *See also* Mental health.
Mental imagery 324, 330, 379, 421
Mental retardation 421–424
  autism 61
  familial retardation 240
  fetal alcohol syndrome 248
  language delay 367
Mental sets 100
Merrill-Palmer scales of mental tests 424
Mesencephalon 110
Mesmer, Franz Anton 424–426, 425 (ill.)
Metapsychology 426
Methylphenidate 54
Meyer, Adolf 426 (ill.), 426–427
Midbrain 110
Middle years 427–428
Midlife. *See* Middle years.
Miescher, Friedrich 173
Milgram, Stanley 428–429, 605
Milgram's obedience experiment 428
Military psychology 429–430
Mill, James 50
Mill, John Stuart 50
Miller, Neal 65
Minimal brain dysfunction 430–431
Minnesota Multiphasic Personality Inventory 431, 495
Minuchin, Salvador 242, 431–432
Mischel, Walter 606
MMPI. *See* Minnesota Multiphasic Personality Inventory.
Mnemonic strategies 433

# N

# O

# P

# Q

# R